A SHAKESPEAREAN GENEALOGY

This chart reflects Shakespeare's history plays and is thus not historically accurate. Many descendants of Henry II and Edward III are omitted. On occasion, Shakespeare combined or simply invented historical figures. These deviations from fact are explained in the notes.

In the chart, the names of Kings and Queens are printed in capitals, and the dates of their reigns are printed in bold. The names of characters appearing in the plays are underlined.

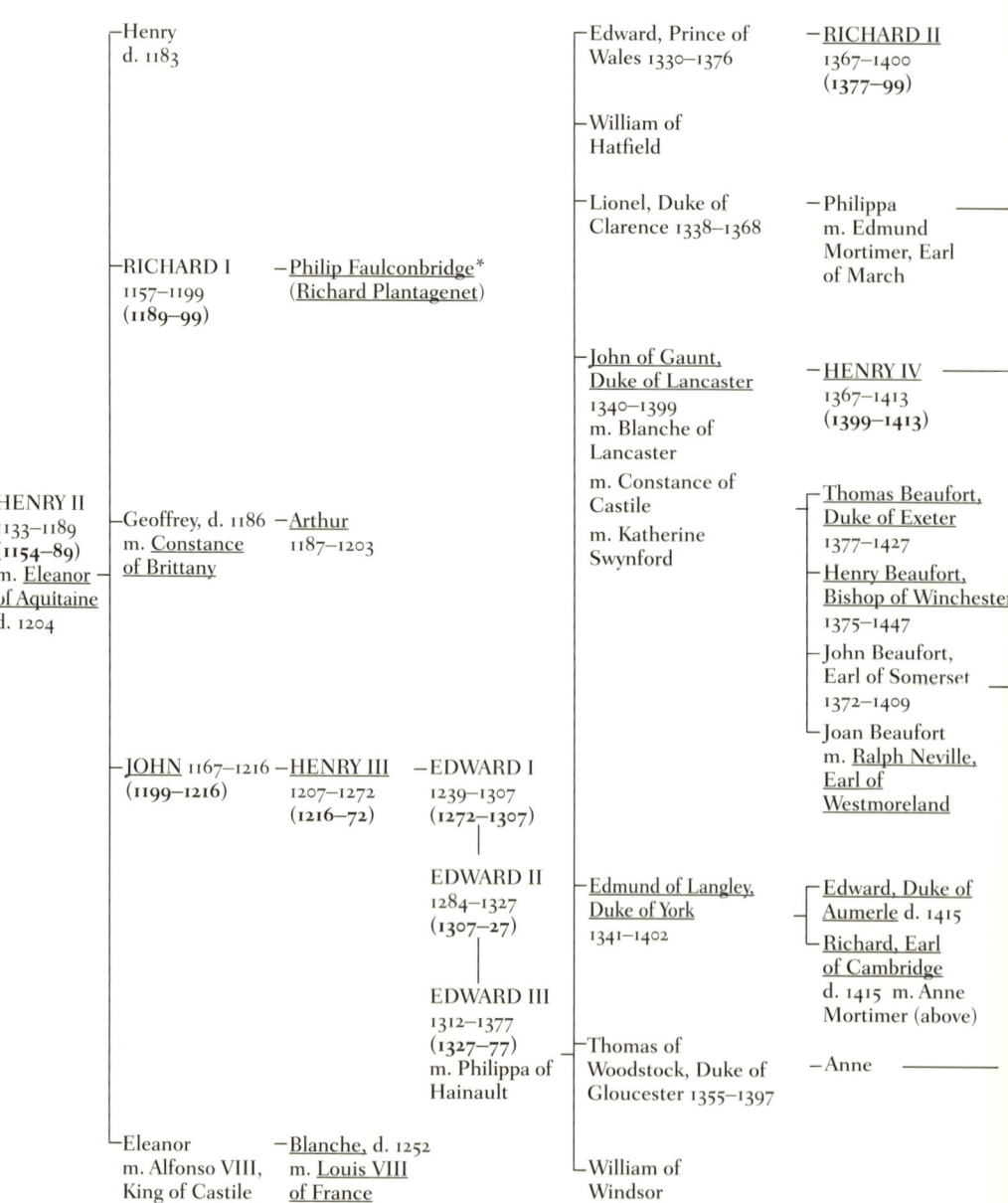

*Philip Faulconbridge, the bastard son of Richard I, had no historical existence. Such a character appears in the play *The Life and Death of King John* and is referred to in passing in Holinshed's *Chronicles*.

† In the character of Edmund Mortimer, Shakespeare combines two historical figures. The Edmund Mortimer who married Catrin, daughter of Owain Glyndŵr, was the grandson of Lionel, Duke of Clarence, and the younger brother of Roger, Earl of March. He died in 1409. Shakespeare combines him with his nephew, the Edmund Mortimer recognized by Richard II as his heir (d. 1424). This second Edmund was the brother of Anne Mortimer and the uncle of Richard Plantagenet.

‡ The character of the Duke of Somerset combines Henry Beaufort with his younger brother Edmund (d. 1471), who succeeded him as Duke.

Elizabeth Mortimer ("Kate") m. Henry Percy ("Hotspur") 1364–1403

Henry, Earl of Northumberland 1394–1455

EDWARD IV 1442–1483 (1461–83) m. Elizabeth Woodville d. 1492

EDWARD V 1470–1483 (1483)

Richard, Duke of York 1472–1483

Elizabeth of York 1465–1503 m. HENRY VII (below)

Edmund, Earl of Rutland 1443–1460

Edmund Mortimer†

George, Duke of Clarence 1449–1478 m. Isabel Neville (below)

Anne Mortimer m. Richard, Earl of Cambridge (below)

Richard Plantagenet, Duke of York 1411–1460 m. Cicely Neville (below)

RICHARD III 1452–1485 (1483–85) m. Anne Neville (below)

Edward, Prince of Wales

HENRY V 1387–1422 (1413–22) m. Catherine 1401–1437

HENRY VI 1421–1471 (1422–61) m. Margaret of Anjou d. 1482

Edward, Prince of Wales 1453–1471 m. Anne Neville (below)

Arthur m. Catherine of Aragon (below)

Thomas, Duke of Clarence d. 1421

Margaret m. James IV of Scotland

James V of Scotland

Mary, Queen of Scots

John of Lancaster, Duke of Bedford 1389–1435

Humphrey, Duke of Gloucester 1391–1447 m. Eleanor Cobham d. 1454

JAMES I 1566–1625 (1603–25)

John Beaufort, Duke of Somerset 1403–1444

Margaret Beaufort m. Edmund Tudor, Earl of Richmond

HENRY VII 1457–1509 (1485–1509) m. Elizabeth of York (above)

HENRY VIII 1491–1547 (1509–47) m. Catherine of Aragon

m. Anne Boleyn

MARY I 1516–1558 (1553–58) m. Philip of Spain

ELIZABETH I 1533–1603 (1558–1603)

Edmund Beaufort, Duke of Somerset 1406–1455

Henry Beaufort, Duke of Somerset 1436–1464‡

m. Jane Seymour

EDWARD VI 1537–1553 (1547–53)

Isabel Neville d. 1476 m. George, Duke of Clarence (above)

m. Anne of Cleves

m. Katherine Howard

Richard Neville, Earl of Salisbury 1400–1460

Richard Neville, Earl of Warwick 1428–1471

John Neville, Marquess of Montague d. 1471

Anne Neville d. 1485 m. Edward, Prince of Wales (above)

m. Katherine Parr

m. RICHARD III (above)

Mary m. Charles Brandon

Frances

Jane Grey 1537–1554

Cicely Neville m. Richard Plantagenet, Duke of York (above)

Humphrey, Duke of Buckingham 1402–1460

Humphrey Stafford d. 1455

Henry, Duke of Buckingham 1454?–1483

Edward, Duke of Buckingham 1478–1521

1377–1625

RICHARD II, 1377–99 RICHARD was the eldest son of EDWARD THE BLACK PRINCE, himself the eldest son of KING EDWARD III, who ruled England from 1327 to 1377. When the BLACK PRINCE died in battle in France in 1376, RICHARD became the legitimate heir to the throne. He ruled from EDWARD's death in 1377 until he was deposed in 1399 by HENRY BOLINGBROKE, the eldest son of JOHN OF GAUNT, DUKE OF LANCASTER. Because he was the fourth son of EDWARD III, GAUNT and his Lancastrian descendants had weaker hereditary claims to the throne than did RICHARD. When deposed, RICHARD had no children to succeed him, but he recognized EDMUND MORTIMER, FIFTH EARL OF MARCH, as his heir presumptive. This MORTIMER was descended from LIONEL, DUKE OF CLARENCE, the third son of EDWARD III, and therefore also had stronger hereditary claims to the throne than did BOLINGBROKE. SHAKESPEARE combined this MORTIMER with his uncle EDMUND MORTIMER, who married OWAIN GLYNDŴR'S DAUGHTER.

HENRY IV, 1399–1413 HENRY BOLINGBROKE, eldest son of JOHN OF GAUNT, seized the throne from RICHARD II in 1399. When HENRY died in 1413, he was succeeded by his eldest son, PRINCE HAL, who became HENRY V.

HENRY V, 1413–22 HENRY V became king in 1413 and reigned until his death in 1422. He was succeeded by his son, HENRY VI.

HENRY VI, 1422–61 HENRY VI was less than one year old when he succeeded his father, HENRY V. In the young king's minority, his uncle HUMPHREY, DUKE OF GLOUCESTER, was named Lord Protector, and the kingdom was ruled by an aristocratic council. HENRY VI assumed personal authority in 1437. He was deposed in 1461 by his third cousin, who was crowned EDWARD IV. HENRY was murdered in 1471.

EDWARD IV, 1461–83 EDWARD, the eldest son of RICHARD, DUKE OF YORK, seized the throne from HENRY VI in 1461. His Yorkist claim to the throne derived from his grandmother, ANNE MORTIMER, who was descended from LIONEL, third son of EDWARD III, and was sister to that EDMUND MORTIMER recognized by RICHARD II as his heir presumptive; EDWARD IV's grandfather, RICHARD, EARL OF CAMBRIDGE, was the son of EDMUND OF LANGLEY, fifth son of EDWARD III. EDWARD IV reigned until his death in 1483. His heir was his eldest son (EDWARD), but the throne was usurped by his brother RICHARD, DUKE OF GLOUCESTER.

RICHARD III, 1483–85 RICHARD III was the youngeer brother of EDWARD IV. After the death of EDWARD IV in 1483, RICHARD prevented the coronation of EDWARD V with a claim of illegitimacy and succeeded to the throne himself. EDWARD and his younger brother, RICHARD, DUKE OF YORK, were murdered in the Tower of London. RICHARD III was killed at the Battle of Bosworth Field in 1485, and the kingdom fell to the victor, HENRY TUDOR, EARL OF RICHMOND.

HENRY VII, 1485–1509 HENRY TUDOR seized the throne from RICHARD III in 1485. He was descended from JOHN OF GAUNT by JOHN's third marriage, with CATHERINE SWYNFORD. He married ELIZABETH, daughter of EDWARD IV, uniting the houses of Lancaster and York. He died in 1509 and was succeeded by his son, HENRY VIII.

HENRY VIII, 1509–47 HENRY was the second son of HENRY VII. His older brother, ARTHUR, died in 1502. HENRY VIII's first wife was CATHERINE OF ARAGON, who bore his daughter MARY. His second wife, ANNE BOLEYN, was the mother of ELIZABETH. His third wife, JANE SEYMOUR, bore him a son, who succeeded to the throne as EDWARD VI after HENRY VIII died in 1547.

EDWARD VI, 1547–53 EDWARD VI was nine years old when he became king. From 1547 to 1549, the realm was governed by a Lord Protector, the DUKE OF SOMERSET; power then passed to JOHN DUDLEY, DUKE OF NORTHUMBERLAND. When EDWARD VI died in 1553, NORTHUMBERLAND attempted unsuccessfully to prevent the succession of MARY TUDOR by installing as queen his daughter-in-law, LADY JANE GREY, a great-granddaughter of HENRY VII.

MARY I, 1553–58 MARY, daughter of HENRY VIII and his first wife, CATHERINE OF ARAGON, came to the throne in 1553. She married KING PHILIP OF SPAIN but died childless. She was succeeded by her half sister, ELIZABETH.

ELIZABETH I, 1558–1603 ELIZABETH, the daughter of HENRY VIII and his second wife, ANNE BOLEYN, became queen after the death of her half sister, MARY, in 1558. She ruled until her death in 1603. She was succeeded by her cousin JAMES.

JAMES I, 1603–1625 JAMES VI OF SCOTLAND became JAMES I OF ENGLAND in 1603. His claim to the throne of England derived from his great-grandmother, MARGARET TUDOR, a daughter of HENRY VII who married JAMES IV OF SCOTLAND. JAMES ruled England and Scotland until his death in 1625; he was succeeded by his son, CHARLES I.

THE NORTON
SHAKESPEARE

BASED ON THE OXFORD EDITION

SECOND EDITION

Histories

The original Oxford Text on which this
edition is based was prepared by

Stanley Wells
Gary Taylor
General Editors

John Jowett
William Montgomery

The Norton Shakespeare, Second Edition, is based on *William Shakespeare: The Complete Works*,
Second Edition, and is published by arrangement with Oxford University Press,
with additional material from W. W. Norton & Company, Inc.

THE NORTON SHAKESPEARE

Based on the Oxford Edition

SECOND EDITION

Histories

Stephen Greenblatt, *General Editor*
HARVARD UNIVERSITY

Walter Cohen
CORNELL UNIVERSITY

Jean E. Howard
COLUMBIA UNIVERSITY

Katharine Eisaman Maus
UNIVERSITY OF VIRGINIA

With an Essay on the Shakespearean stage
by Andrew Gurr

W · W · NORTON & COMPANY · NEW YORK · LONDON

W. W. Norton & Company has been independent since its founding in 1923, when William Warder Norton and Mary D. Herter Norton first published lectures delivered at the People's Institute, the adult education division of New York City's Cooper Union. The Nortons soon expanded their program beyond the Institute, publishing books by celebrated academics from America and abroad. By mid-century, the two major pillars of Norton's publishing program—trade books and college texts—were firmly established. In the 1950s, the Norton family transferred control of the company to its employees, and today—with a staff of four hundred and a comparable number of trade, college, and professional titles published each year—W. W. Norton & Company stands as the largest and oldest publishing house owned wholly by its employees.

Editor: Julia Reidhead
Manuscript editor: Carol Flechner
Electronic media editor: Eileen Connell
Editorial assistant: Rivka Genesen
Production manager: Diane O'Connor
Photo research: Rivka Genesen
Interior design: Antonina Krass
Managing editor, College: Marian Johnson

Copyright © 2008, 1997 by W. W. Norton & Company, Inc.
Text and some commentaries copyright © 1986, 2005 by Oxford University Press

Composition by Binghamton Valley Composition.
Manufacturing by R. R. Donnelley.

The Library of Congress has cataloged the one-volume edition as follows:

Shakespeare, William, 1564–1616.
The Norton Shakespeare / Stephen Greenblatt, general editor ; Walter Cohen, Jean
E. Howard, Katharine Eisaman Maus [editors] ; with an essay on the Shakespearean
stage by Andrew Gurr. — 2nd ed.
p. cm.
"Based on the Oxford edition."
Includes bibliographical references and index.
ISBN 978-0-393-92991-1
I. Greenblatt, Stephen, 1943– II. Cohen, Walter, 1949– III. Howard, Jean E.
(Jean Elizabeth), 1948– IV. Maus, Katharine Eisaman, 1955– V. Gurr, Andrew.
VI. Title.
PR2754.G74 2008
822.3'3—dc22
2007046599

This edition: ISBN 978-0-393-93142-6

W. W. Norton & Company, Inc., 500 Fifth Avenue, New York, NY 10110
www.wwnorton.com

W. W. Norton & Company Ltd., Castle House, 75/76 Wells Street, London W1T 3QT

3 4 5 6 7 8 9 0

Contents

Illustrations

Preface

Shakespeare's principal medium, the drama, was thoroughly collaborative, and it involved as well continual efforts at revision and renewal. It seems appropriate, then, that this edition of his works is itself the result of sustained collaboration and revision. Two lists of editors' names on the title-page spread hint at the collaboration that has brought to fruition the *Norton Shakespeare*. But the title page does not tell the full history of this project. The text on which the *Norton Shakespeare* is based was published in both modern-spelling and original-spelling versions by Oxford University Press, in 1986. Under the general editorship of Stanley Wells and Gary Taylor, the Oxford text was a thorough rethinking of the entire body of Shakespeare's works, the most far-reaching and innovative revision of the traditional canon in centuries. When many classroom instructors who wanted to introduce their students to the works of Shakespeare through a modern text expressed a need for the pedagogical apparatus they have come to expect in an edition oriented toward students, Norton negotiated with Oxford to assemble an editorial team of its own to prepare the necessary teaching materials around the existing Oxford text. Hence ensued a collaboration of two publishers and two editorial teams.

To what extent is this the *Norton Shakespeare* and to what extent the Oxford text? Introductions (both the General Introduction and those to individual plays and poems), footnotes, glosses, bibliographies, genealogies, annals, maps, documents, and illustrations have all been the responsibility of the Norton team. Andrew Gurr's much-admired essay on the London theater in Shakespeare's time, specially commissioned for the *Norton Shakespeare*, has been moved in this second edition to the front matter.

The textual notes and variants derive for the most part from the work of the Oxford team, especially as represented in *William Shakespeare: A Textual Companion* (Oxford University Press, 1987), a remarkably comprehensive explanation of editorial decisions that is herewith strongly recommended to instructors as a valuable companion to this volume. Several of the textual notes—those to *The First Part of Henry the Sixth*, *Various Poems*, *The Two Noble Kinsmen*, *The Merry Wives of Windsor*, *Troilus and Cressida*, *The Sonnets* and "A Lover's Complaint"—have been substantially updated in the current edition, and all Textual Variants are now gathered in an appendix.

The Oxford text is widely available and already well known to scholars. A few words here may help clarify the extent of our fidelity to that text and the nature of the collaboration that has brought about this volume. The Oxford editors have profited from the massive and sustained attention accorded their edition by Shakespeare scholars across the globe, and of course they have continued to participate actively in the ongoing scholarly discussion about the nature of Shakespeare's text. In the reprintings of the Oxford volumes and in various articles over the past years, the Oxford editors have made a number of refinements of the edition they originally published. Such changes have been incorporated silently here. A small number of other changes made by the Norton team, however, were not part of the Oxford editors' design and were only accepted by them after we reached, through lengthy consultation, a mutual understanding about the nature, purpose, and intended audience of this volume. In all such changes, our main concern was for the classroom; we wished to make fully and clearly available the scholarly innovation and freshness of the Oxford text, while at the same time making certain that this was a superbly useful teaching text. It is a pleasure here to record, on behalf of the Norton team, our gratitude for the personal and professional generosity of the Oxford editors in offering advice and entertaining arguments in our common goal of providing the best student Shakespeare for our times. The Norton changes to the Oxford text are various, but in only a few instances are they major. The following brief notes are sufficient to summarize all of these changes, which are also indicated in appropriate play introductions, footnotes, or textual notes.

1. The Oxford editors, along with other scholars, have strenuously argued—in both the Oxford text and elsewhere—that the now-familiar text of *King Lear*, so nearly omnipresent in our classrooms as to seem unquestionably authoritative but in reality dating from the work of Alexander Pope (1723) and Lewis Theobald (1733), represents a wrongheaded conflation of two distinct versions of the play: Shakespeare's original creation as printed in the 1608 Quarto and his substantial revision as printed in the First Folio (1623). The Oxford text, therefore, prints both *The History of King Lear* and *The Tragedy of King Lear*. Norton follows suit, but where Oxford presents these two texts sequentially, we print them on facing pages. While each version may be read independently, and to ensure this we have provided glosses and footnotes for each, the substantial points of difference between the two are immediately apparent and available for comparison. But even many who agree with the scholarly argument for the two texts of *Lear* nevertheless favor making available a conflated text, the text on which innumerable performances of the play have been based and on which a huge body of literary criticism has been written. With the reluctant acquiescence, therefore, of the Oxford editors, we have included a conflated *Lear*, a text that has no part in the Oxford canon and that has been edited by Barbara K. Lewalski of Harvard University rather than by Gary Taylor, the editor of the Oxford *Lears*.

The Norton Shakespeare, then, includes three separate texts of *King Lear*. The reader can compare them, understand the role of editors in constructing the texts we now call Shakespeare's, explore in considerable detail the kinds of decisions that playwrights, editors, and printers make and remake, witness firsthand the historical transformation of what might at first glance seem fixed and unchanging. The *Norton Shakespeare* offers extraordinary access to this supremely brilliant, difficult, compelling play.

2. Among several other plays, *Hamlet* offers similar grounds for objections to the traditional conflation, but both the economics of publishing and the realities of bookbinding—not to mention our recognition of the limited time in the typical undergraduate syllabus—preclude our offering three (or even four) *Hamlets* to match three *Lears*. What we have provided in this edition is a convenient selection of parallel passages that will enable teachers to convey some of the complex, often enigmatic issues, at once stylistic and conceptual, raised by the different texts of the play.

The Oxford text of *Hamlet* was based upon the Folio text, with an appended list of Additional Passages from the Second Quarto (Q2). These additional readings total more than two hundred lines, a significant number, among which are lines that have come to seem very much part of the play as widely received, even if we may doubt that they belong with all the others in any single one of Shakespeare's *Hamlets*. The Norton team, while following the Oxford text, has moved the Q2 passages from the appendix to the body of the play. But in doing so, we have not wanted once again to produce a conflated text. We have therefore indented the Q2 passages, printed them in a different typeface, and numbered them in such a way as to make clear their provenance. Those who wish to read the Folio version of *Hamlet* can thus simply skip over the indented Q2 passages, while at the same time it is possible for readers to see clearly the place that the Q2 passages occupy. We have adopted a similar strategy with several other plays: passages printed in Oxford in appendices are generally printed here in the play texts, though clearly demarcated and not conflated. In the case of *The Taming of the Shrew* and the related quarto text, *The Taming of a Shrew*, however, we have followed Oxford's procedure and left the quarto passages in an appendix, since we believe the texts reflect two distinct plays rather than a revision of one. We have similarly reproduced Oxford's brief appendices to A *Midsummer Night's Dream* and *Henry V,* enabling readers to consider alternative revisions of certain passages.

3. For reasons understood by every Shakespearean (and rehearsed at some length in this volume), the Oxford editors chose to restore the name "Sir John Oldcastle" to the character much better known as Falstaff in *1 Henry IV.* (They made comparable changes in the names of the characters known as Bardolph and Peto.) But for reasons understood by everyone who has presented this play to undergraduates or sampled the centuries of enthusiastic criticism, the Norton editors, with the Oxford editors' gracious agreement, have for this classroom edition opted for the familiar name "Falstaff" (and those of his boon companions), properly noting the change and its significance in the play's introduction.

4. The Oxford editors chose not to differentiate between those stage directions that appeared in the early editions up to and including the Folio and those that have been added by subsequent editors. Instead, in *A Textual Companion* they include separate lists of the original stage directions. These lists are not readily available to readers of the Norton text, whose editors opted instead to bracket all stage directions that derive from editions published after the Folio. Readers can thus easily see which stage directions derive from texts that may bear at least some relation to performances in Shakespeare's time, if not to Shakespeare's own authorship. The Norton policy is more fully explained in the General Introduction.

5. The Oxford editors have newly prepared complete texts of the multiauthored *King Edward III* and *Sir Thomas More,* in which Shakespeare may have had a hand as collaborator. The texts are available online at wwnorton.com/shakespeare. In addition, the *Norton Shakespeare,* Second Edition, continues to print, with a revised introduction, notes, and glosses, passages from *Sir Thomas More* that appear in the surviving manuscript to be in Shakespeare's own handwriting, and we include for the first time an introduction and bibliography to *King Edward III.*

The collaboration with Oxford was obviously essential to the creation of the *Norton Shakespeare.* But in preparing this Second Edition and making it something fresh and engaging, the critically important collaboration has been with the thousands of people who have used the book. Many of these, teachers and students alike, have generously offered helpful suggestions along with praise. Guided by their responses, as well as by recent developments in Shakespeare scholarship, we determined to look afresh at every detail and to make a wide range of changes. The General Introduction and the individual play introductions have been substantially revised, in some cases wholly rewritten, to make them clearer and more accessible. Textual notes throughout have been updated in response to new findings, and there are hundreds of new and fine-tuned notes and glosses, designed to make this edition an even better tool for learning and pleasure. The General Bibliography has been reorganized and extensively updated, with 7 new sections and over 350 new entries. The Selected Bibliographies, too, have been updated as well as newly annotated. A new introduction provides an illuminating guide to the array of maps, three of them archival and three new, showing places important to Shakespeare's plays. The genealogies have been revised, as has been the text/contexts Timeline. New annotated film lists, including over 50 films, now follow the play introductions. Instructors who emphasize films in their courses may wish to assign *Shakespeare and Film: A Norton Guide* by Samuel Crowl, available packaged with the *Norton Shakespeare.* Finally, in response to many requests, we are making the *Norton Shakespeare* available in three different formats: the familiar one-volume clothbound edition, new two-volume chronological splits (*Early Plays and Poems* and *Later Plays*), and four genre paperbacks, each with a new introduction.

With the Second Edition of the *Norton Shakespeare,* the publisher expands its extensive online resource, Norton Literature Online (wwnorton.com/literature). Students who activate the free password in each new copy of the book gain access to an array of general resources, among them a glossary of literary terms, advice on writing about literature and using MLA documentation style, an author portrait gallery, more than 100 maps, and over 90 minutes of recorded readings and musical selections, among them 80 songs by Shakespeare. With their passwords, students also gain access to a site specifically developed to support the *Norton Shakespeare* (wwnorton.com/shakespeare). Based on content prepared by Mark Rose, University of California, Santa Barbara, this Web site invites students to explore six of the most widely taught plays—*The Merchant of Venice, 1 Henry IV, Hamlet, Othello, King Lear,* and *The Tempest*—through different contextual lenses. For each of these plays, the Web site provides materials on the elements of theater, sources, stage history, and critical receptions, as well as the complete Oxford text. Audio clips and stills from classic productions, etchings, photographs, and costume-design illustrations help students appreciate performance aspects of the plays. The student Web site also includes the redesigned "Shakespearean Chronicle, 1558–1616," an illustrated timeline that interweaves three kinds of chronologies illuminating Shakespeare's life and times. As noted above, a password-protected section of the Web site also includes the complete texts of *The Book of Sir Thomas More* and *The Reign of King Edward the Third,* prepared by the editors of the *Oxford Shakespeare.*

The creation of this edition has drawn heavily on the resources, experience, and skill of its remarkable publisher, the independent, employee-owned company W. W. Norton. Our principal guide has been our brilliant editor Julia Reidhead, whose calm intelligence, common sense, and steady focus have been essential in enabling us to reach our goal. With this Second Edition, we were blessed with the characteristically thoughtful oversight of Marian Johnson, managing editor, college department; scrupulous manuscript editing by Carol Flechner; and the assistance of an extraordinary group of Norton staffers: editorial assistant Rivka Genesen, who, among many other things, coordinated the art program; production manager Diane O'Connor; designer Antonina Krass; editor of the *Norton Shakespeare* Web site Eileen Connell; and proofreaders Paula Noonan and Ann Warren.

The *Norton Shakespeare* editors have, in addition, had the valuable—indeed, indispensable—support of a host of undergraduate and graduate research assistants, colleagues, friends, and family. Even a partial listing of those to whom we owe our heartfelt thanks is very long, but we are all fortunate enough to live in congenial and supportive environments, and the edition has been part of our lives for a long time. We owe special thanks for sustained dedication and learning to our principal assistants: Tiffany Alkan, Lianne Habinek, and Emily Peterson. Particular thanks are due to Noah Heringman for his work on the texts assembled in the documents section and for the prefatory notes and comments on those texts; to Philip Schwyzer for preparing the genealogies and the glossary and for conceiving and preparing the (now online) "Shakespearean Chronicle"; and to Holger Schott Syme for reconceiving and extensively updating the General Bibliography. In addition, we are deeply grateful to Ezra Feldman, Francesca Mari, Douglas McQueen-Thomson, Jeffrey Patterson, and Benjamin Woodring. All of these companions, and many more besides, have helped us find in this long collective enterprise what the "Dedicatorie Epistle" to the First Folio promises to its readers: delight. We make the same promise to the readers of our edition and invite them to continue the great Shakespearean collaboration.

STEPHEN GREENBLATT
WALTER COHEN
JEAN E. HOWARD
KATHARINE EISAMAN MAUS

Acknowledgments

Among our many critics, advisers, and friends, the following were of special help in providing critiques for particular plays or of the project as a whole: Janet Adelman (University of California, Berkeley), Joel Altman (University of California, Berkeley), Rebecca Bach (University of Alabama at Birmingham), John Baxter (Dalhousie University), Edward I. Berry (University of Victoria), Timothy Billings (Middlebury College), Bruce Boehrer (Florida State University), Barbara Bono (University at Buffalo, SUNY), Gordon M. Braden (University of Virginia), Douglas Brooks (Texas A&M University), Stephen Buhler (University of Nebraska—Lincoln), Richard Burt (University of Florida), Joseph F. Ceccio (University of Akron), Julie Crawford (Columbia University), Christy Desmet (University of Georgia), Heather Dubrow (University of Wisconsin—Madison), Laurie Ellinghausen (University of Missouri—Kansas City), Chris Fitter (Rutgers, State University of New Jersey), Susan Fraiman (University of Virginia), Daniel Gil (University of Oregon), Miriam Gilbert (University of Iowa), Suzanne Gossett (Loyola University), Elizabeth Hanson (Queen's University), Jim Harner (Texas A&M University), Jonathan Gil Harris (George Washington University), Don Hedrick (Kansas State University), Roze Hentschell (Colorado State University), Clifford Huffman (Stony Brook University, SUNY), John Huntington (University of Illinois at Chicago), Sujata Iyengar (University of Georgia), Kimberly Johnson (Brigham Young University), Coppélia Kahn (Brown University), Sean Keilen (University of Pennsylvania), Theodore B. Leinwand (University of Maryland), Zachary Lesser (University of Pennsylvania), Naomi Liebler (Montclair State University), Joyce MacDonald (University of Kentucky), Leah Marcus (Vanderbilt University), Mark Matheson (University of Utah), Robert Matz (George Mason University), Kristen McDermott (Central Michigan University), Ted McGee (University of Waterloo), Scott McMillin (late of Cornell University), Gordon McMullan (King's College London), John Moore (Pennsylvania State University), Carol Neely (University of Illinois at Urbana-Champaign), Lori Newcomb (University of Illinois at Urbana-Champaign), Karen Newman (New York University), Hillary Nunn (University of Akron), Thomas G. Olsen (SUNY at New Paltz), Jim O'Rourke (Florida State University), Paul Parrish (Texas A&M University), Michael Payne (Bucknell University), Rebecca J. Perederin (University of Virginia), Curtis Perry (Arizona State University), Susan Phillips (Northwestern University), Tanya Pollard (Brooklyn College, CUNY), Kristen Poole (University of Delaware), Arnold Preussner (Truman State University), Phyllis Rackin (University of Pennsylvania), Peter L. Rudnytsky (University of Florida), Benjamin Saunders (University of Oregon), Barbara Sebek (Colorado State University), Tracey Sedinger (University of Northern Colorado), Jyotsna Singh (Michigan State University), Andrew Stott (University at Buffalo, SUNY), Garrett Sullivan (Pennsylvania State University), Ramie Targoff (Brandeis University), Henry Turner (University of Wisconsin—Madison), Martine van Elk (California State University, Long Beach), William N. West (University of Colorado at Boulder), Linda Woodbridge (Pennsylvania State University), Lingui Yang (Texas A&M University).

General Introduction
by
STEPHEN GREENBLATT

"He was not of an age, but for all time!"

The celebration of Shakespeare's genius, eloquently initiated by his friend and rival Ben Jonson, has over the centuries become an institutionalized rite of civility. The person who does not love Shakespeare has made, the rite implies, an incomplete adjustment not simply to a particular culture—English culture of the late sixteenth and early seventeenth centuries—but to "culture" as a whole, the dense network of constraints and entitlements, dreams and practices that links us to nature. Indeed, so absolute is Shakespeare's achievement that he has himself come to seem like great creating nature: the common bond of humankind, the principle of hope, the symbol of the imagination's power to transcend time-bound beliefs and assumptions, peculiar historical circumstances, and specific artistic conventions.

The near-worship that Shakespeare inspires is one of the salient facts about his art. But we must at the same time acknowledge that this art is the product of peculiar historical circumstances and specific conventions, four centuries distant from our own. The acknowledgment is important because Shakespeare the working dramatist did not typically lay claim to the transcendent, visionary truths attributed to him by his most fervent admirers; his characters more modestly say, in the words of the magician Prospero, that their project was "to please" (*The Tempest,* Epilogue, line 13). The starting point, and perhaps the ending point as well, in any encounter with Shakespeare is simply to enjoy him, to savor his imaginative richness, to take pleasure in his infinite delight in language.

"If then you do not like him," Shakespeare's first editors wrote in 1623, "surely you are in some manifest danger not to understand him." Over the years, accommodations have been devised to make liking Shakespeare easier for everyone. When the stage sank to melodrama and light opera, Shakespeare—in suitably revised texts—was there. When the populace had a craving for hippodrama, plays performed entirely on horseback, *Hamlet* was dutifully rewritten and mounted. When audiences went mad for realism, live frogs croaked in productions of *A Midsummer Night's Dream.* When the stage was stripped bare and given over to stark exhibitions of sadistic cruelty, Shakespeare was our contemporary. And when the theater itself had lost some of its cultural centrality, Shakespeare moved effortlessly to Hollywood and the soundstages of the BBC.

This virtually universal appeal is one of the most astonishing features of the Shakespeare phenomenon: plays that were performed before glittering courts thrive in junior-high-school auditoriums; enemies set on destroying one another laugh at the same jokes and weep at the same catastrophes; some of the richest and most complex English verse ever written migrates with spectacular success into German and Italian, Hindi, Swahili, and Japanese. Is there a single, stable, continuous object that underlies all of these migrations and metamorphoses? Certainly not. The global diffusion and long life of Shakespeare's works depend on their extraordinary malleability, their protean capacity to elude definition and escape secure possession. At the same time, they are not without identifiable shared features: across centuries and continents, family resemblances link many of the wildly diverse manifestations of plays such as *Romeo and Juliet, Hamlet,* and *Twelfth Night.* And if there is no clear limit or end point, there is a reasonably clear beginning: the

1

England of the late sixteenth and early seventeenth centuries, when the plays and poems collected in this volume made their first appearance.

An art virtually without end or limit but with an identifiable, localized, historical origin: Shakespeare's achievement defies the facile opposition between transcendent and time-bound. It is not necessary to choose between an account of Shakespeare as the scion of a particular culture and an account of him as a universal genius who created works that continually renew themselves across national and generational boundaries. On the contrary: crucial clues to understanding his art's remarkable power to soar beyond its originary time and place lie in the very soil from which that art sprang.

Shakespeare's World

Life and Death

Life expectancy at birth in early modern England was exceedingly low by our standards: under thirty years old, compared with over seventy today. Infant mortality rates were extraordinarily high, and it is estimated that in the poorer parishes of London only about half the children survived to the age of fifteen, while the children of aristocrats fared only a little better. In such circumstances, some parents must have developed a certain detachment—one of Shakespeare's contemporaries writes of losing "some three or four children"—but there are many expressions of intense grief, so that we cannot assume that the frequency of death hardened people to loss or made it routine.

Still, the spectacle of death, along with that other great threshold experience, birth, must have been far more familiar to Shakespeare and his contemporaries than to ourselves. There was no equivalent in early modern England to our hospitals, and most births and deaths occurred at home. Physical means for the alleviation of pain and suffering were extremely limited—alcohol might dull the terror, but it was hardly an effective anesthetic—and medical treatment was generally both expensive and worthless, more likely to intensify suffering than to lead to a cure. This was a world without a concept of antiseptics, with little actual understanding of disease, with few effective ways of treating earaches or venereal disease, let alone the more terrible instances of what Shakespeare calls "the thousand natural shocks that flesh is heir to."

The worst of these shocks was the bubonic plague, which repeatedly ravaged England, and particularly English towns, until the third quarter of the seventeenth century. The plague was terrifyingly sudden in its onset, rapid in its spread, and almost invariably lethal. Physicians were helpless in the face of the epidemic, though they prescribed amulets,

Bill recording plague deaths in London, 1609.

preservatives, and sweet-smelling substances (on the theory that the plague was carried by noxious vapors). In the plague-ridden year of 1564, the year of Shakespeare's birth, some 254 people died in Stratford-upon-Avon, out of a total population of 800. The year before, some 20,000 Londoners are thought to have died; in 1593, almost 15,000; in 1603, 36,000, or over a sixth of the city's inhabitants. The social effects of these horrible visitations were severe: looting, violence, and despair, along with an intensification of the age's perennial poverty, unemployment, and food shortages. The London plague regulations of 1583, reissued with modifications in later epidemics, ordered that the infected and their households be locked in their homes for a month; that the streets be kept clean; that vagrants be expelled; and that funerals and plays be restricted or banned entirely.

The plague, then, had a direct and immediate impact on Shakespeare's own profession. City officials kept records of the weekly number of plague deaths; when these surpassed a certain number, the theaters were peremptorily closed. The basic idea was not only to prevent contagion but also to avoid making an angry God still angrier with the spectacle of idleness. While restricting public assemblies may in fact have slowed the epidemic, other public policies in times of plague, such as killing the cats and dogs, may have made matters worse (since the disease, as we now know, was spread not by these animals but by the fleas that bred on the black rats that infested the poorer neighborhoods). Moreover, the playing companies, driven out of London by the closing of the theaters, may have carried plague to the provincial towns.

Even in good times, when the plague was dormant and the weather favorable for farming, the food supply in England was precarious. A few successive bad harvests, such as occurred in the mid-1590s, could cause serious hardship, even starvation. Not surprisingly, the poor bore the brunt of the burden: inflation, low wages, and rent increases left large numbers of people with very little cushion against disaster. Further, at its best, the diet of most people seems to have been seriously deficient. The lower classes then, as throughout most of history, subsisted on one or two foodstuffs, usually low in protein. The upper classes disdained green vegetables and milk and gorged themselves on meat. Illnesses that we now trace to vitamin deficiencies were rampant. Some, but not much, relief from pain was provided by the beer that Elizabethans, including children, drank almost incessantly. (Home brewing aside, enough beer was sold in England for every man, woman, and child to have consumed 40 gallons a year.)

Wealth

Despite rampant disease, the population of England in Shakespeare's lifetime was steadily growing, from approximately 3,060,000 in 1564 to 4,060,000 in 1600 and 4,510,000 in 1616. Though the death rate was more than twice what it is in England today, the birthrate was almost three times the current figure. London's population in particular soared, from 60,000 in 1520 to 120,000 in 1550, 200,000 in 1600, and 375,000 half a century later, making it the largest and fastest-growing city not only in England but in all of Europe. Every year in the first half of the seventeenth century, about 10,000 people migrated to London from other parts of England—wages in London tended to be around 50 percent higher than in the rest of the country—and it is estimated that one in eight English people lived in London at some point in their lives. The economic viability of Shakespeare's profession was closely linked to this extraordinary demographic boom: between 1567 and 1642, a theater historian has calculated, the London playhouses were paid close to 50 million visits.

As these visits to the theater indicate, in the capital city and elsewhere a substantial number of English men and women, despite hardships that were never very distant, had money to spend. After the disorder and dynastic wars of the fifteenth century, England in the sixteenth and early seventeenth centuries was for the most part a nation at peace, and with peace came a measure of enterprise and prosperity: the landowning classes busied themselves building great houses, planting orchards and hop gardens, draining marshlands, bringing untilled "wastes" under cultivation. The artisans and laborers who actually accomplished these tasks, although they were generally paid very little, often managed to accumulate something, as did the small freeholding farmers, the yeomen, who are repeatedly celebrated in the period as the backbone of English national independence and well-being. William Harrison's *Description of England* (1577) lovingly itemizes the yeoman's precious possessions: "fair garnish of pewter on his cupboard, with so much more odd vessel going about the house, three or four featherbeds, so many coverlets and carpets of tapestry, a silver salt[cellar], a bowl for wine (if not a whole nest) and a dozen of spoons." There are comparable accounts of the hard-earned acquisitions of the city dwellers—masters and apprentices in small workshops, shipbuilders, wool merchants, clothmakers, chandlers, tradesmen, shopkeepers, along with lawyers, apothecaries, schoolteachers, scriveners, and the like—whose pennies from time to time enriched the coffers of the players.

The chief source of England's wealth in the sixteenth century was its textile industry, an industry that depended on a steady supply of wool. In *The Winter's Tale*, Shakespeare provides a warm, richly comic portrayal of a rural sheepshearing festival, but the increasingly intensive production of wool had in reality its grim side. When a character in Thomas More's *Utopia* (1516) complains that "the sheep are eating the people," he is referring to the practice of enclosure: throughout the sixteenth and early seventeenth centuries, many acres of croplands once farmed in common by rural communities were enclosed with fences by wealthy landowners and turned into pasturage. The ensuing misery, displacement, and food shortages led to repeated riots, some of them violent and bloody, along with a series of government proclamations, but the process of enclosure was not reversed.

The economic stakes were high, and not only for the domestic market. In 1565, woolen cloth alone made up more than three-fourths of England's exports. (The remainder consisted mostly of other textiles and raw wool, with some trade in lead, tin, grain, and skins.) The Company of Merchant Adventurers carried cloth to distant ports on the Baltic and Mediterranean, establishing links with Russia and Morocco (each took about 2 percent of London's cloth in 1597–98). English lead and tin, as well as fabrics, were sold in Tuscany and Turkey, and merchants found a market for Newcastle coal on the island of Malta. In the latter half of the century, London, which handled more than 85 percent of all exports, regularly shipped abroad more than 100,000 woolen cloths a year at a value of at least £750,000. This figure does not include the increasingly important and profitable trade in so-called New Draperies, including textiles that went by such exotic names as bombazines, calamancoes, damazellas, damizes, mockadoes, and virgenatoes. When the Earl of Kent in *King Lear* insults Oswald as a "filthy worsted-stocking knave" (2.2.14–15) or when the aristocratic Biron in *Love's Labour's Lost* declares that he will give up "taffeta phrases, silken terms precise, / Three-piled hyperboles" and woo henceforth "in russet yeas, and honest kersey noes" (5.2.406–07, 413), Shakespeare is assuming that a substantial portion of his audience will be alert to the social significance of fabric.

There is amusing confirmation of this alertness from an unexpected source: the report of a visit made to the Fortune playhouse in London in 1614 by a foreigner, Father Orazio Busino, the chaplain of the Venetian embassy. Father Busino neglected to mention the name of the play he saw, but like many foreigners, he was powerfully struck by the presence of gorgeously dressed women in the audience. In Venice, there was a special gallery for courtesans, but socially respectable women would not have been permitted to attend plays, as they could in England. In London, not only could middle- and upper-class women go to the theater, but they could also wear masks and mingle freely with male spectators and women of ill repute. The bemused cleric was uncertain about the ambiguous social situation in which he found himself:

> These theatres are frequented by a number of respectable and handsome ladies, who come freely and seat themselves among the men without the slightest hesitation. On the evening in question his Excellency and the Secretary were pleased to play me a trick by placing me amongst a bevy of young women. Scarcely was I seated ere a very

elegant dame, but in a mask, came and placed herself beside me. . . . She asked me for my address both in French and English; and, on my turning a deaf ear, she determined to honour me by showing me some fine diamonds on her fingers, repeatedly taking off not fewer than three gloves, which were worn one over the other. . . . This lady's bodice was of yellow satin richly embroidered, her petticoat of gold tissue with stripes, her robe of red velvet with a raised pile, lined with yellow muslin with broad stripes of pure gold. She wore an apron of point lace of various patterns: her head-tire was highly perfumed, and the collar of white satin beneath the delicately-wrought ruff struck me as extremely pretty.

Father Busino may have turned a deaf ear on this "elegant dame" but not a blind eye: his description of her dress is worthy of a fashion designer and conveys something of the virtual clothes cult that prevailed in England in the late sixteenth and early seventeenth centuries, a cult whose major shrine, outside the royal court, was the theater.

Imports, Patents, and Monopolies

England produced some luxury goods, but the clothing on the backs of the most fashionable theatergoers was likely to have come from abroad. By the late sixteenth century, the English were importing substantial quantities of silks, satins, velvets, embroidery, gold and silver lace, and other costly items to satisfy the extravagant tastes of the elite and of those who aspired to dress like the elite. The government tried to put a check on the sartorial ambitions of the upwardly mobile by passing sumptuary laws—that is, laws restricting to the ranks of the aristocracy the right to wear certain of the most precious fabrics. But the very existence of these laws, in practice almost impossible to enforce, only reveals the scope and significance of the perceived problem.

Sumptuary laws were in part a conservative attempt to protect the existing social order from upstarts. Social mobility was not widely viewed as a positive virtue, and moralists repeatedly urged people to stay in their place. Conspicuous consumption that was tolerated, even admired, in the aristocratic elite was denounced as sinful and monstrous in less exalted social circles. English authorities were also deeply concerned throughout the period about the effects of a taste for luxury goods on the balance of trade. One of the principal English imports was wine: the "sherris" whose virtues Falstaff extols in 2 Henry IV came from Xeres in Spain; the malmsey in which poor Clarence is drowned in Richard III was probably made in Greece or in the Canary Islands (from whence came Sir Toby Belch's "cup of canary" in Twelfth Night); and the "flagon of rhenish" that Yorick in Hamlet had once poured on the Gravedigger's head came from the Rhine region of Germany. Other imports included canvas, linen, fish, olive oil, sugar, molasses, dates, oranges and lemons, figs, raisins, almonds, capers, indigo, ostrich feathers, and that increasingly popular drug from the New World, tobacco.

Joint-stock companies were established to import goods for the burgeoning English market. The Merchant Venturers of the city of Bristol (established in 1552) handled great shipments of Spanish sack, the light, dry wine that largely displaced the vintages of Bordeaux and Burgundy when trade with France was disrupted by war. The Muscovy Company (established in 1555) traded English cloth and manufactured goods for Russian furs, oil, and beeswax. The Venice Company and the Turkey Company—uniting in 1593 to form the wealthy Levant Company—brought silk and spices home from Aleppo and carpets from Istanbul. The East India Company (founded in 1600), with its agent at Bantam in Java, brought pepper, cloves, nutmeg, and other spices from east Asia, along with indigo, cotton textiles, sugar, and saltpeter from India. English privateers "imported" American products, especially sugar, fish, and hides, in huge quantities, along with more precious cargoes. In 1592, a privateering expedition principally funded by Sir Walter Ralegh captured a huge Portuguese carrack (sailing ship), the Madre de Dios, in the Azores and brought it back to Dartmouth. The ship, the largest that had ever entered any English port, held 536 tons of pepper, cloves, cinnamon, cochineal, mace, civet, musk, ambergris,

Cannoneer. From *Edward Webbe, . . . His Travailes* (1590).

and nutmeg, as well as jewels, gold, ebony, carpets, and silks. Before order could be established, the English seamen began to pillage this immensely rich prize, and witnesses said they could smell the spices on all the streets around the harbor. Such piratical expeditions were rarely officially sanctioned by the state, but the queen had in fact privately invested £1,800, for which she received about £80,000.

In the years of war with Spain, 1586–1604, the goods captured by the privateers annually amounted to 10 to 15 percent of the total value of England's imports. But organized theft alone could not solve England's balance-of-trade problems. Statesmen were particularly worried that the nation's natural wealth was slipping away in exchange for unnecessary things. In his *Discourse of the Commonweal* (1549), the prominent humanist Sir Thomas Smith exclaims against the importation of such trifles as mirrors, paper, laces, gloves, pins, inkhorns, tennis balls, puppets, and playing cards. And more than a century later, the same fear that England was trading its riches for trifles and wasting away in idleness was expressed by the Bristol merchant John Cary. The solution, Cary argues in "An Essay on the State of England in Relation to Its Trade" (1695), is to expand productive domestic employment. "People are or may be the Wealth of a Nation," he writes, "yet it must be where you find Employment for them, else they are a Burden to it, as the Idle Drone is maintained by the Industry of the laborious Bee, so are all those who live by their Dependence on others, as Players, Ale-House Keepers, Common Fiddlers, and such like, but more particularly Beggars, who never set themselves to work."

Stage players, all too typically associated here with vagabonds and other idle drones, could have replied in their defense that they not only labored in their vocation but also exported their skills abroad: English acting companies routinely traveled overseas and performed as far away as Bohemia. But their labor was not regarded as a productive contribution to the national wealth, and plays were in truth no solution to the trade imbalances that worried authorities.

The government attempted to stem the flow of gold overseas by establishing a patent system initially designed to encourage skilled foreigners to settle in England by granting them exclusive rights to produce particular wares by a patented method. Patents were granted for such things as the making of hard white soap (1561), ovens and furnaces (1563), window glass (1567), sailcloths (1574), drinking glasses (1574), sulphur, brimstone, and oil (1577), armor and horse harness (1587), starch (1588), white writing paper made from rags (1589), aqua vitae and vinegar (1594), playing cards (1598), and mathematical instruments (1598).

Although their ostensible purpose was to increase the wealth of England, encourage technical innovation, and provide employment for the poor, the effect of patents was often the enrichment of a few and the hounding of poor competitors by wealthy monopolists, a group that soon extended well beyond foreign-born entrepreneurs to the favorites of the monarch who vied for the huge profits to be made. "If I had a monopoly out" on folly, the Fool in *King Lear* protests, glancing at the "lords and great men" around him, "they would have part on't." The passage appears only in the quarto version of the play (*History of King Lear* 4.135–36); it may have been cut for political reasons from the Folio. For the issue of monopolies provoked bitter criticism and parliamentary debate for decades. In 1601, Elizabeth was prevailed upon to revoke a number of the most hated monopolies, including aqua vitae and vinegar, bottles, brushes, fish livers, the coarse sailcloth known as poldavis and mildernix, pots, salt, and starch. The whole system was revoked during the reign of James I by an act of Parliament.

Haves and Have-Nots

When in the 1560s Elizabeth's ambassador to France, the humanist Sir Thomas Smith, wrote a description of England, he saw the commonwealth as divided into four sorts of people: "gentlemen, citizens, yeomen artificers, and laborers." At the forefront of the class of gentlemen was the monarch, followed by a very small group of nobles—dukes, marquesses, earls, viscounts, and barons—who either inherited their exalted titles, as the eldest male heirs of their families, or were granted them by the monarch. Under Elizabeth, this aristocratic peerage numbered between 50 and 60 individuals; James's promotions increased the number to nearer 130. Strictly speaking, Smith notes, the younger sons of the nobility were only entitled to be called "esquires," but in common speech they were also called "lords."

Below this tiny cadre of aristocrats in the social hierarchy of gentry were the knights, a title of honor conferred by the monarch, and below them were the "simple gentlemen." Who was a gentleman? According to Smith, "whoever studieth the laws of the realm, who studieth in the universities, who professeth liberal sciences, and to be short, who can live idly and without manual labor, and will bear the port, charge and countenance of a gentleman, he shall be called master . . . and shall be taken for a gentleman." To "live idly and without manual labor": where in Spain, for example, the crucial mark of a gentleman was "blood," in England it was "idleness," in the sense of sufficient income to afford an education and to maintain a social position without having to work with one's hands.

For Smith, the class of gentlemen was far and away the most important in the kingdom. Below were two groups that had at least some social standing and claim to authority: the citizens, or burgesses, those who held positions of importance and responsibility in their cities, and yeomen, farmers with land and a measure of economic independence. At the bottom of the social order was what Smith calls "the fourth sort of men which do not rule." The great mass of ordinary people have, Smith writes, "no voice nor authority in our commonwealth, and no account is made of them but only to be ruled." Still, even they can bear some responsibility, he notes, since they serve on juries and are named to such positions as churchwarden and constable.

In everyday practice, as modern social historians have observed, the English tended to divide the population not into four distinct classes but into two: a very small empowered group—the "richer" or "wiser" or "better" sort—and all the rest who were without much social standing or power, the "poorer" or "ruder" or "meaner" sort. References to the "middle sort of people" remain relatively rare until after Shakespeare's lifetime; these people are absorbed into the rulers or the ruled, depending on speaker and context.

The source of wealth for most of the ruling class, and the essential measure of social status, was landownership, and changes to the social structure in the sixteenth and seventeenth centuries were largely driven by the land market. The property that passed into private hands as the Tudors and early Stuarts sold off confiscated monastic estates and then their own crown lands for ready cash amounted to nearly a quarter of all the land in England. At the same time, the buying and selling of private estates was on the rise throughout the period. Land was bought up not only by established landowners seeking to enlarge their estates but by successful merchants, manufacturers, and urban professionals; even if the taint of vulgar moneymaking lingered around such figures, their heirs would be taken for true gentlemen. The rate of turnover in landownership was great; in many counties, well over half the gentle families in 1640 had appeared since the end of the fifteenth century. The class that Smith called "simple gentlemen" was expanding rapidly: in the fifteenth century, they had held no more than a quarter of the land in the country; but by the later seventeenth century, they controlled almost half. Over the same period, the land held by the great aristocratic magnates held steady at 15 to 20 percent of the total.

Riot and Disorder

London was a violent place in the first half of Shakespeare's career. There were thirty-five riots in the city in the years 1581–1602, twelve of them in the volatile month of June 1595. These included protests against the deeply unpopular lord mayor Sir John Spencer, attempts to release prisoners, anti-alien riots, and incidents of "popular market regulation." There is an unforgettable depiction of a popular uprising in *Coriolanus*, along with many other glimpses in Shakespeare's works, including John Cade's grotesque rebellion in *The First Part of the Contention* (*2 Henry VI*), the plebeian violence in *Julius Caesar*, and Laertes' "riotous head" in *Hamlet*.

The London rioters were mostly drawn from the large mass of poor and discontented apprentices who typically chose as their scapegoats foreigners, prostitutes, and gentlemen's servingmen. Theaters were very often the site of the social confrontations that sparked disorder. For two days running in June 1584, disputes between apprentices and gentlemen triggered riots outside the Curtain Theatre involving up to a thousand participants. On one occasion, a gentleman was said to have exclaimed that "the apprentice was but a rascal, and some there were little better than rogues that took upon them the name of gentlemen, and said the prentices were but the scum of the world." These occasions culminated in attacks by the apprentices on London's law schools, the Inns of Court.

The most notorious and predictable incidents of disorder came on Shrove Tuesday (the Tuesday before the beginning of Lent), a traditional day of misrule when apprentices ran riot. Shrove Tuesday disturbances involved attacks by mobs of young men on the brothels of the South Bank, in the vicinity of the Globe and other public theaters. The city authorities took precautions to keep these disturbances from getting completely out of control but evidently did not regard them as serious threats to public order.

Of much greater concern throughout the Tudor and early Stuart years were the frequent incidents of rural rioting against the enclosure of commons and wasteland by local landlords (and, in the royal forests, by the crown). This form of popular protest was at its height during Shakespeare's career: in the years 1590–1610, the frequency of anti-enclosure rioting doubled from what it had been earlier in Elizabeth's reign.

Although they often became violent, anti-enclosure riots were usually directed not against individuals but against property. Villagers—sometimes several hundred, often

fewer than a dozen—gathered to tear down newly planted hedges. The event often took place in a carnival atmosphere, with songs and drinking, that did not prevent the participants from acting with a good deal of political canniness and forethought. Especially in the Jacobean period, it was common for participants to establish a common fund for legal defense before commencing their assault on the hedges. Women were frequently involved, and on a number of occasions wives alone participated in the destruction of the enclosure, since there was a widespread, though erroneous, belief that married women acting without the knowledge of their husbands were immune from prosecution. In fact, the powerful Court of Star Chamber consistently ruled that both the wives and their husbands should be punished.

Peddler. From Jost Amman, *The Book of Trades* (1568).

Although Stratford was never the scene of serious rioting, enclosure controversies there turned violent more than once in Shakespeare's lifetime. In January 1601, Shakespeare's friend Richard Quiney and others leveled the hedges of Sir Edward Greville, lord of Stratford manor. Quiney was elected bailiff of Stratford in September of that year but did not live to enjoy the office for long. He died from a blow to the head struck by one of Greville's men in a tavern brawl. Greville, responsible for the administration of justice, neglected to punish the murderer.

There was further violence in January 1615, when William Combe's men threw to the ground two local aldermen who were filling in a ditch by which Combe was enclosing common fields near Stratford. The task of filling in the offending ditch was completed the next day by the women and children of Stratford. Combe's enclosure scheme was eventually stopped in the courts. Although he owned land whose value would have been affected by this controversy, Shakespeare took no active role in it, since he had previously come to a private settlement with the enclosers insuring him against personal loss.

Most incidents of rural rioting were small, localized affairs, and with good reason: when confined to the village community, riot was a misdemeanor; when it spread outward to include multiple communities, it became treason, punishable by death. The greatest of the anti-enclosure riots, those in which hundreds of individuals from a large area participated, commonly took place on the eve of full-scale regional rebellions. The largest of these disturbances, Kett's Rebellion, involved some 16,000 peasants, artisans, and townspeople who rose up in 1549 under the leadership of a Norfolk tanner and landowner, Robert Kett, to protest economic exploitation. The agrarian revolts in Shakespeare's lifetime were on a much smaller scale. In the abortive Oxfordshire Rebellion of 1596, a carpenter named Bartholomew Steere attempted to organize a rising against enclosing gentlemen. The optimistic Steere promised his followers that "it was but a month's work to overrun England" and informed them "that the commons long since in Spain did rise and kill all gentlemen . . . and since that time have lived merrily there." Steere expected several hundred men to join him on Enslow Hill on November 21, 1596, for the start of the rising; no more than twenty showed up. They were captured, imprisoned, and tortured. Several were executed, but Steere apparently cheated the hangman by dying in prison.

Rebellions, most often triggered by hunger and oppression, continued into the reign of James I. The Midland Revolt of 1607, which may be reflected in *Coriolanus,* consisted of a string of agrarian risings in the counties of Northamptonshire, Warwickshire, and Leicestershire, involving assemblies of up to 5,000 rebels in various places. The best known of their leaders was John Reynolds, called "Captain Powch" because of the pouch he wore, whose magical contents were supposed to defend the rebels from harm. (According to the chronicler Edmund Howes, when Reynolds was captured and the pouch opened, it contained "only a piece of green cheese.") The rebels, who were called by themselves and others both "Levelers" and "Diggers," insisted that they had no quarrel with the king but only sought an end to injurious enclosures. But Robert Wilkinson, who preached a sermon against the leaders at their trial, credited them with the intention to "level all states as they leveled banks and ditches." Most of the rebels got off relatively lightly, but, along with other ringleaders, Captain Powch was executed.

The Legal Status of Women

Even though England was ruled for over forty years by a powerful woman, the great majority of women in the kingdom had very restricted social, economic, and legal standing. To be sure, a tiny number of influential aristocratic women, such as the formidable Countess of Shrewsbury, Bess of Hardwick, wielded considerable power. But, these rare exceptions aside, women were denied any rightful claim to institutional authority or personal autonomy. When Sir Thomas Smith thinks of how he should describe his country's social order, he declares that "we do reject women, as those whom nature hath made to keep home and to nourish their family and children, and not to meddle with matters abroad, nor to bear office in a city or commonwealth."

Then, with a kind of glance over his shoulder, he makes an exception of those few for whom "the blood is respected, not the age nor the sex": for example, the queen.

English women were not under the full range of crushing constraints that afflicted women in some countries in Europe. Foreign visitors were struck by their relative freedom, as shown, for example, by the fact that respectable women could venture unchaperoned into the streets and attend the theater. Single women, whether widowed or unmarried, could, if they were of full age, inherit and administer land, make a will, sign a contract, possess property, sue and be sued, without a male guardian or proxy. But married women had no such rights under the common law.

Early modern writings about women and the family constantly return to a political model of domination and submission, in which the father justly rules over wife and children as the monarch rules over the state. This conception of a woman's role conveniently ignores the fact that a *majority* of the adult women at any time in Shakespeare's England were not married. They were either widows or spinsters (a term that was not yet pejorative), and thus for the most part managing their own affairs. Even within marriage, women typically had more control over certain spheres than moralizing writers on the family cared to admit. For example, village wives oversaw the production of eggs, cheese, and beer, and sold these goods in the market. As seamstresses, pawnbrokers, secondhand clothing dealers, peddlers, and the like—activities not controlled by the all-male guilds—women managed to acquire some economic power of their own, and, of course, they participated as well in the unregulated, black-market economy of the age and in the underworld of thievery and prostitution.

Women were not in practice as bereft of property as, according to English common law, they should have been. Demographic studies indicate that the inheritance system called primogeniture, the orderly transmission of property from father to eldest male heir, was more often an unfulfilled wish than a reality. Some 40 percent of marriages failed to produce a son, and in such circumstances fathers often left their land to their daughters, rather than to brothers, nephews, or male cousins. In many families, the father died before his male heir was old enough to inherit property, leaving the land, at least temporarily, in the hands of the mother. And while they were less likely than their brothers to inherit land ("real property"), daughters normally inherited a substantial share of their father's personal property (cash and movables).

In fact, the legal restrictions upon women, though severe in Shakespeare's time, actually worsened in subsequent decades. The English common law, the system of law based on court decisions rather than on codified written laws, was significantly less egalitarian in its approach to wives and daughters than were alternative legal codes (manorial, civil, and ecclesiastical) still in place in the late sixteenth century. The eventual triumph of common law stripped women of many traditional rights, slowly driving them out of economically productive trades and businesses.

Limited though it was, the economic freedom of Elizabethan and Jacobean women far exceeded their political and social freedom—the opportunity to receive a grammar-school or university education, to hold office in church or state, to have a voice in public debates, or even simply to speak their mind fully and openly in ordinary conversation. Women who asserted their views too vigorously risked being perceived as shrewish and labeled "scolds." Both urban and rural communities had a horror of scolds. In the Elizabethan period, such women came to be regarded as a threat to public order, to be dealt with by the local authorities. The preferred methods of correction included public humiliation—of the sort Katherine endures in *The Taming of the Shrew*—and such physical abuse as slapping, bridling, and soaking by means of a contraption called the "cucking stool" (or "ducking stool"). This latter punishment originated in the Middle Ages, but its use spread in the sixteenth century, when it became almost exclusively a punishment for women. From 1560 onward, cucking stools were built or renovated in many English provincial towns; between 1560 and 1600, the contraptions were installed by rivers or ponds in Norwich, Bridport, Shrewsbury, Kingston-upon-Thames, Marlborough, Devizes, Clitheroe, Thornbury, and Great Yarmouth.

Such punishment was usually intensified by a procession through the town to the sound of "rough music," the banging together of pots and pans. The same cruel festivity accompanied the "carting" or "riding" of those accused of being whores. In some parts of the country, villagers also took the law into their own hands, publicly shaming women who married men much younger than themselves or who beat or otherwise domineered over their husbands. One characteristic form of these charivaris, or rituals of shaming, was known in the West Country as the Skimmington Ride. Villagers would rouse the offending couple from bed with rough music and stage a raucous pageant in which a man, holding a distaff, would ride backward on a donkey, while his "wife" (another man dressed as a woman) struck him with a ladle. In these cases, the collective ridicule and indignation was evidently directed at least as much at the henpecked husband as at his transgressive wife.

Women and Print

Books published for a female audience surged in popularity in the late sixteenth century, reflecting an increase in female literacy. (It is striking how many of Shakespeare's women are shown reading.) This increase is probably linked to a Protestant longing for direct access to the Scriptures, and the new books marketed specifically for women included devotional manuals and works of religious instruction. But there were also practical guides to such subjects as female education (for example, Giovanni Bruto's *Necessarie, Fit, and Convenient Education of a Young Gentlewoman,* 1598), midwifery (James Guillemeau's *Child-birth; or, The Happy Delivery of Women,* 1612), needlework (Federico di Vinciolo's *New and Singular Patterns and Workes of Linnen,* 1591), cooking (Thomas Dawson's *The Good Husewifes Jewell,* 1587), gardening (Pierre Erondelle's *The French Garden for English Ladyes and Gentlewomen to Walke In,* 1605), and married life (Patrick Hannay's *A Happy Husband; or, Directions for a Maide to Choose Her Mate,* 1619). As the authors' names suggest, many of these works were translations, and almost all were written by men.

Starting in the 1570s, writers and their publishers increasingly addressed works of recreational literature (romance, fiction, and poetry) partially or even exclusively to women. Some books, such as Robert Greene's *Mamillia, a Mirrour or Looking-Glasse for the Ladies of Englande* (1583), directly specified in the title their desired audience. Others, such as Sir Philip Sidney's influential and popular romance *Arcadia* (1590–93), solicited female readership in their dedicatory epistles. The ranks of Sidney's followers eventually included his own niece, Mary Wroth, whose romance *Urania* was published in 1621.

In the literature of Shakespeare's time, women readers were not only wooed but also frequently railed at, in a continuation of a popular polemical genre that had long inspired heated charges and countercharges. Both sides in the polemic generally agreed that it was the duty of women to be chaste, dutiful, shamefast, and silent; the argument was whether women fulfilled or fell short of this proper role. Ironically, then, a modern reader is more likely to find inspiring accounts of courageous women not in the books written in defense of female virtue but in attacks on those who refused to be silent and obedient.

The most famous English skirmish in this controversy took place in a rash of pamphlets at the end of Shakespeare's life. Joseph Swetnam's crude *Araignment of Lewd, Idle, Froward, and Unconstant Women* (1615) provoked three fierce responses attributed to women: Rachel Speght's *A Mouzell [Muzzle] for Melastomus,* Ester Sowernam's *Ester Hath Hang'd Haman,* and Constantia Munda's *Worming of a Mad Dogge,* all 1617. There was also an anonymous play, *Swetnam, the Woman-hater, Arraigned by Women* (1618), in which Swetnam, depicted as a braggart and a lecher, is put on trial by women and made to recant his misogynistic lies.

Prior to the Swetnam controversy, only one English woman, "Jane Anger," had published a defense of women (*Jane Anger, Her Protection for Women,* 1589). Learned women writers in the sixteenth century tended not to become involved in public debate but rather to undertake a project to which it was difficult for even obdurately chauvinistic

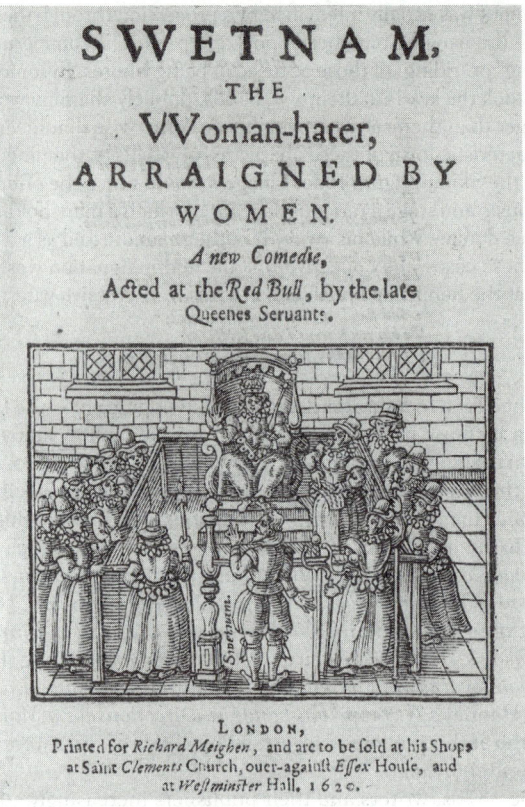

SWETNAM,
THE
Woman-hater,
ARRAIGNED BY
WOMEN.

A new Comedie,

Acted at the *Red Bull*, by the late
Queenes Seruants.

LONDON,
Printed for *Richard Meighen*, and are to be sold at his Shops
at Saint *Clements* Church, ouer-against *Essex* House, and
at *Westminster* Hall. 1 6 2 0.

Title page of *Swetnam, the Woman-hater, Arraigned by Women* (1620), a play written in response to Joseph Swetnam's *The Araignment of Lewd, Idle, Froward and Unconstant Women* (1615); the woodcut depicts the trial of Swetnam in Act 4.

males to object: the translation of devotional literature into English. Thomas More's daughter Margaret More Roper translated Erasmus (*A Devout Treatise upon the Pater Noster*, 1524); Francis Bacon's mother, Anne Cooke Bacon, translated Bishop John Jewel (*An Apologie or Answere in Defence of the Churche of Englande*, 1564); Anne Locke Prowse, a friend of John Knox, translated the *Sermons of John Calvin* in 1560; and Mary Sidney, Countess of Pembroke, completed the metrical version of the Psalms that her brother Sir Philip Sidney had begun. Elizabeth Tudor (the future queen) herself translated, at the age of eleven, Marguerite de Navarre's *Miroir de l'âme pécheresse* (*The Glass of the Sinful Soul*, 1544). The translation was dedicated to her stepmother, Catherine Parr, herself the author of a frequently reprinted book of prayers.

There was in the sixteenth and early seventeenth centuries a social stigma attached to print. Far from celebrating publication, authors, and particularly female authors, often apologized for exposing themselves to the public gaze. Nonetheless, a number of women ventured beyond pious translations circulated in manuscript. Some, including Elizabeth Tyrwhitt, Anne Dowriche, Isabella Whitney, Mary Sidney, and Aemilia Lanyer, composed and published their own poems. Aemilia Lanyer's *Salve Deus Rex Judaeorum*, published in 1611, is a poem in praise of virtuous women, from Eve and the Virgin Mary to her noble patron, the Countess of Cumberland. "A Description of Cookeham," appended to the poem, may be the first English-country-house poem.

The first Tudor woman to translate a play was the learned Jane Lumley, who composed an English version of Euripides' *Iphigenia at Aulis* (c. 1550). The first known original play in English by a woman was by Elizabeth Cary, Viscountess Falkland, whose *Tragedie of Mariam, the Faire Queene of Jewry* was published in 1613. This remarkable play, which was not intended to be performed, includes speeches in defense of women's equality, though the most powerful of these is spoken by the villainous Salome, who schemes to divorce her husband and marry her lover. Cary, who bore eleven children, herself had a deeply troubled marriage, which effectively came to an end in 1625, when, defying her husband's staunchly Protestant family, she openly converted to Catholicism. Her biography was written by one of her four daughters, all of whom became nuns.

Henry VIII and the English Reformation

There had long been serious ideological and institutional tensions in the religious life of England, but officially, at least, England in the early sixteenth century had a single religion, Catholicism, whose acknowledged head was the pope in Rome. In 1517, drawing upon long-standing currents of dissent, Martin Luther, an Augustinian monk and professor of theology at the University of Wittenberg, challenged the authority of the pope and attacked several key doctrines of the Catholic Church. According to Luther, the Church, with its elaborate hierarchical structure centered in Rome, its rich monasteries and convents, and its enormous political influence, had become hopelessly corrupt, a conspiracy of venal priests who manipulated popular superstitions to enrich themselves and amass worldly power. Luther began by vehemently attacking the sale of indulgences—certificates promising the remission of punishments to be suffered in the afterlife by souls sent to purgatory to expiate their sins. These indulgences were a fraud, he argued; purgatory itself had no foundation in the Bible, which in his view was the only legitimate source of religious truth. Christians would be saved not by scrupulously following the ritual practices fostered by the Catholic Church—observing fast days, reciting the ancient Latin prayers, endowing chantries to say prayers for the dead, and so on—but by faith and faith alone.

This challenge, which came to be known as the Reformation, spread and gathered force, especially in northern Europe, where major leaders like the Swiss pastor Huldrych Zwingli and the French theologian John Calvin established institutional structures and elaborated various and sometimes conflicting doctrinal principles. Calvin, whose thought came to be particularly influential in England, emphasized the obligation of governments to implement God's will in the world. He advanced too the doctrine of predestination, by which, as he put it, "God adopts some to hope of life and sentences others to eternal death." God's "secret election" of the saved made Calvin uncomfortable, but his study of the Scriptures had led him to conclude that "only a small number, out of an incalculable multitude, should obtain salvation." It might seem that such a conclusion would lead to passivity or even despair, but for Calvin predestination was a mystery bound up with faith, confidence, and an active engagement in the fashioning of a Christian community.

The Reformation had a direct and powerful impact on those territories, especially in northern Europe, where it gained control. Monasteries were sacked, their possessions seized by princes or sold off to the highest bidder; the monks and nuns, expelled from their cloisters, were encouraged to break their vows of chastity and find spouses, as Luther and his wife, a former nun, had done. In the great cathedrals and in hundreds of smaller churches and chapels, the elaborate altarpieces, bejeweled crucifixes, crystal reliquaries holding the bones of saints, and venerated statues and paintings were attacked as "idols" and often defaced or destroyed. Protestant congregations continued, for the most part, to celebrate the most sacred Christian ritual, the Eucharist, or Lord's Supper, but they did so in a profoundly different spirit from that of the Catholic Church—more as commemoration than as miracle—and they now prayed not in the ancient liturgical Latin but in the vernacular.

"The Pope as Antichrist riding the Beast of the Apocalypse." From *Fierie Tryall of God's Saints* (1611; author unknown).

The Reformation was at first vigorously resisted in England. Indeed, with the support of his ardently Catholic chancellor, Thomas More, Henry VIII personally wrote (or at least lent his name to) a vehement, often scatological attack on Luther's character and views, an attack for which the pope granted him the honorific title "Defender of the Faith." Protestant writings, including translations of the Scriptures into English, were seized by officials of the church and state and burned. Protestants who made their views known were persecuted, driven to flee the country, or arrested, put on trial, and burned at the stake. But the situation changed drastically and decisively when in 1527 Henry decided to seek a divorce from his first wife, Catherine of Aragon, in order to marry Anne Boleyn.

Catherine had given birth to six children, but since only a daughter, Mary, survived infancy, Henry did not have the son he craved. Then as now, the Catholic Church did not ordinarily grant divorce, but Henry's lawyers argued on technical grounds that the marriage was invalid (and, therefore, by extension, that Mary was illegitimate and hence unable to inherit the throne). Matters of this kind were far less doctrinal than diplomatic: Catherine, the daughter of Ferdinand of Aragon and Isabella of Castile, had powerful allies in Rome, and the pope ruled against Henry's petition for a divorce. A series of momentous events followed, as England lurched away from the Church of Rome. In 1531, Henry charged the entire clergy of England with having usurped royal authority in the administration of canon law (the ecclesiastical law that governed faith, discipline, and morals, including such matters as divorce). Under extreme pressure, including the threat of mass confiscations and imprisonment, the Convocation of the English Clergy begged for pardon, made a donation to the royal coffers of over £100,000, and admitted that the king was "supreme head of the English Church and clergy" (modified by the rider "as far as the law of Christ allows"). On May 15 of the next year, the convocation submitted to the demand that the king be the final arbiter of canon law; on the next day, Thomas More resigned his post.

In 1533, Henry's marriage to Catherine was officially declared null and void, and on June 1 Anne Boleyn was crowned queen (a coronation Shakespeare depicts in his late play *All Is True*). The king was promptly excommunicated by the pope, Clement VII. In the following year, the parliamentary Act of Succession confirmed the effects of the divorce and required an oath from all adult male subjects confirming the new dynastic settlement. Thomas More and John Fisher, Bishop of Rochester, were among the small number who refused. The Act of Supremacy, passed later in the year, formally declared the king to be "Supreme Head of the Church in England" and again required an oath to this effect. In 1535 and 1536, further acts made it treasonous to refuse the oath of royal supremacy or, as More had tried to do, to remain silent. The first victims were three Carthusian monks who rejected the oath—"How could the king, a layman," said one of them, "be Head of the Church of England?"—and in May 1535, they were duly hanged, drawn, and quartered. A few weeks later, Fisher and More were convicted and beheaded. Between 1536 and 1539, the monasteries were suppressed and their vast wealth seized by the crown.

Royal defiance of the authority of Rome was a key element in the Reformation but did not by itself constitute the establishment of Protestantism in England. On the contrary, in the same year that Fisher and More were martyred for their adherence to Roman Catholicism, twenty-five Protestants, members of a sect known as Anabaptists, were burned for heresy on a single day. Through most of his reign, Henry remained an equal-opportunity persecutor, ruthless to Catholics loyal to Rome and hostile to some of those who espoused Reformation ideas, though many of these ideas gradually established themselves on English soil.

Even when Henry was eager to do so, it proved impossible to eradicate Protestantism, as it would later prove impossible for his successors to eradicate Catholicism. In large part this tenacity arose from the passionate, often suicidal heroism of men and women who felt that their souls' salvation depended on the precise character of their Christianity. It arose, too, from a mid-fifteenth-century technological innovation that made it almost impossible to suppress unwelcome ideas: the printing press. Early Protestants quickly grasped that with a few clandestine presses they could defy the Catholic authorities and flood the country with their texts. "How many printing presses there be in the world," wrote the Protestant polemicist John Foxe, "so many blockhouses there be against the high castle" of the pope in Rome, "so that either the pope must abolish knowledge and printing or printing at length will root him out." By the century's end, it was the Catholics who were using the clandestine press to propagate their beliefs in the face of Protestant persecution.

The greatest insurrection of the Tudor age was not over food, taxation, or land but over religion. On Sunday, October 1, 1536, stirred up by their vicar, the traditionalist parishioners of Louth in Lincolnshire, in the north of England, rose up in defiance of the ecclesiastical visitation sent to enforce royal supremacy. The rapidly spreading rebellion, which became known as the Pilgrimage of Grace, was led by the lawyer Robert Aske. The city of Lincoln fell to the rebels on October 6, and though it was soon retaken by royal forces, the rebels seized cities and fortifications throughout Yorkshire, Durham, Northumberland, Cumberland, Westmoreland, and northern Lancashire. Carlisle, Newcastle, and a few castles were all that were left to the king in the north. The Pilgrims soon numbered 40,000, led by some of the region's leading noblemen. The Duke of Norfolk, representing the crown, was forced to negotiate a truce, with a promise to support the rebels' demands that the king restore the monasteries, shore up the regional economy, suppress heresy, and dismiss his evil advisers.

The Pilgrims kept the peace for the rest of 1536, on the naive assumption that their demands would be met. But Henry moved suddenly early in 1537 to impose order and capture the ringleaders; 130 people, including lords, knights, heads of religious houses, and, of course, Robert Aske, were executed.

In 1549, two years after the death of Henry VIII, the west and the north of England were the sites of further unsuccessful risings for the restoration of Catholicism. The Western Rising is striking for its blend of Catholic universalism and intense regionalism among people who did not yet regard themselves as English. One of the rebels' articles, protesting against the imposition of the English Bible and religious service, declares, "We the Cornish men (whereof certain of us understand no English) utterly refuse this new English." The rebels besieged but failed to take the city of Exeter. As with almost all Tudor rebellions, the number of those executed in the aftermath of the failed rising was far greater than those killed in actual hostilities.

Henry VIII's Children: Edward, Mary, and Elizabeth

Upon Henry's death in 1547, his ten-year-old son, Edward VI, came to the throne, with his maternal uncle Edward Seymour named as Lord Protector and Duke of Somerset. Both Edward and his uncle were staunch Protestants, and reformers hastened to transform the English Church accordingly. During Edward's reign, Archbishop Thomas Cranmer formulated the forty-two articles of religion that became the core of Anglican orthodoxy and wrote the first Book of Common Prayer, which was officially adopted in 1549 as the basis of English worship services.

Somerset fell from power in 1549 and was replaced as Lord Protector by John Dudley, later Duke of Northumberland. When Edward fell seriously ill, probably of tuberculosis, Northumberland persuaded him to sign a will depriving his half sisters, Mary (the daughter of Catherine of Aragon) and Elizabeth (the daughter of Anne Boleyn), of their claim to royal succession. The Lord Protector was scheming to have his daughter-in-law, the Protestant Lady Jane Grey, a granddaughter of Henry VII, ascend to the throne. But when Edward died in 1553, Mary marshaled support, quickly secured the crown from Lady Jane (who had been titular queen for nine days), and had Lady Jane executed, along with her husband and Northumberland.

Queen Mary immediately took steps to return her kingdom to Roman Catholicism. Even though she was unable to get Parliament to agree to restore church lands seized under Henry VIII, she restored the Catholic Mass, once again affirmed the authority of the pope, and put down a rebellion that sought to depose her. Seconded by her ardently Catholic husband, Philip II, King of Spain, she initiated a series of religious persecutions that earned her (from her enemies) the name "Bloody Mary." Hundreds of Protestants took refuge abroad in cities such as Calvin's Geneva; almost three hundred less fortunate Protestants were condemned as heretics and burned at the stake.

The Family of Henry VIII: An Allegory of the Tudor Succession. By Lucas de Heere (c. 1572). Henry, in the middle, is flanked by Mary to his right, and Edward and Elizabeth to his left.

Mary died childless in 1558, and her younger half sister Elizabeth became queen. Elizabeth's succession had been by no means assured. For if Protestants regarded Henry VIII's marriage to Catherine as invalid and hence deemed Mary illegitimate, so Catholics regarded his marriage to Anne Boleyn as invalid and deemed Elizabeth illegitimate. Henry VIII himself seemed to support both views, since only three years after divorcing Catherine, he beheaded Anne Boleyn on charges of treason and adultery, and urged Parliament to invalidate the marriage. Moreover, though during her sister's reign Elizabeth outwardly complied with the official Catholic religious observance, Mary and her advisers were deeply suspicious, and the young princess's life was in grave danger. Poised and circumspect, Elizabeth warily evaded the traps that were set for her. As she ascended the throne, her actions were scrutinized for some indication of the country's future course. During her coronation procession, when a girl in an allegorical pageant presented her with a Bible in English translation—banned under Mary's reign—Elizabeth kissed the book, held it up reverently, and laid it to her breast; when the abbot and monks of Westminster Abbey came to greet her in broad daylight with candles (a symbol of Catholic devotion) in their hands, she briskly dismissed them with the telling words "Away with those torches! we can see well enough." England had returned to the Reformation.

Many English men and women, of all classes, remained loyal to the old Catholic faith, but English authorities under Elizabeth moved steadily, if cautiously, toward ensuring at least an outward conformity to the official Protestant settlement. Recusants, those who refused to attend regular Sunday services in their parish churches, were fined heavily. Anyone who wished to receive a university degree, to be ordained as a priest in the Church of England, or to be named as an officer of the state had to swear an oath to the royal supremacy. Commissioners were sent throughout the land to confirm that religious services were following the officially approved liturgy and to investigate any reported backsliding into Catholic practice or, alternatively, any attempts to introduce more radical reforms than the queen and her bishops had chosen to embrace. For the Protestant exiles who streamed back were eager not only to undo the damage Mary had done but to carry the Reformation much further. They sought to dismantle the church hierarchy, to purge the calendar of folk customs deemed pagan and the church service of ritual practices deemed superstitious, to dress the clergy in simple garb, and, at the extreme edge, to smash "idolatrous" statues, crucifixes, and altarpieces. Throughout her long reign, however, Elizabeth herself remained cautiously conservative and determined to hold in check what she regarded as the religious zealotry of Catholics, on the one side, and Puritans, on the other.

Shakespeare's plays tap into the ongoing confessional tensions: "Sometimes," Maria in *Twelfth Night* says of the sober, festivity-hating steward Malvolio, "he is a kind of puritan" (2.3.125). But they tend to avoid the risks of direct engagement: "The dev'l a puritan that he is, or anything constantly," Maria adds a moment later, "but a time-pleaser, an affectioned ass" (2.3.131–32). *The Winter's Tale* features a statue that comes to life—exactly the kind of magical image that Protestant polemicists excoriated as Catholic superstition and idolatry—but the play is set in pre-Christian world of the Delphic oracle. And as if this careful distancing might not be enough, the play's ruler goes out of his way to pronounce the wonder legitimate: "If this be magic, let it be an art / Lawful as eating" (5.3.110–11).

In the space of a single lifetime, England had gone officially from Roman Catholicism, to Catholicism under the supreme headship of the English king, to a guarded Protestantism, to a more radical Protestantism, to a renewed and aggressive Roman Catholicism, and finally to Protestantism again. Each of these shifts was accompanied by danger, persecution, and death. It was enough to make some people wary. Or skeptical. Or extremely agile.

The English Bible

Luther had undertaken a fundamental critique of the Catholic Church's sacramental system, a critique founded on the twin principles of salvation by faith alone (*sola fide*) and the absolute primacy of the Bible (*sola scriptura*). *Sola fide* contrasted faith with "works," by which was meant primarily the whole elaborate system of rituals sanctified, conducted, or directed by the priests. Protestants proposed to modify or reinterpret many of these rituals or, as with the rituals associated with purgatory, to abolish them altogether. *Sola scriptura* required direct lay access to the Bible, which meant in practice the widespread availability of vernacular translations. The Roman Catholic Church had not always and everywhere opposed such translations, but it generally preferred that the populace encounter the Scriptures through the interpretations of the priests, trained to read the Latin translation known as the Vulgate. In times of great conflict, this preference for clerical mediation hardened into outright prohibition of vernacular translation and into persecution and book burning.

Zealous Protestants set out, in the teeth of fierce opposition, to put the Bible into the hands of the laity. A remarkable translation of the New Testament, by an English Lutheran named William Tyndale, was printed on the Continent and smuggled into England in 1525; Tyndale's translation of the Pentateuch, the first five books of the Hebrew Bible, followed in 1530. Many copies of these translations were seized and burned, as was the translator himself, but the printing press made it extremely difficult for authorities to eradicate books for which there was a passionate demand. The English Bible was a force that could not be suppressed, and it became, in its various forms, the single most important book of the sixteenth century.

Tyndale's translation was completed by an associate, Miles Coverdale, whose rendering of the Psalms proved to be particularly influential. Their joint labor was the basis for the Great Bible (1539), the first authorized version of the Bible in English, a copy of which was ordered to be placed in every church in the kingdom. With the accession of Edward VI, many editions of the Bible followed, but the process was sharply reversed when Mary came to the throne in 1553. Along with people condemned as heretics, English Bibles were burned in great bonfires.

Marian persecution was indirectly responsible for what would become the most popular as well as most scholarly English Bible, the translation known as the Geneva Bible, prepared, with extensive, learned, and often fiercely polemical marginal notes, by English exiles in Calvin's Geneva and widely diffused in England after Elizabeth came to the throne. In addition, Elizabethan church authorities ordered a careful revision of the Great Bible, and this version, known as the Bishops' Bible, was the one read in the churches. The success of the Geneva Bible in particular prompted those Elizabethan Catholics who now in turn found themselves in exile to bring out a vernacular translation of their own in order to counter the Protestant readings and glosses. This Catholic translation, known as the Rheims Bible, may have been known to Shakespeare, but he seems to have been far better acquainted with the Geneva Bible, and he would also have repeatedly heard the Bishops' Bible read aloud. Scholars have identified over three hundred references to the Bible in Shakespeare's work; in one version or another, the Scriptures had a powerful impact on his imagination.

A Female Monarch in a Male World

In the last year of Mary's reign, 1558, the Scottish Calvinist minister John Knox thundered against what he called "the monstrous regiment of women." When the Protestant Elizabeth came to the throne the following year, Knox and his religious brethren were less inclined to denounce female rulers, but in England as elsewhere in Europe there remained a widespread conviction that women were unsuited to wield power over men. Many men seem to have regarded the capacity for rational thought as exclusively male; women, they assumed, were led only by their passions. While gentlemen mastered the arts of rhetoric and warfare, gentlewomen were expected to display the virtues of silence and good housekeeping. Among upper-class males, the will to dominate others was acceptable and, indeed, admired; the same will in women was condemned as a grotesque and dangerous aberration.

One of the Armada portraits (c. 1588). Note Elizabeth's hand on the globe.

Apologists for the queen countered these prejudices by appealing to historical precedent and legal theory. History offered inspiring examples of just female rulers, notably Deborah, the biblical prophetess who judged Israel. In the legal sphere, crown lawyers advanced the theory of "the king's two bodies." As England's crowned head, Elizabeth's person was mystically divided between her mortal "body natural" and the immortal "body politic." While the queen's natural body was inevitably subject to the failings of human flesh, the body politic was timeless and perfect. In political terms, therefore, Elizabeth's sex was a matter of no consequence, a thing indifferent.

Elizabeth, who had received a fine humanist education and an extended, dangerous lesson in the art of survival, made it immediately clear that she intended to rule in more than name only. She assembled a group of trustworthy advisers, foremost among them William Cecil (later named Lord Burghley, also known as Burleigh), but she insisted on making many of the crucial decisions herself. Like many Renaissance monarchs, Elizabeth was drawn to the idea of royal absolutism, the theory that ultimate power was properly concentrated in her person and, indeed, that God had appointed her to be His deputy in the kingdom. Opposition to her rule, in this view, was not only a political act but also a kind of impiety, a blasphemous grudging against the will of God. Apologists for absolutism contended that God commands obedience even to manifestly wicked rulers whom He has sent to punish the sinfulness of humankind. Such arguments were routinely made in speeches and political tracts and from the pulpits of churches, where they were incorporated into the *First* and *Second Book of Homilies,* which clergymen were required to read out to their congregations.

In reality, Elizabeth's power was not absolute. The government had a network of spies, informers, and agents provocateurs, but it lacked a standing army, a national police force, an efficient system of communication, and an extensive bureaucracy. Above all, the queen had limited financial resources and needed to turn periodically to an independent and often recalcitrant Parliament, which by long tradition had the sole right to levy taxes and to grant subsidies. Members of the House of Commons were elected from their boroughs, not appointed by the monarch, and although the queen had considerable influence over their decisions, she could by no means dictate policy. Under these constraints, Elizabeth ruled through a combination of adroit political maneuvering and imperious command, all the while enhancing her authority in the eyes of both court and country by means of an extraordinary cult of love.

"We all loved her," Elizabeth's godson Sir John Harington wrote, with just a touch of irony, a few years after the queen's death, "for she said she loved us." Ambassadors, courtiers, and parliamentarians all submitted to Elizabeth's cult of love, in which the queen's gender was transformed from a potential liability into a significant asset. Those who approached her generally did so on their knees and were expected to address her with extravagant compliments fashioned from the period's most passionate love poetry; she in turn spoke, when it suited her to do so, in the language of love poetry. The court moved in an atmosphere of romance, with music, dancing, plays, and the elaborate, fancy-dress entertainments called masques. The queen adorned herself in gorgeous clothes and rich jewels. When she went on one of her summer "progresses," ceremonial journeys through her land, she looked like an exotic, sacred image in a religious cult of love, and her noble hosts virtually bankrupted themselves to lavish upon her the costliest pleasures. England's leading artists, such as the poet Edmund Spenser and the painter Nicholas Hilliard, enlisted themselves in the celebration of Elizabeth's mystery, likening her to the goddesses and queens of mythology: Diana, Astraea, Gloriana. Her cult drew its power from cultural discourses that ranged from the secular (her courtiers could pine for her as a cruel Petrarchan mistress) to the sacred (the veneration that under Catholicism had been due to the Virgin Mary could now be directed toward England's semidivine queen).

There was a sober, even grim, aspect to these poetical fantasies: Elizabeth was brilliant at playing one dangerous faction off another, now turning her gracious smiles on one favorite, now honoring his hated rival, now suddenly looking elsewhere and raising an obscure upstart to royal favor. And when she was disobeyed or when she felt that her prerogatives had been challenged, she was capable of an anger that, as Harington put it, "left no doubtings whose daughter she was." Thus, when Sir Walter Ralegh, one of the queen's glittering favorites, married without her knowledge or consent, he found himself promptly imprisoned in the Tower of London. And when the Protestant polemicist John Stubbs ventured to publish a pamphlet stridently denouncing the queen's proposed marriage to the French Catholic Duke of Alençon, Stubbs and his publisher were arrested and had their right hands chopped off. (After receiving the blow, the now prudent Stubbs lifted his hat with his remaining hand and cried, "God save the Queen!")

The queen's marriage negotiations were a particularly fraught issue. When she came to the throne at twenty-five years old, speculation about a suitable match, already widespread, intensified and remained for decades at a fever pitch, for the stakes were high. If Elizabeth died childless, the Tudor line would come to an end. The nearest heir was her cousin Mary, Queen of Scots, a Catholic whose claim was supported by France and by the papacy, and whose penchant for sexual and political intrigue confirmed the worst fears of English Protestants. The obvious way to avert the nightmare was for Elizabeth to marry and produce an heir, and the pressure upon her to do so was intense.

More than the royal succession hinged on the question of the queen's marriage; Elizabeth's perceived eligibility was a vital factor in the complex machinations of international diplomacy. A dynastic marriage between the Queen of England and a foreign ruler would forge an alliance powerful enough to alter the balance of power in Europe. The English court hosted a steady stream of ambassadors from kings and princes eager to win the hand of the royal maiden, and Elizabeth, who prided herself on speaking fluent French and Italian (and on reading Latin and Greek), played her romantic part with exemplary skill, sighing and spinning the negotiations out for months and even years.

Most probably, she never meant to marry any of her numerous foreign (and domestic) suitors. Such a decisive act would have meant the end of her independence, as well as the end of the marriage game by which she played one power off against another. One day she would seem to be on the verge of accepting a proposal; the next, she would vow never to forsake her virginity. "She is a Princess," the French ambassador remarked, "who can act any part she pleases."

The Kingdom in Danger

Beset by Catholic and Protestant extremists, Elizabeth contrived to forge a moderate compromise that enabled her realm to avert the massacres and civil wars that poisoned France and other countries on the Continent. But menace was never far off, and there were constant fears of conspiracy, rebellion, and assassination. Many of the fears swirled around Mary, Queen of Scots, who had been driven from her own kingdom in 1568 by a powerful faction of rebellious nobles and had taken refuge in England. Her presence, under a kind of house arrest, was the source of intense anxiety and helped generate continual rumors of plots. Some of these plots were real enough, others imaginary, still others traps set in motion by the secret agents of the government's intelligence service under the direction of Sir Francis Walsingham. The situation worsened greatly after the St. Bartholomew's Day Massacre of Protestants (Huguenots) in France (August 24, 1572), after Spanish imperial armies invaded the Netherlands in order to stamp out Protestant rebels, and after the assassination there of Europe's other major Protestant leader, William of Orange (1584).

The queen's life seemed to be in even greater danger after Pope Gregory XIII's proclamation in 1580 that the assassination of the great heretic Elizabeth (who had been excommunicated a decade before) would not constitute a mortal sin. The immediate effect of the proclamation was to make existence more difficult for English Catholics, most of whom were loyal to the queen but who fell under grave suspicion. Suspicion was intensified by the clandestine presence of English Jesuits, trained at seminaries abroad and smuggled back into England to serve the Roman Catholic cause. When Elizabeth's spymaster Walsingham unearthed an assassination plot in the correspondence between the Queen of Scots and the Catholic Anthony Babington, the wretched Mary's fate was sealed. After vacillating, a very reluctant Elizabeth signed the death warrant in February 1587, and her cousin was beheaded.

The long-anticipated military confrontation with Catholic Spain was now unavoidable. Elizabeth learned that Philip II, her former brother in law and onetime suitor, was preparing to send an enormous fleet against her island realm. It was to sail to the Netherlands, where a Spanish army would be waiting to embark and invade England. Barring its way was England's small fleet of well-armed and highly maneuverable fighting vessels, backed up by ships from the merchant navy. The Invincible Armada reached English waters in July 1588, only to be routed in one of the most famous and decisive naval battles in European history. Then, in what many viewed as an act of God on behalf of Protestant England, the Spanish fleet was dispersed and all but destroyed by violent storms.

As England braced itself to withstand the invasion that never came, Elizabeth appeared in person to review a detachment of soldiers assembled at Tilbury. Dressed in a white gown and a silver breastplate, she declared that though some among her councillors had urged her not to appear before a large crowd of armed men, she would never fail to trust the loyalty of her faithful and loving subjects. Nor did she fear the Spanish armies. "I know I have the body of a weak and feeble woman," Elizabeth declared, "but I have the heart and stomach of a king, and of England too." In this celebrated speech, Elizabeth displayed many of her most memorable qualities: her self-consciously histrionic command of grand public occasion, her subtle blending of magniloquent rhetoric and the language of love, her strategic appropriation of traditionally masculine qualities, and her great personal courage. "We princes," she once remarked, "are set on stages in the sight and view of all the world."

The English and Otherness

Shakespeare's London had a large population of resident aliens, mainly artisans and merchants and their families, from Portugal, Italy, Spain, Germany, and, above all, France and the Netherlands. Many of these people were Protestant refugees, and they were accorded some legal and economic protection by the government. But they were not always welcome by the local populace. Throughout the sixteenth century, London was the site of repeated demonstrations and, on occasion, bloody riots against the communities of foreign artisans, who were accused of taking jobs away from Englishmen. There was widespread hostility as well toward the Welsh, the Scots, and especially the Irish, whom the English had for centuries been struggling unsuccessfully to subdue. The kings of England claimed to be rulers of Ireland, but in reality they effectively controlled only a small area known as the Pale, extending north from Dublin. The great majority of the Irish people remained stubbornly Catholic and, despite endlessly reiterated English repression, burning of villages, destruction of crops, and massacres, incorrigibly independent.

Shakespeare's *Henry V* (1598–99) seems to invite the audience to celebrate the conjoined heroism of English, Welsh, Scots, and Irish soldiers all fighting together as a "band of brothers" against the French. But such a way of imagining the national community must be set against the tensions and conflicting interests that often set these brothers at each other's throats. As Shakespeare's King Henry realizes, a feared or hated foreign enemy helps at least to mask these tensions, and, indeed, in the face of the Spanish Armada, even the bitter gulf between Catholic and Protestant Englishmen seemed to narrow significantly. But the patriotic alliance was only temporary.

Another way of partially masking the sharp differences in language, belief, and custom among the peoples of the British Isles was to group these people together in contrast to the Jews. Medieval England's Jewish population, the recurrent object of persecution, extortion, and massacre, had been officially expelled by King Edward I in 1290, but Elizabethan England harbored a tiny number of Jews or Jewish converts to Christianity who were treated with suspicion and hostility. One of these was Elizabeth's own physician, Roderigo Lopez, who was tried in 1594 for an alleged plot to poison the queen. Convicted and condemned to the hideous execution reserved for traitors, Lopez went to his death, in the words of the Elizabethan historian William Camden, "affirming that he loved the Queen as well as he loved Jesus Christ; which coming from a man of the Jewish profession moved no small laughter in the standers-by." It is difficult to gauge the meaning here of the phrase "the Jewish profession," used to describe a man who never, as far as we know, professed Judaism, just as it is difficult to gauge the meaning of the crowd's cruel laughter.

Elizabethans appear to have been fascinated by Jews and Judaism but uncertain whether the terms referred to a people, a foreign nation, a set of strange prac-

A Jewish man poisoning a well. From Pierre Boaistuau, *Certaine Secrete Wonders of Nature* (1569).

tices, a living faith, a defunct religion, a villainous conspiracy, or a messianic inheritance. Protestant Reformers brooded deeply on the Hebraic origins of Christianity; government officials ordered the arrest of those "suspected to be Jews"; villagers paid pennies to itinerant fortune-tellers who claimed to be descended from Abraham or masters of cabalistic mysteries; and London playgoers, perhaps including some who laughed at Lopez on the scaffold, enjoyed the spectacle of the downfall of the wicked Barabas in Christopher Marlowe's *Jew of Malta* (c. 1592) and the forced conversion of Shylock in Shakespeare's *Merchant of Venice* (1596–97). Few if any of Shakespeare's contemporaries would have encountered on English soil Jews who openly practiced their religion, though England probably harbored a small number of so-called Marranos, Spanish or Portuguese Jews who had officially converted to Christianity but secretly continued to observe Jewish practices. Jews were not officially permitted to resettle in England until the middle of the seventeenth century, and even then their legal status was ambiguous.

Shakespeare's England also had a small African population whose skin color was the subject of pseudoscientific speculation and theological debate. Some Elizabethans believed that Africans' blackness resulted from the climate of the regions in which they lived, where, as one traveler put it, they were "so scorched and vexed with the heat of the sun, that in many places they curse it when it riseth." Others held that blackness was a curse inherited from their forefather Chus, the son of Ham, who had, according to Genesis, wickedly exposed the nakedness of the drunken Noah. George Best, a proponent of this theory of inherited skin color, reported that "I myself have seen an Ethiopian as black as coal brought into England, who taking a fair English woman to wife, begat a son in all respects as black as the father was, although England were his native country, and an English woman his mother: whereby it seemeth this blackness proceedeth rather of some natural infection of that man."

As the word "infection" suggests, Elizabethans frequently regarded blackness as a physical defect, though the blacks who lived in England and Scotland throughout the sixteenth century were also treated as exotic curiosities. At his marriage to Anne of Denmark, James I entertained his bride and her family by commanding four naked black youths to dance before him in the snow. (The youths died of exposure shortly afterward.) In 1594, in the festivities celebrating the baptism of James's son, a "Black-Moor" entered pulling an elaborately decorated chariot that was, in the original plan, supposed to be drawn in by a lion. There was a black trumpeter in the courts of Henry VII and Henry VIII, while Elizabeth had at least two black servants, one an entertainer and the other a page. Africans became increasingly popular as servants in aristocratic and gentle households in the last decades of the sixteenth century.

peña, El rey desta tierra es muy poderoso porque es señot de cincuenta y quatro islas muy grādes y en cada vna ōstas ay vn rey z todos son obedientes a el/en las sles islas ay muchas maneras de gētes,

En la india ay vna isla en la qual ay y habitan vna manera de gētes las quales son pequeñas de cuerpo y son de muy maluada natura porque ellas ni

Man with head beneath his shoulders. From a Spanish edition of Sir John Mandeville's *Travels*. See *Othello* 1.3.144–45: "and men whose heads / Do grow beneath their shoulders." Such men were occasionally reported by medieval travelers to the East.

An Indian dance. From Thomas Hariot, *A Briefe and True Report of the New Found Land of Virginia* (1590 ed.).

Some of these Africans were almost certainly slaves, though the legal status of slavery in England was ambiguous. In Cartwright's case (1569), the court ruled "that England was too Pure an Air for Slaves to breathe in," but there is evidence that black slaves were owned in Elizabethan and Jacobean England. Moreover, by the mid-sixteenth century, the English had become involved in the profitable trade that carried African slaves to the New World. In 1562, John Hawkins embarked on his first slaving voyage, transporting some three hundred blacks from the Guinea coast to Hispaniola, where they were sold for £10,000. Elizabeth is reported to have said of this venture that it was "detestable, and would call down the Vengeance of Heaven upon the Undertakers." Nevertheless, she invested in Hawkins's subsequent voyages and loaned him ships.

English men and women of the sixteenth century experienced an unprecedented increase in knowledge of the world beyond their island, for a number of reasons. Religious persecution compelled both Catholics and Protestants to live abroad; wealthy gentlemen (and, in at least a few cases, ladies) traveled in France and Italy to view the famous cultural monuments; merchants published accounts of distant lands such as Turkey, Morocco, and Russia; and military and trading ventures took English ships to still more distant shores. In 1496, a Venetian tradesman living in Bristol, John Cabot, was granted a license by Henry VII to sail on a voyage of exploration; with his son Sebastian, he discovered Newfoundland and Nova Scotia. Remarkable feats of seamanship and reconnaissance soon followed: on his ship the *Golden Hind,* Sir Francis Drake circumnavigated the globe in 1579 and laid claim to California on behalf of the queen; a few years later, a ship commanded by Thomas Cavendish also completed a circumnavigation. Sir Martin Frobisher explored bleak Baffin Island in search of a Northwest Passage to the Orient; Sir John Davis explored the west coast of Greenland and discovered the Falkland Islands off the coast of Argentina; Sir Walter Ralegh ventured up the Orinoco Delta, in what is now Venezuela, in search of the mythical land of El Dorado. Accounts of these and other exploits were collected by a clergyman and promoter of empire, Richard Hakluyt, and published as *The Principal Navigations* (1589; expanded edition 1599).

"To seek new worlds for gold, for praise, for glory," as Ralegh characterized such enterprises, was not for the faint of heart: Drake, Cavendish, Frobisher, and Hawkins all died at sea, as did huge numbers of those who sailed under their command. Elizabethans sensible enough to stay at home could do more than read written accounts of their fellow countrymen's far-reaching voyages. Expeditions brought back native plants (including, most famously, tobacco), animals, cultural artifacts, and, on occasion, samples of the native peoples themselves, most often seized against their will. There were exhibitions in London of a kidnapped Eskimo with his kayak and of Virginians with their canoes. Most of these miserable captives, violently uprooted and vulnerable to European diseases, quickly perished, but even in death they were evidently valuable property: when the English will not give one small coin "to relieve a lame beggar," one of the characters in *The Tempest* wryly remarks, "they will lay out ten to see a dead Indian" (2.2.30–31).

Perhaps most nations learn to define what they are by defining what they are not. This negative self-definition is, in any case, what Elizabethans seemed constantly to be doing, in travel books, sermons, political speeches, civic pageants, public exhibitions, and theatrical spectacles of otherness. The extraordinary variety of these exercises (which include public executions and urban riots, as well as more benign forms of curiosity) suggests that the boundaries of national identity were by no means clear and unequivocal. Even peoples whom English writers routinely, viciously stigmatize as irreducibly alien—Italians, Indians, Turks, and Jews—have a surprising instability in the Elizabethan imagination and may appear for brief, intense moments as powerful models to be admired and emulated before they resume their place as emblems of despised otherness.

James I and the Union of the Crowns

Though under great pressure to do so, the aging Elizabeth steadfastly refused to name her successor. It became increasingly apparent, however, that it would be James Stuart, the son of Mary, Queen of Scots, and by the time Elizabeth's health began to fail, several of her principal advisers, including her chief minister, Robert Cecil, had been for several years in secret correspondence with him in Edinburgh. Crowned King James VI of Scotland in 1567 when he was but one year old, Mary's son had been raised as a Protestant by his powerful guardians, and in 1589 he married a Protestant princess, Anne of Denmark. When Elizabeth died on March 24, 1603, English officials reported that on her deathbed the queen had named James to succeed her.

Upon his accession, James—now styled James VI of Scotland and James I of England—made plain his intention to unite his two kingdoms. As he told Parliament in 1604, "What God hath conjoined then, let no man separate. I am the husband, and all of the whole isle is my lawful wife; I am the head and it is my body; I am the shepherd and it is my flock." But the flock was less perfectly united than James optimistically envisioned: English and Scottish were sharply distinct identities, as were Welsh and Cornish and other peoples who were incorporated, with varying degrees of willingness, into the realm.

Fearing that to change the name of the kingdom would invalidate all laws and institutions established under the name of England, a fear that was partly real and partly a cover for anti-Scots prejudice, Parliament balked at James's desire to be called "King of

Funeral procession of Queen Elizabeth. From a watercolor sketch by an unknown artist (1603).

Great Britain" and resisted the unionist legislation that would have made Great Britain a legal reality. Although the English initially rejoiced at the peaceful transition from Elizabeth to her successor, there was a rising tide of resentment against James's advancement of Scots friends and his creation of new knighthoods. Lower down the social ladder, English and Scots occasionally clashed violently on the streets: in July 1603, James issued a proclamation against Scottish "insolencies," and in April 1604, he ordered the arrest of "swaggerers" waylaying Scots in London. The ensuing years did not bring the amity and docile obedience for which James hoped, and, though the navy now flew the Union Jack, combining the Scottish cross of St. Andrew and the English cross of St. George, the unification of the kingdoms remained throughout his reign an unfulfilled ambition.

Unfulfilled as well were James's lifelong dreams of ruling as an absolute monarch. Crown lawyers throughout Europe had long argued that a King, by virtue of his power to make law, must necessarily be above law. But in England, sovereignty was identified not with the King alone or with the people alone but with the "King in Parliament." Against his absolutist ambitions, James faced the crucial power to raise taxes that was vested not in the monarch but in the elected members of the Parliament. He faced as well a theory of republicanism that traced it roots back to ancient Rome and that prided itself on its steadfast and, if necessary, violent resistance to tyranny. Shakespeare's fascination with monarchy is apparent throughout his work, but in his Roman plays in particular, as well as in his long poem *The Rape of Lucrece*, he manifests an intense imaginative interest in the idea of a republic.

The Jacobean Court

With James as with Elizabeth, the royal court was the center of diplomacy, ambition, intrigue, and an intense jockeying for social position. As always in monarchies, proximity to the king's person was a central mark of favor, so that access to the royal bedchamber was one of the highest aims of the powerful, scheming lords who followed James from his sprawling London palace at Whitehall to the hunting lodges and country estates to which he loved to retreat. A coveted office, in the Jacobean as in the Tudor court, was the Groom of the Stool, the person who supervised the disposal of the king's wastes. The officeholder was close to the king at one of his most exposed and vulnerable moments, and enjoyed the further privilege of sleeping on a pallet at the foot of the royal bed and putting on the royal undershirt. Another, slightly less privileged official, the Gentleman of the Robes, dressed the king in his doublet and outer garments.

The royal lifestyle was increasingly expensive. Unlike Elizabeth, James had to maintain separate households for his queen and for the heir apparent, Prince Henry. (Upon Henry's death at the age of eighteen in 1612, his younger brother, Prince Charles, became heir, eventually succeeding his father in 1625.) James was also extremely generous to his friends, amassing his own huge debts in the course of paying off theirs. As early as 1605, he told his principal adviser that "it is a horror to me to think of the height of my place, the greatness of my debts, and the smallness of my means." This smallness notwithstanding, James continued to lavish gifts upon handsome favorites such as the Earl of Somerset, Robert Carr, and the Duke of Buckingham, George Villiers.

The attachment James formed for these favorites was highly romantic. "God so love me," the king wrote to Buckingham, "as I desire only to live in the world for your sake, and that I had rather live banished in any part of the earth with you than live a sorrowful widow's life without you." Such sentiments, not surprisingly, gave rise to widespread rumors of homosexual activities at court. The rumors are certainly plausible, even though the surviving evidence of same-sex relationships, at court or elsewhere, is extremely difficult to interpret. A statute of 1533 made "the detestable and abominable vice of buggery committed with mankind or beast" a felony punishable by death. (English law declined to recognize or criminalize lesbian acts.) The effect of the draconian laws against buggery and sodomy seems to have been to reduce actual prosecutions to the barest minimum: for the next hundred years, there are no known cases of trials resulting in a death sentence for homosexual activity alone. If the legal record is, therefore, unreliable as an index of the extent of homosexual relations, the literary record (including, most famously, the majority of Shakespeare's sonnets) is equally opaque. Any poetic avowal of male-male love may simply be a formal expression of affection based on classical models, or, alternatively, it may be an expression of passionate physical and spiritual love. The interpretive difficulty is compounded by the absence in the period of any clear reference to a homosexual "identity," even though there are many references to same-sex acts and feelings. What is clear is that male friendships at the court of James and elsewhere were suffused with a potential eroticism, at once delightful and threatening, that subsequent periods policed more anxiously.

In addition to the extravagant expenditures on his favorites, James was also the patron of ever more

James I. By John De Critz the Elder (c. 1606).

Two Young Men. By Crispin van den Broeck (c. 1590).

elaborate feasts and masques. Shakespeare's work provides a small glimpse of these in *The Tempest,* with its exotic banquet and its "majestic vision" of mythological goddesses and dancing nymphs and reapers. The actual Jacobean court masques, designed by the great architect, painter, and engineer Inigo Jones, were spectacular, fantastic, technically ingenious, and staggeringly costly celebrations of regal magnificence. With their exquisite costumes and their elegant blend of music, dancing, and poetry, the masques, generally performed by the noble lords and ladies of the court, were deliberately ephemeral exercises in conspicuous expenditure and consumption: by tradition, at the end of the performance, the private audience would rush forward and tear to pieces the gorgeous scenery. And although masques were enormously sophisticated entertainments, often on rather esoteric allegorical themes, they could on occasion collapse into grotesque excess. In a letter of 1606, Sir John Harington describes a masque in honor of the visiting Danish king in which the participants, no doubt toasting their royal majesties, had had too much to drink. A lady playing the part of the Queen of Sheba attempted to present precious gifts, "but, forgetting the steps arising to the canopy, overset her caskets into his Danish Majesty's lap. . . . His Majesty then got up and would dance with the Queen of Sheba; but he fell down and humbled himself before her, and was carried to an inner chamber and laid on a bed." Meanwhile, Harington writes, the masque continued with a pageant of Faith, Hope, and Charity, but Charity could barely keep her balance, while Hope and Faith "were both sick and spewing in the lower hall." This was, we can hope, not a typical occasion.

While the English seem initially to have welcomed James's free-spending ways as a change from the relative parsimoniousness of Queen Elizabeth, they were dismayed by its consequences. Elizabeth had died owing £400,000. In 1608, the royal debt had risen to £1,400,000 and was increasing by £140,000 a year. The money to pay off this debt, or at least to keep it under control, was raised by various means. These included customs farming (leasing the right to collect customs duties to private individuals); the highly unpopular impositions (duties on the import of nonnecessities, such as spices, silks, and currants); the sale of crown lands; the sale of baronetcies; and appeals to an increasingly grudging and recalcitrant Parliament. In 1614, Parliament demanded an end to impositions before it would relieve the king and was angrily dissolved without completing its business.

James's Religious Policy and the Persecution of Witches

Before his accession to the English throne, the king had made known his view of Puritans, the general name for a variety of Protestant sects that were agitating for a radical reform of the Church, the overthrow of its conservative hierarchy of bishops, and the rejection of a large number of traditional rituals and practices. In a book he wrote, *Basilikon Doron* (1599), James denounced "brainsick and heady preachers" who were prepared "to let King, people, law and all be trod underfoot." Yet he was not entirely unwilling to consider religious reforms. In religion, as in foreign policy, he was above all concerned to maintain peace.

On his way south to claim the throne of England in 1603, James was presented with the Millenary Petition (signed by 1,000 ministers), which urged him as "our physician" to heal the disease of lingering "popish" ceremonies. He responded by calling a conference on the ceremonies of the Church of England, which duly took place at Hampton Court Palace in January 1604. The delegates who spoke for reform were moderates, and there was little in the outcome to satisfy Puritans. Nevertheless, while the Church of England continued to cling to such remnants of the Catholic past as wedding rings, square caps, bishops, and Christmas, the conference did produce some reform in the area of ecclesiastical discipline. It also authorized a new English translation of the Bible, known as the King James Bible, which was printed in 1611, too late to have been extensively used by Shakespeare. Along with Shakespeare's works, the King James Bible has probably had the profoundest influence on the subsequent history of English literature.

Having arranged this compromise, James saw his main task as ensuring conformity. He promulgated the 1604 Canons (the first definitive code of canon law since the Reformation), which required all ministers to subscribe to three articles. The first affirmed royal supremacy; the second confirmed that there was nothing in the Book of Common Prayer "contrary to the Word of God" and required ministers to use only the authorized

The "swimming" of a suspected witch (1615).

services; the third asserted that the central tenets of the Church of England were "agreeable to the Word of God." There were strong objections to the second and third articles from those of Puritan leanings inside and outside the House of Commons. In the end, many ministers refused to conform or subscribe to the articles, but only about 90 of them, or 1 percent of the clergy, were deprived of their livings. In its theology and composition, the Church of England was little changed from what it had been under Elizabeth. In hindsight, what is most striking are the ominous signs of growing religious divisions that would by the 1640s burst forth in civil war and the execution of James's son Charles.

James seems to have taken seriously the official claims to the sacredness of kingship, and he certainly took seriously his own theories of religion and politics, which he had printed for the edification of his people. He was convinced that Satan, perpetually warring against God and His representatives on earth, was continually plotting against him. James thought, moreover, that he possessed special insight into Satan's wicked agents, the witches, and in 1597, while King of Scotland, he published his *Daemonology*, a learned exposition of their malign threat to his godly rule. Hundreds of witches, he believed, were involved in a 1590 conspiracy to kill him by raising storms at sea when he was sailing home from Denmark with his new bride.

In the 1590s, Scotland embarked on a virulent witch craze of the kind that had since the fifteenth century repeatedly afflicted France, Switzerland, and Germany, where many thousands of women (and a much smaller number of men) were caught in a nightmarish web of wild accusations. Tortured into lurid confessions of infant cannibalism, night flying, and sexual intercourse with the devil at huge, orgiastic "witches' Sabbaths," the victims had little chance to defend themselves and were routinely burned at the stake.

In England, too, there were witchcraft prosecutions, but on a much smaller scale and with significant differences in the nature of the accusations and the judicial procedures. Witch trials began in England in the 1540s; statutes against witchcraft were enacted in 1542, 1563, and 1604. English law did not allow judicial torture, stipulated lesser punishments in cases of "white magic," and mandated jury trials. Juries acquitted more than half of the defendants in witchcraft trials; in Essex, where the judicial records are particularly extensive, some 24 percent of those accused were executed, while the remainder of those convicted were pilloried and imprisoned or sentenced and reprieved. The accused were generally charged with *maleficium*, an evil deed—usually harming neighbors, causing destructive storms, or killing farm animals—but not with worshipping Satan.

After 1603, when James came to the English throne, he somewhat moderated his enthusiasm for the judicial murder of witches, for the most part defenseless, poor women resented by their neighbors. Although he did nothing to mitigate the ferocity of the ongoing witch hunts in his native Scotland, he did not try to institute Scottish-style persecutions and trials in his new realm. This relative waning of persecutorial eagerness principally reflects the differences between England and Scotland, but it may also bespeak some small, nascent skepticism on James's part about the quality of evidence brought against the accused and about the reliability of the "confessions" extracted from them. It is sobering to reflect that plays like Shakespeare's *Macbeth* (1606), Thomas Middleton's *Witch* (before 1616), and Thomas Dekker, John Ford, and William Rowley's *Witch of Edmonton* (1621) seem to be less the allies of skepticism than the exploiters of fear.

The Playing Field

Cosmic Spectacles

The first permanent, freestanding public theaters in England date only from Shakespeare's own lifetime: a London playhouse, the Red Lion, is mentioned in 1567, and James Burbage's playhouse, The Theatre, was built in 1576. (The innovative use of these new stages, crucial to a full understanding of Shakespeare's achievement, is, in this volume, the subject of a separate essay by the theater historian Andrew Gurr, pages 79–99.) But it is misleading to identify English drama exclusively with these specially constructed playhouses, for in fact there was a rich and vital theatrical tradition in England stretching back for centuries. Many towns in late medieval England were the sites of annual festivals that mounted elaborate cycles of plays depicting the great biblical stories, from the creation of the world to Christ's Passion and its miraculous aftermath. Most of these plays have been lost, but the surviving cycles, such as those from York, are magnificent and complex works of art. They are sometimes called "mystery plays," either because they were performed by the guilds of various crafts (known as "mysteries") or, more likely, because they represented the mysteries of the faith. The cycles were most often performed on the annual feast day instituted in the early fourteenth century in honor of the Corpus Christi, the sacrament of the Lord's Supper, which is perhaps the greatest of these religious mysteries.

The Feast of Corpus Christi, celebrated on the Thursday following Trinity Sunday, helped give the play cycles their extraordinary cultural resonance, but it also contributed to their downfall. For along with the specifically liturgical plays traditionally performed by religious confraternities and the "saints' plays," which depicted miraculous events in the lives of individual holy men and women, the mystery cycles were closely identified with the Catholic Church. Protestant authorities in the sixteenth century, eager to eradicate all remnants of popular Catholic piety, moved to suppress the annual procession of the Host, with its gorgeous banners, pageant carts, and cycle of visionary plays. In 1548, the Feast of Corpus Christi was abolished. Towns that continued to perform the mysteries were under increasing pressure to abandon them. It is sometimes said that the cycles were already dying out from neglect, but recent research has shown that many towns and their guilds were extremely reluctant to give them up. Desperate offers to strip away any traces of Catholic doctrine and to submit the play scripts to the authorities for their approval met with unbending opposition from the government. In 1576, the courts gave York permission to perform its cycle but only if

> in the said play no pageant be used or set forth wherein the Majesty of God the Father, God the Son, or God the Holy Ghost or the administration of either the Sacraments of baptism or of the Lord's Supper be counterfeited or represented, or anything played which tend to the maintenance of superstition and idolatry or which be contrary to the laws of God . . . or of the realm.

Such "permission" was tantamount to an outright ban. The local officials in the city of Norwich, proud of their St. George and the Dragon play, asked if they could at least parade the dragon costume through the streets, but even this modest request was refused. It is likely that as a young man Shakespeare had seen some of these plays: when Hamlet says of a noisy, strutting theatrical performance that it "out-Herods Herod," he is alluding to the famously bombastic role of Herod of Jewry in the mystery plays. But by the century's end, the cycles were no longer performed.

Early English theater was by no means restricted to these civic and religious festivals. Payments to professional and amateur performers appear in early records of towns and aristocratic households, although the terms—"ministralli," "histriones," "mimi," "lusores," and so forth—are not used with great consistency and make it difficult to distinguish among minstrels, jugglers, stage players, and other entertainers. Performers acted in town halls and the halls of guilds and aristocratic mansions, on scaffolds erected in town squares and marketplaces, on pageant wagons in the streets, and in inn yards. By the fifteenth century and probably earlier, there were organized companies of players traveling under noble patronage. Such companies earned a living providing amusement, while enhancing the prestige of the patron.

A description of a provincial performance in the late sixteenth century, written by one R. Willis, provides a glimpse of what seems to have been the usual procedure:

> In the City of Gloucester the manner is (as I think it is in other like corporations) that when the Players of Interludes come to town, they first attend the Mayor to

Panorama of London, showing two theaters, both
round and both flying flags: a flying flag indicated that
a performance was in progress. The Globe is in the
foreground, and the Beargarden or Hope is to the left.

inform him what nobleman's servant they are, and so to get licence for their public
playing; and if the Mayor like the Actors, or would show respect to their Lord and
Master, he appoints them to play their first play before himself and the Aldermen
and common Council of the City and that is called the Mayor's play, where everyone that will come in without money, the Mayor giving the players a reward as he
thinks fit to show respect unto them.

In addition to their take from this "first play," the players would almost certainly have
supplemented their income by performing in halls and inn yards, where they could pass
the hat after the performance or even on some occasions charge an admission fee. It
was no doubt a precarious existence.

The "Interludes" mentioned in Willis's description of the Gloucester performances
are likely plays that were, in effect, staged dialogues on religious, moral, and political
themes. Such works could, like the mysteries, be associated with Catholicism, but they
were also used in the sixteenth century to convey polemical Protestant messages, and
they reached outside the religious sphere to address secular concerns as well. Henry
Medwall's *Fulgens and Lucrece* (c. 1490–1501), for example, pits a wealthy but dissolute nobleman against a virtuous public servant of humble origins, while John Heywood's *Play of the Weather* (c. 1525–33) stages a debate among social rivals, including
a gentleman, a merchant, a forest ranger, and two millers. The structure of such plays
reflects the training in argumentation that students received in Tudor schools and, in
particular, the sustained practice in examining all sides of a difficult question. Some of
Shakespeare's amazing ability to look at critical issues from multiple perspectives may
be traced back to this practice and the dramatic interludes it helped to inspire.

Another major form of theater that flourished in England in the fifteenth century
and continued on into the sixteenth was the morality play. Like the mysteries, moralities addressed questions of the ultimate fate of the soul. They did so, however, not by
rehearsing scriptural stories but by dramatizing allegories of spiritual struggle. Typically,
a person named Human or Mankind or Youth is faced with a choice between a pious
life in the company of such associates as Mercy, Discretion, and Good Deeds and a dissolute life among riotous companions like Lust or Mischief. Plays like *Mankind* (c.
1465–70) and *Everyman* (c. 1495) show how powerful these unpromising-sounding
dramas could be, in part because of the extraordinary comic vitality of the evil character, or Vice, and in part because of the poignancy and terror of an individual's encounter
with death. Shakespeare clearly grasped this power. The hunchbacked Duke of
Gloucester in *Richard III* gleefully likens himself to "the formal Vice, Iniquity." And

when Othello wavers between Desdemona and Iago (himself a Vice figure), his anguished dilemma echoes the fateful choice repeatedly faced by the troubled, vulnerable protagonists of the moralities.

If such plays sound a bit like sermons, it is because they were. Clerics and actors shared some of the same rhetorical skills. It would be misleading to regard churchgoing and playgoing as comparable entertainments, but in attacking the stage, ministers often seemed to regard the professional players as dangerous rivals. The players themselves were generally too discreet to rise to the challenge; it would have been foolhardy to present the theater as the Church's direct competitor. Yet in its moral intensity and its command of impassioned language, the stage frequently emulates and outdoes the pulpit.

Music and Dance

Playacting took its place alongside other forms of public expression and entertainment as well. Perhaps the most important, from the perspective of the theater, were music and dance, since these were directly and repeatedly incorporated into plays. Many plays, comedies and tragedies alike, include occasions that call upon the characters to dance: hence Beatrice and Benedick join the other masked guests at the dance in *Much Ado About Nothing;* in *Twelfth Night,* the befuddled Sir Andrew, at the instigation of the drunken Sir Toby Belch, displays his skill, such as it is, in capering; Romeo and Juliet first see each other at the Capulet ball; the witches dance in a ring around the hideous caldron and perform an "antic round" to cheer Macbeth's spirits; and, in one of Shakespeare's strangest and most wonderful scenes, the drunken Antony in *Antony and Cleopatra* joins hands with Caesar, Enobarbus, Pompey, and others to dance "the Egyptian Bacchanals."

Moreover, virtually all plays in the period, including Shakespeare's, apparently ended with a dance. Brushing off the theatrical gore and changing their expressions from woe to pleasure, the actors in plays like *Hamlet* and *King Lear* would presumably have received the audience's applause and then bid for a second round of applause by performing a stately pavane or a lively jig. Indeed, jigs, with their comical leaping dance steps often accompanied by scurrilous ballads, became so popular that they drew not only large crowds but also official disapproval. A court order of 1612 complained about the "cutpurses and other lewd and ill-disposed persons" who flocked to the theater at the end of every play to be entertained by "lewd jigs, songs, and dances." The players were warned to suppress these disreputable entertainments on pain of imprisonment.

The displays of dancing onstage clearly reflected a widespread popular interest in dancing outside the walls of the playhouse as well. Renaissance intellectuals conjured up visions of the universe as a great cosmic dance, poets figured relations between men and women in terms of popular dance steps, stern moralists denounced dancing as an incitement to filthy lewdness, and, perhaps as significant, men of all classes evidently spent a great deal of time worrying about how shapely their legs looked in tights and how gracefully they could leap. Shakespeare assumes that his audience will be quite familiar with a variety of dances. "For hear me, Hero," Beatrice tells her friend, "wooing, wedding, and repenting is as a Scotch jig, a measure, and a cinquepace" (2.1.60–61). Her speech dwells on the comparison a bit, teasing out its implications, but it still does not make much sense if you do not already know something about the dances and perhaps occasionally venture to perform them yourself.

Closely linked to dancing and even more central to the stage was music, both instrumental and vocal. In the early sixteenth century, the Reformation had been disastrous for sacred music: many church organs were destroyed, choir schools were closed, the glorious polyphonal liturgies sung in the monasteries were suppressed. But by the latter part of the century, new perspectives were reinvigorating English music. Latin Masses were reset in English, and tunes were written for newly translated, metrical psalms. More important for the theater, styles of secular music were developed that emphasized music's link to humanist eloquence, its ability to heighten and to rival rhetorically powerful texts.

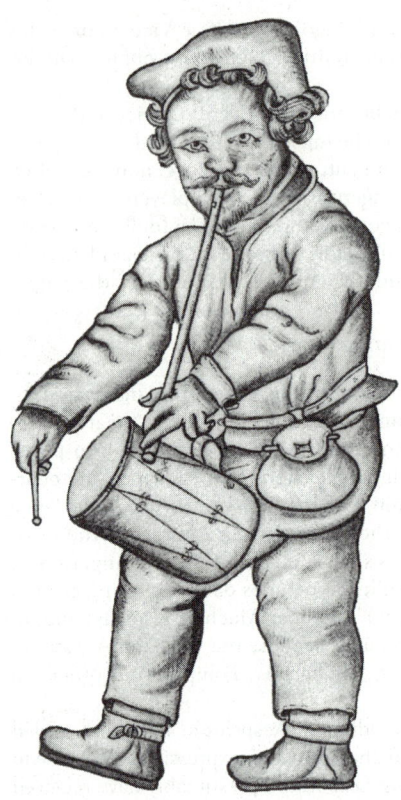

Richard Tarlton. Tarlton was the lead comedian of the Queen's Company from 1583, the year of its founding, until 1588, when he died.

This link is particularly evident in vocal music, at which Elizabethan composers excelled. Renowned composers William Byrd, Thomas Morley, John Dowland, and others wrote a rich profusion of madrigals (part songs for two to eight voices unaccompanied) and ayres (songs for solo voice, generally accompanied by the lute). These works, along with hymns, popular ballads, rounds, catches, and other forms of song, enjoyed immense popularity, not only in the royal court, where musical skill was regarded as an important accomplishment, and in aristocratic households, where professional musicians were employed as entertainers, but also in less exalted social circles. In his *Plaine and Easie Introduction to Practicall Musicke* (1597), Morley tells a story of social humiliation at a failure to perform that suggests that a well-educated Elizabethan was expected to be able to sing at sight. Even if this is an exaggeration in the interest of book sales, there is evidence of impressively widespread musical literacy, reflected in a splendid array of music for the lute, viol, recorder, harp, and virginal, as well as the marvelous vocal music.

Whether it is the aristocratic Orsino luxuriating in the dying fall of an exquisite melody or bully Bottom craving "the tongs and the bones," Shakespeare's characters frequently call for music. They also repeatedly give voice to the age's conviction that there was a deep relation between musical harmony and the harmonies of the well-ordered individual and state. "The man that hath no music in himself," warns Lorenzo in *The Merchant of Venice*, "nor is not moved with concord of sweet sounds, / Is fit for treasons, stratagems, and spoils" (5.1.82–84). This conviction, in turn, reflects a still deeper link between musical harmony and the divinely created harmony of the cosmos. When Ulysses, in *Troilus and Cressida,* wishes to convey the image of universal chaos, he speaks of the untuning of a string (1.3.109).

The playing companies must have regularly employed trained musicians, and many actors (like the actor who in playing Pandarus in *Troilus and Cressida* is supposed to accompany himself on the lute) must have possessed musical skill. Unfortunately, we possess the original settings for very few of Shakespeare's songs, possibly because many of them may have been set to popular tunes of the time that everyone knew and no one bothered to write down.

Alternative Entertainments

Plays, music, and dancing were by no means the only shows in town. There were jousts, tournaments, royal entries, religious processions, pageants in honor of newly installed civic officials or ambassadors arriving from abroad; wedding masques, court masques, and costumed entertainments known as "disguisings" or "mummings"; juggling acts, fortune-tellers, exhibitions of swordsmanship, mountebanks, folk healers, storytellers, magic shows; bearbaiting, bullbaiting, cockfighting, and other blood sports; folk festivals such as Maying, the Feast of Fools, Carnival, and Whitsun Ales. For several years, Elizabethan Londoners were delighted by a trained animal—Banks's Horse—that could, it was thought, do arithmetic and answer questions. And there was always the grim but compelling spectacle of public shaming, mutilation, and execution.

Most English towns had stocks and whipping posts. Drunks, fraudulent merchants, adulterers, and quarrelers could be placed in carts or mounted backward on asses and paraded through the streets for crowds to jeer and throw refuse at. Women accused of being scolds could be publicly muzzled by an iron device called a "brank" or tied to a cucking stool and dunked in the river. Convicted criminals could have their ears cut off, their noses slit, their foreheads branded. Public beheadings (generally reserved for the elite) and hangings were common. In the worst cases, felons were sentenced to be "hanged by the neck, and being alive cut down, and your privy members to be cut off, and your bowels to be taken out of your belly and there burned, you being alive."

Shakespeare occasionally takes note of these alternative entertainments: at the end of *Macbeth,* for example, with his enemies closing in on him, the doomed tyrant declares, "They have tied me to a stake. I cannot fly,/But bear-like I must fight the course" (5.7.1–2). The audience is reminded then that it is witnessing the human equivalent of a popular spectacle—a bear chained to a stake and attacked by fierce dogs—that they could have paid to watch at an arena near the Globe. And when, a few moments later, Macduff enters carrying Macbeth's head, the audience is seeing the theatrical equivalent of the execution of criminals and traitors that they could have also watched in the flesh, as it were, nearby. In a different key, the audiences who paid to see *A Midsummer Night's Dream* or *The Winter's Tale* got to enjoy the comic spectacle of a Maying and a Whitsun Pastoral, while the spectators of *The Tempest* could gawk at what the Folio list of characters calls a "salvage and deformed slave" and to enjoy an aristocratic magician's wedding masque in honor of his daughter.

An Elizabethan hanging.

The Enemies of the Stage

In 1624, a touring company of players arrived in Norwich and requested permission to perform. Permission was denied, but the municipal authorities, "in regard of the honorable respect which this City beareth to the right honorable the Lord Chamberlain," gave the players 20 shillings to get out of town. Throughout the sixteenth and early seventeenth centuries, there are many similar records of civic officials prohibiting performances and then, to appease a powerful patron, paying the actors to take their skills elsewhere. As early as the 1570s, there is evidence that the London authorities, while mindful of the players' influential protectors, were energetically trying to drive the theater out of the city.

Why should what we now regard as one of the undisputed glories of the age have aroused so much hostility? One answer, curiously enough, is traffic: plays drew large audiences—the public theaters could accommodate thousands—and residents objected to the crowds, the noise, and the crush of carriages. Other, more serious concerns were public health and crime. It was thought that numerous diseases, including the dreaded bubonic plague, were spread by noxious odors, and the packed playhouses were obvious breeding grounds for infection. (Patrons often tried to protect themselves by sniffing nosegays or stuffing cloves into their nostrils.) The large crowds drew pickpockets and other scoundrels. On one memorable afternoon, a pickpocket was caught in the act and tied for the duration of the play to one of the posts that held up the canopy above the stage.

Syphilis victim in a tub. Frontispiece to the play *Cornelianum Dolium* (1638), possibly authored by Thomas Randolph. The tub inscription translates as "I sit on the throne of love, I suffer in the tub," and the banner as "Farewell O sexual pleasures and lusts."

The theater was, moreover, a well-known haunt of prostitutes and, it was alleged, a place where innocent maids were seduced and respectable matrons corrupted. It was darkly rumored that "chambers and secret places" adjoined the theater galleries, and in any case, taverns, disreputable inns, and whorehouses were close at hand.

There were other charges as well. Plays were performed in the afternoon and, therefore, drew people, especially the young, away from their work. They were schools of idleness, luring apprentices from their trades, law students from their studies, housewives from their kitchens, and potentially pious souls from the sober meditations to which they might otherwise devote themselves. Wasting their time and money on disreputable shows, citizens exposed themselves to sexual provocation and outright political sedition. Even when the content of plays was morally exemplary—and, of course, few plays were so gratifyingly high-minded—the theater itself, in the eyes of most mayors and aldermen, was inherently disorderly.

The attack on the stage by civic officials was echoed and intensified by many of the age's moralists and religious leaders, especially those associated with Puritanism. While English Protestants earlier in the sixteenth century had attempted to counter the Catholic mystery cycles and saints' plays by mounting their own doctrinally correct dramas, by the century's end a fairly widespread consensus, even among those mildly sympathetic toward the theater, held that the stage and the pulpit were in tension with one another. After 1591, a ban on Sunday performances was strictly enforced, and in 1606, Parliament passed an act imposing a fine of £10 on any person who shall "in any stage-play, interlude, show, May-game, or pageant, jestingly or profanely speak or use the holy name of God, or of Christ Jesus, or of the Holy Ghost, or of the Trinity (which are not to be spoken but with fear and reverence)." If changes in the printed texts are a reliable indication, the players seem to have complied at least to some degree with the ruling. The Folio (1623) text of *Richard III*, for example, omits the Quarto's (1597) four uses of "zounds" (for "God's wounds"), along with a mention of "Christ's dear blood shed for our grievous sins"; "God's my judge" in *The Merchant of Venice* becomes "well I know"; "By Jesu" in *Henry V* becomes a very proper "I say"; and in all the plays, "God" from time to time metamorphoses to "Jove."

But for some of the theater's more extreme critics, these modest expurgations were tiny bandages on a gaping wound. In his huge book *Histriomastix* (1633), William Prynne regurgitates half a century of frenzied attacks on the "sinful, heathenish, lewd, ungodly Spectacles." In the eyes of Prynne and his fellow antitheatricalists, stage plays were part of a demonic tangle of obscene practices proliferating like a cancer in the body of society. It is "manifest to all men's judgments," he writes, that

> effeminate mixed dancing, dicing, stage-plays, lascivious pictures, wanton fashions, face-painting, health-drinking, long hair, love-locks, periwigs, women's curling, powdering and cutting of their hair, bonfires, New-year's gifts, May-games, amorous pastorals, lascivious effeminate music, excessive laughter, luxurious disorderly Christmas-keeping, mummeries . . . [are] wicked, unchristian pastimes.

Given the anxious emphasis on effeminacy, it is not surprising that denunciations of this kind obsessively focused on the use of boy actors to play the female parts. The enemies of the stage charged that theatrical transvestism excited illicit sexual desires, both heterosexual and homosexual.

Since cross-dressing violated a biblical prohibition (Deuteronomy 22:5), religious antitheatricalists attacked it as wicked regardless of its erotic charge; indeed, they often seemed to consider any act of impersonation as inherently wicked. In their view, the theater itself was Satan's domain. Thus a Cambridge scholar, John Greene, reports the sad fate of "a Christian woman" who went to the theater to see a play, "felt, entered in well and sound, but she returned and came forth possessed of the devil. Whereupon certain godly brethren demanded Satan how he durst be so bold, as to enter into her a Christian. Whereto he answered, that *he found her in his own house,* and therefore took possession of her as his own" (italic in original). When the "godly brethren" came to power in the mid-seventeenth century, with the overthrow of Charles I, they saw to it that the playhouses, temporarily shut down in 1642 at the onset of the Civil War, remained closed. The theater did not resume until the restoration of the monarchy in 1660.

Faced with enemies among civic officials and religious leaders, Elizabethan and Jacobean playing companies relied on the protection of their powerful patrons. As the liveried servants of aristocrats or of the monarch, the players could refute the charge that they were mere vagabonds, and they claimed, as a convenient legal fiction, that their public performances were necessary rehearsals in anticipation of those occasions when they would be called upon to entertain their noble masters. But harassment by the mayor and aldermen continued unabated, and the players were forced to build their theaters outside the immediate jurisdiction of the city authorities, either in the suburbs or in the areas known as the "liberties." A liberty was a piece of land within the City of London itself that was not directly subject to the authority of the lord mayor. The most significant of these from the point of view of the theater was the area near St. Paul's Cathedral called "the Blackfriars," where, until the dissolution of the monasteries in 1538, there had been a

Dominican monastery. It was here that in 1608 Shakespeare's company, then called the King's Men, built the indoor playhouse in which they performed during the winter months, reserving the open-air Globe in the suburb of Southwark for their summer performances.

Censorship and Regulation

In addition to those authorities who campaigned to shut down the theater, there were others whose task was to oversee, regulate, and censor it. Given the outright hostility of the former, the latter may have seemed to the London players equivocal allies rather than enemies. After all, plays that passed the censor were at least licensed to be performed and hence conceded to have some limited legitimacy. In April 1559, at the very start of her reign, Queen Elizabeth drafted a proposal that for the first time envisaged a system for the prior review and regulation of plays throughout her kingdom:

> The Queen's Majesty doth straightly forbid all manner interludes to be played either openly or privately, except the same be notified beforehand, and licensed within any city or town corporate, by the mayor or other chief officers of the same, and within any shire, by such as shall be lieutenants for the Queen's Majesty in the same shire, or by two of the Justices of Peace inhabiting within that part of the shire where any shall be played. . . . And for instruction to every of the said officers, her Majesty doth likewise charge every of them, as they will answer: that they permit none to be played wherein either matters of religion or of the governance of the estate of the commonweal shall be handled or treated upon, but by men of authority, learning and wisdom, nor to be handled before any audience, but of grave and discreet persons.

This proposal, which may not have been formally enacted, makes an important distinction between those who are entitled to address sensitive issues of religion and politics—authors "of authority, learning and wisdom" addressing audiences "of grave and discreet persons"—and those who are forbidden to do so.

The London public theater, with its playwrights who were the sons of glovers, shoemakers, and bricklayers and its audiences in which the privileged classes mingled with rowdy apprentices, masked women, and servants, was clearly not a place to which the government wished to grant freedom of expression. In 1581, the Master of the Revels, an official in the lord chamberlain's department whose role had hitherto been to provide entertainment at court, was given an expanded commission. Sir Edmund Tilney, the functionary who held the office, was authorized

> to warn, command, and appoint in all places within this our Realm of England, as well within franchises and liberties as without, all and every player or players with their playmakers, either belonging to any nobleman or otherwise . . . to appear before him with all such plays, tragedies, comedies, or shows as they shall in readiness or mean to set forth, and them to recite before our said Servant or his sufficient deputy, whom we ordain, appoint, and authorize by these presents of all such shows, plays, players, and playmakers, together with their playing places, to order and reform, authorize and put down, as shall be thought meet or unmeet unto himself or his said deputy in that behalf.

What emerged from this commission was in effect a national system of regulation and censorship. One of its consequences was to restrict virtually all licensed theater to the handful of authorized London-based playing companies. These companies would have to submit their plays for official scrutiny, but in return they received implicit, and on occasion explicit, protection against the continued fierce opposition of the local authorities. Plays reviewed and allowed by the Master of the Revels had been deemed fit to be performed before the monarch; how could mere aldermen legitimately claim that such plays should be banned as seditious?

The key question, of course, is how carefully the Master of the Revels scrutinized the plays brought before him either to hear or, more often from the 1590s onward, to peruse. What was Tilney, who served in the office until his death in 1610, or his successor, Sir George Buc, who served from 1610 to 1621, looking for? What did they insist be cut before they would release what was known as the "allowed copy," the only version licensed for performance? Unfortunately, the office books of the Master of the Revels in Shakespeare's time have been lost; what survives is a handful of scripts on which Tilney, Buc, and their assistants jotted their instructions. These suggest that the readings were rather painstaking, with careful attention paid to possible religious, political, and diplomatic repercussions. References, directly or strongly implied, to any living Christian prince or any important English nobleman, gentleman, or government official were particularly sensitive and likely to be struck. Renaissance political life was highly personalized; people in power were exceptionally alert to insult and zealously patrolled the boundaries of their prestige and reputation.

Moreover, the censors knew that audiences and readers were quite adept at applying theatrical representations distanced in time and space to their own world. At a time of riots against resident foreigners, Tilney read *Sir Thomas More*, a play in which Shakespeare probably had a hand, and instructed the players to cut scenes that, even though they were set in 1517, might have had an uncomfortable contemporary resonance. "Leave out the insurrection wholly," Tilney's note reads, "and the cause thereof and begin with Sir Thomas More at the Mayor's sessions, with a report afterwards of his good service done being sheriff of London upon a mutiny against the Lombards only by a short report and not otherwise at your own perils. E. Tilney." Of course, as Tilney knew perfectly well, most plays succeed precisely by mirroring, if only obliquely, their own times, but this particular reflection evidently seemed to him too dangerous or provocative.

The topical significance of a play depends in large measure on the particular moment in which it is performed and on certain features of the performance—for example, a striking resemblance between one of the characters and a well-known public figure—that the script itself will not necessarily disclose to us at this great distance or even to the censor at the time. Hence the Master of the Revels noted angrily of one play performed in 1632 that "there were diverse personated so naturally, both of lords and others of the court, that I took it ill." Hence, too, a play that was deemed allowable when it was first written and performed could return, like a nightmare, to haunt a different place and time. The most famous instance of such a return involves Shakespeare, for on the day before the Earl of Essex's attempted coup against Queen Elizabeth in 1601, someone paid the Lord Chamberlain's Men (the name of Shakespeare's company at the time) 40 shillings to revive their old play about the deposition and murder of Richard II. "I am Richard II," the queen declared. "Know ye not that?" However distressed she was by this performance, the queen significantly did not take out her wrath on the players: neither the playwright nor his company was punished, nor was the Master of the Revels criticized for allowing the play in the first place. It was Essex and several of his key supporters who lost their heads.

Evidence suggests that the Master of the Revels often regarded himself not as the strict censor of the theater but as its friendly guardian, charged with averting catastrophes. He was a bureaucrat concerned less with subversive ideas per se than with potential trouble. That is, there is no record of a dramatist being called to account for his heterodox beliefs; rather, plays were censored if they risked offending influential people, including important foreign allies, or if they threatened to cause public disorder by exacerbating religious or other controversies. The distinction is not a stable one, but it helps to explain the intellectual boldness, power, and freedom of a censored theater in a society in which the perceived enemies of the state were treated mercilessly. Shakespeare could have Lear articulate a searing indictment of social injustice—

> Robes and furred gowns hide all. Plate sin with gold,
> And the strong lance of justice hurtless breaks;
> Arm it in rags, a pygmy's straw does pierce it.
> (4.5.155–57)

—and evidently neither the Master of the Revels nor the courtiers in their robes and furred gowns protested. But when the Spanish ambassador complained about Thomas Middleton's anti-Spanish allegory *A Game at Chess,* performed at the Globe in 1624, the whole theater was shut down, the players were arrested, and the king professed to be furious at his official for licensing the play in the first place and allowing it to be performed for nine consecutive days.

In addition to the system for the licensing of plays for performance, there was also a system for the licensing of plays for publication. At the start of Shakespeare's career, such press licensing was the responsibility of the Court of High Commission, headed by the Archbishop of Canterbury and the Bishop of London. Their deputies, a panel of junior clerics, were supposed to review the manuscripts, granting licenses to those worthy of publication and rejecting any they deemed "heretical, seditious, or unseemly for Christian ears." Without a license, the Stationers' Company, the guild of the book trade, was not supposed to register a manuscript for publication. In practice, as various complaints and attempts to close loopholes attest, some playbooks were printed without a license. In 1607, the system was significantly revised when Sir George Buc began to license plays for the press. When Buc succeeded to the post of Master of the Revels in 1610, the powers to license plays for the stage and the page were vested in one man.

Theatrical Innovations

The theater continued to flourish under this system of regulation after Shakespeare's death; by the 1630s, as many as five playhouses were operating daily in London. When the theater reemerged after the eighteen-year hiatus imposed by Puritan rule, it quickly resumed its cultural importance, but not without a number of significant changes. Major innovations in staging resulted principally from Continental influences on the English artists who accompanied the court of Charles II into exile in France, where they supplied it with masques and other theatrical entertainments.

The institutional conditions and business practices of the two companies chartered by Charles after the Restoration in 1660 also differed from those of Shakespeare's theater. In place of the more collective practice of Shakespeare's company, the Restoration theaters were controlled by celebrated actor-managers who not only assigned themselves starring roles, in both comedy and tragedy, but also assumed sole responsibility for many business decisions, including the setting of their colleagues' salaries. At the same time, the power of the actor-manager, great as it was, was limited by the new importance of outside capital. No longer was the theater, with all of its properties from script to costumes, owned by the "sharers"—that is, by those actors who held shares in the joint-stock company. Instead, entrepreneurs would raise capital for increasingly fantastic sets and stage machinery that could cost as much as £3,000, an astronomical sum, for a single production. This investment, in turn, not only influenced the kinds of new plays written for the theater but helped to transform old plays that were revived, including Shakespeare's.

In his diary entry for August 24, 1661, Samuel Pepys notes that he has been "to the Opera, and there saw Hamlet, Prince of Denmark, done with scenes very well, but above all, Betterton did the prince's part beyond imagination." This is Thomas Betterton's first review, as it were, and it is typical of the enthusiasm he would inspire throughout his fifty-year career on the London stage. Pepys's brief and scattered remarks on the plays he voraciously attended in the 1660s are precious because they are among the few records from the period of concrete and immediate responses to theatrical performances. Modern readers might miss the significance of Pepys's phrase "done with scenes": this production of *Hamlet* was only the third play to use the movable sets first introduced to England by its producer, William Davenant. The central historical fact that makes the productions of this period so exciting is that public theater had been banned altogether for eighteen years until the Restoration of Charles II.

A brief discussion of theatrical developments in the Restoration period will enable us at least to glance longingly at a vast subject that lies outside the scope of this introduction: the rich performance history that extends from Shakespeare's time to our own, involving tens of thousands of productions and adaptations for theater, opera, Broadway musicals, and, of course, films. The scale of this history is vast in space as well as time: as early as 1607, there is a record of a *Hamlet* performed on board an English ship, HMS *Dragon,* off the coast of Sierra Leone, and troupes of English actors performed in the late sixteenth and early seventeenth centuries as far afield as Poland and Bohemia.

William Davenant, who claimed to be Shakespeare's bastard son, had become an expert on stage scenery while producing masques at the court of Charles I, and when the theaters reopened, he set to work on converting an indoor tennis court into a new kind of theater. He designed a broad open platform like that of the Elizabethan stage, but he replaced the relatively shallow space for "discoveries" (tableaux set up in an opening at the center of the stage, revealed by drawing back a curtain) and the "tiring-house" (the players' dressing room) behind this space with one expanded interior, framed by a proscenium arch, in which scenes could be displayed. These elaborately painted scenes could be moved on and off, using grooves on the floor. The perspectival effect for a spectator of one central painted panel with two "wings" on either side was that of three sides of a room. This effect anticipated that of the familiar "picture frame" stage, developed fully in the nineteenth century, and began a subtle shift in theater away from the elaborate verbal descriptions that are so central to Shakespeare and toward the evocative visual poetry of the set designer's art.

Another convention of Shakespeare's stage, the use of boy actors for female roles, gave way to the more complete illusion of women playing women's parts. The king issued a decree in 1662 forcefully permitting, if not requiring, the use of actresses. The royal decree is couched in the language of social and moral reform: the introduction of actresses will require the "reformation" of scurrilous and profane passages in plays, and this, in turn, will help forestall some of the objections that shut the theaters down in 1642. In reality, male theater audiences, composed of a narrower range of courtiers and aristocrats than in Shakespeare's time, met this intended reform with the assumption that the new actresses were fair game sexually; most actresses (with the partial exception of those who married male members of their troupes) were regarded as, or actually became, whores. But despite the social stigma and the fact that their salaries were predictably lower than those of their male counterparts, the stage saw some formidable female stars by the 1680s.

The first recorded appearance of an actress was that of a Desdemona in December 1660. Betterton's Ophelia in 1661 was Mary Saunderson (c. 1637–1712), who became Mrs. Betterton a year later. The most famous Ophelia of the period was Susanna Mountfort, who appeared in that role for the first time at the age of fifteen in 1705. The performance by Mountfort that became legendary occurred in 1720, after a disappointment in love, or so it was said, had driven her mad. Hearing that *Hamlet* was being performed, Mountfort escaped from her keepers and reached the theater, where she concealed herself until the scene in which Ophelia enters in her state of insanity. At this point, Mountfort rushed onto the stage and, in the words of a contemporary, "was in truth Ophelia herself, to the amazement of the performers and the astonishment of the audience."

That the character Ophelia became increasingly and decisively identified with the mad scene owes something to this occurrence, but it is also a consequence of the text used for Restoration performances of *Hamlet.* Having received the performance rights to a good number of Shakespeare's plays, Davenant altered them for the stage in the 1660s, and many of these acting versions remained in use for generations. In the case of *Hamlet,* neither Davenant nor his successors did what they so often did with other plays by Shakespeare—that is, alter the plot radically and interpolate other material. But many of the lines were cut or "improved." The cuts included most of Ophelia's sane speeches, such as her spirited retort to Laertes' moralizing; what remained made her part almost entirely an emblem of "female love melancholy."

Thomas Betterton (1635–1710), the prototype of the actor-manager, who would be the dominant figure in Shakespeare interpretation and in the theater generally through

The Spanish Tragedie:

OR,

Hieronimo is mad againe.

Containing the lamentable end of *Don Horatio*, and *Belimperia*; with the pittifull death of *Hieronimo*.

Newly corrected, amended, and enlarged with new Additions of the *Painters* part, and others, as it hath of late been diuers times acted.

LONDON,

Printed by W. White, for I. White and T. Langley, and are to be sold at their Shop ouer againſt the Sarazens head without New-gate. 1615.

Title page of Thomas Kyd's *Spanish Tragedie* (1615). The first known edition dates from 1592.

the nineteenth century, made Hamlet his premier role. A contemporary who saw his last performance in the part (at the age of seventy-four, a rather old Prince of Denmark) wrote that to *read* Shakespeare's play was to encounter "dry, incoherent, & broken sentences," but that to see Betterton was to "prove" that the play was written "correctly." Spectators especially admired his reaction to the Ghost's appearance in the Queen's bedchamber: "his Countenance . . . thro' the violent and sudden Emotions of Amazement and Horror, turn[ed] instantly on the Sight of his fathers Spirit, as pale as his Neckcloath, when every Article of his Body seem's affected with a Tremor inexpressible." A piece of stage business in this scene, Betterton's upsetting his chair on the Ghost's entrance, became so thoroughly identified with the part that later productions were censured if the actor left it out. This business could very well have been handed down from Richard Burbage, the star of Shakespeare's original production, for Davenant, who had coached Betterton in the role, had known the performances of Joseph Taylor, who had succeeded Burbage in it. It is strangely gratifying to notice that Hamlets on stage and screen still occasionally upset their chairs.

Shakespeare's Life and Art

Playwrights, even hugely successful playwrights, were not ordinarily the objects of popular curiosity in early modern England, and few personal documents survive from Shakespeare's life of the kind that usually give the biographies of artists their appeal: no diary, no letters, private or public, no accounts of his childhood, almost no contemporary gossip, no scandals. Shakespeare's exact contemporary, the great playwright Christopher Marlowe, lived a mere twenty-nine years—he was murdered in 1593—but he left behind tantalizing glimpses of himself in police documents, the memos of high-ranking government officials, and detailed denunciations by sinister double agents. Ben Jonson recorded his opinions and his reading in a remarkable published notebook, *Timber; or, Discoveries Made upon Men and Matter,* and he also shared his views of the world (including some criticisms of his fellow playwright Shakespeare) with a Scottish poet, William Drummond of Hawthornden, who had the wit to jot them down for posterity. From Shakespeare, there is nothing comparable, not even a book with his name scribbled on the cover and a few marginal notes such as we have for Jonson, let alone working notebooks.

Yet Elizabethan England was a record-keeping society, and centuries of archival labor have turned up a substantial number of traces of its greatest playwright and his family. By themselves the traces would have relatively little interest, but in the light of Shakespeare's plays and poems, they have come to seem like precious relics and manage to achieve a considerable resonance.

Shakespeare's Family

William Shakespeare's grandfather Richard farmed land by the village of Snitterfield, near the small, pleasant market town of Stratford-upon-Avon, about 96 miles northwest of London. The playwright's father, John, moved in the mid-sixteenth century to Stratford, where he became a successful glover, landowner, moneylender, and dealer in wool and other agricultural goods. In or about 1557, he married Mary Arden, the daughter of a prosperous and well-connected farmer from the same area, Robert Arden of Wilmcote.

John Shakespeare was evidently highly esteemed by his fellow townspeople, for he held a series of important posts in local government. In 1556, he was appointed ale taster, an office reserved for "able persons and discreet," in 1558 was sworn in as a constable, and in 1561 was elected as one of the town's fourteen burgesses. As burgess, John served as one of the two chamberlains, responsible for administering borough property and revenues. In 1567, he was elected bailiff, Stratford's highest elective office and the equivalent of mayor. Although John Shakespeare signed all official documents with a cross or other sign, it is likely, but not certain, that he knew how to read and write. Mary, who also signed documents only with her mark, is less likely to have been literate.

According to the parish registers, which recorded baptisms and burials, the Shakespeares had eight children, four daughters and four sons, beginning with a daughter Joan born in 1558. A second daughter, Margaret, was born in December 1562 and died a few months later. William Shakespeare ("Gulielmus, filius Johannes Shakespeare"), their first son, was baptized on April 26, 1564. Since there was usually a few days' lapse between birth and baptism, it is conventional to celebrate Shakespeare's birthday on April 23, which happens to coincide with the feast of St. George, England's patron saint, and with the day of Shakespeare's death fifty-two years later.

William Shakespeare had three younger brothers, Gilbert, Richard, and Edmund, and two younger sisters, Joan and Anne. (It was often the custom to recycle a name, so the firstborn Joan must have died before the birth in 1569 of another daughter

"Southeast Prospect of Stratford-upon-Avon, 1746." From *The Gentleman's Magazine* (December 1792).

christened Joan, the only one of the girls to survive childhood.) Gilbert, who died in his forty-fifth year in 1612, is described in legal records as a Stratford haberdasher; Edmund followed William to London and became a professional actor, but evidently of no particular repute. He was only twenty-eight when he died in 1607 and was given an expensive funeral, perhaps paid for by his successful older brother.

At the high point of his public career, John Shakespeare, the father of this substantial family, applied to the Herald's College for a coat of arms, which would have marked his (and his family's) elevation from the ranks of substantial middle-class citizenry to that of the gentry. But the application went nowhere, for soon after he initiated what would have been a costly petitioning process, John apparently fell on hard times. The decline must have begun when William was still living at home, a boy of twelve or thirteen. From 1576 onward, John Shakespeare stopped attending council meetings. He became caught up in costly lawsuits, started mortgaging his land, and incurred substantial debts. In 1586, he was finally replaced on the council; in 1592, he was one of nine Stratford men listed as absenting themselves from church out of fear of being arrested for debt.

The reason for the reversal in John Shakespeare's fortunes is unknown. Some have speculated that it may have stemmed from adherence to Catholicism, since those who remained loyal to the old faith were subject to increasingly vigorous and costly discrimination. But if John Shakespeare was a Catholic, as seems quite possible, it would not necessarily explain his decline, since other Catholics (and Puritans) in Elizabethan Stratford and elsewhere managed to hold on to their offices. In any case, his fall from prosperity and local power, whatever its cause, was not absolute. In 1601, the last year of his life, his name was included among those qualified to speak on behalf of Stratford's rights. And he was by that time entitled to bear a coat of arms, for in 1596, some twenty years after the application to the Herald's office had been initiated, it was successfully renewed. There is no record of who paid for the bureaucratic procedures that made the grant possible, but it is likely to have been John's oldest son William, by that time a highly successful London playwright.

Education

Stratford was a small provincial town, but it had long been the site of an excellent free school, originally established by the Church in the thirteenth century. The main purpose of such schools in the Middle Ages had been to train prospective clerics; since many aristocrats could neither read nor write, literacy by itself conferred no special distinction and was not routinely viewed as desirable. But the situation began to change markedly in the sixteenth century. Protestantism placed a far greater emphasis upon lay literacy: for the sake of salvation, it was crucially important to be intimately acquainted with the Holy Book, and printing made that book readily available. Schools became less strictly bound up with training for the Church and more linked to the general acquisition of "literature," in the sense both of literacy and of cultural knowledge. In keeping with this new emphasis on reading and with humanist educational reform, the school was reorganized during the reign of Edward VI (1547–53). School records from the period have not survived, but it is almost certain that William Shakespeare attended the King's New School, as it was renamed in Edward's honor.

Scholars have painstakingly reconstructed the curriculum of schools of this kind and have even turned up the names and rather impressive credentials of the schoolmasters who taught there when Shakespeare was a student. (Shakespeare's principal teacher was Thomas Jenkins, an Oxford graduate, who received £20 a year and a rent-free house.) A child's education in Elizabethan England began at age four or five with two years at what was called the "petty school," attached to the main grammar school. The little scholars carried a "hornbook," a sheet of paper or parchment framed in wood and covered, for protection, with a transparent layer of horn. On the paper was written

The Cholmondeley sisters, c. 1600–10. This striking image brings to mind Shakespeare's fascination with twinship, both identical (notably in *The Comedy of Errors*) and fraternal (in *Twelfth Night*).

the alphabet and the Lord's Prayer, which were reproduced as well in the slightly more advanced *ABC with the Catechism,* a combination primer and rudimentary religious guide.

After students demonstrated some ability to read, the boys could go on, at about age seven, to the grammar school. Shakespeare's images of the experience are not particularly cheerful. In his famous account of the Seven Ages of Man, Jaques in *As You Like It* describes

> the whining schoolboy with his satchel
> And shining morning face, creeping like snail
> Unwillingly to school.
>
> (2.7.144–46)

The schoolboy would have crept quite early: the day began at 6:00 A.M. in summer and 7:00 A.M. in winter and continued until 5:00 P.M., with very few breaks or holidays.

At the core of the curriculum was the study of Latin, the mastery of which was in effect a prolonged male puberty rite involving much discipline and pain as well as pleasure. A late sixteenth-century Dutchman (whose name fittingly was Batty) proposed that God had created the human buttocks so that they could be severely beaten without risking permanent injury. Such thoughts dominated the pedagogy of the age, so that even an able young scholar, as we might imagine Shakespeare to have been, could scarcely have escaped recurrent flogging.

Shakespeare evidently reaped some rewards for the miseries he probably endured: his works are laced with echoes of many of the great Latin texts taught in grammar schools. One of his earliest comedies, *The Comedy of Errors,* is a brilliant variation on a theme by the Roman playwright Plautus, whom Elizabethan schoolchildren often performed as well as read; and one of his earliest tragedies, *Titus Andronicus,* is heavily indebted to Seneca. These are among the most visible of the classical influences that are often more subtly and pervasively interfused in Shakespeare's works. He seems to have had a particular fondness for *Aesop's Fables,* Apuleius's *Golden Ass,* and above all Ovid's *Metamorphoses.* His learned contemporary Ben Jonson remarked that Shakespeare had "small Latin and less Greek," but from this distance what is striking is not the limits of Shakespeare's learning but rather the unpretentious ease, intelligence, and gusto with which he draws upon what he must have first encountered as laborious study.

Traces of a Life

In November 1582, William Shakespeare, at the age of eighteen, married twenty-six-year-old Anne Hathaway, who came from the village of Shottery, near Stratford. Their first daughter, Susanna, was baptized six months later. This circumstance, along with the fact that Anne was eight years Will's senior, has given rise to a mountain of speculation, all the more lurid precisely because there is no further evidence. Shakespeare depicts in several plays situations in which marriage is precipitated by a pregnancy, but he also registers, in *Measure for Measure* (1.2.125ff.), the Elizabethan belief that a "true contract" of marriage could be legitimately made and then consummated simply by the mutual vows of the couple in the presence of witnesses.

On February 2, 1585, the twins Hamnet and Judith Shakespeare were baptized in Stratford. Hamnet died at the age of eleven, when his father was already living for much of the year in London as a successful playwright. These are Shakespeare's only known children, although the playwright and impressario William Davenant in the mid-seventeenth century claimed to be his bastard son. Since people did not ordinarily advertise their illegitimacy, the claim, though impossible to verify, at least suggests the unusual strength of the Shakespeare's posthumous reputation.

William Shakespeare's father, John, died in 1601; his mother died seven years later. They would have had the satisfaction of witnessing their eldest son's prosperity, and not only from a distance, for in 1597 William purchased New Place, the second largest house in Stratford. In 1607, the playwright's daughter Susanna married a successful and well-known physician, John Hall. The next year, the Halls had a daughter, Elizabeth, Shakespeare's first grandchild. In 1616, the year of Shakespeare's death, his daughter Judith married a vintner, Thomas Quiney, with whom she had three children. Shakespeare's widow, Anne, died in 1623, at the age of sixty-seven. His first-born, Susanna, died at the age of sixty-six in 1649, the year that King Charles I was beheaded by the parliamentary army. Judith lived through Cromwell's Protectorate and on to the Restoration of the monarchy; she died in February 1662, at the age of seventy-seven. By the end of the century, the line of Shakespeare's direct heirs was extinct.

Patient digging in the archives has turned up other traces of Shakespeare's life as a family man and a man of means: assessments, small fines, real-estate deeds, minor actions in court to collect debts. In addition to his fine Stratford house and a large garden and cottage facing it, Shakespeare bought substantial parcels of land in the vicinity. When in *The Tempest* the wedding celebration conjures up a vision of "barns and garners never empty," Shakespeare could have been glancing at what the legal documents record as his own "tithes of corn, grain, blade, and hay" in the fields near Stratford. At some point after 1610, Shakespeare seems to have begun to shift his attention from the London stage to his Stratford properties, although the term "retirement" implies a more decisive and definitive break than appears to have been the case. By 1613, when the Globe Theatre burned down during a performance of *All Is True* (*Henry VIII*), Shakespeare was probably residing for the most part in Stratford, but he retained his financial interest in the rebuilt playhouse and probably continued to have some links to his theatrical colleagues. Still, by this point, his career as a playwright was substantially over. Legal documents from his last years show his main concern to be the protection of his real-estate interests in Stratford.

Half a century after Shakespeare's death, a Stratford vicar and physician, John Ward, noted in his diary that Shakespeare and his fellow poets Michael Drayton and Ben Jonson "had a merry meeting, and it seems drank too hard, for Shakespeare died of a fever there contracted." It is not inconceivable that Shakespeare's last illness was somehow linked, if only coincidentally, to the festivities on the occasion of the wedding in February 1616 of his daughter Judith (who was still alive when Ward made his diary entry). In any case, on March 25, 1616, Shakespeare revised his will, and on April 23 he died. Two days later, he was buried in the chancel of Holy Trinity Church beneath a stone bearing an epitaph he is said to have devised:

> Good friend for Jesus' sake forbear,
> To dig the dust enclosed here:
> Blest be the man that spares these stones,
> And curst be he that moves my bones.

The verses are hardly among Shakespeare's finest, but they seem to have been effective: though bones were routinely dug up to make room for others—a fate imagined with unforgettable intensity in the graveyard scene in *Hamlet*—his own remains were undisturbed. Like other vestiges of sixteenth- and early seventeenth-century Stratford, Shakespeare's grave has for centuries been the object of a tourist industry that borders on a religious cult.

Shakespeare's will has been examined with an intensity befitting this cult; every provision and formulaic phrase, no matter how minor or conventional, has borne a heavy weight of interpretation, none more so than the bequest to his wife, Anne, of only "my second-best bed." Scholars have pointed out that Anne would in any case have been provided for by custom and that the terms are not necessarily a deliberate slight, but the absence of the customary words "my loving wife" or "my well-beloved wife" is difficult to ignore.

Portrait of the Playwright as Young Provincial

The great problem with the surviving traces of Shakespeare's life is not that they are few but that they are dull. Christopher Marlowe was a double or triple agent, accused of brawling, sodomy, and atheism. Ben Jonson, who somehow clambered up from bricklayer's apprentice to classical scholar, served in the army in Flanders, killed a fellow actor in a duel, converted to Catholicism in prison in 1598, and returned to the Church of England in 1610. Provincial real-estate investments and the second-best bed cannot compete with such adventurous lives. Indeed, the relative ordinariness of Shakespeare's social background and life has contributed to a persistent current of speculation that the glover's son from Stratford-upon-Avon was not in fact the author of the plays attributed to him.

The anti-Stratfordians, as those who deny Shakespeare's authorship are sometimes called, almost always propose as the real author someone who came from a higher social class and received a more prestigious education. Francis Bacon, the Earl of Oxford, the Earl of Southampton, even Queen Elizabeth, have been advanced, among many others, as glamorous candidates for the role of clandestine playwright. Several famous people, including Mark Twain and Sigmund Freud, have espoused these theories, though very few scholars have joined them. Since Shakespeare was quite well-known in his own time as the author of the plays that bear his name, there would need to have been an extraordinary conspiracy to conceal the identity of the real master who (the theory goes) disdained to appear in the vulgarity of print or on the public stage. Like many conspiracy theories, the extreme implausibility of this one only seems to increase the fervent conviction of its advocates.

To the charge that a middle-class author from a small town could not have imagined the lives of kings and nobles, one can respond by citing the exceptional qualities that Ben Jonson praised in Shakespeare: "excellent *Phantsie*; brave notions, and gentle expressions." Even in ordinary mortals, the human imagination is a strange faculty; in Shakespeare, it seems to have been uncannily powerful, working its mysterious, transforming effects on everything it touched. His imagination was intensely engaged by what he found in books. He seems throughout his life to have been an intense, voracious reader, and it is fascinating to witness his creative encounters with Raphael Holinshed's *Chronicles of England, Scotlande, and Irelande*, Plutarch's *Lives of the Noble Grecians and Romans*, Ovid's *Metamorphoses*, Montaigne's *Essays*, and the Bible, to name only some of his favorite books. But books were clearly not the only objects of Shakespeare's attention; like most artists, he drew upon the whole range of his life experiences.

To integrate some of the probable circumstances of Shakespeare's early years with the particular shape of the theatrical imagination associated with his name, let us indulge briefly in the biographical daydreams that modern scholarship is supposed to have rendered forever obsolete. The vignettes that follow are conjectural, but they may suggest ways in which his life as we know it found its way into his art.

1. THE GOWN OF OFFICE

Shakespeare was a very young boy—not quite four years old—when the Stratford council elected his father, John, to a year's term as bailiff (the equivalent of mayor). The office, the town's highest, was attended with considerable ceremony. The bailiff and his deputy were entitled to appear in public in furred gowns, attended by leather-clad sergeants bearing maces before them. On Rogation Days (three days of prayer for the harvest, before Ascension Day), they would solemnly pace out the parish boundaries, and they would similarly walk in processions on market and fair days. On Sundays, the sergeants would accompany the bailiff to church, where he would sit with his wife in a front pew, and he would have a comparable seat of honor at sermons in the Guild Chapel.

Public deference was a matter of law as well as custom: any inhabitant who spoke disrespectfully to the bailiff or other town officer was subject to the penalty of three days and three nights in the stocks. Newcomers who sought employment—notably including traveling players who hoped to stage performances—were obliged to obtain the bailiff's permission. In the year that John Shakespeare held office, two such professional playing companies arrived in Stratford. They must have proceeded to the bailiff's house on Henley Street and presented the letters of recommendation, with wax seals, that showed that they were not vagabonds. They would have spoken with more than ordinary deference, since it was the bailiff who would decide whether they would be sent packing or—as was the case—allowed to post their bills announcing the performances. The first of these performances was usually free to all comers. The bailiff would have been expected to attend, for it was his privilege to determine the level of the reward to be paid out of the city coffers; he would, presumably, have been given one of the best seats in the guildhall, where a special stage had been erected. It is impossible to know whether John Shakespeare took his family to these plays, but his little boy would certainly have been aware of what was happening.

On a precocious child (or even, for that matter, on an ordinary child), the effect of his father's office and the elaborate rituals that attended it would be at least threefold. First, the ceremony would convey irresistibly the power of clothes (the gown of office) and of symbols (the mace) to transform identity as if by magic. Second, it would invest the father with immense power, distinction, and importance, awakening what we may call a lifelong dream of high station. And third, pulling slightly against this dream, it would provoke an odd feeling that the father's clothes do not fit, a perception that the office is not the same as the man, and an intimate, firsthand knowledge that when the robes are put off, their wearer is inevitably glimpsed in a far different, less exalted light.

2. PROGRESSES AND ELECTIONS

This second biographical fantasy, slightly less plausible than the first but still quite likely, involves a somewhat older child witnessing two characteristic forms of Elizabethan political ceremony, both of which were well known in the provinces. Queen Elizabeth was fond of going on what were known as "progresses," triumphant ceremonial journeys around her kingdom. Let us imagine that the young Shakespeare—say, in 1574, when he was ten years old—went with his kinsfolk or friends to Warwick, some 8 miles distant, to witness a progress. He would thus have participated as a spectator in an elaborate celebration of charismatic power: the courtiers in their gorgeous clothes, the nervous local officials bedecked in velvets and silks, and at the center, carried in a special litter like a painted idol, the bejeweled queen. Let us imagine further that in addition to being struck by the overwhelming force of this charisma, the boy was struck, too, by the way this force depended paradoxically on a sense that the queen was after all quite human. Elizabeth was in fact fond of calling attention to this peculiar tension between near-divinization and human ordinariness. For example, on this occasion at Warwick (and what follows really happened), after the trembling Recorder, presumably a local civil official of high standing, had made his official welcoming speech, Elizabeth offered her hand to him to be kissed: "Come hither, little Recorder," she said. "It was told me that you would be afraid to look upon me or to speak boldly; but you were not so afraid of me as I was of you; and I now thank you for putting me in mind of my duty." Of course, the charm of this royal "confession" of nervousness depends on its manifest implausibility: it is, in effect, a theatrical performance of humility by someone with immense confidence in her own histrionic power.

A royal progress was not the only form of spectacular political activity that Shakespeare might well have seen in the 1570s; it is still more likely that he would have witnessed parliamentary elections, particularly since his father was qualified to vote. In 1571, 1572, 1575, and 1578, there were shire elections conducted in nearby Warwick, elections that would certainly have attracted well over a thousand voters. These were often memorable events: large crowds came together; there was usually heavy drinking and carnivalesque festivity; and, at the same time, there was enacted, in a very different register from that of the monarchy, a ritual of empowerment. The people, those entitled to vote by virtue of meeting the property and residence requirements, chose their own representatives by giving their votes—their voices—to candidates for office. Here, legislative sovereignty was conferred not by God but by the consent of the community, a consent marked by shouts and applause.

Recent cultural historians have been so fascinated by the evident links between the spectacles of the absolutist monarchy and the theater that they have largely ignored the significance of this alternative public arena, one that generated intense excitement throughout the country. A child who was a spectator at a parliamentary election in the 1570s might well have found the occasion enormously compelling. It is striking, in any case, how often the adult Shakespeare returns to scenes of acclamation and mass consent, and striking, too, how much the theater depends on the soliciting of popular voices.

3. EXORCISMS

A third and final fantasy is even more speculative than the second and involves a controversial claim, which has long been hotly debated—that Shakespeare either was a secret Catholic or was at least raised in a Roman Catholic household in a time of official suspicion and persecution of recusancy. A late seventeenth-century Anglican clergyman, Richard Davies, jotted down in some notes on Shakespeare that "he died a papist." In a modern biographical study, E. A. J. Honigmann convincingly linked several of the schoolmasters who taught in Stratford at the time that Shakespeare would have been a pupil to a network of Catholic families in Lancashire with whom one "William Shakeshafte," possibly a young schoolmaster or player, was connected in the late 1570s or early 1580s.

Exorcism: Nicole Aubry in the cathedral at Laon, 1566.

Catholics in Elizabethan England were not free to practice their religion—any more than Protestants, in Catholic countries, were free to practice theirs—and the beleaguered faithful, beset with spies, came together only at great risk to confess and receive Communion from clandestine priests. Under the circumstances, although a substantial portion of the population may have retained a residual inward loyalty to the traditional faith, the vast majority fell away from outward Catholic practice. After all, the churches, great and small, were now the places of Protestant worship; the innumerable local saints' shrines and pilgrimage sites had been systematically destroyed; the monasteries and convents had been abolished, their property bestowed on royal favorites or sold at bargain prices to local magnates. Seeking a spectacular way to demonstrate the enduring spiritual power and authenticity of the Roman Church, the embattled Counter-Reformers turned to an ancient ritual: exorcism. Devils who possessed the souls of troubled men and women had once been exorcised in public, but now the healing rite had to be conducted in secret, in a barn in a remote village, perhaps, or in the attic of the secluded house of a Catholic loyalist. The danger for those who presided was enormous—brutal interrogation, torture, and an unspeakably horrible execution was the usual fate of the missionary priests who were caught—but the vivid demonstration of the Church's triumph over evil was sufficiently compelling to warrant the risk. For despite the lynx-eyed alertness of the Protestant authorities, Catholics staged a surprising number of clandestine exorcisms, many of which drew substantial crowds.

Accepting for the moment that William Shakespeare was raised in the recusant faith of his father and mother, let us imagine that one day in the early 1580s the young man attended an exorcism of which he had learned through the secret network of the faithful. Here, based on an eyewitness account of such an occasion recently transcribed by Gerard Kilroy, is what he is likely to have seen. At the center of a large room, emptied of other furniture in order to accommodate the many observers, stood a bed. A young woman sat on the bed, and a priest, in clerical vestments, stood over her, preaching a sermon. As he spoke, the woman began to writhe and scream. At first the screams, uttered by a deep voice that could not have been the woman's although it came from her mouth, were not intelligible. Gradually, the bystanders began to make out some of the words, blasphemous oaths—"God's wounds! God's nails!"—followed by menaces, spoken as if by a rabid Protestant: "Popish priests, popish priests, to prison with them and hang them, hang them, hang them." The exorcist held up the Eucharist over the writhing woman, and the screams intensified. "Who are you?" he demanded. "I am Modu," the voice replied. "Depart, Modu!" shouted the priest, bringing the consecrated wafer closer to the demoniac. When that did not succeed in driving the devil out, the priest advanced a chafing dish of fire and brimstone, provoking more shouting and cursing, and then displayed a painting of the Blessed Virgin. "I will not behold or see her," screamed the demonic voice.

The longer the scene continued, the more there was confirmation of the contested tenets of the Catholic faith. The devil admitted that the Virgin Mary was a particularly efficacious intercessor, that purgatory existed, that the wafer, consecrated by the priest, actually was the body and blood of Christ. The devil also revealed that all Protestants were his followers. Finally, under the irresistible force of spiritual compulsion, he agreed to depart forever from the body of the possessed. The departure was difficult: again and again the tormented young woman gaped, as if her mouth were being torn open. She screamed in pain, rose up only to be cast down violently by invisible hands, cried out that she was being drowned, and called upon Jesus and his mother to save her. Only when a sacred relic was placed directly on her flesh did the devil finally leave her.

There is no way to know if William Shakespeare actually witnessed such a scene, but if he did, he would have carried away several indelible impressions: an awareness that strange, alien voices may speak from within ordinary, familiar bodies; an intimation of the immense, cosmic forces that may impinge upon human life; a belief in the possibility of making contact with these forces and compelling them to speak. These are, after all, the foundation stones of great tragedy.

Many years later, Shakespeare brooded about demonic possession when he was writing his greatest tragedy about the presence of evil in the world, *King Lear*. "This is the foul fiend Flibbertigibbet," shouts the madman, Poor Tom; "The Prince of Darkness is a gentleman. Modo he's called, and Mahu" (3.4.103, 127–28). But Poor Tom in that play is faking it; he is actually the noble Edgar, who has disguised himself as a madman in order to escape persecution. Did Shakespeare as a teenager already think that the whole compelling event, in all of its metaphysical weirdness, was a powerful theatrical fraud, a piece of pious propaganda? Perhaps. But if so, he also clearly understood that evil exists, that persecution is real, and that illusion has an irresistible force.

These imaginary portraits of the playwright as a young provincial introduce us to several of the root conditions of the Elizabethan theater. Biographical fantasies, though entirely speculative and playful, are useful in part because some people have found it difficult to conceive how Shakespeare, with his provincial roots and his restricted range of experience, could have so rapidly and completely mastered the central imaginative themes of his times. Moreover, it is sometimes difficult to grasp how seeming abstractions such as market society, monarchical state, and theological doctrine were actually experienced directly by peculiar, distinct individuals. Shakespeare's plays were social and collective events, but they also bore the stamp of a particular artist, one endowed with a remarkable capacity to craft lifelike illusions (what Jonson called "excellent *Phantsie*"), a daring willingness to articulate an original vision ("brave notions"), and a loving command, at once precise and generous, of language ("gentle expressions"). These plays are stitched together from shared cultural experiences, inherited dramatic devices, and the pungent vernacular of the day, but we should not lose sight of the extent to which they articulate an intensely personal vision, a bold shaping of the available materials. Four centuries of feverish biographical speculation, much of it foolish, bears witness to a basic intuition: the richness of these plays, their inexhaustible openness, is the consequence not only of the auspicious collective conditions of the culture but also of someone's exceptional skill, inventiveness, and courage at taking those conditions and making of them something rich and strange.

The Theater of the Nation

What precisely are the collective conditions highlighted by these vignettes? First, the growth of Stratford-upon-Avon, the bustling market town of which John Shakespeare was bailiff, is a small version of a momentous sixteenth-century development that made Shakespeare's career possible: the making of an urban "public." That development obviously depended on adequate numbers; the period experienced a rapid and still unexplained growth in population. With it came an expansion and elaboration of market relations: markets became less periodic, more continuous, and more abstract—centered, that is, not on the familiar materiality of goods but on the liquidity of capital and goods. In practical terms, this meant that it was possible to conceive of the theater not only as festive entertainment for special events—lord mayor's pageants, visiting princes, seasonal festivals, and the like—but as a permanent, year-round business venture. The venture relied on ticket sales—it was an innovation of this period to have money advanced in the expectation of pleasure rather than offered to servants afterward as a reward—and counted on habitual playgoing with a concomitant demand for new plays from competing theater companies: "But that's all one, our play is done," sings Feste at the end of *Twelfth Night* and adds a glance toward the next afternoon's proceeds: "And we'll strive to please you every day" (5.1.394–95).

Second, the royal progress is an instance of what the anthropologist Clifford Geertz has called the Theater State, a state that manifests its power and meaning in exemplary public performances. Professional companies of players, like the one Shakespeare belonged to, understood well that they existed in relation to this Theater State and would, if they were fortunate, be called upon to serve it. Unlike Ben Jonson, Shakespeare did not, as far as we know, write royal entertainments on commission, but his plays were frequently performed before Queen Elizabeth and then before King James and Queen Anne, along with their courtiers and privileged guests. There are many fascinating glimpses of these performances, including a letter from Walter Cope to Robert Cecil, early in James's reign. "Burbage is come," Cope writes, referring to the leading actor of Shakespeare's company, "and says there is no new play that the queen hath not seen, but they have revived an old one, called *Love's Labours Lost*, which for wit and mirth he says will please her exceedingly. And this is appointed to be played tomorrow night at my Lord of Southampton's." Not only would such theatrical performances have given great pleasure—evidently, the queen had already exhausted the company's new offerings—but they conferred prestige upon those who commanded them and those in whose honor they were mounted.

Monarchical power in the period was deeply allied to spectacular manifestations of the ruler's glory and disciplinary authority. The symbology of power depended on regal magnificence, reward, punishment, and pardon, all of which were heavily theatricalized. Indeed, the conspicuous public display does not simply serve the interests of power; on many occasions in the period, power seemed to exist in order to make pageantry possible, as if the nation's identity were only fully realized in theatrical performance. It would be easy to exaggerate this perception: the subjects of Queen Elizabeth and King James were acutely aware of the distinction between shadow and substance. But they were fascinated by the political magic through which shadows could be taken for substantial realities, and the ruling elite was largely complicit in the formation and celebration of a charismatic absolutism. At the same time, the claims of the monarch who professes herself or himself to be not the representative of the nation but its embodiment were set against the counterclaims of the House of Commons. And this institution, too, as we have glimpsed, had its own theatrical rituals, centered on the crowd whose shouts of approval, in heavily stage-managed elections, chose the individuals who would stand for the polity and participate in deliberations held in a hall whose resemblance to a theater did not escape contemporary notice.

Third, illicit exorcism points both to the theatricality of much religious ritual in the late Middle Ages and the Renaissance and to the heightened possibility of secularization. English Protestant authorities banned the medieval mystery plays, along with pilgrimages and other rituals associated with holy shrines and sacred images, but playing companies could satisfy at least some of the popular longings and appropriate aspects of the social energy no longer allowed a theological outlet. That is, official attacks on certain Catholic practices made it more possible for the public theater to appropriate and exploit their allure. Hence, for example, the plays that celebrated the solemn miracle of the Catholic Mass were banned, along with the most elaborate church vestments, but in *The Winter's Tale* Dion can speak in awe of what he witnessed at Apollo's temple:

> I shall report,
> For most it caught me, the celestial habits—
> Methinks I so should term them—and the reverence
> Of the grave wearers. O, the sacrifice—
> How ceremonious, solemn, and unearthly
> It was i'th' off'ring!

(3.1.3–8)

And at the play's end, the statue of the innocent mother breathes, comes to life, and embraces her child.

The theater in Shakespeare's time, then, is intimately bound up with all three crucial cultural formations: the market society, the theater state, and the Church. But it is important to note that the institution is not *identified* with any of them. The theater may be a market phenomenon, but it is repeatedly and bitterly attacked as the enemy of diligent, sober, productive economic activity. Civic authorities generally regarded the theater as a pestilential nuisance, a parasite on the body of the commonwealth, a temptation to students, apprentices, housewives, even respectable merchants to leave their serious business and lapse into idleness and waste. That waste, it might be argued, could be partially recuperated if it went for the glorification of a guild or the entertainment of an important dignitary, but the only group regularly profiting from the theater were the players and their disreputable associates.

For his part, Shakespeare made a handsome profit from the commodification of theatrical entertainment, but he seems never to have written "city comedy"—plays set in London and more or less explicitly concerned with market relations—and his characters express deep reservations about the power of money and commerce: "That smooth-faced gentleman, tickling commodity," Philip the Bastard observes in *King John*, "wins of all, / Of kings, of beggars, old men, young men, maids" (2.1.574, 570–71). We could argue that the smooth-faced gentleman is none other than Shakespeare himself, for his drama famously mingles kings and clowns, princesses and panderers. But the mingling is set against a romantic current of social conservatism: in *Twelfth Night,* the aristocratic heiress Olivia falls in love with someone who appears far beneath her in wealth and social station, but it is revealed that he (and his sister Viola) are of noble blood; in *The Winter's Tale,* Leontes' daughter Perdita is raised as a shepherdess, but her noble nature shines through her humble upbringing, and she marries the Prince of Bohemia; the strange island maiden with whom Ferdinand, son of the King of Naples, falls madly in love in *The Tempest* turns out to be the daughter of the rightful Duke of Milan. Shakespeare pushes against this conservative logic in *All's Well That Ends Well,* but the noble young Bertram violently resists the unequal match thrust upon him by the King, and the play's mood is notoriously uneasy.

Similarly, Shakespeare's theater may have been patronized and protected by the monarchy—after 1603, his company received a royal patent and was known as the King's Men—but it was by no means identical in its interests or its ethos. To be sure, *Richard III* and *Macbeth* incorporate aspects of royal propaganda, but given the realities of censorship, Shakespeare's plays, and the period's drama as a whole, are surprisingly independent and complex in their political vision. There is, in any case, a certain inherent tension between kings and player kings: Elizabeth and James may both have likened themselves to actors onstage, but they were loath to admit their dependence on the applause and money, freely given or freely withheld, of the audience. The charismatic monarch insists that the sacredness of authority resides in the body of the ruler, not in a costume that may be worn and then discarded by an actor. Kings are not *representations* of power—or do not admit that they are—but claim to be the thing itself. The government institution that was actually based on the idea of representation, Parliament, had theatrical elements, as we have seen, but it significantly excluded any audience from its deliberations. And Shakespeare's oblique portraits of parliamentary representatives, the tribunes Sicinius Velutus and Junius Brutus in *Coriolanus,* are anything but flattering.

Finally, the theater drew significant energy from the liturgy and rituals of the late medieval Church, but as Shakespeare's contemporaries widely remarked, the playhouse and the Church were scarcely natural allies. Not only did the theater represent a potential competitor to worship services, and not only did ministers rail against prostitution and other vices associated with playgoing, but theatrical representation itself, even when ostensibly pious, seemed to many to empty out whatever it presented, turning substance into mere show. The theater could and did use the period's deep currents of religious feeling, but it had to do so carefully and with an awareness of conflicting interests.

Shakespeare Comes to London

How did Shakespeare decide to turn his prodigious talents to the stage? When did he make his way to London? How did he get his start? To these and similar questions we have a mountain of speculation but no secure answers. There is not a single surviving record of Shakespeare's existence from 1585, when his twins were baptized in Stratford church, until 1592, when a rival London playwright made an envious remark about him. In the late seventeenth century, the delightfully eccentric collector of gossip John Aubrey was informed that prior to moving to London the young Shakespeare had been a schoolteacher in the country. Aubrey also recorded a story that Shakespeare had been a rather unusual apprentice butcher: "When he killed a calf, he would do it in a high style, and make a speech."

These and other legends, including one that has Shakespeare whipped for poaching game, fill the void until the unmistakable reference in Robert Greene's *Groats-Worth of Witte, Bought with a Million of Repentance* (1592). An inspired hack writer with a university education, a penchant for self-dramatization, a taste for wild living, and a strong streak of resentment, Greene, in his early thirties, was dying in poverty when he penned his last farewell, piously urging his fellow dramatists Christopher Marlowe, Thomas Nashe, and George Peele to abandon the wicked stage before they were brought low, as he had been, by a new arrival: "For there is an upstart crow, beautified with our feathers, that with his 'Tiger's heart wrapped in player's hide' supposes he is as well able to bombast out a blank verse as the best of you, and, being an absolute *Johannes Factotum,* is in his own conceit the only Shake-scene in a country." If "Shake-scene" is not enough to identify the object of his attack, Greene parodies a line from Shakespeare's early play *Richard Duke of York (3 Henry VI):* "O tiger's heart wrapped in a woman's hide!" (1.4.138). Greene is accusing Shakespeare of being an upstart, a plagiarist, an egomaniacal jack-of-all-trades—and, above all perhaps, a popular success.

By 1592, then, Shakespeare had already arrived on the highly competitive London theatrical scene. He was successful enough to be attacked by Greene and, a few months later, defended by Henry Chettle, another hack writer who had seen Greene's manuscript through the press (or, some scholars speculate, had written the attack himself and passed it off as the dying Greene's). Chettle expresses his regret that he did not suppress Greene's diatribe and spare Shakespeare "because myself have seen his demeanor no less civil than he excellent in the quality he professes." Besides, Chettle adds, "divers of worship have reported his uprightness of dealing, which argues his honesty and his facetious [polished] grace in writing that approves his art." "Divers of worship": not only was Shakespeare established as an accomplished writer and actor, but he evidently had aroused the attention and the approbation of several socially prominent people. In Elizabethan England, aristocratic patronage, with the money, protection, and prestige it alone could provide, was probably a professional writer's most important asset.

This patronage, or at least Shakespeare's quest for it, is most visible in the dedications in 1593 and 1594 of his narrative poems *Venus and Adonis* and *The Rape of Lucrece* to the young nobleman Henry Wriothesley, Earl of Southampton. It may be glimpsed as well, perhaps, in the sonnets, with their extraordinary adoration of the fair youth, though the identity of that youth has never been determined. What return Shakespeare got for his exquisite offerings is likewise unknown. We do know that among wits and gallants, the narrative poems won Shakespeare a fine reputation as an immensely stylish and accomplished poet. An amateur play performed at Cambridge University at the end of the sixteenth century, *The Return from Parnassus,* makes fun of this vogue, as a foolish character effusively declares, "I'll worship sweet Mr. Shakespeare, and to honour him will lay his *Venus and Adonis* under my pillow." Many readers at the time may have done so: the poem went through sixteen editions before 1640, more than any other work by Shakespeare.

Patronage was crucially important not only for individual artists but also for the actors, playwrights, and investors who pooled their resources to form professional theater companies. The public playhouses had enemies, especially among civic and religious authorities, who wished greatly to curb performances or to ban them altogether. An act of 1572 included players among those classified as vagabonds, threatening them, therefore, with the horrible punishments meted out to those regarded as economic parasites. The players' escape route was to be nominally enrolled as the servants of high-ranking noblemen. The legal fiction was that their public performances were a kind of rehearsal for the command performances before the patron or the monarch.

When Shakespeare came to London, presumably in the late 1580s, there were more than a dozen of these companies operating under the patronage of various aristocrats.

We do not know for which of these companies, several of which had toured in Stratford, he originally worked, nor whether he began, as legend has it, as a prompter's assistant and then graduated to acting and playwriting. Shakespeare is listed among the actors in Ben Jonson's *Every Man in His Humour* (performed in 1598) and *Sejanus* (performed in 1603), but we do not know for certain what roles he played, nor are there records of any of his other performances. Tradition has it that he played Adam in *As You Like It* and the Ghost in *Hamlet,* but he was clearly not one of the leading actors of the day.

By the 1590s, the number of playing companies in London had been considerably reduced, in part through competition and in part through legislative restriction. (In 1572, knights and gentry lost the privilege of patronizing a troupe of actors; in 1598, justices of the peace lost the power to authorize performances.) By the early years of the seventeenth century, there were usually only three companies competing against one another in any season, along with two children's companies, which were often successful at drawing audiences away from the public playhouses. Shakespeare may initially have been associated with the Earl of Leicester's company or with the company of Ferdinando Stanley, Lord Strange; both groups included actors with whom Shakespeare was later linked. Or he may have belonged to the Earl of Pembroke's Men, since there is evidence that they per-

Edward Alleyn (1566–1626). Artist unknown. Alleyn was the great tragic actor of the Lord Admiral's Men (the principal rival to Shakespeare's company). He was famous especially for playing the great Marlovian heroes.

formed *The Taming of a Shrew* and a version of *Richard Duke of York (3 Henry VI)*. At any event, by 1594, Shakespeare was a member of the Lord Chamberlain's Men, for his name, along with those of Will Kemp (or Kempe) and Richard Burbage, appears on a record of those "servants to the Lord Chamberlain" paid for performance at the royal palace at Greenwich on December 26 and 28. Shakespeare stayed with this company, which during the reign of King James received royal patronage and became the King's Men, for the rest of his career.

Many playwrights in Shakespeare's time worked freelance, moving from company to company as opportunities arose, collaborating on projects, adding scenes to old plays, scrambling from one enterprise to another. But certain playwrights, among them the most successful, wrote for a single company, often agreeing contractually to give that company exclusive rights to their theatrical works. Shakespeare seems to have followed such a pattern. For the Lord Chamberlain's Men, he wrote an average of two plays per year. His company initially performed in The Theatre, a playhouse built in 1576 by an entrepreneurial carpenter, James Burbage, the father of the actor Richard, who was to perform many of

Shakespeare's greatest roles. When in 1597 their lease on this playhouse expired, the Lord Chamberlain's Men passed through a difficult and legally perilous time, but they formed a joint-stock company, raising sufficient capital to lease a site and put up a splendid new playhouse in the suburb of Southwark, on the south bank of the Thames. This playhouse, the Globe, opened in 1599. Shakespeare is listed in the legal agreement as one of the principal investors; and when the company began to use Blackfriars as their indoor playhouse around 1609, he was a major shareholder in that theater as well. The Lord Chamberlain's Men, later the King's Men, dominated the theater scene, and the shares were quite valuable. Then as now, the theater was an extremely risky enterprise—most of those who wrote plays and performed in them made pathetically little money—but Shakespeare was a notable exception. The fine house in Stratford and the coat of arms he succeeded in acquiring were among the fruits of his multiple mastery, as actor, playwright, and investor in the London stage.

The Shakespearean Trajectory

Even though Shakespeare's England was in many ways a record-keeping society, no reliable record survives that details the performances, year by year, in the London theaters. Every play had to be licensed by a government official, the Master of the Revels, but the records kept by the relevant officials from 1579 to 1621, Sir Edmund Tilney and Sir George Buc, have not survived. A major theatrical entrepreneur, Philip Henslowe, kept a careful account of his expenditures, including what he paid for the scripts he commissioned, but unfortunately Henslowe's main business was with the Rose and the Fortune theaters and not with the playhouses at which Shakespeare's company performed. A comparable ledger must have been kept by the shareholders of the Lord Chamberlain's Men, but it has not survived. Shakespeare himself apparently did not undertake to preserve for posterity the sum of his writings, let alone to clarify the chronology of his works or specify which plays he wrote alone and which with collaborators.

The principal source for Shakespeare's works is the 1623 Folio volume of *Mr. William Shakespeares Comedies, Histories, & Tragedies*. Most scholars believe that the editors were careful to include only those plays for which they knew Shakespeare to be the main author. Their edition does not, however, include any of Shakespeare's nondramatic poems, and it omits two plays in which Shakespeare is now thought to have had a significant hand, *Pericles, Prince of Tyre* and *The Two Noble Kinsmen*, along with his probable contribution to the multiauthored *Sir Thomas More*. (A number of other plays were attributed to Shakespeare, both before and after his death, but scholars have not generally accepted any of these into the established canon.) Moreover, the Folio edition does not print the plays in chronological order, nor does it attempt to establish a chronology. We do not know how much time would normally have elapsed between the writing of a play and its first performance, nor, with

IF YOU KNOW NOT ME,
You know no body.
OR,
The troubles of Queene ELIZABETH.

LONDON.
Printed by *B.A.* and *T.F.* for *Nathanaell Butter.* 1632.

Title page of Thomas Heywood's *If You Know Not Me, You Know No Body; or, The Troubles of Queene Elizabeth* (1632 ed.).

a few exceptions, do we know with any certainty the month or even the year of the first performance of any of Shakespeare's plays. The quarto editions of those plays that were published during Shakespeare's lifetime obviously establish a date by which we know a given play had been written, but they give us little more than an end point, because there was likely to be a substantial though indeterminate gap between the first performance of a play and its publication.

With enormous patience and ingenuity, however, scholars have gradually assembled a considerable archive of evidence, both external and internal, for dating the composition of the plays. Besides actual publication, the external evidence includes explicit reference to a play, a record of its performance, or (as in the case of Greene's attack on the "upstart crow") the quoting of a line, though all of these can be maddeningly ambiguous. The most important single piece of external evidence appears in 1598 in *Palladis Tamia,* a long book of jumbled reflections by Francis Meres that includes a survey of the contemporary literary scene. Meres finds that "the sweet, witty soul of Ovid lives in melliflous and honey-tongued Shakespeare, witness his *Venus and Adonis,* his *Lucrece,* his sugered Sonnets among his private friends, etc." Meres goes on to list Shakespeare's accomplishments as a playwright as well:

> As Plautus and Seneca are accounted the best for Comedy and Tragedy among the Latins: so Shakespeare among the English is the most excellent in both kinds for the stage; for Comedy, witness his *Gentlemen of Verona,* his *Errors,* his *Love labors lost,* his *Love labours won,* his *Midsummers night dream,* & his *Merchant of Venice:* for Tragedy his *Richard the 2, Richard the 3, Henry the 4, King John, Titus Andronicus* and his *Romeo and Juliet.*

Meres thus provides a date by which twelve of Shakespeare's plays had definitely appeared (including one, *Love's Labour's Won,* that appears to have been lost or that we know by a different title). Unfortunately, Meres provides no clues about the order of appearance of these plays, and there are no other comparable lists.

Faced with the limitations of the external evidence, scholars have turned to a bewildering array of internal evidence, ranging from datable sources and topical allusions on the one hand to evolving stylistic features (ratio of verse to prose, percentage of rhyme to blank verse, colloquialisms, use of extended similes, and the like) on the other. Thus, for example, a cluster of plays with a high percentage of rhymed verse may follow closely upon Shakespeare's writing of the rhymed poems *Venus and Adonis* and *The Rape of Lucrece* and, therefore, be datable to 1594–95. Similarly, vocabulary overlap probably indicates proximity in composition, so if four or five plays share relatively "rare" vocabulary, it is likely that they were written in roughly the same period. Again, there seems to be a pattern in Shakespeare's use of colloquialisms, with a steady increase from *As You Like It* (1599–1600) to *Coriolanus* (1608), followed in the late romances by a retreat from the colloquial.

More sophisticated computer analysis should provide further guidance in the future, even though the precise order of the plays, still very much in dispute, is never likely to be settled to universal satisfaction. Still, certain broad patterns are now widely accepted. These patterns can be readily grasped in the *Norton Shakespeare,* which presents the plays in the chronological order proposed by the Oxford editors.

Shakespeare began his career, probably in the early 1590s, by writing both comedies and history plays. The attack by Greene suggests that he made his mark with the series of theatrically vital but rather crude plays based on the foreign and domestic broils that erupted during the unhappy reign of the Lancastrian Henry VI. Modern readers and audiences are more likely to find the first sustained evidence of unusual power in *Richard III* (c. 1592), a play that combines a brilliantly conceived central character, a dazzling command of histrionic rhetoric, and an overarching moral vision of English history.

At virtually the same time that he was setting his stamp on the genre of the history play, Shakespeare was writing his first—or first surviving—comedies. Here, there are even fewer signs than in the histories of an apprenticeship: *The Comedy of Errors,* one of his early efforts in this genre, already displays a rare command of the resources of comedy: mistaken identity, madcap confusion, and the threat of disaster, giving way in the end to reconciliation, recovery, and love. Shakespeare's other comedies from the early 1590s, *The Taming of the Shrew, The Two Gentlemen of Verona,* and *Love's Labour's Lost,* are no less remarkable for their sophisticated variations on familiar comic themes, their inexhaustible rhetorical inventiveness, and their poignant intimation, in the midst of festive celebration, of loss.

Successful as are these early histories and comedies, and indicative of an extraordinary theatrical talent, Shakespeare's achievement in the later 1590s would still have been all but impossible to foresee. Starting with *A Midsummer Night's Dream* (c. 1595), Shakespeare wrote an unprecedented series of romantic comedies—*The Merchant of Venice, The Merry Wives of Windsor, Much Ado About Nothing, As You Like It,* and *Twelfth Night* (c. 1602)—whose poetic richness and emotional complexity remain unmatched. In the same period, he wrote a sequence of profoundly searching and ambitious history plays—*Richard II, 1* and *2 Henry IV,* and *Henry V*—which together explore the death throes of feudal England and the birth of the modern nation-state ruled by a charismatic monarch. Both the comedies and histories of this period are marked by their capaciousness, their ability to absorb characters who press up against the outermost boundaries of the genre: the comedy *Merchant of Venice* somehow contains the figure, at once nightmarish and poignant, of Shylock, while the *Henry IV* plays, with their somber vision of crisis in the family and the state, bring to the stage one of England's greatest comic characters, Falstaff.

If in the mid to late 1590s Shakespeare reached the summit of his art in two major genres, he also manifested a lively interest in a third. As early as 1593, he wrote the crudely violent tragedy *Titus Andronicus,* the first of several plays on themes from Roman history, and a year or two later, in *Richard II,* he created in the protagonist a figure who achieves by the play's close the stature of a tragic hero. In the same year that Shakespeare wrote the wonderfully farcical "Pyramus and Thisbe" scene in *A Midsummer Night's Dream,* he probably also wrote the deeply tragic realization of the same story in *Romeo and Juliet.* But once again, the lyric anguish of *Romeo and Juliet* and the tormented self-revelation of *Richard II,* extraordinary as they are, could not have led anyone to predict the next phase of Shakespeare's career, the great tragic dramas that poured forth in the early years of the seventeenth century: *Hamlet, Othello, King Lear, Macbeth, Antony and Cleopatra,* and *Coriolanus.* These plays, written from 1601 to 1607, seem to mark a major shift in sensibility, an existential and metaphysical darkening that many readers think must have originated in a deep personal anguish, perhaps caused by the death of Shakespeare's father, John, in 1601.

Whatever the truth of these speculations—and we have no direct, personal testimony either to support or to undermine them—there appears to have occurred in the same period a shift as well in Shakespeare's comic sensibility. The comedies written between 1601 and 1604, *Troilus and Cressida, All's Well That Ends Well,* and *Measure for Measure,* are sufficiently different from the earlier comedies—more biting in tone, more uneasy with comic conventions, more ruthlessly questioning of the values of the characters and the resolutions of the plots—to have led many twentieth-century scholars to classify them as "problem plays" or "dark comedies." This category has recently begun to fall out of favor, since Shakespeare criticism is perfectly happy to demonstrate that *all* of the plays are "problem plays." But there is another group of plays, among the last Shakespeare wrote, that continue to constitute a distinct category. *Pericles, Cymbeline, The Winter's Tale,* and *The Tempest,* written between 1608 and 1611, when the playwright had developed a remarkably fluid, dreamlike sense of plot and a poetic style that could veer, apparently effortlessly, from the tortured to the ineffably sweet, are known as the "romances." These plays share an interest in the moral and emotional life less of the adolescents who dominate the earlier comedies than of their parents. The romances are deeply concerned with patterns of loss and recovery, suffering and redemption,

despair and renewal. They have seemed to many critics to constitute a deliberate conclusion to a career that began in histories and comedies and passed through the dark
and tormented tragedies.

One effect of the practice of printing Shakespeare's plays in a reconstructed
chronological order, as this edition does, is to produce a kind of authorial plot, a
progress from youthful exuberance and a heroic grappling with history, through psychological anguish and radical doubt, to a mature serenity built upon an understanding of loss. The ordering of Shakespeare's "complete works" in this way reconstitutes
the figure of the author as the beloved hero of his own, lived romance. There are
numerous reasons to treat this romance with considerable skepticism: the precise order
of the plays remains in dispute, the obsessions of the earliest plays crisscross with those
of the last, the drama is a collaborative art form, and the relation between authorial
consciousness and theatrical representation is murky. Yet a longing to identify Shakespeare's personal trajectory, to chart his psychic and spiritual as well as professional
progress, is all but irresistible.

The Fetishism of Dress

Whatever the personal resonance of Shakespeare's own life, his art is deeply
enmeshed in the collective hopes, fears, and fantasies of his time. For example, throughout his plays, Shakespeare draws heavily upon his culture's investment in costume, symbols of authority, visible signs of status—the fetishism of dress he must have witnessed
from early childhood. Disguise in his drama is often assumed to be incredibly effective:
when Henry V borrows a cloak, when Portia dresses in a jurist's robes, when Viola puts
on a young man's suit, it is as if each has become unrecognizable, as if identity resided
in clothing. At the end of *Twelfth Night,* even though Viola's true identity has been disclosed, Orsino continues to call her Cesario; he will do so, he says, until she resumes
her maid's garments, for only then will she be transformed into a woman:

> Cesario, come—
> For so you shall be while you are a man;
> But when in other habits you are seen,
> Orsino's mistress, and his fancy's queen.
> (5.1.372–75)

The pinnacle of this fetishism of costume is the royal crown, for whose identity-
conferring power men are willing to die, but the principle is everywhere from the filthy
blanket that transforms Edgar into Poor Tom to the coxcomb that is the badge of the
licensed fool. Antonio, wishing to express his utter contempt, spits on Shylocks' "Jewish gaberdine," as if the clothing were the essence of the man; Kent, pouring insults on
the loathsome Oswald, calls him a "filthy worsted-stocking knave"; and innocent Innogen, learning that her husband has ordered her murder, thinks of herself as an expensive cast-off dress, destined to be ripped at the seams:

> Poor I am stale, a garment out of fashion,
> And for I am richer than to hang by th' walls
> I must be ripped. To pieces with me!
> (*Cymbeline* 3.4.50–52)

What can be said, thought, felt, in this culture seems deeply dependent on the
clothes one wears—clothes that one is, in effect, *permitted* or *compelled* to wear, since
there is little freedom in dress. Shakespearean drama occasionally represents something like such freedom: after all, Viola in *Twelfth Night* chooses to put off her "maiden
weeds," as does Rosalind, who declares, "We'll have a swashing and a martial outside"
(*As You Like It* 1.3.114). But these choices are characteristically made under the pressure of desperate circumstances, here shipwreck and exile. Part of the charm of Shakespeare's heroines is their ability to transform distress into an opportunity for

self-fashioning, but the plays often suggest that there is less autonomy than meets the eye. What looks like an escape from cultural determinism may be only a deeper form of constraint. We may take, as an allegorical emblem of this constraint, the transformation of the beggar Christopher Sly into a nobleman in the playful Induction to *The Taming of the Shrew*. The transformation seems to suggest that you are free to make of yourself whatever you choose to be—the play begins with the drunken Sly indignantly claiming the dignity of his pedigree ("Look in the Chronicles" [Induction 1.3–4])—but in fact he is only the subject of the mischievous lord's experiment, designed to demonstrate the interwovenness of clothing and identity. "What think you," the lord asks his huntsman,

> if he were conveyed to bed,
> Wrapped in sweet clothes, rings put upon his fingers,
> A most delicious banquet by his bed,
> And brave attendants near him when he wakes—
> Would not the beggar then forget himself?

To which the huntsman replies, in words that underscore the powerlessness of the drunken beggar, "Believe me, lord, I think he cannot choose" (Induction 1.33–38).

Petruccio's taming of Katherine is similarly constructed around an imposition of identity, an imposition closely bound up with the right to wear certain articles of clothing. When the haberdasher arrives with a fashionable lady's hat, Petruccio refuses it over his wife's vehement objections: "This doth fit the time, / And gentlewomen wear such caps as these." "When you are gentle," Petruccio replies, "you shall have one, too, / And not till then" (4.3.69–72). At the play's close, Petruccio demonstrates his authority by commanding his tamed wife to throw down her cap: "Off with that bauble, throw it underfoot" (5.2.126). Here as elsewhere in Shakespeare, acts of robing and disrobing are intensely charged, a charge that culminates in the trappings of monarchy. When Richard II, in a scene that was probably censored from the stage as well as the printed text during the reign of Elizabeth, is divested of his crown and scepter, he experiences the loss as the eradication of his name, the symbolic melting away of his identity:

> Alack the heavy day,
> That I have worn so many winters out
> And know not now what name to call myself!
> O, that I were a mockery king of snow,
> Standing before the sun of Bolingbroke
> To melt myself away in water-drops!
> (4.1.247–52)

When Lear tears off his regal "lendings" in order to reduce himself to the nakedness of the Bedlam beggar, he is expressing not only his radical loss of social identity but the breakdown of his psychic order as well, expressing, therefore, his reduction to the condition of the "poor bare forked animal" that is the primal condition of undifferentiated existence. And when Cleopatra determines to kill herself in order to escape public humiliation in Rome, she magnificently affirms her essential being by arraying herself as she had once done to encounter Antony:

> Show me, my women, like a queen. Go fetch
> My best attires. I am again for Cydnus
> To meet Mark Antony.
> (5.2.223–25)

Such scenes are a remarkable intensification of the everyday symbolic practice of Renaissance English culture, its characteristically deep and knowing commitment to illusion: "I know perfectly well that the woman in her crown and jewels and gorgeous gown is an aging, irascible, and fallible mortal—she herself virtually admits as much—yet I profess that she is the Virgin Queen, timelessly beautiful, wise, and just." Shakespeare understood how close this willed illusion was to the spirit of the theater, to the actors' ability to work on what the chorus in *Henry V* calls the "imaginary forces" of the audience. But there is throughout Shakespeare's works a counterintuition that, while it does not exactly overturn this illusion, renders it poignant, vulnerable, fraught. The "masculine usurp'd attire" that is donned by Viola, Rosalind, Portia, Jessica, and other Shakespeare heroines alters what they can say and do, reveals important aspects of their character, and changes their destiny, but it is, all the same, not theirs and not all of who they are. They have, the plays insist, natures that are neither transformed nor altogether concealed by their dress: "Pray God defend me," exclaims the frightened Viola. "A little thing would make me tell them how much I lack of a man" (*Twelfth Night* 3.4.268–69).

The Paradoxes of Identity

The gap between costume and identity is not simply a matter of what women supposedly lack; virtually all of Shakespeare's major characters, men and women, convey the sense of both a *self-division* and an *inward expansion*. The belief in a complex inward realm beyond costumes and status is a striking inversion of the clothes cult: we know perfectly well that the characters have no inner lives apart from what we see on the stage, and yet we believe that they continue to exist when we do not see them, that they exist apart from their represented words and actions, that they have hidden dimensions. How is this conviction aroused and sustained? In part, it is the effect of what the characters themselves say: "My grief lies all within," Richard II tells Bolingbroke,

> And these external manner of laments
> Are merely shadows to the unseen grief
> That swells with silence in the tortured soul.
> (4.1.285–88)

Similarly, Hamlet, dismissing the significance of his outward garments, declares, "I have that within which passeth show— / These but the trappings and the suits of woe" (1.2.85–86). And the distinction between inward and outward is reinforced throughout this play and elsewhere by an unprecedented use of the aside and the soliloquy.

The soliloquy is a continual reminder in Shakespeare that the inner life is by no means transparent to one's surrounding world. Prince Hal seems open and easy with his mates in Eastcheap, but he has a hidden reservoir of disgust:

> I know you all, and will a while uphold
> The unyoked humour of your idleness.
> Yet herein will I imitate the sun,
> Who doth permit the base contagious clouds
> To smother up his beauty from the world,
> That when he please again to be himself,
> Being wanted he may be more wondered at
> By breaking through the foul and ugly mists
> Of vapours that did seem to strangle him.
> (*1 Henry IV* 1.2.173–81)

"When he please again to be himself": the line implies that identity is a matter of free choice—you decide how much of yourself you wish to disclose—but Shakespeare employs other devices that suggest more elusive and intractable layers of inwardness. There is a peculiar, recurrent lack of fit between costume and character, in fools as in princes, that is not simply a matter of disguise and disclosure. If Hal's true identity is partially "smothered" in the tavern, it is not completely revealed either in his soldier's armor or in his royal robes, nor do his asides reach the bedrock of unimpeachable self-understanding.

Identity in Shakespeare repeatedly slips away from the characters themselves, as it does from Richard II after the deposition scene and from Lear after he has given away his land and from Macbeth after he has gained the crown. The slippage does not mean that they retreat into silence; rather, they embark on an experimental, difficult fashioning of themselves and the world, most often through role-playing. "I cannot do it," says the deposed and imprisoned Richard II. "Yet I'll hammer it out" (5.5.5). This could serve as the motto for many Shakespearean characters: Viola becomes Cesario, Rosalind calls herself Ganymede, Kent becomes Caius, Edgar presents himself as Poor Tom, Hamlet plays the madman that he has partly become, Hal pretends that he is his father and a highwayman and Hotspur and even himself. Even in comedy, these ventures into alternate identities are rarely matters of choice; in tragedy, they are always undertaken under pressure and compulsion. And often enough it is not a matter of role-playing at all, but of a drastic transformation whose extreme emblem is the harrowing madness of Lear and of Leontes.

There is a moment in *Richard II* in which the deposed King asks for a mirror and then, after musing on his reflection, throws it to the ground. The shattering of the glass serves to remind us not only of the fragility of identity in Shakespeare but of its characteristic appearance in fragmentary mirror images. The plays continually generate alternative reflections, identities that intersect with, underscore, echo, or otherwise set off that of the principal character. Hence, Desdemona and Iago are not only important figures in Othello's world, they also seem to embody partially realized aspects of himself; Falstaff and Hotspur play a comparable role in relation to Prince Hal, Fortinbras and Horatio in relation to Hamlet, Gloucester and the Fool in relation to Lear, and so forth. In many of these plays, the complementary and contrasting characters figure in subplots, subtly interwoven with the play's main plot and illuminating its concerns. The note so conspicuously sounded by Fortinbras at the close of *Hamlet*—what the hero might have been, "had he been put on"—is heard repeatedly in Shakespeare and contributes to the overwhelming intensity, poignancy, and complexity of the characters. This is a world in which outward appearance is everything and nothing, in which individuation is at once sharply etched and continually blurred, in which the victims of fate are haunted by the ghosts of the possible, in which everything is simultaneously as it must be and as it need not have been.

Are these antinomies signs of a struggle between contradictory and irreconcilable perspectives in Shakespeare? In certain plays—notably, *Measure for Measure, All's Well That Ends Well, Coriolanus,* and *Troilus and Cressida*—the tension seems both high and entirely unresolved. But Shakespearean contradictions are more often reminiscent of the capacious spirit of Montaigne, who refused any systematic order that would betray his sense of reality. Thus, individual characters are immensely important in Shakespeare—he is justly celebrated for his unmatched skill in the invention of particular dramatic identities, marked with distinct speech patterns, manifested in social status, and confirmed by costume and gesture—but the principle of individuation is not the rock on which his theatrical art is founded. After the masks are stripped away, the pretenses exposed, the claims of the ego shattered, there is a mysterious remainder; as the shamed but irrepressible Paroles declares in *All's Well That Ends Well*, "Simply the thing I am / Shall make me live" (4.3.310–11). Again and again, the audience is made to sense a deeper energy, a source of power that at once discharges itself in individual characters and seems to sweep right through them.

The Poet of Nature

In *The Birth of Tragedy,* Nietzsche called a comparable source of energy that he found in Greek tragedy "Dionysos." But the god's name, conjuring up Bacchic frenzy, does not seem appropriate to Shakespeare. In the late seventeenth and eighteenth centuries, it was more plausibly called Nature: "The world must be peopled," says the delightful Benedick in *Much Ado About Nothing* (2.3.213–14), and there are frequent invocations elsewhere of the happy, generative power that brings couples together—

Jack shall have Jill,
Naught shall go ill,
the man shall have his mare again, and all shall be well.
(*A Midsummer Night's Dream* 3.3.45–47)

—and the melancholy, destructive power that brings all living things to the grave: "Golden lads and girls all must, / As chimney-sweepers, come to dust" (*Cymbeline* 4.2.263–64).

But the celebration of Shakespeare as a poet of nature—often coupled with an inane celebration of his supposedly "natural" (that is, untutored) genius—has its distinct limitations. For Shakespearean art brilliantly interrogates the "natural," refusing to take for granted precisely what the celebrants think is most secure. His comedies are endlessly inventive in showing that love is not simply natural: the playful hint of bestiality in the line quoted above, "the man shall have his mare again" (from a play in which the Queen of the Fairies falls in love with an ass-headed laborer), lightly unsettles the boundaries between the natural and the perverse. These boundaries are called into question throughout Shakespeare's work, from the cross-dressing and erotic crosscurrents that deliciously complicate the lives of the characters in *Twelfth Night* and *As You Like It* to the terrifying violence that wells up from the heart of the family in *King Lear* or from the sweet intimacy of sexual desire in *Othello*. Even the boundary between life and death is not secure, as the ghosts in *Julius Caesar, Hamlet,* and *Macbeth* attest, while the principle of natural death (given its most eloquent articulation by old Hamlet's murderer, Claudius!) is repeatedly tainted and disrupted.

Disrupted, too, is the idea of order that constantly makes its claim, most insistently in the history plays. Scholars have observed the presence in Shakespeare's works of the so-called Tudor myth—the ideological justification of the ruling dynasty as a restoration of national order after a cycle of tragic violence. The violence, Tudor apologists claimed, was divine punishment unleashed after the deposition of the anointed king, Richard II, for God will not tolerate violations of the sanctified order. Traces of this propaganda certainly exist in the histories—Shakespeare may, for all we know, have personally subscribed to its premises—but a closer scrutiny of his plays has disclosed so many ironic reservations and qualifications and subversions as to call into question any straightforward adherence to a political line. The plays manifest a profound fascination with the monarchy and with the ambitions of the aristocracy, but the fascination is never simply endorsement. There is always at least the hint of a slippage between the great figures, whether admirable or monstrous, who stand at the pinnacle of authority and the vast, miscellaneous mass of soldiers, scriveners, ostlers, poets, whores, gardeners, thieves, weavers, shepherds, country gentlemen, sturdy beggars, and the like who make up the commonwealth. And the idea of order, though eloquently articulated (most memorably by Ulysses in *Troilus and Cressida*), is always shadowed by a relentless spirit of irony.

The Play of Language

If neither the individual nor nature nor order will serve, can we find a single comprehensive name for the underlying force in Shakespeare's work? Certainly not. The work is too protean and capacious. But much of the energy that surges through this astonishing body of plays and poems is closely linked to the power of language. Shakespeare was the supreme product of a rhetorical culture, a culture steeped in the arts of persuasion and verbal expressiveness. In 1512, the great Dutch humanist Erasmus published a work called *De copia verborum* that taught its readers how to cultivate "copiousness," verbal richness, in discourse. (Erasmus obligingly provides, as a sample, a list of 144 different ways of saying "Thank you for your letter.") Recommended modes of variation include putting the subject of an argument into fictional form, as well as the use of synonym, substitution, paraphrase, metaphor, metonymy, synecdoche, hyperbole, diminution, and a host of other figures of speech. To change emotional tone, he suggests trying *ironia, interrogatio, admiratio, dubitatio, abominatio*—the possibilities seem infinite.

In Renaissance England, certain syntactic forms or patterns of words known as "figures" (also called "schemes") were shaped and repeated in order to confer beauty or heighten expressive power. Figures were usually known by their Greek and Latin names, though in an Elizabethan rhetorical manual, *The Arte of English Poesie,* George Puttenham made a valiant if short-lived attempt to give them English equivalents, such as "*Hyperbole,* or the Overreacher," "*Ironia,* or the Dry Mock," and "*Ploce,* or the Doubler." Those who received a grammar-school education throughout Europe at almost any point between the Roman Empire and the eighteenth century probably knew by heart the names of up to one hundred such figures, just as they knew by heart their multiplication tables. According to one scholar's count, Shakespeare knew and made use of about two hundred.

As certain grotesquely inflated Renaissance texts attest, lessons from *De copia verborum* and similar rhetorical guides could encourage mere prolixity and verbal self-display. But even though he shared his culture's delight in rhetorical complexity, Shakespeare always understood how to swoop from baroque sophistication to breathtaking simplicity. Moreover, he grasped early in his career how to use figures of speech, tone, and rhythm not only to provide emphasis and elegant variety but also to articulate the inner lives of his characters. Take, for example, these lines from *Othello,* where, as scholars have noted, Shakespeare deftly combines four common rhetorical figures—*anaphora, parison, isocolon,* and *epistrophe*—to depict with painful vividness Othello's psychological torment:

> By the world,
> I think my wife be honest, and think she is not.
> I think that thou art just, and think thou art not.
> I'll have some proof.
>
> (3.3.388–91)

Anaphora is simply the repetition of a word at the beginning of a sequence of sentences or clauses ("I/I"). *Parison* is the correspondence of word to word within adjacent sentences or clauses, either by direct repetition ("think/think") or by the matching of noun with noun, verb with verb ("wife/thou"; "be/art"). *Isocolon* gives exactly the same length to corresponding clauses ("and think she is not/and think thou art not"), and *epistrophe* is the mirror image of *anaphora* in that it is the repetition of a word at the end of a sequence of sentences or clauses ("not/not"). Do we need to know the Greek names for these figures in order to grasp the effectiveness of Othello's lines? Of course not. But Shakespeare and his contemporaries, convinced that rhetoric provided the most natural and powerful means by which feelings could be conveyed to readers and listeners, were trained in an analytical language that helped at once to promote and to account for this effectiveness. In his 1593 edition of *The Garden of Eloquence,* Henry Peacham remarks that *epistrophe* "serveth to leave a word of importance in the end of a sentence, that it may the longer hold the sound in the mind of the hearer," and in *Directions for Speech and Style* (c. 1599), John Hoskins notes that *anaphora* "beats upon one thing to cause the quicker feeling in the audience."

Shakespeare also shared with his contemporaries a keen understanding of the ways that rhetorical devices could be used not only to express powerful feelings but to hide them: after all, the artist who created Othello also created Iago, Richard III, and Lady Macbeth. He could deftly skewer the rhetorical affectations of Polonius in *Hamlet* or the pedant Holophernes in *Love's Labour's Lost.* He could deploy stylistic variations to mark the boundaries not of different individuals but of different social realms; in *A Midsummer Night's Dream,* for example, the blank verse of Duke Theseus is played off against the rhymed couplets of the well-born young lovers, and both in turn contrast with the prose spoken by the artisans. At the same time that he thus marks boundaries between both individuals and groups, Shakespeare shows a remarkable ability to establish unifying patterns of imagery that knit together the diverse strands of his plot and suggest subtle links among characters who may be scarcely aware of how much they share with one another.

One of the hidden links in Shakespeare's own works is the frequent use he makes of a somewhat unusual rhetorical figure called *hendiadys*. An example from the Roman poet Virgil is the phrase *pateris libamus et auro,* "we drink from cups and gold" (*Georgics* 2.192). Rather than serving as an adjective or a dependent noun, as in "golden cups" or "cups of gold," the word "gold" serves as a substantive joined to another substantive, "cups," by a conjunction, "and." Shakespeare uses the figure over three hundred times in all, and since it does not appear in ancient or medieval lists of tropes and schemes and is treated only briefly by English rhetoricians, he may have come upon it directly in Virgil. *Hendiadys* literally means "one through two," though Shakespeare's versions often make us quickly, perhaps only subliminally, aware of the complexity of what ordinarily passes for straightforward perceptions. When Othello, in his suicide speech, invokes the memory of "a malignant and a turbaned Turk," the figure of speech at once associates enmity with cultural difference and keeps them slightly apart. And when Macbeth speaks of his "strange and self-abuse," the *hendiadys* seems briefly to hold both "strange" and "self" up for scrutiny. It would be foolish to make too much of any single feature in Shakespeare's varied and diverse creative achievement, and yet this curious rhetorical scheme has something of the quality of a fingerprint.

But all of his immense rhetorical gifts, though rich, beautiful, and supremely useful, do not adequately convey Shakespeare's relation to language, which is less strictly functional than a total immersion in the arts of persuasion may imply. An Erasmian admiration for copiousness cannot fully explain Shakespeare's astonishing vocabulary of some 25,000 words. (His closest rival among the great English poets of the period was John Milton, with about 12,000 words, and most major writers, let alone ordinary people, have much smaller vocabularies.) This immense word hoard, it is worth noting, was not the result of scanning a dictionary; in the late sixteenth century, there were no English dictionaries of the kind to which we are now accustomed. Shakespeare seems to have absorbed new words from virtually every discursive realm he ever encountered, and he experimented boldly and tirelessly with them. These experiments were facilitated by the very fact that dictionaries as we know them did not exist and by a flexibility in grammar, orthography, and diction that the more orderly, regularized English of the later seventeenth and eighteenth centuries suppressed.

Owing in part to the number of dialects in London, pronunciation was variable, and there were many opportunities for phonetic association between words: the words "bear," "barn," "bier," "bourne," "born," and "barne" could all sound like one another. Homonyms were given greater scope by the fact that the same word could be spelled so many different ways—Christopher Marlowe's name appears in the records as Marlowe, Marloe, Marlen, Marlyne, Merlin, Marley, Marlye, Morley, and Morle—and by the fact that a word's grammatical function could easily shift, from noun to verb, verb to adjective, and so forth. Since grammar and punctuation did not insist on relations of coordination and subordination, loose, nonsyntactic sentences were common, and etymologies were used to forge surprising or playful relations between distant words.

It would seem inherently risky for a popular playwright to employ a vocabulary so far in excess of what most mortals could possibly possess, but Shakespeare evidently counted on his audience's linguistic curiosity and adventurousness, just as he counted on its general and broad-based rhetorical competence. He was also usually careful to provide a context that in effect explained or translated his more arcane terms. For example, when Macbeth reflects with horror on his murderous hands, he shudderingly imagines that even the sea could not wash away the blood; on the contrary, his bloodstained hand, he says, "will rather / The multitudinous seas incarnadine." The meaning of the unfamiliar word "incarnadine" is explained by the next line: "Making the green one red" (2.2.59–61).

What is most striking is not the abstruseness or novelty of Shakespeare's language but its extraordinary vitality, a quality that the playwright seemed to pursue with a kind of passionate recklessness. Perhaps Samuel Johnson was looking in the right direction when he complained that the "quibble," or pun, was "the fatal Cleopatra for which

[Shakespeare] lost the world, and was content to lose it." For the power that continually discharges itself throughout the plays, at once constituting and unsettling everything it touches, is the polymorphous power of language, language that seems both costume and that which lies beneath the costume, personal identity and that which challenges the merely personal, nature and that which enables us to name nature and thereby distance ourselves from it.

Shakespeare's language has an overpowering exuberance and generosity that often resembles the experience of love. Consider, for example, Oberon's description in *A Midsummer Night's Dream* of the moment when he saw Cupid shoot his arrow at the fair vestal: "Thou rememb'rest," he asks Puck,

> Since once I sat upon a promontory
> And heard a mermaid on a dolphin's back
> Uttering such dulcet and harmonious breath
> That the rude sea grew civil at her song
> And certain stars shot madly from their spheres
> To hear the sea-maid's music?
>
> (2.1.148–54)

Here, Oberon's composition of place, lightly alluding to a classical emblem, is infused with a fantastically lush verbal brilliance. This brilliance, the result of masterful alliterative and rhythmical technique, seems gratuitous—that is, it does not advance the plot, but rather exhibits a capacity for display and self-delight that extends from the fairies to the playwright who has created them. The rich music of Oberon's words imitates the "dulcet and harmonious breath" he is intent on recalling, breath that has, in his account, an oddly contradictory effect: it is at once a principle of order, so that the rude sea is becalmed like a lower-class mob made civil by a skilled orator, and a principle of disorder, so that celestial bodies in their fixed spheres are thrown into mad confusion. And this contradictory effect, so intimately bound up with an inexplicable, supererogatory, and intensely erotic verbal magic, is a key to *A Midsummer Night's Dream,* with its exquisite blend of confusion and discipline, lunacy and hierarchical ceremony.

The fairies in this comedy seem to embody a pervasive sense found throughout Shakespeare's work that there is something uncanny about language, something that is not quite human, at least in the conventional and circumscribed sense of the human that dominates waking experience. In the comedies, this intuition is alarming but ultimately benign: Oberon and his followers trip through the great house at the play's close, blessing the bridebeds and warding off the nightmares that lurk in marriage and parenthood. But there is in Shakespeare an alternative, darker vision of the uncanniness of language, a vision also embodied in creatures that test the limits of the human—not the fairies of *A Midsummer Night's Dream* but the weird sisters of *Macbeth*. When in the tragedy's opening scene the witches chant "Fair is foul, and foul is fair" (1.1.10), they unsettle through the simplest and most radical act of linguistic equation (x is y) the fundamental antinomies through which a moral order is established. And when Macbeth appears onstage a few minutes later, his first words unconsciously echo what we have just heard from the witches' mouths: "So foul and fair a day I have not seen" (1.3.36). What is the meaning of this linguistic "unconscious"? On the face of things, Macbeth presumably means only that the day of fair victory is also a day of foul weather, but the fact that he echoes the witches (something that we hear but that he cannot know) intimates an occult link between them, even before their direct encounter. It is difficult, perhaps impossible, to specify exactly what this link signifies—generations of emboldened critics have tried without notable success—but we can at least affirm that its secret lair is in the play's language, like a half-buried pun whose full articulation will entail the murder of Duncan, the ravaging of his kingdom, and Macbeth's own destruction.

Macbeth is haunted by half-buried puns, equivocations, and ambiguous grammatical constructions known as amphibologies. They manifest themselves most obviously in the words of the witches, from the opening exchanges to the fraudulent assurances that deceive Macbeth at the close, but they are also present in his most intimate and private reflections, as in his tortured broodings about his proposed act of treason:

> If it were done when 'tis done, then 'twere well
> It were done quickly. If th'assassination
> Could trammel up the consequence, and catch
> With his surcease success: that but this blow
> Might be the be-all and the end-all, here,
> But here upon this bank and shoal of time,
> We'd jump the life to come.
>
> (1.7.1–7)

The dream is to reach a secure and decisive end, to catch as in a net (hence "trammel up") all of the slippery, unforeseen, and uncontrollable consequences of regicide, to hobble time as one might hobble a horse (another sense of "trammel up"), to stop the flow ("success") of events, to be, as Macbeth later puts it, "settled." But Macbeth's words themselves slip away from the closure he seeks; they slide into one another, trip over themselves, twist and double back and swerve into precisely the sickening uncertainties their speaker most wishes to avoid. And if we sense a barely discernible note of comedy in Macbeth's tortured language, a discordant playing with the senses of the word "done" and the hint of a childish tongue twister in the phrase "catch / With his surcease success," we are in touch with a dark pleasure to which Shakespeare was all his life addicted.

Look again at the couplet from *Cymbeline*: "Golden lads and girls all must, / As chimney-sweepers, come to dust."

The playwright who insinuated a pun into the solemn dirge is the same playwright whose tragic heroine in *Antony and Cleopatra*, pulling the bleeding body of her dying lover into the pyramid, says, "Our strength is all gone into heaviness" (4.16.34). He is the playwright whose Juliet, finding herself alone on the stage, says, "My dismal scene I needs must act alone" (*Romeo and Juliet* 4.3.19), and the playwright who can follow the long, wrenching periodic sentence that Othello speaks, just before he stabs himself, with the remark "O bloody period!" (5.2.366). The point is not merely the presence of puns in the midst of tragedy (as there are stabs of pain in the midst of Shakespearean comedy); it is rather the streak of wildness that they so deliberately disclose, the sublimely indecorous linguistic energy of which Shakespeare was at once the towering master and the most obedient, worshipful servant.

The Dream of the Master Text

Shakespeare and the Printed Book

Ben Jonson's famous tribute to Shakespeare—"He was not of an age, but for all time!"—comes in one of the dedicatory poems to the 1623 First Folio of *Mr. William Shakespeares Comedies, Histories, & Tragedies.* This large, handsome volume, the first collection of Shakespeare's plays, was not, as far as we know, the product of the playwright's own design. We do not even know if he would have approved of the Folio's division of each play into five acts or its organization of the plays into three loose generic categories. Several of the plays grouped among the histories—*Richard Duke of York* (3 *Henry VI*), *Richard II*, and *Richard III*—had been printed separately during Shakespeare's lifetime as tragedies; one of the most famous of his tragedies had appeared as *The History of King Lear.* The Folio editors evidently decided to group together as "histories" only those plays which dealt with English history after the Norman Conquest; hence, *King Lear,* set in ancient Britain, appears with the "tragedies," and so, too, despite its happy ending, does *Cymbeline, King of Britain.* One play, *Troilus and Cressida,* was printed first as a "history," then printed in a second version with a preface that describes it as a "comedy," and then printed in the Folio as a "tragedy." As a fitting

Sixteenth-century printing shop. Engraving by Jan van der Straet. From *Nova Reperta* (1580).

emblem of the confusion, *Troilus and Cressida* does not appear in the Folio title page: apparently included only at the last minute, it was placed, unpaginated, after the last of the histories and the first of the tragedies. Modern readers, who remain perplexed by its genre, may take some consolation from the fact that for Shakespeare and his contemporaries generic boundaries were not hard and fast.

Published seven years after the playwright's death, the Folio was printed by the London printers William and Isaac Jaggard, who were joined in this expensive venture by Edward Blount, John Smethwicke, and William Aspley. It was edited by two of Shakespeare's old friends and fellow actors, John Heminges and Henry Condell, who claimed to be using "True Originall Copies" in the author's own hand. (None of these copies has survived, or, more cautiously, none has to date been found.) Eighteen plays included in the First Folio had already appeared individually in print in the small-format and relatively inexpensive texts called "Quartos" (or, in one case, the still smaller format called "Octavo"); to these, Heminges and Condell added eighteen others never before published: *All's Well That Ends Well, Antony and Cleopatra, As You Like It, The Comedy of Errors, Coriolanus, Cymbeline, All Is True (Henry VIII), Julius Caesar, King John, Macbeth, Measure for Measure, The Taming of the Shrew, The Tempest, Timon of Athens, Twelfth Night, The Two Gentlemen of Verona, The Winter's Tale,* and *1 Henry VI.** None of the

---

*This sketch simplifies several complex questions such as the status of the 1594 Quarto called *The Taming of a Shrew,* sufficiently distinct from the similarly titled Folio text as to constitute for many editors a different play.

plays included in the Folio has dropped out of the generally accepted canon of Shakespeare's works, and only two plays not included in the volume (*Pericles* and *The Two Noble Kinsmen*) have been allowed to join this select company, along with the nondramatic poems. Of the latter, *Venus and Adonis* (1593) and *The Rape of Lucrece* (1594) first appeared during Shakespeare's lifetime in Quartos with dedications from the author to the Earl of Southampton. *Shakespeare's Sonnets* (1609) were apparently printed without his authorization, as were his poems in a collection called *The Passionate Pilgrim* (1599).

Over the centuries, there have been many attempts to discover and authenticate additional works partly or entirely written by Shakespeare. An interesting case has been made for sections of a history play entitled *King Edward the Third* and for some small traces in the eighteenth-century tragicomedy *The Double Falsehood*, allegedly based on a manuscript of the lost Shakespearean play *Cardenio*. *The Norton Shakespeare* includes a poem, "Shall I die?" whose original inclusion in the 1988 *Oxford Shakespeare* provoked vigorous debate and much skepticism. Still more skepticism greeted the attribution to Shakespeare of a long poem called "A Funeral Elegy," printed in an appendix to *The Norton Shakespeare*'s first edition and now dropped in the wake of widespread consensus that the attribution was false. In the future, other claimants will no doubt come forward, but, with the very few additions already noted, the Folio will always remain the foundation of Shakespeare's dramatic canon.

The plays were the property of the theatrical company in which Shakespeare was a shareholder. It was not normally in the interest of such companies to have their scripts circulating in print, at least while the plays were actively in repertory: players evidently feared competition from rival companies and thought that reading might dampen playgoing. Plays were generally sold only when the theaters were temporarily closed by plague, or when the company was in need of capital (four of Shakespeare's plays were published in 1600, presumably to raise money to pay the debts incurred in building the new Globe), or when a play had grown too old to revive profitably. There is no evidence that Shakespeare himself disagreed with this professional caution, no sign that he wished to see his plays in print. Unlike Ben Jonson, who took the radical step of rewriting his own plays for publication in the 1616 folio of his *Works*, Shakespeare evidently was not interested in constituting his plays as a canon. If in the sonnets he imagines his verse achieving a symbolic immortality, this dream apparently did not extend to his plays, at least through the medium of print.

Moreover, there is no evidence that Shakespeare had an interest in asserting authorial rights over his scripts or that he or any other working English playwright had a public "standing," legal or otherwise, from which to do so. (Jonson was ridiculed for his presumption.) There is no indication whatever that he could, for example, veto changes in his scripts or block interpolated scenes or withdraw a play from production if a particular interpretation, addition, or revision did not please him. To be sure, in his advice to the players, Hamlet urges that those who play the clowns "speak no more than is set down for them," but—apart from the question of whether the Prince speaks for the playwright—the play within the play in *Hamlet* is precisely an instance of a script altered to suit a particular occasion. It seems likely that Shakespeare would have routinely accepted the possibility of such alterations. Moreover, he would of necessity have routinely accepted the possibility, and in certain cases the virtual inevitability, of cuts in order to stage his plays in the two to two and one-half hours that was the normal performing time. There is an imaginative generosity in many of Shakespeare's scripts, as if he were deliberately offering his fellow actors more than they could use on any one occasion and, hence, giving them abundant materials with which to reconceive and revivify each play again and again as they or their audiences liked it. The Elizabethan theater, like most theater in our own time, was a collaborative enterprise, and the collaboration almost certainly extended to decisions about selection, trimming, shifts of emphasis, and minor or major revision.

For many years, it was thought that Shakespeare himself did little or no revising. Some recent editors—above all the editors of the *Oxford Shakespeare*, whose texts the

Norton presents—have argued persuasively that there are many signs of authorial revision, even wholesale rewriting. But there is no sign that Shakespeare sought through such revision to bring each of his plays to its "perfect," "final" form. On the contrary, many of the revisions seem to indicate that the scripts remained open texts, that the playwright and his company expected to add, cut, and rewrite as the occasion demanded.

Ralph Waldo Emerson once compared Shakespeare and his contemporary Francis Bacon in terms of the relative "finish" of their work. All of Bacon's work, wrote Emerson, "lies along the ground, a vast unfinished city." Each of Shakespeare's dramas, by contrast, "is perfect, hath an immortal integrity. To make Bacon's work complete, he must live to the end of the world." Recent scholarship suggests that Shakespeare was more like Bacon than Emerson thought. Neither the Folio nor the quarto texts of Shakespeare's plays bear the seal of final authorial intention, the mark of decisive closure that has served, at least ideally, as the guarantee of textual authenticity. We want to believe, as we read the text, "This is the play as Shakespeare himself wanted it read," but there is no license for such a reassuring sentiment. To be "not of an age, but for all time" means in Shakespeare's case not that the plays have achieved a static perfection, but that they are creatively, inexhaustibly unfinished.

That we have been so eager to link certain admired scripts to a single known playwright is closely related to changes in the status of artists in the Renaissance, changes that led to a heightened interest in the hand of the individual creator. Like medieval painting, medieval drama gives us few clues as to the particular individuals who fashioned the objects we admire. We know something about the places in which these objects were made, the circumstances that enabled their creation, the spaces in which they were placed, but relatively little about the particular artists themselves. It is easy to imagine a wealthy patron or a civic authority in the late Middle Ages commissioning a play on a particular subject (appropriate, for example, to a seasonal ritual, a religious observance, or a political festivity) and specifying the date, place, and length of the performance, the number of actors, even the costumes to be used, but it is more difficult to imagine him specifying a particular playwright and still less insisting that the entire play be written by this dramatist alone. Only with the Renaissance do we find a growing insistence on the name of the maker, the signature that heightens the value and even the meaning of the work by implying that it is the emanation of a single, distinct shaping consciousness.

In the case of Renaissance painting, we know that this signature does not necessarily mean that every stroke was made by the master. Some of the work, possibly the greater part of it, may have been done by assistants, with only the faces and a few finishing touches from the hand of the illustrious artist to whom the work is confidently attributed. As the skill of individual masters became more explicitly valued, contracts began to specify how much was to come from the brush of the principal painter. Consider, for example, the Italian painter Luca Signorelli's contract of 1499 for frescoes in Orvieto Cathedral:

> The said master Luca is bound and promises to paint [1] all the figures to be done on the said vault, and [2] especially the faces and all the parts of the figures from the middle of each figure upwards, and [3] that no painting should be done on it without Luca himself being present. . . . And it is agreed [4] that all the mixing of colours should be done by the said master Luca himself.

Such a contract at once reflects a serious cash interest in the characteristic achievement of a particular artist and a conviction that this achievement is compatible with the presence of other hands, provided those hands are subordinate, in the finished work. For paintings on a smaller scale, it was more possible to commission an exclusive performance. Thus, the contract for a small altarpiece by Signorelli's great teacher, Piero della Francesca, specifies that "no painter may put his hand to the brush other than Piero himself."

There is no record of any comparable concern for exclusivity in the English theater. Unfortunately, the contracts that Shakespeare and his fellow dramatists almost certainly signed have not, with one significant exception, survived. But plays written for the professional theater are by their nature an even more explicitly collective art form than paintings; they depend for their full realization on the collaboration of others, and that collaboration may well extend to the fashioning of the script. It seems that some authors may simply have been responsible for providing plots that others then dramatized; still others were hired to "mend" old plays or to supply prologues, epilogues, or songs. A particular playwright's name came to be attached to a certain identifiable style—a characteristic set of plot devices, a marked rhetorical range, a tonality of character—but this name may refer in effect more to a certain product associated with a particular playing company than to the individual artist who may or may not have written most of the script. The one contract whose details do survive, that entered into by Richard Brome and the actors and owners of the Salisbury Court Theatre in 1635, does not stipulate that Brome's plays must be written by him alone or even that he must be responsible for a certain specifiable proportion of each script. Rather, it specifies that the playwright "should not nor would write any play or any part of a play to any other players or playhouse, but apply all his study and endeavors therein for the benefit of the said company of the said playhouse." The Salisbury Court players want rights to everything Brome writes for the stage; the issue is not that the plays associated with his name be exclusively *his* but rather that he be exclusively *theirs*.

Recent textual scholarship, then, has been moving steadily away from a conception of Shakespeare's plays as direct, unmediated emanations from the mind of the author and toward a conception of them as working scripts, composed and continually reshaped as part of a collaborative commercial enterprise in competition with other, similar enterprises. One consequence has been the progressive weakening of the idea of the solitary, inspired genius, in the sense fashioned by Romanticism and figured splendidly in the statue of Shakespeare in the public gardens in Germany's Weimar, the city of Goethe and Schiller: the poet, with his sensitive, expressive face and high domed forehead sitting alone and brooding, a skull at his feet, a long-stemmed rose in his crotch. In place of this projection of German Romanticism, we have now a playwright and sometime actor who is also (to his considerable financial advantage) a major shareholder in the company—the Lord Chamberlain's Men, later the King's Men—to which he loyally supplies for most of his career an average of two plays per year.

These developments are salutary insofar as they direct attention to the actual conditions in which the textual traces that the Folio calls Shakespeare's "Comedies, Histories, & Tragedies" came to be produced, reproduced, consumed, revised, and transmitted to future generations. They highlight elements that Shakespeare shared with his contemporaries, and they insistently remind us that we are encountering scripts written primarily for the stage and not for the study. They make us more attentive to such matters as business cycles, plague rolls, the cost of costumes, government censorship, and urban topography and less concerned with the elusive and enigmatic details of the poet's biography—his supposed youthful escapades and erotic yearnings and psychological crises.

All well and good. But the fact remains that in 1623, seven years after the playwright's death, Heminges and Condell thought they could sell copies of their expensive collection of Shakespeare's plays—"What euer you do," they urge their readers, "buy"—by insisting that their texts were "as he conceiued them." This means that potential readers in the early seventeenth century were already interested in Shakespeare's "conceits"—his "wit," his imagination, and his creative power—and were willing to assign a high value to the products of his particular, identifiable skill, one distinguishable from that of his company and of his rival playwrights. After all, Jonson's tribute praises Shakespeare not as the playwright of the incomparable King's Men but as the equal of Aeschylus, Sophocles, and Euripides. And if we now see Shakespeare's dramaturgy in the context of his contemporaries and of a collective artistic practice, readers continue to have little difficulty recognizing that most of the plays attached to his name tower over those of his rivals.

From Foul to Fair: The Making of the Printed Play

What exactly is a printed play by Shakespeare? Is it like a novel or a poem? Is it like the libretto or the score of an opera? Is it the trace of an absent event? Is it the blueprint of an imaginary structure that will never be completed? Is it a record of what transpired in the mind of a man long dead? We might say cautiously that it is a mechanically reproduced version of what Shakespeare wrote, but unfortunately, with the possible (and disputed) exception of a small fragment from a collaboratively written play called *Sir Thomas More*, virtually nothing Shakespeare actually wrote in his own hand survives. We might propose that it is a printed version of the script that an Elizabethan actor would have held in his hands during rehearsals, but here, too, no such script of a Shakespeare play survives; and besides, Elizabethan actors were evidently not given the whole play to read. To reduce the expense of copying and the risk of unauthorized reproduction, each actor received only his own part, along with the cue lines. (Shakespeare uses this fact to delicious comic effect in *A Midsummer Night's Dream* 3.1.80–88.) Nonetheless, the play certainly existed as a whole, either in the author's original manuscript or in the copy prepared for the government censor or for the company's prompter or stage manager, so we might imagine the text we hold in our hands as a printed copy of one of these manuscripts. But since no contemporary manuscript survives of any of Shakespeare's plays, we cannot verify this hypothesis. And even if we could, we would not have resolved the question of the precise relation of the printed text either to the playwright's imagination or to the theatrical performance by the company to which he belonged.

All of Shakespeare's plays must have begun their textual careers in the form of "foul papers," drafts presumably covered with revisions, crossings-out, and general "blotting." To be sure, Heminges and Condell remark that so great was the playwright's facility that they "have scarce received from him a blot in his papers." This was, however, a routine and conventional compliment in the period. The same claim, made for the playwright John Fletcher in an edition published in 1647, is clearly contradicted by the survival of Fletcher's far-from-unblotted manuscripts. It is safe to assume that, since Shakespeare was human, his manuscripts contained their share of second and third thoughts scribbled in the margins and between the lines. Once complete, this authorial draft would usually have to be written out again, either by the playwright or by a professional scribe employed by the theater company, as "fair copy."

In the hands of the theater company, the fair copy (or sometimes, it seems, the foul papers themselves) would be annotated and transformed into "the book of the play" or the "playbook" (what we would now call a "promptbook"). Shakespeare's authorial draft presumably contained a certain number of stage directions, though these may have been sketchy and inconsistent. The promptbook clarified these and added others, noted theatrical properties and sound effects, and on occasion cut the full text to meet the necessities of performance. The promptbook was presented to the Master of the Revels for licensing, and it incorporated any changes upon which the master insisted. As the editors of the *Oxford Shakespeare* put it, the difference between foul papers and promptbook is the difference between "the text in an as yet individual, private form" and "a socialized text."

But the fact remains that for Shakespeare's plays, we have neither foul papers nor fair copies nor promptbooks. We have only the earliest printed editions of these texts in numerous individual quartos and in the First Folio. (Quartos are so called because each sheet of paper was folded twice, making four leaves or eight pages front and back; folio sheets were folded once, making two leaves or four pages front and back.) From clues embedded in these "substantive" texts—substantive because (with the exception of *The Two Noble Kinsmen*) they date from Shakespeare's own lifetime or from the collected works edited by his associates using, or claiming to use, his own manuscripts—editors attempt to reconstruct each play's journey from manuscript to print. Different plays took very different journeys.

Of the thirty-six plays included in the First Folio, eighteen had previously appeared in quarto editions, some of these in more than one printing. Generations of editors have distinguished between "good Quartos," presumably prepared from the author's own draft or from a scribal transcript of the play (fair copy), and "bad Quartos." The latter category, first formulated as such by A. W. Pollard in 1909, includes, by widespread but not universal agreement, the 1594 version of *The First Part of the Contention* (2 Henry VI), the 1595 *Richard Duke of York* (3 Henry VI), the 1597 *Richard the Third*, the 1597 *Romeo and Juliet*, the 1600 *Henry the Fifth*, the 1602 *Merry Wives of Windsor*, the 1603 *Hamlet*, and *Pericles* (1609). Some editors also regard the 1591 *Troublesome Reign of King John*, the 1594 *Taming of a Shrew*, and the 1608 *King Lear* as bad Quartos, but others have strenuously argued that these are distinct rather than faulty texts, and the whole concept of the bad Quarto has come under increasingly critical scrutiny. The criteria for distinguishing between "good" and "bad" texts are imprecise, and the evaluative terms seem to raise as many questions as they answer. Nevertheless, the striking mistakes, omissions, repetitions, and anomalies in a number of the Quartos require some explanation beyond the ordinary fallibility of scribes and printers.

The explanation most often proposed for suspect Quartos is that they are the products of "memorial reconstruction." The hypothesis, first advanced in 1910 by W. W. Greg, is that a series of features found in what seem to be particularly flawed texts may be traced to the derivation of the copy from the memory of one or more of the actors. Elizabethan actors, Greg observed, often found themselves away from the London theaters—for example, on tour in the provinces during plague periods—and may not on those occasions have had access to the promptbooks they would ordinarily have used. In such circumstances, those in the company who remembered a play may have written down or dictated the text, as best they could, perhaps adapting it for provincial performance. Moreover, unscrupulous actors may have sold such texts to enterprising printers eager to turn a quick profit.

Memorially reconstructed texts tend to be much shorter than those prepared from foul papers or fair copy; they frequently paraphrase or garble lines, drop or misplace speeches and whole scenes, and on occasion fill in the gaps with scraps from other plays. In several cases, scholars think they can detect which roles the rogue actors played, since these parts (and the scenes in which they appear) are reproduced with greater accuracy than the rest of the play. Typically, these roles are minor ones, since the leading parts would be played by actors with a greater stake in the overall financial interest of the company and, hence, less inclination to violate its policy. Thus, for example, editors speculate that the bad Quarto of *Hamlet* (Q1) was provided by the actor playing Marcellus (and doubling as Lucianus). What is often impossible to determine is whether particular differences between a bad Quarto and a good Quarto or Folio text result from the actor's faulty memory or from changes introduced in performance, possibly with the playwright's own consent, or from both. Shakespearean bad Quartos ceased to appear after 1609, perhaps as a result of greater scrutiny by the Master of the Revels, who after 1606 was responsible for licensing plays for publication as well as performance.

The syndicate that prepared the Folio had access to the manuscripts of the King's Men. In addition to the previously published editions of eighteen plays, they made use of scribal transcripts (fair copies), promptbooks, and (more rarely) foul papers. The indefatigable labors of generations of bibliographers, antiquaries, and textual scholars have recovered an extraordinary fund of information about the personnel, finances, organizational structure, and material practices of Elizabethan and Jacobean printing houses, including the names and idiosyncrasies of particular compositors who calculated the page length, set the type, and printed the sheets of the Folio. This impressive scholarship has for the most part intensified respect for the seriousness with which the Folio was prepared and printed, and where the Folio is defective, it has provided plausible readings from the Quartos or proposed emendations to approximate what Shakespeare is likely to have written. But it has not succeeded, despite all its heroic efforts, in transforming the Folio, or any other text, into an unobstructed, clear window into Shakespeare's mind.

The dream of the master text is a dream of transparency. The words on the page should ideally give the reader unmediated access to the astonishing forge of imaginative power that was the mind of the dramatist. Those words welled up from the genius of the great artist, and if the world were not an imperfect place, they would have been set down exactly as he conceived them and transmitted to each of us as a precious inheritance. Such is the vision—at its core closely related to the preservation of the holy text in the great scriptural religions—that has driven many of the great editors who have for centuries produced successive editions of Shakespeare's works. The vision was not yet fully formed in the First Folio, for Heminges and Condell still felt obliged to apologize to their noble patrons for dedicating to them a collection of mere "trifles." But by the eighteenth century, there were no longer any ritual apologies for Shakespeare; instead, there was a growing recognition not only of the supreme artistic importance of his works but also of the uncertain, conflicting, and in some cases corrupt state of the surviving texts. Every conceivable step, it was thought, must be undertaken to correct mistakes, strip away corruptions, return the texts to their pure and unsullied form, and make this form perfectly accessible to readers.

Paradoxically, this feverishly renewed, demanding, and passionate editorial project has produced the very opposite of the transparency that was the dream of the master text. The careful weighing of alternative readings, the production of a textual apparatus, the writing of notes and glosses, the modernizing and regularizing of spelling and punctuation, the insertion of scene divisions, the complex calculation of the process of textual transmission from foul papers to print, the equally complex calculation of the effects that censorship, government regulation, and, above all, theatrical performance had on the surviving documents all make inescapably apparent the fact that we do not have and never will have any direct, unmediated access to Shakespeare's imagination. Every Shakespeare text, from the first that was published to the most recent, has been edited: it has come into print by means of a tangled social process and inevitably exists at some remove from the author.

Heminges and Condell, who knew the author and had access to at least some of his manuscripts, lament the fact that Shakespeare did not live "to have set forth and overseen his own writings." And even had he done so—or, alternatively, even if a cache of his manuscripts were discovered in a Warwickshire attic tomorrow—all of the editorial problems would not be solved, nor would all of the levels of mediation be swept away. Certainly, the entire textual landscape would change. But the written word has strange powers: it seems to hold on to something of the very life of the person who has written it, but it also seems to pry that life loose from the writer, exposing it to vagaries of history and chance independent of those to which the writer was personally subject. Moreover, with the passing of centuries, the language itself and the whole frame of reference within which language and symbols are understood have decisively changed. The most learned modern scholar still lives at a huge experiential remove from Shakespeare's world and, even holding a precious copy of the First Folio in hand, cannot escape having to read across a vast chasm of time what is, after all, an edited text. The rest of us cannot so much as indulge in the fantasy of direct access: our eyes inevitably wander to the glosses and the explanatory notes.

The Oxford Shakespeare

The shattering of the dream of the master text is no cause for despair, nor should it lead us to throw our hands up and declare that one text is as good as another. What it does is to encourage the reader to be actively interested in the editorial principles that underlie the particular edition that he or she is using. It is said that the great artist Brueghel once told a nosy connoisseur who had come to his studio, "Keep your nose out of my paintings; the smell of the paint will poison you." In the case of Shakespeare, it is increasingly important to bring one's nose close to the page, as it were, and sniff the ink. More precisely, it is important to understand the rationale for the choices that the editors have made.

The text of the *Norton Shakespeare* is, with very few changes, that published by the Oxford University Press in 1988 and, in a second edition, in 2005. The *Oxford Shakespeare* was the extraordinary achievement of a team of editors, Stanley Wells, Gary Taylor, John Jowett, and William Montgomery, with Wells and Taylor serving as the general editors. The Oxford editors approached their task with a clear understanding that, as we have seen, all previous texts have been mediated by agents other than Shakespeare; however, they regard this mediation not as a melancholy obstacle intervening between the reader and the "true" Shakespearean text but rather as a constitutive element of this text. The art of the playwright is thoroughly dependent on the craft of go-betweens.

Shakespeare's plays were not written to be circulated in manuscript or printed form among readers. They were written to be performed by the players and, as the preface to the Quarto *Troilus and Cressida* indelicately puts it, "clapper-clawed with the palms of the vulgar." The public was, thus, never meant to be in a direct relationship with the author but in a "triangular relationship" in which the players gave voice and gesture to the author's words. As we have seen, Shakespeare was the master of the unfinished, the perpetually open. And even if we narrow our gaze and try to find only what Shakespeare himself might have regarded as a textual resting point, a place to stop and go on to another play, we have, the Oxford editors point out, a complex task. For whatever Shakespeare wrote was meant from the start to be supplemented by an invisible "paratext" consisting of words spoken by Shakespeare to the actors and by the actors to each other concerning emphasis, stage business, tone, pacing, possible cuts, and so forth. To the extent that this paratext was ever written down, it was recorded in the promptbook. Therefore, in contrast to standard editorial practice, the Oxford editors prefer, when there is a choice, copy based on the promptbook to copy based on the author's own draft. They choose the text immersed in history—that is, in the theatrical embodiment for which it was intended by its author—over the text unstained by the messy, collaborative demands of the playhouse. The closest we can get to Shakespeare's "final" version of a play—understanding that for him as for us there is no true "finality" in a theatrical text—is the latest version of that play performed by his company during his professional life—that is, during the time in which he could still oversee and participate in any cuts and revisions.

This choice does not mean that the Oxford editors are turning away from the very idea of Shakespeare as author. On the contrary, Wells and Taylor are deeply committed to establishing a text that comes as close as possible to the plays as Shakespeare wrote them, but they are profoundly attentive to the fact that he wrote them as a member of a company of players, a company in which he was a shareholder and an actor as well as a writer. "Writing" for the theater, at least for Shakespeare, is not simply a matter of setting words to paper and letting the pages drift away; it is a social process as well as an individual act. The Oxford editors acknowledge that some aspects of this social process may have been frustrating to Shakespeare: he may, for example, have been forced on occasion to cut lines and even whole scenes to which he was attached, or his fellow players may have insisted that they could not successfully perform what he had written, compelling him to make changes he did not welcome. But compromise and collaboration are part of what it means to be in the theater, and Wells and Taylor return again and again to the recognition that Shakespeare was, supremely, a man of the theater.

Is there a tension between the Oxford editors' preference for the performed, fully socialized text and their continued commitment to recovering the text as Shakespeare himself intended it? Yes. The tension is most visible in their determination to strip away textual changes arising from circumstances, such as government censorship, over which Shakespeare had no control. ("We have, wherever possible," they write, put "profanities back in Shakespeare's mouth.") It can be glimpsed as well in the editors' belief, almost a leap of faith, that there was little revision of Shakespeare's plays in his company's revivals between the time of his death and the publication of the Folio. But the tension is mainly a creative one, for it forces them (and, therefore, us) to attend to the playwright's unique imaginative power as well as his social and historical entanglements.

The Oxford editors took a radical stance on a second major issue: the question of authorial revision. Previous editors had generally accepted the fact that Shakespeare practiced revision within individual manuscripts—that is, while he was still in the act of writing a particular play—but they generally rejected the notion that he undertook substantial revisions from one version of a play to another (and, hence, from one manuscript to another). Wells and Taylor point out that six major works (*Hamlet, Othello, 2 Henry IV, King Lear, Richard II,* and *Troilus and Cressida*) survive in two independent substantive sources, both apparently authoritative, with hundreds of significant variant readings. Previous editors have generally sought to deny authority to one edition or another ("faced with two sheep," the Oxford editors observe wryly, "it is all too easy to insist that one *must* be a goat") or have conflated the two versions into a single text in an attempt to reconstruct the ideal, definitive, complete, and perfect version that they imagine Shakespeare must have reached for each of his plays. But if one doubts that Shakespeare ever conceived of his plays as closed, finished entities, if one recalls that he wrote them for the living repertory of the commercial playing company to which he belonged, then the whole concept of the single, authoritative text of each play loses its force. In a startling departure from the editorial tradition, the *Oxford Shakespeare* printed two distinct versions of *King Lear,* quarto and Folio, and the editors glanced longingly at the impractical but alluring possibility of including two texts of *Hamlet, Othello,* and *Troilus.*

The *Oxford Shakespeare* was published in both old-spelling and modern-spelling editions. The former, the first of its kind ever published, raised some reviewers' eyebrows because the project, a critical edition rather than a facsimile, required the modern editors to invent plausible Elizabethan spellings for their emendations and to add stage directions. The modern-spelling edition, which is the basis for Norton's text, is noteworthy for taking the principles of modernization further than they had generally been taken. Gone are such words as "murther," "mushrump," "vild," and "porpentine," which confer on many modern-spelling editions a certain cozy, Olde-English quaintness; Oxford replaces them with "murder," "mushroom," "vile," and "porcupine."

The inclusion of two texts of *King Lear* aroused considerable controversy when the *Oxford Shakespeare* first appeared, although by now the arguments for doing so have received widespread, though not unanimous, scholarly support. Other features remain controversial: "Ancients" Pistol and Iago have been modernized to "Ensigns"; *Henry VIII* has reverted to its performance title *All Is True*; demonic spirits in *Macbeth* sing lyrics written by Thomas Middleton. The white-hot intensity of the debates triggered by the *Oxford Shakespeare*'s editorial choices casts an interesting light on the place of Shakespeare not only in the culture at large but in the psyches of millions of individuals: any alteration, however minor, in a deeply familiar and beloved text, even an alteration based on thoughtful and highly plausible scholarly principles, arouses genuine anxiety. The anxiety in this case was intensified not only by the boldness of certain crucial emendations but also by the fact that the editors' explanations, arguments, and justifications for all their decisions were printed in a separate, massive volume, *William Shakespeare: A Textual Companion.* This formidable, dense volume is an astonishing monument to the seriousness, scholarly rigor, and immense labor of the Oxford editors. Anyone who is interested in pursuing why Shakespeare's words appear as they do in the current edition, anyone who wishes insight into the editors' detailed reasons for making the thousands of decisions required by a project of this kind, should consult the *Textual Companion.*

The Norton Shakespeare

The primary task that the editors of the *Norton Shakespeare* set themselves was to present the modern-spelling Oxford *Complete Works* in a way that would make the text more accessible to modern readers. The *Oxford Shakespeare* prints little more than the text itself: along with one-page introductions to the individual works, it contains a short general introduction, a list of contemporary allusions to Shakespeare, and a brief glossary. But while it is possible to enjoy a Shakespeare play on stage or screen without any assistance beyond the actors' own art, many readers at least since the eighteenth century have found it far more difficult to understand and to savor the texts without some more substantial commentary.

In addition to writing introductions, textual notes, and brief bibliographies for each of the works, the Norton editors provide glosses and footnotes designed to facilitate comprehension. Such is the staggering richness of Shakespeare's language that it is tempting to gloss everything. But there is a law of diminishing returns: too much explanatory whispering at the margins makes it difficult to enjoy what the reader has come for in the first place. Our general policy is to gloss only those words that cannot be found in an ordinary dictionary or whose meanings have altered out of recognition. The glosses attempt to be simple and straightforward, giving multiple meanings for words only when the meanings are essential for making sense of the passages in which they appear. We try not to gloss the same word over and over—it becomes distracting to be told three times on a single page that "an" means "if"—but we also assume that the reader does not have a perfect memory, so after an interval we will gloss the same word again.

Marginal glosses generally refer to a single word or a short phrase. The footnotes paraphrase longer units or provide other kinds of information, such as complex plays on words, significant allusions, textual cruxes, historical and cultural contexts. Here, too, however, we have tried to check the impulse to annotate so heavily that the reader is distracted from the pleasure of the text, and we have avoided notes that provide interpretation, as distinct from information.

Following the works, the Norton editors have provided lists of textual variants. These are variants from the control text only—that is, they do not record all of the variants in all of the substantive texts, nor do they record all of the myriad shifts of meaning that may arise from modernization of spelling and repunctuation. Readers who wish to pursue these interesting, if complex, topics are encouraged to consult the *Textual Companion,* along with the old-spelling *Oxford Shakespeare,* the Norton facsimile of the First Folio, and the quarto facsimiles published by the University of California Press. The *Norton Shakespeare* does provide a convenient list for each play of the different ways the same characters are designated in the speech prefixes in the substantive texts. These variants (for example, Lady Capulet in *Romeo and Juliet* is called, variously, "Lady," "Mother," "Wife," "Old Woman," etc.) often cast an interesting light on the ways a particular character is conceived. Variants as they appear in this edition, as well as their line numbers, are printed in boldface; each is followed by the corresponding reading in the control text, and sometimes the source from which the variant is taken. Further information on readings in substantive texts is given in brackets.

Stage directions pose a complex set of problems for the editors of a one-volume Shakespeare. The printing conventions for the stage directions in sixteenth- and seventeenth-century plays were different from those of our own time. Often all of the entrances for a particular scene are grouped together at the beginning, even though some of the characters clearly do not enter until later; placement in any case seems at times haphazard or simply incorrect. There are moments when the stage directions seem to provide stunning insight into the staging of the plays in Shakespeare's time, other moments when they are absent or misleading. It is difficult to gauge how much the stage directions in the substantive editions reflect Shakespeare's own words or at least decisions. It would seem that he was often relatively careless about them, understanding perhaps that these decisions in any precise sense would be the first to be made and unmade by different productions.

The Oxford editors, like virtually all modern editors, necessarily altered and supplemented the stage directions in their control texts. They decided to mark certain of the stage directions with a special sign to indicate a dubious action or placement, but they did not distinguish between the stage directions that came from the substantive texts and those added in later texts, from the seventeenth century to the present. They referred readers instead to the *Textual Companion,* which provides lists of the exact wording of the stage directions in the substantive texts.

The editors of the *Norton Shakespeare* share a sense of the limitations of the early stage directions and share as well some skepticism about how many of these should be attributed even indirectly to Shakespeare. Hence, we do not routinely differentiate between quarto and Folio stage directions; we do so only when we think it is a significant point. But there is, it seems to us, a real interest in knowing which stage directions come from those editions of the plays published up to the 1623 Folio (and including *The Two Noble Kinsmen,* published shortly thereafter) and which were added when the editors were no longer in contact with Shakespeare's presence or his manuscripts. Therefore, we have placed brackets around all stage directions that were added after the First Folio. Unbracketed stage directions, then, all derive from editions up through the Folio.

The *Norton Shakespeare* has made several other significant departures from the Oxford text. The Oxford editors note that when *1 Henry IV* was first performed, probably in 1596, the character we know as Sir John Falstaff was called Sir John Oldcastle. But in the wake of protests from Oldcastle's descendants, one of whom, William Brooke, tenth Baron Cobham, was Elizabeth I's lord chamberlain, Shakespeare changed the name to "Falstaff" (and probably for similar reasons changed the names of Falstaff's companions, Russell and Harvey, to "Bardolph" and "Peto"). Consistent with their decision not to honor changes that Shakespeare was *compelled* to make by censorship or other forms of pressure, the Oxford editors changed the names back to their initial form. But this decision is a problem for several reasons. It draws perhaps too sharp a distinction between those things that Shakespeare did under social pressure and those he did of his own accord. More seriously, it pulls against the principle of a text that represents the latest performance version of a play during Shakespeare's lifetime: after all, even the earliest quarto title page advertises "the humorous conceits of Sir John Falstaff." And, of course, it asks the reader to ignore completely and radically centuries of response—elaboration, fascination, and love—all focused passionately on Sir John Falstaff. The response is not a modern phenomenon: it began with Shakespeare, who developed the character as Sir John Falstaff in *2 Henry IV* and *The Merry Wives of Windsor.* Norton thus restores the more familiar names.

Another major departure from the Oxford text is Norton's printing of the so-called Additional Passages, especially in *Hamlet.* Consistent with their decision not to conflate quarto and Folio texts, the Oxford editors adhere to their control text for *Hamlet,* the Folio, and print those passages that appear only in the Second Quarto in an appendix at the end of the play. As explained at length in the Textual Note to the play, the Norton editors decided not to follow this course, but instead chose a different way of demarcating the quarto and Folio texts (inserting the quarto passages, indented, in the body of the text), one that makes it easier to see how the quarto passages functioned in a version of the play that Shakespeare also authored.

The *Norton Shakespeare* follows Oxford in printing separate quarto and Folio texts of *King Lear,* to which we have added a conflated version of the play so that readers will have the opportunity to assess for themselves the effects of the traditional editorial practice. Moreover, we have departed from Oxford in printing the quarto and Folio texts of the plays on facing pages, so that their differences can be readily weighed. In the hundreds of changes, some trivial and other momentous, it is possible to glimpse, across what Prospero calls "the dark backward and abysm of time," a thrilling sight: Shakespeare at work.

The Shakespearean Stage
by
ANDREW GURR

Publication by Performance

The curt exchange between the sentries in the first six lines of *Hamlet* tells us that it is very late at night ("'Tis now struck twelve") and that "'tis bitter cold." This opening was staged originally at the Globe in London in broad daylight, at 2 o'clock probably on a hot summer's afternoon. The words required the audience, half of them standing on three sides of the stage platform and all of them as visible to one another as the players were, to imagine themselves watching a scene quite the opposite of what they could see and feel around them. The original mode of staging for a Shakespearean play was utterly different from the cinematic realism we are used to now, where the screen gives us close-ups on a simulacrum of reality, an even more privileged view of the actors' facial twitches than we get in ordinary life. Eloquence then was in words, not facial expressions.

The playgoers of Shakespeare's time knew the plays in forms at which we can only now guess. It is a severe loss. Shakespeare's own primary concept of his plays was as stories "personated" onstage, not as words on a page. He himself never bothered to get his playscripts into print, and more than half of them were not published until seven years after his death, in the First Folio of his plays published as a memorial to him in 1623. His fellow playwright Francis Beaumont called the printing of plays "a second publication"; the first was their showing onstage. Print recorded a set of scripts, written for the original players to teach them what they should speak in the ensemble of the play in production. The only technology then available to record the performances was the written word. If video recordings had existed at that time, our understanding of Shakespeare would be vastly different from what it is today.

Since the texts were composed only to be a record of the words the players were to memorize, we now have to infer how the plays were originally staged largely by guess-work. Shakespeare was himself a player and shareholder in his acting company, and he expected to be present at rehearsals. Consequently, the stage directions in his scripts are distinctly skimpy compared with some of those provided by his fellow playwrights. He was cursory even in noting entrances and exits, let alone how he expected his company to stage the more complex spectacles, such as heaving Antony up to Cleopatra on her monument. There are sometimes hints in the stage directions and more frequently in the words used to describe some of the actions, and knowing what the design of the theater was like is a help as well. Knowing more about how Shakespeare expected his plays to be staged can transform how we think about them. But gaining such knowledge is no easy matter. One of the few certainties is that Shakespeare's plays in modern performance are even more different from the originals than modern printed editions are from the first much-thumbed manuscripts.

The Shakespearean Mindset

The general mindset of the original playgoers, the patterns of thinking and expectation that Tudor culture imposed on Shakespeare's audiences, is not really difficult to identify.

79

It is less easy, though, to pin it down in the sort of detail that tells us what the original concept of staging the plays would have been like. We know that all the original playgoers paid for the privilege of attending the plays and committed themselves willingly to suspend their disbelief in what they were to see. They knew as we do that they were paying to be entertained by fictions. Beyond that, we need reminding today that going to open-air performances in daylight in Shakespeare's time meant being constantly aware that one was in a theater, a place designed to offer illusions. On the one hand, this consciousness of oneself and where one was meant that the players had to do more to hold attention than is needed now, when audiences have nothing but the stage to look at and armchairs to sit in. On the other hand, it made everyone more receptive to extratheatrical tricks, such as Hamlet's reference to "this distracted globe," or Polonius's claim in the same play to have taken the part of Julius Caesar at the university and been killed by Brutus. The regular playgoers at the Globe who recognized Polonius as the man who had played Caesar in Shakespeare's play of the year before, and who recognized Hamlet as the man who had played Brutus, would laugh at this theatrical in-joke. But two scenes later, when Hamlet kills Polonius, they would think of it again, in a different light.

Features of the original mindset such as these are readily identifiable. For others, though, we need to look further, into the design of the theaters and into the staging traditions that they housed and that Shakespeare exploited. Invisibility has a part to play in *A Midsummer Night's Dream* that we can easily underrate, for instance. Invisibility onstage is a theatrical in-joke, an obvious privileging of the audience, which is allowed to see what the characters onstage can't. The impresario Philip Henslowe's inventory of costumes used at the Rose theater in 1597, which lists "a robe for to go invisible," indicates a fictional device that openly expects the willing suspension of the audience's disbelief. In *A Midsummer Night's Dream,* the ostensible invisibility of all the visible fairies emphasizes the theatricality of the whole presentation while pandering to the audience's self-indulgent superiority, the feeling that it knows what is going on better than any character, whether he be Bottom or even Duke Theseus. That prepares us for the mockery of stage realism we get later, in the mechanicals' play in Act 5, and even for the doubt we as willing audience might feel over Theseus's own skepticism about the dangers of imagination that he voices in his speech at the beginning of Act 5.

More to the point, though, it throws into question our readiness to be an audience, since we have ourselves been indulging in just the games of suspending disbelief that the play staged by the mechanicals enters into so unsuccessfully. When Theseus disputes with Hippolyta about the credibility of the lovers' story, he voices the very skepticism—about the lover, the lunatic, and the poet—that any sensible realist in the audience would have been feeling for most of the previous three acts in the forest. The play starts and ends at the court in broad daylight, while the scenes of midsummer madness take place at night in a forest. At the early amphitheaters, all the plays were staged in broad daylight, between 2 and 5 o'clock in the afternoon, and without any persuasive scenery: the two stage posts served as trees onstage. So the play, moving as it does from daylight realism to nocturnal fantasy and back again, with a last challenge to credulity in the mechanicals' burlesque of how to stage a play, has already thoroughly challenged the willing suspension of the viewers' disbelief. *A Midsummer Night's Dream* is a play about nocturnal dreams and fictions that are accepted as truths in broad daylight. It was only a small extension of this game to have the women's parts played by boys, as well as plots in which the girls dressed as boys, to the point where in *As You Like It* Rosalind was played by a boy playing a girl pretending to be a boy playing a girl.

The Shakespeare plays were written for a new and unique kind of playhouse, the Elizabethan amphitheater, which had a distinctive design quite different from modern theaters. Elizabethans knew what the standard features in their theaters stood for, and Shakespeare drew on that knowledge for the staging of his plays. The physical features of the playhouses were a potent element in the ways that the plays were designed for the Elizabethan mindset. When Richard III, the archdeceiver and playactor, appears "aloft between two Bishops" to claim the crown in *Richard III* 3.7, his placing on the stage balcony literally above the crowd on the stage would, even without the accompanying priests, have signified his ironic claim to a social and moral superiority that ought to have matched his elevation. When Richard II comes down from the wall of Flint Castle to the "base court" in *Richard II* 3.3, Elizabethans would have seen his descent as a withdrawal from power and status. These theaters were still new when Shakespeare started to write for them, and their novelty meant that the plays were written more tightly to fit their specific design than the plays of later years, when theatergoing had become a more routine social activity and different kinds of theater were available.

London Playgoing and the Law

This heightened sense of theatricality, or "metatheater," in Shakespearean audiences was far from the only difference in their mindset from that of all modern audiences. Regular playgoing in London only started in the 1570s, and through Shakespeare's earlier years it was always a perilous and precarious activity. The Lord Mayor of London and the mayors of most of England's larger towns hated playgoing and tried to suppress it whenever and wherever it appeared. Playgoing was exciting not only because it was new but because it was dangerous. The hostility of so many authorities to plays meant that they were seen almost automatically as subversive of authority. Paradoxically, the first London companies were only able to establish themselves in London through the active support of Queen Elizabeth and her Privy Council, which tried hard, in the face of constant complaints from the Lord Mayor, to ensure that the best companies would be on hand every Christmas to entertain the Queen's leisure hours. Popular support for playgoing depended on royal protection for the leading companies.

London was by far the largest city in England. Within a few years of Shakespeare's death, it became the largest in Europe. It was generally an orderly place to live, especially in the city itself. Even in the suburbs, where the poorer people had to live, there were not many of the riots and other disorders that preachers always associated with the brothels, animal-baiting arenas, and playhouses clustering there. The reputation that the playhouses gained for promoting riots was not well justified. Any crowd of people was seen by the authorities as a potential riot, and playhouses regularly drew some of the largest crowds that London had yet seen. The city's government was not designed to control large crowds of people. There was no paid police force, and the Lord Mayor was held responsible by the Privy Council, the Queen's governing committee, for any disorders that did occur. So the city authorities found that playgoing challenged their control over their people.

The rapid growth of London did not help the situation. Officially, the city was governed by the Lord Mayor and his council. But he had authority only inside the city, and London now spread through a large suburban area in the adjacent counties of Middlesex to the north and Surrey across the river to the south. Because the court and the national government were housed in London, the Privy Council often intervened in city affairs in its own interests, as well as when orders were needed that covered broader zones than the city itself. The periodic outbreaks of bubonic plague were one clear instance of such a need, because the plague took no notice of parish or city boundaries. The intrusion of the professional companies to play in London provided another. In the early years, they were chronic travelers, and London was simply one of many stopovers. But the Queen enjoyed seeing plays at Christmas, and her council accordingly supported the best companies so that they could perform for her. It protected the playing companies against the hatred of successive Lord Mayors, except when a national emergency such as a plague epidemic erupted. The Privy Council took control then by ordering the 126 parishes in and around London to list all deaths from plague separately from ordinary deaths. Each Thursday, the parish totals were added together. When the total number of deaths from plague in these lists rose above 30 in any one week, the Privy Council closed all places of public assembly. This meant especially the playhouses, which created by far the largest gatherings. When the theaters were closed, the playing companies had to revert to their traditional practice of going on tour to play in the towns through the country, provided that the news of plague did not precede them.

Plague was not the only reason for the government to lay its controlling hand on the companies. From the time the post was inaugurated in 1578, the Master of the Revels controlled all playing. He was executive officer to the Lord Chamberlain, the Privy Council officer responsible for the annual season of royal entertainment and thus, by extension, for the professional playing companies. The Master of the Revels licensed each company and censored its plays. He was expected to cut out any references to religion or affairs of state, and he tried to prevent other offenses by banning the depiction of any living person onstage. After 1594, he issued licenses to the approved London playhouses, too. Later still, the printing of any playbook was allowed only if he gave authority for it. The companies had to accept this tight control because the government was its only protector against the hostile municipal authorities, who included not only the Lord Mayor of London but also the mayors of most of the major towns in the country.

Most mayors had the commercial interest of keeping local employees at work to justify their hostility to playgoing. But across the country, the hostility went much deeper. A large proportion of the population disliked the very idea of playacting. Their reasons, ostensibly religious, were that for actors to pretend to be characters they were unlike in life was a deception and that for boys to dress as women was contrary to what the Bible said. Somewhere beneath this was a more basic fear of pretense and deceit, of people not acting honestly. It put actors into the same category as con men, cheats, and thieves. That was probably one reason why companies of boys acting men's parts were thought rather more tolerable than men pretending to be other kinds of men. The deception involved in boys playing men was more transparent than when men played characters other than themselves. There was also a strong Puritan suspicion about shows of any kind, which looked too much like the Catholic ceremonial that the new Church of England had renounced. Playgoing found much better favor on the Catholic side of English society than on the Puritan side. Different preachers took different positions over the new phenomenon of playgoing. But few would speak in its favor, and most of them openly disapproved of it. Playgoing was an idle pastime, and the devil finds work for idle hands.

In the 1590s, when *Romeo and Juliet* and Shakespeare's histories and early comedies were exciting audiences, only two playhouses and two companies were officially approved by the Queen's Privy Council for the entertainment of London's citizens. The other main forms of paid entertainment were bear- and bullbaiting, which were much harder on the performers than was playing and so could be staged less frequently. The hostility to plays meant that the right to perform was confined to only a few of the most outstanding companies. These few companies were in competition with one another, and this led to a rapid growth in the quality of their offerings. But playacting was always a marginal activity. Paying to enter a specially built theater in order to see professional companies perform plays was still a new phenomenon, and it still met with great opposition from the London authorities. The open-air theaters like the Globe were built out in the suburbs. London as a city had no centrally located playhouses until after the civil war and the restoration of the monarchy, in 1661. And even playing in the city's suburbs, where they were free from the Lord Mayor's control, the companies had to work under the control of the Privy Council. All the great amphitheaters were built either in Middlesex or in Surrey. At the height of their success, in the years after Shakespeare's death, the Privy Council never licensed more than four or five playhouses in London.

Playgoing in London was viewed even by the playgoers as an idle occupation. The largest numbers who went to the Globe were apprentices and artisans taking time off from work, often surreptitiously, and law students from the Inns of Court doing the same. These fugitives were linked with the wealthier kind of idler, "gallants" or rich gentlemen and other men of property, along with soldiers and sailors on leave from the wars, people visiting London from the country on business or pleasure (usually both), and above all the women of London. Women were not expected to be literate, but one did not need to be able to read and write to enjoy hearing and seeing a play. A respectable woman had to make sure she was escorted by a man. He might be a husband or a friend, or her page if she was rich, or her husband's apprentice if she was a middle-class citizen. She might have a mask on, part of standard women's wear outdoors to protect the face against the weather and to assert modesty—and perhaps anonymity. Market women (applewives and fishwives) went to plays in groups. Whores were expected to be there looking for business, especially from the gallants, but they usually had male escorts, too.

The social range of playgoers at the two playhouses approved for use in 1594 was almost complete, stretching from the aristocracy to the poorest workmen and boys. Many people disapproved of plays, but at peak times up to 25,000 a week flocked to see the variety of plays being offered. Prices for playgoing remained much the same throughout the decades up to 1642, when the parliamentary government that was fighting the King closed all the theaters for eighteen years. Until then, one could get standing room at an amphitheater for 1 penny ($\frac{1}{240}$th of a modern pound, roughly 1 cent),

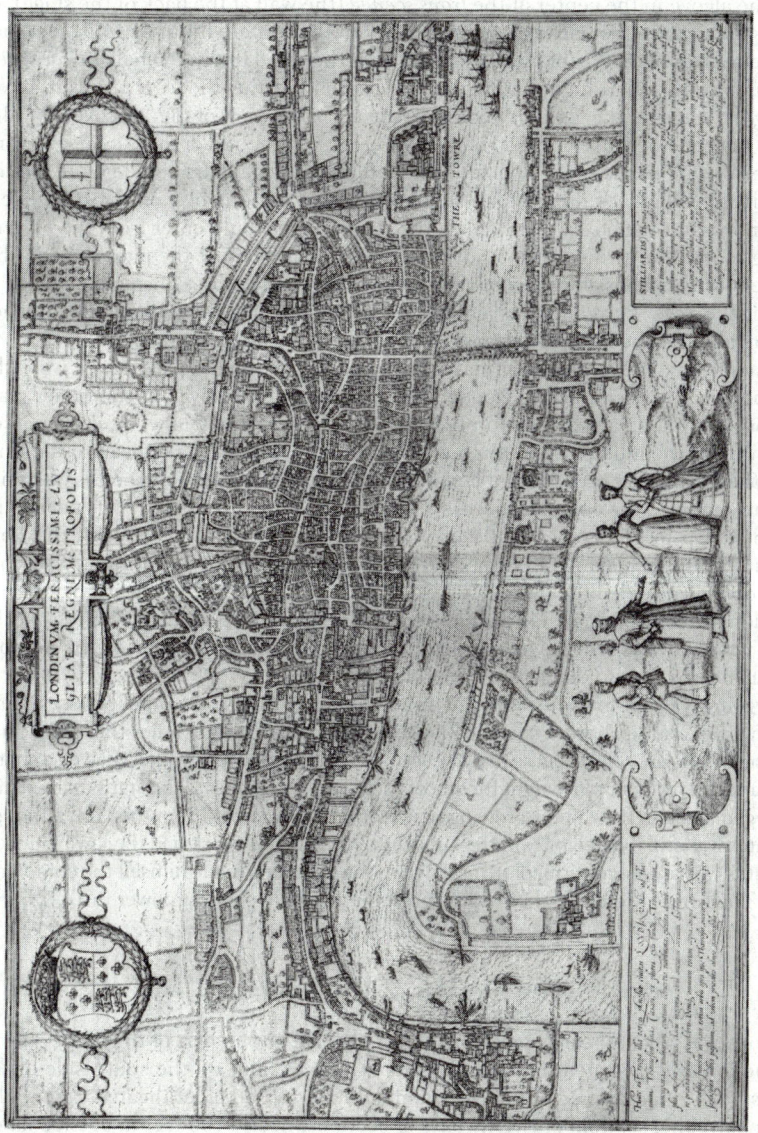

The city of London and its suburbs in 1572.

or a seat on a bench in the roofed galleries for twopence. A seat in a lord's room cost sixpence, which was not much less than a day's wage for a skilled artisan in 1600. The smaller roofed theaters that opened in 1599 were much more expensive. They were called "private" theaters to distinguish them from the "public" open-air amphitheaters, although the claim to privacy was mainly a convenient fiction to escape the controls imposed on the "public" theaters. At the Blackfriars hall theater, sixpence only gained you a seat in the topmost gallery, while a seat in the pit near the stage cost three times that amount and a seat in a box five times, or half a skilled worker's weekly wage.

It was not only the plays and players that were the sights at the playhouses. The richest lords and gallants went to be seen as much as they went to see. At the Globe, the costliest rooms were positioned alongside the balcony "above," over the stage. They were called "lords' rooms," and the playgoers who chose to sit there had a limited view of what went on beneath them. They saw no "discoveries," for instance, such as Portia's three caskets in *The Merchant of Venice,* which were uncovered underneath them inside the alcove in the center of the *frons scenae* (the wall at the back of the stage), or anything other than the backs of the players when they entered. But as audience, they were themselves highly visible, and that was what they paid for. In the hall, or "private," playhouses, with much higher admission prices than at the Globe, there were boxes flanking the stage for the gentry, which gave them a better view of the "discoveries." But at these "select" (because costlier) hall playhouses, where, unlike the Globe, everyone had a seat, some of the most colorful and exhibitionistic gallants could go one better. Up to fifteen gallants could pay for a stool to sit and watch the play on the stage itself, sitting in front of the boxes that flanked the stage. Each would enter from the players' dressing room (the "tiring-house") with his stool in hand before the play started. This gave them the best possible view of the play and easily the most conspicuous place in the audience's eye. Playgoing was a public occasion in which the visibility of audience members allowed them to play almost as large a part as the players.

Through the 1590s, the only permanent and custom-made playhouses were the large open-air theaters. Paying sixpence for a ferry across the river, as the richer playgoers did, or walking across London Bridge to the Rose or the Globe, or else trudging north through the mud of Shoreditch and Finsbury Fields or Clerkenwell to the Theatre or the Fortune in order to see a play, did not have great appeal when it was raining. Consequently, the companies were always trying to secure roofed halls nearer the city center. Up to 1594, they could use city inns, especially in winter, but the Lord Mayor's hostility to playing never made them reliable places for performing. Two constant problems troubled the players throughout these first years of professional theater in London: the city officials' chronic hatred of plays and the periodic visitations of the plague, which always led the government to close the theaters as soon as the number of plague deaths rose to dangerously high levels.

Playgoing was not firmly established in London until the Privy Council chose to protect it in 1594 and to approve specific playhouses for the two companies that it officially sanctioned. By then, Shakespeare had already made his mark. He became a player, a shareholder, and the resident playwright for one of these two companies. That status gained him a privileged place in the rapidly growing new world of playgoing. From then on, although his theater was still located only in the suburbs of the city, his work had the law behind it. That status was amply confirmed in 1603, when the new King made himself the company's patron. The King's Men held their status until the King himself lost power in 1642.

The Design of the Globe

The Globe was Shakespeare's principal playhouse. He put up part of the money for its construction and designed his best plays for it. It was built on the south side of the Thames in 1599, fashioned out of the framing timbers of an older theater. Essentially, it was a polygonal scaffold of twenty bays or sections, nearly 100 feet in outside diameter, making a circle of three levels of galleries that rose to more than 30 feet high, with wooden bench seating and cushions for those who could afford them. This surrounded an open "yard," into which the stage projected.

The yard was over 70 feet in diameter. Nearly half the audience stood on their feet to watch the play from inside this yard, closest to the stage platform. The stage extended out nearly to the middle of the yard, so the actors could stand in the center of the crowd. The uncertain privilege of having standing room in the open air around the stage platform could be bought with the minimal price for admission, 1 penny (about a cent). It had the advantage of proximity to the stage and the players; its disadvantage was keeping you on your feet for the two or three hours of the play, as well as leaving you subject to the weather. If you wanted a seat, or if it rained and you wanted shelter, you paid twice as much to sit in the three ranks of roofed galleries that circled behind the crowd standing in the yard. With some squeezing, the theater could hold over 3,000 people. It was an open-air theater because that gave it a larger capacity than a roofed hall. The drawback of its being open to the weather was more than outweighed by the gain in daylight that shone on stage and spectators alike.

The stage was a great square platform as much as 40 feet wide. It had over it a canopied roof, or "heavens," to protect the players and their expensive costumes from rain. This canopy was held up by two pillars rising through the stage. The stage platform was about 5 feet high and without any protective rails, so that the eyes of the audience in the yard were at the level of the players' feet. At the back of the stage, a wall—the *frons scenae*—stretched across the front of the players' tiring-house, the attiring or dressing room. It had a door on each flank and a wider curtained space in the center, which was used for major entrances and occasionally for set-piece scenes. Above these entry doors was a gallery or balcony, most of which was partitioned into rooms for the wealthiest spectators. A central room "above" was sometimes used in staging: for example, as Juliet's balcony, as the place for Richard III to stand between the bish-

The second Globe, from Wenceslaus Hollar's engraving of the "Long View" of London (1647). The two captions saying "The Globe" and "Beere bayting h." were accidentally transposed in the original. The Globe is the round structure in the center of the picture.

A photograph of the interior framework of the "new" Globe, on the south bank of the Thames in London, showing the general dimensions of the yard and the surrounding galleries.

ops, as the wall of Flint Castle in *Richard II,* and as the wall over the city gates of Harfleur in *Henry V.* After 1608, when Shakespeare's company acquired the Blackfriars consort of musicians, this central gallery room was turned into a curtained-off music room that could double as an "above" when required. Fewer than half of Shakespeare's plays need an "above."

The Original Staging Techniques

Shakespearean staging was emblematic. The "heavens" that covered the stage was the colorful feature from which gods descended to the earth of the stage platform. When Jupiter made his appearance in *Cymbeline,* in clouds of "sulphurous breath" provided by fireworks, he was mounted on an eagle being lowered through a trapdoor in the heavens. The other trapdoor, set in the stage platform itself, symbolized the opposite, a gateway to hell. The large stage trap was the place where the Gravedigger came to work at the beginning of Act 5 of *Hamlet.* It was the cell where Malvolio was imprisoned in *Twelfth Night.* The Shakespearean mindset accepted such conventions automatically.

Shakespeare inherited from Marlowe a tradition of using the stage trap as the dreaded hell's mouth. Barabbas plunges into it in *The Jew of Malta,* and the demons drag the screaming Faustus down it at the end of *Dr. Faustus.* Hell was not a fiction taken lightly by Elizabethans. Edward Alleyn, by far the most famous player of Faustus in the 1590s, wore a cross on his breast while he played the part, as insurance—just in case the fiction turned serious. Tracking the Elizabethan mindset about the stage trapdoor can give us a few warnings of what we might overlook when we come fresh to the plays today.

In the original staging of *Hamlet* at the Globe, the stage trap had two functions. Besides serving as Ophelia's grave, it was the distinctive entry point, not used by any other character, for the Ghost in Act 1. When he tells his son that he is "for the day confined to fast in fires," the first audiences would have already taken the point that he

The Globe as reconstructed in Southwark near the original site in London.

had come up from the underworld. His voice comes from under the stage, telling the soldiers to swear the oath of secrecy that Hamlet lays upon them. The connection between that original entry by the Ghost through the trap and the trap's later use for Ophelia is one we might easily miss. At the start of Act 5, the macabre discussion between the Gravediggers about whether she committed suicide and is, therefore, con-

The *frons scenae* of the new Globe.

A gesture using the language of hats, as shown by the man attending the brothers Browne.

signed to hell gets its sharpest edge from the association of the trap, here the grave being dug for her, with the Ghost's purgatorial fires. More to the point, though, Hamlet, as he eavesdrops on the curtailed burial ceremony, makes the same connection when he discovers that it is the body of Ophelia being so neglectfully interred. He remembers the other apparition that came up through the trap and springs forward in a grotesque parody of the Ghost, crying, "This is I, Hamlet the Dane!" It is a melodramatic claim to be acting a new role, that of his father the dead King. The first audiences would have remembered the ghost of dead King Hamlet using the stage trap at this point more readily than we do now. Hamlet's private knowledge of the Ghost and the trapdoor sets him, as so often happens in the play, at odds with his audience. Consequently, centuries of editors, like the characters onstage, have misread this claim as a declaration that young Hamlet ought to be King.

Since his own name is Hamlet, and since he alone could have made the connection between the Ghost and the trapdoor, he was all too likely to be misunderstood. In the next scene, Osric certainly shows that he understands Hamlet's graveside claim that he is his father's ghost to be a claim that he should now be King of Denmark. That explains why Osric insists on keeping his hat in his hand when he comes to invite Hamlet to duel with Laertes. With equals, an Elizabethan gentleman would doff his hat in greeting and then put it back on. Only in the presence of your master, or as a courtier in the presence of the King, did you keep it in your hand. Osric is trying tactfully to acknowledge what he thinks is Hamlet's lunatic claim to be King. He missed the private connection that Hamlet had made with the trapdoor and his father's ghost. Tudor body language, with its wordless gestures and signals that defined human relations, was an aspect of social life so widely understood that it needed no stage direction. The language of hats was a part of the Shakespearean mindset that we now have to register in footnotes.

Other signifiers are necessarily more elusive. We might take heart from the range of the comments made in *Much Ado About Nothing* 4.1 when Hero is accused and is seen to go red. Each of the viewers—Claudio, Leonato, and Friar Francis—gives a different reading (or "noting") of her blush. Different mindsets lead to visual indicators being read in different ways. Each reading tells as much about the observer as about the thing observed. We might add that since the blush is commented on so extensively, Shakespeare must have been concerned to save the boy playing Hero from the necessity of holding his breath long enough to produce the right visual effect.

Costume was a vital element in the plays, a mute and instant signifier of the scene. If a character entered carrying a candle and dressed in a gown with a nightcap on his head, he had evidently just been roused from bed. Characters who entered wearing cloaks and riding boots and possibly holding a whip had just ended a long journey. York,

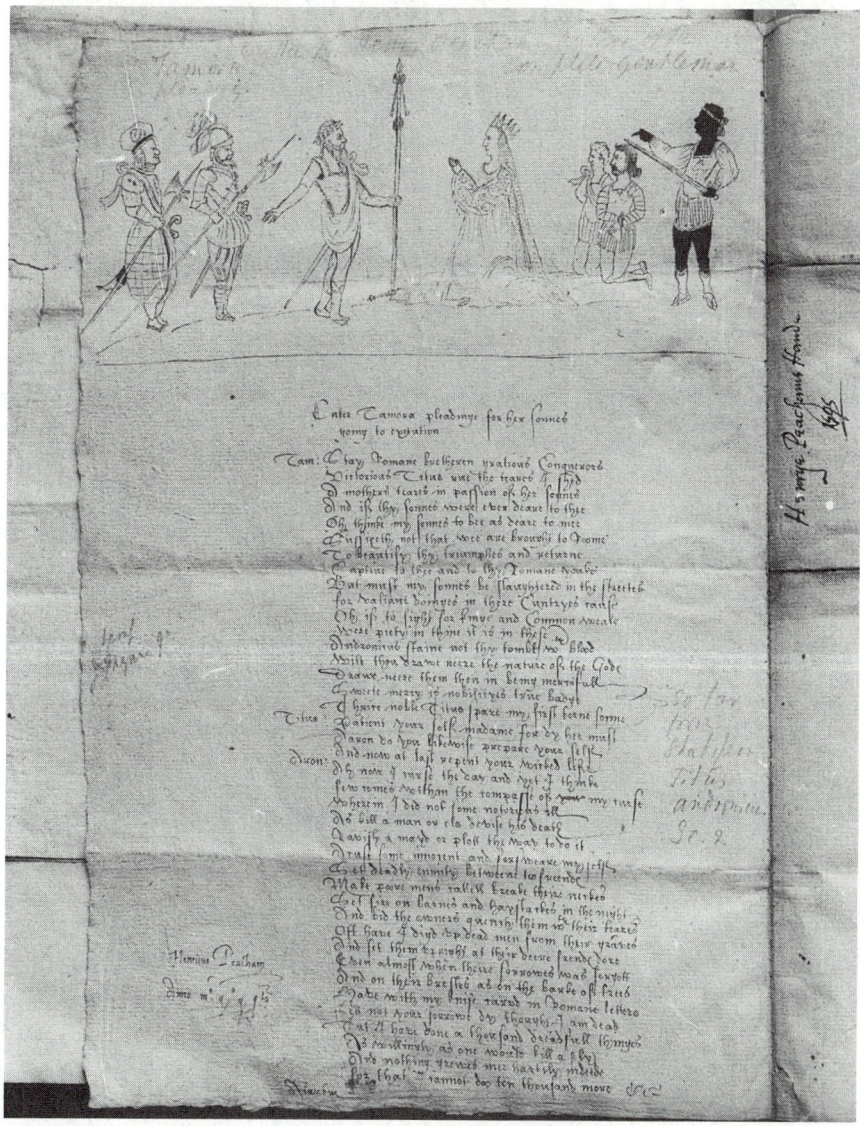

A sketch by Henry Peacham of an early staging of *Titus Andronicus* by Shakespeare's company (1595). Note the attempt at a Roman costume for Titus but not for his soldiers, who carry Tudor halberds, and note Aaron's makeup and wig.

entering in *Richard II* with a gorget (a metal neck plate, the "signs of war about his agèd neck" [2.2.74]), was preparing for battle. Even the women's wigs that the boys wore could be used to indicate the wearer's state of mind. Hair worn loose and unbound meant madness, whether in *Hamlet*'s Ophelia or *Troilus*'s Cassandra.

Comparable audience expectations could be roused by other visual features. Characters with faces blackened and wigs of curly black wool were recognized as Moors,

Johannes de Witt's drawing of the Swan Theatre in 1596, showing two boys playing women greeted by a chamberlain.

alien and dangerous non-Christians. Aaron the Moor in *Titus Andronicus* and the Prince of Morocco in *The Merchant of Venice* acquire that character as soon as they come in view. Othello, by Iago's report and by his own first appearance, takes on the same stereotype. By contrast, Iago is dressed like a simple and honest soldier. Only in the course of Act 1 does it become apparent that it is Othello who is the honest soldier, Iago the un-Christian alien. The play neatly reverses the visual stereotypes of Elizabethan staging. Twentieth-century playgoers miss most of these signals and the ways that the original players used them to show the discrepancy between outward appearance and inner person. As King Lear said, robes and furred gowns hide all.

For *The Merchant of Venice*, Shylock wore his "Jewish gabardine" and may also have put on a false nose, as Alleyn was said to have done for the title role in *The Jew of Malta*. Other national characteristics were noted by features of dress, such as the Irish "strait strossers" (tight trousers) that Macmorris would have worn in *Henry V.* The dress of the women in the plays, who were usually played by boys with unbroken voices, was always a special expense. The records kept by Philip Henslowe, owner of the Rose playhouse and impresario for the rival company to Shakespeare's, show that he paid the author less for the script of *A Woman Killed with Kindness* than he paid the costumer for the heroine's gown.

Women's clothing and the decorums and signals that women's costume contained were very different from those of men and men's clothing. Men frequently used their hats, doffing them to signal friendship and holding them in their hands while speaking to anyone in authority over them. Women's hats were fixed to their heads and were rarely if ever taken off in public. The forms and the language of women's clothes reflected the silent modesty and the quiet voices that men thought proper for women. Women had other devices to signal with, including handkerchiefs, fans, and face masks, and the boys playing the women's parts in the theaters exploited such accessories to the full. A lady out of doors commonly wore a mask to protect her complexion. When Othello is quizzing Emilia in 4.2 about his wife's behavior while she spoke to Cassio, he asks Emilia, who should have been chaperoning her mistress, whether Desdemona had not sent her away "to fetch her fan, her gloves, her mask, nor nothing?" There is little doubt that the boys would have routinely worn masks when they played gentlewomen onstage, and not just at the masked balls in *Romeo and Juliet, Love's Labour's Lost,* and *Much Ado About Nothing.*

Other features of the original staging stemmed from the actor–audience relationship, which differs radically in daylight, when both parties can see one another, from what we are used to in modern, darkened, theaters. An eavesdropping scene onstage, for instance, works rather on the same basis as the "invisible" fairies in *A Midsummer Night's Dream,* where the audience agrees to share the pretense. At the Globe, it also entailed adopting the eavesdropper's perspective. In *Much Ado,* the two games of eavesdropping played on Benedick and Beatrice are chiefly done around the two stage posts. In these scenes, the posts that held up the stage cover, or "heavens," near what we now think of as the front of the stage were round, like the whole auditorium, and their function was to allow things to be seen equally by all of the audience, wherever people might be standing or sitting. Members of the audience, sitting in the surrounding galleries or standing around the stage itself at the Globe or its predecessors, had the two tall painted pillars in their sight all the time, wherever they were in the playhouse. And since the audience was in a complete circle all around the stage, if the stage posts were used for concealment there was always a large proportion of the audience who could see the player trying to hide behind a post. It was a three-dimensional game in which the audience might find itself behind any of the game players, victims or eavesdroppers, complicit in either role.

The first of *Much Ado*'s eavesdropping scenes, 2.3, starts as usual in Shakespeare with a verbal indication of the locality. Benedick tells his boy, "Bring it hither to me in the orchard." So we don't need stage trees to tell us where we are supposed to be. He later hides "in the arbour" to listen to what Don Pedro and the others have set for him; this means concealing himself behind a stage post, closer to the audience than the playactors who are talking about him. Don Pedro asks, "See you where Benedick hath hid himself?" a self-contradiction that confirms the game. When it is Beatrice's turn in her arbor scene, 3.1, she slips into a "bower" behind "this alley," which again signals a retreat behind the prominent stage post. These games are played with both of the eavesdroppers hiding behind the post at the stage edge, while the others do their talking at center stage between the two posts.

Such games of eavesdropping, using the same bits of the stage structure, make a strong visual contrast with all that goes on at what we two-dimensional thinkers, used to the pictorial staging of the cinema, call the "back" of the stage, or upstage—where, for instance, the Friar starts the broken-off wedding and where Claudio and Don Pedro later figure at Leonato's monument. These events are more distant from the audience, less obviously comic and intimate. The close proximity of players to audience in such activities as eavesdropping strongly influenced the audience's feeling of kinship with the different groupings of players.

A multitude of other staging differences can be identified. Quite apart from the fact that the language idioms were more familiar to the playgoers at the original Globe than they are now, all playgoers in 1600, many of them illiterate, were practiced listeners. The speed of speech, even in blank verse, was markedly higher then than the recitation of Shakespeare is today. The original performances of *Hamlet*, if the Folio version reflects what was usually acted, would have run for not much more than two and a half hours (the time quoted by Ben Jonson for a play as long as *Hamlet*), compared with the more than four hours that the full Folio or 1605 quarto text with at least one intermission would take today. Quicker speaking, quicker stage action, no intermissions, and the audience's ability to grasp the language more quickly meant that the plays galloped along. The story, not the verse, carried the thrust of the action. Occasional set speeches, like Hamlet's soliloquies or Gaunt's "sceptred isle" speech in *Richard II,* would be heard, familiar as they already were to many in the audience, like a solo aria in a modern opera. In theory if not in practice, the business of hearing, as "audience" (from the Latin *audire,* "to hear"), was more important than the business of seeing, as "spectators" (from the Latin *spectare,* "to see"). The visual aspects of acting, like scenic staging, are inherently two-dimensional and do not work well when the audience completely surrounds the actors. Most of Shakespeare's fellow writers, notably Jonson, understandably set a higher priority on the audience's hearing their verse than on their seeing what the players did with the lines. The poets wanted listeners, although the players did try to cater to the viewers. Yet for all the games with magic tricks and devils spouting fireworks that were part of the Shakespearean staging tradition, spectacle was a limited resource on the scene-free Elizabethan stage. Shakespeare in this was a poet more than a player. Even in his last and most richly staged plays—*Cymbeline, The Winter's Tale,* and *The Tempest*—he made notably less use of such "spectacles" than did his contemporaries.

One piece of internal evidence about the original staging is Hamlet's advice to the visiting players. In 3.2, before they stage the *Mousetrap* play that he has rewritten for them, he lectures them on what a noble student of the theater then considered to be good acting. He objects first to overacting and second to the clown who ad libs with his own jokes and does not keep to the script. How far this may have been Shakespeare's own view it is impossible to say. Hamlet is an amateur lecturing professionals about how they should do their job. His views are what we would expect an amateur playwright with a liking for plays that are "caviar to the general" to hold. His objections to the clown are noteworthy, because once the original performances ended, the clown would conclude the afternoon's entertainment with a comic song-and-dance jig. Thomas Platter, a young German-speaking Swiss student, went to the Globe in 1599 to see *Julius Caesar.* He reported back home that

> on 21 September after lunch I and my party crossed the river, and there in the playhouse with the thatched roof witnessed an excellent performance of the tragedy of the first emperor Julius Caesar with a cast of about fifteen people. When the play

The hall screen in the Middle Temple Hall, built in 1574. Shakespeare's company staged *Twelfth Night* in this hall in February 1602.

was over they danced marvellously and gracefully together as their custom is, two dressed as men and two as women.[1]

The script for one jig survives, probably played by Will Kemp, who was the Shakespeare company clown until he left just before *Hamlet* came to the Globe. Its story is a bawdy knockabout tale of different men trying to seduce a shopkeeper's wife in rhyming couplets, hiding in a chest from her husband, and beating one another up. There is nothing to say what the audience reaction to such a jig might have been after they had seen a performance of *Julius Caesar* or *Hamlet*. It is possible that the Globe players stopped offering that kind of coda when they acquired the clown who played Feste in *Twelfth Night* in 1601. The song with which Feste ends that play might have become an alternative form of closure, replacing the traditional bawdy jig.

Vigorous and rapid staging was inevitable when the half of the audience closest to the stage had to stand throughout the performance. Shakespeare's plays were distinctive among the other plays of the time for their reliance on verbal sparkle over scenes of battle and physical movement, but even the soliloquies raced along. There was little occasion for long pauses and emoting. Dumb shows, like the players' prelude to the *Mousetrap* play in *Hamlet,* were the nearest that the players came to silent acting. There were no intermissions—apples, nuts, and drink were peddled in the auditorium throughout the performance—and the only "comfort stations" were, for the men, the nearest blank wall; for the women, whatever convenient pots or bottles they might be carrying under their long skirts.

Nor were there any pauses to change scenes. There was no static scenery apart from an emblematic candle to signify a night scene, a bed "thrust out" onto the stage, or the canopied chair of state on which the ruler or judge sat for court scenes. Usually any

---

1. *Thomas Platter's Travels in England* (1599), rendered into English from the German, and with introductory matter by Clare Williams (London: Cape, 1937), p. 166.

special locality would be signaled in the first words of a new scene, but unlocalized scenes were routine. Each scene ended when all the characters left the stage and another set entered. No act breaks appear in the plays before *The Tempest*. *Henry V* marked each act with a Chorus, but even he entered on the heels of the characters from the previous scene. Blue-coated stagehands were a visibly invisible presence onstage. They would draw back the central hangings on the *frons scenae* for a discovery scene, carry on the chair of state on its dais for courtroom scenes, or push out the bed with Desdemona on it for the last act of *Othello*. They served the stage like the house servants with whom the nobility peopled every room in their great houses, silent machines ready to spring into action when needed.

There has been a great deal of speculation about the tiring-house front at the rear of the stage platform: did it look more like an indoor set or an outdoor one, like the hall screen of a great house or palace or like a housefront exterior? In fact, it could easily be either. The upper level of the *frons*, the balconied "above," might equally represent a musicians' gallery, like those in the main hall of a great house, or a city wall under which the central discovery space served as the city gates, as it did for York in *Richard Duke of York* (*3 Henry VI*) 4.8, or *Henry V*'s Harfleur (3.3.78). The "above" could equally be an indoor gallery or an outdoor balcony. The appearance of the stage was everything and nothing, depending on what the play required. Players and playwrights expected the audience members to use their imagination, as they had to with the opening lines of *Hamlet*, or, as the Prologue to *Henry V* put it, to "piece out our imperfections with your thoughts."

Shakespeare's Companies and Their Playhouses

Shakespeare's plays were written for a variety of staging conditions. Until 1594, when he joined a new company under the patronage of the Lord Chamberlain, the Queen's officer responsible for licensing playing companies, poets had written their plays for any kind of playhouse. The Queen's Men, the largest and best company of the 1580s, is on record as playing at the Bell, the Bel Savage, and the Bull inns inside the city, and at the Theatre and the Curtain playhouses in the suburbs. Early in 1594, it completed this sweep of all the available London venues by playing at the Rose. But in that year, the system of playing changed. The Lord Mayor had always objected to players using the city's inns, and in May 1594 he succeeded in securing the Lord Chamberlain's agreement to a total ban. From then on, only the specially built playhouses in the suburbs were available for plays.

The Queen's Men had been set up in 1583, drawn from all the then-existing major companies with the best players. This larger and favored group at first monopolized playing in London. But it was in decline by the early 1590s, and the shortage of companies to perform for the Queen at Christmas led the Lord Chamberlain and his son-in-law, the Lord Admiral, to set up two new companies in its place as a duopoly in May 1594. Shakespeare became a "sharer," or partner, in one of these companies. As part of the same new establishment, his company, the Lord Chamberlain's Men, was allocated the Theatre to perform in, while its partner company in the duopoly, the Lord Admiral's Men, was assigned to the Rose. This was the first time any playing company secured a playhouse officially authorized for its use alone.

The Theatre, originally built in 1576 by James Burbage, father of the leading player of the Lord Chamberlain's company, was in Shoreditch, a suburb to the north of the city. The Rose, built in 1587 by Philip Henslowe, father-in-law of the Lord Admiral's leading player, Edward Alleyn, was in the suburb of Southwark, on the south bank of the Thames. Henslowe's business papers, his accounts, some lists of costumes and other resources, and his "diary," a day-by-day listing of each day's takings and the plays that brought the money in, have survived for the period from 1592 until well into the next decade. Together they provide an invaluable record of how one of the two major companies of the later 1590s, the only rival to Shakespeare's company, operated through these years.[2] Some of Shakespeare's earlier plays, written before he joined the Lord Chamberlain's Men, including *1 Henry VI* and *Titus Andronicus,* were performed at the Rose. After May 1594, the new company acquired all of his early plays; every Shakespeare play through the next three years was written for the Theatre. Its familiarity supplied one sort of resource to the playwright. But the repertory system laid heavy demands on the company.

Henslowe's papers give a remarkable record of the company repertory for these years. Each afternoon, the same team of fifteen or so players would stage a different play. With only two companies operating in London, the demand was for constant change. No play at the Rose was staged more than four or five times in any month, and it was normal to stage a different play on each of the six afternoons of each week that they performed. A new play would be introduced roughly every three weeks—after three weeks of transcribing and learning the new parts; preparing the promptbook, costumes, and properties; and rehearsing in the mornings—while each afternoon, whichever of the established plays had been advertised around town on the playbills would be put on. The leading players had to memorize on average as many as eight hundred lines for each afternoon. Richard Burbage, who played the first Hamlet in 1601, probably had to play Richard III, Orlando in *As You Like It,* and Hamlet on successive afternoons while at the same time learning the part of Duke Orsino and rehearsing the new *Twelfth Night*—and still holding at least a dozen other parts in his head for the rest of the month's program. In the evenings, he might be called on to take the company to perform a different play at court or at a nobleman's house in the Strand. The best companies made a lot of money, but not without constant effort.

The companies were formed rather like guilds, controlled by their leading "sharers." Each senior player shared the company's profits and losses equally with his fellows. Most of the plays have seven or eight major speaking parts for the men, plus two for the boys playing the women. A normal London company had eight or ten sharers, who collectively chose the repertory of plays to be performed, bought the playbooks from the poets, and put up the money for the main company resource of playbooks and costumes (not to mention the wagon and horses for touring when plague forced the London theaters to close). Shakespeare made most of his fortune from his "share," first in his company and later in its two playhouses.

As a playhouse landlord, Henslowe took half of the takings from the galleries each afternoon for his rent, while the players shared all the yard takings and the other half of the gallery money. From their takings, the sharers paid hired hands to take the walk-on parts and to work as stagehands, musicians, bookkeeper or prompter, and "gatherers" at the different entry gates. The leading players also kept the boys who played the women's parts, housing and feeding them as "apprentices" in an imitation of the London livery companies and trades, which ran apprenticeships to train boys to become skilled artisans, or "journeymen." City apprenticeships ran for seven years from the age of seventeen, but the boy players began much younger, because unbroken voices were needed. They graduated to become adult players at an age when the city apprentices were only beginning their training. Most of the "extras," apart from the playing boys, would be left in London whenever the company had to go on tour.

Because the professional companies of the kind that Shakespeare joined all started as traveling groups rather than as companies settled at a single playhouse in London, the years up to 1594 yielded plays that could be staged anywhere. The company might be summoned to play at court, at private houses, or at the halls of the Inns of Court as readily as at inns or innyards or the custom-built theaters themselves. They traveled the country with their plays, using the great halls of country houses, or town guildhalls and local inns, wherever the town they visited allowed them. Consequently, the plays could not demand elaborate resources for staging. In this highly mobile tradition of traveling

2. See *Henslowe's Diary,* ed. R. A. Foakes (Cambridge, Eng.: Cambridge University Press, 1961).

companies, they were written in the expectation of the same basic but minimal features being available at each venue. Besides the stage platform itself, the basic features appear to have been two entry doors, usually a trap in the stage floor, a pair of stage pillars, sometimes a discovery space, and very occasionally a heavens with descent machinery. Apart from these fixtures, properties such as chairs and a table, a canopied throne on a dais, and sometimes a bed were also in regular use, though in a pinch these could be as mobile as the players themselves. The only essential traveling properties were players, playbooks, and costumes.

Once the two authorized companies settled permanently at the Theatre and the Rose in 1594, they slowly lost some of this mobility. The demands of versatility and readiness to make rapid changes now had to be switched from the venues to the plays themselves. A traveling company needed very few plays, since the locations and audiences were always changing. When the venues became fixed, it was the plays that had to keep changing. The Henslowe papers record that the Lord Admiral's Men staged an amazingly varied repertory of plays at the Rose. Shakespeare's company must have been equally versatile. The practice of giving popular plays long runs did not begin until the 1630s, by which time the number of London playhouses had grown to as many as five, all offering their plays each afternoon. Shakespeare's company in London had only the one peer from 1594 until 1600; and only two from then until 1608, aside from the once-weekly plays by the two boy companies, the "little eyases" mentioned in *Hamlet*, that started with the new century.

From May 1594 to April 1597 at the Theatre, in addition to all his earlier plays that he brought to his new company, Shakespeare gave them possibly *Romeo and Juliet* and *King John*, and certainly *Richard II, A Midsummer Night's Dream, 1 Henry IV*, and *The Merchant of Venice*. But then they ran into deep trouble, because they lost the Theatre. In April 1597, its original twenty-one-year lease expired, and the landlord, who disliked plays, refused to let them renew it. Anticipating this, the company's impresario, James Burbage, had built a new theater for them, a roofed place in the Blackfriars near St. Paul's Cathedral. The Blackfriars precinct was a "liberty," free from the Lord Mayor's jurisdiction. But the plan proved a disaster. The rich residents of Blackfriars objected, and the Privy Council stopped the theater from opening. From April 1597, Shakespeare's company had to rent the Curtain, an old neighbor of their now-silent Theatre, and it was there that the next four of Shakespeare's plays—*2 Henry IV, Much Ado About Nothing, The Merry Wives of Windsor*, and probably *Henry V*—were first staged.

In December 1598, losing hope of a new lease for the old Theatre, the Burbage sons had it pulled down and quietly transported its massive framing timbers across the Thames to make the scaffold for the Globe on the river's south bank, near the Rose. Most of their capital was sunk irretrievably into the Blackfriars theater, and they could afford only half the cost of rebuilding. So they raised money as best they could. Some of the company's more popular playbooks were sold to printers, including *Romeo and Juliet, Richard III, Richard II*, and *1 Henry IV*. More to the point, the Burbage brothers raised capital for the building by cutting in five of the leading players, including Shakespeare, and asking them to put up the other half of its cost. The Globe, its skeleton taken from the old Theatre, thus became the first playhouse to be owned by its players, and, within the limits set by the old frame, the first one built to their own design.

For this theater, one-eighth of which he personally owned, Shakespeare wrote his greatest plays: *Julius Caesar, As You Like It, Hamlet, Twelfth Night, Othello, All's Well That Ends Well, Measure for Measure, King Lear, Macbeth, Pericles, Antony and Cleopatra, Coriolanus, Cymbeline, The Winter's Tale*, and most likely *Troilus and Cressida* and *Timon of Athens*. As the first playhouse to be owned by the players who expected to use it, its fittings must have satisfied all the basic needs of Shakespearean staging. At one time or another, the company staged every one of Shakespeare's plays there.

In 1600, a company consisting entirely of boys started using the Blackfriars playhouse that Richard Burbage's father had tried to open four years before. Companies of boy players had a higher social status than the adult professionals, and, playing only in halls, they commanded a more affluent clientele. The boys performed only once a week, and the relative infrequency of their crowds, plus their skills as trained singers (they were choir-school children turned to making money for their choirmasters), proved less offensive to the local residents than a noisy adult company with its drums and trumpets. Leasing the Blackfriars to the boy company made a minor profit for the Burbages, who took the rent for eight years.

In the longer run, though, this arrangement provided a different means for the Burbage–Shakespeare company to advance its career. The boys' eight years of playing in their rented hall playhouse eventually made it possible for the company of adult players to renew Burbage's old plan of 1596. Shakespeare's company had been made the King's Men when James came to the throne in 1603, and their new patron gave them a status that made it impossible for the residents of Blackfriars to prevent them from implementing the original plan. During a lengthy closure of all the theaters because of a plague epidemic in 1608, the boys' manager surrendered his lease of the hall playhouse to the Burbages. They then took possession for their own company of the playhouse that their father had built for them twelve years before. They divided the new playhouse property among the leading players as they had done in 1599 with the Globe.

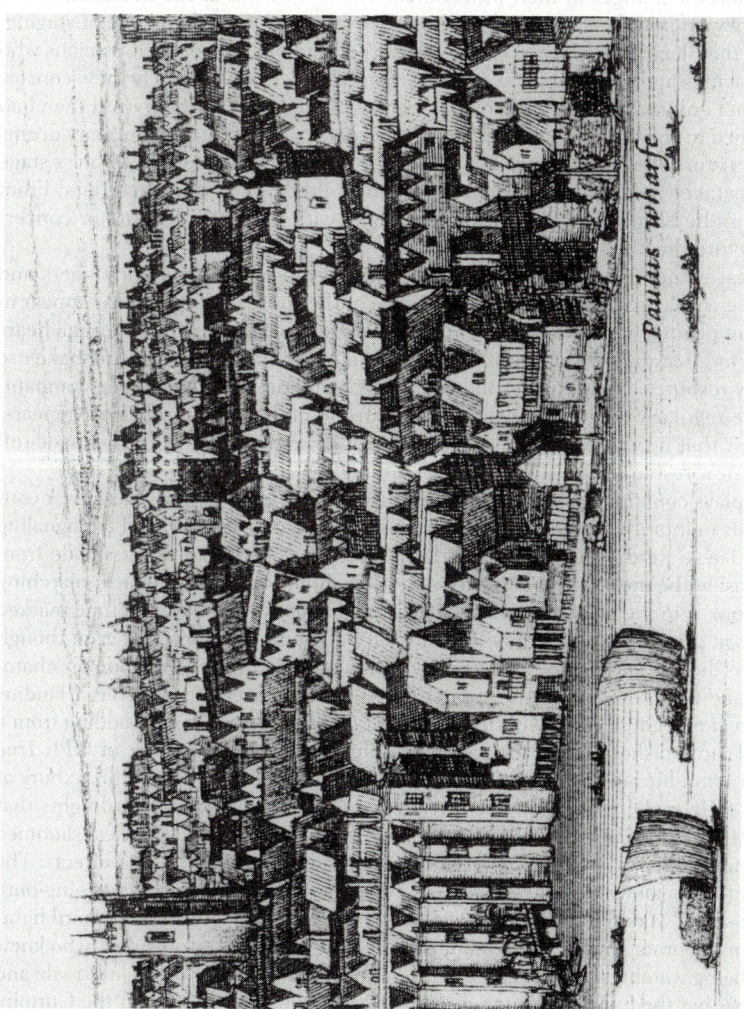

A section from Wenceslaus Hollar's "Long View" of London, printed in 1644. Drawn from a standpoint on the tower of the church that is now Southwark Cathedral, Hollar's view shows the roof of the great hall in which the Blackfriars playhouse was built. It can be seen as the long angled roof with two central chimneys, below and to the east of St. Bride's Church.

They were the King's Men, the leading company in the country, and their status after ten years of playing at the Globe was matched by their wealth. By the time theaters reopened late in 1609, the company had established a new system of playing.

The King's Men now had two playhouses, a large open amphitheater and a much smaller roofed hall. Instead of selling or renting one out and using the other for themselves, they decided to use both in turn, for half of each year. It was a reversion to the old system with the city inns, where through the summer they played in the large open yards and in the winter played at inns with big indoor rooms. This time, though, the company owned both playhouses. Their affluence and their high status are signaled by the fact that they chose to keep one of their playhouses idle while they used the other, despite there now being a shortage of playhouses in London. That affluence was needed in 1613, when the Globe burned down at a performance of *All Is True* (*Henry VIII*) and the company chose the much more expensive option of rebuilding it instead of reverting to the Blackfriars for both winter and summer. That decision, in its way, was the ultimate gesture of affection for their original playhouse. It was a costly gesture, but it meant that the Globe continued in use by the company until all the theaters were closed down by Parliament in 1642.

In 1609, when they reopened after the closure for plague, Shakespeare's company had made several changes in their procedures. The restart was at the Blackfriars, and although they offered the same kind of plays, they began to alter their style of staging. Along with the Blackfriars playhouse, they acquired a famous consort of musicians who played on strings and woodwinds in a music room set over the stage. The new consort was a distinct enhancement of the company's musical resources, which until then had been confined to song, the occasional use of recorders or hautboys, and military drums and trumpets for the scenes with soldiery. In 1608, a central room on the Globe's stage balcony was taken over to serve as a music room like the one at the Blackfriars. From this time on, the King's Men's performances began with a lengthy overture or concert of music before the play.

With that change, the plays themselves now had music to back their singers and provide other sorts of atmospheric effects. Some of the songs and music that appear in the plays not printed until the First Folio of 1623, such as the song that Mariana hears in *Measure for Measure* 4.1, may have been added after Shakespeare's time to make use of this new resource. Shakespeare did use songs, sometimes with string accompaniment, quite regularly in the early plays, but instrumental music hardly ever appears. The last play that he wrote alone, *The Tempest*, was the only one in which he made full use of this new resource.

All the plays containing soldiers and battles used the military drums that in war conveyed signals to infantry formations, as well as the trumpets that were used for signaling to cavalry. These were usually employed for offstage noises, sound effects made from "within" (inside the dressing room or tiring-house behind the stage). Soldiers marching in procession, as in the dead march at the close of *Hamlet*, would have the time marked by an onstage drum. Shakespeare never calls for guns to be fired onstage, even though other writers did, but he did have other noises at his command. A small cannon or "chamber" might be used, fired from the gable-fronted heavens over the stage, as Claudius demands in *Hamlet* and as the Chorus to Act 3 of *Henry V* notes. It was wadding from a ceremonial cannon shot that set the gallery thatch alight at a performance of *All Is True* in July 1613 and burned the Globe to the ground. Stage battles such as Shrewsbury at the end of *1 Henry IV*, written for the Theatre, were accompanied by sword fights that were not the duels of *Hamlet*'s finale but exchanges with broadswords or "foxes" slammed against metal shields or "targets." That action guaranteed emphatic sound effects. The drums and trumpets, with clashes of swords and a great deal of to-ing and fro-ing onto and off the stage, were highlighted in between the shouted dialogue by some hard fighting between the protagonists. The leading players were practiced swordsmen, who knew they were being watched by experts. These were the scenes of "four or five most vile and ragged foils" that the fourth Chorus self-consciously derided in *Henry V* at the Curtain.

The second great reason for noise in the amphitheaters was to mark storm and tempest. Stagehands used the kind of device that Jonson mocked in the Prologue to *Every Man in His Humour,* written for its 1616 publication. His play, wrote Jonson, was free from choruses that wafted you over the seas, "nor rolled bullet heard / To say, it thunders; nor tempestuous drum / Rumbles, to tell you when the storm doth come." For centuries, lead balls rolling down a tin trough were a standard way of making thunder noises in English theaters. The tempest in Act 3 of *King Lear* is heralded several times in the text before a stage direction, "Storm and tempest" (Folio 2.2.450), tells us that it has at last arrived. In 2.2, Cornwall notes its coming twice (Folio 2.2.452, 473). Kent comments on the "Foul weather" in his first line in Act 3, prefaced by the entry stage direction for Act 3, "Storm still," which is repeated for 3.2. Such stage directions appear in both texts (Q has "Storm" for the equivalent Scenes 8, 9, and also at 11, F's 3.4, where F omits any further reference to these noises). These explicit signals indicate that the stagehands provided offstage noises, for all that Lear himself outstorms them with his violent speeches in 3.2.

The main question about the storm scenes in *King Lear* is this: with such consistent emphasis on storm in the language, what was the design behind the stage directions? In the centuries that *Lear* has been restaged, the tempest has been made to roar offstage in a wide variety of ways, often with so much effect that, in the face of complaints that the storm noises made it difficult for the audience to hear the words, some modern productions reduced the storm to solely visual effects, or even left Lear's own raging language to express it unsupported. But the two stage directions indicate that in the original performances the "storm in nature" was not left to Lear himself to convey. The two "Storm still" directions in the Folio suggest a constant rumbling, not the intermittent crashes that might allow Lear to conduct a dialogue with the occasional outbursts of storm noises, as some modern productions have done.

Shakespeare left regrettably few stage directions to indicate the special tricks or properties that he wanted. Curtained beds are called for in *Othello* 5.2 and *Cymbeline* 2.2, and there is the specification "Stocks brought out" in *King Lear* 2.2.132. Small and portable things like papers were a much more common device, from the letters in *The Two Gentlemen of Verona* 1.2.46, 1.3.44, and 2.1.95 to Lear's map at 1.1.35. Across the whole thirty-eight plays, though, there are very few such directions. Shakespeare's economy in preparing his scripts is a major impediment to the modern reader. He hardly ever bothered to note the standard physical gestures, such as kneeling or doffing a hat, and did little more to specify any special effects. Nonetheless, it is important not to imagine elaborate devices or actions where the text does not call for them. On the whole, the demands Shakespeare made of his fellows for staging his plays appear to have been remarkably modest. Since he was a company shareholder, his parsimony may have had a simple commercial motive. Stage properties cost the company money, and one had to be confident of a new play's popularity before investing much in its staging.

There may have been other reasons for avoiding extravagant staging spectacles. Shakespeare made little use of the discovery space until the last plays, for instance, for reasons that we can only guess at. The few definite discoveries in the plays include Portia's caskets in *The Merchant of Venice,* Falstaff sleeping off his sack in *1 Henry IV* 2.5.482, the body of Polonius in *Hamlet,* Hermione's statue in *The Winter's Tale* 5.3.20, and the lovers in *The Tempest* 5.1.173, who are found when discovered to be playing chess. The audience's shock when Hermione moves and comes out of the discovery space onto the main stage is rare in Shakespeare: in every other play, whether comedy or tragedy, the audience knows far more than the characters onstage about what is going on. Shakespeare matched this late innovation in *The Winter's Tale* with his last play, *The Tempest.* After the preliminary and soothing concert by the resident Blackfriars musicians, it opens with a storm at sea so realistic that it includes that peculiarly distinctive stage direction "Enter Mariners, wet" (1.1.46). That startling piece of stage realism turns out straightaway to be not real at all but a piece of stage magic.

HISTORIES

HISTORIES

Shakespearean History
by

JEAN E. HOWARD

In the 1590s, the first decade of his life as an actor and playwright for the London stage, Shakespeare poured much of his energy into dramatizing events from the prior several hundred years of England's past. At this time, he wrote or had a major hand in writing at least eight plays depicting English monarchical history of the late fourteenth and the fifteenth centuries. These included *The First Part of the Contention of the Two Famous Houses of York and Lancaster (2 Henry VI), The True Tragedy of Richard Duke of York and the Good King Henry the Sixth (3 Henry VI), The First Part of Henry the Sixth (1 Henry VI), The Tragedy of King Richard the Third, The Tragedy of King Richard the Second, The History of Henry the Fourth (1 Henry IV), The Second Part of Henry the Fourth (2 Henry IV)*, and *The Life of Henry the Fifth*. Collectively, these plays dramatized the deposition of Richard II, the attempts of Henry IV and Henry V to rule England in the wake of this deposition, the civil war (the so-called War of the Roses) that subsequently broke out between the Lancastrian and Yorkist branches of the Plantagenet family to which Richard belonged, and finally the defeat by Henry Tudor, a Lancastrian, of the Yorkist king, Richard III, at the Battle of Bosworth Field in 1485. During this decade, Shakespeare also wrote *The Life and Death of King John* that examines the reign of the thirteenth-century monarch who struggled to be regarded as the legitimate King of England despite competing claims to that title, and later in his career (1613) he composed *All Is True (Henry VIII)* in collaboration with John Fletcher that dramatizes events from the reign of Henry VIII, the second of the Tudor kings of England. Recently, critics have once again begun to take seriously the possibility that parts of *King Edward the Third* (c. 1596) are also by Shakespeare. It depicts the impressive military victories achieved by the father and grandfather of Richard II over French and Scottish adversaries. In his fascination with dramatizing English history Shakespeare was dealing with events that had had a formative effect on the world in which he lived. When Henry Tudor kills Richard III at Bosworth Field, is crowned King of England, and marries Elizabeth of York, he not only unites the Lancastrian and Yorkist factions, but also inaugurates the Tudor dynasty that held the throne during Shakespeare's own lifetime. Elizabeth I, who ruled England from 1558 to 1603, was the granddaughter of Henry VII.

In these plays about English history, Shakespeare was also giving a distinctive stamp to one of the most important dramatic genres of the 1590s, but one whose exact parameters were somewhat undefined at the time and remain in dispute today. Elizabethan playwrights regularly staged plays based on historical events. Shakespeare's contemporary, Christopher Marlowe, for example, wrote a famous play, *Edward II* (1592), about the ill-fated reign of a fourteenth-century English king that may have sparked Shakespeare's interest in mining late medieval monarchical chronicles for dramatic subjects. Many playwrights, however, did not confine themselves to medieval English materials, but looked to classical Greece and Rome, ancient Britain, or contemporary France for historical subjects. Some plays based on historical events were not labeled as histories. If, for example, they focused on the life of a particular character, as in Shakespeare's own play about Richard III, they might simply be called tragedies. Generic categorizations at the time were fluid, and some plays could be categorized in more than one way. Moreover, historical plays differed widely in form and feel. Some dramas from the mid-sixteenth century, such as John Bale's vehemently anti-Catholic *King Johan* (1538), were often overtly polemical and, in Bale's case, warned against the dangers of the Roman Church to England's well-being. To drive home his point, Bale gave his characters allegorical names such as Sedition, Dissimulation, and Usurped Power (another name for the Pope). Other history plays, such as Thomas Heywood's two-part play on the life of Edward IV (1600), combined a fairly perfunctory depiction of political and military events of Edward's reign with a second, sentimental plot focusing on the suffering of Jane Shore, the citizen wife whom the king seduced. That part of the play feels like a domestic drama of citizen life and competes with the monarchical plot for the audience's attention.

The Elizabethan history play was, therefore, a capacious and somewhat indeterminate genre. The Shakespearean history play is a less elusive entity, partly because of the help given by the 1623 Folio edition of Shakespeare's works, prepared after his death by members of his acting company, the King's Men. There, all of Shakespeare's plays are divided into three categories: comedies, histories, and tragedies. Among the histories, the editors list ten Shakespeare plays, all defined by their subject matter—that is, their focus on monarchical history from post–Norman Conquest England (history about events after 1066). These include *King John* and *Henry VIII* plus the eight plays dealing with the reigns of Richard II to Henry VI. *Edward III*, whose authorship is even debated today, is not included on the list. In retrospect, critics, when speaking of the Elizabethan history play, tend to limit the genre to the kind of play Shakespeare made popular. This a testament to his achievement, but it nonetheless narrows our understanding of the many different kinds of plays that might be considered part of the early modern theater's romance with history.

In formal terms, Shakespeare's histories can be tragic, like *Richard II*, or comic, like *1 Henry IV*. In his own lifetime, at least three of the plays listed in the First Folio as histories were designed as tragedies on the title pages of the quarto or Octavo texts in which they were first published: *The True Tragedy of Richard Duke of York and the Good King Henry the Sixth* (3 *Henry VI*), *The Tragedy of King Richard the Third,* and *The Tragedy of King Richard the Second.* In regard to the latter two plays, each focuses on the rise and fall of a single major figure, unlike other histories in which attention is distributed across a range of characters and that often dramatize only part of a

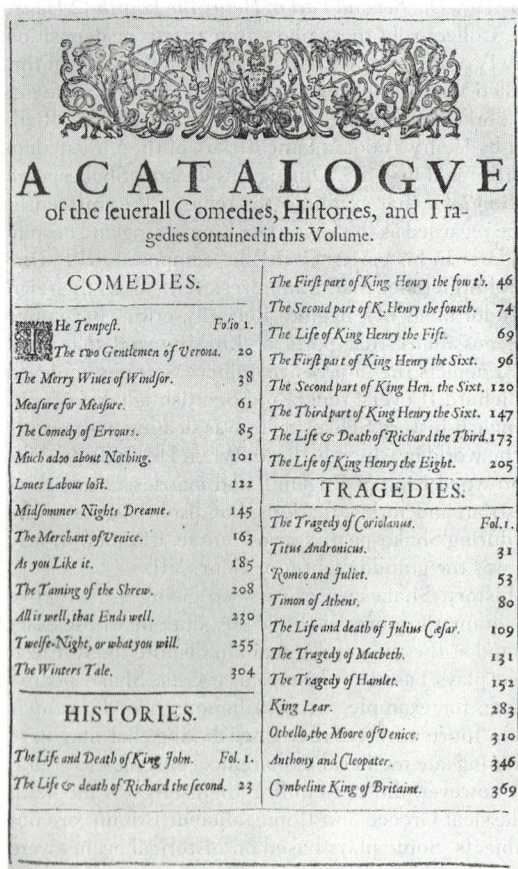

The table of contents of the first folio (1623). Note the division of the plays into the categories of comedies, histories, and tragedies.

particular king's reign. Even though Shakespeare wrote plays about Roman history, such as *Julius Caesar* and *Antony and Cleopatra,* and plays about England's ancient past, such as *Cymbeline* and *King Lear,* they are not typically now grouped with his English histories.

The ambiguities surrounding what was and was not a history play testify to the experimental nature of the genre in Shakespeare's day and the energies it captured. As early as 1592, if contemporary commentators are right, audiences were excited by plays that showed them their national past. Thomas Nashe, writing in that year, praised plays in which "our forefathers valiant acts (that have line long buried in rustie brasse and worm-eaten bookes) are revived, and they themselves raised from the Grave of Oblivion, and brought to pleade their aged Honours in open presence." He goes on to refer to events dramatized in Shakespeare's *1 Henry VI* in which the English hero, Talbot, and his son are killed heroically fighting the French and refusing to flee, even though they are vastly outnumbered. As Nashe says: "How would it have joyed brave *Talbot* (the terror of the French) to thinke that after he had lyne two hundred yeares in his Tombe, he should triumphe againe on the Stage, and have his bones newe embalmed with the teares of ten thousand spectators at least (at severall times), who, in the Tragedian that represents his person, imagine they behold him fresh bleeding?" Here, Nashe imagines Talbot receiving a kind of immortality through drama as his deeds and person are revivified (to his distinct pleasure) again and again on the contemporary stage. Theatergoers, in their turn, were reported to be moved to tears by this vivid reenactment of events two hundred years in the past but retaining the capacity to give pleasure in the present.

But the pleasure of history plays was not without its dangers. Because many history plays dealt with fairly recent historical events, and because audiences might read these plays with an eye to how they covertly commented on contemporary events, dramatists had to be careful about what they dramatized and how. For example, it was forbidden to refer on the stage to current affairs of state or to sitting monarchs and their representatives. Technically, all playbooks had to be submitted to the Office of the Master of the Revels to be reviewed for libelous or dangerous matter before a play could be performed, and sometimes parts of a play were ordered to be excised. A coauthored play on the life of Sir Thomas More, in which Shakespeare is believed to have a hand, provides one such example. This play dramatized what is known as the Ill May Day riots of 1517 against foreign workers in England. Edmund Tilney, then Master of the Revels, wrote on the playbook: "Leave out ye insurrection wholly and ye cause thereof." In the 1590s, there was considerable resentment toward foreign workers in London, and presumably a play that staged an anti-alien riot (even one that had occurred seventy years earlier) was considered too provocative to be allowed. More mysterious is the performance and print history of *Richard II.* In its fourth act, this play shows Richard II's abdication of the throne of England under pressure from his captor, Bolingbroke, soon to be Henry IV. In the First Folio, at least, the play shows these events. In the First Quarto (1597), these lines are missing. No one can definitively explain their absence. Perhaps they were simply added by Shakespeare after the first printing of the play. But it is also possible that this part of the play *did* exist in 1597 but was subject to censorship. We know the play could be controversial. In 1601, when the Earl of Essex led a rebellion against Elizabeth I, his supporters requested Shakespeare's company to perform a play about Richard II on the eve of their great undertaking. By legend, at least, a fearful Elizabeth is supposed to have said: "I am Richard II. Know you not that?" A sitting monarch was always afraid of a usurper, and staging Richard's ignominious descent from the throne could have been considered dangerous matter.

However tricky it was to stage history, Shakespeare's interest in the enterprise was shared with a number of his contemporaries. In the sixteenth century, there was widespread interest in the writing of history and a number of new developments in its practice. For many medieval historians, history was closely linked to theology and revealed God's divine plan for mankind. A providential sense that God was the first cause of historical events remained widespread well into the seventeenth century. However, many historians were also increasingly interested in the role that human actors play in shaping historical events and in the lessons that could be learned from reading accounts of the past. Many of the changes in historical practice originated in Italy as writers like Polydore Vergil began to question medieval historical narratives and to consult archives to determine the causes of historical changes and the circumstances surrounding particular events. In England in the late sixteenth century, an elite group of men, including William Camden, took pride in doing original research into the texts and objects of the past, rather than accepting received wisdom about them. Known as antiquarians, these scholars eschewed a providential view of history, studying antiquity for its own sake and not for its relevance to the present. While they constituted a distinct minority within the writers of history in Shakespeare's lifetime, they nonetheless pointed the way to modern research practices and showed how far some writers could move from the providentialism and reliance on prior authorities that was the dominant mode of medieval historical writing.

In England, the keen interest in the writing of history was probably partly due to the century of warfare and political strife that had preceded the establishment of the Tudor dynasty. Writers were eager to understand and make sense of these past events and to draw lessons from them that would lead to greater stability in the present. In writing his plays, Shakespeare made frequent use of several complex sixteenth-century chronicle histories that surveyed events in the reigns of England's kings. The first, Edward Hall's

The title page of Raphael Holinshed's *Chronicles* (1587 ed.).

The Union of the Two Noble and Illustre Famelies of Lancastre and Yorke (1548), painted a devastating picture of the chaos of the War of the Roses and presented the coming to power of the Tudors as the providential salvation of England. In writing his history plays, Shakespeare frequently drew upon details from Hall, but even more often from Raphael Holinshed's *Chronicles of England, Scotlande, and Irelande,* 2nd ed. (1587). This massive book, especially in the second edition published after Holinshed's death, incorporated writings by William Harrison, Richard Stanyhurst, John Hooker, Abraham Fleming, and many others in addition to Holinshed's own histories. While popularly attributed to a single author, it was in actuality a plural text that included competing accounts of some events and demonstrated an array of styles and modes of historical practice. As was true for the chronicle writers, Shakespeare typically organized his representation of English history through the exploration of a particular king's reign.

Besides these enormous prose chronicles, Shakespeare was probably familiar as well with the practice of humanists writers of the mid-sixteenth century (men of letters dedicated to the revival of classical learning, to the editing and translation of classical texts, and to the reform of contemporary educational practices). The humanists were particularly concerned with the moral purposes to which the reading and writing of history could be put. They felt that reading history could inspire men to virtue and warn them from vice and that kings, for example, should learn from history how to avoid tyrannical deeds. Sir Thomas Elyot, a mid-sixteenth-century humanist interested in the role of education in preparing young men for lives of public service, wrote in his *The Boke Named the Governour* (1531) that "if a noble man do thus seriously and diligently rede histories, I dare affirme there is no study or science for him of equal commoditie and pleasure, havynge regarde to every tyme and age." Roger Ascham, schoolmaster to Elizabeth I, affirmed the utilitarian value of studying history, saying that it "could bring excellent learning and breed staid judgment in taking any like matter in hand." Among the humanist histories important to Shakespeare was Sir Thomas More's *History of King Richard the Thirde* (1513), which served as the basis for the accounts of Richard's reign in Hall and Holinshed. In this psychologically complex work, More included a number of vivid speeches that he attributes to the historical figures he discusses in order to heighten the rhetorical impact of his narrative. One can imagine the effect of this practice on a dramatist like Shakespeare, whose stock in trade was making history live through the speeches of his characters.

The writing of history was, then, in sixteenth-century England in a state of transition and ferment. A number of different assumptions and practices were in play, sometimes within a single work. Particular writers might, for example, intensely explore the human motives and the secular causes of particular events but still insist on the providential design undergirding all earthly actions. Shakespeare was familiar with a number of different kinds of historical texts, and aspects of many of them were incorporated into his plays. But drama was different from prose history. In the early modern period, history and poetry (or poesy), though not always clearly distinguished from one another, were beginning to be disentangled. There was growing consensus that writers of history were less at liberty than poets to embellish facts with fiction or to take liberties with chronology. Edmund Spenser, Shakespeare's contemporary and a fellow poet, described the difference between poets who deal with historical matter and historians primarily in terms of the order of presentation that each must employ. "An historiographer discourseth of affayres orderly as they were donne, accounting as well the times as the actions; but a poet thrusteth into the middest, even where it most concerneth him, and there recoursing to the thinges forepaste, and divining of thinges to come, maketh a pleasing analysis of all." If historians are to begin at the start of a reign and move through to its conclusion, a poet can begin anywhere he wishes and selectively dramatize events of particular interest. This is a practice everywhere evident in Shakespeare's history plays. He begins his play on the reign of Richard III not with Richard's birth, but with a soliloquy, both humorous and chilling, in which the grown prince confesses to the audience his desire for the throne and meditates on how he will snatch it from his older brothers. The play itself dramatizes only a handful of events from Richard's life but does so in a way that follows a tragic trajectory in which Richard schemes and murders his way to power, only to lose his touch and to fall prey to his own hubris and the accumulated anger of those whom he has injured, an ending piously presented as fulfilling the will of heaven.

Sir Philip Sidney, another poet and Shakespeare's contemporary, makes an even sharper distinction between historians and poets. In his *Apology for Poetry*, he defends poetry as superior to history in that historians are bound to tell "the particular truth of things," while historical poets can embellish the historical record, create more perfect examples of vice or virtue than history affords, and, through "the speaking picture" of poetry vividly embody for readers the moral lessons historians less effectively attempt to impart. As Sidney says:

> for whatsoever action, or faction, whatsoever counsel, policy, or war strategem the historian is bound to recite, that may the poet (if he list) with his imitation make his own, beautifying it both for further teaching, and more delighting, as it pleaseth him: having all, from Dante's heaven to his hell, under the authority of his pen.

Shakespeare used the poet's liberty liberally. While many modern readers obtain much of their "knowledge" about fifteenth-century English history from Shakespeare's plays, this may not be smart if those readers want to know what contemporary historians actually believe happened during those bloody decades. Everywhere, Shakespeare treats historical events with the freedom that is the poet's prerogative. He notoriously alters and adds to his sources, compresses into a single year events that took decades, and everywhere assigns speeches to characters that are entirely the creation of his own brain and not of any historical record. For example, a famous scene in one of his early history plays—Act 2, Scene 4, of *1 Henry VI*—is found in no historical record. In it, Shakespeare memorably depicts the followers of the Yorkists plucking white roses from bushes in the Temple Garden in London, while Lancastrians pluck red roses in order to show whose part each group takes in the acrimonious dispute over which branch of the Plantagenet line has a superior claim to the English throne. From this scene, the bloody fiasco of decades of civil war is imagined to have derived. The scene is typical of Shakespeare's practice in that it gives vivid physical embodiment to an abstraction—in this case, the War of the Roses—while allowing the audience to keep straight a large cast of characters by the flower badges that each faction wears.

There are innumerable examples of other occasions when Shakespeare takes liberties with the historical accounts he found in his sources. In his plays about the reign of Henry IV, for example, he makes the king's son, Prince Hal, the same age as Hotspur, the son of the king's former friend and now his great enemy, the Earl of Northumberland. In actuality, Hotspur was more than twenty years older than Hal. But Shakespeare wants to present the two young men as same-age rivals and as a study in contrasts: Hotspur is honor-driven, impetuous, and valiant in war; Hal is a seeming layabout who spends days in a London tavern with low-life companions, rather than at court learning from his father how to rule a kingdom or at war winning the honor Hotspur so strenuously pursues. Hal's father goes so far as to wish that these children had been switched at birth and that Hotspur were his own flesh and blood and heir to his kingdom. While Hal eventually vindicates himself and becomes a successful ruler, a great deal of the dramatic interest of *1 Henry IV* derives from the contrast Shakespeare creates between the chivalric Hotspur and the more calculating son of England's king.

In the *Henry IV* plays, Shakespeare also invents a memorable group of ordinary people who hang out in a London tavern. They aren't found in the chronicle sources; rather, they resemble contemporary residents of Shakespeare's own day. The group includes a tavernkeeper, Mistress Quickly; a woman of dubious virtue appropriately called Doll Tearsheet; a bombastic braggart, Pistol; and other characters suited to the low-life milieu of commercial London. By adding these figures to his account of England's past, Shakespeare greatly increased the social and temporal range of his history plays. This may in part have been done to enhance the appeal of those plays to contemporary theatergoers, who saw in these characters traces of the familiar world in which they lived. But they serve other purposes, including providing an ironic or contrasting perspective on issues broached elsewhere in the play. For example, in *Henry V* a Chorus figure claims that honor motivates all the soldiers who go with Prince Hal, now King Henry V, to fight against the French in pursuit of English claims to French territory. Pistol, however, urges his friends to join the French campaign for quite another reason. "Let us to France, like horseleeches, my boys, / To suck, to suck, the very blood to suck" (2.3.46–47). Pillage and plunder are his goals. The juxtaposition of the Chorus and Pistol undercuts the former's rosy picture of the unity of the English forces and calls attention to the gap between the Chorus's idealized view of the French campaign and the more sordid aspects of its execution. This counterpoint of voices and perspectives, present elsewhere as well, is what gives the play its ironic edge and keeps it from slipping over into a mythologized view of Henry's greatness and the unity of the "band of brothers" that he creates around him. The presence of these low-life characters also reminds the audience that while monarchical history is about monarchs, it affects ordinary people in crucial ways, not all of them beneficial. Some people die in Henry's campaign; some lose their homes; some are turned into scavengers for profit, like Pistol. On the edges of this and other plays, Shakespeare gives glimpses of the effects on the powerless of the events that the chronicles record, and these are nearly always his own invention.

Shakespeare, then, takes a poet's liberty with historical material, drawing repeatedly from prose sources but adding, changing, and embellishing in ways that make the plays more theatrical and more complex. A great deal of ink has been spilled trying to figure out whether Shakespeare himself took a particular view on history's unfolding. Did he see history in providential terms? By contrast, did he view history as a sequence of events motivated entirely by the actions of powerful individuals? Did he believe Tudor mythology that saw in Henry Tudor's defeat of Richard III and marriage to Elizabeth of York the working out of a divine plan for England's salvation after the chaos of civil war and the treasonous deposition of Richard II by Henry Bolingbroke? One difficulty in answering these questions with conviction rests in the considerable differences among his ten or so English histories. Shakespeare came of dramatic age in the 1590s, and his approach to the genre that he helped to make popular changed over time.

The first four plays dealing with the reign of Henry VI and of Richard III— commonly called the first tetralogy—were all written before 1594. They represent some of Shakespeare's very earliest dramatic efforts, and, as was common practice at the time, he may well have written several of them in collaboration with other dramatists. It is not clear that they were intended at first as a unified set of plays, and 2 *Henry VI* was probably written before 1 *Henry VI*. Collectively, they dramatize the origins and devastating effects of the War of the Roses. The three *Henry VI* plays suggest that civil war was largely caused by the weakness of Henry VI and by the self-centeredness of many of the English nobles who put their own private interests before the good of the Commonwealth. In regard to these three plays, it would be too grand, I think, to say that they embody a theory of history. What they reveal is the chaos that overtakes a kingdom that is weakly ruled and the dangerous anomalies that arise in those conditions, including the unprecedented power wielded by Henry's Amazonian queen, Margaret of Anjou, or by the lower-class rebel leader, Jack Cade. *Richard III*, by contrast, most powerfully of any of Shakespeare's histories, articulates a providential view of history's unfolding. Cursed by his victims and haunted by bad dreams, Richard's character is modeled in part on the Vice figure of medieval morality plays. The Vice, always clever and theatrically compelling, nonetheless embodies evil and is at war with virtue and the forces of good. In *Richard III*, the King is finally beaten at Bosworth Field by Henry Tudor, a man presented as Richard's antithesis. A virtuous figure who longs to unite England and end civil strife, he is blessed by dreams predicting his victory over the so-called "dog," Richard, and himself prays that his descendants will "enrich the time to come with smooth-faced peace, / With smiling plenty, and fair prosperous days" (5.8.33–34). Elizabeth I, of course, was one of those descendants. In this particular play, Shakespeare seems to intimate that England has been providentially rescued from chaos by the miraculous appearance of a savior bent on returning England to a state of peace and lawful rule.

King John is something of an anomaly. Set much earlier than Shakespeare's other histories, it deals with the reign of a monarch whom Protestant writers hailed as an early defender of England's freedom from the Church of Rome. There are several sixteenth-century plays dealing with John's reign, but Shakespeare's is distinguished by its relative indifference to the religious questions to which other dramatists devoted most of their attention. Instead, Shakespeare's play focuses with unusual realism on questions of legitimacy. John is a sitting king, but his nephew Arthur, son of his older brother Geoffrey, has a more legitimate dynastic claim to the throne. Arthur, however, is a child, raised in France, and ill suited to rule. The most talented potential claimant to the throne is the Bastard, Falconbridge, the illegitimate son of Richard the Lionheart. In such circumstances, who should rule? The play creates unusually strong parts for women, including Constance, Arthur's mother, and Eleanor, John's mother; and they play major roles in the play's inconclusive, but troubling meditation on the relative weight to be given to bloodlines, talent, and possession of the throne as factors in determining monarchical legitimacy.

The so-called second tetralogy, starting with *Richard II* (1596) and including the two parts of *Henry IV* (1597 and 1598) and *Henry V* (1599), differs in many ways from the plays dealing with the War of the Roses. Although written after those earlier plays, the second tetralogy nonetheless deals with the historical period that preceded the War of the Roses. It provides, in effect, the backstory to those plays. It begins with Richard II's ill-fated reign, including his deposition and death, and then in three successive plays dramatizes the struggles of the Lancastrian kings, Henry IV and Henry V, to maintain their power and win legitimacy in the wake of the deposition of this lawfully anointed king. Although in *Richard II* the Bishop of Carlisle warns that God will punish Richard's enemies, in truth the following three plays focus less on the theme of divine retribution and more on the skills needed for the successful performance of kingship, whatever the route that led to the throne. Prince Hal is an especially vivid example of a figure who, at his first appearance in *1 Henry IV*, does not seem suited to rule. He prefers to jest with Falstaff in

A late sixteenth-century portrait of Henry IV (1367–1413) by an unknown artist. National Portrait Gallery, London.

Mistress Quickly's tavern rather than to attend to statescraft. Gradually, however, Shakespeare reveals the calculation that guides his activities and the benefits that accrue to him from his tavern sojourn, including his ability to speak with any man "in his own language," a gift he finds crucial when he needs to lead common soldiers into battle in France. Prince Hal is a new kind of political being, one whose legitimacy depends less on his dubious genealogical claim to the throne than on the performative skills through which he crafts a public image and carefully manipulates those around him.

The plays in the second tetralogy also broaden their focus beyond that of the court and the nobility to include scenes that depict the common people of the realm, whether Mistress Quickly and Pistol, the Gloucestershire Justices of the Peace Silence and Shallow, or the common footsoldiers Michael Williams and John

Bates. Rather than just a kingdom, the England of the *Henry IV* and *Henry V* plays is also a nation, an entity defined by its status as a bounded territory with various inhabitants whose allegiance must be won and not assumed. In these later histories, Shakespeare displays less a theory of history than a keen interest in how power can be exercised well or badly and the particular skills one needs to be a leader of the many men who comprise the nation.

Henry VIII is different yet again, one of the very last plays Shakespeare's wrote and one dealing with events closest to the period in which he himself lived. Partly a melodrama based on the rise and fall of Henry's chief adviser, Cardinal Wolsey, *Henry VIII* shares features with Shakespeare's late romances in its episodic structure and its happy resolution with the birth of a daughter, Elizabeth, to Henry's second wife, Anne Boleyn. Though unusually sympathetic to the plight of Katherine, Henry's first wife, the play for the most part skates over the difficulties of Henry's long and eventful reign to conclude with the event that for the Tudors was the most important aspect of it: the birth of the woman that was to rule England from 1558 to 1603.

From this diverse body of dramatic material, it is difficult to generalize about Shakespeare's attitudes toward history. But it is clear that he found in the chronicles rich resources that he could use in creating compelling dramas about how power is won and lost, about how ambition for a throne can destroy (in the case of *Richard III*) those who experience it, or (as with Henry V) can sometimes transform a wastrel into a disciplined leader of men. It is often said that theatergoers in Shakespeare's time found his history plays compelling because they played to a general interest in the nation's history at a time, after the defeat of the Spanish Armada in 1588, when England was becoming increasingly self-conscious about its status as a national power alongside the other nations of Europe. London was a thriving commercial center; the Tudors had developed centralized administrative structures for the country; England was establishing trading routes to the East and soon was to be engaged in American colonization; national pride was running high. In such circumstances, it was undoubtedly true that Shakespeare's history plays had considerable popular appeal as windows into the past of a nation in a period of rapid and self-conscious change. Many theatergoers would not have been able to read or, if they could read, would not have been able to afford a book like Holinshed's *Chronicles of England, Scotlande, and Irelande*. Anyone, however, for a small fee could attend the public theater. Shakespeare's history plays reached people from every social class, gender, and level of literacy.

Yet the popular success of these plays also depended on the skill with which

A 1537 ink-and-watercolor portrait of Henry VIII (1491–1547) by Hans Holbein the Younger. National Portrait Gallery, London.

Shakespeare and his collaborators transformed the raw material of their sources into effective drama—the way, that is, they exercised the "liberty" of the poet to shape a pleasing fiction. Examining the range of his history plays reveals, in part, Shakespeare's increasing sophistication with the arts of stagecraft. The early histories have huge casts of characters: in terms of significant parts, there are 32 male characters and 3 women in *1 Henry VI*; 50 men and 4 women in *The First Part of the Contention*; 42 men and 3 women in *The True Tragedy of Richard Duke of York*; and 37 men and 5 women in *The Tragedy of King Richard The Third*. These plays also have complex plots. Yet Shakespeare quickly grew adept at distinguishing between characters and organizing the action through compelling juxtapositions and richly emblematic scenes that crystallize the essence of the action. The Temple Garden scene in *1 Henry VI* in which Yorkists and Lancastrians pluck red and white roses as emblems of their differing monarchical allegiances is one such scene. Amid the chaotic slaughter that dominates *The True Tragedy of Richard Duke of York,* Shakespeare inserts another such scene—Scene 5 of Act 2—in which the weak king, sitting on a molehill away from the battle being waged by his wife's army against his enemies, observes a father carry onstage the body of a man he has slain whom he discovers to be his own son and a son carry on stage the body of a man he has slain whom he discovers to be his father. This allegorical tableau captures the essence of civil war: the killing of son by father, father by son. Meanwhile, the king, who should control civil strife, sits helplessly by, wishing he were a shepherd and not the king of England. While Shakespeare came to eschew such highly emblematic scenes, he nonetheless learned from these complex early histories how to give dramatic shape to complicated narratives and much larger sets of characters than are found in his early comedies written at about the same time.

In *Richard II,* much of the theatrical tension comes from the telling juxtaposition of the poetic, loquacious, and ineffective Richard and his pragmatic, highly effective antagonist Harry Bolingbroke. They are studies in alternative modes of kingship, the one setting in high relief the qualities of the other. As early as *1 Henry VI*, Shakespeare had effectively juxtaposed Lord Talbot, the great English warrior who defends England's claims to French territory, against, on the one hand, the many English nobles, like Suffolk, who selfishly refuse to send him aid and, on the other hand, the French maid, Joan of Arc, who leads the French resistance to his assault on territories in France. Talbot embodies the best of chivalric English values. Unswerving in his service to Henry VI, his steadfastness sets in sharp relief the degeneracy of the other English nobles, while his gender, his nobility, and his fidelity to a code of chivalric honor (even if that means the certain death of himself and his young son) contrasts with the low-born Joan of Arc's femininity, her opportunism, and her desperate attempts to save her life at any cost. Talbot is singled out by Nashe as an especially memorable example of the kind of figure the historical drama could rescue from oblivion; he is also the fulcrum around which Shakespeare builds a play of telling juxtapositions.

By the time he wrote *1* and *2 Henry IV,* Shakespeare had developed what can only be called a rich contrapuntal style of dramatizing history in which the actions of one group of characters mirror, comment upon, and offer other alternatives to the actions of other groups of characters. In *1 Henry IV,* there is a particularly fine example of this dramatic technique. There are three distinct dramatic worlds evoked in this play: the prosaic world of Henry IV, struggling to keep control of his throne; the exotic world of the rebels who oppose him, a group including the Welsh magician Glyndŵr, the bold Scottish warrior the Earl of Douglas, and the hotheaded Hotspur, whose family hails from the wild northern territories of England; and, finally, the world of the Eastcheap tavern, where Falstaff, a fat, down-at-the-heels knight, presides over a festive world of eating, drinking, and practical pranks. The differences among these three worlds starkly dramatize the choices facing the young Prince Hal, who must choose whether he will be, as his actions seem to promise, a truant from the duty-driven world of court or rise to the challenge posed by Hotspur and strive for honor on the field of battle. Must he, if he chooses the path of duty, forfeit the spontaneous pleasures of the tavern, where people make stage plays about kings, using cushions for crowns, without actually having to assume the grinding burdens of the office? With a dramaturgy marvelously free of didacticism, Shakespeare invites the theatergoer to ponder the consequences of choice, to feel as well as to intellectualize what it means to follow one course of life and not another.

It is in his early history plays that Shakespeare also first revealed his magical ability to create characters that are not only memorable, but that do the work of making history intelligible and quietly suggesting the role that individuals play in its making. Everyone, of course, remembers Falstaff, one of the most popular dramatic characters ever created, and the hunchbacked villain Richard III, for whom, as for his father, Shakespeare created some of his first soliloquies, speeches that reveal the working of mind at play and not just a recitation of events. For example, in the middle of *The True Tragedy of Richard Duke of York,* the Duke's son, Richard of Gloucester, having just watched his brother, King Edward, fawn over a low-born woman whom he will soon take to wife, renounces the pleasures of love and declares his intention to seize the crown from this brother.

> Why, I can smile, and murder whiles I smile,
> And cry 'Content!' to that which grieves my heart,
> And wet my cheeks with artificial tears,
> And frame my face to all occasions.
> I'll drown more sailors than the mermaid shall;
> I'll slay more gazers than the basilisk;
> I'll play the orator as well as Nestor,
> Deceive more slyly than Ulysses could,
> And, like a Sinon, take another Troy.
> I can add colours to the chameleon,
> Change shapes with Proteus for advantages,
> And set the murderous Machiavel to school.
> Can I do this, and cannot get a crown?
> Tut, were it farther off, I'll pluck it down.
>
> (3.2.182–95)

This litany of boasting claims captures Richard's hubris and his theatrical bent. He will take his example from the most treacherous figures of history and myth, and outdo them all. But what gives the speech its special character is the dismissive last line. Descending to a colloquial "Tut," breaking the iambic pentameter with an explosive opening syllable, Richard signals that he is prepared to do more than list precedents. He'll "pluck" the crown, no matter what the obstacles.

The early histories, though dominated by men like Richard, also contain some usually vivid roles for women; see especially Joan of Arc in *1 Henry VI;* Margaret of Anjou, who appears in all four plays of the first tetralogy; Constance and Eleanor in *King John;* and Mistress Quickly, Hotspur's wife, Kate, and the French Princess, Catherine, in the second tetralogy. Lingering a moment on Margaret's part shows how Shakespeare embellished his sources to create one of the most memorable women in any of his histories. In all of these plays, patriarchal rule is assumed. The crown passes lineally from father to son; women are vehicles for this reproductive continuity. Margaret of Anjou, however, is much more. At the end of *1 Henry VI,* she is brought from France to be the young Henry VI's bride, largely because her beauty made her irresistibly attractive to Suffolk, one of Henry's nobles and eventually Margaret's openly acknowledged lover. In *Part II,* as King Henry proves utterly incapable of rule, Margaret assumes a greater and greater role in public affairs, actually leading Lancastrian troops into battle against the Yorkist forces and ordering Henry to stay off the battlefield, so disheartening is his impact on his troops. In *Part III,* Henry goes so far as to make a bargain with the Yorkists that, if they will let him retain his crown in his lifetime, he will resign it to them upon his death, in effect disinheriting his young son, Edward. It is at this point that the paradoxical greatness and monstrosity of Margaret is fully revealed. In essence, she becomes the effective ruler of England, directing the course of the war and defending the rights of her son to his royal inheritance; paradoxically, she defends these traditional values while usurping her husband's prerogatives. Enacting what many considered an unnatural role for a woman, she reveals what she sees as the unnatural behavior of the King.

Shakespeare embellishes Margaret's historical role considerably. Early in *The True Tragedy of Richard Duke of York,* Shakespeare creates a scene in which Margaret cruelly exults over Richard, the Yorkist patriarch whom she has captured. In the chronicle sources, her ally, Clifford, cuts off the head of the already dead York, puts a paper crown on that head, and presents it to Margaret. In Shakespeare's version of the scene, York is still alive when brought to Margaret, and she mockingly makes him stand on a molehill, then gives him a napkin dipped in the blood of his youngest son, Rutland, for him to use to dry his tears, and finally has him crowned with the paper crown before herself being one of those who stabs him to death. Throughout this long scene, Margaret jeers and mocks her defeated foe, and he curses her, at one point asserting that she has a "tiger's heart wrapped in a woman's hide!" (1.4.138). Her villainy is impressively over the top, and the scene must have been a memorable one. When Robert Greene, one of Shakespeare's contemporaries, wanted to put down his rival playwright he called him "an upstart Crow, beautified with our feathers, that with his *Tygers hart wrapt in a Players hyde,* supposes he is as well able to bombast out a blanke verse as the best of you." Angry at Shakespeare for borrowing from his work or copying his style ("beautified with our feathers"), Greene uses Shakespeare's own memorable line about Margaret to suggest that Shakespeare himself is an unnatural overreacher. The final act for this crowd-pleasing character occurred in *Richard III,* in which, defeated and stripped of military power, she becomes a prophet of doom, calling down curses on her enemies, including Richard himself.

In his English histories, then, Shakespeare was learning his craft as well as meditating on historical causation and the role of chance and of personality and personal skills in historical events. After the 1590s, his interest in the genre waned, replaced by an intensified commitment to the writing of tragedies that drew on material other than the doings of England's late medieval kings. But in his decade of deep involvement with the English history play, Shakespeare created a body of work unmatched by his contemporaries in the sophistication with which it dramatized the interplay of chance, personality, skill, force, and perhaps even providence in the shaping of history. He began by dramatizing the chaotic War of the Roses and ended his histories of the 1590s by moving backward in time to the heroics of Henry V's French campaign, in the process creating plays strikingly different in form and feel. What remained constant was his commitment to exploring the complexity of events, sometimes looking at the compromises that for him seem to attend the work of rule and sometimes glancing, on the edges of the monarchical narrative, at the lives of ordinary people as they are affected, or not, by the strivings of the powerful. In the process, he created an origin story for his country and a picture of

The head of Margaret of Anjou, depicted on a medal. Victoria and Albert Museum, London.

late medieval England so powerful that we have to remind ourselves today that it is just a fiction, the work of a poet historical.

SELECTED BIBLIOGRAPHY

Calderwood, James L. *Metadrama in Shakespeare's Henriad: Richard II to Henry V.* Berkeley: University of California Press, 1979.

Dutton, Richard, and Jean E. Howard. *A Companion to Shakespeare's Works, II: The Histories.* Malden, Mass.: Blackwell, 2003.

Hodgdon, Barbara. *The End Crowns All: Closure and Contradiction in Shakespeare's Histories.* Princeton: Princeton University Press, 1991.

Howard, Jean E., and Phyllis Rackin. *Engendering a Nation: A Feminist Account of Shakespeare's English Histories.* London: Routledge, 1997.

Levine, Nina S. *Women's Matters: Politics, Gender, and Nation in Shakespeare's Early History Plays.* Newark: University of Delaware Press, 1998.

Levy, F. J. *Tudor Historical Thought.* San Marino, Calif.: Huntington Library, 1967.

Ornstein, Robert. *A Kingdom for a Stage: The Achievement of Shakespeare's History Plays.* Cambridge, Mass.: Harvard University Press, 1972.

Pugliatti, Paola. *Shakespeare the Historian.* Basingstoke, Eng.: Macmillan, 1996.

Rackin, Phyllis. *Stages of History: Shakespeare's English Chronicles.* Ithaca, N.Y.: Cornell University Press, 1990.

Ribner, Irving. *The English History Play in the Age of Shakespeare.* Princeton: Princeton University Press, 1957.

Tillyard, E. M. W. *Shakespeare's History Plays.* London: Chatto & Windus, 1944.

The First Part of the Contention
of the Two Famous Houses
of York and Lancaster
(The Second Part of Henry VI)

What happens to a kingdom when the sitting monarch is too weak to rule effectively? Shakespeare explores this difficult problem in *The First Part of the Contention of the Two Famous Houses of York and Lancaster,* in which Henry VI, crowned when he was nine months old, has never been able to establish control over his realm. As his assertive French wife, Margaret of Anjou, exclaims in exasperation to the Duke of Suffolk, who had wooed her for Henry:

> when in the city Tours
> Thou rann'st a-tilt in honour of my love
> And stol'st away the ladies' hearts of France,
> I thought King Henry had resembled thee
> In courage, courtship, and proportion.
> But all his mind is bent to holiness,
> To number Ave-Maries on his beads.
>
> (1.3.54–60)

Margaret thought she would be marrying a chivalric hero, one adept at the arts of love and war; instead, she finds herself wed to an ineffective, pious man who elsewhere openly expresses his desire to live as a private person rather than as his country's King. Partly as a result of Henry's deficiencies, Margaret grows increasingly independent, conducting a love intrigue with Suffolk and openly defying her husband's wishes. Presented as a sexualized figure of gender disorder, Margaret is as powerful as her husband is weak. Margaret, however, represents but one of the threats to Henry's authority and the well-being of the country. Lacking the strong hand of a powerful monarch to rein them in, Henry's nobles quarrel and threaten civil war, and eventually a group of rebellious commoners storm London, killing all who oppose them. The kingdom slides into chaos.

In the early modern period, the king stood at the top of the social order and was invested with enormous responsibilities. The symbolic head and heart of the body politic, the monarch was enjoined to rule wisely, to care for the welfare of his subjects, and to take counsel from and exert control over the nobility. Some theories of kingship argued that monarchs had their authority from God; rebellion against a sitting monarch was a form of treason punishable by death. Given the centrality of the king to the health of the kingdom and its subjects, an evil or a weak king could have a disastrous impact on the realm. Tyrants—that is, kings who followed their passions, refused to take counsel, and ignored the welfare of their subjects—were anxiously discussed by the political thinkers of the period. Could they ever be overthrown? Must their tyranny be endured? In plays such as *Richard III* and *Macbeth,* Shakespeare dramatized such tyrant kings and in each case showed their deaths at the hands of high-placed subjects. Henry VI poses a different kind of danger. Rather than an evil or personally ambitious monarch, he is simply ineffectual and weak, unable to control the ambition and selfish desires of his nobles or to see to the welfare of his subjects. In effect, *The First Part of the Contention* explores what happens when a kingdom is left rudderless, graphically depicting the brutality let loose when the King is unable to assert his authority, commoners are set against nobles, and nobles begin to destroy one another.

The First Part of the Contention may well be the first English history play Shakespeare wrote (for a fuller discussion of the genre of the history play and Shakespeare's work in that genre, see the introduction to *1 Henry VI*). It has been dated as early as 1591 and exists in two distinct versions: a quarto edition printed in 1594 and a longer version printed in the First Folio in 1623 (for the differences between these two texts, see the Textual Note). Historically, the protracted broils depicted in this and the following play were known as the Wars of the Roses (1455–85) because the House of York, which staked its claim to England's throne through Lionel, Duke of Clarence, third son of Edward III, took a white rose for its emblem, while the House of Lancaster, which claimed the throne through John of Gaunt, fourth son of Edward III, became identified with the red rose. While giving a war the name of a flower might suggest a trivial or symbolic struggle, Shakespeare's plays decisively refute such an idea. Collectively they explore the horror of a kingdom divided against itself.

When read, the play can seem chaotic, a series of violent acts carried out by a bewildering array of characters who rise to the forefront of attention only to disappear quickly from view. But the play is more carefully structured than may at first be apparent. For the first two acts, Henry's weakness is counterbalanced by the strength of Humphrey, Duke of Gloucester, a man who since the King's youth has served as Lord Protector of the realm and who attempts to see that the common people are fairly treated and the quarrelling nobles kept in check. The play reaches a decisive turning point in Act 3 when Gloucester is driven from office by the Queen, Suffolk, York, and the Cardinal Beaufort (who is also the Bishop of Winchester). Once Gloucester is gone, no one can protect the King or the kingdom from the ambition of Richard, Duke of York, the most powerful of the nobles who would supplant Henry. From Act 3 on, York and his minions dominate the action, countered primarily by the equally strong-willed Margaret. In the brutal struggles that follow upon Gloucester's death, one powerful figure after another suffers disgrace or death, including Cardinal Beaufort, Suffolk, and Somerset. York, however, does not fall but, like Margaret, moves with unnerving single-mindedness into the power vacuum created by the King's passivity.

To register the disaster that has overtaken England, Shakespeare relentlessly focuses on the actual human bodies maimed, brutalized, and destroyed by the play's contending forces. The death of Gloucester is exemplary. In *The First Part of the Contention,* he is strangled onstage in his bed; in the Folio version of the play his death occurs offstage. But in both texts, the corpse is eventually displayed to the audience while Warwick recites a grisly

Henry VI, depicted as a child, carried by the Earl of Warwick.

description of the state of the body. In contrast to the paleness of a man who has died peacefully, the good Duke's

> face is black and full of blood;
> His eyeballs further out than when he lived,
> Staring full ghastly like a strangled man;
> His hair upreared; his nostrils stretched with struggling;
> His hands abroad displayed, as one that grasped
> And tugged for life and was by strength subdued.
> Look on the sheets. His hair, you see, is sticking;
> His well-proportioned beard made rough and rugged,
> Like to the summer's corn by tempest lodged.
> It cannot be but he was murdered here.
> The least of all these signs were probable.
> (3.2.168–78)

This terrible inventory of the unnatural state of Gloucester's dead body highlights the marks of his futile struggle for life—the bulging eyes, the disordered hair and beard, the outstretched hands. Warwick's point is that these are *not* the signs of a soul weighed down by sin and unprepared for death, as is true of Cardinal Beaufort, whose death occurs in the next scene; rather, Gloucester's disordered corpse testifies to the horrific and untimely circumstances in which he died.

In this extremely violent play, many other bodies suffer indignity, pain, and death. In Act 4, Suffolk, captured on his flight to France, is beheaded offstage by his captors. His body is then taken to England, where Queen Margaret, in one of the most macabre scenes in Shakespeare, carries his severed head around the court, lamenting her dead lover. Later, the rebels attacking London capture Lord Saye, a supporter of King Henry. After enumerating a catalog of his crimes, including the "crime" of literacy, the followers of Jack Cade, the chief rebel, behead Saye along with his son-in-law. Cade's followers then stick the severed heads on poles and carry them through the streets, grotesquely making them "kiss" at every corner. After five days of living in the woods without food have rendered him too famished to fight effectively, Jack Cade is himself beheaded and his head taken to the King. This is hardly an exhaustive list of the forms of violence depicted in the play. It does not, for example, take account of those slain in battle, such as Somerset, or of the shameful treatment Cade visits upon defeated enemies such as Sir Humphrey Stafford and his brother, whose armor he strips from their corpses before he drags their bodies behind his horse toward London.

Some small portion of this violence displays the monarch's sanctioned power to punish unruly or disobedient subjects. In Elizabethan England, traitors' heads were regularly displayed on London Bridge, and public executions were popular spectacles, showing the King's power over traitors and criminals. In *The First Part of the Contention*, the most spectacular scene of public correction involves Eleanor Cobham, Gloucester's wife. A proud and ambitious woman who hopes to see her husband displace Henry as King of England, Cobham dabbles in the forbidden arts of witchcraft and conjuration, soliciting prophecies about the fate of the King and two of his nobles, Suffolk and Somerset. Such prophecies were considered politically dangerous because they caused uncertainty and unrest among the common people and could be used to foment sedition. They had been specifically banned by Henry VIII, Edward VI, and Elizabeth. Like many famous prophecies, those delivered to Eleanor Cobham are ambiguous. For example, "The Duke yet lives that Henry shall depose, / But him outlive, and die a violent death" (1.4.29–30) can mean either that Henry shall depose a duke or that a duke shall depose Henry. Nor is it entirely clear who shall outlive whom and die a violent death. The ambiguity of such statements was exactly what rulers feared, since under the cover of a benign interpretation they could be used to predict and promote rebellion. For engaging in witchcraft and conjuration as well as for circulating such prophecies, Eleanor Cobham is first shamed—she must walk through London carrying a candle and wearing only a sheet, her crimes listed on a piece of paper pinned to her back—and then banished, and her confederates hanged and burned. The King here appears to be using sanctioned violence to punish dangerously seditious subjects.

Yet in much of the play, the state either fails to control violence or else uses it with questionable justice. Even Eleanor's case is more ambiguous than the above account suggests. She did undeniably dabble in witchcraft, yet she was urged on by people in the employ of Suffolk and the Cardinal, who wished through her acts to disgrace her innocent husband and dislodge him from power. Legally, Eleanor's punishment is just, yet it occurs in a context of chicanery and treachery that the King either does not or will not see until Gloucester, the chief prop of royal justice, has been removed. Between the discovery of Eleanor's witchcraft and her public shaming, the play shows the audience another troubling example of a ritual of justice. Earlier Peter Thump, an apprentice, had accused his master, Horner, of saying that the Duke of York—not Henry—was the rightful ruler of England. Thump had no proof but his own word, and Horner had no defense but denial. To resolve the issue, Gloucester orders a day of combat for the man and master: whoever wins the duel would be assumed to have spoken the truth. Such trials by combat were customary in adjudicating disputes among nobles. But the apprentice is terrified, having no experience with such contests or with the weapons commonly used in them: the sword or lance. As it is dramatized, the trial by combat becomes a parody of justice. Rather than fighting with swords, the two contestants appear with sandbags attached to poles, and Horner is roaring drunk. It is under these conditions that the apprentice kills his master, and the King, who has now taken Gloucester's staff of office from him as the result of Eleanor's treason, seems satisfied that justice has prevailed. But the ludicrous nature of the drunken encounter threatens to empty such traditional rituals of their meaning and legitimacy.

With Gloucester's death, the King's fair and effective control of the machinery of justice and of violence is further compromised. Under the pressure of an enraged commons, Henry *does* banish Suffolk for his role in Gloucester's death, but the King cannot begin to contain the escalating stage violence. In the second half of the play, his loss of control is demonstrated by the spectacular rise to power of the lower-class rebel Jack Cade, one of York's minions. As he marches toward London, Cade boasts that the laws of England are to come from his mouth, and he arrogates to himself the right to kill whom he chooses. The murder of Lord Saye, the death of the clerk of Chartham, the desecration of Stafford's body—these are a mere sampling of events in a brutal career, and the play does not shrink from showing what is cruel and arbitrary in Cade's brief reign of terror. Critics often take Shakespeare's representation of Cade as confirming Elizabethan fears about the dangers of popular rule.

Yet interpreting Cade and his actions is a complicated business. Does Shakespeare create this character simply to discredit popular rebellion, or does he use Cade to articulate the legitimate grievances of the common people and employ Cade's brutality as a disquieting mirror of the brutality of the ruling classes? It is important to remember that Cade is not synonymous with "the commons" in this play. In the opening acts, while he is still in power, Gloucester is presented as a champion of the people and promotes a commonwealth in which the king and nobles care for the needs of the commoners and are responsive to their petitions. The people, in turn, seem confident that their views will be heard by those near the King. For example, in 1.3, three commoners wait with petitions for Gloucester: Peter Thump wishes to report his master's treasonous words about the Duke of York; another man complains that Cardinal Beaufort's man has unlawfully seized his land, house, and wife; a third protests that the Duke of Suffolk has enclosed the commons of Melford. (Enclosures—fencing in land once shared by many for growing food and grazing cattle—were a main cause of rural protest in the sixteenth and seventeenth centuries.) How these commoners behave as political agents registering grievances with those in power is revealing. First, the petitioners believe that they can get redress from the Lord Protector, the figure nearest the King himself. Second, they use peaceful means to obtain their desires. Third, they act from a position of loyalty to their King and his Lord Protector. Thump, in particular, puts himself at personal risk to report an act of treason against Henry. These figures hardly constitute a mob or many-headed monster. Even when they become enraged by Gloucester's murder and demand the banishment of Suffolk, they couch their protest as a desire to protect the King rather than to seize power for themselves.

It is crucial to note, however, that in 1.3 the petitioners are largely thwarted in their appeal for justice because they mistake Suffolk for Gloucester. Suffolk and the Queen are interested in dealing with York's supposed treason because they can use that accusation to prevent York from becoming Regent of France. They ignore the other petitions, one of which details a complaint against Suffolk himself. It is the nobles and not the commoners who fail to exercise their political duties responsibly. Timid and gullible and surrounded by selfish nobles like Suffolk, the King disregards the welfare and the needs of the common people, who are presented in this scene as loyal and orderly actors in a hierarchical commonwealth.

Cade enters the picture only when the one noble—Gloucester—who cares about maintaining this paternal relationship between the commons and the King is about to be killed. At the end of 3.1, York, in soliloquy, reveals his intention to use the army levied against Ireland to further his own political ends; in addition, he will employ the Kentishman Jack Cade as his stalking horse in his move to seize the crown. Cade will pretend to be John Mortimer, a claimant to the throne through the Yorkist line, in order to test the waters for York's own bid for power. Cade is thus never an entirely independent agent of the people; rather, he is at least in part the tool of an ambitious nobleman who employs him because he is stubborn, strong, and impervious to pain. York reports that in battle against the Irish, Cade

> fought so long till that his thighs with darts
> Were almost like a sharp-quilled porcupine;
> And in the end, being rescued, I have seen
> Him caper upright like a wild Morisco,
> Shaking the bloody darts as he his bells.
> (3.1.362–66)

Will Kemp doing his morris dance. From Kemp's *Nine Days' Wonder* (1600).

Morris dancers tied bells to their legs, and these shook and jangled as they danced. The powerful image of the wounded Cade dancing depicts a man endowed with enormous spirit and physical strength. It is worth recalling that one of the most famous clowns of the 1590s, Will Kemp, who may have played the part of Cade, was himself a noted acrobat and dancer; in 1599, he left Shakespeare's company and did a celebrated morris dance from London to Norwich. Skilled and strong, Cade and Kemp suggest both what was feared and what was admired about hardhanded men, some of whom were employed in the London theater industry and some of whom would have been in the audience. In fact, the Cade scenes must have been powerfully charged, because out of this rebel's mouth—along with arbitrary brutality and pompous self-aggrandizement—issues a critique of social and economic inequality that, endowed with a long history, also spoke to living issues in the London of the 1590s.

Historically, Cade's rebellion occurred in 1450, but in portraying it, Shakespeare draws on accounts of many instances of popular social protest. For example, he takes from Raphael Holinshed's *Chronicles of England, Scotland, and Ireland* (1587) details from the Peasants' Revolt of 1381, in which rebels such as Wat Tyler burned London Bridge and attacked the Savoy (John of Gaunt's house) and the Inns of Court, both places of privilege that became a focus for lower-class anger. Other popular uprisings occurred in 1517, when apprentices on Ill May Day attacked foreign workers in the City of London; in 1549 (Kett's Rebellion); and in London itself throughout the decade of the 1590s. Between 1581 and 1602, there were numerous outbreaks of disorder in London directed against various forms of economic hardship, some of which stemmed from disruptions and changes in the English cloth trade that disadvantaged English weavers. Protests also occurred against the high price of commodities such as butter and fish and against the granting of monopolies that put the sale of key goods, such as starch, in the hands of a small group. Apprentices were often involved in and blamed for these riots. Many of Cade's followers in *The First Part of the Contention* are artisans: weavers and butchers. Through Cade, their economic grievances find expression, along with the articulation of an alternative model of social and economic organization much more radically utopian than that implied in Gloucester's hierarchical paternalism.

This tradition of popular radicalism, whose roots went back at least to the fourteenth century, stressed that all men had been equally redeemed by Christ's blood and that there was as much nobility in the labor of an honest man as in the fine silks and the educated speech of a gentleman. A riddle common throughout Europe from the fourteenth century on—"When Adam delved and Eve span, who then was the gentleman?"—suggests the egalitarian purposes for which the Bible could be appropriated. The first man and woman, digging in the earth and spinning cloth, knew no distinctions of rank, simply the dignity of labor. Often, popular protest stressed the value of manual labor, as opposed to the idleness of the rich, and claimed the clouted shoe or hobnailed boot of the rural peasant and the leather apron of the urban laborer as valued emblems of their working lives.

The Cade scenes are filled with references to this egalitarian tradition. In 4.2, when the rebels first describe how Cade means to reform the commonwealth, they make clear that in their view working men, and only working men, should be magistrates and rulers. Referring to Scripture, the second rebel says: "Yet it is said 'Labour in thy vocation'; which is as much to say as 'Let the magistrates be labouring men'; and therefore should we be magistrates" (4.2.14–16). By contrast, the present nobility "scorn to go in leather aprons" (4.2.10–11) and have no respect for handicraftsmen. Part of Cade's success is that he is able to mobilize such artisan anger against the privileges of gentlemen, whether those be conferred by literacy or by inherited wealth. Much of Cade's violence is directed against those who can read and write, like the clerk of Chartham or Lord Saye. Literacy, whether defined as the ability to read or to read and write, was not nearly so widespread as it has since become. These skills were acquired by only a small part of the population, who thereby had certain advantages wherever the reading or writing of documents had importance, such as in courts of law. Cade would not only kill all the lawyers, but he would also punish all those who wrote on parchment, that is, those in control of written documents. He also promises that when he is in charge, bread will be cheap, beer of the highest quality, all material goods enjoyed in common, and all men dressed in a common livery.

It is hardly necessary to point out how often Cade contradicts himself in articulating his vision of a commonwealth of equals and how he undermines the utopian aspirations of the tradition of popular radicalism to which his words repeatedly refer. In his egalitarian commonwealth, Cade, of course, would be King, and from his mouth would come all the laws by which others would live. Women would have no rights in his commonwealth but would be fair game for rape. When a Sergeant complains to Cade that his wife has been ravished by one of Cade's men, Cade authorizes his man to cut out the Sergeant's tongue, cripple him, and then knock out his brains. Cade then invites his followers to enter London, where they will "lustily stand to it" and "take up these commodities following—item, a gown, a kirtle, a petticoat, and a smock" (4.7.134–36). The violence and arbitrary cruelty repeatedly displayed make Cade a frightening figure and one whom even his followers often recognize as a charlatan and a hypocrite.

Yet Cade's personal viciousness does not simply wipe away the power of the social critique to which he intermittently gives voice and which had a history extending far beyond this play. When Cade learns that Lord Saye has his horse covered with an elaborate cloth, he bluntly states a point of view that must have resonated with some in Shakespeare's audience: "Marry, thou ought'st not to let thy horse wear a cloak when honester men than thou go in their hose and doublets" (4.7.42–43). Moreover, Shakespeare gives plenty of evidence in the play that if many commoners feel anger and resentment toward the nobility, many nobility are in their turn full of contempt for the lower classes. Act 4, which is dominated by Cade, opens with the scene in which Suffolk is captured and questioned by the Captain of a ship. Furious that when he reveals himself as the Duke of Suffolk his captors do not free him immediately, Suffolk contemptuously attacks the Captain:

> Obscure and lousy swain, King Henry's blood,
> The honourable blood of Lancaster,
> Must not be shed by such a jady groom.
> (4.1.51–53)

The speech goes on in a similar vein for twelve more lines, making clear the truth of the second rebel's claim that the gentlemen of England do not have much respect for hardhanded men. Nor, after the grisly murder of Gloucester, can it be thought that only the common people have the capacity for lawless violence. In short, the play dramatizes many instances of class-based antagonisms rooted in the unequal distribution of wealth and cultural capital.

This complicated political drama seems unequivocally to confirm only one principle: the absence of a strong and just king leaves the commonwealth at risk, but at risk not solely from its most disenfranchised members. Cade, who offers the most radical critique of social inequality, is personally vilified and discredited within the play; but it is arguable that the larger context for his grim saturnalia of violence is the unspeakable selfishness of the English nobles. Many of them—York, Suffolk, Winchester—are everything Cade accuses the nobility of being. Moreover, though Cade is killed in this play, civil war does not vanish with his death, because the ambition and selfishness of these English nobles have not been contained. York still lives, and it will take Shakespeare another two plays to trace the destructive legacy of his ambition.

Some critics have suggested that given the venality of many of the nobles and the cruelty and hypocrisy of Cade, the play privileges the point of view of Alexander Iden, the landowning gentleman who kills Cade. Iden is well worth scrutiny. A property holder, a man who has built a brick wall around his garden, Iden also has charitable impulses. He "sends the poor well pleasèd from [his] gate" and at first does not want to fight with Cade, a "poor famished man" (4.9.21, 41). Does Iden's garden represent an

The houses of York and Lancaster depicted as two parts of a rosebush conjoined, by the marriage of Henry VII and Elizabeth of York, to form the Tudor dynasty. Title page to Edward Halle's (or Hall's) *Union of the Two Noble and Illustre Famelies of Lancastre & Yorke* (1550 ed.).

English Eden? Shakespeare sounds several evocative notes through the creation of this figure. Iden conjures up the virtues of rural England as opposed to the values of the corrupt court or the rampaging urban artisans. And he anticipates the emergence of the bourgeois property holder as the backbone of the nation. But Iden is not the dominant force in the political landscape of the play, nor, despite his seeming independence, are his loyalties in doubt. When he learns who the poor famished man really is, Iden is glad to have killed Cade; and when he delivers the rebel's head to King Henry, he receives a knighthood in return. The independent property holder is certainly the King's man and no friend to those who would level the social order and make property common. How deeply Shakespeare—the man from rural Stratford who eventually became a major property holder in that town—idealized Iden, or replicated his political stance, is a matter for debate.

JEAN E. HOWARD

TEXTUAL NOTE

The play commonly known as *2 Henry VI* existed in two versions in the early modern period. In 1594, a quarto version (Q) entitled *The First Part of the Contention of the Two Famous Houses of York and Lancaster* was published; it was followed in 1600 and 1619 by two other quartos based on the first. In 1623, a version of the play about a third longer than Q was included in the First Folio (F), where it was entitled *The Second Part of Henry VI*. The relationship between these two texts is one of the vexed issues in Shakespearean scholarship. In the 1920s, several scholars proposed that Q had been prepared by several actors who had performed in a London production of the play and had reconstructed as much of the script as they could remember. The stage directions in Q are unusually full, indicating the quarto's probable theatrical origins. It may derive, indirectly, from the promptbook prepared for either a London performance or a provincial tour.

Recently, some scholars have questioned whether memorial reconstruction (actors piecing together scripts from memory) provides an adequate explanation for the differences so often found among variant texts that survive for many early modern plays. In particular, Steven Urkowitz has argued that the 1594 Quarto of this play is not a product of memorial reconstruction but is Shakespeare's early version, which he later revised. Urkowitz maintains that both the 1594 and the 1623 texts were prepared by Shakespeare, even though they differ from one another in important ways. He argues, for example, that Queen Margaret is a fiercer and more assertive figure in F than in Q. Urkowitz urges that each version of the play be studied on its own. Other textual editors argue that many people—actors, compositors, censors, scribes—may have had a hand in altering a play as it moved onto the stage or into print. Shakespeare may not himself have been responsible for all the differences we now perceive between quarto and Folio texts; nonetheless, the existing texts are distinct entities and should be examined separately rather than conflated into one amalgamated version.

The Oxford edition of the play adheres to the view, dominant since the 1920s, that the quarto is, indeed, a memorial reconstruction of some version of the Folio text, probably a version that had been abridged and otherwise revised on its way from the authorial "foul papers" on which F is based to the promptbook that lies behind Q. Therefore, while F serves as the primary control text, the Oxford edition, like most others, uses many of Q's stage directions to clarify playhouse practice. More controversially, the Oxford edition also assumes that in preparing the Folio text, the compositors who set type drew on the printed quarto versions in some places, probably because the manuscript serving as the basis of F was occasionally illegible or hard to use. At five points (indicated in the Textual Variants), the Oxford editors use Q rather than F as control text. At other points, they follow the quarto placement of particular events, interpolate material found only in Q, or replace Folio material with quarto material when they believe that the changes represent authorial revisions to the version of the Folio text on which Q was based. The Oxford editors also retain the title used for the 1594 Quarto on the grounds that it is more descriptive of the play's content than the blander

Second Part of Henry VI, and because it is the title by which the play was probably known during Shakespeare's own lifetime.

The Oxford text differs, then, in many ways from modern texts based more exclusively on F. One striking change occurs at the beginning of 3.2: the Oxford edition follows Q in showing the actual murder of Gloucester onstage; F only shows the murderers running from the scene of the crime. The Oxford text also incorporates some quarto material about the Cade rebellion not found in F. These additions, lines 116–31 and 134–36 of 4.7, report the burning of London Bridge, the rape of a Sergeant's wife by one of Cade's men, and Cade's own boast that he will lead his men in sexual assaults upon the women of the city. Together, they darken further F's depiction of Cade's lawlessness. Another substantive change involves the Oxford editors' choice to print the quarto version of the final fight between York and Clifford (5.3.20–30) rather than the Folio version. The two differ markedly in tone; Q stresses the enmity of York and Clifford, F their mutual respect and chivalric honor. This edition prints both, providing the Folio version as an inset passage, and this juxtaposition affords an excellent opportunity to examine one of the important places where F and Q diverge.

The Oxford text in two places follows Q's ordering of particular incidents. In 1.4, a scene involving conjuration, F has a spirit deliver prophecies concerning the fate of several characters—the King, Suffolk, Somerset. York then breaks in upon the scene, seizes the written transcription of the prophecies, and reads them out a second time. The Oxford editors, however, follow Q: when York breaks into the scene of conjuration, he does *not* read the prophecies aloud, an act that seems theatrically redundant. Rather, they are read aloud by King Henry in the next scene (2.1.177–87), when the conjuring episode is reported to him. Similarly, in Act 5, the Oxford edition follows Q in having the final fight between Richard and Somerset occur as 5.2, right before Clifford's battle with York, rather than placing Somerset's death later as young Clifford is bearing off the body of his dead father. The quarto arrangement thus puts maximum emphasis on York's triumph over old Clifford, King Henry's champion.

The Oxford edition differs from most modern texts in one other interesting way. At the beginning of 4.2 in F, two minor characters are listed as Bevis and John Holland. Most editors assume that these are the names of actual players, George Bevis and John Holland, who at some time acted in the play, rather than of fictional characters, yet they use these names as speech prefixes. In the Oxford text, Bevis and Holland are designated, as in Q, simply as "rebels."

Scene numbers follow most modern editions, except that the Oxford edition makes one continuous scene of what are traditionally Scenes 7 and 8 of Act 4, Cade's attack on London and his encounter with Buckingham and Clifford. Oxford also divides Act 5 into five scenes rather than the usual three. Placing the fight between Richard and Somerset after Scene 1 requires setting that fight off as 5.2. In addition, the Oxford editors believe that the stage is cleared after the encounter in which York kills old Clifford, whose body is carried off by his son. Henry and Margaret's ensuing flight from the battlefield is thus set off as a separate scene, 5.4.

SELECTED BIBLIOGRAPHY

Carroll, William. "Theories of Kingship in Shakespeare's England." *A Companion to Shakespeare's Works.* Vol. II: *The Histories.* Ed. Richard Dutton and Jean E. Howard. Malden, Mass.: Blackwell, 2003. 125–45. Lays out the main ideas circulating in early modern England and Scotland about the powers and duties of the king as well as limits to his power.

Cartelli, Thomas. "Jack Cade in the Garden: Class Consciousness and Class Conflict in *2 Henry VI.*" *Enclosure Acts: Sexuality, Property, and Culture in Early Modern England.* Ed. Richard Burt and John Michael Archer. Ithaca, N. Y.: Cornell University Press, 1994. 48–64. Explores the class-based antagonism between Jack Cade and members of the propertied elite, including Alexander Iden, into whose garden the starving Cade intrudes.

Fitter, Chris. "Emergent Shakespeare and the Politics of Protest: *2 Henry VI* in Historical Contexts." *English Literary History* 72 (2005): 129–58. Discusses the connections between the play and political events in Shakespeare's own lifetime and argues for Shakespeare's radical political leanings.

Greenblatt, Stephen. "Murdering Peasants: Status, Genre, and the Representation of Rebellion." *Representations* no. 1 (1983): 1–29. Explores the difficulties of representing early modern popular insurrection and the ideological instability of such representations.

Helgerson, Richard. "Staging Exclusion." *Forms of Nationhood: The Elizabethan Writing of England.* Chicago: University of Chicago Press, 1992. 195–245. Argues that through a predominantly negative representation of Cade and through a focus on the consolidation of monarchical rule, Shakespeare was instrumental in disrupting the traditional link between the theater and popular revolt.

Howard, Jean E., and Phyllis Rackin. *"Henry VI, Part II." Engendering a Nation: A Feminist Account of Shakespeare's English Histories.* London: Routledge, 1997. 65–82. Examines the relationship between political disorder and gender disorder with special attention paid to Queen Margaret, King Henry, Eleanor Cobham, and Jack Cade.

Knowles, Ronald. "The Farce of History: Miracle, Combat, and Rebellion in *2 Henry VI*." *The Yearbook of English Studies* 21 (1991): 168–86. Examines the dramatic techniques of ironic juxtaposition, mirroring, and parody through which Shakespeare staged historical events and processes.

Manley, Lawrence. "From Strange's Men to Pembroke's Men: *2 Henry VI* and *The First Part of the Contention*." *Shakespeare Quarterly* 54 (2003): 253–87. Argues that the Quarto is a revision of some version of the longer Folio text and that this revision, which includes a harsher treatment of Eleanor Cobham, sprang from the play's transfer from Lord Strange's Men to Pembroke's Men.

Patterson, Annabel. "The Peasant's Toe: Popular Culture and Popular Pressure." *Shakespeare and the Popular Voice.* Cambridge, Mass.: Blackwell, 1989. 32–51. Argues that there was a cultural tradition of popular protest in Shakespeare's England to which his representation of Jack Cade is indebted.

Urkowitz, Steven. "'If I Mistake in These Foundations Which I Build Upon': Peter Alexander's Textual Analysis of *Henry VI Parts 2 and 3*." *English Literary Renaissance* 18 (1988): 230–56. Refutes the idea of memorial reconstruction—that is, that the Quarto is a text derived from actors' memories of performance—and, instead, sees the Folio text as Shakespeare's purposeful revision of the Quarto.

FILM

Henry VI, Part Two. 1983. Dir. Jane Howell. UK/USA. Sumptuously costumed but tepid BBC-TV production with Julia Foster as Margaret, David Burke as Gloucester, Peter Benson as Henry VI, and Trevor Peacock as Cade.

The First Part of the Contention
of the Two Famous Houses
# of York and Lancaster
(The Second Part of Henry VI)

THE PERSONS OF THE PLAY

Of the King's Party

KING HENRY VI
QUEEN MARGARET
William de la Pole, Marquis, later Duke, of SUFFOLK, the Queen's lover
Duke Humphrey of GLOUCESTER, the Lord Protector, the King's uncle
Dame Eleanor Cobham, the DUCHESS of Gloucester
CARDINAL BEAUFORT, Bishop of Winchester, Gloucester's uncle
   and the King's great-uncle
Duke of BUCKINGHAM
Duke of SOMERSET
Old Lord CLIFFORD
YOUNG CLIFFORD, his son

Of the Duke of York's Party

Duke of YORK
EDWARD, Earl of March ⎱ his sons
Crookback RICHARD ⎰
Earl of SALISBURY
Earl of WARWICK, his son

The petitions and the combat

Two or three PETITIONERS
Thomas HORNER, an armourer
PETER Thump, his man
Three NEIGHBOURS, who drink to Horner
Three PRENTICES, who drink to Peter

The conjuration

Sir John HUME ⎱ priests
John SOUTHWELL ⎰
Margery Jordan, a WITCH
Roger BOLINGBROKE, a conjurer
ASNATH, a spirit

The false miracle

Simon SIMPCOX
SIMPCOX'S WIFE
The MAYOR of Saint Albans
Aldermen of Saint Albans
A BEADLE of Saint Albans
Townsmen of Saint Albans

Eleanor's penance

Gloucester's SERVANTS
Two SHERIFFS of London
Sir John STANLEY
HERALD

The murder of Gloucester

Two MURDERERS
COMMONS

The murder of Suffolk

CAPTAIN of a ship
MASTER of that ship
The Master's MATE
Walter WHITMORE
Two GENTLEMEN

The Cade Rebellion

Jack CADE, a Kentishman suborned by the Duke of York
Dick the BUTCHER ⎫
Smith the WEAVER ⎪
A Sawyer ⎬ Cade's followers
JOHN ⎪
REBELS ⎭
Emmanuel, the CLERK of Chatham ⎫
Sir Humphrey STAFFORD ⎪
STAFFORD'S BROTHER ⎪
Lord SAYE ⎬ those who die at the rebels' hands
Lord SCALES ⎪
Matthew Gough ⎪
A SERGEANT ⎭
Three or four CITIZENS of London
Alexander IDEN, an esquire of Kent, who kills Cade

Others

VAUX, a messenger
A POST
MESSENGERS
A SOLDIER
Attendants, guards, servants, soldiers, falconers

1.1

Flourish° of trumpets, then hautboys.° Enter, at one   Fanfare / oboes
door, KING HENRY *and Humphrey Duke of* GLOUCESTER,
the Duke of SOMERSET, *the Duke of* BUCKINGHAM, CAR-
DINAL BEAUFORT, *and others. Enter, at the other door,*
the Duke of YORK, *and the Marquis of* SUFFOLK, *and*
QUEEN MARGARET, *and the Earl[s] of* SALISBURY *and*
WARWICK[1]

1.1 Location: The palace, London.
1. This stage direction, like many others, is modeled primarily upon that in Q. Many editors believe Q is based
indirectly on a promptbook and closely reflects play-

house practice. In F, Salisbury, Warwick, Gloucester, and
Beaufort enter with the King, while Somerset and Buckingham enter with the Queen, Suffolk, and York.

SUFFOLK [*kneeling before* KING HENRY]   As by your high imperial majesty
    I had in charge° at my depart° for France,   *was charged / departure*
    As Procurator° to your excellence,   *deputy*
    To marry Princess Margaret for your grace,°   *on your behalf*
5   So, in the famous ancient city Tours,
    In presence of the Kings of France and Sicil,[2]
    The Dukes of Orléans, Calaber,° Bretagne, and Alençon,   *Calabria*
    Seven earls, twelve barons, and twenty reverend bishops,
    I have performed my task and was espoused,
10   And humbly now upon my bended knee,
    In sight of England and her lordly peers,
    Deliver up my title in the Queen
    To your most gracious hands, that are the substance
    Of that great shadow° I did represent—   *image (of royalty)*
15   The happiest° gift that ever marquis[3] gave,   *most fortunate; best*
    The fairest queen that ever king received.
KING HENRY   Suffolk, arise. Welcome, Queen Margaret.
    I can express no kinder° sign of love   *more natural*
    Than this kind° kiss.   *affectionate*
        [*He kisses her*]
                 O Lord that lends me life,
20   Lend me a heart replete with thankfulness!
    For thou hast given me in this beauteous face
    A world of earthly blessings to my soul,
    If sympathy° of love unite our thoughts.   *mutual feeling*
QUEEN MARGARET   Th'excess of love I bear unto your grace
25   Forbids me to be lavish of my tongue
    Lest I should speak more than beseems a woman.
    Let this suffice: my bliss is in your liking,°   *your affection for me*
    And naught can make poor Margaret miserable
    Unless the frown of mighty England's King.[4]
29.1   QUEEN MARGARET   *Great King of England, and my gracious lord,*
        The mutual conference° that my mind hath had—   *intimate talk*
        By day, by night; waking, and in my dreams;
        In courtly company, or at my beads°—   *while praying*
29.5   *With you, mine alder liefest° sovereign,*   *entirely most precious*
        Makes me the bolder to salute my king
        With ruder terms, such as my wit affords
        And overjoy of heart doth minister.°   *suggest*
30   KING HENRY   Her sight did ravish, but her grace in speech,
    Her words yclad° with wisdom's majesty,   *clad*
    Makes me from wond'ring° fall to weeping joys,   *admiring*
    Such is the fullness of my heart's content.
    Lords, with one cheerful voice, welcome my love.

---

2. Sicily. Queen Margaret's father, René, the Duke of
Anjou, was Sicily's king in name only.
3. A nobleman ranking below a duke and above an earl.
In *1 Henry VI,* Suffolk holds the rank of earl; here
he appears as a marquis; later in this scene, Henry
will make him a duke for his service as royal marriage

broker.
4. Oxford adopts the 1594 Quarto version of the
Queen's initial speech, lines 24–29; the Folio version,
which follows as an indented passage (lines 29.1–29.8),
may be the author's original draft.

35 LORDS *kneel*[*ing*]   Long live Queen Margaret, England's happiness.
QUEEN MARGARET   We thank you all.
                    Flourish. [*They all rise*]
SUFFOLK [*to* GLOUCESTER]   My Lord Protector, so it please your grace,
        Here are the articles of contracted peace
        Between our sovereign and the French King Charles,
40   For eighteen months concluded by consent.
GLOUCESTER (*reads*)   Imprimis:° it is agreed between the French   *First*
        King Charles and William de la Pole, Marquis of Suffolk,
        ambassador for Henry, King of England, that the said Henry
        shall espouse the Lady Margaret, daughter unto René, King
45   of Naples, Sicilia, and Jerusalem, and crown her Queen of
        England, ere the thirtieth of May next ensuing.
            Item:° it is further agreed between them that the duchy of   *Likewise*
        Anjou and the county of Maine shall be released and delivered
        to the King her fa—
                    Duke Humphrey [GLOUCESTER] *lets* [*the paper*] *fall*[5]
KING HENRY   Uncle, how now?
50 GLOUCESTER   Pardon me, gracious lord.
        Some sudden qualm° hath struck me at the heart   *illness; fear*
        And dimmed mine eyes that I can read no further.
KING HENRY [*to* CARDINAL BEAUFORT]   Uncle of Winchester,
        I pray read on.
CARDINAL BEAUFORT [*reads*]   Item: it is further agreed between
55   them that the duchy of Anjou and the county of Maine shall
        be released and delivered to the King her father, and she sent
        over of° the King of England's own proper° cost and charges,   *at / personal*
        without dowry.
KING HENRY   They please us well. [*To* SUFFOLK] Lord Marquis,
        kneel down.
                    [SUFFOLK *kneels*]
60 We here create thee first Duke of Suffolk,
        And gird thee with the sword.
                    [SUFFOLK *rises*]
                        Cousin[6] of York,
        We here discharge your grace from being regent
        I'th' parts° of France till term of eighteen months   *(English) regions*
        Be full° expired. Thanks uncle Winchester,   *fully*
65   Gloucester, York, and Buckingham, Somerset,
        Salisbury, and Warwick.
        We thank you all for this great favour done
        In entertainment° to my princely Queen.   *welcome*
        Come, let us in, and with all speed provide
70   To see her coronation be performed.
                    Exeunt KING [HENRY], QUEEN [MARGARET],
                    and Suffolk. GLOUCESTER *stays all the rest*
GLOUCESTER   Brave peers of England, pillars of the state,
        To you Duke Humphrey must unload his grief,

5. In subsequent stage directions, "Humphrey" will often be silently changed to "Gloucester." As with many directions, this one appears only in Q, not in F.

6. A form of address customarily used by English monarchs to nobles.

Your grief, the common grief of all the land.
What—did my brother Henry° spend his youth,   *Henry V*
His valour, coin, and people in the wars?
Did he so often lodge in open field
In winter's cold and summer's parching heat
To conquer France, his true inheritance?[7]
And did my brother Bedford toil his wits
To keep by policy° what Henry got?   *political skill*
Have you yourselves, Somerset, Buckingham,
Brave York, Salisbury, and victorious Warwick,
Received deep scars in France and Normandy?
Or hath mine uncle Beaufort and myself,
With all the learnèd Council of the realm,
Studied so long, sat in the Council House
Early and late, debating to and fro,
How France and Frenchmen might be kept in awe,°   *obedience*
And had his highness in his infancy
Crownèd in Paris in despite of foes?
And shall these labours and these honours die?
Shall Henry's conquest, Bedford's vigilance,
Your deeds of war, and all our counsel die?
O peers of England, shameful is this league,
Fatal this marriage, cancelling your fame,
Blotting your names from books of memory,
Razing the characters° of your renown,   *Erasing the records*
Defacing monuments of conquered France,
Undoing all, as° all had never been!   *as though*

CARDINAL BEAUFORT Nephew, what means this passionate discourse,
This peroration° with such circumstance?[8]   *rhetorical speech*
For France, 'tis ours; and we will keep it still.° *always*

GLOUCESTER Ay, uncle, we will keep it if we can—
But now it is impossible we should.
Suffolk, the new-made duke that rules the roast,°   *roost*
Hath given the duchy of Anjou and Maine
Unto the poor King René, whose large style°   *exalted title*
Agrees not with the leanness of his purse.

SALISBURY Now by the death of Him that died for all,[9]
These counties were the keys of Normandy—
But wherefore weeps Warwick, my valiant son?

WARWICK For grief that they are past recovery.
For were there hope to conquer them again
My sword should shed hot blood, mine eyes no tears.
Anjou and Maine? Myself did win them both!
Those provinces these arms of mine did conquer—
And are the cities that I got with wounds
Delivered up again with peaceful words?
Mort Dieu![1]

YORK For Suffolk's duke, may he be suffocate,°   *choked (a pun)*
That dims the honour of this warlike isle!

7. England laid claim to France throughout the fourteenth century, and Henry V won the title "heir of
France" with the Treaty of Troyes in 1420. See *Henry V*
1.1.85–90.

8. Such long-winded formality; so many details.
9. An oath equivalent to "by Christ's death."
1. God's death (French oath).

France should have torn and rent my very heart
Before I would have yielded to this league.
I never read but° England's kings have had   *I have always read that*
125 Large sums of gold and dowries with their wives—
And our King Henry gives away his own,
To match with° her that brings no vantages.°   *wed / profits (dowry)*
    GLOUCESTER   A proper jest, and never heard before,
    That Suffolk should demand a whole fifteenth²
130 For costs and charges in transporting her!
    She should have stayed in France and starved in France
    Before—
    CARDINAL BEAUFORT   My lord of Gloucester, now ye grow too hot!
    It was the pleasure of my lord the King.
135 GLOUCESTER   My lord of Winchester, I know your mind.
    'Tis not my speeches that you do mislike,
    But 'tis my presence that doth trouble ye.
    Rancour will out. Proud prelate, in thy face
    I see thy fury. If I longer stay
140 We shall begin our ancient bickerings—
    But I'll be gone, and give thee leave to speak.
    Lordings,° farewell, and say when I am gone,   *My lords*
    I prophesied France will be lost ere long.   *Exit*
    CARDINAL BEAUFORT   So, there goes our Protector in a rage.
145 'Tis known to you he is mine enemy;
    Nay more, an enemy unto you all,
    And no great friend, I fear me, to the King.
    Consider, lords, he is the next of blood³
    And heir apparent to the English crown.
150 Had Henry got an empire by his marriage,
    And all the wealthy kingdoms of the west,⁴
    There's reason he° should be displeased at it.   *(Gloucester)*
    Look to it, lords—let not his smoothing° words   *flattering*
    Bewitch your hearts. Be wise and circumspect.
155 What though the common people favour him,
    Calling him 'Humphrey, the good Duke of Gloucester',
    Clapping their hands and crying with loud voice
    'Jesu maintain your royal excellence!'
    With 'God preserve the good Duke Humphrey!'
160 I fear me, lords, for all this flattering gloss,°   *fair appearance*
    He will be found a dangerous Protector.
    BUCKINGHAM   Why should he then protect our sovereign,
    He being of age⁵ to govern of himself?
    Cousin of Somerset, join you with me,
165 And all together, with the Duke of Suffolk,
    We'll quickly hoist° Duke Humphrey from his seat.   *remove*
    CARDINAL BEAUFORT   This weighty business will not brook° delay—   *permit*
    I'll to the Duke of Suffolk presently.°   *Exit*   *immediately*

---

2. A tax of one-fifteenth of the value of personal property.
3. Because Henry VI did not yet have children, the heir
to the throne was Gloucester, his father's brother.
4. An anachronistic reference to the European conquest of the Americas.

5. Henry VI being old enough. At the time represented
in this scene, the historical King was twenty-four and
Gloucester was no longer Protector. Shakespeare here
as elsewhere alters his sources.

SOMERSET   Cousin of Buckingham, though Humphrey's pride
170   And greatness of his place be grief to us,
        Yet let us watch the haughty Cardinal;
        His insolence is more intolerable
        Than all the princes in the land beside.
        If Gloucester be displaced, he'll be Protector.
175 BUCKINGHAM   Or° thou or I, Somerset, will be Protector,   *Either*
        Despite Duke Humphrey or the Cardinal.
                  Exeunt BUCKINGHAM *and* SOMERSET
SALISBURY   Pride went before, ambition follows him.[6]
        While these do labour for their own preferment,°   *advancement*
        Behoves it us to labour for the realm.
180   I never saw but Humphrey Duke of Gloucester
        Did bear him like a noble gentleman.
        Oft have I seen the haughty Cardinal,
        More like a soldier than a man o'th' church,
        As stout° and proud as° he were lord of all,   *arrogant / as if*
185   Swear like a ruffian, and demean° himself   *conduct*
        Unlike the ruler of a commonweal.
        Warwick, my son, the comfort of my age,
        Thy deeds, thy plainness,° and thy housekeeping°   *honesty / hospitality*
        Hath won thee greatest favour of the commons,
190   Excepting none but good Duke Humphrey.
        And, brother York,[7] thy acts in Ireland,
        In bringing them to civil discipline,°   *civilized order*
        Thy late exploits done in the heart of France,
        When thou wert Regent for our sovereign,
195   Have made thee feared and honoured of the people.
        The reverence of° mine age and Neville's name[8]   *respect for*
        Is of no little force if I command.
        Join we together for the public good,
        In what we can to bridle° and suppress   *restrain*
200   The pride of Suffolk and the Cardinal
        With Somerset's and Buckingham's ambition;
        And, as we may, cherish° Duke Humphrey's deeds   *encourage*
        While they do tend° the profit of the land.   *promote*
WARWICK   So God help Warwick, as he loves the land,
205   And common profit of his country!
YORK   And so says York, [*aside*] for he hath greatest cause.
SALISBURY   Then let's away, and look unto the main.[9]
WARWICK   Unto the main? O, father, Maine is lost!
        That Maine which by main° force Warwick did win,   *overwhelming*
210   And would have kept so long as breath did last!
        Main chance, father, you meant—but I meant Maine,
        Which I will win from France or else be slain.
            Exeunt WARWICK *and* SALISBURY. *Manet*° YORK   *Remains*
YORK   Anjou and Maine are given to the French,
        Paris is lost, the state of Normandy
215   Stands on a tickle° point now they are gone;   *an unstable*
        Suffolk concluded on the articles,

---

6. A variation on the proverb "Pride goes before and shame comes after." Salisbury seems to refer to the Cardinal, who exited first, as "pride" and to Buckingham and Somerset as "ambition."
7. York was actually Salisbury's brother-in-law, having married Salisbury's sister Cicely.
8. Neville was the family name of the Earl of Salisbury and of his son, Warwick.
9. And consider the principal matter at stake. A gambling term, with subsequent puns on the several meanings of "main," including wordplay on "Maine," a French province lost in Suffolk's treaty.

The peers agreed, and Henry was well pleased
To change two dukedoms for a duke's fair daughter.
I cannot blame them all—what is't to them?
220   'Tis thine[1] they give away and not their own!
Pirates may make cheap pennyworths of° their pillage,   *sell at a low price*
And purchase friends, and give to courtesans,
Still° revelling like lords till all be gone,   *Continually*
Whileas the seely° owner of the goods   *While the helpless*
225   Weeps over them, and wrings his hapless° hands,   *unlucky*
And shakes his head, and, trembling, stands aloof,
While all is shared and all is borne away,
Ready to starve and dare not touch his own.
So York must sit and fret and bite his tongue,
230   While his own lands are bargained for and sold.
Methinks the realms of England, France, and Ireland
Bear that proportion° to my flesh and blood   *relation*
As did the fatal brand Althaea burnt
Unto the prince's heart of Calydon.[2]
235   Anjou and Maine both given unto the French!
Cold° news for me—for I had hope of France,   *Unwelcome*
Even as I have of fertile England's soil.
A day will come when York shall claim his own,
And therefore I will take the Nevilles' parts,[3]
240   And make a show of love to proud Duke Humphrey,
And, when I spy advantage,° claim the crown,   *opportunity*
For that's the golden mark° I seek to hit.   *target*
Nor shall proud Lancaster[4] usurp my right,
Nor hold the sceptre in his childish fist,
245   Nor wear the diadem upon his head
Whose church-like humours° fits not for a crown.   *pious temperament*
Then, York, be still a while till time do serve.
Watch° thou, and wake when others be asleep,   *Stay awake*
To pry into the secrets of the state—
250   Till Henry, surfeit° in the joys of love   *sickened from excess*
With his new bride and England's dear-bought queen,
And Humphrey with the peers be fall'n at jars.°   *into contention*
Then will I raise aloft the milk-white rose,[5]
With whose sweet smell the air shall be perfumed,
255   And in my standard° bear the arms of York,   *military flag*
To grapple with the house of Lancaster;
And force perforce° I'll make him yield the crown,   *by violent coercion*
Whose bookish rule hath pulled fair England down.   *Exit*

1.2

Enter Duke Humphrey [of GLOUCESTER] *and his wife*
Eleanor [the DUCHESS]
DUCHESS   Why droops my lord, like over-ripened corn°   *grain*
Hanging the head at Ceres' plenteous load?[1]

---

1. It is your own (York is addressing himself and referring to his claim to the throne).
2. Althaea, mother of Meleager, Prince of Calydon,
was told by the Fates that her son would live only as
long as a log burning in the fire at his birth. She
snatched the log from the flames, but later, when
Meleager killed her brothers, Althaea returned the log
to the fire and Meleager's heart stopped beating. See
Ovid, *Metamorphoses* 8.

3. And therefore will I ally myself with Salisbury and
Warwick.
4. Henry VI was also Duke of Lancaster.
5. The emblem of the Yorkists; the red rose was the
Lancastrian emblem.
1.2 Location: The Duke of Gloucester's house, London.
1. At the rich harvest of Ceres (the Roman goddess of
agriculture and the harvest).

Why doth the great Duke Humphrey knit his brows,
As frowning at the favours of the world?
5 Why are thine eyes fixed to the sullen earth,
Gazing on that which seems to dim thy sight?
What seest thou there? King Henry's diadem,
Enchased° with all the honours of the world?   *Adorned*
If so, gaze on, and grovel on thy face[2]
10 Until thy head be circled with the same.
Put forth thy hand, reach at the glorious gold.
What, is't too short? I'll lengthen it with mine;
And having both together heaved° it up,   *raised*
We'll both together lift our heads to heaven
15 And never more abase our sight so low
As to vouchsafe one glance unto the ground.
GLOUCESTER   O Nell, sweet Nell, if thou dost love thy lord,
Banish the canker° of ambitious thoughts!   *ulcer*
And may that hour when I imagine ill
20 Against my king and nephew, virtuous Henry,
Be my last breathing in this mortal world!
My troublous dream this night° doth make me sad.   *this past night*
DUCHESS   What dreamed my lord? Tell me and I'll requite it
With sweet rehearsal° of my morning's dream.[3]   *recital*
25 GLOUCESTER   Methought this staff, mine office-badge° in court,   *symbol of my position*
Was broke in twain—by whom I have forgot,
But, as I think, it was by th' Cardinal—
And on the pieces of the broken wand
Were placed the heads of Edmund, Duke of Somerset,
30 And William de la Pole, first Duke of Suffolk.
This was my dream—what it doth bode, God knows.
DUCHESS   Tut, this was nothing but an argument°   *a proof*
That he that breaks a stick of Gloucester's grove
Shall lose his head for his presumption.
35 But list° to me, my Humphrey, my sweet duke: *listen*
Methought I sat in seat of majesty
In the cathedral church of Westminster,
And in that chair° where kings and queens are crowned,   *throne*
Where Henry and Dame Margaret kneeled to me,
40 And on my head did set the diadem.
GLOUCESTER   Nay, Eleanor, then must I chide outright.
Presumptuous dame! Ill-nurtured° Eleanor!   *Ill-bred*
Art thou not second woman in the realm,
And the Protector's wife beloved of him?
45 Hast thou not worldly pleasure at command
Above the reach or compass of thy thought?
And wilt thou still be hammering° treachery   *devising*
To tumble down thy husband and thyself
From top of honour to disgrace's feet?
50 Away from me, and let me hear no more!
DUCHESS   What, what, my lord? Are you so choleric°   *hot-tempered*
With Eleanor for telling but her dream?
Next time I'll keep my dreams unto myself
And not be checked.°   *rebuked*

2. Crawl on the ground (perhaps to seek supernatural   3. Morning dreams were popularly believed to be true.
aid).

55 GLOUCESTER   Nay, be not angry; I am pleased again.
        Enter a MESSENGER
  MESSENGER   My Lord Protector, 'tis his highness' pleasure
        You do prepare to ride unto Saint Albans,
        Whereas° the King and Queen do mean to hawk.   *Where*
  GLOUCESTER   I go. Come, Nell, thou wilt ride with us?
60 DUCHESS   Yes, my good lord, I'll follow presently.°   *immediately*
        Exeunt GLOUCESTER [*and the* MESSENGER]
        Follow I must; I cannot go before
        While Gloucester bears this base° and humble mind.   *servile*
        Were I a man, a duke, and next of blood,
        I would remove these tedious stumbling blocks
65   And smooth my way upon their headless necks.
        And, being a woman, I will not be slack
        To play my part in fortune's pageant.[4]
        [*Calling within*]   Where are you there? Sir John![5] Nay, fear not man.
        We are alone. Here's none but thee and I.
        Enter Sir John HUME
70 HUME   Jesus preserve your royal majesty.
  DUCHESS   What sayst thou? 'Majesty'? I am but 'grace'.[6]
  HUME   But by the grace of God and Hume's advice
        Your grace's title shall be multiplied.
  DUCHESS   What sayst thou, man? Hast thou as yet conferred
75   With Margery Jordan, the cunning witch[7] of Eye,
        With Roger Bolingbroke, the conjuror?
        And will they undertake to do me good?
  HUME   This they have promisèd: to show your highness
        A spirit raised from depth of underground
80   That shall make answer to such questions
        As by your Grace shall be propounded him.
  DUCHESS   It is enough. I'll think upon the questions.
        When from Saint Albans we do make return,
        We'll see these things effected to the full.
85   Here, Hume [*giving him money*], take this reward. Make merry, man,
        With thy confederates in this weighty cause.   *Exit*
  HUME   Hume must make merry with the Duchess' gold;
        Marry,[8] and shall. But how now, Sir John Hume?
        Seal up your lips, and give no words but mum;
90   The business asketh silent secrecy.
        Dame Eleanor gives gold to bring the witch.
        Gold cannot come amiss were she a devil.
        Yet have I gold flies from another coast[9]—
        I dare not say from the rich Cardinal
95   And from the great and new-made Duke of Suffolk,
        Yet I do find it so; for, to be plain,
        They, knowing Dame Eleanor's aspiring humour,°   *ambitious nature*
        Have hired me to undermine the Duchess,

---

4. In Roman mythology, the goddess Fortune symbolized the element of chance in human life and was often depicted with a rudder (as the pilot of destiny), wings, or a wheel. Here Fortune is imagined as directing a medieval play ("pageant") or leading a ceremonial procession.
5. Priests were commonly addressed as "sir."
6. The appropriate title for a duchess.
7. Cunning women, sometimes prosecuted for witchcraft, were familiar village figures who made a living by telling fortunes, healing sicknesses, making love potions, and finding lost objects.
8. By the Virgin Mary (a mild oath).
9. I have gold that comes from another quarter.

And buzz° these conjurations in her brain.   *whisper*
100   They say 'A crafty knave does need no broker',°   *middleman; agent*
Yet am I Suffolk and the Cardinal's broker.
Hume, if you take not heed you shall go near
To call them both a pair of crafty knaves.
Well, so it stands; and thus, I fear, at last
105   Hume's knavery will be the Duchess' wrack,°   *ruin*
And her attainture° will be Humphrey's fall.   *conviction*
Sort° how it will, I shall have gold for all.   *Exit*   *Turn out*

1.3

Enter PETER, *the armourer's man,*° [*with*] *two or three*   *apprentice*
[*other*] PETITIONERS

FIRST PETITIONER   My masters, let's stand close. My Lord Pro-
tector will come this way by and by and then we may deliver
our supplications in the quill.°   *as a group*
SECOND PETITIONER   Marry, the Lord protect him, for he's a
5   good man, Jesu bless him.
Enter the Duke of SUFFOLK *and* QUEEN [MARGARET]
FIRST PETITIONER   Here a° comes, methinks, and the Queen   *he*
with him. I'll be the first, sure.¹
[*He goes to meet* SUFFOLK *and the* QUEEN]
SECOND PETITIONER   Come back, fool—this is the Duke of Suf-
folk and not my Lord Protector.
10   SUFFOLK [*to the* FIRST PETITIONER]   How now, fellow²—wouldst
anything with me?
FIRST PETITIONER   I pray, my lord, pardon me—I took ye for my
Lord Protector.
QUEEN MARGARET [*seeing his supplication, she reads*]   'To my
15   Lord Protector'—are your supplications to his lordship? Let
me see them.
[*She takes First Petitioner's supplication*]
What is thine?
FIRST PETITIONER   Mine is, an't° please your grace, against   *if it*
John Goodman, my lord Cardinal's man, for keeping my
20   house and lands and wife and all from me.
SUFFOLK   Thy wife too? That's some wrong indeed. [*To the* SEC-
OND PETITIONER]   What's yours?
[*He takes the supplication*]
What's here? [*Reads*] 'Against the Duke of Suffolk for enclos-
ing the commons³ of Melford'! [*To the* SECOND PETITIONER]
25   How now, Sir Knave?
SECOND PETITIONER   Alas, sir, I am but a poor petitioner of our
whole township.
PETER [*offering his petition*]   Against my master, Thomas
Horner, for saying that the Duke of York was rightful heir to
30   the crown.

1.3 Location: The palace, London.
1. In F, these lines are assigned to Peter, but lines
12–13 suggest they are spoken by the First Petitioner,
who here pushes himself forward to get the attention of
the Queen and Suffolk (whom he believes to be
Gloucester).

2. A common form of address to a social inferior.
3. Fencing in for private use land once used by the entire
community. The practice of enclosure, which benefited
landowners while forcing into poverty the lower classes
who had farmed the land, was a chronic source of unrest
in many regions in early modern England.

QUEEN MARGARET   What sayst thou? Did the Duke of York say
   he was rightful heir to the crown?
PETER   That my master was? No, forsooth, my master said that
   he was and that the King was an usurer.
35 QUEEN MARGARET   An usurper thou wouldst say.
PETER   Ay, forsooth—an usurper.
SUFFOLK [*calling within*]   Who is there?
       Enter [a] servant
   Take this fellow in and send for his master with a pursuivant°   *an officer*
   presently. [*To* PETER] We'll hear more of your matter before
40   the King.   *Exit* [*the servant*] *with* [PETER] *the armourer's man*
QUEEN MARGARET [*to the* PETITIONERS]   And as for you that love to be protected
   Under the wings of our Protector's grace,
   Begin your suits anew and sue to him.
       [*She*] *tears the supplication*[4]
   Away, base cullions![5] Suffolk, let them go.
45 ALL PETITIONERS   Come, let's be gone.   *Exeunt* PETITIONERS
QUEEN MARGARET   My lord of Suffolk, say, is this the guise?°   *custom*
   Is this the fashions in the court of England?
   Is this the government of Britain's isle,
   And this the royalty of Albion's° king?   *England's*
50   What, shall King Henry be a pupil still
   Under the surly Gloucester's governance?
   Am I a queen in title and in style,°   *form of address*
   And must be made a subject to a duke?
   I tell thee, Pole, when in the city Tours
55   Thou rann'st a-tilt[6] in honour of my love
   And stol'st away the ladies' hearts of France,
   I thought King Henry had resembled thee
   In courage, courtship,° and proportion.[7]   *courtly manners*
   But all his mind is bent to holiness,
60   To number Ave-Maries on his beads.[8]
   His champions are the prophets and apostles,[9]
   His weapons holy saws° of sacred writ,   *sayings*
   His study is his tilt-yard,° and his loves   *jousting arena*
   Are brazen images of canonizèd saints.
65   I would the college of the cardinals
   Would choose him Pope, and carry him to Rome,
   And set the triple crown° upon his head—   *papal crown*
   That were a state fit for his holiness.
SUFFOLK   Madam, be patient—as I was cause
70   Your highness came to England, so will I
   In England work your grace's full content.
QUEEN MARGARET   Beside the haught° Protector have we Beaufort   *arrogant*
   The imperious churchman, Somerset, Buckingham,
   And grumbling York; and not the least of these
75   But can do more in England than the King.

---

4. In Q, Suffolk is the one who "tears the papers." This is one of the places where F gives more initiative to Margaret than does Q.
5. Lowborn rascals. "Cullion" comes from the Italian word *coglioni*, meaning "testicles."
6. You took part in a jousting tournament.
7. Physical grace; physique.

8. Referring to a Roman Catholic devotion in which a string of beads (a rosary) is used to keep track of prayers said in a particular sequence. Among the prayers are "Ave Maria," or "Hail Mary," addressed to the Virgin Mary.
9. A champion stood in for the King at jousts and tournaments. Margaret scornfully suggests that Henry VI makes holy men rather than real warriors his champions.

SUFFOLK   And he of these that can do most of all
　　　Cannot do more in England than the Nevilles:
　　　Salisbury and Warwick are no simple peers.
QUEEN MARGARET   Not all these lords do vex me half so much
80　　As that proud dame, the Lord Protector's wife.
　　　She sweeps it through the court with troops of ladies
　　　More like an empress than Duke Humphrey's wife.
　　　Strangers in court do take her for the queen.
　　　She bears a duke's revenues on her back,°　　　　　　　　　　*wears costly clothing*
85　　And in her heart she scorns our poverty.
　　　Shall I not live to be avenged on her?
　　　Contemptuous° base-born callet° as she is,　　　　　　　*Despicable / whore*
　　　She vaunted 'mongst her minions° t'other day　　　　　　　　　*followers*
　　　The very train of her worst-wearing° gown　　　　　　　　　　*poorest*
90　　Was better worth° than all my father's lands,　　　　　　　*worth more*
　　　Till Suffolk gave two dukedoms° for his daughter.　　　　*(Maine and Anjou)*
SUFFOLK   Madam, myself have limed a bush[1] for her,
　　　And placed a choir of such enticing birds
　　　That she will light° to listen to their lays,°　　　　　　*perch / songs*
95　　And never mount to trouble you again.
　　　So let her rest; and, madam, list to me,
　　　For I am bold to counsel you in this:
　　　Although we fancy not the Cardinal,
　　　Yet must we join with him and with the lords
100　　Till we have brought Duke Humphrey in disgrace.
　　　As for the Duke of York, this late complaint[2]
　　　Will make but little for his benefit.
　　　So one by one we'll weed them all at last,
　　　And you yourself shall steer the happy helm.
　　　　　　Sound a sennet.° Enter KING HENRY, [*with*] *the Duke*　　　*trumpet call*
　　　　　　of YORK *and the Duke of* SOMERSET *on both sides,*
　　　　　　whispering with him. [*Also*] *enter Duke Humphrey*
　　　　　　[*of* GLOUCESTER], *Dame Eleanor the* DUCHESS
　　　　　　[*of Gloucester*], *the Duke of* BUCKINGHAM,
　　　　　　the Earl[*s*] *of* SALISBURY *and* WARWICK, *and* CARDINAL
　　　　　　[BEAUFORT *Bishop*] *of Winchester*
105　KING HENRY   For my part, noble lords, I care not which:
　　　Or° Somerset or York, all's one to me.　　　　　　　　　　*Either*
YORK   If York have ill demeaned° himself in France　　　　　　*conducted*
　　　Then let him be denied the regentship.
SOMERSET   If Somerset be unworthy of the place,
110　　Let York be regent—I will yield to him.
WARWICK   Whether your grace be worthy, yea or no,
　　　Dispute not that: York is the worthier.
CARDINAL BEAUFORT   Ambitious Warwick, let thy betters speak.
WARWICK   The Cardinal's not my better in the field.°　　　　*in battle*
115　BUCKINGHAM   All in this presence are thy betters, Warwick.
WARWICK   Warwick may live to be the best of all.
SALISBURY   Peace, son; [*to* BUCKINGHAM] and show some reason,
　　　　　Buckingham,
　　　Why Somerset should be preferred in this.

---

1. Have set a trap. Elizabethans caught birds by smear-
ing bushes and twigs with a sticky substance known as
birdlime.

2. This recent complaint. Suffolk means that Peter's
claim against his master casts doubt on York's loyalty to
the King.

QUEEN MARGARET   Because the King, forsooth, will have it so.

120 GLOUCESTER   Madam, the King is old enough himself
To give his censure.° These are no women's matters.   judgment
QUEEN MARGARET   If he be old enough, what needs your grace
To be Protector of his excellence?
GLOUCESTER   Madam, I am Protector of the realm,
125 And at his pleasure will resign my place.
SUFFOLK   Resign it then, and leave thine insolence.
Since thou wert king—as who is king but thou?—
The commonwealth hath daily run to wrack,
The Dauphin³ hath prevailed beyond the seas,
130 And all the peers and nobles of the realm
Have been as bondmen to thy sovereignty.
CARDINAL BEAUFORT [to GLOUCESTER]   The commons hast thou
racked,° the clergy's bags   overtaxed
Are lank and lean with thy extortions.
SOMERSET [to GLOUCESTER]   Thy sumptuous buildings⁴ and thy wife's attire
135 Have cost a mass of public treasury.
BUCKINGHAM [to GLOUCESTER]   Thy cruelty in execution
Upon offenders hath exceeded law
And left thee to the mercy of the law.
QUEEN MARGARET [to GLOUCESTER]   Thy sale of offices and
towns in France—
140 If they were known, as the suspect° is great—   suspicion
Would make thee quickly hop without thy head.⁵
                                    Exit GLOUCESTER
         QUEEN [MARGARET] lets fall her fan⁶
[To the DUCHESS] Give me my fan—what, minion,° can ye not?   hussy
         She gives the DUCHESS a box on the ear
I cry you mercy,° madam! Was it you?   beg your pardon
DUCHESS   Was't I? Yea, I it was, proud Frenchwoman!
145 Could I come near your beauty with my nails,
I'd set my ten commandments° in your face.   (ten fingers)
KING HENRY   Sweet aunt, be quiet—'twas against her will.°   unintentional
DUCHESS   Against her will? Good King, look to't in time!
She'll pamper thee and dandle thee like a baby,
150 Though in this place most master⁷ wear no breeches,
She shall not strike Dame Eleanor unrevenged!   Exit
BUCKINGHAM [aside to CARDINAL BEAUFORT]   Lord Cardinal, I
will follow Eleanor
And listen after Humphrey how he proceeds.
She's tickled° now, her fury needs no spurs—   vexed
155 She'll gallop far enough to her destruction.   Exit
         Enter Duke Humphrey [of GLOUCESTER]
GLOUCESTER   Now, lords, my choler being overblown°   dispelled
With walking once about the quadrangle,
I come to talk of commonwealth affairs.
As for your spiteful false objections,

---

3. "Dauphin" was the title of the oldest son of the French King, but here it refers to the French King himself, Charles VII, and bears witness to the fact that England did not acknowledge Charles's right to the throne.
4. Probably a reference to Greenwich Palace. In 1437,

Gloucester obtained a grant to expand the old manor, which he lent to Henry VI and Margaret for their honeymoon.
5. Proverbial expression meaning to be beheaded.
6. In Q, the Queen lets fall a glove, not a fan.
7. The one most in control (the Queen).

160 Prove them, and I lie open to the law.
But God in mercy so deal with my soul
As I in duty love my King and country.
But to the matter that we have in hand—
I say, my sovereign, York is meetest° man   *the most suitable*
165 To be your regent in the realm of France.
SUFFOLK   Before we make election,° give me leave   *a choice*
To show some reason of no little force
That York is most unmeet of any man.
YORK   I'll tell thee, Suffolk, why I am unmeet:
170 First, for° I cannot flatter thee in pride;   *because*
Next, if I be appointed for the place,
My lord of Somerset will keep me here
Without discharge,° money, or furniture,°   *payment / equipment*
Till France be won into the Dauphin's hands.
175 Last time I danced attendance on his will[8]
Till Paris was besieged, famished, and lost.
WARWICK   That can I witness, and a fouler fact°   *deed*
Did never traitor in the land commit.
SUFFOLK   Peace, headstrong Warwick.
180 WARWICK   Image of pride, why should I hold my peace?
Enter [guarded, HORNER *the] armourer and [*PETER*] his
man*
SUFFOLK   Because here is a man accused of treason—
Pray God the Duke of York excuse himself!
YORK   Doth anyone accuse York for a traitor?
KING HENRY   What mean'st thou, Suffolk? Tell me, what are these?
185 SUFFOLK   Please it your majesty, this is the man
[*He indicates* PETER]
That doth accuse his master [*indicating* HORNER] of high treason.
His words were these: that Richard Duke of York
Was rightful heir unto the English crown,
And that your majesty was an usurper.
190 KING HENRY [*to* HORNER]   Say, man, were these thy words?
HORNER   An't shall please your majesty, I never said nor
thought any such matter. God is my witness, I am falsely
accused by the villain.
PETER [*raising his hands*]   By these ten bones,° my lords, he did   *(ten fingers)*
195 speak them to me in the garret one night as we were scouring
my lord of York's armour.
YORK   Base dunghill villain and mechanical,°   *manual laborer*
I'll have thy head for this thy traitor's speech!
[*To* KING HENRY]   I do beseech your royal majesty,
200 Let him have all the rigour of the law.
HORNER   Alas, my lord, hang me if ever I spake the words. My
accuser is my prentice, and when I did correct him for his
fault the other day, he did vow upon his knees he would be
even with me. I have good witness of this, therefore, I beseech
205 your majesty, do not cast away° an honest man for a villain's   *destroy*
accusation.

---

8. I did as he wished. York refers to events depicted in *1 Henry VI*, specifically to Somerset's failure to supply him
with reinforcements during the wars in France. See *1 Henry VI* 4.3.9–11.

KING HENRY [*to* GLOUCESTER]   Uncle, what shall we say to this in law?

GLOUCESTER   This doom,° my lord, if I may judge by case: judgment
　　Let Somerset be regent o'er the French,
210　　Because in York this breeds suspicion.⁹
　　[*Indicating* HORNER *and* PETER] And let these have a day
　　　　appointed them
　　For single combat in convenient place,
　　For he [*indicating* HORNER] hath witness of his servant's malice.
　　This is the law, and this Duke Humphrey's doom.

215 KING HENRY   Then be it so. [*To* SOMERSET] My lord of Somerset,
　　We make you regent o'er the realm of France
　　There to defend our rights 'gainst foreign foes.

SOMERSET   I humbly thank your royal majesty.

HORNER   And I accept the combat willingly.

220 PETER [*to* GLOUCESTER]   Alas, my lord, I cannot fight; for God's
　　sake, pity my case! The spite of man prevaileth against me.
　　O Lord, have mercy upon me—I shall never be able to fight a
　　blow! O Lord, my heart!

GLOUCESTER   Sirrah,¹ or° you must fight or else be hanged.   either

225 KING HENRY   Away with them to prison, and the day
　　Of combat be the last of the next month.
　　Come, Somerset, we'll see thee sent away.   *Flourish. Exeunt*

1.4

Enter Margery Jordan, a WITCH; *Sir John* HUME
[*and John* SOUTHWELL, *two priests*]; *and Roger*
BOLINGBROKE, *a conjuror*¹

HUME   Come, my masters, the Duchess, I tell you, expects per-
　　formance of your promises.

BOLINGBROKE   Master Hume, we are therefore° provided. Will   *for that purpose*
　　her ladyship behold and hear our exorcisms?°   *conjuring of spirits*

5 HUME   Ay, what else? Fear you not her courage.

BOLINGBROKE   I have heard her reported to be a woman of an
　　invincible spirit. But it shall be convenient, Master Hume,
　　that you be by her, aloft, while we be busy below. And so, I
　　pray you, go in God's name and leave us.   *Exit* HUME

10　　Mother Jordan, be you prostrate and grovel on the earth.
　　　　She lies down upon her face.
　　　　Enter Eleanor [*the* DUCHESS *of Gloucester*] *aloft*
　　John Southwell, read you and let us to our work.

DUCHESS   Well said, my masters, and welcome all. To this gear°   *business*
　　the sooner the better.
　　　　[*Enter* HUME *aloft*]

BOLINGBROKE   Patience, good lady—wizards know their times.

15　　Deep night, dark night, the silent of the night,
　　The time of night when Troy was set on fire,²
　　The time when screech-owls cry and bandogs° howl,   *chained watchdogs*

---

9. Because this matter casts doubt on York's loyalty.
1. A common form of address to a social inferior.
1.4 Location: Gloucester's garden, London.
1. Neither Q nor F names John Southwell as one of the two priests in this scene, but he is named in dialogue at line 11. Q has Eleanor enter at the beginning of the scene; F, as here, has her enter aloft a few lines into the scene. After Hume's exit at line 9, he must reenter aloft

at some point to attend Eleanor. This entry is not marked, but having Hume reenter after line 13 leaves enough time for him to exit the stage at line 9 and make an entrance above.
2. Virgil's *Aeneid*, Book 2, describes how the Greeks, having entered Troy through treachery, set fire to the ancient city.

And spirits walk, and ghosts break up° their graves—   *burst open*
That time best fits the work we have in hand.

20   Madam, sit you, and fear not. Whom we raise
We will make fast within a hallowed verge.°   *magic circle*
Here do the ceremonies belonging,[3] and make the
circle. SOUTHWELL *reads 'Coniuro te',[4] &c. It thunders*
and lightens terribly, then the spirit [ASNATH][5] *riseth*

ASNATH   Adsum.°   *I am here*
WITCH   Asnath,
By the eternal God whose name and power
25   Thou tremblest at, answer that° I shall ask,   *what*
For till thou speak, thou shalt not pass from hence.
ASNATH   Ask what thou wilt, that° I had said and done.   *would that*
BOLINGBROKE [*reads*] 'First, of the King: what shall of him
become?'
ASNATH   The Duke yet lives that Henry shall depose,
30   But him outlive, and die a violent death.[6]
        [*As the spirit speaks,* SOUTHWELL *writes the answer*]
BOLINGBROKE [*reads*] 'Tell me what fate awaits the Duke of Suffolk.'
ASNATH   By water shall he die, and take his end.
BOLINGBROKE [*reads*] 'What shall betide the Duke of Somerset?'
ASNATH   Let him shun castles. Safer shall he be
35   Upon the sandy plains than where castles mounted° stand.   *on mountains*
Have done—for more I hardly can endure.
BOLINGBROKE   Descend to darkness and the burning lake!
False° fiend, avoid!°   *Treacherous / be gone*
        Thunder and lightning. [*The spirit*] *sinks down again*[7]
38.1   BOLINGBROKE *Then down, I say, unto the damnèd pool*
Where Pluto[8] in his fiery wagon° sits   *chariot*
Riding, amidst the singed and parchèd smokes,
The roads of Ditis by the River Styx.[9]
38.5   *There howl and burn for ever in those flames.*
Rise, Jordan, rise and stay° thy charming spells—   *halt*
Zounds,° we are betrayed!   *By God's wounds (oath)*
        Enter the Duke[s] *of* YORK *and* BUCKINGHAM *with their guard,* [*among them*
        Sir Humphrey STAFFORD] *and break in*
YORK   Lay hands upon these traitors and their trash.
        [BOLINGBROKE, SOUTHWELL, *and Jordan are taken pris-*
        oner. BUCKINGHAM *takes the writings from*
        BOLINGBROKE *and* SOUTHWELL]
40   [*To Jordan*] Beldam,° I think we watched you at an inch.°   *Witch / closely*
[*To the* DUCHESS] What, madam, are you there? The King
and common weal
Are deep indebted for this piece of pains.°   *your trouble*

---

3. The rituals necessary (for conjuring spirits).
4. I conjure you (Latin), the beginning of a spell.
5. An anagram of "Sathan," a variant form of "Satan."
Demons were supposed to be invoked by anagrams.
6. *The . . . death:* Like many prophecies, this one is
ambiguous. The syntax of the first line can mean that
there lives a duke whom Henry shall depose or who
shall depose Henry. The duke is probably York, who in
Richard Duke of York (*3 Henry VI*) forces Henry to
entail the crown to York rather than to Henry's own son,
thus symbolically deposing him. York, however, dies a
violent death after the Battle of Wakefield, and Henry
outlives him. But Henry also dies a violent death, murdered in the Tower of London by the Duke of York's son,
Richard, Duke of Gloucester, who eventually becomes
King Richard III.
7. For lines 37–38, Q substitutes the following
indented passage (lines 38.1–38.7); it may record a
revision made in rehearsal to cover the spirit's descent.
8. In classical mythology, the god of the infernal regions.
9. The river of Hades over which Charon ferried the
dead.

My lord Protector will, I doubt it not,
  See you well guerdoned° for these good deserts.   *rewarded*
DUCHESS Not half so bad as thine to England's king,
45 Injurious° Duke, that threatest where's no cause.   *Abusive*
BUCKINGHAM True, madam, none at all—
    [*He raises the writings*]
                        what call you this?
    [*To his men*] Away with them. Let them be clapped up close°   *imprisoned securely*
  And kept asunder. [*To the* DUCHESS] You, madam, shall with us.
50 Stafford, take her to thee.
                 [*Exeunt* STAFFORD *and others to the* DUCHESS
                                 and HUME *above*]
We'll see your trinkets here all forthcoming.[1]
All away!
                Exeunt [*below, Jordan,* SOUTHWELL, *and*
            BOLINGBROKE, *guarded, and, above,* HUME *and*
            the DUCHESS *guarded by* STAFFORD *and others.*
                          YORK *and* BUCKINGHAM *remain*]
YORK Lord Buckingham, methinks you watched her well.
  A pretty plot,° well chosen to build upon.   *trick; plot of ground*
55 Now pray, my lord, let's see the devil's writ.
    [BUCKINGHAM *gives him the writings*]
  What have we here?
    [*He*] *reads* [*the writings*]
                  Why, this is just°   *precisely*
  Aio Aeacidam, Romanos vincere posse.[2]
  These oracles are hardily° attained   *with difficulty*
  And hardly understood. Come, come, my lord,
60 The King is now in progress towards Saint Albans;
  With him the husband of this lovely lady.
  Thither goes these news as fast as horse can carry them—
  A sorry breakfast for my lord Protector.
BUCKINGHAM Your grace shall give me leave, my lord of York,
65 To be the post° in hope of his reward.   *messenger*
YORK [*returning the writings to* BUCKINGHAM] At your pleasure,
    my good lord.   *Exit* BUCKINGHAM
[*Calling within*] Who's within there, ho!
    Enter a SERVINGMAN
Invite my lords of Salisbury and Warwick
To sup with me tomorrow night. Away.   *Exeunt* [*severally*]°   *separately*

2.1

Enter KING [HENRY], QUEEN [MARGARET] *with her hawk
on her fist, Duke Humphrey* [*of* GLOUCESTER],
CARDINAL [BEAUFORT], *and* [*the Duke of*] SUFFOLK, *with
falconers hollering*

QUEEN MARGARET Believe me, lords, for flying at the brook°   *hawking for waterfowl*
  I saw not better sport these seven years' day;
  Yet, by your leave, the wind was very high,
  And, ten to one, old Joan had not gone out.[1]

---

1. We'll see that your worthless goods (the conjuring paraphernalia) are produced as evidence against you.
2. I say that you, descendant of Aeacus, the Romans can conquer. A famously ambiguous response by an oracle to King Pyrrhus's question about whether he would conquer Rome.
2.1 Location: St. Albans.
1. The hawk named "Old Joan" would probably not have flown because of the high wind.

KING HENRY [*to* GLOUCESTER]   But what a point,[2] my lord, your falcon made,
5   And what a pitch° she flew above the rest!   *height*
          To see how God in all his creatures works!
          Yea, man and birds are fain° of climbing high.   *fond*
SUFFOLK   No marvel, an it like° your majesty,   *if it please*
          My Lord Protector's hawks do tower so well;
10   They know their master loves to be aloft,°   *to rule over others*
          And bears his thoughts above his falcon's pitch.[3]
GLOUCESTER   My lord, 'tis but a base ignoble mind
          That mounts no higher than a bird can soar.
CARDINAL BEAUFORT   I thought as much; he would be above the clouds.
15   GLOUCESTER   Ay, my lord Cardinal, how think you by that?
          Were it not good your grace could fly to heaven?
KING HENRY   The treasury of everlasting joy.
CARDINAL BEAUFORT [*to* GLOUCESTER]   Thy heaven is on earth;
          thine eyes and thoughts
20   Beat on° a crown, the treasure of thy heart,   *Think obsessively about*
          Pernicious Protector, dangerous peer,
          That smooth'st it so with° King and common weal!   *Who so flatters*
GLOUCESTER   What, Cardinal? Is your priesthood grown peremptory?
          Tantaene animis caelestibus irae?[4]
25   Churchmen so hot? Good uncle, hide such malice
          With some holiness—can you do it?
SUFFOLK   No malice, sir, no more than well becomes°   *is appropriate to*
          So good° a quarrel and so bad a peer.   *just*
GLOUCESTER   As who, my lord?
SUFFOLK   Why, as you, my lord—
30   An't like your lordly Lord's Protectorship.
GLOUCESTER   Why, Suffolk, England knows thine insolence.
QUEEN MARGARET   And thy ambition, Gloucester.
KING HENRY   I prithee peace,
          Good Queen, and whet not on° these furious peers—   *do not encourage*
          For blessèd are the peacemakers on earth.[5]
35   CARDINAL BEAUFORT   Let me be blessèd for the peace I make
          Against this proud Protector with my sword.
          [GLOUCESTER *and* CARDINAL BEAUFORT *speak privately to*
          one another]
GLOUCESTER   Faith, holy uncle, would't were come to that.
CARDINAL BEAUFORT   Marry, when thou dar'st.
GLOUCESTER   Dare? I tell thee, priest,
          Plantagenets[6] could never brook° the dare!   *tolerate*
40   CARDINAL BEAUFORT   I am Plantagenet as well as thou,
          And son to John of Gaunt.

---

2. High position to which hawks fly to await prey.
3. Alluding to Gloucester's heraldic crest, which consisted of a falcon with a maiden's head. Suffolk is accusing Gloucester of overweening ambition.
4. Quoting Virgil's *Aeneid* 1.11, "Can there be such anger in heavenly minds?"
5. Quoting Jesus' Sermon on the Mount (Matthew 5:9).
6. "Plantagenet" was a name given the kings descended from Geoffrey, Count of Anjou, and Matilda, daughter of Henry I, thought to derive from the Latin words for

"a sprig of broom," which Geoffrey wore in his cap. Gloucester, a grandson of John of Gaunt, was a Plantagenet. John of Gaunt was Beaufort's father, but Beaufort's mother, Catherine Swynford, gave birth to him and his brothers before she married Gaunt; this explains why Gloucester calls Beaufort a bastard (line 42). Historically, the Beauforts, though eventually legitimated, were barred from any claim to the throne. The lines referring to Beaufort's bastardy, 38–43, appear only in Q and not in F.

GLOUCESTER   In bastardy.

CARDINAL BEAUFORT   I scorn thy words.

GLOUCESTER   Make up no factious numbers for the matter,[7]

45   In thine own person answer thy abuse.°   insult; offense

CARDINAL BEAUFORT   Ay, where thou dar'st not peep; an if° thou dar'st,   an if = if
        This evening on the east side of the grove.

KING HENRY   How now, my lords?

CARDINAL BEAUFORT [aloud]   Believe me, cousin Gloucester,
        Had not your man put up° the fowl so suddenly,   raised; startled
        We had had more sport. [Aside to GLOUCESTER] Come with thy

50   two-hand sword.

GLOUCESTER [aloud]   True, uncle.
        [Aside to CARDINAL BEAUFORT] Are ye advised?° The east side   agreed
        of the grove.

CARDINAL BEAUFORT [aside to GLOUCESTER]
        I am with you.

KING HENRY   Why, how now, uncle Gloucester?

GLOUCESTER   Talking of hawking, nothing else, my lord.
        [Aside to the CARDINAL] Now, by God's mother, priest, I'll shave

55   your crown[8] for this,
        Or all my fence° shall fail.   skill in fencing

CARDINAL BEAUFORT [aside to GLOUCESTER]
                            Medice, teipsum[9]—
        Protector, see to't well; protect yourself.

KING HENRY   The winds grow high; so do your stomachs,° lords.   tempers
        How irksome is this music to my heart!

60   When such strings jar,[1] what hope of harmony?
        I pray, my lords, let me compound° this strife.   settle
                Enter one crying 'a miracle'

GLOUCESTER   What means this noise?
        Fellow, what miracle dost thou proclaim?

ONE   A miracle, a miracle!

65   SUFFOLK   Come to the King—tell him what miracle.

ONE [to KING HENRY]   Forsooth, a blind man at Saint Alban's shrine[2]
        Within this half-hour hath received his sight
        A man that ne'er saw in his life before.

KING HENRY   Now God be praised, that to believing souls

70   Gives light in darkness, comfort in despair!
                Enter the MAYOR of Saint Albans and his brethren
                [aldermen] with music, bearing the man [SIMPCOX]
                between two in a chair. [Enter SIMPCOX'S WIFE
                and other townsmen with them]

CARDINAL BEAUFORT   Here comes the townsmen on° procession   in
        To present your highness with the man.
                [The townsmen kneel]

KING HENRY   Great is his comfort in this earthly vale,
        Although by sight his sin be multiplied.[3]

GLOUCESTER [to the townsmen]   Stand by, my masters, bring

75   him near the King.

---

7. Call in no supporters for this quarrel.
8. Alluding to a tonsure, or a shaved circular patch, often seen on the heads of religious men.
9. Physician, (heal) thyself (see Luke 4:23).

1. When instruments such as these grow discordant.
2. A shrine to the first British martyr, who was beheaded by the Romans for giving sanctuary to Christians.
3. Although his sight will lead him into more temptation.

His highness' pleasure is to talk with him.
          [*They rise and bear* SIMPCOX *before the* KING]
KING HENRY [*to* SIMPCOX]   Good fellow, tell us here the circumstance,
     That we for thee may glorify the Lord.
     What, hast thou been long blind and now restored?
SIMPCOX   Born blind, an't please your grace.
80 SIMPCOX'S WIFE   Ay, indeed, was he.
SUFFOLK   What woman is this?
SIMPCOX'S WIFE   His wife, an't like your worship.
GLOUCESTER   Hadst thou been his mother
     Thou couldst have better told.
KING HENRY [*to* SIMPCOX]   Where wert thou born?
85 SIMPCOX   At Berwick,[4] in the north, an't like your grace.
KING HENRY   Poor soul, God's goodness hath been great to thee.
     Let never day nor night unhallowed° pass,   *unblessed*
     But still° remember what the Lord hath done.   *continually*
QUEEN MARGARET [*to* SIMPCOX]   Tell me, good fellow, cam'st
          thou here by chance,
90   Or of devotion to this holy shrine?
SIMPCOX   God knows, of pure devotion, being called
     A hundred times and oftener, in my sleep,
     By good Saint Alban, who said, 'Simon, come;
     Come offer° at my shrine and I will help thee.'   *make an offering*
95 SIMPCOX'S WIFE   Most true, forsooth, and many time and oft
     Myself have heard a voice to call him so.
CARDINAL BEAUFORT [*to* SIMPCOX]
     What, art thou lame?
SIMPCOX   Ay, God almighty help me.
SUFFOLK   How cam'st thou so?
SIMPCOX   A fall off of a tree.
SIMPCOX'S WIFE [*to* SUFFOLK]
     A plum tree,[5] master.
GLOUCESTER   How long hast thou been blind?
SIMPCOX   O, born so, master.
100 GLOUCESTER   What, and wouldst climb a tree?
SIMPCOX   But that° in all my life, when I was a youth.   *Only that once*
SIMPCOX'S WIFE [*to* GLOUCESTER]   Too true—and bought his
          climbing very dear.
GLOUCESTER [*to* SIMPCOX]   Mass,° thou loved'st plums well   *By the Mass (an oath)*
          that wouldst venture so.
SIMPCOX   Alas, good master, my wife desired some damsons,°   *tiny plums; testicles*
105   And made me climb with danger of my life.
GLOUCESTER [*aside*]   A subtle knave, but yet it shall not serve.
     [*To* SIMPCOX] Let me see thine eyes: wink° now, now open   *close your eyes*
     them. In my opinion yet thou seest not well.
SIMPCOX   Yes, master, clear as day, I thank God and Saint Alban.
110 GLOUCESTER   Sayst thou me so? [*Pointing*] What colour is this cloak of?
SIMPCOX   Red, master; red as blood.
GLOUCESTER   Why, that's well said.
     [*Pointing*] And his cloak?
SIMPCOX   Why, that's green.

---

4. Town on the Scottish border, far from St. Albans.   5. Slang for "female thighs and genitals."

GLOUCESTER [*pointing*]   And what colour's
     His hose?
SIMPCOX   Yellow, master; yellow as gold.
GLOUCESTER   And what colour's my gown?
SIMPCOX   Black, sir; coal-black, as jet.°   *glossy black stone*
115 KING HENRY   Why, then, thou know'st what colour jet is of?
SUFFOLK   And yet I think jet did he never see.
GLOUCESTER   But cloaks and gowns before this day, a many.°   *a multitude*
SIMPCOX'S WIFE   Never before this day in all his life.
GLOUCESTER   Tell me, sirrah, what's my name?
120 SIMPCOX   Alas, master, I know not.
GLOUCESTER [*pointing*]   What's his name?
SIMPCOX   I know not.
GLOUCESTER [*pointing*]   Nor his?
SIMPCOX   No, truly, sir.
125 GLOUCESTER [*pointing*]   Nor his name?
SIMPCOX   No indeed, master.
GLOUCESTER   What's thine own name?
SIMPCOX   Simon[6] Simpcox, an it please you, master.
GLOUCESTER   Then, Simon, sit thou there the lying'st knave
130   In Christendom. If thou hadst been born blind
     Thou mightst as well have known our names as thus
     To name the several colours we do wear.
     Sight may distinguish colours, but suddenly
     To nominate° them all—it is impossible.   *name*
135   Saint Alban here hath done a miracle.
     Would you not think his cunning° to be great   *skill*
     That could restore this cripple to his legs again?
SIMPCOX   O master, that you could!
GLOUCESTER [*to the* MAYOR *and aldermen*]   My masters of Saint
     Albans, have you not
140   Beadles[7] in your town, and things called whips?
MAYOR   We have, my lord, an if it please your grace.
GLOUCESTER   Then send for one presently.°   *immediately*
MAYOR [*to a townsman*]   Sirrah, go fetch the beadle hither
     straight.   *Exit one*
GLOUCESTER   Bring me a stool.
          [*A stool is brought*]
     [*To* SIMPCOX]   Now, sirrah, if you mean
145   To save yourself from whipping, leap me° o'er   *for me*
     This stool and run away.
SIMPCOX   Alas, master,
     I am not able even to stand alone.
     You go about to torture me in vain.
          Enter a BEADLE *with whips*
GLOUCESTER   Well, sirrah, we must have you find your legs.
150   [*To the* BEADLE] Whip him till he leap over that same stool.
BEADLE   I will, my lord.
          [*To* SIMPCOX] Come on, sirrah, off with your doublet quickly.

---

6. Q and F both call the character "Sander Simpcox" at this point. At line 93 of F, however, Simpcox refers to himself as "Simon." It has been proposed that "Sander" was the name of an actor who played the part of Simpcox, that his name entered Q at this point, and that this portion of F derives from Q.
7. Minor parish officials who administered punishment to vagabonds and those guilty of petty offenses.

SIMPCOX   Alas, master, what shall I do? I am not able to stand.
 After the BEADLE *hath hit him once, he leaps over the*
 stool and runs away. [*Some of the townsmen*] *follow*
 and cry, 'A miracle! A miracle!'
 KING HENRY   O God, seest thou this and bear'st so long?

155 QUEEN MARGARET   It made me laugh to see the villain run!
 GLOUCESTER [*to the* BEADLE]   Follow the knave, and take this
  drab° away.   *slut*
 SIMPCOX'S WIFE   Alas, sir, we did it for pure need.° *out of utter poverty*
        [*Exit the* BEADLE *with the* WIFE]
 GLOUCESTER [*to the* MAYOR]   Let them be whipped through
  every market-town
 Till they come to Berwick, from whence they came.
    Exeunt [*the*] MAYOR [*and any remaining townsmen*]

160 CARDINAL BEAUFORT   Duke Humphrey has done a miracle today.
 SUFFOLK   True: made the lame to leap and fly away.
 GLOUCESTER   But you have done more miracles than I—
 You made, in a day, my lord, whole towns to fly.[8]
    Enter the Duke of BUCKINGHAM
 KING HENRY   What tidings with our cousin Buckingham?

165 BUCKINGHAM   Such as my heart doth tremble to unfold.
 A sort of naughty persons, lewdly bent,[9]
 Under the countenance and confederacy° *protection and complicity*
 Of Lady Eleanor, the Protector's wife,
 The ringleader and head of all this rout,
170 Have practised° dangerously against your state, *plotted*
 Dealing with witches and with conjurors,
 Whom we have apprehended in the fact,° *in the very act*
 Raising up wicked spirits from under ground,
 Demanding of King Henry's life and death
175 And other° of your highness' Privy Council. *other members*
 And here's the answer the devil did make to them.
    [BUCKINGHAM *gives* KING HENRY *the writings*][1]
 KING HENRY [*reads*]   'First of the King: what shall of him become?
 The Duke yet lives that Henry shall depose,
 But him outlive and die a violent death.'
180 God's will be done in all. Well, to the rest.
 [*Reads*] 'Tell me what fate awaits the Duke of Suffolk?
 By water shall he die, and take his end.'
 SUFFOLK [*aside*]   By water must the Duke of Suffolk die?
 It must be so, or else the devil doth lie.
185 KING HENRY [*reads*]   'What shall betide the Duke of Somerset?
 Let him shun castles. Safer shall he be
 Upon the sandy plains than where castles mounted stand.'
 CARDINAL BEAUFORT [*to* GLOUCESTER]   And so, my Lord
  Protector, by this means
 Your lady is forthcoming° yet at London. *in custody*
190 [*Aside to* GLOUCESTER] This news, I think, hath turned your
  weapon's edge.°   *blunted your sword*

---

8. Referring to the French towns Suffolk gave away
when he arranged Henry's marriage to Margaret.
9. A gang of evil people, wickedly inclined.
1. Neither Q nor F directs Buckingham to hand Henry
the prophecies, but he clearly must do so if, as in Q,

Henry is to read them out at this point. Lines 177–87
follow the substance of York's reading of the prophecies
in F's 1.4, but they have been reconstructed by the
Oxford editors to fit their quarto placement here. For
details, see the Textual Variants.

'Tis like, my lord, you will not keep your hour.[2]
GLOUCESTER   Ambitious churchman, leave° to afflict my heart.   *cease*
Sorrow and grief have vanquished all my powers,
And, vanquished as I am, I yield to thee
195   Or to the meanest groom.°   *poorest servant*
KING HENRY   O God, what mischiefs work the wicked ones,
Heaping confusion on their own heads thereby!
QUEEN MARGARET   Gloucester, see here the tainture° of thy nest,   *defilement*
And look thyself be faultless, thou wert best.
200   GLOUCESTER   Madam, for myself, to heaven I do appeal,
How I have loved my King and common weal;
And for my wife, I know not how it stands.
Sorry I am to hear what I have heard.
Noble she is, but if she have forgot
205   Honour and virtue and conversed° with such   *consulted*
As, like to pitch, defile nobility,
I banish her my bed and company,[3]
And give her as a prey to law and shame
That hath dishonoured Gloucester's honest name.
210   KING HENRY   Well, for this night we will repose us here;
Tomorrow toward London back again,
To look into this business thoroughly,
And call these foul offenders to their answers,
And poise° the cause in justice' equal scales,   *weigh*
215   Whose beam stands sure,[4] whose rightful cause prevails.

Flourish. Exeunt

2.2

Enter the Duke of YORK *and the Earls of* SALISBURY
and WARWICK

YORK   Now, my good lords of Salisbury and Warwick,
Our simple supper ended, give me leave
In this close walk° to satisfy myself   *secluded path*
In craving your opinion of my title,
5   Which is infallible, to England's crown.
SALISBURY   My lord, I long to hear it out at full.
WARWICK   Sweet York, begin, and if thy claim be good,
The Nevilles are thy subjects to command.
YORK   Then thus:
10   Edward the Third, my lords, had seven sons:
The first, Edward the Black Prince, Prince of Wales;
The second, William of Hatfield; and the third,
Lionel Duke of Clarence; next to whom
Was John of Gaunt, the Duke of Lancaster;
15   The fifth was Edmund Langley, Duke of York;
The sixth was Thomas of Woodstock, Duke of Gloucester;
William of Windsor was the seventh and last.
Edward the Black Prince died before his father
And left behind him Richard, his only son,

---

2. Appointment (for the duel previously arranged between Gloucester and Cardinal Beaufort).
3. Echoing the language of church law, which permitted marital separation "from bed and board" in cases of adultery, heresy, and cruelty.

4. Whose bar (from which the two scales are suspended) is perfectly balanced and therefore allows accurate measurements.
2.2 Location: The Duke of York's garden, London.

20   Who, after Edward the Third's death, reigned as king
      Till Henry Bolingbroke, Duke of Lancaster,
      The eldest son and heir of John of Gaunt,
      Crowned by the name of Henry the Fourth,
      Seized on the realm, deposed the rightful king,
25   Sent his poor queen to France from whence she came,
      And him to Pomfret; where, as well you know,
      Harmless Richard was murdered traitorously.
    WARWICK [to SALISBURY]   Father, the Duke of York hath told the truth;
      Thus got the house of Lancaster the crown.
30 YORK   Which now they hold by force and not by right;
      For Richard, the first son's heir, being dead,
      The issue of the next son should have reigned.
    SALISBURY   But William of Hatfield died without an heir.
    YORK   The third son, Duke of Clarence, from whose line
35   I claim the crown, had issue Phillipe, a daughter,
      Who married Edmund Mortimer, Earl of March;[1]
      Edmund had issue, Roger, Earl of March;
      Roger had issue, Edmund, Anne and Eleanor.
    SALISBURY   This Edmund, in the reign of Bolingbroke,
40   As I have read, laid claim unto the crown,
      And, but for Owain Glyndŵr, had been king,
      Who kept him in captivity till he died.
      But to the rest.
    YORK   His eldest sister, Anne,
      My mother, being heir unto the crown,
45   Married Richard, Earl of Cambridge, who was son
      To Edmund Langley, Edward the Third's fifth son.
      By her I claim the kingdom: she was heir
      To Roger, Earl of March, who was the son
      Of Edmund Mortimer, who married Phillipe,
50   Sole daughter unto Lionel, Duke of Clarence.
      So if the issue of the elder son
      Succeed before the younger, I am king.
    WARWICK   What plain proceedings is more plain than this?
      Henry doth claim the crown from John of Gaunt,
55   The fourth son; York claims it from the third:
      Till Lionel's issue fails, John's should not reign.
      It fails not yet, but flourishes in thee
      And in thy sons, fair slips of such a stock.[2]
      Then, father Salisbury, kneel we together,
60   And in this private plot° be we the first   plot of ground
      That shall salute our rightful sovereign
      With honour of his birthright to the crown.
    SALISBURY and WARWICK [kneeling]   Long live our sovereign
          Richard, England's king!
    YORK   We thank you, lords;

---

1. Like Raphael Holinshed and Edward Hall, whose chronicles Shakespeare used as sources for this play, Shakespeare conflates Edmund Mortimer, the fifth Earl of March, who was named heir to the throne by Richard II, with his uncle of the same name who was captured by Glyndŵr, a Welsh lord Shakespeare was later to depict in *1 Henry IV* as a rebel against the King. Although Shakespeare here says Glyndŵr kept Mortimer imprisoned until he died, in *1 Henry IV* he follows the chronicles in having Mortimer eventually marry Glyndŵr's daughter.
2. Fair cuttings of such a tree.

[SALISBURY *and* WARWICK *rise*]

      but I am not your king

65 Till I be crowned, and that° my sword be stained   *until*
 With heart-blood of the house of Lancaster—
 And that's not suddenly to be performed,
 But with advice° and silent secrecy.   *deliberation*
 Do you, as I do, in these dangerous days,
70 Wink at° the Duke of Suffolk's insolence,   *Ignore*
 At Beaufort's pride, at Somerset's ambition,
 At Buckingham, and all the crew of them,
 Till they have snared the shepherd of the flock,
 That virtuous prince, the good Duke Humphrey.
75 'Tis that they seek, and they, in seeking that,
 Shall find their deaths, if York can prophesy.
SALISBURY My lord, break off—we know your mind at full.
WARWICK My heart assures me that the Earl of Warwick
 Shall one day make the Duke of York a king.
80 YORK And Neville, this I do assure myself—
 Richard shall live to make the Earl of Warwick
 The greatest man in England but the King.   *Exeunt*

2.3

  Sound trumpets. Enter KING HENRY *and state,° with*   *persons of rank*
  guard, to banish the DUCHESS: KING HENRY *and* QUEEN
  [MARGARET], *Duke Humphrey [of* GLOUCESTER], *the*
  Duke of SUFFOLK *and the Duke of* BUCKINGHAM,
  CARDINAL [BEAUFORT], *and, led with officers, Dame*
  Eleanor Cobham [the DUCHESS, *Margery Jordan the*
  WITCH, *John* SOUTHWELL *and Sir John* HUME *the two*
  priests, and Roger BOLINGBROKE *the conjuror]; then*
  enter to them the Duke of YORK *and the Earls of*
  SALISBURY *and* WARWICK[1]

KING HENRY [*to the* DUCHESS] Stand forth, Dame Eleanor
 Cobham, Gloucester's wife.
  [*She comes forward*]
 In sight of God and us your guilt is great;
 Receive the sentence of the law for sins
 Such as by God's book are adjudged to death.[2]
 [*To the* WITCH, SOUTHWELL, HUME, *and* BOLINGBROKE] You
5   four, from hence to prison back again;
 From thence, unto the place of execution.
 The witch in Smithfield[3] shall be burned to ashes,
 And you three shall be strangled° on the gallows.   *hanged*
    [*Exeunt* WITCH, SOUTHWELL, HUME, *and*
         BOLINGBROKE, guarded]
 [*To the* DUCHESS] You, madam, for° you are more nobly born,   *because*
10 Despoilèd° of your honour in your life,   *Deprived*
 Shall, after three days' open penance done,
 Live in your country here in banishment

2.3 Location: A London hall of justice.
1. F's stage direction simply reads "Sound Trumpets. Enter the King and State, with Guard to banish the Duchess." Q does not mention Jordan, the two priests, or Bolingbroke, but F clearly requires them.
2. *Receive . . . death*: alluding to Exodus 22:18: "Thou shalt not suffer a witch to live." At times throughout Elizabeth's reign, witch hunts were conducted and laws against witchcraft strictly enforced.
3. Famous as the site in London where heretics were burned.

With Sir John Stanley in the Isle of Man.[4]
DUCHESS Welcome is banishment; welcome were my death.
15 GLOUCESTER Eleanor, the law, thou seest, hath judgèd thee;
I cannot justify° whom the law condemns.   *excuse*
                    Exit [the DUCHESS, guarded]
Mine eyes are full of tears, my heart of grief.
Ah, Humphrey, this dishonour in thine age
Will bring thy head with sorrow to the grave.
20 [*To* KING HENRY] I beseech your majesty, give me leave to go.
Sorrow would° solace, and mine age would ease.   *desires*
KING HENRY Stay, Humphrey Duke of Gloucester. Ere thou go,
Give up thy staff.[5] Henry will to himself
Protector be; and God shall be my hope,
25 My stay, my guide, and lantern to my feet.
And go in peace, Humphrey, no less beloved
Than when thou wert Protector to thy King.
QUEEN MARGARET I see no reason why a king of years°   *who is of age*
Should be to be° protected like a child.   *need to be*
30 God and King Henry govern England's helm!
Give up your staff, sir, and the King his° realm.   *the king's*
GLOUCESTER My staff? Here, noble Henry, is my staff.
As willingly do I the same resign
As erst° thy father Henry made it mine;   *formerly*
35 And even as willing at thy feet I leave it
As others would ambitiously receive it.
          [*He lays the staff at King Henry's feet*]
Farewell, good King. When I am dead and gone,
May honourable peace attend thy throne.   *Exit*
QUEEN MARGARET Why, now is Henry King and Margaret Queen,
40 And Humphrey Duke of Gloucester scarce himself,
That bears so shrewd a maim;[6] two pulls° at once—   *pluckings; tugs*
His lady banished and a limb° lopped off.   *(his staff)*
          [*She picks up the staff*]
This staff of honour raught,° there let it stand   *seized*
Where it best fits to be, in Henry's hand.
          [*She gives the staff to* KING HENRY]
45 SUFFOLK Thus droops this lofty pine and hangs his sprays;°   *branches*
Thus Eleanor's pride dies in her youngest days.°   *in its youth*
YORK Lords, let him go. Please it your majesty,
This is the day appointed for the combat,
And ready are the appellant° and defendant—   *challenger*
50 The armourer and his man—to enter the lists,°   *dueling area*
So please your highness to behold the fight.
QUEEN MARGARET Ay, good my lord, for purposely therefor
Left I the court to see this quarrel tried.
KING HENRY A° God's name, see the lists and all things fit;   *In*
55 Here let them end it, and God defend the right.
YORK I never saw a fellow worse bestead,°   *prepared*
Or more afraid to fight, than is the appellant,
The servant of this armourer, my lords.

---

4. An island off England's northwest coast.
5. Emblem of his office as Protector.
6. Who endures so painful a mutilation.

Enter at one door [HORNER] *the armourer and his*
NEIGHBOURS, *drinking to him so much that he is*
drunken; and he enters with a drum[mer] before him
and [carrying] his staff with a sandbag fastened to it.
[Enter] at the other door [PETER] *his man, [also] with*
a drum[mer] and [a staff with] sandbag, and PRENTICES
drinking to him

FIRST NEIGHBOUR [*offering drink to* HORNER]   Here, neighbour
60   Horner, I drink to you in a cup of sack,° and fear not, neigh-   *sherry*
bour, you shall do well enough.
SECOND NEIGHBOUR [*offering drink to* HORNER]   And here,
neighbour, here's a cup of charneco.°   *port*
THIRD NEIGHBOUR [*offering drink to* HORNER]   Here's a pot of
65   good double° beer, neighbour, drink and be merry, and fear   *extra-strong*
not your man.
HORNER [*accepting the offers of drink*]   Let it come,° i'faith I'll   *Pass it around*
pledge you all, and a fig[7] for Peter.
FIRST PRENTICE [*offering drink to* PETER]   Here, Peter, I drink to
70   thee, and be not afeard.
SECOND PRENTICE [*offering drink to* PETER]   Here, Peter, here's
a pint of claret wine for thee.
THIRD PRENTICE [*offering drink to* PETER]   And here's a quart for
me, and be merry, Peter, and fear not thy master. Fight for
75   credit° of the prentices!   *the honor*
PETER [*refusing the offers of drink*]   I thank you all. Drink and
pray for me, I pray you, for I think I have taken my last
draught in this world. Here, Robin, an if° I die, I give thee my   *an if = if*
apron; and, Will, thou shalt have my hammer; and here, Tom,
80   take all the money that I have. O Lord bless me, I pray God,
for I am never able to deal with my master, he hath learned so
much fence° already.   *fencing skill*
SALISBURY   Come, leave your drinking, and fall to blows.
[*To* PETER] Sirrah, what's thy name?
85   PETER   Peter, forsooth.
SALISBURY   Peter? What more?
PETER   Thump.
SALISBURY   Thump! Then see that thou thump thy master well.
HORNER   Masters, I am come hither, as it were, upon my man's
90   instigation, to prove him a knave and myself an honest man;
and touching the Duke of York, I will take my death° I never   *stake my life on it*
meant him any ill, nor the King, nor the Queen; and therefore,
Peter, have at thee° with a downright° blow.   *I come at thee / vertical*
YORK   Dispatch; this knave's tongue begins to double.°   *to slur his words*
Sound trumpets [an] alarum to the combatants.[8]
They fight and PETER *hits* [HORNER] *on the head and*
strikes him down
95   HORNER   Hold, Peter, hold—I confess, I confess treason.
                                           He dies
YORK [*to an attendant, pointing to* HORNER]   Take away his
weapon. [*To* PETER] Fellow, thank God and the good wine in
thy master's wame.°   *belly*

---

7. Slang for "vulva"; hence, an obscene insult. It was
typically accompanied by a gesture in which the thumb
was thrust between two closed fingers or into the
mouth.
8. In F, the line "Sound Trumpets, Alarum to the Combatants" is spoken by York as part of his prior speech.

PETER *He kneels down*[9]   O God, have I overcome mine enemy
100   in this presence? O, Peter, thou hast prevailed in right.
KING HENRY [*to attendants, pointing to* HORNER] Go, take hence
            that traitor from our sight,
        For by his death we do perceive his guilt.
        And God in justice hath revealed to us
        The truth and innocence of this poor fellow,
105   Which he° had thought to have murdered wrongfully.   *Whom he (Horner)*
        [*To* PETER] Come, fellow, follow us for thy reward.
            Sound a flourish. Exeunt [some carrying HORNER'*s body*]

                                    2.4
            Enter Duke Humphrey [of GLOUCESTER] *and his men*
            in mourning cloaks[1]
GLOUCESTER   Thus sometimes hath the brightest day a cloud;
        And after summer evermore succeeds°   *follows*
        Barren winter, with his wrathful nipping° cold;   *biting*
        So cares and joys abound as seasons fleet.°   *fly by*
5   Sirs, what's o'clock?
SERVANT   Ten, my lord.
GLOUCESTER   Ten is the hour that was appointed me
        To watch the coming of my punished Duchess;
        Uneath° may she endure the flinty streets,   *Scarcely*
10   To tread them with her tender-feeling feet.
        Sweet Nell, ill can thy noble mind abrook°   *endure*
        The abject° people gazing on thy face   *lowly born*
        With envious° looks, laughing at thy shame,   *spiteful*
        That erst did follow thy proud chariot wheels
15   When thou didst ride in triumph through the streets.
        But soft, I think she comes; and I'll prepare
        My tear-stained eyes to see her miseries.
            Enter the DUCHESS, *Dame Eleanor Cobham, barefoot,*
            [*with*] *a white sheet about her, written verses pinned*
            on her back[2] [*and carrying a*] *wax candle in her hand;*
            [*she is*] *accompanied with the [two]* SHERIFFS
            of London, and Sir John STANLEY, *and officers with*
            bills and halberds[3]
SERVANT [*to* GLOUCESTER]   So please your grace, we'll take her°   *rescue her by force*
        from the sheriffs.
GLOUCESTER   No, stir not for your lives, let her pass by.
20 DUCHESS   Come you, my lord, to see my open shame?
        Now thou dost penance too. Look how they gaze,
        See how the giddy multitude do point
        And nod their heads, and throw their eyes on thee.
        Ah, Gloucester, hide thee from their hateful° looks,   *full of hate*
25   And, in thy closet° pent up, rue my shame,   *private chamber*
        And ban° thine enemies—both mine and thine.   *curse*
GLOUCESTER   Be patient, gentle Nell; forget this grief.
DUCHESS   Ah, Gloucester, teach me to forget myself;
        For whilst I think I am thy married wife,

---

9. Only Q records, "He [Peter] kneels down," just as Q,
and not F, indicates, "He [Horner] dies" (line 95).
2.4 Location: A London street.
1. Hooded black garments worn to funerals to express
sorrow.

2. Eleanor's offenses were presumably detailed in
these verses.
3. Both bills and halberds were long-handled weapons.
Bills had a curved blade, halberds an axlike blade with
a spike at the back.

30   And thou a prince, Protector of this land,
      Methinks I should not thus be led along,
      Mailed up[4] in shame, with papers on my back,
      And followed with a rabble that rejoice
      To see my tears and hear my deep-fet groans.[5]
35   The ruthless flint doth cut my tender feet,
      And when I start,° the envious people laugh,   *flinch*
      And bid me be advisèd how I tread.
      Ah, Humphrey, can I bear this shameful yoke?
      Trowest° thou that e'er I'll look upon the world,   *Believeth*
40   Or count them happy that° enjoys the sun?   *who*
      No, dark shall be my light, and night my day;
      To think upon my pomp shall be my hell.
      Sometime I'll say I am Duke Humphrey's wife,
      And he a prince and ruler of the land;
45   Yet so he ruled, and such a prince he was,
      As he stood by whilst I, his forlorn Duchess,
      Was made a wonder and a pointing stock°   *an object of scorn*
      To every idle rascal° follower.   *lowborn*
      But be thou mild and blush not at my shame,
50   Nor stir at nothing till the axe of death
      Hang over thee, as sure it shortly will.
      For Suffolk, he that can do all in all
      With her° that hateth thee and hates us all,   *(Margaret)*
      And York, and impious Beaufort that false priest,
55   Have all limed bushes[6] to betray thy wings,
      And fly thou how thou canst, they'll tangle thee.
      But fear not thou until thy foot be snared,
      Nor never seek prevention of° thy foes.   *safeguards against*
GLOUCESTER   Ah, Nell, forbear; thou aimest all awry.
60   I must offend before I be attainted,°   *condemned for treason*
      And had I twenty times so many foes,
      And each of them had twenty times their power,
      All these could not procure me any scathe°   *harm*
      So long as I am loyal, true, and crimeless.
65   Wouldst have me rescue thee from this reproach?
      Why, yet thy scandal were not wiped away,
      But I in danger for the breach of law.
      Thy greatest help is quiet, gentle Nell.
      I pray thee sort° thy heart to patience.   *adapt*
70   These few days' wonder will be quickly worn.[7]
            Enter a HERALD
HERALD   I summon your grace to his majesty's parliament
      holden° at Bury[8] the first of this next month.   *to be held*
GLOUCESTER   And my consent ne'er asked herein before?
      This is close° dealing. Well, I will be there.   *Exit* HERALD   *secret*
75   My Nell, I take my leave; and, Master Sheriff,
      Let not her penance exceed the King's commission.
FIRST SHERIFF   An't please your grace, here my commission stays,°   *ends*

---

4. Enveloped: a term from falconry that describes the
condition of a hawk wrapped in cloth so as to prevent
its flying away.
5. Moans fetched from deep within me.

6. Coated bushes with birdlime (see note to 1.3.92).
7. What was marveled at for a few days will soon be
forgotten.
8. Bury St. Edmunds, a town in Suffolk.

And Sir John Stanley is appointed now
To take her with him to the Isle of Man.

80   GLOUCESTER   Must you, Sir John, protect° my lady here?   *keep in custody*
STANLEY   So am I given in charge, may't please your grace.
GLOUCESTER   Entreat° her not the worse in that° I pray   *Treat / just because*
You use her well. The world may laugh again,
And I may live to do you kindness if
85   You do it her. And so, Sir John, farewell.
            [GLOUCESTER *begins to leave*]
DUCHESS   What, gone, my lord, and bid me not farewell?
GLOUCESTER   Witness my tears—I cannot stay to speak.
            Exeunt GLOUCESTER *and his men*
DUCHESS   Art thou gone too? All comfort go with thee,
For none abides with me. My joy is death—
90   Death, at whose name I oft have been afeard,
Because I wished this world's eternity.°   *immortality on earth*
Stanley, I prithee go and take me hence.
I care not whither, for I beg no favour,
Only convey me where thou art commanded.
95   STANLEY   Why, madam, that is to the Isle of Man,
There to be used according to your state.°   *rank; condition*
DUCHESS   That's bad enough, for I am but reproach;°   *in a state of shame*
And shall I then be used reproachfully?
STANLEY   Like to a duchess and Duke Humphrey's lady,
100   According to that state you shall be used.
DUCHESS   Sheriff, farewell, and better than I fare,
Although thou hast been conduct° of my shame.   *conductor*
FIRST SHERIFF   It is my office, and, madam, pardon me.
DUCHESS   Ay, ay, farewell—thy office is discharged.
            [*Exeunt* SHERIFFS]
105   Come, Stanley, shall we go?
STANLEY   Madam, your penance done, throw off this sheet,
And go we to attire you for our journey.
DUCHESS   My shame will not be shifted⁹ with my sheet—
No, it will hang upon my richest robes
110   And show itself, attire me how I can.
Go, lead the way, I long to see my prison.   *Exeunt*

3.1

Sound a sennet. Enter to the parliament: enter two
heralds before, then the Duke[s] of BUCKINGHAM *and*
SUFFOLK, *and then the Duke of* YORK *and* CARDINAL
[BEAUFORT], *and then* KING [HENRY] *and* QUEEN [MAR-
GARET,] *and then the Earl[s]* OF SALISBURY *and* WAR-
WICK [*with attendants*]

KING HENRY   I muse° my lord of Gloucester is not come   *am surprised*
'Tis not his wont° to be the hindmost man,   *habit*
Whate'er occasion keeps him from us now.
QUEEN MARGARET   Can you not see, or will ye not observe,
5   The strangeness of his altered countenance?
With what a majesty he bears himself?

9. Changed, with a pun on "shifted" as meaning "put   **3.1** Location: A great hall, Bury St. Edmunds.
on new undergarments."

How insolent of late he is become?
How proud, how peremptory, and unlike himself?
We know the time since° he was mild and affable,   *We remember when*
10 And if we did but glance a far-off look,
Immediately he was upon his knee,
That all the court admired him for° submission.   *was amazed at his*
But meet him now, and be it in the morn
When everyone will give the time of day,°   *say good morning*
15 He knits his brow, and shows an angry eye,
And passeth by with stiff unbowèd knee,
Disdaining° duty that to us belongs.   *Not paying*
Small curs are not regarded when they grin,°   *snarl; show the teeth*
But great men tremble when the lion roars—
20 And Humphrey is no little man in England.
First, note that he is near you in descent,
And, should you fall, he is the next will mount.°   *mount the throne*
Meseemeth then it is no policy,°   *not prudent*
Respecting° what a rancorous mind he bears   *Considering*
25 And his advantage following your decease,
That he should come about your royal person,
Or be admitted to your highness' Council.
By flattery hath he won the commons' hearts,
And when he please to make commotion,°   *incite rebellion*
30 'Tis to be feared they all will follow him.
Now 'tis the spring, and weeds are shallow-rooted;
Suffer° them now, and they'll o'ergrow the garden,   *Tolerate*
And choke the herbs for want of husbandry.
The reverent care I bear unto my lord
35 Made me collect° these dangers in the Duke.   *deduce*
If it be fond,° call it a woman's fear;   *foolish*
Which fear, if better reasons can supplant,
I will subscribe° and say I wronged the Duke.   *concur*
My lord of Suffolk, Buckingham, and York,
40 Reprove° my allegation if you can,   *Refute*
Or else conclude my words effectual.°   *decisive*
SUFFOLK   Well hath your highness seen into this Duke,
And had I first been put to speak my mind,
I think I should have told your grace's tale.
45 The Duchess by his subornation,°   *instigation*
Upon my life, began her devilish practices;
Or if he were not privy to those faults,°   *crimes*
Yet by reputing° of his high descent,   *boasting*
As next the King he was successive heir,
50 And such high vaunts° of his nobility,   *boasts*
Did instigate the bedlam¹ brainsick Duchess
By wicked means to frame° our sovereign's fall.   *devise*
Smooth runs the water where the brook is deep,
And in his simple show° he harbours treason.   *outward appearance*
55 The fox barks not when he would steal the lamb.
[*To* KING HENRY] No, no, my sovereign, Gloucester is a man
Unsounded° yet, and full of deep deceit.   *Unfathomed*

---

1. Insane (a shortened form of "Bethlehem Hospital," a notorious asylum maintained by the City of London).

CARDINAL BEAUFORT [*to* KING HENRY]   Did he not, contrary to
    form of law,
    Devise strange° deaths for small offences done?   *cruel; illegal*
60   YORK [*to* KING HENRY]   And did he not, in his Protectorship,
    Levy great sums of money through the realm
    For soldiers' pay in France, and never sent it,
    By means whereof the towns each day revolted?
    BUCKINGHAM [*to* KING HENRY]   Tut, these are petty faults to°   *compared to*
    faults unknown,
65   Which time will bring to light in smooth Duke Humphrey.
    KING HENRY   My lords, at once:° the care you have of us   *once and for all*
    To mow down thorns that would annoy our foot
    Is worthy praise, but shall I speak my conscience?
    Our kinsman Gloucester is as innocent
70   From meaning treason to our royal person
    As is the sucking lamb or harmless dove.
    The Duke is virtuous, mild, and too well given
    To dream on evil or to work my downfall.
    QUEEN MARGARET   Ah, what's more dangerous than this fond
    affiance?°   *foolish confidence*
75   Seems he a dove? His feathers are but borrowed,
    For he's disposèd as the hateful raven.
    Is he a lamb? His skin is surely lent him,
    For he's inclined as is the ravenous wolf.[2]
    Who cannot steal a shape that means deceit?[3]
80   Take heed, my lord, the welfare of us all
    Hangs on the cutting short that fraudful° man.   *treacherous*
          Enter the Duke of SOMERSET
    SOMERSET [*kneeling before* KING HENRY]   All health unto my
    gracious sovereign.
    KING HENRY   Welcome, Lord Somerset. What news from France?
    SOMERSET   That all your interest in those territories
85   Is utterly bereft you—all is lost.
    KING HENRY   Cold news, Lord Somerset; but God's will be done.
          [SOMERSET *rises*]
    YORK [*aside*]   Cold news for me, for I had hope of France,
    As firmly as I hope for fertile England.
    Thus are my blossoms blasted° in the bud,   *withered*
90   And caterpillars eat my leaves away.
    But I will remedy this gear° ere long,   *business*
    Or sell my title for a glorious grave.
          Enter Duke Humphrey [of] GLOUCESTER
    GLOUCESTER [*kneeling before* KING HENRY]   All happiness unto
    my lord the King.
    Pardon, my liege, that I have stayed° so long.   *delayed*
95   SUFFOLK   Nay, Gloucester, know that thou art come too soon
    Unless thou wert more loyal than thou art.
    I do arrest thee of high treason here.
    GLOUCESTER [*rising*]   Well, Suffolk's Duke, thou shalt not see me blush,
    Nor change my countenance for this arrest.

---

2. *Is he . . . wolf*: alluding to the Sermon on the Mount, which warns of "false prophets, which come to you in sheep's clothing, but inwardly they are ravening wolves". (Matthew 7:15).

3. Who that intends to deceive cannot assume an appropriate disguise?

100 A heart unspotted is not easily daunted.
The purest spring is not so free from mud
As I am clear from treason to my sovereign.
Who can accuse me? Wherein am I guilty?
YORK 'Tis thought, my lord, that you took bribes of France,
105 And, being Protector, stayed° the soldiers' pay,   *withheld*
By means whereof his highness hath lost France.
GLOUCESTER Is it but thought so? What are they that think it?
I never robbed the soldiers of their pay,
Nor ever had one penny bribe from France.
110 So help me God, as I have watched the night,°   *stayed up all night*
Ay, night by night, in studying good for England,
That doit° that e'er I wrested from the King,   *a coin of little value*
Or any groat° I hoarded to my use,   *a coin worth 4 pence*
Be brought against me at my trial day!
115 No: many a pound of mine own proper store,°   *personal fortune*
Because I would not tax the needy commons,
Have I dispursèd° to the garrisons,   *paid*
And never asked for restitution.
CARDINAL BEAUFORT It serves you well, my lord, to say so much.
120 GLOUCESTER I say no more than truth, so help me God.
YORK In your Protectorship you did devise
Strange tortures for offenders, never heard of,
That° England was defamed by° tyranny.   *So that / was infamous for*
GLOUCESTER Why, 'tis well known that whiles I was Protector
125 Pity was all the fault that was in me,
For I should° melt at an offender's tears,   *would*
And lowly words were ransom for their fault.
Unless it were a bloody murderer,
Or foul felonious thief that fleeced poor passengers,°   *travelers*
130 I never gave them condign° punishment.   *well-deserved*
Murder, indeed—that bloody sin—I tortured
Above the felon or what trespass else.[4]
SUFFOLK My lord, these faults are easy,° quickly answerèd,   *slight*
But mightier crimes are laid unto your charge
135 Whereof you cannot easily purge yourself.
I do arrest you in his highness' name,
And here commit you to my good lord Cardinal
To keep until your further time of trial.
KING HENRY My lord of Gloucester, 'tis my special hope
140 That you will clear yourself from all suspense.°   *suspicion*
My conscience tells me you are innocent.
GLOUCESTER Ah, gracious lord, these days are dangerous.
Virtue is choked with foul ambition,
And charity chased hence by rancour's hand.
145 Foul subornation[5] is predominant,
And equity exiled° your highness' land.   *exiled from*
I know their complot° is to have my life,   *plot*
And if my death might make this island happy
And prove the period° of their tyranny,   *mark the end*
150 I would expend it with all willingness.
But mine is made the prologue to their play,

4. More than any other kind of crime.   5. Instigating others to commit crimes, including perjury.

For thousands more that yet suspect no peril
Will not conclude their plotted tragedy.
Beaufort's red sparkling eyes blab his heart's malice,
155 And Suffolk's cloudy brow his stormy hate;
Sharp Buckingham unburdens with his tongue
The envious load that lies upon his heart;
And doggèd° York that reaches at the moon, *currish; determined*
Whose overweening arm I have plucked back,
160 By false accuse° doth level° at my life. *accusation / aim*
[*To* QUEEN MARGARET] And you, my sovereign lady, with the rest,
Causeless have laid disgraces on my head,
And with your best endeavour have stirred up
My liefest liege° to be mine enemy. *dearest sovereign*
165 Ay, all of you have laid your heads together—
Myself had notice of your conventicles°— *secret meetings*
And all to make away my guiltless life.
I shall not want° false witness to condemn me, *lack*
Nor store of treasons to augment my guilt.
170 The ancient proverb will be well effected:
'A staff is quickly found to beat a dog'.
CARDINAL BEAUFORT [*to* KING HENRY]   My liege, his railing is intolerable.
If those that care to keep your royal person
From treason's secret knife and traitor's rage
175 Be thus upbraided, chid, and rated at,° *berated; scolded*
And the offender granted scope of speech,
'Twill make them cool in zeal unto your grace.
SUFFOLK [*to* KING HENRY]   Hath he not twit° our sovereign lady here *upbraided*
With ignominious words, though clerkly couched,° *cleverly phrased*
180 As if she had subornèd some to swear
False allegations to o'erthrow his state?° *high position*
QUEEN MARGARET   But I can give the loser leave to chide.
GLOUCESTER   Far truer spoke than meant. I lose indeed;
Beshrew° the winners, for they played me false! *Curse*
185 And well such losers may have leave to speak.
BUCKINGHAM [*to* KING HENRY]   He'll wrest the sense,° and hold *distort the meaning*
us here all day.
Lord Cardinal, he is your prisoner.
CARDINAL BEAUFORT [*to some of his attendants*]   Sirs, take
away the Duke and guard him sure.
GLOUCESTER   Ah, thus King Henry throws away his crutch
190 Before his legs be firm to bear his body.
Thus is the shepherd beaten from thy side,
And wolves are gnarling° who shall gnaw thee first. *snarling*
Ah, that my fear were false; ah, that it were!
For, good King Henry, thy decay° I fear. *ruin*
        Exit GLOUCESTER, [*guarded by*] *the Cardinal's men*
195 KING HENRY   My lords, what to your wisdoms seemeth best
Do or undo, as if ourself were here.
QUEEN MARGARET   What, will your highness leave the Parliament?
KING HENRY   Ay, Margaret, my heart is drowned with grief,
Whose flood begins to flow within mine eyes,
200 My body round engirt with misery;
For what's more miserable than discontent?
Ah, uncle Humphrey, in thy face I see

The map of honour, truth, and loyalty;
And yet, good Humphrey, is the hour to come
205 That e'er I proved thee false, or feared thy faith.°   *doubted your loyalty*
What louring° star now envies thy estate,   *gloomy*
That these great lords and Margaret our Queen
Do seek subversion of thy harmless life?
Thou never didst them wrong, nor no man wrong.
210 And as the butcher takes away the calf,
And binds the wretch, and beats it when it strains,
Bearing it to the bloody slaughterhouse,
Even so remorseless have they borne him hence;
And as the dam° runs lowing up and down,   *mother*
215 Looking the way her harmless young one went,
And can do naught but wail her darling's loss;
Even so myself bewails good Gloucester's case
With sad unhelpful tears, and with dimmed eyes
Look after him, and cannot do him good,°   *give him help*
220 So mighty are his vowèd enemies.
His fortunes I will weep, and 'twixt each groan,
Say 'Who's a traitor? Gloucester, he is none'.
                   Exeunt KING, SALISBURY, *and* WARWICK
QUEEN MARGARET   Free° lords, cold snow melts with the sun's hot beams.   *Noble*
Henry my lord is cold in great affairs,
225 Too full of foolish pity; and Gloucester's show
Beguiles him as the mournful crocodile
With sorrow snares relenting passengers,⁶
Or as the snake rolled in a flow'ring bank
With shining chequered slough° doth sting a child   *skin*
230 That for the beauty thinks it excellent.
Believe me, lords, were none more wise than I—
And yet herein I judge mine own wit good—
This Gloucester should be quickly rid the world
To rid us from the fear we have of him.
235 CARDINAL BEAUFORT   That he should die is worthy policy;
But yet we want a colour° for his death.   *pretext*
'Tis meet he be condemned by course of law.
SUFFOLK   But, in my mind, that were no policy.
The King will labour still° to save his life,   *continually*
240 The commons haply° rise to save his life;   *perhaps*
And yet we have but trivial argument°   *evidence*
More than mistrust° that shows him worthy death.   *Other than suspicion*
YORK   So that, by this, you would not have him die?
SUFFOLK   Ah, York, no man alive so fain as I.
245 YORK [*aside*]   'Tis York that hath more reason for his death.
[*Aloud*] But my lord Cardinal, and you my lord of Suffolk,
Say as you think, and speak it from your souls.
Were't not all one an empty° eagle were set   *a hungry*
To guard the chicken from a hungry kite,°   *bird of prey*
250 As place Duke Humphrey for the King's Protector?

6. Compassionate travelers. Sixteenth-century natural historians claimed that crocodiles moaned and wept in order to lure sympathetic humans to their death.

QUEEN MARGARET   So the poor chicken should be sure of death.

SUFFOLK   Madam, 'tis true; and were't not madness then

To make the fox surveyor° of the fold,   *guardian*

Who being accused a crafty murderer,

His guilt should be but idly posted over°   *foolishly ignored*

Because his purpose is not executed?

No—let him die in that he is a fox,

By nature proved an enemy to the flock,

Before his chaps° be stained with crimson blood,   *jaws*

As Humphrey, proved by reasons, to my liege.[7]

And do not stand on quillets° how to slay him;   *subtle distinctions*

Be it by gins,° by snares, by subtlety,   *traps*

Sleeping or waking, 'tis no matter how,

So he be dead; for that is good conceit°   *a good idea*

Which mates° him first that first intends deceit.   *checkmates; kills*

QUEEN MARGARET   Thrice-noble Suffolk, 'tis resolutely spoke.

SUFFOLK   Not resolute, except° so much were done;   *unless*

For things are often spoke and seldom meant;

But that° my heart accordeth with my tongue,   *to show that*

Seeing the deed is meritorious,

And to preserve my sovereign from his foe,

Say but the word and I will be his priest.[8]

CARDINAL BEAUFORT   But I would have him dead, my lord of Suffolk,

Ere you can take due orders for a priest.[9]

Say you consent and censure° well the deed,   *approve*

And I'll provide his executioner;

I tender so the safety of my liege.

SUFFOLK   Here is my hand; the deed is worthy doing.

QUEEN MARGARET   And so say I.

YORK   And I. And now we three have spoke it,

It skills not greatly who impugns our doom.[1]

Enter a POST

POST   Great lord, from Ireland am I come amain°   *in haste*

To signify that rebels there are up°   *up in arms*

And put the Englishmen unto the sword.

Send succours, lords, and stop the rage betime,°   *promptly*

Before the wound do grow uncurable;

For, being green,° there is great hope of help.   [*Exit*]   *fresh*

CARDINAL BEAUFORT   A breach that craves a quick expedient stop!

What counsel give you in this weighty cause?

YORK   That Somerset be sent as regent thither.

'Tis meet° that lucky ruler be employed—   *fit (said scornfully)*

Witness the fortune he hath had in France.

SOMERSET   If York, with all his far-fet° policy,   *cunning*

Had been the regent there instead of me,

He never would have stayed in France so long.

YORK   No, not to lose it all as thou hast done.

I rather would have lost my life betimes

---

7. Just as Humphrey proved (to be a fox or enemy) to
Henry.
8. I will kill him. Suffolk alludes to the priest's role
in administering the sacrament of last rites to dying

Christians.
9. Can become a priest; can arrange to have a priest
there.
1. It doesn't matter who questions our decision.

Than bring a burden of dishonour home
By staying there so long till all were lost.
300 Show me one scar charactered° on thy skin.   *inscribed*
Men's flesh preserved so whole do seldom win.
QUEEN MARGARET Nay, then, this spark will prove a raging fire
If wind and fuel be brought to feed it with.
No more, good York; sweet Somerset, be still.
305 Thy fortune, York, hadst thou been regent there,
Might happily° have proved far worse than his.   *perhaps*
YORK What, worse than naught? Nay, then a shame take all!
SOMERSET And, in the number,° thee that wishest shame.   *among them*
CARDINAL BEAUFORT My lord of York, try what your fortune is.
310 Th'uncivil kerns of Ireland² are in arms
And temper clay° with blood of Englishmen.   *moisten the earth*
To Ireland will you lead a band of men
Collected choicely, from each county some,
And try your hap° against the Irishmen?   *luck*
315 YORK I will, my lord, so please his majesty.
SUFFOLK Why, our authority is his consent,
And what we do establish he confirms.
Then, noble York, take thou this task in hand.
YORK I am content. Provide me soldiers, lords,
320 Whiles I take order° for mine own affairs.   *arrange*
SUFFOLK A charge, Lord York, that I will see performed.
But now return we to the false Duke Humphrey.
CARDINAL BEAUFORT No more of him—for I will deal with him
That henceforth he shall trouble us no more.
325 And so, break off; the day is almost spent.
Lord Suffolk, you and I must talk of that event.
YORK My lord of Suffolk, within fourteen days
At Bristol I expect my soldiers;
For there I'll ship them all for Ireland.
330 SUFFOLK I'll see it truly done, my lord of York.

Exeunt. Manet YORK³

330.1 YORK *Let me have some bands of chosen soldiers,*
And York shall try his fortune 'gainst those kerns.
QUEEN MARGARET *York, thou shalt. My lord of Buckingham,*
Let it be your charge to muster up such soldiers
330.5 *As shall suffice him in these needful wars.*
BUCKINGHAM *Madam, I will, and levy such a band*
As soon shall overcome those Irish rebels.
But, York, where shall those soliders stay° for thee   *wait*
YORK *At Bristol I will expect them ten days hence.*
330.10 BUCKINGHAM *Then thither shall they come, and*
so farewell.   *Exit*
YORK *Adieu, my lord of Buckingham.*
QUEEN MARGARET *Suffolk, remember what you have to do—*
And you, Lord Cardinal—concerning Duke Humphrey.

---

2. Barbaric Irish foot soldiers or rebels. Kerns were the most numerous, poorest, and most lightly armed of the Irish soldiers who fought against the English during Elizabeth's reign. Many Elizabethan writers described the Irish as an inferior, uncivilized "race" and used the term "kern" to signify all Irish opponents of England.

3. The entire debate on Duke Humphrey's death in 3.1 is handled differently by Q and F. Oxford retains F's version of the debate, but Q may represent authorial revision. The following indented Q lines (330.1–330.15), roughly corresponding to lines 310–30, are of particular interest because they supply Buckingham with speeches for this latter part of the scene.

'Twere good that you did see to it in time.

330.15 Come, let us go, that it may be performed.

Exeunt all. Manet YORK

YORK Now, York, or never, steel thy fearful thoughts,

And change misdoubt° to resolution. *fear*

Be that thou hop'st to be, or what thou art

Resign to death; it is not worth th'enjoying.

335 Let pale-faced fear keep° with the mean-born° man *dwell / lowborn*

And find no harbour in a royal heart.

Faster than springtime showers comes thought on thought,

And not a thought but thinks on dignity.° *high estate (kingship)*

My brain, more busy than the labouring spider,

340 Weaves tedious° snares to trap mine enemies. *laborious*

Well, nobles, well: 'tis politicly done

To send me packing with an host of men.

I fear me° you but warm the starvèd° snake, *I am afraid / frozen*

Who, cherished in your breasts, will sting your hearts.

345 'Twas men I lacked, and you will give them me.

I take it kindly. Yet be well assured

You put sharp weapons in a madman's hands.

Whiles I in Ireland nurse a mighty band,

I will stir up in England some black storm

350 Shall blow ten thousand souls to heaven or hell,

And this fell° tempest shall not cease to rage *ferocious*

Until the golden circuit° on my head *crown*

Like to the glorious sun's transparent beams

Do calm the fury of this mad-bred flaw.[4]

355 And for a minister° of my intent, *an agent*

I have seduced a headstrong Kentishman,

John Cade of Ashford,

To make commotion,° as full well he can, *rebellion*

Under the title of John Mortimer.[5]

360 In Ireland have I seen this stubborn Cade

Oppose himself against a troop of kerns,

And fought so long till that his thighs with darts[6]

Were almost like a sharp-quilled porcupine;

And in the end, being rescued, I have seen

365 Him caper° upright like a wild Morisco,[7] *leap*

Shaking the bloody darts as he° his bells. *as would the dancer*

Full often like a shag-haired[8] crafty kern

Hath he conversèd with the enemy

And, undiscovered, come to me again

370 And given me notice of their villainies.

This devil here shall be my substitute,

For that° John Mortimer, which now is dead, *Because*

In face, in gait, in speech, he doth resemble.

By this I shall perceive the commons' mind,

---

4. This storm ("flaw") created by madness.
5. The Mortimers are the family line by which York claims the crown. See York's account of his claim in 2.2.10–52.
6. Light spears or arrows, the weapons for which kerns were known.
7. A Moor who converted to Christianity; a morris dancer. Deriving from the Spanish word for "Moor," the morris dance was originally a Spanish dance that reenacted Christian battles with Moors. From the fifteenth century, it was associated with English popular festivals and was usually performed by men with bells attached to their legs who carried sticks and wore costumes from English folklore.
8. Alluding to the popular notion that the Irish grew "glibs," or long, thick bangs, in order to disguise themselves and escape punishment for their crimes.

375 How they affect° the house and claim of York.   *like*
Say he be taken, racked,⁹ and torturèd—
I know no pain they can inflict upon him
Will make him say I moved him to those arms.
Say that he thrive, as 'tis great like° he will—   *very likely*
380 Why then from Ireland come I with my strength
And reap the harvest which that coistrel° sowed.   *base fellow*
For Humphrey being dead, as he shall be,
And Henry put apart, the next for me.   *Exit*

3.2

The curtains [are] drawn [apart, revealing] Duke
Humphrey [of GLOUCESTER] *in his bed [with] two men*
*lying on his breast, smothering him in his bed*¹
FIRST MURDERER [*to the* SECOND MURDERER] Run to my lord
        of Suffolk—let him know
We have dispatched the Duke as he commanded.
SECOND MURDERER O that it were to do!² What have we done?
Didst ever hear a man so penitent?
        Enter the Duke of SUFFOLK
5 FIRST MURDERER Here comes my lord.
SUFFOLK Now, sirs, have you dispatched this thing?
FIRST MURDERER Ay, my good lord, he's dead.
SUFFOLK Why, that's well said. Go, get you to my house.
I will reward you for this venturous° deed.   *dangerous*
10 The King and all the peers are here at hand.
Have you laid fair° the bed? Is all things well,   *rearranged*
According as I gave directions?
FIRST MURDERER 'Tis, my good lord.
SUFFOLK Then draw the curtains close; away, be gone!
        Exeunt [the] MURDERERS [*drawing the curtains as they leave*]
        Sound trumpets, then enter KING [HENRY] *and* QUEEN
        [MARGARET], CARDINAL [BEAUFORT], *the Duke of* SOM-
        ERSET, [*and*] *attendants*
15 KING HENRY [*to* SUFFOLK] Go call our uncle to our presence straight.°   *immediately*
Say we intend to try his grace today
If° he be guilty, as 'tis publishèd.   *To find whether*
SUFFOLK I'll call him presently,° my noble lord.   *Exit*   *at once*
KING HENRY Lords, take your places; and, I pray you all,
20 Proceed no straiter° 'gainst our uncle Gloucester   *more severely*
Than from true evidence, of good esteem,°   *worthy of belief*
He be approved in practice culpable.°   *determined guilty*
QUEEN MARGARET God forbid any malice should prevail
That faultless may condemn a noble man!³
25 Pray God he may acquit him° of suspicion!   *himself*
KING HENRY I thank thee, Meg. These words content me much.
        Enter SUFFOLK
How now? Why look'st thou pale? Why tremblest thou?
Where is our uncle? What's the matter, Suffolk?

---

9. Tortured by having one's limbs fastened to a frame
that stretched the body.
3.2 Location: Gloucester's bedchamber and an adjoining room of state, Bury St. Edmunds.
1. F's stage direction reads, "Enter two or three
running over the Stage, from the Murder of Duke

Humfrey." Q, by contrast, indicates that the actual
smothering of Gloucester is shown onstage.
2. Would that it were still to be done (so that it could
remain undone).
3. That may condemn a noble man who is blameless.

SUFFOLK   Dead in his bed, my lord—Gloucester is dead.

30   QUEEN MARGARET   Marry, God forfend!°   *forbid*

CARDINAL BEAUFORT   God's secret judgement. I did dream tonight°   *last night*
    The Duke was dumb and could not speak a word.

                KING HENRY *falls [to the ground]*[4]

QUEEN MARGARET   How fares my lord? Help, lords—the King is
        dead!

SOMERSET   Rear° up his body; wring him by the nose.[5]   *Raise*

35   QUEEN MARGARET   Run, go, help, help! O Henry, ope thine eyes!

SUFFOLK   He doth revive again. Madam, be patient.

KING HENRY   O heavenly God!

QUEEN MARGARET   How fares my gracious lord?

SUFFOLK   Comfort, my sovereign; gracious Henry, comfort.

KING HENRY   What, doth my lord of Suffolk comfort me?

40   Came he right now° to sing a raven's note[6]   *a moment ago*
    Whose dismal tune bereft° my vital powers;   *robbed me of*
    And thinks he that the chirping of a wren,
    By crying comfort from a hollow° breast   *an insincere*
    Can chase away the first-conceivèd° sound?   *previously perceived*

45   Hide not thy poison with such sugared words.
        [*He begins to rise.* SUFFOLK *offers to assist him*]
    Lay not thy hands on me—forbear, I say!
    Their touch affrights me as a serpent's sting.
    Thou baleful messenger, out of my sight!
    Upon thy eyeballs murderous tyranny

50   Sits in grim majesty to fright the world.
    Look not upon me, for thine eyes are wounding—
    Yet do not go away. Come, basilisk,[7]
    And kill the innocent gazer with thy sight.
    For in the shade° of death I shall find joy;   *shadow*

55   In life, but double death, now Gloucester's dead.

QUEEN MARGARET   Why do you rate° my lord of Suffolk thus?   *chide*
    Although the Duke was enemy to him,
    Yet he most Christian-like laments his death.
    And for myself, foe as he was to me,

60   Might liquid tears, or heart-offending° groans,   *heart-wounding*
    Or blood-consuming[8] sighs recall his life,
    I would be blind with weeping, sick with groans,
    Look pale as primrose with blood-drinking sighs,
    And all to have the noble Duke alive.

65   What know I how the world may deem° of me?   *judge*
    For it is known we were but hollow friends,
    It may be judged I made the Duke away.
    So shall my name with slander's tongue be wounded
    And princes' courts be filled with my reproach.

70   This get I by his death. Ay me, unhappy,
    To be a queen, and crowned with infamy.

KING HENRY   Ah, woe is me for Gloucester, wretched man!

---

4. In Q, the stage direction reads, "The King falls in a sound" (swoon). F reads, "King sounds."
5. This was thought to revive circulation and restore consciousness.
6. According to popular superstition, an omen of death.

7. A mythical reptile, hatched from a cock's egg, whose look was supposed to be fatal.
8. It was popularly believed that each sigh or groan drew a drop of blood from the heart.

QUEEN MARGARET Be woe° for me, more wretched than he is.   *woeful; sorry*
What, dost thou turn away and hide thy face?
75I am no loathsome leper—look on me!
What, art thou, like the adder, waxen deaf?⁹
Be poisonous too and kill thy forlorn queen.
Is all thy comfort shut in Gloucester's tomb?
Why, then Queen Margaret was ne'er thy joy.
80Erect his statuë and worship it,
And make my image but an alehouse sign.¹
Was I for this nigh wrecked upon the sea,
And twice by awkward° winds from England's bank°   *unfavorable / shore*
Drove back again unto my native clime?
85What boded this, but° well forewarning winds   *but that*
Did seem to say, 'Seek not a scorpion's nest,
Nor set no footing on this unkind shore'.
What did I then, but cursed the gentle gusts
And he that loosed them forth their brazen caves,²
90And bid them blow towards England's blessèd shore,
Or turn our stern upon a dreadful rock.
Yet Aeolus would not be a murderer,
But left that hateful office unto thee.
The pretty vaulting° sea refused to drown me,   *bounding*
95Knowing that thou wouldst have me drowned on shore
With tears as salt as sea through thy unkindness.
The splitting rocks cow'red in the sinking sands,³
And would not dash me with their ragged sides,
Because thy flinty heart, more hard than they,
100Might in thy palace perish° Margaret.   *destroy*
As far as I could ken° thy chalky cliffs,   *see*
When from thy shore the tempest beat us back,
I stood upon the hatches° in the storm,   *deck*
And when the dusky sky began to rob
105My earnest-gaping° sight of thy land's view,   *earnestly peering*
I took a costly jewel from my neck—
A heart it was, bound in with diamonds—
And threw it towards thy land. The sea received it,
And so I wished thy body might my heart.
110And even with this I lost fair England's view,
And bid mine eyes be packing° with my heart,   *be gone*
And called them blind and dusky spectacles°   *instruments of sight*
For losing ken of Albion's° wishèd coast.   *England's*
How often have I tempted Suffolk's tongue—
115The agent of thy foul inconstancy—
To sit and witch° me, as Ascanius⁴ did,   *bewitch*
When he to madding° Dido would unfold   *going mad (with love)*
His father's acts, commenced in burning Troy!
Am I not witched like her? Or thou not false like him?
120Ay me, I can no more.° Die, Margaret,   *my strength fails*

9. Alluding to the belief that adders stopped up their ears to resist attempts to charm them.
1. Inns and shops in Elizabethan London were usually distinguished by signs bearing images rather than words.
2. Referring to Aeolus, whom Zeus appointed ruler of the winds, which he kept in caves. *brazen:* strong (as brass).

3. Rocks that ordinarily break ships into pieces crouched down fearfully in the sands where ships usually sink.
4. In Book 1 of the *Aeneid*, Venus sends Cupid in the form of Ascanius, son of Aeneas, to bewitch Dido, Queen of Carthage, and inflame her with love for Aeneas.

For Henry weeps that thou dost live so long.

Noise within. Enter the Earls of WARWICK *and*
SALISBURY, [*with*] *many* COMMONS

WARWICK [*to* KING HENRY]   It is reported, mighty sovereign,
That good Duke Humphrey traitorously is murdered
By Suffolk and the Cardinal Beaufort's means.

125   The commons, like an angry hive of bees
That want° their leader, scatter up and down   *lack*
And care not who they sting in his revenge.
Myself have calmed their spleenful° mutiny,   *angry*
Until they hear the order° of his death.   *manner*

130   KING HENRY   That he is dead, good Warwick, 'tis too true.
But how he died God knows, not Henry.
Enter his chamber, view his breathless corpse,
And comment then upon° his sudden death.   *And then explain*

WARWICK   That shall I do, my liege.—Stay, Salisbury,

135   With the rude multitude till I return.

Exeunt [WARWICK *at one door,*] SALISBURY [*and*
COMMONS *at another*][5]

KING HENRY   O thou that judgest all things, stay° my thoughts,   *restrain*
My thoughts that labour to persuade my soul
Some violent hands were laid on Humphrey's life.
If my suspect° be false, forgive me God,   *suspicion*

140   For judgement only doth belong to thee.
Fain would I go to chafe his paly° lips   *pale*
With twenty thousand kisses, and to drain°   *rain; let fall*
Upon his face an ocean of salt tears,
To tell my love unto his dumb, deaf trunk,°   *body*

145   And with my fingers feel his hand unfeeling.°   *which lacks feeling*
But all in vain are these mean obsequies,°   *funeral rites*

[*Enter*] WARWICK [*who*] *draws* [*apart*] *the curtains and*
shows GLOUCESTER [*dead*] *in his bed. Bed put forth*

And to survey his dead and earthy image,
What were it but to make my sorrow greater?

WARWICK   Come hither, gracious sovereign, view this body.

150   KING HENRY   That is to see how deep my grave is made:
For with his soul fled all my worldly solace,
For seeing him I see my life° in death.   *that my life will end*

WARWICK   As surely as my soul intends to live
With that dread King° that took our state° upon Him   *(Christ)/condition*

155   To free us from his Father's wrathful curse,
I do believe that violent hands were laid
Upon the life of this thrice-famèd° Duke.   *very famous*

SUFFOLK   A dreadful oath, sworn with a solemn tongue!
What instance° gives Lord Warwick for his vow?   *evidence*

160   WARWICK   See how the blood is settled in his face.
Oft have I seen a timely-parted ghost[6]
Of ashy semblance, meagre, pale, and bloodless,

---

5. Q has Salisbury exit at this point, while the dialogue
in F and Q indicates that Warwick also leaves the stage.
He must return to reveal Gloucester's corpse at line
146. Some editors have suggested that Salisbury stays

onstage with the Commons here, but at line 243 he is
directed to enter, and it appears that the Commons are
also then offstage. Both must have exited at some point.
6. The corpse of someone who died a natural death.

Being all descended to the labouring heart;[7]
Who, in the conflict that it holds with death,
165   Attracts the same° for aidance° 'gainst the enemy;   *(the blood)/aid*
Which, with the heart, there cools, and ne'er returneth
To blush and beautify the cheek again.
But see, his face is black and full of blood;
His eyeballs further out than when he lived,
170   Staring full ghastly like a strangled man;
His hair upreared; his nostrils stretched with struggling;
His hands abroad displayed,° as one that grasped   *spread wide*
And tugged for life and was by strength subdued.
Look on the sheets. His hair, you see, is sticking;
175   His well-proportioned beard made rough and rugged,
Like to the summer's corn by tempest lodged.°   *beaten down*
It cannot be but he was murdered here.
The least of all these signs were probable.°   *sufficient proof*
SUFFOLK   Why, Warwick, who should do the Duke to death?
180   Myself and Beaufort had him in protection,
And we, I hope, sir, are no murderers.
WARWICK   But both of you were vowed Duke Humphrey's foes,
[*To* CARDINAL BEAUFORT] And you, forsooth, had the good
Duke to keep.°   *guard*
'Tis like you would not feast him like a friend;
185   And 'tis well seen he found an enemy.
QUEEN MARGARET   Then you, belike,° suspect these noblemen   *perchance*
As guilty of Duke Humphrey's timeless° death?   *untimely*
WARWICK   Who finds the heifer dead and bleeding fresh,
And sees fast° by a butcher with an axe,   *near*
190   But will suspect 'twas he that made the slaughter?
Who finds the partridge in the puttock's° nest   *kite's (bird of prey)*
But may imagine how the bird was dead,°   *killed*
Although the kite soar with unbloodied beak?
Even so suspicious is this tragedy.
195   QUEEN MARGARET   Are you the butcher, Suffolk? Where's your knife?
Is Beaufort termed a kite? Where are his talons?
SUFFOLK   I wear no knife to slaughter sleeping men.
But here's a vengeful sword, rusted with ease,°   *lack of use*
That shall be scourèd in his rancorous heart
200   That° slanders me with murder's crimson badge.   *Who*
Say, if thou dar'st, proud Lord of Warwickshire,
That I am faulty in Duke Humphrey's death.
                    Exit CARDINAL [BEAUFORT *assisted by* SOMERSET]
WARWICK   What dares not Warwick, if false Suffolk dare him?
QUEEN MARGARET   He dares not calm his contumelious° spirit,   *insolent*
205   Nor cease to be an arrogant controller,°   *critic; slanderer*
Though Suffolk dare him twenty thousand times.
WARWICK   Madam, be still, with reverence may I say,
For every word you speak in his behalf
Is slander to your royal dignity.
210   SUFFOLK   Blunt-witted lord, ignoble in demeanour!
If ever lady wronged her lord so much,
Thy mother took into her blameful bed
Some stern° untutored churl, and noble stock   *rough*

7. The blood having all drained into the palpitating heart.

Was graffed with crabtree slip, whose fruit thou art,[8]
215   And never of the Nevilles' noble race.
WARWICK   But that the guilt of murder bucklers° thee   *shields*
        And I should rob the deathsman° of his fee,   *executioner*
        Quitting° thee thereby of ten thousand shames,   *Freeing*
        And that my sovereign's presence makes me mild,[9]
220   I would, false murd'rous coward, on thy knee
        Make thee beg pardon for thy passèd° speech,   *just uttered*
        And say it was thy mother that thou meant'st—
        That thou thyself wast born in bastardy!
        And after all this fearful homage° done,   *cowardly submission*
225   Give thee thy hire° and send thy soul to hell,   *reward*
        Pernicious blood-sucker of sleeping men!
SUFFOLK   Thou shalt be waking while I shed thy blood,
        If from this presence° thou dar'st go with me.   *the King's presence*
WARWICK   Away, even now, or I will drag thee hence.
230   Unworthy though thou art, I'll cope° with thee,   *fight*
        And do some service to Duke Humphrey's ghost.
                            Exeunt SUFFOLK *and* WARWICK
KING HENRY   What stronger breastplate than a heart untainted?
        Thrice is he armed that hath his quarrel just;
        And he but naked, though locked up in steel,°   *armored*
235   Whose conscience with injustice is corrupted.
COMMONS (*within*)   Down with Suffolk! Down with Suffolk![1]
QUEEN MARGARET   What noise is this?
            Enter SUFFOLK *and* WARWICK *with their weapons drawn*
KING HENRY   Why, how now, lords? Your wrathful weapons drawn
        Here in our presence? Dare you be so bold?
240   Why, what tumultuous clamour have we here?
SUFFOLK   The trait'rous Warwick with the men of Bury
        Set all upon me, mighty sovereign!
COMMONS [*within*]   Down with Suffolk! Down with Suffolk!
            Enter from [*the* COMMONS] *the Earl of* SALISBURY
SALISBURY [*to the* COMMONS, *within*]   Sirs, stand apart. The
            King shall know your mind.
        [*To* KING HENRY] Dread lord, the commons send you word
245   by me
        Unless Lord Suffolk straight be done to death,
        Or banishèd° fair England's territories,   *banished from*
        They will by violence tear him from your palace
        And torture him with grievous ling'ring death.
250   They say, by him the good Duke Humphrey died;
        They say, in him they fear your highness' death;
        And mere° instinct of love and loyalty,   *pure*
        Free from a stubborn opposite° intent,   *antagonistic*
        As being thought to contradict your liking,[2]
255   Makes them thus forward in° his banishment.   *insistent upon*

---

8. *noble . . . art:* into the trunk of a great tree was inserted a cutting, or "slip," from an inferior, wild one, and you are the result. The analogy puns on "stock" as meaning "an aristocratic line of descent" and implies that the pedigree has been tainted. "Noble stock" may also refer to the trunk of a noblewoman's body into which a worthless "slip," such as the penis of a lowborn man, has been inserted.

9. It was illegal to draw weapons in the King's presence.
1. In Q, this line is printed inside a longer stage direction: "Exit Warwick and Suffolk, and then all the Commons within, cries, down with Suffolk, down with Suffolk. And then enter again, the Duke of Suffolk and Warwick, with their weapons drawn."
2. That might be thought to contradict your wishes.

They say, in care of your most royal person,
That if your highness should intend to sleep,
And charge that no man should disturb your rest
In pain of your dislike, or pain of death,
260 Yet, notwithstanding such a strait° edict,   strict
Were there a serpent seen with forkèd tongue,
That slily glided towards your majesty,
It were but necessary you were waked,
Lest, being suffered° in that harmful slumber,   permitted to remain
265 The mortal worm° might make the sleep eternal.   deadly serpent
And therefore do they cry, though you forbid,
That they will guard you, whe'er° you will or no,   whether
From such fell° serpents as false Suffolk is,   cruel
With whose envenomèd and fatal sting
270 Your loving uncle, twenty times his worth,
They say, is shamefully bereft of life.
COMMONS (*within*)   An answer from the King, my lord of Salisbury!
SUFFOLK   'Tis like° the commons, rude unpolished hinds,°   probable / boors
Could send such message to their sovereign.
275 But you, my lord, were glad to be employed,
To show how quaint° an orator you are.   skilled
But all the honour Salisbury hath won
Is that he was the Lord Ambassador
Sent from a sort° of tinkers[3] to the King.   gang
280 COMMONS (*within*)   An answer from the King, or we will all break in!
KING HENRY   Go, Salisbury, and tell them all from me
I thank them for their tender loving care,
And had I not been 'cited° so by them,   urged
Yet did I purpose as they do entreat;
285 For sure my thoughts do hourly prophesy
Mischance unto my state by Suffolk's means.
And therefore by His° majesty I swear,   (God's)
Whose far unworthy deputy I am,
He shall not breathe° infection in this air   breathe out; spread
290 But three days longer, on the pain of death.   *Exit* SALISBURY
QUEEN MARGARET [*kneeling*]   O Henry, let me plead for gentle°   noble
          Suffolk.
KING HENRY   Ungentle Queen, to call him gentle Suffolk.
No more, I say! If thou dost plead for him
Thou wilt but add increase unto my wrath.
295 Had I but said, I would have kept my word;
But when I swear, it is irrevocable.
[*To* SUFFOLK] If after three days' space thou here beest found
On any ground that I am ruler of,
The world shall not be ransom for thy life.
300 Come, Warwick; come, good Warwick, go with me.
I have great matters to impart to thee.
          Exeunt KING [HENRY] *and* WARWICK [*with attendants*
               who draw the curtains as they leave]. Manent°   Remain
               QUEEN [MARGARET] *and* SUFFOLK

---

3. Tinkers were usually itinerant pot menders and were synonymous with vagrants and gypsies.

QUEEN MARGARET [*rising*]   Mischance and sorrow go along with you!
    Heart's discontent and sour affliction
    Be playfellows to keep you company!
305   There's two of you, the devil make a third,
    And threefold vengeance tend upon your steps!
SUFFOLK   Cease, gentle Queen, these execrations,
    And let thy Suffolk take his heavy° leave.   *sorrowful*
QUEEN MARGARET   Fie, coward woman[4] and soft-hearted wretch!
310   Hast thou not spirit to curse thine enemies?
SUFFOLK   A plague upon them! Wherefore° should I curse them?   *Why*
    Could curses kill, as doth the mandrake's groan,[5]
    I would invent as bitter searching° terms,   *piercing*
    As curst, as harsh, and horrible to hear,
315   Delivered strongly through my fixèd° teeth,   *clenched*
    With full as many signs of deadly hate,
    As lean-faced envy[6] in her loathsome cave.
    My tongue should stumble in mine earnest words;
    Mine eyes should sparkle like the beaten flint;
320   My hair be fixed on end, as one distraught;
    Ay, every joint should seem to curse and ban.°   *curse*
    And, even now, my burdened heart would break
    Should I not curse them. Poison be their drink!
    Gall,° worse than gall, the daintiest that they taste!   *Bile (a bitter fluid)*
325   Their sweetest shade a grove of cypress trees![7]
    Their chiefest prospect° murd'ring basilisks![8]   *view*
    Their softest touch as smart° as lizards' stings!   *sharp*
    Their music frightful as the serpent's hiss,
    And boding screech-owls[9] make the consort° full!   *group of musicians*
330   All the foul terrors in dark-seated hell—
QUEEN MARGARET   Enough, sweet Suffolk, thou torment'st thyself,
    And these dread curses, like the sun 'gainst glass,
    Or like an overchargèd gun, recoil
    And turn the force of them upon thyself.
335 SUFFOLK   You bade me ban, and will you bid me leave?°   *stop*
    Now by this ground that I am banished from,
    Well could I curse away a winter's night,
    Though standing naked on a mountain top,
    Where biting cold would never let grass grow,
340   And think it but a minute spent in sport.
QUEEN MARGARET   O let me entreat thee cease. Give me thy hand,
    That I may dew it with my mournful tears;
    Nor let the rain of heaven wet this place
    To wash away my woeful monuments.°   *signs of grief (tears)*
    [*She kisses his palm*]
345   O, could this kiss be printed in thy hand
    That thou mightst think upon these lips by the seal,°   *imprint*

---

4. In calling Suffolk a woman, Margaret questions his manhood. The pun in the next line on "spirit" as meaning "semen" as well as "courage" continues Margaret's assault on Suffolk's masculinity.
5. It was popularly believed that the mandrake—an herb whose root was thought to resemble a man and to grow wherever the semen of a man executed for murder had fallen—killed humans with its dreadful scream

when it was uprooted.
6. Envy was traditionally described as an emaciated woman. See Ovid, *Metamorphoses* 2.949ff.
7. From ancient times, trees associated with death. Frequently planted in graveyards, their wood was used for coffins.
8. See note to line 52 above.
9. Thought to be harbingers of death.

Through whom° a thousand sighs are breathed for thee!   *which (her lips)*
So get thee gone, that I may know my grief.
'Tis but surmised whiles thou art standing by,
350 As one that surfeits° thinking on a want.°   *gorges / famine*
I will repeal thee,° or, be well assured,   *win your recall*
Adventure to be banishèd° myself.   *Risk banishment*
And banishèd I am, if but from thee.
Go, speak not to me; even now be gone!
355 O, go not yet. Even thus two friends condemned
Embrace, and kiss, and take ten thousand leaves,
Loather a hundred times to part than die.
Yet now farewell, and farewell life with thee.
SUFFOLK   Thus is poor Suffolk ten times banishèd—
360 Once by the King, and three times thrice by thee.
'Tis not the land I care for, wert thou thence,
A wilderness is populous enough,
So Suffolk had thy heavenly company.
For where thou art, there is the world itself,
365 With every several° pleasure in the world;   *distinct*
And where thou art not, desolation.
I can no more. Live thou to joy° thy life;   *enjoy*
Myself no joy in naught but that thou liv'st.
      Enter VAUX
QUEEN MARGARET   Whither goes Vaux so fast? What news, I prithee?
370 VAUX   To signify unto his majesty
That Cardinal Beaufort is at point of death.
For suddenly a grievous sickness took him
That makes him gasp, and stare, and catch the air,
Blaspheming God and cursing men on earth.
375 Sometime he talks as if Duke Humphrey's ghost
Were by his side; sometime he calls the King,
And whispers to his pillow as to him
The secrets of his over-chargèd° soul;   *overburdened*
And I am sent to tell his majesty
380 That even now he cries aloud for him.
QUEEN MARGARET   Go tell this heavy message to the King.
      Exit VAUX
Ay me! What is this world? What news are these?
But wherefore grieve I at an hour's poor loss[1]
Omitting° Suffolk's exile, my soul's treasure?   *Ignoring*
385 Why only, Suffolk, mourn I not for thee,
And with the southern clouds[2] contend in tears—
Theirs for the earth's increase, mine for my sorrow's?
Now get thee hence. The King, thou know'st, is coming.
If thou be found by° me, thou art but dead.   *near*
390 SUFFOLK   If I depart from thee, I cannot live.
And in thy sight to die, what were it else
But like a pleasant slumber in thy lap?[3]
Here could I breathe my soul into the air,

---

1. Alluding to the Cardinal's old age and suggesting that
he has in any case but a short time (an hour) to live.
2. It was generally thought that rain came from the
south.
3. Punning on "die in thy lap" as meaning "have an
orgasm while in your embrace."

As mild and gentle as the cradle babe
395 Dying with mother's dug° between his lips;   *nipple*
Where, from° thy sight, I should be raging mad,   *out of*
And cry out for thee to close up mine eyes,
To have thee with thy lips to stop my mouth,
So shouldst thou either turn° my flying soul   *return to me*
400 Or I should breathe it, so, into thy body—
        [*He kisseth her*]
And then it lived in sweet Elysium.[4]
By thee to die were but to die in jest;[5]
From thee to die were torture more than death.
O, let me stay, befall what may befall!
405 QUEEN MARGARET Away. Though parting be a fretful corrosive,°   *painful remedy*
It is applièd to a deathful° wound.   *deadly*
To France, sweet Suffolk. Let me hear from thee.
For wheresoe'er thou art in this world's Globe
I'll have an Iris[6] that shall find thee out.
410 SUFFOLK I go.
QUEEN MARGARET And take my heart with thee.
        She kisseth him
SUFFOLK A jewel, locked into the woefull'st cask°   *casket*
That ever did contain a thing of worth.
Even as a splitted barque,° so sunder° we—   *boat / part*
This way fall I to death.
415 QUEEN MARGARET   This way for me.   *Exeunt* [*severally*]

3.3

Enter KING [HENRY *and the Earls of*] SALISBURY
and WARWICK. *Then the curtains be drawn* [*revealing*]
CARDINAL [BEAUFORT] *in his bed raving and staring as*
if he were mad

KING HENRY [*to* CARDINAL BEAUFORT] How fares my lord? Speak, Beaufort,
    to thy sovereign.
CARDINAL BEAUFORT If thou beest death, I'll give thee England's treasure
    Enough to purchase such another island,
    So° thou wilt let me live and feel no pain.   *If*
5 KING HENRY Ah, what a sign it is of evil life
    Where death's approach is seen so terrible.
WARWICK Beaufort, it is thy sovereign speaks to thee.
CARDINAL BEAUFORT Bring me unto my trial when you will.
    Died he° not in his bed? Where should he die?   *(Gloucester)*
10 Can I make men live whe'er° they will or no?   *whether*
    O, torture me no more—I will confess.
    Alive again? Then show me where he is.
    I'll give a thousand pound to look upon him.
    He hath no eyes! The dust hath blinded them.
15 Comb down his hair—look, look: it stands upright,
    Like lime twigs[1] set to catch my wingèd soul.

---

4. In classical mythology, the paradise where blessed souls dwelled.
5. To die near you or by means of you is not really to die (with a continuing pun on "die" as meaning "attain orgasm").

6. In Greek mythology, Iris was a messenger of the gods, particularly of Hera.
3.3 Location: The Cardinal's bedchamber, London.
1. Twigs smeared with birdlime. See note to 1.3.92.

    Give me some drink, and bid the apothecary
    Bring the strong poison that I bought of him.
KING HENRY   O Thou eternal mover of the heavens,°   (God)
20   Look with a gentle eye upon this wretch.
    O, beat away the busy meddling fiend
    That lays strong siege unto this wretch's soul,
    And from his bosom purge this black despair.
WARWICK   See how the pangs of death do make him grin.°   bare his teeth
25 SALISBURY   Disturb him not; let him pass peaceably.
KING HENRY   Peace to his soul, if God's good pleasure be.
    Lord Card'nal, if thou think'st on heaven's bliss,
    Hold up thy hand, make signal of thy hope.
            CARDINAL [BEAUFORT] *dies*
    He dies and makes no sign. O God, forgive him.
30 WARWICK   So bad a death argues a monstrous life.
KING HENRY   Forbear to judge, for we are sinners all.
    Close up his eyes and draw the curtain close,
    And let us all to meditation.°   prayer
            Exeunt [drawing the curtains. The bed is removed]

4.1

Alarums within, and the chambers° *be discharged like as*   small cannon
it were a fight at sea. And then enter the CAPTAIN *of the*
ship, the MASTER, *the Master's mate,* Walter WHITMORE[1]
and others. [With them, as their prisoners,] the Duke of
SUFFOLK, *disguised [and two* GENTLEMEN]
CAPTAIN   The gaudy, blabbing, and remorseful day[2]
    Is crept into the bosom of the sea;
    And now loud-howling wolves arouse the jades[3]
    That drag the tragic melancholy night;
    Who, with their drowsy, slow, and flagging wings
5   Clip° dead men's graves, and from their misty jaws   Embrace
    Breathe foul contagious darkness in the air.
    Therefore bring forth the soldiers of our prize,°   captured ship
    For whilst our pinnace° anchors in the downs,°   small ship / anchorage
    Here shall they make their ransom on the sand,
10   Or with their blood stain this discoloured shore.[4]
    Master, [*pointing to the* FIRST GENTLEMAN] this prisoner freely give I thee,
    [*To the* MATE] And thou, that art his mate, make boot of this.[5]
         [*He points to the* SECOND GENTLEMAN]
    [*To Walter* WHITMORE] The other [*pointing to* SUFFOLK],
        Walter Whitmore, is thy share.
FIRST GENTLEMAN [*to the* MASTER]   What is my ransom, Master,
15   let me know.
MASTER   A thousand crowns, or else lay down your head.
MATE [*to the* SECOND GENTLEMAN] And so much shall you give,
        or off goes yours.

4.1 Location: At sea off the Kentish coast.
1. Q's stage direction reads, "Water Whickmore," anticipating the later play on "Walter" and "Water."
2. The garish, telltale (revealing secrets of the dark), and guilty day.
3. Usually worn-out cart horses, here an allusion to the

dragons of Hecate that, according to classical mythology, drew Night's chariot.
4. Or discolor this shore with their blood.
5. Make a profit from (the ransom of) this second prisoner.

CAPTAIN [*to both the* GENTLEMEN]   What, think you much to
     pay two thousand crowns,
    And bear the name and port° of gentlemen?   *demeanor*
20 WHITMORE   Cut both the villains' throats! [*To* SUFFOLK] For die you shall.
    The lives of those which we have lost in fight
    [   ]⁶
    Be counterpoised° with such a petty sum.   *Be compensated*
FIRST GENTLEMAN [*to the* MASTER]   I'll give it, sir, and therefore
     spare my life.
SECOND GENTLEMAN [*to the* MATE]   And so will I, and write
25   home for it straight.
WHITMORE [*to* SUFFOLK]   I lost mine eye in laying the prize aboard,° *boarding the ship*
    And therefore to revenge it, shalt thou die—
    And so should these, if I might have my will.
CAPTAIN   Be not so rash; take ransom; let him live.
30 SUFFOLK   Look on my George⁷—I am a gentleman.
    Rate° me at what thou wilt, thou shalt be paid.   *Value*
WHITMORE   And so am I; my name is Walter⁸ Whitmore.
      [SUFFOLK] *starteth*
    How now—why starts thou? What doth thee affright?
SUFFOLK   Thy name affrights me, in whose sound is death.
35   A cunning man did calculate my birth,⁹
    And told me that by 'water' I should die.
    Yet let not this make thee be bloody-minded;
    Thy name is Gualtier,¹ being rightly sounded.
WHITMORE   Gualtier or Walter—which it is I care not.
40   Never yet did base dishonour blur our name
    But with our sword we wiped away the blot.
    Therefore, when merchant-like I sell revenge,
    Broke be my sword, my arms° torn and defaced,   *coat of arms*
    And I proclaimed a coward through the world.
45 SUFFOLK   Stay, Whitmore; for thy prisoner is a prince,
    The Duke of Suffolk, William de la Pole.
WHITMORE   The Duke of Suffolk muffled up in rags?
SUFFOLK   Ay, but these rags are no part of the Duke.
    Jove sometime went disguised, and why not I?
50 CAPTAIN   But Jove was never slain as thou shalt be.
SUFFOLK   Obscure and lousy° swain, King Henry's blood,²   *lice-infested*
    The honourable blood of Lancaster,
    Must not be shed by such a jady groom.³
    Hast thou not kissed thy hand° and held my stirrup? *(a gesture of servility)*
55   Bare-headed plodded by my foot-cloth mule⁴
    And thought thee happy when I shook° my head?   *nodded*
    How often hast thou waited at my cup,
    Fed from my trencher,° kneeled down at the board°   *platter / table*
    When I have feasted with Queen Margaret?

6. A line appears to be missing from F at this point, probably one indicating that the ransom demanded can never compensate for the lives lost in battle.
7. Alluding to the image of St. George and the dragon on the insignia of the Order of the Garter, the highest order of English knighthood.
8. "Walter" was usually pronounced "water." The spirit Asnath, conjured by Roger Bolingbroke, had predicted that Suffolk should die by "water" (see 1.4.32).
9. An astrologer cast my horoscope.
1. French for "Walter."
2. A dubious claim: Suffolk's mother was a distant cousin to Henry VI.
3. Servant in charge of horses; contemptible fellow.
4. The animal used to bear the large, richly ornamented cloth displayed in royal processions.

60	Remember it, and let it make thee crestfall'n,[5]	
	Ay, and allay this thy abortive° pride,	*monstrous*
	How in our voiding lobby° hast thou stood	*antechamber*
	And duly waited for my coming forth?	
	This hand of mine hath writ° in thy behalf,	*written testimonials*
65	And therefore shall it charm° thy riotous tongue.	*silence*

WHITMORE Speak, Captain—shall I stab the forlorn swain?° *wretched peasant*

CAPTAIN First let my words stab him as he hath me.

SUFFOLK Base slave, thy words are blunt° and so art thou. *harmless*

CAPTAIN Convey him hence and, on our longboat's side,
Strike off his head.

70 SUFFOLK   Thou dar'st not for thy own.

CAPTAIN Pole—

SUFFOLK   Pole?[6]

CAPTAIN   Ay, kennel,° puddle, sink,° whose filth *open gutter / cesspool*
and dirt
Troubles the silver spring where England drinks,
Now will I dam up this thy yawning mouth
For swallowing the treasure of the realm.

75 Thy lips that kissed the Queen shall sweep the ground,
And thou that smiledst at good Duke Humphrey's death
Against the senseless° winds shalt grin in vain, *unfeeling*
Who in contempt shall hiss at thee again.
And wedded be thou to the hags of hell,
80 For daring to affy° a mighty lord *betroth*
Unto the daughter of a worthless king,
Having neither subject, wealth, nor diadem.
By devilish policy art thou grown great,
And like ambitious Sylla,[7] overgorged
85 With gobbets° of thy mother's° bleeding heart. *chunks / (England's)*
By thee Anjou and Maine were sold to France,
The false revolting° Normans, thorough° thee, *rebellious / because of*
Disdain to call us lord, and Picardy
Hath slain their governors, surprised our forts,
90 And sent the ragged soldiers, wounded, home.
The princely Warwick, and the Nevilles all,
Whose dreadful swords were never drawn in vain,
As hating thee, are rising up in arms;
And now the house of York, thrust from the crown,
95 By shameful murder of a guiltless king[8]
And lofty, proud, encroaching tyranny,
Burns with revenging fire, whose hopeful colours
Advance° our half-faced sun,[9] striving to shine, *Display*
Under the which is writ, '*Invitis nubibus*'.° *In spite of clouds*
100 The commons here in Kent are up in arms,
And, to conclude, reproach and beggary
Is crept into the palace of our King,

---

5. Humble; deprived of a "crest" (coat of arms).
6. The fact that Suffolk's family name could be pronounced "pool" leads to the punning insults that follow. Lines 71–72 are garbled in F (see Textual Variants). Oxford's reconstruction assumes that abbreviations for "Suffolk" and "Lieutenant" were misread as "Sir" and "Lord" by those who set type from the Folio manuscript.
7. The Roman dictator Lucius Cornelius Sulla (138–78

B.C.E.), notorious for drawing up lists of enemies whom he executed or banished.
8. Alluding to the deposition and murder of Richard II, which allowed the Lancastrian branch of the royal family to seize the throne. Shakespeare dramatizes these events in *Richard II*.
9. A sun emerging above clouds was the badge of Edward III and his successor, Richard II.

And all by thee. [*To* WHITMORE] Away, convey him hence.

SUFFOLK   O that I were a god, to shoot forth thunder

105   Upon these paltry, servile, abject drudges.
Small things make base men proud. This villain here,
Being captain of a pinnace, threatens more
Than Bargulus, the strong Illyrian pirate.[1]
Drones° suck not eagles' blood, but rob beehives.   *Beetles; parasites*

110   It is impossible that I should die
By such a lowly vassal as thyself.
Thy words move rage, and not remorse in me.

CAPTAIN   But my deeds, Suffolk, soon shall stay thy rage.

SUFFOLK   I go of message° from the Queen to France—   *as messenger*

115   I charge thee, waft° me safely cross the Channel!   *convey*

CAPTAIN   Walter—

WHITMORE   Come, Suffolk, I must waft thee to thy death.

SUFFOLK   *Paene gelidus timor occupat artus*[2]—
It is thee I fear.

120   WHITMORE   Thou shalt have cause to fear before I leave thee.
What, are ye daunted now? Now will ye stoop?

FIRST GENTLEMAN [*to* SUFFOLK]   My gracious lord, entreat
him—speak him fair.

SUFFOLK   Suffolk's imperial tongue is stern and rough,
Used to command, untaught to plead for favour.

125   Far be it we should honour such as these
With humble suit. No, rather let my head
Stoop to the block than these knees bow to any
Save to the God of heaven and to my king;
And sooner dance upon a bloody pole[3]

130   Than stand uncovered to the vulgar groom.
True nobility is exempt from fear;
More can I bear than you dare execute.

CAPTAIN   Hale° him away, and let him talk no more.   *Drag*

SUFFOLK   Come, 'soldiers', show what cruelty ye can,

135   That this my death may never be forgot.
Great men oft die by vile Besonians;[4]
A Roman sworder and banditto° slave   *cutthroat and lawless*
Murdered sweet Tully; Brutus' bastard hand[5]
Stabbed Julius Caesar; savage islanders

140   Pompey the Great;[6] and Suffolk dies by pirates.

Exit WHITMORE *with* SUFFOLK

CAPTAIN   And as for these whose ransom we have set,
It is our pleasure one of them depart.
[*To the* SECOND GENTLEMAN] Therefore, come you with us and
[*to his men, pointing* to *the* FIRST GENTLEMAN] let him go.

Exeunt. Manet the FIRST GENTLEMAN

1. An ancient pirate alluded to in Ciero's *De Officiis* (*On Public Duties*), a text much used in Elizabethan schools.
2. Cold fear seizes my limbs almost entirely (perhaps alluding to Virgil, *Aeneid* 7.446; Lucan, *Pharsalia* 1,246; or both).
3. Punning on his name ("Pole") and on Elizabethan slang for "head" ("poll"), Suffolk alludes to the fact that heads of executed criminals were set upon poles in public places. Londoners would often pass by such poles as they crossed the bridge on their way to the theaters in

Southwark.
4. Base fellows. From the Spanish word *bisoño*, meaning "recruit": foot soldiers were usually poor commoners.
5. Brutus, who helped murder Caesar, was rumored to have been his illegitimate son. *Tully:* the Roman orator Cicero, who was in fact murdered by Roman soldiers.
6. Alluding either to Plutarch's claim that the Egyptians who murdered this Roman general were led by one born on the island of Chios or to the tradition that Pompey was murdered on the island of Lesbos.

Enter WHITMORE *with* [*Suffolk's head and*] *body*

WHITMORE   There let his head and lifeless body lie,

145   Until the Queen his mistress bury it.   *Exit*

FIRST GENTLEMAN   O barbarous and bloody spectacle!

His body will I bear unto the King.

If he revenge it not, yet will his friends;

So will the Queen, that living held him dear.

[*Exit with Suffolk's head and body*]

4.2

Enter two REBELS *with long staves*[1]

FIRST REBEL   Come and get thee a sword, though made of a
    lath;[2] they have been up° these two days.   *in revolt*

SECOND REBEL   They have the more need to sleep now then.

FIRST REBEL   I tell thee, Jack Cade the clothier[3] means to dress
5   the commonwealth, and turn it,[4] and set a new nap upon it.[5]

SECOND REBEL   So he had need, for 'tis threadbare. Well, I say it
    was never merry world in England since gentlemen came up.°   *came into fashion*

FIRST REBEL   O, miserable age! Virtue is not regarded in handi-
    craftsmen.°   *artisans*

10   SECOND REBEL   The nobility think scorn to go in leather
    aprons.°   *(workers' attire)*

FIRST REBEL   Nay more, the King's Council are no good
    workmen.

SECOND REBEL   True; and yet it is said 'Labour in thy vocation';
15   which is as much to say as 'Let the magistrates be labouring
    men'; and therefore should we be magistrates.

FIRST REBEL   Thou hast hit it; for there's no better sign of a
    brave° mind than a hard° hand.   *fine / calloused*

SECOND REBEL   I see them! I see them! There's Best's son, the
20   tanner of Wingham—

FIRST REBEL   He shall have the skins of our enemies to make
    dog's leather[6] of.

SECOND REBEL   And Dick the butcher—

FIRST REBEL   Then is sin struck down like an ox, and iniquity's
25   throat cut like a calf.

SECOND REBEL   And Smith the weaver—

FIRST REBEL   Argo,[7] their thread of life is spun.

SECOND REBEL   Come, come, let's fall in with them.

    Enter Jack CADE, *Dick* [*the*] BUTCHER, *Smith the*
    WEAVER, *a sawyer,* [*and a drummer,*] *with infinite num-*
    bers, [*all*] *with long staves*

CADE   We, John Cade, so termed of° our supposed father—   *named for*

30   BUTCHER [*to his fellows*]   Or rather of stealing a cade° of   *barrel*
    herrings.

CADE   For our enemies shall fall before us,[8] inspired with the
    spirit of putting down kings and princes—command silence!

4.2 Location: Blackheath, Kent.
1. Staves are mentioned only in the Q stage directions
and dialogue, and may reflect performance.
2. A strip of wood commonly used as a sword or dagger
by the Vice figure in English morality plays.
3. Clothiers, or textile workers, were involved in
a number of uprisings throughout the sixteenth
century.

4. Turn it inside out (as a way of renewing old cloth),
with a secondary sense of inverting the social hierarchy.
5. Improve its surface texture, probably by brushing
the outer fibers ("nap") of the cloth; reform it.
6. Inferior leather used in glove making.
7. A variant form of *ergo*, Latin for "therefore."
8. Borrowing biblical language and punning on the
Latin *cadere*, meaning "fall."

BUTCHER   Silence!

35 CADE   My father was a Mortimer—

BUTCHER [*to his fellows*]   He was an honest man and a good bricklayer.[9]

CADE   My mother a Plantagenet—

BUTCHER [*to his fellows*]   I knew her well, she was a midwife.

40 CADE   My wife descended of the Lacys[1]—

BUTCHER [*to his fellows*]   She was indeed a pedlar's daughter and sold many laces.

WEAVER [*to his fellows*]   But now of late, not able to travel with her furred pack,[2] she washes bucks[3] here at home.

45 CADE   Therefore am I of an honourable house.

BUTCHER [*to his fellows*]   Ay, by my faith, the field is honourable, and there was he born, under a hedge; for his father had never a house but the cage.°   prison

CADE   Valiant I am—

50 WEAVER [*to his fellows*]   A° must needs, for beggary is valiant.[4]   He

CADE   I am able to endure much—

BUTCHER [*to his fellows*]   No question of that, for I have seen him whipped[5] three market days together.

CADE   I fear neither sword nor fire.

55 WEAVER [*to his fellows*]   He need not fear the sword, for his coat is of proof.[6]

BUTCHER [*to his fellows*]   But methinks he should stand in fear of fire, being burned i'th' hand for stealing of sheep.[7]

CADE   Be brave, then, for your captain is brave and vows refor-
60 mation. There shall be in England seven halfpenny loaves sold for a penny, the three-hooped pot shall have ten hoops,[8] and I will make it felony to drink small° beer. All the realm shall   weak
be in° common, and in Cheapside[9] shall my palfrey° go to   held in / saddle horse
grass. And when I am king, as king I will be—

65 ALL CADE'S FOLLOWERS   God save your majesty!

CADE   I thank you good people!—there shall be no money. All
shall eat and drink on my score,° and I will apparel them all   at my expense
in one livery that they may agree like brothers, and worship
me their lord.

70 BUTCHER   The first thing we do let's kill all the lawyers.

CADE   Nay, that I mean to do. Is not this a lamentable thing that
of the skin of an innocent lamb should be made parchment?
That parchment, being scribbled o'er, should undo a man?
Some say the bee stings, but I say 'tis the bee's wax.° For   sealing wax
75 I did but seal[1] once to a thing, and I was never mine own man
since. How now? Who's there?

Enter [some bringing forth] the CLERK *of Chatham*

WEAVER   The Clerk of Chatham—he can write and read and
cast account.°   do arithmetic

---

9. Punning on "Mortimer" and "mortarer" (meaning "builder").
1. The family name of the earls of Lincoln.
2. Not able to travel with her peddler's pack made of skins with the hair turned outward; not able to make a living ("travail") with her sexual organs.
3. She washes laundry; she absolves ("washes") cuckolds (husbands with horns, like bucks) of their shame by helping them get even with their unfaithful wives.
4. Worthy of praise; sturdy. The Weaver is referring ironically to the fact that Elizabethan poor laws made it

illegal to give alms to able-bodied, or "valiant," beggars.
5. The usual punishment for vagabonds.
6. Impenetrable (from dirt?); well worn.
7. Thieves were branded on one hand with a "T" for "thief."
8. "Hoops," or regularly spaced bands on pots, were used for measuring. Cade means that for the price of a three-hooped pot (about a quart), one will receive over three times that amount.
9. Elizabethan London's chief commercial district.
1. Sign and seal (a legal document).

CADE   O, monstrous!

80   WEAVER   We took him setting of boys' copies.[2]

CADE   Here's a villain.

WEAVER   He's a book in his pocket with red letters[3] in't.

CADE   Nay, then he is a conjuror!

BUTCHER   Nay, he can make obligations° and write court hand.[4]   *bonds*

85   CADE   I am sorry for't. The man is a proper° man, of mine   *handsome*
honour. Unless I find him guilty, he shall not die. Come
hither, sirrah, I must examine thee. What is thy name?

CLERK   Emmanuel.

BUTCHER   They use to write that on the top of letters[5]—'twill go

90   hard with you.

CADE   Let me alone. [*To the* CLERK] Dost thou use to write thy
name? Or hast thou a mark[6] to thyself like an honest plain-
dealing man?

CLERK   Sir, I thank God I have been so well brought up that I

95   can write my name.

ALL CADE'S FOLLOWERS   He hath confessed—away with him!
He's a villain and a traitor.

CADE   Away with him, I say, hang him with his pen and inkhorn
about his neck.   *Exit one with the* CLERK

Enter [a MESSENGER*]*[7]

100   MESSENGER   Where's our general?

CADE   Here I am, thou particular[8] fellow.

MESSENGER   Fly, fly, fly! Sir Humphrey Stafford and his brother
are hard by with the King's forces.

CADE   Stand, villain, stand—or I'll fell thee down. He shall be

105   encountered with a man as good as himself. He is but a
knight, is a?

MESSENGER   No.[9]

CADE   To equal him I will make myself a knight presently.
[*He kneels and knights himself*]
Rise up, Sir John Mortimer.
[*He rises*]

110   Now have at him!

Enter Sir Humphrey STAFFORD *and his brother,*
with [a] drum[mer] and soldiers

STAFFORD [*to Cade's followers*]   Rebellious hinds,° the filth and   *peasants*
scum of Kent,
Marked for the gallows, lay your weapons down;
Home to your cottages, forsake this groom.
The King is merciful, if you revolt.°   *turn against Cade*

STAFFORD'S BROTHER [*to Cade's followers*]   But angry, wrathful,

115   and inclined to blood,
If you go forward. Therefore, yield or die.

CADE [*to his followers*]   As for these silken-coated slaves, I pass° not.   *care*
It is to you, good people, that I speak,

---

2. Preparing writing exercises for schoolboys. Village
clerks often doubled as schoolmasters.
3. Alluding to the red printing in almanacs and
primers.
4. The script used for legal documents.
5. The name, which means "God is with us," commonly appeared on legal documents.

6. Those who were illiterate often "signed" documents
by using distinctive marks.
7. Q calls this figure "Tom," F "Michael."
8. Private (as opposed to "general" in the previous line).
9. No, nothing but a knight. The Messenger is replying
to the negative implied in the prior sentence: "He is
nothing but a knight, is he?"

Over whom, in time to come, I hope to reign—
120   For I am rightful heir unto the crown.
STAFFORD   Villain, thy father was a plasterer
    And thou thyself a shearman,[1] art thou not?
CADE   And Adam was a gardener.
STAFFORD'S BROTHER   And what of that?
CADE   Marry, this: Edmund Mortimer, Earl of March,
125   Married the Duke of Clarence' daughter, did he not?
STAFFORD   Ay, sir.
CADE   By her he had two children at one birth.
STAFFORD'S BROTHER   That's false.
CADE   Ay, there's the question—but I say 'tis true.
130   The elder of them, being put to nurse,
    Was by a beggar-woman stol'n away,
    And, ignorant of his birth and parentage,
    Became a bricklayer when he came to age.
    His son am I—deny it an° you can.   *if*
135 BUTCHER   Nay, 'tis too true—therefore he shall be king.
WEAVER   Sir, he made a chimney in my father's house, and the
    bricks are alive at this day to testify. Therefore deny it not.
STAFFORD [*to Cade's followers*]   And will you credit this base drudge's words
    That speaks he knows not what?
140 ALL CADE'S FOLLOWERS   Ay, marry, will we—therefore get ye gone.
STAFFORD'S BROTHER   Jack Cade, the Duke of York hath taught you this.
CADE [*aside*]   He lies, for I invented it myself.
    [*Aloud*] Go to, sirrah[2]—tell the King from me that for his
    father's sake, Henry the Fifth, in whose time boys went to
145   span-counter° for French crowns,[3] I am content he shall   *played a game of toss*
    reign; but I'll be Protector over him.
BUTCHER   And, furthermore, we'll have the Lord Saye's[4] head
    for selling the dukedom of Maine.
CADE   And good reason, for thereby is England maimed, and
150   fain to go with a staff, but that my puissance° holds it up.   *power*
    Fellow-kings, I tell you that that Lord Saye hath gelded the
    commonwealth, and made it an eunuch, and, more than that,
    he can speak French, and therefore he is a traitor!
STAFFORD   O gross and miserable ignorance!
155 CADE   Nay, answer if you can: the Frenchmen are our enemies;
    go to, then, I ask but this—can he that speaks with the tongue
    of an enemy be a good counsellor or no?
ALL CADE'S FOLLOWERS   No, no—and therefore we'll have his
    head!
STAFFORD'S BROTHER [*to* STAFFORD]   Well, seeing gentle words
160   will not prevail,
    Assail them with the army of the King.
STAFFORD   Herald, away, and throughout every town
    Proclaim them traitors that are up with Cade;

1. One who cuts the nap from cloth during its manufacture.
2. Term used to address inferiors.
3. Alluding to Henry V's conquest of France. "French
crowns" might refer to French coins, kings, kingdoms,
or the bald heads that were symptomatic of the venereal
diseases blamed on the French.
4. *Lord Saye:* James Fiennes, Treasurer of England,
was associated with Suffolk in the loss of Anjou and
Maine.

That those which fly before the battle ends
165 May, even in their wives' and children's sight,
Be hanged up for° example at their doors.   *to make an*
And you that be the King's friends, follow me!
        Exeunt [the] STAFFORD[s] *and his men [their soldiers]*
CADE   And you that love the commons, follow me!
Now show yourselves men—'tis for liberty.
170 We will not leave one lord, one gentleman—
Spare none but such as go in clouted shoon,°   *hobnailed shoes*
For they are thrifty honest men, and such
As would, but that they dare not, take our parts.
BUTCHER   They are all in order, and march toward us.
175 CADE   But then are we in order when we are
Most out of order.° Come, march forward!   *rebellious*
                                                        Exeunt

4.3

Alarums to the fight; [excursions,]° wherein both the   *skirmishes*
STAFFORDS *are slain. Enter Jack* CADE, [*Dick the*
BUTCHER,] *and the rest*
CADE   Where's Dick, the butcher of Ashford?
BUTCHER   Here, sir.
CADE   They fell before thee like sheep and oxen, and thou
behaved'st thyself as if thou hadst been in thine own slaughter-
5 house. Therefore, thus will I reward thee—the Lent shall be
as long again as it is. Thou shalt have licence to kill for a hundred, lacking one.[1]
BUTCHER   I desire no more.
CADE   And to speak truth, thou deserv'st no less.
        [*He apparels himself in the Staffords' armour*]
10 This monument of the victory will I bear, and the bodies shall
be dragged at my horse heels till I do come to London, where
we will have the Mayor's sword borne before us.
BUTCHER   If we mean to thrive and do good, break open the
jails and let out the prisoners.
15 CADE   Fear not° that, I warrant thee. Come, let's march towards   *Don't worry about*
London.   *Exeunt [dragging the Staffords' bodies]*

4.4

Enter KING [HENRY] *reading a supplication*, QUEEN
[MARGARET] *with Suffolk's head, the Duke of*
BUCKINGHAM, *and the Lord* SAYE, *with others*
QUEEN MARGARET [*aside*]   Oft have I heard that grief softens the mind,
And makes it fearful and degenerate;
Think, therefore, on revenge, and cease to weep.
But who can cease to weep and look on this?
5 Here may his head lie on my throbbing breast,
But where's the body that I should embrace?

4.3 Location: Scene continues.
1. Butchers were not permitted to slaughter meat during the forty-day period before Easter during
which Christians were to avoid eating flesh) except by
special license to provide food for the ill. Cade promises

the Butcher that he will have such a license and that
Lent will be twice as long as it is now. *Thou . . . one*:
You can kill ninety-nine animals, or serve ninety-nine
customers.
4.4 Location: The palace, London.

BUCKINGHAM [*to* KING HENRY]   What answer makes your grace
    to the rebels' supplication?
KING HENRY   I'll send some holy bishop to entreat,
    For God forbid so many simple souls
10   Should perish by the sword. And I myself,
    Rather than bloody war shall cut them short,
    Will parley° with Jack Cade their general.   *speak*
    But stay, I'll read it over once again.
      [*He*] *read*[*s*]
QUEEN MARGARET [*to* Suffolk's head]   Ah, barbarous villains!
    Hath this lovely face
15   Ruled like a wandering planet over me,[1]
    And could it not enforce them to relent,
    That were unworthy to behold the same?
KING HENRY   Lord Saye, Jack Cade hath sworn to have thy head.
SAYE   Ay, but I hope your highness shall have his.
KING HENRY [*to* QUEEN MARGARET]   How now, madam? Still
20   lamenting and mourning
    Suffolk's death?
    I fear me, love, if that I had been dead,
    Thou wouldest not have mourned so much for me.
QUEEN MARGARET   No, my love, I should not mourn, but die for thee.
      Enter a MESSENGER [*in haste*]
25 KING HENRY   How now? What news? Why com'st thou in such haste?
MESSENGER   The rebels are in Southwark[2]—fly, my lord!
    Jack Cade proclaims himself Lord Mortimer,
    Descended from the Duke of Clarence' house,
    And calls your grace usurper, openly,
30   And vows to crown himself in Westminster.
    His army is a ragged multitude
    Of hinds and peasants, rude and merciless.
    Sir Humphrey Stafford and his brother's death
    Hath given them heart and courage to proceed.
35   All scholars, lawyers, courtiers, gentlemen,
    They call false caterpillars° and intend their death.   *treacherous parasites*
KING HENRY   O, graceless° men; they know not what they do.[3]   *sinful*
BUCKINGHAM   My gracious lord, retire to Kenilworth°   (*a royal castle*)
    Until a power be raised to put them down.
40 QUEEN MARGARET   Ah, were the Duke of Suffolk now alive
    These Kentish rebels would be soon appeased!°   *made peaceful*
KING HENRY   Lord Saye, the trait'rous rabble hateth thee—
    Therefore away with us to Kenilworth.
SAYE   So might your grace's person be in danger.
45   The sight of me is odious in their eyes,
    And therefore in this city will I stay
    And live alone as secret as I may.
      Enter another MESSENGER
SECOND MESSENGER [*to* KING HENRY]   Jack Cade hath almost gotten
    London Bridge;

---

1. It was popularly believed that influences from the stars ("wandering planets") determined the fate of those born under them.
2. A suburb of London (in Shakespeare's time, the site of brothels and theaters).
3. An echo of Jesus' words on the cross to those who crucified and mocked him. See Luke 23:34.

    The citizens fly and forsake their houses;
50   The rascal people, thirsting after prey,
    Join with the traitor; and they jointly swear
    To spoil° the city and your royal court.   *plunder*
BUCKINGHAM [*to* KING HENRY] Then linger not, my lord; away,
    take horse!
KING HENRY Come, Margaret. God, our hope, will succour us.
QUEEN MARGARET [*aside*] My hope is gone, now Suffolk is
55   deceased.
KING HENRY [*to* SAYE] Farewell, my lord. Trust not the Kentish
    rebels.
BUCKINGHAM [*to* SAYE] Trust nobody, for fear you be betrayed.
SAYE The trust I have is in mine innocence,
    And therefore am I bold and resolute.
                      Exeunt [SAYE *at one door, the rest at another*]

4.5

Enter the Lord SCALES *upon the Tower, walking.*
Enter three or four CITIZENS *below*

SCALES How now? Is Jack Cade slain?
FIRST CITIZEN No, my lord Scales,[1] nor likely to be slain, for he
    and his men have won the bridge, killing all those that did
    withstand them. The Lord Mayor craveth aid of your honour
5   from the Tower to defend the city from the rebels.
SCALES Such aid as I can spare you shall command,
    But I am troubled here with them myself.
    The rebels have essayed° to win the Tower.   *attempted*
    Get you to Smithfield,[2] there to gather head,°   *raise forces*
10   And thither will I send you Matthew Gough.
    Fight for your king, your country, and your lives!
    And so, farewell, for I must hence again.
                    Exeunt [SCALES *above, the* CITIZENS *below*]

4.6

Enter Jack Cade, [*the* WEAVER, *the* BUTCHER,] *and the*
rest. [CADE] *strikes his sword on London Stone*[1]

CADE Now is Mortimer lord of this city. And, here sitting upon
    London Stone, I charge and command that, of the city's cost,
    the Pissing Conduit[2] run nothing but claret wine this first
    year of our reign. And now henceforward it shall be treason
5   for any that calls me otherwise than Lord Mortimer.
              Enter a SOLDIER, *running*
SOLDIER Jack Cade, Jack Cade!
CADE Zounds,° knock him down there!   *God's wounds (an oath)*
        They kill him
BUTCHER If this fellow be wise, he'll never call ye Jack Cade
    more; I think he hath a very fair warning.
        [*He takes a paper from the soldier's body and reads it*]
10   My lord, there's an army gathered together in Smithfield.

4.5 Location: The Tower, London.
1. Thomas de Scales fought with Talbot in France and was charged by the King with the defense of the Tower.
2. Area just outside London's walls and to the northwest.
4.6 Location: Cannon Street, London.

1. An ancient stone found in Cannon Street and famous as a London landmark.
2. The nickname for Little Conduit, a fountain used by lower-class Londoners as a water supply.

CADE   Come then, let's go fight with them—but first, go on and
set London Bridge afire, and, if you can, burn down the Tower
too. Come, let's away.   *Exeunt*

4.7

Alarums. [Excursions, wherein] Matthew GOUGH *is
slain, and all the rest [of his men] with him. Then enter
Jack* CADE *with his company [among them the* BUTCHER,
the WEAVER, *and* JOHN, *a rebel]*

CADE   So, sirs, now go some and pull down the Savoy;[1] others
to th' Inns of Court[2]—down with them all.

BUTCHER   I have a suit unto your lordship.

CADE   Be it a lordship, thou shalt have it for that word.

5   BUTCHER   Only that the laws of England may come out of your
mouth.

JOHN [*aside to his fellows*]   Mass, 'twill be sore° law then, for he   harsh
was thrust in the mouth with a spear, and 'tis not whole yet.

WEAVER [*aside to* JOHN]   Nay, John, it will be stinking law, for his
10   breath stinks with eating toasted cheese.

CADE   I have thought upon it—it shall be so. Away! Burn all
the records of the realm. My mouth shall be the Parliament
of England.

JOHN [*aside to his fellows*]   Then we are like to have biting°   severe
15   statutes unless his teeth be pulled out.

CADE   And henceforward all things shall be in common.

            Enter a MESSENGER

MESSENGER   My lord, a prize, a prize! Here's the Lord Saye
which sold the towns in France. He that made us pay one-and-
twenty fifteens and one shilling to the pound the last subsidy.[3]

            Enter a rebel with the Lord SAYE[4]

20   CADE   Well, he shall be beheaded for it ten times. [*To* SAYE] Ah,
thou say, thou serge—nay, thou buckram lord![5] Now art thou
within point-blank° of our jurisdiction regal. What canst thou   within reach
answer to my majesty for giving up of Normandy unto Moun-
sieur Basimecu,[6] the Dauphin of France? Be it known unto
25   thee by these presence,[7] even the presence of Lord Mortimer,
that I am the besom° that must sweep the court clean of such   broom
filth as thou art. Thou hast most traitorously corrupted the
youth of the realm in erecting a grammar school; and,
whereas before, our forefathers had no other books but the
30   score and the tally,[8] thou hast caused printing to be used and,
contrary to the King his° crown and dignity, thou hast built a   the King's
paper-mill.[9] It will be proved to thy face that thou hast men

---

4.7 Location: Smithfield; London.
1. An anachronistic reference to the London residence
of the Duke of Lancaster, which was burned down during a 1381 uprising and not rebuilt until 1505.
2. The buildings where London's lawyers were trained
and lived.
3. He who made us pay very high personal property taxes
in the last tax assessment. A "fifteen" was a levy of one-
fifteenth of the property value; "twenty-one fifteens"
would be a tax in excess of the value of the property itself.
4. F and Q both read, "Enter George." As elsewhere,
the Oxford editors change what is assumed to be an
actor's name to the generic "a rebel."
5. Say was an expensive silk fabric, serge a durable

woolen fabric often worn by the lower classes, and
buckram a coarse linen also worn by the poor.
6. Punning on *baise mon cul*, French for "kiss my ass."
7. "These presents" was a legal term meaning "the
present document," a phrase that begins many legal
writings of the period. Cade, however, means "in the
presence of the King, who declares the law."
8. A rudimentary device for keeping track of financial
transactions. Sticks were marked, or "scored," split into
two pieces, and then divided between the debtor and
creditor. Each half was called a "tally."
9. Printing presses and paper mills were not in fact established in England until late in the fifteenth century.
Under Elizabeth, they were subject to strict regulation.

about thee that usually talk of a noun and a verb and such
abominable words as no Christian ear can endure to hear.
35 Thou hast appointed justices of peace to call poor men before
them about matters they were not able to answer. Moreover,
thou hast put them in prison, and, because they could not
read,[1] thou hast hanged them when indeed only for that
cause° they have been most worthy to live. Thou dost ride on   *for that reason alone*
40 a foot-cloth,[2] dost thou not?
SAYE What of that?
CADE Marry, thou ought'st not to let thy horse wear a cloak
when honester men than thou go in° their hose and doublets.   *wear only*
BUTCHER And work in their shirts, too; as myself, for example,
45 that am a butcher.
SAYE You men of Kent.
BUTCHER What say you of Kent?
SAYE Nothing but this—'tis *bona terra, mala gens.*[3]
CADE *Bonum terrum*—zounds, what's that?
50 BUTCHER He speaks French.
FIRST REBEL No, 'tis Dutch.
SECOND REBEL No, 'tis Out-talian, I know it well enough.
SAYE Hear me but speak, and bear me where you will.
Kent, in the commentaries Caesar writ,
55 Is termed the civil'st° place of all this isle;   *most civilized*
Sweet is the country, because full of riches;
The people liberal,° valiant, active, wealthy;   *generous*
Which makes me hope you are not void of pity.
I sold not Maine, I lost not Normandy;
60 Yet to recover them would lose my life.
Justice with favour° have I always done,   *leniency*
Prayers and tears have moved me—gifts could never.
When have I aught° exacted at your hands,   *anything*
But to maintain the King, the realm, and you?
65 Large gifts have I bestowed on learnèd clerks°   *scholars*
Because my book preferred me to[4] the King,
And seeing ignorance is the curse of God,
Knowledge the wing wherewith we fly to heaven.
Unless you be possessed with devilish spirits,
70 You cannot but forbear to murder me.
This tongue hath parleyed unto° foreign kings   *negotiated with*
For your behoof°—   *behalf*
CADE Tut, when struck'st thou one blow in the field?°   *battlefield*
SAYE Great men have reaching hands.[5] Oft have I struck
75 Those that I never saw, and struck them dead.
REBEL O monstrous coward! What, to come behind folks?
SAYE These cheeks are pale for watching for your good—
CADE Give him a box o'th' ear, and that will make 'em red again.
        [*One of the rebels strikes* SAYE]
SAYE Long sitting° to determine poor men's causes   *(as a judge)*
80 Hath made me full of sickness and diseases.

---

1. Read Latin. By demonstrating reading knowledge of Latin, a person charged with a crime in early modern England could plead "benefit of clergy" and thereby be excused from hanging.
2. An ornamented cloth hung over the back of a horse and reaching to the ground on each side.
3. A good land, a bad people.

4. Because my own education brought me to the attention of the King (and improved my social position).
5. A variation on the classical proverb "Kings have long hands," suggesting that monarchs and influential people such as lord Saye have influence that causes much to happen even when they are not present.

CADE   Ye shall have a hempen caudle,⁶ then, and the health
    o'th' hatchet.°   *executioner's ax*

BUTCHER [*to* SAYE]   Why dost thou quiver, man?

SAYE   The palsy, and not fear, provokes me.

85 CADE   Nay, he nods at us as who should say 'I'll be even with
    you'. I'll see if his head will stand steadier on a pole or no.
    Take him away, and behead him.

SAYE   Tell me wherein have I offended most?
    Have I affected wealth or honour? Speak.

90   Are my chests filled up with extorted gold?
    Is my apparel sumptuous to behold?
    Whom have I injured, that ye seek my death?
    These hands are free from guiltless bloodshedding,
    This breast from harbouring foul deceitful thoughts.

95   O let me live!

CADE [*aside*]   I feel remorse in myself with his words, but I'll bri-
    dle it. He shall die an it be but for pleading so well for his life.
    [*Aloud*] Away with him—he has a familiar° under his tongue;   *demon*
    he speaks not a God's name. Go, take him away, I say, to the
100 Standard⁷ in Cheapside, and strike off his head presently;° and   *immediately*
    then go to Mile End Green—break into his son-in-law's house,
    Sir James Cromer, and strike off his head, and bring them both
    upon two poles hither.

ALL CADE'S FOLLOWERS   It shall be done!

105 SAYE   Ah, countrymen, if, when you make your prayers,
    God should be so obdurate as yourselves,
    How would it fare with your departed souls?
    And therefore yet relent and save my life!

CADE   Away with him, and do as I command ye!
                 Exeunt [the BUTCHER *and] one or two*
                             with the Lord SAYE

110 The proudest peer in the realm shall not wear a head on his
    shoulders unless he pay me tribute. There shall not a maid be
    married but she shall pay to me her maidenhead,⁸ ere they
    have it. Married men shall hold of me *in capite*.⁹ And we
    charge and command that their wives be as free° as heart can   *sexually available*
115 wish or tongue can tell.
              Enter a REBEL

REBEL   O captain, London Bridge is afire!

CADE   Run to Billingsgate and fetch pitch and flax and
    quench it.
              Enter the BUTCHER *and a* SERGEANT

SERGEANT   Justice, justice, I pray you, sir, let me have justice of
120 this fellow here.

CADE   Why, what has he done?

SERGEANT   Alas, sir, he has ravished° my wife.   *raped*

BUTCHER [*to* CADE]   Why, my lord, he would have 'rested° me   *arrested*
    and I went and entered my action in his wife's proper house.¹

---

6. Caudel was a warm gruel, but "a hempen caudel" was a slang term for "hangman's noose."
7. A water conduit in Cheapside often used as a place of execution.
8. Alluding to a supposed feudal practice by which a lord had the right to sleep with the bride of any of his vassals on the night of her wedding.
9. A Latin phrase indicating property held by grant directly from the king, with a pun on *caput* (Latin for "head") as slang for "maidenhead."
1. Stated my case in his wife's own house; had sex in his wife's own body.

125 CADE Dick, follow thy suit in her common place.² [*To the*
SERGEANT] You whoreson° villain, you are a sergeant—you'll   *bastard*
take any man by the throat for twelve pence, and 'rest a man
when he's at dinner, and have him to prison ere the meat be
out of his mouth. [*To the* BUTCHER] Go, Dick, take him hence:
130 cut out his tongue for cogging,° hough° him for running, and,   *deception / cripple*
to conclude, brain him with his own mace.°   *staff of office*

Exit [the BUTCHER] with the SERGEANT

REBEL My lord, when shall we go to Cheapside and take up
commodities upon our bills?³
CADE Marry, presently. He that will lustily stand to it⁴ shall go
135 with me and take up these commodities following—item, a
gown, a kirtle, a petticoat, and a smock.⁵
ALL CADE'S FOLLOWERS O brave!

Enter two with the Lord Saye's head and Sir James
Cromer's upon two poles

CADE But is not this braver? Let them kiss one another, for they
loved well when they were alive.

[The two heads are made to kiss]

140 Now part them again, lest they consult about the giving up
of some more towns in France. Soldiers, defer the spoil°   *destruction; plunder*
of the city until night. For with these borne before us
instead of maces will we ride through the streets, and at
every corner have them kiss. Away!

Exeunt [two with the heads. The others begin to follow]

145 Up Fish Street! Down Saint Magnus' Corner!⁶ Kill and
knock down! Throw them into Thames!

Sound a parley

What noise is this? Dare any be so bold to sound retreat or
parley when I command them kill?

Enter the Duke of BUCKINGHAM and old Lord CLIFFORD

BUCKINGHAM Ay, here they be that dare and will disturb thee!
150 Know, Cade, we come ambassadors from the King
Unto the commons, whom thou hast misled,
And here pronounce free pardon to them all
That will forsake thee and go home in peace.
CLIFFORD What say ye, countrymen, will ye relent
155 And yield to mercy whilst 'tis offered you,
Or let a rebel lead you to your deaths?
Who loves the King and will embrace his pardon,
Fling up his cap and say 'God save his majesty'.
Who hateth him and honours not his father,
160 Henry the Fifth, that made all France to quake,
Shake he his weapon at us,° and pass by.   *Defy us*

They [fling up their caps and] forsake CADE

ALL CADE'S FOLLOWERS God save the King! God save the King!
CADE What, Buckingham and Clifford, are ye so brave?° [*To*   *arrogant*
the rabble] And you, base peasants, do ye believe him? Will
165 you needs be hanged with your pardons about your necks?

---

2. Pursue your sexual desire in her vagina; pursue your
legal suit in her meetinghouse.
3. And acquire goods on credit or by means of our
weapons ("bills"); and rape women, punning on "commodity" as meaning "female sexual organs" and "bills"
as meaning "penises."
4. Apply himself manfully; have an erection.
5. Slang terms for "female sexual organs."
6. Place at the north end of London Bridge opposite
Southwark.

Hath my sword, therefore, broke through London gates that
you should leave me at the White Hart[7] in Southwark?
I thought ye would never have given out° these arms till you   *abandoned*
had recovered your ancient freedom. But you are all recreants
170   and dastards,° and delight to live in slavery to the nobility. Let   *traitors and cowards*
them break your backs with burdens, take your houses over
your heads, ravish your wives and daughters before your
faces. For me, I will make shift for one,° and so God's curse   *take care of myself*
light upon you all.
175 ALL CADE'S FOLLOWERS   We'll follow Cade! We'll follow Cade!
        They run to CADE *again*
  CLIFFORD   Is Cade the son of Henry the Fifth
That thus you do exclaim you'll go with him?
Will he conduct you through the heart of France
And make the meanest° of you earls and dukes?   *lowest born*
180   Alas, he hath no home, no place to fly to,
Nor knows he how to live but by the spoil—
Unless by robbing of your friends and us.
Were't not a shame that whilst you live at jar°   *at odds*
The fearful° French, whom you late vanquishèd,   *timid*
185   Should make a start° o'er seas and vanquish you?   *rouse themselves*
Methinks already in this civil broil
I see them lording it in London streets,
Crying '*Villiago!*'[8] unto all they meet.
Better ten thousand base-born Cades miscarry°   *meet disaster*
190   Than you should stoop unto a Frenchman's mercy.
To France! To France! And get what you have lost!
Spare England, for it is your native coast.
Henry hath money; you are strong and manly;
God on our side, doubt not of victory.
195 ALL CADE'S FOLLOWERS   A Clifford!° A Clifford! We'll follow   *To Clifford*
the King and Clifford!
        [*They forsake* CADE]
  CADE [*aside*]   Was ever feather so lightly blown to and fro as this
multitude? The name of Henry the Fifth hales° them to   *draws*
an hundred mischiefs, and makes them leave me desolate.
200   I see them lay their heads together to surprise° me. My sword   *capture*
make way for me, for here is no staying. [*Aloud*] In despite of
the devils and hell, have through° the very middest of you!   *here I come through*
And heavens and honour be witness that no want of resolu-
tion in me, but only my followers' base and ignominious trea-
205   sons, makes me betake me to my heels.
        He runs through them with his staff, and flies away
  BUCKINGHAM   What, is he fled? Go, some, and follow him,
And he that brings his head unto the King
Shall have a thousand crowns for his reward.
                Exeunt some of them [*after* CADE]
[*To the remaining rebels*] Follow me, soldiers, we'll devise a mean°   *way*
210   To reconcile you all unto the King.   *Exeunt*

---

7. An inn, with a pun on the coward's "white heart"   8. A variation on the Italian word for "coward."
(because drained of its blood or spirit).

4.8

Sound trumpets. Enter KING HENRY, QUEEN
[MARGARET], *and* [*the Duke of*] SOMERSET
on the terrace

KING HENRY   Was ever King that joyed° an earthly throne   *enjoyed*
And could command no more content than I?
No sooner was I crept out of my cradle
But I was made a king at nine months old.

5   Was never subject longed to be a king
As I do long and wish to be a subject.

Enter the Duke of BUCKINGHAM *and* [*Lord*] CLIFFORD
[*on the terrace*]

BUCKINGHAM [*to* KING HENRY]   Health and glad tidings to your majesty.
KING HENRY   Why, Buckingham, is the traitor Cade surprised?
Or is he but retired to make him strong?

Enter [*below*] *multitudes with halters¹ about their
necks*

10   CLIFFORD   He is fled, my lord, and all his powers do yield,
And humbly thus with halters on their necks
Expect° your highness' doom° of life or death.   *Await / sentence*
KING HENRY   Then, heaven, set ope° thy everlasting gates   *open*
To entertain my vows of thanks and praise.

15   [*To the multitudes below*] Soldiers, this day have you redeemed your lives,
And showed how well you love your prince and country.
Continue still° in this so good a mind,   *always*
And Henry, though he be infortunate,°   *unlucky*
Assure yourselves will never be unkind.

20   And so, with thanks and pardon to you all,
I do dismiss you to your several countries.°   *different regions*
ALL CADE'S FORMER FOLLOWERS   God save the King! God save
the King!   [*Exeunt multitudes below*]

Enter a MESSENGER [*on the terrace*]

MESSENGER [*to* KING HENRY]   Please it your grace to be advertisèd°   *informed*
25   The Duke of York is newly come from Ireland,
And with a puissant and a mighty power
Of galloglasses and stout Irish kerns²
Is marching hitherward in proud array,
And still proclaimeth, as he comes along,

30   His arms are only to remove from thee
The Duke of Somerset, whom he terms a traitor.
KING HENRY   Thus stands my state,° 'twixt Cade and York distressed,   *condition*
Like to a ship that, having scaped a tempest,
Is straightway calmed° and boarded with a pirate.   *becalmed*

35   But now is Cade driven back, his men dispersed,
And now is York in arms to second° him.   *support*
I pray thee, Buckingham, go and meet him,
And ask him what's the reason of these arms.

4.8 Location: Kenilworth Castle.
1. Cade's followers wore nooses as a sign of their
submission.

2. See note to 3.1.310. *galloglasses*: professional Irish
mercenary soldiers who were usually armed with axes
and rode on horseback.

Tell him I'll send Duke Edmund° to the Tower;   *Somerset*
40   And, Somerset, we will commit thee thither,
Until his army be dismissed from him.
SOMERSET   My lord, I'll yield myself to prison willingly,
Or unto death, to do my country good.
KING HENRY [*to* BUCKINGHAM]   In any case, be not too rough in terms,°   *language*
45   For he is fierce and cannot brook° hard language.   *endure*
BUCKINGHAM   I will, my lord, and doubt not so to deal
As all things shall redound unto your good.
KING HENRY   Come, wife, let's in and learn to govern better;
For yet° may England curse my wretched reign.   *up until now*

                     Flourish. Exeunt

4.9

    Enter Jack CADE[1]
CADE   Fie on ambitions; fie on myself that have a sword and yet
am ready to famish. These five days have I hid me in these
woods and durst not peep out, for all the country is laid° for   *set with traps*
me. But now am I so hungry that if I might have a lease of my
5   life for a thousand years, I could stay° no longer. Wherefore   *delay*
o'er a brick wall have I climbed into this garden to see if I can
eat grass or pick a sallet° another while, which is not amiss to   *salad*
cool a man's stomach° this hot weather. And I think this word   *hunger; anger*
'sallet' was born to do me good; for many a time, but for a
10   sallet,° my brain-pan had been cleft with a brown bill;[2] and   *helmet*
many a time, when I have been dry, and bravely marching, it
hath served me instead of a quart pot to drink in; and now the
word 'sallet' must serve me to feed on.
    [*He*] *lies down picking of herbs and eating them.*
    Enter [*Sir*] *Alexander* IDEN *and* [*five of*] *his men*
IDEN   Lord, who would live turmoilèd° in the court   *harried*
15   And may enjoy such quiet walks as these?
This small inheritance my father left me
Contenteth me, and worth a monarchy.
I seek not to wax great by others' waning,
Or gather wealth I care not with what envy;
20   Sufficeth that° I have maintains my state,   *that what*
And sends the poor well pleasèd° from my gate.   *(with their alms)*
    [CADE *rises to his knees*]
CADE [*aside*]   Zounds, here's the lord of the soil come to seize
me for a stray° for entering his fee-simple[3] without leave. [*To*   *trespasser*
IDEN] A villain, thou wilt betray me and get a thousand crowns
25   of the king by carrying my head to him; but I'll make thee eat
iron like an ostrich[4] and swallow my sword like a great pin, ere
thou and I part.

4.9 Location: Alexander Iden's garden, in Kent.
1. Q's stage direction indicates that Jack Cade enters at one door and Alexander Iden and his men at another. Q's version of this scene is shorter than F's and makes clear what F only implies: that Iden is accompanied by attendants. The presence of these figures makes Cade's offer to fight Iden seem the more courageous. In Q, Iden enters unarmed, orders one of his men to fetch his

sword, and chivalrously orders them to stand aside while he fights Cade. In F, Iden presumably enters armed.
2. A long-handled weapon with an axlike blade. The brown color is from blood or varnish.
3. Property that belonged forever to its owner and his or her heirs; on it, stray animals could legally be seized.
4. It was popularly believed that ostriches ate iron.

IDEN   Why, rude companion,° whatsoe'er thou be,   *lowborn fellow*
    I know thee not. Why then should I betray thee?
30   Is't not enough to break into my garden,
    And, like a thief, to come to rob my grounds,
    Climbing my walls in spite of me the owner,
    But thou wilt brave° me with these saucy terms?   *taunt*
CADE   Brave thee? Ay, by the best blood that ever was
35   broached°—and beard° thee too! Look on me well—I have eat   *shed / defy*
    no meat these five days, yet come thou and thy five men, an
    if I do not leave you all as dead as a doornail I pray God I may
    never eat grass more.
IDEN   Nay, it shall ne'er be said while England stands
40   That Alexander Iden, an esquire of Kent,
    Took odds° to combat a poor famished man.   *advantage*
    Oppose thy steadfast gazing eyes to mine—
    See if thou canst outface me with thy looks.
    Set limb to limb, and thou art far the lesser—
45   Thy hand is but a finger to my fist,
    Thy leg a stick comparèd with this truncheon.°   *thick staff (his leg)*
    My foot shall fight with all the strength thou hast,
    And if mine arm be heavèd in the air,
    Thy grave is digged already in the earth.
50   As for words, whose greatness answers words,[5]
    Let this my sword report what speech forbears.
    [*To his men*] Stand you all aside.
CADE   By my valour, the most complete° champion that ever I   *accomplished*
    heard. [*To his sword*] Steel, if thou turn the edge° or cut not   *fail to cut*
55   out the burly-boned clown in chines° of beef ere thou sleep in   *roasts*
    thy sheath, I beseech God on my knees thou mayst be turned
    to hobnails.
        [*CADE stands.*] *Here they fight, and* CADE *falls down*
    O, I am slain! Famine and no other hath slain me! Let ten
    thousand devils come against me, and give me but the ten
60   meals I have lost, and I'd defy them all. Wither, garden, and
    be henceforth a burying place to all that do dwell in this
    house, because the unconquered soul of Cade is fled.
IDEN   Is't Cade that I have slain, that monstrous traitor?
    Sword, I will hallow thee for this thy deed
65   And hang thee o'er my tomb when I am dead.
    Ne'er shall this blood be wipèd from thy point
    But thou shalt wear it as a herald's coat
    To emblaze the honour that thy master got.[6]
CADE   Iden, farewell, and be proud of thy victory. Tell Kent
70   from me she hath lost her best man, and exhort all the world
    to be cowards. For I, that never feared any, am vanquished by
    famine, not by valour.   *He dies*
IDEN   How much thou wrong'st me, heaven be my judge.
    Die, damnèd wretch, the curse of her that bore thee!
75   And [*stabbing him again*] as I thrust thy body in with my sword,[7]
    So wish I I might thrust thy soul to hell.

---

5. This line may be corrupt. It may mean "As for words, I whose might more than matches your words."
6. *But . . . got:* Just as a device on a herald's coat proclaims his lord's identity and status, so the blood on Iden's sword proclaims the fame he has won for killing Cade.
7. As I thrust my sword into your body.

Hence will I drag thee headlong° by the heels   *head downward*
Unto a dunghill, which shall be thy grave,
And there cut off thy most ungracious head,
80   Which I will bear in triumph to the King,
Leaving thy trunk for crows to feed upon.

Exeunt [with the body]

5.1

Enter the Duke of YORK *and his army of Irish*
with [a] drum[mer] and soldiers [bearing] colours

YORK   From Ireland thus comes York to claim his right,
And pluck the crown from feeble Henry's head.
Ring, bells, aloud; burn, bonfires, clear and bright,
To entertain° great England's lawful king.   *welcome*
5   Ah, *sancta maiestas!*° Who would not buy thee dear?   *sacred majesty*
Let them obey that knows not how to rule;
This hand was made to handle naught but gold.
I cannot give due action to my words,
Except° a sword or sceptre balance it.   *Unless*
10   A sceptre shall it have, have I° a sword,   *as sure as I have*
On which I'll toss the fleur-de-lis of France.[1]

Enter the Duke of BUCKINGHAM

[*Aside*] Whom have we here? Buckingham to disturb me?
The King hath sent him sure—I must dissemble.
BUCKINGHAM   York, if thou meanest well, I greet thee well.
15   YORK   Humphrey of Buckingham, I accept thy greeting.
Art thou a messenger, or come of pleasure?
BUCKINGHAM   A messenger from Henry, our dread liege,
To know the reason of these arms° in peace;   *armed men*
Or why thou, being a subject as I am,
20   Against thy oath and true allegiance sworn,
Should raise so great a power without his leave,
Or dare to bring thy force so near the court?
YORK [*aside*]   Scarce can I speak, my choler is so great.
O, I could hew up rocks and fight with flint,
25   I am so angry at these abject terms;°   *insulting words*
And now, like Ajax Telamonius,[2]
On sheep or oxen could I spend my fury.
I am far better born than is the King,
More like a king, more kingly in my thoughts;
30   But I must make fair weather° yet a while,   *pretend to be mild*
Till Henry be more weak and I more strong.
[*Aloud*] Buckingham, I prithee pardon me,
That I have given no answer all this while;
My mind was troubled with deep melancholy.
35   The cause why I have brought this army hither
Is to remove proud Somerset from the King,
Seditious to his grace and to the state.
BUCKINGHAM   That is too much presumption on thy part;
But if thy arms be to no other end,

5.1 Location: The remainder of the play takes place in
an open field between St. Albans and London.
1. On which I'll impale the national emblem of France,
the lily flower.

2. A Greek hero of the Trojan War who went mad and
slaughtered a flock of sheep, taking them to be his
Greek enemies.

40   The King hath yielded unto thy demand:
        The Duke of Somerset is in the Tower.
    YORK   Upon thine honour, is he prisoner?
    BUCKINGHAM   Upon mine honour, he is prisoner.
    YORK   Then, Buckingham, I do dismiss my powers.
45   Soldiers, I thank you all; disperse yourselves;
        Meet me tomorrow in Saint George's field³
        You shall have pay and everything you wish.   *Exeunt soldiers*
        [*To* BUCKINGHAM] And let my sovereign, virtuous Henry,
        Command° my eldest son—nay, all my sons—   *Demand*
50   As pledges of my fealty and love.
        I'll send them all as willing as I live.
        Lands, goods, horse, armour, anything I have
        Is his to use, so° Somerset may die.   *provided that*
    BUCKINGHAM   York, I commend this kind° submission.   *natural; proper*
55   We twain will go into his highness' tent.
                Enter KING HENRY *and attendants*
    KING HENRY   Buckingham, doth York intend no harm to us,
        That thus he marcheth with thee arm in arm?
    YORK   In all submission and humility
        York doth present himself unto your highness.
60 KING HENRY   Then what intends these forces thou dost bring?
    YORK   To heave the traitor Somerset from hence,
        And fight against that monstrous rebel Cade,
        Who since I heard to be discomfited.°   *defeated*
                Enter IDEN *with Cade's head*
    IDEN   If one so rude° and of so mean condition°   *uncultivated / low rank*
65   May pass into the presence of a king,
        [*Kneeling*] Lo, I present your grace a traitor's head,
        The head of Cade, whom I in combat slew.
    KING HENRY   The head of Cade? Great God, how just art thou!
        O let me view his visage, being dead,
70   That living wrought me such exceeding trouble.
        Tell me, my friend, art thou the man that slew him?
    IDEN [*rising*]   Iwis,° an't like° your majesty.   *Truly / if it please*
    KING HENRY   How art thou called? And what is thy degree?°   *rank*
    IDEN   Alexander Iden, that's my name;
75   A poor esquire⁴ of Kent that loves his king.
    BUCKINGHAM [*to* KING HENRY]   So please it you, my lord, 'twere not amiss
        He were created knight for his good service.
    KING HENRY   Iden, kneel down.
                [IDEN *kneels and* KING HENRY *knights him*]
                        Rise up a knight.
                [IDEN *rises*]
        We give thee for reward a thousand marks,
80   And will° that thou henceforth attend on us.   *command*
    IDEN   May Iden live to merit such a bounty,
        And never live but true unto his liege.   *Exit*
                Enter Queen [MARGARET] *and the Duke of* SOMERSET
    KING HENRY   See, Buckingham, Somerset comes wi'th' Queen.
        Go bid her hide him quickly from the Duke.

---

3. One of the main drill grounds for Elizabethan militia, located south of the Thames.

4. A member of the gentry ranking just below a knight.

85 QUEEN MARGARET For thousand Yorks he shall not hide his head,
But boldly stand and front° him to his face.   *confront*
YORK How now? Is Somerset at liberty?
Then, York, unloose thy long imprisoned thoughts,
And let thy tongue be equal with thy heart.
90 Shall I endure the sight of Somerset?
False King, why hast thou broken faith with me,
Knowing how hardly I can brook abuse?⁵
'King' did I call thee? No, thou art not king;
Not fit to govern and rule multitudes,
95 Which dar'st not—no, nor canst not—rule a traitor.
That head of thine doth not become a crown;
Thy hand is made to grasp a palmer's° staff,   *pilgrim's*
And not to grace an aweful° princely sceptre.   *awe-inspiring*
That gold must round engird these brows of mine,
100 Whose smile and frown, like to Achilles' spear,
Is able with the change to kill and cure.⁶
Here is a hand to hold a sceptre up,
And with the same to act° controlling laws.   *enact*
Give place! By heaven, thou shalt rule no more
105 O'er him whom heaven created for thy ruler.
SOMERSET O monstrous traitor! I arrest thee, York,
Of capital treason 'gainst the King and crown.
Obey, audacious traitor; kneel for grace.
YORK [*to an attendant*] Sirrah, call in my sons to be my bail.
                                                    [*Exit attendant*]
110 I know, ere they will have me go to ward,°   *into custody*
They'll pawn° their swords for my enfranchisement.°   *pledge / freedom*
QUEEN MARGARET [*to* BUCKINGHAM] Call hither Clifford; bid
    him come amain,°   *at once*
To say if that the bastard boys of York
Shall be the surety for their traitor father. [*Exit* BUCKINGHAM]
115 YORK O blood-bespotted Neapolitan,⁷
Outcast of Naples, England's bloody scourge!
The sons of York, thy betters in their birth,
Shall be their father's bail, and bane° to those   *destruction*
That for my surety will refuse the boys.
            Enter at one door York's sons EDWARD *and crookback*
            RICHARD *with [a] drum[mer] and soldiers*⁸
120 See where they come. I'll warrant they'll make it good.
            Enter at the other door CLIFFORD *and his son, with [a]*
            drum[mer] and soldiers
QUEEN MARGARET And here comes Clifford to deny their bail.
CLIFFORD [*kneeling before* KING HENRY] Health and all happi-
    ness to my lord the King.
            [*He rises*]
YORK I thank thee, Clifford. Say, what news with thee?
Nay, do not fright us with an angry look—

---

5. Knowing with what difficulty I can tolerate deception.
6. Telephus, wounded by Achilles' spear, was cured by rust from that same spear.
7. Margaret's father claimed the throne of Naples. Elizabethan writers typically associated Italy with sexual vice, criminality, and the evils of Roman Catholicism.

8. This spectacular double entry of York's sons, followed by Clifford and his son, each accompanied by drummer and soldiers, is indicated only in Q. F's stage directions read, "Enter Edward and Richard" and "Enter Clifford."

125   We are thy sovereign, Clifford; kneel again.
        For thy mistaking so, we pardon thee.
        CLIFFORD   This is my king, York; I do not mistake.
        But thou mistakes me much to think I do.
        [*To* KING HENRY] To Bedlam⁹ with him! Is the man grown mad?
130   KING HENRY   Ay, Clifford, a bedlam° and ambitious humour°   *mad / disposition*
        Makes him oppose himself against his king.
        CLIFFORD   He is a traitor; let him to the Tower,
        And chop away that factious pate° of his.   *rebellious head*
        QUEEN MARGARET   He is arrested, but will not obey.
135   His sons, he says, shall give their words for him.
        YORK [*to* EDWARD *and* RICHARD]   Will you not, sons?
        EDWARD   Ay, noble father, if our words will serve.
        RICHARD   And if words will not, then our weapons shall.
        CLIFFORD   Why, what a brood of traitors have we here!
140   YORK   Look in a glass,° and call thy image so.   *mirror*
        I am thy king, and thou a false-heart traitor.
        Call hither to the stake my two brave bears,
        That with the very shaking of their chains,
        They may astonish these fell-lurking° curs.¹   *savagely waiting*
145   [*To an attendant*] Bid Salisbury and Warwick come to me.
                                          [*Exit attendant*]
        Enter the Earls of WARWICK *and* SALISBURY *with* [*a*]
        drum[*mer*] *and soldiers*
        CLIFFORD   Are these thy bears? We'll bait thy bears to death,
        And manacle the bearherd° in their chains,   *bear keeper (York)*
        If thou dar'st bring them to the baiting place.°   *bear pit*
        RICHARD   Oft have I seen a hot o'erweening° cur   *overconfident*
150   Run back and bite,° because he was withheld;   *(his keeper)*
        Who, being suffered with° the bear's fell° paw,   *injured by / savage*
        Hath clapped his tail between his legs and cried;
        And such a piece of service will you do,
        If you oppose yourselves° to match Lord Warwick.   *undertake*
155   CLIFFORD   Hence, heap of wrath, foul indigested lump,
        As crooked in thy manners as thy shape!²
        YORK   Nay, we shall heat you thoroughly anon.°   *soon*
        CLIFFORD   Take heed, lest by your heat you burn yourselves.
        KING HENRY   Why, Warwick, hath thy knee forgot to bow?
160   Old Salisbury, shame to thy silver hair,
        Thou mad misleader of thy brainsick son!
        What, wilt thou on thy deathbed play the ruffian,
        And seek for sorrow with thy spectacles?°   *eyes; eyeglasses*
        O, where is faith? O, where is loyalty?
165   If it be banished from the frosty head,
        Where shall it find a harbour in the earth?
        Wilt thou go dig a grave to find out° war,   *in seeking out*
        And shame thine honourable age with blood?

---

9. The shortened name of a London lunatic asylum. See note to 3.1.51.
1. York refers to the Elizabethan sport of bearbaiting, in which a tame bear was chained to a stake and set upon with dogs. Warwick's family crest depicted a bear chained to a staff. See below, lines 200–1.

2. *foul . . . shape*: alluding to the fact that Richard of Gloucester was deformed from birth (he was a hunchback) and to the notion that bears are born as formless lumps and licked into shape by their mothers. *indigested*: ill-formed.

Why, art thou old and want'st° experience?   *lack*
170   Or wherefore dost abuse it if thou hast it?
    For shame in duty bend thy knee to me,
    That bows unto the grave with mickle° age.   *much*
SALISBURY   My lord, I have considered with myself
    The title of this most renownèd Duke,
175   And in my conscience do repute his grace
    The rightful heir to England's royal seat.
KING HENRY   Hast thou not sworn allegiance unto me?
SALISBURY   I have.
KING HENRY   Canst thou dispense with heaven for[3] such an oath?
180 SALISBURY   It is great sin to swear unto a sin,
    But greater sin to keep a sinful oath.
    Who can be bound by any solemn vow
    To do a murd'rous deed, to rob a man,
    To force a spotless virgin's chastity,
185   To reave° the orphan of his patrimony,   *bereave*
    To wring the widow from her customed right,[4]
    And have no other reason for this wrong
    But that he was bound by a solemn oath?
QUEEN MARGARET   A subtle traitor needs no sophister.°   *expert in false reasoning*
KING HENRY [*to an attendant*]   Call Buckingham, and bid him
190   arm himself.   [*Exit attendant*]
YORK [*to* KING HENRY]   Call Buckingham and all the friends thou hast,
    I am resolved for death or dignity.°   *(the crown)*
CLIFFORD   The first, I warrant thee, if dreams prove true.
WARWICK   You were best to go to bed and dream again,
195   To keep you from the tempest of the field.
CLIFFORD   I am resolved to bear a greater storm
    Than any thou canst conjure up today—
    And that I'll write upon thy burgonet°   *helmet*
    Might I but know thee by thy household badge.°   *family crest*
200 WARWICK   Now by my father's badge, old Neville's crest,[5]
    The rampant bear chained to the ragged° staff,   *jagged*
    This day I'll wear aloft° my burgonet,   *on top of*
    As on a mountain top the cedar shows
    That keeps his leaves in spite of any storm,
205   Even to affright thee with the view thereof.
CLIFFORD   And from thy burgonet I'll rend thy bear,
    And tread it under foot with all contempt,
    Despite the bearherd that protects the bear.
YOUNG CLIFFORD   And so to arms, victorious father,
210   To quell the rebels and their complices.°   *accomplices*
RICHARD   Fie, charity, for shame! Speak not in spite—
    For you shall sup with Jesu Christ tonight.
YOUNG CLIFFORD   Foul stigmatic,[6] that's more than thou canst tell.
RICHARD   If not in heaven, you'll surely sup in hell.

               Exeunt [*severally*]

---

3. Can you win dispensation from heaven for breaking.
4. Her traditional right to a portion of her husband's estate.
5. The Neville badge was actually a bull. Warwick inherited the badge of a bear from his father-in-law, Richard Beauchamp.
6. One branded with the mark of crime, as Richard is "branded" with deformity.

5.2

[An alehouse sign: a castle.] Alarums to the battle. Then
enter the Duke of SOMERSET *and* RICHARD *fighting.*
RICHARD *kills* [SOMERSET] *under the sign*

RICHARD   So lie thou there—
For underneath an alehouse' paltry sign,
The Castle in Saint Albans, Somerset
Hath made the wizard famous in his death.[1]
5   Sword, hold thy temper;[2] heart, be wrathfull still—
Priests pray for enemies, but princes kill.
Exit [with Somerset's body. The sign is removed]

5.3

Alarum again. Enter the Earl of WARWICK

WARWICK   Clifford of Cumberland, 'tis Warwick calls!
An if thou dost not hide thee from the bear,
Now, when the angry trumpet sounds alarum,
And dead° men's cries do fill the empty air,   *dying*
5   Clifford I say, come forth and fight with me!
Proud northern lord, Clifford of Cumberland,
Warwick is hoarse with calling thee to arms!
CLIFFORD [*within*]   Warwick, stand still; and stir not till I come.
Enter [the Duke of] YORK
WARWICK   How now, my noble lord? What, all afoot?°   *not on horseback*
10   YORK   The deadly-handed Clifford slew my steed.
But match to match I have encountered him,
And made a prey for carrion kites and crows
Even of the bonny beast he loved so well.
Enter [Lord] CLIFFORD
WARWICK [*to* CLIFFORD]   Of one or both of us the time is come.
15   YORK   Hold, Warwick—seek thee out some other chase,°   *game*
For I myself must hunt this deer to death.
WARWICK   Then nobly, York; 'tis for a crown thou fight'st.
[*To* CLIFFORD] As I intend, Clifford, to thrive today,
It grieves my soul to leave thee unassailed.   *Exit*
20   YORK   Clifford, since we are singled here alone,
Be this the day of doom to one of us.
For know my heart hath sworn immortal hate
To thee and all the house of Lancaster.
CLIFFORD   And here I stand and pitch my foot to thine,
25   Vowing not to stir till thou or I be slain.
For never shall my heart be safe at rest
Till I have spoiled° the hateful house of York.   *stripped of honor*
Alarums. They fight. YORK *kills* CLIFFORD
YORK   Now, Lancaster, sit sure—thy sinews shrink.°   *powers fail*
Come, fearful° Henry, grovelling on thy face—   *timid*
30   Yield up thy crown unto the prince of York.[1]   *Exit*
30.1   CLIFFORD   *What seest thou in me, York? Why dost thou pause?*
YORK   *With thy brave bearing° should I be in love,*   *fine appearance*

5.2 Location: Scene continues.
1. Somerset's death under the sign of the Castle Inn confirms the spirit's warning that he shun castles (see 1.4.34–36). *in his:* by his (Somerset's).
2. Retain the resiliency of steel.

5.3 Location: Scene continues.
1. Oxford adopts Q's version of the confrontation between Clifford and York at lines 20–30; the F version, an edited text of which follows in the indented passage (lines 30.1–30.12), may be the author's original draft.

> But that thou art so fast mine enemy.

CLIFFORD Nor should thy prowess want° praise and esteem,   lack

30.5 But that 'tis shown ignobly and in treason.

YORK So let it help me now against thy sword,

> As I in justice and true right express it.

CLIFFORD My soul and body on the action both.²

YORK A dreadful lay.° Address° thee instantly.   wager / Prepare

30.10 CLIFFORD La fin couronne les oeuvres.³

> *Alarums. They fight.* YORK *kills* CLIFFORD

YORK Thus war hath given thee peace, for thou art still.

> Peace with his soul, heaven, if it be thy will.   Exit

> *Alarums, then enter* YOUNG CLIFFORD

YOUNG CLIFFORD Shame and confusion, all is on the rout!°   in disorderly retreat

Fear frames° disorder, and disorder wounds   gives rise to

Where it should guard. O, war, thou son of hell,

Whom angry heavens do make their minister,

35 Throw in the frozen° bosoms of our part°   cowardly / faction

Hot coals of vengeance! Let no soldier fly!

He that is truly dedicate° to war   dedicated

Hath no self-love; nor he that loves himself

Hath not essentially, but by circumstance,°   merely by accident

The name of valour.

> [*He sees his father's body*]

40   O, let the vile world end,

And the premisèd° flames of the last day   foreordained

Knit earth and heaven together.

Now let the general trumpet blow his blast,⁴

Particularities° and petty sounds   Individual affairs

45 To cease! Wast thou ordainèd, dear father,

To lose thy youth in peace, and to achieve

The silver livery of advisèd° age,   wise

And in thy reverence and thy chair-days,° thus   old age

To die in ruffian battle? Even at this sight

50 My heart is turned to stone, and while 'tis mine

It shall be stony. York not our old men spares;

No more will I their babes. Tears virginal

Shall be to me even as the dew to fire,⁵

And beauty that the tyrant oft reclaims°   calms the tyrant

55 Shall to my flaming wrath be oil and flax.

Henceforth I will not have to do with pity.

Meet I an infant of the house of York,

Into as many gobbets° will I cut it   lumps of flesh

As wild Medea young Absyrtus did.⁶

60 In cruelty will I seek out my fame.

Come, thou new ruin of old Clifford's house,

> *He takes* [*his father's body*] *up on his back*

As did Aeneas old Anchises bear,⁷

---

2. I wager both my soul and body on the outcome of
this fight (action).
3. The end crowns the works (French).
4. Young Clifford is evoking doomsday, when a trumpet
will summon everyone to judgment (see 1 Corinthians
15:52).
5. Dew was popularly believed to make fire burn more
fiercely.

6. According to classical mythology, as Medea fled over
the sea with her lover, Jason, she murdered her brother
Absyrtus and scattered bits of his body on the waves so
that her father would stop to collect the fragments and
be delayed in his pursuit of her.
7. In Virgil's *Aeneid* 2.707–29, Aeneas carries his aged
father, Anchises, on his back in their escape from the
burning city of Troy.

So bear I thee upon my manly shoulders.
But then Aeneas bare a living load,
65   Nothing so heavy as these woes of mine.   [*Exit with the body*]

5.4

Alarums again. Then enter three or four bearing the
Duke of BUCKINGHAM *wounded to his tent. Alarums*
still. Enter KING [HENRY], QUEEN [MARGARET], *and*
others

QUEEN MARGARET   Away, my lord! You are slow. For shame, away!
KING HENRY   Can we outrun the heavens?° Good Margaret, stay.   *escape our fate*
QUEEN MARGARET   What are you made of? You'll nor° fight nor fly.   *neither*
   Now is it manhood, wisdom, and defence,
5   To give the enemy way, and to secure us°   *save ourselves*
   By what° we can, which° can no more but fly.   *whatever means / who*
     Alarum afar off
   If you be ta'en, we then should see the bottom
   Of all our fortunes; but if we haply scape°—   *by chance escape*
   As well we may if not° through your neglect—   *if we don't fail*
10   We shall to London get where you are loved,
   And where this breach now in our fortunes made
   May readily be stopped.
     Enter [YOUNG] CLIFFORD
YOUNG CLIFFORD [*to* KING HENRY]   But that my heart's on future
     mischief set,
   I would speak blasphemy ere° bid you fly;   *before I would*
15   But fly you must; uncurable discomfit°   *irreversible defeat*
   Reigns in the hearts of all our present parts.°   *remaining forces*
   Away for your relief, and we will live
   To see their day and them our fortune give.[1]
   Away, my lord, away!   *Exeunt*

5.5

Alarum. Retreat. Enter the Duke of YORK, [*his sons*
EDWARD *and*] RICHARD, *and soldiers*, [*including a*]
drum[*mer*] *and* [*some bearing*] *colours*

YORK [*to* EDWARD *and* RICHARD]   How now, boys! Fortunate this
     fight hath been,
   I hope, to us and ours for England's good
   And our great honour, that so long we lost
   Whilst faint-heart Henry did usurp our rights.
5   Of Salisbury, who can report of him?
   That winter° lion who in rage forgets   *aged*
   Agèd contusions and all brush of time,[1]
   And, like a gallant in the brow° of youth,   *prime*
   Repairs° him with occasion.° This happy day   *Revives / action*
10   Is not itself, nor have we won one foot
   If Salisbury be lost.
RICHARD   My noble father,

5.4 Location: Scene continues.
1. *we . . . give:* we will survive to see a day of victory like
theirs and to make them suffer misfortunes like ours.

5.5 Location: Scene continues.
1. Bruises of old age and all assaults of time.

Three times today I holp° him to his horse;   helped
Three times bestrid him;[2] thrice I led him off,
Persuaded him from any further act;
15 But still° where danger was, still there I met him,   always
And like rich hangings in a homely° house,   humble
So was his will in his old feeble body.
        Enter [the Earls of] SALISBURY *and* [WARWICK]
EDWARD [*to* YORK]   See, noble father, where they both do come—
The only props unto the house of York!
20 SALISBURY   Now, by my sword, well hast thou fought today;
By th' mass, so did we all. I thank you, Richard.
God knows how long it is I have to live,
And it hath pleased him that three times today
You have defended me from imminent death.
25 Well, lords, we have not got that which we have[3]—
'Tis not enough our foes are this time fled,
Being opposites of such repairing nature.[4]
YORK   I know our safety is to follow them,
For, as I hear, the King is fled to London,
30 To call a present court of Parliament.
Let us pursue him ere the writs° go forth.   summons to Parliament
What says Lord Warwick, shall we after them?
WARWICK   After them? Nay, before them if we can!
Now by my hand, lords, 'twas a glorious day!
35 Saint Albans battle won by famous York
Shall be eternized° in all age to come.   immortalized
Sound drums and trumpets, and to London all,
And more such days as these to us befall! [*Flourish.*] *Exeunt*

---

2. Stood over the fallen Salisbury to protect him.   4. Since they are enemies who can quickly recover
3. We have not secured what we have won.   what they have lost.

Richard Duke of York (3 Henry VI)

There are two Richards in the play known in its octavo version as *The True Tragedy of Richard Duke of York and the Good King Henry the Sixth* (3 *Henry VI*). As the play begins, the title character, Richard of York, is leading an attempt to seize the English throne from Henry VI, the Lancastrian King. This Richard is killed at the end of the first act, and it is his tragic death to which the play's title refers. He, however, has four sons: Edward, Edmund (known as the Earl of Rutland), George, and Richard. This second Richard, who eventually acquires the title Duke of Gloucester, is a hunchback; and much of the play chronicles his attempts to continue his father's efforts to seize the English throne. Near the end of the play, this second Richard meditates on his condition:

> Then, since the heavens have shaped my body so,
> Let hell make crooked my mind to answer it.
> I had no father, I am like no father;
> I have no brother, I am like no brother;
> And this word, 'love', which greybeards call divine,
> Be resident in other men like one another
> And not in me—I am myself alone.
>
> (5.6.78–84)

This chilling pronouncement places Richard outside kinship networks, even though his two older brothers, Edward and George, are very much alive; and it exempts him from ordinary bonds of human affection.

Claiming to know nothing of love, Richard blames his isolation on his deformity. He is not "like" other men, not like his brothers, because heaven has shaped his body crookedly. This is a convenient explanation for villainy and alienation. But the play's exploration of deformity and its relationship to the breakdown of social order and emotional bonds is more complex than Richard here allows. Is Richard's hunchback the cause of his villainy or merely its outward sign? Are his villainy and deformity unique or simply the most tangible manifestation of a social deformity that reaches far beyond this single character? Richard's hump invites such questions, but the answers must be sought by broadly surveying the dramatic world in which Richard is placed.

Richard Duke of York is one of the most ambitious of Shakespeare's history plays simply in terms of the historical matter it covers. It is in part a continuation of *The First Part of the Contention of the Two Famous Houses of York and Lancaster* (2 *Henry VI*), the play in which Shakespeare began to dramatize the Wars of the Roses between the Lancastrian descendants of Edward III, who took the red rose for their symbol, and his Yorkist descendants, who claimed the white. In the struggles between these two branches of the family, the Yorkists asserted that Henry VI's grandfather, Henry IV, had illegitimately usurped the throne from Richard II, the son of Edward III's oldest male offspring, Edward, the Black Prince. Even though the Lancastrians could claim the throne through John of Gaunt, Edward III's fourth son, the Yorkists felt that they had a superior claim as descendants of the third son, Lionel, Duke of Clarence, and his daughter Philippa. In *Richard Duke of York*, Shakespeare depicts many of the most significant military encounters stemming from the struggle between the two branches of the family, stretching from the Battle of Wakefield (1460), in which the Duke of York

205

was captured and killed by the Lancastrian forces of Henry VI, to the Battle of Tewkesbury in 1471, in which Edward, the eldest son of Richard Duke of York, decisively defeated the Lancastrian army. It is after the latter battle, and Richard Duke of Gloucester's subsequent murder of Henry VI in the Tower of London, that the hunchbacked Richard speaks his chilling lines about having no father and no brother.

As with all his history plays, Shakespeare's *Richard Duke of York* takes many liberties with its historical sources, in this case Raphael Holinshed's *Chronicles of England, Scotland, and Ireland* (1587 edition) and Edward Hall's *Union of the Two Noble and Illustre [Illustrious] Famelies of Lancastre & Yorke* (1548). Many historical events are simply omitted or conflated with other events, and aspects of the historical record are altered for dramatic or thematic purposes. For example, at the time of the Battle of Wakefield, at which Richard Duke of York was killed, his son Richard was only seven years old. But in Shakespeare's play, he is a grown man who himself participates in the battle and after it vows revenge for his father's death. Moreover, that death is handled with grim originality. In Hall, Clifford decapitates York, then puts a paper crown on his severed head and presents it on a pole to Margaret, Henry VI's warlike queen. In Holinshed, Clifford verbally torments York before beheading him. But in none of the sources does Margaret dominate the scene as she does in Shakespeare's play. In *Richard Duke of York*, she taunts York ferociously and—a detail found in none of the sources—to wipe his tears gives him a handkerchief that has been dipped in the blood of Rutland, York's twelve-year-old son, who had been butchered by Clifford earlier in the same battle. Eventually both Margaret and Clifford stab York, and Margaret orders his head displayed on the gates of the city of York. This act is typical of Margaret's audacity throughout the play. The only character to appear in all four of Shakespeare's first histories (*The First Part of the Contention [2 Henry VI], Richard Duke of York [3 Henry VI], 1 Henry VI,* and *Richard III*), Margaret dominates much of the action of this one. Fiercely protective of her son's rights and skilled as both general and diplomat, she is unmatched as a publicly powerful figure by any of the female characters in Shakespeare's later histories.

The scene in which Margaret tortures York and he excoriates her as an Amazonian whore must have been riveting theater. In September of 1592, Robert Greene, a rival playwright, published *Greene's Groats-worth of Wit,* in which he makes fun of Shakespeare by parodying a line from this scene. Richard at one point exclaims of Margaret, "O tiger's heart wrapped in a woman's hide!" (1.4.138). Greene writes of Shakespeare that "there is an upstart Crow, beautified with our feathers, that with his *Tiger's heart wrapt in a Player's hide,* supposes he is as well able to bombast out a blank verse as the best of you: and being an absolute *Johannes fac totum* [jack-of-all-trades], is in his own conceit the onely Shakes-scene in a country." Greene, who had a university education, clearly resented Shakespeare, who did not but who was

Seventeenth-century ornamental halberd from southern Germany.

nonetheless having considerable theatrical success. Greene accuses Shakespeare either of appropriating his work or of acting in his dramas ("beautified with our feathers") and of thinking too well of himself and his many theatrical skills. Particularly striking is Greene's own appropriation of Richard's line about Margaret to apply to Shakespeare. Implicitly, Greene suggests that there is something as unnatural and presumptuous in Shakespeare's theatrical ambition as in the cruelty and ambition of Henry's manlike Queen. At the same time, this appropriative gesture pays tribute, however grudging, to Shakespeare's skill as a writer of memorable dialogue. Affronted by Shakespeare's success, Greene nonetheless grants his rival the homage of parody. The lines have another value as well. Although *Richard Duke of York* was first printed in a shortened octavo version in 1595, Greene's comments suggest that some version of the play had been staged or was circulating in manuscript by late summer of 1592 (see Textual Note).

This early play, then, may have brought Shakespeare contemporary notoriety. It certainly shows his boldness in adopting chronicle history to fit the requirements of the theater. And while some critics have seen *Richard Duke of York* as flawed, evidencing Shakespeare's weariness with his dramatization of the Wars of the Roses or his inability to shape so much matter into coherent form, theatrical productions of this play attest to its viability on the stage. The vicious energies of hate and ambition that propel the play make its enactment an intense and exhausting experience. The vigorous stage battles, the soaring rhetorical duels between the contending factions, the centrality of the ruthless Margaret, the emergence of the alienated Richard, Duke of Gloucester as the brooding antihero—these are elements that, particularly in the post–World War II period, have led to many memorable productions, productions that emphasize a once-civil world spiraling vertiginously toward chaos.

But the play is also more than the sum of its memorable parts. When Richard asserts, "I am myself alone," his chosen isolation follows from the play's carefully orchestrated dramatization of the breakdown of social order, particularly as epitomized in the breakdown of family ties. From its inception, the Wars of the Roses, a continuing civil war, was also a family feud in that it pitted the Lancastrian and Yorkist descendants of Edward III against one another. But in the prior play, *The First Part of the Contention*, members of each family line and their followers typically remained loyal to their faction. Family lineage was a source of pride and identity. One sees this also in *1 Henry VI* in the idealized relationship between the English hero Lord Talbot and his son John. John aspires in all respects to emulate his father, and the two of them die together in battle defending England and the honor of their family name. In *Richard Duke of York,* by contrast, family bonds are hideously fragile; and when they break, chaos ensues. Unflinching in its depiction of emotional and physical violence, the play examines the forms of monstrous individualism that emerge when the social identities provided by networks of kinship and feudal loyalty no longer exert their hold. In effect, *Richard Duke of York* depicts the radical separation of self from defining social networks as a species of monstrosity.

The signal event in the play's treatment of the sundering of family bonds is King Henry's startling offer, at the beginning of Act 1, to entail the crown to Richard, Duke of York in exchange for Henry's right to hold the throne during his lifetime. Henry has a son, Prince Edward, and his act negates his son's right to the throne. It also transforms the crown of England from a symbol of lineal succession into an alienable property. The immediate consequence is that Henry's supporters turn from him in disgust and his wife, Queen Margaret, proclaims:

> I here divorce myself
> Both from thy table, Henry, and thy bed,
> Until that act of Parliament be repealed
> Whereby my son is disinherited.
>
> (1.1.248–51)

Suddenly, Edward is *her* son, not Henry's; and soon thereafter she is raising an army to lead against the Yorkists. Many in the play describe Margaret's acts as unnatural, yet they

Edward IV (1442–1483). Probably painted during his reign; artist unknown.

follow from Henry's feckless negation of his role as guarantor of his son's succession. It was a truism of the early modern gender system that unmanly men, unnatural in their weakness, opened the door to a corresponding anomaly, the manlike woman. Margaret is represented as such a figure, taking Henry's place both at the head of his army and also as champion of young Edward's lineal rights. In both roles, the Queen is highly effective for much of the play. Though demonized, Margaret embodies strengths that contradict the patriarchal view that women are inherently weaker than men and therefore less suited to have dominion either in the state or in the household.

Occasionally, especially in his early plays, Shakespeare wrote what Hereward T. Price called "mirror scenes," that is, scenes that are separate from the main line of plot development but that symbolically encapsulate, or mirror, some of the play's chief thematic concerns. In *Richard Duke of York,* 2.5 is such a scene. Having given command of his army to Clifford and Margaret, Henry sits contemplatively upon a molehill while the Battle of Towton proceeds without him. Voicing his longing for the simplicity of a pastoral life, Henry suddenly sees a soldier carry onstage a man he has killed. It turns out to be the soldier's father, who was forced to serve with the Yorkist forces, while the son had been impressed into King Henry's service. The King then observes a second soldier carry onstage a man *he* has killed. It turns out to be the soldier's son. The scene schematically underscores one of the play's primary emblems of social disintegration: namely, the severing of bonds between father and son, son and father, leaving nothing to replace these bonds but individual rapaciousness. In both instances, the killers of the dead men have brought the bodies onstage to search them for money—"some store of crowns" (2.5.57) and "gold" (80). The ironic power of the scene is heightened, of course, because its central events are witnessed and lamented by King Henry, who has already disinherited his own son and as King is the symbolic fountainhead from which the familial disorder before him flows.

But the most interesting variation on the theme of dissevered families is embodied in the persons of Richard, Duke of York and his four sons: Edward, George, Richard, and Rutland. At the beginning of the play, the Yorks constitute an unusually integrated unit. Richard's sons support their father and urge him to seize the crown. Before he is captured at the Battle of Wakefield, Richard praises his offspring, assuming that in the battle "they have demeaned themselves / Like men born to renown by life or death" (1.4.7–8). At Wakefield, one of Richard's sons, the young Rutland, is killed. Just before the remaining three sons learn that their father has also died as a consequence of that battle, they praise him, as he has praised them. No one is more gracious than young Richard, who says, "Methinks 'tis prize enough to be his son" (2.1.20). At that moment, three suns appear in the heavens, each distinct, and then these suns join together.

The pun on "suns/sons" seems to lead Edward to interpret this odd spectacle to mean that the three sons of Richard,

> Each one already blazing by our meeds,
> Should notwithstanding join our lights together
> And over-shine the earth as this the world.
>
> (2.1.36–38)

He then pledges to have three suns emblazoned on his shield.

Like all portents, the exact significance of this one is unclear. To Edward, it seems to imply the unwavering unity of the three sons of York. Yet Richard, who is to be as devastated as any of them by the news of their father's death, treats Edward's assertion that he will wear three suns on his shields as the occasion for a joke that distances him from his brother. "Nay, bear three daughters— by your leave I speak it— / You love the breeder better than the male" (2.1.41–42). With the death of the powerful patriarch, Richard, Duke of York, fraternal rivalry quickly replaces fraternal unity, and broken allegiances multiply. When Edward insists on marrying a commoner, the widow Lady Elizabeth Gray, War-

"My ashes, as the phoenix, may bring forth / A bird that will revenge upon you all" (1.4.36–37). From Geffrey Whitney, *A Choice of Emblemes* (1586).

wick, who is Edward's strongest supporter and who has been sent to France to secure a French bride for Edward, turns against him in disgust. George temporarily abandons his brother, marries Warwick's daughter, and joins the Lancastrian cause. Richard, always outwardly loyal, privately vows to hack his way to the throne and displace both of his brothers in the process.

With ties of kinship and loyalty broken, nothing remains but the sheer exertion of individual will. Richard emerges as both the most fascinating and the most horrific character in the second half of the play because his will is indomitable and his desires unchecked by any moral constraints. The audience probably registers this fact most decisively during the bravura soliloquy that Richard speaks after he and George have watched—and obscenely commented upon—Edward's wooing of Lady Gray. Soliloquies, in which a character speaks to himself but is overheard by the theater audience, help create the illusion of interiority and inner subjectivity. Perhaps goaded by jealousy at the sight of Edward's successful wooing of Lady Gray, Richard in his soliloquy both reveals his frustrations and desires and hardheadedly maps a future course. In quick succession, he contemplates the number of people who before him have claims on the throne; resigns himself to seek instead the pleasures of courtship and love; despairs, since his deformed body prevents him from being loved; resolves therefore to seek the crown at any cost; and vows to change himself into any imaginable persona necessary to achieve his end. The soliloquy is long (3.2.124–95) and relentless. Richard tracks his argument like a bloodhound, registering his predicament with memorably vivid language.

> And yet I know not how to get the crown,
> For many lives stand between me and home.
> And I—like one lost in a thorny wood,

> That rends the thorns and is rent with the thorns,
> Seeking a way and straying from the way,
> Not knowing how to find the open air,
> But toiling desperately to find it out—
> Torment myself to catch the English crown.
>   (3.2.172–79)

Struggle and frustration are evident in the repetitions of this passage. Seeking, straying, toiling, Richard is in constant motion, throwing himself against impossible barriers. The crown eludes him, yet he goes on. He is by turns attractive and frightening.

Many prototypes are drawn upon to create this distinctive character. His "individuality" does not emerge from nowhere but depends on Shakespeare's skillful appropriation of prior dramatic resources. Richard's characterization owes much, for example, to the striving, overreaching stage heroes created by Shakespeare's early rival Christopher Marlowe. Like Marlowe's Tamburlaine, Richard makes his heaven "to dream upon the crown" (3.2.168) and stops at nothing to achieve that goal. In part, he is also fashioned after the Vice figure from the medieval religious drama. The Vice was the character—often witty and quite disconcertingly entertaining—who embodied the principle of evil and tried to compel others to sin. Richard's witty asides, as much as his aggression and lack of scruple, reveal his kinship to the Vice. Perhaps this character's strongest association, however, is with the figure of the stage Machiavel, whom Richard himself evokes at the end of his soliloquy. The historical Niccolò Machiavelli was an Italian political philosopher whose influential book *The Prince* pragmatically rather than moralistically detailed the tactics and principles that made for successful government in the modern world. In the popular imagination, he came to stand for the hypocrisy and political cunning associated with Protestant England's symbolic enemy, Catholic Italy.

Sharing affinities with each of these figures but not fully modeled on any of them, Richard functions in Shakespeare's play to suggest what emerges when one no longer acknowledges the primacy of the identities constructed by the words "son" and "brother." In a society that defined people in terms of their place within family structures and social hierarchies, to separate oneself from those structures and hierarchies risked being read as monstrous and unnatural. Richard is riveting precisely because he seems so autonomous and so indifferent to the bonds and loyalties—to family and to king—that supposedly hold his society together and constrain the actions of its members. Though not the only one in the play whose ambition corrodes ties of blood and allegiance, Richard most fully epitomizes ambition's deforming effects. One way to read Richard's crooked back is as a physical sign of his unnatural inner being. Yet it is also true that to Richard his crooked body is the cause of (or at least the excuse for) his behavior. In modern psychological terms, he is compensating for a handicap in the only way he can. But it is a measure of Shakespeare's distance from us that such a reading of Richard's deformity is countered by another that emphasizes the moral significance of physical signs and is deeply ambivalent about the very idea of the socially autonomous individual.

Marriage is one way to incorporate individuals into social structures, but in *Richard Duke of York* the breakdown of social bonds is both caused and symbolized by its disorderly marriages. In the feudal world depicted in most of Shakespeare's early history plays, marriages in noble or monarchical families were primarily premised not on love but on dynastic convenience. Wives were to be chosen for the dowry or the territory or the alliances they brought with them. To marry for love was viewed as dangerous because it introduced irrational passion into what was supposed to be a rational choice and threatened the husband's control of himself and of his spouse. In marrying the widow Lady Gray, Edward makes such a passion-driven marriage and thereby nearly loses control of the kingdom. By his actions, he forfeits Warwick's loyalty and temporarily that of his brother George. King Henry had also made an irrational match in marrying the dowerless Margaret (see *The First Part of the Contention* 1.1). In *Richard Duke of York*, this initial lack of control finds its consequence in Henry's inability to govern Margaret and in the increasingly topsy-turvy nature of their marriage.

The end of the play, however, refocuses on the marriage of Edward and Lady Gray to bring a tenuous and highly ironized sense of resolution to the play's action. In the final scene, King Edward admires the son to which his wife, now Queen Elizabeth, has given birth and invites his brothers Richard and Clarence to do the same. The ambience is domestic in a modern way. This is a marriage of affection more than utility. Edward calls the babe "Ned" (5.7.16) and his wife "Bess" (15), the nicknames suggesting intimacy. But if Edward thinks this cozy domesticity, so pleasing to him but so politically ill advised, can reestablish the Yorkist dynasty and center it on him and his descendants, the presence of Richard signals otherwise. Leaning down to kiss the babe, Richard says, "And that I love the tree from whence thou sprang'st, / Witness the loving kiss I give the fruit" (31–32). The tree he refers to is, of course, the family of York, the family tree from which he himself springs. But then, in an aside, he adds: "To say the truth, so Judas kissed his master, / And cried 'All hail!' whenas he meant all harm" (33–34). For Richard to cast himself as the betrayer of Christ bodes badly for the happy family: Edward, Ned, and Bess. To late twentieth-century audiences and theatergoers, the King's doting attention to his wife and son may make him seem quite modern and quite human. Yet viewed historically and in its dramatic context, the King's behavior also signals his weakness, his propensity to let his affections overrule his reason. Fixated on his Ned and his Bess, he seems oblivious to the threat posed by his alienated, thoroughly undomestic brother.

Richard Duke of York ends, then, with a scene that underscores the tenuousness of Edward's purchase on power and threatens a renewal of civil war and family strife. The play's imaginative landscape is dominated by those willful, monstrous individuals such as Richard and Margaret who thrive amid the chaos of a disintegrating society. Few can oppose them, most especially not "the good King Henry," a man disastrously unsuited to play a monarch's part. Hovering on the periphery of this play's action and killed before its final scene, Henry is gradually transformed into a mere observer of the public world around him. Saintly and detached, he comes to represent the antithesis of Richard's surging, self-centered ambition, finally serving almost as choric commentator and as prophet. He predicts, for example, that Henry, Earl of Richmond (later Henry VII) will be England's savior (4.7.68–76), and he predicts (5.6.37–43) that many will come to curse the hunchbacked Richard (later Richard III). But hope for release from Richard's evil lies far in the future, and Henry's increasing saintliness neither erases his responsibility for civil war nor solves the immediate problem of secular rule. Neither saints nor monsters are particularly suited to govern other men. Edward is neither and so seems more fit to rule; yet he is unable to control, or even to recognize, his brother's villainy. *Richard Duke of York* feels so grim because its compelling depiction of the unraveling of England's social fabric suggests little about how that fabric can once again be rewoven.

JEAN E. HOWARD

TEXTUAL NOTE

In 1595, *The True Tragedy of Richard Duke of York and the Good King Henry the Sixth* was published in an octavo volume, and the same text appeared in quarto format in 1600. In 1602, control of the play fell to Thomas Pavier, who in 1619 issued another, edited, quarto version. Both of these quartos are based on the Octavo of 1595 (O) and have no independent textual authority. In 1623, a play approximately one thousand lines longer than any of these early texts appeared in Shakespeare's First Folio (F) under the title *The third part of Henry the Sixt*. While some scholars believe that the 1595 Octavo text is an early draft of the play included in the First Folio, the Oxford editors follow the majority of editors since the 1920s in assuming that the Octavo is a memorial reconstruction of an abridged and revised version of the Folio text. (For a discussion of theories of memorial reconstruction, see the Textual Note to *The First Part of the Contention [2 Henry VI]*.) Consequently, the control text for *Richard Duke of York* is F, though the Oxford editors have retained the title used in the Octavo text on the theory that that was the title by which the play was probably known during Shakespeare's lifetime. They assume that the manuscript used for setting the Folio copy was the author's "foul papers," which had not been marked up for theatrical performance, because F contains a number of vague and unspecific stage directions as well as a high proportion of musical cues. Interestingly, several speeches bear actor's names (Gabriel, Sinklo, Humfrey) rather than characters' (Messenger [1.2.49] and First Gamekeeper and Second Gamekeeper [3.1]). The Octavo text, however, is believed to have been based on the promptbook for a theatrical production and contains important stage directions and perhaps some authorial revisions that occurred between the play's foul-papers stage and the promptbook. In some cases, when Octavo staging seems preferable to that suggested in F, this edition has rearranged dialogue or speech assignments to accord with such staging. These changes are marked in the notes and Textual Variants.

The Oxford text employs the standard act and scene divisions into which the play was divided in the eighteenth century, with two exceptions. A new scene is marked at 4.3.27, indicating that the stage is cleared between the time Edward's guards fly from his tent and Edward is subsequently brought onstage as a captive. And at the very end of Act 4, Scene 10 is introduced to separate Henry's conversation with Warwick about Edward's return from the Low Countries from his subsequent conversation with Exeter before he is surprised and seized by Edward and Richard, Duke of Gloucester.

SELECTED BIBLIOGRAPHY

Bergeron, David. "The Play-Within-the-Play in 3 *Henry VI*." *Tennessee Studies in Literature* 22 (1977): 37–47. Examines four instances of Shakespeare's early use of the play within the play in 3 *Henry VI*.

Berman, Ronald. "Fathers and Sons in the *Henry VI* Plays." *Shakespeare Quarterly* 13 (1962): 487–97. Explores the disruption of relations between fathers and sons, kings and subjects under conditions of war and unstable monarchy.

Carroll, D. Allen. "Greene's 'Upstart Crow' Passage: A Survey of Commentary." *Research Opportunities in Renaissance Drama* 28 (1985): 111–27. Explores the possible meanings of Robert Greene's attack on Shakespeare as an "upstart Crow," a phrase used in Shakespeare's play to describe Queen Margaret.

Champion, Larry. "Developmental Structure in Shakespeare's Early Histories: The Perspective of 3 *Henry VI*." *Studies in Philology* 76 (1979): 218–38. Argues that the play reveals Shakespeare's increasing technical sophistication and mastery of dramatic structure.

Hunt, Maurice. "Unnaturalness in Shakespeare's 3 *Henry VI*." *English Studies: A Journal of English Language and Literature* 80 (1999): 146–67. Links Shakespeare's play to Thomas Sackville and Thomas Norton's earlier tragedy, *Gorboduc,* as each explores the motif of unnatural behavior and its political consequences.

Kahn, Coppélia. " 'The Shadow of the Male': Masculine Identity in the History Plays." *Man's Estate: Masculine Identity in Shakespeare.* Berkeley: University of California Press, 1981. 47–81. Argues that in the early history plays masculine identity emerges primarily from emulation of or rivalry with the father.

Leggatt, Alexander. "Henry VI." *Shakespeare's Political Drama: The History Plays and the Roman Plays.* London: Routledge, 1988. 1–31. Explores the undermining of heroism and the breakdown of social order in the three plays featuring Henry VI.

Levine, Nina S. "Ruling Women and the Politics of Gender in 2 and 3 *Henry VI.*" *Women's Matters: Politics, Gender, and Nation in Shakespeare's Early History Plays.* Newark: University of Delaware Press, 1998. 68–96. Argues that in 3 *Henry VI* the misogyny surrounding Margaret's representation is tempered by her role in fighting for her son's succession to the throne and her defense of the English national interest.

Loehlin, James N. "Brecht and the Rediscovery of *1 Henry VI.*" *Shakespeare's History Plays: Performance, Translation and Adaptation in Britain and Abroad.* Ed. Ton Hoenselaars. Cambridge: Cambridge University Press, 2004. 133–50. Examines the role of Bertolt Brecht's dramatic theory on the resurgence of interest in performing the Henry VI plays after 1960.

Williamson, Marilyn L. "'When Men Are Rul'd by Women': Shakespeare's First Tetralogy." *Shakespeare Studies* 19 (1987): 41–59. Explores how strong female characters such as Margaret become scapegoats for the chaos of civil war.

FILM

The Tragedy of Richard the Third. 1983. Dir. Jane Howell. UK/USA. 112 min. A BBC-TV production with Julia Foster as Margaret and Peter Benson as a bookish and ineffectual Henry VI. (Released as *Richard III* in the United Kingdom.)

The True Tragedy of Richard Duke of York and the Good King Henry the Sixth

THE PERSONS OF THE PLAY

Of the King's Party

KING HENRY VI
QUEEN MARGARET
PRINCE EDWARD, their son
Duke of SOMERSET
Duke of EXETER
Earl of NORTHUMBERLAND
Earl of WESTMORLAND
Lord CLIFFORD
Lord Stafford
SOMERVILLE
Henry, young Earl of Richmond
A SOLDIER who has killed his father
A HUNTSMAN who guards King Edward

The Divided House of Neville

Earl of WARWICK, first of York's party, later of Lancaster's
Marquis of MONTAGUE, his brother, of York's party
Earl of OXFORD, their brother-in-law, of Lancaster's party
Lord HASTINGS, their brother-in-law, of York's party

Of the Duke of York's Party

Richard Plantagenet, Duke of YORK
EDWARD, Earl of March, his son, later Duke of York and KING
    EDWARD IV
LADY GRAY, a widow, later Edward's wife and queen
Earl RIVERS, her brother
GEORGE, Edward's brother, later Duke OF CLARENCE
RICHARD, Edward's brother, later Duke OF GLOUCESTER
Earl of RUTLAND, Edward's brother
Rutland's TUTOR, a chaplain
SIR JOHN Mortimer, York's uncle
Sir Hugh Mortimer, his brother
Duke of NORFOLK
Sir William Stanley
Earl of Pembroke
Sir John MONTGOMERY
A NOBLEMAN
TWO GAMEKEEPERS
Three WATCHMEN, who guard King Edward's tent
LIEUTENANT of the Tower

The French

KING LOUIS

LADY BONA, his sister-in-law

Lord Bourbon, the French High Admiral

Others

A SOLDIER who has killed his son

A SECOND SOLDIER who has killed his father

Mayor of Coventry

MAYOR of York

Aldermen of York

Soldiers, messengers, and attendants

1.1

[*A chair of state.*]¹ *Alarum.*° *Enter Richard Plantagenet,*   Call to arms
Duke of YORK, [*his two sons*] EDWARD, *Earl of March,*
[*and*] *Crookback*° RICHARD, *the Duke of* NORFOLK,   hunchback
[*the*] *Marquis* [*of*] MONTAGUE, [*and*] *the Earl of*
WARWICK, *with drum*[*mers*] *and soldiers.* [*They all*
wear] *white roses*² *in their hats*

WARWICK   I wonder how the King escaped our hands?

YORK   While we pursued the horsemen of the north,
He slyly stole away and left his men;
Whereat the great lord of Northumberland,
5   Whose warlike ears could never brook retreat,³
Cheered up the drooping army; and himself,
Lord Clifford, and Lord Stafford, all abreast,
Charged our main battle's° front, and, breaking in,   army's
Were by the swords of common soldiers slain.⁴

10   EDWARD   Lord Stafford's father, Duke of Buckingham,
Is either slain or wounded dangerous.°   dangerously
I cleft his beaver° with a downright° blow.   helmet visor / vertical
That this is true, father, behold his blood.
[*He shows a bloody sword*]

MONTAGUE [*to* YORK]   And, brother,⁵ here's the Earl of Wiltshire's blood,
[*He shows a bloody sword*]
15   Whom I encountered as the battles joined.

RICHARD [*to Somerset's head, which he shows*]
Speak thou for me, and tell them what I did.

YORK   Richard hath best deserved of all my sons.
[*To the head*] But is your grace dead, my lord of Somerset?

1.1 Location: The Parliament House, London.
1. Although neither O nor F indicates a chair or a raised platform ("a state"), Warwick's lines at 22–27, King Henry's at 50–51, and the stage direction at 32 ("They go up") all suggest that both stage properties are required here. Since the play focuses on the struggle for the English throne, it is fitting that it open with a vacant chair of state.
2. Emblem of the Yorkists. This play depicts part of what is called the Wars of the Roses between the Yorkists, who wore the white rose, and the Lancastrians, who wore the red rose. For Shakespeare's dramatization of the origin of this convention, see *1 Henry VI* 2.4. In O, when the Lancastrian faction enters at line 49, below,

they wear red roses. Both here and at line 49, F's stage directions make no mention of roses. O concludes this direction "with Drum and Soldiers, with white Roses in their hats," leaving ambiguous whether the roses are worn by the soldiers alone or by the entire party.
3. Could never endure hearing the trumpet call signaling retreat.
4. Shakespeare names York (rather than a common soldier) as the person who killed Clifford at several points later in the play. *The First Part of the Contention* (2 *Henry VI*) dramatizes this death in 5.3.
5. The historical Montague was York's nephew. He was also, as Shakespeare suggests elsewhere in this play, Warwick's brother.

NORFOLK Such hap have all the line of John of Gaunt.[6]

20 RICHARD Thus do I hope to shake King Henry's head.
 [*He holds aloft the head, then throws it down*]

WARWICK And so do I, victorious prince of York.
 Before I see thee seated in that throne
 Which now the house of Lancaster usurps,
 I vow by heaven these eyes shall never close.

25 This is the palace of the fearful° King,   *frightened*
 And this [*pointing to the chair of state*], the regal seat—possess it, York,
 For this is thine, and not King Henry's heirs'.

YORK Assist me then, sweet Warwick, and I will,
 For hither we have broken in by force.

30 NORFOLK We'll all assist you—he that flies shall die.

YORK Thanks, gentle° Norfolk. Stay by me, my lords   *noble*
 And soldiers—stay, and lodge by me this night.
 They go up [*upon the state*]

WARWICK And when the King comes, offer him no violence
 Unless he seek to thrust you out perforce.°   *by force*
 [*The soldiers withdraw*][7]

35 YORK The Queen this day here holds her Parliament,
 But little thinks we shall be of her council;
 By words or blows here let us win our right.

RICHARD Armed as we are, let's stay within this house.

WARWICK 'The Bloody Parliament' shall this be called,
40 Unless Plantagenet, Duke of York, be king,
 And bashful Henry deposed, whose cowardice
 Hath made us bywords° to our enemies.   *objects of scorn*

YORK Then leave me not, my lords. Be resolute—
 I mean to take possession of my right.

45 WARWICK Neither the King nor he that loves him best—
 The proudest he that holds up° Lancaster—   *supports*
 Dares stir a wing if Warwick shake his bells.[8]
 I'll plant Plantagenet,[9] root him up who dares.
 Resolve thee, Richard—claim the English crown.
 [YORK *sits in the chair.*]
 Flourish.° *Enter* KING HENRY, [*Lord*] CLIFFORD,   *Trumpet fanfare*
 the Earl of NORTHUMBERLAND, *the Earl of*
 WESTMORLAND, *the Duke of* EXETER, *and the rest.*
 [*They all wear*] *red roses in their hats*

50 KING HENRY My lords, look where the sturdy° rebel sits—   *stubborn*
 Even in the chair of state! Belike he means,
 Backed by the power of Warwick, that false peer,
 To aspire unto the crown and reign as king.
 Earl of Northumberland, he slew thy father—

---

6. May all the descendants of John of Gaunt have the same fate. John of Gaunt held the title Duke of Lancaster; Somerset was his grandson, and Henry VI his great-grandson. The Yorkists contended that John of Gaunt's son Henry IV had usurped Richard II's crown.

7. Neither F nor O indicates when the soldiers leave the stage, but we can assume that they do leave since they are given a reentrance at line 170.

8. If Warwick makes a move. Elizabethans attached bells to the legs of falcons in order to further frighten the falcon's prey; Warwick is comparing himself to such a threatening bird.

9. Richard, Duke of York was also called Richard Plantagenet. The Plantagenets were the medieval dynasty that began to rule England in 1154, when Henry II assumed the throne. The Yorkist and Lancastrian families were both descended from this dynasty.

55　And thine, Lord Clifford—and you both have vowed revenge
　　On him, his sons, his favourites, and his friends.
NORTHUMBERLAND　If I be not, heavens be revenged on me.
CLIFFORD　The hope thereof makes Clifford mourn in steel.[1]
WESTMORLAND　What, shall we suffer this? Let's pluck him down.
60　My heart for anger burns—I cannot brook it.
KING HENRY　Be patient, gentle Earl of Westmorland.
CLIFFORD　Patience is for poltroons,° such as he [*indicating* YORK].　　　*cowards*
　　He durst not sit there had your father lived.
　　My gracious lord, here in the Parliament
65　Let us assail the family of York.
NORTHUMBERLAND　Well hast thou spoken, cousin,° be it so.　　　*kinsman*
KING HENRY　Ah, know you not the city° favours them,　　　*(London)*
　　And they have troops of soldiers at their beck?°　　　*absolute command*
EXETER　But when the Duke is slain, they'll quickly fly.
70　KING HENRY　Far be the thought of this from Henry's heart,
　　To make a shambles° of the Parliament House.　　　*slaughterhouse*
　　Cousin of Exeter, frowns, words, and threats
　　Shall be the war that Henry means to use.
　　[*To* YORK] Thou factious° Duke of York, descend my throne　　　*rebellious*
75　And kneel for grace and mercy at my feet.
　　I am thy sovereign.
YORK　　　　　　I am thine.
EXETER　For shame, come down—he made thee Duke of York.
YORK　It was mine inheritance, as the earldom[2] was.
EXETER　Thy father was a traitor to the crown.[3]
80　WARWICK　Exeter, thou art a traitor to the crown
　　In following this usurping Henry.
CLIFFORD　Whom should he follow but his natural king?
WARWICK　True, Clifford, and that's Richard Duke of York.
KING HENRY [*to* YORK]　And shall I stand and thou sit in my throne?
85　YORK　It must and shall be so—content thyself.
WARWICK [*to* KING HENRY]　Be Duke of Lancaster, let him be king.
WESTMORLAND　He is both king and Duke of Lancaster—
　　And that, the Lord of Westmorland shall maintain.
WARWICK　And Warwick shall disprove it. You forget
90　That we are those which chased you from the field,
　　And slew your fathers, and, with colours° spread,　　　*flags*
　　Marched through the city to the palace gates.
NORTHUMBERLAND　Yes, Warwick, I remember it to my grief,
　　And, by his soul, thou and thy house shall rue it.
95　WESTMORLAND [*to* YORK]　Plantagenet, of thee, and these thy sons,
　　Thy kinsmen, and thy friends, I'll have more lives
　　Than drops of blood were in my father's veins.
CLIFFORD [*to* WARWICK]　Urge it no more, lest that, instead of words,
　　I send thee, Warwick, such a messenger
100　As shall revenge his death before I stir.

1. In armor (rather than the black cloaks that were conventionally worn by mourners).
2. The earldom of March, which York inherited from his mother and through which he claimed the throne.
3. York's father, the Earl of Cambridge, was executed for treason (see *Henry V* 2.2).

WARWICK [*to* YORK]   Poor Clifford, how I scorn his worthless threats.

YORK [*to* KING HENRY]   Will you we° show our title to the crown?   *Do you wish us to*

 If not, our swords shall plead it in the field.

KING HENRY   What title hast thou, traitor, to the crown?

105 Thy father was, as thou art, Duke of York;⁴

 Thy grandfather, Roger Mortimer, Earl of March.

 I am the son of Henry the Fifth,

 Who made the Dauphin⁵ and the French to stoop

 And seized upon their towns and provinces.

110 WARWICK   Talk not of France, sith° thou hast lost it all.   *since*

KING HENRY   The Lord Protector⁶ lost it, and not I.

 When I was crowned, I was but nine months old.

RICHARD   You are old enough now, and yet,° methinks, you lose.   *and even now*

 [*To* YORK] Father, tear the crown from the usurper's head.

115 EDWARD [*to* YORK]   Sweet father, do so—set it on your head.

MONTAGUE [*to* YORK]   Good brother, as thou lov'st and honour'st arms,

 Let's fight it out and not stand cavilling thus.

RICHARD   Sound drums and trumpets, and the King will fly.

YORK   Sons, peace!

NORTHUMBERLAND⁷   Peace, thou—and give King Henry leave°   *permission*

120 to speak.

KING HENRY   Ah, York, why seekest thou to depose me?

 Are we not both Plantagenets by birth,

 And from two brothers lineally descent?

 Suppose by right and equity thou be king—

124.1 KING HENRY   *Peace, thou—and give King Henry leave to*

   speak.

  WARWICK   *Plantagenet shall speak first—hear him, lords,*

   And be you silent and attentive too,

   For he that interrrupts him shall not live.

  KING HENRY [*to* YORK]   *Think'st thou that I will leave my*

124.5   *kingly throne,*

125 Think'st thou that I will leave my Kingly throne,

 Wherein my grandsire and my father sat?

 No—first shall war unpeople this my realm;

 Ay, and their colours, often borne in France,

 And now in England to our heart's great sorrow,

130 Shall be my winding-sheet.° Why faint you,⁸ lords?   *burial shroud*

 My title's good, and better far than his.

WARWICK   Prove it, Henry, and thou shalt be king.

KING HENRY   Henry the Fourth by conquest got the crown.

YORK   'Twas by rebellion against his king.°   *(Richard II)*

135 KING HENRY [*aside*] I know not what to say—my title's weak.

---

4. In fact, the historical York's father was not the Duke of York. York inherited that title from his uncle (Edward).

5. Title of the oldest son of the French King.

6. Humphrey, Duke of Gloucester, was Lord Protector during Henry VI's youth and, as such, had oversight of the King and kingdom. His downfall is dramatized in *The First Part of the Contention* (2 *Henry VI*).

7. For lines 120–25, Oxford follows O. F. assigns line 120 to King Henry, then gives three lines to Warwick and has Henry begin again at 125, omitting the Octavo

passage here printed as 121–24. For the F version, see the inset passage that follows (lines 124.1–124.5). Critics such as Steven Urkowitz have argued that the difference here between O and F indicates two different views of Henry's character, and they treat O and F as completely separate texts, with O composed first. Here as elsewhere, Oxford takes these Octavo lines as an authorial revision that occurred sometime between the play's foul-paper stage and the subsequent prompt-book.

8. Why do you lose heart?

    [*To* YORK] Tell me, may not a king adopt an heir?

YORK   What then?

KING HENRY   An if° he may, then am I lawful king—   *An if = If*

    For Richard, in the view of many lords,

140   Resigned the crown to Henry the Fourth,

    Whose heir my father was, and I am his.

YORK   He rose against him,° being° his sovereign,   *(Richard) / who was*

    And made him to resign his crown perforce.

WARWICK   Suppose, my lords, he did it unconstrained—

145   Think you 'twere prejudicial to his crown?°   *his claim to the throne*

EXETER   No, for he could not so resign his crown

    But° that the next heir should succeed and reign.   *Without ensuring*

KING HENRY   Art thou against us, Duke of Exeter?

EXETER   His° is the right, and therefore pardon me.   *(York's)*

150 YORK   Why whisper you, my lords, and answer not?

EXETER [*to* KING HENRY]   My conscience tells me he is lawful king.

KING HENRY [*aside*] All will revolt from me and turn to him.

NORTHUMBERLAND [*to* YORK]   Plantagenet, for all the claim thou lay'st,

    Think not that Henry shall be so deposed.

155 WARWICK   Deposed he shall be, in despite° of all.   *spite*

NORTHUMBERLAND   Thou art deceived— 'tis not thy southern power

    Of Essex, Norfolk, Suffolk, nor of Kent,

    Which makes thee thus presumptuous and proud,

    Can set the Duke up° in despite of me.   *(on the throne)*

160 CLIFFORD   King Henry, be thy title right or wrong,

    Lord Clifford vows to fight in thy defence.

    May that ground gape and swallow me alive

    Where I shall kneel to him that slew my father.

KING HENRY   O, Clifford, how thy words revive my heart!

165 YORK   Henry of Lancaster, resign thy crown.

    What mutter you, or what conspire you, lords?

WARWICK   Do right unto this princely Duke of York,

    Or I will fill the house with armèd men

    And over the chair of state, where now he sits,

170   Write up his title with usurping blood.[9]

        He stamps with his foot and the soldiers

        show themselves

KING HENRY   My lord of Warwick, hear me but one word—

    Let me for this my lifetime reign as king.

YORK   Confirm the crown to me and to mine heirs,

    And thou shalt reign in quiet while thou liv'st.

175 KING HENRY   I am content. Richard Plantagenet,

    Enjoy the kingdom after my decease.

CLIFFORD   What wrong is this unto the prince your son?

WARWICK   What good is this to England and himself?

WESTMORLAND   Base, fearful, and despairing Henry.

180 CLIFFORD   How hast thou injured both thyself and us?

WESTMORLAND   I cannot stay to hear these articles.°   *terms of agreement*

NORTHUMBERLAND   Nor I.

CLIFFORD   Come, cousin, let us tell the Queen these news.

---

9. With the blood of Henry, whom Warwick considers a usurper.

WESTMORLAND [*to* KING HENRY]   Farewell, faint-hearted and
    degenerate king,
185   In whose cold blood no spark of honour bides.°   *lives*
                           Exit [*with his soldiers*]¹
NORTHUMBERLAND [*to* KING HENRY]   Be thou a prey unto the
    house of York,
   And die in bands° for this unmanly deed.   *fetters*
                           Exit [*with his soldiers*]
CLIFFORD [*to* KING HENRY]   In dreadful war mayst thou be overcome,
   Or live in peace, abandoned and despised.
                           Exit [*with his soldiers*]
190   WARWICK [*to* KING HENRY]   Turn this way, Henry, and regard them not.
EXETER [*to* KING HENRY]   They seek revenge and therefore will not yield.
KING HENRY   Ah, Exeter.
WARWICK   Why should you sigh, my lord?
KING HENRY   Not for myself, Lord Warwick, but my son,
   Whom I unnaturally shall disinherit.
195   But be it as it may. [*To* YORK] I here entail°   *bequeath*
   The crown to thee and to thine heirs for ever,
   Conditionally, that here thou take thine oath
   To cease this civil war, and whilst I live
   To honour me as thy king and sovereign,
200   And nor by treason nor hostility
   To seek to put me down and reign thyself.
YORK   This oath I willingly take and will perform.
WARWICK   Long live King Henry. [*To* YORK] Plantagenet, embrace him.
    [YORK *descends.* HENRY *and* YORK *embrace*]
KING HENRY [*to* YORK]   And long live thou, and these thy forward° sons. *precocious*
205   YORK   Now York and Lancaster are reconciled.
EXETER   Accursed be he that seeks to make them foes.
    *Sennet.*² *Here* [York's *train*] *comes down* [*from the state*]³
YORK [*to* KING HENRY]   Farewell, my gracious lord, I'll to my castle.⁴
        Exeunt YORK *and his sons* [EDWARD *and*
             RICHARD, *with soldiers*]
WARWICK   And I'll keep London with my soldiers.
                Exit [*with soldiers*]
NORFOLK   And I to Norfolk with my followers.
                Exit [*with soldiers*]
210   MONTAGUE   And I unto the sea from whence I came.
                Exit [*with soldiers*]
KING HENRY   And I with grief and sorrow to the court.
    [KING HENRY *and* EXETER *turn to leave.*]
    Enter QUEEN [MARGARET] *and* PRINCE [EDWARD]
EXETER   Here comes the Queen, whose looks bewray° her anger. *reveal*
   I'll steal away.

---

1. F gives no exit for Westmorland, Northumberland, or Clifford; O marks a separate exit for each, as here. Each man is probably followed out by his soldiers.
2. Trumpet notes signaling a procession.
3. F's "Here they come down" again indicates that a state is required for the scene.
4. Sandal, located near Wakefield in Yorkshire.

KING HENRY   Exeter, so will I.
QUEEN MARGARET   Nay, go not from me—I will follow thee.
215   KING HENRY   Be patient, gentle Queen, and I will stay.
QUEEN MARGARET   Who can be patient in such extremes?
        Ah, wretched man, would I had died a maid
        And never seen thee, never borne thee son,
        Seeing thou hast proved so unnatural a father.
220   Hath he deserved to lose his birthright thus?
        Hadst thou but loved him half so well as I,
        Or felt that pain° which I did for him once,   *(labor pains)*
        Or nourished him as I did with my blood,
        Thou wouldst have left thy dearest heart-blood there
225   Rather than have made that savage Duke thine heir
        And disinherited thine only son.
PRINCE EDWARD   Father, you cannot disinherit me.
        If you be king, why should not I succeed?
KING HENRY   Pardon me, Margaret; pardon me, sweet son—
230   The Earl of Warwick and the Duke enforced me.
QUEEN MARGARET   Enforced thee? Art thou king, and wilt be forced?
        I shame° to hear thee speak! Ah, timorous wretch,   *am ashamed*
        Thou hast undone thyself, thy son, and me,
        And giv'n unto the house of York such head[5]
235   As thou shalt reign but by their sufferance.
        To entail him and his heirs unto the crown—
        What is it, but to make thy sepulchre
        And creep into it far before thy time?
        Warwick is Chancellor and the Lord of Calais;
240   Stern Falconbridge commands the narrow seas;°   *(Straits of Dover)*
        The Duke° is made Protector of the Realm;   *(York)*
        And yet shalt thou be safe? Such safety finds
        The trembling lamb environèd° with wolves.   *surrounded*
        Had I been there, which am a seely° woman,   *helpless*
245   The soldiers should have tossed me on their pikes°   *axlike weapons*
        Before I would have granted° to that act.   *assented*
        But thou preferr'st thy life before thine honour.
        And seeing thou dost, I here divorce myself
        Both from thy table, Henry, and thy bed,[6]
250   Until that act of Parliament be repealed
        Whereby my son is disinherited.
        The northern lords that have forsworn thy colours
        Will follow mine, if once they see them spread—
        And spread they shall be, to thy foul disgrace
255   And the utter ruin of the house of York.
        Thus do I leave thee. [*To* PRINCE EDWARD] Come, son, let's away.
        Our army is ready—come, we'll after them.
KING HENRY   Stay, gentle Margaret, and hear me speak.
QUEEN MARGARET   Thou hast spoke too much already.
        [*To* PRINCE EDWARD]   Get thee gone.

5. Such freedom to act. To give a horse its head means
to loosen its reins and let it go where it will.
6. *I here . . . bed*: echoing the language of church law,

which permitted marital separation "from bed and
board" in cases of adultery, heresy, and cruelty.

260   KING HENRY   Gentle son Edward, thou wilt stay with me?
      QUEEN MARGARET   Ay, to be murdered by his enemies.
      PRINCE EDWARD [*to* KING HENRY]   When I return with victory
            from the field,
            I'll see your grace. Till then, I'll follow her.
      QUEEN MARGARET   Come, son, away—we may not linger thus.
                                    [*Exit with* PRINCE EDWARD][7]
265   KING HENRY   Poor Queen, how love to me and to her son
            Hath made her break out into terms of rage.
            Revenged may she be on that hateful Duke,
            Whose haughty spirit, wingèd with desire,
            Will coast° my crown, and, like an empty° eagle,   *attack / a hungry*
270   Tire° on the flesh of me and of my son.   *Feed ravenously*
            The loss of those three lords torments my heart.
            I'll write unto them and entreat them fair.°   *courteously*
            Come, cousin, you shall be the messenger.
      EXETER   And I, I hope, shall reconcile them all.
                                            Flourish. Exeunt[8]

                              1.2
                  Enter RICHARD, EDWARD [*Earl of March*],
                  and [*the Marquis of*] MONTAGUE
      RICHARD   Brother, though I be youngest give me leave.°   *allow me (to speak)*
      EDWARD   No, I can better play the orator.
      MONTAGUE   But I have reasons strong and forcible.
                  Enter the Duke of YORK
      YORK   Why, how now, sons and brother—at a strife?
5   What is your quarrel? How began it first?
      EDWARD   No quarrel, but a slight contention.
      YORK   About what?
      RICHARD   About that which concerns your grace and us—
            The crown of England, father, which is yours.
10   YORK   Mine, boy? Not till King Henry be dead.
      RICHARD   Your right depends not on his life or death.
      EDWARD   Now you are heir—therefore enjoy it now.
            By giving the house of Lancaster leave to breathe,°   *permission to rest*
            It will outrun you, father, in the end.
15   YORK   I took an oath that he should quietly reign.
      EDWARD   But for a kingdom any oath may be broken.
            I would break a thousand oaths to reign one year.
      RICHARD [*to* YORK]   No—God forbid your grace should be forsworn.
      YORK   I shall be if I claim by open war.
20   RICHARD   I'll prove the contrary, if you'll hear me speak.
      YORK   Thou canst not, son—it is impossible.
      RICHARD   An oath is of no moment° being not took   *consequence*
            Before a true and lawful magistrate
            That hath authority over him that swears.
25   Henry had none, but did usurp the place.
            Then, seeing 'twas he that made you to depose,°   *swear an oath*

---

7. O omits the Queen's last line and has her exit at line   "Flourish" before Richard's entrance in the next line.
261, Prince Edward at 263.   1.2 Location: York's castle, Sandal (in Yorkshire).
8. F marks a single exit for Exeter here and places the

Your oath, my lord, is vain and frivolous.
Therefore to arms—and, father, do but think
How sweet a thing it is to wear a crown,
30   Within whose circuit° is Elysium[1]   *circumference*
And all that poets feign° of bliss and joy.   *imagine*
Why do we linger thus? I cannot rest
Until the white rose that I wear be dyed
Even in the luke-warm blood of Henry's heart.
35 YORK   Richard, enough! I will be king or die.
        [*To* MONTAGUE] Brother, thou shalt to London presently°   *at once*
        And whet on Warwick to this enterprise.
        Thou, Richard, shalt to the Duke of Norfolk
        And tell him privily° of our intent.   *secretly*
40   You, Edward, shall to Edmund Brook, Lord Cobham,
        With whom the Kentishmen will willingly rise.°   *rebel; take arms*
        In them I trust, for they are soldiers
        Witty, courteous, liberal, full of spirit.
        While you are thus employed, what resteth more°   *what else remains*
45   But that I seek occasion how to rise,
        And yet the King not privy to my drift,°   *aware of my intent*
        Nor any of the house of Lancaster.
                    Enter a MESSENGER
        But stay, what news? Why com'st thou in such post?°   *haste*
    MESSENGER   The Queen, with all the northern earls and lords,
50   Intend here to besiege you in your castle.
        She is hard by with twenty thousand men,
        And therefore fortify your hold,° my lord.   *castle*
    YORK   Ay, with my sword. What—think'st thou that we fear them?
        Edward and Richard, you shall stay with me;
55   My brother Montague shall post to London.
        Let noble Warwick, Cobham, and the rest,
        Whom we have left protectors of the King,
        With powerful policy° strengthen themselves,   *cunning*
        And trust not simple Henry nor his oaths.
60 MONTAGUE   Brother, I go—I'll win them, fear it not.
        And thus most humbly I do take my leave.   *Exit*
                    Enter SIR JOHN *Mortimer and his brother Sir Hugh*
    YORK   Sir John and Sir Hugh Mortimer, mine uncles,
        You are come to Sandal in a happy° hour.   *fortunate*
        The army of the Queen mean to besiege us.
65 SIR JOHN   She shall not need, we'll meet her in the field.
    YORK   What, with five thousand men?
    RICHARD   Ay, with five hundred, father, for a need.°   *if necessary*
        A woman's general—what should we fear?
                    A march [*sounds*] *afar off*
    EDWARD   I hear their drums. Let's set our men in order,
70   And issue forth and bid them battle straight.°   *at once*
    YORK [*to* SIR JOHN *and Sir Hugh*]   Five men to twenty—though
            the odds be great,
        I doubt not, uncles, of our victory.
        Many a battle have I won in France

---

1. In classical mythology, the paradise where blessed souls dwelled.

Whenas° the enemy hath been ten to one—   *When*
75   Why should I not now have the like success?   *Exeunt*

1.3

Alarums, and then enter the young Earl of RUTLAND
and his TUTOR [*a chaplain*]

RUTLAND   Ah, whither shall I fly to scape° their hands?   *escape*
    Enter [*Lord*] CLIFFORD [*with soldiers*]
    Ah, tutor, look where bloody Clifford comes.
CLIFFORD [*to the* TUTOR]   Chaplain, away—thy priesthood saves thy life.
5   Whose father slew my father—he shall die.
TUTOR   And I, my lord, will bear him company.
CLIFFORD   Soldiers, away with him.
TUTOR   Ah, Clifford, murder not this innocent child
    Lest thou be hated both of° God and man.   *Exit* [*guarded*]   *by*
    [RUTLAND *falls to the ground*]
10   CLIFFORD   How now—is he dead already?
    Or is it fear that makes him close his eyes?
    I'll open them.
RUTLAND [*reviving*]   So looks the pent-up° lion o'er the wretch   *caged*
    That trembles under his devouring paws,
15   And so he walks, insulting° o'er his prey,   *scornfully triumphing*
    And so he comes to rend his limbs asunder.
    Ah, gentle Clifford, kill me with thy sword
    And not with such a cruel threat'ning look.
    Sweet Clifford, hear me speak before I die.
20   I am too mean° a subject for thy wrath.   *lowly*
    Be thou revenged on men, and let me live.
CLIFFORD   In vain thou speak'st, poor boy. My father's blood
    Hath stopped the passage where thy words should enter.
RUTLAND   Then let my father's blood open it again.
25   He is a man, and, Clifford, cope° with him.   *fight*
CLIFFORD   Had I thy brethren here, their lives and thine
    Were not revenge sufficient for me.
    No—if I digged up thy forefathers' graves,
    And hung their rotten coffins up in chains,
30   It could not slake° mine ire nor ease my heart.   *lessen*
    The sight of any of the house of York
    Is as a fury to torment my soul.
    And till I root out their accursèd line,
    And leave not one alive, I live in hell.
35   Therefore—
RUTLAND   O, let me pray before I take my death.
    [*Kneeling*] To thee I pray: sweet Clifford, pity me.
CLIFFORD   Such pity as my rapier's point affords.
RUTLAND   I never did thee harm—why wilt thou slay me?
CLIFFORD   Thy father hath.
40   RUTLAND   But 'twas ere I was born.
    Thou hast one son—for his sake pity me,
    Lest in revenge thereof, sith° God is just,   *since*

1.3 Location: A battlefield between Sandal and Wakefield.

He be as miserably slain as I.
Ah, let me live in prison all my days,
45 And when I give occasion of offence,
Then let me die, for now thou hast no cause.
CLIFFORD No cause? Thy father slew my father, therefore die.
     [*He stabs him*]
RUTLAND *Dii faciant laudis summa sit ista tuae.*[1]   [*He dies*]
CLIFFORD Plantagenet—I come, Plantagenet!
50 And this thy son's blood cleaving to my blade
Shall rust upon my weapon till thy blood,
Congealed with this, do make me wipe off both.
     Exit [*with Rutland's body and soldiers*][2]

1.4

Alarum. Enter Richard Duke of YORK
YORK The army of the Queen hath got° the field;   won
My uncles[1] both are slain in rescuing me;
And all my followers to the eager foe
Turn back,° and fly like ships before the wind,   *Turn their backs*
5 Or lambs pursued by hunger-starvèd wolves.
My sons—God knows what hath bechancèd° them.   *happened to*
But this I know—they have demeaned° themselves   *conducted*
Like men born to renown by life or death.
Three times did Richard make a lane to me,
10 And thrice cried, 'Courage, father, fight it out!'
And full as oft came Edward to my side,
With purple falchion° painted to the hilt   *curved sword*
In blood of those that had encountered him.
And when the hardiest warriors did retire,
15 Richard cried, 'Charge and give no foot of ground!'
[   ][2]
And cried 'A crown or else a glorious tomb!
A sceptre or an earthly sepulchre!'
With this, we charged again—but out, alas—
20 We bodged° again, as I have seen a swan   *gave way*
With bootless° labour swim against the tide   *fruitless*
And spend her strength with over-matching° waves.   *against too powerful*
     A short alarum within
Ah, hark—the fatal followers do pursue,
And I am faint and cannot fly their fury;
25 And were I strong, I would not shun their fury.
The sands° are numbered that makes up my life.   *(of the hourglass)*
Here must I stay, and here my life must end.
     Enter QUEEN [MARGARET, *Lord*] CLIFFORD, [*the Earl of*]
     NORTHUMBERLAND, [*and*] *the young* PRINCE [EDWARD,
     with] *soldiers*
Come bloody Clifford, rough Northumberland—
I dare your quenchless fury to more rage!

---

1. "The gods grant that this may be the height of your
glory" (Ovid, *Heroides* 2.66).
2. Although no Folio or Octavo stage direction indicates whether any soldiers are present during this scene,
Clifford's command at line 7 makes it clear that some,
at least, escort the tutor offstage. Some may remain to
exit here. Oxford notes that "the question, unresolvable,

is an important one, for it asks, essentially, whether Clifford's murder of Rutland is witnessed by anyone."
1.4 Location: Scene continues.
1. Sir John and Sir Hugh Mortimer.
2. It has been conjectured that this missing line
referred to Edward, who, like his brother Richard, may
have cried out encouragement to York's forces.

30 I am your butt,° and I abide your shot.   *target (in archery)*
NORTHUMBERLAND Yield to our mercy, proud Plantagenet.
CLIFFORD Ay, to such mercy as his ruthless arm,
    With downright payment,³ showed unto my father.
    Now Phaëton hath tumbled from his car,⁴
35 And made an evening at the noontide prick.⁵
YORK My ashes, as the phoenix,⁶ may bring forth
    A bird° that will revenge upon you all,   *child*
    And in that hope I throw mine eyes to heaven,
    Scorning whate'er you can afflict me with.
40 Why come you not? What—multitudes, and fear?
CLIFFORD So cowards fight when they can fly no further;
    So doves do peck the falcon's piercing talons;
    So desperate thieves, all hopeless of their lives,
    Breathe out invectives 'gainst the officers.
45 YORK O, Clifford, but bethink thee once again,
    And in thy thought o'errun° my former time,   *review*
    And, if thou canst for blushing, view this face
    And bite thy tongue, that slanders him with cowardice
    Whose frown hath made thee faint and fly ere this.
50 CLIFFORD I will not bandy with thee word for word,
    But buckle° with thee blows twice two for one.   *join in close combat*
        [*He draws his sword*]
QUEEN MARGARET Hold, valiant Clifford: for a thousand causes
    I would prolong a while the traitor's life.
    Wrath makes him deaf—speak thou, Northumberland.
55 NORTHUMBERLAND Hold, Clifford—do not honour him so much
    To prick thy finger though to wound his heart.
    What valour were it when a cur doth grin°   *show its teeth*
    For one to thrust his hand between his teeth
    When he might spurn° him with his foot away?   *kick*
60 It is war's prize to take all vantages,°   *opportunities*
    And ten to one is no impeach of valour.⁷
        [*They*] *fight and take* [YORK]
CLIFFORD Ay, ay, so strives the woodcock with the gin.⁸
NORTHUMBERLAND So doth the cony° struggle in the net.   *rabbit*
YORK So triumph thieves upon their conquered booty,
65 So true° men yield, with robbers so o'ermatched.   *honest*
NORTHUMBERLAND [*to the* QUEEN] What would your grace have
        done unto him now?
QUEEN MARGARET Brave warriors, Clifford and Northumberland,
    Come make him stand upon this molehill here,
    That wrought° at mountains with outstretchèd arms   *reached*
70 Yet parted but° the shadow with his hand.   *only*
    [*To* YORK] What—was it you that would be England's king?
    Was't you that revelled in our Parliament,

---

3. Alluding to the "downright," or vertical, sword stroke
that York used to kill Clifford's father in *The First Part
of the Contention*.
4. Phaeton, in classical mythology, was the son of
Phoebus (the sun god) and nearly set the world on fire
when he attempted to drive his father's chariot ("car,"
the sun). Zeus hurled a thunderbolt, and Phaeton fell
blazing to his death. This is one of the play's many allusions to the fact that the sun was an emblem of the
house of York. See note to 2.1.40.
5. The noon mark on a sundial.
6. A mythological bird that periodically built an elaborate funeral pyre, set itself on fire, and was reborn from
its own ashes.
7. And for ten to fight with one does not call our bravery into question.
8. Trap. *woodcock*: a bird reputed to lack brains and
thus easily caught in traps.

	And made a preachment° of your high descent?	*sermon*
	Where are your mess of° sons to back you now?	*group of four*
75	The wanton Edward and the lusty George?	
	And where's that valiant crookback prodigy,°	*marvel; monster*
	Dickie, your boy, that with his grumbling voice	
	Was wont to cheer his dad in mutinies?	
	Or with the rest where is your darling Rutland?	
80	Look, York, I stained this napkin° with the blood	*handkerchief*
	That valiant Clifford with his rapier's point	
	Made issue from the bosom of thy boy.	
	And if thine eyes can water for his death,	
	I give thee this to dry thy cheeks withal.°	*with*
85	Alas, poor York, but that I hate thee deadly	
	I should lament thy miserable state.	
	I prithee, grieve, to make me merry, York.	
	What—hath thy fiery heart so parched thine entrails°	*inner organs*
	That not a tear can fall for Rutland's death?	
90	Why art thou patient, man? Thou shouldst be mad,	
	And I, to make thee mad, do mock thee thus.	
	Stamp, rave, and fret, that I may sing and dance.	
	Thou wouldst be fee'd,° I see, to make me sport.	*paid*
	York cannot speak unless he wear a crown.	
95	[*To her men*] A crown for York, and, lords, bow low to him.	
	Hold you his hands whilst I do set it on.	
	[*She puts a paper crown on York's head*]	
	Ay, marry, sir, now looks he like a king,	
	Ay, this is he that took King Henry's chair,	
	And this is he was his adopted heir.	
100	But how is it that great Plantagenet	
	Is crowned so soon and broke his solemn oath?	
	As I bethink me, you should not be king	
	Till our King Henry had shook hands with death.	
	And will you pale° your head in Henry's glory,	*enclose*
105	And rob his temples of the diadem	
	Now, in his life, against your holy oath?	
	O 'tis a fault too, too, unpardonable.	
	Off with the crown,	
	[*She knocks it from his head*]	
	and with the crown his head,	
	And whilst we breathe,° take time to do him dead.°	*rest / kill him*
110	CLIFFORD That is my office for my father's sake.	
	QUEEN MARGARET Nay, stay—let's hear the orisons° he makes.	*prayers*
	YORK She-wolf of France, but worse than wolves of France,	
	Whose tongue more poisons than the adder's tooth—	
	How ill-beseeming° is it in thy sex	*unbecoming*
115	To triumph like an Amazonian trull[9]	
	Upon their woes whom fortune captivates!°	*subdues*
	But that° thy face is visor-like,[1] unchanging,	*Were it not that*
	Made impudent with use of evil deeds,	
	I would essay,° proud Queen, to make thee blush.	*attempt*

9. In the manner of an Amazonian whore. Amazons were a tribe of mythical warrior women who governed themselves and lived separate from men. Sometimes they were accused of sexual impropriety because to beget offspring they would mate with men they had conquered but did not marry.

1. Masklike; fixed in expression like the frontpiece of a helmet. Perhaps alluding to the practice of prostitutes who wore masks.

120   To tell thee whence thou cam'st, of whom derived,
       Were shame enough to shame thee— wert thou not shameless.
       Thy father bears the type° of King of Naples,   *title*
       Of both the Sicils,[2] and Jerusalem—
       Yet not so wealthy as an English yeoman.[3]
125   Hath that poor monarch taught thee to insult?
       It needs not, nor it boots° thee not, proud Queen,   *profits*
       Unless the adage must be verified
       That beggars mounted run their horse to death.
       'Tis beauty that doth oft make women proud—
130   But, God he knows, thy share thereof is small;
       'Tis virtue that doth make them most admired—
       The contrary doth make thee wondered at;
       'Tis government° that makes them seem divine—   *self-control*
       The want thereof makes thee abominable.
135   Thou art as opposite to every good
       As the antipodes[4] are unto us,
       Or as the south to the septentrion.[5]
       O tiger's heart wrapped in a woman's hide!
       How couldst thou drain the life-blood of the child
140   To bid the father wipe his eyes withal,
       And yet be seen to bear a woman's face?
       Women are soft, mild, pitiful,° and flexible—   *full of pity*
       Thou stern, obdurate, flinty, rough, remorseless.
       Bidd'st thou me rage? Why, now thou hast thy wish.
145   Wouldst have me weep? Why, now thou hast thy will.
       For raging wind blows up incessant showers,
       And when the rage allays° the rain begins.   *abates*
       These tears are my sweet Rutland's obsequies,
       And every drop cries vengeance for his death
150   'Gainst thee, fell° Clifford, and thee, false Frenchwoman.   *cruel*
       NORTHUMBERLAND   Beshrew° me, but his passions move me so   *Curse*
       That hardly can I check my eyes from tears.
       YORK   That face of his the hungry cannibals
       Would not have touched, would not have stained with blood—
155   But you are more inhuman, more inexorable,
       O, ten times more than tigers of Hyrcania.[6]
       See, ruthless Queen, a hapless° father's tears.   *an unlucky*
       This cloth thou dipped'st in blood of my sweet boy,
       And I with tears do wash the blood away.
160   Keep thou the napkin and go boast of this,
       And if thou tell'st the heavy° story right,   *sorrowful*
       Upon my soul the hearers will shed tears,
       Yea, even my foes will shed fast-falling tears
       And say, 'Alas, it was a piteous deed'.
165   There, take the crown—and with the crown, my curse:
       And in thy need such comfort come to thee
       As now I reap at thy too cruel hand.
       Hard-hearted Clifford, take me from the world.
       My soul to heaven, my blood upon your heads.

---

2. Naples and Sicily (known as the Kingdom of the   5. North. The word refers to the seven stars that make
Two Sicilies).   up the Great Bear constellation.
3. Landowner below the rank of gentleman.   6. Region in ancient Persia known for the cruelty of its
4. People living on the opposite side of the world.   tigers (see *Aeneid* 4.366–67).

170 NORTHUMBERLAND   Had he been slaughter-man to all my kin,
    I should not, for my life, but weep with him,
    To see how inly° sorrow gripes his soul.   *inward*
QUEEN MARGARET   What—weeping-ripe,° my lord Northumberland?   *ready to weep*
    Think but upon the wrong he did us all,
175 And that will quickly dry thy melting tears.
CLIFFORD   Here's for my oath, here's for my father's death.
            [*He stabs* YORK]
QUEEN MARGARET   And here's to right our gentle-hearted King.
            [*She stabs* YORK]
YORK   Open thy gate of mercy, gracious God—
    My soul flies through these wounds to seek out thee.
                                                              [*He dies*]
180 QUEEN MARGARET   Off with his head and set it on York gates,
    So York may overlook the town of York.
                              Flourish. Exeunt [*with York's body*]

2.1

    [A] *march. Enter* EDWARD [*Earl of March*]
    and RICHARD, *with* [*a*] *drum*[*mer*] *and soldiers*
EDWARD   I wonder how our princely father scaped,
    Or whether he be scaped away or no
    From Clifford's and Northumberland's pursuit.
    Had he been ta'en we should have heard the news;
5   Had he been slain we should have heard the news;
    Or had he scaped, methinks we should have heard
    The happy tidings of his good escape.
    How fares my brother? Why is he so sad?
RICHARD   I cannot joy until I be resolved
10 Where our right valiant father is become.°   *has betaken himself*
    I saw him in the battle range about,
    And watched him how he singled Clifford forth.
    Methought he bore him in the thickest troop,
    As doth a lion in a herd of neat;°   *cattle*
15 Or as a bear encompassed round with dogs,
    Who having pinched° a few and made them cry,   *bitten*
    The rest stand all aloof and bark at him.
    So fared our father with his enemies;
    So fled his enemies my warlike father.
20 Methinks 'tis prize enough to be his son.
            Three suns appear in the air[1]
    See how the morning opes her golden gates
    And takes her farewell of the glorious sun.
    How well resembles it the prime of youth,
    Trimmed° like a younker° prancing to his love!   *Dressed up / young man*
25 EDWARD   Dazzle mine eyes, or do I see three suns?
RICHARD   Three glorious suns, each one a perfect sun;
    Not separated with the racking° clouds,   *drifting*
    But severed in a pale clear-shining sky.
            [*The three suns begin to join*]

2.1. Location: Fields near the border, or marches, between Wales and England.
1. This stage direction appears in O, which may have been based on a theatrical promptbook (see Textual Note). It suggests that the acting company who performed the play had some kind of artificial "suns" they used as properties for this scene.

See, see—they join, embrace, and seem to kiss,
30 As if they vowed some league inviolable.
Now are they but one lamp, one light, one sun.
In this the heaven figures° some event.   *prefigures*
EDWARD   'Tis wondrous strange, the like yet never heard of.
I think it cites° us, brother, to the field,   *urges*
35 That we, the sons of brave Plantagenet,
Each one already blazing by our meeds,°   *merits*
Should notwithstanding join our lights together
And over-shine the earth as this° the world.   *this phenomenon*
Whate'er it bodes, henceforward will I bear
40 Upon my target three fair-shining suns.²
RICHARD   Nay, bear three daughters—by your leave I speak it—
You love the breeder° better than the male.   *childbearer; woman*
      Enter one blowing³
But what art thou whose heavy looks foretell
Some dreadful story hanging on thy tongue?
45 MESSENGER   Ah, one that was a woeful looker-on
Whenas° the noble Duke of York was slain—   *When*
Your princely father and my loving lord.
EDWARD   O, speak no more, for I have heard too much.
RICHARD   Say how he died, for I will hear it all.
50 MESSENGER   Environèd° he was with many foes,   *Surrounded*
And stood against them as the hope of Troy⁴
Against the Greeks that would have entered Troy.
But Hercules⁵ himself must yield to odds;
And many strokes, though with a little axe,
55 Hews down and fells the hardest-timbered oak.
By many hands your father was subdued,
But only slaughtered by the ireful arm
Of unrelenting Clifford and the Queen,
Who crowned the gracious Duke in high despite,°   *in great contempt*
60 Laughed in his face, and when with grief he wept,
The ruthless Queen gave him to dry his cheeks
A napkin steepèd in the harmless blood
Of sweet young Rutland, by rough Clifford slain;
And after many scorns, many foul taunts,
65 They took his head, and on the gates of York
They set the same; and there it doth remain,
The saddest spectacle that e'er I viewed.
EDWARD   Sweet Duke of York, our prop to lean upon,
Now thou art gone, we have no staff, no stay.°   *support*
70 O Clifford, boist'rous° Clifford—thou hast slain   *savage*
The flower of Europe for his chivalry,
And treacherously hast thou vanquished him—
For hand to hand he would have vanquished thee.
Now my soul's palace° is become a prison.   *(my body)*
75 Ah, would she° break from hence that this my body   *(my soul)*
Might in the ground be closèd up in rest.

---

2. As elsewhere, Shakespeare here slightly changes his sources. In Holinshed's *Chronicles,* Edward chose the sun as his badge because he had seen three suns join in one before the Battle of Mortimer's Cross, which he won. *target*: shield.
3. Blowing a horn as messengers did to announce themselves.
4. *hope of Troy*: Hector, a mighty warrior in Homer's *Iliad,* who defended the city of Troy against Greek invaders.
5. A mythic hero of enormous physical strength and courage.

For never henceforth shall I joy again—
Never, O never, shall I see more joy.
RICHARD   I cannot weep, for all my body's moisture
80   Scarce serves to quench my furnace-burning heart;
Nor can my tongue unload my heart's great burden,
For selfsame wind° that I should speak withal   breath
Is kindling coals that fires all my breast,
And burns me up with flames that tears would quench.
85   To weep is to make less the depth of grief;
Tears, then, for babes—blows and revenge for me!
Richard, I bear thy name; I'll venge° thy death   revenge
Or die renownèd by attempting it.
EDWARD   His name that valiant Duke hath left with thee,
90   His dukedom and his chair⁶ with me is left.
RICHARD   Nay, if thou be that princely eagle's bird,
Show thy descent by gazing 'gainst the sun:⁷
For 'chair and dukedom', 'throne and kingdom' say—
Either that is thine or else thou wert not his.
       March. Enter the Earl of WARWICK *[and the] Marquis*
       [of] MONTAGUE, *with drum[mers], [an] ensign,*
       and soldiers
95   WARWICK   How now, fair lords? What fare?° What news abroad?   success
RICHARD   Great lord of Warwick, if we should recount
Our baleful° news, and at each word's deliverance   deadly
Stab poniards° in our flesh till all were told,   daggers
The words would add more anguish than the wounds.
100   O valiant lord, the Duke of York is slain.
EDWARD   O Warwick, Warwick! That Plantagenet,
Which held thee dearly as his soul's redemption,
Is by the stern Lord Clifford done to death.
WARWICK   Ten days ago I drowned these news in tears.
105   And now, to add more measure to your woes,
I come to tell you things sith° then befall'n.   since
After the bloody fray at Wakefield fought,
Where your brave father breathed his latest° gasp,   last
Tidings, as swiftly as the posts° could run,   messengers
110   Were brought me of your loss and his depart.°   death
I then in London, keeper of the King,
Mustered my soldiers, gathered flocks of friends,
And, very well appointed° as I thought,   equipped
Marched toward Saint Albans to intercept the Queen,
115   Bearing the King in my behalf along—
For by my scouts I was advertisèd°   informed
That she was coming with a full intent
To dash our late° decree in Parliament   recent
Touching King Henry's oath and your succession.
120   Short tale to make, we at Saint Albans met,
Our battles° joined, and both sides fiercely fought;   armies
But whether 'twas the coldness of the King,
Who looked full gently on his warlike queen,
That robbed my soldiers of their heated spleen,°   fiery passion
125   Or whether 'twas report of her success,

6. Seat of his authority as Duke.   birds, were supposed to be able to gaze unblinkingly at
7. Eagles, described by Elizabethans as the king of   the sun.

Or more than common fear of Clifford's rigour—
Who thunders to his captains blood and death—
I cannot judge; but, to conclude with truth,
Their weapons like to lightning came and went;
130   Our soldiers', like the night-owl's lazy flight,
Or like an idle thresher with a flail,[8]
Fell gently down, as if they struck their friends.
I cheered them up with justice of our cause,
With promise of high pay, and great rewards.
135   But all in vain. They had no heart to fight,
And we in them no hope to win the day.
So that we fled—the King unto the Queen,
Lord George your brother, Norfolk, and myself
In haste, post-haste, are come to join with you.
140   For in the Marches° here we heard you were,   *Welsh borders*
Making another head° to fight again.   *Raising another army*

EDWARD   Where is the Duke of Norfolk, gentle Warwick?
And when came George from Burgundy to England?

WARWICK   Some six miles off the Duke is with his soldiers;
145   And for your brother—he was lately sent
From your kind aunt, Duchess of Burgundy,[9]
With aid of soldiers to this needful war.

RICHARD   'Twas odd belike[1] when valiant Warwick fled.
Oft have I heard his praises in pursuit,°   *(of enemies)*
150   But ne'er till now his scandal of retire.[2]

WARWICK   Nor now my scandal, Richard, dost thou hear—
For thou shalt know this strong right hand of mine
Can pluck the diadem from faint° Henry's head   *weak*
And wring the aweful° sceptre from his fist,   *awe-inspiring*
155   Were he as famous and as bold in war
As he is famed for mildness, peace, and prayer.

RICHARD   I know it well, Lord Warwick—blame me not.
'Tis love I bear thy glories make me speak.
But in this troublous time what's to be done?
160   Shall we go throw away our coats of steel,
And wrap our bodies in black mourning gowns,
Numb'ring our Ave-Maries with our beads?[3]
Or shall we on the helmets of our foes
Tell our devotion[4] with revengeful arms?
165   If for the last, say 'ay', and to it, lords.

WARWICK   Why, therefore Warwick came to seek you out,
And therefore comes my brother Montague.
Attend me, lords. The proud insulting Queen,
With Clifford and the haught° Northumberland,   *haughty*
170   And of their feather many more proud birds,
Have wrought° the easy-melting King like wax.   *worked on*
[*To* EDWARD] He swore consent to your succession,

8. Threshers beat grain from wheat with specially designed sticks, or "flails."
9. According to the chronicles, both George and Richard were sent for safety to the court of Philip of Burgundy; his wife, the Duchess of Burgundy, whom Warwick mentions, was a granddaughter of John of Gaunt.
1. The odds must have been much against him.
2. Defamation or condemnation of him for retreating

(from his enemies).
3. Rosary beads are used in Roman Catholic devotion for keeping track of the prayers one has said, including "Ave Marias" ("Hail Marys"), prayers addressed to the Virgin Mary.
4. Proclaim the object of our devotion (York), with a pun on "telling" as meaning "counting," which is what one does when saying the rosary.

His oath enrollèd° in the Parliament.   *officially recorded*
And now to London all the crew are gone,
175 To frustrate both his oath and what beside
May make against° the house of Lancaster.   *be unfavorable to*
Their power, I think, is thirty thousand strong.
Now, if the help of Norfolk and myself,
With all the friends that thou, brave Earl of March,⁵
180 Amongst the loving Welshmen canst procure,
Will but amount to five-and-twenty thousand,
Why, *via*,° to London will we march,   *onward*
And once again bestride our foaming steeds,
And once again cry 'Charge!' upon our foes—
185 But never once again turn back and fly.
RICHARD   Ay, now methinks I hear great Warwick speak.
Ne'er may he live to see a sunshine day
That cries 'Retire!' if Warwick bid him stay.
EDWARD   Lord Warwick, on thy shoulder will I lean,
190 And when thou fail'st—as God forbid the hour—
Must Edward fall, which peril heaven forfend!°   *forbid*
WARWICK   No longer Earl of March, but Duke of York;
The next degree° is England's royal throne—   *step*
For King of England shalt thou be proclaimed
195 In every borough as we pass along,
And he that throws not up his cap for joy,
Shall for the fault make forfeit of his head.
King Edward, valiant Richard, Montague—
Stay we no longer dreaming of renown,
200 But sound the trumpets and about our task.
RICHARD   Then, Clifford, were thy heart as hard as steel,
As thou hast shown it flinty by thy deeds,
I come to pierce it or to give thee mine.
EDWARD   Then strike up drums—God and Saint George°   *patron saint of England*
for us!
Enter a MESSENGER
205 WARWICK   How now? What news?
MESSENGER   The Duke of Norfolk sends you word by me
The Queen is coming with a puissant° host,   *powerful*
And craves your company for speedy counsel.
WARWICK   Why then it sorts.° Brave warriors, let's away.   *is fitting*
[*March.*] *Exeunt*

2.2

[*York's head is thrust out, above.*]¹
Flourish. Enter KING [HENRY], QUEEN [MARGARET],
[*Lord*] CLIFFORD, [*the Earl of*] NORTHUMBERLAND,
and young PRINCE EDWARD, *with* [*a*] drum[*mer*]
and trumpet[*er*]s
QUEEN MARGARET   Welcome, my lord, to this brave town of York.
Yonder's the head of that arch-enemy
That sought to be encompassed with your crown.

---

5. The title by which Edward and his father before him
laid claim to the throne of England. See line 192 and
note to 1.1.78.
2.2. Location: Before the walls of York.
1. Neither F nor O indicates in stage directions that

York's head is displayed above the stage, but Queen
Margaret's words in lines 2–4 and King Henry's
response suggest that it remains visible, perhaps (as
Oxford proposes) until 2.6.110.

Doth not the object cheer your heart, my lord?
5 KING HENRY   Ay, as the rocks cheer them that fear their wreck.
To see this sight, it irks my very soul.
Withhold revenge, dear God—'tis not my fault,
Nor wittingly have I infringed my vow.
CLIFFORD   My gracious liege,° this too much lenity   *sovereign*
10 And harmful pity must be laid aside.
To whom do lions cast their gentle looks?
Not to the beast that would usurp their den.
Whose hand is that the forest bear doth lick?
Not his that spoils° her young before her face.   *takes as prey*
15 Who scapes the lurking serpent's mortal sting?
Not he that sets his foot upon her back.
The smallest worm will turn, being trodden on,
And doves will peck in safeguard of their brood.
Ambitious York did level° at thy crown,   *aim*
20 Thou smiling while he knit his angry brows.
He, but a duke, would have his son a king,
And raise° his issue° like a loving sire;   *raise in rank / offspring*
Thou, being a king, blest with a goodly son,
Didst yield consent to disinherit him,
25 Which argued thee a most unloving father.
Unreasonable creatures° feed their young,   *Animals*
And though man's face be fearful to their eyes,
Yet, in protection of their tender ones,
Who hath not seen them, even with those wings
30 Which sometime they have used with fearful flight,
Make war with him that climbed unto their nest,
Offering their own lives in their young's defence?
For shame, my liege, make them your precedent!
Were it not pity that this goodly boy
35 Should lose his birthright by his father's fault,
And long hereafter say unto his child
'What my great-grandfather and grandsire got
My careless father fondly° gave away'?   *foolishly*
Ah, what a shame were this! Look on the boy,
40 And let his manly face, which promiseth
Successful fortune, steel thy melting heart
To hold thine own and leave thine own with him.
KING HENRY   Full well hath Clifford played the orator,
Inferring° arguments of mighty force.   *Offering*
45 But, Clifford, tell me—didst thou never hear
That things ill got had ever bad success?°   *outcome*
And happy always was it for that son
Whose father for his hoarding went to hell?
I'll leave my son my virtuous deeds behind,
50 And would my father had left me no more.
For all the rest is held at such a rate°   *cost*
As brings a thousandfold more care to keep
Than in possession any jot of pleasure.
Ah, cousin York, would thy best friends did know
55 How it doth grieve me that thy head is here.
QUEEN MARGARET   My lord, cheer up your spirits—our foes are nigh,
And this soft courage makes your followers faint.°   *lose heart*
You promised knighthood to our forward° son.   *precocious*

Unsheathe your sword and dub² him presently.°   *at once*

60   Edward, kneel down.

      [PRINCE EDWARD *kneels*]

KING HENRY   Edward Plantagenet, arise a knight—

And learn this lesson: draw thy sword in right.

PRINCE EDWARD [*rising*]   My gracious father, by your kingly leave,

I'll draw it as apparent° to the crown,   *heir*

65   And in that quarrel° use it to the death.   *cause*

CLIFFORD   Why, that is spoken like a toward° prince.   *bold*

      Enter a MESSENGER

MESSENGER   Royal commanders, be in readiness—

For with a band of thirty thousand men

Comes Warwick backing of° the Duke of York;³   *supporting*

70   And in the towns, as they do march along,

Proclaims him king, and many fly to him.

Darraign your battle,° for they are at hand.   *Deploy your troops*

CLIFFORD [*to* KING HENRY]   I would your highness would depart

    the field—

The Queen hath best success when you are absent.

QUEEN MARGARET [*to* KING HENRY]   Ay, good my lord, and leave

75   us to our fortune.

KING HENRY   Why, that's my fortune too—therefore I'll stay.

NORTHUMBERLAND   Be it with resolution then to fight.

PRINCE EDWARD [*to* KING HENRY]   My royal father, cheer these

    noble lords

And hearten those that fight in your defence.

80   Unsheathe your sword, good father; cry 'Saint George!'°   *England's patron saint*

    March. Enter EDWARD [*Duke of York, the Earl of*] WAR-

    WICK, RICHARD, [GEORGE,⁴ *the Duke of*]

    NORFOLK, [*the Marquis of*] MONTAGUE, *and soldiers*

EDWARD   Now, perjured Henry, wilt thou kneel for grace,

And set thy diadem upon my head—

Or bide° the mortal° fortune of the field?   *wait for / fatal*

QUEEN MARGARET   Go rate° thy minions,° proud insulting boy!   *chide / favorites*

85   Becomes it thee to be thus bold in terms

Before thy sovereign and thy lawful king?

EDWARD   I am his king, and he should bow his knee.

I was adopted heir by his consent.

GEORGE [*to* QUEEN MARGARET]   Since when his oath is broke—

    for, as I hear,

90   You that are king, though he do wear the crown,

Have caused him by new act of Parliament

To blot our brother out, and put his own son in.

CLIFFORD   And reason too—

Who should succeed the father but the son?

95   RICHARD   Are you there, butcher? O, I cannot speak!

CLIFFORD   Ay, crookback, here I stand to answer thee,

Or any he the proudest of thy sort.°   *gang*

RICHARD   'Twas you that killed young Rutland, was it not?

CLIFFORD   Ay, and old York, and yet not satisfied.

---

2. Confer the rank of knight by the ceremony of striking the shoulder with a sword.
3. Edward has now assumed the title Duke of York
after the death of his father at Margaret's hands.

4. Here and elsewhere, F's stage directions read
"Clarence" rather than "George." The Duke of Clarence
is the title he eventually assumes.

100	RICHARD For God's sake, lords, give signal to the fight.	
	WARWICK What sayst thou, Henry, wilt thou yield the crown?	
	QUEEN MARGARET Why, how now, long-tongued Warwick, dare	
	you speak?	
	When you and I met at Saint Albans last,	
	Your legs did better service than your hands.	
105	WARWICK Then 'twas my turn to fly—and now 'tis thine.	
	CLIFFORD You said so much before, and yet you fled.	
	WARWICK 'Twas not your valour, Clifford, drove me thence.	
	NORTHUMBERLAND No, nor your manhood that durst make you stay.	
	RICHARD Northumberland, I hold thee reverently.°	*in respect*
110	Break off the parley, for scarce I can refrain	
	The execution of my big-swoll'n heart[5]	
	Upon that Clifford, that cruel child-killer.	
	CLIFFORD I slew thy father—call'st thou him a child?	
	RICHARD Ay, like a dastard° and a treacherous coward,	*base coward*
115	As thou didst kill our tender brother Rutland.	
	But ere sun set I'll make thee curse the deed.	
	KING HENRY Have done with words, my lords, and hear me speak.	
	QUEEN MARGARET Defy them, then, or else hold close thy lips.	
	KING HENRY I prithee give no limits to my tongue—	
120	I am a king, and privileged to speak.	
	CLIFFORD My liege, the wound that bred this meeting here	
	Cannot be cured by words—therefore be still.	
	RICHARD Then, executioner, unsheathe thy sword.	
	By him that made us all, I am resolved	
125	That Clifford's manhood lies upon his tongue.°	*exists only in words*
	EDWARD Say, Henry, shall I have my right or no?	
	A thousand men have broke their fasts today	
	That ne'er shall dine unless thou yield the crown.	
	WARWICK [*to* KING HENRY] If thou deny,° their blood upon thy head;	*refuse*
130	For York in justice puts his armour on.	
	PRINCE EDWARD If that be right which Warwick says is right,	
	There is no wrong, but everything is right.	
	RICHARD Whoever got° thee, there thy mother stands—	*sired*
	For, well I wot,° thou hast thy mother's tongue.	*know*
135	QUEEN MARGARET But thou art neither like thy sire nor dam,	
	But like a foul misshapen stigmatic,[6]	
	Marked by the destinies[7] to be avoided,	
	As venom° toads or lizards' dreadful stings.	*poisonous*
	RICHARD Iron of Naples, hid with English gilt,[8]	
140	Whose father bears the title of a king—	
	As if a channel° should be called the sea—	*gutter*
	Sham'st thou not, knowing whence thou art extraught,°	*descended*
	To let thy tongue detect° thy base-born heart?	*reveal*

---

5. From acting passionately. Passions were supposed to cause the heart to swell.
6. A deformed person; a criminal marked by means of an iron brand for his or her crime.
7. The Fates, three goddesses in classical mythology thought to determine the course of a person's life.

8. You cheap product of Naples, hiding under the gold veneer of an English marriage. Since Naples is synonymous in many Elizabethan texts with prostitution and venereal disease, "iron" may also refer to the metal noses allegedly worn by wealthy people to disguise the disfiguring effects of syphilis.

EDWARD   A wisp of straw⁹ were° worth a thousand crowns   *would be*
145   To make this shameless callet° know herself.   *whore*
      Helen of Greece was fairer far than thou,
      Although thy husband may be Menelaus;¹
      And ne'er was Agamemnon's brother° wronged   *(Menelaus)*
      By that false woman, as this king by thee.
150   His father° revelled in the heart of France,   *(Henry V)*
      And tamed the King, and made the Dauphin² stoop;
      And had he matched° according to his state,°   *(Henry VI) wed / rank*
      He might have kept that glory to this day.
      But when he took a beggar to his bed,
155   And graced thy poor sire with his bridal day,³
      Even then that sunshine brewed a shower for him
      That washed his father's fortunes forth of° France,   *out of*
      And heaped sedition on his crown at home.
      For what hath broached this tumult but thy pride?
160   Hadst thou been meek, our title° still had slept,   *claim to the throne*
      And we, in pity of the gentle King,
      Had slipped° our claim until another age.   *postponed*
GEORGE [*to* QUEEN MARGARET]   But when we saw our sunshine
            made thy spring,
      And that thy summer bred us no increase,°   *harvest*
165   We set the axe to thy usurping root.
      And though the edge hath something° hit ourselves,   *to some extent*
      Yet know thou, since we have begun to strike,
      We'll never leave till we have hewn thee down,
      Or bathed thy growing with our heated bloods.
170   EDWARD [*to* QUEEN MARGARET]   And in this resolution I defy thee,
      Not willing any longer conference
      Since thou deniest the gentle King to speak.
      Sound trumpets—let our bloody colours wave!
      And either victory, or else a grave!
175   QUEEN MARGARET   Stay, Edward.
      EDWARD   No, wrangling woman, we'll no longer stay—
      These words will cost ten thousand lives this day.
                    [*Flourish. March.*] *Exeunt* [EDWARD *and his men*
                        at one door and QUEEN MARGARET *and her men*
                                        at another door]⁴

                              2.3
            Alarum. Excursions.° *Enter* [*the Earl of*] WARWICK¹   *Skirmishes*
WARWICK   Forespent° with toil, as runners with a race,   *Exhausted*
      I lay me down a little while to breathe;°   *rest*
      For strokes received, and many blows repaid,

---

9. Being made to wear or hold straw was a practice by which women were marked as scolds in public shaming rituals.
1. The Trojan War was said to have begun because the Greek Helen, the most beautiful woman in the world, betrayed her husband, Menelaus, and eloped with the Trojan warrior Paris.
2. The French King's oldest son, later Charles VII of France.
3. And brought honor to your impoverished father by marrying you.

4. Oxford proposes that Edward and Margaret and their men exit at separate stage doors to indicate symbolically their enmity. F and O read simply "Exeunt omnes."
2.3 Location: The remaining scenes in Act 2 take place in the fields near York.
1. While Shakespeare does not specify the locale, the events in this and the following three scenes resemble those associated with a battle waged at Towton in Yorkshire in 1461.

Have robbed my strong-knit° sinews of their strength,   *powerful*

5   And, spite of spite,° needs must I rest a while.   *come what may*

Enter EDWARD [*the Duke of York*] *running*

EDWARD   Smile, gentle heaven, or strike, ungentle° death!   *ignoble*

For this world frowns, and Edward's sun[2] is clouded.

WARWICK   How now, my lord, what hap?° What hope of good?   *fortune*

Enter GEORGE [*running*]

GEORGE   Our hap is loss, our hope but sad despair;

10   Our ranks are broke, and ruin follows us.

What counsel give you? Whither shall we fly?

EDWARD   Bootless° is flight—they follow us with wings,   *Useless*

And weak we are, and cannot shun pursuit.

Enter RICHARD, *running*

RICHARD   Ah, Warwick, why hast thou withdrawn thyself?

15   Thy brother's[3] blood the thirsty earth hath drunk,

Broached° with the steely point of Clifford's lance.   *Set flowing*

And in the very pangs of death he cried,

Like to a dismal clangour heard from far,

'Warwick, revenge—brother, revenge my death!'

20   So, underneath the belly of their steeds

That stained their fetlocks in his smoking° blood,   *steaming*

The noble gentleman gave up the ghost.

WARWICK   Then let the earth be drunken with our blood.

I'll kill my horse, because I will not fly.

25   Why stand we like soft-hearted women here,

Wailing our losses, whiles the foe doth rage;

And look upon,° as if the tragedy   *on*

Were played in jest by counterfeiting actors?

[*Kneeling*]   Here, on my knee, I vow to God above

30   I'll never pause again, never stand still,

Till either death hath closed these eyes of mine

Or fortune given me measure of revenge.

EDWARD [*kneeling*] O, Warwick, I do bend my knee with thine,

And in this vow do chain my soul to thine.

35   And, ere my knee rise from the earth's cold face,

I throw my hands, mine eyes, my heart to Thee,°   *(God)*

Thou setter up and plucker down of kings,[4]

Beseeching Thee, if with Thy will it stands°   *agrees*

That to my foes this body must be prey,

40   Yet that Thy brazen gates of heaven may ope

And give sweet passage to my sinful soul.

[*They rise*]

Now, lords, take leave until we meet again,

Where'er it be, in heaven or in earth.

RICHARD   Brother, give me thy hand; and, gentle° Warwick,   *noble*

45   Let me embrace thee in my weary arms.

I, that did never weep, now melt with woe

That winter should cut off our springtime so.

WARWICK   Away, away! Once more, sweet lords, farewell.

GEORGE   Yet let us all together to our troops,

50   And give them leave° to fly that will not stay;   *permission*

---

2. Good fortune, alluding to the sun as Edward's emblem.
3. Warwick's half brother, the Bastard of Salisbury.

4. Echoing a biblical description of God in Daniel 2:21. See also 3.3.157, where Margaret calls Warwick the "setter-up and puller-down of kings."

And call them pillars that will stand to° us;   *by*
And, if we thrive, promise them such rewards
As victors wear at the Olympian games.[5]
This may plant courage in their quailing breasts,
55   For yet is hope of life and victory.
Forslow° no longer—make we hence amain.°   *Exeunt*   *Delay / speedily*

2.4

Alarums. Excursions. Enter RICHARD *at one door*
and [Lord] CLIFFORD *at the other*

RICHARD   Now, Clifford, I have singled thee alone[1]
Suppose this arm is for the Duke of York,
And this for Rutland, both bound to revenge,
Wert thou environed° with a brazen wall.   *surrounded*
5   CLIFFORD   Now, Richard, I am with thee here alone.
This is the hand that stabbed thy father York,
And this the hand that slew thy brother Rutland,
And here's the heart that triumphs in their death
And cheers these hands that slew thy sire and brother
10   To execute the like upon thyself—
And so, have at thee!
They fight. [The Earl of] WARWICK *comes and rescues*
RICHARD. *[Lord]* CLIFFORD *flies*
RICHARD   Nay, Warwick, single out some other chase°—   *prey*
For I myself will hunt this wolf to death.   *Exeunt*

2.5

Alarum. Enter KING HENRY

KING HENRY   This battle fares like to the morning's war,[1]
When dying clouds contend with growing light,
What time° the shepherd, blowing of° his nails,   *When / on*
Can neither call it perfect day nor night.
5   Now sways it this way like a mighty sea
Forced by the tide to combat with the wind,
Now sways it that way like the selfsame sea
Forced to retire by fury of the wind.
Sometime the flood prevails, and then the wind;
10   Now one the better, then another best—
Both tugging to be victors, breast to breast,
Yet neither conqueror nor conquerèd.
So is the equal poise° of this fell° war.   *balance / deadly*
Here on this molehill[2] will I sit me down.
15   To whom God will, there be the victory.
For Margaret my queen, and Clifford, too,
Have chid me from the battle, swearing both
They prosper best of all when I am thence.
Would I were dead, if God's good will were so—
20   For what is in this world but grief and woe?

5. The Olympian Games in ancient Greece were festivals that included athletic contests. Victors were presented with garlands of olive leaves.
2.4
1. I have isolated you from the herd (a hunting
term).

2.5
1. In O, King Henry's ensuing fifty-four-line soliloquy
as found in F is reduced to thirteen lines, perhaps
shortened for performance.
2. See 1.4.68, where Richard, Duke of York is made to
stand on a molehill before his death.

O God! Methinks it were a happy life
To be no better than a homely swain.°   *simple shepherd*
To sit upon a hill, as I do now;
To carve out dials quaintly,° point by point,   *sundials artfully*
25 Thereby to see the minutes how they run:
How many makes the hour full complete,
How many hours brings about° the day,   *completes*
How many days will finish up the year,
How many years a mortal man may live.
30 When this is known, then to divide the times:
So many hours must I tend my flock,
So many hours must I take my rest,
So many hours must I contemplate,
So many hours must I sport myself,
35 So many days my ewes have been with young,
So many weeks ere the poor fools will ean,°   *give birth*
So many years ere I shall shear the fleece.
So minutes, hours, days, weeks, months, and years,
Passed over to the end they° were created,   *for which they*
40 Would bring white hairs unto a quiet grave.
Ah, what a life were this! How sweet! How lovely!
Gives not the hawthorn bush a sweeter shade
To shepherds looking on their seely° sheep   *innocent*
Than doth a rich embroidered canopy
45 To kings that fear their subjects' treachery?
O yes, it doth—a thousandfold it doth.
And to conclude, the shepherd's homely curds,
His cold thin drink out of his leather bottle,
His wonted° sleep under a fresh tree's shade,   *customary*
50 All which secure and sweetly he enjoys,
Is far beyond a prince's delicates,°   *delicacies*
His viands° sparkling in a golden cup,   *food*
His body couchèd in a curious° bed,   *an ornate*
When care, mistrust, and treason waits on him.
         Alarum. Enter at one door a SOLDIER *with a dead man
         in his arms.* [KING HENRY *stands apart*]³
55 SOLDIER   Ill blows the wind that profits nobody.
This man, whom hand to hand I slew in fight,
May be possessèd with some store of crowns;°   *coins*
And I, that haply° take them from him now,   *by chance*
May yet ere night yield both my life and them
60 To some man else, as this dead man doth me.
         [*He removes the dead man's helmet*]
Who's this? O God! It is my father's face
Whom in this conflict I, unwares, have killed.
O, heavy times, begetting such events!
From London by the King was I pressed forth;⁴
65 My father, being the Earl of Warwick's man,°   *servant*

3. Here Oxford adopts a combination of Folio and
Octavo staging. F indicates a simultaneous entrance, at
two different doors, of a "Son that hath kill'd his
Father" and a "Father that hath kill'd his Son." O, as
here, designates both figures as simply "a soldier with a
dead man in his arms" and "another soldier with a dead
man," and gives them entrances at lines 54 and 78,
respectively, but without mention of two doors. In O,
the relationship between the living and the dead is
revealed through the dialogue only.
4. Forcibly enlisted. Because England had no standing army until the latter half of the seventeenth
century, many soldiers in Elizabethan England were
conscripts.

Came on the part° of York, pressed by his master;   *side*°
    And I, who at his hands received my life,
    Have by my hands of life bereavèd him.
    Pardon me, God, I knew not what I did;
70   And pardon, father, for I knew not thee.
    My tears shall wipe away these bloody marks,
    And no more words till they have flowed their fill.
        [He weeps]
KING HENRY   O piteous spectacle! O bloody times!
    Whiles lions war and battle for their dens,
75   Poor harmless lambs abide their enmity.
    Weep, wretched man, I'll aid thee tear for tear;
    And let our hearts and eyes, like civil war,
    Be blind with tears, and break, o'erchargèd° with grief.   *overburdened*
        Enter at another door another SOLDIER *with a dead*
        man [in his arms]
SECOND SOLDIER   Thou that so stoutly hath resisted me,
80   Give me thy gold, if thou hast any gold—
    For I have bought it with an hundred blows.
        [He removes the dead man's helmet]
    But let me see: is this our foeman's° face?   *enemy's*
    Ah, no, no, no—it is mine only son!
    Ah, boy, if any life be left in thee,
85   Throw up thine eye! *[Weeping]* See, see, what showers arise,
    Blown with the windy tempest of my heart,
    Upon thy wounds, that kills mine eye and heart!
    O, pity, God, this miserable age!
    What stratagems,° how fell,° how butcherly,   *violent acts / cruel*
90   Erroneous,° mutinous, and unnatural,   *Criminal*
    This deadly quarrel daily doth beget!
    O boy, thy father gave thee life too soon,
    And hath bereft thee of thy life too late!°   *recently*
KING HENRY   Woe above woe! Grief more than common grief!
95   O that my death would stay° these ruthful° deeds!   *stop / pitiful*
    O, pity, pity, gentle heaven, pity!
    The red rose and the white are on his face,
    The fatal colours of our striving houses;
    The one his purple blood right well resembles,
100   The other his pale cheeks, methinks, presenteth.
    Wither one rose, and let the other flourish—
    If you contend, a thousand lives must wither.
FIRST SOLDIER   How will my mother for a father's death
    Take on with° me, and ne'er be satisfied!   *Rage against*
105 SECOND SOLDIER   How will my wife for slaughter of my son
    Shed seas of tears, and ne'er be satisfied!
KING HENRY   How will the country for these woeful chances°   *events*
    Misthink° the King, and not be satisfied!   *Think ill of*
FIRST SOLDIER   Was ever son so rued a father's death?
110 SECOND SOLDIER   Was ever father so bemoaned his son?
KING HENRY   Was ever king so grieved for subjects' woe?
    Much is your sorrow, mine ten times so much.
FIRST SOLDIER *[to his father's body]*   I'll bear thee hence where
    I may weep my fill.
        Exit [at one door] with [the body of] his father

SECOND SOLDIER [*to his son's body*]   These arms of mine shall be
    thy winding sheet;°   *shroud*
115 My heart, sweet boy, shall be thy sepulchre,
    For from my heart thine image ne'er shall go.
    My sighing breast shall be thy funeral bell,
    And so obsequious° will thy father be,   *dutiful in mourning*
    E'en for the loss of thee, having no more,
120 As Priam[5] was for all his valiant sons.
    I'll bear thee hence, and let them fight that will—
    For I have murdered where I should not kill.

            Exit [at another door] with [the body of] his son

KING HENRY   Sad-hearted men, much overgone° with care,   *overcome*
    Here sits a king more woeful than you are.

       Alarums. Excursions. Enter PRINCE EDWARD[6]

125 PRINCE EDWARD   Fly, father, fly—for all your friends are fled,
    And Warwick rages like a chafèd° bull!   *an angered*
    Away—for death doth hold us in pursuit!

       Enter QUEEN [MARGARET]

QUEEN MARGARET   Mount you, my lord—towards Berwick[7] post
    amain.°   *ride speedily*
    Edward and Richard, like a brace° of greyhounds   *pair*
130 Having the fearful flying hare in sight,
    With fiery eyes sparkling for very wrath,
    And bloody steel grasped in their ireful hands,
    Are at our backs—and therefore hence amain.°   *at full speed*

       Enter EXETER

EXETER   Away—for vengeance comes along with them!
135 Nay—stay not to expostulate°—make speed—   *argue*
    Or else come after. I'll away before.
KING HENRY   Nay, take me with thee, good sweet Exeter.
    Not that I fear to stay, but love to go
    Whither the Queen intends. Forward, away.   *Exeunt*

2.6

    A loud alarum. Enter [Lord] CLIFFORD, *wounded with*
    an arrow in his neck

CLIFFORD   Here burns my candle out—ay, here it dies,
    Which, whiles it lasted, gave King Henry light.
    O Lancaster, I fear thy overthrow
    More than my body's parting with my soul!
5 My love and fear° glued many friends to thee—   *Love and fear of me*
    And, now I fall, thy tough commixture[1] melts,
    Impairing Henry, strength'ning misproud° York.   *arrogant*
    The common people swarm like summer flies,
    And whither fly the gnats but to the sun?[2]
10 And who shines now but Henry's enemies?
    O Phoebus, hadst thou never given consent
    That Phaëton[3] should check° thy fiery steeds,   *manage*

---

5. King of Troy during the Trojan War. His fifty sons, of whom Hector was one, were killed defending the city.
6. F indicates a single entrance for "the Queen, the Prince, and Exeter" at line 124, and they speak in the order Prince-Queen-Exeter; O has Margaret enter first, then Prince Edward, and finally Exeter. Oxford follows O and divides the entrances, but places them in F's order of speech.

7. Berwick-upon-Tweed, a village near Scotland in Northumberland.
2.6
1. The compound of love and fear that I commanded.
2. Alluding to the sun as Edward's emblem. See note to 2.1.40.
3. The son of Phoebus, god of the sun. See note to 1.4.34.

	Thy burning car° never had scorched the earth!	*chariot*
	And, Henry, hadst thou swayed° as kings should do,	*ruled*
15	Or as thy father and his father did,	
	Giving no ground unto the house of York,	
	They never then had sprung like summer flies;	
	I and ten thousand in this luckless realm	
	Had left no mourning widows for our death;	
20	And thou this day hadst kept thy chair° in peace.	*throne*
	For what doth cherish° weeds, but gentle air?	*nurture*
	And what makes robbers bold, but too much lenity?	
	Bootless are plaints,° and cureless are my wounds;	*Useless are pleas*
	No way to fly, nor strength to hold out flight;	
25	The foe is merciless and will not pity,	
	For at their hands I have deserved no pity.	
	The air hath got into my deadly wounds,	
	And much effuse° of blood doth make me faint.	*effusion*
	Come York and Richard, Warwick and the rest—	
30	I stabbed your fathers' bosoms; split my breast.	

       [*He faints.*]
       Alarum and retreat. Enter EDWARD [*Duke of York, his*
       brothers] GEORGE *and* RICHARD, [*the Earl of*] WARWICK,
       [*the Marquis of*] MONTAGUE, *and soldiers*[4]

EDWARD   Now breathe we, lords—good fortune bids us pause,
And smooth the frowns of war with peaceful looks.
Some troops pursue the bloody-minded Queen,
That led calm Henry, though he were a king,

35	As doth a sail filled with a fretting° gust	*blowing fitfully*
	Command an argosy° to stem° the waves.	*a merchant ship / resist*

But think you, lords, that Clifford fled with them?
WARWICK   No—'tis impossible he should escape;
   For, though before his face I speak the words,
40   Your brother Richard marked him for the grave.
   And whereso'er he is, he's surely dead.
       CLIFFORD *groans*
EDWARD   Whose soul is that which takes her heavy leave?[5]
RICHARD   A deadly groan, like life and death's departing.
EDWARD [*to* RICHARD]   See who it is.
       [RICHARD *goes to* CLIFFORD]
                        And now the battle's ended,
45   If friend or foe, let him be gently used.

	RICHARD Revoke that doom° of mercy, for 'tis Clifford;	*sentence*
	Who not contented that he lopped the branch	
	In hewing Rutland when his leaves put forth,	
	But set his murd'ring knife unto the root	
50	From whence that tender spray° did sweetly spring—	*shoot*

I mean our princely father, Duke of York.
WARWICK   From off the gates of York fetch down the head,
   Your father's head, which Clifford placèd there.
   Instead whereof let this supply the room[6]—

---

4. In F, the order of names in the stage direction ends with "Montague and Clarence" (George) placed after "Soldiers." The peculiarity of listing these noble figures last may suggest that they were added as an afterthought. Montague does not speak during the scene. Neither he nor George is indicated in O's stage directions, in which George speaks the same lines as in F.
5. In F, lines 42 and 43 and half of line 44 are assigned to Richard. O divides them as here. Oxford, as elsewhere, argues that this is an instance of authorial revision between foul papers and promptbook.
6. Let Clifford's head take its place.

55   Measure for measure[7] must be answerèd.°   *given in return*

EDWARD   Bring forth that fatal screech-owl to our house,[8]
That nothing sung but death to us and ours.
        [CLIFFORD *is dragged forward*]
Now death shall stop his dismal threat'ning sound
And his ill-boding° tongue no more shall speak.   *doom-promising*

60 WARWICK   I think his understanding is bereft.°   *destroyed*
Speak, Clifford, dost thou know who speaks to thee?
Dark cloudy death o'ershades his beams of life,
And he nor° sees nor hears us what we say.   *neither*

RICHARD   O, would he did—and so perhaps he doth.

65 'Tis but his policy to counterfeit,
Because he would avoid such bitter taunts
Which in the time of death he gave our father.

GEORGE   If so thou think'st, vex him with eager° words.   *bitter*

RICHARD   Clifford, ask mercy and obtain no grace.

70 EDWARD   Clifford, repent in bootless penitence.

WARWICK   Clifford, devise excuses for thy faults.

GEORGE   While we devise fell° tortures for thy faults.   *cruel*

RICHARD   Thou didst love York, and I am son to York.

EDWARD   Thou pitied'st Rutland—I will pity thee.

75 GEORGE   Where's Captain Margaret to fence° you now?   *protect*

WARWICK   They mock thee, Clifford—swear as thou wast wont.

RICHARD   What, not an oath? Nay, then, the world goes hard
When Clifford cannot spare his friends an oath.
I know by that he's dead—and, by my soul,

80 If this right hand would buy but two hours' life
That I, in all despite, might rail at him,
This hand° should chop it off, and with the issuing blood   *(his left hand)*
Stifle° the villain whose unstanchèd° thirst   *Choke / insatiable*
York and young Rutland could not satisfy.

85 WARWICK   Ay, but he's dead. Off with the traitor's head,
And rear it in the place your father's stands.
And now to London with triumphant march,
There to be crownèd England's royal king;
From whence shall Warwick cut the sea to France,

90 And ask the Lady Bona[9] for thy queen.
So shalt thou sinew° both these lands together.   *tie firmly*
And, having France thy friend, thou shalt not dread
The scattered foe that hopes to rise again,
For though they cannot greatly sting to hurt,

95 Yet look to have them buzz to offend thine ears.
First will I see the coronation,
And then to Brittany I'll cross the sea
To effect this marriage, so it please my lord.

EDWARD   Even as thou wilt, sweet Warwick, let it be.

100 For in thy shoulder° do I build my seat,   *with your support*
And never will I undertake the thing
Wherein thy counsel and consent is wanting.
Richard, I will create thee Duke of Gloucester,

---

7. Alluding to the strict rule of justice described in Mark 4:24: "With what measure ye mete, it shall be measured unto you."
8. Bring forth that creature ominous to our house.

Screech owls were traditionally thought to be harbingers of death.
9. The sister-in-law of King Louis XI of France and daughter of Louis, Duke of Savoy.

And George, of Clarence; Warwick, as ourself,
105 Shall do and undo as him pleaseth best.
RICHARD   Let me be Duke of Clarence, George of Gloucester—
For Gloucester's dukedom is too ominous.[1]
WARWICK   Tut, that's a foolish observation—
Richard, be Duke of Gloucester. Now to London
110 To see these honours in possession.
                                    Exeunt. [York's head is removed]

3.1

Enter two [GAME]KEEPERS, with crossbows in their hands
FIRST GAMEKEEPER   Under this thick-grown brake° we'll shroud   thicket
        ourselves,
For through this laund° anon the deer will come,   clearing
And in this covert will we make our stand,
Culling the principal° of all the deer.   *Selecting the best*
5 SECOND GAMEKEEPER   I'll stay above the hill, so both may shoot.
FIRST GAMEKEEPER   That cannot be—the noise of thy crossbow
Will scare the herd, and so my shoot is lost.
Here stand we both, and aim we at the best.°   *as well as we can*
And, for° the time shall not seem tedious,   *so that*
10 I'll tell thee what befell me on a day
In this self place where now we mean to stand.
FIRST GAMEKEEPER   Here comes a man—let's stay till he be past.
        [They stand apart.]
        Enter KING HENRY, disguised, with a prayer-book
KING HENRY   From Scotland am I stolen, even of° pure love,   *out of*
To greet mine own land with my wishful° sight.   *longing*
15 No, Harry, Harry—'tis no land of thine.
Thy place is filled, thy sceptre wrung from thee,
Thy balm washed off wherewith thou wast anointed.
No bending knee will call thee Caesar° now,   *emperor*
No humble suitors press to speak for right,°   *beg for justice*
20 No, not a man comes for redress of° thee—   *from*
For how can I help them and not myself?
FIRST GAMEKEEPER *[to the SECOND GAMEKEEPER]*   Ay, here's a
        deer whose skin's a keeper's fee:[1]
This is the quondam° king—let's seize upon him.   *former*
KING HENRY   Let me embrace thee, sour adversity,
25 For wise men say it is the wisest course.
SECOND GAMEKEEPER *[to the FIRST GAMEKEEPER]*   Why linger
        we? Let us lay hands upon him.
FIRST GAMEKEEPER *[to the SECOND GAMEKEEPER]*   Forbear
        awhile—we'll hear a little more.
KING HENRY   My queen and son are gone to France for aid,
And, as I hear, the great commanding Warwick
30 Is thither gone to crave the French King's sister
To wife for Edward. If this news be true,
Poor Queen and son, your labour is but lost—
For Warwick is a subtle orator,
And Louis a prince soon won with moving words.

1. Referring to the fact that three previous Dukes of
Gloucester had suffered violent deaths.
3.1 Location: A forest in northern England near the
Scottish border.
1. Traditionally, hunters presented the horns and skin
of a captured deer to the park's gamekeeper.

35 By this account, then, Margaret may win him—
    For she's a woman to be pitied much.
    Her sighs will make a batt'ry° in his breast,   *a breach*
    Her tears will pierce into a marble heart,
    The tiger will be mild whiles she doth mourn,
40 And Nero² will be tainted° with remorse   *touched*
    To hear and see her plaints,° her brinish° tears.   *pleas / salty*
    Ay, but she's come to beg; Warwick to give.
    She on his left side, craving aid for Henry;
    He on his right, asking a wife for Edward.
45 She weeps and says her Henry is deposed,
    He smiles and says his Edward is installed;
    That she, poor wretch, for grief can speak no more,
    Whiles Warwick tells his title,³ smooths the wrong,
    Inferreth° arguments of mighty strength,   *Presents*
50 And in conclusion wins the King from her
    With promise of his sister and what else
    To strengthen and support King Edward's place.
    O, Margaret, thus 'twill be; and thou, poor soul,
    Art then forsaken, as thou went'st forlorn.
    SECOND GAMEKEEPER [*coming forward*] Say, what art thou that
55   talk'st of kings and queens?
    KING HENRY   More than I seem, and less than I was born to:
    A man at least, for less I should not be;
    And men may talk of kings, and why not I?
    SECOND GAMEKEEPER   Ay, but thou talk'st as if thou wert a king.
60 KING HENRY   Why, so I am, in mind—and that's enough.
    SECOND GAMEKEEPER   But if thou be a king, where is thy crown?
    KING HENRY   My crown is in my heart, not on my head;
    Not decked with diamonds and Indian stones,°   *pearls*
    Nor to be seen. My crown is called content—
65 A crown it is that seldom kings enjoy.
    SECOND GAMEKEEPER   Well, if you be a king crowned with content,
    Your crown content and you must be contented
    To go along with us—for, as we think,
    You are the king King Edward hath deposed,
70 And we his subjects sworn in all allegiance
    Will apprehend you as his enemy.
    KING HENRY   But did you never swear and break an oath?
    SECOND GAMEKEEPER   No—never such an oath, nor will not now.
    KING HENRY   Where did you dwell when I was King of England?
75 SECOND GAMEKEEPER   Here in this country, where we now remain.
    KING HENRY   I was anointed king at nine months old,
    My father and my grandfather were kings,
    And you were sworn true subjects unto me—
    And tell me, then, have you not broke your oaths?
80 FIRST GAMEKEEPER   No, for we were subjects but° while you were king.   *only*
    KING HENRY   Why, am I dead? Do I not breathe a man?
    Ah, simple men, you know not what you swear.
    Look as I blow this feather from my face,

---

2. A notoriously cruel Roman Emperor.   3. While Warwick asserts Edward's claim to the throne.

And as the air blows it to me again,
85 Obeying with° my wind when I do blow,   *Submitting to*
And yielding to another when it blows,
Commanded always by the greater gust—
Such is the lightness° of you common men.   *fickleness*
But do not break your oaths, for of that sin
90 My mild entreaty shall not make you guilty.
Go where you will, the King shall be commanded;
And be you kings, command, and I'll obey.
FIRST GAMEKEEPER We are true subjects to the King, King Edward.
KING HENRY So would you be again to Henry,
95 If he were seated as King Edward is.
FIRST GAMEKEEPER We charge you, in God's name and in the King's,
To go with us unto the officers.
KING HENRY In God's name, lead; your king's name be obeyed;
And what God will, that let your king perform;
100 And what he will I humbly yield unto.   *Exeunt*

3.2

Enter KING EDWARD, [RICHARD *Duke* OF] GLOUCESTER,
[GEORGE *Duke* OF] CLARENCE, *and the* LADY GRAY
KING EDWARD Brother of Gloucester, at Saint Albans field
This lady's husband, Sir Richard Gray, was slain,
His lands then seized on by the conqueror.
Her suit is now to repossess those lands,
5 Which we in justice cannot well deny,
Because in quarrel of the house of York
The worthy gentleman did lose his life.
RICHARD OF GLOUCESTER Your highness shall do well to grant her suit—
It were dishonour to deny it her.
10 KING EDWARD It were no less; but yet I'll make a pause.
RICHARD OF GLOUCESTER [*aside to* GEORGE] Yea, is it so?
I see the lady hath a thing° to grant   *(sexual) favor*
Before the King will grant her humble suit.
GEORGE OF CLARENCE [*aside to* RICHARD] He knows the game;
     how true he keeps the wind!¹
15 RICHARD OF GLOUCESTER [*aside to* GEORGE] Silence.
KING EDWARD [*to* LADY GRAY] Widow, we will consider of your suit;
And come some other time to know our mind.
LADY GRAY Right gracious lord, I cannot brook° delay.   *tolerate*
May it please your highness to resolve me now,
20 And what your pleasure° is shall satisfy me.   *will; sexual desire*
RICHARD OF GLOUCESTER [*aside to* GEORGE] Ay, widow? Then
     I'll warrant° you all your lands   *guarantee*
An if° what pleases him shall pleasure you.   *An if = If*

3.2 Location: The palace, London.
1. "The game" suggests the "sport" of hunting animals or of pursuing sex partners, as well as the objects of both pursuits. Hounds "keep the wind" by keeping the prey against the wind so that it does not catch the scent of the hunter and run away. Clarence implies that Edward pursues Lady Gray with similar skill. The following lines are full of sexual wordplay that Clarence and Richard clearly intend, but that Lady Gray probably does not.

Fight closer, or, good faith, you'll catch a blow.[2]

GEORGE OF CLARENCE [*aside to* RICHARD]   I fear° her not unless   *fear for*
      she chance to fall.[3]

RICHARD OF GLOUCESTER [*aside to* GEORGE]   God forbid that!
25   For he'll take vantages.°   *opportunities*

KING EDWARD [*to* LADY GRAY]   How many children hast thou,
      widow? Tell me.

GEORGE OF CLARENCE [*aside to* RICHARD]   I think he means to
      beg a child of her.[4]

RICHARD OF GLOUCESTER [*aside to* GEORGE]   Nay, whip me
      then—he'll rather give her two.

LADY GRAY [*to* KING EDWARD]   Three, my most gracious lord.

RICHARD OF GLOUCESTER [*aside*]   You shall have four, an° you'll   *if*
30   be ruled by him.

KING EDWARD [*to* LADY GRAY]   'Twere pity they should lose their
      father's lands.

LADY GRAY   Be pitiful, dread lord, and grant it them.

KING EDWARD [*to* RICHARD *and* GEORGE]   Lords, give us leave°—   *leave us alone*
      I'll try this widow's wit.

RICHARD OF GLOUCESTER [*aside to* GEORGE]   Ay, good leave
      have you; for you will have leave,
35   Till youth take leave and leave you to the crutch.[5]
            [RICHARD *and* GEORGE *stand apart*]

KING EDWARD [*to* LADY GRAY]   Now tell me, madam, do you love
      your children?

LADY GRAY   Ay, full as dearly as I love myself.

KING EDWARD   And would you not do much to do them good?

LADY GRAY   To do them good I would sustain some harm.
40 KING EDWARD   Then get your husband's lands, to do them good.

LADY GRAY   Therefore I came unto your majesty.

KING EDWARD   I'll tell you how these lands are to be got.

LADY GRAY   So shall you bind me to your highness' service.

KING EDWARD   What service wilt thou do me, if I give them?
45 LADY GRAY   What you command, that rests in me to do.

KING EDWARD   But you will take exceptions to my boon.°   *request*

LADY GRAY   No, gracious lord, except° I cannot do it.   *unless*

KING EDWARD   Ay, but thou canst do what I mean to ask.

LADY GRAY   Why, then, I will do what your grace commands.

RICHARD OF GLOUCESTER [*to* GEORGE]   He plies her hard, and
50   much rain wears the marble.

GEORGE OF CLARENCE   As red as fire! Nay, then her wax must
      melt.

LADY GRAY [*to* KING EDWARD]   Why stops my lord? Shall I not
      hear my task?

KING EDWARD   An easy task—'tis but to love a king.

LADY GRAY   That's soon performed, because I am a subject.

---

2. Fight nearer to avoid his thrusts. Conflating sexual
slang and the language of dueling, Richard puns on
"blow" as meaning both "hit" and "sexual thrust."
3. Stumble; submit to sex.
4. To ask her to bear him a child; to petition for
guardianship of one of her children. English monarchs
generated income by gaining control of wealthy orphans

from the Court of Wards and Liveries and arranging
their marriages in ways profitable to the monarch.
5. *Ay . . . crutch:* Yes, we will leave you alone, for you
will take liberties (with Lady Gray) until your youth
departs and leaves you walking on crutches (too old for
love). The multiple puns in these lines include "crutch"
as a play on "crotch."

55 KING EDWARD   Why, then, thy husband's lands I freely give thee.

LADY GRAY [*curtsies*]   I take my leave, with many thousand thanks.

RICHARD OF GLOUCESTER [*to* GEORGE]   The match is made—she
    seals it with a curtsy.

KING EDWARD [*to* LADY GRAY]   But stay thee—'tis the fruits of
    love I mean.

LADY GRAY   The fruits of love *I* mean, my loving liege.

60 KING EDWARD   Ay, but I fear me in another sense.
    What love think'st thou I sue so much to get?

LADY GRAY   My love till death, my humble thanks, my prayers—
    That love which virtue begs and virtue grants.

KING EDWARD   No, by my troth, I did not mean such love.

65 LADY GRAY   Why, then, you mean not as I thought you did.

KING EDWARD   But now you partly may perceive my mind.

LADY GRAY   My mind will never grant what I perceive
    Your highness aims at, if I aim aright.°   *guess correctly*

KING EDWARD   To tell thee plain, I aim to lie with thee.

70 LADY GRAY   To tell *you* plain, I had rather lie in prison.

KING EDWARD   Why, then, thou shalt not have thy husband's
    lands.

LADY GRAY   Why, then, mine honesty° shall be my dower;   *chastity*
    For by that loss I will not purchase them.

KING EDWARD   Therein thou wrong'st thy children mightily.

75 LADY GRAY   Herein your highness wrongs both them and me.
    But, mighty lord, this merry inclination
    Accords not with the sadness° of my suit.   *seriousness*
    Please you dismiss me either with ay or no.

KING EDWARD   Ay, if thou wilt say 'ay' to my request;

80   No, if thou dost say 'no' to my demand.

LADY GRAY   Then, no, my lord—my suit is at an end.

RICHARD OF GLOUCESTER [*to* GEORGE]   The widow likes him
    not—she knits her brows.

GEORGE OF CLARENCE   He is the bluntest wooer in Christendom.

KING EDWARD [*aside*]   Her looks doth argue° her replete with modesty;   *prove*

85   Her words doth show her wit incomparable;
    All her perfections challenge° sovereignty.   *lay claim to*
    One way or other, she is for a king;
    And she shall be my love or else my queen.
    [*To* LADY GRAY] Say that King Edward take thee for his queen?

90 LADY GRAY   'Tis better said than done, my gracious lord.
    I am a subject fit to jest withal,
    But far unfit to be a sovereign.

KING EDWARD   Sweet widow, by my state° I swear to thee   *kingship*
    I speak no more than what my soul intends,

95   And that is to enjoy thee for my love.

LADY GRAY   And that is more than I will yield unto.
    I know I am too mean to be your queen,
    And yet too good to be your concubine.

KING EDWARD   You cavil,° widow—I did mean my queen.   *object frivolously*

100 LADY GRAY   'Twill grieve your grace my sons should call you father.

KING EDWARD   No more than when my daughters call thee mother.
    Thou art a widow and thou hast some children;
    And, by God's mother, I, being but a bachelor,
    Have other some.° Why, 'tis a happy thing   *some others*

105   To be the father unto many sons.
        Answer no more, for thou shalt be my queen.
    RICHARD OF GLOUCESTER [*to* GEORGE]   The ghostly father°   *priest*
        now hath done his shrift.[6]
    GEORGE OF CLARENCE   When he was made a shriver, 'twas for
        shift.[7]
    KING EDWARD [*to* RICHARD *and* GEORGE]   Brothers, you muse°   *wonder*
        what chat we two have had.
           [RICHARD *and* GEORGE *come forward*]
    RICHARD OF GLOUCESTER   The widow likes it not, for she looks
110   very sad.
    KING EDWARD   You'd think it strange if I should marry her.
    GEORGE OF CLARENCE   To who, my lord?
    KING EDWARD   Why, Clarence, to myself.
    RICHARD OF GLOUCESTER   That would be ten days' wonder at
        the least.
    GEORGE OF CLARENCE   That's a day longer than a wonder lasts.[8]
115   RICHARD OF GLOUCESTER   By so much is the wonder in extremes.°   *exceedingly great*
    KING EDWARD   Well, jest on, brothers—I can tell you both
      Her suit is granted for her husband's lands.
           Enter a NOBLEMAN
    NOBLEMAN   My gracious lord, Henry your foe is taken
      And brought as prisoner to your palace gate.
120   KING EDWARD   See that he be conveyed unto the Tower—
      [*To* RICHARD *and* GEORGE] And go we, brothers, to the man
        that took him,
      To question of his apprehension.
      [*To* LADY GRAY] Widow, go you along. [*To* RICHARD *and* GEORGE]
        Lords, use her honourably.
                   Exeunt. Manet° RICHARD   *Remains*
    RICHARD OF GLOUCESTER   Ay, Edward will use women honourably.
125   Would he were wasted, marrow, bones, and all,[9]
      That from his loins no hopeful branch may spring
      To cross° me from the golden time I look for.   *keep*
      And yet, between my soul's desire and me—
      The lustful Edward's title burièd°—   *eliminated*
130   Is Clarence, Henry, and his son young Edward,
      And all the unlooked-for° issue of their bodies,   *unforeseen*
      To take their rooms° ere I can place myself.   *places*
      A cold premeditation° for my purpose.   *A discouraging prospect*
      Why, then, I do but dream on sovereignty
135   Like one that stands upon a promontory
      And spies a far-off shore where he would tread,
      Wishing his foot were equal with his eye,[1]
      And chides the sea that sunders him from thence,
      Saying he'll lade° it dry to have his way—   *empty*
140   So do I wish° the crown being so far off,   *wish for*
      And so I chide the means that keeps me from it,

---

6. Has heard her confession and given absolution.
7. It was for a purpose; it was in order to gain access to her undergarments ("shift").
8. Referring to the proverbial expression "nine day's wonder," something that for a short while causes a sensation.

9. Would he were destroyed by disease. Elizabethan medical theory held that syphilis attacked the bones, affected male "mettle," or semen, and caused sterility.
1. Wishing he were able to attain what his eye sees.

And so I say I'll cut the causes off,
Flattering me with impossibilities.
My eye's too quick, my heart o'erweens° too much,   *presumes*
145 Unless my hand and strength could equal them.
Well, say there is no kingdom then for Richard—
What other pleasure can the world afford?
I'll make my heaven in a lady's lap,
And deck my body in gay ornaments,
150 And 'witch° sweet ladies with my words and looks.   *bewitch*
O, miserable thought! And more unlikely
Than to accomplish° twenty golden crowns.   *obtain*
Why, love forswore° me in my mother's womb,   *abandoned*
And, for° I should not deal in her soft laws,   *so that*
155 She did corrupt frail nature with some bribe
To shrink mine arm up like a withered shrub,
To make an envious° mountain on my back—   *a detested*
Where sits deformity to mock my body—
To shape my legs of an unequal size,
160 To disproportion me in every part,
Like to a chaos,° or an unlicked bear whelp²   *formless mass*
That carries no impression like the dam.³
And am I then a man to be beloved?
O, monstrous fault, to harbour such a thought!
165 Then, since this earth affords no joy to me
But to command, to check,° to o'erbear° such   *rebuke / dominate*
As are of better person° than myself,   *appearance*
I'll make my heaven to dream upon the crown,
And whiles I live, t'account this world but hell,
170 Until my misshaped trunk that bears this head
Be round impalèd° with a glorious crown.   *enclosed*
And yet I know not how to get the crown,
For many lives stand between me and home.°   *(my goal)*
And I—like one lost in a thorny wood,
175 That rends the thorns and is rent with the thorns,
Seeking a way and straying from the way,
Not knowing how to find the open air,
But toiling desperately to find it out—
Torment myself to catch the English crown.
180 And from that torment I will free myself,
Or hew my way out with a bloody axe.
Why, I can smile, and murder whiles I smile,
And cry 'Content!' to that which grieves my heart,
And wet my cheeks with artificial tears,
185 And frame my face to all occasions.
I'll drown more sailors than the mermaid⁴ shall;
I'll slay more gazers than the basilisk;⁵
I'll play the orator as well as Nestor,⁶
Deceive more slyly than Ulysses⁷ could,

---

2. Alluding to the popular belief that bears were born as formless lumps and licked into shape by their mothers.
3. That does not resemble its mother.
4. A fabulous marine monster, resembling a woman, who sang sweet songs to lure sailors onto the rocks and to their death.

5. A mythical reptile, hatched from a cock's egg, whose look was supposed to be fatal.
6. The Greek King and aged counselor present at the siege of Troy, famous for his skill in speech.
7. The Greek warrior famous for his cunning, hero of Homer's *Odyssey*.

190   And, like a Sinon,[8] take another Troy.
      I can add colours to the chameleon,[9]
      Change shapes with Proteus[1] for advantages,
      And set the murderous Machiavel[2] to school.
      Can I do this, and cannot get a crown?
195   Tut, were it farther off, I'll pluck it down.   *Exit*

3.3

[Two chairs of state.][1] Flourish. Enter KING LOUIS
[of France], his sister the LADY BONA, *[Lord]* Bourbon
his admiral, PRINCE EDWARD, QUEEN MARGARET,
and the Earl of OXFORD. LOUIS *[goes up upon the*
state,] sits, and riseth up again

KING LOUIS   Fair Queen of England, worthy Margaret,
      Sit down with us. It ill befits thy state
      And birth that thou shouldst stand while Louis doth sit.
QUEEN MARGARET   No, mighty King of France, now Margaret
5   Must strike her sail° and learn a while to serve   *humble herself*
      Where kings command. I was, I must confess,
      Great Albion's° queen in former golden days,   *England's*
      But now mischance hath trod my title down,
      And with dishonour laid me on the ground,
10   Where I must take like seat unto my fortune[2]
      And to my humble state conform myself.
KING LOUIS   Why, say, fair Queen, whence springs this deep despair?
QUEEN MARGARET   From such a cause as fills mine eyes with tears
      And stops my tongue, while heart is drowned in cares.
15   KING LOUIS   Whate'er it be, be thou still like thyself,
      And sit thee by our side.
                      Seats her by him
                                 Yield not thy neck
      To fortune's yoke, but let thy dauntless mind
      Still ride in triumph over all mischance.
      Be plain, Queen Margaret, and tell thy grief.
20   It shall be eased if France° can yield relief.   *the King of France*
QUEEN MARGARET   Those gracious words revive my drooping
            thoughts,
      And give my tongue-tied sorrows leave to speak.
      Now, therefore, be it known to noble Louis
      That Henry, sole possessor of my love,
25   Is of° a king become a banished man,   *Instead of*

---

8. Like a treacherous man. According to Virgil, Sinon's lies convinced the Trojans to accept as a gift the wooden horse in which the Greek soldiers who later sacked Troy were concealed.
9. A reptile able to change the color of its skin in order to blend into its surroundings.
1. A Greek sea god who was able to assume different shapes at will.
2. Niccolò Machiavelli (1469–1527), an Italian political philosopher popularly known in England as a depraved advocate of political cunning and ruthlessness.
3.3 Location: The King's palace, France.
1. Louis's request for Margaret to "sit down with us" at line 2 suggests that at least two chairs of state are required, possibly three (including one for Lady Bona).
2. Where I must take a position in keeping with my fortune.

And forced to live in Scotland a forlorn,°   *an outcast*
While proud ambitious Edward, Duke of York,
Usurps the regal title and the seat
Of England's true-anointed lawful King.
30 This is the cause that I, poor Margaret,
With this my son, Prince Edward, Henry's heir,
Am come to crave thy just and lawful aid.
An if thou fail us all our hope is done.
Scotland hath will to help, but cannot help;
35 Our people and our peers are both misled,
Our treasure seized, our soldiers put to flight,
And, as thou seest, ourselves in heavy plight.
KING LOUIS Renownèd Queen, with patience calm the storm,
While we bethink a means to break it off.
40 QUEEN MARGARET The more we stay,° the stronger grows our foe. *delay*
KING LOUIS The more I stay, the more I'll succour thee.
QUEEN MARGARET O, but impatience waiteth on° true sorrow. *attends*
   Enter [the Earl of] WARWICK
And see where comes the breeder of my sorrow.
KING LOUIS What's he approacheth boldly to our presence?
45 QUEEN MARGARET Our Earl of Warwick, Edward's greatest friend.
KING LOUIS Welcome, brave Warwick. What brings thee to France?
   He descends. She ariseth
QUEEN MARGARET *[aside]* Ay, now begins a second storm to rise,
For this is he that moves both wind and tide.
WARWICK *[to* KING LOUIS*]* From worthy Edward, King of Albion,
50 My lord and sovereign, and thy vowèd friend,
I come in kindness and unfeignèd love,
First, to do greetings to thy royal person,
And then, to crave a league of amity,°   *friendship*
And lastly, to confirm that amity
55 With nuptial knot, if thou vouchsafe to grant
That virtuous Lady Bona, thy fair sister,
To England's King in lawful marriage.
QUEEN MARGARET *[aside]* If that go forward, Henry's hope is done.
WARWICK *(to [*LADY*]* BONA*)* And, gracious madam, in our King's behalf
60 I am commanded, with your leave and favour,
Humbly to kiss your hand, and with my tongue
To tell the passion of my sovereign's heart,
Where fame, late ent'ring at his heedful ears,
Hath placed thy beauty's image and thy virtue.
65 QUEEN MARGARET King Louis and Lady Bona, hear me speak
Before you answer Warwick. His demand
Springs not from Edward's well-meant honest love,
But from deceit, bred by necessity.
For how can tyrants safely govern home
70 Unless abroad they purchase° great alliance?   *obtain*
To prove him tyrant this reason may suffice—
That Henry liveth still; but were he dead,
Yet here Prince Edward stands, King Henry's son.
Look, therefore, Louis, that by this league and marriage
75 Thou draw not on thy danger and dishonour,
For though usurpers sway the rule° a while,   *wield power*
Yet heav'ns are just and time suppresseth wrongs.

WARWICK   Injurious° Margaret.   *Insulting*
PRINCE EDWARD   And why not 'Queen'?
WARWICK   Because thy father Henry did usurp,
80   And thou no more art prince than she is queen.
OXFORD   Then Warwick disannuls° great John of Gaunt,   *cancels*
     Which did subdue the greatest part of Spain;
     And, after John of Gaunt, Henry the Fourth,
     Whose wisdom was a mirror to the wisest;
85   And, after that wise prince, Henry the Fifth,
     Who by his prowess conquerèd all France.
     From these our Henry lineally descends.
WARWICK   Oxford, how haps it in this smooth discourse
     You told not how Henry the Sixth hath lost
90   All that which Henry the Fifth had gotten?
     Methinks these peers of France should smile at that.
     But for the rest, you tell a pedigree
     Of threescore and two years³—a silly° time   *trifling*
     To make prescription for a kingdom's worth.⁴
95   OXFORD   Why, Warwick, canst thou speak against thy liege,
     Whom thou obeyedest thirty and six years,
     And not bewray° thy treason with a blush?   *reveal*
WARWICK   Can Oxford, that did ever fence the right,°   *defend justice*
     Now buckler° falsehood with a pedigree?   *shield*
100   For shame—leave Henry, and call Edward king.
OXFORD   Call him my king by whose injurious doom°   *insulting judgment*
     My elder brother, the Lord Aubrey Vere,⁵
     Was done to death? And more than so, my father,
     Even in the downfall° of his mellowed years,   *decline*
105   When nature brought him to the door of death?
     No, Warwick, no—while life upholds this arm,
     This arm upholds the house of Lancaster.
WARWICK   And I the house of York.
KING LOUIS   Queen Margaret, Prince Edward, and Oxford,
110   Vouchsafe, at our request, to stand aside
     While I use further conference° with Warwick.   *talk further*
          [QUEEN MARGARET *comes down from the state and,*
          with PRINCE EDWARD *and* OXFORD, *stands apart*]⁶
QUEEN MARGARET   Heavens grant that Warwick's words bewitch him not.
KING LOUIS   Now, Warwick, tell me even upon thy conscience,
     Is Edward your true king? For I were loath
115   To link with him that were not lawful chosen.
WARWICK   Thereon I pawn my credit and mine honour.
KING LOUIS   But is he gracious in the people's eye?
WARWICK   The more that⁷ Henry was unfortunate.
KING LOUIS   Then further, all dissembling set aside,
120   Tell me for truth the measure of his love
     Unto our sister Bona.

---

3. Meaning the sixty-two years between 1399, when   5. Eldest son of the twelfth Earl of Oxford, John de
Henry IV deposed Richard II, and 1461, when Henry   Vere. Both were executed for treason by the Yorkists in
VI was deposed by Edward.   1462.
4. To make a claim based on custom for something as   6. F's stage direction reads "They stand aloof."
valuable as a kingdom.   7. The more (gracious) because.

WARWICK   Such it seems
    As may beseem° a monarch like himself.   *befit*
    Myself have often heard him say and swear
    That this his love was an eternal plant,
125   Whereof the root was fixed in virtue's ground,
    The leaves and fruit maintained with beauty's sun,
    Exempt from envy, but not from disdain,[8]
    Unless the Lady Bona quit° his pain.°   *end / (by loving him)*
KING LOUIS [*to* LADY BONA]   Now, sister, let us hear your firm resolve.
130 LADY BONA   Your grant, or your denial, shall be mine.
    (*To* WARWICK) Yet I confess that often ere this day,
    When I have heard your king's desert° recounted,   *merit*
    Mine ear hath tempted judgement to desire.
KING LOUIS [*to* WARWICK]   Then, Warwick, thus—our sister
        shall be Edward's.
135   And now, forthwith, shall articles be drawn
    Touching the jointure° that your king must make,   *marriage settlement*
    Which with her dowry shall be counterpoised.°   *equally balanced*
    [*To* QUEEN MARGARET] Draw near, Queen Margaret, and be a
        witness
    That Bona shall be wife to the English king.
      [QUEEN MARGARET, PRINCE EDWARD, *and* OXFORD *come*
      forward]
140 PRINCE EDWARD   To Edward, but not to the English king.
QUEEN MARGARET   Deceitful Warwick—it was thy device
    By this alliance to make void my suit!
    Before thy coming Louis was Henry's friend.
KING LOUIS   And still is friend to him and Margaret.
145   But if your title to the crown be weak,
    As may appear by Edward's good success,
    Then 'tis but reason that I be released
    From giving aid which late° I promisèd.   *recently*
    Yet shall you have all kindness at my hand
150   That your estate requires and mine can yield.
WARWICK [*to* QUEEN MARGARET]   Henry now lives in Scotland at his ease,
    Where having nothing, nothing can he lose.
    And as for you yourself, our quondam° queen,   *former*
    You have a father able to maintain you,
155   And better 'twere you troubled him than France.
QUEEN MARGARET   Peace, impudent and shameless Warwick, peace!
    Proud setter-up and puller-down of kings!
    I will not hence till, with my talk and tears,
    Both full of truth, I make King Louis behold
160   Thy sly conveyance° and thy lord's false love,   *deceit*
        POST° *blowing a horn within*   *Messenger*
    For both of you are birds of selfsame feather.
KING LOUIS   Warwick, this is some post to us or thee.
        Enter the POST
POST (*to* WARWICK)   My lord ambassador, these letters are for you,

8. Exempt from malice, but not exempt from (being hurt by) her disdain for him.

Sent from your brother Marquis Montague;
165 (*To* LOUIS) These from our King unto your majesty;
(*To* [QUEEN] MARGARET) And, madam, these for you, from
whom I know not.
         They all read their letters
OXFORD [*to* PRINCE EDWARD]   I like it well that our fair Queen and mistress
Smiles at her news, while Warwick frowns at his.
PRINCE EDWARD   Nay, mark how Louis stamps° as he were   *(his foot)*
nettled.°   *angry*
170 I hope all's for the best.
KING LOUIS   Warwick, what are thy news? And yours, fair Queen?
QUEEN MARGARET   Mine, such as fill my heart with unhoped joys.
WARWICK   Mine, full of sorrow and heart's discontent.
KING LOUIS   What! Has your king married the Lady Gray?
175 And now to soothe° your forgery° and his,   *smooth over / deceit*
Sends me a paper to persuade me patience?
Is this th'alliance that he seeks with France?
Dare he presume to scorn us in this manner?
QUEEN MARGARET   I told your majesty as much before—
180 This proveth Edward's love and Warwick's honesty.
WARWICK   King Louis, I here protest in sight of heaven
And by the hope I have of heavenly bliss,
That I am clear from this misdeed of Edward's,
No more my king, for he dishonours me,
185 But most himself, if he could see his shame.
Did I forget that by the house of York
My father came untimely to his death?⁹
Did I let pass th'abuse done to my niece?¹
Did I impale him° with the regal crown?   *encircle his head*
190 Did I put Henry from his native right?
And am I guerdoned° at the last with shame?   *rewarded*
Shame on himself, for my desert is honour.
And to repair my honour, lost for him,
I here renounce him and return to Henry.
195 [*To* QUEEN MARGARET]   My noble Queen, let former grudges pass,
And henceforth I am thy true servitor.°   *servant*
I will revenge his wrong to Lady Bona
And replant Henry in his former state.
QUEEN MARGARET   Warwick, these words have turned my hate to love,
200 And I forgive and quite forget old faults,
And joy that thou becom'st King Henry's friend.
WARWICK   So much his friend, ay, his unfeignèd friend,
That if King Louis vouchsafe to furnish us
With some few bands of chosen soldiers,
205 I'll undertake to land them on our coast
And force the tyrant from his seat by war.

---

9. Actually, Warwick's father, the Earl of Salisbury of *The First Part of the Contention*, was executed by the Lancastrians. Perhaps Warwick means that his father would not have died in the Yorkist cause had the Yorkists never tried to seize the throne.
1. Holinshed's *Chronicles* reports that while visiting Warwick's house, Edward attempted to sexually assault his host's daughter or niece.

'Tis not his new-made bride shall succour him.
And as for Clarence, as my letters tell me,
He's very likely now to fall from° him _desert_
210 For matching° more for wanton lust than honour, _marrying_
Or than for strength and safety of our country.
LADY BONA [_to_ KING LOUIS]   Dear brother, how shall Bona be revenged,
But by thy help to this distressèd Queen?
QUEEN MARGARET [_to_ KING LOUIS]   Renownèd Prince, how shall
poor Henry live
215 Unless thou rescue him from foul despair?
LADY BONA [_to_ KING LOUIS]   My quarrel and this English
Queen's are one.
WARWICK   And mine, fair Lady Bona, joins with yours.
KING LOUIS   And mine with hers, and thine, and Margaret's.
Therefore at last I firmly am resolved:
220 You shall have aid.
QUEEN MARGARET   Let me give humble thanks for all at once.
KING LOUIS [_to the_ POST]   Then, England's messenger, return in post° _haste_
And tell false Edward, thy supposèd king,
That Louis of France is sending over masquers²
225 To revel it with him and his new bride.
Thou seest what's passed, go fear° thy king withal.° _frighten / with it_
LADY BONA [_to the_ POST]   Tell him, in hope he'll prove a widower shortly,
I'll wear the willow garland³ for his sake.
QUEEN MARGARET [_to the_ POST]   Tell him my mourning weeds° _apparel_
are laid aside,
230 And I am ready to put armour on.
WARWICK [_to the_ POST]   Tell him from me that he hath done me wrong,
And therefore I'll uncrown him ere't be long.
[_Giving money_] There's thy reward—be gone.   _Exit_ POST
KING LOUIS   But, Warwick, thou and Oxford, with five thousand men,
235 Shall cross the seas and bid false Edward battle;
And, as occasion serves, this noble Queen
And Prince shall follow with a fresh supply.
Yet, ere thou go, but answer me one doubt:
What pledge have we of thy firm loyalty?
240 WARWICK   This shall assure my constant loyalty:
That if our Queen and this young Prince agree,
I'll join mine eldest daughter⁴ and my joy
To him forthwith in holy wedlock bands.
QUEEN MARGARET   Yes, I agree, and thank you for your motion.° _proposal_
245 [_To_ PRINCE EDWARD] Son Edward, she is fair and virtuous,
Therefore delay not. Give thy hand to Warwick,
And with thy hand thy faith irrevocable
That only Warwick's daughter shall be thine.
PRINCE EDWARD   Yes, I accept her, for she well deserves it,

---

2. The actors in courtly revels and entertainments that were often staged to celebrate the marriages of members of the Elizabethan aristocracy.
3. Token of a forsaken lover.
4. The historical Edward was betrothed (but never married) to Warwick's second daughter, Anne. She eventually married Richard Duke of York (later Richard III). Warwick's eldest daughter married George of Clarence.

250 And here to pledge my vow I give my hand.
　　　　　　He gives his hand to WARWICK
KING LOUIS   Why stay we now? These soldiers shall be levied,
　　And thou, Lord Bourbon, our high admiral,
　　Shall waft° them over with our royal fleet.　　　　　　*convey by water*
　　I long till Edward fall by war's mischance
255　For mocking marriage with a dame of France.
　　　　　　　　　　　　　　　Exeunt. Manet WARWICK
WARWICK   I came from Edward as ambassador,
　　But I return his sworn and mortal foe.
　　Matter of marriage was the charge he gave me,
　　But dreadful war shall answer his demand.
260　Had he none else to make a stale° but me?　　　　　　*laughingstock*
　　Then none but I shall turn his jest to sorrow.
　　I was the chief that raised him to the crown,
　　And I'll be chief to bring him down again.
　　Not that I pity Henry's misery,
265　But seek revenge on Edward's mockery.　　　　　*Exit*

4.1

Enter RICHARD [*Duke* OF GLOUCESTER, GEORGE
Duke OF] CLARENCE, [*the Duke of*] SOMERSET, *and*
[*the Marquis of*] MONTAGUE
RICHARD OF GLOUCESTER   Now tell me, brother Clarence, what think you
　　Of this new marriage with the Lady Gray?
　　Hath not our brother made a worthy choice?
GEORGE OF CLARENCE   Alas, you know 'tis far from hence to France;
5　How could he stay° till Warwick made return?　　　　　　*wait*
SOMERSET   My lords, forbear this talk—here comes the King.
　　　　　　Flourish. Enter KING EDWARD, *the* LADY GRAY [*his*]
　　　　　　Queen, [*the Earl of*] *Pembroke,* [*and the Lords*]
　　　　　　Stafford [*and*] HASTINGS. *Four stand on one side* [*of*
　　　　　　the King], *and four on the other*
RICHARD OF GLOUCESTER   And his well-chosen bride.
GEORGE OF CLARENCE   I mind° to tell him plainly what I think.　　　　　　*intend*
KING EDWARD   Now, brother of Clarence, how like you our choice,
10　That you stand pensive, as half-malcontent?°　　　　　*partly discontented*
GEORGE OF CLARENCE   As well as Louis of France, or the Earl
　　of Warwick,
　　Which° are so weak of courage and in judgement　　　　　　*Who*
　　That they'll take no offence at our abuse.°　　　　　　*insult*
KING EDWARD   Suppose they take offence without a cause—
15　They are but Louis and Warwick; I am Edward,
　　Your king and Warwick's, and must have my will.°　　　*way; sexual desire*
RICHARD OF GLOUCESTER   And you shall have your will,
　　　　because our king.
　　Yet hasty marriage seldom proveth well.
KING EDWARD   Yea, brother Richard, are you offended too?
RICHARD OF GLOUCESTER   Not I, no—God forbid that I should
20　　　wish them severed

4.1 Location: The palace, London.

Whom God hath joined together. Ay, and 'twere pity
To sunder them that yoke° so well together. *who are coupled*

KING EDWARD Setting your scorns and your mislike° aside, *displeasure*
Tell me some reason why the Lady Gray

25 Should not become my wife and England's queen.
And you too, Somerset and Montague,
Speak freely what you think.

GEORGE OF CLARENCE Then this is my opinion: that King Louis
Becomes your enemy for mocking him

30 About the marriage of the Lady Bona.

RICHARD OF GLOUCESTER And Warwick, doing what you gave in charge,
Is now dishonourèd by this new marriage.

KING EDWARD What if both Louis and Warwick be appeased
By such invention° as I can devise? *scheme*

35 MONTAGUE Yet, to have joined with France in such alliance
Would more have strengthened this our commonwealth
'Gainst foreign storms than any home-bred marriage.

HASTINGS Why, knows not Montague that of itself
England is safe, if true within itself?

40 MONTAGUE But the safer when 'tis backed with France.

HASTINGS 'Tis better using France than trusting France.
Let us be backed with God and with the seas
Which he hath giv'n for fence impregnable,
And with their helps only° defend ourselves. *alone*

45 In them and in ourselves our safety lies.

GEORGE OF CLARENCE For this one speech Lord Hastings well deserves
To have the heir of the Lord Hungerford.[1]

KING EDWARD Ay, what of that? It was my will and grant—
And for this once my will shall stand for law.

RICHARD OF GLOUCESTER And yet, methinks, your grace hath

50 not done well
To give the heir and daughter of Lord Scales
Unto the brother[2] of your loving bride.
She better would have fitted me or Clarence,
But in° your bride you bury° brotherhood. *because of / forget*

GEORGE OF CLARENCE Or else you would not have bestowed

55 the heir
Of the Lord Bonville on your new wife's son,° *(Sir Thomas Gray)*
And leave your brothers to go speed elsewhere.

KING EDWARD Alas, poor Clarence, is it for a wife
That thou art malcontent? I will provide thee.

GEORGE OF CLARENCE In choosing for yourself you showed

60 your judgement,
Which being shallow, you shall give me leave
To play the broker° in mine own behalf, *marriage broker*
And to that end I shortly mind to leave you.

KING EDWARD Leave me, or tarry. Edward will be king,

65 And not be tied unto his brother's will.

---

1. To marry a rich heiress. Clarence is objecting to the
Queen's upstart relatives, such as Hastings, being given
wealthy marriage partners.
2. That is, Anthony Woodville, second Earl Rivers.

LADY GRAY My lords, before it pleased his majesty
To raise my state to title of a queen,
Do me but right, and you must all confess
That I was not ignoble of descent—
70 And meaner° than myself have had like fortune.³   *people of lower rank*
But as this title honours me and mine,
So your dislikes, to whom I would be pleasing,
Doth cloud my joys with danger° and with sorrow.   *apprehension*
KING EDWARD My love, forbear to fawn upon° their frowns.   *be abject before*
75 What danger or what sorrow can befall thee
So long as Edward is thy constant friend,
And their true sovereign, whom they must obey?
Nay, whom they shall obey, and love thee too—
Unless they seek for hatred at my hands,
80 Which if they do, yet will I keep thee safe,
And they shall feel the vengeance of my wrath.
RICHARD OF GLOUCESTER [*aside*] I hear, yet say not much, but
        think the more.
        Enter [the] POST [*from France*]
KING EDWARD Now, messenger, what letters or what news from France?
POST My sovereign liege, no letters and few words,
85 But such as I, without your special pardon,
Dare not relate.
KING EDWARD Go to, we pardon thee. Therefore, in brief,
Tell me their words as near as thou canst guess° them.   *approximate*
What answer makes King Louis unto our letters?
90 POST At my depart these were his very words:
'Go tell false Edward, thy supposèd king,
That Louis of France is sending over masquers
To revel it with him and his new bride.'
KING EDWARD Is Louis so brave? Belike° he thinks me Henry.   *Perhaps*
95 But what said Lady Bona to my marriage?
POST These were her words, uttered with mild disdain:
'Tell him in hope he'll prove a widower shortly,
I'll wear the willow garland for his sake.'
KING EDWARD I blame not her, she could say little less;
100 She had the wrong. But what said Henry's queen?
For I have heard that she was there in place.
POST 'Tell him', quoth she, 'my mourning weeds are done,
And I am ready to put armour on.'
KING EDWARD Belike she minds to play the Amazon.⁴
105 But what said Warwick to these injuries?
POST He, more incensed against your majesty
Than all the rest, discharged me with these words:
'Tell him from me that he hath done me wrong,
And therefore I'll uncrown him ere't be long.'
110 KING EDWARD Ha! Durst the traitor breathe out so proud words?
Well, I will arm me, being thus forewarned.
They shall have wars and pay for their presumption.
But say, is Warwick friends with Margaret?

---

3. In fact, the historical Lady Gray was the first com-   4. Legendary warrior woman. See note to 1.4.115.
moner to become Queen of England.

POST   Ay, gracious sovereign, they are so linked in friendship
115   That young Prince Edward marries Warwick's daughter.
GEORGE OF CLARENCE   Belike the elder; Clarence will have the younger.
Now, brother King, farewell, and sit you fast,
For I will hence to Warwick's other daughter,
That, though I want° a kingdom, yet in marriage   *lack*
120   I may not prove inferior to yourself.
You that love me and Warwick, follow me.

Exit CLARENCE, *and* SOMERSET *follows*

RICHARD OF GLOUCESTER   Not I—[*aside*] my thoughts aim at a
further matter.
I stay not for the love of Edward, but the crown.
KING EDWARD   Clarence and Somerset both gone to Warwick?
125   Yet am I armed against the worst can happen,
And haste is needful in this desp'rate case.
Pembroke and Stafford, you in our behalf
Go levy men and make prepare° for war.   *preparation*
They are already, or quickly will be, landed.
130   Myself in person will straight follow you.

Exeunt Pembroke and Stafford

But ere I go, Hastings and Montague,
Resolve my doubt. You twain, of all the rest,
Are near'st to Warwick by blood and by alliance.
Tell me if you love Warwick more than me.
135   If it be so, then both depart to him—
I rather wish you foes than hollow° friends.   *false*
But if you mind to hold your true obedience,
Give me assurance with some friendly vow
That I may never have you in suspect.°   *under suspicion*
140   MONTAGUE   So God help Montague as he proves true.
HASTINGS   And Hastings as he favours Edward's cause.
KING EDWARD   Now, brother Richard, will you stand by us?
RICHARD OF GLOUCESTER   Ay, in despite of all that shall withstand you.
KING EDWARD   Why, so. Then am I sure of victory.
145   Now, therefore, let us hence and lose no hour
Till we meet Warwick with his foreign power.°   *Exeunt*   *army*

4.2

Enter [the Earls of] WARWICK *and* OXFORD *in England,
with French soldiers*

WARWICK   Trust me, my lord, all hitherto° goes well.   *thus far*
The common sort by numbers swarm to us.

Enter [the Dukes of] CLARENCE *and* SOMERSET

But see where Somerset and Clarence comes.
Speak suddenly, my lords, are we all friends?
5   GEORGE OF CLARENCE   Fear not that, my lord.
WARWICK   Then, gentle Clarence, welcome unto Warwick—
And welcome, Somerset. I hold it cowardice
To rest mistrustful where a noble heart
Hath pawned° an open hand in sign of love,   *pledged*

4.2 Location: Fields near Warwick.

10   Else might I think that Clarence, Edward's brother,
    Were but a feignèd friend to our proceedings.
    But come, sweet Clarence, my daughter shall be thine.
    And now what rests° but, in night's coverture,°   remains / shadow
    Thy brother being carelessly encamped,
15   His soldiers lurking° in the towns about,   idling
    And but attended by a simple guard,
    We may surprise and take him at our pleasure?
    Our scouts have found the adventure very easy;
    That, as Ulysses and stout Diomed
20   With sleight° and manhood° stole to Rhesus' tents   stealth / bravery
    And brought from thence the Thracian fatal steeds,[1]
    So we, well covered with the night's black mantle,
    At unawares° may beat down Edward's guard   Suddenly
    And seize himself—I say not 'slaughter him',
25   For I intend but only to surprise° him.   capture
    You that will follow me to this attempt,
    Applaud the name of Henry with your leader.
        They all cry 'Henry'
    Why, then, let's on our way in silent sort,°   manner
    For Warwick and his friends, God and Saint George!°   patron saint of England
                                                    Exeunt

4.3

Enter three WATCHMEN, *to guard the King's
[Edward's] tent*

FIRST WATCHMAN   Come on, my masters, each man take his stand.°   post
    The King by this is set him down° to sleep.   settled (in a chair)
SECOND WATCHMAN   What, will he not to bed?
FIRST WATCHMAN   Why, no—for he hath made a solemn vow
5   Never to lie and take his natural rest
    Till Warwick or himself be quite suppressed.°   vanquished
SECOND WATCHMAN   Tomorrow then belike shall be the day,
    If Warwick be so near as men report.
THIRD WATCHMAN   But say, I pray, what nobleman is that
10   That with the King here resteth in his tent?
FIRST WATCHMAN   'Tis the Lord Hastings, the King's chiefest friend.
THIRD WATCHMAN   O, is it so? But why commands the King
    That his chief followers lodge in towns about him,
    While he himself keeps° in the cold field?   lodges
15   SECOND WATCHMAN   'Tis the more honour, because more dangerous.
THIRD WATCHMAN   Ay, but give me worship° and quietness—   dignity
    I like it better than a dangerous honour.
    If Warwick knew in what estate° he° stands,   condition / (Edward)
    'Tis to be doubted° he would waken him.   feared
20   FIRST WATCHMAN   Unless our halberds[1] did shut up° his passage.   bar
SECOND WATCHMAN   Ay, wherefore else guard we his royal tent

---

1. The Greek warriors Ulysses and Diomedes captured
the horses of the Thracian prince Rhesus in a night
raid, after an oracle predicted that Troy would not fall
to the Greeks as long as the horses of Rhesus grazed
on the plains of Troy (see *The Iliad*, Book 10). *fatal:*
fateful.
4.3 Location: King Edward's camp near Warwick.
1. Long-handled weapons with axlike blades.

But to defend his person from night-foes?
Enter [the Earl of] WARWICK, [GEORGE Duke of]
CLARENCE, [the Earl of] OXFORD, [and the Duke of]
SOMERSET, and French soldiers. Silent all
WARWICK   This is his tent—and see where stand his guard.
Courage, my masters—honour now or never!
25   But follow me, and Edward shall be ours.
FIRST WATCHMAN   Who goes there?
SECOND WATCHMAN   Stay or thou diest.
         WARWICK and the rest all cry 'Warwick, Warwick!'
         and set upon the guard, who fly, crying 'Arm, arm!' WAR-
         WICK and the rest follow them

4.4

[With] the drum[mer] playing and trumpet[er] sound-
ing, enter [the Earl of] WARWICK, [the Duke of]
SOMERSET, and the rest bringing the KING [EDWARD]
out in his gown, sitting in a chair. RICHARD [Duke of
GLOUCESTER] and [Lord] HASTINGS flies over the stage
SOMERSET   What are they that fly there?
WARWICK   Richard and Hastings—let them go. Here is the Duke.
KING EDWARD   'The Duke'! Why, Warwick, when we parted,
Thou calledst me king.
WARWICK   Ay, but the case is altered.[1]
5   When you disgraced me in my embassade,°   *diplomatic mission*
Then I degraded you from being king,
And come now to create you Duke of York.
Alas, how should you govern any kingdom
That know not how to use ambassadors,
10   Nor how to be contented with one wife,
Nor how to use your brothers brotherly,
Nor how to study for the people's welfare,
Nor how to shroud° yourself from enemies?   *conceal*
KING EDWARD [*seeing GEORGE*]   Yea, brother of Clarence, art
thou here too?
15   Nay, then, I see that Edward needs must down.°   *must fall*
Yet, Warwick, in despite of all mischance,
Of thee thyself and all thy complices,
Edward will always bear himself as king.
Though fortune's malice overthrow my state,°   *sovereignty*
20   My mind exceeds the compass of her wheel.[2]
WARWICK   Then, for his° mind, be Edward England's king.   *in his (Edward's)*
         [*WARWICK*] *takes off [Edward's] crown*
But Henry now shall wear the English crown,
And be true king indeed, thou but the shadow.
My lord of Somerset, at my request,
25   See that, forthwith, Duke Edward be conveyed
Unto my brother, Archbishop of York.
When I have fought with Pembroke and his fellows,
I'll follow you, and tell what answer
Louis and the Lady Bona send to him.

4.4 Location: Scene continues.
1. Proverbial for "things have changed."
2. My thoughts escape the control of fortune. The

goddess Fortune was often depicted turning a wheel on
which human destinies both rose and fell, sometimes
coming full circle.

30   Now for a while farewell, good Duke of York.
                  They [begin to] lead [EDWARD] out forcibly
     KING EDWARD   What fates impose, that men must needs abide.°   *endure*
       It boots not to resist both wind and tide.³
                                  Exeunt some with EDWARD
     OXFORD   What now remains, my lords, for us to do
       But march to London with our soldiers?
35   WARWICK   Ay, that's the first thing that we have to do—
       To free King Henry from imprisonment
       And see him seated in the regal throne.   *Exeunt*

4.5

      Enter [Earl] RIVERS *and [his sister,]* LADY GRAY
      [Edward's queen]
     RIVERS   Madam, what makes you in this sudden change?¹
     LADY GRAY   Why, brother Rivers, are you yet to learn
       What late misfortune is befall'n King Edward?
     RIVERS   What? Loss of some pitched battle against Warwick?
5   LADY GRAY   No, but the loss of his own royal person.
     RIVERS   Then is my sovereign slain?
     LADY GRAY   Ay, almost slain—for he is taken prisoner,
       Either betrayed by falsehood of his guard
       Or by his foe surprised at unawares,
10   And, as I further have to understand,
       Is new committed to the Bishop of York,
       Fell° Warwick's brother, and by that° our foe.   *Cruel / therefore*
     RIVERS   These news, I must confess, are full of grief.
       Yet, gracious madam, bear it as you may.
15   Warwick may lose, that now hath won the day.
     LADY GRAY   Till then fair hope must hinder life's decay,
       And I the rather° wean me from despair   *I am the more obliged to*
       For love of Edward's offspring in my womb.
       This is it that makes me bridle° passion   *control*
20   And bear with mildness my misfortune's cross.
       Ay, ay, for this I draw in many a tear
       And stop the rising of blood-sucking² sighs,
       Lest with my sighs or tears I blast° or drown   *blight*
       King Edward's fruit, true heir to th'English crown.
25   RIVERS   But, madam, where is Warwick then become?°   *gone*
     LADY GRAY   I am informèd that he comes towards London
       To set the crown once more on Henry's head.
       Guess thou the rest—King Edward's friends must down.
       But to prevent the tyrant's violence—
30   For trust not him that hath once broken faith—
       I'll hence forthwith unto the sanctuary,³
       To save at least the heir of Edward's right.
       There shall I rest secure from force and fraud.
       Come, therefore, let us fly while we may fly.
35   If Warwick take us, we are sure to die.   *Exeunt*

---

3. Compare with 3.3.48, where Margaret says that Warwick "moves both wind and tide." *boots*: profits.
4.5 Location: The palace, London.
1. What is the reason for this sudden change of mind?

2. It was popularly believed that each sigh consumed a drop of blood from the heart.
3. Place that by law conferred immunity from arrest.

4.6

Enter RICHARD [*Duke of* GLOUCESTER], *Lord*
HASTINGS, *and Sir William Stanley* [*with soldiers*]

RICHARD OF GLOUCESTER Now my lord Hastings and Sir
  William Stanley,
  Leave off to wonder why I drew you hither
  Into this chiefest thicket of the park.°   *hunting grounds*
  Thus stands the case: you know our King, my brother,
5 Is prisoner to the Bishop here, at whose hands
  He hath good usage and great liberty,
  And, often but attended with weak guard,
  Comes hunting this way to disport° himself.   *amuse*
  I have advertised° him by secret means   *informed*
10 That if about this hour he make this way
  Under the colour° of his usual game,°   *pretext / hunting*
  He shall here find his friends with horse and men
  To set him free from his captivity.

Enter KING EDWARD *and a* HUNTSMAN *with him*

HUNTSMAN This way, my lord—for this way lies the game.
15 KING EDWARD Nay, this way, man—see where the huntsmen stand.
  Now, brother of Gloucester, Lord Hastings, and the rest,
  Stand you thus close° to steal the Bishop's deer?   *concealed*
RICHARD OF GLOUCESTER Brother, the time and case requireth haste.
  Your horse stands ready at the park corner.
20 KING EDWARD But whither shall we then?
HASTINGS To Lynn,[1] my lord,
  And shipped from thence to Flanders.
RICHARD OF GLOUCESTER [*aside*] Well guessed, believe me—for
  that was my meaning.
KING EDWARD Stanley, I will requite thy forwardness.°   *reward your zeal*
RICHARD OF GLOUCESTER But wherefore stay we? 'Tis no time
25 to talk.
KING EDWARD Huntsman, what sayst thou? Wilt thou go along?
HUNTSMAN Better do so than tarry and be hanged.
RICHARD OF GLOUCESTER Come then, away—let's have no more ado.
KING EDWARD Bishop, farewell—shield thee from Warwick's frown,
30 And pray that I may repossess the crown.   *Exeunt*

4.7

Flourish. Enter [*the Earl of*] WARWICK *and* [GEORGE
Duke of] CLARENCE *with the crown. Then* [*enter*] KING
HENRY, [*the Earl of*] OXFORD, [*the Duke of*] SOMERSET,
[*with*] *young Henry Earl of Richmond,* [*the Marquis of*]
MONTAGUE, *and* [*the*] LIEUTENANT [*of the Tower*]

KING HENRY Master Lieutenant, now that God and friends
  Have shaken Edward from the regal seat
  And turned my captive state to liberty,

4.6 Location; The Archbishop of York's park or hunting
ground, Yorkshire.

1. King's Lynn, a town on the Norfolk coast.
4.7 Location: The Tower, London.

My fear to hope, my sorrows unto joys,
5   At our enlargement° what are thy due fees?¹   *release*
LIEUTENANT   Subjects may challenge° nothing of their sovereigns—   *demand*
    But if an humble prayer may prevail,
    I then crave pardon of your majesty.
KING HENRY   For what, Lieutenant? For well using me?
10   Nay, be thou sure I'll well requite thy kindness,
    For that it made my prisonment a pleasure—
    Ay, such a pleasure as encagèd birds
    Conceive when, after many moody thoughts,
    At last by notes of household harmony
15   They quite forget their loss of liberty.
    But, Warwick, after God, thou sett'st me free,
    And chiefly therefore I thank God and thee.
    He was the author, thou the instrument.
    Therefore, that I may conquer fortune's spite
20   By living low,° where fortune cannot hurt me,   *humbly*
    And that the people of this blessèd land
    May not be punished with my thwarting stars,²
    Warwick, although my head still wear the crown,
    I here resign my government to thee,
25   For thou art fortunate in all thy deeds.
WARWICK   Your grace hath still° been famed for virtuous,   *always*
    And now may seem as wise as virtuous
    By spying and avoiding fortune's malice,
    For few men rightly temper with the stars.³
30   Yet in this one thing let me blame your grace:
    For choosing me when Clarence is in place.
GEORGE OF CLARENCE   No, Warwick, thou art worthy of the sway,°   *rule*
    To whom the heav'ns in thy nativity⁴
    Adjudged an olive branch and laurel crown,⁵
35   As likely to be blest in peace and war.
    And therefore I yield thee my free consent.
WARWICK   And I choose Clarence only° for Protector.⁶   *alone*
KING HENRY   Warwick and Clarence, give me both your hands.
    Now join your hands, and with your hands your hearts,
40   That no dissension hinder government.
    I make you both Protectors of this land,
    While I myself will lead a private life
    And in devotion spend my latter days,
    To sin's rebuke and my creator's praise.
45 WARWICK   What answers Clarence to his sovereign's will?
GEORGE OF CLARENCE   That he consents, if Warwick yield consent,
    For on thy fortune I repose myself.
WARWICK   Why, then, though loath, yet must I be content.

---

1. Wealthy prisoners paid fees for special food and services.
2. My bad luck. Stars were believed to emit influences that might either favor or thwart the actions of individuals.
3. Because not many men correctly conform to or come to terms with their fate.

4. The precise position of the stars at one's birth was held to determine the course of one's life.
5. Symbols of peace and victory, respectively.
6. The title of an individual given charge of the kingdom while the monarch is absent, incapacitated, or a youth.

We'll yoke together, like a double shadow
50 To Henry's body, and supply° his place—   *take*
   I mean in bearing weight of government—
   While he enjoys the honour and his ease.
   And, Clarence, now then it is more than needful
   Forthwith that Edward be pronounced a traitor,
55 And all his lands and goods be confiscate.
GEORGE OF CLARENCE   What else? And that succession be
         determined.
WARWICK   Ay, therein Clarence shall not want his part.[7]
KING HENRY   But with the first of all your chief affairs,
   Let me entreat—for I command no more—
60 That Margaret your queen and my son Edward
   Be sent for, to return from France with speed.
   For, till I see them here, by doubtful fear
   My joy of liberty is half eclipsed.
GEORGE OF CLARENCE   It shall be done, my sovereign, with all speed.
65 KING HENRY   My lord of Somerset, what youth is that
   Of whom you seem to have so tender care?
SOMERSET   My liege, it is young Henry, Earl of Richmond.[8]
KING HENRY   Come hither, England's hope.
         [KING HENRY] *lays his hand on* [Richmond's] *head*
                                 If secret powers
   Suggest but truth to my divining° thoughts,   *prophesying*
70 This pretty lad will prove our country's bliss.
   His looks are full of peaceful majesty,
   His head by nature framed to wear a crown,
   His hand to wield a sceptre, and himself
   Likely in time to bless a regal throne.
75 Make much of him, my lords, for this is he
   Must help you more than you are hurt by me.
         Enter a POST
WARWICK   What news, my friend?
POST   That Edward is escapèd from your brother°   *(the Archbishop of York)*
   And fled, as he hears since, to Burgundy.
80 WARWICK   Unsavoury news—but how made he escape?
POST   He was conveyed by Richard Duke of Gloucester
   And the Lord Hastings, who attended him
   In secret ambush on the forest side
   And from the Bishop's huntsmen rescued him—
85 For hunting was his daily exercise.
WARWICK   My brother was too careless of his charge.
   [*To* KING HENRY]   But let us hence, my sovereign, to provide
   A salve for any sore that may betide.°   *occur*
         Exeunt. Manent° SOMERSET, RICHMOND, *and* OXFORD   *Remain*
SOMERSET [*to* OXFORD]   My lord, I like not of this flight of Edward's,

---

7. George of Clarence would be next in line to the
throne if the Lancastrian claim were dismissed and
Edward pronounced a traitor. want: lack.
8. Somerset's nephew was the future Henry VII, the
founder of the Tudor dynasty. The Wars of the Roses,
represented in this play and in *The First Part of the Contention*, ended upon his accession to the throne,
depicted at the end of *Richard III*.

90 For doubtless Burgundy will yield him help,
    And we shall have more wars before't be long.
    As Henry's late presaging prophecy
    Did glad my heart with hope of this young Richmond,
    So doth my heart misgive me, in these conflicts,
95 What may befall him, to his harm and ours.
    Therefore, Lord Oxford, to prevent the worst,
    Forthwith we'll send him hence to Brittany,
    Till storms be past of civil enmity.
    OXFORD Ay, for if Edward repossess the crown,
100   'Tis like that Richmond with the rest shall down.°   *fall*
    SOMERSET It shall be so—he shall to Brittany.
    Come, therefore, let's about it speedily.   *Exeunt*

4.8

Flourish. Enter [KING] EDWARD, RICHARD [*Duke* OF
GLOUCESTER], *and* [*Lord*] HASTINGS, *with a troop of
Hollanders*

KING EDWARD   Now, brother Richard, Lord Hastings, and the rest,
    Yet thus far fortune maketh us amends,
    And says that once more I shall interchange
    My wanèd° state for Henry's regal crown.   *diminished*
5   Well have we passed and now repassed the seas
    And brought desirèd help from Burgundy.
    What then remains, we being thus arrived
    From Ravenspurgh¹ haven before the gates of York,
    But that we enter, as into our dukedom?
        [HASTINGS *knocks at the gates of York*]
10 RICHARD OF GLOUCESTER   The gates made fast? Brother, I like not this.
    For many men that stumble at the threshold
    Are well foretold that danger lurks within.
    KING EDWARD   Tush, man, abodements° must not now affright us.   *omens*
    By fair or foul means we must enter in,
15 For hither will our friends repair to us.
    HASTINGS   My liege, I'll knock once more to summon them.
        [*He knocks.*]
        Enter, on the walls, the MAYOR *of York, and his Brethren*
        [*aldermen*]
    MAYOR   My lords, we were forewarnèd of your coming,
    And shut the gates for safety of ourselves—
    For now we owe allegiance unto Henry.
20 KING EDWARD   But, Master Mayor, if Henry be your king,
    Yet Edward at the least is Duke of York.
    MAYOR   True, my good lord, I know you for no less.
    KING EDWARD   Why, and I challenge nothing but my dukedom,
    As being well content with that alone.
    RICHARD OF GLOUCESTER [*aside*]   But when the fox hath once
25   got in his nose,

4.8 Location: Outside the walls of York.   1. Town on the coast of Yorkshire.

He'll soon find means to make the body follow.

HASTINGS   Why, Master Mayor, why stand you in a doubt?
Open the gates—we are King Henry's friends.

MAYOR   Ay, say you so? The gates shall then be opened.
     [They] descend²

RICHARD OF GLOUCESTER   A wise stout° captain, and soon   *valiant*
30   persuaded.

HASTINGS   The good old man would fain° that all were well,   *wish*
So 'twere not long of him;³ but being entered,
I doubt not, I, but we shall soon persuade
Both him and all his brothers unto reason.
     Enter [below] the MAYOR *and two aldermen*

35 KING EDWARD   So, Master Mayor, these gates must not be shut
But in the night or in the time of war.
What—fear not, man, but yield me up the keys,
     *[*KING EDWARD*] takes [some] keys [from the* MAYOR*]*
For Edward will defend the town and thee,
And all those friends that deign° to follow me.   *are willing*
     March. Enter Sir John MONTGOMERY *with [a]*
     drum[mer] and soldiers

40 RICHARD OF GLOUCESTER   Brother, this is Sir John Montgomery,
Our trusty friend, unless I be deceived.

KING EDWARD   Welcome, Sir John—but why come you in arms?

MONTGOMERY   To help King Edward in his time of storm,
As every loyal subject ought to do.

45 KING EDWARD   Thanks, good Montgomery, but we now forget
Our title to the crown, and only claim
Our dukedom till God please to send the rest.

MONTGOMERY   Then fare you well, for I will hence again.
I came to serve a king and not a duke.

50   Drummer, strike up, and let us march away.
     The drum[mer] begins to [sound a] march

KING EDWARD   Nay, stay, Sir John, a while, and we'll debate
By what safe means the crown may be recovered.

MONTGOMERY   What talk you of debating? In few words,
If you'll not here proclaim yourself our king

55   I'll leave you to your fortune and be gone
To keep them back that come to succour you.
Why shall we fight, if you pretend° no title?   *claim*

RICHARD OF GLOUCESTER *[to* KING EDWARD*]* Why, brother,
     wherefore stand you on nice points?⁴

KING EDWARD   When we grow stronger, then we'll make our claim.

60   Till then 'tis wisdom to conceal our meaning.

HASTINGS   Away with scrupulous wit!° Now arms must rule.   *reasoning*

RICHARD OF GLOUCESTER   And fearless minds climb soonest unto crowns.
Brother, we will proclaim you out of hand,
The bruit° thereof will bring you many friends.   *news*

65 KING EDWARD   Then be it as you will, for 'tis my right,

---

2. F's stage direction reads "He descends," as if only the Mayor comes down from the walls.

3. So long as he is not held responsible.

4. Why do you dwell on such overly precise distinctions?

And Henry but usurps the diadem.
MONTGOMERY   Ay, now my sovereign speaketh like himself,
  And now will I be Edward's champion.
HASTINGS   Sound trumpet, Edward shall be here proclaimed.
  [*To* MONTGOMERY]⁵
70 Come, fellow soldier, make thou proclamation.
    Flourish
MONTGOMERY   Edward the Fourth, by the grace of God King of
  England and France, and Lord of Ireland—
  And whosoe'er gainsays° King Edward's right,   *denies*
  By this I challenge him to single fight.
    [*He*] *throws down his gauntlet*⁶
75 ALL   Long live Edward the Fourth!
KING EDWARD   Thanks, brave Montgomery, and thanks unto you all.
  If fortune serve me I'll requite° this kindness.   *repay*
  Now, for this night, let's harbour here in York;
  And when the morning sun shall raise his car°   *chariot*
80 Above the border of this horizon,
  We'll forward towards Warwick and his mates.
  For well I wot° that Henry is no soldier.   *know*
  Ah, froward° Clarence, how evil it beseems thee   *perverse*
  To flatter Henry and forsake thy brother!
85 Yet, as we may, we'll meet both thee and Warwick.
  Come on, brave soldiers—doubt not of the day
  And, that once gotten, doubt not of large pay.   *Exeunt*

4.9

Flourish. Enter KING [HENRY, *the Earl of*] WARWICK,
[*the Marquis of*] MONTAGUE, [GEORGE *Duke of*]
CLARENCE, *and* [*the Earl of*] OXFORD¹
WARWICK   What counsel, lords? Edward from Belgia,°   *the Low Countries*
  With hasty° Germans and blunt° Hollanders,   *rash / merciless*
  Hath passed in safety through the narrow seas,
  And with his troops doth march amain° to London,   *at full speed*
5 And many giddy people flock to him.
KING HENRY   Let's levy men and beat him back again.
GEORGE OF CLARENCE   A little fire is quickly trodden out,
  Which, being suffered, rivers cannot quench.
WARWICK   In Warwickshire I have true-hearted friends,
10 Not mutinous in peace, yet bold in war.
  Those will I muster up. And thou, son° Clarence,   *son-in-law*
  Shalt stir in Suffolk, Norfolk, and in Kent,
  The knights and gentlemen to come with thee.
  Thou, brother Montague, in Buckingham,
15 Northampton, and in Leicestershire shalt find
  Men well inclined to hear what thou command'st.
  And thou, brave Oxford, wondrous well beloved

---

5. F assigns lines 71–72 to a "Soul⟨dier⟩" and 73–74 to
Montgomery; O omits line 70 and the following stage
direction and assigns all the lines to Montgomery.
6. Throwing down a gaunlet, or glove, was a medieval
rite of chivalry. To pick it up was to accept a challenge
to duel.

4.9 Location: The Bishop of London's palace.
1. F includes Somerset at this entrance and does not
mark a scene division here or at line 32. Somerset has
no lines in this scene. Oxford omits him until the stage
direction at 5.1.71, begins a new scene (4.10) after
4.9.32, and places Exeter's entrance there.

In Oxfordshire, shalt muster up thy friends.
My sovereign, with the loving citizens,
20 Like to his island girt in with the ocean,
Or modest Dian² circled with her nymphs,
Shall rest in London till we come to him.
Fair lords, take leave and stand not to reply.
Farewell, my sovereign.
25 KING HENRY Farewell, my Hector,³ and my Troy's true hope.
GEORGE OF CLARENCE In sign of truth, I kiss your highness'
        hand.
        [*He kisses King Henry's hand*]
KING HENRY Well-minded Clarence, be thou fortunate.
MONTAGUE Comfort, my lord, and so I take my leave.
        [*He kisses King Henry's hand*]
OXFORD And thus I seal my truth° and bid adieu.   affirm my loyalty
        [*He kisses King Henry's hand*]
30 KING HENRY Sweet Oxford, and my loving Montague,
And all at once,° once more a happy farewell. [*Exit*]   together
WARWICK Farewell, sweet lords—let's meet at Coventry.
                                    Exeunt [*severally*]°   separately

4.10

[*Enter* KING HENRY *and the Duke of* EXETER]
KING HENRY Here at the palace will I rest a while.
Cousin of Exeter, what thinks your lordship?
Methinks the power that Edward hath in field
Should not be able to encounter mine.
5 EXETER The doubt° is that he will seduce the rest.   fear
KING HENRY That's not my fear. My meed° hath got° me fame.   merit / won
I have not stopped mine ears to their demands,
Nor posted off° their suits with slow delays.   postponed
My pity hath been balm to heal their wounds,
10 My mildness hath allayed their swelling griefs,
My mercy dried their water-flowing tears.
I have not been desirous of their wealth,
Nor much oppressed them with great subsidies,°   taxes
Nor forward of° revenge, though they much erred.   eager for
15 Then why should they love Edward more than me?
No, Exeter, these graces challenge grace;°   claim favor
And when the lion fawns upon the lamb,
The lamb will never cease to follow him.
        *Shout within 'A Lancaster'[, 'A York']*¹
EXETER Hark, hark, my lord—what shouts are these?
        Enter [KING] EDWARD *and* [RICHARD *Duke* OF
        GLOUCESTER, *with*] *soldiers*
20 KING EDWARD Seize on the shame-faced° Henry—bear him hence,   timid
And once again proclaim us King of England.

2. The goddess of the moon, of hunting, and of chastity, often depicted presiding over a circle of virginal nymphs in the forest. Queen Elizabeth was sometimes represented as Diana.
3. The greatest warrior of Troy, killed when the Greeks conquered the city (see note to 2.1.51). By one legendary account, London was founded as a second Troy by Brutus (or Brute), a Trojan who conquered Albion and renamed it Britain.
4.10 Location: Scene continues.
1. F indicates "A Lancaster, A Lancaster"; Oxford's emendation suggests offstage conflict between the two armies.

You are the fount that makes small brooks to flow.
Now stops thy spring—my sea shall suck them dry,
And swell so much the higher by their ebb.
25 Hence with him to the Tower—let him not speak.
        Exeunt [some] with KING HENRY *[and* EXETER]
And lords, towards Coventry bend we our course,
Where peremptory° Warwick now remains.   *overbearing*
The sun shines hot, and, if we use delay,
Cold biting winter mars our hoped-for hay.°   *expected harvest*
30 RICHARD OF GLOUCESTER   Away betimes,° before his forces join,   *quickly*
And take the great-grown traitor unawares.
Brave warriors, march amain towards Coventry.   *Exeunt*

5.1

Enter [the Earl of] WARWICK, *the Mayor of Coventry,*
two MESSENGERS, *and others upon the walls*[1]
WARWICK   Where is the post that came from valiant Oxford?
      [The FIRST MESSENGER *steps forward]*
How far hence is thy lord, mine honest fellow?
FIRST MESSENGER   By this° at Dunsmore,[2] marching hitherward.   *By now*
WARWICK   How far off is our brother Montague?
5 Where is the post that came from Montague?
      [The SECOND MESSENGER *steps forward]*
SECOND MESSENGER   By this at Da'ntry,[3] with a puissant° troop.   *powerful*
      Enter SOMERVILLE *[to them, above]*
WARWICK   Say, Somerville—what says my loving son?
And, by thy guess, how nigh is Clarence now?
SOMERVILLE   At Southam[4] I did leave him with his forces,
10 And do expect him here some two hours hence.
      [A march afar off]
WARWICK   Then Clarence is at hand—I hear his drum.
SOMERVILLE   It is not his, my lord. Here Southam lies.[5]
The drum your honour hears marcheth from Warwick.
WARWICK   Who should that be? Belike,° unlooked-for friends.   *Perhaps*
15 SOMERVILLE   They are at hand, and you shall quickly know.
      Flourish. Enter [below KING] EDWARD, *[and]* RICHARD
      [Duke OF GLOUCESTER, *with]* soldiers
KING EDWARD   Go, trumpet, to the walls, and sound a parley.[6]
      [Sound a parley]
RICHARD OF GLOUCESTER   See how the surly Warwick mans the wall.
WARWICK   O, unbid° spite—is sportful° Edward come?   *unwelcome / lecherous*
Where slept our scouts, or how are they seduced,
20 That we could hear no news of his repair?°   *approach*

5.1 Location: Before the walls of Coventry.
1. This entire scene was probably played with War-wick's party in the gallery above the main stage and King Edward and Richard of Gloucester below, looking upward in lines 16–17 and throughout. In stage directions following lines 59, 67, and 72, first Oxford, then the Marquis of Montague, and then the Duke of Somerset enter. They may enter above to Warwick or, more probably, enter below, cross the stage, and then exit through a stage door as if "into the city" and thus out of view. F gives each an entrance but no exit; O marks both an entrance and an exit for each.
2. Dunsmore Heath, between Coventry and Daventry.
3. Daventry, a Northamptonshire town about 20 miles southeast of Coventry.
4. A town about 10 miles southeast of Coventry.
5. Southam is in this direction.
6. A trumpet signal requesting a conference between warring troops.

KING EDWARD   Now, Warwick, wilt thou ope the city gates,
     Speak gentle words, and humbly bend thy knee,
     Call Edward king, and at his hands beg mercy?
     And he shall pardon thee these outrages.
25   WARWICK   Nay, rather, wilt thou draw thy forces hence,
     Confess who set thee up and plucked thee down,
     Call Warwick patron, and be penitent?
     And thou shalt still remain the Duke of York.
RICHARD OF GLOUCESTER   I thought at least he would have said 'the King'.
30   Or did he make the jest against his will?
WARWICK   Is not a dukedom, sir, a goodly gift?
RICHARD OF GLOUCESTER   Ay, by my faith, for a poor earl[7] to give.
     I'll do thee service for so good a gift.
WARWICK   'Twas I that gave the kingdom to thy brother.
35   KING EDWARD   Why then, 'tis mine, if but by Warwick's gift.
WARWICK   Thou art no Atlas[8] for so great a weight;
     And, weakling, Warwick takes his gift again;
     And Henry is my king, Warwick his subject.
KING EDWARD   But Warwick's king is Edward's prisoner,
40   And, gallant Warwick, do but answer this:
     What is the body when the head is off?
RICHARD OF GLOUCESTER   Alas, that Warwick had no more forecast,°   *anticipated*
     But whiles he thought to steal the single ten,[9]
     The king was slyly fingered° from the deck.   *stolen*
45   [*To* WARWICK]   You left poor Henry at the Bishop's palace,
     And ten to one you'll meet him in the Tower.
KING EDWARD   'Tis even so—[*to* WARWICK] yet you are Warwick still.
RICHARD OF GLOUCESTER   Come, Warwick, take the time°—   *seize the moment*
       kneel down, kneel down.
     Nay, when? Strike now, or else the iron cools.[1]
50   WARWICK   I had rather chop this hand off at a blow,
     And with the other fling it at thy face,
     Than bear so low a sail° to strike to thee.   *be so humble as*
KING EDWARD   Sail how thou canst, have wind and tide thy friend,
     This hand, fast wound about thy coal-black hair,
55   Shall, whiles thy head is warm and new cut off,
     Write in the dust this sentence with thy blood:
     'Wind-changing° Warwick now can change no more'.   *Fickle*
       Enter [the Earl of] OXFORD, *with [a] drum[mer]*
       and soldiers [bearing] colours°   *flags*
WARWICK   O cheerful colours! See where Oxford comes.
OXFORD   Oxford, Oxford, for Lancaster!
       [OXFORD *and his men pass over the stage and*
                   exeunt into the city]
RICHARD OF GLOUCESTER [*to* KING EDWARD]   The gates are
60   open—let us enter too.
KING EDWARD   So other foes may set upon our backs?
     Stand we in good array, for they no doubt

---

7. Dukes are higher in rank than earls.
8. In Greek mythology, a giant who bore the weight of the heavens on his shoulders.
9. Alluding to the conventions of card games in which

the ten is valuable, but less so than the king. *single:* mere.
1. Referring to the proverb "Strike while the iron is hot," with a pun on "strike" as meaning "to lower a sail" or "to yield."

Will issue out again and bid us battle.
If not, the city being but of small defence,
65 We'll quickly rouse² the traitors in the same.
WARWICK [to OXFORD, within] O, welcome, Oxford—for we want° thy help.   need
    Enter [the Marquis of] MONTAGUE with [a]
    drum[mer] and soldiers [bearing] colours
MONTAGUE Montague, Montague, for Lancaster!
    [MONTAGUE and his men pass over the stage and
                            exeunt into the city]
RICHARD OF GLOUCESTER Thou and thy brother both shall
    bye° this treason   atone for
    Even with the dearest blood your bodies bear.
70 KING EDWARD The harder matched, the greater victory.
    My mind presageth happy gain and conquest.
    Enter [the Duke of] SOMERSET with [a] drum[mer]
    and soldiers [bearing] colours
SOMERSET Somerset, Somerset, for Lancaster!
    [SOMERSET and his men pass over the stage
    and exeunt into the city]
RICHARD OF GLOUCESTER Two of thy name, both dukes of Somerset,
    Have sold their lives unto the house of York—
75 And thou shalt be the third, an° this sword hold.³   if
    Enter [GEORGE Duke of] CLARENCE with [a]
    drum[mer] and soldiers [bearing] colours
WARWICK And lo, where George of Clarence sweeps along,
    Of force enough to bid his brother battle;
    With whom an upright zeal to right° prevails   for justice
    More than the nature of a brother's love.
80 GEORGE OF CLARENCE Clarence, Clarence, for Lancaster!
KING EDWARD Et tu, Brute⁴—wilt thou stab Caesar too?
    [To a trumpeter] A parley, sirra,⁵ to George of Clarence.
    Sound a parley. RICHARD [OF GLOUCESTER] and
    [GEORGE OF] CLARENCE whisper together
WARWICK Come, Clarence, come—thou wilt if Warwick call.
GEORGE OF CLARENCE Father of Warwick, know you what this means?
    [He] takes his red rose out of his hat and throws
    it at WARWICK
85 Look—here I throw my infamy at thee!
    I will not ruinate my father's house,
    Who gave his blood to lime° the stones together,   cement
    And set up Lancaster. Why, trowest thou,° Warwick,   do you believe
    That Clarence is so harsh, so blunt,° unnatural,   uncivilized
90 To bend the fatal instruments of war
    Against his brother and his lawful king?
    Perhaps thou wilt object° my holy oath.   invoke

2. A hunting term meaning "to surprise creatures in their lair."
3. Richard addresses Edmund, the fourth Duke of Somerset. The defection of his older brother Henry, the third Duke, from Edward's cause is described in 4.1 and 4.2. Richard threw the head of their father, the second Duke, across the stage in the play's first scene.
4. "You, too, Brutus": Julius Caesar's exclamation when he realized that his friend was one of the conspirators to his murder.
5. Fellow: a customary form of address to a social inferior.

To keep that oath were more impiety
Than Jephthah, when he sacrificed his daughter.[6]
95   I am so sorry for my trespass made
That, to deserve well at my brothers' hands,
I here proclaim myself thy mortal foe,
With resolution, wheresoe'er I meet thee—
As I will meet thee, if thou stir abroad°—   (*outside Coventry*)
100   To plague thee for thy foul misleading me.
And so, proud-hearted Warwick, I defy thee,
And to my brothers turn my blushing cheeks.
[*To* KING EDWARD] Pardon me, Edward—I will make amends.
[*To* RICHARD] And, Richard, do not frown upon my faults,
105   For I will henceforth be no more unconstant.
KING EDWARD   Now welcome more, and ten times more beloved,
Than if thou never hadst deserved our hate.
RICHARD OF GLOUCESTER [*to* GEORGE] Welcome, good
        Clarence—this is brother-like.
WARWICK [*to* GEORGE]   O, passing° traitor—perjured and unjust!   *unsurpassed*
110   KING EDWARD   What, Warwick, wilt thou leave the town and fight?
Or shall we beat the stones about thine ears?
WARWICK [*aside*]   Alas, I am not cooped° here for defence.   *shut up*
[*To* KING EDWARD] I will away towards Barnet[7] presently,
And bid thee battle, Edward, if thou dar'st.
115   KING EDWARD   Yes, Warwick—Edward dares, and leads the way.
Lords, to the field—Saint George and victory!
        Exeunt [*below* KING EDWARD *and his company*].
        March. [*The Earl of*] WARWICK *and his company*
                                [*descend and*] *follow*

5.2

Alarum and excursions. Enter [KING] EDWARD
bringing forth [*the Earl of*] WARWICK, *wounded*
KING EDWARD   So lie thou there. Die thou, and die our fear—
For Warwick was a bug° that feared° us all.   *goblin / frightened*
Now, Montague, sit fast°—I seek for thee   *be on guard*
That Warwick's bones may keep thine company.   *Exit*
5   WARWICK   Ah, who is nigh? Come to me, friend or foe,
And tell me who is victor, York or Warwick?
Why ask I that? My mangled body shows,
My blood, my want of strength, my sick heart shows,
That I must yield my body to the earth
10   And by my fall the conquest to my foe.
Thus yields the cedar[1] to the axe's edge,
Whose arms gave shelter to the princely eagle,[2]
Under whose shade the ramping lion[3] slept,

6. Alluding to the biblical story in which Jephthah, an Israelite leader, kills his daughter in fulfillment of a vow. He swore that if he were victorious in battle, he would sacrifice to God whoever first met him from his house when he returned from the battlefield (see Judges 11).
7. Shakespeare treats this town, which is about 10 miles north of London and 75 miles southeast of Coventry, as though it were near Coventry.
5.2 Location: Near Barnet.
1. Often regarded as the king of evergreens and thus a

symbol of sovereignty.
2. Probably referring to Richard, Duke of York. In 2.1.91, his son Richard refers to the Duke of York as a "princely eagle." The eagle was often described as the king of birds.
3. Under whose protection Henry VI rested. A reference both to the lion as king of the animal world and to the Lancastrian coat of arms, which showed three lions rampant or reared on their hind legs.

Whose top-branch over-peered° Jove's spreading tree[4]   *rose above*
15   And kept low shrubs from winter's powerful wind.
      These eyes, that now are dimmed with death's black veil,
      Have been as piercing as the midday sun
      To search the secret treasons of the world.
      The wrinkles in my brows, now filled with blood,
20   Were likened oft to kingly sepulchres—
      For who lived king, but I could dig his grave?
      And who durst smile when Warwick bent his brow?
      Lo now my glory smeared in dust and blood.
      My parks,° my walks, my manors that I had,   *hunting grounds*
25   Even now forsake me, and of all my lands
      Is nothing left me but my body's length.
      Why, what is pomp, rule, reign, but earth and dust?
      And, live how we can, yet die we must.
              Enter [the Earl of] OXFORD and [the Duke of] SOMERSET
SOMERSET   Ah, Warwick, Warwick—wert thou as we are,
30   We might recover all our loss again.
      The Queen from France hath brought a puissant power.°   *powerful army*
      Even now we heard the news. Ah, couldst thou fly!
WARWICK   Why, then I would not fly. Ah, Montague,
      If thou be there, sweet brother, take my hand,
35   And with thy lips keep in my soul a while.[5]
      Thou lov'st me not—for, brother, if thou didst,
      Thy tears would wash this cold congealèd blood
      That glues my lips and will not let me speak.
      Come quickly, Montague, or I am dead.
40 SOMERSET   Ah, Warwick—Montague hath breathed his last,
      And to the latest gasp cried out for Warwick,
      And said 'Commend me to my valiant brother.'
      And more he would have said, and more he spoke,
      Which sounded like a canon in a vault,
45   That mote° not be distinguished; but at last   *might*
      I well might hear, delivered with a groan,
      'O, farewell, Warwick.'
WARWICK   Sweet rest his soul. Fly, lords, and save yourselves—
      For Warwick bids you all farewell, to meet in heaven. *He dies*
50 OXFORD   Away, away—to meet the Queen's great power!
              Here they bear away [Warwick's] body. Exeunt

5.3

      Flourish. Enter KING EDWARD in triumph, with
      RICHARD [*Duke* OF GLOUCESTER, GEORGE *Duke of*]
      CLARENCE, *and soldiers*
KING EDWARD   Thus far our fortune keeps an upward course,
      And we are graced with wreaths of victory.
      But in the midst of this bright-shining day
      I spy a black suspicious threatening cloud
5   That will encounter with our glorious sun
      Ere he attain his easeful western bed.
      I mean, my lords, those powers that the Queen

---

4. Jove's tree, according to Virgil, was the oak, the king
of deciduous trees.
5. Kiss me. Many Elizabethans believed the soul

escaped through the mouth at death.
5.3 Location: Scene continues.

Hath raised in Gallia° have arrived our coast,   *France*
And, as we hear, march on to fight with us.
10 GEORGE OF CLARENCE   A little gale will soon disperse that cloud,
And blow it to the source from whence it came.
Thy very beams will dry those vapours up,
For every cloud engenders not a storm.
RICHARD OF GLOUCESTER   The Queen is valued° thirty thousand   *estimated to be*
strong,
15 And Somerset, with Oxford, fled to her.
If she have time to breathe,° be well assured,   *gather her strength*
Her faction will be full as strong as ours.
KING EDWARD   We are advertised° by our loving friends   *informed*
That they do hold their course toward Tewkesbury.¹
20 We, having now the best at Barnet field,
Will thither straight, for willingness rids way²—
And, as we march, our strength will be augmented
In every county as we go along.
Strike up the drum, cry 'Courage!'; and away.
[*Flourish. March.*] *Exeunt*

5.4

Flourish. March. Enter QUEEN [MARGARET], PRINCE
EDWARD, [*the Duke of*] SOMERSET, [*the Earl of*]
OXFORD, *and soldiers*
QUEEN MARGARET   Great lords, wise men ne'er sit and wail their loss,
But cheerly° seek how to redress their harms.   *cheerfully*
What though the mast be now blown overboard,
The cable broke, the holding-anchor¹ lost,
5 And half our sailors swallowed in the flood?
Yet lives our pilot° still. Is't meet that he   *(Henry)*
Should leave the helm and, like a fearful lad,
With tearful eyes add water to the sea,
And give more strength to that which hath too much,
10 Whiles, in his moan,° the ship splits on the rock   *state of grief*
Which industry and courage might have saved?
Ah, what a shame; ah, what a fault were this.
Say Warwick was our anchor—what of that?
And Montague our top-mast—what of him?
15 Our slaughtered friends the tackles²—what of these?
Why, is not Oxford here another anchor?
And Somerset another goodly mast?
The friends of France our shrouds³ and tacklings?
And, though unskilful, why not Ned° and I   *(her son Edward)*
20 For once allowed the skilful pilot's charge?°   *responsibility*
We will not from the helm to sit and weep,
But keep our course, though the rough wind say no,
From shelves° and rocks that threaten us with wreck.   *sandbanks*
As good to chide the waves as speak them fair.

1. A town in Gloucestershire.
2. For eagerness to travel makes the journey seem
shorter.
5.4 Location: Fields near Tewkesbury.
1. The anchor meant to stabilize the ship by taking

hold of the sea bottom.
2. Ropes and pulleys used for raising and lowering
sails.
3. Ropes that brace and support the mast.

25   And what is Edward but a ruthless sea?
      What Clarence but a quicksand of deceit?
      And Richard but a raggèd° fatal rock?   *jagged*
      All these the enemies to our poor barque.°   *ship*
      Say you can swim—alas, 'tis but a while;
30   Tread on the sand—why, there you quickly sink;
      Bestride the rock—the tide will wash you off,
      Or else you famish. That's a threefold death.
      This speak I, lords, to let you understand,
      If° case some one of you would fly from us,   *In*
35   That there's no hoped-for mercy with the brothers York
      More than with ruthless waves, with sands, and rocks.
      Why, courage then—what cannot be avoided
      'Twere childish weakness to lament or fear.
      PRINCE EDWARD   Methinks a woman of this valiant spirit
40   Should, if a coward heard her speak these words,
      Infuse his breast with magnanimity°   *great courage*
      And make him, naked,° foil° a man at arms.   *unarmed / defeat*
      I speak not this as doubting any here—
      For did I but suspect a fearful man,
45   He should have leave to go away betimes,°   *at once*
      Lest in our need he might infect another
      And make him of like spirit to himself.
      If any such be here—as God forbid—
      Let him depart before we need his help.
50   OXFORD   Women and children of so high a courage,
      And warriors faint°—why, 'twere perpetual shame!   *fainthearted*
      O brave young Prince, thy famous grandfather°   *(Henry V)*
      Doth live again in thee! Long mayst thou live
      To bear his image and renew his glories!
55   SOMERSET   And he that will not fight for such a hope,
      Go home to bed, and like the owl by day,
      If he arise, be mocked and wondered at.
      QUEEN MARGARET   Thanks, gentle Somerset; sweet Oxford, thanks.
      PRINCE EDWARD   And take his thanks that yet° hath nothing else.   *who as yet*
            Enter a MESSENGER
60   MESSENGER   Prepare you, lords, for Edward is at hand
      Ready to fight—therefore be resolute.
      OXFORD   I thought no less. It is his policy
      To haste thus fast to find us unprovided.°   *unprepared*
      SOMERSET   But he's deceived; we are in readiness.
65   QUEEN MARGARET   This cheers my heart, to see your forwardness.
      OXFORD   Here pitch our battle°—hence we will not budge.   *deploy our army*
            Flourish and march. Enter KING EDWARD, RICHARD
            [*Duke* OF GLOUCESTER], *and* [GEORGE *Duke* OF]
            CLARENCE, [*with*] *soldiers*
      KING EDWARD [*to his followers*]   Brave followers, yonder stands
            the thorny wood
      Which, by the heavens' assistance and your strength,
      Must by the roots be hewn up yet ere night.
70   I need not add more fuel to your fire,
      For well I wot° ye blaze to burn them out.   *know*
      Give signal to the fight, and to it, lords.

QUEEN MARGARET [*to her followers*]   Lords, knights, and
    gentlemen—what I should say
  My tears gainsay;° for every word I speak   *hinder*
75 Ye see I drink the water of my eye.
  Therefore, no more but this: Henry your sovereign
  Is prisoner to the foe, his state usurped,
  His realm a slaughter-house, his subjects slain,
  His statutes cancelled, and his treasure spent—
80 And yonder is the wolf that makes this spoil.
  You fight in justice; then in God's name, lords,
  Be valiant, and give signal to the fight.
        Alarum, retreat, excursions. Exeunt

5.5

Flourish. Enter [KING] EDWARD, RICHARD [DUKE OF
GLOUCESTER, *and* GEORGE *Duke* OF] CLARENCE, [*with*]
QUEEN [MARGARET, *the Earl of*] OXFORD, [*and the Duke
of*] SOMERSET [*guarded*]

KING EDWARD   Now here a period of° tumultuous broils.   *an end to*
  Away with Oxford to Hames Castle[1] straight;
  For Somerset, off with his guilty head.
  Go bear them hence—I will not hear them speak.
5 OXFORD   For my part, I'll not trouble thee with words.
                            Exit [*guarded*]
SOMERSET   Nor I, but stoop with patience to my fortune.
                            Exit [*guarded*]
QUEEN MARGARET   So part we sadly in this troublous world
  To meet with joy in sweet Jerusalem.[2]
KING EDWARD   Is proclamation made that who finds Edward
10 Shall have a high reward and he his life?
RICHARD OF GLOUCESTER   It is, and lo where youthful Edward
  comes.
    Enter PRINCE [EDWARD, *guarded*]
KING EDWARD   Bring forth the gallant—let us hear him speak.
  What, can so young a thorn begin to prick?
  Edward, what satisfaction° canst thou make   *amends*
15 For bearing arms, for stirring up my subjects,
  And all the trouble thou hast turned me to?
PRINCE EDWARD   Speak like a subject, proud ambitious York.[3]
17.1   ALL THE LANCASTER PARTY   *Saint George for Lancaster!*
    Alarums to the battle. [*The house of*] *York flies, then
    the chambers°* [*are*] *discharged. Then enter* KING   *small cannon*
    [EDWARD, GEORGE OF] CLARENCE, *and* [RICHARD OF]
    GLOUCESTER, *and* [*their followers; they*] *make a great
    shout, and cry 'For York! For York!' Then* QUEEN [MAR-
    GARET], PRINCE [EDWARD], OXFORD *and* SOMERSET
    [*are all*] *taken* [*prisoner. Flourish,*] *and enter all
    again*

5.5 Location: Scene continues.
1. Hammes Castle, near Calais.
2. Referring to heaven, which is described as the new
Jerusalem in Revelation 21:2.

3. O abridges 5.4.82–5.5.17 and may reflect authorial
revision. An edited text of the abridged passage is given
as the inset passage that follows (lines 17.1–17.10).

KING EDWARD   *Now here a period of° tumultuous broils*   an end to
    Away with Oxford to Hames Castle straight;
    For Somerset, off with his guilty head.
17.5   *Go, bear them hence—I will not hear them speak.*
OXFORD   *For my part, I'll not trouble thee with words.*
                                  Exit [guarded]
SOMERSET   *Nor I, but stoop with patience to my death.*
                                  Exit [guarded]
KING EDWARD *[to PRINCE EDWARD]* *Edward, what*
    satisfaction° canst thou make   amends
    For stirring up my subjects to rebellion?
17.10   PRINCE EDWARD   *Speak like a subject, proud ambitious York.*
    Suppose that I am now my father's mouth—
    Resign thy chair, and where I stand, kneel thou,
20   Whilst I propose the self-same words to thee,
    Which, traitor, thou wouldst have me answer to.
QUEEN MARGARET   Ah, that thy father had been so resolved.
RICHARD OF GLOUCESTER   That you might still have worn the petticoat
    And ne'er have stolen the breech° from Lancaster.   trousers
25   PRINCE EDWARD   Let Aesop[4] fable in a winter's night—
    His currish riddles sorts not with this place.[5]
RICHARD OF GLOUCESTER   By heaven, brat, I'll plague ye for that word.
QUEEN MARGARET   Ay, thou wast born to be a plague to men.
RICHARD OF GLOUCESTER   For God's sake take away this captive scold.
30   PRINCE EDWARD   Nay, take away this scolding crookback° rather.   hunchback
KING EDWARD   Peace, wilful boy, or I will charm° your tongue.   silence with a spell
GEORGE OF CLARENCE *[to PRINCE EDWARD]*   Untutored lad,
    thou art too malapert.°   saucy
PRINCE EDWARD   I know my duty—you are all undutiful.
    Lascivious Edward, and thou, perjured George,
35   And thou, misshapen Dick—I tell ye all
    I am your better, traitors as ye are,
    And thou usurp'st my father's right and mine.
KING EDWARD   Take that, the likeness of this railer° here.   scold (Margaret)
    [KING EDWARD] stabs [PRINCE EDWARD]
RICHARD OF GLOUCESTER   Sprawl'st thou?[6] Take that, to end thy agony.
    RICHARD stabs [PRINCE EDWARD]
40   GEORGE OF CLARENCE   And there's for twitting me with perjury.
    [GEORGE] stabs [PRINCE EDWARD, who dies]
QUEEN MARGARET   O, kill me too!
RICHARD OF GLOUCESTER   Marry,[7] and shall.
    [He] offers to kill her
KING EDWARD   Hold, Richard, hold—for we have done too much.
RICHARD OF GLOUCESTER   Why should she live to fill the world
    with words?
    [QUEEN MARGARET faints]

---

4. An ancient storyteller famous for his fables about animals. Like Richard, he reputedly was physically deformed. *fable:* tell tales.
5. His mean and cynical comments are not welcome here.
6. Do you convulse in the agonies of death?
7. A mild oath invoking the name of the Virgin Mary.

KING EDWARD   What—doth she swoon? Use means for her recovery.
RICHARD OF GLOUCESTER [*aside to* GEORGE]   Clarence, excuse
45   me to the King my brother.
    I'll hence to London on a serious matter.
    Ere ye come there, be sure° to hear some news.   *expect*
GEORGE OF CLARENCE [*aside to* RICHARD]   What? What?
50 RICHARD OF GLOUCESTER [*aside to* GEORGE]   The Tower, the Tower.
                                                      Exit
QUEEN MARGARET   O Ned, sweet Ned—speak to thy mother, boy.
    Canst thou not speak? O traitors, murderers!
    They that stabbed Caesar shed no blood at all,
    Did not offend, nor were not worthy blame,
55   If this foul deed were by to equal it.°   *to compare with it*
    He was a man—this, in respect,° a child;   *in comparison*
    And men ne'er spend their fury on a child.
    What's worse than murderer that I may name it?
    No, no, my heart will burst an if I speak;
60   And I will speak that so my heart may burst.
    Butchers and villains! Bloody cannibals!
    How sweet a plant have you untimely cropped!
    You have no children, butchers; if you had,
    The thought of them would have stirred up remorse.
65   But if you ever chance to have a child,
    Look in his youth to have him so cut off
    As, deathsmen, you have rid° this sweet young Prince!   *killed*
KING EDWARD   Away with her—go, bear her hence perforce.
QUEEN MARGARET   Nay, never bear me hence—dispatch° me here.   *kill*
70   Here sheathe thy sword—I'll pardon thee my death.
    What? Wilt thou not? Then, Clarence, do it thou.
GEORGE OF CLARENCE   By heaven, I will not do thee so much ease.
QUEEN MARGARET   Good Clarence, do; sweet Clarence, do thou do it.
GEORGE OF CLARENCE   Didst thou not hear me swear I would not do it?
75 QUEEN MARGARET   Ay, but thou usest° to forswear thyself.   *are accustomed*
    'Twas sin before, but now 'tis charity.
    What, wilt thou not? Where is that devil's butcher,
    Hard-favoured° Richard? Richard, where art thou?   *Ugly*
    Thou art not here. Murder is thy alms-deed°—   *act of charity*
80   Petitioners for blood thou ne'er putt'st back.°   *you never turn away*
KING EDWARD   Away, I say—I charge ye, bear her hence.
QUEEN MARGARET   So come to you and yours as to this Prince!
                                              Exit [*guarded*]
KING EDWARD   Where's Richard gone?
GEORGE OF CLARENCE   To London all in post° [—*aside*] and as I guess,   *haste*
85   To make a bloody supper in the Tower.
KING EDWARD   He's sudden if a thing comes in his head.
    Now march we hence. Discharge the common sort°   *ordinary soldiers*
    With pay and thanks, and let's away to London,
    And see our gentle Queen how well she fares.
90   By this° I hope she hath a son for me.   *Exeunt*   *By now*

5.6

Enter on the walls [KING] HENRY VI, [*reading a book,*]
RICHARD [*Duke* OF GLOUCESTER, *and*] *the* LIEUTENANT
[*of the Tower*][1]

RICHARD OF GLOUCESTER   Good day, my lord. What, at your
   book so hard?

KING HENRY   Ay, my good lord—'my lord', I should say, rather.
   'Tis sin to flatter; 'good' was little better.°   *(than flattery)*
   'Good Gloucester' and 'good devil' were alike,

5   And both preposterous°—therefore not 'good lord'.   *unnatural*

RICHARD OF GLOUCESTER [*to the* LIEUTENANT]   Sirrah,° leave us   *Fellow*
   to ourselves. We must confer.   [*Exit* LIEUTENANT]

KING HENRY   So flies the reckless° shepherd from the wolf;   *careless*
   So first the harmless sheep doth yield his fleece,
   And next his throat unto the butcher's knife.

10   What scene of death hath Roscius[2] now to act?

RICHARD OF GLOUCESTER   Suspicion always haunts the guilty mind;
   The thief doth fear each bush an officer.

KING HENRY   The bird that hath been limèd[3] in a bush
   With trembling wings misdoubteth° every bush.   *fears*

15   And I, the hapless male° to one sweet bird,°   *father / child*
   Have now the fatal object in my eye
   Where my poor young was limed, was caught and killed.

RICHARD OF GLOUCESTER   Why, what a peevish° fool was that of Crete,   *silly*
   That taught his son the office of a fowl![4]

20   And yet, for all his wings, the fool was drowned.

KING HENRY   I, Daedalus; my poor boy, Icarus;
   Thy father, Minos,[5] that denied our course;
   The sun that seared the wings of my sweet boy,
   Thy brother Edward;[6] and thyself, the sea,

25   Whose envious gulf did swallow up his life.
   Ah, kill me with thy weapon, not with words!
   My breast can better brook° thy dagger's point   *tolerate*
   Than can my ears that tragic history.
   But wherefore dost thou come? Is't for my life?

30   RICHARD OF GLOUCESTER   Think'st thou I am an executioner?

KING HENRY   A persecutor I am sure thou art;
   If murdering innocents be executing,
   Why, then thou art an executioner.

RICHARD OF GLOUCESTER   Thy son I killed for his presumption.

35   KING HENRY   Hadst thou been killed when first thou didst presume,
   Thou hadst not lived to kill a son of mine.

5.6 Location: The Tower, London.
1. The precise setting is ambiguous. F's stage directions indicate that the scene takes place "on the Walls," O's that it occurs "in the Tower." Richard's first line makes clear that Henry is reading, which may mean he is in an inner chamber. His murder could be staged in a small alcove at the back of the main stage, on the walls (up in the gallery), or in full view on the main stage.
2. An ancient Roman actor (actually best known as a comedian) whom many Elizabethans cited as the archetype of a great tragedian.

3. Caught with birdlime, a sticky substance smeared on twigs.
4. Alluding to the myth of Daedalus, who, in order to escape imprisonment in Crete, designed wings made of wax and feathers for himself and his son Icarus. When Icarus flew too near the sun, the wax melted, and he fell to his death in the sea.
5. The King of Crete who imprisoned Daedalus and Icarus.
6. Referring to the sun insignia associated with Edward.

And thus I prophesy: that many a thousand
Which now mistrust no parcel of my fear,[7]
And many an old man's sigh, and many a widow's,
40 And many an orphan's water-standing° eye—   *flooded with tears*
Men for their sons', wives for their husbands',
Orphans for their parents' timeless° death—   *untimely*
Shall rue the hour that ever thou wast born.
The owl shrieked at thy birth—an evil sign;
45 The night-crow[8] cried, aboding° luckless time;   *foretelling*
Dogs howled, and hideous tempests shook down trees;
The raven rooked her° on the chimney's top;   *crouched*
And chatt'ring pies° in dismal discords sung.   *magpies*
Thy mother felt more than a mother's pain,
50 And yet brought forth less than a mother's hope—
To wit, an indigested° and deformèd lump,   *a shapeless*
Not like the fruit of such a goodly tree.
Teeth hadst thou in thy head when thou wast born,[9]
To signify thou cam'st to bite the world;
55 And if the rest be true which I have heard
Thou cam'st—
RICHARD   I'll hear no more. Die, prophet, in thy speech,
     He stabs him
For this, amongst the rest, was I ordained.
KING HENRY   Ay, and for much more slaughter after this.
60 O, God forgive my sins, and pardon thee.   *He dies*
RICHARD OF GLOUCESTER   What—will the aspiring blood of
       Lancaster
Sink in the ground? I thought it would have mounted.
See how my sword weeps for the poor King's death.
O, may such purple° tears be alway shed   *blood-red*
65 From those that wish the downfall of our house!
If any spark of life be yet remaining,
Down, down to hell, and say I sent thee thither—
     [*He*] *stabs him again*
I that have neither pity, love, nor fear.
Indeed, 'tis true that Henry told me of,
70 For I have often heard my mother say
I came into the world with my legs forward.
Had I not reason, think ye, to make haste,
And seek their ruin that usurped our right?
The midwife wondered and the women cried
75 'O, Jesus bless us, he is born with teeth!'—
And so I was, which plainly signified
That I should snarl and bite and play the dog.
Then, since the heavens have shaped my body so,
Let hell make crooked my mind to answer° it.   *match*
80 I had no father, I am like no father;
I have no brother, I am like no brother;
And this word, 'love', which greybeards call divine,
Be resident in men like one another
And not in me—I am myself alone.

---

7. Who do not share any of my fears.
8. A mythical bird supposed to be an evil omen.

9. Richard III was popularly believed to have been born
with teeth, a physical sign of his monstrous character.

85   Clarence, beware; thou kept'st me from the light—
     But I will sort° a pitchy° day for thee.   *arrange / dark*
     For I will buzz° abroad such prophecies   *whisper*
     That Edward shall be fearful of his life,
     And then, to purge his fear, I'll be thy death.
90   Henry and his son are gone; thou, Clarence, art next;
     And by one and one I will dispatch the rest,
     Counting myself but bad till I be best.
     I'll throw thy body in another room
     And triumph, Henry, in thy day of doom. *Exit [with the body]*

5.7

[A chair of state.] Flourish. Enter KING EDWARD, [LADY
GRAY *his*] *Queen,* [GEORGE *Duke* OF] CLARENCE, RICH-
ARD [*Duke* OF GLOUCESTER, *the Lord*] HASTINGS, *a
nurse, [carrying the infant] Prince* [Edward], *and
attendants*

KING EDWARD   Once more we sit in England's royal throne,
     Repurchased with the blood of enemies.
     What valiant foemen, like to autumn's corn,
     Have we mowed down in tops° of all their pride!   *at the peak*
5   Three dukes of Somerset, threefold renowned
     For hardy and undoubted° champions;   *fearless*
     Two Cliffords, as the father and the son;
     And two Northumberlands—two braver men
     Ne'er spurred their coursers° at the trumpet's sound.   *warhorses*
10   With them, the two brave bears, Warwick and Montague,[1]
     That in their chains fettered the kingly lion
     And made the forest tremble when they roared.
     Thus have we swept suspicion° from our seat°   *worry / throne*
     And made our footstool of security.
15   [*To* LADY GRAY] Come hither, Bess, and let me kiss my boy.
        [*The nurse brings forth the infant prince.* KING
        EDWARD *kisses him*]
     Young Ned, for thee, thine uncles and myself
     Have in our armours watched° the winter's night,   *stayed awake during*
     Went all afoot in summer's scalding heat,
     That thou mightst repossess the crown in peace;
20   And of our labours thou shalt reap the gain.
RICHARD OF GLOUCESTER [*aside*]   I'll blast° his harvest, an your   *wither*
     head were laid;[2]
     For yet I am not looked on° in the world.   *noticed*
     This shoulder was ordained so thick to heave;
     And heave it shall some weight or break my back.
25   Work thou the way, and thou shalt execute.[3]
KING EDWARD   Clarence and Gloucester, love my lovely queen;
     And kiss your princely nephew, brothers, both.
GEORGE OF CLARENCE   The duty that I owe unto your majesty
     I seal upon the lips of this sweet babe.
        [*He kisses the infant prince*]
30   LADY GRAY   Thanks, noble Clarence—worthy brother, thanks.

5.7 Location: The Palace, London.
1. The coat of arms of these brothers included the
image of a bear chained to a staff.

2. Once your head is laid in the grave.
3. Devise a way, (my head), and you, (shoulder and
hand), shall carry it out.

RICHARD OF GLOUCESTER   And that I love the tree° from whence   (family of York)
    thou sprang'st,
Witness the loving kiss I give the fruit.
    [He kisses the infant prince]
[Aside] To say the truth, so Judas kissed his master,
And cried 'All hail!' whenas he meant all harm.[4]
35 KING EDWARD   Now am I seated as my soul delights,
Having my country's peace and brothers' loves.
GEORGE OF CLARENCE   What will your grace have done with
    Margaret?
René her father, to the King of France
Hath pawned the Sicils° and Jerusalem,   Naples and Sicily
40 And hither have they sent it° for her ransom.   (the money raised)
KING EDWARD   Away with her, and waft her° hence to France.   convey her by water
And now what rests° but that we spend the time   remains
With stately triumphs,° mirthful comic shows,   festivals
Such as befits the pleasure of the court?
45 Sound drums and trumpets—farewell, sour annoy!°   bitter troubles
For here, I hope, begins our lasting joy.   [Flourish.] Exeunt

---

4. Judas, identifying Jesus to the officers eager to arrest him, greeted him with a kiss and the salutation "All hail."
whenas: when.

The First Part of Henry the Sixth

Battles dominate *1 Henry VI*. Set in the fifteenth century, the play depicts England's attempts to retain a military and political foothold in France. Orléans, Rouen, Angiers (modern Angers), Bordeaux—the English and French clash at each place, spilling vast amounts of blood to assert control over the territories to which each laid claim. The English claimed parts of France both by treaty and by inheritance. In 1360, the English King, Edward III, was granted sovereignty over Calais and Bordeaux by the Treaty of Bretigny, which concluded part of what came to be known as the Hundred Years' War. This same Edward, from whom Henry VI was descended, also claimed the French Crown itself through his mother, Isabella, the daughter of Philip IV of France. Philip's three sons died without producing male heirs, but Isabella, married to Edward II of England, gave birth to Edward III, who vigorously pursued both the Crown and the territory of France. In the fifteenth century, his great-grandson, Henry V, renewed these efforts and achieved remarkable military successes at Harfleur and Agincourt (see Shakespeare's *Henry V* for an account of his reign). His son, Henry VI, struggled to retain what his father had won.

In this struggle, depicted in the present play, England has one incomparable hero, the valiant Lord Talbot, who fights with such ferocity that the French flee at the very sound of his name. In 1592, probably just a few months after the play was first performed, Thomas Nashe, Shakespeare's contemporary (and himself a playwright who may have had a hand in the composition of the play—see Textual Note), wrote: "How would it have joyed brave Talbot (the terror of the French) to think that after he had lain two hundred yeares in his tomb, he should triumph again on the stage, and have his bones new embalmed with the tears of ten thousand spectators at least (at several times), who, in the Tragedian that represents his person, imagine they behold him fresh bleeding?" This comment—which imagines the long-dead Talbot cheered by the thought of having his mighty victories and lamentable death played again and again—forms part of Nashe's extended defense of stage plays. While many Elizabethan writers attacked the theater as a place of idleness where lies and lewd stories were circulated, Nashe used plays like *1 Henry VI* to argue for the value of the stage, partly because of its role in preserving the memory of England's glorious heroes. As Nashe says, "For the subject of them (for the most part) it is borrowed out of our English Chronicles, wherein our forefathers' valiant acts (that have lain long buried in rusty brass and worm-eaten books) are revived, and they themselves raised from the grave of oblivion, and brought to plead their aged honors in open presence." For Nashe, Talbot is one of those worthy forefathers, pleased to be resurrected in the person of an English actor.

Shakespeare was instrumental in creating the vogue in the 1590s for stage plays based on events from the reigns of England's former monarchs. The division of the 1623 First Folio into histories, comedies, and tragedies indicates that the plays dealing with English history were perceived as a distinct and important group of works. From the beginning of his career until 1599, when *Henry V* was first acted, Shakespeare contributed to the writing of at least eight plays based loosely on the reigns of English Kings from Richard II, who was deposed in 1399, to Henry VII, who assumed the English throne in 1485 after the Battle of Bosworth Field; in addition, there was one play on the reign of King John (1199–1216). Some of these plays chronicle the English wars in France. And some depict the lengthy struggle, known as the Wars of the Roses, between two branches of England's royal family for possession of the English throne:

on one side of this struggle were the Lancastrians, who wore the red rose as their badge; on the other side were the Yorkists, who wore the white. Both groups claimed descent from King Edward III. (For charts showing the genealogies of the Lancastrians and the Yorkists, see the endpapers at back.) The Battle of Bosworth Field ended this civil strife when Henry Tudor, a descendant of John of Gaunt, Duke of Lancaster, defeated Richard III, the last of the Yorkist Kings, and then married Elizabeth of York, the daughter of an earlier Yorkist King, Edward IV. Henry Tudor thus united the red rose and the white, and the Tudors ruled England until 1603, when Elizabeth I, granddaughter of Henry VII, died without issue. It was during the final years of Elizabeth's reign that Shakespeare wrote his history plays.

Many have speculated about why these plays about England's past became so popular. Nashe gives us a clue when he emphasizes their role in celebrating martial heroes and in creating for the common people a collective memory of their national past. In the sixteenth century, many chronicle histories of England were written, such as Edward Hall's *Union of the Two Noble and Illustre Famelies of Lancastre & Yorke* (1548) and Raphael Holinshed's *Chronicles of England, Scotland, and Ireland;* the second edition of Holinshed, published in 1587, was used extensively by Shakespeare in composing his history plays. These prose chronicles, in fact, may have been some of the "worm-eaten" books from which Nashe imagined Talbot being revived for a more pleasurable life on the stage. The theater, unlike obscure and musty texts, made a version of English history accessible even to those who could not read. For a penny, a common person could go to the theater, stand in the pit, and thrill to the exploits of Talbot, the embodiment of English martial valor. Dramatized history thus contributed to an emerging sense of national identity that depended not only on allegiance to a monarch, but also on pride in a shared English culture, language, and identity. The theater played a role in constructing this shared identity, providing ordinary people with riveting representations of a common national past.

In the early 1590s, there were good reasons why arousing patriotic sentiment for an English military hero like Talbot might have been popular. In 1588, England had, with the help of bad weather, repulsed an attack by the Spanish Armada, an invasion fleet sent by Europe's most powerful Catholic power, Spain. This victory had encouraged many English people to feel that their country should play a more active role in supporting the Protestant powers of Europe against their Catholic enemies. In 1591–92, Elizabeth had with some reluctance sent her charismatic nobleman the Earl of Essex into France to aid Henry IV of Navarre and the French Protestant faction. In this campaign, Essex participated in a struggle for control of the city of Rouen. We can date *1 Henry VI* to sometime in 1592 both because Nashe's comments on Talbot were published that year and because the play seems to refer to this French campaign. It depicts fifteenth-century Englishmen invading French soil—and attacking Rouen—at the very moment an English army was once again before the city's walls. Many in England might thus have seen in Talbot an image of their contemporary champion, the dashing Earl of Essex.

Shakespeare was involved in writing two more plays on the reign of Henry VI; in the First Folio, these were entitled, respectively, *The Second Part of Henry the Sixth* and *The Third Part of Henry the Sixth.* These two plays, however, were also published in earlier Octavo or quarto versions, where they bore the titles *The First Part of the Contention of the Two Famous Houses of York and Lancaster* and *The True Tragedy of Richard Duke of York and the Good King Henry the Sixth.* No one is certain whether these plays were written before or after *1 Henry VI,* although the Oxford editors believe they precede *Part 1.* Whatever the exact order of composition, these three plays represent Shakespeare's earliest efforts in the history genre. They were quickly followed by *Richard III,* about the Yorkist monarchs Edward IV and Richard III, who pushed their way to the throne after Henry VI and his son had been killed. This completed Shakespeare's treatment of the reign of Henry VI and of the bloody civil war that erupted during it. Only later in the decade did Shakespeare dramatize the events leading up to Henry VI's kingship. These

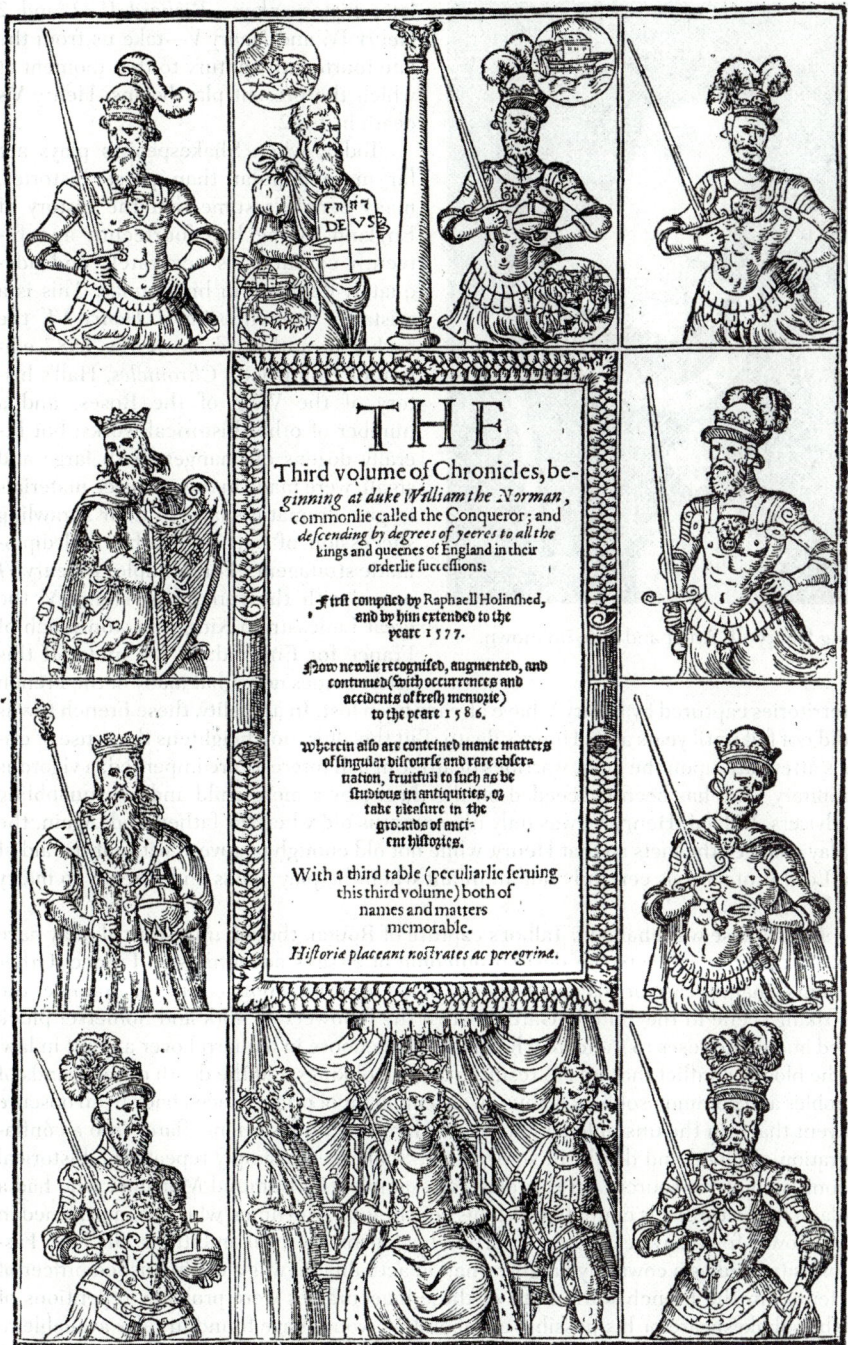

The title page of the third volume of Raphael Holinshed's *Chronicles* (1587 ed.).

King Henry VI. Artist and date unknown.

later history plays—*Richard II, 1* and *2 Henry IV*, and *Henry V*—take us from the late fourteenth century to that moment at which the present play begins: Henry V's death in 1422.

Today, when Shakespeare's plays are far more popular than prose histories, many people assume that the history of England in the late fourteenth and fifteenth centuries is accurately and adequately depicted in his dramas. This is a mistake. In composing *1 Henry VI*, the author or authors drew on the 1587 edition of Holinshed's *Chronicles*, Hall's history of the Wars of the Roses, and a number of other historical works; but literally dozens of changes, both large and small, were made in these source materials to give dramatic shape to their sprawling succession of battles, deaths, and diplomatic stratagems. For example, *1 Henry VI* opens with the funeral of Henry V, the great Lancastrian King who won much of France for England. In the midst of this scene comes news that many of the French territories captured by Henry V have already been lost. In actuality, these French towns did not fall until years after Henry's death. But the alteration heightens the sense of crisis attendant upon the great warrior's death. English interests are imperiled; a vigorous military King has been succeeded on the throne by a mere child and his squabbling advisers. Indeed, Henry VI was only nine months old when his father died. Again, the play changes the facts so that Henry, while not old enough to govern without the aid of a Lord Protector, is certainly not an infant when the play opens and is ready to marry when it ends.

Much else was changed. Talbot's capture of Rouen, though unhistorical, may have been added to indicate the desired outcome of Essex's adventures in France. Other events Shakespeare or his collaborators made up from whole cloth: for example, the striking scene in the Temple Garden when the followers of York and Somerset pluck red and white roses to indicate whose side they choose in a quarrel over a point in law. The bloody conflict that was to result in the fall of kings and the death of thousands of nobles and common soldiers is thus given a moment of origin, traced back to an obscure event that—in the unstable conditions of Henry's tenuous reign—flares into a conflagration of blood and death. In some cases, Shakespeare simply repeats the historical confusion of his sources. In this play, for example, the Edmund Mortimer who had a claim to the throne is conflated with his cousin John Mortimer, who was imprisoned in the Tower for many years for supporting his kinsman's royal ambitions. Sir John Fastolf is treated as a cowardly knight, when in actuality he was a distinguished officer of Henry's in the French wars. Both of these inaccuracies were probably repetitions of what Shakespeare or his possible collaborators would have found in texts available to them. (Later, a cowardly character named Falstaff appears in Shakespeare's *1* and *2 Henry IV* and in *The Merry Wives of Windsor*.)

Indisputably, the play depicts events neither exactly as they were presented in the chronicles nor as a modern historian might present them. In turning historical materials into effective drama, Shakespeare or his collaborators gave one of many possible shapes to the welter of events recorded in the various sources. Many have tried to discern what Shakespeare's "philosophy of history" could have been. Did he, for example, subscribe to the view expressed in Edward Hall's history that the turmoil of the fifteenth century was God's punishment for Henry IV's crime in deposing a rightful King, Richard II—a crime for which England paid in blood for over a hundred years? Or did he take a more secular view of history, in which events unfold as they do because of human choices and actions rather than because of God's intervention? One must read the plays to decide about these questions, and the answers may differ from play to play. An early and possibly a collaborative work, *1 Henry VI* does not necessarily adopt a single point of view toward why historical events unfold as they do. Unlike some of Shakespeare's other history plays, such as *Richard III,* this one contains very little language suggesting that an angry God is punishing England for Henry IV's earlier deposition of Richard II. Rather, events seem to unfold as a direct consequence of human decisions and human rivalries. That demons actually appear to Joan of Arc in Act V, however, complicates matters. Their presence suggests the existence of a supernatural realm that has some influence, however ambiguous, on the course of human affairs.

In dramatic terms, *1 Henry VI* is structured by juxtaposing two conflicts. In the foreground is the struggle between the French and English forces in France. The English, led by Talbot, clash repeatedly with the army of Charles, the French Dauphin. He, in turn, is given aid throughout much of the play by a remarkable figure: the martial maid, Joan of Arc. But a counterpoint to the struggle between French and English emerges by way of the feuding the play depicts among the English nobility. These two lines of action impinge on one another, as the internal squabbling among the English leaders keeps them from giving proper support to their soldiers in the field, eventually allowing Joan and Charles to kill Talbot before the walls of Bordeaux.

If the play has a message to deliver to the English, it would seem to be that petty rivalries and divisions among the English nobility can destroy England from within. As the boy King says to his quarreling nobles, Gloucester and Winchester,

> Believe me, lords, my tender years can tell
> Civil dissension is a viperous worm
> That gnaws the bowels of the commonwealth.
> (3.1.72–74)

The play seldom lets the audience forget about this worm. As early as the first scene, Winchester, whose status as bishop and then later as cardinal connects him to the Church of Rome, quarrels with Gloucester, who has been appointed the Protector of the Realm—that is, the one who effectively holds royal power while the King is still a child. Secular and religious authority clash, and the rent that this causes in the fabric of the commonwealth finds visual embodiment in the several arguments and stage fights that break out between Winchester's tawny-clothed followers and Gloucester's blue-coated serving men. This striking visual juxtaposition of the two factions vividly reveals the cankerworm of civil dissension at work. The red and white roses worn by the followers, respectively, of Somerset and York serve the same purpose, splitting England into two parties just when a united front is needed to sustain the French wars. Young Henry, although aware of the danger of civil dissension, can do little to stop it. On the one hand, he empowers Richard of York by returning to him the lands and titles taken from his father, the Earl of Cambridge, who had been accused of treason; and on the other hand, he decides to wear the red rose of the House of Lancaster. Striving, perhaps, for even-handedness, he inadvertently encourages the dissension he would suppress.

Yet to modern readers, perhaps the most interesting part of the play is not its demonstration of the dangers of civil dissension but its handling of the opposition between Talbot, terror of the French, and Joan, scourge of the English. In contrast to the rivalrous and selfish nobles who surround the young Henry, Talbot is the epitome of the unselfish heroism that Nashe found so compelling. Like a good feudal lord, he lives to serve his King in battle, an arena in which he repeatedly confirms his noble lineage and demonstrates his masculinity. Captured by the French when stabbed in the back by "a base Walloon" (an inhabitant of a French-speaking province now in Belgium), he nonetheless so terrifies his captors that they keep a guard of armed bowmen around him even when he sleeps. Talbot embodies the play's nostalgia for an idealized feudal world in which the values of valor and loyalty are shared by a community of men and passed on by them to their sons. In this regard, the play quite possibly spoke to a longing on the part of some of Elizabeth's subjects to be ruled once more by a king, not by an aging female monarch. When *1 Henry VI* was written, Elizabeth, no longer young and with no heir, was entering the fourth decade of her long reign. The play seems to tap into a yearning for a return to masculine rule and martial values.

In France, Talbot is surrounded by other great English warriors: most notably Salisbury, who dies at the siege of Orléans, and Bedford, who, though sick and dying, insists on being carried in a chair to the battlefield at Rouen in order to give courage to his men. Perhaps most touchingly, at Bordeaux, where the warring English nobles refuse to send him aid, Talbot is joined on the battlefield by his son John, a fledgling warrior come to learn from his father the skills and the values of the warrior class he aspires to join. Urged to flee, he refuses, certain that flight would prove him both effeminate and baseborn. Instead, he is initiated into the rites of manhood by shedding blood and sustaining wounds in what can only be described as an erotics of battle. Having rescued him from the Bastard of Orléans, his father says:

> When from the Dauphin's crest thy sword struck fire
> It warmed thy father's heart with proud desire
> Of bold-faced victory. Then leaden age,
> Quickened with youthful spleen and warlike rage,
> Beat down Alençon, Orléans, Burgundy,
> And from the pride of Gallia rescued thee.
> The ireful Bastard Orléans, that drew blood
> From thee, my boy, and had the maidenhood
> Of thy first fight, I soon encounterèd,
> And interchanging blows, I quickly shed
> Some of his bastard blood. . . .
>
> (4.6.10–20)

Young Talbot, shedding blood in his first battle, is compared to a young girl who bleeds during her first experience of intercourse. The cut and thrust of battle is thus imaged as a sexual encounter in which the goal is to penetrate the body and shed the blood of one's enemy. Young Talbot's willingness to participate in such struggles, no matter how inevitable his ultimate defeat, signifies the purity of his lineage and blood. Bound together by a code of chivalric values and by the rites of blood, Talbot, his son, and Bedford, Salisbury, and those who fight with them upon the fields of France embody the heroism Nashe suggested would stir the hearts of English theatergoers. By play's end, however, all these warriors are dead. With young Talbot's premature slaughter on the plains of Bordeaux, the bright flame of English chivalry flickers out. England passes into the hands of mere politicians and rivalrous churchmen who, if they fight, fight not for king and country but for their own particular interests.

The English in this play are defeated in part because of their failure to live up to and support their own best ideals as embodied in the figure of Talbot. Their defeat, however, also owes much to Talbot's chief antagonist, Joan of Arc, in Shakespeare's play a magnetic and complicated figure. Depending on the vantage point from which she is viewed, Joan is a holy maid sent by God to aid her country, a servant of the devil, or a deceitful whore. When the Bastard of Orléans first introduces her to the Dauphin, he calls Joan a holy maid and a prophet, and after she both sees through the Dauphin's trick to substitute René for himself and defeats the Dauphin in single combat, he proclaims her an Amazon (one of the legendary race of women warriors) and a Deborah (an Old Testament prophet and judge who accompanied an Israelite army against their Canaanite oppressors). These comparisons suggest how highly the French at first value their female champion. For a time, Joan seems possessed of uncanny powers. Not only does she recognize the Dauphin without ever having seen him before, but, perhaps more remarkably, she seems to suck away the great Talbot's strength, leaving him confused and ashamed before the walls of Orléans.

The English respond to this powerful but disarmingly down-to-earth peasant girl by calling her a witch and a whore. Much of their language concerning Joan is filled with bawdy double meanings, beginning with their play on the word *pucelle*, meaning "maid" or "virgin" in French, but sounding like "puzzel," English slang for "whore." From the first time he meets her in battle, Talbot assumes that Joan's powers can come only from witchcraft, rather than from a heavenly or merely human source. Joan's circumstances invite this kind of denigration. She is an unmarried woman who has turned

Fifteenth-century Franco-Flemish portrait of Joan of Arc.

soldier and assumed the garments of a man. In the early modern period, to dress like a man was often read as a violation of woman's assigned place in the gender hierarchy and an indication of the cross-dresser's uncontrolled will and appetites. Such women were easily assumed to be sexually transgressive, as well as vulnerable to the temptations of the devil.

Even Elizabeth, the unmarried Queen, was subject to endless rumors concerning her sexuality. Some whispered that she had had bastard children with the Earl of Leicester, some that her hymen was so thick that no man could penetrate her. The virgin and the whore, the heaven-sent exception and the unnatural monster—the one could easily be turned into the other. While it seems implausible that Joan was constructed explicitly to remind spectators of the English Queen, nonetheless the shepherd girl serves as a lightning rod to capture some of the ambivalent emotions attached to the Queen and to the idea of powerful public women more generally. Occasionally Joan is portrayed in language echoing that used of Elizabeth. Charles, for example, calls her Astraea's daughter—that is, daughter of the goddess of justice—a title often applied to Elizabeth. Several critics have argued that Joan's battlefield exploits recall the stories circulated about Elizabeth in 1588, when she was said to have appeared in armor before her troops at Tilbury as they prepared to go into battle against the Spanish. Having the body of a woman but the role and the clothing of a man, each of these women could incite reverence but also demonization. Anomalies, they could be read as criminals or fiends rather than as miraculous exceptions to their cultures' expectations concerning virtuous women.

Shakespeare's Joan is built of contradictions. At first, she seems a miracle worker who speaks confidently of her role as servant of "God's mother" (1.3.57) and savior of France. At times, she demonstrates Amazonian strength and shrewd military leadership. At other times, she speaks with the sharp tongue and pragmatic realism of a shepherd girl. When, for example, the English herald delivers an extended eulogy over the body of Talbot on the plains of Bordeaux, Joan interrupts him: "Him that thou magnifi'st with all these titles / Stinking and flyblown lies here at our feet" (4.7.75–76). Elsewhere, having persuaded Burgundy to leave his alliance with Talbot and rejoin the French side, she remarks with irony: "Done like a Frenchman—[aside] turn and turn again" (3.7.85).

The greatest shift in the presentation of Joan, however, occurs in Act 5, when she unexpectedly dwindles into a frightened and ineffectual practitioner of witchcraft. Summoning demons, she offers to let them suck her blood in return for doing her bidding. They refuse, leaving her vainly attempting to save herself from burning by pleading pregnancy. This diminished Joan of the last act—who, when directly depicted as a witch, is presented as an impotent one—seems deployed in part to bring the play to a closure acceptable to English pride. Talbot may have been defeated, but Joan is not allowed to win the war or even to live. This ending also echoes historical fact. The English handed the actual Joan of Arc over to the Inquisition, and, found guilty of heresy and witchcraft, she was burned in May 1431.

Joan's connection with witchcraft also capitalizes on the widespread interest in the phenomenon in the early 1590s. In 1591, accounts had reached England of the Scottish King James's prosecution of witches; and some had dared to hint that Elizabeth herself had used witchcraft to defeat the Spanish Armada. Several English treatises had been published in the 1580s debating whether witches were indeed the servants of the devil or were simply people, usually old women, scapegoated by their communities or deluded into thinking they had powers they actually lacked. The play, of course, doesn't settle the matter, giving us a Joan whose success against the English could have either a supernatural cause or a more mundane origin in her own strength, cleverness, and ability to inspire others. And while she does summon demons in the last act, they fail to aid her.

But Joan is not the only woman in 1 Henry VI. There are two others: the Countess of Auvergne and Margaret of Anjou, both French and both allied to Joan in the threat they pose to English manhood. While the play certainly highlights the political and military damage done to England by dissension among the English nobility, it also constructs women, especially French women, as a source of danger to England and her male leaders. While no English women appear in 1 Henry VI, three French women play important roles, and all threaten English interests. Joan almost ousts the English from France. The Countess of Auvergne attempts to imprison Talbot in her castle. Margaret conquers men's hearts by her great beauty, causing Henry VI to accept the dowerless Margaret as his bride, despite his promise to marry another woman. Suffolk, the King's retainer, has already fallen prey to her charms, setting up the possibility that, Joan gone, yet another French woman will cause rivalries and dissension in England.

In the warrior culture idealized in the person of Talbot, women would not seem to figure very importantly, except perhaps as mothers who give birth to sons who will continue the lineage and the values of the fathers. But 1 Henry VI depicts a more complicated reality. It shows, for example, how a potential wife, like Margaret, can incite uncontrollable desires in men and so become much more than a vehicle for reproduction or a pawn in a dynastic settlement. It also shows that some men, like the French of this play, seem unable to be martial heroes without the extraordinary and exceptional help of a woman. And it acknowledges that sometimes fathers don't beget sons worthy of the paternal name, as seems to be the case with Henry VI. Sometimes women must fill the void left by masculine failings; occasionally, as with Elizabeth I, a woman must even become King. 1 Henry VI puts all of these complex and contradictory knowledges in play. While it creates heroes for men weary of feminine rule, in the process it also acknowledges the potential weaknesses of men, the occasional failures of the patriarchal gender system to function as it should, and the sometimes surprising and terrifying powers of women. As it turns out, Nashe painted too simple a picture of the history plays. They are not only about the valiant acts of "our forefathers" but also about the failings of less admirable Englishmen and indeed about the actions of women, some of whom, though foreign, seem to have spoken to anxieties generated very close to home.

Jean E. Howard

TEXTUAL NOTE

The only text of *1 Henry VI* is found in the First Folio (F) of 1623. Using several types of stylistic and metrical evidence, the Oxford editors have returned to an existing editorial tradition of assigning authorship to several dramatists. Much of Act 1, they believe, was written by Thomas Nashe; Shakespeare is assigned only 2.4, the scene in the Temple Garden in which the followers of York and Somerset pluck the white roses and the red, and 4.2 through 4.7.32, the battle scenes at Bordeaux in which Talbot and his son meet their deaths after being denied aid by the quarreling English nobles. While the identities of other collaborators are suggested with less certainty, Robert Greene and George Peele are possibilities. Other contemporary textual critics, who attribute the entire play to Shakespeare, feel that the kinds of textual evidence used to adduce multiple authorship are unreliable for work produced so early in Shakespeare's career and discern no marked differences between the quality of this and other plays attributed to him in the early 1590s.

Act and scene divisions are incomplete in the Folio text and may not be theatrical in origin. The Oxford editors have divided the text in Acts 1, 3, and 5 into more scenes than are found in most modern editions. Generally, additional scenes are marked at points during a battle when the stage appears momentarily to be clear of all characters, the traditional indication in the Renaissance theater that one scene has ended and another begun. Thus, during the battle for Orléans, what are traditionally designated as 1.2 and 1.4 are each divided into two shorter scenes (1.2–1.3 and 1.5–1.6); during the struggle for Rouen, the scene traditionally designated as 3.2 is divided into five parts (3.2–3.6); and during the battle for Angiers, 5.3 is divided in this text into three scenes (5.3–5.5).

In addition, the Oxford editors have disposed of what has long been a confusion in F concerning whether Winchester is a cardinal for the whole duration of the play or is elevated to cardinal in Act 5. In Act 1, he is referred to both as a bishop and as a cardinal. The Oxford editors have taken the liberty of deleting or altering all Act 1 references to Winchester as a cardinal. Thus, for example, at 1.4.41, the Oxford text refers to Winchester's "purple robes," while F refers to his "scarlet robes," the color traditionally worn by cardinals.

SELECTED BIBLIOGRAPHY

Hodgdon, Barbara. "Enclosing Contention: *1, 2,* and *3 Henry VI.*" *The End Crowns All: Closure and Contradiction in Shakespeare's History.* Princeton: Princeton University Press, 1991. 44–99. Analyzes techniques for creating or disrupting dramatic closure in Shakespeare's early histories.

Jackson, Gabriele Bernhard. "Topical Ideology: Witches, Amazons, and Shakespeare's Joan of Arc." *English Literary Renaissance* 18 (1988): 40–65. Examines the contradictory aspects of the characterization of Joan of Arc, arguing that she is represented both as a positive force and analogue of Queen Elizabeth and also as a witch and strumpet.

Knowles. Ric. "The First Tetralogy in Performance." *A Companion to Shakespeare's Works.* Vol. II: *The Histories.* Ed. Richard Dutton and Jean E. Howard. Malden, Mass.: Blackwell, 2003. 263–86. Discusses key theatrical performances of Shakespeare's earliest history plays, including *1 Henry VI.*

Lee, Patricia-Ann. "Reflections of Power: Margaret of Anjou and the Dark Side of Queenship." *Renaissance Quarterly* 39 (1986): 183–217. Analyzes how the historical Margaret was represented not only in Shakespeare's plays but in the historical chronicles of the fifteenth and sixteenth centuries.

Rackin, Phyllis. *Stages of History: Shakespeare's English Chronicles.* Ithaca, N.Y.: Cornell University Press, 1990. 146–200. Discusses how women in Shakespeare's English history plays subvert and challenge the masculine writing of history.

Riggs, David. *Shakespeare's Heroical Histories: Henry VI and Its Literary Tradition.* Cambridge, Mass.: Harvard University Press, 1971. 93–139. Explores the deterioration of heroic ideals in Shakespeare's early English histories with special attention paid to the opposition of Talbot, the English hero, and Joan of Arc, his French antithesis.

Saccio, Peter. *Shakespeare's English Kings: History, Chronicle, and Drama.* 2nd ed. New York: Oxford University Press, 2000. 90–113. Discusses the differences between the historical events of Henry VI's reign and Shakespeare's representation of them.

Taylor, Gary. "Shakespeare and Others: The Authorship of *Henry the Sixth, Part I.*" *Medieval and Renaissance Drama in England* 7 (1995) : 145–205. Lays out evidence for his view that *1 Henry VI* was collaboratively written.

Tricomi, Albert. "Joan la Pucelle and the Inverted Saints Play in *1 Henry VI.*" *Renaissance and Reformation* 25 (2001): 5–31. Reads *1 Henry VI* as a Reformation critique of Joan of Arc as a false prophet who incites men to idolatry and of *1 Henry VI* as an inversion of a Catholic saint's play.

Walsh, Brian. "'Unkind Division': The Double Absence of Performing History in *1 Henry VI.*" *Shakespeare Quarterly* 55 (2004): 119–47. Discusses the role of performance in evoking, but never fully capturing, the historical past to which *1 Henry VI* refers.

FILM

Henry VI, Part One. 1983. Dir. Jane Howell. UK/USA. 112 min. A BBC-TV production featuring Trevor Peacock as Talbot, Peter Benson as Henry VI, and Brenda Blethyn as Joan. Lavish costumes and some strong performances in a textually faithful version of the play.

The First Part of Henry the Sixth

THE PERSONS OF THE PLAY

The English

KING HENRY VI
Duke of GLOUCESTER, Lord Protector, uncle of King Henry
Duke of BEDFORD, Regent of France
Duke of EXETER
Bishop of WINCHESTER (later Cardinal), uncle of King Henry
Duke of SOMERSET
RICHARD PLANTAGENET, later DUKE OF YORK, and Regent of France
Earl of WARWICK
Earl of SALISBURY
Earl of SUFFOLK
Lord TALBOT
JOHN Talbot
Edmund MORTIMER
Sir William GLASDALE
Sir Thomas GARGRAVE
Sir John FASTOLF
Sir William LUCY
WOODVILLE, Lieutenant of the Tower of London
MAYOR of London
VERNON
BASSET
A LAWYER
A LEGATE and ambassadors
Messengers, warders and keepers of the Tower of London,
    servingmen, officers, captains, soldiers, heralds, watch

The French

CHARLES, Dauphin of France
RENÉ, Duke of Anjou, King of Naples
MARGARET, his daughter
Duke of ALENÇON
BASTARD of Orléans
Duke of BURGUNDY, uncle of King Henry
GENERAL of the French garrison at Bordeaux
COUNTESS of Auvergne
MASTER GUNNER of Orléans
A BOY, his son
JOAN la Pucelle
A SHEPHERD, father of Joan
Porter, French sergeant, French sentinels, French scout,
    French herald, the Governor of Paris, fiends, and soldiers

1.1

Dead march.° Enter the funeral of King Henry the   *Funeral march*
Fifth, attended on by the Duke of BEDFORD *(Regent of*
France), the Duke of GLOUCESTER *(Protector), the Duke*
of EXETER, *[the Earl of]* WARWICK, *the Bishop of* WIN-
CHESTER, *and the Duke of* SOMERSET

BEDFORD   Hung be the heavens with black![1] Yield, day, to night!
    Comets, importing° change of times and states,   *foretelling*
    Brandish your crystal tresses[2] in the sky,
    And with them scourge the bad revolting° stars   *rebellious*
5   That have consented unto Henry's death—
    King Henry the Fifth, too famous to live long.[3]
    England ne'er lost a king of so much worth.
GLOUCESTER   England ne'er had a king until his time.
    Virtue° he had, deserving to command.   *Merit; power*
10   His brandished sword did blind men with his° beams.   *its*
    His arms spread wider than a dragon's wings.
    His sparkling eyes, replete with wrathful fire,
    More dazzled and drove back his enemies
    Than midday sun, fierce bent against their faces.
15   What should I say? His deeds exceed all speech.
    He ne'er lift up his hand but conquerèd.[4]
EXETER   We mourn in black; why mourn we not in blood?°   *by shedding blood*
    Henry is dead, and never shall revive.
    Upon a wooden coffin we attend,
20   And death's dishonourable victory
    We with our stately presence glorify,
    Like captives bound to a triumphant car.°   *chariot*
    What, shall we curse the planets of mishap,
    That plotted thus our glory's overthrow?
25   Or shall we think the subtle-witted French
    Conjurers and sorcerers, that, afraid of him,
    By magic verses have contrived his end?
WINCHESTER   He was a king blest of the King of Kings.[5]
    Unto the French, the dreadful judgement day
30   So dreadful will not be as was his sight.
    The battles of the Lord of Hosts[6] he fought.
    The Church's prayers made him so prosperous.°   *successful*
GLOUCESTER   The Church? Where is it? Had not churchmen prayed,[7]
    His thread of life had not so soon decayed.°   *grown weak*
35   None do you like but an effeminate prince,
    Whom like a schoolboy you may overawe.
WINCHESTER   Gloucester, whate'er we like, thou art Protector,[8]
    And lookest to command the Prince and realm.

1.1 Location: Westminster Abbey, England.
1. Alluding to the theatrical practice, when a tragedy was to be performed, of hanging black draperies from the "heavens," or roof projecting over the stage.
2. Flash your bright hair (the tails of the comets).
3. Henry V, the English conqueror of France who is the subject of a later play by Shakespeare, lived from 1387 until 1422. The assertion that he was too famous to live long may refer to the popular belief that jealous fate (the stars of line 4) prematurely cut down those whose fame became too great.

4. He never lifted up his hand (in battle) without conquering.
5. The name for God in biblical descriptions of the Last Judgment (see Revelation 19:16).
6. Another biblical name for God (see Psalms 24:10, Isaiah 13:13).
7. Punning on "preyed" and implying that Winchester conspired against the King.
8. Ruler of the kingdom during the King's youth. (Henry VI was an infant when his father died.)

Thy wife⁹ is proud: she holdeth thee in awe,°   *overawes or rules you*
40   More than God or religious churchmen may.
GLOUCESTER   Name not religion, for thou lov'st the flesh,
     And ne'er throughout the year to church thou go'st,
     Except it be to pray against thy foes.
BEDFORD   Cease, cease these jars,° and rest your minds in peace.   *discords*
45   Let's to the altar. Heralds, wait on us.°   *attend us*
     [*Exeunt* WARWICK, SOMERSET, *and heralds with coffin*]¹
     Instead of gold, we'll offer up our arms—
     Since arms avail not, now that Henry's dead.
     Posterity, await for° wretched years,   *expect*
     When, at their mothers' moistened eyes, babes shall suck,²
50   Our isle be made a marish° of salt tears,   *marsh*
     And none but women left to wail the dead.
     Henry the Fifth, thy ghost I invocate:
     Prosper this realm; keep it from civil broils;°   *wars*
     Combat with adverse planets in the heavens.
55   A far more glorious star thy soul will make
     Than Julius Caesar³ or bright—
               Enter a MESSENGER
MESSENGER   My honourable lords, health to you all.
     Sad tidings bring I to you out of France,
     Of loss, of slaughter, and discomfiture.
60   Guyenne, Compiègne, Rouen, Rheims, Orléans,
     Paris, Gisors, Poitiers are all quite lost.
BEDFORD   What sayst thou, man, before dead Henry's corpse?
     Speak softly, or the loss of those great towns
     Will make him burst his lead° and rise from death.   *lead lining of coffin*
65   GLOUCESTER [*to the* MESSENGER]   Is Paris lost? Is Rouen yielded up?
     If Henry were recalled to life again,
     These news would cause him once more yield the ghost.°   *to die*
EXETER [*to the* MESSENGER]   How were they lost? What
               treachery was used?
MESSENGER   No treachery, but want° of men and money.   *lack*
70   Amongst the soldiers this is mutterèd:
     That here you maintain several factions,
     And whilst a field° should be dispatched and fought,   *an army; battle*
     You are disputing of° your generals.   *about*
     One would have ling'ring wars, with little cost;
75   Another would fly swift, but wanteth wings;
     A third thinks, without expense at all,
     By guileful fair words peace may be obtained.
     Awake, awake, English nobility!
     Let not sloth dim your honours new-begot.
80   Cropped° are the flower-de-luces⁴ in your arms;   *Plucked*

9. Eleana Cobham. Accused of pride and overweening ambition, she is found guilty of witchcraft in *The First Part of the Contention*.
1. F does not indicate when the funeral procession exits. If it exits now rather than at the end of the scene, then Henry's coffin is not onstage when the messengers from France arrive; but the actors carrying the coffin would have more time to prepare for their parts in the battle scene in 1.2.
2. When babies are fed only with their mother's tears.
3. According to Roman tradition, Caesar's soul was turned into a shining star (Ovid's *Metamorphoses*) or comet (Suetonius) after his murder.
4. English name for the French national emblem, the fleur-de-lis (lily flower), which appeared in the English coat of arms and signified the English claim to the French throne. By the Treaty of Troyes (1420), Henry V was named heir to the French King Charles VI, but Henry died shortly before Charles; at Charles's death, the French throne passed to his son, the Dauphin, leading to the renewed struggles between the French and English depicted here.

Of England's coat,° one half is cut away.   [*Exit*]   coat of arms
EXETER   Were our tears wanting to this funeral,
These tidings would call forth her° flowing tides.   (England's)
BEDFORD   Me they concern; Regent⁵ I am of France.
85   Give me my steelèd coat. I'll fight for France.
Away with these disgraceful wailing robes!
[*He removes his mourning robe*]
Wounds will I lend the French, instead of eyes,
To weep⁶ their intermissive° miseries.   temporarily interrupted
Enter to them another MESSENGER [*with letters*]
SECOND MESSENGER   Lords, view these letters, full of bad mischance.
90   France is revolted from the English quite,
Except some petty towns of no import.
The Dauphin⁷ Charles is crownèd king in Rheims;
The Bastard of Orléans⁸ with him is joined;
René, Duke of Anjou, doth take his part;
95   The Duke of Alençon flyeth to his side.   *Exit*
EXETER   The Dauphin crownèd King? All fly to him?
O whither shall *we* fly from this reproach?
GLOUCESTER   We will not fly, but to our enemies' throats.
Bedford, if thou be slack, I'll fight it out.
100   BEDFORD   Gloucester, why doubt'st thou of my forwardness?
An army have I mustered in my thoughts,
Wherewith already France is overrun.
Enter another MESSENGER
THIRD MESSENGER   My gracious lords, to add to your laments,
Wherewith you now bedew King Henry's hearse,
105   I must inform you of a dismal° fight   disastrous
Betwixt the stout° Lord Talbot⁹ and the French.   brave
WINCHESTER   What, wherein Talbot overcame—is't so?
THIRD MESSENGER   O no, wherein Lord Talbot was o'erthrown.
The circumstance I'll tell you more at large.°   in greater detail
110   The tenth of August last, this dreadful° lord,   fear-inspiring
Retiring from the siege of Orléans,
Having full scarce° six thousand in his troop,   barely
By three-and-twenty thousand of the French
Was round encompassèd and set upon.
115   No leisure had he to enrank° his men.   to set in battle lines
He wanted pikes¹ to set before his archers—
Instead whereof, sharp stakes plucked out of hedges
They pitchèd in the ground confusèdly,
To keep the horsemen off from breaking in.
120   More than three hours the fight continuèd,

5. Ruler in the King's absence.
6. *Wounds . . . weep:* I will give the French wounds, so that they will weep blood (from the wounds, instead of tears from the eyes).
7. Charles VII (1403–1461) held the title of Dauphin (heir to the French throne) until he became King in 1422. Historically, his coronation at Reims did not occur until 1429.
8. Jean, Count of Dunois (1403–1468), illegitimate son of the Duke of Orléans and nephew of King Charles VI.
9. John Talbot, first Earl of Shrewsbury (1388–1453) and perhaps the most celebrated English military hero of his day, was captured by the French at the Battle of Patay, the "dismal fight" described here.
1. He lacked ironbound stakes (normally set in the ground in front of archers to protect against attacking cavalry).

Where valiant Talbot above human thought
Enacted wonders with his sword and lance.
Hundreds he sent to hell, and none durst stand° him;   face
Here, there, and everywhere, enraged he slew.
125   The French exclaimed the devil was in arms:
All the whole army stood agazed on° him.   astonished at
His soldiers, spying his undaunted spirit,
'A° Talbot! A Talbot!' cried out amain,°   To / strongly
And rushed into the bowels of the battle.
130   Here had the conquest fully been sealed up,
If Sir John Fastolf² had not played the coward.
He, being in the vanguard placed behind,³
With purpose to relieve and follow them,
Cowardly fled, not having struck one stroke.
135   Hence grew the general wrack° and massacre.   destruction
Enclosèd were they with° their enemies.   by
A base Walloon,⁴ to win the Dauphin's grace,
Thrust Talbot with a spear into the back—
Whom all France, with their chief assembled strength,
140   Durst not presume to look once in the face.
BEDFORD   Is Talbot slain then? I will slay myself,
For living idly here in pomp and ease
Whilst such a worthy leader, wanting aid,
Unto his dastard foemen° is betrayed.   enemies
145   THIRD MESSENGER   O no, he lives, but is took prisoner,
And Lord Scales with him, and Lord Hungerford;
Most of the rest slaughtered, or took likewise.
BEDFORD   His ransom there is none but I shall pay.
I'll hale the Dauphin headlong from his throne;
150   His crown shall be the ransom of my friend.
Four of their lords I'll change° for one of ours.   exchange (kill)
Farewell, my masters; to my task will I.
Bonfires in France forthwith I am to make,
To keep our great Saint George's feast⁵ withal.
155   Ten thousand soldiers with me I will take,
Whose bloody deeds shall make all Europe quake.
THIRD MESSENGER   So you had need. Fore Orléans, besieged,
The English army is grown weak and faint.
The Earl of Salisbury craveth supply,°   reinforcements
160   And hardly keeps his men from mutiny,
Since they, so few, watch such a multitude.   [Exit]
EXETER   Remember, lords, your oaths to Henry sworn:
Either to quell the Dauphin utterly,
Or bring him in obedience to your yoke.
165   BEDFORD   I do remember it, and here take my leave
To go about my preparation.   Exit

2. Shakespeare follows a doubtful historical tradition
here. Even though in some chronicles depicted as a
coward, Sir John Fastolf (1378?–1459) was actually a
distinguished soldier and officer of Henry V in the
French wars. For this character's relationship with
the cowardly knight Falstaff in (1 and 2) Henry IV, see
the Introduction to 1 Henry IV.

3. He being stationed in the rear of the vanguard.
4. Inhabitant of a French-speaking province in what is
now southern Belgium.
5. The feast day of St. George, England's patron saint,
April 23, was traditionally celebrated with bonfires.
Bedford suggests that he will celebrate it every day with
military victories over the French.

GLOUCESTER   I'll to the Tower[6] with all the haste I can,
 To view th'artillery and munition,
 And then I will proclaim young Henry king.   *Exit*
170 EXETER   To Eltham[7] will I, where the young King is,
 Being ordained his special governor,
 And for his safety there I'll best devise.   *Exit*
WINCHESTER   Each hath his place and function to attend;
 I am left out; for me, nothing remains.
175 But long I will not be Jack-out-of-office.[8]
 The King from Eltham I intend to steal,
 And sit at chiefest stern° of public weal.   *Exit*   (*as steersman*)

1.2

Sound a flourish.° Enter CHARLES [*the Dauphin, the*   *fanfare of trumpets*
Duke of] ALENÇON, *and* RENÉ [*Duke of Anjou*], *march-*
ing with drum[*mer*] *and soldiers*

CHARLES   Mars his true moving—even as in the heavens,
 So in the earth—to this day is not known.[1]
 Late° did he shine upon the English side;   *Recently*
 Now we are victors: upon us he smiles.
5 What towns of any moment° but we have?   *importance*
 At pleasure here we lie near Orléans
 Otherwhiles° the famished English, like pale ghosts,   *Occasionally*
 Faintly besiege us one hour in a month.
ALENÇON   They want their porrage° and their fat bull beeves. *porridge; stew*
10 Either they must be dieted° like mules,   *fed*
 And have their provender tied to their mouths,
 Or piteous they will look, like drownèd mice.
RENÉ   Let's raise the siege. Why live we idly here?
 Talbot is taken, whom we wont° to fear.   *were accustomed*
15 Remaineth none but mad-brained Salisbury,
 And he may well in fretting spend his gall:°   *exhaust his anger*
 Nor° men nor money hath he to make war.   *Neither*
CHARLES   Sound, sound, alarum!° We will rush on them. (*the call to arms*)
 Now for the honour of the forlorn[2] French,
20 Him I forgive my death that killeth me
 When he sees me go back one foot or flee.   *Exeunt*

1.3

Here alarum. They [*the French*] *are beaten back by the*
English with great loss. Enter CHARLES [*the Dauphin,*
the Duke of] ALENÇON, *and* RENÉ [*Duke of Anjou*]

CHARLES   Who ever saw the like? What men have I?
 Dogs, cowards, dastards! I would ne'er have fled,
 But that they left me 'midst my enemies.
RENÉ   Salisbury is a desperate homicide.
5 He fighteth as one weary of his life.
 The other lords, like lions wanting food,
 Do rush upon us as their hungry prey.°   *prey to their hunger*

---

6. The Tower of London, which served as both a royal
residence and an arsenal.
7. Another royal residence, located south of London.
8. Proverbial for someone who had been dismissed
from a job.
1.2 Location: Near Orléans, France.

1. The precise nature of the planet Mars's orbit was a
subject of debate until Johannes Kepler described it in
1609. Mars, the god of war, was known for his unpre-
dictability.
2. Performing their duty at the risk of death.
1.3 Location: Near Orléans.

ALENÇON   Froissart,[1] a countryman of ours, records
    England all Olivers and Rolands[2] bred
10 During the time Edward the Third did reign.
    More truly now may this be verified,
    For none but Samsons and Goliases[3]
    It sendeth forth to skirmish. One to ten?
    Lean raw-boned rascals,° who would e'er suppose   *thin, inferior deer*
15 They had such courage and audacity?
CHARLES   Let's leave this town, for they are hare-brained slaves,
    And hunger will enforce them to be more eager.°   *fierce*
    Of old I know them: rather with their teeth
    The walls they'll tear down, than forsake the siege.
20 RENÉ   I think by some odd gimmers[4] or device
    Their arms are set, like clocks, still to strike on,
    Else ne'er could they hold out so as they do.
    By my consent we'll even let them alone.
ALENÇON   Be it so.
          Enter the BASTARD *of Orléans*
25 BASTARD   Where's the Prince Dauphin? I have news for him.
CHARLES   Bastard of Orléans, thrice welcome to us.
BASTARD   Methinks your looks are sad, your cheer appalled.°   *countenance made pale*
    Hath the late overthrow wrought this offence?
    Be not dismayed, for succour is at hand.
30 A holy maid hither with me I bring,
    Which, by a vision sent to her from heaven,
    Ordainèd is to raise this tedious siege
    And drive the English forth° the bounds of France.   *out of*
    The spirit of deep prophecy she hath,
35 Exceeding the nine sibyls of old Rome.[5]
    What's past and what's to come she can descry.
    Speak: shall I call her in? Believe my words,
    For they are certain and unfallible.
CHARLES   Go call her in.   *[Exit* BASTARD*]*[6]
          But first, to try her skill,
40 René stand thou as Dauphin in my place
    Question her proudly; let thy looks be stern.
    By this means shall we sound° what skill she hath.   *test*
      Enter [the BASTARD *of Orléans with]* JOAN *[la]*
      Pucelle[7] *[armed]*
RENÉ *[as Charles]*   Fair maid, is't thou wilt do these wondrous feats?
JOAN   René, is't thou that thinkest to beguile me?
45 Where is the Dauphin? *[To* CHARLES*]* Come, come from behind.
    I know thee well, though never seen before.
    Be not amazed. There's nothing hid from me.
    In private will I talk with thee apart.

---

1. Jean Froissart, author of a history of medieval France and England.
2. The most famous of Charlemagne's knights.
3. The biblical warriors Samson and Goliath were noted for their exceptional strength.
4. Gimmals, mechanical parts for transmitting motion (as in clockwork).
5. Sibyls were women in antiquity possessing the power of prophecy, perhaps "nine" here because of confusion with the nine prophetic books offered to Tarquin, the ruler of Rome, by the Cumaean Sibyl.
6. F does not indicate who brings in Joan, but it seems likely that it is the Bastard himself rather than a servant.
7. French for "the maid" or "the virgin." Joan of Arc (1412–1431) was celebrated by the French as the "Maid of Orléans" after she fought in the battle depicted here. A formidable warrior, she eventually became a prisoner of the English and was burned alive for heresy.

Stand back you lords, and give us leave awhile.
  [RENÉ, ALENÇON *and* BASTARD *stand apart*]
RENÉ [*to* ALENÇON *and* BASTARD] She takes upon her bravely, at
50   first dash.[8]
JOAN   Dauphin, I am by birth a shepherd's daughter,
  My wit untrained in any kind of art.
  Heaven and our Lady gracious° hath it pleased   (the Virgin Mary)
  To shine on my contemptible estate.
55 Lo, whilst I waited on my tender lambs,
  And to sun's parching heat displayed my cheeks,
  God's mother deignèd to appear to me,
  And in a vision, full of majesty,
  Willed me to leave my base vocation
60 And free my country from calamity.
  Her aid she promised, and assured success.
  In complete glory she revealed herself—
  And whereas I was black[9] and swart° before,   dark; swarthy
  With those clear rays which she infused° on me   shed
65 That beauty am I blest with, which you may see.
  Ask me what question thou canst possible,
  And I will answer unpremeditated.
  My courage try by combat, if thou dar'st,
  And thou shalt find that I exceed my sex.
70 Resolve on° this: thou shalt be fortunate,   Be sure of
  If thou receive me for thy warlike mate.°   co-worker; lover
CHARLES   Thou hast astonished me with thy high terms.°   lofty phrases
  Only this proof ° I'll of thy valour make: test
  In single combat thou shalt buckle° with me.   contend; make love
75 An if° thou vanquishest, thy words are true;   An if = If
  Otherwise, I renounce all confidence.
JOAN   I am prepared. Here is my keen-edged sword,
  Decked with five flower-de-luces on each side—
  The which at Touraine, in Saint Katherine's[1] churchyard,
80 Out of a great deal of old iron I chose forth.
CHARLES   Then come a° God's name. I fear no woman.   in
JOAN   And while I live, I'll ne'er fly from a man.
        Here they fight and JOAN [la] *Pucelle overcomes*
CHARLES   Stay, stay thy hands! Thou art an Amazon,[2]
  And fightest with the sword of Deborah.[3]
85 JOAN   Christ's mother helps me, else I were too weak.
CHARLES   Whoe'er helps thee, 'tis thou that must help me.
  Impatiently I burn with thy desire.°   with desire for you
  My heart and hands thou hast at once subdued.
  Excellent Pucelle if thy name be so,
90 Let me thy servant,° and not sovereign be.   lover
  'Tis the French Dauphin sueth to thee thus.
JOAN   I must not yield to any rites of love,
  For my profession's sacred from above.
  When I have chasèd all thy foes from hence,
95 Then will I think upon a recompense.

8. She plays her part well from the start.
9. Dark-skinned (probably from the sun).
1. Patroness of young maidens and female students;
reputed to be the holiest of Christ's virgins.
2. One of the tribe of legendary female warriors
claimed by Herodotus to live in Scythia.
3. An Old Testament prophet and judge who accompanied Barak as he led a victorious Israelite army
against the Canaanites (see Judges 4–5).

CHARLES Meantime, look gracious on thy prostrate thrall.

RENÉ [*to the other lords apart*] My lord, methinks, is very long
    in talk.

ALENÇON Doubtless he shrives this woman to her smock,[4]

    Else ne'er could he so long protract his speech.

100 RENÉ Shall we disturb him, since he keeps no mean?°   *moderation*

ALENÇON He may mean more than we poor men do know.

    These women are shrewd tempters with their tongues.

RENÉ [*to* CHARLES] My lord, where are you? What devise° you on?   *decide*

    Shall we give o'er Orléans, or no?

105 JOAN Why, no, I say. Distrustful recreants,°   *cowards*

    Fight till the last gasp; I'll be your guard.

CHARLES What she says, I'll confirm. We'll fight it out.

JOAN Assigned am I to be the English scourge.[5]

    This night the siege assurèdly I'll raise.

110   Expect Saint Martin's summer, halcyon's days,[6]

    Since I have entered into these wars.

    Glory is like a circle in the water,

    Which never ceaseth to enlarge itself

    Till, by broad spreading, it disperse to naught.

115   With Henry's death, the English circle ends.

    Dispersèd are the glories it included.

    Now am I like that proud insulting° ship   *exultant*

    Which Caesar and his fortune bore at once.[7]

CHARLES Was Mohammed inspirèd with a dove?[8]

120   Thou with an eagle[9] art inspirèd then.

    Helen,[1] the mother of great Constantine,

    Nor yet Saint Philip's daughters[2] were like thee.

    Bright star of Venus,° fall'n down on the earth,   *Roman goddess of love*

    How may I reverently worship thee enough?

125 ALENÇON Leave off delays, and let us raise the siege.

RENÉ Woman, do what thou canst to save our honours.

    Drive them from Orléans, and be immortalized.

CHARLES Presently° we'll try. Come, let's away about it.   *Immediately*

    No prophet will I trust, if she prove false.   *Exeunt*

1.4

Enter [the Duke of] GLOUCESTER, *with his* SERVINGMEN
[in blue coats][1]

GLOUCESTER I am come to survey the Tower this day.

    Since Henry's death, I fear there is conveyance.°   *dishonesty*

    Where be these warders,° that they wait not here?   *guards*

    [A SERVINGMAN *knocketh on the gates*]

---

4. Hears her confession completely; examines her intimately (to her "smock," or undergarments).
5. An individual sent by God to punish sin.
6. A period of unseasonable calm (the sea was thought to grow calm in December so that halcyons, or kingfishers, could build their nests upon it). *Saint Martin's summer*: Indian summer (St. Martin's Day falls on November 11).
7. According to Plutarch, an anxious sea captain was calmed when Caesar told him that his ship contained both Caesar and Caesar's natural good fortune.
8. Mohammed was the prophet and founder of Islam. Some Elizabethans claimed he was a fraud who fooled followers into thinking he was divinely inspired by training a dove to take seeds from his ear. Christians saw the dove as an incarnation of the Holy Spirit.
9. Attribute of the apostle St. John and hence a symbol of divine inspiration; also an aggressive enemy of the dove.
1. St. Helena, the mother of the emperor who made Christianity the official religion of the Roman Empire, was said to have been led by a vision to discover Jesus' cross and sepulcher.
2. Four virgins noted in the New Testament (Acts 21:9) for their powers of prophecy.
1.4 Location: The Tower of London.
1. The typical attire of Elizabethan servants.

Open the gates: 'tis Gloucester that calls.

FIRST WARDER [*within the Tower*]   Who's there that knocketh so

5   imperiously?

GLOUCESTER'S FIRST MAN   It is the noble Duke of Gloucester.

SECOND WARDER [*within the Tower*]   Whoe'er he be, you may

        not be let in.

GLOUCESTER'S FIRST MAN   Villains,° answer you so the Lord   Scoundrels; peasants

        Protector?

FIRST WARDER [*within the Tower*]   The Lord protect him, so we

        answer him.

10   We do no otherwise than we are willed.°   *commanded*

GLOUCESTER   Who willèd you? Or whose will stands, but mine?

        There's none Protector of the realm but I.

        [*To* SERVINGMEN] Break up the gates. I'll be your warrantize.°   surety; authorization

        Shall I be flouted thus by dunghill grooms?

            Gloucester's men rush at the Tower gates

WOODVILLE[2] [*within the Tower*][3]   What noise is this? What

15   traitors have we here?

GLOUCESTER   Lieutenant, is it you whose voice I hear?

        Open the gates! Here's Gloucester, that would enter.

WOODVILLE [*within the Tower*]   Have patience, noble duke:

        I may not open.

        My lord of Winchester forbids.

20   From him I have express commandèment

        That thou, nor none of thine, shall be let in.

GLOUCESTER   Faint-hearted Woodville! Prizest him fore me?—

        Arrogant Winchester, that haughty prelate,

        Whom Henry, our late sovereign, ne'er could brook?°   *tolerate*

25   Thou art no friend to God or to the King.

        Open the gates, or I'll shut thee out shortly.

SERVINGMEN   Open the gates unto the Lord Protector,

        Or we'll burst them open, if that you come not quickly.

            Enter, to the [Lord] Protector at the Tower gates, [the

            Bishop of] WINCHESTER *and his men in tawny coats*[4]

WINCHESTER   How now, ambitious vizier![5] What means this?

GLOUCESTER   Peeled° priest, dost thou command me to be   *Shaven; tonsured*

30   shut out?

WINCHESTER   I do, thou most usurping proditor,°   *traitor*

        And not 'Protector', of the King or realm.

GLOUCESTER   Stand back, thou manifest conspirator.

        Thou that contrived'st to murder our dead lord,

35   Thou that giv'st whores indulgences to sin,[6]

        If thou proceed in this thy insolence—

WINCHESTER   Nay, stand thou back! I will not budge a foot.

---

2. Richard Woodville (died c. 1441) was a loyal follower of the Lancastrian King Henry VI. His granddaughter Elizabeth married the Yorkist King Edward IV
in 1464, a marriage Shakespeare depicts in *Richard III*.
3. The original stage direction at 1.4.14 reads:
"Gloucester's men rush at the Tower gates, and
Woodville the Lieutenant speaks within." The First and
Second Warders most likely also speak here from within
the Tower, but it is unclear whether they speak from the
upper stage or from behind some stage device suggesting a grate or window.

4. Typically worn by attendants of important churchmen.
5. A high state official in the Turkish Empire, which
Elizabethans frequently denounced as barbaric.
6. In 1426, Gloucester charged Winchester with
attempting to have King Henry V ("our dead lord")
killed. He here also accuses Winchester of encouraging
prostitution, referring to the revenues that the Bishop
of Winchester collected from the brothels on the south
bank of the Thames (where, in Shakespeare's time,
many theaters were also located).

This be Damascus,[7] be thou cursèd Cain,
To slay thy brother Abel, if thou wilt.
40 GLOUCESTER   I will not slay thee, but I'll drive thee back.
Thy purple robes, as a child's bearing-cloth,°   *christening gown*
I'll use to carry thee out of this place.
WINCHESTER   Do what thou dar'st, I beard° thee to thy face.   *defy*
GLOUCESTER   What, am I dared and bearded to my face?
45   Draw, men, for all this privilegèd place.[8]
     [*All draw their swords*]
Blue coats to tawny coats!—Priest, beware your beard.
I mean to tug it, and to cuff you soundly.
Under my feet I'll stamp thy bishop's mitre.
In spite of Pope, or dignities of church,
50   Here by the cheeks I'll drag thee up and down.
WINCHESTER   Gloucester, thou wilt answer this before the Pope.
GLOUCESTER   Winchester goose! I cry, 'A rope, a rope!'[9]
[*To his* SERVINGMEN] Now beat them hence. Why do you let them stay?
[*To* WINCHESTER] Thee I'll chase hence, thou wolf in sheep's array.
55   Out, tawny coats! Out, cloakèd hypocrite!
     Here Gloucester's men beat out the Bishop's men.[1] *Enter*
     in the hurly-burly the MAYOR *of London and his Officers*
MAYOR   Fie, lords!—that you, being supreme magistrates,
Thus contumeliously° should break the peace.   *contemptuously*
GLOUCESTER   Peace, mayor, thou know'st little of my wrongs.
Here's Beaufort—that regards nor° God nor king—   *neither*
60   Hath here distrained° the Tower to his use.   *seized*
WINCHESTER [*to* MAYOR]   Here's Gloucester—a foe to citizens,
One that still motions° war, and never peace,   *who always advocates*
O'ercharging your free purses[2] with large fines°—   *taxes*
That seeks to overthrow religion,
65   Because he is Protector of the realm,
And would have armour here out of the Tower
To crown himself king and suppress the Prince.
GLOUCESTER   I will not answer thee with words but blows.
     Here they [*the factions*] *skirmish again*
MAYOR   Naught rests° for me, in this tumultuous strife,   *is left*
70   But to make open proclamation.
Come, officer, as loud as e'er thou canst, cry.
OFFICER   All manner of men, assembled here in arms this day
against God's peace and the King's, we charge and command
you in his highness' name to repair to your several dwelling
75   places, and not to wear, handle, or use any sword, weapon, or
dagger henceforward, upon pain of death.
     [*The skirmishes cease*]
GLOUCESTER   Bishop, I'll be no breaker of the law.
But we shall meet and break our minds° at large.   *express our views*

WINCHESTER   Gloucester, we'll meet to thy cost, be sure.
80   Thy heart-blood I will have for this day's work.
MAYOR   I'll call for clubs,³ if you will not away.
         [*Aside*] This bishop is more haughty than the devil.
GLOUCESTER   Mayor, farewell. Thou dost but what thou mayst.
WINCHESTER   Abominable Gloucester, guard thy head,
85   For I intend to have it ere long.

                              Exeunt [*both factions severally*]°   separately
MAYOR [*to* OFFICERS]   See the coast cleared, and then we will depart.—
         Good God, these nobles should such stomachs° bear!   angry tempers
         I myself fight not once in forty year.   *Exeunt*

1.5

Enter the MASTER GUNNER *of Orléans and his* BOY
MASTER GUNNER   Sirrah,¹ thou know'st how Orléans is besieged,
         And how the English have the suburbs won.
BOY   Father, I know, and oft have shot at them;
         Howe'er, unfortunate, I missed my aim.
5   MASTER GUNNER   But now thou shalt not. Be thou ruled by me.
         Chief Master Gunner am I of this town;
         Something I must do to procure me grace.°   honor
         The Prince's spials° have informèd me   spies
         How the English, in the suburbs close entrenched,
10   Wont,° through a secret grate of iron bars   Are accustomed
         In yonder tower, to overpeer the city,
         And thence discover how with most advantage
         They may vex us with shot or with assault.
         To intercept this inconvenience,°   harm
15   A piece of ordnance 'gainst° it I have placed,   directed toward
         And even these three days have I watched, if I could see them.
         Now do thou watch, for I can stay no longer.
         If thou spy'st any, run and bring me word,
         And thou shalt find me at the governor's.
20   BOY   Father, I warrant you, take you no care°—   don't worry
                              Exit [MASTER GUNNER *at one door*]
         I'll never trouble you, if I may spy them.
                              Exit [*at the other door*]

1.6

Enter [*the Earl of*] SALISBURY *and* [*Lord*] TALBOT
[*above*] *on the turrets with others* [*among them
Sir Thomas* GARGRAVE *and Sir William* GLASDALE]
SALISBURY   Talbot, my life, my joy, again returned?
         How wert thou handled, being prisoner?
         Or by what means got'st thou to be released?
         Discourse, I prithee, on this turret's top.
5   TALBOT   The Duke of Bedford had a prisoner,
         Called the brave Lord Ponton de Santrailles;
         For him was I exchanged and ransomèd.

---

3. I'll shout for London apprentices to bring their clubs   1. Normally used to address social inferiors, but here
and quell this riot. "Prentices and clubs" was a common   used to address the Master Gunner's young son.
rallying cry.   **1.6** Location: Tower before the walls of Orléans.
1.5 Location: Orléans.

	But with a baser man-of-arms° by far	*soldier of lower rank*
	Once in contempt they would have bartered me—	
10	Which I, disdaining, scorned, and cravèd death	
	Rather than I would be so pilled esteemed.°	*so cheaply valued*
	In fine,° redeemed I was, as I desired.	*In short*
	But O, the treacherous Fastolf wounds my heart,	
	Whom with my bare fists I would execute	
15	If I now had him brought into my power.	

SALISBURY Yet tell'st thou not how thou wert entertained.°   *treated*

	TALBOT With scoffs and scorns and contumelious taunts.	
	In open market place produced they me,	
	To be a public spectacle to all.	
20	'Here', said they, 'is the terror of the French,	
	The scarecrow that affrights our children so.'	
	Then broke I from the officers that led me	
	And with my nails digged stones out of the ground	
	To hurl at the beholders of my shame.	
25	My grisly countenance made others fly.	
	None durst come near, for fear of sudden death.	
	In iron walls they deemed me not secure:	
	So great fear of my name 'mongst them were spread	
	That they supposed I could rend bars of steel	
30	And spurn° in pieces posts of adamant.[1]	*kick*
	Wherefore a guard of chosen shot° I had	*selected marksmen*
	That walked about me every minute while;°	*constantly*
	And if I did but stir out of my bed,	
	Ready they were to shoot me to the heart.	

The BOY [*passes over the stage*] *with a linstock*[2]

	SALISBURY I grieve to hear what torments you endured.	
35	But we will be revenged sufficiently.	
	Now it is supper time in Orléans.	
	Here, through this grate, I count each one,	
	And view the Frenchmen how they fortify.	
40	Let us look in: the sight will much delight thee.—	
	Sir Thomas Gargrave and Sir William Glasdale,	
	Let me have your express° opinions	*precise*
	Where is best place to make our batt'ry next.	

[*They look through the grate*]

GARGRAVE I think at the north gate, for there stands Lou.°   *fortress of St. Lou*

45	GLASDALE And I here, at the bulwark of the Bridge.	
	TALBOT For aught I see, this city must be famished°	*starved out*
	Or with light skirmishes enfeeblèd.	

Here they° shoot [*off chambers within*] *and* SALISBURY   *(the French)*
[*and* GARGRAVE] *fall down*

SALISBURY O Lord have mercy on us, wretched sinners!

GARGRAVE O Lord have mercy on me, woeful man!

50	TALBOT What chance is this that suddenly hath crossed us?	
	Speak, Salisbury—at least, if thou canst, speak.	
	How far'st thou, mirror° of all martial men?	*best example*
	One of thy eyes and thy cheek's side struck off?	

---

1. A legendary stony substance said to be impregnable.
2. F's stage direction reads: "Enter the Boy with a linstock." He probably does not stay onstage, however, but passes from one side to the other on his way to light the charge that will strike down Salisbury and Gargrave. *linstock*: a stick used to hold a lighted match or torch for firing cannon.

Accursèd tower! Accursèd fatal hand
55   That hath contrived this woeful tragedy!
In thirteen battles Salisbury o'ercame;
Henry the Fifth he first trained to the wars;
Whilst any trump did sound or drum struck up
His sword did ne'er leave striking in the field.
60   Yet liv'st thou, Salisbury? Though thy speech doth fail,
One eye thou hast to look to heaven for grace.
The sun with one eye vieweth all the world.
Heaven, be thou gracious to none alive
If Salisbury wants° mercy at thy hands.—   lacks
65   Sir Thomas Gargrave, hast thou any life?
Speak unto Talbot. Nay, look up to him.—
Bear hence his body; I will help to bury it.
                    [Exit one with Gargrave's body]
Salisbury, cheer thy spirit with this comfort:
Thou shalt not die whiles°—   until
70   He beckons with his hand, and smiles on me,
As who should say, 'When I am dead and gone,
Remember to avenge me on the French.'
Plantagenet, I will—and like thee, Nero,[3]
Play on the lute, beholding the towns burn.
75   Wretched shall France be only in° my name.   at the mere sound of
                    Here an alarum, and it thunders and lightens
What stir is this? What tumult's in the heavens?
Whence cometh this alarum and the noise?
                    Enter a MESSENGER
MESSENGER   My lord, my lord, the French have gathered head.°   assembled an army
The Dauphin, with one Joan la Pucelle joined,
80   A holy prophetess new risen up,
Is come with a great power° to raise the siege.   army
                    Here SALISBURY lifteth himself up and groans
TALBOT   Hear, hear, how dying Salisbury doth groan!
It irks his heart he cannot be revenged.
Frenchmen, I'll be a Salisbury to you.
85   Pucelle or pucelle,[4] Dauphin or dog-fish,[5]
Your hearts I'll stamp out with my horse's heels
And make a quagmire of your mingled brains.—
Convey me° Salisbury into his tent,   for me
And then we'll try what these dastard Frenchmen dare.
                    Alarum. Exeunt [carrying SALISBURY]

1.7

Here an alarum again, and [Lord] TALBOT pursueth the
Dauphin and driveth him. Then enter JOAN [la] Pucelle
driving Englishmen before her [and exeunt]. Then enter
[Lord] TALBOT
TALBOT   Where is my strength, my valour, and my force?
Our English troops retire; I cannot stay them.
A woman clad in armour chaseth men.

---

3. Talbot here compares himself with Nero, the
emperor who played music while he watched Rome
burn. Salisbury was a descendant of the Plantagenet
dynasty, which ruled England from 1154 to 1485.
4. Talbot puns on the French word for "virgin" (pucelle),

which sounds like the English slang for "slut" ("puzzel").
5. Punning on the Elizabethan spelling of "dauphin"
as "dolphin": hence the taunt that the Dauphin is a
"dog-fish".
1.7 Location: In and before Orléans.

Enter [JOAN *la*] *Pucelle*
Here, here she comes. [*To* JOAN] I'll have a bout¹ with thee.

5 Devil or devil's dam,° I'll conjure thee.   *mother*
Blood will I draw on thee—thou art a witch²—
And straightway give thy soul to him thou serv'st.

JOAN Come, come, 'tis only I that must disgrace thee.
Here they fight

TALBOT Heavens, can you suffer hell so to prevail?
10 My breast I'll burst with straining of my courage°   *vital energy*
And from my shoulders crack my arms asunder
But I will° chastise this high-minded° strumpet.   *If I do not / arrogant*
They fight again

JOAN Talbot, farewell. Thy hour is not yet come.
I must go victual° Orléans forthwith.   *supply with provisions*
A short alarum, then [*the French pass over the stage
and*] *enter the town with soldiers*

15 O'ertake me if thou canst. I scorn thy strength.
Go, go, cheer up thy hungry-starvèd° men.   *starving to death*
Help Salisbury to make his testament.
This day is ours, as many more shall be.   *Exit* [*into the town*]

TALBOT My thoughts are whirlèd like a potter's wheel.
20 I know not where I am nor what I do.
A witch by fear, not force, like Hannibal³
Drives back our troops and conquers as she lists.
So bees with smoke and doves with noisome° stench   *noxious*
Are from their hives and houses driven away.
25 They called us, for our fierceness, English dogs;
Now, like to whelps, we crying run away.
A short alarum. [*Enter English soldiers*]
Hark, countrymen: either renew the fight
Or tear the lions out of England's coat.°   *coat of arms*
Renounce your style;° give sheep in lions' stead.⁴   *distinguishing mark*
30 Sheep run not half so treacherous° from the wolf,   *cowardly*
Or horse or oxen from the leopard,
As you fly from your oft-subduèd slaves.
Alarum. Here another skirmish
It will not be. Retire into your trenches.
You all consented unto Salisbury's death,
35 For none would strike a stroke in his revenge.°   *in revenge of his death*
Pucelle is entered into Orléans
In spite of us or aught that we could do.   [*Exeunt Soldiers*]
O would I were to die with Salisbury!
The shame hereof will make me hide my head.
*Exit. Alarum. Retreat*⁵

1.8
Flourish. Enter on the walls [JOAN *la*] *Pucelle,* [CHARLES
the] *Dauphin,* RENÉ [*Duke of Anjou, the Duke of*]
ALENÇON *and* [*French*] *Soldiers* [*with colours*]

JOAN Advance° our waving colours on the walls;   *Raise*
Rescue is Orléans from the English.

---

1. Fight; sexual encounter. Much of the speech to and about Joan has sexual overtones.
2. Whoever drew blood from a witch was supposed to be protected from her magic.
3. The Carthaginian military leader who once put to

flight his Roman enemies by tying firebrands to the horns of two thousand oxen.
4. Display (on your coat of arms) sheep instead of lions.
5. A trumpet call to signal a retreat.
1.8 Location: Scene continues.

Thus Joan la Pucelle hath performed her word.
CHARLES Divinest creature, Astraea's[1] daughter,
5   How shall I honour thee for this success?
Thy promises are like Adonis' garden,[2]
That one day bloomed and fruitful were the next.
France, triumph in thy glorious prophetess!
Recovered is the town of Orléans.
10   More blessèd hap° did ne'er befall our state.   event
RENÉ Why ring not out the bells aloud throughout the town?
Dauphin, command the citizens make bonfires
And feast and banquet in the open streets
To celebrate the joy that God hath given us.
15 ALENÇON All France will be replete with mirth and joy
When they shall hear how we have played the men.°   acted like men
CHARLES 'Tis Joan, not we, by whom the day is won—
For which I will divide my crown with her,
And all the priests and friars in my realm
20   Shall in procession sing her endless praise.
A statelier pyramid to her I'll rear
Than Rhodope's[3] of Memphis ever was.
In memory of her, when she is dead
Her ashes, in an urn more precious
25   Than the rich-jewelled coffer of Darius,[4]
Transported shall be at high festivals
Before the kings and queens of France.
No longer on Saint Denis° will we cry,   patron saint of France
But Joan la Pucelle shall be France's saint.
30   Come in, and let us banquet royally
After this golden day of victory.

Flourish. Exeunt

2.1

Enter [on the walls] a [French] SERGEANT *of a band,
with two* SENTINELS
SERGEANT Sirs, take your places and be vigilant.
If any noise or soldier you perceive
Near to the walls, by some apparent° sign   obvious
Let us have knowledge at the court of guard.°   guardroom
A SENTINEL Sergeant, you shall.   [*Exit* SERGEANT]
5   Thus are poor servitors,
When others sleep upon their quiet beds,
Constrained to watch in darkness, rain, and cold.
Enter [Lord] TALBOT, *[the Dukes of]* BEDFORD *and* BUR-
GUNDY *[and soldiers], with scaling ladders, their drums
beating a dead march*[1]
TALBOT Lord regent, and redoubted° Burgundy—   distinguished
By whose approach the regions of Artois,
10   Wallon, and Picardy are friends to us[2]—

1. Greek goddess of justice; she lived on earth during the Golden Age but fled to the heavens during the corruption of the Iron Age. Queen Elizabeth I was often compared to Astraea.
2. A mythical garden noted for its fertility and described by Spenser in *The Faerie Queene*.
3. A Greek courtesan who married the King of Memphis (city in Egypt) and reputedly built the third pyramid.
4. A jeweled treasure chest that Alexander allegedly won from the Persian King Darius III and used to store the works of Homer.
2.1 Location: In and before Orléans.
1. Either a funeral march for Salisbury or the muffled march that signifies a secret attack.
2. By . . . us: during Henry V's reign, the Duke of Burgundy became an English ally and won support for the English from the French and Netherlandish regions to which Talbot refers.

This happy night the Frenchmen are secure,°   *overconfident*
Having all day caroused and banqueted.
Embrace we then this opportunity,
As fitting best to quittance° their deceit,   *repay*
15   Contrived by art° and baleful sorcery.   *craftiness*
BEDFORD   Coward of France!³ How much he wrongs his fame,°   *reputation*
Despairing of his own arms' fortitude,
To join with witches and the help of hell.
BURGUNDY   Traitors have never other company.
20   But what's that 'Pucelle' whom they term so pure?
TALBOT   A maid, they say.
BEDFORD   A maid? And be so martial?
BURGUNDY   Pray God she prove not masculine ere long.⁴
If underneath the standard of the French⁵
She carry armour⁶ as she hath begun—
25   TALBOT   Well, let them practise and converse⁷ with spirits.
God is our fortress, in whose conquering name
Let us resolve to scale their flinty bulwarks.
BEDFORD   Ascend, brave Talbot. We will follow thee.
TALBOT   Not all together. Better far, I guess,
30   That we do make our entrance several ways—
That, if it chance the one of us do fail,
The other yet may rise against their force.⁸
BEDFORD   Agreed. I'll to yon corner.
BURGUNDY   And I to this.
                    [*Exeunt severally* BEDFORD *and* BURGUNDY
                                    with some soldiers]⁹
TALBOT   And here will Talbot mount, or make his grave.
35   Now, Salisbury, for thee, and for the right
Of English Henry, shall this night appear
How much in duty I am bound to both.
             [TALBOT *and his soldiers scale the walls*]
SENTINELS   Arm! Arm! The enemy doth make assault!
ENGLISH SOLDIERS   Saint George! A Talbot!¹   [*Exeunt above.*]
             [*Alarum*] *The French* [*soldiers*] *leap o'er the walls in*
             their shirts [*and exeunt*]. *Enter several ways* [*the*]
             BASTARD [*of Orléans, the Duke of*] ALENÇON, [*and*] RENÉ
             [*Duke of Anjou*], *half ready and half unready*²
40   ALENÇON   How now, my lords? What, all unready so?
BASTARD   Unready? Ay, and glad we scaped so well.
RENÉ   'Twas time, I trow,° to wake and leave our beds,   *believe*
Hearing alarums at our chamber doors.
ALENÇON   Of all exploits since first I followed arms
45   Ne'er heard I of a warlike enterprise
More venturous or desperate than this.

3. The Dauphin.
4. She does not turn out to be a man; she does not turn out to be carrying a male child. The following lines are full of sexual innuendoes.
5. French ensign; French penis.
6. Wear armor; bear the weight of an armed man (in intercourse).
7. Scheme and talk; have sex and be intimate.
8. May scale the walls despite French resistance.
9. The staging of this scene is complex. Bedford and Burgundy may stay onstage and attack different parts of the tiring-house wall, or, as here, they may exit in

several directions and fight offstage.
1. To Talbot. This cry is included in the actual stage directions in F, but here it is assigned to nameless "English soldiers" (see also line 79).
2. In this complicated piece of stage business, Talbot's men ascend ladders to the upper stage, which represents the walls of Orléans. They there surprise French soldiers, some of whom leap down from the upper to the lower stage as if fleeing from Orléans. On the lower stage, the fleeing and defeated French nobles debate their plight. *half ready and half unready*: half dressed and half undressed.

BASTARD   I think this Talbot be a fiend of hell.
RENÉ   If not of hell, the heavens sure favour him.
ALENÇON   Here cometh Charles. I marvel how he sped.°   *fared*

Enter CHARLES [*the Dauphin*] *and* JOAN [*la Pucelle*]

50 BASTARD   Tut, holy Joan³ was his defensive guard.
CHARLES [*to* JOAN]   Is this thy cunning,° thou deceitful dame?   *skill; sorcery*
Didst thou at first, to flatter us withal,
Make us partakers of a little gain
That now our loss might be ten times so much?
55 JOAN   Wherefore is Charles impatient with his friend?
At all times will you have my power alike?
Sleeping or waking must I still prevail,
Or will you blame and lay the fault on me?—
Improvident° soldiers, had your watch been good,   *Negligent*
60 This sudden mischief never could have fall'n.
CHARLES   Duke of Alençon, this was your default,
That, being captain of the watch tonight,
Did look no better to that weighty charge.
ALENÇON   Had all your quarters been as safely kept
65 As that whereof I had the government,
We had not been thus shamefully surprised.
BASTARD   Mine was secure.
RENÉ   And so was mine, my lord.
CHARLES   And for myself, most part of all this night
Within her° quarter and mine own precinct   *(Joan's)*
70 I was employed in passing to and fro
About relieving of the sentinels.
Then how or which way should they first break in?
JOAN   Question, my lords, no further of the case,
How or which way. 'Tis sure they found some place
75 But weakly guarded, where the breach was made.
And now there rests° no other shift° but this—   *remains / device*
To gather our soldiers, scattered and dispersed,
And lay new platforms° to endamage them.   *plots; schemes*

Alarum. Enter [*an* ENGLISH] SOLDIER

ENGLISH SOLDIER   A Talbot! A Talbot!

They [*the French*] *fly, leaving their clothes behind*

80 ENGLISH SOLDIER   I'll be so bold to take what they have left.
The cry of 'Talbot' serves me for a sword,
For I have loaden me with many spoils,
Using no other weapon but his name.   *Exit* [*with spoils*]

2.2

Enter [*Lord*] TALBOT, [*the Dukes of*] BEDFORD [*and*]
BURGUNDY [*a* CAPTAIN, *and soldiers*]

BEDFORD   The day begins to break and night is fled,
Whose pitchy mantle overveiled the earth.
Here sound retreat and cease our hot pursuit.

Retreat [*is sounded*]

TALBOT   Bring forth the body of old Salisbury
5 And here advance it° in the market place,   *raise it up (on a bier)*

---

3. A reference to her sexual availability; "hole" was   2.2 Location: Within Orléans.
slang for "vagina."

The middle centre of this cursèd town.   [*Exit one or more*]
Now have I paid my vow unto his soul:
For every drop of blood was° drawn from him   *that was*
There hath at least five Frenchmen died tonight.
10   And that hereafter ages may behold
What ruin happened in revenge of him,
Within their chiefest temple I'll erect
A tomb, wherein his corpse shall be interred—
Upon the which, that everyone may read,
15   Shall be engraved the sack of Orléans,
The treacherous manner of his mournful death,
And what a terror he had been to France.
But, lords, in all our bloody massacre
I muse° we met not with the Dauphin's grace,   *wonder*
20   His new-come champion, virtuous[1] Joan of Arc,
Nor any of his false confederates.
BEDFORD   'Tis thought, Lord Talbot, when the fight began,
Roused on the sudden from their drowsy beds,
They did amongst the troops of armèd men
25   Leap o'er the walls for refuge in the field.
BURGUNDY   Myself, as far as I could well discern
For smoke and dusky vapours of the night,
Am sure I scared the Dauphin and his trull,°   *whore*
When arm-in-arm they both came swiftly running,
30   Like to a pair of loving turtle-doves
That could not live asunder day or night.
After that things are set in order here,
We'll follow them with all the power we have.
        Enter a MESSENGER
MESSENGER   All hail, my lords! Which of this princely train
35   Call ye the warlike Talbot, for his acts
So much applauded through the realm of France?
TALBOT   Here is the Talbot. Who would speak with him?
MESSENGER   The virtuous lady, Countess of Auvergne,
With modesty admiring thy renown,
40   By me entreats, great lord, thou wouldst vouchsafe
To visit her poor castle where she lies,°   *dwells*
That she may boast she hath beheld the man
Whose glory fills the world with loud report.°   *acclaim; din of war*
BURGUNDY   Is it even so? Nay, then I see our wars
45   Will turn unto a peaceful comic sport,
When ladies crave to be encountered with.
You may not, my lord, despise her gentle suit.°   *well-bred request*
TALBOT   Ne'er trust me then, for when a world of men
Could not prevail with all their oratory,
50   Yet hath a woman's kindness overruled.—
And therefore tell her I return great thanks,
And in submission will attend on her.—
Will not your honours bear me company?
BEDFORD   No, truly, 'tis more than manners will.°   *etiquette allows*
55   And I have heard it said, 'Unbidden guests

---

1. Full of virtue or manly courage; chaste (said ironically).

Are often welcomest when they are gone'.

TALBOT   Well then, alone—since there's no remedy—
I mean to prove° this lady's courtesy.   test
Come hither, captain.
          [*He*] *whispers*
                    You perceive my mind?
60   CAPTAIN   I do, my lord, and mean° accordingly.   intend to act
                              Exeunt [*severally*]

                    2.3
          Enter [*the*] COUNTESS [*of Auvergne and her* PORTER]
COUNTESS   Porter, remember what I gave in charge,°   I commanded
And when you have done so, bring the keys to me.
PORTER   Madam, I will.   *Exit*
COUNTESS   The plot is laid. If all things fall out right,
5   I shall as famous be by this exploit
As Scythian Tomyris[1] by Cyrus' death.
Great is the rumour° of this dreadful° knight,   fame / fear-inspiring
And his achievements of no less account.
Fain° would mine eyes be witness with mine ears,   Gladly
10   To give their censure° of these rare° reports.   opinion / remarkable
          Enter MESSENGER *and* [*Lord*] TALBOT
MESSENGER   Madam, according as your ladyship desired,
By message craved, so is Lord Talbot come.
COUNTESS   And he is welcome. What, is this the man?
MESSENGER   Madam, it is.
COUNTESS   Is this the scourge[2] of France?
15   Is this the Talbot, so much feared abroad
That with his name the mothers still their babes?
I see report is fabulous and false.
I thought I should have seen some Hercules,[3]
A second Hector,[4] for his grim aspect°   appearance
20   And large proportion of his strong-knit limbs.
Alas, this is a child, a seely° dwarf.   feeble
It cannot be this weak and writhled° shrimp   wrinkled
Should strike such terror to his enemies.
TALBOT   Madam, I have been bold to trouble you.
25   But since your ladyship is not at leisure,
I'll sort some other time to visit you.
          [*He is going*]
COUNTESS [*to* MESSENGER]   What means he now? Go ask him
          whither he goes.
MESSENGER   Stay, my Lord Talbot, for my lady craves
To know the cause of your abrupt departure.
30   TALBOT   Marry,[5] for that° she's in a wrong belief,   because
I go to certify her Talbot's here.
          Enter PORTER *with keys*
COUNTESS   If thou be he, then art thou prisoner.
TALBOT   Prisoner? To whom?

2.3 Location: The Countess's castle, Auvergne.
1. Asian queen who, in revenge for her son's death, killed the Persian King Cyrus and kept his head in a wineskin filled with human blood.
2. Individual sent by God to punish sin. Joan describes
herself as "the English scourge" at 1.3.108.
3. Mythical hero famous for his immense strength.
4. Greatest of the Trojan warriors, celebrated in Homer's *Iliad*.
5. By the Virgin Mary, a mild oath.

COUNTESS   To me, bloodthirsty lord;
    And for that cause I trained° thee to my house.   *enticed*
35   Long time thy shadow° hath been thrall° to me,   *image / slave*
    For in my gallery thy picture hangs;
    But now the substance shall endure the like,
    And I will chain these legs and arms of thine
    That hast by tyranny these many years
40   Wasted our country, slain our citizens,
    And sent our sons and husbands captive°—   *into captivity*
TALBOT Ha, ha, ha!
COUNTESS Laughest thou, wretch? Thy mirth shall turn to moan.
TALBOT I laugh to see your ladyship so fond°   *foolish*
45   To think that you have aught but Talbot's shadow
    Whereon to practise your severity.
COUNTESS Why? Art not thou the man?
TALBOT I am indeed.
COUNTESS Then have I substance too.
50 TALBOT No, no, I am but shadow of myself.
    You are deceived; my substance is not here.
    For what you see is but the smallest part
    And least proportion of humanity.[6]
    I tell you, madam, were the whole frame[7] here,
55   It is of such a spacious lofty pitch°   *height*
    Your roof were not sufficient to contain't.
COUNTESS This is a riddling merchant for the nonce.[8]
    He will be here, and yet he is not here.
    How can these contrarieties agree?
60 TALBOT That will I show you presently.°   *immediately*
    [*He*] *winds° his horn.* [*Within,*] *drums strike up; a peal*   *blows*
    of ordnance. Enter [*English*] *soldiers*
    How say you, madam? Are you now persuaded
    That Talbot is but shadow of himself?
    These are his substance, sinews, arms, and strength,
    With which he yoketh your rebellious necks,
65   Razeth your cities and subverts° your towns,   *overthrows*
    And in a moment makes them desolate.
COUNTESS Victorious Talbot, pardon my abuse.°   *error; deception*
    I find thou art no less than fame hath bruited,°   *proclaimed*
    And more than may be gathered by thy shape.
70   Let my presumption not provoke thy wrath,
    For I am sorry that with reverence
    I did not entertain° thee as thou art.   *receive*
TALBOT Be not dismayed, fair lady, nor misconster°   *misconstrue*
    The mind of Talbot, as you did mistake
75   The outward composition of his body.
    What you have done hath not offended me;
    Nor other satisfaction do I crave
    But only, with your patience,° that we may   *permission*
    Taste of your wine and see what cates° you have: *delicacies*
80   For soldiers' stomachs always serve them well.

---

6. Smallest part of the whole man (and, by implication,   7. The entire structure of my body (and of my army).
of the whole army that constitutes Talbot's military   8. This is a dealer in riddles as occasion requires.
presence).

COUNTESS   With all my heart; and think me honourèd
    To feast so great a warrior in my house.   *Exeunt*

2.4

[*A rose brier.*] *Enter* RICHARD PLANTAGENET, [*the Earl
of*] WARWICK, [*the Duke of*] SOMERSET, [*William de la*]
Pole [*the Earl of* SUFFOLK], *and others* [VERNON, *and a*
LAWYER]

RICHARD PLANTAGENET   Great lords and gentlemen, what
    means this silence?
    Dare no man answer in a case of truth?

SUFFOLK   Within the Temple hall we were° too loud.   *would have been*
    The garden here is more convenient.

5 RICHARD PLANTAGENET   Then say at once if I maintained the truth;
    Or else was wrangling Somerset in th'error?

SUFFOLK   Faith, I have been a truant° in the law,   *neglectful of study*
    And never yet could frame° my will to it,   *adapt*
    And therefore frame the law unto my will.

10 SOMERSET   Judge you, my lord of Warwick, then between us.

WARWICK   Between two hawks, which flies the higher pitch,°   *height*
    Between two dogs, which hath the deeper mouth,°   *voice*
    Between two blades, which bears the better temper,[1]
    Between two horses, which doth bear him best,

15   Between two girls, which hath the merriest eye,
    I have perhaps some shallow spirit of judgement;
    But in these nice° sharp quillets° of the law,   *precise / distinctions*
    Good faith, I am no wiser than a daw.[2]

RICHARD PLANTAGENET   Tut, tut, here is a mannerly forbearance.

20   The truth appears so naked on my side
    That any purblind° eye may find it out.   *half-blind*

SOMERSET   And on my side it is so well apparelled,
    So clear, so shining, and so evident,
    That it will glimmer through a blind man's eye.

25 RICHARD PLANTAGENET   Since you are tongue-tied and so loath to speak,
    In dumb significants° proclaim your thoughts.   *silent gestures*
    Let him that is a true-born gentleman
    And stands upon the honour of his birth,
    If he suppose that I have pleaded truth,[3]

30   From off this briar pluck a white rose[4] with me.
        [*He plucks a white rose*]

SOMERSET   Let him that is no coward nor no flatterer,
    But dare maintain the party° of the truth,   *side*
    Pluck a red rose[5] from off this thorn with me.
        [*He plucks a red rose*]

2.4 Location: The Temple Garden, near the Middle and Inner Temple, two buildings that housed the London law schools known as the Inns of Court.
1. *the better temper*: this refers to the degree of hardness attained by a steel sword blade when it is tempered (that is, heated to a required temperature and then plunged into cold liquid).
2. Jackdaw (a proverbially stupid bird).
3. Presented the case for truth according to proper procedures. (This scene contains many legal terms.)

4. Badge of the House of York. In the mid-fifteenth century, two branches of the Plantagenet dynasty, the Yorkists and the Lancastrians, fought what was termed the Wars of the Roses over who would hold the English throne. Shakespeare invented this scene to provide a point of origin for the quarrel that grew into the civil wars he depicted in his plays on the reigns of Henry VI, Edward IV, and Richard III.
5. Badge of the House of Lancaster.

WARWICK I love no colours,° and without all colour		*hues; pretenses*
35	Of base insinuating flattery	
	I pluck this white rose with Plantagenet.	

SUFFOLK   I pluck this red rose with young Somerset,
And say withal° I think he held the right.   *besides*

VERNON   Stay, lords and gentlemen, and pluck no more
40   Till you conclude that he upon whose side
The fewest roses from the tree are cropped
Shall yield° the other in the right opinion.   *concede*

SOMERSET   Good Master Vernon, it is well objected.°   *urged*
If I have fewest, I subscribe° in silence.   *submit*

45   RICHARD PLANTAGENET   And I.

VERNON   Then for the truth and plainness of the case
I pluck this pale and maiden blossom here,
Giving my verdict on the white rose' side.

SOMERSET   Prick not your finger as you pluck it off,
50   Lest, bleeding, you do paint the white rose red,
And fall on my side so against your will.

VERNON   If I, my lord, for my opinion° bleed,   *conviction*
Opinion° shall be surgeon to my hurt   *Reputation*
And keep me on the side where still I am.

55   SOMERSET   Well, well, come on! Who else?

LAWYER   Unless my study and my books be false,
The argument you held was wrong in law;
In sign whereof I pluck a white rose too.

RICHARD PLANTAGENET   Now Somerset, where is your argument?

60   SOMERSET   Here in my scabbard, meditating that°   *thinking of what*
Shall dye your white rose in a bloody red.

RICHARD PLANTAGENET   Meantime your cheeks do counterfeit° our roses,   *imitate*
For pale they look with fear, as witnessing
The truth on our side.

SOMERSET   No, Plantagenet,
65   'Tis not for fear, but anger, that thy cheeks
Blush for pure shame to counterfeit our roses,
And yet thy tongue will not confess thy error.

RICHARD PLANTAGENET   Hath not thy rose a canker,° Somerset?   *cankerworm; grub*

SOMERSET   Hath not thy rose a thorn, Plantagenet?

70   RICHARD PLANTAGENET   Ay, sharp and piercing, to maintain his° truth,   *its*
Whiles thy consuming canker eats his falsehood.

SOMERSET   Well, I'll find friends to wear my bleeding roses,
That shall maintain what I have said is true,
Where false Plantagenet dare not be seen.

75   RICHARD PLANTAGENET   Now, by this maiden blossom in my hand,
I scorn thee and thy fashion,° peevish boy.   *sort*

SUFFOLK   Turn not thy scorns this way, Plantagenet.

RICHARD PLANTAGENET   Proud Pole,[6] I will, and scorn both him
and thee.

SUFFOLK   I'll turn my part thereof into thy throat.[7]

80   SOMERSET   Away, away, good William de la Pole.

---

6. The Duke of Suffolk's family name.   7. I'll throw the slanders back into your throat.

We grace° the yeoman[8] by conversing with him.   *do honor to*

WARWICK   Now, by God's will, thou wrong'st him, Somerset.
   His grandfather was Lionel Duke of Clarence,
   Third son to the third Edward, King of England.[9]

85   Spring crestless° yeomen from so deep a root?   *without a coat of arms*

RICHARD PLANTAGENET   He bears him on the place's privilege,[1]
   Or durst not for his craven° heart say thus.   *cowardly*

SOMERSET   By him that made me, I'll maintain my words
   On any plot of ground in Christendom.

90   Was not thy father, Richard Earl of Cambridge,
   For treason executed in our late king's days?
   And by his treason stand'st not thou attainted,[2]
   Corrupted, and exempt° from ancient gentry?   *excluded*
   His trespass yet lives guilty in thy blood,

95   And till thou be restored[3] thou art a yeoman.

RICHARD PLANTAGENET   My father was attachèd, not attainted;[4]
   Condemned to die for treason, but no traitor—
   And that I'll prove on better men than Somerset,
   Were growing time once ripened to my will.[5]

100   For your partaker° Pole, and you yourself,   *As for your ally*
   I'll note you in my book of memory,
   To scourge you for this apprehension.°   *opinion*
   Look to it well, and say you are well warned.

SOMERSET   Ah, thou shalt find us ready for thee still,

105   And know us by these colours for thy foes,
   For these my friends, in spite of° thee, shall wear.   *in contempt of*

RICHARD PLANTAGENET   And, by my soul, this pale and angry rose,
   As cognizance° of my blood-drinking hate,   *an emblem*
   Will I forever, and my faction, wear

110   Until it wither with me to my grave,
   Or flourish to the height of my degree.°   *noble rank*

SUFFOLK   Go forward, and be choked with thy ambition.
   And so farewell until I meet thee next.   *Exit*

SOMERSET   Have with thee,° Pole.—Farewell, ambitious Richard.   *Let us go*
                                               Exit

115 RICHARD PLANTAGENET   How I am braved,° and must perforce endure it!   *insulted*

WARWICK   This blot that they object° against your house   *allege*
   Shall be wiped out in the next parliament,
   Called for the truce of° Winchester and Gloucester.   *to make peace between*
   An if° thou be not then created York,   *An if=If*

120   I will not live to be accounted Warwick.
   Meantime, in signal of my love to thee,

---

8. A man, below the rank of gentleman, holding a small estate. (Richard Plantagenet lost his lands and titles when Henry V executed his father, Richard, Earl of Cambridge, for treason.)
9. Clarence was actually Richard's great-great-grandfather on his mother's side. Edmund, Duke of York, fifth son of Edward III, was his paternal grandfather; thus Richard could trace his descent from Edward III through both his mother and his father.
1. He takes advantage of the safety provided by a privileged place. Quarreling with drawn weapons was prohibited in some precincts, but the Temple, though

originally founded as a religious house, was not one of them.
2. Condemned for treason. One so convicted lost his estate and property. His blood was declared "corrupted" (see line 93), so he could neither inherit nor transmit property and titles.
3. Are given back your lands and titles.
4. Was arrested, not convicted. Plantagenet implies that his father's execution was illegal because there was no parliamentary bill of attainder.
5. If the unfolding of time brings me my desire.

Against proud Somerset and William Pole,
Will I upon thy party wear this rose.
And here I prophesy: this brawl today,
125 Grown to this faction° in the Temple garden,   *conflict*
Shall send, between the red rose and the white,
A thousand souls to death and deadly night.
RICHARD PLANTAGENET   Good Master Vernon, I am bound to you,
That you on my behalf would pluck a flower.
130 VERNON   In your behalf still will I wear the same.
LAWYER   And so will I.
RICHARD PLANTAGENET   Thanks, gentles.
Come, let us four to dinner. I dare say
This quarrel will drink blood another day.
           Exeunt. [*The rose brier is removed*]

2.5

Enter [*Edmund*] MORTIMER, *brought in a chair*
[*by his* KEEPERS][1]
MORTIMER   Kind keepers of my weak decaying age,
Let dying Mortimer here rest himself.
Even like a man new-halèd° from the rack,[2]   *newly dragged*
So fare my limbs with long imprisonment;
5 And these grey locks, the pursuivants° of death,   *heralds*
Argue the end of Edmund Mortimer,[3]
Nestor-like[4] agèd in an age of care.
These eyes, like lamps whose wasting oil is spent,
Wax dim, as drawing to their exigent;°   *end*
10 Weak shoulders, overborne with burdening grief,
And pithless° arms, like to a withered vine   *strengthless*
That droops his° sapless branches to the ground.   *its*
Yet are these feet—whose strengthless stay° is numb,   *support*
Unable to support this lump of clay—
15 Swift-wingèd with desire to get a grave,
As witting° I no other comfort have.   *knowing*
But tell me, keeper, will my nephew come?
KEEPER   Richard Plantagenet, my lord, will come.
We sent unto the Temple, unto his chamber,
20 And answer was returned that he will come.
MORTIMER   Enough. My soul shall then be satisfied.
Poor gentleman, his wrong° doth equal mine.   *(wrong done to him)*
Since Henry Monmouth° first began to reign—   *(Henry V)*
Before whose glory I was great in arms—
25 This loathsome sequestration° have I had;   *imprisonment*

2.5 Location: A cell in the Tower of London.
1. F's stage direction reads: "Enter Mortimer, brought in in a Chair and Jailors."
2. Instrument of torture on which the victim's body was stretched.
3. As in the sources that Shakespeare probably used, several historical Mortimers are conflated here. In 1385, Richard II declared Roger Mortimer, fourth Earl of March, his heir. When Roger died in battle in 1398, his claim passed to Edmund Mortimer, fifth Earl of March and uncle of Richard Plantagenet, who in turn inherited the Mortimer claim to the throne. It was Edmund's cousin Sir John Mortimer, however, who lay imprisoned in the Tower until 1424, when he was executed for advocating Edmund's claim to the throne.
4. Like Nestor, the aged Homeric hero and adviser famous for his wisdom.

And even since then hath Richard been obscured,
Deprived of honour and inheritance.
But now the arbitrator of despairs,
Just Death, kind umpire of men's miseries,
30   With sweet enlargement° doth dismiss me hence.   release
I would his° troubles likewise were expired,   (Richard's)
That so he might recover what was lost.
          Enter RICHARD [PLANTAGENET]
KEEPER   My lord, your loving nephew now is come.
MORTIMER   Richard Plantagenet, my friend, is he come?
35   RICHARD PLANTAGENET   Ay, noble uncle, thus ignobly used:
Your nephew, late° despisèd Richard, comes.   recently
MORTIMER [*to* KEEPERS]   Direct mine arms I may embrace his neck
And in his bosom spend my latter° gasp.   final
O tell me when my lips do touch his cheeks,
40   That I may kindly give one fainting kiss.
          [*He embraces* RICHARD]
And now declare, sweet stem from York's great stock,°   trunk
Why didst thou say of late thou wert despised?
RICHARD PLANTAGENET   First lean thine agèd back against mine arm,
And in that ease I'll tell thee my dis-ease.°   trouble
45   This day in argument upon a case
Some words there grew 'twixt Somerset and me;
Among which terms he used his lavish tongue
And did upbraid me with my father's death;
Which obloquy° set bars before my tongue,   disgrace
50   Else with the like I had requited him.
Therefore, good uncle, for my father's sake,
In honour of a true Plantagenet,
And for alliance'° sake, declare the cause   kinship's
My father, Earl of Cambridge, lost his head.
55   MORTIMER   That cause, fair nephew, that imprisoned me,
And hath detained me all my flow'ring youth
Within a loathsome dungeon, there to pine,
Was cursèd instrument of his decease.
RICHARD PLANTAGENET   Discover° more at large what cause that was,   Explain
60   For I am ignorant and cannot guess.
MORTIMER   I will, if that my fading breath permit
And death approach not ere my tale be done.
Henry the Fourth, grandfather to this King,
Deposed his nephew° Richard, Edward's son,   kinsman (here, cousin)
65   The first begotten and the lawful heir
Of Edward king, the third of that descent;
During whose° reign the Percies of the north,   (Henry IV's)
Finding his usurpation most unjust,
Endeavoured my advancement to the throne.
70   The reason moved° these warlike lords to this   that moved
Was for that°—young King Richard thus removed,   Was because
Leaving no heir begotten of his body—
I was the next° by birth and parentage,   (in line for the throne)
For by my mother I derivèd° am   descended
75   From Lionel Duke of Clarence, the third son
To King Edward the Third—whereas the King
From John of Gaunt doth bring his pedigree,

Being but fourth of that heroic line.
But mark: as in this haughty° great attempt   *lofty*
80 They labourèd to plant the rightful heir,
I lost my liberty, and they their lives.
Long after this, when Henry the Fifth,
Succeeding his father Bolingbroke, did reign,
Thy father, Earl of Cambridge then, derived
85 From famous Edmund Langley, Duke of York,
Marrying my sister that thy mother was,
Again, in pity of my hard distress,
Levied an army, weening° to redeem   *intending*
And have installed me in the diadem;°   *crown*
90 But, as the rest, so fell that noble earl,
And was beheaded. Thus the Mortimers,
In whom the title rested, were suppressed.
RICHARD PLANTAGENET   Of which, my lord, your honour is the last.
MORTIMER   True, and thou seest that I no issue have,
95 And that my fainting words do warrant° death.   *promise*
Thou art my heir. The rest I wish thee gather°—   *infer*
But yet be wary in thy studious° care.   *diligent*
RICHARD PLANTAGENET   Thy grave admonishments prevail with me.
But yet methinks my father's execution
100 Was nothing less than bloody tyranny.
MORTIMER   With silence, nephew, be thou politic.°   *prudent*
Strong-fixèd is the house of Lancaster,
And like a mountain, not to be removed.
But now thy uncle is removing° hence,   *departing*
105 As princes do their courts, when they are cloyed°   *sickened*
With long continuance in a settled place.
RICHARD PLANTAGENET   O uncle, would some part of my young years
Might but redeem the passage of your age.
MORTIMER   Thou dost then wrong me, as that slaughterer doth
110 Which giveth many wounds when one will kill.
Mourn not, except° thou sorrow for my good.   *unless*
Only give order for my funeral.
And so farewell, and fair be all thy hopes,
And prosperous be thy life in peace and war.   *Dies*
115 RICHARD PLANTAGENET   And peace, no war, befall thy parting soul.
In prison hast thou spent a pilgrimage,
And like a hermit overpassed° thy days.   *spent*
Well, I will lock his counsel in my breast,
And what I do imagine, let that rest.
120 Keepers, convey him hence, and I myself
Will see his burial better than his life.[5]
                    Exeunt [KEEPERS *with Mortimer's body*]
Here dies the dusky torch of Mortimer,
Choked with° ambition of the meaner sort.[6]   *by*
And for° those wrongs, those bitter injuries,   *And as for*

---

5. *better than his life:* more sumptuous than the life he   6. *meaner sort:* people of lower rank (referring to Bol-
led (in prison).   ingbroke and his line).

125   Which Somerset hath offered to my house,
        I doubt not but with honour to redress.
        And therefore haste I to the Parliament,
        Either to be restorèd to my blood,°   *inherited rights*
        Or make mine ill th'advantage of my good.[7]   ***Exit***

3.1

Flourish. Enter [young] KING [HENRY],[1] *[the Dukes of]*
EXETER, *[and]* GLOUCESTER, *[the Bishop of]*
WINCHESTER, *[the Duke of]* SOMERSET, *[and the Earl*
of] SUFFOLK, *[with red roses, the Earl of]* WARWICK,
[and] RICHARD PLANTAGENET *[with white roses].*[2]
GLOUCESTER *offers to put up a bill;*° WINCHESTER   *written statement*
snatches it, tears it

  WINCHESTER   Com'st thou with deep premeditated lines?
        With written pamphlets studiously devised?
        Humphrey of Gloucester, if thou canst accuse,
        Or aught intend'st to lay unto my charge,
5   Do it without invention,° suddenly,   *premeditated design*
        As I with sudden and extemporal speech
        Purpose to answer what thou canst object.°   *lay to my charge*
  GLOUCESTER   Presumptuous priest, this place° commands my patience,   *(Parliament)*
        Or thou shouldst find thou hast dishonoured me.
10   Think not, although in writing I preferred°   *set out*
        The manner of thy vile outrageous crimes,
        That therefore I have forged, or am not able
        Verbatim° to rehearse the method of my pen.[3]   *Orally*
        No, prelate, such is thy audacious wickedness,
15   Thy lewd,° pestiferous,° and dissentious pranks,   *base / deadly*
        As very° infants prattle of thy pride.   *That even*
        Thou art a most pernicious usurer,[4]
        Froward° by nature, enemy to peace,   *Perverse*
        Lascivious, wanton, more than well beseems
20   A man of thy profession and degree.°   *rank*
        And for° thy treachery, what's more manifest?—   *And as for*
        In that thou laid'st a trap to take my life,
        As well at London Bridge as at the Tower.
        Beside, I fear me, if thy thoughts were sifted,°   *closely examined*
25   The King thy sovereign is not quite exempt
        From envious malice of thy swelling heart.
  WINCHESTER   Gloucester, I do defy thee.—Lords, vouchsafe
        To give me hearing what I shall reply.
        If I were covetous, ambitious, or perverse,
30   As he will have me, how am I so poor?
        Or how haps it I seek not to advance
        Or raise myself, but keep my wonted° calling?   *customary*

---

7. Or turn the injuries I have suffered to my advantage.
3.1 Location: The Parliament House, London.
1. The historical Henry VI was five years old at the time of this Parliament in 1327. In this scene, Shakespeare refers to the King's "tender years" but does not specify his age.
2. F does not mention that roses are worn in this scene, but in 2.4 the rival factions promised to wear them forever. This edition indicates their presence throughout

the ensuing action.
3. To recount the order of the argument I wrote.
4. Alluding to the fact that Winchester's wealth was partly derived from his use of a papal bull and partly from the Southwark brothels (see 1.4.35 and note). In *Measure for Measure*, Shakespeare refers to prostitution as one of the "two usuries" (3.1.263). Moneylending bred illicit offspring and financial profit.

And for dissension, who preferreth peace
More than I do?—except I be provoked.
35 No, my good lords, it is not that offends;
It is not that that hath incensed the Duke.
It is because no one should sway° but he,　　　　　　　　　　　*rule*
No one but he should be about the King—
And that engenders thunder in his breast
40 And makes him roar these accusations forth.
But he shall know I am as good—
GLOUCESTER　　As good?—
Thou bastard of my grandfather.[5]
WINCHESTER　　Ay, lordly sir; for what are you, I pray,
45 But one imperious° in another's throne?　　　　　　　　　*ruling*
GLOUCESTER　　Am I not Protector, saucy priest?
WINCHESTER　　And am not I a prelate of the Church?
GLOUCESTER　　Yes—as an outlaw in a castle keeps°　　　　*dwells*
And useth it to patronage° his theft.　　　　　　　　　　*protect*
WINCHESTER　　Unreverent Gloucester.
50 GLOUCESTER　　　　　　　　　　Thou art reverend
Touching° thy spiritual function, not thy life.　　*With regard to*
WINCHESTER　　Rome shall remedy this.
GLOUCESTER[6]　　　　　　　　　Roam thither then.
WARWICK [to WINCHESTER]　　My lord, it were your duty to forbear.
SOMERSET　　Ay, so° the bishop be not overborne:°　　*as long as / overruled*
55 Methinks my lord° should be religious,°　　　*(Gloucester) / pious*
And know the office° that belongs to such.°　　　*duty / (prelates)*
WARWICK　　Methinks his lordship° should be humbler.　　*(Winchester)*
It fitteth not a prelate so to plead.°　　　　　　　　　　*wrangle*
SOMERSET　　Yes, when his holy state is touched so near.°　*affected so directly*
60 WARWICK　　State holy or unhallowed, what of that?
Is not his grace Protector to the King?
RICHARD PLANTAGENET [aside]　　Plantagenet, I see, must hold his tongue,
Lest it be said, 'Speak, sirrah,[7] when you should;
Must your bold verdict intertalk° with lords?'　　*hold opinion; converse*
65 Else would I have a fling at Winchester.
KING HENRY　　Uncles of Gloucester and of Winchester,
The special watchmen of our English weal,°　　　　*well-being; state*
I would prevail, if prayers might prevail,
To join your hearts in love and amity.
70 O what a scandal is it to our crown
That two such noble peers as ye should jar!°　　　　　　　*quarrel*
Believe me, lords, my tender years can tell
Civil dissension is a viperous worm
That gnaws the bowels of the commonwealth.
　　　　A noise within
75 SERVINGMEN [within]　　Down with the tawny coats![8]
KING HENRY　　What tumult's this?
WARWICK　　　　　　　　　　An uproar, I dare warrant,

---

5. Winchester was born an illegitimate son of Gloucester's grandfather, John of Gaunt, though later he was
made legitimate by an act of Parliament.
6. F assigns this line to Warwick, but giving it to
Gloucester further heightens the antipathy between
Winchester and the Lord Protector.

7. Term used to address social inferiors.
8. Again, this line is included as part of the stage directions in F and is here plausibly assigned to "Servingmen." The same is true at line 78, where F's stage
direction reads: "A noise again, Stones, Stones."

Begun through malice of the Bishop's men.
    A noise again
SERVINGMEN [*within*]   Stones, stones!
    Enter [*the*] MAYOR [*of London*]
MAYOR   O my good lords, and virtuous Henry,
80   Pity the city of London, pity us!
    The Bishop and the Duke of Gloucester's men,
    Forbidden late° to carry any weapon,   *lately*
    Have filled their pockets full of pebble stones
    And, banding themselves in contrary parts,°   *opposing parties*
85   Do pelt so fast at one another's pate
    That many have their giddy brains knocked out.
    Our windows are broke down in every street,
    And we for fear compelled to shut our shops.
    Enter in skirmish, with bloody pates[*, Winchester's*
    SERVINGMEN *in tawny coats and Gloucester's in blue*
    coats]
KING HENRY   We charge you, on allegiance to ourself,
90   To hold your slaught'ring hands and keep the peace.
    [*The skirmish ceases*]
    Pray, Uncle Gloucester, mitigate this strife.
FIRST SERVINGMAN   Nay, if we be forbidden stones, we'll fall to
    it with our teeth.
SECOND SERVINGMAN   Do what ye dare, we are as resolute.
    Skirmish again
95 GLOUCESTER   You of my household, leave this peevish broil,°   *this foolish fight*
    And set this unaccustomed° fight aside.   *unusual; disorderly*
THIRD SERVINGMAN   My lord, we know your grace to be a man
    Just and upright and, for your royal birth,
    Inferior to none but to his majesty;
100   And ere that° we will suffer such a prince,   *And before*
    So kind a father of the commonweal,
    To be disgracèd° by an inkhorn mate,°   *insulted / scribbler*
    We and our wives and children all will fight
    And have our bodies slaughtered by thy foes.
105 FIRST SERVINGMAN   Ay, and the very parings of our nails
    Shall pitch a field⁹ when we are dead.
    [*They*] *begin* [*to skirmish*] *again*
GLOUCESTER   Stay, stay, I say!
    An if you love me as you say you do,
    Let me persuade you to forbear a while.
KING HENRY   O how this discord doth afflict my soul!
110   Can you, my lord of Winchester, behold
    My sighs and tears, and will not once relent?
    Who should be pitiful° if you be not?   *merciful*
    Or who should study to prefer° a peace,   *propose*
    If holy churchmen take delight in broils?
115 WARWICK   Yield, my lord Protector; yield, Winchester—
    Except you mean with obstinate repulse°   *refusal*
    To slay your sovereign and destroy the realm.
    You see what mischief—and what murder, too—
    Hath been enacted through your enmity.
120   Then be at peace, except° ye thirst for blood.   *unless*

---

9. Shall fortify a battlefield (usually with defensive wood or iron stakes).

WINCHESTER   He shall submit, or I will never yield.

GLOUCESTER   Compassion on the King commands me stoop,
Or I would see his heart out ere the priest
Should ever get that privilege of° me.   *advantage over*

125   WARWICK   Behold, my lord of Winchester, the Duke
Hath banished moody° discontented fury,   *sullen*
As by his smoothèd brows it doth appear.
Why look you still so stern and tragical?

GLOUCESTER   Here, Winchester, I offer thee my hand.

130   KING HENRY [*to* WINCHESTER]   Fie, Uncle Beaufort! I have heard you preach
That malice was a great and grievous sin;
And will not you maintain the thing you teach,
But prove a chief offender in the same?

WARWICK   Sweet King! The Bishop hath a kindly gird.°   *a gentle rebuke*

135   For shame, my lord of Winchester, relent.
What, shall a child instruct you what to do?

WINCHESTER   Well, Duke of Gloucester, I will yield to thee
Love for thy love, and hand for hand I give.

GLOUCESTER [*aside*]   Ay, but I fear me with a hollow° heart.   *an insincere*

140   [*To the others*] See here, my friends and loving countrymen,
This token serveth for a flag of truce
Betwixt ourselves and all our followers.
So help me God, as I dissemble not.

WINCHESTER   So help me God [*aside*] as I intend it not.

145   KING HENRY   O loving uncle, kind Duke of Gloucester,
How joyful am I made by this contract!
[*To* SERVINGMEN] Away, my masters, trouble us no more,
But join in friendship as your lords have done.

FIRST SERVINGMAN   Content. I'll to the surgeon's.

150   SECOND SERVINGMAN   And so will I.

THIRD SERVINGMAN   And I will see what physic° the tavern   *medicine*
affords.

Exeunt [*the* MAYOR *and* SERVINGMEN]

WARWICK   Accept this scroll, most gracious sovereign,
Which in the right of Richard Plantagenet

155   We do exhibit to your majesty.

GLOUCESTER   Well urged, my lord of Warwick—for, sweet prince,
An if your grace mark every circumstance,
You have great reason to do Richard right,
Especially for those occasions°   *reasons*

160   At Eltham Place I told your majesty.

KING HENRY   And those occasions, uncle, were of force.—
Therefore, my loving lords, our pleasure is
That Richard be restorèd to his blood.

WARWICK   Let Richard be restorèd to his blood.

165   So shall his father's wrongs be recompensed.

WINCHESTER   As will the rest, so willeth Winchester.

KING HENRY   If Richard will be true,° not that alone   *loyal*
But all the whole inheritance I give
That doth belong unto the house of York,

170   From whence you spring by lineal descent.[1]

---

1. *But . . . descent*: The King restores Richard not only to the earldom of Cambridge (inherited from his father) but also to the dukedom of York (inherited from his uncle).

RICHARD PLANTAGENET   Thy humble servant vows obedience
And humble service till the point of death.
KING HENRY   Stoop then, and set your knee against my foot.
[RICHARD *kneels*]
And in reguerdon° of that duty done,   *reward*
175   I gird thee with the valiant sword of York.
Rise, Richard, like a true Plantagenet,
And rise created princely Duke of York.
RICHARD DUKE OF YORK [*rising*]   And so thrive Richard, as thy
      foes may fall;
And as my duty springs, so perish they
180   That grudge one thought° against your majesty.   *hold any grudges*
ALL BUT RICHARD AND SOMERSET   Welcome, high prince, the
         mighty Duke of York!
SOMERSET [*aside*]   Perish, base prince, ignoble Duke of York!
GLOUCESTER   Now will it best avail your majesty
To cross the seas and to be crowned in France.
185   The presence of a king engenders love
Amongst his subjects and his loyal friends,
As it disanimates° his enemies.   *discourages*
KING HENRY   When Gloucester says the word, King Henry goes,
For friendly counsel cuts off many foes.
190   GLOUCESTER   Your ships already are in readiness.
                  Sennet.[2] *Exeunt. Manet*° EXETER   *Remains*
EXETER   Ay, we may march in England or in France,
Not seeing what is likely to ensue.
This late° dissension grown betwixt the peers   *recent*
Burns under feignèd ashes of forgèd love,
195   And will at last break out into a flame.
As festered members° rot but by degree   *parts of the body*
Till bones and flesh and sinews fall away,
So will this base and envious discord breed.
And now I fear that fatal prophecy
200   Which, in the time of Henry named the Fifth,
Was in the mouth of every sucking babe:
That 'Henry born at Monmouth° should win all,   *(Henry V)*
And Henry born at Windsor° should lose all'—   *(Henry VI)*
Which is so plain that Exeter doth wish
205   His days may finish, ere that hapless time.   *Exit*

3.2

*Enter [*JOAN *la] Pucelle, disguised, with four [French]*
SOLDIERS *with sacks upon their backs*
JOAN   These are the city gates, the gates of Rouen,
Through which our policy° must make a breach.   *trickery*
Take heed. Be wary how you place your words.
Talk like the vulgar° sort of market men   *common*
5   That come to gather money for their corn.°   *grain*
If we have entrance, as I hope we shall,
And that° we find the slothful watch but weak,   *if*

---

2. Trumpet notes that accompany a procession.   **3.2.** Location: In and around Rouen, France.

I'll by a sign give notice to our friends,
That Charles the Dauphin may encounter them.
10 A SOLDIER Our sacks shall be a mean° to sack the city,   *means*
And we be lords and rulers over Rouen.
Therefore we'll knock.
        [*They*] *knock*
WATCH [*within*] Qui là?°   *Who is there*
JOAN   *Paysans, la pauvre gens de France:*[1]
Poor market folks that come to sell their corn.
15 WATCH [*opening the gates*] Enter, go in. The market bell is rung.
JOAN [*aside*] Now, Rouen, I'll shake thy bulwarks to the ground.
                                                                              Exeunt

3.3

Enter CHARLES [*the Dauphin, the*] BASTARD
[*of Orléans, the Duke of*] ALENÇON[, RENÉ *Duke of*
Anjou, and French soldiers]

CHARLES Saint Denis bless this happy stratagem,
And once again we'll sleep secure in Rouen.
BASTARD Here entered Pucelle and her practisants.°   *conspirators*
Now she is there, how will she specify
5   'Here is the best and safest passage in'?
RENÉ By thrusting out a torch from yonder tower—
Which, once discerned, shows that her meaning is:
No way to that, for weakness, which she entered.[1]
        Enter [JOAN *la*] *Pucelle on the top, thrusting out a torch*
        burning
JOAN Behold, this is the happy wedding torch
10   That joineth Rouen unto her countrymen,
But burning fatal to the Talbonites.°   *followers of Talbot*
BASTARD See, noble Charles, the beacon of our friend.
The burning torch in yonder turret stands.
CHARLES Now shine it° like a comet of revenge,   *may it shine*
15   A prophet to the fall of all our foes!
RENÉ Defer no time; delays have dangerous ends.
Enter and cry, 'The Dauphin!', presently,°   *at once*
And then do execution on the watch.°   *Alarum.* [*Exeunt*]   *then kill the guards*

3.4

An alarum. [*Enter Lord*] TALBOT *in an excursion°*   *a skirmish*
TALBOT France, thou shalt rue this treason with thy tears,
If Talbot but survive thy treachery.
Pucelle, that witch, that damnèd sorceress,
Hath wrought this hellish mischief unawares,°   *unexpectedly*
5   That hardly we escaped the pride of France.[1]   *Exit*

---

1. Peasants, the poor folk of France.
3.3 Location: Scene continues.
1. No entrance is as weakly guarded as the one she entered.

3.4 Location: Scene continues.
1. That only with difficulty we escaped the princely power of France.

3.5

An alarum. Excursions. [The Duke of] BEDFORD
brought in sick, in a chair. Enter [Lord] TALBOT and
[the Duke of] BURGUNDY, without; within,[1] *[JOAN la]*
Pucelle, CHARLES [the Dauphin, the] BASTARD
[of Orléans, the Duke of ALENÇON], and RENÉ [Duke
of Anjou] on the walls

JOAN   Good morrow gallants. Want ye corn for bread?
   I think the Duke of Burgundy will fast
   Before he'll buy again at such a rate.
   'Twas full of darnel.° Do you like the taste?   *weeds*
5 BURGUNDY   Scoff on, vile fiend and shameless courtesan.
   I trust ere long to choke thee with thine own,°   *your own bread*
   And make thee curse the harvest of that corn.
CHARLES   Your grace may starve, perhaps, before that time.
BEDFORD   O let no words, but deeds, revenge this treason.
10 JOAN   What will you do, good graybeard? Break a lance
   And run a-tilt at° death within a chair?   *joust with*
TALBOT   Foul fiend of France, and hag of all despite,°   *most despicable*
   Encompassed with thy lustful paramours,
   Becomes it thee to taunt his valiant age
15   And twit with cowardice a man half dead?
   Damsel, I'll have a bout° with you again,   *fight; sexual struggle*
   Or else let Talbot perish with this shame.
JOAN   Are ye so hot,° sir?—Yet, Pucelle, hold thy peace.   *angry; lustful*
   If Talbot do but thunder, rain will follow.
      They [the English] whisper together in counsel
20   God speed the parliament; who shall be the Speaker?
TALBOT   Dare ye come forth and meet us in the field?
JOAN   Belike your lordship takes us then for fools,
   To try if that our own be ours or no.
TALBOT   I speak not to that railing Hecate[2]
25   But unto thee, Alençon, and the rest.
   Will ye, like soldiers, come and fight it out?
ALENÇON   Seignieur, no.
TALBOT   Seignieur, hang! Base muleteers° of   *Lowborn mule drivers*
   France,
   Like peasant footboys do they keep° the walls   *stay near*
   And dare not take up arms like gentlemen.
30 JOAN   Away, captains, let's get us from the walls,
   For Talbot means no goodness by his looks.
   Goodbye, my lord. We came but to tell you
   That we are here.   *Exeunt [French] from the walls*
TALBOT   And there will we be, too, ere it be long,
35   Or else reproach be Talbot's greatest fame.
   Vow Burgundy, by honour of thy house,
   Pricked on° by public wrongs sustained in France,   *Urged on*
   Either to get the town again or die.
   And I—as sure as English Henry lives,
40   And as his father here was conqueror;[3]

3.5 Location: Scene continues.
1. The stage directions suggest that Talbot's party is on the main stage; Joan's party may appear on the upper stage gallery.
2. In classical mythology, the goddess of night and the underworld and the patron of witchcraft.
3. Henry V had captured Rouen in 1419.

As sure as in this late° betrayèd town   *recently*
Great Cœur-de-lion's heart was buried[4]—
So sure I swear to get the town or die.

BURGUNDY   My vows are equal partners with thy vows.

45   TALBOT   But ere we go, regard this dying prince,
The valiant Duke of Bedford. [*To* BEDFORD] Come, my lord,
We will bestow you in some better place,
Fitter for sickness and for crazy° age.   *feeble*

BEDFORD   Lord Talbot, do not so dishonour me.
50   Here will I sit before the walls of Rouen,
And will be partner of your weal° or woe.   *happiness*

BURGUNDY   Courageous Bedford, let us now persuade you.

BEDFORD   Not to be gone from hence; for once I read
That stout Pendragon,[5] in his litter sick,
55   Came to the field and vanquishèd his foes.
Methinks I should revive the soldiers' hearts,
Because I ever found them as myself.

TALBOT   Undaunted spirit in a dying breast!
Then be it so; heavens keep old Bedford safe.
60   And now no more ado, brave Burgundy,
But gather we our forces out of hand,°   *at once*
And set upon our boasting enemy.   *Exit* [*with* BURGUNDY]
An alarum. Excursions. Enter Sir John FASTOLF
and a CAPTAIN

CAPTAIN   Whither away, Sir John Fastolf, in such haste?

FASTOLF   Whither away? To save myself by flight.
65   We are like to have the overthrow° again.   *to be defeated*

CAPTAIN   What, will you fly, and leave Lord Talbot?

FASTOLF   Ay, all the Talbots in the world, to save my life.   *Exit*

CAPTAIN   Cowardly knight, ill fortune follow thee!   *Exit*
Retreat. Excursions. [JOAN *la*] *Pucelle,* ALENÇON,
and CHARLES *fly*

BEDFORD   Now, quiet soul, depart when heaven please,
70   For I have seen our enemies' overthrow.
What is the trust or strength of foolish man?
They that of late were daring with their scoffs
Are glad and fain° by flight to save themselves.   *eager*
BEDFORD *dies, and is carried in by two in his chair*

3.6

An alarum. Enter [*Lord*] TALBOT, [*the Duke of*]
BURGUNDY, *and the rest* [*of the English soldiers*]

TALBOT   Lost and recovered in a day again!
This is a double honour, Burgundy;
Yet heavens have glory for this victory!

BURGUNDY   Warlike and martial Talbot, Burgundy
5   Enshrines thee in his heart, and there erects
Thy noble deeds as valour's monuments.

TALBOT   Thanks, gentle° Duke. But where is Pucelle now?   *noble*
I think her old familiar° is asleep.   *attendant demon*

---

4. According to Holinshed's *Chronicles*, Richard
Cœur-de-Lion (the Lion-Hearted), who ruled England
from 1189 to 1199, willed that his heart be buried in
Rouen as a sign of his love for the city.

5. Uther Pendragon, the father of King Arthur. This
story is told in Geoffrey of Monmouth's history of
Britain (*Historia Regum Britanniae*). stout: brave.
3.6 Location: Scene continues.

Now where's the Bastard's braves,° and Charles his gleeks?°   *boasts / Charles's jests*
10 What, all amort?° Rouen hangs her head for grief   *dispirited*
That such a valiant company are fled.
Now will we take some order° in the town,   *establish order*
Placing therein some expert officers,
And then depart to Paris, to the King,
15 For there young Henry with his nobles lie.°   *lives*
BURGUNDY   What wills Lord Talbot pleaseth Burgundy.
TALBOT   But yet, before we go, let's not forget
The noble Duke of Bedford late deceased,
But see his exequies° fulfilled in Rouen.   *funeral rites*
20 A braver soldier never couchèd° lance;   *leveled (for attack)*
A gentler heart did never sway in court.
But kings and mightiest potentates must die,
For that's the end of human misery.   *Exeunt*

3.7

Enter CHARLES [*the Dauphin, the*] BASTARD [*of Orléans,
the Duke of*] ALENÇON, [JOAN *la*] *Pucelle* [*and French
soldiers*]

JOAN   Dismay not, princes, at this accident,
Nor grieve that Rouen is so recoverèd.
Care° is no cure, but rather corrosive,°   *Sorrow / destructive*
For things that are not to be remedied.
5 Let frantic° Talbot triumph for a while,   *mad*
And like a peacock sweep along his tail;
We'll pull his plumes and take away his train,°   *peacock's tail; army*
If Dauphin and the rest will be but ruled.
CHARLES   We have been guided by thee hitherto,
10 And of thy cunning had no diffidence.°   *doubt*
One sudden foil° shall never breed distrust.   *defeat*
BASTARD [*to* JOAN]   Search out thy wit for secret policies,°   *stratagems*
And we will make thee famous through the world.
ALENÇON [*to* JOAN]   We'll set thy statue in some holy place
15 And have thee reverenced like a blessèd saint.
Employ thee then, sweet virgin, for our good.
JOAN   Then thus it must be; this doth Joan devise:
By fair persuasions mixed with sugared words
We will entice the Duke of Burgundy
20 To leave the Talbot and to follow us.
CHARLES   Ay, marry, sweeting,° if we could do that   *(a lover's nickname)*
France were no place for Henry's warriors,
Nor should that nation boast it so with us,
But be extirpèd° from our provinces.   *rooted out*
25 ALENÇON   For ever should they be expulsed from France
And not have title of an earldom here.
JOAN   Your honours shall perceive how I will work
To bring this matter to the wishèd end.
     Drum sounds afar off
Hark, by the sound of drum you may perceive
30 Their powers are marching unto Paris-ward.°   *toward Paris*
     Here sound an English march

3.7 Location: Plains near Rouen.

There goes the Talbot, with his colours spread,°   *flags unfurled*
And all the troops of English after him.
    [*Here sound a*] *French march*
Now in the rearward comes the Duke and his;
Fortune in favour° makes him lag behind.   *as a favor to us*
35   Summon a parley.[1] We will talk with him.
    Trumpets sound a parley
CHARLES [*calling*]   A parley with the Duke of Burgundy.
    [*Enter the Duke of* BURGUNDY]
BURGUNDY   Who craves a parley with the Burgundy?
JOAN   The princely Charles of France, thy countryman.
BURGUNDY   What sayst thou, Charles?—for I am marching hence.
40   CHARLES   Speak, Pucelle, and enchant him with thy words.
JOAN   Brave Burgundy, undoubted° hope of France,   *certain*
    Stay. Let thy humble handmaid speak to thee.
BURGUNDY   Speak on, but be not over-tedious.
JOAN   Look on thy country, look on fertile France,
45   And see the cities and the towns defaced
    By wasting ruin of the cruel foe.
    As looks the mother on her lowly babe
    When death doth close his tender-dying° eyes,   *young-dying*
    See, see the pining malady of France;
50   Behold the wounds, the most unnatural wounds,
    Which thou thyself hast given her woeful breast.
    O turn thy edgèd sword another way,
    Strike those that hurt, and hurt not those that help.
    One drop of blood drawn from thy country's bosom
55   Should grieve thee more than streams of foreign gore.
    Return thee, therefore, with a flood of tears,
    And wash away thy country's stainèd spots.[2]
BURGUNDY [*aside*]   Either she hath bewitched me with her words,
    Or nature makes me suddenly relent.
60   JOAN   Besides, all French and France exclaims on° thee,   *denounces*
    Doubting thy birth and lawful progeny.°   *ancestry*
    Who join'st thou with but with a lordly nation
    That will not trust thee but for profit's sake?
    When Talbot hath set footing once in France
65   And fashioned thee that instrument of ill,
    Who then but English Henry will be lord,
    And thou be thrust out like a fugitive?
    Call we to mind, and mark but this for proof:
    Was not the Duke of Orléans thy foe?
70   And was he not in England prisoner?
    But when they heard he was thine enemy
    They set him free, without his ransom paid,
    In spite of Burgundy and all his friends.[3]
    See, then, thou fight'st against thy countrymen,
75   And join'st with them will be thy slaughtermen.
    Come, come, return; return, thou wandering lord,

---

1. Sound a trumpet to request a conference.
2. And wash away the spots of blood that defile your country.
3. The historical Orléans was not released by the English until five years after Burgundy abandoned the English alliance.

Charles and the rest will take thee in their arms.

BURGUNDY [*aside*] I am vanquishèd.[4] These haughty° words of hers   *lofty*
Have battered me like roaring cannon-shot
80   And made me almost yield upon my knees.
[*To the others*] Forgive me, country, and sweet countrymen;
And lords, accept this hearty kind embrace.
My forces and my power of men are yours.
So farewell, Talbot. I'll no longer trust thee.
85   JOAN Done like a Frenchman—[*aside*] turn and turn again.
CHARLES Welcome, brave Duke. Thy friendship makes us fresh.
BASTARD And doth beget new courage in our breasts.
ALENÇON Pucelle hath bravely played her part in this,
And doth deserve a coronet of gold.
90   CHARLES Now let us on, my lords, and join our powers,
And seek how we may prejudice° the foe.   *Exeunt*   *hurt*

3.8

[*Flourish.*] *Enter* KING [HENRY, *the Duke of*] GLOUCES-
TER, [*the Bishop of*] WINCHESTER, [*the Duke of*] EXE-
TER; [RICHARD DUKE OF] YORK, [*the Earl of*] WARWICK,
[*and* VERNON *with white roses; the Earl of*] SUFFOLK,
[*the Duke of*] SOMERSET [*and* BASSET *with red roses*]. *To
them, with his soldiers,* [*enter Lord*] TALBOT

TALBOT My gracious prince and honourable peers,
Hearing of your arrival in this realm
I have a while given truce unto my wars
To do my duty° to my sovereign;   *give homage*
5   In sign whereof, this arm that hath reclaimed
To your obedience fifty fortresses,
Twelve cities, and seven walled towns of strength,
Beside five hundred prisoners of esteem,°   *noble rank*
Lets fall his sword before your highness' feet,
10   And with submissive loyalty of heart
Ascribes the glory of his conquest got
First to my God, and next unto your grace.
[*He kneels*][1]
KING HENRY Is this the Lord Talbot, uncle Gloucester,
That hath so long been resident in France?
15   GLOUCESTER Yes, if it please your majesty, my liege.
KING HENRY [*to* TALBOT] Welcome, brave captain and victorious lord.
When I was young—as yet I am not old—
I do remember how my father said
A stouter champion never handled sword.
20   Long since we were resolvèd° of your truth,°   *convinced / loyalty*
Your faithful service and your toil in war,
Yet never have you tasted our reward,
Or been reguerdoned° with so much as thanks,   *rewarded*
Because till now we never saw your face.

---

4. The historical Burgundy did not return to the
French side until four years after Joan's death.
3.8 Location: The palace, Paris.

1. F does not indicate when Talbot kneels, but he must
do so: at line 25, he is urged to "stand up."

Therefore stand up,
            [TALBOT *rises*]
25   and for these good deserts
We here create you Earl of Shrewsbury;
And in our coronation take your place.²
                    Sennet. Exeunt. Manent° VERNON *and* BASSET   *Remain*
VERNON   Now sir, to you that were so hot° at sea,   *angry*
Disgracing of these colours° that I wear   *this badge (the rose)*
30 In honour of my noble lord of York,
Dar'st thou maintain the former words thou spak'st?
BASSET   Yes, sir, as well as you dare patronage°   *defend*
The envious barking of your saucy tongue
Against my lord the Duke of Somerset.
35 VERNON   Sirrah, thy lord I honour as he is.
BASSET   Why, what is he?—as good a man as York.
VERNON   Hark ye, not so. In witness, take ye that.
            [VERNON] *strikes him*
BASSET   Villain, thou know'st the law of arms³ is such
That whoso draws a sword 'tis present° death,   *immediate*
40 Or else this blow should broach° thy dearest blood.   *tap (as a wine vat)*
But I'll unto his majesty and crave
I may have liberty° to venge this wrong,   *permission*
When thou shalt see I'll meet thee to thy cost.
VERNON   Well, miscreant,° I'll be there as soon as you,   *villain*
45 And after meet you sooner than you would.°   *Exeunt*   *would wish*

4.1

[*Flourish.*] *Enter* KING [HENRY, *the Duke of*]
GLOUCESTER, [*the Bishop of*] WINCHESTER, [*the Duke*
of] EXETER, [RICHARD DUKE OF] YORK, [*and the Earl of*]
WARWICK, [*with white roses; the Earl of*] SUFFOLK, [*and*
the Duke of] SOMERSET, [*with red roses; Lord*] TALBOT,
and [*the*] Governor [*of Paris*]
GLOUCESTER   Lord Bishop, set the crown upon his head.
WINCHESTER   God save King Henry, of that name the sixth!
            [WINCHESTER *crowns the* KING]
GLOUCESTER   Now, Governor of Paris, take your oath
That you elect° no other king but him;   *acknowledge*
5 Esteem none friends but such as are his friends,
And none your foes but such as shall pretend°   *propose*
Malicious practices against his state.
This shall ye do, so help you righteous God.
            Enter [*Sir John*] FASTOLF [*with a letter*]
FASTOLF   My gracious sovereign, as I rode from Calais
10 To haste unto your coronation
A letter was delivered to my hands,
            [*He presents the letter*]
Writ to your grace from th' Duke of Burgundy.
TALBOT   Shame to the Duke of Burgundy and thee!
I vowed, base knight, when I did meet thee next,

---

2. The historical Talbot was created Earl of Shrewsbury in 1442, more than ten years after Henry's coronation.

3. The law that forbade fighting near a royal residence (see also 1.4.45 and 2.4.86).
4.1 Location: The palace, Paris.

15   To tear the Garter[1] from thy craven's° leg,   *coward's*
        [*He tears it off*]
        Which I have done because unworthily
        Thou wast installèd in that high degree.—
        Pardon me, princely Henry and the rest.
        This dastard° at the battle of Patay   *coward*
20   When but in all° I was six thousand strong,   *When all told*
        And that the French were almost ten to one,
        Before we met, or that a stroke was given,
        Like to a trusty° squire did run away;   *faithful (here ironic)*
        In which assault we lost twelve hundred men.
25   Myself and divers gentlemen beside
        Were there surprised and taken prisoners.
        Then judge, great lords, if I have done amiss,
        Or whether that such cowards ought to wear
        This ornament of knighthood: yea or no?
30 GLOUCESTER   To say the truth, this fact° was infamous   *deed*
        And ill beseeming any common man,
        Much more a knight, a captain and a leader.
    TALBOT   When first this order was ordained, my lords,
        Knights of the Garter were of noble birth,
35   Valiant and virtuous, full of haughty° courage,   *lofty*
        Such as were grown to credit° by the wars;   *fame*
        Not fearing death nor shrinking for distress,
        But always resolute in most extremes.°   *in greatest extremities*
        He then that is not furnished in this sort°   *not endowed like this*
40   Doth but usurp the sacred name of knight,
        Profaning this most honourable order,
        And should—if I were worthy to be judge—
        Be quite degraded,° like a hedge-born swain[2]   *reduced in rank*
        That doth presume to boast of gentle° blood.   *noble*
    KING HENRY [*to* FASTOLF]   Stain to thy countrymen, thou hear'st
45   thy doom.°   *sentence*
        Be packing, therefore, thou that wast a knight.
        Henceforth we banish thee on pain of death.   [*Exit* FASTOLF]
        And now, my Lord Protector, view the letter
        Sent from our uncle, Duke of Burgundy.[3]
    GLOUCESTER   What means his grace that he hath changed his
50   style?°   *form of address*
        No more but plain and bluntly 'To the King'?
        Hath he forgot he is his sovereign?
        Or doth this churlish superscription°   *rude address*
        Pretend° some alteration in good will?   *Indicate*
55   What's here? 'I have upon especial cause,
        Moved with compassion of my country's wrack°   *destruction*
        Together with the pitiful complaints
        Of such as your oppression feeds upon,
        Forsaken your pernicious faction
60   And joined with Charles, the rightful King of France.'
        O monstrous treachery! Can this be so?

---

1. A ribbon, worn below the left knee, signifying membership in the Order of the Garter, the highest rank of English knighthood.
2. A lowly or illegitimate country person.
3. Henry VI's uncle, the Duke of Bedford, married Burgundy's sister Anne.

That in alliance, amity, and oaths
There should be found such false dissembling guile?

KING HENRY   What? Doth my uncle Burgundy revolt?

65   GLOUCESTER   He doth, my lord, and is become your foe.

KING HENRY   Is that the worst this letter doth contain?

GLOUCESTER   It is the worst, and all, my lord, he writes.

KING HENRY   Why then, Lord Talbot there shall talk with him
And give him chastisement for this abuse.

70   [*To* TALBOT] How say you, my lord? Are you not content?

TALBOT   Content, my liege? Yes. But that I am prevented,°   *anticipated*
I should have begged I might have been employed.

KING HENRY   Then gather strength and march unto him straight.°   *at once*
Let him perceive how ill we brook° his treason,   *tolerate*

75   And what offence it is to flout his friends.

TALBOT   I go, my lord, in heart desiring still°   *always*
You may behold confusion of your foes.   [*Exit*]

Enter VERNON [*wearing a white rose,*] *and* BASSET [*wearing a red rose*]

VERNON [*to* KING HENRY]   Grant me the combat,° gracious   *permission to duel*
sovereign.

BASSET [*to* KING HENRY]   And me, my lord; grant me the combat, too.

RICHARD DUKE OF YORK [*to* KING HENRY, *pointing to* VERNON]

80   This is my servant;° hear him, noble Prince.   *follower*

SOMERSET [*to* KING HENRY, *pointing to* BASSET]   And this is mine,
sweet Henry; favour him.

KING HENRY   Be patient, lords, and give them leave to speak.
Say, gentlemen, what makes you thus exclaim,
And wherefore crave you combat, or with whom?

85   VERNON   With him, my lord; for he hath done me wrong.

BASSET   And I with him; for he hath done me wrong.

KING HENRY   What is that wrong whereof you both complain?
First let me know, and then I'll answer you.

BASSET   Crossing the sea from England into France,

90   This fellow here with envious carping tongue
Upbraided me about the rose I wear,
Saying the sanguine° colour of the leaves°   *blood-red / petals*
Did represent my master's blushing cheeks
When stubbornly he did repugn° the truth   *reject*

95   About a certain question[4] in the law
Argued betwixt the Duke of York and him,
With other vile and ignominious terms;
In confutation of which rude reproach,
And in defence of my lord's worthiness,

100   I crave the benefit of law of arms.[5]

VERNON   And that is my petition, noble lord;
For though he seem with forgèd quaint conceit°   *false cunning words*
To set a gloss° upon his bold intent,   *good appearance*
Yet know, my lord, I was provoked by him,

105   And he first took exceptions at this badge,
Pronouncing that the paleness of this flower
Bewrayed° the faintness of my master's heart.   *Revealed*

---

4. The "certain question" apparently concerns the
question of York's succession to the throne and the
attainder of his father. See 2.4 and 2.5.45–129.
5. The right to decide the matter in a duel.

RICHARD DUKE OF YORK   Will not this malice, Somerset, be left?°   *put aside*
SOMERSET   Your private grudge, my lord of York, will out,
110   Though ne'er so cunningly you smother it.
KING HENRY   Good Lord, what madness rules in brainsick men
   When for so slight and frivolous a cause
   Such factious emulations° shall arise?   *divisive jealousies*
   Good cousins both of York and Somerset,
115   Quiet yourselves, I pray, and be at peace.
RICHARD DUKE OF YORK   Let this dissension first be tried by fight,
   And then your highness shall command a peace.
SOMERSET   The quarrel toucheth none but us alone;
   Betwixt ourselves let us decide it then.
120 RICHARD DUKE OF YORK   There is my pledge.[6] Accept it, Somerset.
VERNON [*to* KING HENRY]   Nay, let it rest where it began at first.[7]
BASSET [*to* KING HENRY]   Confirm it so, mine honourable lord.
GLOUCESTER   Confirm it so? Confounded be your strife,
   And perish ye with your audacious prate!°   *prattling*
125   Presumptuous vassals, are you not ashamed
   With this immodest clamorous outrage
   To trouble and disturb the King and us?
   And you, my lords, methinks you do not well
   To bear with their perverse objections,°   *accusations*
130   Much less to take occasion° from their mouths   *the opportunity*
   To raise a mutiny betwixt yourselves.
   Let me persuade you take a better course.
EXETER   It grieves his highness. Good my lords, be friends.
KING HENRY   Come hither, you that would be combatants.
135   Henceforth I charge you, as you love our favour,
   Quite to forget this quarrel and the cause.
   And you, my lords, remember where we are—
   In France, amongst a fickle wavering nation.
   If they perceive dissension in our looks,
140   And that within ourselves we disagree,
   How will their grudging stomachs° be provoked   *resentful tempers*
   To wilful disobedience, and rebel!
   Beside, what infamy will there arise
   When foreign princes shall be certified°   *informed*
145   That for a toy,° a thing of no regard,   *trifle*
   King Henry's peers and chief nobility
   Destroyed themselves and lost the realm of France!
   O, think upon the conquest of my father,
   My tender years, and let us not forgo
150   That for a trifle that was bought with blood.[8]
   Let me be umpire in this doubtful° strife.   *uncertain*
   I see no reason, if I wear this rose,
     [*He takes a red rose*]
   That anyone should therefore be suspicious
   I more incline to Somerset than York.
155   Both are my kinsmen, and I love them both.

---

6. A glove or gauntlet thrown down in a duel.
7. Let the quarrel remain with me and Basset, who began it.

8. *let . . . blood:* let us not lose for a trifle what was bought with blood (that is, let us not lose France).

As well they may upbraid me with my crown
Because, forsooth, the King of Scots is crowned.
But your discretions better can persuade
Than I am able to instruct or teach,
160   And therefore, as we hither came in peace,
So let us still continue peace and love.
Cousin of York, we institute° your grace   *appoint*
To be our regent in these parts of France;
And good my lord of Somerset, unite
165   Your troops of horsemen with his bands of foot,°   *infantry*
And like true subjects, sons of your progenitors,
Go cheerfully together and digest°   *dissipate*
Your angry choler on your enemies.
Ourself, my Lord Protector, and the rest,
170   After some respite, will return to Calais,
From thence to England, where I hope ere long
To be presented by your victories
With Charles, Alençon, and that traitorous rout.°   *rabble*
          [*Flourish.*] *Exeunt. Manent* YORK, WARWICK,
                                   VERNON, [*and*] EXETER
WARWICK   My lord of York, I promise you, the King
175   Prettily, methought, did play the orator.
RICHARD DUKE OF YORK   And so he did; but yet I like it not
In that he wears the badge of Somerset.
WARWICK   Tush, that was but his fancy; blame him not.
I dare presume, sweet Prince, he thought no harm.
180   RICHARD DUKE OF YORK   An if I wist° he did—but let it rest.   *If I knew for certain*
Other affairs must now be managèd. *Exeunt. Manet* EXETER
EXETER   Well didst thou, Richard, to suppress thy voice;
For had the passions of thy heart burst out
I fear we should have seen deciphered° there   *revealed*
185   More rancorous spite, more furious raging broils,
Than yet can be imagined or supposed.
But howsoe'er, no simple man that sees
This jarring discord of nobility,
This shouldering of each other in the court,
190   This factious bandying° of their favourites,°   *quarreling / followers*
But that° it doth presage some ill event.°   *But sees that / outcome*
'Tis much when sceptres are in children's hands,
But more when envy breeds unkind° division: *unnatural*
There comes the ruin, there begins confusion.   *Exit*

4.2

          Enter [*Lord*] TALBOT *WITH* [*a*] *trump*[*eter*] *and*
          drum[*mer and soldiers*] *before Bordeaux*
TALBOT   Go to the gates of Bordeaux, trumpeter.
Summon their general unto the wall.
          [*The trumpeter*] *sounds* [*a parley*]. *Enter* [*French*]
          GENERAL, *aloft*
English John Talbot, captain, calls you forth,
Servant in arms to Harry King of England;
5   And thus he would:° open your city gates,   *desires*
Be humble to us, call my sovereign yours

4.2 Location: Before Bordeaux.

And do him homage as obedient subjects,
And I'll withdraw me and my bloody power.
But if you frown upon this proffered peace,
10   You tempt the fury of my three attendants—
Lean famine, quartering° steel, and climbing fire—   *dismembering*
Who in a moment even° with the earth   *level*
Shall lay your stately and air-braving° towers   *air-defying; lofty*
If you forsake the offer of their love.
15   GENERAL   Thou ominous and fearful owl[1] of death,
Our nation's terror and their bloody scourge,
The period° of thy tyranny approacheth.   *end*
On us thou canst not enter but by death,
For I protest we are well fortified
20   And strong enough to issue out and fight.
If thou retire, the Dauphin well appointed°   *equipped*
Stands with the snares of war to tangle thee.
On either hand thee° there are squadrons pitched[2]   *On both sides of you*
To wall thee from the liberty of flight,
25   And no way canst thou turn thee for redress
But death doth front thee with apparent spoil,[3]
And pale destruction meets thee in the face.
Ten thousand French have ta'en the sacrament[4]
To fire their dangerous artillery
30   Upon no Christian soul but English Talbot.
Lo, there thou stand'st, a breathing valiant man
Of an invincible unconquered spirit.
This is the latest° glory of thy praise,   *final*
That I thy enemy due° thee withal,   *endow*
35   For ere the glass° that now begins to run   *hourglass*
Finish the process of his° sandy hour,   *progress of its*
These eyes that see thee now well colourèd°   *in good health*
Shall see thee withered, bloody, pale, and dead.
          Drum afar off
Hark, hark, the Dauphin's drum, a warning bell,
40   Sings heavy music to thy timorous soul,
And mine shall ring thy dire departure out.[5]   *Exit*
TALBOT   He fables not. I hear the enemy.
Out, some light horsemen, and peruse their wings.°   *survey their flanks*
          [*Exit one or more*]
O negligent and heedless° discipline,   *careless*
45   How are we parked° and bounded in a pale!°—   *enclosed / fenced area*
A little herd of England's timorous deer
Mazed with[6] a yelping kennel of French curs.
If we be English deer, be then in blood,°   *vigorous*
Not rascal-like[7] to fall down with a pinch,°   *nip (from hounds)*
50   But rather, moody-mad° and desperate stags,   *enraged*
Turn on the bloody hounds with heads of steel
And make the cowards stand aloof at bay.
Sell every man his life as dear as mine

---

1. The owl's cry was thought to portend evil or death (see Ovid's *Metamorphoses* 10.521–52 and *Macbeth* 2.2.3).
2. Arranged on the field for battle.
3. But death confronts you with obvious destruction.
4. Have received the Christian sacrament of Holy

Communion (as a way of confirming their oaths).
5. And my drum—the alarm signal given when the general's army is to "issue out and fight" (line 20) against Talbot—shall signal your death.
6. Bewildered by; trapped in maze with.
7. Not like lean, worthless deer.

And they shall find dear° deer of us, my friends.   *costly*
55 God and Saint George,° Talbot and England's right,   *England's patron saint*
    Prosper our colours in this dangerous fight!   [*Exeunt*]

4.3

Enter a MESSENGER *that meets* [*the* DUKE OF] YORK.
Enter [RICHARD DUKE OF] YORK *with* [*a*] *trumpet*[*er*] *and
many soldiers*

RICHARD DUKE OF YORK   Are not the speedy scouts returned again
    That dogged° the mighty army of the Dauphin?   *tracked*
MESSENGER   They are returned, my lord, and give it out
    That he is marched to Bordeaux with his power
5   To fight with Talbot. As he marched along,
    By your espials° were discoverèd   *spies*
    Two mightier troops than that the Dauphin led,
    Which joined with him and made their march for Bordeaux.
RICHARD DUKE OF YORK   A plague upon that villain Somerset
10 That thus delays my promisèd supply
    Of horsemen that were levied for this siege!
    Renownèd Talbot doth expect my aid,
    And I am louted° by a traitor villain   *made a fool of*
    And cannot help the noble chevalier.
15 God comfort him in this necessity;
    If he miscarry,° farewell wars in France!   *come to harm*
        Enter another messenger [*Sir William* LUCY]
LUCY[1]   Thou princely leader of our English strength,
    Never so needful on the earth of France,
    Spur to the rescue of the noble Talbot,
20 Who now is girdled with a waste° of iron   *vast expanse; belt*
    And hemmed about with grim destruction.
    To Bordeaux, warlike Duke; to Bordeaux, York,
    Else farewell Talbot, France, and England's honour.
RICHARD DUKE OF YORK   O God, that Somerset, who in proud heart
25 Doth stop my cornets,° were in Talbot's place!   *troops of cavalry*
    So should we save a valiant gentleman
    By forfeiting a traitor and a coward.
    Mad ire and wrathful fury makes me weep,
    That thus we die while remiss° traitors sleep.   *idle; negligent*
30 LUCY   O, send some succour to the distressed lord.
RICHARD DUKE OF YORK   He dies, we lose; I break my warlike word;
    We mourn, France smiles; we lose, they daily get,
    All 'long° of this vile traitor Somerset.   *because*
LUCY   Then God take mercy on brave Talbot's soul,
35 And on his son young John, who two hours since
    I met in travel toward his warlike father.
    This seven years did not Talbot see his son,
    And now they meet where both their lives are done.
RICHARD DUKE OF YORK   Alas, what joy shall noble Talbot have
40 To bid his young son welcome to his grave?

4.3 Location: An unspecified field in France.
1. In F, this and the subsequent three speeches assigned to Lucy are spoken by "Second Messenger" and "Messenger." However, at line 43, York addresses the speaker as "Lucy."

Away—vexation almost stops my breath
That sundered friends greet in the hour of death.
Lucy, farewell. No more my fortune can°   *can do*
But curse the cause I cannot aid the man.
45   Maine, Blois, Poitiers, and Tours are won away
'Long all° of Somerset and his delay.   *Exeunt [all but* LUCY]   *All because*
LUCY   Thus while the vulture of sedition
Feeds in the bosom of such great commanders,
Sleeping neglection° doth betray to loss   *Careless disregard*
50   The conquest of our scarce-cold conqueror,[2]
That ever-living man of memory[3]
Henry the Fifth. Whiles they each other cross,
Lives, honours, lands, and all hurry to loss.   *[Exit]*[4]

4.4

Enter [the Duke of] SOMERSET *with his army*
SOMERSET *[to a* CAPTAIN]   It is too late, I cannot send them now.
This expedition was by York and Talbot
Too rashly plotted. All our general force
Might with a sally of the very town
5   Be buckled with.[1] The over-daring Talbot
Hath sullied all his gloss of former honour
By this unheedful, desperate, wild adventure.
York set him on to fight and die in shame
That, Talbot dead, great York might bear the name.°   *claim preeminence*
    [Enter LUCY]
10   CAPTAIN   Here is Sir William Lucy, who with me
Set from our o'ermatched forces forth for aid.
SOMERSET   How now, Sir William, whither were you sent?
LUCY   Whither, my lord? From bought and sold[2] Lord Talbot,
Who, ringed about with bold adversity,
15   Cries out for noble York and Somerset
To beat assailing death from his weak legions;
And whiles the honourable captain there
Drops bloody sweat from his war-wearied limbs
And, unadvantaged,° ling'ring looks for rescue,   *disadvantaged*
20   You his false hopes, the trust of England's honour,
Keep off aloof with worthless emulation.°   *rivalry*
Let not your private discord keep away
The levied succours° that should lend him aid,   *reinforcements*
While he, renownèd noble gentleman,
25   Yield up his life unto a world of ° odds.   *immense*
Orléans the Bastard, Charles, and Burgundy,
Alençon, René, compass him about,
And Talbot perisheth by your default.
SOMERSET   York set him on; York should have sent him aid.

---

2. The conquest made by our recently dead conqueror.
(The events of this scene actually took place thirty-one
years after the death of the historical Henry V.)
3. That man who will live forever in memory.
4. F does not mark Lucy's exit at this point. Conceivably, he stays onstage as Somerset enters to him.
4.4 Location: Scene continues.
1. *All . . . with:* Our entire army might be engaged by

an attack simply from the French garrison in the town
(without taking into account the other French forces
coming as reinforcements).
2. *bought and sold:* a proverbial expression meaning
"betrayed," perhaps alluding to the biblical account of
Christ's betrayal by his disciple Judas for forty pieces of
silver.

30 LUCY   And York as fast upon your grace exclaims,
        Swearing that you withhold his levied horse
        Collected for this expedition.
   SOMERSET   York lies. He might have sent° and had the horse.   *sent for*
        I owe him little duty and less love,
35   And take foul scorn° to fawn on him by sending.   *find it disgraceful*
   LUCY   The fraud of England, not the force of France,
        Hath now entrapped the noble-minded Talbot.
        Never to England shall he bear his life,
        But dies betrayed to fortune by your strife.
40 SOMERSET   Come, go. I will dispatch the horsemen straight.°   *immediately*
        Within six hours they will be at his aid.
   LUCY   Too late comes rescue. He is ta'en or slain,
        For fly he could not if he would have fled,
        And fly would Talbot never, though he might.
45 SOMERSET   If he be dead, brave Talbot, then adieu.
   LUCY   His fame lives in the world, his shame in you.
                                                    Exeunt [*severally*]

                              4.5
              Enter [*Lord*] TALBOT *and his son* [JOHN]
   TALBOT   O young John Talbot, I did send for thee
        To tutor thee in stratagems of war,
        That Talbot's name might be in thee revived
        When sapless° age and weak unable limbs   *withered*
5   Should bring thy father to his drooping chair.[1]
        But O—malignant and ill-boding stars!—
        Now thou art come unto a feast of death,
        A terrible and unavoided° danger.   *unavoidable*
        Therefore, dear boy, mount on my swiftest horse,
10   And I'll direct thee how thou shalt escape
        By sudden flight. Come, dally not, be gone.
   JOHN   Is my name Talbot, and am I your son,
        And shall I fly? O, if you love my mother,
        Dishonour not her honourable name
15   To make a bastard and a slave of me.
        The world will say he is not Talbot's blood
        That basely fled when noble Talbot stood.
   TALBOT   Fly to revenge my death if I be slain.
   JOHN   He that flies so will ne'er return again.
20 TALBOT   If we both stay, we both are sure to die.
   JOHN   Then let me stay and, father, do you fly.
        Your loss is great; so your regard° should be.   *concern for yourself*
        My worth unknown, no loss is known in me.
        Upon my death the French can little boast;
25   In yours they will: in you all hopes are lost.
        Flight cannot stain the honour you have won,
        But mine it will, that no exploit have done.
        You fled for vantage,° everyone will swear,   *military advantage*
        But if I bow, they'll say it was for fear.
30   There is no hope that ever I will stay
        If the first hour I shrink and run away.

____

4.5 Location: Battlefield near Bordeaux.
1. Chair where he sits wearily, as his strength and life decline.

Here on my knee I beg mortality°   *death*
Rather than life preserved with infamy.
TALBOT   Shall all thy mother's hopes lie in one tomb?
35   JOHN   Ay, rather than I'll shame my mother's womb.
TALBOT   Upon my blessing I command thee go.
JOHN   To fight I will, but not to fly the foe.
TALBOT   Part of thy father may be saved in thee.
JOHN   No part of him but will be shamed in me.
40   TALBOT   Thou never hadst renown, nor canst not lose it.
JOHN   Yes, your renownèd name—shall flight abuse it?
TALBOT   Thy father's charge° shall clear thee from that stain.   *order*
JOHN   You cannot witness for me, being slain.°   *if you are slain*
        If death be so apparent,° then both fly.   *appear so likely*
45   TALBOT   And leave my followers here to fight and die?
        My age° was never tainted with such shame.   *life*
JOHN   And shall my youth be guilty of such blame?
        No more can I be severed from your side
        Than can yourself your self in twain divide.
50   Stay, go, do what you will: the like do I,
        For live I will not if my father die.
TALBOT   Then here I take my leave of thee, fair son,
        Born to eclipse° thy life this afternoon.   *extinguish*
        Come, side by side together live and die,
55   And soul with soul from France to heaven fly.   *Exeunt*

4.6

*Alarum. Excursions, wherein [Lord] Talbot's son [*JOHN*]
is hemmed about [by French soldiers] and* TALBOT
rescues him. [The English drive off the French]
TALBOT   Saint George° and victory! Fight, soldiers, fight!   *patron saint of England*
        The Regent[1] hath with Talbot broke his word,
        And left us to the rage of France his° sword.   *(France's)*
        Where is John Talbot? [*To* JOHN] Pause and take thy breath.
5   I gave thee life, and rescued thee from death.
JOHN   O twice my father, twice am I thy son:
        The life thou gav'st me first was lost and done
        Till with thy warlike sword, despite of fate,
        To my determined° time thou gav'st new date.°   *exactly defined / limit*
10   TALBOT   When from the Dauphin's crest thy sword struck fire
        It warmed thy father's heart with proud desire
        Of bold-faced victory. Then leaden age,
        Quickened with youthful spleen° and warlike rage,   *courage*
        Beat down Alençon, Orléans, Burgundy,
15   And from the pride of Gallia° rescued thee.   *France*
        The ireful Bastard Orléans, that drew blood
        From thee, my boy, and had the maidenhood
        Of thy first fight,[2] I soon encountèred,
        And interchanging blows, I quickly shed
20   Some of his bastard blood, and in disgrace°   *disdain*
        Bespoke him thus: 'Contaminated, base,
        And misbegotten blood I spill of thine,

4.6 Location: Scene continues.
1. York, who was appointed regent at 4.1.162–63.
2. *that drew . . . fight:* an allusion to the notion that a

woman bleeds during her first experience of heterosexual intercourse. So young Talbot has bled during his
first battle.

Mean° and right poor, for that pure blood of mine　　　　　*Base*
Which thou didst force from Talbot, my brave boy.'
25　Here, purposing° the Bastard to destroy,　　　　*as I was intending*
Came in strong rescue. Speak thy father's care:
Art thou not weary, John? How dost thou fare?
Wilt thou yet leave the battle, boy, and fly,
Now thou art sealed° the son of chivalry?　　　　*confirmed*
30　Fly to revenge my death when I am dead;
The help of one stands me in little stead.°　　　　*does me little good*
O, too much folly is it, well I wot,°　　　　*knew*
To hazard all our lives in one small boat.
If I today die not with Frenchmen's rage,
35　Tomorrow I shall die with mickle° age.　　　　*great*
By me they nothing gain, and if I stay
'Tis but the short'ning of my life one day.
In thee thy mother dies, our household's name,
My death's revenge, thy youth, and England's fame.
40　All these and more we hazard by thy stay;
All these are saved if thou wilt fly away.
JOHN　The sword of Orléans hath not made me smart;°　　　　*suffer*
These words of yours draw life-blood from my heart.
On that advantage,[3] bought with such a shame,
45　To save a paltry life and slay bright fame,
Before young Talbot from old Talbot fly
The coward horse that bears me fall° and die;　　　　*may it fall*
And like me° to the peasant boys of France,　　　　*compare me*
To be shame's scorn and subject of mischance![4]
50　Surely, by all the glory you have won,
An if I fly I am not Talbot's son.
Then talk no more of flight; it is no boot.°　　　　*use; profit*
If son to Talbot, die at Talbot's foot.
TALBOT　Then follow thou thy desp'rate sire of Crete,
55　Thou Icarus;[5] thy life to me is sweet.
If thou wilt fight, fight by thy father's side,
And commendable proved, let's die in pride.　　　　*Exeunt*

4.7

Alarum. Excursions. Enter old [Lord] TALBOT *led*
[by a SERVANT*]*
TALBOT　Where is my other life? Mine own is gone.
O where's young Talbot, where is valiant John?
Triumphant death smeared with captivity,°　　　　*the blood of captives*
Young Talbot's valour makes me smile at thee.
5　When he perceived me shrink° and on my knee,　　　　*weaken*
His bloody sword he brandished over me,
And like a hungry lion did commence
Rough deeds of rage and stern impatience.
But when my angry guardant° stood alone,　　　　*protector*
10　Tend'ring° my ruin and assailed of none,　　　　*Concerned for*

3. For the sake of that advantage (of safety).
4. To be an ashamed object of scorn and a victim of misfortune.
5. According to classical mythology, Icarus and his father, Daedalus, tried to escape imprisonment in Crete using artificial wings of feathers and wax. Daedalus succeeded, but Icarus flew too close to the sun and died.
4.7 Location: Scene continues.

Dizzy-eyed fury and great rage of heart
Suddenly made him from my side to start
Into the clust'ring battle° of the French,   *crowded ranks*
And in that sea of blood my boy did drench°   *drown*
15   His over-mounting spirit; and there died
My Icarus, my blossom, in his pride.
      Enter [English soldiers] with John Talbot['s body], borne
SERVANT   O my dear lord, lo where your son is borne.
TALBOT   Thou antic° death, which laugh'st us here to scorn,   *grotesquely grinning*
Anon° from thy insulting tyranny,   *Soon*
20   Coupled in bonds of perpetuity,
Two Talbots wingèd through the lither° sky   *yielding*
In thy despite shall scape mortality.
[To JOHN] O thou whose wounds become hard-favoured death,[1]
Speak to thy father ere thou yield thy breath.
25   Brave° death by speaking, whether he will or no;   *Defy*
Imagine him a Frenchman and thy foe.—
Poor boy, he smiles, methinks, as who° should say   *as one who*
'Had death been French, then death had died today'.
Come, come, and lay him in his father's arms.
      [Soldiers lay JOHN *in Talbot's arms]*
30   My spirit can no longer bear these harms.
Soldiers, adieu. I have what I would have,
Now my old arms are young John Talbot's grave.
      [He] dies. [Alarum. Exeunt soldiers leaving the bodies]
      Enter CHARLES *[the Dauphin, the dukes of]* ALENÇON
      [and] BURGUNDY, *[the]* BASTARD *[of Orléans], and [*JOAN
      la] Pucelle
CHARLES   Had York and Somerset brought rescue in,
We should have found a bloody day of this.
35   BASTARD   How the young whelp of Talbot's,[2] raging wood,°   *mad*
Did flesh his puny sword[3] in Frenchmen's blood!
JOAN   Once I encountered[4] him, and thus I said:
'Thou maiden[5] youth, be vanquished by a maid.'
But with a proud, majestical high scorn
40   He answered thus: 'Young Talbot was not born
To be the pillage of a giglot° wench.'   *plunder of a wanton*
So rushing in the bowels° of the French,   *center*
He left me proudly, as unworthy fight.
BURGUNDY   Doubtless he would have made a noble knight.
45   See where he lies inhearsèd° in the arms   *(as in a coffin)*
Of the most bloody nurser of his harms.[6]
BASTARD   Hew them to pieces, hack their bones asunder,
Whose life was England's glory, Gallia's° wonder.   *France's*
CHARLES   O no, forbear; for that which we have fled
50   During the life, let us not wrong it dead.
      Enter [Sir William] LUCY *[with a French herald]*
LUCY   Herald, conduct me to the Dauphin's tent

---

1. Whose wounds make ugly death attractive.
2. The young puppy of Talbot's (John Talbot). The Bastard is punning on "talbot" as the name for a kind of hunting dog.
3. Plunged in his inexperienced sword for the first time, with a sexual wordplay: plunged in his inexperienced or

diminutive penis for the first time.
4. Another bawdy pun: "encounter" may mean "to meet sexually."
5. Virginal; inexperienced in battle.
6. Person who taught him to harm his enemies; person who caused his injuries.

To know who hath obtained the glory of the day.
CHARLES   On what submissive message art thou sent?
LUCY   Submission, Dauphin? 'Tis a mere° French word.   *pure*
55   We English warriors wot° not what it means.   *know*
I come to know what prisoners thou hast ta'en,
And to survey the bodies of the dead.
CHARLES   For prisoners ask'st thou? Hell our prison is.⁷
But tell me whom thou seek'st.
60   LUCY   But where's the great Alcides⁸ of the field,
Valiant Lord Talbot, Earl of Shrewsbury,
Created for his rare success in arms
Great Earl of Wexford, Waterford, and Valence,
Lord Talbot of Goodrich and Urchinfield,
65   Lord Strange of Blackmere, Lord Verdun of Alton,
Lord Cromwell of Wingfield, Lord Furnival of Sheffield,
The thrice victorious lord of Falconbridge,
Knight of the noble order of Saint George,
Worthy⁹ Saint Michael and the Golden Fleece,
70   Great *Maréhal*° to Henry the Sixth   *commander in chief*
Of all his wars within the realm of France?
JOAN   Here's a silly, stately style° indeed.   *list of titles*
The Turk,° that two-and-fifty kingdoms hath,   *Sultan of Turkey*
Writes not so tedious a style as this.
75   Him that thou magnifi'st with all these titles
Stinking and flyblown° lies here at our feet.   *putrified*
LUCY   Is Talbot slain, the Frenchmen's only scourge,
Your kingdom's terror and black Nemesis?¹
O, were mine eye-balls into bullets turned,
80   That I in rage might shoot them at your faces!
O, that I could but call these dead to life!—
It were enough to fright the realm of France.
Were but his picture left amongst you here
It would amaze° the proudest of you all.   *terrify*
85   Give me their bodies, that I may bear them hence
And give them burial as beseems° their worth.   *as is appropriate to*
JOAN [*to* CHARLES]   I think this upstart is old Talbot's ghost,
He speaks with such a proud commanding spirit.
For God's sake let him have them. To keep them here
90   They would but stink and putrefy the air.
CHARLES   Go, take their bodies hence.
LUCY   I'll bear them hence, but from their ashes shall be reared
A phoenix² that shall make all France afeard.
CHARLES   So we be rid of them, do with them what thou wilt.
            [*Exeunt* LUCY *and herald with the bodies*]
95   And now to Paris in this conquering vein.
All will be ours, now bloody Talbot's slain.   *Exeunt*

7. Charles implies that the French have killed their enemies (sent them to hell) rather than taking prisoners.
8. Hercules (a descendant of Alcaeus), the hero of
classical mythology, famous for performing difficult
feats of strength and bravery.
9. Worthy of; equal in value to. The Order of St.
Michael was a French chivalric order established in

1469, after the events of the play occurred. The Order
of the Golden Fleece was formed in Burgundy in 1430.
1. The Greek goddess of avenging justice.
2. A legendary bird that was said to live five hundred
years, burn itself to ashes, and then be reborn from the
ashes.

5.1

Sennet. Enter KING [HENRY, *the Dukes of*]
    GLOUCESTER, *and* EXETER [*and others*]

KING HENRY [*to* GLOUCESTER]   Have you perused the letters from the Pope,
    The Emperor, and the Earl of Armagnac?
GLOUCESTER   I have, my lord, and their intent is this:
    They humbly sue unto your excellence
5   To have a godly peace concluded of
    Between the realms of England and of France.
KING HENRY   How doth your grace affect their motion?°   *like their proposal*
GLOUCESTER   Well, my good lord, and as the only means
    To stop effusion° of our Christian blood   *spilling*
10   And 'stablish quietness on every side.
KING HENRY   Ay, marry, uncle; for I always thought
    It was both impious and unnatural
    That such immanity° and bloody strife   *barbarity*
    Should reign among professors of one faith.
15 GLOUCESTER   Beside, my lord, the sooner to effect
    And surer bind this knot of amity,
    The Earl of Armagnac, near knit° to Charles—   *closely related*
    A man of great authority in France—
    Proffers his only daughter to your grace
20   In marriage, with a large and sumptuous dowry.
KING HENRY   Marriage, uncle? Alas, my years are young,
    And fitter is my study and my books
    Than wanton dalliance with a paramour.
    Yet call th'ambassadors,   [*Exit one or more*]
                              and as you please,
25   So let them have their answers every one.
    I shall be well content with any choice
    Tends° to God's glory and my country's weal.°   *That tends / welfare*

Enter [*the Bishop of*] WINCHESTER, [*now in cardinal's*
habit,] *and three ambassadors* [*one a Papal* LEGATE]

EXETER [*aside*]   What, is my lord of Winchester installed
    And called unto a cardinal's degree?
30   Then I perceive that will be verified
    Henry the Fifth did sometime° prophesy: *at one time*
    'If once he come to be a cardinal,
    He'll make his cap° co-equal with the crown.'   *(a cardinal's red hat)*
KING HENRY   My lords ambassadors, your several suits
35   Have been considered and debated on.
    Your purpose is both good and reasonable,
    And therefore are we certainly resolved
    To draw° conditions of a friendly peace,   *draft*
    Which by my lord of Winchester we mean
40   Shall be transported presently to France.
GLOUCESTER [*to ambassadors*]   And for the proffer of my lord your master,
    I have informed his highness so at large°   *in full*
    As,° liking of the lady's virtuous gifts,   *That*
    Her beauty, and the value of her dower,
45   He doth intend she shall be England's queen.

5.1 Location: The palace, London.

KING HENRY [*to ambassadors*]   In argument° and proof of which   *As evidence*
    contract
  Bear her this jewel, pledge of my affection.
  [*To* GLOUCESTER] And so, my lord Protector, see them guarded
  And safely brought to Dover, wherein shipped,°   *where once embarked*
50 Commit them to the fortune of the sea.
        Exeunt [*severally all but* WINCHESTER *and* LEGATE]
WINCHESTER   Stay, my lord legate; you shall first receive
  The sum of money which I promisèd
  Should be delivered to his holiness
  For clothing me in these grave ornaments.°   *solemn robes of office*
55 LEGATE   I will attend upon your lordship's leisure.   [*Exit*][1]
WINCHESTER   Now Winchester will not submit, I trow,°   *trust*
  Or be inferior to the proudest peer.
  Humphrey of Gloucester, thou shalt well perceive
  That nor° in birth or for authority   *neither*
60 The Bishop will be overborne° by thee.   *overruled*
  I'll either make thee stoop and bend thy knee,
  Or sack this country with a mutiny.°   *Exit*   *an open revolt*

5.2

Enter CHARLES [*the Dauphin reading a letter,*
the Dukes of] BURGUNDY [*and*] ALENÇON, [*the*]
BASTARD [*of Orléans*], RENÉ [*Duke of Anjou*], *and* JOAN
[*la Pucelle*]

CHARLES   These news, my lords, may cheer our drooping spirits.
  'Tis said the stout° Parisians do revolt   *valiant*
  And turn again unto the warlike French.
ALENÇON   Then march to Paris, royal Charles of France,
5 And keep not back your powers in dalliance.°   *idleness*
JOAN   Peace be amongst them if they turn to us;
  Else, ruin combat with their palaces![1]
        Enter [*a*] SCOUT
SCOUT   Success unto our valiant general,
  And happiness to his accomplices.°   *allies*
10 CHARLES   What tidings send our scouts? I prithee speak.
SCOUT   The English army, that divided was
  Into two parties, is now conjoined in one,[2]
  And means to give you battle presently.°   *immediately*
CHARLES   Somewhat too sudden, sirs, the warning is;
15 But we will presently provide for them.
BURGUNDY   I trust the ghost of Talbot is not there.
JOAN   Now he is gone, my lord, you need not fear.[3]
  Of all base passions, fear is most accursed.
  Command the conquest, Charles, it shall be thine;
20 Let Henry fret and all the world repine.°   *complain*
CHARLES   Then on, my lords; and France be fortunate!   *Exeunt*

---

1. The legate may leave at this point, but there is no
exit marked in F. He may simply step to the side while
Winchester makes his final speech and then exit with
the prelate.

5.2 Location: Plains in Anjou, France.
1. Otherwise, let ruin destroy their palaces.
2. In other words, York and Suffolk have joined forces.
3. F assigns this line to Burgundy.

5.3

Alarum. Excursions. Enter JOAN [*la*] *Pucelle*

JOAN   The Regent° conquers, and the Frenchmen fly.   (*Richard Duke of York*)
       Now help, ye charming° spells and periapts,°   *magic / amulets*
       And ye choice spirits that admonish° me   *forewarn*
       And give me signs of future accidents.°   *events*
              Thunder
5   You speedy helpers, that are substitutes°   *deputies*
       Under the lordly monarch of the north,[1]
       Appear, and aid me in this enterprise.
              Enter Fiends
       This speed and quick appearance argues° proof   *offers*
       Of your accustomed° diligence to me.   *customary*
10   Now, ye familiar spirits[2] that are culled
       Out of the powerful regions under earth,
       Help me this once, that France may get the field.°   *win the battle*
              They walk and speak not
       O, hold me not with silence overlong!
       Where I was wont to feed you with my blood,[3]
15   I'll lop a member° off and give it you   *limb*
       In earnest° of a further benefit,   *As an advance payment*
       So you do condescend to help me now.
              They hang their heads
       No hope to have redress? My body shall
       Pay recompense if you will grant my suit.
              They shake their heads
20   Cannot my body nor blood-sacrifice
       Entreat you to your wonted furtherance?°   *usual assistance*
       Then take my soul—my body, soul, and all—
       Before that England give the French the foil.°   *defeat*
              They depart
       See, they forsake me. Now the time is come
25   That France must vail her lofty-plumèd crest[4]
       And let her head fall into England's lap.
       My ancient° incantations are too weak,   *former*
       And hell too strong for me to buckle° with.   *fight; do combat*
       Now, France, thy glory droopeth to the dust.   *Exit*

5.4

Excursions. [The Dukes of] BURGUNDY *and* YORK *fight*
*hand to hand. [The] French fly. [*JOAN *la Pucelle*
is taken]

RICHARD DUKE OF YORK   Damsel of France, I think I have you fast.
       Unchain your spirits now with spelling° charms,   *conjuring*
       And try if they can gain your liberty.
       A goodly prize, fit for the devil's grace![1]
5   [*To his soldiers*] See how the ugly witch doth bend her brows,°   *scowls*
       As if with Circe[2] she would change my shape.

5.3 Location: Before Angiers (i.e., Angers), France.
1. The devil and his demons were frequently associated with the north.
2. Attendant spirits that could be summoned by a witch; often they inhabited the bodies of animals.
3. Witches were thought to have extra nipples with which they fed their familiars, or attendant spirits.

4. Must lower her high-feathered helmet.
5.4 Location: Scene continues.
1. Fit for his grace, the devil (said sarcastically).
2. According to Greek mythology, a witch who seduced Odysseus and turned his men into swine (see Homer, *Odyssey* 10).

JOAN   Changed to a worser shape thou canst not be.

RICHARD DUKE OF YORK   O, Charles the Dauphin is a proper° man.   *handsome*
  No shape but his can please your dainty° eye.   *fastidious*

10 JOAN   A plaguing mischief light on Charles and thee,
  And may ye both be suddenly surprised
  By bloody hands in° sleeping on your beds!   *while*

RICHARD DUKE OF YORK   Fell banning° hag, enchantress, hold   *Fierce cursing*
  thy tongue.

JOAN   I prithee give me leave to curse awhile.

RICHARD DUKE OF YORK   Curse, miscreant,° when thou comest   *heretic*
15 to the stake.   *Exeunt*

5.5

Alarum. Enter [the Earl of] SUFFOLK *with* MARGARET
in his hand°   *led by the hand*

SUFFOLK   Be what thou wilt, thou art my prisoner.
  [He] gazes on her
  O fairest beauty, do not fear nor fly,
  For I will touch thee but with reverent hands,
  And lay them gently on thy tender side.

5 I kiss these fingers for eternal peace.
  Who art thou? Say, that I may honour thee.

MARGARET   Margaret my name, and daughter to a king,
  The King of Naples,[1] whosoe'er thou art.

SUFFOLK   An earl I am, and Suffolk am I called.

10 Be not offended, nature's miracle,
  Thou art allotted° to be ta'en by me.   *destined*
  So doth the swan his downy cygnets save,°   *young swans protect*
  Keeping them prisoner underneath his wings.
  Yet if this servile usage° once offend,   *treatment as a slave*
15 Go, and be free again, as Suffolk's friend.
    She is going
  O stay! *[Aside]* I have no power to let her pass.
  My hand would free her, but my heart says no.
  As plays the sun upon the glassy stream,
  Twinkling another counterfeited° beam,   *reflected*
20 So seems this gorgeous beauty to mine eyes.
  Fain would I woo her, yet I dare not speak.
  I'll call for pen and ink, and write my mind.
  Fie, de la Pole,[2] disable° not thyself!   *disparage*
  Hast not a tongue? Is she not here to hear?
25 Wilt thou be daunted at a woman's sight?[3]
  Ay, beauty's princely majesty is such
  Confounds° the tongue, and makes the senses rough.°   *That it confuses / dull*

MARGARET   Say, Earl of Suffolk—if thy name be so—
  What ransom must I pay before I pass?
30 For I perceive I am thy prisoner.

SUFFOLK *[aside]*   How canst thou tell she will deny° thy suit   *refuse*

5.5 Location: Scene continues.
1. That is, the René of earlier scenes, Duke of Anjou and also titular King of Naples and Sicily.
2. Suffolk's family name.
3. At the sight of a woman; at a woman's gaze.

Before thou make a trial of her love?

MARGARET   Why speak'st thou not? What ransom must I pay?

SUFFOLK [*aside*]   She's beautiful, and therefore to be wooed;

35   She is a woman, therefore to be won.

MARGARET   Wilt thou accept of ransom, yea or no?

SUFFOLK [*aside*]   Fond° man, remember that thou hast a wife;   *Foolish*

Then how can Margaret be thy paramour?°   *mistress*

MARGARET [*aside*]   I were best to leave him, for he will not hear.

40   SUFFOLK [*aside*]   There° all is marred; there lies a cooling card.[4]   *By that fact*

MARGARET [*aside*]   He talks at random; sure the man is mad.

SUFFOLK [*aside*]   And yet a dispensation[5] may be had.

MARGARET   And yet I would that you would answer me.

SUFFOLK [*aside*]   I'll win this Lady Margaret. For whom?

45   Why, for my king—tush, that's a wooden[6] thing.

MARGARET [*aside*]   He talks of wood. It is some carpenter.

SUFFOLK [*aside*]   Yet so my fancy° may be satisfied,   *love*

And peace establishèd between these realms.

But there remains a scruple° in that too,   *an objection*

50   For though her father be the King of Naples,

Duke of Anjou and Maine, yet is he poor,

And our nobility will scorn the match.

MARGARET   Hear ye, captain? Are you not at leisure?

SUFFOLK [*aside*]   It shall be so, disdain they ne'er so much.

55   Henry is youthful, and will quickly yield.

[*To* MARGARET] Madam, I have a secret to reveal.

MARGARET [*aside*]   What though I be enthrallèd,° he seems a knight   *taken captive*

And will not any way dishonour me.

SUFFOLK   Lady, vouchsafe to listen° what I say.   *listen to*

60   MARGARET [*aside*]   Perhaps I shall be rescued by the French,

And then I need not crave his courtesy.

SUFFOLK   Sweet madam, give me hearing in a cause.

MARGARET [*aside*]   Tush, women have been captivate[7] ere now.

SUFFOLK   Lady, wherefore talk you so?

65   MARGARET   I cry you mercy, 'tis but *quid* for *quo*.°   *tit for tat*

SUFFOLK   Say, gentle Princess, would you not suppose

Your bondage happy to be° made a queen?   *if you were to be*

MARGARET   To be a queen in bondage is more vile

Than is a slave in base servility,°   *slavery*

For princes should be free.

70   SUFFOLK   And so shall you,

If happy England's royal king be free.

MARGARET   Why, what concerns his freedom unto me?

SUFFOLK   I'll undertake to make thee Henry's queen,

To put a golden sceptre in thy hand,

75   And set a precious crown upon thy head,

If thou wilt condescend° to be my—   *agree*

MARGARET   What?

SUFFOLK   His love.

MARGARET   I am unworthy to be Henry's wife.

---

4. An obstacle; literally, a card that, when played, dashes the hopes of one's opponent.
5. Special permission from the Pope to dissolve a marriage.
6. Stupid (referring either to King Henry or to his own scheme to woo Margaret).
7. Have been taken prisoner; have fallen in love against their will.

SUFFOLK No, gentle madam, I unworthy am
80 To woo so fair a dame to be his wife
    [*Aside*] And have no portion° in the choice myself.—   *share*
    How say you, madam; are ye so content?
MARGARET An if my father please, I am content.
SUFFOLK Then call our captains and our colours forth,
    [*Enter captains, colours, and trumpeters*]
85 And, madam, at your father's castle walls
    We'll crave a parley to confer with him.
        Sound [a parley]. Enter RENÉ [*Duke of Anjou*]
        on the walls
    See, René, see thy daughter prisoner.
RENÉ To whom?
SUFFOLK   To me.
RENÉ   Suffolk, what remedy?
    I am a soldier, and unapt° to weep   *unsuited*
90 Or to exclaim on° fortune's fickleness.   *complain of*
SUFFOLK Yes, there is remedy enough, my lord.
    Assent, and for thy honour give consent
    Thy daughter shall be wedded to my king,
    Whom I with pain have wooed and won thereto;
95 And this her easy-held° imprisonment   *easily endured*
    Hath gained thy daughter princely liberty.
RENÉ Speaks Suffolk as he thinks?
SUFFOLK   Fair Margaret knows
    That Suffolk doth not flatter, face° or feign.   *deceive*
RENÉ Upon thy princely warrant° I descend   *guarantee*
100 To give thee answer of thy just demand.
SUFFOLK And here I will expect° thy coming.   *await*
                        [*Exit* RENÉ *above*]
        Trumpets sound. Enter RENÉ
RENÉ Welcome, brave Earl, into our territories.
    Command in Anjou what your honour pleases.
SUFFOLK Thanks, René, happy for° so sweet a child,   *fortunate in having*
105 Fit to be made companion with a king,
    What answer makes your grace unto my suit?
RENÉ Since thou dost deign to woo her little worth
    To be the princely bride of such a lord,
    Upon condition I may quietly
110 Enjoy mine own, the countries Maine and Anjou,
    Free from oppression or the stroke of war,
    My daughter shall be Henry's, if he please.
SUFFOLK That is her ransom. I deliver her,
    And those two counties° I will undertake   *domains of a count*
115 Your grace shall well and quietly enjoy.
RENÉ And I again° in Henry's royal name,   *in return*
    As deputy unto that gracious king,
    Give thee her hand for sign of plighted faith.°   *a marriage pledge*
SUFFOLK René of France, I give thee kingly thanks,
120 Because this is in traffic° of a king.   *business*
    [*Aside*] And yet methinks I could be well content
    To be mine own attorney in this case.[8]
    [*To* RENÉ] I'll over then to England with this news,

8. To act on my own behalf in this instance, with a pun on "case" as slang for "vagina."

And make this marriage to be solemnized.
125   So farewell, René; set this diamond safe
      In golden palaces, as it becomes.°   *as befits it*
RENÉ   I do embrace thee as I would embrace
      The Christian prince King Henry, were he here.
MARGARET [*to* SUFFOLK]   Farewell, my lord. Good wishes, praise, and prayers
130   Shall Suffolk ever have of Margaret.
          She is going
SUFFOLK   Farewell, sweet madam; but hark you, Margaret—
      No princely commendations° to my king?   *greetings*
MARGARET   Such commendations as becomes a maid,
      A virgin, and his servant, say to him.
135 SUFFOLK   Words sweetly placed, and modestly directed.
          [*She is going*]
      But madam, I must trouble you again—
      No loving token to his majesty?
MARGARET   Yes, my good lord: a pure unspotted heart,
      Never yet taint° with love, I send the King.   *tinged*
140 SUFFOLK   And this withal.°   *in addition*
          [*He*] kiss[*es*] *her*
MARGARET   That for thyself; I will not so presume
      To send such peevish° tokens to a king.   *trifling*
          [*Exeunt* RENÉ *and* MARGARET]
SUFFOLK [*aside*]   O, wert thou for myself!—but Suffolk, stay.
      Thou mayst not wander in that labyrinth.⁹
145   There Minotaurs and ugly treasons lurk.
      Solicit° Henry with her wondrous praise.   *Entice*
      Bethink thee on her virtues that surmount,
      Mad° natural graces that extinguish° art.   *Extravagant / eclipse*
      Repeat their semblance¹ often on the seas,
150   That when thou com'st to kneel at Henry's feet
      Thou mayst bereave° him of his wits with wonder.   *Exeunt*   *dispossess*

5.6

      Enter [RICHARD DUKE OF] YORK, [*the Earl of*]
      WARWICK, [*and a*] SHEPHERD
RICHARD DUKE OF YORK   Bring forth that sorceress condemned
      to burn.
          [*Enter* JOAN *la Pucelle guarded*]¹
SHEPHERD   Ah, Joan, this kills thy father's heart outright.
      Have I sought° every country far and near,   *searched*
      And now it is my chance to find thee out°   *discover you*
5   Must I behold thy timeless° cruel death?   *untimely*
      Ah Joan, sweet daughter Joan, I'll die with thee.
JOAN   Decrepit miser,° base ignoble wretch,   *miserable person*
      I am descended of a gentler° blood.   *more aristocratic*
      Thou art no father nor no friend° of mine.   *kinsman*
10 SHEPHERD   Out, out!—My lords, an't please you, 'tis not so.

---

9. A maze built by Daedalus for King Minos of Crete, who kept in it the Minotaur (a monster born from Queen Pasiphaë's sexual encounter with a bull).
1. Recall the image or description of her virtues.
5.6 Location: Camp of the Duke of York, France.

1. In F, Joan is included in the list of those who enter at the beginning of this scene, but it makes sense to have her enter after York commands that she be brought forth.

I did beget her, all the parish knows.
Her mother liveth yet, can testify
She was the first fruit of my bach'lorship.²
WARWICK [*to* JOAN]   Graceless,° wilt thou deny thy parentage?   *Depraved person*
RICHARD DUKE OF YORK   This argues° what her kind of life hath   *testifies to*
15   been—
Wicked and vile; and so her death concludes.°   *confirms; ends*
SHEPHERD   Fie, Joan, that thou wilt be so obstacle.³
God knows thou art a collop° of my flesh,   *slice*
And for thy sake have I shed many a tear.
20   Deny me not, I prithee, gentle Joan.
JOAN   Peasant, avaunt! [*To the English*] You have suborned⁴ this man
Of purpose to obscure my noble birth.
SHEPHERD [*to the English*]   'Tis true I gave a noble⁵ to the priest
The morn that I was wedded to her mother.
25   [*To* JOAN] Kneel down, and take my blessing, good my girl.
Wilt thou not stoop? Now cursèd be the time
Of thy nativity. I would the milk
Thy mother gave thee when thou sucked'st her breast
Had been a little ratsbane° for thy sake.   *rat poison*
30   Or else, when thou didst keep° my lambs afield,   *tend*
I wish some ravenous wolf had eaten thee.
Dost thou deny thy father, cursèd drab?°   *whore*
[*To the English*] O burn her, burn her! Hanging is too good.
                                                                        Exit
RICHARD DUKE OF YORK [*to guards*]   Take her away, for she hath
        lived too long,
35   To fill the world with vicious qualities.
JOAN   First let me tell you whom you have condemned:
Not one begotten of a shepherd swain,
But issued from the progeny of kings;
Virtuous and holy, chosen from above
40   By inspiration of celestial grace
To work exceeding° miracles on earth.   *exceptional*
I never had to do with wicked spirits.
But you that are polluted with your lusts,
Stained with the guiltless blood of innocents,
45   Corrupt and tainted with a thousand vices—
Because you want° the grace that others have,   *lack*
You judge it straight° a thing impossible   *immediately*
To compass° wonders but by help of devils.   *accomplish*
No, misconceivèd⁶ Joan of Arc hath been
50   A virgin from her tender infancy,
Chaste and immaculate in very thought,
Whose maiden-blood thus rigorously effused°   *cruelly shed*
Will cry for vengeance at the gates of heaven.
RICHARD DUKE OF YORK   Ay, ay, [*to guards*] away with her to execution.
55   WARWICK [*to guards*]   And hark ye, sirs: because she is a maid,
Spare for no faggots. Let there be enough.

---

2. The first child I had as an unmarried man.
3. Obstinate. This use of "obstacle" suggests the shepherd's country dialect.
4. Hired to give false evidence.

5. English gold coin worth about one-third of a pound.
6. Misunderstood, with a pun on "misconceived" as "miscreated in the womb."

Place barrels of pitch upon the fatal stake,
That so her torture may be shortenèd.[7]

JOAN   Will nothing turn° your unrelenting hearts?   *change*
60   Then Joan, discover° thine infirmity,   *reveal*
That warranteth by law to be thy privilege:[8]
I am with child, ye bloody homicides.
Murder not then the fruit within my womb,
Although ye hale° me to a violent death.   *drag*
RICHARD DUKE OF YORK   Now heaven forfend—the holy maid
65   with child?
WARWICK [*to* JOAN]   The greatest miracle that e'er ye wrought.
Is all your strict preciseness° come to this?   *propriety*
RICHARD DUKE OF YORK   She and the Dauphin have been
        ingling.°   *having sex; dallying*
I did imagine° what would be her refuge.°   *wonder / last defense*
70   WARWICK   Well, go to, we will have no bastards live,
Especially since Charles must father it.
JOAN   You are deceived. My child is none of his.
It was Alençon[9] that enjoyed my love.
RICHARD DUKE OF YORK   Alençon, that notorious Machiavel?[1]
75   It dies an if it had a thousand lives.
JOAN   O give me leave, I have deluded you.
'Twas neither Charles nor yet the Duke I named,
But René King of Naples that prevailed.
WARWICK   A married man?—That's most intolerable.
80   RICHARD DUKE OF YORK   Why, here's a girl; I think she knows not well—
There were so many—whom she may accuse.
WARWICK   It's sign she hath been liberal° and free.   *generous; promiscuous*
RICHARD DUKE OF YORK   And yet forsooth she is a virgin pure!
[*To* JOAN] Strumpet, thy words condemn thy brat and thee.
85   Use no entreaty, for it is in vain.
JOAN   Then lead me hence; with whom I leave my curse.
May never glorious sun reflex° his beams   *throw*
Upon the country where you make abode,
But darkness and the gloomy shade of death
90   Environ you till mischief° and despair   *misfortune*
Drive you to break your necks or hang yourselves.
        Enter [*the Bishop of* WINCHESTER, *now*] *Cardinal*
RICHARD DUKE OF YORK [*to* JOAN]   Break thou in pieces, and
        consume° to ashes,   *burn away*
Thou foul accursèd minister of hell.   [*Exit* JOAN, *guarded*]
WINCHESTER   Lord Regent, I do greet your excellence
95   With letters of commission from the King.
For know, my lords, the states of Christendom,
Moved with remorse of° these outrageous broils,   *pity for*
Have earnestly implored a general peace
Betwixt our nation and the aspiring French,

---

7. The orders for wood and pitch are meant to ensure either that Joan will die quickly as a result of asphyxiation from the smoke, rather than from the flames themselves, or that she will die swiftly from the intensity of the fire.
8. The legal right of a pregnant woman to postpone her execution until after she has given birth.
9. Jean, second Duke of Alençon, was cousin to Charles, the Dauphin.
1. Scheming politician. Niccolò Machiavelli (1469–1527), author of *The Prince*, became associated with principles of cunning statecraft.

100 And here at hand the Dauphin and his train
Approacheth to confer about some matter.
RICHARD DUKE OF YORK   Is all our travail° turned to this effect?   *labor*
After the slaughter of so many peers,
So many captains, gentlemen, and soldiers
105 That in this quarrel have been overthrown
And sold their bodies for their country's benefit,
Shall we at last conclude effeminate peace?
Have we not lost most part of all the towns
By treason, falsehood, and by treachery,
110 Our great progenitors had conquerèd?
O Warwick, Warwick, I foresee with grief
The utter loss of all the realm of France!
WARWICK   Be patient, York. If we conclude a peace
It shall be with such strict and severe covenants
115 As° little shall the Frenchmen gain thereby.   *That*

Enter CHARLES [*the Dauphin, the Duke of*] ALENÇON,
[*the*] BASTARD [*of Orléans, and*] RENÉ [*Duke of Anjou*]

CHARLES   Since, lords of England, it is thus agreed
That peaceful truce shall be proclaimed in France,
We come to be informèd by yourselves
What the conditions of that league° must be.   *treaty*
120 RICHARD DUKE OF YORK   Speak, Winchester; for boiling choler° chokes   *anger*
The hollow passage of my poisoned voice
By sight of these our baleful° enemies.   *deadly*
WINCHESTER   Charles and the rest, it is enacted thus:
That, in regard° King Henry gives consent,   *since*
125 Of mere° compassion and of lenity,°   *Out of pure / mildness*
To ease your country of distressful war
And suffer° you to breathe in fruitful peace,   *allow*
You shall become true liegemen[2] to his crown.
And, Charles, upon condition thou wilt swear
130 To pay him tribute and submit thyself,
Thou shalt be placed as viceroy under him,
And still enjoy thy regal dignity.
ALENÇON   Must he be then as shadow of himself?—
Adorn his temples with a coronet,[3]
135 And yet in substance and authority
Retain but privilege of a private man?
This proffer is absurd and reasonless.
CHARLES   'Tis known already that I am possessed
With more than half the Gallian° territories,   *French*
140 And therein reverenced for their lawful king.
Shall I, for lucre° of the rest° unvanquished,   *gain / rest that are*
Detract so much from that prerogative
As to be called but° viceroy of the whole?   *merely*
No, lord ambassador, I'll rather keep
145 That which I have than, coveting for more,
Be cast° from possibility of all.   *excluded*
RICHARD DUKE OF YORK   Insulting Charles, hast thou by secret means
Used intercession to obtain a league

2. Those bound to serve a feudal lord; faithful subjects.   3. Small crown worn by nobles.

And, now the matter grows to compromise,° *toward resolution*
150 Stand'st thou aloof upon comparison?[4]
Either accept the title thou usurp'st,
Of benefit° proceeding from our king *As a benefaction*
And not of any challenge of desert,[5]
Or we will plague thee with incessant wars.
155 RENÉ [*aside to* CHARLES] My lord, you do not well in obstinacy
To cavil[6] in the course of this contract.
If once it be neglected,° ten to one *disregarded*
We shall not find like opportunity.
ALENÇON [*aside to* CHARLES] To say the truth, it is your policy° *astute course*
160 To save your subjects from such massacre
And ruthless slaughters as are daily seen
By our proceeding in hostility;
And therefore take this compact of a truce,
Although you break it when your pleasure serves.
165 WARWICK How sayst thou, Charles? Shall our condition stand?
CHARLES It shall,
Only reserved° you claim no interest *With the reservation*
In any of our towns of garrison.° *fortified towns*
RICHARD DUKE OF YORK Then swear allegiance to his majesty,
170 As thou art knight, never to disobey
Nor be rebellious to the crown of England,
Thou nor thy nobles, to the crown of England.
[*They swear*]
So, now dismiss your army when ye please.
Hang up your ensigns, let your drums be still;
175 For here we entertain a solemn peace. *Exeunt*

5.7

Enter [the Earl of] SUFFOLK, in conference with KING
[HENRY, *and the Dukes of*] GLOUCESTER *and* EXETER
KING HENRY [*to* SUFFOLK] Your wondrous rare description, noble Earl,
Of beauteous Margaret hath astonished me.
Her virtues gracèd with external gifts
Do breed love's settled° passions in my heart, *unchanging*
5 And like as rigour° of tempestuous gusts *violent force*
Provokes° the mightiest hulk° against the tide, *Drives / ship*
So am I driven by breath of her renown° *word of her fame*
Either to suffer shipwreck or arrive
Where I may have fruition of her love.
10 SUFFOLK Tush, my good lord, this superficial tale
Is but a preface of her worthy praise.° *the praise she deserves*
The chief perfections of that lovely dame,
Had I sufficient skill to utter them,
Would make a volume of enticing lines
15 Able to ravish any dull conceit;° *imagination*
And, which is more, she is not so divine,
So full° replete with choice of all delights, *fully*
But with as humble lowliness of mind
She is content to be at your command—

---

4. Do you hold off in order to quibble about the terms? 6. To raise frivolous objections.
5. And not by any claim of inherent right. 5.7 Location: The palace, London.

20 Command, I mean, of virtuous chaste intents,
    To love and honour Henry as her lord.
    KING HENRY   And otherwise will Henry ne'er presume.
    [*To* GLOUCESTER] Therefore, my lord Protector, give consent
    That Marg'ret may be England's royal queen.
25 GLOUCESTER   So should I give consent to flatter sin.
    You know, my lord, your highness is betrothed
    Unto another lady of esteem.[1]
    How shall we then dispense with that contract
    And not deface your honour with reproach?
30 SUFFOLK   As doth a ruler with unlawful oaths,
    Or one that, at a triumph[2] having vowed
    To try his strength, forsaketh yet the lists[3]
    By reason of his adversary's odds.
    A poor earl's daughter is unequal odds,
35 And therefore may be broke[4] without offence.
    GLOUCESTER   Why, what, I pray, is Margaret more than that?
    Her father is no better than an earl,
    Although in glorious titles he excel.
    SUFFOLK   Yes, my lord; her father is a king,
40 The King of Naples and Jerusalem,
    And of such great authority in France
    As his alliance will confirm our peace
    And keep the Frenchmen in allegiance.
    GLOUCESTER   And so the Earl of Armagnac may do,
45 Because he is near kinsman unto Charles.
    EXETER   Beside, his wealth doth warrant° a liberal dower,   *guarantee*
    Where René sooner will receive than give.
    SUFFOLK   A dower, my lords? Disgrace not so your King
    That he should be so abject, base, and poor
50 To choose for wealth and not for perfect love.
    Henry is able to enrich his queen,
    And not to seek a queen to make him rich.
    So worthless peasants bargain for their wives,
    As market men for oxen, sheep, or horse.
55 Marriage is a matter of more worth
    Than to be dealt in by attorneyship.°   *proxy*
    Not whom *we* will but whom his grace affects°   *desires*
    Must be companion of his nuptial bed.
    And therefore, lords, since he affects her most,
60 That most of all these reasons bindeth us:
    In our opinions she should be preferred.
    For what is wedlock forcèd° but a hell,   *enforced marriage*
    An age of discord and continual strife,
    Whereas the contrary bringeth bliss,
65 And is a pattern° of celestial peace.   *an example*
    Whom should we match with Henry, being a king,
    But Margaret, that is daughter to a king?
    Her peerless feature° joinèd with her birth°   *form / high rank*
    Approves her° fit for none but for a king.   *Confirms that she is*
70 Her valiant courage and undaunted spirit,

---

1. The daughter of the Earl of Armagnac (see 5.1.15–20).
2. Tournament or combat between two opponents on horseback and armed with lances.
3. *forsaketh yet the lists:* nevertheless leaves the tournament grounds.
4. That is, the marriage pledge may be broken.

More than in women commonly is seen,
Will answer our hope in issue of a king.[5]
For Henry, son unto a conqueror,
Is likely to beget more conquerors
75 If with a lady of so high resolve°   determination
As is fair Margaret he be linked in love.
Then yield, my lords, and here conclude with me:
That Margaret shall be queen, and none but she.
   KING HENRY   Whether it be through force of your report,
80 My noble lord of Suffolk, or for that°   or because
My tender youth was never yet attaint°   infected
With any passion of inflaming love,
I cannot tell; but this I am assured:
I feel such sharp dissension in my breast,
85 Such fierce alarums° both of hope and fear,   alarms
As I am sick with working of my thoughts.
Take therefore shipping; post,° my lord, to France;   hasten
Agree to any covenants, and procure
That Lady Margaret do vouchsafe° to come   promise
90 To cross the seas to England and be crowned
King Henry's faithful and anointed queen.
For your expenses and sufficient charge,°   money to spend
Among the people gather up a tenth.[6]
Be gone, I say; for till you do return
95 I rest perplexèd° with a thousand cares.   I remain troubled
   [To GLOUCESTER] And you, good uncle, banish all offence.°   hostility
If you do censure me by what you were,[7]
Not what you are, I know it will excuse
This sudden execution of my will.
100 And so conduct me where from° company   away from
I may revolve and ruminate my grief.[8]   Exit [with EXETER]
   GLOUCESTER   Ay, grief, I fear me, both at first and last.   Exit
   SUFFOLK   Thus Suffolk hath prevailed, and thus he goes
As did the youthful Paris[9] once to Greece,
105 With hope to find the like event° in love,   the same outcome
But prosper better than the Trojan did.
Margaret shall now be queen and rule the King;
But I will rule both her, the King, and realm.   Exit

---

5. Will satisfy our hopes by bringing forth a king.
6. A tax of 10 percent on income or property.
7. If you judge me by how you behaved when you were young.
8. I may return again and again in my mind to my grief.

9. According to Greek mythology, Paris went to Greece from Troy and abducted Helen, the wife of Menelaus. This act was said to have brought about the Trojan War, in which Paris was killed.

Richard III

Among the very few anecdotes about Shakespeare that date from his own lifetime is a ribald story recorded in 1602 in the diary of a London law student, John Manningham:

> Upon a time when Burbage played Richard III there was a citizen grew so far in liking with him, that before she went from the play she appointed him to come that night unto her by the name of Richard III. Shakespeare, overhearing their conclusion, went before, was entertained and at his game ere Burbage came. The message being brought that Richard III was at the door, Shakespeare caused return to be made that William the Conqueror was before Richard III.

Like most stories about celebrities, this one probably says more about those who circulated it than about those it describes. But it does at least suggest that Richard Burbage, the famous actor who first played Richard III (as well as such parts as Romeo and Hamlet), had not by virtue of his villainous role lost all of his glamour. Indeed, it is striking that Richard—the "elvish-marked, abortive, rooting hog" (1.3.225), the "poisonous bunch-backed toad" (1.3.244), the heartless cur sent, as he himself puts it, "deformed" and "unfinished" (1.1.20) into the world—has seemed weirdly and compellingly attractive to generations of playgoers. From the start, the play seems to have aroused intense interest: first performed in 1592 or 1593, *Richard III* was published in quarto no fewer than five times during Shakespeare's lifetime.

What can account for this attraction? It is not an obvious feature in the chronicle histories upon which Shakespeare relied, nor does Richard seem to have a comparable allure in another play of unknown authorship that dates from the same period, *The True Tragedy of Richard III*. In these works, Richard figures as the pitiless, treacherous villain of what has been called the "Tudor Myth"—that is, the officially sanctioned account of the origin and legitimacy of the Tudor dynasty. That dynasty was founded by Henry, Earl of Richmond, who defeated Richard III at the Battle of Bosworth Field (1485), reigned until his death in 1509 as Henry VII, and was the grandfather of Queen Elizabeth (1533–1603). It is hardly surprising that the new regime, whose claim to the throne was somewhat shaky, would wish to discredit the old. Modern historians emphasize Richard's solid administrative skills; Tudor apologists depict Richard not merely as venal or unscrupulous but as a monster of evil, a creature whose moral viciousness was vividly stamped on his twisted body.

The principal literary source for this spectacularly partisan depiction was not a piece of simple propaganda but an unusually subtle and complex *History of King Richard the Third* (c. 1513) by the great humanist Thomas More. Later sixteenth-century historians, notably Edward Halle in *The Union of the Two Noble and Illustre Fameilies of Lancastre & Yorke* (1548) and Raphael Holinshed in *The Chronicles of England, Scotland, and Ireland* (1577, revised in 1587), followed closely in More's wake, repeating many of the details that Shakespeare in turn borrowed: Richard's habit of gnawing his lip, for example, or his restlessness, or the rumor that he was born with teeth. More and his followers deftly interwove three distinct explanatory accounts of Richard's behavior: political, psychological, and metaphysical. As a politician (a word with nasty connotations in the Renaissance), More's Richard is a particularly cunning player in a corrupt world, a schemer plotting to seize power and destroy all real or potential rivals. Psychologically, he is a strange blend of courage, wit, skillful dissembling, and fathomless malice. And on the metaphysical plane, he is a horrible instrument of God's wrath, a virtual devil incarnate.

Most sixteenth-century historians and chroniclers were, by our standards, far more interested in conveying moral meanings than in impartially recounting facts. Shakespeare allowed himself an even greater latitude, freely reshaping and condensing his historical materials in order to heighten dramatic effect and to intensify the political, psychological, and metaphysical dimensions of his villainous antihero. The play compresses events that in reality occurred over a long period of time, so that, for example, Richard's murderous plot against his brother George, Duke of Clarence (1478), is cleverly twined around his cynical courtship of Lady Anne (1472), which is in turn depicted as occurring during the funeral procession of King Henry (1471). The historical Lady Anne had only been betrothed to King Henry's son Edward, but Shakespeare writes as if she had actually been married to him; likewise, he folds Richmond's unsuccessful attempt to invade England in 1483 into his successful invasion of 1485, and he has old Queen Margaret, who was not even in England during most of the events that the play depicts, haunting the royal court like a bitter, half-crazed Greek tragic chorus.

Manipulating the insecurities, factional rivalries, and ambitions of everyone around him, Shakespeare's Richard is a consummate portrait of what sixteenth-century Englishmen termed a "machiavel"—that is, a person who acts on the immoral advice allegedly offered by the Florentine humanist Niccolò Machiavelli in *The Prince* (written in 1513, first printed in 1532). According to the period's lurid and grossly distorted account of this advice, Machiavelli had counseled princes to lie, cheat, and murder under the cover of hypocritical professions of virtue and piety. "I count Religion but a childish Toy," declares the character called Machevil, who speaks the prologue to Marlowe's *Jew of Malta* (c. 1590). Shakespeare's Richard, at first terrified by the apparition of the ghosts in Act 5, rallies to express comparable sentiments: "Conscience is but a word that cowards use, / Devised at first to keep the strong in awe" (5.6.39–40). These are sentiments that, for the most part, Richard keeps to himself—or, rather, shares only with the audience in a succession of gleeful asides—for he is highly skilled at assuming the pose of religious faith. Aided by his fellow hypocrite Buckingham, Richard appears in a memorable scene, prayer book in hand, miming "devotion and right Christian zeal" (3.7.103) while cynically stage-managing the supposedly popular call for his coronation.

Shakespeare's vision of Richard as a consummate role-player goes back to a brilliant sketch of the same character in one of the three earlier plays he had written on fifteenth-century English history. Taken together, these plays—*The First Part of Henry the Sixth, The First Part of the Contention of the Two Famous Houses of York and Lancaster* (2 Henry VI), and *The True Tragedy of Richard Duke of York and the Good King Henry the Sixth* (3 Henry VI)— depict the chaotic, violent struggle known as the Wars of the Roses, between two noble houses, the Lancastrians and the Yorkists. At the close of *Richard Duke of York* (3 Henry VI), the Yorkist faction, led by the Duke of York's three surviving sons (Edward, George, and Richard), has triumphed. The last Lancastrian

Richard III. Portrait by unknown artist (c. 1590).

king, Henry VI, has been killed, and Richard's eldest brother has been crowned King Edward IV. But a shadow is cast across this decisive Yorkist victory by the ruthless and unsatisfied ambition of Richard.

Even though it can stand (and be performed) entirely on its own, *Richard III* may be regarded as the fourth part of a tetralogy, for it picks up directly from the turbulent events depicted in *Richard Duke of York* and, more particularly, from the project Richard announces in a long soliloquy. He declares that since nature has seen fit to deform his body and so exclude him from sensual pleasures, he will instead pursue the crown. "I can add colours to the chameleon," he boasts, "change shapes with Proteus for advantages, / And set the murderous Machiavel to school" (*Richard Duke of York* 3.2.191–93). Here Shakespeare is beginning to psychologize the machiavel, to provide inner motives for his violent ambition and his compulsive shape changing. *Richard III* continues and intensifies this process: as his opening soliloquy suggests, Richard feels that from birth he has been cruelly cheated by dissembling nature. Deprived of the normal satisfactions of nurturing and kindness—it is as if his mother's womb itself had rejected him—he tries to find compensatory satisfaction in cruelty and dissembling of his own. He seeks not only vengeance against an unloving world but also the pleasure of cherishing himself. Yet at the end, in a vigorous if crude moment of self-analysis, he discovers that even self-love eludes him: "I love myself. Wherefore? . . . O no, alas, I rather hate myself" (5.5.141–43).

Richard's self-hatred is psychologically revealing—evidently, he has internalized the loathing that he inspires in virtually everyone around him—but it is not simply generated from within: there is, the play's characters continually imply, a divinely sanctioned, objective moral order independent of both individuals and society, and by the fixed norms of this order Richard *is* hateful. It is possible for villains like Richard or the murderers of Clarence to close their ears to the admonitions of conscience, but all human actions are part of a larger design and will ultimately be judged by a heavenly power. From this higher perspective, Richard's deformity is less the *cause* of his evil nature than its *sign*. Similarly, the ghosts in Act 5 are not merely psychological projections but metaphysical emissaries. The dead do not simply rot and disappear, nor do they survive only in the memories and dreams of the living: they are an ineradicable presence, a part of the structure of reality, an uncanny age group capable of blessing and cursing. Richard tries to shake off their condemnation, as earlier he had jauntily deflected Margaret's elaborate curse, but their words bring beads of sweat to his trembling flesh. For while he may tell himself that his victims' words are merely the impotent weapons of the powerless, he cannot escape the play's pervasive sense that there is something eerie and disturbing about curses, as if through incantatory verbal ritual they magically touch the hidden order of things.

Despite Richard's disruptive mockery and unceremonious violence, an atmosphere of ritual lingers over much of *Richard III*, tingeing the rhetorically elaborate expressions of grief and

Henry VII. Portrait by Michael Sittow (1505).

"For they account his head upon the bridge" (3.2.67). London Bridge adorned with the heads of traitors. From Claes Jansz. Visscher, *Londinum florentissima Britanniae urbs* (1625).

anger, solemnizing formal ceremonies, and shaping the perceptions of the guilt-ridden characters. Although the play gives us historical figures with psychological motivations and political stratagems, often we seem less in the secular world of disenchanted politics than in the world of classical tragedy or medieval rite. Thus, for example, Clarence's terrible nightmare just before his murder recalls the hell of the Roman playwright Seneca and, still more, the hell of fourteenth-century Christian painting, with its howling fiends and damned souls. Clarence is haunted by the sense of an unappeasable God preparing to punish him for his crimes, and his dream discloses what he does not yet consciously know: that the agent of divine retribution is his own brother, Richard.

This ritual process—the inexorable working out, through the agency of Richard, of retributive justice or (as ancient tragedians personified it) Nemesis—is best conveyed perhaps by the chorus of grief-crazed women, above all by old Queen Margaret, who identifies Richard as "hell's black intelligencer" (4.4.71), or secret agent. In a series of stiff antiphonal laments (4.4.35ff.), Margaret (the widow of the slain Henry VI), Queen Elizabeth (the widow of Edward IV), and the Duchess of York (the widowed mother of Edward and his brothers, including Richard) tease out the strict eye-for-an-eye logic of the action. And at one startling moment, Richard himself comes close to acknowledging his role within this scheme: he likens himself to "the formal Vice, Iniquity" (3.1.82).

The character called the Vice is an inheritance of the medieval morality play: the busy enemy of mankind, the Vice was at once the agent of hell and the tool of divine providence, a master plotter and a puppet in a play that is not of his own making. Yet this fixed place in the divine plan did not preclude his acquiring an extraordinary theatrical power and resourcefulness, qualities that Shakespeare would later exploit in characters as different (and as magnificent) as Falstaff and Iago. Shakespeare constructs Richard out of many elements in the Vice tradition: a jaunty use of asides, a delight in sharing his schemes with the audience, a grotesque appearance, a penchant for disguise, a manic energy and humor, and a wickedly engaging ability to defer though not finally to escape well-deserved punishment. Richard's own allusion to the Vice calls attention to yet another element, a skill in playing with the doubleness of words and exploiting the slipperiness of language: "Thus like the formal Vice, Iniquity, / I moralize two meanings in one word" (3.1.82–83). *Richard III* puts the demonic master of this vicious skill on display and, in the end, stages his destruction: in a sense, the ritual that lingers over the play is an exorcism.

But, of course, *Richard III* is not in fact a ritual, and Shakespeare's subtle blending of psychological, metaphysical, and political perspectives carefully suspends any determination of their relative significance in the events he dramatizes. The psychological development of Richard is arrested by the intimation that psychology is itself the tool of a supernatural scheme; the supernatural is subverted (at least until the ghost scene) by the Machiavellian subordination of religion to power politics; but power politics is itself undermined by the suggestion that individuals act in the grip not of rational calculation but of psychological pressures and passions over which they have little or no control. The complex interplay of forces is reflected perhaps in an ambiguity about the play's genre: first appearing in print as *The Tragedy of King Richard the Third*, it was rechristened in the First Folio as one of Shakespeare's history plays, *The Life & Death of Richard the Third*.

That these multiple perspectives do not simply cancel each other out is the result of the extraordinary theatrical force of Richard himself. Only *Hamlet*, of all Shakespeare's plays, is comparably dominated by a single character, and only *Macbeth* is comparably structured around an evil hero. (The villains Richard most anticipates—Philip the Bastard in *King John*, Don John in *Much Ado About Nothing*, Iago in *Othello*, and Edmund in *King Lear*—are all at varying degrees of distance from the main protagonist.) Without for a moment concealing from the audience Richard's appalling, monstrous evil, Shakespeare makes his villain immensely captivating. In large part, his allure derives from what Keats called the "gusto," the overwhelming liveliness, of Shakespeare's characters: "Your eyes drop millstones when fools' eyes fall tears," says Richard to the murderers; "I like you, lads" (1.3.351–52). The startling frankness of this villainy has a comic charge, a charge renewed in the open wickedness of his plans for unsuspecting Hastings—"Chop off his head" (3.1.190)—or for the innocent young princes: "I wish the bastards dead" (4.2.19). There is gusto in Richard's slyness as well as in his frankness, a slyness that also is often comic: "So wise so young, they say, do never live long" (3.1.79).

The allure of such moments seems to be bound up with the allure of the theater itself, with its capacity for emotional intensification, surprise, deception, and heightened energy. The religious enemies of the theater in Shakespeare's age charged that this energy was essentially erotic—the playhouse, they complained, aroused sexual desire—and before dismissing their charges as preposterous, we might recall the comic anecdote from John Manningham's diary with which this introduction began. Shakespeare himself in *Richard III* seems to play with the seductive power of theatrical performance in the bizarre scene in which Richard successfully courts Lady Anne over the body of her father-in-law, the King, whom he has murdered: "Was ever woman in this humour wooed?" Richard exults; "Was ever woman in this humour won?" (1.2.215–16). Richard's wooing has nothing to do with tenderness, affection, sympathy, or even physical attraction; we witness an aggressive male assault upon Lady Anne's rooted, eloquently expressed, and eminently justified fear and loathing. Here, as elsewhere, Richard gets what he wants because he possesses greater power to control the scenario: more than Anne, more than anyone, he knows how to initiate action, conceal motives, threaten, intimidate, and hurt. He has killed Anne's husband as well as her father-in-law; he will, when she has served his purpose, kill Anne too. Anne knows this well enough—"Ill rest betide the chamber where thou liest" (1.2.112)—but she virtually invents uncertainties to mask the calculating murderousness she herself has perceived with cold clarity: "I would I knew thy heart," she muses, seconds after she has thoroughly inventoried Richard's villainous heart (1.2.180).

Anne is shallow, corruptible, naively ambitious, and, above all, frightened—all qualities that help to account for her spectacular surrender—but the scene's theatrical power rests less upon a depiction of her character than upon the spectacle of Richard's restless aggression transformed during the rapid-fire exchange of one-liners (called in rhetoric *stichomythia*) into a perverse form of sexual provocation and of Anne's verbal violence transformed, in spite of itself, into an erotic response. In light of this transformation, the misshapen Richard's celebration of his sexual attractiveness—

> I do mistake my person all this while.
> Upon my life she finds, although I cannot,
> Myself to be a marv'lous proper man—

is not wholly ironic, even if he himself thinks it is (1.2.239–50).

Eros has not been excluded from Richard's career; it has found a new and compelling form in his energetic, witty, and murderous chafing against the obstacles in his path. These obstacles are not simply set in opposition to his desire; rather they virtually constitute it, for it is the extent of his distance from power that generates Richard's craving for it. His politics, and hence the sexuality implied by that politics, is transgressive; it thrives on the violation of social and natural bonds. His is the psychology of the rapist, and the character in Shakespeare closest to Richard III is the rapist Tarquin (in *The Rape of Lucrece*), whose lust is excited precisely by the barriers he is forced to overcome. This chafing structure is why the violent verbal assaults upon Richard, most intense from the women in the play, seem only to intensify his aggressive energies. It is perhaps also why Richard seems to lose much of his erotic power as soon as he has established himself on the throne. When the obstacles in his path to the crown have been removed, when there is no legitimate authority to transgress, the erotic quality of his ambition immediately begins to wane.

The play has allowed Richard to be a perverse erotic champion—a role probably possible only in this highly theatrical vision of history—but the desire he embodies cannot be integrated into any viable social or natural order; nor does it constitute a coherent, stable inner life. By the play's end, he seems a hollow man, a set of theatrical masks that project grotesque shadows upon the world. Fittingly, when "shadows," in the form of those he has murdered, return to terrify him, he can only express his fear in histrionic terms, staging a miniature dialogue with himself and then imagining his conscience as the audience, with its thousand tongues condemning him for a villain.

Richard's manifest theatricality is only the extreme form of a theatricality diffused throughout the play. Virtually all of the speeches—lamentation, cursing, debate, persuasion—are cast as self-conscious performances: "What means this scene of rude impatience?" asks the Duchess of York; Queen Elizabeth replies, "To mark an act of tragic violence" (2.2.38–39). Moreover, there is a pervasive sense that the characters exist as figures in someone else's play: through most of the performance, they are figures, without knowing it, in Richard's play, but Richard himself is a figure in another play, larger than himself. That larger play is at once the drama of history, scripted (as Tudor ideology claimed) by God, and the historical drama or tragedy, scripted by Shakespeare. If the script obliges all of the characters to display the power of divine providence, it obliges them at the same time to display the power of the theater. For if the stage pays homage to the state, it also makes the state into a histrionic spectacle on the public stage. *Richard III* manages to imply that the whole vast enterprise of Tudor power exists to make this play, and the theater in which it is performed, possible.

STEPHEN GREENBLATT

TEXTUAL NOTE

Richard III first appeared in quarto (Q1) in 1597, without the playwright's name but with a very full title page:

> THE TRAGEDY OF King Richard the third. Containing, His treacherous Plots against his brother Clarence: the pittiefull murther of his iunocent nephewes: his tyrannicall vsurpation: with the whole course of his detested life, and most deserued death. As it hath beene lately Acted by the Right honourable the Lord Chamberlaine his seruants AT LONDON Printed by Valentine Sims, for Andrew Wise, dwelling in Paules Chu[r]chyard, at the Signe of the Angell. 1597.

The play proved to be a popular one: so much so that five more quarto versions came out before the appearance of the First Folio (F) in 1623. These quarto editions (Q2–Q6) can claim no textual authority, because of their means of composition; each was based on the text of the one immediately preceding it. Each not only carried forward, therefore, the accumulated errors of its predecessors but added some of its own. The main editorial questions revolve, then, about the authority of, and the relationship between, Q1 and F.

Certainly the quarto text influenced F. But the hundreds of differences between the two suggest that a further source, an independent manuscript, was also used in the construction of F. The Oxford editor Gary Taylor believes that this manuscript was probably a transcript, presumably done by a scribe, of Shakespeare's "foul papers," that is, a version of the play in Shakespeare's own hand, with whatever additions, corrections, and revisions he may have inserted in the course of its composition.

It appears that neither Q nor F derives directly from Shakespeare's own manuscript. It has, however, been proposed that Q, the shorter text, might represent a first draft of the play. Gary Taylor rejects this hypothesis. In his view, Q is a "bad" Quarto—that is, one reconstructed from memory of the play as performed. If so, it is a surprisingly thorough reconstruction, carried out, probably, not by one or two renegade players of minor roles but by Shakespeare's company itself, or rather by those members to hand when the reconstructed text was being written down. Some part of the company on tour in the provinces, for example, could have found itself without a prompt copy of *Richard III.* A text hurriedly assembled in such circumstances might be substantially complete, except for gaps in the minor roles, which would have been played by hired men. Such gaps, showing up as omissions and textual variants, do in fact occur in the quarto version of the play and therefore lend support to Taylor's theory. Given that the passages Q omits tend to slow down the dramatic action and that its only substantial additional passage is a particularly impressive one (the "clock" dialogue, 4.2.101–20), it seems to follow that Q is a later text—one more theatrically attuned, one trimmed of some superfluous bulk. Hence, Oxford adopts a substantial number of the quarto variants.

Other omissions appear to show the effects of censorship. The exclamation "Zounds" ("by His wounds") appears four times in Q but not in F, as does a reference to "Christ's dear blood shed for our grievous sins." The name "God," however, appears frequently in both texts. Political rather than purely religious concerns seem to have caused a further omission. Hastings's lines at the conclusion of 3.4, in which he prophesies "the fearful'st time" in a coming "miserable England," could well be seen as unsettling to an audience that laid great store by prophecy. These lines do not appear in F. But what of the inclusion only in Q of the "clock" dialogue mentioned above? In fact, this seeming anomaly (it is the only major passage not in F) adds weight to the early F hypothesis. The very singular nature of this passage leads Oxford to see it as "an inspired afterthought." No political considerations—far less theatrical ones—could justify its deletion. We might also note that in what was an already very long play, Shakespeare might have been more inclined to deletion than to addition.

F, we can see, is closer to its sources, Halle and Holinshed, and is manifestly the superior text. Many passages are better crafted in meter and meaning than their quarto counterparts. F, then, is the control text for substantive readings. Recalling, however, that the quarto reconstruction would have taken place at a time when Shakespeare himself was active in the company and may have had a hand in revision for the stage, an unusually large number of departures from the control text have been retained. The reader is thus presented, we hope, with the play in its most fully realized theatrical form.

In this edition, Folio passages that were omitted from Q and relegated in the *Oxford Shakespeare* to an appendix are printed inset and in italics.

SELECTED BIBLIOGRAPHY

Burnett, Mark Thornton. "'Monsters' and 'Molas': Body Politics in *Richard III.*" *Constructing "Monsters" in Shakespearean Drama and Early Modern Culture.* New York: Palgrave Macmillan, 2002. 65–94. Fluctuating between images of monsters shaped and unfinished, Richard represents the anxieties of a barren Tudor line seeking new political form.

Carroll, William. " 'The Form of Law': Ritual and Succession in *Richard III*." *True Rites and Maimed Rites: Ritual and Anti-Ritual in Shakespeare and His Age*. Ed. Linda Woodbridge and Edward Berry. Urbana: University of Illinois Press, 1992. 203–19.

Howard, Jean E., and Phyllis Rackin. "Weak Kings, Warrior Women, and the Assault on Dynastic Authority." *Engendering a Nation: A Feminist Account of Shakespeare's English Histories*. London: Routledge, 1997. 100–18. Shifting from history to tragedy, *Richard III* ennobles and disempowers women as passive emblems of pity, while Richard appropriates their seductive theatrical energy.

Hunter, Robert G. *Shakespeare and the Mystery of God's Judgments*. Athens: University of Georgia Press, 1976. Poised between Augustinian and Calvinist conceptions of God's will, Richard's seemingly contradictory status as a tragic figures acting in a providential frame generates the complexity of Shakespeare's art.

Marche, Stephen. "Mocking Dead Bones: Historical Memory and the Theater of the Dead in *Richard III*." *Comparative Drama* 37.1 (2003): 37–57. The play's ambivalent generic status—between tragedy and history—is reflected in Richard's tragic inability to overcome history by silencing the dead who challenge his shaping narrative.

Moulton, Ian Frederick. " 'A Monster Great Deformed': The Unruly Masculinities of *Richard III*." *Shakespeare Quarterly* 47.3 (1996): 251–68. Shakespeare both critiques and celebrates masculine aggression, revealing the incoherence of masculinity as an early modern cultural concept.

Rossiter, A. P. *Angel with Horns, and Other Shakespeare Lectures*. Ed. Graham Storey. New York: Theatre Arts Books, 1961. Richard's demonic appeal as God's avenging angel makes the play less moral history than comic history built on paradoxical irony and inversion.

Targoff, Ramie. " 'Dirty' Amens: Devotion, Applause, and Consent in *Richard III*." *Renaissance Drama* 31 (2002): 61–84. The question of what constitutes true consent on the part of the English toward their King can be tracked through the play's odd use of the liturgical term "Amen," which both Richard and Richmond solicit in different ways from their audiences in order to legitimate their rule.

Torey, Michael. " 'The Plain Devil and Dissembling Looks': Ambivalent Physiognomy and Shakespeare's *Richard III*." *English Literary Renaissance* 30.2 (2000): 123–53. Richard's ability to deceive his victims and manipulate his corporal image complicates the seeming intelligibility of his deformity.

Wheeler, Richard P. "History, Character, and Conscience in *Richard III*." *Comparative Drama* 5 (1971–72): 301–21. The play dramatizes the struggle between divine and profane views of history, between conscience and egoism, that troubled the late Elizabethan era.

FILMS

Richard III. 1912. Dir. André Calmettes and James Keane. USA. 55 min. The silent film version, with Robert Gemp as Edward IV and Frederick Warde as Richard.

Richard III. 1955. Dir. Laurence Olivier. UK. 161 min. A deformed and morally twisted yet seductively charismatic Richard, played by Olivier, with John Gielgud as Clarence.

Richard III. 1995. Dir. Richard Loncraine. UK/USA. 104 min. Richard as a sly and ruthless fascist dictator in a stylishly corrupt 1930s Britain. Ian McKellan is Richard, Robert Downey, Jr. is Lord Rivers.

Looking for Richard. 1996. Dir. Al Pacino. USA. 111 min. Part adaptation, part behind-the-scenes documentary about bringing the Shakespeare play to modern audiences. With Pacino playing Richard and Kevin Spacey playing Buckingham.

The Tragedy of
King Richard the Third

THE PERSONS OF THE PLAY

KING EDWARD IV
DUCHESS OF YORK, his mother
PRINCE EDWARD
Richard, the young Duke of YORK } his sons
George, Duke of CLARENCE
RICHARD, Duke of GLOUCESTER, later KING RICHARD III } his brothers
Clarence's SON
Clarence's DAUGHTER
QUEEN ELIZABETH, King Edward's wife
Anthony Woodeville, Earl RIVERS, her brother
Marquis of DORSET }
Lord GRAY } her sons
Sir Thomas VAUGHAN
GHOST OF KING HENRY VI
QUEEN MARGARET, his widow
GHOST OF PRINCE EDWARD, his son
LADY ANNE, Prince Edward's widow
William, LORD HASTINGS, Lord Chamberlain
Lord STANLEY, Earl of Derby, his friend
HENRY EARL OF RICHMOND, later KING HENRY VII, Stanley's son-in-law
Earl of OXFORD }
Sir James BLUNT } Richmond's followers
Sir Walter HERBERT }
Duke of BUCKINGHAM }
Duke of NORFOLK }
Sir Richard RATCLIFFE }
Sir William CATESBY } Richard Gloucester's followers
Sir James TYRRELL }
Two MURDERERS }
A PAGE }
CARDINAL
BISHOP OF ELY
John, a PRIEST
SIR CHRISTOPHER, a Priest
Sir Robert BRACKENBURY, Lieutenant of the Tower of London
Lord MAYOR of London
A SCRIVENER
Hastings, a PURSUIVANT
SHERIFF
Aldermen and Citizens
Attendants, two bishops, messengers, soldiers

1.1

Enter RICHARD *Duke of* GLOUCESTER[1]

RICHARD GLOUCESTER   Now is the winter of our discontent
    Made glorious summer by this son of York;[2]
    And all the clouds that loured° upon our house°   *glowered / family*
    In the deep bosom of the ocean buried.
5   Now are our brows bound with victorious wreaths,
    Our bruisèd arms° hung up for monuments,°   *armor / memorials*
    Our stern alarums° changed to merry meetings,   *call to arms*
    Our dreadful marches to delightful measures.°   *dances*
    Grim-visaged war hath smoothed his wrinkled front,°   *forehead*
10   And now—instead of mounting barbèd° steeds   *armored*
    To fright the souls of fearful adversaries—
    He capers[3] nimbly in a lady's chamber
    To the lascivious pleasing of a lute.
    But I, that am not shaped for sportive° tricks   *amorous*
15   Nor made to court an amorous looking-glass,
    I that am rudely stamped[4] and want° love's majesty   *lack*
    To strut before a wanton ambling nymph,
    I that am curtailed of this fair proportion,°   *shape*
    Cheated of feature° by dissembling nature,   *good appearance*
20   Deformed, unfinished, sent before my time
    Into this breathing world scarce half made up—
    And that so lamely and unfashionable°   *badly formed*
    That dogs bark at me as I halt° by them—   *limp*
    Why, I in this weak piping[5] time of peace
25   Have no delight to pass away the time,
    Unless to spy my shadow in the sun
    And descant on° mine own deformity.   *remark upon*
    And therefore since I cannot prove° a lover   *prove to be*
    To entertain these fair well-spoken days,
30   I am determinèd° to prove a villain   *resolved; fated*
    And hate the idle pleasures of these days.
    Plots have I laid, inductions[6] dangerous,
    By drunken prophecies, libels and dreams
    To set my brother Clarence[7] and the King
35   In deadly hate the one against the other.
    And if King Edward be as true and just
    As I am subtle false and treacherous,
    This day should Clarence closely be mewed up°   *caged (like a hawk)*
    About a prophecy which says that 'G'[8]
40   Of Edward's heirs the murderer shall be.

        Enter [George Duke of] CLARENCE, *guarded, and [Sir*
        Robert] BRACKENBURY

    Dive, thoughts, down to my soul: here Clarence comes.
    Brother, good day. What means this armèd guard
    That waits upon your grace?

1.1 Location: A street in London.
1. Pronounced "Gloster."
2. *son of York:* Edward IV, son of Richard, Duke of York; with wordplay on Edward's emblem, a sun in splendor.
3. In court dances, men often made "capers," or showy leaps; also suggests a sexual escapade.
4 Roughly, imperfectly shaped (alluding to the stamping of a coin with an image).
5. Characterized by the music of a peaceful shepherd's

flute: shrill-voiced, like women or children.
6. Initial moves, prologues.
7. George, Duke of Clarence, Richard, Duke of Gloucester, and King Edward IV were brothers; Clarence, being older than Richard, would become King if Edward and his heirs died.
8. Which Edward interprets as "George," but which could—and does—mean "Gloucester."

CLARENCE His majesty,
Tend'ring° my person's safety, hath appointed *Caring about*
45 This conduct° to convey me to the Tower.⁹ *escort*
RICHARD GLOUCESTER Upon what cause?
CLARENCE Because my name is George.
RICHARD GLOUCESTER Alack, my lord, that fault is none of yours.
He should for that commit your godfathers.¹
Belike° his majesty hath some intent *Probably*
50 That you should be new-christened in the Tower.
But what's the matter, Clarence? May I know?
CLARENCE Yea, Richard, when I know—for I protest
As yet I do not. But as I can learn
He hearkens after prophecies and dreams,
55 And from the cross-row° plucks the letter 'G' *alphabet*
And says a wizard told him that by 'G'
His issue° disinherited should be. *children*
And for my name of George begins with 'G',
It follows in his thought that I am he.
60 These, as I learn, and suchlike toys° as these, *trifles*
Hath moved his highness to commit° me now. *arrest*
RICHARD GLOUCESTER Why, this it is when men are ruled by women.
'Tis not the King that sends you to the Tower;
My Lady Gray,² his wife—Clarence, 'tis she
65 That tempts him to this harsh extremity.
Was it not she, and that good man of worship³
Anthony Woodeville her brother there,
That made him send Lord Hastings to the Tower,
From whence this present day he is delivered?
70 We are not safe, Clarence; we are not safe.
CLARENCE By heaven, I think there is no man secure
But the Queen's kindred, and night-walking heralds° *secret go-betweens*
That trudge betwixt the King and Mrs Shore.⁴
Heard ye not what an humble suppliant
75 Lord Hastings was for his delivery?
RICHARD GLOUCESTER Humbly complaining to her deity⁵
Got my Lord Chamberlain⁶ his liberty.
I'll tell you what: I think it is our way,° *strategy*
If we will keep in favour with the King,
80 To be her men and wear her livery.⁷
The jealous, o'erworn widow⁸ and herself,° *(Jane Shore)*
Since that our brother dubbed them⁹ gentlewomen,
Are mighty gossips° in our monarchy. *busybodies*
BRACKENBURY I beseech your graces both to pardon me.
85 His majesty hath straitly given in charge° *has strictly ordered*

---

9. Tower of London, used to house noble prisoners as well as (in Elizabethan England) traitors and political agitators.
1. The godfather was responsible for the naming of a newborn child.
2. A sarcastic reference to the Queen, widow of Sir John Gray before her marriage to the King. Her maiden name was Elizabeth Woodeville (also Woodville).
3. Honor (here, a sarcastic phrase, more appropriate to a solid, middle-class citizen than to the Queen's brother, Anthony Woodeville, who succeeded his father as Earl Rivers).
4. Jane Shore, wife of a London goldsmith. Her liaison

with Edward was notorious. *Mrs*: Mistress (here in both the polite and the abusive sense).
5. Jane Shore (ironically, by analogy with "her majesty").
6. Hastings's title. According to Shakespeare's sources, Jane Shore became his mistress when her affair with the King ended.
7. Servants ("men") in noble households wore the colors ("livery") of the family.
8. The Queen, a widow before she married Edward IV. *o'erworn*: faded.
9. Invested them with the status of (usually used of knights). Richard grossly exaggerates the lowly status of the Queen's family before her marriage.

That no man shall have private conference,
Of what degree soever,[1] with your brother.

RICHARD GLOUCESTER   Even so. An't° please your worship, Brackenbury,   *If it*
You may partake of anything we say.
90   We speak no treason, man. We say the King
Is wise and virtuous, and his noble Queen
Well struck° in years, fair, and not jealous.   *advanced*
We say that Shore's wife hath a pretty foot,
A cherry lip,
95   A bonny eye, a passing° pleasing tongue,   *an exceedingly*
And that the Queen's kin are made gentlefolks.
How say you, sir? Can you deny all this?

BRACKENBURY   With this, my lord, myself have naught° to do.   *nothing*

RICHARD GLOUCESTER   Naught[2] to do with Mrs Shore? I tell thee, fellow:
100   He that doth naught with her—excepting one—
Were best to do it secretly alone.

BRACKENBURY   What one, my lord?

RICHARD GLOUCESTER   Her husband, knave. Wouldst thou betray me?

BRACKENBURY   I beseech your grace to pardon me, and do withal°   *moreover*
105   Forbear your conference with the noble Duke.

CLARENCE   We know thy charge, Brackenbury, and will obey.

RICHARD GLOUCESTER   We are the Queen's abjects,° and must obey.   *base subjects*
Brother, farewell. I will unto the King,
And whatsoe'er you will employ me in—
110   Were it to call King Edward's widow° 'sister'—   *(Queen Elizabeth)*
I will perform it to enfranchise° you.   *free*
Meantime, this deep disgrace in brotherhood
Touches me dearer[3] than you can imagine.

CLARENCE   I know it pleaseth neither of us well.

115   RICHARD GLOUCESTER   Well, your imprisonment shall not be long.
I will deliver you or lie for you.[4]
Meantime, have patience.

CLARENCE   I must perforce.° Farewell.   *of necessity*

Exeunt CLARENCE[, BRACKENBURY, *and guard, to the Tower*]

RICHARD GLOUCESTER   Go tread the path that thou shalt ne'er return.
Simple plain Clarence, I do love thee so
120   That I will shortly send thy soul to heaven,
If heaven will take the present at° our hands.   *from*
But who comes here? The new-delivered° Hastings?   *newly released*

Enter LORD HASTINGS [*from the Tower*]

LORD HASTINGS   Good time of day unto my gracious lord.

RICHARD GLOUCESTER   As much unto my good Lord Chamberlain.
125   Well are you welcome to the open air.
How hath your lordship brooked° imprisonment?   *tolerated*

LORD HASTINGS   With patience, noble lord, as prisoners must.
But I shall live, my lord, to give them thanks
That were the cause of my imprisonment.

130   RICHARD GLOUCESTER   No doubt, no doubt—and so shall Clarence too,
For they that were your enemies are his,
And have prevailed as much on him as you.

1. *no . . . soever*: that is, despite Richard's high rank ("degree"), he must not speak with the prisoner.
2. Wickedness; here, specifically sexual intercourse.
3. Wounds me more, but also (as a hidden meaning), implicates me more.
4. In prison, in place of Clarence (with a pun on "lie" as "tell falsehoods about"). "Deliver" and "lie for" rhyme.

LORD HASTINGS More pity that the eagles should be mewed
    While kites° and buzzards prey at liberty.   *scavenger birds*
135 RICHARD GLOUCESTER What news abroad?°   *circulating*
LORD HASTINGS No news so bad abroad as this at home:
    The King is sickly, weak, and melancholy,
    And his physicians fear° him mightily.   *fear for*
RICHARD GLOUCESTER Now by Saint Paul, that news is bad indeed.
140   O he hath kept an evil diet° long,   *way of life*
    And overmuch consumed his royal person.[5]
    'Tis very grievous to be thought upon.
    Where is he? In his bed?
LORD HASTINGS   He is.
RICHARD GLOUCESTER Go you before and I will follow you.
                                   Exit HASTINGS
145   He cannot live, I hope, and must not die
    Till George be packed with post-haste° up to heaven.   *by express*
    I'll in to urge his hatred more to Clarence,
    With lies well steeled° with weighty arguments.   *made strong*
    And if I fail not in my deep intent,
150   Clarence hath not another day to live—
    Which done, God take King Edward to his mercy
    And leave the world for me to bustle in.
    For then I'll marry Warwick's youngest daughter.[6]
    What though I killed her husband and her father?[7]
155   The readiest way to make the wench amends
    Is to become her husband and her father,
    The which will I: not all so much for love,
    As for another secret close intent,°   *private purpose*
    By marrying her, which I must reach unto.
160   But yet I run before my horse to market.
    Clarence still breathes, Edward still lives and reigns;
    When they are gone, then must I count my gains.   *Exit*

1.2

Enter [gentlemen, bearing] the corpse of [King] Henry VI
[in an open coffin], with halberdiers[1] to guard it,
    LADY ANNE *being the mourner*
LADY ANNE Set down, set down your honourable load,
    If honour may be shrouded in a hearse,°   *an open coffin*
    Whilst I a while obsequiously° lament   *mournfully*
    Th'untimely fall of virtuous Lancaster.[2]
    [They set the coffin down]
5   Poor key-cold[3] figure of a holy king,
    Pale ashes of the house of Lancaster,
    Thou bloodless remnant of that royal blood:
    Be it lawful that I invocate thy ghost[4]
    To hear the lamentations of poor Anne,
10   Wife to thy Edward, to thy slaughtered son,

---

5. And has been weakened by extravagant living.
6. Lady Anne Neville, who had been betrothed (but not married) to Edward, Prince of Wales, the son of King Henry VI. Shakespeare, however, writes of Anne as Edward's widow.
7. *her father:* Henry VI (father-in-law).
1.2 Location: A street in London.
1. Men carrying halberds (a spearlike weapon with a

blade as well as a point).
2. Henry VI, of the house of Lancaster, was deposed and murdered by the Yorkists. The dynastic quarrel dates from the deposition of Richard II and is dramatized in Shakespeare's three *Henry VI* plays.
3. Proverbial for "cold as death."
4. Conjuring of spirits was generally condemned. *invocate:* invoke.

Stabbed by the selfsame hand that made these wounds.
Lo, in these windows[5] that let forth thy life,
I pour the helpless° balm of my poor eyes.   *useless*
O cursèd be the hand that made these holes,

15   Cursèd the blood that let this blood from hence,
Cursèd the heart that had the heart to do it.
More direful hap betide° that hated wretch   *fate befall*
That makes us wretched by the death of thee
Than I can wish to wolves, to spiders, toads,

20   Or any creeping venomed thing that lives.
If ever he have child, abortive° be it,   *incompletely formed*
Prodigious,° and untimely brought to light,   *Monstrous*
Whose ugly and unnatural aspect°   *appearance*
May fright the hopeful mother at the view,

25   And that be heir to his unhappiness.[6]
If ever he have wife, let her be made
More miserable by the death of him
Than I am made by my young lord and thee.[7]—
Come now towards Chertsey° with your holy load,   *monastery near London*

30   Taken from Paul's[8] to be interrèd there,
      [*The gentlemen lift the coffin*]
And still as° you are weary of this weight   *Whenever*
Rest you, whiles I lament King Henry's corpse.
      Enter RICHARD *Duke of* GLOUCESTER

RICHARD GLOUCESTER [*to the gentlemen*] Stay, you that bear
    the corpse, and set it down.
LADY ANNE What black magician conjures up this fiend

35   To stop devoted charitable deeds?
RICHARD GLOUCESTER [*to the gentlemen*] Villains,° set down   *Scoundrels; peasants*
    the corpse, or by Saint Paul
I'll make a corpse of him that disobeys.
HALBERDIER My lord, stand back and let the coffin pass.
RICHARD GLOUCESTER Unmannered dog, stand thou when I command.

40   Advance[9] thy halberd higher than my breast,
Or by Saint Paul I'll strike thee to my foot
And spurn° upon thee, beggar, for thy boldness.   *kick*
      [*They set the coffin down*]
LADY ANNE [*to gentlemen and halberdiers*] What, do you tremble?
    Are you all afraid?
Alas, I blame you not, for you are mortal,

45   And mortal eyes cannot endure the devil.—
Avaunt,° thou dreadful minister of hell.   *Be gone*
Thou hadst but power over his mortal body;
His soul thou canst not have; therefore be gone.
RICHARD GLOUCESTER Sweet saint, for charity be not so cursed.°   *bad-tempered*

50 LADY ANNE Foul devil, for God's sake hence and trouble us not,
For thou hast made the happy earth thy hell,
Filled it with cursing cries and deep exclaims.
If thou delight to view thy heinous deeds,
Behold this pattern° of thy butcheries.—   *example*

55   O gentlemen, see, see! Dead Henry's wounds

---

5. Stab wounds (possibly referring to the custom of opening the windows to let a dying soul pass).
6. Evil nature; ill fortune.
7. By the deaths of Prince Edward and King Henry VI.
8. St. Paul's, cathedral of the City of London.
9. Raise upright (rather than hold it pointing at Richard).

Ope their congealèd mouths and bleed afresh.[1]—
Blush, blush, thou lump of foul deformity,
For 'tis thy presence that ex-hales° this blood   *calls forth*
From cold and empty veins where no blood dwells.
60   Thy deed, inhuman and unnatural,
Provokes this deluge supernatural.[2]
O God, which this blood mad'st, revenge his death.
O earth, which this blood drink'st, revenge his death.
Either heav'n with lightning strike the murd'rer dead,
65   Or earth gape open wide and eat him quick°   *alive*
As thou dost swallow up this good king's blood,
Which his hell-governed arm hath butcherèd.
    RICHARD GLOUCESTER   Lady, you know no rules of charity,
Which renders good for bad, blessings for curses.
70   LADY ANNE   Villain, thou know'st no law of God nor man.
No beast so fierce but knows some touch of pity.
    RICHARD GLOUCESTER   But I know none, and therefore am no beast.
    LADY ANNE   O wonderful, when devils tell the truth![3]
    RICHARD GLOUCESTER   More wonderful, when angels are so angry.
75   Vouchsafe,° divine perfection of a woman,   *Grant*
Of these supposèd crimes to give me leave
By circumstance° but to acquit myself.   *detailed argument*
    LADY ANNE   Vouchsafe, diffused[4] infection of a man,
Of these known evils but to give me leave
80   By circumstance t'accuse thy cursèd self.
    RICHARD GLOUCESTER   Fairer than tongue can name thee, let me have
Some patient leisure to excuse myself.
    LADY ANNE   Fouler than heart can think thee, thou canst make
No excuse current° but to hang thyself.   *valid*
85   RICHARD GLOUCESTER   By such despair I should accuse myself.
    LADY ANNE   And by despairing shalt thou stand excused,
For doing worthy vengeance on thyself
That didst unworthy slaughter upon others.
    RICHARD GLOUCESTER   Say that I slew them not.
    LADY ANNE   Then say they were not slain.
90   But dead they are—and, devilish slave, by thee.
    RICHARD GLOUCESTER   I did not kill your husband.
    LADY ANNE   Why, then he is alive.
    RICHARD GLOUCESTER   Nay, he is dead, and slain by Edward's hand.
    LADY ANNE   In thy foul throat thou liest. Queen Margaret saw
Thy murd'rous falchion° smoking in his blood,[5]   *curved sword*
95   The which thou once didst bend against° her breast,   *turn toward*
But that thy brothers beat aside the point.
    RICHARD GLOUCESTER   I was provokèd by her sland'rous tongue,
That laid their guilt upon my guiltless shoulders.
    LADY ANNE   Thou wast provokèd by thy bloody mind,
100   That never dream'st on aught° but butcheries.   *anything*
Didst thou not kill this king?
    RICHARD GLOUCESTER   I grant ye.

---

1. A murdered victim's wounds were supposed to bleed
again in the presence of the murderer.
2. Q, F: most unnatural. The emendation underscores
Anne's call (in the next line) for divine intervention.
3. That is, Richard is a devil, not man or beast.

4. Misshapen, but also an infection whose harmful
effects are dispersed widely.
5. In *Richard Duke of York* (3 *Henry VI*) 5.5, King
Edward stabbed the Prince first, and Richard followed.

LADY ANNE   Dost grant me, hedgehog?[6] Then God grant me, too,
Thou mayst be damnèd for that wicked deed.
O he was gentle, mild, and virtuous.

105 RICHARD GLOUCESTER   The better for the King of Heaven that hath him.

LADY ANNE   He *is* in heaven, where thou shalt never come.

RICHARD GLOUCESTER   Let him thank me that holp° that to send him thither,   helped
For he was fitter for that place than earth.

LADY ANNE   And thou unfit for any place but hell.

110 RICHARD GLOUCESTER   Yes, one place else, if you will hear me name it.

LADY ANNE   Some dungeon.

RICHARD GLOUCESTER   Your bedchamber.

LADY ANNE   Ill rest betide° the chamber where thou liest.   befall

RICHARD GLOUCESTER   So will it, madam, till I lie with you.

LADY ANNE   I hope so.

RICHARD GLOUCESTER   I know so. But gentle Lady Anne,
115 To leave this keen encounter of our wits
And fall something into a slower method,[7]
Is not the causer of the timeless° deaths   untimely
Of these Plantagenets,[8] Henry and Edward,
As blameful as the executioner?

120 LADY ANNE   Thou wast the cause of that accursed effect.

RICHARD GLOUCESTER   Your beauty was the cause of that effect—
Your beauty that did haunt me in my sleep
To undertake the death of all the world
So I might live one hour in your sweet bosom.

125 LADY ANNE   If I thought that, I tell thee, homicide,°   murderer
These nails should rend that beauty from my cheeks.

RICHARD GLOUCESTER   These eyes could not endure sweet beauty's wreck.
You should not blemish it if I stood by.
As all the world is cheerèd by the sun,
130 So I by that: it is my day, my life.

LADY ANNE   Black night o'ershade thy day, and death thy life.

RICHARD GLOUCESTER   Curse not thyself, fair creature: thou art both.

LADY ANNE   I would I were, to be revenged on thee.[9]

RICHARD GLOUCESTER   It is a quarrel most unnatural,
135 To be revenged on him that loveth you.

LADY ANNE   It is a quarrel just and reasonable,
To be revenged on him that killed my husband.

RICHARD GLOUCESTER   He that bereft thee, lady, of thy husband,
Did it to help thee to a better husband.

140 LADY ANNE   His better doth not breathe upon the earth.

RICHARD GLOUCESTER   He lives that loves thee better than he° could.   (Edward)

LADY ANNE   Name him.

RICHARD GLOUCESTER   Plantagenet.

LADY ANNE   Why, that was he.

RICHARD GLOUCESTER   The selfsame name, but one of better nature.

LADY ANNE   Where is he?

RICHARD GLOUCESTER   Here.
                    She spits at him
                    Why dost thou spit at me?

145 LADY ANNE   Would it were mortal poison for thy sake.

---

6. Term of abuse applied to someone who pays no attention to others' feelings; alluding to Richard's humped back and his heraldic badge, the boar.
7. And argue somewhat less hastily.
8. The royal house from which both Lancastrians, including Henry and his son Edward, and Yorkists, including Richard himself, descended.
9. That is, if Anne were Richard's day and his life, she could end both and thus be revenged on him.

RICHARD GLOUCESTER   Never came poison from so sweet a place.

LADY ANNE   Never hung poison on a fouler toad.[1]
  Out of my sight! Thou dost infect mine eyes.

RICHARD GLOUCESTER   Thine eyes, sweet lady, have infected mine.

150   LADY ANNE   Would° they were basilisks[2] to strike thee dead.   *I wish that*

RICHARD GLOUCESTER   I would they were, that I might die at once,°   *once and for all*
  For now they kill me with a living death.
  Those eyes of thine from mine have drawn salt tears,
  Shamed their aspects° with store of childish drops.[3]   *appearance*

154.1   *These eyes, which never shed remorseful tear—*
      No, when my father York and Edward[4] wept
      To hear the piteous moan that Rutland[5] made
      When black-faced° Clifford shook his sword at him;   *threatening*

154.5   *Nor when thy warlike father° like a child*   *(Warwick)*
      Told the sad story of my father's death
      And twenty times made pause to sob and weep,
      That all the standers-by had wet their cheeks
      Like trees bedashed with rain. In that sad time

154.10   *My manly eyes did scorn an humble tear,*
      And what these sorrows could not thence exhale°   *draw out*
      Thy beauty hath, and made them blind with weeping.

155   I never sued° to friend nor enemy;   *petitioned*
  My tongue could never learn sweet smoothing° word;   *flattering*
  But now thy beauty is proposed my fee,°   *recompense*
  My proud heart sues and prompts my tongue to speak.
      She looks scornfully at him
  Teach not thy lip such scorn, for it was made

160   For kissing, lady, not for such contempt.
  If thy revengeful heart cannot forgive,
      [*He kneels and offers her his sword*]
  Lo, here I lend thee this sharp-pointed sword,
  Which if thou please to hide in this true breast
  And let the soul forth that adoreth thee,

165   I lay it naked to the deadly stroke
  And humbly beg the death upon my knee.
      He lays his breast open;° she offers° at [it] with his sword   *bare / thrusts*
  Nay, do not pause, for I did kill King Henry;
  But 'twas thy beauty that provokèd me.
  Nay, now dispatch: 'twas I that stabbed young Edward;

170   But 'twas thy heavenly face that set me on.
      She lets fall the sword
  Take up the sword again, or take up me.

LADY ANNE   Arise, dissembler.
      [*He rises*]
                Though I wish thy death,
  I will not be thy executioner.

RICHARD GLOUCESTER   Then bid me kill myself, and I will do it.

LADY ANNE   I have already.

175   RICHARD GLOUCESTER   That was in thy rage.
  Speak it again, and even with the word

---

1. Toads were popularly regarded as "ugly and ven- omous" (*As You Like It* 2.1.13).
2. Legendary monsters, supposed to kill with a glance.
3. The indented passage that follows, 154.1–154.12, appears only in F.

4. His brother, now the King.
5. Historically, Rutland was Richard's older brother. Shakespeare unhistorically makes him a child. His death is dramatized in *Richard Duke of York* 1.3–2.1.

This hand—which for thy love did kill thy love—
Shall, for thy love, kill a far truer love.
To both their deaths shalt thou be accessary.

180 LADY ANNE   I would I knew thy heart.

RICHARD GLOUCESTER   'Tis figured in my tongue.

LADY ANNE   I fear me both are false.

RICHARD GLOUCESTER   Then never man was true.

LADY ANNE   Well, well, put up your sword.

185 RICHARD GLOUCESTER   Say then my peace is made.

LADY ANNE   That shalt thou know hereafter.

RICHARD GLOUCESTER   But shall I live in hope?

LADY ANNE   All men, I hope, live so.

RICHARD GLOUCESTER   Vouchsafe° to wear this ring.   *Consent*

190 LADY ANNE   To take is not to give.⁶

RICHARD GLOUCESTER   Look how my ring encompasseth° thy finger;   *encircles*
Even so thy breast encloseth my poor heart.
Wear both of them, for both of them are thine.
And if thy poor devoted servant° may   *lover*

195 But beg one favour at thy gracious hand,
Thou dost confirm his happiness for ever.

LADY ANNE   What is it?

RICHARD GLOUCESTER   That it may please you leave these sad designs°   *affairs*
To him that hath most cause to be a mourner,

200 And presently° repair to Crosby House,⁷   *at once*
Where—after I have solemnly interred
At Chertsey monast'ry this noble king,
And wet his grave with my repentant tears—
I will with all expedient° duty see you.   *prompt*

205 For divers unknown° reasons, I beseech you   *various secret*
Grant me this boon.°   *favor*

LADY ANNE   With all my heart—and much it joys me, too,
To see you are become so penitent.
Tressell and Berkeley, go along with me.

RICHARD GLOUCESTER   Bid me farewell.

210 LADY ANNE   'Tis more than you deserve.⁸
But since you teach me how to flatter you,
Imagine I have said farewell already.   *Exeunt two with* ANNE

RICHARD GLOUCESTER   Sirs, take up the corpse.

GENTLEMAN   Towards Chertsey, noble lord?

RICHARD GLOUCESTER   No, to Blackfriars; there attend° my coming.   *await*
                          Exeunt [with] corpse. Manet° GLOUCESTER   *Remains*

215 Was ever woman in this humour° wooed?   *mood; manner*
Was ever woman in this humour won?
I'll have her, but I will not keep her long.
What, I that killed her husband and his father,
To take her in her heart's extremest hate,

220 With curses in her mouth, tears in her eyes,
The bleeding witness of my hatred by,
Having God, her conscience, and these bars° against me,   *obstacles*
And I no friends to back my suit withal
But the plain devil and dissembling looks—

225 And yet to win her, all the world to nothing?° Ha!   *against such odds*

---

6. To take your ring is not to give myself.   8. That is, to fare well is more than you deserve.
7. One of Richard's London residences.

    Hath she forgot already that brave prince,
    Edward her lord, whom I some three months since
    Stabbed in my angry mood at Tewkesbury?
    A sweeter and a lovelier gentleman,
230 Framed in the prodigality of nature,⁹
    Young, valiant, wise, and no doubt right royal,
    The spacious world cannot again afford°—   *provide*
    And will she yet abase° her eyes on me,   *lower; humble*
    That cropped the golden prime¹ of this sweet prince
235 And made her widow to a woeful bed?
    On me, whose all not equals Edward's moiety?°   *half*
    On me, that halts° and am misshapen thus?   *limp*
    My dukedom to a beggarly *denier*,²
    I do mistake my person all this while.
240 Upon my life she finds, although I cannot,
    Myself to be a marv'lous proper° man.   *handsome*
    I'll be at charges for° a looking-glass   *I'll buy*
    And entertain° a score or two of tailors   *hire*
    To study fashions to adorn my body.
245 Since I am crept in° favour with myself,   *into*
    I will maintain it with some little cost.
    But first I'll turn yon fellow in his grave,
    And then return lamenting to my love.
    Shine out, fair sun, till I have bought a glass,
250 That I may see my shadow as I pass.   *Exit*

1.3

Enter QUEEN [ELIZABETH], *Lord* RIVERS, [*Marquis* DORSET],
  and Lord GRAY
RIVERS [*to* ELIZABETH] Have patience, madam. There's no doubt his majesty
  Will soon recover his accustomed health.
GRAY [*to* ELIZABETH] In that you brook it ill,° it makes him worse. *take it badly*
  Therefore, for God's sake entertain good comfort,
5 And cheer his grace with quick° and merry eyes.   *lively*
QUEEN ELIZABETH If he were dead, what would betide on° me?   *befall*
RIVERS¹ No other harm but loss of such a lord.
QUEEN ELIZABETH The loss of such a lord includes all harms.
GRAY The heavens have blessed you with a goodly son
10 To be your comforter when he is gone.
QUEEN ELIZABETH Ah, he is young, and his minority
  Is put unto the trust of Richard Gloucester,
  A man that loves not me—nor none of you.
RIVERS Is it concluded° he shall be Protector?   *officially decreed*
15 QUEEN ELIZABETH It is determined,° not concluded yet;   *decided*
  But so it must be, if the King miscarry.°   *die*
    Enter [*the Duke of*] BUCKINGHAM *and* [*Lord* STANLEY
    Earl of] *Derby*
GRAY Here come the Lords of Buckingham and Derby.
BUCKINGHAM [*to* ELIZABETH] Good time of day unto your royal grace.
STANLEY [*to* ELIZABETH] God make your majesty joyful, as you have been.

---

9. Made when nature in its gift giving was being lavish.
1. Springtime (Richard "cropped," or harvested, Edward's life prematurely).
2. French coin, one-twelfth of a sou (extremely little).

to: against (as in betting).
1.3 Location: The royal palace of Westminster.
1. F: Gray. Rivers's role in the conversation is far fuller in Q than in F (see lines 30, 54).

20 QUEEN ELIZABETH   The Countess Richmond,[2] good my lord of Derby,
　　　To your good prayer will scarcely say 'Amen'.
　　　Yet, Derby—notwithstanding she's your wife,
　　　And loves not me—be you, good lord, assured
　　　I hate not you for her proud arrogance.
25 STANLEY   I do beseech you, either not believe
　　　The envious° slanders of her false accusers　　　　　　　　　*malicious*
　　　Or, if she be accused on true report,
　　　Bear with her weakness, which I think proceeds
　　　From wayward° sickness, and no grounded malice.　　　*not easily treated*
30 RIVERS   Saw you the King today, my lord of Derby?
　　　STANLEY   But° now the Duke of Buckingham and I　　　　　　*Just*
　　　Are come from visiting his majesty.
　　　QUEEN ELIZABETH   With likelihood of his amendment,° lords?　　*recovery*
　　　BUCKINGHAM   Madam, good hope: his grace speaks cheerfully.
35 QUEEN ELIZABETH   God grant him health. Did you confer with him?
　　　BUCKINGHAM   Ay, madam. He desires to make atonement°　　　*reconciliation*
　　　Between the Duke of Gloucester and your brothers,
　　　And between them and my Lord Chamberlain,°　　　　　　*(Hastings)*
　　　And sent to warn° them to his royal presence.　　　　　　*summon*
40 QUEEN ELIZABETH   Would all were well! But that will never be.
　　　I fear our happiness is at the height.[3]

　　　　　Enter RICHARD [*Duke of*] GLOUCESTER [*and* LORD
　　　　　HASTINGS]

　　　RICHARD GLOUCESTER   They do me wrong, and I will not endure it.
　　　Who are they that complain unto the King
　　　That I forsooth am stern and love them not?
45 By holy Paul, they love his grace but lightly
　　　That fill his ears with such dissentious rumours.
　　　Because I cannot flatter and look fair,
　　　Smile in men's faces, smooth,° deceive, and cog,°　　　　　*flatter / cheat*
　　　Duck with French nods[4] and apish° courtesy,　　　　*imitative; clumsy*
50 I must be held a rancorous enemy.
　　　Cannot a plain man live and think no harm,
　　　But thus his simple truth must be abused
　　　With° silken, sly, insinuating jacks?°　　　　　　　　　*By / nobodies*
　　　RIVERS   To whom in all this presence° speaks your grace?　*present company*
55 RICHARD GLOUCESTER   To thee, that hast nor honesty nor grace.
　　　When have I injured thee? When done thee wrong?
　　　Or thee? Or thee? Or any of your faction?
　　　A plague upon you all! His royal grace—
　　　Whom God preserve better than you would wish—
60 Cannot be quiet scarce a breathing while[5]
　　　But you must trouble him with lewd° complaints.　　　　　*ignorant*
　　　QUEEN ELIZABETH   Brother of Gloucester, you mistake the matter.
　　　The King—on his own royal disposition,°　　　　　　　　*inclination*
　　　And not provoked by any suitor else—
65 Aiming belike° at your interior hatred,　　　　　　　*Guessing probably*
　　　That in your outward action shows itself
　　　Against my children, brothers, and myself,

2. Lady Margaret Beaufort, Lord Stanley's wife, was (by an earlier marriage) the mother of Henry Tudor, Earl of Richmond, who at play's end succeeds Richard and becomes Henry VII. As a descendant of the house of Lancaster, she was unlikely to have friendly feelings toward the Yorkist King Edward IV or his family.
3. At its highest point on Fortune's proverbial wheel, and thus about to decline.
4. *French nods*: elaborate bows.
5. Long enough to catch his breath.

Makes[6] him to send, that he may learn the ground
Of your ill will, and thereby to remove it.

70 RICHARD GLOUCESTER   I cannot tell. The world is grown so bad
That wrens make prey where eagles dare not perch.
Since every jack became a gentleman,
There's many a gentle person made a jack.

QUEEN ELIZABETH   Come, come, we know your meaning, brother Gloucester.
75 You envy my advancement, and my friends'.
God grant we never may have need of you.

RICHARD GLOUCESTER   Meantime, God grants that I have need of you.
Our brother° is imprisoned by your means,   (Clarence)
Myself disgraced, and the nobility
80 Held in contempt, while great promotions
Are daily given to ennoble those
That scarce some two days since were worth a noble.[7]

QUEEN ELIZABETH   By him° that raised me to this care-full height   (God)
From that contented hap° which I enjoyed,   fortune; lot
85 I never did incense his majesty
Against the Duke of Clarence, but have been
An earnest advocate to plead for him.
My lord, you do me shameful injury
Falsely to draw me in these vile suspects.°   suspicions

90 RICHARD GLOUCESTER   You may deny that you were not the mean°   instigation
Of my Lord Hastings' late imprisonment.

RIVERS   She may, my lord, for—

RICHARD GLOUCESTER   She may, Lord Rivers; why, who knows not so?
She may do more, sir, than denying that.
95 She may help you to many fair preferments,°   lucrative positions
And then deny her aiding hand therein,
And lay those honours on[8] your high desert.
What may she not? She may—ay, marry,[9] may she.

RIVERS   What 'marry, may she'?

100 RICHARD GLOUCESTER   What marry, may she? Marry with a king:
A bachelor, and a handsome stripling,° too.   young man
Iwis your grandam had a worser match.[1]

QUEEN ELIZABETH   My lord of Gloucester, I have too long borne
Your blunt upbraidings and your bitter scoffs.
105 By heaven, I will acquaint his majesty
Of those gross taunts that oft I have endured.
I had rather be a country servant-maid
Than a great queen, with this condition:
To be so baited,° scorned, and stormèd at.   provoked
        Enter old QUEEN MARGARET[2] [*unseen behind them*]
110 Small joy have I in being England's queen.

QUEEN MARGARET [*aside*]   And lessened be that small, God I beseech him.
Thy honour, state,° and seat° is due to me.   rank / throne

RICHARD GLOUCESTER [*to* ELIZABETH]   What? Threat you me
        with telling of the King?
Tell him, and spare not. Look what° I have said,   Whatever

---

6. The grammatical subject is still "the King."
7. Gold coin, worth one-third of a pound sterling.
8. And attribute those honors to.
9. Indeed (originally, an oath on the Virgin Mary), with pun in nest line on "wed."
1. Your mother (and the Queen's) was born of a less

distinguished union. *Iwis*: Assuredly (already archaic).
2. Historically, Margaret—widow of the Lancastrian King Henry VI—was held prisoner in England for five years after her husband's defeat at the Battle of Tewkesbury and then exiled to France.

115   I will avouch't in presence of the King.

        I dare adventure to be° sent to th' Tower.   *I risk being*

        'Tis time to speak; my pains³ are quite forgot.

        QUEEN MARGARET [*aside*]   Out, devil! I remember them too well.

        Thou killed'st my husband Henry in the Tower,

120   And Edward, my poor son, at Tewkesbury.

        RICHARD GLOUCESTER [*to* ELIZABETH]   Ere you were queen—

            ay, or your husband king—

        I was a packhorse° in his great affairs,   *beast of burden*

        A weeder-out of his proud adversaries,

        A liberal rewarder of his friends.

125   To royalize his blood, I spent mine own.

        QUEEN MARGARET [*aside*]   Ay, and much better blood than his or thine.

        RICHARD GLOUCESTER [*to* ELIZABETH]   In all which time you

            and your husband Gray

        Were factious° for the house of Lancaster;   *partisan*

        And Rivers, so were you.—Was not your husband

130   In Margaret's battle° at Saint Albans slain?⁴   *army*

        Let me put in your minds, if you forget,

        What you have been ere this, and what you are;

        Withal,° what I have been, and what I am.   *In addition; also*

        QUEEN MARGARET [*aside*]   A murd'rous villain, and so still thou art.

135   RICHARD GLOUCESTER   Poor Clarence did forsake his father⁵ Warwick—

        Ay, and forswore himself, which Jesu pardon—

        QUEEN MARGARET [*aside*]   Which God revenge!

        RICHARD GLOUCESTER   To fight on Edward's party° for the crown,   *side*

        And for his meed,° poor lord, he is mewed up.   *reward*

140   I would to God my heart were flint like Edward's,

        Or Edward's soft and pitiful like mine.

        I am too childish-foolish for this world.

        QUEEN MARGARET [*aside*]   Hie° thee to hell for shame, and leave this world,   *Hurry*

        Thou cacodemon;° there thy kingdom is.   *evil spirit*

145   RIVERS   My lord of Gloucester, in those busy days

        Which here you urge° to prove us enemies,   *recall*

        We followed then our lord, our sovereign king.

        So should we you, if you should be our king.

        RICHARD GLOUCESTER   If I should be? I had rather be a pedlar.

150   Far be it from my heart, the thought thereof.

        QUEEN ELIZABETH   As little joy, my lord, as you suppose

        You should enjoy, were you this country's king,

        As little joy may you suppose in me,

        That I enjoy being the queen thereof.

155   QUEEN MARGARET [*aside*]   Ah, little joy enjoys the queen thereof,

        For I am she, and altogether joyless.

        I can no longer hold me patient.

            [*She comes forward*]

        Hear me, you wrangling pirates, that fall out

        In sharing that which you have pilled° from me.   *pillaged*

160   Which of you trembles not that looks on me?

        If not that I am Queen, you bow like subjects;

---

3. Efforts, trouble (on the King's behalf).
4. Queen Elizabeth's first husband, Sir John Gray, died fighting for the Lancastrian faction.
5. Father-in-law. Clarence married Warwick's daughter Isabella, sister of this play's Lady Anne, and for a time defied his brothers by supporting the Lancastrian faction. He "forswore himself" (line 136) by returning to fight for the Yorkish faction.

Yet that by you deposed, you quake like rebels.[6]
[*To* RICHARD] Ah, gentle villain,[7] do not turn away.

RICHARD GLOUCESTER   Foul wrinkled witch, what mak'st thou°   *what are you doing*
    in my sight?

165   QUEEN MARGARET   But repetition° of what thou hast marred: *recounting*
    That will I make before I let thee go.[8]

166.1   RICHARD GLOUCESTER   *Wert thou not banishèd on pain of death?*
      QUEEN MARGARET   *I was, but I do find more pain in banishment*
      Than death can yield me here by my abode.
    A husband and a son thou ow'st to me,
    [*To* ELIZABETH] And thou a kingdom; [*to the rest*] all of you allegiance.
    This sorrow that I have by right is yours,
170   And all the pleasures you usurp are mine.

RICHARD GLOUCESTER   The curse my noble father laid on thee—
    When thou didst crown his warlike brows with paper,
    And with thy scorns° drew'st rivers from his eyes,   *mocking speeches*
    And then, to dry them, gav'st the duke a clout°   *rag; handkerchief*
175   Steeped in the faultless° blood of pretty Rutland[9]—   *innocent*
    His curses then, from bitterness of soul
    Denounced against thee, are all fall'n upon thee,
    And God, not we, hath plagued thy bloody deed.

QUEEN ELIZABETH [*to* MARGARET]   So just is God to right the innocent.

LORD HASTINGS [*to* MARGARET]   O 'twas the foulest deed to slay
180   that babe,°   *(Rutland)*
    And the most merciless that e'er was heard of.

RIVERS [*to* MARGARET]   Tyrants themselves wept when it was reported.

DORSET [*to* MARGARET]   No man but prophesied revenge for it.

BUCKINGHAM [*to* MARGARET]   Northumberland, then present, wept to see it.

185   QUEEN MARGARET   What? Were you snarling all before I came,
    Ready to catch each other by the throat,
    And turn you all your hatred now on me?
    Did York's dread curse prevail so much with heaven
    That Henry's death, my lovely Edward's death,
190   Their kingdom's loss, my woeful banishment,
    Should all but answer for° that peevish brat?   *Should merely equal*
    Can curses pierce the clouds and enter heaven?
    Why then, give way, dull clouds, to my quick° curses!   *lively*
    Though not by war, by surfeit° die your king,   *high living*
195   As ours by murder to make him a king.
    [*to* ELIZABETH] Edward thy son, that now is Prince of Wales,
    For Edward my son, that was Prince of Wales,
    Die in his youth by like° untimely violence.   *similarly*
    Thyself, a queen, for me that was a queen,
200   Outlive thy glory like my wretched self.
    Long mayst thou live—to wail thy children's death,
    And see another, as I see thee now,
    Decked° in thy rights, as thou art 'stalled° in mine.   *Dressed / installed*
    Long die thy happy days before thy death,
205   And after many lengthened hours of grief
    Die, neither mother, wife, nor England's queen.—

---

6. *If . . . rebels:* Even if you do not bow because I am Queen, at least you tremble like rebels because you deposed me.
7. Well-born peasant; kindly scoundrel.
8. The indented passage that follows, 166.1–166.3, appears only in F.
9. This is dramatized in *Richard Duke of York* 1.4.80–96, in which Margaret crowns the Duke of York with a paper crown and waves a handkerchief dipped in his son Rutland's blood in front of his eyes.

Rivers and Dorset, you were standers-by,
And so wast thou, Lord Hastings,[1] when my son
Was stabbed with bloody daggers. God I pray him,
210 That none of you may live his natural age,
But by some unlooked° accident cut off.   *unlooked-for*
RICHARD GLOUCESTER   Have done thy charm,° thou hateful,   *spell; curse*
    withered hag.
QUEEN MARGARET   And leave out thee? Stay, dog, for thou shalt hear me.
If heaven have any grievous plague in store
215 Exceeding those that I can wish upon thee,
O let them keep it till thy sins be ripe,
And then hurl down their indignation
On thee, the troubler of the poor world's peace.
The worm of conscience still begnaw thy soul.
220 Thy friends suspect for° traitors while thou liv'st,   *to be*
And take deep traitors for thy dearest friends.
No sleep close up that deadly eye of thine,
Unless it be while some tormenting dream
Affrights thee with a hell of ugly devils.
225 Thou elvish-marked, abortive, rooting hog,[2]
Thou that wast sealed° in thy nativity   *stamped*
The slave of nature[3] and the son of hell,
Thou slander of thy heavy° mother's womb,   *sorrowful*
Thou loathèd issue of thy father's loins,
230 Thou rag of honour, thou detested—
RICHARD GLOUCESTER   Margaret.
QUEEN MARGARET   Richard.
RICHARD GLOUCESTER   Ha?
QUEEN MARGARET   I call thee not.
RICHARD GLOUCESTER   I cry thee mercy° then, for I did think   *I beg your pardon*
That thou hadst called me all these bitter names.
235 QUEEN MARGARET   Why so I did, but looked for no reply.
O let me make the period° to my curse.   *full stop; finish*
RICHARD GLOUCESTER   'Tis done by me, and ends in 'Margaret'.
QUEEN ELIZABETH [*to* MARGARET]   Thus have you breathed your
    curse against yourself.
QUEEN MARGARET   Poor painted Queen, vain flourish[4] of my fortune,
240 Why strew'st thou sugar on that bottled° spider   *bottle-shaped; swollen*
Whose deadly web ensnareth thee about?
Fool, fool, thou whet'st a knife to kill thyself.
The day will come that thou shalt wish for me
To help thee curse this poisonous bunch-backed° toad.   *hunchbacked*
245 LORD HASTINGS   False-boding° woman, end thy frantic curse,   *Falsely prophesying*
Lest to thy harm thou move our patience.
QUEEN MARGARET   Foul shame upon you, you have all moved mine.
RIVERS   Were you well served, you would be taught your duty.
QUEEN MARGARET   To serve me well you all should do me duty.°   *show me deference*
250 Teach me to be your queen, and you my subjects:
O serve me well, and teach yourselves that duty.
DORSET   Dispute not with her: she is lunatic.

---

1. Rivers, Dorset, and Hastings were not present at Prince Edward's murder at Tewkesbury as dramatized in *Richard Duke of York* 5.5, but they are in the chronicles that served as Shakespeare's sources. The Prince, in fact, was slain by unknown combatants during the battle.

2. Richard's emblem was the white boar. *elvish-marked*: deformed by evil fairies. *abortive*: misshapen.
3. Because he was deformed from birth.
4. *painted*: counterfeit, with play on "use of cosmetics." *vain flourish*: empty, meaningless decoration.

QUEEN MARGARET   Peace, master Marquis, you are malapert.°   *impertinent*
Your fire-new stamp of honour is scarce current.[5]
255   O that your young nobility could judge
What 'twere to lose it and be miserable.
They that stand high have many blasts to shake them,
And if they fall they dash themselves to pieces.
RICHARD GLOUCESTER   Good counsel, marry!—Learn it, learn it, Marquis.
260   DORSET   It touches you, my lord, as much as me.
RICHARD GLOUCESTER   Ay, and much more; but I was born so high.
Our eyrie[6] buildeth in the cedar's top,
And dallies with the wind, and scorns the sun.
QUEEN MARGARET   And turns the sun to shade. Alas, alas!
265   Witness my son, now in the shade of death,
Whose bright outshining beams thy cloudy wrath
Hath in eternal darkness folded up.
Your eyrie buildeth in our eyrie's nest.—
O God that seest it, do not suffer it;
270   As it was won with blood, lost be it so.
RICHARD GLOUCESTER   Peace, peace! For shame, if not for charity.
QUEEN MARGARET   Urge neither charity nor shame to me.
Uncharitably with me have you dealt,
And shamefully my hopes by you are butchered.
275   My charity is outrage; life, my shame;°   *my life is one of shame*
And in that shame still live my sorrow's rage.
BUCKINGHAM   Have done, have done.
QUEEN MARGARET   O princely Buckingham, I'll kiss thy hand
In sign of league and amity with thee.
280   Now fair befall° thee and thy noble house!   *good fortune to*
Thy garments are not spotted with our blood,
Nor thou within the compass° of my curse.   *scope*
BUCKINGHAM   Nor no one here, for curses never pass
The lips of those that breathe them in the air.[7]
285   QUEEN MARGARET   I will not think but they ascend the sky
And there awake God's gentle sleeping peace.
O Buckingham, take heed of yonder dog.
    [*She points at* RICHARD]
Look when he fawns, he bites; and when he bites,
His venom tooth will rankle[8] to the death.
290   Have naught to do with him; beware of him;
Sin, death, and hell have set their marks on him,
And all their ministers attend on him.
RICHARD GLOUCESTER   What doth she say, my lord of Buckingham?
BUCKINGHAM   Nothing that I respect, my gracious lord.
295   QUEEN MARGARET   What, dost thou scorn me for my gentle counsel,
And soothe the devil that I warn thee from?
O but remember this another day,
When he shall split thy very heart with sorrow,
And say, 'Poor Margaret was a prophetess'.—
300   Live each of you the subjects to his hate,
And he to yours, and all of you to God's.   *Exit*
HASTINGS   My hair doth stand on end to hear her curses.

5. Your recently acquired title is not yet secure (as newly minted coins that have not yet achieved common currency).
6. Eagle's brood (the sons of York).

7. *curses . . . air:* it is as if curses were never spoken or afflict only the curser.
8. Will cause a wound that will fester.

RIVERS   And so doth mine. I muse why she's at liberty.
RICHARD GLOUCESTER   I cannot blame her, by God's holy mother.
305   She hath had too much wrong, and I repent
My part thereof that I have done to her.
QUEEN ELIZABETH   I never did her any, to my knowledge.
RICHARD GLOUCESTER   Yet you have all the vantage of her wrong.[9]
I was too hot° to do somebody good,   *eager*
310   That° is too cold° in thinking of it now.   *Who / ungrateful*
Marry, as for Clarence, he is well repaid:
He is franked up to fatting[1] for his pains.
God pardon them that are the cause thereof.
RIVERS   A virtuous and a Christian-like conclusion,
315   To pray for them that have done scathe° to us.   *harm*
RICHARD GLOUCESTER   So do I ever—(*speaks to himself*) being well advised:
For had I cursed now, I had cursed myself.
        Enter [Sir William] CATESBY
CATESBY   Madam, his majesty doth call for you,
And for your grace, and you my gracious lords.
320   QUEEN ELIZABETH   Catesby, I come.—Lords, will you go with me?
RIVERS   We wait upon your grace.   *Exeunt. Manet* RICHARD
RICHARD GLOUCESTER   I do the wrong, and first begin to brawl.°   *complain; protest*
The secret mischiefs that I set abroach°   *set in motion*
I lay unto the grievous charge of[2] others.
325   Clarence, whom I indeed have cast in darkness,
I do beweep to many simple gulls°—   *credulous fools*
Namely to Derby, Hastings, Buckingham—
And tell them, ''Tis the Queen and her allies
That stir the King against the Duke my brother'.
330   Now they believe it, and withal whet me
To be revenged on Rivers, Dorset, Gray;
But then I sigh, and with a piece of scripture
Tell them that God bids us do good for evil;
And thus I clothe my naked villainy
335   With odd old ends,° stol'n forth of Holy Writ,   *old bits and pieces*
And seem a saint when most I play the devil.
        Enter two MURDERERS
But soft, here come my executioners.—
How now, my hardy, stout, resolvèd° mates!   *resolute*
Are you now going to dispatch this thing?
340   A MURDERER   We are, my lord, and come to have the warrant,
That we may be admitted where he is.
RICHARD GLOUCESTER   Well thought upon; I have it here about me.
        [*He gives them the warrant*]
When you have done, repair° to Crosby Place.   *return*
But sirs, be sudden° in the execution,   *swift*
345   Withal obdurate; do not hear him plead,
For Clarence is well spoken, and perhaps
May move your hearts to pity, if you mark° him.   *listen to*
A MURDERER   Tut, tut, my lord, we will not stand to prate.
Talkers are no good doers. Be assured,
350   We go to use our hands, and not our tongues.

9. All the benefits acquired as a result of the wrong she   2. I make into a serious accusation against.
has suffered.
1. He is penned up to fatten (for slaughter, like a pig).

RICHARD GLOUCESTER   Your eyes drop millstones when fools'
    eyes fall° tears.   *let fall*
  I like you, lads. About your business straight.°   *straightaway*
  Go, go, dispatch.
MURDERERS   We will, my noble lord.
    Exeunt [RICHARD *at one door, the* MURDERERS *at another*]

1.4

Enter [*George Duke of*] CLARENCE [*and Sir Robert*
BRACKENBURY[1]]

BRACKENBURY   Why looks your grace so heavily° today?   *melancholy*
CLARENCE   O I have passed a miserable night,
  So full of fearful dreams, of ugly sights,
  That as I am a Christian faithful man,
5 I would not spend another such a night
  Though 'twere to buy a world of happy days,
  So full of dismal terror was the time.
BRACKENBURY   What was your dream, my lord? I pray you, tell me.
CLARENCE   Methoughts that I had broken from the Tower,
10 And was embarked to cross to Burgundy,
  And in my company my brother Gloucester,
  Who from my cabin tempted me to walk
  Upon the hatches;[2] there we looked toward England,
  And cited up° a thousand heavy times   *recalled*
15 During the wars of York and Lancaster
  That had befall'n us. As we paced along
  Upon the giddy footing of the hatches,
  Methought that Gloucester stumbled, and in falling
  Struck me—that sought to stay° him—overboard   *steady*
20 Into the tumbling billows of the main.
  O Lord! Methought what pain it was to drown,
  What dreadful noise of waters in my ears,
  What sights of ugly death within my eyes.
  Methoughts I saw a thousand fearful wrecks,
25 Ten thousand men that fishes gnawed upon,
  Wedges of gold, great ouches,[3] heaps of pearl,
  Inestimable° stones, unvalued° jewels,   *Countless / invaluable*
  All scattered in the bottom of the sea.
  Some lay in dead men's skulls; and in those holes
30 Where eyes did once inhabit, there were crept—
  As 'twere in scorn of eyes—reflecting gems,
  Which wooed the slimy bottom of the deep
  And mocked the dead bones that lay scattered by.
BRACKENBURY   Had you such leisure in the time of death,
35 To gaze upon these secrets of the deep?
CLARENCE   Methought I had, and often did I strive
  To yield the ghost,° but still° the envious° flood   *To die / always / malicious*
  Stopped-in° my soul and would not let it forth   *Stopped up*
  To find the empty, vast, and wand'ring air,
40 But smothered it within my panting bulk,°   *body*
  Who° almost burst to belch it in the sea.   *Which*

1.4 Location: In the Tower of London.
1. F gives this part to an anonymous keeper, Brackenbury not entering until line 72.
2. Planks laid across the hold of a ship, forming a temporary deck.
3. Gold or silver brooches set with jewels. Q, F: anchors.

BRACKENBURY Awaked you not in this sore agony?

CLARENCE No, no, my dream was lengthened after life.[4]

O then began the tempest to my soul!

45 I passed, methought, the melancholy flood,[5]
With that sour ferryman which poets write of,
Unto the kingdom of perpetual night.
The first that there did greet my stranger soul
Was my great father-in-law, renownèd Warwick,

50 Who cried aloud, 'What scourge° for perjury   punishment
Can this dark monarchy afford false Clarence?'
And so he vanished. Then came wand'ring by
A shadow[6] like an angel, with bright hair,
Dabbled in blood, and he shrieked out aloud,

55 'Clarence is come: false, fleeting,° perjured Clarence,   fickle
That stabbed me in the field by Tewkesbury.
Seize on him, furies![7] Take him unto torment!'
With that, methoughts a legion of foul fiends
Environed° me, and howlèd in mine ears   Surrounded

60 Such hideous cries that with the very noise
I trembling waked, and for a season after
Could not believe but that I was in hell,
Such terrible impression made my dream.

BRACKENBURY No marvel, lord, though° it affrighted you;   that

65 I am afraid, methinks, to hear you tell it.

CLARENCE Ah, Brackenbury, I have done these things,
That now give evidence against my soul,
For Edward's sake; and see how he requites me.[8]

68.1 *O God! If my deep prayers cannot appease thee*
But thou wilt be avenged on my misdeeds,
Yet execute thy wrath in me alone.
O spare my guiltless wife and my poor children.
Keeper, I pray thee, sit by me awhile.

70 My soul is heavy, and I fain would° sleep.   I desire to

BRACKENBURY I will, my lord. God give your grace good rest.

[CLARENCE *sleeps*]

Sorrow breaks seasons and reposing hours,[9]
Makes the night morning and the noontide night.
Princes have but their titles for their glories,

75 An outward honour for an inward toil,
And for unfelt imaginations[1]
They often feel a world of restless cares;
So that, between their titles and low name,
There's nothing differs but the outward fame.

Enter two MURDERERS

80 FIRST MURDERER Ho, who's here?

BRACKENBURY What wouldst thou, fellow? And how cam'st thou hither?

SECOND MURDERER I would speak with Clarence, and I came
hither on my legs.

4. My dream also depicted my fate after death.
5. The river Styx, across which Charon (the "sour ferryman" of the next line) ferried souls to Hades, the classical hell.
6. Shade, ghost (Edward, Prince of Wales—son of Henry VI, and Clarence's brother-in-law—whom Clarence helped to murder; see *Richard Duke of York* 5.5.40).
7. In Greek mythology, female spirits who enacted vengeance for blood crimes against relatives.
8. The indented passage that follows, 68.1–68.4, appears only in F. *requites*: repays.
9. Sorrow disrupts life's normal rhythms and disregards the hours appropriate to sleep.
1. *for unfelt imaginations*: "for the sake of imaginary and unreal gratifications" (Dr. Johnson).

BRACKENBURY What, so brief?

85 FIRST MURDERER 'Tis better, sir, than to be tedious. [*To* SECOND
 MURDERER] Let him see our commission,° and talk no more. *authorization*
 [BRACKENBURY] *reads*

BRACKENBURY I am in this commanded to deliver
 The noble Duke of Clarence to your hands.
 I will not reason what is meant hereby,

90 Because I will be° guiltless of the meaning. *wish to be*
 There lies the Duke asleep, and there the keys.
 [*He throws down the keys*]
 I'll to the King and signify to him
 That thus I have resigned to you my charge.° *responsibility*

FIRST MURDERER You may, sir; 'tis a point of wisdom. Fare you

95 well.   *Exit* [BRACKENBURY]

SECOND MURDERER What, shall I stab him as he sleeps?

FIRST MURDERER No. He'll say 'twas done cowardly, when he
 wakes.

SECOND MURDERER Why, he shall never wake until the great

100 judgement day.

FIRST MURDERER Why, then he'll say we stabbed him sleeping.

SECOND MURDERER The urging of that word 'judgement' hath
 bred a kind of remorse in me.

FIRST MURDERER What, art thou afraid?

105 SECOND MURDERER Not to kill him, having a warrant, but to
 be damned for killing him, from the which no warrant can
 defend me.

FIRST MURDERER I thought thou hadst been resolute.

SECOND MURDERER So I am—to let him live.

110 FIRST MURDERER I'll back to the Duke of Gloucester and tell
 him so.

SECOND MURDERER Nay, I pray thee. Stay a little. I hope this
 passionate humour° of mine will change. It was wont to hold *compassionate mood*
 me but while one tells° twenty. *counts*
 [*He counts to twenty*]

115 FIRST MURDERER How dost thou feel thyself now?

SECOND MURDERER Some certain dregs of conscience are yet
 within me.

FIRST MURDERER Remember our reward, when the deed's done.

SECOND MURDERER 'Swounds,° he dies. I had forgot the reward. *By God's wounds*

120 FIRST MURDERER Where's thy conscience now?

SECOND MURDERER O, in the Duke of Gloucester's purse.

FIRST MURDERER When he opens his purse to give us our
 reward, thy conscience flies out.

SECOND MURDERER 'Tis no matter. Let it go. There's few or

125 none will entertain° it. *host; employ*

FIRST MURDERER What if it come to thee again?

SECOND MURDERER I'll not meddle with it. It makes a man a coward. A man cannot steal but it accuseth him. A man cannot
 swear but it checks him. A man cannot lie with his neighbour's

130 wife but it detects him. 'Tis a blushing, shamefaced spirit, that
 mutinies in a man's bosom. It fills a man full of obstacles. It
 made me once restore a purse of gold that by chance I found.
 It beggars any man that keeps it. It is turned out of towns and
 cities for a dangerous thing, and every man that means to live

135 well endeavours to trust to himself and live without it.

FIRST MURDERER 'Swounds, 'tis even now at my elbow, persuading me not to kill the Duke.

SECOND MURDERER Take the devil in thy mind, and believe him°   (*conscience*)
not: he would insinuate with thee but to make thee sigh.[2]

140 FIRST MURDERER I am strong framed; he cannot prevail with
me.

SECOND MURDERER Spoke like a tall° man that respects thy rep-
utation. Come, shall we fall to work?   *valiant*

FIRST MURDERER Take him on the costard with the hilts of thy
145 sword, and then throw him into the malmsey butt[3] in the next
room.

SECOND MURDERER O excellent device!—and make a sop[4] of
him.

FIRST MURDERER Soft,° he wakes.   *Hush*

150 SECOND MURDERER Strike!

FIRST MURDERER No, we'll reason with him.

CLARENCE Where art thou, keeper? Give me a cup of wine.

SECOND MURDERER You shall have wine enough, my lord, anon.

CLARENCE In God's name, what art thou?

FIRST MURDERER   A man, as you are.

155 CLARENCE But not as I am, royal.

FIRST MURDERER Nor you as we are, loyal.

CLARENCE Thy voice is thunder, but thy looks are humble.

FIRST MURDERER My voice is now the King's;[5] my looks, mine own.

CLARENCE How darkly and how deadly dost thou speak.
160 Your eyes do menace me. Why look you pale?
Who sent you hither? Wherefore do you come?

SECOND MURDERER To, to, to—

CLARENCE   To murder me.

BOTH MURDERERS   Ay, ay.

CLARENCE You scarcely have the hearts to tell me so,
And therefore cannot have the hearts to do it.
165 Wherein, my friends, have I offended you?

FIRST MURDERER Offended us you have not, but the King.

CLARENCE I shall be reconciled to him again.

SECOND MURDERER Never, my lord; therefore prepare to die.

CLARENCE Are you drawn forth° among a world of men   *selected from*
170 To slay the innocent? What is my offence?
Where is the evidence that doth accuse me?
What lawful quest° have given their verdict up   *jury*
Unto the frowning judge, or who pronounced
The bitter sentence of poor Clarence' death?
175 Before I be convict by course of law,
To threaten me with death is most unlawful.
I charge you, as you hope to have redemption
By Christ's dear blood, shed for our grievous sins,
That you depart and lay no hands on me.
180 The deed you undertake is damnable.

FIRST MURDERER What we will do, we do upon command.

SECOND MURDERER And he that hath commanded is our king.

CLARENCE Erroneous vassals,° the great King of Kings   *Misguided subjects*

---

2. *he . . . sight:* he (conscience) would ingratiate himself with you simply to cause you grief.
3. Wine barrel (malmsey is a strong, sweet wine).

costard: head (literally, a large apple).
4. Piece of bread or wafer soaked in wine.
5. I am now acting on the King's command.

Hath in the table of his law° commanded   *the Ten Commandments*
185   That thou shalt do no murder. Will you then
       Spurn at his edict, and fulfil a man's?
       Take heed, for he holds vengeance in his hand
       To hurl upon their heads that break his law.
SECOND MURDERER   And that same vengeance doth he hurl on thee,
190   For false forswearing, and for murder too.
       Thou didst receive the sacrament[6] to fight
       In quarrel of° the house of Lancaster.   *On the side of*
FIRST MURDERER   And, like a traitor to the name of God,
       Didst break that vow, and with thy treacherous blade
195   Unripped'st the bowels of thy sov'reign's son.[7]
SECOND MURDERER   Whom thou wast sworn to cherish and defend.
FIRST MURDERER   How canst thou urge God's dreadful law to us,
       When thou hast broke it in such dear degree?
CLARENCE   Alas, for whose sake did I that ill deed?
200   For Edward, for my brother, for his sake.
       He sends ye not to murder me for this,
       For in that sin he is as deep as I.
       If God will be avengèd for the deed,
       O know you yet, he doth it publicly.
205   Take not the quarrel from his pow'rful arm;
       He needs no indirect or lawless course
       To cut off those that have offended him.
FIRST MURDERER   Who made thee then a bloody minister°   *agent*
       When gallant springing° brave Plantagenet,°   *sprightly / (Edward)*
210   That princely novice,° was struck dead by thee?   *youth*
CLARENCE   My brother's love,° the devil, and my rage.   *My love for my brother*
FIRST MURDERER   Thy brother's love, our duty, and thy faults
       Provoke us hither now to slaughter thee.
CLARENCE   If you do love my brother, hate not me.
215   I am his brother, and I love him well.
       If you are hired for meed,° go back again,   *reward*
       And I will send you to my brother Gloucester,
       Who shall reward you better for my life
       Than Edward will for tidings of my death.
220 SECOND MURDERER   You are deceived. Your brother Gloucester hates you.
CLARENCE   O no, he loves me, and he holds me dear.
       Go you to him from me.
FIRST MURDERER   Ay, so we will.
CLARENCE   Tell him, when that our princely father York
       Blessed his three sons with his victorious arm,
225   And charged us from his soul to love each other,
       He little thought of this divided friendship.
       Bid Gloucester think of this, and he will weep.
FIRST MURDERER   Ay, millstones, as he lessoned° us to weep.   *taught*
CLARENCE   O do not slander him, for he is kind.[8]
230 FIRST MURDERER   As snow in harvest. Come, you deceive yourself.
       'Tis he that sends us to destroy you here.
CLARENCE   It cannot be, for he bewept my fortune,

---

6. Take communion and in doing so swear by the body   Henry VI.
of God.   8. He is full of natural feelings (and hence a loving
7. That is, Prince Edward, son of the then sovereign, brother).

And hugged me in his arms, and swore with sobs
That he would labour° my delivery.   *work for*

235 FIRST MURDERER   Why, so he doth, when he delivers you
From this earth's thraldom to the joys of heaven.
SECOND MURDERER   Make peace with God, for you must die, my lord.
CLARENCE   Have you that holy feeling in your souls
To counsel me to make my peace with God,
240 And are you yet to your own souls so blind
That you will war with God by murd'ring me?
O sirs, consider: they that set you on
To do this deed will hate you for the deed.
SECOND MURDERER [*to* FIRST]   What shall we do?
CLARENCE   Relent? and save your souls.
245 FIRST MURDERER   Relent? No. 'Tis cowardly and womanish.
CLARENCE   Not to relent is beastly, savage, devilish.—
My friend, I spy some pity in thy looks.
O if thine eye be not a flatterer,°   *deceiver (of Clarence)*
Come thou on my side, and entreat for me.
250 A begging prince, what beggar pities not?
Which of you, if you were a prince's son,
Being pent° from liberty as I am now,   *restrained*
If two such murderers as yourselves came to you,
Would not entreat for life? As you would beg
255 Were you in my distress—
SECOND MURDERER   Look behind you, my lord!
FIRST MURDERER (*He stabs* [CLARENCE]) Take that, and that! If
        all this will not serve,
I'll drown you in the malmsey butt within.
                                             Exit [*with Clarence's body*]
SECOND MURDERER   A bloody deed, and desperately dispatched!
260 How fain,° like Pilate, would I wash my hands   *gladly*
Of this most grievous, guilty murder done.
            Enter FIRST MURDERER
FIRST MURDERER   How now? What mean'st thou, that thou help'st me not?
By heaven, the Duke shall know how slack you have been.
SECOND MURDERER   I would he knew that I had saved his brother.
265 Take thou the fee, and tell him what I say,
For I repent me that the Duke is slain.   *Exit*
FIRST MURDERER   So do not I. Go, coward as thou art.—
Well, I'll go hide the body in some hole
Till that the Duke give order for his burial.
270 And, when I have my meed, I will away,
For this will out,⁹ and then I must not stay.   *Exit*

2.1

Flourish.° Enter KING [EDWARD], *sick,* QUEEN [ELIZA-   *Trumpet call*
BETH], *Lord Marquis* DORSET, [*Lord*] RIVERS, [LORD]
HASTINGS, [*Sir William*] CATESBY, [*the Duke of*] BUCK-
INGHAM [*and Lord Gray*]
KING EDWARD   Why, so! Now have I done a good day's work.
You peers, continue this united league.
I every day expect an embassage
From my redeemer to redeem me hence,

9. "Murder will out" was proverbial.   2.1 Location: The palace, London.

5   And more in peace my soul shall part to heaven
        Since I have made my friends at peace on earth.
        Hastings and Rivers, take each other's hand.
        Dissemble not[1] your hatred; swear your love.
    RIVERS   By heaven, my soul is purged from grudging hate,
10   And with my hand I seal my true heart's love.
        [He takes Hastings' hand]
    LORD HASTINGS   So thrive I,° as I truly swear the like.   *May I prosper*
    KING EDWARD   Take heed you dally° not before your king,   *trifle*
        Lest he that is the supreme King of Kings
        Confound° your hidden falsehood, and award°   *Defeat / cause*
15   Either of you to be the other's end.[2]
    LORD HASTINGS   So prosper I, as I swear perfect love.
    RIVERS   And I, as I love Hastings with my heart.
    KING EDWARD *[to ELIZABETH]*   Madam, yourself is not exempt from this,
        Nor your son Dorset;—Buckingham, nor you.
20   You have been factious one against the other.
        Wife, love Lord Hastings, let him kiss your hand—
        And what you do, do it unfeignedly.
    QUEEN ELIZABETH *[giving HASTINGS her hand to kiss]*   There,
        Hastings. I will never more remember
        Our former hatred: so thrive I, and mine.°   *my family*
25   KING EDWARD   Dorset, embrace him. Hastings, love Lord Marquis.
    DORSET   This interchange of love, I here protest,°   *affirm*
        Upon my part shall be inviolable.
    LORD HASTINGS   And so swear I.
        [They embrace]
    KING EDWARD   Now, princely Buckingham, seal thou this league
30   With thy embracements to my wife's allies,
        And make me happy in your unity.
    BUCKINGHAM *[to ELIZABETH]*   Whenever Buckingham doth turn his hate
        Upon your grace, but° with all duteous love   *nor*
        Doth cherish you and yours, God punish me
35   With hate in those where I expect most love.
        When I have most need to employ a friend,
        And most assurèd that he is a friend,
        Deep,° hollow, treacherous, and full of guile   *Crafty*
        Be he unto me. This do I beg of heaven,
40   When I am cold in love to you or yours.
        [They] embrace
    KING EDWARD   A pleasing cordial,° princely Buckingham,   *health-giving drink*
        Is this thy vow unto my sickly heart.
        There wanteth now our brother Gloucester here,
        To make the blessèd period° of this peace.   *conclusion*
        Enter [Sir Richard] RATCLIFFE *and [*RICHARD *Duke of]*
        GLOUCESTER
45   BUCKINGHAM   And in good time,
        Here comes Sir Richard Ratcliffe and the Duke.
    RICHARD GLOUCESTER   Good morrow to my sovereign King and Queen.—
        And princely peers, a happy time of day.
    KING EDWARD   Happy indeed, as we have spent the day.
50   Brother, we have done deeds of charity,
        Made peace of enmity, fair love of hate,

---

1. Do not merely disguise.   2. Each of you to cause the death of the other.

Between these swelling wrong-incensèd³ peers.
RICHARD GLOUCESTER   A blessèd labour, my most sovereign lord.
Among this princely heap° if any here,   *company*
55   By false intelligence° or wrong surmise,   *information*
Hold me a foe,
If I unwittingly or in my rage
Have aught committed that is hardly borne°   *is deeply resented*
By any in this presence, I desire
60   To reconcile me to his friendly peace.
'Tis death to me to be at enmity.
I hate it, and desire all good men's love.—
First, madam, I entreat true peace of you,
Which I will purchase with my duteous service.—
65   Of you, my noble cousin Buckingham,
If ever any grudge were lodged between us.—
Of you, Lord Rivers, and Lord Gray of you,
That all without desert° have frowned on me.—   *entirely without cause*
Dukes, earls, lords, gentlemen, indeed of all!
70   I do not know that Englishman alive
With whom my soul is any jot at odds
More than the infant that is born tonight.
I thank my God for my humility.
QUEEN ELIZABETH   A holy day shall this be kept hereafter.
75   I would to God all strifes were well compounded.°—   *resolved*
My sovereign lord, I do beseech your highness
To take our brother Clarence to your grace.
RICHARD GLOUCESTER   Why, madam, have I offered love for this,
To be so flouted° in this royal presence?   *mocked*
80   Who knows not that the gentle Duke is dead?
           They all start
You do him injury to scorn his corpse.⁴
RIVERS⁵   Who knows not he is dead? Who knows he is?
QUEEN ELIZABETH   All-seeing heaven, what a world is this?
BUCKINGHAM   Look I so pale, Lord Dorset, as the rest?
85   DORSET   Ay, my good lord, and no one in the presence°   *(of the King)*
But his red colour hath forsook his cheeks.
KING EDWARD   Is Clarence dead? The order was reversed.
RICHARD GLOUCESTER   But he, poor man, by your first order died,
And that a wingèd Mercury⁶ did bear;
90   Some tardy cripple bore the countermand,
That came too lag° to see him burièd.   *late*
God grant that some, less noble and less loyal,
Nearer in bloody thoughts, but not in blood,⁷
Deserve not worse than wretched Clarence did,
95   And yet go current from suspicion.⁸
           Enter [Lord STANLEY] Earl of Derby
STANLEY [*kneeling*]   A boon,° my sovereign, for my service done.   *favor*
KING EDWARD   I pray thee, peace! My soul is full of sorrow.
STANLEY   I will not rise, unless your highness hear me.

---

3. *swelling:* inflated with anger and pride. *wrong-incensèd:* mistakenly provoked; provoked by wrongs, injuries.
4. *to scorn his corpse:* by (supposedly) speaking ironically of him.
5. F assigns this line to King Edward.

6. The speedy messenger of the gods in classical mythology.
7. That is, nearer to bloody plots than was the innocent Clarence, but not so near the King in blood (another dig at the Queen's upstart relatives).
8. And yet are accepted at face value without suspicion.

KING EDWARD   Then say at once, what is it thou requests?
100 STANLEY   The forfeit, sovereign, of my servant's life,[9]
            Who slew today a riotous gentleman,
            Lately attendant on the Duke of Norfolk.
        KING EDWARD   Have I a tongue to doom° my brother's death,   *order*
            And shall that tongue give pardon to a slave?
105   My brother slew no man; his fault was thought;
            And yet his punishment was bitter death.
            Who sued to me for him? Who in my wrath
            Kneeled at my feet, and bid me be advised?°   *consider carefully*
            Who spoke of brotherhood? Who spoke of love?
110   Who told me how the poor soul did forsake
            The mighty Warwick and did fight for me?
            Who told me, in the field at Tewkesbury,
            When Oxford had me down, he rescued me,
            And said, 'Dear brother, live, and be a king'?
115   Who told me, when we both lay in the field,
            Frozen almost to death, how he did lap° me   *wrap*
            Even in his garments, and did give himself
            All thin° and naked to the numb-cold night?   *thinly clad*
            All this from my remembrance brutish wrath
120   Sinfully plucked, and not a man of you
            Had so much grace to put it in my mind.
            But when your carters° or your waiting vassals   *cart drivers*
            Have done a drunken slaughter, and defaced
            The precious image[1] of our dear redeemer,
125   You straight° are on your knees for 'Pardon, pardon!'—   *straightaway*
            And I, unjustly too, must grant it you.
            But, for my brother, not a man would speak,
            Nor I, ungracious, speak unto myself
            For him, poor soul. The proudest of you all
130   Have been beholden to him in his life,
            Yet none of you would once beg for his life.
            O God, I fear thy justice will take hold
            On me—and you, and mine, and yours, for this.—
            Come, Hastings, help me to my closet.°   *private (bed)room*
135   Ah, poor Clarence!   *Exeunt some with* KING *and* QUEEN
        RICHARD GLOUCESTER   This is the fruits of rashness. Marked you not
            How that the guilty kindred of the Queen
            Looked pale, when they did hear of Clarence' death?
            O, they did urge it still unto the King.
140   God will revenge it. Come, lords, will you go
            To comfort Edward with our company?
        BUCKINGHAM   We wait upon your grace.   *Exeunt*

2.2

Enter the old DUCHESS OF YORK *with the two children of*
Clarence[1]

BOY   Good grannam, tell us, is our father dead?
DUCHESS OF YORK   No, boy.
GIRL   Why do you weep so oft, and beat your breast,

---

9. That is, the release of his servant from a sentence of
death.
1. A man, thought to be created in God's image.

2.2 Location: The palace, London.
1. Edward and Margaret Plantagenet (not to be confused
with King Edward, Prince Edward, or Queen Margaret).

And cry, 'O Clarence, my unhappy son'?

5   BOY   Why do you look on us and shake your head,
And call us orphans, wretches, castaways,
If that our noble father were alive?
DUCHESS OF YORK   My pretty cousins,° you mistake me both.   *kinsmen*
I do lament the sickness of the King,
10   As loath to lose him, not your father's death.
It were lost sorrow to wail one that's lost.
BOY   Then you conclude, my grannam, he is dead.
The King mine uncle is to blame for this.
God will revenge it—whom I will importune°   *beg*
15   With earnest prayers, all to that effect.
GIRL   And so will I.
DUCHESS OF YORK   Peace, children, peace! The King doth love you well.
Incapable° and shallow innocents,   *Uncomprehending*
You cannot guess who caused your father's death.
20   BOY   Grannam, we can. For my good uncle Gloucester
Told me the King, provoked to it by the Queen,
Devised impeachments° to imprison him,   *charges*
And when my uncle told me so he wept,
And pitied me, and kindly kissed my cheek,
25   Bade me rely on him as on my father,
And he would love me dearly as his child.
DUCHESS OF YORK   Ah, that deceit should steal such gentle shapes,°   *appearances*
And with a virtuous visor° hide deep vice!   *mask*
He is my son, ay, and therein my shame;
30   Yet from my dugs° he drew not this deceit.   *breasts*
BOY   Think you my uncle did dissemble, grannam?
DUCHESS OF YORK   Ay, boy.
BOY   I cannot think it. Hark, what noise is this?
            Enter QUEEN [ELIZABETH] *with her hair about her ears*[2]
QUEEN ELIZABETH   Ah, who shall hinder me to wail and weep?
35   To chide my fortune, and torment myself?
I'll join with black despair against my soul,
And to myself become an enemy.
DUCHESS OF YORK   What means this scene of rude° impatience?   *violent*
QUEEN ELIZABETH   To mark an act of tragic violence.
40   Edward, my lord, thy son, our king, is dead.[3]
Why grow the branches when the root is gone?
Why wither not the leaves that want° their sap?   *lack*
If you will live, lament; if die, be brief,
That our swift-wingèd souls may catch the King's,
45   Or like obedient subjects follow him
To his new kingdom of ne'er-changing night.
DUCHESS OF YORK   Ah, so much interest° have I in thy sorrow   *right to share*
As I had title[4] in thy noble husband.
I have bewept a worthy husband's[5] death,
50   And lived with looking on his images.°   *likenesses (his sons)*
But now two mirrors[6] of his princely semblance

2. Disheveled hair was a conventional expression of grief
on the Elizabethan stage. F adds "Rivers and Dorset after
her" and gives them lines to speak later in the scene.
3. Shakespeare is telescoping events. Edward actually
died some five years after Clarence.

4. Legal right (as Edward's mother, the Duchess of York
has a right to mourn).
5. The Duke of York (whose death is dramatized in
Richard Duke of York).
6. Clarence and King Edward.

Are cracked in pieces by malignant death,
And I for comfort have but one false glass,°   *(Richard)*
That grieves me when I see my shame in him.
55 Thou art a widow, yet thou art a mother,
And hast the comfort of thy children left.
But death hath snatched my husband from mine arms
And plucked two crutches from my feeble hands,
Clarence and Edward. O what cause have I,
60 Thine being but a moiety° of my moan,   *half*
To overgo° thy woes, and drown thy cries?   *exceed*
BOY [*to* ELIZABETH]   Ah, aunt, you wept not for our father's death.
How can we aid you with our kindred tears?°   *tears of relatives*
DAUGHTER [*to* ELIZABETH]   Our fatherless distress was left unmoaned;
65 Your widow-dolour° likewise be unwept.   *widow's grief*
QUEEN ELIZABETH   Give me no help in lamentation.
I am not barren to bring forth complaints.[7]
All springs reduce[8] their currents to mine eyes,
That I, being governed by the wat'ry moon,
70 May send forth plenteous tears to drown the world.
Ah, for my husband, for my dear Lord Edward!
CHILDREN   Ah, for our father, for our dear Lord Clarence!
DUCHESS OF YORK   Alas, for both, both mine, Edward and Clarence!
QUEEN ELIZABETH   What stay° had I but Edward, and he's gone?   *support*
75 CHILDREN   What stay had we but Clarence, and he's gone?
DUCHESS OF YORK   What stays had I but they, and they are gone?
QUEEN ELIZABETH   Was never widow had so dear° a loss!   *grievous*
CHILDREN   Were never orphans had so dear a loss!
DUCHESS OF YORK   Was never mother had so dear a loss!
80 Alas, I am the mother of these griefs.
Their woes are parcelled;° mine is general.   *inclusive*
She for an Edward weeps, and so do I;
I for a Clarence weep, so doth not she.
These babes for Clarence weep, and so do I;
85 I for an Edward weep, so do not they.
Alas, you three on me, threefold distressed,
Pour all your tears. I am your sorrow's nurse,
And I will pamper° it with lamentation.[9]   *(over)feed*
88.1   DORSET   *Comfort, dear mother. God is much displeased*
       That you take with unthankfulness his doing.
       In common worldly things 'tis called ungrateful
       With dull unwillingness to pay a debt
88.5   *Which with a bounteous hand was kindly lent;*
       Much more to be thus opposite with° heaven   *in opposition to*
       For it requires° the royal debt it lent you.   *calls back*
    RIVERS   *Madam, bethink you like a careful mother*
       Of the young Prince your son. Send straight for him;
88.10   *Let him be crowned. In him your comfort lives.*
       Drown desperate sorrow in dead Edward's grave
       And plant your joys in living Edward's throne.

---

7. I can deliver my own lamentations.
8. Lead back (as to the sea, which is governed by the moon).

9. The indented passage that follows, 88.1–88.12, appears only in F.

Enter RICHARD *[Duke of]* GLOUCESTER, *the [Duke of]*
BUCKINGHAM, *[Lord* STANLEY *Earl of]* Derby, *[*LORD*]*
HASTINGS, *and [Sir Richard]* RATCLIFFE

RICHARD GLOUCESTER [*to* ELIZABETH]   Sister, have comfort. All of us have cause

90   To wail the dimming of our shining star,
      But none can help our harms by wailing them.—
      Madam, my mother, I do cry you mercy.°   *I beg your pardon*
      I did not see your grace. Humbly on my knee
      I crave your blessing.
95   DUCHESS OF YORK   God bless thee, and put meekness in thy breast,
      Love, charity, obedience, and true duty.
      RICHARD GLOUCESTER   Amen. [*Aside*] 'And make me die a good old man.'
      That is the butt-end° of a mother's blessing;   *conclusion*
      I marvel that her grace did leave it out.
100   BUCKINGHAM   You cloudy° princes and heart-sorrowing peers   *sad; raining (tears)*
      That bear this heavy mutual load of moan,°   *lamentation*
      Now cheer each other in each other's love.
      Though we have spent our harvest of this king,
      We are to reap the harvest of his son.
105   The broken rancour[1] of your high-swoll'n hearts
      But lately° splinted, knit, and joined together,   *Only recently*
      Must gently be preserved, cherished, and kept.
      Meseemeth° good that, with some little train,°   *I think it / entourage*
      Forthwith from Ludlow[2] the young Prince be fet°   *fetched*
110   Hither to London to be crowned our king.[3]
110.1   RIVERS   *Why with some little train, my lord of Buckingham?*
            BUCKINGHAM   *Marry, my lord, lest by a multitude°*   *large entourage*
            The new-healed wound of malice should break out,
            Which would be so much the more dangerous
110.5   *By how much the estate is green and yet ungoverned.[4]*
            Where every horse bears his commanding rein[5]
            And may direct his course as please himself°   *as he pleases*
            As well the fear of harm as harm apparent°   *as actual harm*
            In my opinion ought to be prevented.
110.10   RICHARD GLOUCESTER   *I hope the King made peace with all of us,*
            And the compact is firm and true in me.
            RIVERS   *And so in me, and so I think in all.*
            Yet since it is but green, it should be put
            To no apparent likelihood of breach,
110.15   *Which haply° by much company might be urged.*   *perhaps*
            Therefore I say, with noble Buckingham,
            That it is meet° so few should fetch the Prince.   *fitting*
      HASTINGS   *And so say I.*
      RICHARD GLOUCESTER   Then be it so, and go we to determine
      Who they shall be that straight shall post° to Ludlow.—   *ride speedily*
      Madam, and you my sister, will you go
      To give your censures° in this weighty business?   *opinions*
115   QUEEN ELIZABETH *and* DUCHESS OF YORK   With all our hearts.
                 Exeunt. Manent RICHARD *and* BUCKINGHAM

---

1. Bitterness that caused you to be divided (unnaturally, like a broken limb).
2. Royal castle in Shropshire, near the Welsh border,
where Prince Edward, as Prince of Wales, was staying.
3. The indented passage that follows, 110.1–110.18,

appears only in F.
4. *By . . . ungoverned*: Considering that the government is newly established and not yet in full control.
5. *bears . . . rein*: takes charge of the rein that should
restrain him.

BUCKINGHAM   My lord, whoever journeys to the Prince,
    For God's sake let not us two stay at home,
    For by the way I'll sort° occasion,   *find*
    As index° to the story we late° talked of,   *prologue / lately*
120   To part the Queen's proud kindred from the Prince.
RICHARD GLOUCESTER   My other self, my counsel's consistory,°   *council chamber*
    My oracle, my prophet, my dear cousin!
    I, as a child, will go by thy direction.
    Towards Ludlow then, for we'll not stay behind.   *Exeunt*

2.3

Enter one CITIZEN *at one door and another at the other*
FIRST CITIZEN   Good morrow, neighbour. Whither away so fast?
SECOND CITIZEN   I promise° you, I scarcely know myself.   *assure*
    Hear you the news abroad?
FIRST CITIZEN   Yes, that the King is dead.
SECOND CITIZEN   Ill news, by'r Lady;° seldom comes the better.[1]   *by the Virgin Mary*
5   I fear, I fear, 'twill prove a giddy° world.   *mad*
    Enter another CITIZEN
THIRD CITIZEN   Neighbours, God speed.
FIRST CITIZEN   Give you good morrow, sir.
THIRD CITIZEN   Doth the news hold of good King Edward's death?
SECOND CITIZEN   Ay, sir, it is too true. God help the while.
THIRD CITIZEN   Then, masters,° look to see a troublous world.   *sirs*
10 FIRST CITIZEN   No, no, by God's good grace his son shall reign.
THIRD CITIZEN   Woe to that land that's governed by a child.
SECOND CITIZEN   In him there is a hope of government,
    Which in his nonage council under him,[2]
    And in his full and ripened years himself,
15   No doubt shall then, and till then, govern well.
FIRST CITIZEN   So stood the state when Henry the Sixth
    Was crowned in Paris but at nine months old.
THIRD CITIZEN   Stood the state so? No, no, good friends, God wot.°   *knows*
    For then this land was famously enriched
20   With politic,° grave counsel;° then the King   *astute / advisers*
    Had virtuous uncles to protect his grace.
FIRST CITIZEN   Why, so hath this, both by his father and mother.
THIRD CITIZEN   Better it were they all came by his father,
    Or by his father there were none at all.
25   For emulation° who shall now be near'st[3]   *competition*
    Will touch us all too near, if God prevent not.
    O full of danger is the Duke of Gloucester,
    And the Queen's sons and brothers haught° and proud.   *haughty*
    And were they° to be ruled, and not to rule,   *(both factions)*
30   This sickly land might solace° as before.   *prosper*
FIRST CITIZEN   Come, come, we fear the worst. All will be well.
THIRD CITIZEN   When clouds are seen, wise men put on their cloaks;
    When great leaves fall, then winter is at hand;
    When the sun sets, who doth not look for night?
35   Untimely storms make men expect a dearth.

2.3 Location: A street in London.
1. Things rarely change for the better (proverbial).
2. The Privy Council governing in his name during the
years of his minority.
3. Most influential with the King.

All may be well, but if God sort° it so   ordain
'Tis more than we deserve, or I expect.
SECOND CITIZEN   Truly the hearts of men are full of fear.
You cannot reason° almost with a man   converse
40   That looks not heavily and full of dread.
THIRD CITIZEN   Before the days of change still is it so.
By a divine instinct men's minds mistrust°   suspect
Ensuing danger, as by proof° we see   experience
The water swell before a boist'rous storm.
45   But leave it all to God. Whither away?
SECOND CITIZEN   Marry, we were sent for to the justices.
THIRD CITIZEN   And so was I. I'll bear you company.   *Exeunt*

2.4

Enter [Lord] CARDINAL, *young [Duke of]* YORK, QUEEN
[ELIZABETH], *and the [old]* DUCHESS OF YORK

CARDINAL   Last night, I hear, they lay them at Northampton.
At Stony Stratford[1] they do rest tonight.
Tomorrow, or next day, they will be here.
DUCHESS OF YORK   I long with all my heart to see the Prince.
5   I hope he is much grown since last I saw him.
QUEEN ELIZABETH   But I hear, no. They say my son of York
Has almost overta'en him in his growth.
YORK   Ay, mother, but I would not have it so.
DUCHESS OF YORK   Why, my young cousin, it is good to grow.
10   YORK   Grandam, one night as we did sit at supper,
My uncle Rivers talked how I did grow
More than my brother. 'Ay', quoth my nuncle° Gloucester,   uncle (colloquial)
'Small herbs have grace; gross weeds do grow apace'.°   rapidly
And since, methinks I would not grow so fast,
15   Because sweet flow'rs are slow, and weeds make haste.
DUCHESS OF YORK   Good faith, good faith, the saying did not hold°   hold true
In him that did object° the same to thee.   argue
He was the wretched'st thing when he was young,
So long a-growing, and so leisurely,
20   That if his rule were true he should be gracious.
CARDINAL   Why, so no doubt he is, my gracious madam.
DUCHESS OF YORK   I hope he is, but yet let mothers doubt.
YORK   Now, by my troth, if I had been remembered,
I could have given my uncle's grace a flout[2]
25   To touch his growth, nearer than he touched° mine.   hit
DUCHESS OF YORK   How, my young York? I pray thee, let me hear it.
YORK   Marry, they say my uncle grew so fast
That he could gnaw a crust at two hours old.
'Twas full two years ere I could get a tooth.
30   Grannam, this would have been a biting jest.
DUCHESS OF YORK   I pray thee, pretty York, who told thee this?
YORK   Grannam, his nurse.
DUCHESS OF YORK   His nurse? Why, she was dead ere thou wast born.
YORK   If 'twere not she, I cannot tell who told me.

2.4 Location: The palace, London.   2. *if . . . flout:* if I had been told this, I could have
1. Town in Buckinghamshire (south of Northampton).   taunted my noble uncle.
F reverses the order of the towns.

35 QUEEN ELIZABETH   A parlous° boy! Go to,³ you are too shrewd.°   *mischievous / sharp*
   CARDINAL   Good madam, be not angry with the child.
   QUEEN ELIZABETH   Pitchers have ears.⁴
                    Enter [Marquis] DORSET
   CARDINAL   Here comes your son, Lord Dorset.
        What news, Lord Marquis?
   DORSET   Such news, my lord,
        As grieves me to report.
   QUEEN ELIZABETH   How doth the Prince?
   DORSET   Well, madam, and in health.
40 DUCHESS OF YORK   What is thy news then?
   DORSET   Lord Rivers and Lord Gray are sent to Pomfret,⁵
        And with them Thomas Vaughan, prisoners.
   DUCHESS OF YORK   Who hath committed them?
   DORSET   The mighty dukes,
        Gloucester and Buckingham.
   CARDINAL   For what offence?
45 DORSET   The sum of all I can,° I have disclosed.   *know*
        Why or for what the nobles were committed
        Is all unknown to me, my gracious lord.
   QUEEN ELIZABETH   Ay me! I see the ruin of our house.
        The tiger now hath seized the gentle hind.°   *doe*
50   Insulting tyranny begins to jet°   *encroach; strut*
        Upon the innocent and aweless⁶ throne.
        Welcome destruction, blood, and massacre!
        I see, as in a map, the end of all.
   DUCHESS OF YORK   Accursèd and unquiet wrangling days,
55   How many of you have mine eyes beheld?
        My husband lost his life to get the crown,
        And often up and down my sons were tossed,
        For me to joy and weep their gain and loss.
        And being seated,° and domestic broils°   *enthroned / disorders*
60   Clean overblown,° themselves the conquerors   *Completely ended*
        Make war upon themselves, brother to brother,
        Blood to blood, self against self. O preposterous
        And frantic outrage, end thy damnèd spleen,°   *malice*
        Or let me die, to look on death no more.
65 QUEEN ELIZABETH [*to* YORK]   Come, come, my boy, we will to sanctuary.⁷—
        Madam, farewell.
   DUCHESS OF YORK   Stay, I will go with you.
   QUEEN ELIZABETH   You have no cause.
   CARDINAL [*to* ELIZABETH]   My gracious lady, go,
        And thither bear your treasure and your goods.
        For my part, I'll resign° unto your grace   *hand over*
70   The seal⁸ I keep, and so betide° to me   *and so may it happen*
        As well I tender° you and all of yours.   *care for*
        Go, I'll conduct you to the sanctuary.   *Exeunt*

---

3. Expression of disapproval.
4. Proverbially said of children who overhear remarks made by adults: "Little pitchers have big ears."
5. Modern Pontefract, in west Yorkshire, site of the castle where Richard II was murdered.
6. Not able to command respect (because the King is so young).

7. Anyone, including criminals, could claim the protection of the church ("sanctuary") and thus immunity from civil law, initially for forty days. The Queen sought sanctuary at Westminster Abbey.
8. An engraved stamp, signifying the authority of the bearer, used to authenticate legal documents; here, the Great Seal of England.

3.1[1]

The Trumpets sound. Enter young PRINCE [EDWARD],
the Dukes of GLOUCESTER *and* BUCKINGHAM, *Lord* CAR-
DINAL, *with others* [*including Lord* STANLEY *Earl of*
Derby and Sir William CATESBY]

BUCKINGHAM   Welcome, sweet Prince, to London, to your chamber.[2]

RICHARD GLOUCESTER [*to* PRINCE EDWARD]   Welcome, dear
    cousin, my thoughts' sovereign.°   *ruler of my thoughts*
The weary way hath made you melancholy.

PRINCE EDWARD   No, uncle, but our crosses[3] on the way
5 Have made it tedious, wearisome, and heavy.
I want° more uncles here to welcome me.   *lack; desire*

RICHARD GLOUCESTER   Sweet Prince, the untainted virtue of your years
Hath not yet dived into the world's deceit,
Nor more can you distinguish of a man
10 Than of his outward show, which God he knows
Seldom or never jumpeth° with the heart.   *coincides*
Those uncles[4] which you want were dangerous.
Your grace attended to their sugared words,
But looked not on the poison of their hearts.
15 God keep you from them, and from such false friends.

PRINCE EDWARD   God keep me from false friends; but they were none.

Enter Lord MAYOR [*and his train*]

RICHARD GLOUCESTER   My lord, the Mayor of London comes to greet you.

MAYOR [*kneeling to* PRINCE EDWARD]   God bless your grace with
    health and happy days.

PRINCE EDWARD   I thank you, good my lord, and thank you all.—
20 I thought my mother and my brother York
Would long ere this have met us on the way.
Fie, what a slug° is Hastings, that he hastes not   *sluggard*
To tell us whether they will come or no.

Enter LORD HASTINGS

BUCKINGHAM   In happy time here comes the sweating lord.

25 PRINCE EDWARD [*to* HASTINGS]   Welcome, my lord. What, will
    our mother come?

LORD HASTINGS   On what occasion° God he knows, not I,   *For what reason*
The Queen your mother, and your brother York,
Have taken sanctuary. The tender° Prince   *young; affectionate*
Would fain have° come with me to meet your grace,   *Would have liked to*
30 But by his mother was perforce° withheld.   *forcibly*

BUCKINGHAM   Fie, what an indirect and peevish° course   *perverse*
Is this of hers!—Lord Cardinal, will your grace
Persuade the Queen to send the Duke of York
Unto his princely brother presently?°—   *immediately*
35 If she deny, Lord Hastings, go with him,
And from her jealous° arms pluck him perforce.   *suspicious; mistrustful*

CARDINAL   My lord of Buckingham, if my weak oratory
Can from his mother win the Duke of York,

3.1 Location: A street in London.
1. Either because of defects in the original manuscript or because of blunders in the printing house, the text of this scene, up to line 148, is exceptionally corrupt and has been editorially reconstructed.
2. Capital (London was known as *camera regis*, "the King's chamber").

3. Referring to the arrests of his uncle and half-brothers on the journey.
4. Of the two arrested, only Rivers, being Elizabeth's brother, was Prince Edward's real uncle; Gray, a son by Elizabeth's previous marriage, was therefore actually half brother to the Prince.

Anon° expect him. But if she be obdurate   *Very soon*
40 To mild entreaties, God in heaven forbid
We should infringe the sacred privilege
Of blessèd sanctuary. Not for all this land
Would I be guilty of so deep a sin.
BUCKINGHAM   You are too senseless-obstinate, my lord,
45 Too ceremonious° and traditional.   *rule-bound*
Weigh it not with the grossness° of this age.   *coarseness*
You break not sanctuary in seizing him.
The benefit thereof is always granted
To those whose dealings have deserved the place,
50 And those who have the wit to claim the place.
This prince hath neither claimed it nor deserved it,
And therefore, in my mind, he cannot have it.
Then taking him from thence that 'longs not there,[5]
You break thereby no privilege nor charter.
55 Oft have I heard of 'sanctuary men',[6]
But 'sanctuary children' ne'er till now.
CARDINAL   My lord, you shall o'errule my mind for once.—
Come on, Lord Hastings, will you go with me?
LORD HASTINGS   I come, my lord.
60 PRINCE EDWARD   Good lords, make all the speedy haste you may.—
Exeunt CARDINAL *and* HASTINGS
Say, uncle Gloucester, if our brother come,
Where shall we sojourn° till our coronation?   *stay*
RICHARD GLOUCESTER   Where it seems best unto your royal self.
If I may counsel you, some day or two
65 Your highness shall repose you at the Tower,[7]
Then where you please and shall be thought most fit
For your best health and recreation.
PRINCE EDWARD   I do not like the Tower of any place.°—   *of all places*
Did Julius Caesar build that place, my lord?
70 BUCKINGHAM   He did, my gracious lord, begin that place,
Which since succeeding ages have re-edified.°   *built further*
PRINCE EDWARD   Is it upon record, or else reported[8]
Successively from age to age, he built it?
BUCKINGHAM   Upon record, my gracious liege.
75 PRINCE EDWARD   But say, my lord, it were not registered,°   *documented*
Methinks the truth should live from age to age,
As 'twere retailed° to all posterity   *related orally*
Even to the general all-ending day.°   *Day of Judgment*
RICHARD GLOUCESTER [*aside*]   So wise so young, they say, do
never live long.
80 PRINCE EDWARD   What say you, uncle?
RICHARD GLOUCESTER   I say, 'Without characters° fame lives long'.   *writing*
[*Aside*] Thus like the formal Vice, Iniquity,[9]
I moralize two meanings in one word.[1]
PRINCE EDWARD   That Julius Caesar was a famous man:

5. Taking the Prince from a place he has not claimed as sanctuary.
6. Criminals seeking to avoid prosecution.
7. It was customary for Kings of England (before James II) to spend the night before their coronation in the Tower, it being a royal palace and one of the strongest fortresses in the country. But Edward fears its other aspect, as a prison.
8. Is it on written record or otherwise told orally.
9. The conventional Vice figure, called Iniquity, who in sixteenth-century morality plays symbolized all of the vices.
1. As the Vice often did, Richard makes the same phrase have a double meaning.

85 With what his valour did t'enrich his wit,
His wit set down to make his valour live.[2]
Death made no conquest of this conqueror,
For yet he lives in fame though not in life.
I'll tell you what, my cousin Buckingham.

90 BUCKINGHAM   What, my good lord?
PRINCE EDWARD   An if° I live until I be a man,   *An if = If*
I'll win our ancient right[3] in France again,
Or die a soldier, as I lived a king.
RICHARD GLOUCESTER [*aside*]   Short summers lightly have a
forward spring.[4]

      Enter young [Duke of] YORK, [LORD] HASTINGS, *and*
      [*Lord*] CARDINAL

95 BUCKINGHAM   Now in good time, here comes the Duke of York.
PRINCE EDWARD   Richard of York, how fares our loving brother?
YORK   Well, my dread[5] lord—so must I call you now.
PRINCE EDWARD   Ay, brother, to our grief, as it is yours.
Too late° he died that might have kept that title,   *recently*
100 Which by his death hath lost much majesty.
RICHARD GLOUCESTER   How fares our noble cousin, Lord of York?
YORK   I thank you, gentle uncle, well. O, my lord,
You said that idle° weeds are fast in growth;   *useless*
The Prince, my brother, hath outgrown me far.
105 RICHARD GLOUCESTER   He hath, my lord.
YORK   And therefore is he idle?
RICHARD GLOUCESTER   O my fair cousin, I must not say so.
YORK   He is more beholden to you then than I.
RICHARD GLOUCESTER   He may command me as my sovereign,
But you have power in me as a kinsman.
110 YORK   I pray you, uncle, render me this dagger.
RICHARD GLOUCESTER   My dagger, little cousin? With all my heart.
PRINCE EDWARD   A beggar, brother?
YORK   Of my kind uncle that I know will give,
It being but a toy° which is no grief to give.   *trifle*
115 RICHARD GLOUCESTER   A greater gift than that I'll give my cousin.
YORK   A greater gift? O, that's the sword to it.[6]
RICHARD GLOUCESTER   Ay, gentle cousin, were it light enough.
YORK   O, then I see you will part but° with light° gifts.   *only / trivial*
In weightier things you'll say a beggar nay.
120 RICHARD GLOUCESTER   It is too heavy for your grace to wear.
YORK   I'd weigh it lightly, were it heavier.[7]
RICHARD GLOUCESTER   What, would you have my weapon, little lord?
YORK   I would, that I might thank you as you call me.
RICHARD GLOUCESTER   How?
125 YORK   Little.
PRINCE EDWARD   My lord of York will still be cross° in talk.— *perverse; quarrelsome*
Uncle, your grace knows how to bear with him.
YORK   You mean to bear me, not to bear with me.—
Uncle, my brother mocks both you and me.

---

2. *With . . . live:* The same valorous deeds that enlivened Caesar's writing were themselves made immortal by his retelling of them.
3. Right to the throne (claimed by Henry V and his son Henry VI).
4. Proverbial: Those who die young ("forward") are

often ("lightly") precocious.
5. Held in awe (a common formula for addressing a king).
6. *to it:* that is, to the dagger (the sword is to the dagger as the greater gift is to the lesser).
7. I'd consider it of little value, even if it were heavier.

130   Because that I am little like an ape,
        He thinks that you should bear me on your shoulders.[8]
    BUCKINGHAM   With what a sharp, prodigal wit[9] he reasons.
        To mitigate the scorn he gives his uncle,
        He prettily and aptly taunts himself.
135   So cunning and so young is wonderful.°   *a cause of wonder*
    RICHARD GLOUCESTER [*to* PRINCE EDWARD]   My lord, will't
            please you pass along?
        Myself and my good cousin Buckingham
        Will° to your mother to entreat of her   *Will go*
        To meet you at the Tower and welcome you.
140   YORK [*to* PRINCE EDWARD]   What, will you go unto the Tower, my lord?
    PRINCE EDWARD   My Lord Protector needs will have it so.
    YORK   I shall not sleep in quiet at the Tower.
    RICHARD GLOUCESTER   Why, what should you fear there?
    YORK   Marry, my uncle Clarence' angry ghost.
145   My grannam told me he was murdered there.
    PRINCE EDWARD   I fear no uncles dead.
    RICHARD GLOUCESTER   Nor none that live, I hope.
    PRINCE EDWARD   An if they[1] live, I hope I need not fear.
        [*To* YORK] But come, my lord, and with a heavy heart,
        Thinking on them, go we unto the Tower.
        A sennet.[2]

              Exeunt. Manent RICHARD, BUCKINGHAM, *and* CATESBY
    BUCKINGHAM [*to* RICHARD]   Think you, my lord, this little prating°   *chattering*
150   York
        Was not incensèd° by his subtle mother   *incited*
        To taunt and scorn you thus opprobriously?
    RICHARD GLOUCESTER   No doubt, no doubt. O, 'tis a parlous° boy,   *shrewd*
        Bold, quick, ingenious, forward, capable.
155   He is all the mother's, from the top to toe.
    BUCKINGHAM   Well, let them rest.—Come hither, Catesby. Thou art sworn
        As deeply° to effect what we intend   *cunningly*
        As closely° to conceal what we impart.   *secretly*
        Thou know'st our reasons, urged upon the way.[3]
160   What think'st thou? Is it not an easy matter
        To make Lord William Hastings of our mind,[4]
        For the instalment° of this noble duke   *enthroning*
        In the seat royal of this famous isle?
    CATESBY   He for his father's sake so loves the Prince[5]
165   That he will not be won to aught against him.
    BUCKINGHAM   What think'st thou then of Stanley?° Will not he?   *(Earl of Derby)*
    CATESBY   He will do all-in-all as Hastings doth.
    BUCKINGHAM   Well then, no more but this. Go, gentle Catesby,
        And, as it were far off, sound thou Lord Hastings
170   How he doth stand affected to our purpose.[6]
170.1   *And summon him tomorrow to the Tower*
          To sit about° the coronation.   *To discuss in council*
        If thou dost find him tractable° to us,   *compliant*

8. Alluding to Richard's hunched back, which is compared to the saddle worn by jesters who carried monkeys about at carnivals and fairs.
9. A nimble wit (intelligence); a wit both sharp and prodigal (abundant or excessive).
1. Richard meant himself; Edward refers to Rivers and Gray.

2. Trumpet notes to signal a procession.
3. On the journey from London to Ludlow.
4. To have Hastings share in our opinion.
5. Hastings loves the Prince as the son of the beloved King Edward.
6. The following indented passage, 170.1–170.2, appears only in F. *stand affected to:* regard, like.

Encourage him, and tell him all our reasons.
If he be leaden, icy, cold, unwilling,
Be thou so too, and so break off your talk,
175 And give us notice of his inclination,
For we tomorrow hold divided counsels,[7]
Wherein thyself shalt highly° be employed.   *importantly*
RICHARD GLOUCESTER   Commend me to Lord William.° Tell   *(Hastings)*
        him, Catesby,
His ancient knot[8] of dangerous adversaries
180 Tomorrow are let blood° at Pomfret Castle,   *are executed*
And bid my lord, for joy of this good news,
Give Mrs Shore[9] one gentle kiss the more.
BUCKINGHAM   Good Catesby, go effect this business soundly.°   *thoroughly; well*
CATESBY   My good lords both, with all the heed I can.
185 RICHARD GLOUCESTER   Shall we hear from you, Catesby, ere we sleep?
CATESBY   You shall, my lord.
RICHARD GLOUCESTER   At Crosby House,° there shall you find   *(Richard's residence)*
        us both.   *Exit* CATESBY
BUCKINGHAM   My lord, what shall we do if we perceive
Lord Hastings will not yield to our complots?°   *plots*
190 RICHARD GLOUCESTER   Chop off his head. Something we will determine.
And look when° I am king, claim thou of me   *And as soon as*
The earldom of Hereford, and all the movables[1]
Whereof the King my brother was possessed.
BUCKINGHAM   I'll claim that promise at your grace's hand.
195 RICHARD GLOUCESTER   And look° to have it yielded with all kindness.   *And expect*
Come, let us sup betimes,° that afterwards   *early*
We may digest our complots in some form.[2]   *Exeunt*

3.2

Enter a MESSENGER *to the door of* LORD HASTINGS
MESSENGER [*knocking*]   My lord, my lord!
LORD HASTINGS [*within*]   Who knocks?
MESSENGER   One from Lord Stanley.
        Enter LORD HASTINGS
LORD HASTINGS   What is't o'clock?
MESSENGER   Upon the stroke of four.
LORD HASTINGS   Cannot my Lord Stanley sleep these tedious nights?
MESSENGER   So it appears by that I have to say.
5 First he commends him to your noble self.
LORD HASTINGS   What then?
MESSENGER   Then certifies° your lordship that this night   *assures*
He dreamt the boar had razèd off his helm.[1]
Besides, he says there are two councils kept,
10 And that may be determined at the one
Which may make you and him to rue at° th'other.   *regret*
Therefore he sends to know your lordship's pleasure,
If you will presently° take horse with him,   *immediately*

---

7. There will be two separate council meetings, one public to plan the Prince's coronation, the other private to plot Richard's seizing of the crown.
8. Conspiracy, with additional meaning of "tumor," picked up in the next line in the image of bloodletting as medical treatment.
9. After Edward's death, Jane Shore (see 1.1.71–77) became Hastings's mistress.

1. Personal as opposed to real property: furnishings, rather than land.
2. We may break plans down into an orderly system (with pun on "digest").
3.2 Location: Outside Lord Hastings's house, in London.
1. He dreamed the boar (Richard's emblem) had sheared off his helmet (figuratively, cut off his head).

And with all speed post with him toward the north
15   To shun the danger that his soul divines.°   *prophesies*
LORD HASTINGS   Go, fellow, go, return unto thy lord.
     Bid him not fear the separated councils.
     His honour and myself are at the one,
     And at the other is my good friend Catesby,
20   Where nothing can proceed that toucheth° us   *concerns; harms*
     Whereof I shall not have intelligence.°   *secret information*
     Tell him his fears are shallow, without instance.°   *evidence*
     And for his dreams, I wonder he's so simple,°   *childish*
     To trust the mock'ry of unquiet slumbers.
25   To fly the boar before the boar pursues
     Were to incense the boar to follow us,
     And make pursuit where he did mean° no chase.   *intend*
     Go, bid thy master rise, and come to me,
     And we will both together to the Tower,
30   Where he shall see the boar will use us kindly.[2]
MESSENGER   I'll go, my lord, and tell him what you say.   *Exit*
       Enter CATESBY
CATESBY   Many good morrows to my noble lord.
LORD HASTINGS   Good morrow, Catesby. You are early stirring.
     What news, what news, in this our tott'ring state?
35 CATESBY   It is a reeling° world indeed, my lord,   *an unstable*
     And I believe will never stand upright
     Till Richard wear the garland of the realm.
LORD HASTINGS   How? 'Wear the garland'? Dost thou mean the crown?
CATESBY   Ay, my good lord.
40 LORD HASTINGS   I'll have this crown° of mine cut from my shoulders   *head*
     Before I'll see the crown so foul misplaced.
     But canst thou guess that he doth aim at it?
CATESBY   Ay, on my life, and hopes to find you forward°   *a strong supporter*
     Upon his party° for the gain thereof—   *On his side*
45   And thereupon he sends you this good news:
     That this same very day your enemies,
     The kindred of the Queen, must die at Pomfret.
LORD HASTINGS   Indeed I am no mourner for that news,
     Because they have been still my adversaries.
50   But that I'll give my voice on Richard's side
     To bar my master's heirs in true descent,
     God knows I will not do it, to the death.[3]
CATESBY   God keep your lordship in that gracious mind!
LORD HASTINGS   But I shall laugh at this a twelvemonth hence:
55   That they which brought me in my master's hate,[4]
     I live to look upon their tragedy.
     Well, Catesby, ere a fortnight make me older,
     I'll send some packing that yet think not on't.
CATESBY   'Tis a vile thing to die, my gracious lord,
60   When men are unprepared, and look not for it.
LORD HASTINGS   O monstrous, monstrous! And so falls it out
     With Rivers, Vaughan, Gray—and so 'twill do
     With some men else, that think themselves as safe

---

2. Gently (but also, with unintended irony, character-istically).
3. Even at the risk of death.

4. That those (Rivers, Vaughan, and Gray) who turned King Edward against me.

As thou and I, who as thou know'st are dear
65 To princely Richard and to Buckingham.
CATESBY The Princes both make high account of° you—   *highly esteem*
[*Aside*] For they account° his head upon the bridge.⁵   *expect*
LORD HASTINGS I know they do, and I have well deserved it.

Enter Lord STANLEY

Come on, come on, where is your boar-spear,⁶ man?
70 Fear you the boar, and go so unprovided?⁷
STANLEY My lord, good morrow.—Good morrow, Catesby.—
You may jest on, but by the Holy Rood°   *Cross*
I do not like these several° councils, I.   *separate*
LORD HASTINGS My lord, I hold my life as dear as you do yours,
75 And never in my days, I do protest,
Was it so precious to me as 'tis now.
Think you, but° that I know our state secure,   *if it were not*
I would be so triumphant as I am?
STANLEY The lords at Pomfret, when they rode from London,
80 Were jocund,° and supposed their states were sure,°   *merry / secure*
And they indeed had no cause to mistrust;
But yet you see how soon the day o'ercast.°   *became overcast*
This sudden stab of rancour I misdoubt.⁸
Pray God, I say, I prove a needless coward.
85 What, shall we toward the Tower? The day is spent.⁹
LORD HASTINGS Come, come, have with you!° Wot° you what,   *I'll go with you / Know*
my lord?
Today the lords you talked of are beheaded.
STANLEY They for their truth° might better wear their heads   *honesty*
Than some that have accused them wear their hats.°   *retain their offices*
90 But come, my lord, let us away.

Enter a PURSUIVANT [*named*] *Hastings*¹

LORD HASTINGS Go on before; I'll follow presently.

Exeunt STANLEY *and* CATESBY

Well met, Hastings. How goes the world with thee?
PURSUIVANT The better that your lordship please° to ask.   *is pleased*
LORD HASTINGS I tell thee, man, 'tis better with me now
95 Than when I met thee last, where now we meet.
Then was I going prisoner to the Tower,
By the suggestion° of the Queen's allies;   *incitement*
But now, I tell thee—keep it to thyself—
This day those enemies are put to death,
100 And I in better state than e'er I was.
PURSUIVANT God hold it² to your honour's good content.
LORD HASTINGS Gramercy,° Hastings. There, drink that for me.   *Many thanks*

He throws him his purse

PURSUIVANT God save your lordship.   *Exit*

Enter a PRIEST

---

5. London Bridge (where the heads of traitors were displayed high on poles).
6. Specialized hunting spear with a crossbar to prevent the impaled boar's tusks from wounding the hunter.
7. Do you fear the boar, and (yet) go unprepared?
8. I mistrust such sudden attacks (as those that befell Rivers, Vaughan, and Gray).
9. It's getting late (in the morning). The scene had opened at 4:00 A.M.
1. F omits his name (taken from Holinshed's *Chroni-*

cles), here and in the dialogue. The name may be important in calling attention to the significance of Lord Hastings's own name: the word means either "someone who hurries" (here, to his destruction) or "a fruit that ripens early or before its time." *pursuivant:* state messenger with authority to execute warrants (particularly of treason). Figuratively, a pursuivant was any summoner or messenger.
2. May God maintain your prosperity.

PRIEST Well met, my lord. I am glad to see your honour.
105 LORD HASTINGS I thank thee, good Sir³ John, with all my heart.
I am in your debt for your last exercise.°   *sermon*
Come the next sabbath, and I will content you.⁴
    He whispers in his ear.
    Enter BUCKINGHAM
BUCKINGHAM What, talking with a priest, Lord Chamberlain?
Your friends at Pomfret, they do need the priest;
110 Your honour hath no shriving work⁵ in hand.
LORD HASTINGS Good faith, and when I met this holy man
The men you talk of came into my mind.
What, go you toward the Tower?
BUCKINGHAM I do, my lord, but long I cannot stay there;
115 I shall return before your lordship thence.
LORD HASTINGS Nay, like enough, for I stay dinner⁶ there.
BUCKINGHAM [*aside*] And supper° too, although thou⁷ know'st it not.   *evening meal*
Come, will you go?
LORD HASTINGS   I'll wait upon° your lordship.   *Exeunt*   *attend; go with*

3.3

Enter Sir Richard RATCLIFFE *with halberdiers carrying*
Lords RIVERS, GRAY, *and [Sir Thomas]* VAUGHAN *to*
*death at Pomfret*¹
RIVERS Sir Richard Ratcliffe, let me tell thee this:
Today shalt thou behold a subject die
For truth, for duty, and for loyalty.
GRAY [*to* RATCLIFFE] God bless the Prince from all the pack of you!
5 A knot° you are of damnèd bloodsuckers.   *group*
VAUGHAN [*to* RATCLIFFE] You live, that shall cry woe for° this   *shall regret*
    hereafter.
RATCLIFFE Dispatch.° The limit of your lives is out.   *Be quick*
RIVERS O Pomfret, Pomfret! O thou bloody prison,
Fatal and ominous to noble peers!
10 Within the guilty closure° of thy walls,   *enclosure*
Richard the Second here was hacked to death,
And, for more slander to thy dismal seat,²
We give to thee our guiltless blood to drink.
GRAY Now Margaret's curse is fall'n upon our heads,
15 For standing by when Richard stabbed her son.
RIVERS Then cursed she Hastings; then cursed she Buckingham;
Then cursed she Richard. O remember, God,
To hear her prayer for them as now for us.
And for° my sister and her princely sons,   *as for*
20 Be satisfied, dear God, with our true blood,
Which, as thou know'st, unjustly must be spilt.
RATCLIFFE Make haste: the hour of death is expiate.°   *fully come*
RIVERS Come, Gray; come, Vaughan; let us here embrace.
Farewell, until we meet again in heaven.   *Exeunt*

---

3. Courteous title of respect for clergymen.
4. I will pay your "debt" with a donation.
5. Confession and absolution (here, before execution).
6. I stay for dinner (eaten at about 11:00 A.M.).
7. Here, used contemptuously, as opposed to the formal "you" in line 118.

3.3 Location: Pontefract Castle.
1. Q has an extra opening line for this scene: RATCLIFFE Come, bring forth the prisoners.
2. And, in order to increase the notoriety of this gloomy place.

3.4

*Enter [the Duke of] BUCKINGHAM, [Lord STANLEY Earl
of] Derby, [LORD] HASTINGS, BISHOP OF ELY, [the Duke
of] NORFOLK, [Sir William CATESBY,]¹ with others at a
table*

LORD HASTINGS   Now, noble peers, the cause why we are met

Is to determine of° the coronation.   decide upon

In God's name, speak: when is the royal day?

BUCKINGHAM   Is all things ready for that solemn time?

5   STANLEY   It is, and wants but nomination.°   naming the day

BISHOP OF ELY   Tomorrow, then, I judge a happy° day.   suitable

BUCKINGHAM   Who knows the Lord Protector's mind herein?

Who is most inward° with the noble Duke?   intimate

BISHOP OF ELY   Your grace, methinks, should soonest know his mind.

10   BUCKINGHAM   We know each other's faces. For° our hearts,   As for

He knows no more of mine than I of yours,

Or I of his, my lord, than you of mine.—

Lord Hastings, you and he are near in love.

LORD HASTINGS   I thank his grace; I know he loves me well.

15   But for his purpose in the coronation,

I have not sounded him,° nor he delivered   sounded him out

His gracious pleasure any way therein.

But you, my honourable lords, may name the time,

And in the Duke's behalf I'll give my voice,°   vote

20   Which I presume he'll take in gentle part.°   he'll graciously approve

Enter [RICHARD Duke of] GLOUCESTER

BISHOP OF ELY   In happy time, here comes the Duke himself.

RICHARD GLOUCESTER   My noble lords, and cousins all, good morrow.

I have been long a sleeper, but I trust

My absence doth neglect no great design²

25   Which by my presence might have been concluded.

BUCKINGHAM   Had not you come upon your cue, my lord,

William Lord Hastings had pronounced your part—

I mean, your voice, for crowning of the King.

RICHARD GLOUCESTER   Than my Lord Hastings no man might be bolder.³

30   His lordship knows me well, and loves me well.—

My lord of Ely, when I was last in Holborn⁴

I saw good strawberries in your garden there.

I do beseech you send for some of them.

BISHOP OF ELY   Marry, and will, my lord, with all my heart.   *Exit*

35   RICHARD GLOUCESTER   Cousin of Buckingham, a word with you.

[*Aside*] Catesby hath sounded Hastings in° our business,   in respect to

And finds the testy gentleman so hot

That he will lose his head ere give consent

His 'master's child'—as worshipful° he terms it—   reverentially

40   Shall lose the royalty° of England's throne.   sovereignty

BUCKINGHAM   Withdraw yourself a while; I'll go with you.

Exeunt [RICHARD and BUCKINGHAM]⁵

STANLEY   We have not yet set down this day of triumph.

3.4 Location: The Tower of London.
1. F has Ratcliffe and Lovell (Sir Thomas Lovell; see
4.4.449) instead of Catesby.
2. My absence delays no important project.
3. No one could more confidently speak for me than

Lord Hastings; but also, no one could be more presumptuous.
4. The Bishop of Ely's official London residence.
5. Q keeps Buckingham on, and changes "I'll go with
you" to "I'll follow you."

Tomorrow, in my judgement, is too sudden,
For I myself am not so well provided°   *well equipped*
45   As else I would be, were the day prolonged.°   *further off*
     Enter BISHOP OF ELY
BISHOP OF ELY   Where is my lord, the Duke of Gloucester?
    I have sent for these strawberries.
LORD HASTINGS   His grace looks cheerfully and smooth° this morning.   *untroubled*
    There's some conceit° or other likes° him well,   *thought / pleases*
50   When that he bids good morrow with such spirit.
    I think there's never a man in Christendom
    Can lesser hide his love or hate than he,
    For by his face straight° shall you know his heart.   *immediately*
STANLEY   What of his heart perceive you in his face
55   By any likelihood° he showed today?   *appearance*
LORD HASTINGS   Marry, that with no man here he is offended—
    For were he, he had shown it in his looks.
STANLEY   I pray God he be not.
     Enter RICHARD[6] *and* BUCKINGHAM
RICHARD GLOUCESTER   I pray you all, tell me what they deserve
60   That do conspire my death with devilish plots
    Of damnèd witchcraft, and that have prevailed
    Upon my body with their hellish charms?
LORD HASTINGS   The tender love I bear your grace, my lord,
    Makes me most forward in this princely presence
65   To doom th'offenders, whatsoe'er they be.
    I say, my lord, they have deservèd death.
RICHARD GLOUCESTER   Then be your eyes the witness of their evil:
    See how I am bewitched. Behold, mine arm
    Is like a blasted sapling withered up.
70   And this is° Edward's wife, that monstrous witch,   *this is the work of*
    Consorted° with that harlot, strumpet Shore,   *In league with*
    That by their witchcraft thus have markèd me.
LORD HASTINGS   If they have done this deed, my noble lord—
RICHARD GLOUCESTER   'If'? Thou protector of this damnèd strumpet,
75   Talk'st thou to me of 'ifs'? Thou art a traitor.—
    Off with his head. Now, by Saint Paul I swear,
    I will not dine until I see the same.
    Some see it done.
    The rest that love me, rise and follow me.
     Exeunt. Manent CATESBY[7] *with* HASTINGS
80   LORD HASTINGS   Woe, woe for England! Not a whit for me,
    For I, too fond,° might have prevented this.   *foolish*
    Stanley did dream the boar did raze our helms,
    But I did scorn it and disdain to fly.
    Three times today my footcloth horse[8] did stumble,
85   And started when he looked upon the Tower,
    As° loath to bear me to the slaughterhouse.   *As though*
    O now I need the priest that spake to me.
    I now repent I told the pursuivant,
    As too triumphing,° how mine enemies   *exulting*

---

6. According to Holinshed, "He returned into the chamber . . . with a wonderful sour, angry countenance, knitting the brows, frowning and fretting, and gnawing on his lips."

7. F calls for Ratcliffe and Lovell.
8. Horse draped with a richly ornamented covering reaching almost to the ground.

90   Today at Pomfret bloodily were butchered,
     And I myself secure in grace and favour.
     O Margaret, Margaret! Now thy heavy curse
     Is lighted on poor Hastings' wretched head.
     CATESBY   Come, come, dispatch: the Duke would be at dinner.
95   Make a short shrift;° he longs to see your head.   *confession (to a priest)*
     LORD HASTINGS   O momentary grace of mortal men,
     Which we more hunt for than the grace of God.
     Who builds his hope in th'air of your good looks[9]
     Lives like a drunken sailor on a mast,
100 Ready with every nod[1] to tumble down
     Into the fatal bowels of the deep.[2]
     CATESBY   Come, come, dispatch. 'Tis bootless to exclaim.°   *pointless to protest*
     LORD HASTINGS   O bloody Richard! Miserable England!
     I prophesy the fearful'st time to thee
105 That ever wretched age hath looked upon.—
     Come lead me to the block; bear him my head.
     They smile at me, who shortly shall be dead.   *Exeunt*

3.5

     Enter RICHARD *Duke of* GLOUCESTER *and* [*the Duke of*]
       BUCKINGHAM *in rotten*° *armour, marvellous ill-favoured*°   *rusty / ugly*
     RICHARD GLOUCESTER   Come, cousin, canst thou quake and change thy
       colour?
     Murder thy breath in middle of a word?
     And then again begin, and stop again,
     As if thou wert distraught and mad with terror?
5   BUCKINGHAM   Tut, I can counterfeit the deep tragedian,
     Tremble and start at wagging of a straw,[1]
     Speak, and look back, and pry° on every side,   *peer*
     Intending° deep suspicion; ghastly looks   *Suggesting*
     Are at my service, like enforcèd smiles,
10   And both are ready in their offices[2]
     At any time to grace my stratagems.
       Enter the [*Lord*] MAYOR
     RICHARD GLOUCESTER [*aside to* BUCKINGHAM]   Here comes the Mayor.
     BUCKINGHAM [*aside to* RICHARD]   Let me alone to entertain him.—Lord Mayor—
     RICHARD GLOUCESTER [*calling as to one within*]   Look to the drawbridge there!
15   BUCKINGHAM   Hark, a drum!
     RICHARD GLOUCESTER [*calling as to one within*]   Catesby, o'erlook°   *look (out) over*
       the walls!
     BUCKINGHAM   Lord Mayor, the reason we have sent—
     RICHARD GLOUCESTER   Look back, defend thee! Here are enemies.
     BUCKINGHAM   God and our innocence defend and guard us.
       Enter [*Sir William*] CATESBY[3] *with Hastings' head*
20   RICHARD GLOUCESTER   O, O, be quiet! It is Catesby.
     CATESBY   Here is the head of that ignoble traitor,
       The dangerous and unsuspected Hastings.
     RICHARD GLOUCESTER   So dear I loved the man that I must weep.

---

9. *Who . . . looks:* Anyone who puts his faith in your
seemingly favorable glances.
1. Complex play on words: Ready as he dozes off; as the
ship rolls; as the monarch, whose "good looks" upheld
him, condemns him with a silent nod.
2. Lines 102–7 appear only in F. Censorship or the fear
of censorship may well be why Hastings's ominous pre-

diction was omitted from Q.
3.5 Location: The Tower of London.
1. Act startled by the least movement or gesture.
2. Both are eager to perform their functions.
3. F calls for Ratcliffe and Lovell, and brings on
Catesby earlier, with the Mayor.

I took him for the plainest° harmless creature   *most manifestly*

25 That breathed upon the earth, a Christian,

Made him my book° wherein my soul recorded   *diary*

The history of all her secret thoughts.

So smooth he daubed his vice with show of virtue

That, his apparent open guilt omitted—

30 I mean, his conversation[4] with Shore's wife—

He lived from all attainture of suspect.[5]

BUCKINGHAM The covert'st sheltered° traitor that ever lived. *The most hidden*

[*To the* MAYOR] Would you imagine, or almost believe—

Were't not that, by great preservation,[6]

35 We live to tell it—that the subtle traitor

This day had plotted in the Council house

To murder me and my good lord of Gloucester?

MAYOR Had he done so?

RICHARD GLOUCESTER What, think you we are Turks or infidels,

40 Or that we would against the form of law

Proceed thus rashly in the villain's death

But that the extreme peril of the case,

The peace of England, and our persons' safety,

Enforced us to this execution?

45 MAYOR Now fair befall you, he deserved his death,

And your good graces both have well proceeded,°   *acted*

To warn false traitors from the like° attempts.   *similar*

I never looked for better at his hands

After he once fell in with Mrs Shore.

50 RICHARD GLOUCESTER[7] Yet had not we determined he should die,

Until your lordship came to see his end,

Which now the loving haste of these our friends°— *(Catesby and Buckingham)*

Something against our meanings°—have prevented; *intentions*

Because, my lord, we would have had you hear

55 The traitor speak, and timorously confess

The manner and the purpose of his treason,

That you might well have signified the same

Unto the citizens, who haply° may   *perhaps*

Misconster us in him,[8] and wail his death.

60 MAYOR But, my good lord, your graces' word shall serve

As well as° I had seen and heard him speak. *As well as = As if*

And do not doubt, right noble princes both,

But° I'll acquaint our duteous citizens   *That*

With all your just proceedings in this cause.°   *action*

65 RICHARD GLOUCESTER And to that end we wished your lordship here,

T'avoid the censures of the carping° world.   *overcritical*

BUCKINGHAM Which, since you come too late of our intent,° *for what we intended*

Yet witness° what you hear we did intend,   *bear witness to*

And so, my good Lord Mayor, we bid farewell. *Exit* MAYOR

70 RICHARD GLOUCESTER Go after; after, cousin Buckingham!

The Mayor towards Guildhall[9] hies him in all post;° *haste*

There, at your meetest vantage of the time,[1]

Infer° the bastardy of Edward's children.   *Allege*

Tell them how Edward put to death a citizen

---

4. Intercourse (in both senses).
5. He lived free from all taint of suspicion.
6. By the most fortunate preservation (of our lives).
7. F assigns this speech and the two preceding lines to

Buckingham.
8. Misunderstand our treatment of him.
9. Center of municipal government in London.
1. At your most appropriate and advantageous moment.

75 Only for saying he would make his son
'Heir to the Crown'—meaning indeed, his house,°   *tavern*
Which by the sign thereof was termèd so.
Moreover, urge his hateful luxury°   *lasciviousness*
And bestial appetite in change of lust,[2]
80 Which stretched unto their servants, daughters, wives,
Even where° his raging eye, or savage heart,   *Wherever*
Without control, listed° to make a prey.   *desired*
Nay, for a need, thus far come near my person:[3]
Tell them, when that my mother went with child
85 Of that insatiate Edward,[4] noble York,
My princely father, then had wars in France,
And by true computation of the time
Found that the issue° was not his begot—   *offspring*
Which well appearèd in his lineaments,°   *features*
90 Being nothing like the noble Duke my father.
Yet touch this sparingly, as 'twere far off,
Because, my lord, you know my mother lives.
BUCKINGHAM   Doubt not, my lord, I'll play the orator
As if the golden fee[5] for which I plead
95 Were for myself. And so, my lord, adieu.   *[He starts to go]*
RICHARD GLOUCESTER   If you thrive well, bring them to Baynard's Castle,[6]
Where you shall find me well accompanied
With reverend fathers and well-learnèd bishops.
BUCKINGHAM   I go, and towards three or four o'clock
100 Look for the news that the Guildhall affords.[7]   *Exit*
100.1   KING RICHARD   *Go, Lovell, with all speed to Doctor Shaw;*
[To RATCLIFFE] Go thou to Friar Penker.[8] Bid them both
Meet me within this hour at Baynard's Castle.
    [Exeunt LOVELL and RATCLIFFE]
RICHARD GLOUCESTER   Now will I in, to take some privy order[9]
To draw the brats of Clarence[1] out of sight,
And to give notice that no manner[2] person
Have any° time recourse unto the Princes.   *Exeunt*   *at any*

3.6

Enter a SCRIVENER° *with a paper in his hand*   *scribe*
SCRIVENER   Here is the indictment of the good Lord Hastings,
Which in a set hand fairly is engrossed,[1]
That it may be today read o'er in Paul's[2]—
And mark how well the sequel° hangs together: *sequence of events*
5 Eleven hours I have spent to write it over,
For yesternight by Catesby was it sent me;
The precedent° was full as long a-doing;   *rough draft*
And yet, within these five hours, Hastings lived,

---

2. In continually shifting the object of his lust.
3. *for . . . person:* if necessary, impugn even to this extent my own honor (by implying that his mother was unfaithful).
4. *went . . . Edward:* was pregnant with dissolute Edward. *insatiate:* impossible to satisfy.
5. The crown (punning on "lawyer's fee").
6. Richard's stronghold, between Blackfriars and London Bridge.
7. The indented passage that follows, 100.1–100.3, appears only in F.
8. Dr. Shaw, brother to the Lord Mayor, and Friar Perkins, provincial of the Augustinian Order, were prominent clerics who made public speeches supporting Richard's claim to the throne.
9. To make some secret arrangements.
1. The two children seen in 2.2.
2. No kind of (in other words, of whatever status or importance).
3.6 Location: Somewhere in London.
1. Which is written in official script (as opposed to a draft copy) and in the format of a legal document.
2. St. Paul's Cathedral, which served as a secular as well as sacred gathering place.

Untainted,° unexamined, free, at liberty.   *Unaccused*
10   Here's a good world the while! Who is so gross°   *stupid*
That cannot see this palpable device?°   *obvious stratagem*
Yet who so bold but says he sees it not?
Bad is the world, and all will come to naught,°   *wickedness; nothing*
When such ill dealing must be seen in thought.³   *Exit*

3.7

Enter RICHARD [*Duke of*] GLOUCESTER *at one door and*
[*the Duke of*] BUCKINGHAM *at another*

RICHARD GLOUCESTER   How now, how now! What say the citizens?
BUCKINGHAM   Now, by the holy mother of our Lord,
The citizens are mum, say not a word.
RICHARD GLOUCESTER   Touched you° the bastardy of Edward's   *Did you touch on*
children?
5   BUCKINGHAM   I did, with his contract with Lady Lucy,¹
And his contract by deputy² in France,
Th'insatiate greediness of his desire,
And his enforcement° of the city wives,   *violation*
His tyranny for trifles, his own bastardy—
10   As being got° your father then in France,   *conceived*
And his resemblance,° being not like the Duke.   *appearance*
Withal, I did infer your lineaments°—   *lineage*
Being the right idea° of your father   *true image*
Both in your face³ and nobleness of mind;
15   Laid open all your victories in Scotland,⁴
Your discipline in war, wisdom in peace,
Your bounty, virtue, fair humility—
Indeed, left nothing fitting for your purpose
Untouched or slightly handled° in discourse.   *lightly mentioned*
20   And when mine oratory grew toward end,
I bid them that did love their country's good
Cry 'God save Richard, England's royal king!'
RICHARD GLOUCESTER   And did they so?
BUCKINGHAM   No, so God help me. They spake not a word,
25   But, like dumb statues or breathing stones,
Stared each on other and looked deadly pale—
Which, when I saw, I reprehended them,
And asked the Mayor, what meant this wilful silence?
His answer was, the people were not used
30   To be spoke to but by the Recorder.°   *(a city official)*
Then he was urged to tell my tale again:
'Thus saith the Duke . . . thus hath the Duke inferred'°—   *asserted*
But nothing spoke in warrant from himself.°   *on his own authority*
When he had done, some followers of mine own,
35   At lower end of the Hall, hurled up their caps,

---

3. Must be perceived but not spoken of.
3.7 Location: Baynard's Castle.
1. Lady Elizabeth Lucy bore Edward a child. If, as
Buckingham alleges, there had been a formal engagement between them, Edward's subsequent marriage to
Elizabeth Gray would have been ruled invalid. His children by that marriage would have been bastards and
hence ineligible to inherit the throne.
2. The Earl of Warwick, as deputy, had contracted with
Louis XI of France for the marriage of Edward to Bona

of Savoy, the French queen's sister (see *Richard Duke
of York* 3.3).
3. Q, F: forme. The Oxford editors observe that since
Richard is prominently deformed, "form" is inappropriate; in the chronicles, it is Richard's *face* that is compared with his father's.
4. In 1482, as leader of an English expeditionary force
against the Scots, Richard had advanced all the way to
Edinburgh.

And some ten voices cried 'God save King Richard!'
And thus I took the vantage of° those few: *opportunity presented by*
'Thanks, gentle citizens and friends', quoth I;
'This general applause and cheerful shout
40 Argues your wisdoms and your love to Richard'—
And even here brake off and came away.
RICHARD GLOUCESTER What tongueless blocks were they!
     Would they not speak?
BUCKINGHAM⁵ No, by my troth, my lord.
RICHARD GLOUCESTER Will not the Mayor then, and his brethren, come?
45 BUCKINGHAM The Mayor is here at hand. Intend° some fear;   *Pretend*
Be not you spoke with, but by mighty suit;⁶
And look you get a prayer book in your hand,
And stand between two churchmen, good my lord,
For on that ground I'll build a holy descant.⁷
50 And be not easily won to our request.
Play the maid's part:⁸ still answer 'nay'—and take it.
RICHARD GLOUCESTER I go. An if you plead as well for them
As I can say nay to thee for myself,
No doubt we'll bring it to a happy issue.
     [*One knocks within*]
55 BUCKINGHAM Go, go, up to the leads!⁹ The Lord Mayor knocks.—
                                  Exit [RICHARD]
     Enter the [*Lord*] MAYOR, [*aldermen,*] *and citizens*
Welcome, my lord. I dance attendance° here.   *am kept waiting*
I think the Duke will not be spoke withal.
     Enter CATESBY
Now Catesby, what says your lord to my request?
CATESBY He doth entreat your grace, my noble lord,
60 To visit him tomorrow, or next day.
He is within with two right reverend fathers,
Divinely bent to meditation,
And in no worldly suits would he be moved,
To draw him from his holy exercise.
65 BUCKINGHAM Return, good Catesby, to the gracious Duke.
Tell him myself, the Mayor, and aldermen,
In deep designs, in matter of great moment,
No less importing than¹ our general good,
Are come to have some conference with his grace.
70 CATESBY I'll signify so much unto him straight.   *Exit*
BUCKINGHAM Ah ha! My lord, this prince is not an Edward.
He is not lolling on a lewd day-bed,
But on his knees at meditation;
Not dallying with a brace° of courtesans,   *pair*
75 But meditating with two deep° divines;   *profoundly learned*
Not sleeping to engross° his idle body,   *fatten*
But praying to enrich his watchful° soul.   *vigilant*
Happy were England would this virtuous prince
Take on his grace the sovereignty thereof.
80 But, sure I fear, we shall not win him to it.

5. F omits this line.
6. Do not let them speak with you unless they beg you.
7. Comment; improvised musical variation, usually the highest part. *ground:* basis; musical theme or air, often the bass line.
8. Keep refusing, but at the same time take whatever is offered (proverbial, with sexual innuendo).
9. Flat roof covered with lead.
1. Of no less significance than.

MAYOR   Marry, God defend° his grace should say us nay.   *forbid*
BUCKINGHAM   I fear he will. Here Catesby comes again.
            Enter CATESBY
        Now Catesby, what says his grace?
CATESBY   He wonders to what end you have assembled
85   Such troops of citizens to come to him,
        His grace not being warned thereof before.
        He fears, my lord, you mean no good to him.
BUCKINGHAM   Sorry I am my noble cousin should
        Suspect me that I mean no good to him.
90   By heaven, we come to him in perfect love,
        And so once more return and tell his grace.   *Exit* CATESBY
        When holy and devout religious men
        Are at their beads,° 'tis much to draw them thence.   *prayers*
        So sweet is zealous contemplation.
            Enter RICHARD *aloft, between two bishops.* [*Enter*
            CATESBY *below*]
95 MAYOR   See where his grace stands 'tween two clergymen.
BUCKINGHAM   Two props of virtue for a Christian prince,
        To stay him from the fall of vanity;[2]
        And see, a book of prayer in his hand—
        True ornaments to know[3] a holy man.—
100   Famous Plantagenet, most gracious prince,
        Lend favourable ear to our request,
        And pardon us the interruption
        Of thy devotion and right Christian zeal.
RICHARD GLOUCESTER   My lord, there needs no such apology.
105   I do beseech your grace to pardon me,
        Who, earnest in the service of my God,
        Deferred the visitation of my friends.
        But leaving this, what is your grace's pleasure?
BUCKINGHAM   Even that, I hope, which pleaseth God above,
110   And all good men of this ungoverned isle.
RICHARD GLOUCESTER   I do suspect I have done some offence
        That seems disgracious° in the city's eye,   *displeasing*
        And that you come to reprehend my ignorance.
BUCKINGHAM   You have, my lord. Would it might please your grace
115   On our entreaties to amend your fault.
RICHARD GLOUCESTER   Else wherefore breathe I in a Christian land?[4]
BUCKINGHAM   Know then, it is your fault that you resign
        The supreme seat, the throne majestical,
        The sceptred office of your ancestors,
120   Your state of fortune[5] and your due of birth,
        The lineal glory of your royal house,
        To the corruption of a blemished stock,[6]
        Whiles in the mildness of your sleepy° thoughts—   *contemplative*
        Which here we waken to our country's good—
125   The noble isle doth want her proper° limbs: *lack her own*
        Her face defaced with scars of infamy,
        Her royal stock graft with ignoble plants
        And almost shouldered in° the swallowing gulf   *shoved into*

2. To prevent him from falling into the sin of vanity.
3. *True . . . know*: Prayer books (and also, perhaps, the
clergymen) by which to recognize.
4. Why else do I lead a Christian life?

5. The position that fortune has given you.
6. Edward's "family tree" is degraded by bastardy and
immorality.

Of dark forgetfulness and deep oblivion,
130 Which to recure° we heartily solicit   restore
Your gracious self to take on you the charge
And kingly government of this your land—
Not as Protector, steward, substitute,
Or lowly factor° for another's gain,   agent
135 But as successively,° from blood to blood,   in order of succession
Your right of birth, your empery,° your own.   absolute dominion
For this, consorted° with the citizens,   together
Your very worshipful° and loving friends,   respectful
And by their vehement instigation,
140 In this just cause come I to move your grace.
RICHARD GLOUCESTER   I cannot tell if to depart in silence
Or bitterly to speak in your reproof
Best fitteth my degree° or your condition.[7]   rank
143.1   *If not to answer, you might haply° think*   *perhaps*
              Tongue-tied ambition, not replying, yielded°   *agreed*
              To bear the golden yoke of sovereignty,
              Which fondly° you would here impose on me.   *foolishly*
143.5   *If to reprove you for this suit of yours,*
              So seasoned° with your faithful love to me,   *made palatable*
              Then on the other side I checked° my friends.   *rebuked*
              Therefore to speak, and to avoid the first,
              And then in speaking not to incur the last,
143.10   *Definitively thus I answer you.*
Your love deserves my thanks; but my desert,
145 Unmeritable,° shuns your high request.   Undeserving
First, if all obstacles were cut away
And that my path were even° to the crown,   smooth
As the ripe revenue and due of birth,
Yet so much is my poverty of spirit,
150 So mighty and so many my defects,
That I would rather hide me from my greatness—
Being a barque to brook° no mighty sea—   a boat to endure
Than in my greatness covet to be hid,[8]
And in the vapour of my glory smothered.
155 But God be thanked, there is no need of me,
And much I need° to help you, were there need.   lack (ability)
The royal tree hath left us royal fruit,
Which, mellowed by the stealing hours of time,
Will well become the seat of majesty
160 And make, no doubt, us happy by his reign.
On him I lay that° you would lay on me,   what
The right and fortune of his happy° stars,   auspicious
Which God defend that I should wring from him.
BUCKINGHAM   My lord, this argues conscience in your grace,
165 But the respects thereof are nice and trivial,[9]
All circumstances well consider è d.
You say that Edward is your brother's son;
So say we, too—but not by Edward's wife.
For first was he contract° to Lady Lucy—   betrothed

---

7. Social rank. The indented passage that follows,   9. But the reasons you advance are nit-picking (thus,
143.1–143.10, appears only in F.   overscrupulous).
8. Than desire to be enveloped by my greatness.

170   Your mother lives a witness to his vow¹—
    And afterward, by substitute,° betrothed   *proxy*
    To Bona, sister to the King of France.
    These both put off, a poor petitioner,
    A care-crazed mother to a many sons,
175   A beauty-waning and distressèd widow
    Even in the afternoon of her best days,
    Made prize and purchase° of his wanton eye,   *booty*
    Seduced the pitch and height of his degree²
    To base declension° and loathed bigamy.   *degradation*
180   By her in his unlawful bed he got
    This Edward, whom our manners° call the Prince.   *we in politeness*
    More bitterly could I expostulate,
    Save that for reverence to some alive³
    I give a sparing limit to my tongue.
185   Then, good my lord, take to your royal self
    This proffered benefit° of dignity—   *bestowal*
    If not to bless us and the land withal,
    Yet to draw forth° your noble ancestry   *to rescue*
    From the corruption of abusing times,
190   Unto a lineal, true-derivèd course.
    MAYOR [*to* RICHARD]   Do, good my lord; your citizens entreat you.
    BUCKINGHAM [*to* RICHARD]   Refuse not, mighty lord, this proffered love.
    CATESBY [*to* RICHARD]   O make them joyful: grant their lawful suit.
    RICHARD GLOUCESTER   Alas, why would you heap this care on me?
195   I am unfit for state and majesty.
    I do beseech you, take it not amiss.
    I cannot, nor I will not, yield to you.
    BUCKINGHAM   If you refuse it—as, in love and zeal,
    Loath to depose the child, your brother's son,
200   As well we know your tenderness of heart
    And gentle, kind, effeminate remorse,⁴
    Which we have noted in you to your kindred,
    And equally indeed to all estates°—   *social classes*
    Yet know, whe'er° you accept our suit or no,   *whether*
205   Your brother's son shall never reign our king,
    But we will plant some other in the throne,
    To the disgrace and downfall of your house.
    And in this resolution here we leave you.—
    Come, citizens. 'Swounds,° I'll entreat no more.   *By God's wounds*
210   RICHARD GLOUCESTER   O do not swear, my lord of Buckingham.
                   Exeunt [BUCKINGHAM *and some others*]
    CATESBY   Call him again, sweet prince. Accept their suit.
    ANOTHER⁵   If you deny them, all the land will rue° it.   *suffer for*
    RICHARD GLOUCESTER   Will you enforce° me to a world of cares?   *condemn*
    Call them again.   [*Exit one or more*]
                    I am not made of stone,
215   But penetrable to your kind entreats,°   *entreaties*
    Albeit against my conscience and my soul.

---

1. Buckingham draws attention to the Duchess of York's objection to her son Edward's marriage to Elizabeth Gray; Edward's supposed betrothals (see notes to lines 5–6), along with the fact of Elizabeth's widowhood, are put forward as evidence that the marriage should be considered bigamous and hence the offspring illegitimate.
2. Drew him down from the eminence appropriate to his noble rank.
3. Richard's own mother, the Duchess of York.
4. And natural, tender pity (feelings thought of at that time as primarily feminine).
5. One of the remaining citizens, city officials, or bishops. In F, Catesby speaks this line.

Enter BUCKINGHAM *and the rest*

Cousin of Buckingham, and sage, grave men,
Since you will buckle fortune on my back,
To° bear her burden, whe'er I will or no,   To make me
220   I must have patience to endure the load.
But if black scandal or foul-faced reproach
Attend the sequel of your imposition,°   what you impose on me
Your mere° enforcement shall acquittance° me   outright / acquit
From all the impure blots and stains thereof;
225   For God doth know, and you may partly see,
How far I am from the desire of this.
MAYOR   God bless your grace! We see it, and will say it.
RICHARD GLOUCESTER   In saying so, you shall but say the truth.
BUCKINGHAM   Then I salute you with this royal title:
230   Long live kind Richard, England's worthy king!
ALL BUT RICHARD[6]   Amen.
BUCKINGHAM   Tomorrow may it please you to be crowned?
RICHARD GLOUCESTER   Even when you please, for you will have it so.
BUCKINGHAM   Tomorrow then, we will attend your grace.
235   And so, most joyfully, we take our leave.
RICHARD GLOUCESTER [*to the bishops*]   Come, let us to our holy work again.—
Farewell, my cousin. Farewell, gentle friends.
        Exeunt [RICHARD *and bishops above, the rest below*]

4.1

Enter QUEEN [ELIZABETH], *the* [*old*] DUCHESS OF YORK,
and Marquis DORSET *at one door;* [LADY] ANNE *Duchess
of Gloucester* [*with Clarence's daughter*] *at another door*

DUCHESS OF YORK   Who meets us here? My niece° Plantagenet,   granddaughter
Led in° the hand of her kind aunt of Gloucester?   by
Now for° my life, she's wand'ring to the Tower,   upon
On pure heart's love, to greet the tender° Prince.—   young
Daughter,° well met.   Daughter-in-law
5   LADY ANNE   God give your graces both
A happy and a joyful time of day.
QUEEN ELIZABETH   As much to you, good sister.° Whither away?   sister-in-law
LADY ANNE   No farther than the Tower, and—as I guess—
Upon the like devotion° as yourselves: devout duty
10   To gratulate° the gentle princes there.   greet
QUEEN ELIZABETH   Kind sister, thanks. We'll enter all together—
        Enter [*from the Tower* BRACKENBURY] *the Lieutenant*
And in good time, here the Lieutenant comes.
Master Lieutenant, pray you by your leave,
How doth the Prince, and my young son of York?
15   BRACKENBURY   Right well, dear madam. By your patience,
I may not suffer° you to visit them.   permit
The King hath strictly charged the contrary.
QUEEN ELIZABETH   The King? Who's that?
BRACKENBURY   I mean, the Lord Protector.
QUEEN ELIZABETH   The Lord protect him from that kingly title.[1]
20   Hath he set bounds° between their love and me?   barriers

---

1. May God prevent Richard from acquiring the title of
King.

I am their mother; who shall bar me from them?

DUCHESS OF YORK   I am their father's mother; I will see them.

LADY ANNE   Their aunt I am in law, in love their mother;
Then bring me to their sights. I'll bear thy blame,
25   And take thy office from thee on my peril.[2]

BRACKENBURY   No, madam, no; I may not leave it° so.   *give up my office*
I am bound by oath, and therefore pardon me.   *Exit*

    Enter Lord STANLEY [*Earl of Derby*]

STANLEY   Let me but meet you ladies one hour hence,
And I'll salute your grace of York as mother
30   And reverend looker-on° of two fair queens.[3]   *beholder*
[*To* ANNE] Come, madam, you must straight to Westminster,[4]
There to be crownèd Richard's royal queen.

QUEEN ELIZABETH   Ah, cut my lace asunder,[5] that my pent heart
May have some scope to beat, or else I swoon
35   With this dead-killing news.

LADY ANNE   Despiteful tidings! O unpleasing news!

DORSET [*to* ANNE]   Be of good cheer.—Mother, how fares your grace?

QUEEN ELIZABETH   O Dorset, speak not to me. Get thee gone.
Death and destruction dogs thee at thy heels.
40   Thy mother's name is ominous to children.[6]
If thou wilt outstrip death, go cross the seas,
And live with Richmond from[7] the reach of hell.
Go, hie thee! Hie thee from this slaughterhouse,
Lest thou increase the number of the dead,
45   And make me die the thrall° of Margaret's curses: *slave*
'Nor mother, wife, nor counted° England's Queen'.   *regarded as*

STANLEY   Full of wise care is this your counsel, madam.
[*To* DORSET] Take all the swift advantage of the hours.
You shall have letters from me to my son°   *stepson (Richmond)*
50   In your behalf, to meet you on the way.
Be not ta'en tardy by unwise delay.

DUCHESS OF YORK   O ill-dispersing° wind of misery!   *misfortune-scattering*
O my accursèd womb, the bed° of death!   *birthplace*
A cockatrice[8] hast thou hatched to the world,
55   Whose unavoided eye is murderous.

STANLEY [*to* ANNE]   Come, madam, come. I in all haste was sent.

LADY ANNE   And I in all unwillingness will go.
O would to God that the inclusive verge°   *enclosing rim*
Of golden metal that must round° my brow   *encircle*
60   Were red-hot steel, to sear me to the brains.
Anointed let me be with deadly venom,[9]
And die ere men can say 'God save the Queen'.

QUEEN ELIZABETH   Go, go, poor soul. I envy not thy glory.
To feed my humour,° wish thyself no harm.   *To humor me*
65   LADY ANNE   No? Why? When he that is my husband now
Came to me as I followed Henry's corpse,
When scarce the blood was well washed from his hands,

---

2. And take on the responsibilities of your position at my own risk.
3. Elizabeth, widow of Edward IV, and Anne, wife of Richard III.
4. To Westminster Abbey, where English monarchs are traditionally crowned.
5. Elizabethan women wore tightly laced bodices.

6. The fact that you are my son places you in danger.
7. Away from. Henry Tudor, Earl of Richmond, had fled to Brittany in 1472, when Edward IV secured his grasp on the throne.
8. Basilisk (see note to 1.2.150).
9. Instead of the holy oil used in the ceremony of coronation.

Which issued from my other angel husband
And that dear saint which then I weeping followed—
70   O when, I say, I looked on Richard's face,
This was my wish: 'Be thou', quoth I, 'accursed
For making me, so young, so old a widow,[1]
And when thou wedd'st, let sorrow haunt thy bed;
And be thy wife—if any be so mad—
75   More miserable made by the life of thee
Than thou hast made me by my dear lord's death.'
Lo, ere I can repeat this curse again,
Within so small a time, my woman's heart
Grossly° grew captive to his honey words   *Stupidly*
80   And proved the subject of mine own soul's curse,
Which hitherto hath held mine eyes from rest—
For never yet one hour in his bed
Did I enjoy the golden dew of sleep,
But with his timorous° dreams was still° awaked.   *fearful / continually*
85   Besides, he hates me for° my father Warwick,   *because of*
And will, no doubt, shortly be rid of me.
QUEEN ELIZABETH   Poor heart, adieu. I pity thy complaining.°   *lamenting*
LADY ANNE   No more than with my soul I mourn for yours.
DORSET   Farewell, thou woeful welcomer of glory.
90   LADY ANNE   Adieu, poor soul, that tak'st thy leave of it.
DUCHESS OF YORK [*to* DORSET] Go thou to Richmond, and good fortune guide thee.
  [*To* ANNE, STANLEY, *and Clarence's daughter*] Go thou to Richard, and good angels
    tend thee.
  [*To* ELIZABETH] Go thou to sanctuary, and good thoughts possess thee.
  I to my grave, where peace and rest lie with me.
95   Eighty odd years of sorrow have I seen,
And each hour's joy racked with a week of teen.[2]   [*Exit*]
96.1   QUEEN ELIZABETH   *Stay: yet look back with me unto the Tower.—*
      Pity, you ancient stones, those tender babes,
      Whom envy° hath immured within your walls.   *malice; jealousy*
      Rough cradle for such little pretty ones,
96.5   *Rude ragged nurse, old sullen playfellow*
      For tender princes: use my babies well.
      So foolish sorrow bids your stones farewell.   *Exeunt*

4.2

    Sound a sennet. Enter [KING] RICHARD *in pomp,* [*the
    Duke of*] BUCKINGHAM, [*Sir William*] CATESBY, *other
    nobles*[1] [*and a* PAGE]
KING RICHARD   Stand all apart.°—Cousin of Buckingham.   *aside*
BUCKINGHAM   My gracious sovereign?
KING RICHARD   Give me thy hand.
    Sound [*a sennet*]. *Here he ascendeth the throne*
  Thus high by thy advice
5   And thy assistance is King Richard seated.
But shall we wear these glories for a day?
Or shall they last, and we rejoice in them?
BUCKINGHAM   Still° live they, and for ever let them last.   *Perpetually*

---

1. Doomed to a long life of widowhood.
2. Grief. The indented passage that follows,
96.1–96.7, appears only in F; the other characters
remain onstage.
4.2 Location: The palace, London.
1. In F, specifically Ratcliffe and Lovell.

KING RICHARD   Ah, Buckingham, now do I play the touch,[2]
10   To try if thou be current° gold indeed.   *real, genuine*
      Young Edward lives. Think now what I would speak.
BUCKINGHAM   Say on, my loving lord.
KING RICHARD   Why, Buckingham, I say I would be king.
BUCKINGHAM   Why, so you are, my thrice-renownèd liege.
15   KING RICHARD   Ha? Am I king? 'Tis so. But Edward lives.
BUCKINGHAM   True, noble prince.
KING RICHARD   O bitter consequence,°   *conclusion; retort*
      That Edward still should live 'true noble prince'.
      Cousin, thou wast not wont° to be so dull.   *accustomed*
      Shall I be plain? I wish the bastards dead,
20   And I would have it immediately performed.
      What sayst thou now? Speak suddenly,° be brief.   *at once*
BUCKINGHAM   Your grace may do your pleasure.
KING RICHARD   Tut, tut, thou art all ice. Thy kindness freezes.
      Say, have I thy consent that they shall die?
25   BUCKINGHAM   Give me some little breath, some pause, dear lord,
      Before I positively speak in this.
      I will resolve° you herein presently.°   *Exit*   *answer / shortly*
CATESBY [*to another, aside*]   The King is angry. See, he gnaws his lip.
KING RICHARD [*aside*]   I will converse with iron-witted fools
30   And unrespective° boys. None are for me   *unobservant*
      That look into me with considerate° eyes.   *critical*
      High-reaching° Buckingham grows circumspect.—   *Ambitious*
      Boy.
PAGE   My lord?
35   KING RICHARD   Know'st thou not any whom corrupting gold
      Will tempt unto a close° exploit of death?   *secret*
PAGE   I know a discontented gentleman,
      Whose humble means match not his haughty spirit.
      Gold were as good as twenty orators,
40   And will no doubt tempt him to anything.
KING RICHARD   What is his name?
PAGE   His name, my lord, is Tyrrell.
KING RICHARD   I partly know the man. Go call him hither, boy.
                                        Exit [PAGE]
      [*Aside*] The deep-revolving,° witty° Buckingham   *deeply scheming / clever*
      No more shall be the neighbour to my counsels.
45   Hath he so long held out° with me untired,   *kept up*
      And stops he now for breath? Well, be it so.
            Enter [*Lord*] STANLEY [*Earl of*] *Derby*
      How now, Lord Stanley? What's the news?
STANLEY   Know, my loving lord,
      The Marquis Dorset, as I hear, is fled
50   To Richmond, in those parts beyond the seas
      Where he abides.
KING RICHARD   Come hither, Catesby. [*Aside to* CATESBY] Rumour it abroad
      That Anne, my wife, is very grievous sick.
      I will take order for her keeping close.[3]
55   Enquire me out some mean-born gentleman,
      Whom I will marry straight to Clarence' daughter.

---

2. Touchstone: a means of testing gold.   3. I will arrange to have her kept out of sight.

The boy[4] is foolish,° and I fear not him.   *simpleminded*
Look how thou dream'st. I say again, give out
That Anne, my queen, is sick, and like to die.
60   About it, for it stands me much upon°   *is very important to me*
To stop all hopes whose growth may damage me.
                                    [*Exit* CATESBY]
[*Aside*] I must be married to my brother's daughter,[5]
Or else my kingdom stands on brittle glass.
Murder her brothers, and then marry her?
65   Uncertain way of gain, but I am in
So far in blood that sin will pluck on° sin.   *incite*
Tear-falling pity dwells not in this eye.—
            Enter [*Sir James*] TYRRELL; [*he kneels*]
Is thy name Tyrrell?
TYRRELL   James Tyrrell, and your most obedient subject.
KING RICHARD   Art thou indeed?
70   TYRRELL   Prove° me, my gracious lord.   *Test*
KING RICHARD   Dar'st thou resolve to kill a friend of mine?
TYRRELL   Please you,° but I had rather kill two enemies.   *If you wish*
KING RICHARD   Why there thou hast it: two deep enemies,
Foes to my rest, and my sweet sleep's disturbers,
75   Are they that I would have thee deal upon.°   *set to work upon*
Tyrrell, I mean those bastards in the Tower.
TYRRELL   Let me have open means to come[6] to them,
And soon I'll rid you from the fear of them.
KING RICHARD   Thou sing'st sweet music. Hark, come hither, Tyrrell.
80   Go, by this token. Rise, and lend thine ear.
            [RICHARD] *whispers in his ear*
'Tis no more but so.° Say it is done,   *That's all*
And I will love thee, and prefer° thee for it.   *promote*
TYRRELL   I will dispatch it straight.
KING RICHARD   Shall we hear from thee, Tyrrell, ere we sleep?[7]
            Enter BUCKINGHAM
85   TYRRELL   Ye shall, my lord.   *Exit*
BUCKINGHAM   My lord, I have considered in my mind
The late request that you did sound me in.
KING RICHARD   Well, let that rest. Dorset is fled to Richmond.
BUCKINGHAM   I hear the news, my lord.
90   KING RICHARD   Stanley, he° is your wife's son. Well, look to it.   *(Richmond)*
BUCKINGHAM   My lord, I claim the gift, my due by promise,
For which your honour and your faith is pawned:
Th'earldom of Hereford, and the movables
Which you have promisèd I shall possess.
95   KING RICHARD   Stanley, look to your wife. If she convey
Letters to Richmond, you shall answer it.°   *for it*
BUCKINGHAM   What says your highness to my just request?
KING RICHARD   I do remember me, Henry the Sixth
Did prophesy that Richmond should be king,
100   When Richmond was a little peevish boy.
A king . . . perhaps . . . perhaps.[8]
BUCKINGHAM   My lord?

---

4. Clarence's eldest son, Edward, Earl of Warwick.
5. To Edward's daughter, Elizabeth of York, who was later to unite the two houses by becoming queen to the Lancastrian Henry VII, formerly the Earl of Richmond.
6. Let me have free access.
7. F omits this and the following line.
8. The passage that follows, lines 101–119, appears only in Q.

KING RICHARD   How chance the prophet could not at that time
 Have told me, I being by, that I should kill him?
BUCKINGHAM   My lord, your promise for the earldom.
105 KING RICHARD   Richmond? When last I was at Exeter,
 The Mayor in courtesy showed me the castle,
 And called it 'Ruge-mount'⁹—at which name I started,
 Because a bard of Ireland¹ told me once
 I should not live long after I saw 'Richmond'.
110 BUCKINGHAM   My lord?
KING RICHARD   Ay? What's o'clock?
BUCKINGHAM   I am thus bold to put your grace in mind
 Of what you promised me.
KING RICHARD   But what's o'clock?
BUCKINGHAM   Upon the stroke of ten.
115 KING RICHARD   Well, let it strike!
BUCKINGHAM   Why 'let it strike'?
KING RICHARD   Because that, like a jack,² thou keep'st the stroke
 Betwixt thy begging and my meditation.
 I am not in the giving vein today.
120 BUCKINGHAM   Why then resolve me,° whe'er you will or no?   answer me resolutely
KING RICHARD   Thou troublest me. I am not in the vein.°   mood
     Exit [RICHARD, *followed by all but* BUCKINGHAM]
BUCKINGHAM   And is it thus? Repays he my deep° service   *i.e., rendered at great risk*
 With such contempt? Made I him king for this?
 O let me think on Hastings, and be gone
125 To Brecon,° while my fearful head is on.   *manor house in Wales*
         Exit [*at another door*]

4.3

Enter Sir [*James*] TYRRELL
TYRRELL   The tyrannous and bloody act is done—
 The most arch° deed of piteous massacre   *preeminent*
 That ever yet this land was guilty of.
 Dighton and Forrest,¹ whom I did suborn°   *induce*
5 To do this piece of ruthless butchery,
 Albeit they were fleshed² villains, bloody dogs,
 Melted with tenderness and mild compassion,
 Wept like two children in their deaths' sad story.³
 'O thus', quoth Dighton, 'lay the gentle babes';
10 'Thus, thus', quoth Forrest, 'girdling° one another   *embracing*
 Within their alabaster° innocent arms.   *marble-white*
 Their lips were four red roses on a stalk,
 And in their summer beauty kissed each other.
 A book of prayers on their pillow lay,
15 'Which once', quoth Forrest, 'almost changed my mind.
 But O, the devil'—there the villain stopped,
 When° Dighton thus told on, 'We smotherèd   *At which point*
 The most replenishéd° sweet work of nature,   *complete*

---

9. Redhill (but punning on "Richmond").
1. Celtic bards, or poets, were also considered prophets.
2. A Jack was the mechanical figure who appeared to strike the hours in early clocks. By clockwork reiterations of his suit, Richard suggests, Buckingham is behaving like an annoying beggar and interfering with Richard's "meditation."
4.3 Location: The palace, London.

1. For the murder of the princes, Tyrrell recruited his servant, John Dighton, along with Myles Forrest and two others.
2. Experienced in killing; applied to hounds that had been fed part of their first kill in order to give them a taste for blood.
3. Wept in telling the sad story of the Princes' deaths.

That from the prime° creation e'er she framed.'   *first*
20   Hence both are gone,° with conscience and remorse.   *overcome*
They could not speak, and so I left them both,
To bear this tidings to the bloody king.
        Enter KING RICHARD
And here he comes.—All health, my sovereign lord.
KING RICHARD   Kind Tyrrell, am I happy in thy news?
25   TYRRELL   If to have done the thing you gave in charge
Beget your happiness,⁴ be happy then,
For it is done.
KING RICHARD   But didst thou see them dead?
TYRRELL   I did, my lord.
KING RICHARD   And buried, gentle Tyrrell?
TYRRELL   The chaplain of the Tower hath buried them;
30   But where, to say the truth, I do not know.
KING RICHARD   Come to me, Tyrrell, soon, at after-supper,°   *dessert*
When thou shalt tell the process° of their death.   *story*
Meantime, but think how I may do thee good,
And be inheritor of thy desire.⁵
Farewell till then.
35   TYRRELL   I humbly take my leave.   *Exit*
KING RICHARD   The son of Clarence have I pent° up close.   *locked*
His daughter meanly have I matched in marriage.⁶
The sons of Edward sleep in Abraham's bosom,⁷
And Anne, my wife, hath bid this world goodnight.
40   Now, for° I know the Breton⁸ Richmond aims   *because*
At young Elizabeth, my brother's daughter,
And by that knot° looks proudly o'er the crown,   *marriage; alliance*
To her go I, a jolly thriving wooer⁹—
        Enter [Sir Richard] RATCLIFFE¹ *[running]*
RATCLIFFE   My lord.
45   KING RICHARD   Good news or bad, that thou com'st in so bluntly?
RATCLIFFE   Bad news, my lord. Ely° is fled to Richmond,   *(Bishop of Ely)*
And Buckingham, backed with the hardy Welshmen,
Is in the field, and still his power increaseth.
KING RICHARD   Ely with Richmond troubles me more near°   *deeply*
50   Than Buckingham and his rash-levied strength.°   *hastily raised army*
Come, I have learned that fearful commenting
Is leaden servitor² to dull delay.
Delay leads impotent and snail-paced beggary.°   *ruin*
Then fiery expedition° be my wing: *speed*
55   Jove's Mercury,³ an herald for a king.
Go, muster men. My counsel is my shield.⁴
We must be brief, when traitors brave the field.⁵   *Exeunt*

4. *If . . . happiness:* If it pleases you to have accomplished what you ordered done.
5. *but . . . desire:* you have only to think what you want of me, and you will possess it.
6. I have married off to a poor man.
7. In heaven (see Luke 16:22–23).
8. Person from Brittany; Richmond spent fourteen years in exile there before returning to England to face Richard III in 1485.
9. It was widely rumored that Anne was poisoned in order to facilitate a plan by Richard to marry Elizabeth,

sister to the missing princes; modern historians believe that these allegations are probably untrue. Richard's alleged actions regarding Clarence's son and daughter (lines 36–37) are certainly untrue.
1. Q calls for Catesby.
2. *fearful . . . servitor:* frightened talk is the sluggish attendant.
3. The swift messenger of the gods.
4. *My . . . shield:* I do not talk, but arm myself to fight. *counsel:* adviser.
5. When traitors defy (us on) the battlefield.

4.4

Enter old QUEEN MARGARET

QUEEN MARGARET   So now prosperity begins to mellow°   *ripen*
And drop into the rotten mouth of death.
Here in these confines slyly have I lurked
To watch the waning of mine enemies.

5   A dire induction° am I witness to,   *prologue (as to a play)*
And will to France, hoping the consequence°   *conclusion (as of a play)*
Will prove as bitter, black, and tragical.

Enter the [old] DUCHESS OF YORK *and* QUEEN [ELIZABETH]

Withdraw thee, wretched Margaret. Who comes here?

QUEEN ELIZABETH   Ah, my poor princes! Ah, my tender babes!

10   My unblown° flowers, new-appearing sweets!°   *unopened / blooms*
If yet your gentle souls fly in the air,
And be not fixed in doom perpetual,[1]
Hover about me with your airy wings
And hear your mother's lamentation.

15   QUEEN MARGARET [*aside*]   Hover about her, say that right for right
Hath dimmed your infant morn to agèd night.[2]

DUCHESS OF YORK[3]   So many miseries have crazed° my voice   *cracked*
That my woe-wearied tongue is still and mute.
Edward Plantagenet, why art thou dead?

20   QUEEN MARGARET [*aside*]   Plantagenet doth quit° Plantagenet;   *pay for (the deeds of)*
Edward for Edward pays a dying debt.[4]

QUEEN ELIZABETH   Wilt thou, O God, fly from such gentle lambs
And throw them in the entrails of the wolf?
When° didst thou sleep, when such a deed was done?   *Whenever (up until now)*

25   QUEEN MARGARET [*aside*]   When holy Harry[5] died, and my sweet son.

DUCHESS OF YORK   Dead life, blind sight, poor mortal living ghost,[6]
Woe's scene, world's shame, grave's due by life usurped,[7]
Brief abstract° and record of tedious days,   *epitome; summary*
Rest thy unrest on England's lawful earth,

30   Unlawfully made drunk with innocents' blood.

[*They sit*]

QUEEN ELIZABETH   Ah that thou[8] wouldst as soon afford a grave
As thou canst yield a melancholy seat.
Then would I hide my bones, not rest them here.
Ah, who hath any cause to mourn but we?

35   QUEEN MARGARET [*coming forward*]   If ancient sorrow be most reverend,
Give mine the benefit of seniory,[9]
And let my griefs frown on the upper hand.[1]
If sorrow can admit society,
Tell o'er° your woes again by viewing mine.   *Count; narrate*

40   I had an Edward, till a Richard killed him;
I had a husband, till a Richard killed him.

4.4 Location: Before the palace.
1. *fixed in doom perpetual*: assigned by an irrevocable
sentence to your final place of punishment or reward.
2. *right for . . . night*: evenhanded justice has destroyed
the bright hopes of your young lives.
3. Q places this after line 34 (making it the last speech
before Margaret's intervention) and omits lines 20–21.
4. A debt for which payment is death. *Edward for
Edward*: Prince Edward (Elizabeth's son) for Prince
Edward (Margaret's son, whose murder is dramatized in
Richard Duke of York).

5. Henry VI (Margaret's husband).
6. *mortal living ghost*: a dead person doomed to exist
among the living.
7. *graves . . . usurped*: person who ought to be dead,
unlawfully alive.
8. Here, Elizabeth is addressing the earth directly.
9. Seniority; Q1–5 have "signorie," F "signeurie,"
which suggests that Margaret may mean "sovereignty"
or "lordship" ("seigniory").
1. *frown . . . hand*: have precedence in mourning.

[*To* ELIZABETH] Thou hadst an Edward, till a Richard killed him;
Thou hadst a Richard,[2] till a Richard killed him.
DUCHESS OF YORK [*rising*] I had a Richard too, and thou didst kill him;
45   I had a Rutland too,[3] thou holpst to kill him.
QUEEN MARGARET   Thou hadst a Clarence too, and Richard killed him.
From forth the kennel of thy womb hath crept
A hell-hound that doth hunt us all to death:
That dog that had his teeth before his eyes,[4]
50   To worry° lambs and lap their gentle blood;   *tear apart*
That foul defacer of God's handiwork,
That reigns in gallèd° eyes of weeping souls;   *sore (from crying)*
That excellent grand tyrant of the earth
Thy womb let loose to chase us to our graves.
55   O upright, just, and true-disposing God,
How do I thank thee that this charnel[5] cur
Preys on the issue° of his mother's body,   *offspring*
And makes her pewfellow° with others' moan.   *companion at church*
DUCHESS OF YORK   O Harry's wife, triumph not in my woes.
60   God witness with me, I have wept for thine.
QUEEN MARGARET   Bear with me. I am hungry for revenge,
And now I cloy me° with beholding it.   *gorge myself*
Thy Edward, he is dead, that killed my Edward;
Thy other Edward dead, to quite° my Edward;   *requite*
65   Young York, he is but boot,[6] because both they
Matched not the high perfection of my loss;
Thy Clarence, he is dead, that stabbed my Edward,
And the beholders of this frantic° play—   *insane*
Th'adulterate° Hastings, Rivers, Vaughan, Gray— *adulterous*
70   Untimely smothered° in their dusky graves.   *buried*
Richard yet lives, hell's black intelligencer,°   *spy*
Only reserved their factor[7] to buy souls
And send them thither; but at hand, at hand
Ensues his piteous and unpitied end.
75   Earth gapes, hell burns, fiends roar, saints pray,
To have him suddenly conveyed from hence.
Cancel his bond of life, dear God, I plead,
That I may live and say, 'The dog is dead'.
QUEEN ELIZABETH   O thou didst prophesy the time would come
80   That I should wish for thee to help me curse
That bottled spider, that foul bunch-backed toad.
QUEEN MARGARET   I called thee then 'vain flourish of my fortune';
I called thee then, poor shadow,° 'painted queen'[8]— *semblance*
The presentation° of but what I was,   *copy*
85   The flattering index° of a direful pageant,° *prologue / play*
One heaved a-high to be hurled down below,
A mother only mocked with two fair babes,
A dream of what thou wast, a garish flag

---

2. Edward and Richard were Queen Elizabeth's two sons (smothered in the Tower).
3. Her husband (Richard, Duke of York) and youngest son; both deaths are dramatized in Act 1 of *Richard Duke of York*.
4. His enemies rumored that the savage Richard was born with teeth.

5. Of the charnel house or tomb. Q, F print "carnal."
6. He is thrown in simply to make the bargain even.
7. *Only . . . factor:* Retained (or preserved from death) only in order to serve as hell's agent. *their:* the demonic inhabitants of hell.
8. See 1.3.239.

To be the aim of every dangerous shot,[9]
90 A sign° of dignity, a breath, a bubble,   mere symbol
A queen in jest, only to fill the scene.
Where is thy husband now? Where be thy brothers?
Where are thy two sons? Wherein dost thou joy?
Who sues, and kneels, and says 'God save the Queen'?
95 Where be the bending° peers that flattered thee?   bowing; yielding
Where be the thronging troops that followed thee?
Decline[1] all this, and see what now thou art:
For happy wife, a most distressèd widow;
For joyful mother, one that wails the name;
100 For queen, a very caitiff,° crowned with care;   wretch
For one being sued to, one that humbly sues;
For she that scorned at me, now scorned of° me;   by
For she being feared of all, now fearing one;
For she commanding all, obeyed of none.
105 Thus hath the course of justice whirled about,
And left thee but a very prey to time,
Having no more but thought of what thou wert
To torture thee the more, being what thou art.
Thou didst usurp my place, and dost thou not
110 Usurp the just proportion of my sorrow?
Now thy proud neck bears half my burdened° yoke—   burdensome
From which, even here, I slip my weary head,
And leave the burden of it all on thee.
Farewell, York's wife, and queen of sad mischance.
115 These English woes shall make me smile in France.
QUEEN ELIZABETH [*rising*]   O thou, well skilled in curses, stay a while,
And teach me how to curse mine enemies.
QUEEN MARGARET   Forbear to sleep the nights, and fast the days;
Compare dead happiness with living woe;
120 Think that thy babes were sweeter than they were,
And he that slew them fouler than he is.
Bett'ring° thy loss makes the bad causer worse.   Magnifying
Revolving° this will teach thee how to curse.   Musing on
QUEEN ELIZABETH   My words are dull. O quicken° them with   enliven; sharpen
thine!
QUEEN MARGARET   Thy woes will make them sharp and pierce
125 like mine.   *Exit*
DUCHESS OF YORK   Why should calamity be full of words?
QUEEN ELIZABETH   Windy attorneys to their client woes,[2]
Airy recorders of intestate joys,[3]
Poor breathing° orators of miseries.   speaking
130 Let them have scope. Though what they will impart
Help nothing else, yet do they ease the heart.
DUCHESS OF YORK   If so, then be not tongue-tied; go with me,
And in the breath of bitter words let's smother
My damnèd son, that thy two sweet sons smothered.
[*A march within*]
135 The trumpet sounds. Be copious in exclaims.°   exclamation

9. *garish . . . shot:* bearer of a brightly colored standard   2. Words are long-winded pleaders for the sufferings
who draws the enemy fire.   that have hired them.
1. Recite in order with the proper endings (as a noun   3. Words record joys that have died without bequeath-
in Latin grammar).   ing anything.

Enter KING RICHARD *and his train marching with*
drummers and trumpeters

KING RICHARD   Who intercepts me in my expedition?°   *haste; march*
DUCHESS OF YORK   O, she that might have intercepted thee,
By strangling thee in her accursèd womb,
From all the slaughters, wretch, that thou hast done.

140   QUEEN ELIZABETH   Hid'st thou that forehead with a golden crown,
Where should be branded—if that right were right—
The slaughter of the prince that owed° that crown,   *rightfully owned*
And the dire death of my poor sons and brothers?
Tell me, thou villain-slave, where are my children?

145   DUCHESS OF YORK   Thou toad, thou toad, where is thy brother Clarence?
And little Ned Plantagenet his son?
QUEEN ELIZABETH   Where is the gentle Rivers, Vaughan, Gray?
DUCHESS OF YORK   Where is kind Hastings?
KING RICHARD [*to his train*]   A flourish, trumpets! Strike
alarum,° drums!   *Call to arms*
150   Let not the heavens hear these tell-tale women
Rail on the Lord's anointed. Strike, I say!
Flourish. Alarums
[*To the women*] Either be patient and entreat me fair,°   *treat me courteously*
Or with the clamorous report° of war   *noise*
Thus will I drown your exclamations.

155   DUCHESS OF YORK   Art thou my son?
KING RICHARD   Ay, I thank God, my father, and yourself.
DUCHESS OF YORK   Then patiently hear my impatience.
KING RICHARD   Madam, I have a touch of your condition,°   *temperament*
That cannot brook the accent° of reproof.   *abide the language*
DUCHESS OF YORK   O let me speak!
160   KING RICHARD   Do, then; but I'll not hear.
DUCHESS OF YORK   I will be mild and gentle in my words.
KING RICHARD   And brief, good mother, for I am in haste.
DUCHESS OF YORK   Art thou so hasty? I have stayed° for thee,   *waited*
God knows, in torment and in agony—
165   KING RICHARD   And came I not at last to comfort you?
DUCHESS OF YORK   No, by the Holy Rood,° thou know'st it well.   *Cross*
Thou cam'st on earth to make the earth my hell.
A grievous burden was thy birth to me;
Tetchy° and wayward was thy infancy;   *Irritable*
170   Thy schooldays frightful,° desp'rate, wild, and furious;   *frightening*
Thy prime° of manhood daring, bold, and venturous;   *beginning*
Thy age confirmed,° proud, subtle, sly, and bloody;   *settled maturity*
More mild, but yet more harmful; kind in hatred.[4]
What comfortable hour canst thou name
175   That ever graced me[5] in thy company?
KING RICHARD   Faith, none but Humphrey Hewer,[6] that called your grace
To breakfast once, forth° of my company.   *out*
If I be so disgracious° in your eye,   *unpleasing*
Let me march on, and not offend you, madam.—
Strike up the drum.
180   DUCHESS OF YORK   I pray thee, hear me speak.

---

4. Concealing hatred under cover of kindness.
5. Gave me pleasure; but Richard interprets as "called me by the title 'your grace.'"
6. A proper name, based on "ewer" (a servant who waits at table), but also suggesting "huer" (someone who makes a hue or cry) and playing on "hour" (line 174). Proverbially, "to dine with Duke Humphrey" was not to dine at all.

KING RICHARD   You speak too bitterly.

DUCHESS OF YORK   Hear me a word,
For I shall never speak to thee again.

KING RICHARD   So.

DUCHESS OF YORK   Either thou wilt die by God's just ordinance
185   Ere from this war thou turn° a conqueror,   *return*
Or I with grief and extreme age shall perish,
And never more behold thy face again.
Therefore take with thee my most heavy curse,
Which in the day of battle tire thee more
190   Than all the complete armour that thou wear'st.
My prayers on the adverse party° fight,   *opposite side*
And there the little souls of Edward's children
Whisper° the spirits of thine enemies,   *Whisper to*
And promise them success and victory.
195   Bloody thou art, bloody will be thy end;
Shame serves° thy life, and doth thy death attend.   *Exit*   *accompanies*

QUEEN ELIZABETH   Though far more cause, yet much less spirit to curse
Abides in me; I say 'Amen' to all.

KING RICHARD   Stay, madam. I must talk a word with you.

200   QUEEN ELIZABETH   I have no more sons of the royal blood
For thee to slaughter. For my daughters, Richard,
They shall be praying nuns, not weeping queens,
And therefore level not to hit their lives.[7]

KING RICHARD   You have a daughter called Elizabeth,
205   Virtuous and fair, royal and gracious.

QUEEN ELIZABETH   And must she die for this? O let her live,
And I'll corrupt her manners,° stain her beauty,   *morals*
Slander myself as false to Edward's bed,
Throw over her the veil of infamy.
210   So° she may live unscarred of bleeding slaughter,   *Provided that*
I will confess she was not Edward's daughter.

KING RICHARD   Wrong not her birth. She is a royal princess.

QUEEN ELIZABETH   To save her life I'll say she is not so.

KING RICHARD   Her life is safest only in her birth.[8]

215   QUEEN ELIZABETH   And only in that safety died her brothers.

KING RICHARD   Lo, at their births good stars were opposite.°   *adverse*

QUEEN ELIZABETH   No, to their lives ill friends were contrary.°   *opposed*

KING RICHARD   All unavoided° is the doom° of destiny—   *unavoidable / sentence*

QUEEN ELIZABETH   True, when avoided grace[9] makes destiny.
220   My babes were destined to a fairer death,
If grace had blessed thee with a fairer life.[1]

221.1   *KING RICHARD   You speak as if that I had slain my cousins.*

            QUEEN ELIZABETH   Cousins indeed, and by their uncle cozened°   *cheated*
            Of comfort, kingdom, kindred, freedom, life.
            Whose hand soever lanced their tender hearts,
221.5   *Thy head all indirectly gave direction.[2]*
            No doubt the murd'rous knife was dull and blunt
            Till it was whetted on thy stone-hard heart
            To revel in the entrails of my lambs.
            But that still° use of grief makes wild grief tame,   *Except that continual*

---

7. And therefore do not take aim to kill them.
8. Her life is safe only because of her high birth.
9. When a man who has rejected God's grace (that is, Richard).

1. The indented passage that follows, 221.1–221.14, appears only in F.
2. *Whose . . . direction:* No matter who killed them, it was you, though indirectly, who caused it.

221.10

> *My tongue should to thy ears not name my boys*
> *Till that my nails were anchored in thine eyes—*
> *And I in such a desp'rate bay³ of death,*
> *Like a poor barque° of sails and tackling reft,°*   boat / deprived
> *Rush all to pieces on thy rocky bosom.*

KING RICHARD   Madam, so thrive I in my enterprise
And dangerous success of bloody wars,
As I intend more good to you and yours

225   Than ever you or yours by me were harmed.⁴
QUEEN ELIZABETH   What good is covered with the face of heaven,⁵
To be discovered, that can do me good?
KING RICHARD   Th'advancement of your children, gentle lady.
QUEEN ELIZABETH   Up to some scaffold, there to lose their heads.

230   KING RICHARD   Unto the dignity and height of fortune,
The high imperial type° of this earth's glory.   symbol
QUEEN ELIZABETH   Flatter my sorrow with report of it.
Tell me what state, what dignity, what honour,
Canst thou demise° to any child of mine?   transmit

235   KING RICHARD   Even all I have—ay, and myself and all,
Will I withal endow a child of thine,
So° in the Lethe⁶ of thy angry soul   If
Thou drown the sad remembrance of those wrongs,
Which thou supposest I have done to thee.

240   QUEEN ELIZABETH   Be brief, lest that the process° of thy kindness   story
Last longer telling° than thy kindness' date.°   in the telling / duration
KING RICHARD   Then know that, from my soul,⁷ I love thy daughter.
QUEEN ELIZABETH   My daughter's mother thinks that with her soul.
KING RICHARD   What do you think?

245   QUEEN ELIZABETH   That thou dost love my daughter *from* thy soul;
So *from* thy soul's love didst thou love her brothers,
And *from* my heart's love I do thank thee for it.
KING RICHARD   Be not so hasty to confound° my meaning.   deliberately misconstrue
I mean, that *with* my soul I love thy daughter,

250   And do intend to make her queen of England.
QUEEN ELIZABETH   Well then, who dost thou mean shall be her king?
KING RICHARD   Even he that makes her queen. Who else should be?
QUEEN ELIZABETH   What, thou?
KING RICHARD   Even so. How think you of it?
QUEEN ELIZABETH   How canst thou woo her?
KING RICHARD   That would I learn of you,

255   As one being best acquainted with her humour.°   temperament
QUEEN ELIZABETH   And wilt thou learn of me?
KING RICHARD   Madam, with all my heart.
QUEEN ELIZABETH   Send to her, by the man that slew her brothers,
A pair of bleeding hearts; thereon engrave
'Edward' and 'York'; then haply° will she weep.   perhaps

260   Therefore present to her—as sometimes° Margaret   once
Did to thy father, steeped in Rutland's blood⁸—
A handkerchief which, say to her, did drain

---

3. Inlet; the situation of a cornered animal when it
turns to face its hunters.
4. *Madam . . . harmed:* (I pray) that the success of my
upcoming battles be as certain as is my intention to do
to you more good in the future than I have done you
harm in the past. *success:* consequence.

5. What good is there on earth.
6. A river in the underworld whose waters induced forgetfulness.
7. With all my soul (but Queen Elizabeth takes it as
"separated from," "at variance with").
8. Dramatized in *Richard Duke of York* 1.4.

The purple sap° from her sweet brother's body,   *blood*
And bid her wipe her weeping eyes withal.°   *with it*
265   If this inducement move her not to love,
Send her a letter of thy noble deeds.
Tell her thou mad'st away her uncle Clarence,
Her uncle Rivers—ay, and for her sake
Mad'st quick conveyance with° her good aunt Anne.   *Got rid of*
270   KING RICHARD   You mock me, madam. This is not the way
To win your daughter.
QUEEN ELIZABETH   There is no other way,
Unless thou couldst put on some other shape,
And not be Richard, that hath done all this.[9]

273.1   KING RICHARD   *Say that I did all this for love of her.*
QUEEN ELIZABETH   *Nay, then indeed she cannot choose but hate thee,*
Having bought love with such a bloody spoil.°   *slaughter*
KING RICHARD   *Look what° is done cannot be now amended.*   *Whatever*
273.5   *Men shall deal° unadvisedly sometimes,*   *act*
Which after-hours gives leisure to repent.
If I did take the kingdom from your sons,
To make amends I'll give it to your daughter.
If I have killed the issue of your womb,
273.10   *To quicken your increase[1] I will beget*
Mine issue of your blood upon your daughter.
A grandam's name is little less in love
Than is the doting title of a mother.
They are as children but one step below,
273.15   *Even of your mettall,° of your very blood:*   *spirit*
Of all one pain, save for a night of groans
Endured of her for whom you bid like sorrow.[2]
Your children were vexation to your youth,
But mine shall be a comfort to your age.
273.20   *The loss you have is but a son being king,*
And by that loss your daughter is made queen.
I cannot make you what amends I would,
Therefore accept such kindness as I can.°   *can give*
Dorset your son, that with a fearful soul
273.25   *Leads discontented steps in foreign soil,*
This fair alliance quickly shall call home
To high promotions and great dignity.
The king that calls your beauteous daughter wife,
Familiarly shall call thy Dorset brother.
273.30   *Again shall you be mother to a king,*
And all the ruins of distressful times
Repaired with double riches of content.
What? We have many goodly days to see.
The liquid drops of tears that you have shed
273.35   *Shall come again, transformed to orient° pearl,*   *shining*
Advantaging° their loan with interest   *Augmenting*
Of ten times double gain of happiness.
Go then, my mother, to thy daughter go.
Make bold her bashful years with your experience.

9. The indented passage that follows, 273.1–273.55,   2. *Of all . . . sorrow:* Originating from a single bout of
appears only in F.   labor (Elizabeth's), with the addition of just one more
1. To give (new) life to your offspring.   night of pain by the daughter you bore.

273.40   Prepare her ears to hear a wooer's tale.
                 Put in her tender heart th'aspiring flame
                 Of golden sovereignty. Acquaint the Princess
                 With the sweet silent hours of marriage joys.
                 And when this arm of mine hath chastisèd
273.45   The petty rebel, dull-brained Buckingham,
                 Bound with triumphant garlands will I come
                 And lead thy daughter to a conqueror's bed—
                 To whom I will retail° my conquest won,   relate
                 And she shall be sole victoress: Caesar's Caesar.
273.50   QUEEN ELIZABETH   What were I best to say? Her father's brother
                 Would° be her lord?° Or shall I say her uncle?   Wishes to / husband
                 Or he that slew her brothers and her uncles?
                 Under what title shall I woo for thee,
                 That God, the law, my honour, and her love
273.55   Can make seem pleasing to her tender years?
          KING RICHARD   Infer° fair England's peace by this alliance.   Give as a reason
275   QUEEN ELIZABETH   Which she shall purchase with still-lasting° war.   perpetual
          KING RICHARD   Tell her the King, that may command, entreats.
          QUEEN ELIZABETH   That at her hands which the King's King° forbids.   (God)
          KING RICHARD   Say she shall be a high and mighty queen.
          QUEEN ELIZABETH   To vail° the title,° as her mother doth.   yield / (of Queen)
280   KING RICHARD   Say I will love her everlastingly.
          QUEEN ELIZABETH   But how long shall that title 'ever' last?
          KING RICHARD   Sweetly in force unto her fair life's end.
          QUEEN ELIZABETH   But how long fairly° shall her sweet life last?   without foul play
          KING RICHARD   As long as heaven and nature lengthens it.
285   QUEEN ELIZABETH   As long as hell and Richard likes of it.
          KING RICHARD   Say I, her sovereign, am her subject love.
          QUEEN ELIZABETH   But she, your subject, loathes such sovereignty.
          KING RICHARD   Be eloquent in my behalf to her.
          QUEEN ELIZABETH   An honest tale speeds° best being plainly told.   succeeds
290   KING RICHARD   Then plainly to her tell my loving tale.
          QUEEN ELIZABETH   Plain and not honest is too harsh a style.[3]
          KING RICHARD   Your reasons are too shallow and too quick.[4]
          QUEEN ELIZABETH   O no, my reasons are too deep and dead—
                 Too deep and dead, poor infants, in their graves.
295   KING RICHARD   Harp not on that string, madam. That is past.
          QUEEN ELIZABETH   Harp on it still shall I, till heart-strings break.
          KING RICHARD   Now by my George, my garter,[5] and my crown—
          QUEEN ELIZABETH   Profaned, dishonoured, and the third usurped.
          KING RICHARD   I swear—
          QUEEN ELIZABETH   By nothing, for this is no oath.
300   Thy George, profaned, hath lost his° holy honour;   its
                 Thy garter, blemished, pawned his lordly virtue;
                 Thy crown, usurped, disgraced his kingly glory.
                 If something thou wouldst swear to be believed,
                 Swear then by something that thou hast not wronged.
          KING RICHARD   Then by myself—
305   QUEEN ELIZABETH   Thy self is self-misused.
          KING RICHARD   Now by the world—

3. The plain style (as in the proverb "Truth is plain"),   on "quick" as "alive."
unless it is truth telling, will be too harsh; lies need   5. A garter and a jeweled pendant with the figure of St.
elaborate decoration.   George were parts of the insignia of the Order of the
4. Rash, ill considered; but Elizabeth's response plays   Garter, the highest order of knighthood.

QUEEN ELIZABETH	'Tis full of thy foul wrongs.
KING RICHARD	My father's death—
QUEEN ELIZABETH	Thy life hath that dishonoured.
KING RICHARD	Why then, by God—
QUEEN ELIZABETH	God's wrong is most of all.

If thou didst fear to break an oath with him,
310 The unity the King my husband made[6]
Thou hadst not broken, nor my brothers died.
If thou hadst feared to break an oath by him,
Th'imperial metal circling now thy head
Had graced the tender temples of my child,
315 And both the princes had been breathing here,
Which now—two tender bedfellows for dust—
Thy broken faith hath made the prey for worms.
What canst thou swear by now?

KING RICHARD   The time to come.

QUEEN ELIZABETH   That thou hast wrongèd in the time o'erpast,
320 For I myself have many tears to wash
Hereafter time,° for time past wronged by thee.   *The future*
The children live, whose fathers thou hast slaughtered—
Ungoverned youth,[7] to wail it in their age.°   *when they grow older*
The parents live, whose children thou hast butchered—
325 Old barren plants, to wail it with° their age.   *along with*
Swear not by time to come, for that thou hast
Misused ere used, by times ill-used o'erpast.[8]

KING RICHARD   As I intend[9] to prosper and repent,
So thrive I in my dangerous affairs
330 Of hostile arms—myself myself confound,°   *may I ruin myself*
Heaven and fortune bar me happy hours,
Day yield me not thy light nor night thy rest;
Be opposite, all planets of good luck,
To my proceeding—if, with dear heart's love,
335 Immaculate devotion, holy thoughts,
I tender° not thy beauteous, princely daughter.   *love*
In her consists my happiness and thine.
Without her follows—to myself and thee,
Herself, the land, and many a Christian soul—
340 Death, desolation, ruin, and decay.
It cannot be avoided but by this;
It will not be avoided but by this.
Therefore, good-mother°—I must call you so—   *mother-in-law*
Be the attorney of my love to her.
345 Plead what I will be, not what I have been;
Not my deserts, but what I will deserve.
Urge the necessity and state of times,°   *state of affairs*
And be not peevish-fond° in great designs.   *foolishly obstinate*

QUEEN ELIZABETH   Shall I be tempted of the devil thus?
350 KING RICHARD   Ay, if the devil tempt you to do good.

QUEEN ELIZABETH   Shall I forget myself to be myself?[1]

KING RICHARD   Ay, if yourself 's remembrance wrong yourself.

---

6. The "reconciliation" staged in 2.1 between Queen
Elizabeth and her enemies.
7. Youth without a father's guidance.
8. *thou . . . o'erpast:* you have, by the continuing effects
of your past crimes, misused the future even before it

comes to pass.
9. *As I intend:* the formulation has the force of "I swear
that as I intend."
1. Am I to overlook all wrongs done me in order to
become Queen Mother (as I already have been)?

QUEEN ELIZABETH   Yet thou didst kill my children.
KING RICHARD   But in your daughter's womb I bury them,
355   Where, in that nest of spicery,[2] they will breed
Selves of themselves, to your recomfiture.°   *consolation*
QUEEN ELIZABETH   Shall I go win my daughter to thy will?
KING RICHARD   And be a happy mother by the deed.
QUEEN ELIZABETH   I go. Write to me very shortly,
360   And you shall understand from me her mind.
KING RICHARD   Bear her my true love's kiss,
      [*He kisses her*]
                                          and so farewell—
                          Exit [ELIZABETH]
Relenting fool, and shallow, changing woman.
      Enter [*Sir Richard*] RATCLIFFE
How now, what news?
RATCLIFFE   Most mighty sovereign, on the western coast
365   Rideth a puissant° navy. To our shores   *mighty*
Throng many doubtful, hollow-hearted friends,
Unarmed and unresolved, to beat them back.
'Tis thought that Richmond is their° admiral,   *(the navy's)*
And there they hull,° expecting but the aid   *drift; wait*
370   Of Buckingham to welcome them ashore.
KING RICHARD   Some light-foot° friend post° to the Duke of   *swift-footed / hasten*
      Norfolk.
Ratcliffe thyself, or Catesby—where is he?[3]
CATESBY   Here, my good lord.
KING RICHARD   Catesby, fly to the Duke.
CATESBY   I will, my lord, with all convenient° haste.   *due*
375   KING RICHARD   Ratcliffe, come hither. Post to Salisbury;
When thou com'st thither—[*to* CATESBY] dull, unmindful villain,
Why stay'st thou here, and goest not to the Duke?
CATESBY   First, mighty liege, tell me your highness' pleasure:
What from your grace I shall deliver to him?
380   KING RICHARD   O true, good Catesby. Bid him levy straight
The greatest strength and power that he can make,°   *raise*
And meet me suddenly° at Salisbury.   *without delay*
CATESBY   I go.   *Exit*
RATCLIFFE   What, may it please you, shall I do at Salisbury?
385   KING RICHARD   Why, what wouldst thou do there before I go?
RATCLIFFE   Your highness told me I should post before.
KING RICHARD   My mind is changed.
      Enter Lord STANLEY
                          Stanley, what news with you?
STANLEY   None, good my liege, to please you with the hearing,
Nor none so bad but well may be reported.
390   KING RICHARD   Hoyday,° a riddle! Neither good nor bad.   *(an exclamation)*
Why need'st thou run so many mile about
When thou mayst tell thy tale the nearest° way?   *most direct*
Once more, what news?
STANLEY   Richmond is on the seas.
KING RICHARD   There let him sink, and be the seas on him.
395   White-livered° renegade, what doth he there?   *Cowardly*

2. Fragrant spices—in contrast to the stench of other burial places; the spices on the phoenix's pyre. *nest:* place where eggs are hatched, but also specifically the nest or pyre on which the legendary phoenix burned itself and then rose from its own ashes.
3. Parts of lines 373–74 appear only in F.

STANLEY   I know not, mighty sovereign, but by guess.

KING RICHARD   Well, as you guess?

STANLEY   Stirred up by Dorset, Buckingham, and Ely,
   He makes for England, here to claim the crown.

400 KING RICHARD   Is the chair° empty? Is the sword unswayed?   *throne*
   Is the King dead? The empire° unpossessed?   *state*
   What heir of York is there alive but we?
   And who is England's king but great York's heir?
   Then tell me, what makes he° upon the seas?   *what is he doing*

405 STANLEY   Unless for that, my liege, I cannot guess.

KING RICHARD   Unless for that° he comes to be your liege,   *because*
   You cannot guess wherefore the Welshman⁴ comes.
   Thou wilt revolt and fly to him, I fear.

STANLEY   No, my good lord, therefore mistrust me not.

410 KING RICHARD   Where is thy power then? To beat him back,
   Where be thy tenants and thy followers?
   Are they not now upon the western shore,
   Safe-conducting the rebels from their ships?

STANLEY   No, my good lord, my friends are in the north.

415 KING RICHARD   Cold friends to me. What do they in the north,
   When they should serve their sovereign in the west?

STANLEY   They have not been commanded, mighty King.
   Pleaseth° your majesty to give me leave,   *If it please*
   I'll muster up my friends and meet your grace
420   Where and what time your majesty shall please.

KING RICHARD   Ay, ay, thou wouldst be gone to join with Richmond.
   But I'll not trust thee.

STANLEY   Most mighty sovereign,
   You have no cause to hold my friendship doubtful.
   I never was, nor never will be, false.

425 KING RICHARD   Go then and muster men—but leave behind
   Your son George Stanley. Look your heart be firm,
   Or else his head's assurance is but frail.

STANLEY   So deal with him as I prove true to you.   *Exit*
       Enter a MESSENGER

MESSENGER   My gracious sovereign, now in Devonshire,
430   As I by friends am well advertisèd,°   *well informed*
   Sir Edward Courtenay and the haughty prelate,
   Bishop of Exeter, his elder brother,
   With many more confederates are in arms.
       Enter another MESSENGER

SECOND MESSENGER   In Kent, my liege, the Guildfords are in arms,
435   And every hour more competitors°   *associates*
   Flock to the rebels, and their power grows strong.
       Enter another MESSENGER

THIRD MESSENGER   My lord, the army of great Buckingham—

KING RICHARD   Out on ye, owls!⁵ Nothing but songs of death?
       He striketh him
   There, take thou that, till thou bring better news.

440 THIRD MESSENGER   The news I have to tell your majesty
   Is that, by sudden flood and fall of water,°   *rain*
   Buckingham's army is dispersed and scattered,
   And he himself wandered away alone,

---

4. Richmond's grandfather, Owen Tudor, was Welsh.   5. The cry of the owl was thought to portend evil.

No man knows whither.

KING RICHARD   I cry thee mercy.°—   *I beg your pardon*
445   Ratcliffe, reward him for the blow I gave him.—
       Hath any well-advisèd° friend proclaimed   *foresighted*
       Reward to him that brings the traitor in?

THIRD MESSENGER   Such proclamation hath been made, my lord.

                    Enter another MESSENGER

FOURTH MESSENGER   Sir Thomas Lovell and Lord Marquis Dorset—
450   'Tis said, my liege—in Yorkshire are in arms.
       But this good comfort bring I to your highness:
       The Breton navy is dispersed by tempest.
       Richmond in Dorsetshire sent out a boat
       Unto the shore, to ask those on the banks
455   If they were his assistants,° yea or no?   *allies*
       Who answered him they came from Buckingham
       Upon his party.° He, mistrusting them,   *faction*
       Hoist sail and made his course again for Bretagne.°   *Brittany*

KING RICHARD   March on, march on, since we are up in arms,
460   If not to fight with foreign enemies,
       Yet to beat down these rebels here at home.

                    Enter CATESBY

CATESBY   My liege, the Duke of Buckingham is taken.
       That is the best news. That the Earl of Richmond
       Is with a mighty power landed at Milford[6]
465   Is colder tidings, yet they must be told.

KING RICHARD   Away, towards Salisbury! While we reason° here,   *talk*
       A royal battle might be won and lost.
       Someone take order Buckingham be brought
       To Salisbury. The rest march on with me.   *Flourish. Exeunt*

                              4.5

             Enter [Lord STANLEY *Earl of] Derby and* SIR CHRISTO-
             PHER *[a priest]*

STANLEY   Sir Christopher, tell Richmond this from me:
       That in the sty of this most deadly boar
       My son George Stanley is franked up in hold.[1]
       If I revolt, off goes young George's head.
5   The fear of that holds off my present aid.
       But tell me, where is princely Richmond now?

SIR CHRISTOPHER   At Pembroke, or at Ha'rfordwest[2] in Wales.

STANLEY   What men of name° resort to him?   *rank*

SIR CHRISTOPHER   Sir Walter Herbert, a renownèd soldier,
10   Sir Gilbert Talbot, Sir William Stanley,[3]
       Oxford, redoubted° Pembroke,[4] Sir James Blunt,   *dreaded*
       And Rhys-ap-Thomas with a valiant crew,
       And many other of great name and worth—
       And towards London do they bend their power,°   *lead their troops*

6. Milford Haven, a large, deep natural harbor on the Welsh coast, far enough from centers of population to be ideal for an invading army. The events of Richmond's successful invasion at Milford in 1485 are telescoped, in the mouths of the four messengers, with those of his unsuccessful rebellion against Richard two years earlier.

4.5 Location: A private place, perhaps Derby's house.
1. Is shut up (in a sty) in custody.
2. Haverford West, town at the northern end of Milford Haven. Pembroke was the county town of Pembrokeshire, situated on Milford Haven.
3. Lord Stanley, the Earl of Derby's brother.
4. Jasper Tudor, Richmond's uncle.

15   If by the way they be not fought withal.
STANLEY   Well, hie° thee to thy lord. Commend me to him.   *hasten*
      Tell him the Queen hath heartily consented
      He should espouse Elizabeth her daughter.
      My letter will resolve him of my mind.[5]
20   Farewell.   *Exeunt [severally]*

5.1

*Enter [the Duke of] BUCKINGHAM with halberdiers, led
[by a SHERIFF] to execution*
BUCKINGHAM   Will not King Richard let me speak with him?
SHERIFF   No, my good lord, therefore be patient.
BUCKINGHAM   Hastings, and Edward's children, Gray and Rivers,
      Holy King Henry and thy fair son Edward,
5   Vaughan, and all that have miscarrièd°   *died*
      By underhand, corrupted, foul injustice:
      If that your moody, discontented souls[1]
      Do through the clouds behold this present hour,
      Even for revenge mock my destruction.
10   This is All-Souls' day,[2] fellow, is it not?
SHERIFF   It is.
BUCKINGHAM   Why then All-Souls' day is my body's doomsday.
      This is the day which, in King Edward's time,
      I wished might fall on me,[3] when I was found
15   False to his children and his wife's allies.°   *kinsmen*
      This is the day wherein I wished to fall
      By the false faith of him whom most I trusted.
      This, this All-Souls' day to my fearful soul
      Is the determined respite of my wrongs.[4]
20   That high all-seer which I dallied with
      Hath turned my feignèd prayer on my head,
      And given in earnest what I begged in jest.
      Thus doth he force the swords of wicked men
      To turn their own points in their masters' bosoms.
25   Thus Margaret's curse falls heavy on my neck.
      'When he', quoth she, 'shall split thy heart with sorrow,
      Remember Margaret was a prophetess.'[5]
      Come lead me, officers, to the block of shame.
      Wrong hath but wrong, and blame the due of blame.   *Exeunt*

5.2

*Enter [HENRY EARL OF] RICHMOND [with a letter, the
Earl of] OXFORD, [Sir James] BLUNT, [Sir Walter] HER-
BERT, and others, with drum and colours*
HENRY EARL OF RICHMOND   Fellows in arms, and my most loving friends,
      Bruised underneath the yoke of tyranny,
      Thus far into the bowels° of the land   *center*

5. Will make my intentions clear to him.
5.1 Location: Salisbury.
1. Because they are unable to rest in peace until their violent deaths have been avenged. *moody:* angry.
2. November 2, the day on which the Roman Catholic Church intercedes for all Christian souls and on which spirits were supposed to walk (as in the following scenes at Shrewsbury).
3. See Buckingham's prophetic speech in 2.1.32–40.
4. Is the preordained ending of my wrongdoing (but alluding to the more usual significance of All Souls' Day, "preordained final rest from suffering"). *respite:* day to which something is postponed.
5. See 1.3.298–99.
5.2 Location: Near Tamworth in Staffordshire.

Have we marched on without impediment,
5 And here receive we from our father[1] Stanley
Lines of fair comfort and encouragement.
The wretched, bloody, and usurping boar,
That spoils your summer fields and fruitful vines,
Swills your warm blood like wash,° and makes his trough   *pig fodder*
10 In your inbowelled° bosoms, this foul swine   *disemboweled*
Lies now even in the centry° of this isle,   *center; sentry post*
Near to the town of Leicester, as we learn.
From Tamworth thither is but one day's march.
In God's name, cheerly° on, courageous friends,   *cheerfully*
15 To reap the harvest of perpetual peace
By this one bloody trial of sharp war.
OXFORD   Every man's conscience is a thousand swords
To fight against this guilty homicide.°   *murderer*
HERBERT   I doubt not but his friends will turn to us.
20 BLUNT   He hath no friends but what are friends for fear,
Which in his dearest° need will fly from him.   *most extreme*
HENRY EARL OF RICHMOND   All for our vantage.° Then, in God's   *advantage*
     name, march.
True hope is swift, and flies with swallows' wings;
Kings it makes gods, and meaner° creatures kings.   *baser*

                              Exeunt [marching]

                                 5.3
         Enter KING RICHARD *in arms, with [the Duke of]* NOR-
         FOLK, *[Sir Richard]* RATCLIFFE, *Sir William* [CATESBY,
         and others][1]
KING RICHARD   Here pitch our tent, even here in Bosworth field.
     [*Soldiers begin to pitch a tent*]
   Why, how now, Catesby? Why look you so sad?
CATESBY   My heart is ten times lighter than my looks.
KING RICHARD   My lord of Norfolk.
NORFOLK   Here, most gracious liege.
5 KING RICHARD   Norfolk, we must have knocks.° Ha, must we not?   *blows*
NORFOLK   We must both give and take, my loving lord.
KING RICHARD   Up with my tent! Here will I lie tonight.
   But where tomorrow? Well, all's one for that.°   *it makes no difference*
   Who hath descried° the number of the traitors?   *discerned*
10 NORFOLK   Six or seven thousand is their utmost power.
KING RICHARD   Why, our battalia° trebles that account.°   *army / number*
   Besides, the King's name is a tower of strength,
   Which they upon the adverse faction want.°   *lack*
   Up with the tent! Come, noble gentlemen,
15 Let us survey the vantage of the ground.[2]
   Call for some men of sound direction.°   *military judgment*
   Let's lack no discipline, make no delay—
   For, lords, tomorrow is a busy day.   *Exeunt [at one door]*

---

1. Stepfather (Richmond was the son of Edmund Tudor
and Margaret Beaufort; Lord Stanley, Earl of Derby, was
his mother's third husband). *our*: royal plural.
5.3 Location: The rest of the play takes place on
Bosworth Field.

1. Instead of Catesby, the stage direction in F has the
Earl of Surrey, who speaks with Richard at line 3.
2. *vantage of the ground*: military advantages offered by
the spot chosen for battle.

5.4

Enter [at another door HENRY EARL OF] RICHMOND,
[Sir James BLUNT,] *Sir William Brandon, [the Earl of]*
OXFORD, *[Marquis]* DORSET *[and others]*[1]

HENRY EARL OF RICHMOND   The weary sun hath made a golden set,
    And by the bright track of his fiery car[2]
    Gives token of a goodly day tomorrow.
    Sir William Brandon, you shall bear my standard.
5   The Earl of Pembroke keeps° his regiment;   *stays with*
    Good Captain Blunt, bear my good night to him,
    And by the second hour in the morning
    Desire the Earl to see me in my tent.
    Yet one thing more, good Captain, do for me:
10   Where is Lord Stanley quartered, do you know?
BLUNT   Unless I have mista'en his colours much,
    Which well I am assured I have not done,
    His regiment lies half a mile, at least,
    South from the mighty power of the King.
15 HENRY EARL OF RICHMOND   If without peril it be possible,
    Sweet Blunt, make some good means to speak with him,
    And give him from me this most needful note.
BLUNT   Upon my life, my lord, I'll undertake it.
    And so God give you quiet rest tonight.
HENRY EARL OF RICHMOND   Good night, good Captain Blunt.
                        [Exit BLUNT]
20   Come, gentlemen.
    Give me some ink and paper in my tent.
    I'll draw the form and model° of our battle,   *plan*
    Limit° each leader to his several charge,°   *Appoint / separate duty*
    And part° in just proportion our small power.   *divide*
25   Let us consult upon tomorrow's business.
    Into my tent: the dew is raw and cold.
                    They withdraw into the tent

5.5

[A table brought in.] Enter KING RICHARD, *[Sir
Richard]* RATCLIFFE, *[the Duke of]* NORFOLK, *[Sir
William]* CATESBY *[and others]*

KING RICHARD   What is't o'clock?
CATESBY   It's supper-time, my lord. It's nine o'clock.
KING RICHARD   I will not sup tonight. Give me some ink and paper.
    What, is my beaver easier° than it was?   *my helmet visor looser*
5   And all my armour laid into my tent?
CATESBY   It is, my liege, and all things are in readiness.
KING RICHARD   Good Norfolk, hie thee° to thy charge.   *hasten*
    Use careful watch; choose trusty sentinels.
NORFOLK   I go, my lord.
10 KING RICHARD   Stir with the lark tomorrow, gentle Norfolk.
NORFOLK   I warrant° you, my lord.   *Exit*   *assure; guarantee*
KING RICHARD   Catesby.
CATESBY   My lord?

5.4
1. Although Q and F are silent on the question of how many tents are onstage at the end of this scene, most editors direct these attendants to pitch another for Richmond during the following dialogue. Oxford and Dorset are specified in F but not in Q, which calls only for "the lords."
2. Chariot (of the sun god Phoebus).
5.5

KING RICHARD   Send out a pursuivant-at-arms°   *one who attends a herald*
    To Stanley's regiment. Bid him bring his power°   *forces*
    Before sun-rising, lest his son George fall
15 Into the blind cave of eternal night.   [*Exit* CATESBY]
    Fill me a bowl of wine. Give me a watch.[1]
    Saddle white Surrey[2] for the field tomorrow.
    Look that my staves° be sound, and not too heavy.   *lance shafts*
    Ratcliffe.
20 RATCLIFFE   My lord?
    KING RICHARD   Saw'st thou the melancholy Lord Northumberland?
    RATCLIFFE   Thomas the Earl of Surrey and himself,
        Much about cockshut° time, from troop to troop   *twilight*
        Went through the army, cheering up the soldiers.
25 KING RICHARD   So, I am satisfied. Give me some wine.
        I have not that alacrity of spirit,
        Nor cheer of mind, that I was wont to have.
            [*The wine is brought*]
        Set it down. Is ink and paper ready?
    RATCLIFFE   It is, my lord.
    KING RICHARD   Leave me. Bid my guard watch.
30   About the mid of night come to my tent,
        Ratcliffe, and help to arm me. Leave me, I say.
            Exit RATCLIFFE [*with others.* RICHARD *writes, and later sleeps*]
            Enter [*Lord* STANLEY *Earl of*] *Derby to* HENRY EARL
            OF] RICHMOND [*and the lords*] *in his tent*
    STANLEY   Fortune and victory sit on thy helm!°   *helmet*
    HENRY EARL OF RICHMOND   All comfort that the dark night can afford
        Be to thy person, noble father-in-law.°   *stepfather*
35   Tell me, how fares our loving mother?
    STANLEY   I, by attorney,° bless thee from thy mother,   *by proxy*
        Who prays continually for Richmond's good.
        So much for that. The silent hours steal on,
        And flaky° darkness breaks within the east.   *streaked with light*
40   In brief—for so the season° bids us be—   *time of day*
        Prepare thy battle early in the morning,
        And put thy fortune to th'arbitrement°   *determination; verdict*
        Of bloody strokes and mortal-sharing[3] war.
        I, as I may—that which I would, I cannot—
45   With best advantage will deceive the time,[4]
        And aid thee in this doubtful shock° of arms.   *this uncertain clash*
        But on thy side I may not be too forward—
        Lest, being seen, thy brother,° tender° George,   *stepbrother / young*
        Be executed in his father's sight.
50   Farewell. The leisure° and the fearful time   *time available*
        Cuts off the ceremonious vows of love
        And ample interchange of sweet discourse,
        Which so long sundered friends should dwell upon.
        God give us leisure for these rights of love.
55   Once more, adieu. Be valiant, and speed well.

---

1. Probably a watch light (a slow-burning candle, to write by); possibly a special guard (see line 29).
2. The chroniclers report that Richard was mounted on a "great white course," but the name is Shakespeare's.
3. Apportioning to mortals their lot; shearing or cutting down mortals. Q has "mortal staring," giving the commonplace image of war as both evil-looking and able to cause damage with its glance (like a basilisk).
4. *as . . . time:* as best I can—for I cannot fight openly on your side—I will mislead Richard.

HENRY EARL OF RICHMOND   Good lords, conduct him to his regiment.
I'll strive with° troubled thoughts to take a nap,   *despite*
Lest leaden slumber peise° me down tomorrow,   *weigh*
When I should mount with wings of victory.
60   Once more, good night, kind lords and gentlemen.
            Exeunt [STANLEY *and the lords*]. *Manet* RICHMOND
            [RICHMOND *kneels*]
O thou, whose captain I account myself,
Look on my forces with a gracious eye.
Put in their hands thy bruising irons° of wrath,   *swords*
That they may crush down with a heavy fall
65   Th'usurping helmets of our adversaries.
Make us thy ministers of chastisement,
That we may praise thee in the victory.
To thee I do commend my watchful° soul,   *alert*
Ere I let fall the windows° of mine eyes.   *eyelids*
70   Sleeping and waking, O defend me still!   [*He*] *sleeps*
            Enter the GHOST OF *young* PRINCE EDWARD [*above*]⁵
GHOST OF PRINCE EDWARD (*to* RICHARD)   Let me sit heavy on
      thy soul tomorrow,
Prince Edward, son to Henry the Sixth.⁶
Think how thou stabbedst me in my prime of youth
At Tewkesbury. Despair, therefore, and die.
75   (*To* RICHMOND) Be cheerful, Richmond, for the wrongèd souls
Of butchered princes fight in thy behalf.
King Henry's issue,° Richmond, comforts thee.   [*Exit*]⁷   *offspring*
            Enter [*above*] *the* GHOST OF [KING] HENRY VI
GHOST OF KING HENRY (*to* RICHARD)   When I was mortal, my
      anointed° body   (*with sacred oil*)
By thee was punchèd full of deadly holes.
80   Think on the Tower⁸ and me. Despair and die.
Harry the Sixth bids thee despair and die.
(*To* RICHMOND) Virtuous and holy, be thou conqueror.
Harry that prophesied⁹ thou shouldst be king
Comforts thee in thy sleep. Live and flourish!   [*Exit*]
            Enter [*above*] *the* GHOST OF [*George Duke of*] CLARENCE
85   GHOST OF CLARENCE [*to* RICHARD]   Let me sit heavy on thy soul tomorrow,
I that was washed to death with fulsome° wine,   *sickening*
Poor Clarence, by thy guile betrayed to death.
Tomorrow in the battle think on me,
And fall° thy edgeless sword. Despair and die.   *drop*
90   (*To* RICHMOND) Thou offspring of the house of Lancaster,
The wrongèd heirs of York do pray for thee.
Good angels guard thy battle.° Live and flourish!   [*Exit*]   *army*
            Enter [*above*] *the* GHOSTS OF [*Lords*] RIVERS, GRAY, *and*
            [*Sir Thomas*] VAUGHAN
GHOST OF RIVERS [*to* RICHARD]   Let me sit heavy on thy soul tomorrow,
Rivers that died at Pomfret. Despair and die.
95   GHOST OF GRAY [*to* RICHARD]   Think upon Gray, and let thy soul despair.

---

5. Q, F do not specify how or where the ghosts enter.
6. Line not present in Q, F; it is added here because Edward is the one character not seen previously, and it is possible that information originally intended as dialogue ended up as the stage direction when the text was printed.
7. Exits not given in Q, F. The ghosts could exeunt together at the end.

8. Where Henry VI was supposedly murdered.
9. See *Richard Duke of York* 4.7, in which King Henry (sometimes "Harry"), declaring the young Richmond "England's hope," foresees Richmond's accession to the throne and the beginning of what was to become the Tudor dynasty.

GHOST OF VAUGHAN [*to* RICHARD]   Think upon Vaughan, and with guilty fear
Let fall thy pointless lance. Despair and die.
ALL THREE (*to* RICHMOND)   Awake, and think our wrongs in Richard's bosom
Will conquer him. Awake, and win the day!   [*Exeunt* GHOSTS]
      Enter [*above*] *the* GHOSTS OF THE *two young* PRINCES
GHOSTS OF THE PRINCES (*to* RICHARD)   Dream on thy cousins,¹
100   smothered in the Tower.
Let us be lead within thy bosom, Richard,
And weigh thee down to ruin, shame, and death.
Thy nephews' souls bid thee despair and die.
(*To* RICHMOND) Sleep, Richmond, sleep in peace and wake in joy.
105   Good angels guard thee from the boar's annoy.
Live, and beget a happy race of kings!
Edward's unhappy sons do bid thee flourish. [*Exeunt* GHOSTS]
      Enter [*above*] *the* GHOST OF *Lord* HASTINGS²
GHOST OF HASTINGS [*to* RICHARD]   Bloody and guilty, guiltily awake,
And in a bloody battle end thy days.
110   Think on Lord Hastings, then despair and die.
(*To* RICHMOND) Quiet, untroubled soul, awake, awake!
Arm, fight, and conquer for fair England's sake.   [*Exit*]
      Enter [*above*] *the* GHOST OF LADY ANNE
GHOST OF LADY ANNE (*to* RICHARD)   Richard, thy wife, that wretched Anne thy wife,
That never slept a quiet hour with thee,
115   Now fills thy sleep with perturbations.
Tomorrow in the battle think on me,
And fall thy edgeless sword. Despair and die.
(*To* RICHMOND) Thou quiet soul, sleep thou a quiet sleep.
Dream of success and happy victory.
120   Thy adversary's wife doth pray for thee.   [*Exit*]
      Enter [*above*] *the* GHOST [OF *the Duke*] *of* BUCKINGHAM
GHOST OF BUCKINGHAM (*to* RICHARD)   The first was I that helped thee to the crown;
The last was I that felt thy tyranny.
O in the battle think on Buckingham,
And die in terror of thy guiltiness!
125   Dream on, dream on, of bloody deeds and death;
Fainting,° despair; despairing, yield thy breath.   *Losing heart*
(*To* RICHMOND) I died for hope³ ere I could lend thee aid.
But cheer thy heart, and be thou not dismayed.
God and good angels fight on Richmond's side,
130   And Richard falls in height of all his pride.   [*Exit*]
      RICHARD *starteth up out of a dream*
KING RICHARD   Give me another horse! Bind up my wounds!
Have mercy, Jesu!—Soft, I did but dream.
O coward conscience, how dost thou afflict me?
The lights burn blue.⁴ It is now dead midnight.
135   Cold fearful drops stand on my trembling flesh.
What do I fear? Myself? There's none else by.
Richard loves Richard; that is, I am I.
Is there a murderer here? No. Yes, I am.
Then fly! What, from myself? Great reason. Why?

1. Nephews ("cousins" was a term used for any kins-   3. I died hoping I could aid you.
men).   4. Thought to indicate the presence of ghosts.
2. Q has him enter before the princes, as he had died
before them.

140 Lest I revenge. Myself upon myself?
Alack, I love myself. Wherefore?° For any good   *Why*
That I myself have done unto myself?
O no, alas, I rather hate myself
For hateful deeds committed by myself.

145 I am a villain. Yet I lie: I am not.
Fool, of thyself speak well.—Fool, do not flatter.
My conscience hath a thousand several° tongues,   *separate*
And every tongue brings in a several tale,
And every tale condemns me for a villain.

150 Perjury, perjury, in the high'st degree![5]
Murder, stern murder, in the dir'st degree!
All several sins, all used in each degree,
Throng to the bar,° crying all, 'Guilty, guilty!'   *(of the court)*
I shall despair.[6] There is no creature loves me,

155 And if I die no soul will pity me.
Nay, wherefore should they?—Since that I myself
Find in myself no pity to myself.
Methought the souls of all that I had murdered
Came to my tent, and every one did threat

160 Tomorrow's vengeance on the head of Richard.

        Enter RATCLIFFE

RATCLIFFE   My lord?
KING RICHARD   'Swounds, who is there?
RATCLIFFE   My lord, 'tis I. The early village cock
        Hath twice done salutation to the morn.
165 Your friends are up, and buckle on their armour.
KING RICHARD   O Ratcliffe, I have dreamed a fearful dream.
        What thinkest thou, will all our friends prove true?
RATCLIFFE   No doubt, my lord.
KING RICHARD   Ratcliffe, I fear, I fear.
RATCLIFFE   Nay, good my lord, be not afraid of shadows.°   *illusions; ghosts*
170 KING RICHARD   By the Apostle Paul, shadows tonight
        Have struck more terror to the soul of Richard
        Than can the substance of ten thousand soldiers
        Armèd in proof° and led by shallow Richmond.   *impenetrable armor*
        'Tis not yet near day. Come, go with me.
175 Under our tents I'll play the eavesdropper,
        To see if any mean to shrink from me.

        Exeunt RICHARD *and* RATCLIFFE
        Enter the lords to [HENRY EARL OF] RICHMOND, *sitting*
        in his tent

LORDS   Good morrow, Richmond.
HENRY EARL OF RICHMOND   Cry mercy,° lords and watchful   *Beg your pardon*
        gentlemen,
        That you have ta'en a tardy sluggard here.
180 A LORD   How have you slept, my lord?
HENRY EARL OF RICHMOND   The sweetest sleep and fairest
        boding° dreams   *most propitious*
        That ever entered in a drowsy head
        Have I since your departure had, my lords.

---

5. Every kind of sin, from least to most wicked.
6. Despair was considered the only unforgivable sin; see 1.2.85–88.

Methought their souls whose bodies Richard murdered
185   Came to my tent and cried on[7] victory.
I promise you, my soul is very jocund°   *joyful*
In the remembrance of so fair a dream.
How far into the morning is it, lords?
  A LORD   Upon the stroke of four.
190   HENRY EARL OF RICHMOND   Why then, 'tis time to arm, and give direction.
          His oration to his soldiers
Much that I could say, loving countrymen,
The leisure° and enforcement of the time   *time available*
Forbids to dwell on. Yet remember this:
God and our good cause fight upon our side.
195   The prayers of holy saints and wrongèd souls,
Like high-reared bulwarks, stand before our forces.
Richard except,° those whom we fight against   *excepted*
Had rather have us win than him they follow.
For what is he they follow? Truly, friends,
200   A bloody tyrant and a homicide;
One raised in blood, and one in blood established;[8]
One that made means° to come by what he hath,   *that contrived*
And slaughtered those that were the means to help him;
A base, foul stone, made precious by the foil[9]
205   Of England's chair, where he is falsely set;[1]
One that hath ever been God's enemy.
Then if you fight against God's enemy,
God will, in justice, ward° you as his soldiers.   *guard*
If you do sweat to put a tyrant down,
210   You sleep in peace, the tyrant being slain.
If you do fight against your country's foes,
Your country's foison° pays your pains the hire.   *abundance*
If you do fight in safeguard of your wives,
Your wives shall welcome home the conquerors.
215   If you do free your children from the sword,
Your children's children quites° it in your age.   *requites*
Then, in the name of God and all these rights,
Advance° your standards! Draw your willing swords!   *Raise*
For me, the ransom of this bold attempt
220   Shall be my cold corpse on the earth's cold face;[2]
But if I thrive,° to gain of my attempt,   *succeed*
The least of you shall share his part thereof.
Sound, drums and trumpets, bold and cheerfully!
God and Saint George!° Richmond and victory!   *patron saint of England*
      [*Exeunt to the sound of drums and trumpets*]

5.6

Enter KING RICHARD, [*Sir Richard*] RATCLIFFE, [*Sir
William*] CATESBY [*and others*]

KING RICHARD   What said Northumberland, as touching° Richmond?   *regarding*
RATCLIFFE   That he was never trainèd up in arms.

---

7. And called out (a hunting term); here, urged me on to.
8. *One raised . . . established:* One who has come to the throne by bloodshed and has held it through further bloodshed.
9. Metal leaf was often placed under a jewel as a part of its setting, in order to increase its radiance.
1. Of the throne of England, on which he is wrongly placed; with a pun on "being set like a jewel."
2. *the ransom . . . face:* the only ransom I will give them is my dead body.
5.6

KING RICHARD   He said the truth. And what said Surrey then?

RATCLIFFE   He smiled and said, 'The better for our purpose.'

5   KING RICHARD   He was in the right, and so indeed it is.

Clock strikes

Tell the clock there.[1] Give me a calendar.°   *an almanac*

Who saw the sun today?

[*A book is brought*]

RATCLIFFE   Not I, my lord.

KING RICHARD   Then he disdains to shine, for by the book°   *(the almanac)*

He should have braved° the east an hour ago.   *made resplendent*

10   A black day will it be to somebody.

Ratcliffe.

RATCLIFFE   My lord?

KING RICHARD   The sun will not be seen today.

The sky doth frown and lour° upon our army.   *glower*

I would these dewy tears were from° the ground.   *gone from*

15   Not shine today—why, what is that to me

More than to Richmond? For the selfsame heaven

That frowns on me looks sadly upon him.

Enter [*the Duke of*] NORFOLK

NORFOLK   Arm, arm, my lord! The foe vaunts° in the field.   *flaunts his strength*

KING RICHARD   Come, bustle, bustle! Caparison° my horse.   *Put the trappings on*

[RICHARD *arms*]

20   Call up Lord Stanley, bid him bring his power.°   [*Exit one*]   *forces*

I will lead forth my soldiers to the plain,

And thus my battle° shall be orderèd.   *army*

My forward° shall be drawn out all in length,   *front rank*

Consisting equally of horse and foot,

25   Our archers placèd strongly in the midst.

John Duke of Norfolk, Thomas Earl of Surrey,

Shall have the leading of this multitude.

They thus directed,° we ourself will follow   *positioned*

In the main battle, whose puissance° on both sides   *power*

30   Shall be well wingèd° with our chiefest horse.°   *flanked / best cavalry*

This, and Saint George to boot![2] What think'st thou, Norfolk?

NORFOLK   A good direction, warlike sovereign.

He showeth him a paper

This paper found I on my tent this morning.

[*He reads*]

'Jackie of Norfolk be not too bold,

35   For Dickon thy master is bought and sold.'[3]

KING RICHARD   A thing devisèd by the enemy.—

Go, gentlemen, each man unto his charge.

Let not our babbling dreams affright our souls.

Conscience is but a word that cowards use,

40   Devised at first to keep the strong in awe.

Our strong arms be our conscience; swords, our law.

March on, join° bravely! Let us to't, pell mell—   *join battle*

If not to heaven, then hand in hand to hell.

His oration to his army

What shall I say, more than I have inferred?°   *put forward*

45   Remember whom you are to cope withal:°   *with*

---

1. Count the clock's strokes.
2. *and . . . boot:* with the aid of our patron saint as a bonus.

3. Is betrayed. *Jackie of Norfolk:* John, Duke of Norfolk. *Dickon:* Dick (that is, Richard).

A sort° of vagabonds, rascals and runaways,   *gang*
A scum of Bretons and base lackey° peasants,   *lowly*
Whom their o'ercloyèd° country vomits forth   *nauseously overfull*
To desperate ventures and assured destruction.
50   You sleeping safe, they bring to you unrest;
You having lands and blessed with beauteous wives,
They would distrain° the one, distain° the other.   *confiscate / dishonor*
And who doth lead them, but a paltry fellow?
Long kept in Bretagne at our mother's⁴ cost;
55   A milksop; one that never in his life
Felt so much cold as over shoes in snow.⁵
Let's whip⁶ these stragglers o'er the seas again,
Lash hence these overweening rags of France,
These famished beggars, weary of their lives,
60   Who—but for° dreaming on this fond° exploit—   *were it not for / foolish*
For want of means,° poor rats, had hanged themselves.   *livelihood*
If we be conquered, let *men* conquer us,
And not these bastard Bretons, whom our fathers
Have in their own land beaten, bobbed,° and thumped,   *pounded*
65   And in record left them the heirs of shame.⁷
Shall these enjoy our lands? Lie with our wives?
Ravish our daughters?
          Drum afar off
                              Hark, I hear their drum.
Fight, gentlemen of England! Fight, bold yeomen!
Draw, archers, draw your arrows to the head!
70   Spur your proud horses hard, and ride in blood!
Amaze the welkin° with your broken staves!   *sky*
          Enter a MESSENGER
What says Lord Stanley? Will he bring his power?
MESSENGER   My lord, he doth deny° to come.   *refuse*
KING RICHARD   Off with young George's head!
75 NORFOLK   My lord, the enemy is past the marsh.
After the battle let George Stanley die.
KING RICHARD   A thousand hearts are great within my bosom.
Advance our standards! Set upon our foes!
Our ancient word° of courage, fair Saint George,   *battle cry*
80   Inspire us with the spleen° of fiery dragons.   *anger*
Upon them! Victory sits on our helms!°   *Exeunt*   *helmets*

5.7

Alarum. Excursions.° Enter [*Sir William*] CATESBY   *Military sallies*
CATESBY [*calling*]¹   Rescue, my lord of Norfolk! Rescue, rescue!
[*To a soldier*] The King enacts more wonders than a man,²
Daring an opposite° to every danger.   *to oppose himself*
His horse is slain, and all on foot he fights,
5   Seeking for Richmond in the throat of death.
[*Calling*] Rescue, fair lord, or else the day is lost!

---

4. Apparently from a misprint in Holinshed, which should have read "brother's" (that is, Richard's brother-in-law, Charles, Duke of Burgundy, who supported Richmond in exile). Possibly: to the detriment of England, the mother country.
5. *as . . . snow*: as one who walks in snow that covers the tops of his shoes.

6. English vagabonds were whipped out of the parish by a local official.
7. And gave them a shameful record in history.
5.7
1. Some editors bring Norfolk onstage, although the stage directions do not call for him in either Q or F.
2. More wonders than seems possible for a man.

Alarums. Enter [KING] RICHARD

KING RICHARD   A horse! A horse! My kingdom for a horse!

CATESBY   Withdraw, my lord. I'll help you to a horse.

KING RICHARD   Slave, I have set my life upon a cast,[3]

10   And I will stand the hazard of the die.
I think there be six Richmonds[4] in the field.
Five have I slain today, instead of him.
A horse! A horse! My kingdom for a horse!   [*Exeunt*]

5.8

Alarum. Enter [KING] RICHARD [*at one door*] *and*
[HENRY EARL OF] RICHMOND [*at another*]. *They fight.*
RICHARD *is slain.* [*Exit* RICHMOND.] *Retreat*[1] *and flour-
ish. Enter* [HENRY EARL OF] RICHMOND *and* [*Lord* STAN-
LEY *Earl of*] *Derby, with divers other lords* [*and soldiers*]

HENRY EARL OF RICHMOND   God and your arms be praised, victorious friends!
The day is ours. The bloody dog is dead.

STANLEY [*bearing the crown*]   Courageous Richmond, well hast
thou acquit° thee.   acquitted; conducted
Lo, here this long usurpèd royalty[2]

5   From the dead temples of this bloody wretch
Have I plucked off, to grace thy brows withal.°   with
Wear it, enjoy it, and make much of it.
        [*He sets the crown on Henry's head*]

KING HENRY VII   Great God of heaven, say 'Amen' to all.
But tell me—young George Stanley, is he living?

10   STANLEY   He is, my lord, and safe in Leicester town,
Whither, if it please you, we may now withdraw us.

KING HENRY VII   What men of name are slain on either side?

STANLEY [*reads*]   John Duke of Norfolk, Robert Brackenbury,
Walter Lord Ferrers, and Sir William Brandon.

15   KING HENRY VII   Inter their bodies as becomes their births.°   befits their rank
Proclaim a pardon to the soldiers fled
That in submission will return to us,
And then—as we have ta'en the sacrament[3]—
We will unite the white rose and the red.[4]

20   Smile, heaven, upon this fair conjunction,°   union
That long have frowned upon their enmity.
What traitor hears me and says not 'Amen'?
England hath long been mad, and scarred herself;
The brother blindly shed the brother's blood;

25   The father rashly slaughtered his own son;
The son, compelled, been butcher to the sire;
All that divided York and Lancaster,
United in their dire division.[5]
O now let Richmond and Elizabeth,

30   The true succeeders of each royal house,
By God's fair ordinance° conjoin together,   decree

---

3. A throw of the die (one of a pair of dice) in line 10.
4. In addition to Richmond, five other men dressed and armed to resemble him (a common safety measure).
5.8
1. A trumpet signal for (Richard's) men to retire.
2. Emblem of sovereignty; here, the crown.
3. Referring to the oath, taken by Richmond in the cathedral at Rheims, that he would marry Princess

Elizabeth as soon as he was crowned.
4. The badges of the Yorkist (white) and Lancastrian (red) factions. The marriage of Richmond (Lancastrian) and Princess Elizabeth (Yorkist) brought to an end the so-called Wars of the Roses, dramatized in the three *Henry VI* plays.
5. Joined by hatred, having nothing in common but mutual antagonism.

And let their heirs—God, if his will be so—
Enrich the time to come with smooth-faced peace,
With smiling plenty, and fair prosperous days.

35 Abate° the edge of traitors, gracious Lord,   *Blunt*
That would reduce° these bloody days again   *bring back*
And make poor England weep forth streams of blood.
Let them not live to taste this land's increase,°   *prosperity*
That would with treason wound this fair land's peace.

40 Now civil wounds are stopped; peace lives again.
That she may long live here, God say 'Amen'.

                              [*Flourish.*] *Exeunt*

The Reign of
King Edward the Third

Did Shakespeare write *The Reign of King Edward the Third*? The jury is out, but the Oxford editors have come to believe that he wrote at least part of it. In that view, they are joined by an increasing number of scholars who find in this chronicle history traces of the issues that preoccupied Shakespeare in his early years as a dramatist, as well as a number of lines and scenes that recall other plays and poems he authored both in the early 1590s and later in his career, including *The Rape of Lucrece,* the sonnets, *The Life of Henry V,* and *Measure for Measure. Edward III,* written entirely in verse, was first printed in 1596, with a second edition appearing in 1599, but the title page gave no indication of authorship, only that *"it hath bin sundrie times plaied about the Citie of London."* Many scholars believe that it was first performed by Lord Pembroke's Men, a company that staged several of Shakespeare's early plays before he became a member of the Lord Chamberlain's Men in 1594. In 1656, two printers attributed *Edward III* to Shakespeare in a list of printed plays, but the list has many errors. In 1760, Shakespearean editor and scholar Edward Capell seconded the idea but admitted that there was little external evidence to support it. He, however, provided the first modern version of the text, leaving it to readers to decide the authorship question on their own. Seldom acted, until recent years the play has not been included in collected editions of Shakespeare's works.

The tide, however, has begun to turn. *King Edward III* has been given several recent stage productions, mostly notably by the Royal Shakespeare Company in 2002; and it is now printed in several collected editions of Shakespeare's works, including the second edition of the *Oxford Shakespeare* upon which the *Norton Shakespeare* is based. (For the complete text of the play, go to wwnorton.com/shakespeare.) What caused this new willingness to entertain the possibility that the play is in part or in its entirety by Shakespeare? First, scholars have increasingly realized that a number of early modern plays were collaboratively written, including some traditionally assigned to Shakespeare such as *Pericles, The Two Noble Kinsmen,* and a number of his early history plays. Why, then, exclude *King Edward III,* which, on stylistic and thematic grounds, seems to many scholars to contain several scenes indicating Shakespeare's authorship? While only a few scholars believe the play to be entirely his, a number find it likely that he had a hand in those parts involving the Countess of Salisbury and possibly some involving Prince Edward. The Oxford editors assign the bulk of Scene 2, all of Scenes 3 and 12, and possibly Scene 13 to Shakespeare. Second, the play, which most scholars believe was written between 1590 and 1594, mirrors many of Shakespeare's preoccupations during that time. Its central characters are the great Plantagenet king, Edward III, and his oldest son, Edward the Black Prince; its central action their heroic conquest of France. Throughout the 1590s, Shakespeare wrote about the aftermath of this king's reign as, after the Black Prince's early death, the Yorkist and Lancastrian branches of the Plantagenet family began a bitter fight over the crown, in the process losing effective control of England's French territories. In most of Shakespeare's other history plays, Edward III and his eldest son are revered as exemplars of English chivalry and military prowess. It is plausible, then, to think that Shakespeare would have been drawn to the direct dramatization of the king so often alluded to in his other histories.

Whether or not the play is in part by Shakespeare, *King Edward III* is an interesting and highly patriotic example of dramatized English history, a genre popular throughout

THE
RAIGNE OF
KING EDVVARD
the third:

As it hath bin sundrie times plaied about the Citie of London.

LONDON,
Printed for Cuthbert Burby.
1 5 9 6.

The title page for *The Raigne of King Edward the Third* (1596) gives no indication of who wrote the play.

the 1590s. Written in the wake of the destruction of the Spanish Armada in 1588, an event to which the play several times alludes, it presents England as a nearly invincible military force. As the action opens, Scottish forces have invaded England's northern borders, and Edward III has been insultingly summoned to France to pay tribute to its king. By play's end, Edward has captured both David, King of Scotland, and Jean of Valois, King of France, and he has triumphed in the great naval battle of Sluys as well as in land battles at Crécy, Poitiers, and Calais, a series of events that historically took place over a number of years but are here conveniently collapsed into one continuous arc of action.

Particular attention is paid to the exploits of Prince Edward, who, a little like Prince Hal of the *Henry IV* plays, is shown growing into his role as military hero and prospective monarch. Before the all-important Battle of Crécy, to mark the significance of the Prince's participation in it, his father ritualistically invests his son with the accoutrements of knighthood:

> And, Ned, because this battle is the first
> That ever yet thou fought'st in pitched field,
> As ancient custom is of martialists
> To dub thee with the type of chivalry,
> In solemn manner we will give thee arms.
> Come, therefore, heralds; orderly bring forth
> A strong attirement for the Prince my son.
> (Scene 6, lines 171–77)

The Prince is then ceremoniously given a coat of armor, and then a helmet, a lance, a shield, and finally the honor of leading the vanguard in the coming battle. In the midst of that battle, when the Prince is surrounded by an overwhelming number of foes, the English nobles plead with King Edward to rescue him. Edward refuses. Demonstrating a species of "tough love," he says that the Prince's courage and skill are being tested and that he must fight this battle by himself, whatever the outcome. Miraculously, the Prince returns to his father in triumph *"bearing in his hand his shivered lance. The body of the King of Bohemia is borne before, wrapped in the colours of Bohemia"* (after Scene 8, line 60). This induction into the ways of chivalry recalls *1 Henry VI* and the exploits of the English hero, Talbot, and his son John, although in that play these mighty English warriors are slain by the French, but only after making a remarkable account of themselves against great odds; and it looks ahead to *Henry V* and King Henry's miraculous victory over the French at Agincourt. Not mentioned in this play, but probably known to many in the audience, was the fact that Edward III established the Order of the Garter, a chivalric institution that honored England's most distinguished warrior nobles. In the play, King Edward, his son, and his chief officers all come to embody Garter values of honor, courage, and military prowess.

The stage deeds of Edward and his son must have been memorable. They were explicitly recalled by Thomas Heywood in *An Apology for Actors* (1612), when he exclaims:

> What English Prince should hee behold the true portrature of that famous King *Edward* the third, foraging France, taking so great a King captive in his owne country, quartering the English Lyons with the French Flower-delyce, ... would not bee suddenly Inflam'd with so royall a spectacle, being made apt and fit for the like atchievement. So of *Henry* the fift.

The play clearly could make an impression on spectators, and its consistent emphasis on the overconfidence and pride of the French allowed for easy identification with the courageous and ultimately victorious English forces.

King Edward III's opening scenes, however, offer more complex pleasures, and those scenes are the ones most often attributed to Shakespeare. Edward III does not start the play as a paragon of virtue, even though he is a mighty warrior. Moving north to repel the Scots, who have besieged the castle where the Countess of Salisbury is ensconced, Edward falls swiftly and irrevocably in love with her, despite the fact that both he and she have spouses and children. In several remarkable encounters in which he pursues and she resists, the author dramatizes a moral struggle between two equally matched antagonists. In the end, she prevails, after threatening to kill herself should Edward insist on making her violate her marriage vows. As if waking from a dream, he says:

> Even by that power I swear, that gives me now
> The power to be ashamèd of myself,
> I never mean to part my lips again
> In any words that tends to such a suit.
> Arise, true English lady, whom our isle
> May better boast of than ever Roman might
> Of her, whose ransacked treasury hath tasked
> The vain endeavour of so many pens.
> Arise, and be my fault thy honour's fame
> Which after-ages shall enrich thee with.
> (Scene 3, lines 186–95)

A homegrown Lucrece, the Countess is Edward's ideal of an English lady, her chastity the guarantor of the purity of English bloodlines and, finally, the spur to Edward's own sense of honor. Prior to this moment, however, the play has vividly depicted the psychological torment of a man caught in the throes of a passion he can't control, a passion that draws him from affairs of state and very nearly makes him willing to murder his own wife and the Countess's husband. It is only after Edward overcomes this passion, with the Countess's help, that he is able to lead his army to France. Self-conquest seems the prerequisite for military conquest.

Interestingly, this part of the play contains its only memorably comic character, the hapless Lodowick, secretary to King Edward, who is commanded by the King to pen a letter to the Countess expressing Edward's passion. Lodowick is not much of a love poet and seems completely flummoxed by the task. After he ekes out a few lines, the King critiques them roundly, especially for commending the Countess's chastity, for, as he says, "I had rather have her chased than chaste!" (Scene 2, line 320), and for likening her to the moon when Edward would have her likened to the sun. The scene is both a sly comment on the frustrations of writing poetry at somebody else's command and also a lovely example of the ironic tonal juxtapositions so often found in early modern drama, especially drama by Shakespeare. The King is wrapped up in his own passion, forgetful of all the world, and both the grandeur and the dangerous self-absorption of his passion are highlighted through the contrast provided by the commonsensical, non-lyrical voice of his secretary just trying to do a job. Edward is in raptures over his beloved; Lodowick needs the facts: "To whom, my lord, shall I direct my style?" (Scene 2, line 246); "Write I to a woman?" (Scene 2, line 261). "Of what condition or estate she is / 'Twere requisite that I should know, my lord" (Scene 2, lines 265–66). Eventually, in frustration, the King grabs Lodowick's pen and paper, and vows to write the letter himself.

As the Countess of Salisbury scenes predict, throughout *Edward III* English women are given unusually powerful roles. Salisbury may be the English Lucrece, but the play's most striking embodiment of female power is Queen Philippa, Edward's wife, who, though pregnant, actively takes part in the suppression of the Scots while her husband is in France. As one lord describes her, she, "big with child, was every day in arms" (Scene 10, line 45). At the end of the play, she appears in France, still pregnant, for the moment when the Scottish and French kings both surrender to Edward. In *King Edward III*, women can be warriors without causing scandal. While the central battles in France make war seem an affair between men, the edges of the text suggest that this is not so, that women, too, can be warriors, and important ones.

Their key role in dynastic continuity is equally acknowledged. Edward's claim to

France rests on his mother's status as the only direct heir of the French King, King Philippe. As the Comte d'Artois says, she

> Was all the daughters that this Philippe had,
> Whom afterward your father took to wife.
> And from the fragrant garden of her womb
> Your gracious self, the flower of Europe's hope,
> Derivèd is inheritor to France.
> (Scene 1, lines 12–16)

The womb as a fragrant garden is a striking image, suggesting the beauty of his mother's fecundity, which in this instance has brought forth "the flower of Europe's hope" and secured that son a kingdom. Edward's wife, in turn, has brought forth heirs, in this play exemplified by the Black Prince, upon whose face his mother's image is vividly stamped. Looking at his young son while adulterously pursuing the Countess of Salisbury, Edward exclaims: "O, how his mother's face, / Modelled in his, corrects my strayed desire, / And rates my heart, and chides my thievish eye, / Who, being rich enough in seeing her, / Yet seek elsewhere" (Scene 3, lines 74–78). Rather than passive matter molded by the active father's impress, the mother in this instance has shaped the features of her son. Bearing his father's name, he bears his mother's face. It is women like the Countess whose chastity guarantees the purity of bloodlines and women like Edward's mother and wife who make dynastic lineage possible. The pregnant Philippa's appearance onstage at the end of the play brings together in one body the powerful martial and procreative roles that women in this play exemplify.

If *King Edward III* is primarily concerned with establishing English claims to French territory, its treatment of the Scots may be one factor in its seeming disappearance from print and stage at the end of the sixteenth century. The Scots are depicted as craven opportunists who besiege Roxburgh Castle, the Countess of Salisbury's home, and invade the northern shires of England once Edward's attention turns toward France. The Countess fears their "rough insulting barbarism" and the "vile, uncivil, skipping jigs" in which they will "bray forth" their imagined conquest of her castle (Scene 2, lines 9, 12, 13). Despite their boasting, however, the Scots run away when Edward unexpectedly appears to lift the siege of the castle. Later, these same Scots are defeated by English forces led by Queen Philippa, and the dramatist invents an unhistorical scene in which David, their King, is brought to France to be part of Edward's spectacle of conquest. It might not be surprising if, under a Scottish king like James I, who ascended the English throne in 1603, canny theater companies who wished to avoid his displeasure might have ceased to make *King Edward III* an active part of their repertory. Whatever the cause, the play fell from sight for most of the four hundred years following its first appearance in the 1590s. Now, however, it is available for all to judge what hand Shakespeare may have had—if any—in its composition, but also simply as another interesting example of how the early modern playwrights told the story of their nation's past.

JEAN E. HOWARD

SELECTED BIBLIOGRAPHY

Cahill, Patricia. "Biopower in the English Pale: Generation and Genocide in *King Edward III*." *Unto the Breach: Martial Formations, Historical Trauma, and the Early Modern Stage*. London: Oxford University Press, 2008. Argues that the play by indirection is concerned with the conquest of Ireland and with the military and procreative strategies by which that conquest could be achieved.

Conlan, J. P. "Shakespeare's *Edward III*: A Consolation for English Recusants." *Comparative Drama* 35.2 (2001): 177–207. Proposes that the play critiques the persecution of recusants after the English defeat of the Spanish Armada in 1588.

Melchiori, Giorgio, ed. *King Edward III*. Cambridge: Cambridge University Press, 1998. The introduction to this edition discusses the play's date of composition, the authorship question, and matters of style, theme, and dramatic structure.

———. *Shakespeare's Garter Plays: "Edward III" to "Merry Wives of Windsor."* Newark: University of Delaware Press, 1994. Argues that because the historical Edward III founded the Order of the Garter and because *King Edward III* deals with the theme of honor and the education of princes, it should be grouped with five other Shakespeare plays preoccupied with the Order and its values.

Metz, G. Harold, ed. *Sources of Four Plays Ascribed to Shakespeare: "The Reign of King Edward III," "Sir Thomas More," "The History of Cardenio," "The Two Noble Kinsmen."* Columbia: University of Missouri Press, 1989. Summarizes scholarship on the play and provides primary source material from Jean Froissart, Raphael Holinshed, and William Painter.

Proudfoot, Richard. "*The Reign of Edward III* (1596) and Shakespeare." *Proceedings of the British Academy* 71 (1985): 159–85. Discusses many aspects of the play, including arguing that it has a three-part structure and was first performed by Lord Pembroke's Men.

Rackin, Phyllis. "Women's Roles in the Elizabethan History Plays." *The Cambridge Companion to Shakespeare's History Plays.* Ed. Michael Hattaway. Cambridge: Cambridge University Press, 2002. 71–85. Questioning Shakespeare's authorship of *King Edward III*, Rackin argues that, unlike most of Shakespeare's history plays, it shows women who are both virtuous and powerful in the persons of the Countess of Salisbury and Queen Philippa.

Sams, Eric, ed. *Shakespeare's "Edward III."* New Haven: Yale University Press, 1996. Argues strenuously that Shakespeare was the author of *Edward III* because of parallels to other Shakespeare plays and poems, and on the basis of diction, versification, imagery, and so forth.

Richard II

In the first scene of *Richard II,* two armed noblemen face each other before the royal throne. They hurl insults at one another, their deadly antagonism barely held in check by the formality of the occasion. This is an "appeal for treason," a kind of trial already archaic in Shakespeare's time, in which plaintiff and defendant present their cases in their own persons before the king, who instantly dispenses justice. The structure of the situation suggests what the men themselves insist upon: that one lies and one tells the truth, that one is a traitor and one a true subject. But even while we are implicitly asked to judge between rival claims, we have no way of knowing what has happened or whom to trust.

In the ensuing scenes, we learn that Bolingbroke and Mowbray are fighting about the murder of Thomas of Woodstock, the uncle of King Richard II. Apparently Bolingbroke knows that Richard secretly ordered Woodstock's death. Since he cannot say so, he picks Richard's agent Mowbray as his target, for Woodstock had been in Mowbray's safekeeping. Meanwhile, Mowbray, likewise unable to blame the true culprit openly, is outraged at being called a traitor when it was his allegiance to Richard that led him to acquiesce in the killing.

This is a far more tangled situation than the simple yes-or-no structure of the appeal for treason or, several scenes later, the "trial by combat" could allow anyone to acknowledge. Moreover, the King's participation in the crime upon which he is supposed to be passing judgment obviously compromises his impartiality. The institution of the appeal for treason is premised on the assumptions that, as Richard himself states emphatically, the king has no part in his subjects' quarrels and that it is in his best interests to have the truth revealed. Here, neither assumption is correct. The ceremonies of royal authority so colorfully staged in the first few scenes turn out to be inconclusive, postponing rather than confronting real sources of discord.

As the play continues, we come to realize that the confusion of the first few scenes, a confusion Shakespeare forces his audience momentarily to share, results from an intractable problem in a system of monarchical government. Since the king's subjects are obliged to obey him, it is not clear how, short of direct divine intervention, his follies or vices may be checked. To admit that subjects have a right to judge or even to remove their king threatens the stability of the realm, since any subject, discontented for any reason, might incite a revolt. But to allow the king to have his own way no matter what opens the way to tyranny.

The proper extent of a monarch's power was a crucial, and unresolved, political issue in sixteenth- and early seventeenth-century England, when first the Tudors and then the Stuarts struggled to extend their traditional prerogatives. A few decades after Shakespeare's death, disagreement about the nature of royal authority would provoke the English Civil War. In the 1590s, when Shakespeare was writing his history plays, the lines of stress upon which the country would eventually fracture were already apparent, even though the disasters to come would not have seemed inevitable.

When Shakespeare wrote about the medieval reign of Richard II, in other words, he saw the conflicts of that reign through the lens of the late sixteenth century. His meticulous re-creation of antiquated judicial processes did not conceal from audiences in his own time the contemporary relevance of the play. In all sixteenth-century texts and perhaps in performance, the lines in which Richard gives up his crown were omitted; many scholars theorize that this episode was considered too inflammatory to print or stage. When the Earl of Essex rebelled against Elizabeth I in 1601, some of his supporters cited Richard's reign as providing a historical precedent for the deposition of a monarch. They paid Shakespeare's company to perform a play about Richard's reign—almost certainly Shakespeare's play—in an attempt to rally supporters to their cause. "I am Richard II," snapped the furious Queen. "Know you not that?"

To acknowledge the contemporary relevance of Richard's reign is not to claim that Shakespeare wrote his play purely as a means of commenting obliquely on the policies of Elizabeth I. Rather, the urgent contemporary task of defining a nation-state led Shakespeare to an extended historical inquiry into the institution of the English monarchy, an inquiry of which *Richard II* is a part. By looking at points at which the normal order of royal succession is challenged, Shakespeare illuminates interesting inconsistencies in Renaissance theories of kingship and political authority. Several years earlier, he had written the three *Henry VI* plays and *Richard III,* which while not originally conceived as a series eventually constituted what critics call the "first tetralogy": a group of plays that together present a continuous chronicle of the long Wars of the Roses in the fifteenth century. Soon after finishing *Richard III,* Shakespeare began writing another group of history plays, the "second tetralogy," which backtrack in time to treat the origins of the conflicts he had already brought to the stage.

As he had for his earlier history plays, Shakespeare turned to Raphael Holinshed's *Chronicles of England, Scotland, and Ireland* (1587). There he found in the reign of Richard II a remote cause of the war to be waged many years hence. Richard II was grandson of Edward III, whose formidable precedent haunts all the plays of the second tetralogy. King Edward had five sons who survived to adulthood, but his eldest, Edward the Black Prince, predeceased him. The Black Prince left a son of his own, however, the future Richard II, to whom the throne descended after Edward III's death. At the time of his accession, Richard was ten years old, and during his adolescence his powerful uncles, the younger brothers of the Black Prince, administered his kingdom on his behalf. After Richard reached young adulthood and began to rule in his own name, he found it difficult to gain the respect of his uncles, experienced middle-aged men who had become accustomed to command. His own rashness and ineffectuality only compounded his troubles. Shakespeare's play opens upon the young Richard, already complicit in the murder of one of his uncles; the remaining uncles, who scorn Richard's maladroit rule but realize they owe allegiance to him; and Richard's cousins Bolingbroke and Northumberland, who are more willing than their elders to act on the recognition of the ruler's weakness.

Early in the play, Richard reacts to Bolingbroke's veiled challenge by exiling him; shortly thereafter, he confiscates Bolingbroke's estate. When, exasperated, Bolingbroke invades England and successfully seizes the crown from his cousin, his action neatly ruptures two traditional sources of royal authority. Unquestionably, Bolingbroke is the more astute tactician, the more effective leader. Richard, however, is equally undoubtedly the rightful heir of Edward III, and as such has been anointed king in a sacred coronation ceremony. Thus

Richardus ii. From John Rastell, *The Pastyme of People* (1529).

"Like perspectives, which, rightly gazed upon, / Show nothing but confusion; eyed awry, / Distinguish form" (*Richard II* 2.2.18–20). The most famous Renaissance example of such a "perspective" or anamorphic picture is Hans Holbein's *The Ambassadors* (1533); when the painting is viewed from the side ("awry"), the elongated object in the foreground reveals itself to be a skull.

one character has all the advantages when considered from a material and practical point of view, while the other derives his claim to authority from the more abstract principle of divinely sanctioned hereditary right.

Shakespeare imagines the division between the two men not merely as a political issue but as a question of character. A vivid sense of Bolingbroke's personality emerges in his confrontation with Mowbray. Mowbray harps on Bolingbroke's lies, laments the damage Bolingbroke's accusation has done to his reputation, and experiences Bolingbroke's verbal accusation as a physical attack: he is "pierced to the soul with slander's venomed spear" (1.1.171). Bolingbroke, by contrast, trusts not words but physical strength: "What my tongue speaks my right-drawn sword may prove," he stoutly declares (1.1.46). Tellingly, his word "right" conflates his proficiency as a warrior with the uprightness of his cause, suggesting that he does not care to recognize the potential difference. Likewise, Bolingbroke repeatedly speaks of making his words *good*, by which he means backing them up by force. As a corollary, he is suspicious or dismissive of anything that seems merely imaginary, verbal, or abstract. When his father, Gaunt, encourages him to reconcile himself to his exile by renaming it an educational tour or a pleasure junket, Bolingbroke replies:

> O, who can hold a fire in his hand
> By thinking on the frosty Caucasus,
> Or cloy the hungry edge of appetite
> By bare imagination of a feast . . . ?
>   (1.3.257–60)

As the play proceeds, this insistence on material facts rather than words or imagination comes to seem entirely characteristic of a man who has no legal claim on the throne, but who takes it because he is able to do so.

Unlike Bolingbroke, Richard is an inept manager of practical affairs. In the first act, most of his powerful kinfolk let him literally get away with murder; but in the second act, it becomes clear that they will not tolerate his infringement of property rights. Medieval kings were expected to cover most of the expenses of government from their own large estates, but to raise additional funds Richard "farms out" the realm—that is, grants the power to tax to private individuals who can confiscate subjects' property virtually as they please, provided the king gets a share of the spoils. Not surprisingly, such legalized theft produces widespread resentment. For the upper aristocracy, the last straw is Richard's seizure of the duchy of Lancaster upon John of Gaunt's death: the encroachment seems to them worse than homicide, because it directly threatens the social structure upon which their status depends. Inherited property distinguishes noblemen from "men of no name": in fact, noble names are derived from property, the lands of Lancaster, Gloucester, York, Northumberland, and so forth. In *Richard II*, both social disruptions and identity crises are marked by a struggle over such titles and the power they signify. Bolingbroke, returning to England, insists on being called "Lancaster," not "Hereford"; Northumberland presumptuously forgets to call Richard "King"; Richard himself laments, upon his deposition, that "I must nothing be . . . I have no name, no title" (4.1.191, 245).

Although technically aristocrats did not own their land outright but held it in trust from the sovereign, by Richard's time Magna Carta protected the right of property holders to pass their lands to their heirs. Only a conviction for treason could forfeit the family claim. Ironically, at the moment Richard commandeers the Lancastrian estates, Bolingbroke is apparently on the verge of invading England with an armed force, so he is actually a traitor and Richard could eventually have appropriated his property in a perfectly legal manner. But Richard's characteristic neglect of proper procedure makes Bolingbroke's return seem a response to dispossession and thus turns the nobility toward the rebel cause.

Richard does not imagine that he must earn the respect of the people he governs, or balance his budget, or follow laws. He does not believe that his authority depends on the consent of the governed or on the effective manipulation of material resources. Whereas Bolingbroke thinks of power as emanating from "below"—from the King's subjects, from the deployment of material resources—Richard thinks of it as descending from "above," from the God whose representative on earth he was born to be. His assertion in 3.2.50–53 is entirely characteristic:

> Not all the water in the rough rude sea
> Can wash the balm from an anointed king.
> The breath of worldly men cannot depose
> The deputy elected by the Lord.

Later in the same scene, deserted by all but a few supporters, he exclaims: "Is not the King's name forty thousand names? / Arm, arm, my name!" (3.2.81–82). What Richard needs now, of course, is not names but soldiers, but he deliberately refuses to acknowledge the difference.

Richard's drastic impracticalities derive from his conviction that the God who put him on the throne is immanent in the created universe and vigilant in defense of His deputy. Richard is not unique in this conviction: the assumption that God intervenes continuously in human affairs in order to guarantee just outcomes underlies the ritual of the trial by combat as it is staged in 1.3. The way spirit informs and controls the material world can render "dead matter" sympathetic to human beings. "This earth shall have a feeling," Richard claims (3.2.24). Thus he is confident that the earth will put toads in the way of traitors, and that angels will rush to save a king in trouble.

Medieval histories are full of such narratives: the ground opens up and swallows an atheist; lightning strikes a perjurer dead.

By Shakespeare's time, the trial by combat had been discredited and the conception of the world to which Richard adheres was beginning to seem obsolete. Some thinkers were increasingly discarding anthropocentric ways of thinking and conceiving of the material world as something alien to human consciousness, ruled by purely physical laws of cause and effect. This change in mentality affected historians, who were subjecting long-accepted myths to critical scrutiny; scientists, who began to place a new value on empirical experimentation; and theologians, who were becoming more skeptical of the continuation of miracles in postbiblical times. Political theorists such as Machiavelli pragmatically insisted on describing political power as it really was exercised, and not as God or moral scruples might dictate that it ought to be exercised. The pragmatic Bolingbroke, then, is associated with a new, effective, but not necessarily moral or satisfying way of thinking about the manipulation of men and matter.

Richard's assumptions about the world and his place in it turn out to be wrong. His naïveté about the relationship of language and power, spirit and matter, leaves him vulnerable to Bolingbroke's assault. Bolingbroke's supplanting of Richard, then, might be seen not merely as a personal or even a political victory, but as the uprooting of one worldview by another. Whether this displacement represents an advance or a deterioration is, however, another question. The second part of the play, in which Bolingbroke emerges victorious, reexamines the nature of the conflict between the two men and the principles they represent.

In a pivotal scene in Act 3, Bolingbroke, Northumberland, and York approach the castle in which Richard has sequestered himself. When Richard finally emerges on the battlements, Bolingbroke exclaims:

> See, see, King Richard doth himself appear,
> As doth the blushing discontented sun
> From out the fiery portal of the east
> When he perceives the envious clouds are bent
> To dim his glory and to stain the track
> Of his bright passage to the occident.
>
> (3.3.61–66)

Bolingbroke is untypically eloquent here, but interestingly, his extended simile works against his own interests. The comparison between king and sun, a traditional figure of speech, implies that the king is both unique and indispensable. Rebels are not rival suns; they are transient clouds that the mighty king will eventually burn away. Even while he mutinies against Richard's misgovernment, Bolingbroke seems unable to escape a conservative conception of monarchy in which rebellion is a form of envy doomed to failure.

Bolingbroke's linguistic slip suggests that it may be easier to amass an army and seize the throne than to put aside one's inherited convictions about the nature of royal authority. Bolingbroke does not have an alternative vocabulary in which to justify his own behavior. Thus, throughout the play, it is hard to be sure whether he is cunningly concealing his true motives or simply incapable of articulating them even to himself. In the opening scenes, although Richard recognizes Bolingbroke's challenge to his authority, Bolingbroke himself seems a bit obtuse about his own purposes, as if his accusation of Mowbray were merely an effect of his sturdy loyalty to Richard. Likewise, it is unclear whether he initially realizes that his return from exile commits him not merely to regaining the Lancastrian estates but to a more thorough attack on Richard's sovereignty. Bolingbroke never appears before us, alone or in company, to ponder his own conduct and motives. In this regard, he differs not only from the obsessively self-reflective Richard but from other Shakespearean usurpers: Richard III, Macbeth, Hamlet's Claudius.

In Act 4, however unable he may be to justify the grounds of his own authority, Bolingbroke—now King Henry IV—astutely recognizes that he must convince his subjects that he is legitimately entitled to the crown. Henry needs, somehow, to transfer to himself that mysterious sense of royal sanctity in which Richard initially places so much confidence and to which Henry has no plausible claim. Henry and his followers thus attempt to paper over his gross procedural breach with procedural punctiliousness. Richard cannot be summarily imprisoned or executed; rather, he must seem voluntarily and publicly to resign his sovereignty to Henry.

Unfortunately for Henry, he is not good at managing such rituals, while Richard is in his element. In 4.1, Richard masterfully seizes the symbolic initiative from the apparent victors. "Now mark me how I will undo myself," he announces (line 193).

> I give this heavy weight from off my head,
> And this unwieldy sceptre from my hand,
> The pride of kingly sway from out my heart.
> With mine own tears I wash away my balm,
> With mine own hands I give away my crown,
> With mine own tongue deny my sacred state,
> With mine own breath release all duteous oaths.
> All pomp and majesty I do forswear.
> My manors, rents, revenues I forgo.
> My acts, decrees, and statutes I deny.
>
> (lines 194–203)

Richard's actions and words here are meant to recall a coronation ceremony, in which the king is invested with the crown and scepter as his insignia of office, anointed with balm as a sign that he is God's chosen, promised the allegiance of his subjects, given formal title to the royal domains. One of the main points of this ceremony is its permanence: it cannot be undone. By referring to this ritual at the moment of his deposition, Richard implies that giving up the crown is an impossible act, a kind of absurdity. Moreover, reversing the ceremonies—taking off the crown rather than putting it on, relinquishing rather than accepting the scepter—suggests a special scandal. In medieval and early modern Europe, as among some fundamentalist religious groups today, reversing beneficent ceremonies supposedly evoked their diabolical opposites. One called up devils by reciting Scripture passages backward, or bound oneself to Satan by performing an inversion of baptismal rites. Richard's enthusiastic self-dramatization of his plight does not quell doubts about the legitimacy of the usurpation, but encourages those doubts. Immediately after Richard departs, his friends begin to conspire on his behalf; and although their plot is eventually crushed, Henry's reign will never be quiet thereafter.

As the play proceeds, the view of politics associated with Bolingbroke, a view that initially seems hardheaded and realistic, begins to seem not very practical after all. An acceptable social order requires more than the brute force Henry deploys so expertly. It requires a common set of ideas and practices, a common language and attitude, a set of rituals—all the immaterial abstractions Henry had originally been inclined to disregard.

Just as Shakespeare, over the course of the play, alters our view of the political dilemma represented by the rebellion, so he manipulates our outlook on its main characters. As soon as Richard has lost his throne, we need no longer evaluate him in terms of his effectiveness as a ruler. Immediately his talents seem more obvious, his faults less reprehensible. Richard's extraordinary poetic and introspective gifts allow him to analyze his own situation with a delicacy and insight of which Bolingbroke is entirely incapable. He is acutely aware of the figure he cuts to the only audience that matters to him, himself; in fact, his self-destructive behavior might be seen as an unconscious quest for the expressive opportunities provided only by misery. Always preoccupied with analogies between kingship and godhead, Richard identifies more and more, as the play

Death of Phaeton. From Antonio Tempesta, *Ovid's "Metamorphoses"* (1606).

continues, with the suffering Christ, consoling himself with the comparison and deriving from it a certain sad grandeur. Obviously Richard's particular strengths are intrinsically connected to his weaknesses, but that does not mean that those strengths are negligible. They are especially hard to ignore in a *play*, in which poetic language, symbolic thought, and the effective deployment of spectacle are central concerns.

Our shifting view of Richard has produced, in both Shakespeare's time and our own, a certain ambiguity as to the play's genre. When Shakespeare's friends and fellow actors compiled his works in the First Folio, they grouped *Richard II* with the history plays—understandably, since it concerns itself with problems of rule and the legitimacy of rulers, is based on historical materials, and inaugurates a series of plays that deals with the reigns of three successive kings. Yet in its earliest printed version the play was called "The Tragedie of Richard II," a title that suggests a focus not on the fate of a nation but on the disastrous career of a fascinating, flawed individual.

Richard's case encourages us to reflect on the way the politics and the values of political life—the dominant concerns of history plays—constrain our evaluation of him. In *Richard II*, Shakespeare uses female characters to suggest the possibility of an alternative perspective on the events he depicts. In the second scene, the Duchess of Gloucester urges Gaunt to revenge Thomas of Woodstock, her husband and his brother. Gaunt refuses: in his view, the subject's duty to his monarch must outweigh his obligation to his kin. Their conversation reminds us that England's political crisis is also a familial disaster, and that construing it as one rather than the other has important consequences.

Throughout the play, the men, like Gaunt, tend to subordinate domestic concerns to civic ones, family bonds to the all-important relationship between king and subject. The women, like the Duchess of Gloucester, do the opposite. Although the historical Richard was married to a ten-year-old queen, Shakespeare makes Isabella a mature young woman and invents touching, wholly nonfactual scenes in which she intuitively senses her husband's trouble, then discovers the usurpation in a garden and suffers through an imposed parting from her husband. The pathos of these scenes derives from the Queen's utter helplessness. She is imagined as Richard's wife, a domestic function, not England's Queen, a public one. All her responses are thus founded on her singleminded loyalty to the marital tie, as sharply distinguished from the bonds of politics. "Banish us both, and send the King with me," she begs Northumberland, when he informs them that she will be exiled and her husband kept under house arrest in England. "That were some love, but little policy," Northumberland replies (5.1.83, 84). The last thing Bolingbroke needs is a legitimate child of Richard's to confuse his claims on the throne even more. But the Queen fails to grasp Northumberland's meaning, because she does not understand "policy"—that is, politics. It is not her sphere.

The difference between civic and domestic domains also appears in the scenes immediately following, which stage a dispute between the Duke and Duchess of York over their son, Aumerle. Here again Shakespeare altered his sources, unhistorically making Aumerle an only child and the Duchess his natural mother. Having discovered that Aumerle is involved in a plot to kill the new Henry IV and reinstate Richard, York feels bound to inform Henry of the treason. He puts what he sees as his civic duty above the ties of blood. The Duchess is outraged. "Wilt thou not hide the trespass of thine own?" she asks. "Have we more sons? Or are we like to have?" (5.2.89–90). For her, the familial relationship takes precedence over the public one.

This dividing of the "public" male role from the "private" female role is hardly a Shakespearean invention. But Shakespeare puts that division of perspective to thematic use in *Richard II*. In 2.2, when Isabella has a presentiment of ruin, Bushy tries to console her in an elaborate speech about perspective glasses and "anamorphic" paintings. These two Renaissance inventions encourage speculation about the difference between the "right" or "centered" way of seeing and an oblique outlook from which shapes look very different. Of course, Isabella's inexplicable presentiment of disaster turns out to be more apt than her male companions' optimism. Perhaps the women's different perspective implies that the history play's focus on traditionally masculine political concerns may exclude whole realms of human experience.

In the fifth act, Richard—weeping, enclosed, suffering, and excluded from authority—finds himself in the position the play has defined as a feminine one. Politically marginalized, he nonetheless dominates the closing moments of the play, first by his powerful soliloquizing and later by his courageous defiance of his murderers. In some respects, the final scenes of *Richard II* recall its opening. What seems to be a simple opposition turns out to be far more complex, as categories of expedience and impracticality, power and weakness, right and wrong mutate and change places. Once again, the apparent conclusion of a conflict merely postpones its resolution. The *Henry IV* plays will stage the aftermath.

KATHARINE EISAMAN MAUS

TEXTUAL NOTE

The first printed version of *Richard II* was a Quarto published in 1597 (Q1). The quality of the text is good, and most scholars have assumed that it was printed either directly from Shakespeare's manuscript or (because the stage directions are very brief) from a transcript of Shakespeare's manuscript not designed to provide the basis for theatrical performance. Two more Quartos, printed in 1598 (Q2 and Q3), mention Shakespeare as the author of the play on their title pages. In 1608, a fourth Quarto appeared (Q4), and in 1615, a fifth (Q5); each Quarto seems based on the one that had appeared before it. However, Q4 was the first to print the "new additions of the parliament scene, and the deposing of King Richard," scenes not present in the earlier Quartos.

The First Folio of 1623 (F) text was probably printed with reference to a promptbook, because it has much more detailed stage directions than the quarto texts. Editors disagree, however, over whether this promptbook text was based on Shakespeare's manuscript or on a corrected copy of Q1 or Q3. F includes a version of the abdication scene that is different, and better, than the one in Q4 and Q5. F omits some lines that are present in Q1, and there are also a number of single-word divergences between the two texts. In cases where only a single line is missing, the deletion may represent a compositor's error, so the Oxford editors have followed Q1. In cases where more substantial passages have been excluded, the editors assume that Shakespeare himself was responsible; these passages are indented in the text.

The most important difference between Q1 and F is F's inclusion of the deposition scene. Some scholars have argued that Elizabeth's censors considered the passage too provocative to stage and insisted that it be deleted; after Elizabeth's death, it was possible to reinstate the offending material. Others argue that Shakespeare revised the play during the first decade of the seventeenth century and wrote the deposition scene at that time.

The Oxford editors have generally based their text on Q1, except for the deposition scene, where they have followed F. They have, however, assimilated many of F's more complete stage directions and many of its single-word variants from Q1, when in the editors' opinion those variants represent Shakespeare's revisions to his own text rather than compositorial corruptions.

SELECTED BIBLIOGRAPHY

Calderwood, James L. "*Richard II* and the Fall of Speech." *Shakespearean Metadrama: The Argument of the Play in "Titus Andronicus," "Love's Labour's Lost," "Romeo and Juliet," and "Richard II."* Minneapolis: University of Minnesota Press, 1971. 149–86. The transfer of power from Richard to Bolingbroke as a version of Shakespeare's move from lyric stylization to a sparer dramatic language.

Doran, Madeline. "Imagery in *Richard II* and *Henry IV*." *Modern Language Review* 37 (1942): 113–22. Changes in handling metaphor and simile as key to the differences between *Richard II* and *Henry IV, Part 1*.

Gaudet, Paul. "The 'Parasitical Counselors' in Shakespeare's *Richard II*: A Problem in Dramatic Interpretation." *Shakespeare Quarterly* 33 (1982): 142–54. Bushy, Bagot, and Greene: innocent or guilty?

Hamilton, Donna. "The State of Law in *Richard II*." *Shakespeare Quarterly* 34 (1983): 5–17. The relation between monarchy and law in *Richard II* and in early modern political theory.

Kantorowicz, Ernst H. Chapter 2. *The King's Two Bodies: A Study in Mediaeval Political Theology*. Princeton: Princeton University Press, 1957. 24–41. Theory of kingship in *Richard II*.

Kastan, David. "Proud Majesty Made a Subject: Shakespeare and the Spectacle of Rule." *Shakespeare Quarterly* 37 (1986): 459–75. Theatrical representation destabilizes kingship in *Richard II*.

McMillin, Scott. "*Richard II*: Eyes of Sorrow, Eyes of Desire." *Shakespeare Quarterly* 35 (1984): 40–52. An impulse to self-expressiveness is at odds with the exercise of political power in *Richard II*.

Moore, Jeanie Grant. "Queen of Sorrow, King of Grief: Reflections and Perspectives in *Richard II*." *In Another Country: Feminist Perspectives on Renaissance Drama*. Ed. Dorothea Kehler and Susan Baker. Metuchen, N.J.: Scarecrow Press, 1991. 19–35. Special attention to imagery of mirrors and anamorphic pictures.

Saccio, Peter. *Shakespeare's English Kings: History, Chronicle, and Drama*. 2nd ed. New York: Oxford University Press, 2000. 17–35. Succinct account of the historical background to Shakespeare's play.

Tillyard, E. M. W. *Shakespeare's History Plays*. London: Chatto & Windus, 1944. 244–63. *Richard II* shows the transition from the medieval to the modern world.

Zitner, Sheldon. "Aumerle's Conspiracy." *Studies in English Literature* 14 (1974): 238–57. The importance of the Aumerle scenes for the end of *Richard II*.

FILM

King Richard the Second. 1978. Dir. David Giles, UK. 158 mins. In this BBC-TV production, Derek Jacobi as an effeminate Richard II confronts Jon Finch as the calculating Bolingbroke. John Gielgud is a notable John of Gaunt.

The Tragedy of King Richard
the Second

The Persons of the Play

KING RICHARD II
The QUEEN, his wife
JOHN OF GAUNT, Duke of Lancaster, Richard's uncle
Harry BOLINGBROKE, Duke of Hereford, John of Gaunt's son,
   later KING HENRY IV
DUCHESS OF GLOUCESTER, widow of Gaunt's and York's brother
Duke of YORK, King Richard's uncle
DUCHESS OF YORK
Duke of AUMERLE, their son
Thomas MOWBRAY, Duke of Norfolk
GREEN ⎫
BAGOT ⎬ followers of King Richard
BUSHY ⎭
Percy, Earl of NORTHUMBERLAND ⎫
HARRY PERCY, his son   ⎬ of Bolingbroke's party
Lord ROSS   ⎪
Lord WILLOUGHBY   ⎭
Earl of SALISBURY ⎫
BISHOP OF CARLISLE ⎬ of King Richard's party
Sir Stephen SCROPE ⎭
Lord BERKELEY
Lord FITZWALTER
Duke of SURREY
ABBOT OF WESTMINSTER
Sir Piers EXTON
LORD MARSHAL
HERALDS
CAPTAIN of the Welsh army
LADIES attending the Queen
GARDENER
Gardener's MEN
Exton's MEN
KEEPER of the prison at Pomfret
GROOM of King Richard's stable
Lords, soldiers, attendants

1.1

Enter KING RICHARD, JOHN OF GAUNT, *with* [*the* LORD
MARSHAL], *other nobles, and attendants*
KING RICHARD Old John of Gaunt,[1] time-honoured Lancaster,
   Hast thou according to thy oath and bond
   Brought hither Henry Hereford, thy bold son,
   Here to make good the boist'rous late appeal,°   *violent recent accusation*

1.1. Location: Windsor Castle.
1. Named after his birthplace, Ghent (in Flanders); his title was Duke of Lancaster. He was fifty-eight years old.

5   Which then our leisure² would not let us hear,
    Against the Duke of Norfolk, Thomas Mowbray?
    JOHN OF GAUNT   I have, my liege.
    KING RICHARD   Tell me moreover, hast thou sounded° him   *inquired of*
    If he appeal the Duke on ancient malice³
10 Or worthily, as a good subject should,
    On some known ground of treachery in him?
    JOHN OF GAUNT   As near as I could sift° him on that argument,°   *discover from / topic*
    On some apparent° danger seen in him   *manifest*
    Aimed at your highness, no inveterate malice.
    KING RICHARD   Then call them to our presence.
                                                    [*Exit one or more*]
15   Face to face
    And frowning brow to brow, ourselves will hear
    The accuser and the accusèd freely speak.
    High-stomached° are they both and full of ire;   *Haughty*
    In rage, deaf as the sea, hasty as fire.
            Enter BOLINGBROKE [*Duke of Hereford*], *and* MOWBRAY
            [*Duke of Norfolk*]
20 BOLINGBROKE   Many years of happy days befall
    My gracious sovereign, my most loving liege!
    MOWBRAY   Each day still better others' happiness,⁴
    Until the heavens, envying earth's good hap,°   *fortune*
    Add an immortal title to your crown!
25 KING RICHARD   We thank you both. Yet one but flatters us,
    As well appeareth by the cause you come,
    Namely, to appeal each other of high treason.
    Cousin of Hereford, what dost thou object°   *charge*
    Against the Duke of Norfolk, Thomas Mowbray?
30 BOLINGBROKE   First—heaven be the record to my speech—
    In the devotion of a subject's love,
    Tend'ring° the precious safety of my Prince,   *Having care for*
    And free from other misbegotten hate,
    Come I appellant° to this princely presence.   *as accuser*
35 Now, Thomas Mowbray, do I turn to thee;
    And mark my greeting° well, for what I speak   *address*
    My body shall make good upon this earth,
    Or my divine° soul answer it in heaven.   *Immortal*
    Thou art a traitor and a miscreant,
40 Too good° to be so, and too bad to live,   *wellborn*
    Since the more fair and crystal is the sky,
    The uglier seem the clouds that in it fly.
    Once more, the more to aggravate the note,°   *emphasize the reproach*
    With a foul traitor's name stuff I thy throat,
45 And wish, so please my sovereign, ere I move
    What my tongue speaks my right-drawn sword may prove.
    MOWBRAY   Let not my cold words here accuse my zeal.°   *cast doubt on my loyalty*
    'Tis not the trial of a woman's war,
    The bitter clamour of two eager° tongues,   *sharp*
50 Can arbitrate⁵ this cause betwixt us twain.
    The blood is hot that must be cooled for this.

---

2. That is, lack of leisure. Richard uses the royal "we."   4. May each day be better than the last.
3. Out of long-standing enmity.   5. Judge (without implying compromise).

Yet can I not of such tame patience boast
As to be hushed and naught at all to say.
First, the fair reverence of your highness curbs me
55 From giving reins and spurs to my free speech,
Which else would post° until it had returned   *ride fast*
These terms of treason doubled down his throat.
Setting aside his high blood's royalty,[6]
And let him be° no kinsman to my liege,   *And as if he were*
60 I do defy him, and I spit at him,
Call him a slanderous coward and a villain;
Which to maintain I would allow him odds,
And meet him, were I tied° to run afoot   *obliged*
Even to the frozen ridges of the Alps,
65 Or any other ground inhabitable,
Wherever Englishman durst set his foot.
Meantime let this defend my loyalty:
By all my hopes, most falsely doth he lie.
BOLINGBROKE [*throwing down his gage*][7] Pale trembling coward,
      there I throw my gage,
70 Disclaiming here the kindred of[8] the King,
And lay aside my high blood's royalty,
Which fear, not reverence, makes thee to except.°   *set aside*
If guilty dread have left thee so much strength
As to take up mine honour's pawn,° then stoop.   *(the gage)*
75 By that, and all the rites of knighthood else,
Will I make good against thee, arm to arm,
What I have spoke or thou canst worse devise.
MOWBRAY [*taking up the gage*]   I take it up,[9] and by that sword I swear
      Which gently laid my knighthood on my shoulder,
80 I'll answer thee in any fair degree°   *honorable manner*
Or chivalrous design of knightly trial;
And when I mount, alive may I not light°   *dismount*
If I be traitor or unjustly fight!
KING RICHARD [*to* BOLINGBROKE]   What doth our cousin lay to
      Mowbray's charge?
85 It must be great that can inherit us°   *make us have*
So much as of a thought of ill in him.
BOLINGBROKE   Look what I speak, my life shall prove it true:
That Mowbray hath received eight thousand nobles°   *gold coins*
In name of lendings° for your highness' soldiers,   *As advances on pay*
90 The which he hath detained for lewd employments,°   *improper uses*
Like a false traitor and injurious villain.
Besides I say, and will in battle prove,
Or° here or elsewhere, to the furthest verge°   *Either / horizon*
That ever was surveyed by English eye,
95 That all the treasons for these eighteen years[1]
Complotted° and contrivèd in this land   *Plotted*
Fetch° from false Mowbray their first head° and spring.   *Derive / source*
Further I say, and further will maintain
Upon his bad life, to make all this good,

---

6. Bolingbroke as well as Richard was a grandson of
Edward III.
7. Pledge to combat—probably a glove.

8. The privilege of kinship with.
9. Thereby accepting the challenge.
1. Since the Peasants' Revolt of 1381.

100   That he did plot the Duke of Gloucester's death,[2]
    Suggest° his soon-believing° adversaries,   *Incite / credulous*
    And consequently,° like a traitor-coward,   *subsequently*
    Sluiced° out his innocent soul through streams of blood;   *Let flow*
    Which blood, like sacrificing Abel's,[3] cries
105   Even from the tongueless caverns of the earth
    To me for justice and rough chastisement.
    And, by the glorious worth of my descent,
    This arm shall do it or this life be spent.
    KING RICHARD   How high a pitch[4] his resolution soars!
110   Thomas of Norfolk, what sayst thou to this?
    MOWBRAY   O, let my sovereign turn away his face,
    And bid his ears a little while be deaf,
    Till I have told this slander of his blood°   *disgrace to his ancestry*
    How God and good men hate so foul a liar!
115   KING RICHARD   Mowbray, impartial are our eyes and ears.
    Were he my brother, nay, my kingdom's heir,
    As he is but my father's brother's son,
    Now by my sceptre's awe I make a vow
    Such neighbour-nearness to our sacred blood
120   Should nothing privilege him, nor partialize°   *bias*
    The unstooping firmness of my upright soul.
    He is our subject, Mowbray; so art thou.
    Free speech and fearless I to thee allow.
    MOWBRAY   Then, Bolingbroke, as low as to thy heart
125   Through the false passage of thy throat thou liest!
    Three parts of that receipt° I had for Calais   *money received*
    Disbursed I duly to his highness' soldiers.
    The other part reserved I by consent,
    For that my sovereign liege was in my debt
130   Upon remainder of a dear account[5]
    Since last I went to France to fetch his queen.
    Now swallow down that lie. For Gloucester's death,
    I slew him not, but to my own disgrace
    Neglected my sworn duty in that case.[6]
135   For you, my noble lord of Lancaster,
    The honourable father to my foe,
    Once did I lay an ambush for your life,
    A trespass that doth vex my grievèd soul;
    But ere I last received the Sacrament
140   I did confess it, and exactly° begged   *expressly*
    Your grace's pardon, and I hope I had it.
    This is my fault. As for the rest appealed,°   *accused*
    It issues from the rancour of a villain,
    A recreant° and most degenerate° traitor,   *faithless / cowardly*
145   Which in myself° I boldly will defend,   *my own person*
          [*He throws down his gage*]
    And interchangeably° hurl down my gage   *reciprocally*

---

2. Thomas of Woodstock, Duke of Gloucester, was mysteriously murdered while in the custody of Mowbray. Richard had reason to hate him; earlier Woodstock had attempted to curtail the young King's power by placing authority in the hands of a royal council, of which Woodstock was the head.
3. In Genesis 4, Cain murders his brother Abel

because God prefers Abel's offering of sheep to Cain's fruits of the ground.
4. Highest point of a falcon's flight.
5. For the balance of a large sum.
6. Mowbray is circumspect here; in the next scene, Gaunt and the Duchess assert less ambiguously that Richard ordered him to kill Woodstock.

Upon this overweening traitor's foot,
To prove myself a loyal gentleman
Even in the best blood chambered° in his bosom;   *enclosed*
150 In haste whereof° most heartily I pray   *To hasten which*
Your highness to assign our trial day.
[BOLINGBROKE *takes up the gage*]
KING RICHARD   Wrath-kindled gentlemen, be ruled by me.
Let's purge this choler without letting blood.[7]
This we prescribe, though no physician:
155 Deep malice[8] makes too deep incision;
Forget, forgive, conclude,° and be agreed;   *come to terms*
Our doctors say this is no time to bleed.
Good uncle, let this end where it begun.
We'll calm the Duke of Norfolk, you your son.
160 JOHN OF GAUNT   To be a make-peace shall become my age.
Throw down, my son, the Duke of Norfolk's gage.[9]
KING RICHARD   And, Norfolk, throw down his.
JOHN OF GAUNT   When, Harry, when?
Obedience bids I should not bid again.
KING RICHARD   Norfolk, throw down! We bid; there is no boot.°   *help for it*
165 MOWBRAY [*kneeling*]   Myself I throw, dread sovereign, at thy foot.
My life thou shalt command, but not my shame.
The one my duty owes, but my fair name,
Despite of death that lives upon my grave,
To dark dishonour's use thou shalt not have.
170 I am disgraced, impeached, and baffled[1] here,
Pierced to the soul with slander's venomed spear,
The which no balm can cure but his heart blood
Which breathed° this poison.   *uttered*
KING RICHARD   Rage must be withstood.
Give me his gage. Lions make leopards tame.[2]
175 MOWBRAY [*standing*]   Yea, but not change his spots.[3] Take but my shame,
And I resign my gage. My dear dear lord,
The purest treasure mortal times° afford   *earthly lives*
Is spotless reputation; that away,
Men are but gilded loam, or painted clay.
180 A jewel in a ten-times barred-up chest
Is a bold spirit in a loyal breast.
Mine honour is my life. Both grow in one.°   *united*
Take honour from me, and my life is done.
Then, dear my liege, mine honour let me try.°   *put to the test*
185 In that I live, and for that will I die.
KING RICHARD   Cousin, throw down your gage. Do you begin.
BOLINGBROKE   O God defend my soul from such deep sin!
Shall I seem crest-fallen in my father's sight?
Or with pale beggar-fear impeach my height°   *disgrace my rank*
190 Before this out-dared dastard?° Ere my tongue   *coward*
Shall wound my honour with such feeble wrong,
Or sound so base a parle,° my teeth shall tear   *trumpet call for a truce*
The slavish motive° of recanting fear,   *instrument (the tongue)*

---

7. Let's expel the bile (thought to be the physiological cause of anger) without bloodletting (in combat; as a medical remedy).
8. Enmity; virulence (of a disease).
9. As a gesture of reconciliation.

1. Publicly stripped of knighthood (a chivalric term).
2. Lions were the King's emblem; leopards were Mowbray's. Heraldic banners are likely to be displayed onstage in this scene.
3. Leopard spots; stains of reproach.

And spit it bleeding in his° high disgrace   *its*
195   Where shame doth harbour, even in Mowbray's face.

                                        Exit [JOHN OF] GAUNT

KING RICHARD   We were not born to sue, but to command;
        Which since we cannot do to make you friends,
        Be ready, as your lives shall answer it,
        At Coventry upon Saint Lambert's day.°   *September 17*
200   There shall your swords and lances arbitrate
        The swelling difference of your settled hate.
        Since we cannot atone° you, we shall see   *reconcile*
        Justice design the victor's chivalry.⁴
        Lord Marshal, command our officers-at-arms
205   Be ready to direct these home alarms.°   *Exeunt*   *domestic disturbances*

                                        1.2

        Enter JOHN OF GAUNT [*Duke of Lancaster*], *with*
        DUCHESS OF GLOUCESTER

JOHN OF GAUNT   Alas, the part I had in Gloucester's blood¹
        Doth more solicit me than your exclaims°   *exclamations*
        To stir against the butchers of his life.
        But since correction lieth in² those hands
5   Which made the fault that we cannot correct,
        Put we our quarrel to the will of heaven,
        Who, when they see the hours ripe on earth,
        Will rain hot vengeance on offenders' heads.
DUCHESS OF GLOUCESTER   Finds brotherhood in thee no sharper spur?
10   Hath love in thy old blood no living fire?
        Edward's° seven sons, whereof thyself art one,   *Edward III's*
        Were as seven vials of his sacred blood,
        Or seven fair branches springing from one root.
        Some of those seven are dried by nature's course,
15   Some of those branches by the destinies cut;
        But Thomas, my dear lord, my life, my Gloucester,
        One vial full of Edward's sacred blood,
        One flourishing branch of his most royal root,
        Is cracked, and all the precious liquor spilt;
20   Is hacked down, and his summer leaves all faded
        By envy's° hand and murder's bloody axe.   *hatred's*
        Ah, Gaunt, his blood was thine! That bed, that womb,
        That mettle,° that self° mould that fashioned thee,   *substance / same*
        Made him a man; and though thou liv'st and breathest,
25   Yet art thou slain in him. Thou dost consent
        In some large measure to thy father's death
        In that thou seest thy wretched brother die,
        Who was the model of thy father's life.
        Call it not patience, Gaunt, it is despair.
30   In suff'ring thus thy brother to be slaughtered
        Thou show'st the naked° pathway to thy life,   *defenseless; obvious*
        Teaching stern murder how to butcher thee.
        That which in mean° men we entitle patience   *common*
        Is pale cold cowardice in noble breasts.

---

4. Indicate the victor in knightly combat.   Gaunt's younger brother.
1.2 Location: John of Gaunt's house.   2. Since punishment depends on (Gaunt blames
1. Thomas of Woodstock, Duke of Gloucester, was   Richard for Woodstock's death).

35 What shall I say? To safeguard thine own life
The best way is to venge° my Gloucester's death. *avenge*
JOHN OF GAUNT   God's is the quarrel; for God's substitute,
His deputy anointed in his sight,
Hath caused his death; the which if wrongfully,
40 Let heaven revenge, for I may never lift
An angry arm against his minister.° *agent*
DUCHESS OF GLOUCESTER   Where then, alas, may I complain myself?
JOHN OF GAUNT   To God, the widow's champion and defence.
DUCHESS OF GLOUCESTER   Why then, I will. Farewell, old Gaunt.
45 Thou goest to Coventry, there to behold
Our cousin° Hereford and fell° Mowbray fight. *Kinsman / ruthless*
O, set my husband's wrongs on Hereford's spear,
That it may enter butcher Mowbray's breast!
Or if misfortune miss the first career,³
50 Be Mowbray's sins so heavy in his bosom
That they may break his foaming courser's back
And throw the rider headlong in the lists,
A caitiff,° recreant° to my cousin Hereford! *A wretch / yielding*
Farewell, old Gaunt. Thy sometimes° brother's wife *former*
55 With her companion, grief, must end her life.
JOHN OF GAUNT   Sister, farewell. I must to Coventry.
As much good stay with thee as go with me.
DUCHESS OF GLOUCESTER   Yet one word more. Grief boundeth⁴
    where it falls,
Not with the empty hollowness, but weight.⁵
60 I take my leave before I have begun,
For sorrow ends not when it seemeth done.
Commend me to thy brother, Edmund York.
Lo, this is all.—Nay, yet depart not so!
Though this be all, do not so quickly go.
65 I shall remember more. Bid him—ah, what?—
With all good speed at Pleshey⁶ visit me.
Alack, and what shall good old York there see
But empty lodgings° and unfurnished walls, *rooms*
Unpeopled offices,° untrodden stones, *servants' quarters*
70 And what hear there for welcome but my groans?
Therefore commend me; let him not come there
To seek out sorrow that dwells everywhere.
Desolate, desolate will I hence and die.
The last leave of thee takes my weeping eye. *Exeunt [severally]°* *separately*

1.3

Enter LORD MARSHAL *[with officers setting out chairs],*
and Duke [of] AUMERLE

LORD MARSHAL   My lord Aumerle, is Harry Hereford armed?
AUMERLE   Yea, at all points,° and longs to enter in. *completely*
LORD MARSHAL   The Duke of Norfolk, sprightfully° and bold, *spiritedly*
Stays° but the summons of the appellant's° trumpet. *Awaits / accuser's*
5 AUMERLE   Why then, the champions are prepared, and stay
For nothing but his majesty's approach.

3. If (Mowbray's) downfall fail to occur at the first
encounter.
4. Rebounds (causing further sound; the Duchess
apologizes for continuing to speak).

5. Not because it is hollow, like a bouncing ball, but
because it is heavy.
6. Gloucester's house in Essex.
1.3 Location: The lists (tournament arena) at Coventry.

The trumpets sound, and KING [RICHARD] *enters with*
[JOHN OF] GAUNT, BUSHY, BAGOT, GREEN, *and other*
nobles. When they are set, enter MOWBRAY *Duke of Nor-*
folk, defendant, in arms, and a HERALD [*to Mowbray*]

KING RICHARD   Marshal, demand of yonder champion
The cause of his arrival here in arms.
Ask him his name, and orderly° proceed   according to the rules
10   To swear him in the justice of his cause.
LORD MARSHAL [*to* MOWBRAY]   In God's name and the King's,
    say who thou art,
And why thou com'st thus knightly clad in arms,
Against what man thou com'st, and what thy quarrel.
Speak truly on thy knighthood and thy oath,
15   As so defend thee heaven and thy valour!
MOWBRAY   My name is Thomas Mowbray, Duke of Norfolk,
Who hither come engagèd by my oath—
Which God defend° a knight should violate—   forbid
Both to defend my loyalty and truth
20   To God, my king, and my succeeding issue,
Against the Duke of Hereford that appeals me;
And by the grace of God and this mine arm
To prove him, in defending of myself,
A traitor to my God, my king, and me.
25   And as I truly fight, defend me heaven!
    [*He sits.*]
    The trumpets sound. Enter [BOLINGBROKE] *Duke of*
    Hereford, appellant, in armour, and HERALD
KING RICHARD   Marshal, ask yonder knight in arms
Both who he is and why he cometh hither
Thus plated in habiliments of war;[1]
And formally, according to our law,
30   Depose° him in the justice of his cause.   Take testimony from
LORD MARSHAL [*to* BOLINGBROKE]   What is thy name? And
    wherefore com'st thou hither
Before King Richard in his royal lists?
Against whom comest thou? And what's thy quarrel?
Speak like a true knight, so defend thee heaven!
35   BOLINGBROKE   Harry of Hereford, Lancaster, and Derby
Am I, who ready here do stand in arms
To prove by God's grace and my body's valour
In lists on Thomas Mowbray, Duke of Norfolk,
That he is a traitor foul and dangerous
40   To God of heaven, King Richard, and to me.
And as I truly fight, defend me heaven!
    [*He sits*]
LORD MARSHAL   On pain of death, no person be so bold
Or daring-hardy as to touch the lists
Except the Marshal and such officers
45   Appointed to direct these fair designs.°   procedures
BOLINGBROKE [*standing*]   Lord Marshal, let me kiss my sovereign's hand
And bow my knee before his majesty,
For Mowbray and myself are like two men
That vow a long and weary pilgrimage;

---

1. Wearing plated battle armor.

50   Then let us take a ceremonious leave
    And loving farewell of our several° friends.   *respective*
    LORD MARSHAL [*to* KING RICHARD]   The appellant in all duty
        greets your highness,
    And craves to kiss your hand and take his leave.
    KING RICHARD   We will descend and fold him in our arms.
        [*He descends from his seat and embraces* BOLINGBROKE]
55   Cousin of Hereford, as° thy cause is just,   *insofar as*
    So be thy fortune in this royal fight.
    Farewell, my blood, which if today thou shed,
    Lament we may, but not revenge thee dead.
    BOLINGBROKE   O, let no noble eye profane° a tear   *misuse*
60   For me if I be gored with Mowbray's spear.
    As confident as is the falcon's flight
    Against a bird do I with Mowbray fight.
    [*To the* LORD MARSHAL] My loving lord, I take my leave of you;
    [*To* AUMERLE] Of you, my noble cousin, Lord Aumerle;
65   Not sick, although I have to do with death,
    But lusty,° young, and cheerly drawing breath.   *vigorous*
    Lo, as at English feasts, so I regreet°   *greet*
    The daintiest[2] last, to make the end most sweet.
    [*To* GAUNT, *kneeling*] O thou, the earthly author of my blood,
70   Whose youthful spirit in me regenerate°   *reborn*
    Doth with a two-fold vigour lift me up
    To reach at victory above my head,
    Add proof° unto mine armour with thy prayers,   *invulnerability*
    And with thy blessings steel° my lance's point,   *harden*
75   That it may enter Mowbray's waxen° coat   *(that is, soft)*
    And furbish new the name of John a Gaunt
    Even in the lusty haviour° of his son.   *conduct*
    JOHN OF GAUNT   God in thy good cause make thee prosperous!
    Be swift like lightning in the execution,
80   And let thy blows, doubly redoubled,
    Fall like amazing° thunder on the casque°   *stupefying / helmet*
    Of thy adverse pernicious enemy.
    Rouse up thy youthful blood, be valiant, and live.
    BOLINGBROKE [*standing*]   Mine innocence and Saint George
        to thrive!
85   MOWBRAY [*standing*]   However God or fortune cast my lot,
    There lives or dies, true to King Richard's throne,
    A loyal, just, and upright gentleman.
    Never did captive with a freer heart
    Cast off his chains of bondage and embrace
90   His golden uncontrolled enfranchisement°   *unrestrained liberation*
    More than my dancing soul doth celebrate
    This feast of battle with mine adversary.
    Most mighty liege, and my companion peers,
    Take from my mouth the wish of happy years.
95   As gentle and as jocund as to jest°   *take part in revels*
    Go I to fight. Truth hath a quiet breast.
    KING RICHARD   Farewell, my lord. Securely° I espy   *Confidently*
    Virtue with valour couchèd[3] in thine eye.—
    Order the trial, Marshal, and begin.

---

2. Finest thing, like a dessert.   3. Lodged; aimed in readiness (like a lance).

100   LORD MARSHAL   Harry of Hereford, Lancaster, and Derby,
       Receive thy lance; and God defend the right!
         [*An officer bears a lance to* BOLINGBROKE]
      BOLINGBROKE   Strong as a tower in hope, I cry 'Amen!'°   *from Psalm 61:3*
      LORD MARSHAL [*to an officer*]   Go bear this lance to Thomas,
       Duke of Norfolk.
         [*An officer bears a lance to* MOWBRAY]
     FIRST HERALD   Harry of Hereford, Lancaster, and Derby
105   Stands here for God, his sovereign, and himself,
       On pain to be found false and recreant,
       To prove the Duke of Norfolk, Thomas Mowbray,
       A traitor to his God, his king, and him,
       And dares him to set forward to the fight.
110   SECOND HERALD   Here standeth Thomas Mowbray, Duke of Norfolk,
       On pain to be found false and recreant,
       Both to defend himself and to approve°   *prove*
       Henry of Hereford, Lancaster, and Derby
       To God his sovereign and to him disloyal,
115   Courageously and with a free desire
       Attending but the signal to begin.
      LORD MARSHAL   Sound trumpets, and set forward combatants!
         [*A charge is sounded.*]
         [KING RICHARD *throws down his warder*]°   *staff*
       Stay, the King hath thrown his warder down.
      KING RICHARD   Let them lay by their helmets and their spears,
120   And both return back to their chairs again.
         [BOLINGBROKE *and* MOWBRAY *disarm and sit*]
       [*To the nobles*] Withdraw with us, and let the trumpets sound
       While we return° these dukes what we decree.   *Until we deliver to*
         A long flourish° [*during which* KING RICHARD *and his*   *extended trumpet call*
         nobles withdraw and hold council, then come forward.
         KING RICHARD *addresses* BOLINGBROKE *and* MOWBRAY]
       Draw near, and list what with our council we have done.
       For that° our kingdom's earth should not be soiled   *Because*
125   With that dear blood which it hath fosterèd,
       And for° our eyes do hate the dire aspect°   *because / spectacle*
       Of civil wounds ploughed up with neighbours' swords,[4]
127.1   *And for we think the eagle-wingèd pride*
          Of sky-aspiring and ambitious thoughts
          With rival-hating envy set on you°   *malice set you on*
          To wake our peace, which in our country's cradle
127.5   *Draws the sweet infant breath of gentle sleep,*
       Which, so roused up with boist'rous untuned drums,
       With harsh-resounding trumpets' dreadful bray,
130   And grating shock of wrathful iron arms,
       Might from our quiet confines fright fair peace
       And make us wade even in our kindred's blood,
       Therefore we banish you our territories.
       You, cousin Hereford, upon pain° of life,   *loss*
135   Till twice five summers have enriched our fields
       Shall not regreet° our fair dominions,   *greet again*
       But tread the stranger° paths of banishment.   *foreign*

---

4. The following indented passage (lines 127.1–127.5) appears in Q1 but not in F. Shakespeare probably deleted it as part of his limited revisions to the text.

BOLINGBROKE   Your will be done. This must my comfort be:
That sun that warms you here shall shine on me,
140 And those his golden beams to you here lent
Shall point on me and gild my banishment.
KING RICHARD   Norfolk, for thee remains a heavier doom,°   *sentence*
Which I with some unwillingness pronounce.
The sly° slow hours shall not determinate°   *stealthy / bring to an end*
145 The dateless limit° of thy dear° exile.   *limitless period / grievous*
The hopeless word of 'never to return'
Breathe I against thee, upon pain of life.
MOWBRAY   A heavy sentence, my most sovereign liege,
And all unlooked-for from your highness' mouth.
150 A dearer merit,° not so deep a maim°   *better reward / an injury*
As to be cast forth in the common air,
Have I deservèd at your highness' hands.
The language I have learnt these forty years,
My native English, now I must forgo,
155 And now my tongue's use is to me no more
Than an unstringèd viol° or a harp,   *six-stringed instrument*
Or like a cunning° instrument cased up,   *skillfully made*
Or, being open, put into his hands
That knows no touch to tune the harmony.
160 Within my mouth you have enjailed my tongue,
Doubly portcullised° with my teeth and lips,   *Shut in by an iron gate*
And dull unfeeling barren ignorance
Is made my jailer to attend on me.
I am too old to fawn upon a nurse,
165 Too far in years to be a pupil now.
What is thy sentence then but speechless death,
Which robs my tongue from breathing native breath?
KING RICHARD   It boots° thee not to be compassionate.°   *helps / sorrowful*
After our sentence, plaining° comes too late.   *lamenting*
170 MOWBRAY   Then thus I turn me from my country's light,
To dwell in solemn shades of endless night.
KING RICHARD   Return again, and take an oath with thee.
[*To both*] Lay on our royal sword your banished hands.
Swear by the duty that you owe to God—
175 Our part therein[5] we banish with yourselves—
To keep the oath that we administer.
You never shall, so help you truth and God,
Embrace each other's love in banishment,
Nor never look upon each other's face,
180 Nor never write, regreet, nor reconcile
This low'ring tempest of your home-bred hate,
Nor never by advisèd° purpose meet   *deliberated*
To plot, contrive, or complot any ill
'Gainst us, our state, our subjects, or our land.
BOLINGBROKE   I swear.
185 MOWBRAY   And I, to keep all this.
BOLINGBROKE   Norfolk, so far as to mine enemy
By this time, had the King permitted us,
One of our souls had wandered in the air,

---

5. Your allegiance to me as God's deputy.

Banished this frail sepulchre of our flesh,
190 As now our flesh is banished from this land.
Confess thy treasons ere thou fly the realm.
Since thou hast far to go, bear not along
The clogging° burden of a guilty soul.   *encumbering*
MOWBRAY   No, Bolingbroke, if ever I were traitor,
195 My name be blotted from the book of life,°   *eternal life*
And I from heaven banished as from hence.
But what thou art, God, thou, and I do know,
And all too soon I fear the King shall rue.
Farewell, my liege. Now no way can I stray:°   *lose my way*
200 Save back to England, all the world's my way.   *Exit*
KING RICHARD   Uncle, even in the glasses° of thine eyes   *windows*
I see thy grievèd heart. Thy sad aspect°   *appearance*
Hath from the number of his banished years
Plucked four away. [*To* BOLINGBROKE] Six frozen winters spent,
205 Return with welcome home from banishment.
BOLINGBROKE   How long a time lies in one little word!
Four lagging winters and four wanton° springs   *luxuriant*
End in a word: such is the breath of kings.
JOHN OF GAUNT   I thank my liege that in regard of me
210 He shortens four years of my son's exile.
But little vantage° shall I reap thereby,   *profit*
For ere the six years that he hath to spend
Can change their moons and bring their times about,
My oil-dried lamp and time-bewasted° light   *extinguished by time*
215 Shall be extinct with age and endless night.
My inch of taper will be burnt and done,
And blindfold[6] death not let me see my son.
KING RICHARD   Why, uncle, thou hast many years to live.
JOHN OF GAUNT   But not a minute, King, that thou canst give.
220 Shorten my days thou canst with sudden sorrow,
And pluck nights from me, but not lend a morrow.
Thou canst help time to furrow me with age,
But stop no wrinkle in his pilgrimage.
Thy word is current° with him for my death,   *valid*
225 But dead, thy kingdom cannot buy my breath.
KING RICHARD   Thy son is banished upon good advice,
Whereto thy tongue a party verdict[7] gave.
Why at our justice seem'st thou then to lour?°   *frown*
JOHN OF GAUNT   Things sweet to taste prove in digestion sour.
230 You urged me as a judge, but I had rather
You would have bid me argue like a father.
Alas, I looked when° some of you should say   *I expected that*
I was too strict to make mine own away,
But you gave leave to my unwilling tongue
235 Against my will to do myself this wrong.[8]
235.1   *O, had't been a stranger, not my child,*
         To smooth° his fault I should have been more mild.   *To gloss over*
         A partial slander° sought I to avoid,   *A suspicion of partiality*
         And in the sentence my own life destroyed.

---

6. Because death's emblem is a hooded figure or an
eyeless skull, and because the dead cannot see.
7. A share in the joint verdict.

8. The following indented passage (lines 235.1–235.4)
appears only in Q1.

KING RICHARD   Cousin, farewell; and uncle, bid him so.
　　　Six years we banish him, and he shall go.
　　　　　　　Flourish. Exeunt [all but AUMERLE, *the* LORD MARSHAL,
　　　　　　　JOHN OF GAUNT, *and* BOLINGBROKE]
AUMERLE [*to* BOLINGBROKE]   Cousin, farewell. What presence
　　　must not know,⁹
　　　From where you do remain° let paper show.　　　　　[*Exit*]　　　　　　stay
LORD MARSHAL [*to* BOLINGBROKE]   My lord, no leave take I, for
240　　　I will ride
　　　As far as land will let me by your side.
JOHN OF GAUNT [*to* BOLINGBROKE]   O, to what purpose dost
　　　thou hoard thy words,
　　　That thou return'st no greeting to thy friends?
BOLINGBROKE   I have too few to take my leave of you,
245　　　When the tongue's office° should be prodigal　　　　　　function
　　　To breathe the abundant dolour of the heart.
JOHN OF GAUNT   Thy grief is but thy absence for a time.
BOLINGBROKE   Joy absent, grief is present for that time.
JOHN OF GAUNT   What is six winters? They are quickly gone.
250　BOLINGBROKE   To men in joy, but grief makes one hour ten.
JOHN OF GAUNT   Call it a travel that thou tak'st for pleasure.
BOLINGBROKE   My heart will sigh when I miscall it so,
　　　Which finds it an enforcèd pilgrimage.
JOHN OF GAUNT   The sullen passage of thy weary steps
255　　　Esteem as foil¹ wherein thou art to set
　　　The precious jewel of thy home return.²
256.1　　　BOLINGBROKE   *Nay, rather every tedious stride I make*
　　　　　Will but remember° what a deal° of world　　　remind me / an extent
　　　　　I wander from the jewels that I love.
　　　　　Must I not serve a long apprenticehood
256.5　　　*To foreign passages, and in the end,*
　　　　　Having my freedom, boast of nothing else
　　　　　But that I was a journeyman³ to grief?
　　　　　JOHN OF GAUNT   *All places that the eye of heaven° visits*　　sun; God's presence
　　　　　Are to a wise man ports and happy havens.
256.10　　　*Teach thy necessity to reason thus;*
　　　　　There is no virtue like necessity.
　　　　　Think not the King did banish thee,
　　　　　But thou the King. Woe doth the heavier sit
　　　　　Where it perceives it is but faintly° borne.　　　　　faintheartedly
256.15　　　*Go, say I sent thee forth to purchase° honour,*　　　　acquire
　　　　　And not the King exiled thee; or suppose
　　　　　Devouring pestilence hangs in our air
　　　　　And thou art flying to a fresher clime.
　　　　　Look what° thy soul holds dear, imagine it　　　　　Whatever
256.20　　　*To lie that way thou goest, not whence thou com'st.*
　　　　　Suppose the singing birds musicians,
　　　　　The grass whereon thou tread'st the presence strewed,⁴
　　　　　The flowers fair ladies, and thy steps no more
　　　　　Than a delightful measure° or a dance;　　　　　　a stately dance

---

9. What you cannot tell me personally because of your
absence.
1. Thin metal against which jewels were set to enhance
their luster.

2. The following indented passage (lines 256.1–256.26)
appears only in Q1.
3. Person who has finished an apprenticeship.
4. The royal presence chamber strewn with rushes.

256.25   *For gnarling° sorrow hath less power to bite*   snarling
                The man that mocks at it and sets it light.°   values it lightly
        BOLINGBROKE   O, who can hold a fire in his hand
                By thinking on the frosty Caucasus,[5]
                Or cloy the hungry edge of appetite
260   By bare imagination of a feast,
                Or wallow naked in December snow
                By thinking on fantastic° summer's heat?   imagined
                O no, the apprehension of the good
                Gives but the greater feeling to the worse.
265   Fell sorrow's tooth doth never rankle° more   irritate
                Than when he bites, but lanceth[6] not the sore.
        JOHN OF GAUNT   Come, come, my son, I'll bring thee on thy way.
                Had I thy youth and cause, I would not stay.°   linger
        BOLINGBROKE   Then England's ground, farewell. Sweet soil, adieu,
270   My mother and my nurse that bears me yet!
                Where'er I wander, boast of this I can:
                Though banished, yet a trueborn Englishman.   *Exeunt*

                                    1.4
                Enter KING [RICHARD] *with* GREEN *and* BAGOT *at one*
                     door, and the Lord AUMERLE *at another*
        KING RICHARD   We did observe.[1]—Cousin Aumerle,
                How far brought you high Hereford on his way?
        AUMERLE   I brought high Hereford, if you call him so,
                But to the next highway, and there I left him.
5   KING RICHARD   And say, what store of parting tears were shed?
        AUMERLE   Faith, none for me,° except the north-east wind,   my part
                Which then grew bitterly against our faces,
                Awaked the sleeping rheum,° and so by chance   tears
                Did grace our hollow parting with a tear.
10   KING RICHARD   What said our cousin when you parted with him?
        AUMERLE   'Farewell.' And for° my heart disdained that my tongue   because
                Should so profane the word, that[2] taught me craft
                To counterfeit oppression of such grief
                That words seemed buried in my sorrow's grave.
15   Marry,° would the word 'farewell' have lengthened hours   Indeed
                And added years to his short banishment,
                He should have had a volume of farewells;
                But since it would not, he had none of me.
        KING RICHARD   He is our cousin, cousin;[3] but 'tis doubt,
20   When time shall call him home from banishment,
                Whether our kinsman come to see his friends.°   relatives
                Ourself and Bushy, Bagot here, and Green
                Observed his courtship to the common people,
                How he did seem to dive into their hearts
25   With humble and familiar courtesy,
                What reverence he did throw away on slaves,
                Wooing poor craftsmen with the craft of smiles
                And patient underbearing° of his fortune,   enduring

---

5. Mountain range between the Black and Caspian seas.   2. His heart. Unwilling to give Hereford good wishes
6. Probes (to release the pus from an abscess).   insincerely, Aumerle pretends to be overwhelmed with
1.4 Location: The court.   grief.
1. The scene begins in mid-conversation; the King is   3 Richard, Bolingbroke, and Aumerle were sons of
replying to a remark by Bagot or Green.   three brothers.

As 'twere to banish their affects with him.[4]
30 Off goes his bonnet° to an oysterwench.   *cap*
A brace of draymen° bid God speed him well,   *A couple of cart drivers*
And had the tribute of his supple knee
With 'Thanks, my countrymen, my loving friends',
As were our England in reversion[5] his,
35 And he our subjects' next degree in hope.
GREEN   Well, he is gone, and with him go these thoughts.
Now for the rebels which stand out in Ireland.
Expedient manage° must be made, my liege,   *Hasty arrangements*
Ere further leisure yield them further means
40 For their advantage and your highness' loss.
KING RICHARD   We will ourself in person to this war,
And for° our coffers with too great a court   *because*
And liberal largess are grown somewhat light,
We are enforced to farm our royal realm,[6]
45 The revenue whereof shall furnish us
For our affairs in hand. If that come short,
Our substitutes° at home shall have blank charters,[7]   *deputies*
Whereto, when they shall know what men are rich,
They shall subscribe them° for large sums of gold,   *write down their names*
50 And send them after to supply our wants;
For we will make for Ireland presently.°   *at once*
      Enter BUSHY
Bushy, what news?
BUSHY   Old John of Gaunt is grievous sick, my lord,
Suddenly taken, and hath sent post-haste
55 To entreat your majesty to visit him.
KING RICHARD   Where lies he?
BUSHY   At Ely House.
KING RICHARD   Now put it, God, in his physician's mind
To help him to his grave immediately.
60 The lining[8] of his coffers shall make coats
To deck our soldiers for these Irish wars.
Come, gentlemen, let's all go visit him.
Pray God we may make haste and come too late!   *Exeunt*

2.1

    Enter JOHN OF GAUNT [*Duke of Lancaster*], *sick,* [*carried*
    in a chair], *with Duke of* YORK
JOHN OF GAUNT   Will the King come, that I may breathe my last
In wholesome counsel to his unstaid° youth?   *unruly*
YORK   Vex not yourself, nor strive not with your breath,
For all in vain comes counsel to his ear.
5 JOHN OF GAUNT   O, but they say the tongues of dying men
Enforce attention, like deep harmony.
Where words are scarce they are seldom spent in vain,
For they breathe truth that breathe their words in pain.
He that no more must say is listened more
10 Than they whom youth and ease have taught to glose.°   *talk speciously*

---

4. As if taking their affections with him into exile.
5. A legal term for property that reverts to the original
owner on the expiring of a contract.
6. To lease the King's right to tax.
7. Documents enabling the King to raise money by

forced loans; the deputies can fill in the blanks with any
amount they see fit.
8. Contents (playing on "lining cloth").
2.1 Location: Ely House.

More are men's ends marked than their lives before.
    The setting sun, and music at the close,
As the last taste of sweets, is sweetest last,
Writ in remembrance more than things long past.

15   Though Richard my life's counsel would not hear,
My death's sad tale may yet undeaf his ear.
    YORK   No, it is stopped with other, flattering sounds,
As praises of whose taste the wise are feared,°   *wary*
Lascivious metres to whose venom sound

20   The open ear of youth doth always listen,
Report of fashions in proud Italy,
Whose manners still° our tardy-apish[1] nation   *always*
Limps after in base imitation.
Where doth the world thrust forth a vanity—

25   So° it be new there's no respect° how vile—   *Provided / regard for*
That is not quickly buzzed into his ears?
Then all too late comes counsel, to be heard
Where will doth mutiny with wit's regard.[2]
Direct not him whose way himself will choose:

30   'Tis breath thou lack'st, and that breath wilt thou lose.
    JOHN OF GAUNT   Methinks I am a prophet new-inspired,
And thus, expiring, do foretell of him.
His rash, fierce blaze of riot° cannot last,   *wastefulness*
For violent fires soon burn out themselves.

35   Small showers last long, but sudden storms are short.
He tires betimes° that spurs too fast betimes.   *soon*
With eager feeding food doth choke the feeder.
Light vanity, insatiate cormorant,[3]
Consuming means, soon preys upon itself.

40   This royal throne of kings, this sceptred isle,
This earth of majesty, this seat of Mars,°   *war god's dwelling*
This other Eden, demi-paradise,
This fortress built by nature for herself
Against infection° and the hand of war,   *disease; depravity*

45   This happy breed of men, this little world,
This precious stone set in the silver sea,
Which serves it in the office° of a wall,   *function*
Or as a moat defensive to a house
Against the envy° of less happier lands;   *malice*

50   This blessèd plot, this earth, this realm, this England,
This nurse, this teeming womb of royal kings,
Feared by their breed[4] and famous by their birth,
Renownèd for their deeds as far from home
For Christian service and true chivalry[5]

55   As is the sepulchre, in stubborn Jewry,[6]
Of the world's ransom, blessèd Mary's son;
This land of such dear souls, this dear dear land,
Dear for her reputation through the world,
Is now leased out—I die pronouncing it—

60   Like to a tenement° or pelting° farm.   *rental property / worthless*
England, bound in with the triumphant sea,

---

1. Imitative but outmoded.
2. Where willfulness overthrows sound judgment.
3. Glutton (literally, a bird that swallows fish whole).
4. For their inherited valor.

5. Alluding to the English kings' accomplishments in the Crusades.
6. Judaea, stubborn in its resistance to Christianity.

Whose rocky shore beats back the envious siege
Of wat'ry Neptune, is now bound in with shame,
With inky blots and rotten parchment bonds.[7]
65   That England that was wont to conquer others
Hath made a shameful conquest of itself.
Ah, would the scandal vanish with my life,
How happy then were my ensuing death!

Enter KING [RICHARD], QUEEN, [*Duke of*] AUMERLE,
BUSHY, GREEN, BAGOT, [*Lord*] ROSS, *and* [*Lord*]
WILLOUGHBY

YORK   The King is come. Deal mildly with his youth,
70   For young hot colts, being reined, do rage the more.
QUEEN   How fares our noble uncle Lancaster?
KING RICHARD   What comfort, man? How is't with agèd Gaunt?
JOHN OF GAUNT   O, how that name befits my composition!°   *constitution*
Old Gaunt indeed, and gaunt in being old.
75   Within me grief hath kept a tedious fast,
And who abstains from meat° that is not gaunt?   *food*
For sleeping England long time have I watched.°   *stayed awake*
Watching breeds leanness, leanness is all gaunt.
The pleasure that some fathers feed upon
80   Is my strict fast: I mean my children's looks.[8]
And therein fasting, hast thou made me gaunt.
Gaunt am I for the grave, gaunt as a grave,
Whose hollow womb inherits naught but bones.
KING RICHARD   Can sick men play so nicely° with their names?   *subtly*
85   JOHN OF GAUNT   No, misery makes sport to mock itself.
Since thou dost seek to kill my name in me,[9]
I mock my name, great King, to flatter thee.
KING RICHARD   Should dying men flatter with those that live?
JOHN OF GAUNT   No, no, men living flatter those that die.
90   KING RICHARD   Thou now a-dying sayst thou flatt'rest me.
JOHN OF GAUNT   O no: thou diest, though I the sicker be.
KING RICHARD   I am in health; I breathe, and see thee ill.
JOHN OF GAUNT   Now He that made me knows I see thee ill:
Ill in myself to see, and in thee seeing ill.[1]
95   Thy deathbed is no lesser than thy land,
Wherein thou liest in reputation sick;
And thou, too careless patient as thou art,
Committ'st thy anointed body to the cure
Of those physicians[2] that first wounded thee.
100   A thousand flatterers sit within thy crown,
Whose compass° is no bigger than thy head,   *circumference*
And yet, encagèd in so small a verge,[3]
The waste[4] is no whit lesser than thy land.
O, had thy grandsire with a prophet's eye
105   Seen how his son's son should destroy his sons,
From forth° thy reach he would have laid thy shame,   *out of*
Deposing thee before thou wert possessed,[5]
Which art possessed° now to depose thyself.   *in a diabolical frenzy*

---

7. Richard's "blank charters."
8. Since Bolingbroke is exiled.
9. Destroy my family (by exiling Bolingbroke).
1. Too ill to see well, and seeing evil in you.
2. Richard's favorites, or his own bad impulses.

3. Area; distance of 12 miles around the court, to which special rules applied.
4. Destruction (specifically, injury done to a property by a tenant); waist, narrowest part.
5. In possession of the crown.

Why, cousin,° wert thou regent° of the world   *kinsman / ruler*
110   It were a shame to let this land by lease.
But, for thy world, enjoying but this land,⁶
Is it not more than shame to shame it so?
Landlord of England art thou now, not king.
Thy state of law⁷ is bondslave to the law,
115   And—
KING RICHARD   And thou, a lunatic lean-witted fool,
Presuming on an ague's privilege,°   *the privilege of the sick*
Dar'st with thy frozen° admonition   *rigid; caused by a chill*
Make pale our cheek, chasing the royal blood
120   With fury from his native residence.°   *its natural place*
Now by my seat's° right royal majesty,   *throne's*
Wert thou not brother to great Edward's son,⁸
This tongue that runs so roundly° in thy head   *freely*
Should run thy head from thy unreverent shoulders.
125   JOHN OF GAUNT   O, spare me not, my brother Edward's son,
For that I was his father Edward's son.
That blood already, like the pelican,⁹
Hast thou tapped out¹ and drunkenly caroused.
My brother Gloucester, plain well-meaning soul—
130   Whom fair befall in heaven 'mongst happy souls—
May be a precedent and witness good
That thou respect'st not spilling° Edward's blood.   *don't hesitate to spill*
Join with the present sickness that I have,
And thy unkindness be like crookèd age,
135   To crop° at once a too-long withered flower.   *cut*
Live in thy shame, but die not shame with thee.²
These words hereafter thy tormentors be.
[*To attendants*] Convey me to my bed, then to my grave.
Love they to live that love and honour have.
Exit [*carried in a chair*]
140   KING RICHARD   And let them die that age and sullens° have,   *sulks*
For both hast thou, and both become the grave.
YORK   I do beseech your majesty impute his words
To wayward sickliness and age in him.
He loves you, on my life, and holds you dear
145   As Harry Duke of Hereford, were he here.
KING RICHARD   Right, you say true: as Hereford's love, so his.³
As theirs, so mine; and all be as it is.
Enter [*Earl of*] NORTHUMBERLAND
NORTHUMBERLAND   My liege, old Gaunt commends him to your majesty.
KING RICHARD   What says he?
NORTHUMBERLAND   Nay, nothing: all is said.
150   His tongue is now a stringless instrument.
Words, life, and all, old Lancaster hath spent.
YORK   Be York the next that must be bankrupt so!
Though death be poor, it ends a mortal woe.
KING RICHARD   The ripest fruit first falls, and so doth he.

---

6. Since this realm alone constitutes your world.
7. Legal status (as landlord, not King).
8. Edward the Black Prince, Edward III's son and Richard's father.
9. A mother pelican was thought to wound her breast so her ungrateful young could feed on her blood.

1. Let run as from a barrel tap.
2. May your shame outlive you.
3. York claims that Gaunt loves Richard as much as he loves his own son; Richard deliberately misconstrues York to mean Gaunt loves Richard as much as Hereford does.

<pre>
155   His time is spent; our pilgrimage must be.°   continue
      So much for that. Now for our Irish wars.
      We must supplant those rough rug-headed kerns,⁴
      Which live like venom where no venom else
      But only they have privilege to live.⁵
160   And for° these great affairs do ask some charge,⁶   because
      Towards our assistance we do seize to us
      The plate, coin, revenues, and movables°   personal property
      Whereof our uncle Gaunt did stand possessed.
  YORK How long shall I be patient? Ah, how long
165   Shall tender° duty make me suffer wrong?   scrupulous
      Not Gloucester's death, nor Hereford's banishment,
      Nor Gaunt's rebukes, nor England's private wrongs,⁷
      Nor the prevention of poor Bolingbroke
      About his marriage,⁸ nor my own disgrace,
170   Have ever made me sour my patient cheek,
      Or bend one wrinkle° on my sovereign's face.   one frown
      I am the last of noble Edward's sons,
      Of whom thy father, Prince of Wales, was first.
      In war was never lion raged more fierce,
175   In peace was never gentle lamb more mild,
      Than was that young and princely gentleman.
      His face thou hast, for even so looked he,
      Accomplished with the number of thy hours.°   When he was your age
      But when he frowned it was against the French,
180   And not against his friends. His noble hand
      Did win what he did spend, and spent not that
      Which his triumphant father's hand had won.
      His hands were guilty of no kindred blood,
      But bloody with the enemies of his kin.
185   O, Richard, York is too far gone with grief,
      Or else he never would compare between.
  KING RICHARD Why uncle, what's the matter?
  YORK   O my liege,
      Pardon me if you please; if not, I, pleased
      Not to be pardoned, am content withal.°   nevertheless
190   Seek you to seize and grip into your hands
      The royalties⁹ and rights of banished Hereford?
      Is not Gaunt dead? And doth not Hereford live?
      Was not Gaunt just? And is not Harry true?
      Did not the one deserve to have an heir?
195   Is not his heir a well-deserving son?
      Take Hereford's rights away, and take from Time
      His° charters and his customary rights   Its
      Let not tomorrow then ensue° today;   follow
      Be not thyself, for how art thou a king
200   But by fair sequence and succession?
      Now afore God—God forbid I say true!—
      If you do wrongfully seize Hereford's rights,
      Call in° the letters patents that he hath   Revoke
</pre>

---

4. Shaggy Irish foot soldiers.
5. Alluding to the legend that St. Patrick drove snakes out of Ireland.
6. Do demand some expenditure.
7. Wrongs committed against private individuals.

8. Richard intervened against Bolingbroke's proposed marriage to the King of France's cousin.
9. Privileges granted by a king through "letters patents" (line 203).

By his attorneys general to sue

205 His livery, and deny his offered homage,[1]
You pluck° a thousand dangers on your head,   *pull*
You lose a thousand well-disposèd hearts,
And prick my tender patience to those thoughts
Which honour and allegiance cannot think.

210 KING RICHARD   Think what you will, we seize into our hands
His plate, his goods, his money, and his lands.
YORK   I'll not be by the while.[2] My liege, farewell.
What will ensue hereof there's none can tell.
But by bad courses may be understood

215 That their events° can never fall out good.   *Exit*   *outcomes*
KING RICHARD   Go, Bushy, to the Earl of Wiltshire straight.
Bid him repair° to us to Ely House   *go*
To see° this business. Tomorrow next   *attend to*
We will for Ireland, and 'tis time, I trow.°   *think*

220 And we create, in absence of ourself,
Our uncle York Lord Governor of England;
For he is just and always loved us well.—
Come on, our Queen; tomorrow must we part.
Be merry, for our time of stay is short.

Flourish. Exeunt KING [RICHARD], QUEEN[, AUMERLE,
GREEN, *and* BAGOT *at one door,* BUSHY *at another door*].
Manent° NORTHUMBERLAND, WILLOUGHBY, *and* ROSS   *Remain*

225 NORTHUMBERLAND   Well, lords, the Duke of Lancaster is dead.
ROSS   And living too, for now his son is Duke.
WILLOUGHBY   Barely in title, not in revenues.
NORTHUMBERLAND   Richly in both, if justice had her right.
ROSS   My heart is great,° but it must break with silence   *full of emotion*

230 Ere't be disburdened with a liberal° tongue.   *unrestrained*
NORTHUMBERLAND   Nay, speak thy mind, and let him ne'er
speak more
That speaks thy words again to do thee harm.
WILLOUGHBY   Tends that that thou wouldst speak to[3] the Duke
of Hereford?
If it be so, out with it boldly, man.

235 Quick is mine ear to hear of good towards him.
ROSS   No good at all that I can do for him,
Unless you call it good to pity him,
Bereft and gelded of his patrimony.
NORTHUMBERLAND   Now afore God, 'tis shame such wrongs are borne

240 In him, a royal prince, and many more
Of noble blood in this declining land.
The King is not himself, but basely led
By flatterers; and what they will inform
Merely in° hate 'gainst any of us all,   *Purely out of*

245 That will the King severely prosecute
'Gainst us, our lives, our children, and our heirs.
ROSS   The commons° hath he pilled° with grievous taxes,   *common people / stripped*
And quite lost their hearts. The nobles hath he fined
For ancient quarrels, and quite lost their hearts.

---

1. The letters patents allow Hereford, through his
legal representatives ("attorneys general"), to make a
legal claim for the inheritance of his land ("sue" for
delivery), provided he swears allegiance to the King

("offers homage").
2. Present during the seizure.
3. Does what you would say concern.

250   WILLOUGHBY   And daily new exactions are devised,
         As blanks, benevolences,° and I wot° not what.   *forced loans / know*
         But what, a' God's name, doth become of this?°   *this money*
       NORTHUMBERLAND   Wars hath not wasted it; for warred he hath not,
         But basely yielded upon compromise
255   That which his ancestors achieved with blows.[4]
         More hath he spent in peace than they in wars.
       ROSS   The Earl of Wiltshire hath the realm in farm.[5]
       WILLOUGHBY   The King's grown bankrupt like a broken man.
       NORTHUMBERLAND   Reproach and dissolution hangeth over him.
260   ROSS   He hath not money for these Irish wars,
         His burdenous taxations notwithstanding,
         But by the robbing of the banished Duke.
       NORTHUMBERLAND   His noble kinsman. Most degenerate King!
         But, lords, we hear this fearful tempest sing,
265   Yet seek no shelter to avoid the storm.
         We see the wind sit sore° upon our sails,   *blow hard*
         And yet we strike[6] not, but securely° perish.   *heedlessly*
       ROSS   We see the very wreck that we must suffer,
         And unavoided° is the danger now   *unavoidable*
270   For suffering° so the causes of our wreck.   *enduring*
       NORTHUMBERLAND   Not so: even through the hollow eyes° of death   *eye sockets*
         I spy life peering; but I dare not say
         How near the tidings of our comfort is.
       WILLOUGHBY   Nay, let us share thy thoughts, as thou dost ours.
275   ROSS   Be confident to speak, Northumberland.
         We three are but thyself, and, speaking so,
         Thy words are but as thoughts. Therefore be bold.
       NORTHUMBERLAND   Then thus. I have from Port le Blanc,
         A bay in Brittaine,[7] received intelligence
280   That Harry Duke of Hereford, Reinold Lord Cobham,
         Thomas son and heir to the Earl of Arundel[8]
         That late broke from the Duke of Exeter,
         His[9] brother, Archbishop late° of Canterbury,   *until recently*
         Sir Thomas Erpingham, Sir Thomas Ramston,
285   Sir John Norbery,
         Sir Robert Waterton, and Francis Coint,
         All these well furnished by the Duke of Brittaine
         With eight tall ships, three thousand men of war,°   *soldiers*
         Are making hither with all due expedience,
290   And shortly mean to touch our northern shore.
         Perhaps they had ere this, but that they stay
         The first departing of the King[1] for Ireland.
         If then we shall shake off our slavish yoke,
         Imp out[2] our drooping country's broken wing,
295   Redeem from broking pawn° the blemished crown,   *pawnbrokers*
         Wipe off the dust that hides our sceptre's gilt,
         And make high majesty look like itself,
         Away with me in post° to Ravenspurgh.[3]   *speedily*

---

4. Referring to the ceding of Brest, a city in western France, to the Duke of Brittany.
5. *in farm:* on lease (as in 1.4.44–46).
6. Lower sails; deliver blows.
7. Brittany, in northwest France.
8. An editorial approximation of a line missing from early texts. Shakespeare's source states that Arundel's son escaped from Exeter's custody.
9. The Earl of Arundel's.
1. *they stay . . . King:* they wait for the King to depart first.
2. Engraft new feathers on (from falconry).
3. Then a port on the river Humber, in Yorkshire.

But if you faint,° as fearing to do so,   *are fainthearted*
300   Stay, and be secret, and myself will go.
  ROSS   To horse, to horse! Urge doubts to them that fear.
  WILLOUGHBY   Hold out my horse,° and I will first be there.   *If my horse holds up*

                                                    Exeunt

2.2

Enter the QUEEN, BUSHY, [*and*] BAGOT
  BUSHY   Madam, your majesty is too much sad.[1]
    You promised when you parted with the King
    To lay aside life-harming heaviness°   *melancholy*
    And entertain° a cheerful disposition.   *assume*
5   QUEEN   To please the King I did; to please myself
    I cannot do it. Yet I know no cause
    Why I should welcome such a guest as grief,
    Save bidding farewell to so sweet a guest
    As my sweet Richard. Yet again, methinks
10   Some unborn sorrow, ripe in fortune's womb,
    Is coming towards me; and my inward soul
    At nothing trembles. With something it grieves
    More than with parting from my lord the King.
  BUSHY   Each substance of a grief hath twenty shadows
15   Which shows like grief itself but is not so.
    For sorrow's eye, glazèd with blinding tears,
    Divides one thing entire to many objects—
    Like perspectives, which, rightly gazed upon,
    Show nothing but confusion; eyed awry,
20   Distinguish form.[2] So your sweet majesty,
    Looking awry upon your lord's departure,
    Find shapes° of grief more than himself to wail,°   *images / bewail*
    Which, looked on as it is, is naught but shadows
    Of what it is not. Then, thrice-gracious Queen,
25   More than your lord's departure weep not: more is not seen,
    Or if it be, 'tis with false sorrow's eye,
    Which for things true weeps things imaginary.
  QUEEN   It may be so, but yet my inward soul
    Persuades me it is otherwise. Howe'er it be,
30   I cannot but be sad: so heavy-sad
    As thought—on thinking on no thought I think[3]–
    Makes me with heavy nothing faint and shrink.
  BUSHY   'Tis nothing but conceit,° my gracious lady.   *imagination*
  QUEEN   'Tis nothing less:[4] conceit is still° derived   *always*
35   From some forefather grief; mine is not so;
    For nothing hath begot my something° grief—   *substantial*
    Or something hath the nothing that I grieve[5]—
    'Tis in reversion that I do possess[6]—

2.2. Location: Windsor Castle.
1. Shakespeare makes Richard's queen a mature young woman; the historical Isabella was married to Richard at seven years and was ten at the time of Bolingbroke's invasion.
2. *For . . . from:* Bushy compares the Queen's eye first to a perspective glass that multiplies one image into many, then to a perspective picture that looks distorted unless viewed at an angle ("awry").
3. *As thought . . . think:* a difficult line. The Oxford

editors adopt the Q1 version, "thought"; other editors adopt the F version, "though," which is hardly less obscure. The Queen is playing with the paradox that her premonition, a thought of nothing, or "no thought," is nonetheless almost physically oppressive.
4. Anything but conceit.
5. Or the grief that I feel apparently over nothing actually has some cause.
6. It will come at a later date (that is, her grief anticipates its occasion).

But what it is that is not yet known what,
40   I cannot name; 'tis nameless woe, I wot.

            Enter GREEN

GREEN   God save your majesty, and well met, gentlemen.
    I hope the King is not yet shipped for Ireland.
QUEEN   Why hop'st thou so? 'Tis better hope he is,
    For his designs crave° haste, his haste good hope.   *need*
45   Then wherefore dost thou hope he is not shipped?
GREEN   That he, our hope, might have retired his power,°   *brought back his forces*
    And driven into despair an enemy's hope,
    Who strongly hath set footing in this land.
    The banished Bolingbroke repeals° himself,   *recalls from exile*
50   And with uplifted arms° is safe arrived   *weapons*
    At Ravenspurgh.
QUEEN   Now God in heaven forbid!
GREEN   Ah madam, 'tis too true! And, that is worse,
    The Lord Northumberland, his son young Harry Percy,
    The Lords of Ross, Beaumont, and Willoughby,
55   With all their powerful friends, are fled to him.
BUSHY   Why have you not proclaimed Northumberland,
    And all the rest, revolted faction-traitors?°   *treasonous conspirators*
GREEN   We have; whereupon the Earl of Worcester
    Hath broke his staff,[7] resigned his stewardship,
60   And all the household servants fled with him
    To Bolingbroke.
QUEEN   So, Green, thou art the midwife to my woe,
    And Bolingbroke my sorrow's dismal heir.
    Now hath my soul brought forth her prodigy,°   *monstrous birth; portent*
65   And I, a gasping new-delivered mother,
    Have woe to woe, sorrow to sorrow joined.
BUSHY   Despair not, madam.
QUEEN   Who shall hinder me?
    I will despair, and be at enmity
    With cozening° hope. He° is a flatterer,   *cheating / (Hope)*
70   A parasite, a keeper-back of death,
    Who° gently would dissolve° the bonds of life,   *(Death) / loosen*
    Which false hope lingers in extremity.

            Enter [Duke of] YORK [wearing a gorget][8]

GREEN   Here comes the Duke of York.
QUEEN   With signs of war about his agèd neck.
75   O, full of careful business° are his looks!   *anxious preoccupation*
    Uncle, for God's sake speak comfortable° words.   *comforting*
YORK   Should I do so, I should belie my thoughts.
    Comfort's in heaven, and we are on the earth,
    Where nothing lives but crosses,° cares, and grief.   *misfortunes*
80   Your husband, he is gone to save far off,
    Whilst others come to make him lose at home.
    Here am I, left to underprop his land,
    Who, weak with age, cannot support myself.
    Now comes the sick hour that his surfeit made.
85   Now shall he try° his friends that flattered him.   *test*

            Enter a [SERVINGMAN]

---

7. Symbolically resigning his office as lord steward of   brother.
the King's household. Worcester is Northumberland's   8. Piece of armor protecting the throat.

SERVINGMAN My lord, your son was gone before I came.

YORK He was? Why so, go all which way it will.

    The nobles they are fled. The commons° they are cold,   *common people*

    And will, I fear, revolt on Hereford's side.

90   Sirrah, get thee to Pleshey, to my sister° Gloucester.   *sister-in-law*

    Bid her send me presently° a thousand pound—   *immediately*

    Hold; take my ring.[9]

SERVINGMAN My lord, I had forgot to tell your lordship,

    Today as I came by I callèd there—

95   But I shall grieve you to report the rest.

YORK What is't, knave?°   *fellow*

SERVINGMAN An hour before I came, the Duchess died.

YORK God for his mercy, what a tide of woes

    Comes rushing on this woeful land at once!

100   I know not what to do. I would to God,

    So my untruth° had not provoked him to it,   *disloyalty*

    The King had cut off my head with my brother's.

    What, are there no posts° dispatched for Ireland?   *fast messengers*

    How shall we do for money for these wars?

105   *[To the* QUEEN*]* Come, sister—cousin, I would say; pray pardon me.[1]

    [To the SERVINGMAN*]* Go, fellow, get thee home. Provide some carts,

    And bring away the armour that is there. *[Exit* SERVINGMAN*]*

    Gentlemen, will you go muster men?

    If I know how or which way to order these affairs

110   Thus disorderly thrust into my hands,

    Never believe me. Both are my kinsmen.

    T'one is my sovereign, whom both my oath

    And duty bids defend; t'other again

    Is my kinsman, whom the King hath wronged,

115   Whom conscience and my kindred bids to right.

    Well, somewhat we must do. *[To the* QUEEN*]* Come, cousin,

    I'll dispose of° you.—   *make arrangements for*

    Gentlemen, go muster up your men,

    And meet me presently at Berkeley Castle.[2]

120   I should to Pleshey too, but time will not permit.

    All is uneven,

    And everything is left at six and seven.°   *in confusion*

        Exeunt Duke [of YORK *and]* QUEEN.

        Manent BUSHY, GREEN *[and* BAGOT*]*

BUSHY The wind sits fair[3] for news to go for Ireland,

    But none returns. For us to levy power

125   Proportionable to the enemy

    Is all unpossible.

GREEN Besides, our nearness to the King in love

    Is near° the hate of those love not the King.   *Implies*

BAGOT And that is the wavering commons; for their love

130   Lies in their purses, and whoso empties them

    By so much fills their hearts with deadly hate.

BUSHY Wherein the King stands generally condemned.

BAGOT If judgement lie in them,° then so do we,   *is in the people's hands*

    Because we ever have been near the King.

---

9. As proof that he comes with York's authorization.   2. In Gloucestershire, in western England.
1. The Duchess's death is uppermost in York's mind.   3. The wind blows from a favorable direction.

135 GREEN   Well, I will for refuge straight to Bristol Castle.
      The Earl of Wiltshire is already there.
   BUSHY   Thither will I with you; for little office°   service
      Will the hateful commoners perform for us,
      Except like curs to tear us all to pieces.
140   [*To* BAGOT] Will you go along with us?
   BAGOT   No, I will to Ireland, to his majesty.
      Farewell: if heart's presages be not vain
      We three here part that ne'er shall meet again.
   BUSHY   That's as York thrives⁴ to beat back Bolingbroke.
145 GREEN   Alas, poor Duke, the task he undertakes
      Is numb'ring sands and drinking oceans dry.
      Where one on his side fights, thousands will fly.
   BAGOT   Farewell at once, for once, for all and ever.
   BUSHY   Well, we may meet again.
   BAGOT   I fear me never.
            Exeunt [BUSHY *and* GREEN *at one door,*
                              and BAGOT *at another door*]

2.3

            Enter [BOLINGBROKE *Duke of Lancaster and*] *Hereford,*
            and [*the Earl of*] NORTHUMBERLAND
   BOLINGBROKE   How far is it, my lord, to Berkeley now?
   NORTHUMBERLAND   Believe me, noble lord,
      I am a stranger here in Gloucestershire.
      These high wild hills and rough uneven ways
5   Draws out our miles and makes them wearisome;
      And yet your fair discourse hath been as sugar,
      Making the hard way sweet and delectable.
      But I bethink me what a weary way
      From Ravenspurgh to Cotswold¹ will be found
10   In° Ross and Willoughby, wanting° your company,   By / lacking
      Which I protest hath very much beguiled
      The tediousness and process° of my travel.   tedious course
      But theirs is sweetened with the hope to have
      The present benefit which I possess;
15   And hope to joy is little less in joy
      Than hope enjoyed. By this° the weary lords   this expectation
      Shall make their way seem short as mine hath done
      By sight of what I have: your noble company.
   BOLINGBROKE   Of much less value is my company
      Than your good words.
            Enter HARRY PERCY
20   But who comes here?
   NORTHUMBERLAND   It is my son, young Harry Percy,²
      Sent from my brother Worcester, whencesoever.°   wherever he may be
      Harry, how fares your uncle?°   Worcester
   HARRY PERCY   I had thought, my lord, to have learned his
            health of you.
25 NORTHUMBERLAND   Why, is he not with the Queen?
   HARRY PERCY   No, my good lord; he hath forsook the court,

4. That depends on York's success.
2.3 Location: Gloucestershire.
1. Hilly part of Gloucestershire.

2. Shakespeare makes Harry Percy, the Hotspur of
1 Henry IV, a boy here; the historical Percy was two
years older than Bolingbroke.

Broken his staff of office, and dispersed
The household of the King.

NORTHUMBERLAND   What was his reason?
He was not so resolved when last we spake together.

30 HARRY PERCY   Because your lordship was proclaimèd traitor.
But he, my lord, is gone to Ravenspurgh
To offer service to the Duke of Hereford,
And sent me over by Berkeley to discover
What power the Duke of York had levied there,
35 Then with directions to repair to Ravenspurgh.

NORTHUMBERLAND   Have you forgot the Duke of Hereford, boy?³

HARRY PERCY   No, my good lord, for that is not forgot
Which ne'er I did remember. To my knowledge,
I never in my life did look on him.

40 NORTHUMBERLAND   Then learn to know him now. This is the Duke.

HARRY PERCY   My gracious lord, I tender you my service,
Such as it is, being tender, raw, and young,
Which elder days shall ripen and confirm
To more approvèd° service and desert.   *more fully demonstrated*

45 BOLINGBROKE   I thank thee, gentle Percy, and be sure
I count myself in nothing else so happy
As in a° soul rememb'ring my good friends;   *my*
And as my fortune ripens with thy love,
It shall be still thy true love's recompense.
50 My heart this covenant makes; my hand thus seals it.
            [*He gives* PERCY *his hand*]

NORTHUMBERLAND   How far is it to Berkeley, and what stir°   *activity*
Keeps good old York there with his men of war?

HARRY PERCY   There stands the castle, by yon tuft of trees,
Manned with three hundred men, as I have heard,
55 And in it are the Lords of York, Berkeley, and Seymour,
None else of name° and noble estimate.°   *title / reputation*
            Enter [*Lord*] ROSS *and* [*Lord*] WILLOUGHBY

NORTHUMBERLAND   Here come the Lords of Ross and Willoughby,
Bloody with spurring, fiery red with haste.

BOLINGBROKE   Welcome, my lords. I wot° your love pursues   *know*
60 A banished traitor. All my treasury
Is yet but unfelt° thanks, which, more enriched,   *immaterial*
Shall be your love and labour's recompense.

ROSS   Your presence makes us rich, most noble lord.

WILLOUGHBY   And far surmounts our labour to attain it.

65 BOLINGBROKE   Evermore thank's the exchequer⁴ of the poor,
Which till my infant fortune comes to years°   *of age*
Stands for° my bounty.   *in place of*
            Enter BERKELEY
                    But who comes here?

NORTHUMBERLAND   It is my lord of Berkeley, as I guess.

BERKELEY   My lord of Hereford, my message is to you.

70 BOLINGBROKE   My lord, my answer is to 'Lancaster',⁵
And I am come to seek that name in England,

---

3. Northumberland scolds his son for not greeting Bo-   5. I only reply to the title of Lancaster (which Richard
lingbroke respectfully.   took away).
4. Gratitude is always the treasury.

And I must find that title in your tongue
Before I make reply to aught you say.
BERKELEY   Mistake me not, my lord, 'tis not my meaning
75   To raze one title of your honour out.
To you, my lord, I come—what lord you will—
From the most gracious regent of this land,
The Duke of York, to know what pricks you on°   *incites you*
To take advantage of the absent time°   *time of absence*
80   And fright our native peace with self-borne⁶ arms.
        Enter [Duke of] YORK
BOLINGBROKE   I shall not need transport my words by you.
Here comes his grace in person.—My noble uncle!
        [He kneels]
YORK   Show me thy humble heart, and not thy knee,
Whose duty is deceivable° and false.   *deceptive*
85   BOLINGBROKE   My gracious uncle—
YORK   Tut, tut, grace me no grace, nor uncle me no uncle.
I am no traitor's uncle, and that word 'grace'
In an ungracious mouth is but profane.
Why have those banished and forbidden legs
90   Dared once to touch a dust° of England's ground?   *speck*
But then more 'why': why have they dared to march
So many miles upon her peaceful bosom,
Frighting her pale-faced villages with war
And ostentation° of despisèd arms?   *display*
95   Com'st thou because the anointed King is hence?
Why, foolish boy, the King is left behind,
And in my loyal bosom lies his power.
Were I but now the lord of such hot youth
As when brave Gaunt, thy father, and myself
100   Rescued the Black Prince, that young Mars of men,
From forth the ranks of many thousand French,
O then how quickly should this arm of mine,
Now prisoner to the palsy, chastise thee
And minister correction° to thy fault!   *administer punishment*
105   BOLINGBROKE   My gracious uncle, let me know my fault.
On what condition stands it and wherein?⁷
YORK   Even in condition of the worst degree:
In gross rebellion and detested treason.
Thou art a banished man, and here art come
110   Before the expiration of thy time
In braving° arms against thy sovereign.   *defiant*
BOLINGBROKE   *[standing]*   As I was banished, I was banished Hereford;
But as I come, I come for Lancaster.
And, noble uncle, I beseech your grace,
115   Look on my wrongs with an indifferent° eye.   *impartial*
You are my father, for methinks in you
I see old Gaunt alive. O then, my father,
Will you permit that I shall stand condemned
A wandering vagabond, my rights and royalties
120   Plucked from my arms perforce and given away
To upstart unthrifts?° Wherefore was I born?   *spendthrifts*

---

6. Borne for oneself, not for the King; borne against   7. What is its nature, and in what does it consist?
fellow countrymen.

If that my cousin King be King in England,
It must be granted I am Duke of Lancaster.
You have a son, Aumerle my noble kinsman.
125 Had you first died and he been thus trod down,
He should have found his uncle Gaunt a father
To rouse his wrongs and chase them to the bay.[8]
I am denied to sue my livery[9] here,
And yet my letters patents give me leave.
130 My father's goods are all distrained° and sold,   *confiscated*
And these and all are all amiss employed.
What would you have me do? I am a subject,
And I challenge law;° attorneys are denied me;   *demand my rights*
And therefore personally I lay my claim
135 To my inheritance of free descent.°   *legal succession*
NORTHUMBERLAND   The noble Duke hath been too much abused.
ROSS   It stands your grace upon[1] to do him right.
WILLOUGHBY   Base men by his endowments° are made great.   *property*
YORK   My lords of England, let me tell you this.
140 I have had feeling of my cousin's wrongs,
And laboured all I could to do him right.
But in this kind° to come, in braving arms,   *manner*
Be his own carver,[2] and cut out his way
To find out right with wrong[3]—it may not be.
145 And you that do abet him in this kind
Cherish rebellion, and are rebels all.
NORTHUMBERLAND   The noble Duke hath sworn his coming is
But for his own, and for the right of that
We all have strongly sworn to give him aid;
150 And let him never see joy that breaks that oath.
YORK   Well, well, I see the issue° of these arms.   *consequence*
I cannot mend it, I must needs confess,
Because my power° is weak and all ill-left.   *army*
But if I could, by Him that gave me life,
155 I would attach° you all, and make you stoop   *arrest*
Unto the sovereign mercy of the King.
But since I cannot, be it known to you
I do remain as neuter.° So fare you well—   *neutral*
Unless you please to enter in the castle
160 And there repose you for this night.
BOLINGBROKE   An offer, uncle, that we will accept.
But we must win° your grace to go with us   *persuade*
To Bristol Castle, which they say is held
By Bushy, Bagot, and their complices,°   *accomplices*
165 The caterpillars° of the commonwealth,   *devourers*
Which I have sworn to weed and pluck away.
YORK   It may be I will go with you—but yet I'll pause,
For I am loath to break our country's laws.
Nor° friends nor foes, to me welcome you are.   *Neither*
170 Things past redress are now with me past care.   *Exeunt*

---

8. *rouse*: startle an animal from its cover. *bay*: point
where the animal turns on its pursuers.
9. See note to 2.1.205.

1. It is incumbent on your grace.
2. Help himself to meat (instead of waiting to be served).
3. To illegally obtain what he deserves.

2.4

Enter Earl of SALISBURY *and a* WELSH CAPTAIN

WELSH CAPTAIN My lord of Salisbury, we have stayed° ten days,   *waited*
And hardly° kept our countrymen together,   *with difficulty*
And yet we hear no tidings from the King.
Therefore we will disperse ourselves. Farewell.
5 SALISBURY Stay yet another day, thou trusty Welshman.
The King reposeth all his confidence in thee.
WELSH CAPTAIN 'Tis thought the King is dead. We will not stay.
The bay trees in our country are all withered,
And meteors fright the fixèd stars of heaven.
10 The pale-faced moon looks bloody on the earth,[1]
And lean-looked prophets whisper fearful change.
Rich men look sad, and ruffians dance and leap;
The one in fear to lose what they enjoy,
The other to enjoy° by rage and war.   *hoping to profit*
15 These signs forerun the death or fall of kings.
Farewell. Our countrymen are gone and fled,
As well assured Richard their king is dead.   *Exit*
SALISBURY Ah, Richard! With the eyes of heavy mind
I see thy glory, like a shooting star,
20 Fall to the base earth from the firmament.
Thy sun sets weeping in the lowly west,
Witnessing° storms to come, woe, and unrest.   *Testifying to*
Thy friends are fled to wait upon thy foes,
And crossly° to thy good all fortune goes.   *Exit*   *adversely*

3.1

Enter BOLINGBROKE [*Duke of Lancaster and Hereford,*
Duke of] YORK, [*Earl of*] NORTHUMBERLAND, [*Lord*]
ROSS, [HARRY] PERCY, [*and Lord*] WILLOUGHBY

BOLINGBROKE Bring forth these men.
[*Enter*] BUSHY *and* GREEN, [*guarded as*] *prisoners*
Bushy and Green, I will not vex° your souls,   *afflict*
Since presently° your souls must part your bodies,   *immediately*
With too much urging° your pernicious lives,   *emphasizing*
5 For 'twere no charity. Yet to wash your blood
From off my hands, here in the view of men
I will unfold some causes of your deaths.
You have misled a prince, a royal king,
A happy° gentleman in blood and lineaments,[1]   *fortunate*
10 By you unhappied and disfigured clean.°   *utterly*
You have, in manner,° with your sinful hours   *so to speak*
Made a divorce betwixt his queen and him,
Broke the possession of a royal bed,
And stained the beauty of a fair queen's cheeks
15 With tears drawn from her eyes by your foul wrongs.[2]
Myself—a prince by fortune of my birth,
Near to the King in blood, and near in love
Till you did make him misinterpret me—
Have stooped my neck under your injuries,

2.4 Location: A camp in Wales.
1. Holinshed records the first of these omens (line 8); the others are poetic commonplaces.
3.1 Location: Before Bristol Castle.

1. In descent and qualities.
2. Bolingbroke implies that Bushy and Green had homosexual relations with Richard; Holinshed claims that they procured female paramours for him.

20   And sighed my English breath in foreign clouds,°   *air*
      Eating the bitter bread of banishment,
      Whilst you have fed upon my signories,°   *estates*
      Disparked my parks³ and felled my forest woods,
      From my own windows torn my household coat,⁴
25   Razed° out my imprese,° leaving me no sign,   *Scraped / heraldic emblem*
      Save men's opinions and my living blood,
      To show the world I am a gentleman.
      This and much more, much more than twice all this,
      Condemns you to the death.—See them delivered over
30   To execution and the hand of death.
BUSHY   More welcome is the stroke of death to me
      Than Bolingbroke to England.
GREEN   My comfort is that heaven will take our souls,
      And plague injustice with the pains of hell.
35 BOLINGBROKE   My lord Northumberland, see them dispatched.
      [*Exit* NORTHUMBERLAND, *with* BUSHY *and* GREEN, *guarded*]
      Uncle, you say the Queen is at your house.
      For God's sake, fairly° let her be intreated.°   *courteously / treated*
      Tell her I send to her my kind commends.°   *greetings*
      Take special care my greetings be delivered.
40 YORK   A gentleman of mine I have dispatched
      With letters of your love to her at large.°   *fully described*
BOLINGBROKE   Thanks, gentle uncle.—Come, lords, away,
      To fight with Glyndŵr⁵ and his complices.
      A while to work, and after, holiday.   *Exeunt*

3.2

      Drums. Flourish. Enter [KING] RICHARD, [*Duke of*]
      AUMERLE, [BISHOP OF] CARLISLE, *and soldiers* [*with*]
      colours°   *flags*
KING RICHARD   Harlechly Castle call they this at hand?
AUMERLE   Yea, my lord. How brooks° your grace the air   *enjoys*
      After your late° tossing on the breaking seas?   *recent*
KING RICHARD   Needs must° I like it well. I weep for joy   *Necessarily*
5   To stand upon my kingdom once again.
      [*He touches the ground*]
      Dear earth, I do salute thee with my hand,
      Though rebels wound thee with their horses' hoofs.
      As a long-parted mother with her child
      Plays fondly with her tears, and smiles in meeting,
10   So, weeping, smiling, greet I thee my earth,
      And do thee favours with my royal hands.
      Feed not thy sovereign's foe, my gentle earth,
      Nor with thy sweets° comfort his ravenous sense;¹   *bounty*
      But let thy spiders that suck up thy venom²
15   And heavy-gaited toads³ lie in their way,
      Doing annoyance to the treacherous feet
      Which with usurping steps do trample thee.
      Yield stinging nettles to mine enemies,

3. Put my hunting lands to other use.
4. Removed the stained glass bearing my coat of arms.
5. This character appears in *1 Henry IV* and is perhaps
to be identified with the Welsh captain of 2.4.
3.2 Location: Near Harlech Castle, on the coast of

Gwynedd, Wales.
1. Appetite; intention.
2. It was thought that spiders drew their venom from
the earth.
3. Also thought to be poisonous.

And when they from thy bosom pluck a flower

20 Guard it, I pray thee, with a lurking adder,

Whose double° tongue may with a mortal touch   *forked*

Throw death upon thy sovereign's enemies.—

Mock not my senseless conjuration,[4] lords.

This earth shall have a feeling, and these stones

25 Prove armèd soldiers, ere her native king°   *King entitled by birth*

Shall falter under foul rebellion's arms.

BISHOP OF CARLISLE   Fear not, my lord. That power that made you king

Hath power to keep you king in spite of all.[5]

28.1   *The means that heavens yield must be embraced*

      And not neglected; else° heaven would,   *otherwise*

      And we will not: heaven's offer we refuse,

      The proffered means of succour and redress.

AUMERLE   He means, my lord, that we are too remiss,

30 Whilst Bolingbroke, through our security,°   *overconfidence*

Grows strong and great in substance and in friends.

KING RICHARD   Discomfortable° cousin, know'st thou not   *Disheartening*

That when the searching eye of heaven is hid

Behind the globe, that lights the lower world,

35 Then thieves and robbers range abroad unseen

In murders and in outrage bloody here;

But when from under this terrestrial ball

He fires° the proud tops of the eastern pines,   *lights up*

And darts his light through every guilty hole,

40 Then murders, treasons, and detested sins,

The cloak of night being plucked from off their backs,

Stand bare and naked, trembling at themselves?

So when this thief, this traitor, Bolingbroke,

Who all this while hath revelled in the night

45 Whilst we were wand'ring with the Antipodes,

Shall see us rising in our throne, the east,[6]

His treasons will sit blushing in his face,

Not able to endure the sight of day,

But, self-affrighted, tremble at his sin.

50 Not all the water in the rough rude sea

Can wash the balm° from an anointed king.   *oil of consecration*

The breath of worldly men cannot depose

The deputy elected by the Lord.

For every man that Bolingbroke hath pressed°   *drafted*

55 To lift shrewd° steel against our golden crown,   *wicked; sharp*

God for his Richard hath in heavenly pay

A glorious angel. Then if angels fight,

Weak men must fall; for heaven still° guards the right.   *always*

      Enter [Earl of] SALISBURY

Welcome, my lord. How far off lies your power?

60 SALISBURY   Nor nea'er° nor farther off, my gracious lord,   *Neither nearer*

Than this weak arm. Discomfort guides my tongue,

And bids me speak of nothing but despair.

One day too late, I fear me, noble lord,

Hath clouded all thy happy days on earth.

---

4. Injunction addressed to an insentient being (the earth).

5. The following indented passage (lines 28.1–28.4) appears only in QI.

6. *That when . . . east:* Richard compares the sun ("the searching eye of heaven," line 33), the antipodes, or "lower world" on the other side of the globe, to himself leaving England to visit Ireland. Unlike the sun, however, Richard arrives from the west.

65   O, call back yesterday, bid time return,
        And thou shalt have twelve thousand fighting men.
        Today, today, unhappy day too late,
        Overthrows thy joys, friends, fortune, and thy state;°   *prosperity; nation*
        For all the Welshmen, hearing thou wert dead,
70   Are gone to Bolingbroke, dispersed, and fled.
        AUMERLE   Comfort, my liege. Why looks your grace so pale?
        KING RICHARD   But now° the blood of twenty thousand men   *A moment ago*
        Did triumph° in my face, and they are fled;   *shine*
        And till so much blood thither come again
75   Have I not reason to look pale and dead?
        All souls that will be safe fly from my side,
        For time hath set a blot upon my pride.
        AUMERLE   Comfort, my liege. Remember who you are.
        KING RICHARD   I had forgot myself. Am I not King?
80   Awake, thou sluggard majesty, thou sleep'st!
        Is not the King's name forty thousand names?
        Arm, arm, my name! A puny subject strikes
        At thy great glory. Look not to the ground,
        Ye favourites of a king: are we not high?
85   High be our thoughts. I know my uncle York
        Hath power enough to serve our turn.
                        Enter SCROPE
                                                        But who comes here?
        SCROPE   More health and happiness betide my liege
        Than can my care-tuned⁷ tongue deliver° him.   *offer*
        KING RICHARD   Mine ear is open and my heart prepared.
90   The worst is worldly loss thou canst unfold.
        Say, is my kingdom lost? Why 'twas my care,°   *trouble*
        And what loss is it to be rid of care?
        Strives Bolingbroke to be as great as we?
        Greater he shall not be. If he serve God
95   We'll serve Him too, and be his fellow so.⁸
        Revolt our subjects? That we cannot mend.
        They break their faith to God as well as us.
        Cry° woe, destruction, ruin, loss, decay: *Though you may cry*
        The worst is death, and death will have his° day.   *its*
100   SCROPE   Glad am I that your highness is so armed
        To bear the tidings of calamity.
        Like an unseasonable stormy day,
        Which makes the silver rivers drown their shores
        As if the world were all dissolved to tears,
105   So high above his limits° swells the rage   *bounds; banks*
        Of Bolingbroke, covering your fearful° land   *alarmed*
        With hard bright steel, and hearts harder than steel.
        Whitebeards have armed their thin and hairless scalps
        Against thy majesty. Boys with women's voices
110   Strive to speak big, and clap their female° joints   *weak*
        In stiff unwieldy arms° against thy crown.   *armor*
        Thy very beadsmen⁹ learn to bend their bows
        Of double-fatal¹ yew against thy state.

---

7. Tuned to the key sorrow.   praying for their benefactors' souls.
8. Be Bolingbroke's equal in that regard.   1. Because yew is poisonous, and its wood was used to
9. Poor elderly men who received charity in return for   make bows.

Yea, distaff-women° manage rusty bills[2]   *spinners*
115 Against thy seat.° Both young and old rebel,   *throne*
And all goes worse than I have power to tell.
KING RICHARD   Too well, too well thou tell'st a tale so ill.
Where is the Earl of Wiltshire? Where is Bagot?[3]
What is become of Bushy, where is Green,
120 That they have let the dangerous enemy
Measure our confines[4] with such peaceful° steps?   *unopposed*
If we prevail, their heads shall pay for it.
I warrant they have made peace with Bolingbroke.
SCROPE   Peace have they made with him indeed, my lord.
125 KING RICHARD   O villains, vipers damned without redemption!
Dogs easily won to fawn on any man!
Snakes in my heart-blood warmed, that sting my heart!
Three Judases, each one thrice-worse than Judas![5]
Would they make peace? Terrible hell make war
130 Upon their spotted° souls for this offence!   *blemished*
SCROPE   Sweet love, I see, changing his property,°   *its quality*
Turns to the sourest and most deadly hate.
Again uncurse their souls. Their peace is made
With heads, and not with hands. Those whom you curse
135 Have felt the worst of death's destroying wound,
And lie full low, graved in the hollow ground.
AUMERLE   Is Bushy, Green, and the Earl of Wiltshire dead?
SCROPE   Ay, all of them at Bristol lost their heads.
AUMERLE   Where is the Duke my father, with his power?
140 KING RICHARD   No matter where. Of comfort no man speak.
Let's talk of graves, of worms and epitaphs,
Make dust our paper, and with rainy eyes
Write sorrow on the bosom of the earth.
Let's choose executors and talk of wills—
145 And yet not so, for what can we bequeath
Save our deposèd° bodies to the ground?   *dethroned; prostrate*
Our lands, our lives, and all are Bolingbroke's;
And nothing can we call our own but death,
And that small model[6] of the barren earth
150 Which serves as paste[7] and cover to our bones.
[*Sitting*] For God's sake, let us sit upon the ground,
And tell sad stories of the death of kings—
How some have been deposed, some slain in war,
Some haunted by the ghosts they have deposed,
155 Some poisoned by their wives, some sleeping killed,
All murdered. For within the hollow crown
That rounds° the mortal temples of a king   *encircles*
Keeps Death his court; and there the antic° sits,   *jester*
Scoffing his state[8] and grinning at his pomp,
160 Allowing him a breath, a little scene,
To monarchize,° be feared, and kill with looks,[9]   *play the monarch*
Infusing him with self and vain conceit,[1]
As if this flesh which walls about our life

2. Spiked axes on long shafts.
3. Bagot is not one of the "three Judases" (line 128) actually executed by Bolingbroke; he reappears in 4.1.
4. Travel over our territories.
5. Disciple who betrayed Jesus.
6. Microcosm (the body); enveloping shape (the grave).
7. Pastry shell (also known as "coffin").
8. Mocking the King's regality.
9. Order executions with a glance.
1. Instilling in him vain ideas about himself.

Were brass impregnable; and humoured thus,[2]
165 Comes at the last, and with a little pin
Bores through his castle wall; and farewell, king.
Cover your heads,[3] and mock not flesh and blood
With solemn reverence. Throw away respect,
Tradition, form, and ceremonious duty,
170 For you have but mistook me all this while.
I live with bread, like you; feel want,
Taste grief, need friends. Subjected thus,[4]
How can you say to me I am a king?
BISHOP OF CARLISLE My lord, wise men ne'er wail their present woes,
175 But presently prevent the ways to wail.[5]
To fear the foe, since fear oppresseth° strength,   suppresses
Gives in your weakness strength unto your foe;
And so your follies fight against yourself.
Fear, and be slain. No worse can come to fight;°   in fighting
180 And fight and die is death destroying death,[6]
Where fearing dying pays death servile breath.
AUMERLE My father hath a power.° Enquire of him,   an army
And learn to make a body of a limb.
KING RICHARD [standing] Thou chid'st me well. Proud Boling-
broke, I come
185 To change blows with thee for our day of doom.[7]
This ague-fit° of fear is overblown.°   chill / blown over
An easy task it is to win our own.
Say, Scrope, where lies our uncle with his power?
Speak sweetly, man, although thy looks be sour.
190 SCROPE Men judge by the complexion° of the sky   appearance
The state and inclination of the day.
So may you by my dull and heavy eye
My tongue hath but a heavier tale to say.
I play the torturer by small and small°   little by little
195 To lengthen out the worst that must be spoken.
Your uncle York is joined with Bolingbroke,
And all your northern castles yielded up,
And all your southern gentlemen° in arms   men of rank
Upon his faction.
KING RICHARD   Thou hast said enough.
200 [To AUMERLE] Beshrew° thee, cousin, which didst lead me forth   Woe to
Of that sweet way I was in to despair.
What say you now? What comfort have we now?
By heaven, I'll hate him everlastingly
That bids me be of comfort any more.
205 Go to Flint Castle;° there I'll pine away.   Welsh castle near Chester
A king, woe's slave, shall kingly woe obey.
That power I have, discharge, and let them go
To ear° the land that hath some hope to grow;   till
For I have none. Let no man speak again
210 To alter this, for counsel is but vain.
AUMERLE My liege, one word.
KING RICHARD   He does me double wrong

2. And Death having thus amused himself.
3. Replace your hats (do not respectfully remain bare-
headed).
4. Made a subject to such needs (with pun).

5. But immediately vanquish the causes of grief.
6. To die fighting is to destroy death's power by dying.
7. To exchange blows with you in order to determine
our fates.

That wounds me with the flatteries of his tongue.
Discharge my followers. Let them hence away
From Richard's night to Bolingbroke's fair day.   *Exeunt*

3.3

Enter BOLINGBROKE [*Duke of Lancaster and Hereford,*
Duke of] YORK, [*Earl of*] NORTHUMBERLAND, [*and sol-*
diers] *with drum and colours*

BOLINGBROKE   So that by this intelligence° we learn   *information*
    The Welshmen are dispersed, and Salisbury
    Is gone to meet the King, who lately landed
    With some few private friends upon this coast.
5   NORTHUMBERLAND   The news is very fair and good, my lord.
    Richard not far from hence hath hid his head.
    YORK   It would beseem the Lord Northumberland
    To say 'King Richard'. Alack the heavy day
    When such a sacred king should hide his head!
10 NORTHUMBERLAND   Your grace mistakes. Only to be brief
    Left I his title out.
    YORK   The time hath been,
    Would you have been so brief with him, he would
    Have been so brief with you to shorten you,
    For taking so the head,[1] your whole head's length.
15 BOLINGBROKE   Mistake not, uncle, further than you should.
    YORK   Take not, good cousin, further than you should,
    Lest you mistake° the heavens are over our heads.   *forget*
    BOLINGBROKE   I know it, uncle, and oppose not myself
    Against their will.
            Enter [HARRY] PERCY [*and a trumpeter*]
                    But who comes here?
20 Welcome, Harry. What, will not this castle yield?
    HARRY PERCY   The castle royally is manned, my lord,
    Against thy entrance.
    BOLINGBROKE   Royally?
    Why, it contains no king.
    HARRY PERCY   Yes, my good lord,
    It doth contain a king. King Richard lies
25 Within the limits of yon lime and stone,
    And with him are the Lord Aumerle, Lord Salisbury,
    Sir Stephen Scrope, besides a clergyman
    Of holy reverence; who, I cannot learn.
    NORTHUMBERLAND   O, belike° it is the Bishop of Carlisle.   *probably*
30 BOLINGBROKE [*to* NORTHUMBERLAND]   Noble lord,
    Go to the rude ribs° of that ancient castle;   *rough walls*
    Through brazen trumpet send the breath of parley
    Into his ruined ears,° and thus deliver.   *its battered loopholes*
    Henry Bolingbroke
35 Upon his knees doth kiss King Richard's hand,
    And sends allegiance and true faith of heart
    To his most royal person, hither come
    Even at his feet to lay my arms and power,
    Provided that my banishment repealed°   *revoked*
40 And lands restored again be freely granted.

3.3 Location: Before Flint Castle.   1. For omitting the title thus; for acting without restraint.

If not, I'll use the advantage of my power,
And lay° the summer's dust with showers of blood   *make settle*
Rained from the wounds of slaughtered Englishmen;
The which how far off from the mind of Bolingbroke
45   It is such crimson tempest should bedrench
The fresh green lap of fair King Richard's land,
My stooping duty° tenderly shall show.   *submissive kneeling*
Go, signify as much, while here we march
Upon the grassy carpet of this plain.
50   Let's march without the noise of threat'ning drum,
That from this castle's tottered° battlements   *dilapidated*
Our fair appointments° may be well perused.   *equipment*
Methinks King Richard and myself should meet
With no less terror than the elements
55   Of fire and water° when their thund'ring shock   *lightning and rain*
At meeting tears the cloudy cheeks of heaven.
Be he the fire, I'll be the yielding water.
The rage be his, whilst on the earth I rain°   *(punning on "reign"?)*
My waters: on the earth, and not on him.—
60   March on, and mark King Richard, how he looks.
          [*They march about the stage; then* BOLINGBROKE, YORK,
          PERCY, *and soldiers stand at a distance from the walls;*
          NORTHUMBERLAND *and a trumpeter advance to the*
          walls.] *The trumpets sound* [*a*] *parley without, and* [*an*]
          answer within; then a flourish [*within.* KING] RICHARD
          appeareth on the walls,[2] [*with* BISHOP OF] CARLISLE,
          [*Duke of*] AUMERLE, SCROPE, [*and Earl of*] SALISBURY
See, see, King Richard doth himself appear,
As doth the blushing[3] discontented sun
From out the fiery portal of the east
When he perceives the envious° clouds are bent   *malicious*
65   To dim his glory and to stain the track
Of his bright passage to the occident.
YORK   Yet looks he like a king. Behold, his eye,
As bright as is the eagle's, lightens forth[4]
Controlling majesty. Alack, alack for woe
70   That any harm should stain so fair a show!
KING RICHARD [*to* NORTHUMBERLAND]   We are amazed; and
          thus long have we stood
To watch° the fearful bending of thy knee,   *wait for*
Because we thought ourself thy lawful king.
An if° we be, how dare thy joints forget   *An if = If*
75   To pay their aweful° duty to our presence?   *reverential*
If we be not, show us the hand of God
That hath dismissed us from our stewardship.
For well we know no hand of blood and bone
Can grip° the sacred handle of our sceptre,   *seize*
80   Unless he do profane, steal, or usurp.
And though you think that all—as you have done—
Have torn° their souls by turning them from us,   *ruined (by disloyalty)*
And we are barren and bereft of friends,

---

2. That is, on the balcony of the tiring-house at the back of the stage.
3. Red (proverbially, a red morning sky anticipates bad weather).
4. Flashes out (the eagle is a traditional royal symbol).

Yet know my master, God omnipotent,
85   Is mustering in his clouds on our behalf
Armies of pestilence; and they shall strike
Your children yet unborn and unbegot,
That lift your vassal hands against my head
And threat° the glory of my precious crown.   threaten
90   Tell Bolingbroke, for yon methinks he is,
That every stride he makes upon my land
Is dangerous treason. He is come to open
The purple testament° of bleeding war;   blood-red document
But ere the crown he looks for live in peace
95   Ten thousand bloody crowns° of mothers' sons   heads
Shall ill become the flower of England's face,⁵
Change the complexion of her maid-pale° peace   innocent white
To scarlet indignation, and bedew
Her pastures' grass with faithful English blood.
NORTHUMBERLAND [kneeling]   The King of heaven forbid our
100   lord the King
Should so with civil and uncivil⁶ arms
Be rushed upon. Thy thrice-noble cousin
Harry Bolingbroke doth humbly kiss thy hand,
And by the honourable tomb he swears,
105   That stands upon your royal grandsire's° bones,   (Edward III's)
And by the royalties of both your bloods,
Currents that spring from one most gracious head,°   source
And by the buried hand of warlike Gaunt,
And by the worth and honour of himself,
110   Comprising all that may be sworn or said,
His coming hither hath no further scope°   aim
Than for his lineal royalties,° and to beg   hereditary rights
Enfranchisement° immediate on his knees;   Recall from exile
Which on thy royal party° granted once,   part
115   His glittering arms he will commend° to rust,   commit
His barbèd° steeds to stables, and his heart   armed
To faithful service of your majesty.
This swears he as he is a prince and just,
And as I am a gentleman I credit° him.   believe
120   KING RICHARD   Northumberland, say thus the King returns:°   replies
His noble cousin is right welcome hither,
And all the number of his fair demands
Shall be accomplished without contradiction.
With all the gracious utterance thou hast,
125   Speak to his gentle hearing kind commends.°   regards
        [NORTHUMBERLAND and the trumpeter return to
        BOLINGBROKE]
[To AUMERLE] We do debase ourself, cousin, do we not,
To look so poorly° and to speak so fair?   abjectly
Shall we call back Northumberland, and send
Defiance to the traitor, and so die?
130   AUMERLE   No, good my lord, let's fight with gentle words
Till time lend friends, and friends their helpful swords.
KING RICHARD   O God, O God, that e'er this tongue of mine,
That laid the sentence of dread banishment

5. Blooming surface of England; faces of England's   6. Of the same country and violent; playing on "civil"
choicest youth.   as "peaceful" and "uncivil" as "alien."

On yon proud man, should take it off again
135 With words of sooth!° O, that I were as great   *soothing words*
As is my grief, or lesser than my name,
Or that I could forget what I have been,
Or not remember what I must be now!
Swell'st thou, proud heart? I'll give thee scope to beat,
140 Since foes have scope to beat both thee and me.
        [NORTHUMBERLAND *advances to the walls*]
   AUMERLE   Northumberland comes back from Bolingbroke.
   KING RICHARD   What must the King do now? Must he submit?
The King shall do it. Must he be deposed?
The King shall be contented. Must he lose
145 The name of King? A° God's name, let it go.   *In*
I'll give my jewels for a set of beads,°   *rosary*
My gorgeous palace for a hermitage,
My gay apparel for an almsman's° gown,   *a beggar's*
My figured° goblets for a dish of wood,   *engraved*
150 My sceptre for a palmer's° walking staff,   *pilgrim's*
My subjects for a pair of carvèd saints,
And my large kingdom for a little grave,
A little, little grave, an obscure grave;
Or I'll be buried in the King's highway,°   *(as suicides were)*
155 Some way of common trade° where subjects' feet   *passage*
May hourly trample on their sovereign's head,
For on my heart they tread now, whilst I live,
And buried once, why not upon my head?
Aumerle, thou weep'st, my tender-hearted cousin.
160 We'll make foul weather with despisèd tears.
Our sighs and they shall lodge° the summer corn,   *beat down*
And make a dearth° in this revolting° land.   *famine / rebellious*
Or shall we play the wantons° with our woes,   *we frolic*
And make some pretty match° with shedding tears;   *clever game*
165 As thus to drop them still° upon one place   *continually*
Till they have fretted° us a pair of graves   *eroded for*
Within the earth, and therein laid? 'There lies
Two kinsmen digged their graves with weeping eyes.'
Would not this ill do well? Well, well, I see
170 I talk but idly° and you mock at me.   *foolishly*
Most mighty prince, my lord Northumberland,
What says King Bolingbroke? Will his majesty
Give Richard leave to live till Richard die?
You make a leg,° and Bolingbroke says 'Ay'.   *an obeisance*
175 NORTHUMBERLAND   My lord, in the base court° he doth attend   *outer courtyard*
To speak with you. May it please you to come down?
   KING RICHARD   Down, down I come like glist'ring Phaethon,[7]
Wanting the manage° of unruly jades.[8]   *Lacking control*
In the base court: base court where kings grow base
180 To come at traitors' calls, and do them grace.°   *favor them*
In the base court, come down: down court, down King,
For night-owls shriek where mounting larks should sing.
        [*Exeunt* KING RICHARD *and his party*]

---

7. In Greek mythology, the son of the sun god. He attempted to drive his father's sun chariot but was too weak to control the horses; Zeus, king of the gods, struck him down with a thunderbolt to prevent him from destroying the earth.
8. Horses (contemptuous).

[NORTHUMBERLAND *returns to* BOLINGBROKE]

BOLINGBROKE What says his majesty?

NORTHUMBERLAND   Sorrow and grief of heart

Makes him speak fondly,° like a frantic° man.   *foolishly / an insane*

[*Enter* KING RICHARD *and his party below*]

Yet he is come.

185 BOLINGBROKE   Stand all apart,

And show fair duty to his majesty.

He kneels down

My gracious lord.

KING RICHARD Fair cousin, you debase your princely knee

To make the base earth proud with kissing it.

190 Me rather had° my heart might feel your love   *I had rather*

Than my unpleased eye see your courtesy.

Up, cousin, up. Your heart is up, I know,

Thus high at least,⁹ although your knee be low.

BOLINGBROKE My gracious lord, I come but for mine own.

195 KING RICHARD Your own is yours, and I am yours, and all.

BOLINGBROKE So far be mine, my most redoubted° lord,   *dreaded*

As my true service shall deserve your love.

KING RICHARD Well you deserve. They well deserve to have

That know the strong'st and surest way to get.

[BOLINGBROKE *rises*]

200 [*To* YORK] Uncle, give me your hands. Nay, dry your eyes.

Tears show their love, but want their remedies.°   *do no good*

[*To* BOLINGBROKE] Cousin, I am too young to be your father,

Though you are old enough to be my heir.

What you will have I'll give, and willing too;

205 For do we must what force will have us do.

Set on towards London, cousin: is it so?

BOLINGBROKE Yea, my good lord.

KING RICHARD   Then I must not say no.

Flourish. Exeunt.

3.4

Enter the QUEEN *with her two* LADIES

QUEEN What sport shall we devise here in this garden,

To drive away the heavy thought of care?

FIRST LADY Madam, we'll play at bowls.°   *lawn bowling*

QUEEN 'Twill make me think the world is full of rubs,¹

5 And that my fortune runs against the bias.²

SECOND LADY Madam, we'll dance.

QUEEN My legs can keep no measure° in delight   *dance step*

When my poor heart no measure° keeps in grief;   *moderation*

Therefore no dancing, girl. Some other sport.

10 FIRST LADY Madam, we'll tell tales.

QUEEN Of sorrow or of joy?

FIRST LADY Of either, madam.

QUEEN Of neither, girl.

For if of joy, being altogether wanting,

15 It doth remember° me the more of sorrow.   *remind*

9. Richard touches his crown.
3.4 Location: The Duke of York's garden.
1. Impediments (a term from the game of bowls).

2. Runs askew. *bias:* literally, a lead weight in the bowl
that makes it run smoothly.

Or if of grief, being altogether had,°   *possessed*
It adds more sorrow to my want of joy.
For what I have I need not to repeat,
And what I want it boots° not to complain.   *helps*
SECOND LADY   Madam, I'll sing.
20 QUEEN   'Tis well that thou hast cause;
But thou shouldst please me better wouldst thou weep.
SECOND LADY   I could weep, madam, would it do you good.
QUEEN   And I could sing, would weeping do me good,
And never borrow any tear of thee.

        Enter a GARDENER *and two* [MEN]

25 But stay; here come the gardeners.
Let's step into the shadow of these trees.
My wretchedness unto a row of pins³
They will talk of state, for everyone doth so
Against° a change. Woe is forerun with woe.   *In anticipation of*
    [*The* QUEEN *and her* LADIES *stand apart*]
30 GARDENER [*to* FIRST MAN]   Go, bind thou up young dangling apricots
Which, like unruly children, make their sire
Stoop with oppression of their prodigal° weight.   *excessive*
Give some supportance to the bending twigs.
[*To* SECOND MAN] Go thou, and, like an executioner,
35 Cut off the heads of too fast-growing sprays
That look too lofty in our commonwealth.
All must be even° in our government.   *equal*
You thus employed, I will go root away
The noisome° weeds which without profit suck   *harmful*
40 The soil's fertility from wholesome flowers.
FIRST MAN   Why should we, in the compass of a pale,⁴
Keep law and form and due proportion,
Showing as in a model our firm estate,°   *stable government*
When our sea-wallèd garden, the whole land,
45 Is full of weeds, her fairest flowers choked up,
Her fruit trees all unpruned, her hedges ruined,
Her knots⁵ disordered, and her wholesome herbs
Swarming with caterpillars?
GARDENER   Hold thy peace.
He that hath suffered° this disordered spring   *permitted*
50 Hath now himself met with the fall of leaf.
The weeds which his broad spreading leaves did shelter,
That seemed in eating him to hold him up,
Are plucked up, root and all, by Bolingbroke—
I mean the Earl of Wiltshire, Bushy, Green.
SECOND MAN   What, are they dead?
55 GARDENER   They are; and Bolingbroke
Hath seized the wasteful King. O, what pity is it
That he had not so trimmed and dressed° his land   *cultivated*
As we this garden! We at time of year°   *in season*
Do wound the bark, the skin of our fruit trees,⁶
60 Lest, being over-proud in° sap and blood,   *excessively swollen with*
With too much riches it confound° itself.   *ruin*

---

3. I'll bet my great wretchedness against a trivial row
of pins.
4. In the limits of a fenced enclosure.

5. Intricate flower beds; social bonds.
6. *Do . . . trees:* this restricts the tree's food supply,
encouraging fruit buds to form.

Had he done so to great and growing men,
They might have lived to bear, and he to taste,
Their fruits of duty. Superfluous branches
65 We lop away, that bearing boughs may live.
Had he done so, himself had borne° the crown,[7]   *retained*
Which waste of idle hours hath quite thrown down.
FIRST MAN   What, think you then the King shall be deposed?
GARDENER   Depressed° he is already, and deposed   *Brought low*
70 'Tis doubt° he will be. Letters came last night   *feared*
To a dear friend of the good Duke of York's
That tell black tidings.
QUEEN   O, I am pressed to death through want of speaking![8]
     [*She comes forward*]
Thou, old Adam's[9] likeness, set to dress° this garden,   *cultivate*
75 How dares thy harsh rude° tongue sound this unpleasing news?   *ignorant*
What Eve, what serpent hath suggested° thee   *tempted*
To make a second fall of cursèd man?
Why dost thou say King Richard is deposed?
Dar'st thou, thou little better thing than earth,
80 Divine° his downfall? Say where, when, and how   *Prophesy*
Cam'st thou by this ill tidings? Speak, thou wretch!
GARDENER   Pardon me, madam. Little joy have I
To breathe this news, yet what I say is true.
King Richard he is in the mighty hold
85 Of Bolingbroke. Their fortunes both are weighed.
In your lord's scale is nothing but himself
And some few vanities that make him light.
But in the balance of great Bolingbroke,
Besides himself, are all the English peers,
90 And with that odds he weighs King Richard down.
Post° you to London and you will find it so.   *Hasten*
I speak no more than everyone doth know.
QUEEN   Nimble mischance that art so light of foot,
Doth not thy embassage° belong to me,   *message*
95 And am I last that knows it? O, thou think'st
To serve me last, that I may longest keep
Thy sorrow in my breast. Come, ladies, go
To meet at London London's king in woe.
What, was I born to this, that my sad look
100 Should grace the triumph° of great Bolingbroke?   *triumphal procession*
Gard'ner, for telling me these news of woe,
Pray God the plants thou graft'st may never grow.
             Exit [*with her* LADIES]
GARDENER   Poor Queen, so that° thy state might be no worse   *if as a result*
I would my skill were subject to thy curse.
105 Here did she fall° a tear. Here in this place   *drop*
I'll set a bank of rue,[1] sour herb-of-grace.
Rue even for ruth° here shortly shall be seen   *pity*
In the remembrance of a weeping queen.   *Exeunt*

---

7. Playing on the "crown" of a tree.
8. In medieval and Renaissance England, indicted persons who refused to plead guilty or not guilty were killed with weights laid on the stomach.
9. Adam was the first gardener.
1. Herb associated with compassion and repentance.

4.1

Enter, as to Parliament, BOLINGBROKE [*Duke of Lan-
caster and Hereford, Duke of*] AUMERLE, [*Earl of*]
NORTHUMBERLAND, [HARRY] PERCY, [*Lord*] FITZWALTER,
[*Duke of*] SURREY, [BISHOP OF] CARLISLE, [*and the*]
ABBOT OF WESTMINSTER

BOLINGBROKE   Call forth Bagot.

Enter BAGOT, [*with*] *officers*

                       Now, Bagot, freely speak thy mind:
What thou dost know of noble Gloucester's death,
Who wrought it with[1] the King, and who performed
The bloody office° of his timeless° end.   *deed / untimely*

5 BAGOT   Then set before my face the Lord Aumerle.

BOLINGBROKE [*to* AUMERLE]   Cousin, stand forth, and look
    upon that man.

        [AUMERLE *stands forth*]

BAGOT   My lord Aumerle, I know your daring tongue
Scorns to unsay° what once it hath delivered.   *deny*
In that dead° time when Gloucester's death was plotted *fatal; dark*

10 I heard you say 'Is not my arm of length,°   *long enough*
That reacheth from the restful English court
As far as Calais, to mine uncle's head?'
Amongst much other talk that very time[2]
I heard you say that you had rather refuse

15 The offer of an hundred thousand crowns
Than° Bolingbroke's return to England,   *Than accept*
Adding withal° how blest this land would be   *besides*
In this your cousin's death.

AUMERLE   Princes and noble lords,
What answer shall I make to this base man?

20 Shall I so much dishonour my fair stars°   *honorable birth*
On equal terms to give him chastisement?[3]
Either I must, or have mine honour soiled
With the attainder° of his slanderous lips.   *accusation*

        [*He throws down his gage*]

There is my gage, the manual seal of death

25 That marks thee out for hell. I say thou liest,
And will maintain° what thou hast said is false *will uphold in combat*
In thy heart blood, though being all too base
To stain the temper[4] of my knightly sword.

BOLINGBROKE   Bagot, forbear. Thou shalt not take it up.

30 AUMERLE   Excepting one,° I would he° were the best *(Bolingbroke) / (Bagot)*
In all this presence that hath moved° me so.   *angered*

FITZWALTER   If that thy valour stand on sympathy,[5]
There is my gage, Aumerle, in gage to thine.

        [*He throws down his gage*]

By that fair sun which shows me where thou stand'st,

35 I heard thee say, and vauntingly° thou spak'st it,   *boastfully*
That thou wert cause of noble Gloucester's death.
If° thou deny'st it twenty times, thou liest,   *Even if*

4.1 Location: Westminster Hall.
1. Who persuaded; who collaborated with.
2. *that very time:* inconsistent, since Gloucester was
killed long before Bolingbroke's exile.

3. Punishment (a lord could refuse to fight a lowborn
man in the trial by combat).
4. Quality (literally, "hardness").
5. Insists on equality of rank.

And I will turn thy falsehood to thy heart,
Where it was forgèd, with my rapier's point.

40   AUMERLE   Thou dar'st not, coward, live to see that day.

FITZWALTER   Now by my soul, I would it were this hour.

AUMERLE   Fitzwalter, thou art damned to hell for this.

HARRY PERCY   Aumerle, thou liest. His honour is as true
In this appeal° as thou art all unjust;   *accusation*

45   And that thou art so, there I throw my gage
      [*He throws down his gage*]
To prove it on thee to the extremest point
Of mortal breathing. Seize it if thou dar'st.

AUMERLE   An if I do not, may my hands rot off,
And never brandish more° revengeful steel   *again*

50   Over the glittering helmet of my foe.[6]

50.1   ANOTHER LORD   *I task the earth to the like, forsworn Aumerle,*
        And spur thee on with full as many lies°   *accusations of lying*
        As may be hollowed° in thy treacherous ear   *shouted*
        From sun to sun.° There is my honour's pawn.   *sunrise to sunset*

50.5   *Engage it to[7] the trial if thou darest.*
        [*He throws down his gage*]
      AUMERLE   *Who sets° me else? By heaven, I'll throw[8] at all.*   *challenges (in gambling)*
      I have a thousand spirits in one breast
      To answer twenty thousand such as you.

SURREY   My lord Fitzwalter, I do remember well
The very time Aumerle and you did talk.

FITZWALTER   'Tis very true. You were in presence° then,   *were present*
And you can witness with me this is true.

55   SURREY   As false, by heaven, as heaven itself is true.

FITZWALTER   Surrey, thou liest.

SURREY   Dishonourable boy,
That lie shall lie so heavy on my sword
That it shall render vengeance and revenge,
Till thou, the lie-giver, and that lie do lie

60   In earth as quiet as thy father's skull;
In proof whereof, there is my honour's pawn.
      [*He throws down his gage*]
Engage it to the trial if thou dar'st.

FITZWALTER   How fondly dost thou spur a forward horse!
If I dare eat, or drink, or breathe, or live,

65   I dare meet Surrey in a wilderness
And spit upon him whilst I say he lies,
And lies, and lies.[9] There is my bond of faith
To tie thee to my strong correction.
As I intend to thrive in this new world,

70   Aumerle is guilty of my true appeal.°   *accusation*
Besides, I heard the banished Norfolk° say   *(Mowbray)*
That thou, Aumerle, didst send two of thy men
To execute the noble Duke at Calais.

AUMERLE   Some honest Christian trust me with° a gage.   *lend me*
      [*He takes another's gage and throws it down*]

---

6. The following indented passage (lines 50.1–50.8)   8. Defeat (as by throwing dice).
appears only in Q1.   9. Fitzwalter may throw down another gage here.
7. Accept it as a pledge ("gage") for.

75   That Norfolk lies, here do I throw down this,
     If he may be repealed,° to try his honour.   *recalled from exile*
    BOLINGBROKE   These differences shall all rest under gage[1]
     Till Norfolk be repealed. Repealed he shall be,
     And, though mine enemy, restored again
80   To all his lands and signories.° When he is returned,   *estates*
     Against Aumerle we will enforce his trial.
    BISHOP OF CARLISLE   That honourable day shall never be seen.
     Many a time hath banished Norfolk fought
     For Jesu Christ in glorious Christian field,[2]
85   Streaming the ensign of the Christian cross
     Against black pagans, Turks, and Saracens;
     And, toiled° with works of war, retired himself   *exhausted*
     To Italy, and there at Venice gave
     His body to that pleasant country's earth,
90   And his pure soul unto his captain, Christ,
     Under whose colours he had fought so long.
    BOLINGBROKE   Why, Bishop of Carlisle, is Norfolk dead?
    BISHOP OF CARLISLE   As surely as I live, my lord.
    BOLINGBROKE   Sweet peace conduct his sweet soul to the bosom
95   Of good old Abraham![3] Lords appellants,
     Your differences° shall all rest under gage   *disputes*
     Till we assign you to your days of trial.
          Enter [Duke of] YORK
    YORK   Great Duke of Lancaster, I come to thee
     From plume-plucked° Richard, who with willing soul   *humbled*
100   Adopts thee heir, and his high sceptre yields
     To the possession of thy royal hand.
     Ascend his throne, descending now from him,
     And long live Henry, of that name the fourth!
    BOLINGBROKE   In God's name I'll ascend the regal throne.
105 BISHOP OF CARLISLE   Marry, God forbid!
     Worst° in this royal presence may I speak,   *Least worthy*
     Yet best beseeming° me to speak the truth.   *fitting (as a clergyman)*
     Would God that any in this noble presence
     Were enough noble to be upright judge
110   Of noble Richard. Then true noblesse° would   *nobility*
     Learn° him forbearance from so foul a wrong.   *Teach*
     What subject can give sentence on his king?
     And who sits here that is not Richard's subject?
     Thieves are not judged but° they are by° to hear,   *except when / present*
115   Although apparent° guilt be seen in them;   *obvious*
     And shall the figure° of God's majesty,   *image*
     His captain, steward, deputy elect,°   *chosen*
     Anointed, crownèd, planted many years,
     Be judged by subject and inferior breath,
120   And he himself not present? O, forfend° it, God,   *prohibit*
     That in a Christian climate souls refined[4]
     Should show so heinous, black, obscene° a deed!   *odious*
     I speak to subjects, and a subject speaks
     Stirred up by God thus boldly for his king.

---

1. Shall remain as standing challenges.
2. In battle for the Christian cause.
3. *the bosom . . . Abraham*: that is, heavenly rest; see
Luke 16:22.
4. Spiritually improved; aristocratic.

125   My lord of Hereford here, whom you call king,
       Is a foul traitor to proud Hereford's king;
       And, if you crown him, let me prophesy
       The blood of English shall manure the ground,
       And future ages groan for this foul act.
130   Peace shall go sleep with Turks and infidels,
       And in this seat° of peace tumultuous wars   *region; throne*
       Shall kin with kin and kind with kind confound.⁵
       Disorder, horror, fear, and mutiny
       Shall here inhabit, and this land be called
135   The field of Golgotha⁶ and dead men's skulls.
       O, if you rear this house against this house°   *(Lancaster against York)*
       It will the woefullest division prove
       That ever fell upon this cursèd earth!
       Prevent, resist it; let it not be so,
140   Lest child, child's children, cry against you woe.
       NORTHUMBERLAND   Well have you argued, sir, and for your pains
       Of capital treason we arrest you here.
       My lord of Westminster, be it your charge
       To keep him safely till his day of trial.⁷
145   May it please you, lords, to grant the Commons' suit?⁸
       BOLINGBROKE   Fetch hither Richard, that in common° view   *public*
       He may surrender.⁹ So we shall proceed
       Without suspicion.
       YORK   I will be his conduct.°   *Exit*   *escort*
       BOLINGBROKE   Lords, you that here are under our arrest,
150   Procure your sureties for your days of answer.¹
       Little are we beholden to your love,
       And little looked for° at your helping hands.   *expected*
            Enter RICHARD *and* [*Duke of*] YORK [*with attendants*
            bearing the crown and sceptre]
       RICHARD   Alack, why am I sent for to a king
       Before I have shook off the regal thoughts
155   Wherewith I reigned? I hardly yet have learned
       To insinuate, flatter, bow, and bend my knee.
       Give sorrow leave awhile to tutor me
       To this submission. Yet I well remember
       The favours° of these men. Were they not mine?   *faces; benefits*
160   Did they not sometime cry 'All hail!' to me?
       So Judas did to Christ. But He in twelve
       Found truth in all but one; I, in twelve thousand, none.
       God save the King! Will no man say 'Amen'?
       Am I both priest and clerk?² Well then, Amen.
165   God save the King, although I be not he.
       And yet Amen, if heaven do think him me.
       To do what service am I sent for hither?
       YORK   To do that office° of thine own good will   *task; ceremony*
       Which tired majesty did make thee offer:

---

5. Shall destroy kinsman by fellow kinsman and countryman by fellow countryman.
6. Place of Christ's crucifixion, the name of which
means "place of dead men's skulls."
7. The passage that follows, to line 308, is not included
in the earliest texts. See Textual Note.
8. The House of Commons' request that Richard

should have judgment passed on him.
9. Abdicate (the legitimacy of the Commons' suit
depended on Richard's having given up the crown and
thus his royal immunity from prosecution).
1. Procure persons guaranteeing your appearance on
the day of trial.
2. Priest's assistant who utters the responses to prayers.

170   The resignation of thy state and crown
    To Henry Bolingbroke.
   RICHARD [*to an attendant*] Give me the crown. [*To* BOLINGBROKE]
     Here, cousin, seize the crown.
    Here, cousin. On this side my hand, on that side thine.
    Now is this golden crown like a deep well

175   That owes° two buckets filling one another,[3]   *has*
    The emptier ever dancing in the air,
    The other down, unseen, and full of water.
    That bucket down and full of tears am I,
    Drinking my griefs, whilst you mount up on high.

180 BOLINGBROKE I thought you had been willing to resign.
   RICHARD My crown I am, but still my griefs are mine.
    You may my glories and my state° depose,   *royal status*
    But not my griefs; still° am I king of those.   *permanently*
   BOLINGBROKE Part of your cares you give me with your crown.

185 RICHARD Your cares set up do not pluck my cares down.
    My care is loss of care by old care done;
    Your care is gain of care by new care won.[4]
    The cares I give I have, though given away;
    They 'tend° the crown, yet still with me they stay. *attend; accompany*

190 BOLINGBROKE Are you contented to resign the crown?
   RICHARD Ay, no; no, ay; for I must nothing be;[5]
    Therefore no, no, for I resign to thee.
    Now mark me how I will undo° myself.   *ruin; strip*
    I give this heavy weight from off my head,
     [BOLINGBROKE *accepts the crown*]

195   And this unwieldy sceptre from my hand,
     [BOLINGBROKE *accepts the sceptre*]
    The pride of kingly sway from out my heart.
    With mine own tears I wash away my balm,
    With mine own hands I give away my crown,
    With mine own tongue deny my sacred state,° *divine right to be King*

200   With mine own breath release all duteous oaths.° *oaths of allegiance*
    All pomp and majesty I do forswear.
    My manors, rents, revenues I forgo.
    My acts, decrees, and statutes I deny.°   *repudiate*
    God pardon all oaths that are broke to me.

205   God keep all vows unbroke are made to thee.
    Make me, that nothing have, with nothing grieved,[6]
    And thou with all pleased, that hast all achieved.
    Long mayst thou live in Richard's seat to sit,
    And soon lie Richard in an earthy pit.

210   'God save King Henry,' unkinged Richard says,
    'And send him many years of sunshine° days.'   *sunny*
    What more remains?
   NORTHUMBERLAND [*giving* RICHARD *papers*]
        No more but that you read°   *read aloud*
    These accusations and these grievous crimes
    Committed by your person and your followers

---

3. That is, the raising of one causing the other to descend and fill.

4. *Your cares . . . won:* an extended wordplay on "care": Your assuming cares of state does not relieve me of grief. I mourn the loss of responsibility, by lack of dili-gence in the past; you concern yourself with gaining responsibility, won by effort.

5. Playing on "ay" (yes) and "I": since I am no thing, then "I," that is, "ay," is "no."

6. Grieved at nothing; grieved at having nothing.

215	Against the state and profit° of this land,	*established prosperity*
	That by confessing them, the souls of men	
	May deem that you are worthily deposed.	
	RICHARD Must I do so? And must I ravel out	
	My weaved-up follies? Gentle Northumberland,	
220	If thy offences were upon record,	
	Would it not shame thee in so fair a troop°	*company*
	To read a lecture° of them? If thou wouldst,	*give a public reading*
	There shouldst thou find one heinous article	
	Containing the deposing of a king	
225	And cracking the strong warrant of an oath,	
	Marked with a blot, damned in the book of heaven.	
	Nay, all of you that stand and look upon	
	Whilst that my wretchedness doth bait[7] myself,	
	Though some of you, with Pilate, wash your hands,[8]	
230	Showing an outward pity, yet you Pilates	
	Have here delivered me to my sour° cross,	*bitter*
	And water cannot wash away your sin.	
	NORTHUMBERLAND My lord, dispatch.° Read o'er these articles.	*hurry up*
	RICHARD Mine eyes are full of tears; I cannot see.	
235	And yet salt water blinds them not so much	
	But they can see a sort° of traitors here.	*pack*
	Nay, if I turn mine eyes upon myself	
	I find myself a traitor with the rest,	
	For I have given here my soul's consent	
240	T'undeck the pompous° body of a king,	*splendidly dressed*
	Made glory base and sovereignty a slave,	
	Proud majesty a subject, state° a peasant.	*royalty*
	NORTHUMBERLAND My lord—	
	RICHARD No lord of thine, thou haught°-insulting man,	*haughty*
245	Nor no man's lord. I have no name, no title,	
	No, not that name was given me at the font,	
	But 'tis usurped. Alack the heavy day,	
	That I have worn so many winters out	
	And know not now what name to call myself!	
250	O, that I were a mockery king of snow,	
	Standing before the sun of Bolingbroke	
	To melt myself away in water-drops!	
	Good king, great king—and yet not greatly good—	
	An if my word be sterling° yet in England,	*valid (like currency)*
255	Let it command a mirror hither straight,°	*immediately*
	That it may show me what a face I have,	
	Since it is bankrupt of his° majesty.	*its*
	BOLINGBROKE Go some of you and fetch a looking-glass.	

                              [Exit one or more]

	NORTHUMBERLAND Read o'er this paper while the glass° doth	*until the mirror*
	come.	
260	RICHARD Fiend, thou torment'st me ere I come to hell.	
	BOLINGBROKE Urge it no more, my lord Northumberland.	
	NORTHUMBERLAND The Commons will not then be satisfied.	
	RICHARD They shall be satisfied. I'll read enough	
	When I do see the very book indeed	

---

7. Torment (as in bearbaiting).
8. Pilate, Jesus' judge, washed his hands to signify his disclaiming of responsibility for the death sentence he imposed at the request of the Jews.

265   Where all my sins are writ, and that's myself.
             Enter one with a glass
    Give me that glass, and therein will I read.
      [RICHARD *takes the glass and looks in it*]
    No deeper wrinkles yet? Hath sorrow struck
    So many blows upon this face of mine
    And made no deeper wounds? O flatt'ring glass,
270   Like to my followers in prosperity,
    Thou dost beguile me! Was this face the face
    That every day under his household roof
    Did keep ten thousand men? Was this the face
    That like the sun did make beholders wink?°   *shut their eyes*
275   Is this the face which faced⁹ so many follies,
    That was at last outfaced° by Bolingbroke?   *stared down*
    A brittle glory shineth in this face.
    As brittle as the glory is the face,
             [*He shatters the glass*]
    For there it is, cracked in an hundred shivers.
280   Mark, silent King, the moral of this sport:
    How soon my sorrow hath destroyed my face.
    BOLINGBROKE   The shadow¹ of your sorrow hath destroyed
    The shadow° of your face.   *image*
    RICHARD   Say that again:
    'The shadow of my sorrow'—ha, let's see.
285   'Tis very true: my grief lies all within,
    And these external manner of laments
    Are merely shadows to the unseen grief
    That swells with silence in the tortured soul.
    There lies the substance, and I thank thee, King,
290   For thy great bounty that not only giv'st
    Me cause to wail, but teachest me the way
    How to lament the cause. I'll beg one boon,°   *favor*
    And then be gone and trouble you no more.
    Shall I obtain it?
    BOLINGBROKE   Name it, fair cousin.
295   RICHARD   Fair cousin? I am greater than a king;
    For when I was a king my flatterers
    Were then but subjects; being now a subject,
    I have a king here to my flatterer.
    Being so great, I have no need to beg.
300   BOLINGBROKE   Yet ask.
    RICHARD   And shall I have?
    BOLINGBROKE   You shall.
    RICHARD   Then give me leave to go.
    BOLINGBROKE   Whither?
305   RICHARD   Whither you will, so° I were from your sights.   *provided that*
    BOLINGBROKE   Go some of you, convey° him to the Tower.   *conduct*
    RICHARD   O good, 'convey'!° Conveyors are you all,   *steal*
    That rise thus nimbly by a true king's fall.
                    [*Exit, guarded*]
    BOLINGBROKE   On Wednesday next we solemnly set down

---

9. Countenanced; adorned (as a garment trimmed with "facings").
1. Darkness; outward display; image, reflection; un- happiness (Richard plays on the word's various meanings in the following passage).

310 Our coronation. Lords, prepare yourselves.
Exeunt. Manent [ABBOT OF] WESTMINSTER,
[BISHOP OF] CARLISLE, [*and*] AUMERLE

ABBOT OF WESTMINSTER   A woeful pageant have we here beheld.
BISHOP OF CARLISLE   The woe's to come, the children yet unborn
Shall feel this day as sharp to them as thorn.
AUMERLE   You holy clergymen, is there no plot
315 To rid the realm of this pernicious blot?
ABBOT OF WESTMINSTER   My lord, before I freely speak my
mind herein,
You shall not only take the sacrament[2]
To bury mine intents,[3] but also to effect
Whatever I shall happen to devise.
320 I see your brows are full of discontent,
Your hearts of sorrow, and your eyes of tears.
Come home with me to supper. I will lay
A plot shall show us all a merry day.   *Exeunt*

5.1

Enter the QUEEN *with her* LADIES
QUEEN   This way the King will come. This is the way
To Julius Caesar's ill-erected Tower,[1]
To whose flint bosom my condemnèd lord
Is doomed a prisoner by proud Bolingbroke.
5 Here let us rest, if this rebellious earth
Have any resting for her true king's queen.
Enter RICHARD, *and guard*
But soft,° but see—or rather do not see—   wait
My fair rose wither. Yet look up, behold,
That you in pity may dissolve to dew,
10 And wash him fresh again with true-love tears.—
Ah, thou the model where old Troy did stand![2]
Thou map° of honour, thou King Richard's tomb,   epitome
And not King Richard! Thou most beauteous inn:
Why should hard-favoured° grief be lodged in thee,   ugly; unfortunate
15 When triumph is become an alehouse[3] guest?
RICHARD   Join not with grief, fair woman, do not so,
To make my end too sudden. Learn, good soul,
To think our former state a happy dream,
From which awaked, the truth of what we are
20 Shows us but this. I am sworn brother, sweet,
To grim necessity, and he and I
Will keep a league till death. Hie° thee to France,   Hasten
And cloister thee in some religious house.°   convent
Our holy lives must win a new world's° crown,   (heaven's)
25 Which our profane hours here have stricken down.
QUEEN   What, is my Richard both in shape and mind
Transformed and weakenèd? Hath Bolingbroke
Deposed thine intellect? Hath he been in thy heart?
The lion dying thrusteth forth his paw

---

2. A solemn oath, accompanied by the rite of Communion.
3. To keep my intentions secret.
5.1 Location: A street near the Tower of London.
1. The Tower of London (popularly thought to have

been built by Caesar). *ill-erected:* poorly built; erected
for evil ends.
2. The pattern of fallen greatness, like Troy.
3. Poorer class of lodging (referring to Bolingbroke)
than an "inn."

30   And wounds the earth, if nothing else, with rage
       To be° o'erpowered; and wilt thou, pupil-like,   *At being*
       Take the correction, mildly kiss the rod,
       And fawn on rage with base humility,
       Which art a lion and the king of beasts?
35 RICHARD   A king of beasts[4] indeed! If aught but beasts,
       I had been still a happy king of men.
       Good sometimes° Queen, prepare thee hence for France.   *former*
       Think I am dead, and that even here thou tak'st,
       As from my death-bed, thy last living leave.
40   In winter's tedious nights, sit by the fire
       With good old folks, and let them tell thee tales
       Of woeful ages long ago betid;[5]
       And ere thou bid goodnight, to quit their griefs°   *repay their sad tales*
       Tell thou the lamentable fall of me,
45   And send the hearers weeping to their beds;
       Forwhy the senseless brands will sympathize[6]
       The heavy accent of thy moving[7] tongue,
       And in compassion weep the fire out;
       And some° will mourn in ashes, some coal black,   *(firebrands)*
50   For the deposing of a rightful king.
            Enter [Earl of] NORTHUMBERLAND
    NORTHUMBERLAND   My lord, the mind of Bolingbroke is changed.
       You must to Pomfret,° not unto the Tower.   *castle in Yorkshire*
       And, madam, there is order ta'en[8] for you.
       With all swift speed you must away to France.
55 RICHARD   Northumberland, thou ladder wherewithal
       The mounting Bolingbroke ascends my throne,
       The time shall not be many hours of age
       More than it is ere foul sin, gathering head,
       Shall break into corruption.[9] Thou shalt think,
60   Though he divide the realm and give thee half,
       It is too little helping[1] him to all.
       He shall think that thou, which know'st the way
       To plant unrightful kings, wilt know again,
       Being ne'er so little urged another way,
65   To pluck him headlong from the usurpèd throne.
       The love of wicked friends converts to fear,
       That fear to hate, and hate turns one or both
       To worthy° danger and deservèd death.   *severe*
    NORTHUMBERLAND   My guilt be on my head, and there an end.[2]
70   Take leave and part,° for you must part° forthwith.   *separate / depart*
    RICHARD   Doubly divorced! Bad men, you violate
       A twofold marriage: 'twixt my crown and me,
       And then betwixt me and my married wife.
       [*To the* QUEEN] Let me unkiss the oath 'twixt thee and me—
75   And yet not so, for with a kiss 'twas made.
       Part us, Northumberland: I towards the north,
       Where shivering cold and sickness pines the clime;°   *afflicts the region*

---

4. Lion (Richard's emblem); ruler of beastly men.
5. Woe that happened long ago.
6. Because even the insentient firewood will respond
empathetically.
7. Physically and emotionally.
8. Arrangements have been made.
9. Pus (the image is of a swelling abscess). *Henry IV,*

Parts 1 and 2, the sequels to *Richard II,* dramatize
Northumberland's rebellion against "the mounting Bolingbroke."
1. *helping:* since you helped.
2. Recalling the cry of the Jews at Jesus' trial: "His
death be upon our heads, and the heads of our children."

My queen to France, from whence set forth in pomp
She came adornèd hither like sweet May,
80   Sent back like Hallowmas° or short'st of day.³   *November 1*
QUEEN   And must we be divided? Must we part?
RICHARD   Ay, hand from hand, my love, and heart from heart.
QUEEN   Banish us both, and send the King with me.
NORTHUMBERLAND   That were some love, but little policy.°   *but politically naive*
85 QUEEN   Then whither he goes, thither let me go.
RICHARD   So two together weeping make one woe.
    Weep thou for me in France, I for thee here.
    Better far off than, near, be ne'er the nea'er.⁴
    Go count thy way with sighs, I mine with groans.
90 QUEEN   So longest way shall have the longest moans.
RICHARD   Twice for one step I'll groan, the way being short,
    And piece the way out° with a heavy heart.   *lengthen the way*
    Come, come, in wooing sorrow let's be brief,
    Since, wedding it, there is such length in grief.
95   One kiss shall stop our mouths, and dumbly° part.   *silently*
    Thus give I mine, and thus take I thy heart.
    [*They kiss*]
QUEEN   Give me mine own again. 'Twere no good part⁵
    To take on me to keep and kill thy heart.
    [*They kiss*]
    So now I have mine own again, be gone,
100   That I may strive to kill it with a groan.
RICHARD   We make woe wanton⁶ with this fond delay.
    Once more, adieu. The rest let sorrow say.
        Exeunt [RICHARD, *guarded, and* NORTHUMBERLAND *at*
        one door, the QUEEN *and her* LADIES *at another door*]

5.2

Enter DUKE *and* DUCHESS OF YORK
DUCHESS OF YORK   My lord, you told me you would tell the rest,
    When weeping made you break the story off,
    Of our two cousins'° coming into London.   *kinsmen's*
YORK   Where did I leave?
DUCHESS OF YORK   At that sad stop, my lord,
5   Where rude misgoverned° hands from windows' tops°   *unruly / upper windows*
    Threw dust and rubbish on King Richard's head.
YORK   Then, as I said, the Duke, great Bolingbroke,
    Mounted upon a hot and fiery steed,
    Which his aspiring rider¹ seemed to know,
10   With slow but stately pace kept on his course,
    Whilst all tongues cried 'God save thee, Bolingbroke!'
    You would have thought the very windows spake,
    So many greedy looks of young and old
    Through casements darted their desiring eyes
15   Upon his visage, and that all the walls
    With painted imagery² had said at once,
    'Jesu preserve thee! Welcome, Bolingbroke!'

3. Winter solstice.
4. Better to be far away than to be near but never nearer to our happiness.
5. It would not be good of me.
6. We make our woe unrestrained; we make a sport of our grief.
5.2 Location: The Duke of York's house.
1. Object of "seemed to know."
2. Painted cloths that were hung on walls in pageants; figures in these sometimes had "speech bubbles."

Whilst he, from the one side to the other turning,
Bare-headed, lower than his proud steed's neck,
20 Bespake° them thus: 'I thank you, countrymen',   *Addressed*
And thus still doing, thus he passed along.
DUCHESS OF YORK Alack, poor Richard! Where rode he the whilst?
YORK As in a theatre the eyes of men,
After a well-graced actor leaves the stage,
25 Are idly bent on him that enters next,
Thinking his prattle to be tedious,
Even so, or with much more contempt, men's eyes
Did scowl on gentle Richard. No man cried 'God save him!'
No joyful tongue gave him his welcome home;
30 But dust was thrown upon his sacred head,
Which with such gentle sorrow he shook off,
His face still combating° with tears and smiles,   *continually struggling*
The badges° of his grief and patience,   *emblems*
That had not God for some strong purpose steeled
35 The hearts of men, they must perforce have melted,
And barbarism itself have pitied him.
But heaven hath a hand in these events,
To whose high will we bound our calm contents.³
To Bolingbroke are we sworn subjects now,
40 Whose state and honour I for aye allow.°   *forever acknowledge*
     Enter [Duke of] AUMERLE
DUCHESS OF YORK Here comes my son Aumerle.
YORK   Aumerle that was;⁴
But that is lost for being Richard's friend,
And, madam, you must call him 'Rutland' now.
I am in Parliament pledge for his truth°   *guarantor of his loyalty*
45 And lasting fealty° to the new-made King.   *fidelity*
DUCHESS OF YORK Welcome, my son. Who are the violets now
That strew the green lap of the new-come spring?
AUMERLE Madam, I know not, nor I greatly care not.
God knows I had as lief° be none as one.   *had rather*
50 YORK Well, bear you well in this new spring of time,
Lest you be cropped° before you come to prime.   *cut*
What news from Oxford? Hold these jousts and triumphs?°   *processions*
AUMERLE For aught I know, my lord, they do.
YORK You will be there, I know.
55 AUMERLE If God prevent it not, I purpose so.
YORK What seal is that that hangs without thy bosom?⁵
Yea, look'st thou pale? Let me see the writing.
AUMERLE My lord, 'tis nothing.
YORK   No matter, then, who see it.
I will be satisfied. Let me see the writing.
60 AUMERLE I do beseech your grace to pardon me.
It is a matter of small consequence,
Which for some reasons I would not have seen.
YORK Which for some reasons, sir, I mean to see.
I fear, I fear!
DUCHESS OF YORK What should you fear?

3. Bound ourselves to be calmly contented.
4. Aumerle has been deprived of his dukedom; he remains Earl of Rutland.
5. The document is in Aumerle's doublet, with the seal on a visibly dangling slip of attached paper.

65 'Tis nothing but some bond that he is entered into
For gay apparel 'gainst° the triumph day.   *in time for*
YORK Bound to himself?[6] What doth he with a bond
That he is bound to? Wife, thou art a fool.
Boy, let me see the writing.
70 AUMERLE I do beseech you, pardon me. I may not show it.
YORK I will be satisfied. Let me see it, I say.
        He plucks it out of [Aumerle's] bosom, and reads it
Treason, foul treason! Villain, traitor, slave!
DUCHESS OF YORK What is the matter, my lord?
YORK Ho, who is within there? Saddle my horse.—
75 God for his mercy, what treachery is here!
DUCHESS OF YORK Why, what is it, my lord?
YORK Give me my boots, I say. Saddle my horse.—
Now by mine honour, by my life, my troth,
I will appeach° the villain.   *accuse*
80 DUCHESS OF YORK What is the matter?
YORK Peace, foolish woman.
DUCHESS OF YORK I will not peace. What is the matter, son?
AUMERLE Good mother, be content. It is no more
Than my poor life must answer.
DUCHESS OF YORK   Thy life answer?
85 YORK Bring me my boots. I will unto the King.
        His man enters with his boots
DUCHESS OF YORK Strike him,° Aumerle! Poor boy, thou art   *(the servant)*
        amazed.°   *distraught*
[*To York's man*] Hence, villain! Never more come in my sight.
YORK Give me my boots, I say.
DUCHESS OF YORK   Why, York, what wilt thou do?
Wilt thou not hide the trespass of thine own?
90 Have we more sons?[7] Or are we like to have?
Is not my teeming date° drunk up with time?   *my period of childbearing*
And wilt thou pluck my fair son from mine age,
And rob me of a happy mother's name?
Is he not like thee? Is he not thine own?
95 YORK Thou fond,° mad woman,   *foolish*
Wilt thou conceal this dark conspiracy?
A dozen of them here have ta'en the sacrament,
And interchangeably set down their hands[8]
To kill the King at Oxford.
DUCHESS OF YORK   He shall be none.°   *not be one of them*
100 We'll keep him here, then what is that to him?
YORK Away, fond woman! Were he twenty times my son
I would appeach him.
DUCHESS OF YORK   Hadst thou groaned° for him   *suffered labor pains*
As I have done thou wouldst be more pitiful.
But now I know thy mind: thou dost suspect
105 That I have been disloyal to thy bed,
And that he is a bastard, not thy son.
Sweet York, sweet husband, be not of that mind.
He is as like thee as a man may be,

6. If Aumerle had signed a bond to borrow money, the
creditor would have the bond.
7. Actually, Aumerle had a brother and a sister, and the

Duchess of York, the Duke's second wife, was Aumerle's
stepmother.
8. And mutually committed themselves in writing.

Not like to me or any of my kin,
And yet I love him.

110 YORK   Make way, unruly woman.

Exit [with his man]

DUCHESS OF YORK After, Aumerle! Mount thee upon his horse.
Spur, post,° and get before him to the King,   *Ride fast*
And beg thy pardon ere he do accuse thee.
I'll not be long behind—though I be old,
115 I doubt not but to ride as fast as York—
And never will I rise up from the ground
Till Bolingbroke have pardoned thee. Away, be gone!

Exeunt [severally]

5.3

Enter BOLINGBROKE, [*crowned* KING HENRY,] *with*
[HARRY] PERCY, *and other nobles*

KING HENRY Can no man tell of my unthrifty son?[1]
'Tis full three months since I did see him last.
If any plague hang over us, 'tis he.
I would to God, my lords, he might be found.
5 Enquire at London 'mongst the taverns there,
For there, they say, he daily doth frequent
With unrestrainèd loose companions—
Even such, they say, as stand in narrow lanes
And beat our watch° and rob our passengers°—   *watchmen / wayfarers*
10 Which he, young wanton and effeminate° boy,   *pleasure-seeking*
Takes on° the point of honour to support   *Makes it*
So dissolute a crew.

HARRY PERCY My lord, some two days since,° I saw the Prince,   *ago*
And told him of these triumphs held at Oxford.

15 KING HENRY And what said the gallant?

HARRY PERCY His answer was he would unto the stews,°   *brothels*
And from the common'st creature pluck a glove,
And wear it as a favour,[2] and with that
He would unhorse the lustiest° challenger.   *most vigorous*

20 KING HENRY As dissolute as desperate.° Yet through both   *reckless*
I see some sparks of better hope, which elder days
May happily[3] bring forth.

Enter [Duke of] AUMERLE, *amazed*

                      But who comes here?

AUMERLE Where is the King?

KING HENRY What means our cousin that he stares and looks so wildly?

25 AUMERLE [*kneeling*] God save your grace! I do beseech your majesty
To have some conference with your grace alone.

KING HENRY [*to lords*] Withdraw yourselves, and leave us here alone.

[Exeunt all but KING HENRY *and* AUMERLE]

What is the matter with our cousin now?

AUMERLE For ever may my knees grow° to the earth,   *be fixed*
30 My tongue cleave to the roof within my mouth,
Unless a pardon ere I rise or speak.

KING HENRY Intended or committed was this fault?

5.3 Location: Windsor Castle.   2. Lady's gift to a knight that is worn in combat.
1. Henry's oldest son is Prince Hal of *1* and *2 Henry IV*,   3. Perhaps; with good fortune.
later King Henry V. *unthrifty*: dissolute.

If on the first,° how heinous e'er it be,   *If only intended*
To win thy after-love I pardon thee.

35   AUMERLE[*rising*]   Then give me leave that I may turn the key,
That no man enter till my tale be done.

KING HENRY   Have thy desire.

     [AUMERLE *locks the door.*]

     The Duke of YORK *knocks at the door and crieth*

YORK [*within*]   My liege, beware! Look to thyself!
Thou hast a traitor in thy presence there.

     [KING HENRY *draws his sword*]

KING HENRY [*to* AUMERLE]   Villain, I'll make thee safe.°   *harmless*

40   AUMERLE   Stay° thy revengeful hand! Thou hast no cause to fear.   *Restrain*

YORK [*knocking within*]   Open the door, secure° foolhardy King!   *overconfident*
Shall I for° love speak treason[4] to thy face?   *out of*
Open the door, or I will break it open.

     [KING HENRY *opens the door.*] *Enter* [*Duke of*] YORK

KING HENRY   What is the matter, uncle? Speak,
45   Recover breath, tell us how near is danger,
That we may arm us to encounter it.

YORK   Peruse this writing here, and thou shalt know
The treason that my haste[5] forbids me show.°   *explain*

     [*He gives* KING HENRY *the paper*]

AUMERLE   Remember, as thou read'st, thy promise past.
50   I do repent me. Read not my name there.
My heart is not confederate with my hand.°   *signature*

YORK   It was, villain, ere thy hand did set it down.
I tore it° from the traitor's bosom, King.   *(the bond)*
Fear, and not love, begets his penitence.
55   Forget to pity him, lest pity prove
A serpent that will sting thee to the heart.

KING HENRY   O, heinous, strong, and bold conspiracy!
O loyal father of a treacherous son!
Thou sheer,° immaculate, and silver fountain,   *clear*
60   From whence this stream through muddy passages
Hath held his current and defiled himself,
Thy overflow of good converts to bad,
And thy abundant goodness shall excuse
This deadly° blot in thy digressing[6] son.   *damnable; death-dealing*

65   YORK   So shall my virtue be his vice's bawd,
And he shall spend mine honour with his shame,
As thriftless sons their scraping fathers' gold.
Mine honour lives when his dishonour dies,
Or my shamed life in his dishonour lies.
70   Thou kill'st me in his life: giving him breath
The traitor lives, the true man's put to death.

DUCHESS OF YORK [*within*]   What ho, my liege, for God's sake let me in!

KING HENRY   What shrill-voiced suppliant makes this eager cry?

DUCHESS OF YORK [*within*]   A woman, and thy aunt, great King; 'tis I.
75   Speak with me, pity me! Open the door!
A beggar begs that never begged before.

KING HENRY   Our scene is altered from a serious thing,
And now changed to 'The Beggar and the King'.°   *(the name of a ballad)*

---

4. Disrespectfully criticize (as "secure" and "foolhardy").   6. Diverging from course (as of a stream); transgressing.
5. York is out of breath.

My dangerous cousin, let your mother in.
80   I know she is come to pray for your foul sin.
           [AUMERLE *opens the door.*] *Enter* DUCHESS [OF YORK]
YORK   If thou do pardon, whosoever pray,
    More sins for this forgiveness prosper may.
    This festered joint° cut off, the rest rest sound.   *infected limb*
    This let alone will all the rest confound.°   *destroy*
DUCHESS OF YORK [*kneeling*]   O King, believe not this
85   hard-hearted man.
    Love loving not itself, none other can.[7]
YORK   Thou frantic woman, what dost thou make° here?   *do*
    Shall thy old dugs° once more a traitor rear?   *breasts*
DUCHESS OF YORK   Sweet York, be patient.—Hear me, gentle liege.
KING HENRY   Rise up, good aunt.
90 DUCHESS OF YORK   Not yet, I thee beseech.
    Forever will I kneel upon my knees,
    And never see day that the happy sees,
    Till thou give joy, until thou bid me joy
    By pardoning Rutland, my transgressing boy.
95 AUMERLE [*kneeling*]   Unto° my mother's prayers I bend my knee.   *In support of*
YORK [*kneeling*]   Against them both my true joints bended be.
    Ill mayst thou thrive if thou grant any grace.
DUCHESS OF YORK   Pleads he in earnest? Look upon his face.
    His eyes do drop no tears, his prayers are in jest.
100   His words come from his mouth; ours from our breast.
    He prays but faintly, and would be denied;
    We pray with heart and soul, and all beside.
    His weary joints would gladly rise, I know;
    Our knees shall kneel till to the ground they grow.
105   His prayers are full of false hypocrisy;
    Ours of true zeal and deep integrity.
    Our prayers do outpray his; then let them have
    That mercy which true prayer ought to have.
KING HENRY   Good aunt, stand up.
DUCHESS OF YORK   Nay, do not say 'Stand up'.
110   Say 'Pardon' first, and afterwards 'Stand up'.
    An if° I were thy nurse, thy tongue to teach,   *An if = If*
    'Pardon' should be the first word of thy speech.
    I never longed to hear a word till now.
    Say 'Pardon', King. Let pity teach thee how.
115   The word is short, but not so short as sweet;
    No word like 'Pardon' for kings' mouths so meet.°   *fit*
YORK   Speak it in French, King: say 'Pardonnez-moi'.[8]
DUCHESS OF YORK   Dost thou teach pardon pardon to destroy?[9]
    Ah, my sour° husband, my hard-hearted lord   *harsh*
120   That sets the word itself against the word!
    Speak 'Pardon' as 'tis current in our land;
    The chopping[1] French we do not understand.
    Thine eye begins to speak; set thy tongue there;
    Or in thy piteous heart plant thou thine ear,
125   That hearing how our plaints and prayers do pierce,

---

7. If one does not love one's own flesh and blood, one
can love no one else (not even the King).
8. "Excuse me," a polite refusal.

9. Rhymes with "moi" in anglicized pronunciation.
1. Logic-chopping, changing the meaning.

      Pity may move thee 'Pardon' to rehearse.°   *recite*

KING HENRY   Good aunt, stand up.

DUCHESS OF YORK   I do not sue to stand.

      Pardon is all the suit I have in hand.

KING HENRY   I pardon him as God shall pardon me.

         [YORK *and* AUMERLE *rise*]

130 DUCHESS OF YORK   O, happy vantage° of a kneeling knee!   *gain; position*

      Yet am I sick for fear. Speak it again.

      Twice saying pardon doth not pardon twain,°   *divide*

      But makes one pardon strong.

KING HENRY   I pardon him

      With all my heart.

DUCHESS OF YORK [*rising*]   A god on earth thou art.

135 KING HENRY   But for our trusty brother-in-law[2] and the Abbot,

      With all the rest of that consorted° crew,   *confederated*

      Destruction straight shall dog them at the heels.

      Good uncle, help to order several powers°   *forces*

      To Oxford, or where'er these traitors are.

140   They shall not live within this world, I swear,

      But I will have them if I once know where.

      Uncle, farewell; and cousin, so adieu.

      Your mother well hath prayed; and prove you true.°   *loyal*

DUCHESS OF YORK   Come, my old[3] son. I pray God make thee new.

                Exeunt [KING HENRY *at one door*; YORK,

                    DUCHESS OF YORK, *and* AUMERLE

                       at another door]

5.4

      Enter Sir Piers EXTON, *and* [MEN]

EXTON   Didst thou not mark the King, what words he spake?

      'Have I no friend will rid me of this living fear?'

      Was it not so?

FIRST MAN   Those were his very words.

EXTON   'Have I no friend?' quoth he. He spake it twice,

5   And urged it twice together, did he not?

SECOND MAN   He did.

EXTON   And speaking it, he wishtly° looked on me,   *intently*

      As who° should say 'I would thou wert the man   *As if he*

      That would divorce this terror from my heart',

10   Meaning the King at Pomfret. Come, let's go.

      I am the King's friend, and will rid° his foe.   *Exeunt*   *will get rid of*

5.5

      Enter RICHARD, *alone*

RICHARD   I have been studying how I may compare

      This prison where I live unto the world;

      And for because the world is populous,

      And here is not a creature but myself,

5   I cannot do it. Yet I'll hammer° it out.   *work*

      My brain I'll prove the female° to my soul,   *(that is, receptive)*

      My soul the father, and these two beget

2. The Duke of Exeter and Earl of Huntingdon, husband of Bolingbroke's sister; like Aumerle, he had been deprived of his dukedom.

3. Unregenerate (recalling the baptism service: "O merciful God, grant that the old Adam in this child may be so buried that the new man may be raised up in him").

5.4 Location: Windsor Castle.

5.5 Location: Pomfret Castle.

A generation of still-breeding° thoughts;   *ever-breeding*
And these same thoughts people this little world
10 In humours[1] like the people of this world.°   *(the real world)*
For no thought is contented. The better sort,
As thoughts of things divine, are intermixed
With scruples,° and do set the faith itself   *doubts*
Against the faith,[2] as thus: 'Come, little ones',[3]
15 And then again,
'It is as hard to come as for a camel
To thread the postern of a small needle's eye.'[4]
Thoughts° tending to ambition, they do plot   *Other thoughts*
Unlikely wonders:° how these vain weak nails   *miracles*
20 May tear a passage through the flinty ribs
Of this hard world, my ragged° prison walls;   *rugged*
And for they cannot, die in their own pride.°   *prime of life; arrogance*
Thoughts tending to content° flatter themselves   *contentment*
That they are not the first of fortune's slaves,
25 Nor shall not be the last—like seely° beggars,   *simpleminded*
Who, sitting in the stocks, refuge[5] their shame
That many have, and others must, set there;
And in this thought they find a kind of ease,
Bearing their own misfortunes on the back
30 Of such as have before endured the like.
Thus play I in one person many people,
And none contented. Sometimes am I king;
Then treason makes me wish myself a beggar,
And so I am. Then crushing penury
35 Persuades me I was better when a king.
Then am I kinged again, and by and by
Think that I am unkinged by Bolingbroke,
And straight° am nothing. But whate'er I be,   *at once*
Nor I, nor any man that but° man is,   *merely*
40 With nothing shall be pleased till he be eased
With being nothing.
       The music plays
                   Music do I hear.
Ha; ha; keep time! How sour sweet music is
When time is broke and no proportion kept.
So is it in the music of men's lives.
45 And here have I the daintiness of ear
To check° time broke in a disordered string;°   *rebuke / string instrument*
But for the concord° of my state and time   *harmony*
Had not an ear to hear my true time broke.
I wasted time, and now doth time waste me,
50 For now hath time made me his numb'ring clock.[6]
My thoughts are minutes, and with sighs they jar
Their watches° on unto mine eyes, the outward watch[7]   *periods of vigil*
Whereto my finger, like a dial's point,°   *clock's hand*

1. Temperaments; caprices.
2. *the faith . . . faith*: scriptural passage against scriptural passage.
3. From Matthew 19:14, Mark 10:14, and Luke 18:25, implying the ease of obtaining salvation.
4. Adapting Matthew 19:24, Mark 10:25, or Luke 18:25, which describe the unlikeliness of the rich reaching heaven.
5. Find refuge for; rationalize.
6. Clock that counts hours and minutes, not an hourglass.
7. Clockface; mind's external watcher.

Is pointing still° in cleansing them from tears.[8]   *always*
55 Now, sir, the sounds that tell what hour it is
   Are clamorous groans that strike upon my heart,
   Which is the bell. So sighs, and tears, and groans
   Show minutes, hours, and times. But my time
   Runs posting° on in Bolingbroke's proud joy,   *speeding*
60 While I stand fooling here, his jack of the clock.[9]
   This music mads° me. Let it sound no more,   *maddens*
   For though it have holp° madmen to their wits,   *helped*
   In me it seems it will make wise men mad.
      [*The music ceases*]
   Yet blessing on his heart that gives it me,
65 For 'tis a sign of love, and love to Richard
   Is a strange brooch° in this all-hating world.   *rare ornament*
      Enter a GROOM *of the stable*
GROOM   Hail, royal Prince!
RICHARD   Thanks, noble peer.
   The cheapest of us is ten groats too dear.[1]
   What art thou, and how com'st thou hither,
70 Where no man never comes but that sad dog
   That brings me food to make misfortune live?
GROOM   I was a poor groom of thy stable, King,
   When thou wert king; who, travelling towards York,
   With much ado at length have gotten leave
75 To look upon my sometimes° royal master's face.   *former*
   O, how it erned° my heart when I beheld   *grieved*
   In London streets, that coronation day,
   When Bolingbroke rode on roan Barbary,
   That horse that thou so often hast bestrid,
80 That horse that I so carefully have dressed!°   *groomed*
RICHARD   Rode he on Barbary? Tell me, gentle friend,
   How went he under him?
GROOM   So proudly as if he disdained the ground.
RICHARD   So proud that Bolingbroke was on his back.
85 That jade° hath eat bread from my royal hand;   *nag*
   This hand hath made him proud with clapping° him.   *patting*
   Would he not stumble, would he not fall down—
   Since pride must have a fall—and break the neck
   Of that proud man that did usurp his back?
90 Forgiveness, horse! Why do I rail on thee,
   Since thou, created to be awed by man,
   Wast born to bear? I was not made a horse,
   And yet I bear a burden like an ass,
   Spur-galled[2] and tired by jauncing° Bolingbroke.   *rough-riding*
      Enter KEEPER *to* RICHARD, *with meat*
95 KEEPER [*to* GROOM]   Fellow, give place.° Here is no longer stay.   *leave*
   RICHARD [*to* GROOM]   If thou love me, 'tis time thou wert away.
   GROOM   What my tongue dares not, that my heart shall say.
                                                         Exit
   KEEPER   My lord, will't please you to fall to?

8. Wiping tears from my eyes.
9. Manikin that strikes the clock's bell.
1. You have overpriced the cheaper of us (me, a prisoner) in calling me "royal." The difference between the
coins "royal" (10 shillings) and "noble" (6 shillings 8
pence) is "ten groats" (40 pence). In other words, we
are equal in worth.
2. Made sore by spurring.

RICHARD   Taste of it first,[3] as thou art wont to do.
100   KEEPER   My lord, I dare not. Sir Piers of Exton,
     Who lately came from the King, commands the contrary.
RICHARD [*striking the* KEEPER]   The devil take Henry of Lancaster and thee!
     Patience is stale, and I am weary of it.
KEEPER   Help, help, help!
     EXTON *and his* [*men*] *rush in*
105   RICHARD   How now! What means death in this rude assault?
     [*He seizes a weapon from a man, and kills him*]
     Villain, thy own hand yields thy death's instrument.
     [*He kills another*]
     Go thou, and fill another room in hell.
     Here EXTON *strikes him down*
RICHARD   That hand shall burn in never-quenching fire
     That staggers thus my person.° Exton, thy fierce hand   *thus makes me stagger*
110   Hath with the King's blood stained the King's own land.
     Mount, mount, my soul; thy seat° is up on high,   *residence*
     Whilst my gross flesh sinks downward, here to die. [*He dies*]
EXTON   As full of valour as of royal blood.
     Both have I spilt. O, would the deed were good!
115   For now the devil that told me I did well
     Says that this deed is chronicled in hell.
     This dead King to the living King I'll bear.
     Take hence the rest, and give them burial here.
          Exeunt [EXTON *with Richard's body at one door, and*
               his men with the other bodies at another door]

5.6

Flourish. Enter [KING HENRY] *with* [*Duke of*] YORK, *with
other lords and attendants*
KING HENRY   Kind uncle York, the latest news we hear
     Is that the rebels have consumed with fire
     Our town of Ci'cester° in Gloucestershire;   *Cirencester*
     But whether they be ta'en or slain we hear not.
          Enter [*Earl of*] NORTHUMBERLAND
5   Welcome, my lord. What is the news?
NORTHUMBERLAND   First, to thy sacred state wish I all happiness.
     The next news is, I have to London sent
     The heads of Salisbury, Spencer, Blunt, and Kent.
     The manner of their taking may appear
10   At large discoursèd° in this paper here.   *Narrated in full*
          [*He gives the paper to* KING HENRY]
KING HENRY   We thank thee, gentle Percy, for thy pains,
     And to thy worth will add right worthy° gains.   *valuable; well-deserved*
          Enter Lord FITZWALTER
FITZWALTER   My lord, I have from Oxford sent to London
     The heads of Brocas and Sir Bennet Seely,
15   Two of the dangerous consorted° traitors   *confederated*
     That sought at Oxford thy dire overthrow.
KING HENRY   Thy pains, Fitzwalter, shall not be forgot.
     Right noble is thy merit, well I wot.°   *know*
          Enter HARRY PERCY [*with the* BISHOP OF] CARLISLE
          [*guarded*]

3. To make sure it is not poisoned.   5.6 Location: Windsor Castle.

HARRY PERCY   The grand conspirator Abbot of Westminster,
20   With clog° of conscience and sour melancholy,   *burden*
    Hath yielded up his body to the grave.
    But here is Carlisle living, to abide
    Thy kingly doom° and sentence of his pride.   *judgment*
KING HENRY   Carlisle, this is your doom.
25   Choose out some secret place, some reverent room
    More than thou hast,¹ and with it joy° thy life.   *enjoy*
    So as thou liv'st in peace, die free from strife.
    For though mine enemy thou hast ever been,
    High sparks of honour in thee have I seen.
           Enter EXTON *with [his men bearing] a coffin*
30 EXTON   Great King, within this coffin I present
    Thy buried fear. Herein all breathless lies
    The mightiest of thy greatest enemies,
    Richard of Bordeaux, by me hither brought.
KING HENRY   Exton, I thank thee not, for thou hast wrought
35   A deed of slander° with thy fatal hand   *disgrace*
    Upon my head and all this famous land.
EXTON   From your own mouth, my lord, did I this deed.
KING HENRY   They love not poison that do poison need;
    Nor do I thee. Though I did wish him dead,
40   I hate the murderer, love him murderèd.
    The guilt of conscience take thou for thy labour,
    But neither my good word nor princely favour.
    With Cain² go wander through the shades of night,
    And never show thy head by day nor light.
           [*Exeunt* EXTON *and his men*]
45   Lords, I protest my soul is full of woe
    That blood should sprinkle me to make me grow.
    Come mourn with me for what I do lament,
    And put on sullen black incontinent.°   *immediately*
    I'll make a voyage to the Holy Land
50   To wash this blood off from my guilty hand.
    March sadly after. Grace my mournings here
    In weeping after this untimely bier.   *Exeunt* [*with the coffin*]

---

1. More reverent than the prison cell you inhabit now.
2. After Cain murdered his brother Abel, he was condemned to be a vagabond (Genesis 4:14).

The Life and Death of King John

Historical narrative often attributes meaning to history. *The Life and Death of King John* (1596) does not. Although it focuses on historical process, on how events fit together over time, it suggests the larger significance of John's reign (1199–1216) only in disorienting fashion. The plot promises more coherence than it delivers; the apparent trajectory of events repeatedly proves illusory; seemingly decisive moments turn out to be mere episodes in the open-ended, ironic, unpredictable movement of history. The play thus breaks with the providential conclusion to Shakespeare's first tetralogy (four related plays on English history) provided by *Richard III* (1592–93) and, more generally, with the moralizing strategy of Renaissance humanist historians. A transitional work, it moves Shakespeare closer to the pragmatic, secular political thinking of Niccolò Machiavelli and to the concerns with the problematic relationship between hereditary legitimacy and fitness to rule characteristic of his second tetralogy, from *Richard II* to *Henry V* (1595–99).

The logic of the plot is to undermine logic, to frustrate expectation, to reveal the uncertain relationship between intention and outcome in a world that offers only fragments of an overarching consolation—religious or otherwise—for the frequent futility of human endeavor. The basic antagonisms arise from John's efforts to retain the crown and its overseas French territories. John faces challenges from the French, ostensibly acting on behalf of his young nephew Arthur, whose hereditary claim to the throne is stronger, and from the Catholic Church, with which John is also at odds. These conflicts repeatedly take surprising turns. The first-act struggle over inheritance between the Bastard and his younger half brother Robert Falconbridge leads to the unexpected conclusion that illegitimate birth is no barrier to legitimate inheritance. Even more surprisingly, the Bastard quickly renounces that inheritance. Similarly, when the English and French battle to a stalemate in seeking the loyalty of Angers, they join forces to level the town to punish its autonomy and then instead resolve to end their quarrel—sparing the town—through a cynical political marriage. But this resolution proves as transitory as the previous ones when Pandolf, the papal legate, excommunicates John, and France, as a result, repudiates the deal.

Although John now seems in trouble, his ensuing military triumph shifts his fortunes. Yet by ordering the murder of Arthur, he undermines his own position. It looks as if John will be rescued from the consequences of his crime when Hubert, the executioner, spares Arthur. But Arthur dies attempting to escape, an accident the English lords interpret as murder. Their defection to the invading French army apparently seals John's fate. Even though John submits to the Pope to eliminate the invasion's rationale, this tactic has no effect. But when the lords learn that the Dauphin, son of the French king, plans to kill them after securing the English throne, they return to John.

The war itself is marked less by climactic battles than by both sides' careless habit of losing their armies at sea: nature, too, subverts expectations. But even this does not save John. Hated by the English clergy for his earlier extortions from the monasteries, he is poisoned by a vengeful monk. This outcome lacks dramatic logic: the pillaging of the monasteries is undramatized and given very little weight; royal resistance to Catholic domination is viewed positively if peripherally; John has been reconciled with Rome; and he is apparently dying of a fever even before his poisoning. Finally, Prince Henry, the King's young son, is conveniently produced just as peace breaks out between England and France. Accordingly, the orthodox ending, in which the legitimate heir succeeds his father, feels highly contingent. And this feeling is reinforced by the characters'

The coronation of King John. From Matthew of Westminster, *Flores Historiarum* (late thirteenth or early fourteenth century).

routine repudiation of their oaths, by shifts in dramatic register—from long public, ceremonial set pieces to rapidly shifting, increasingly private introspective scenes—and by the numerous unexplained acts whose significance remains obscure.

This view of history, in which the meaning of events proves unstable and problematic, is of a piece with Shakespeare's treatment of his sources, his major characters, his central themes, and his possible allusions to contemporary Elizabethan politics, as well as with the play's later theatrical fortunes. *King John*'s closest analogue is the anonymous play *The Troublesome Reign of John, King of England* (published 1591). Most critics believe it to be Shakespeare's primary source rather than the other way around; but regardless of the chronology (on which see the Textual Note), comparison of the two works is instructive. If *The Troublesome Reign* is the earlier work, as is assumed here, it relies in part on Raphael Holinshed's *Chronicles of England, Scotland, and Ireland* (second edition, 1587), the nonfictional narrative of English history on which Shakespeare himself drew extensively during the 1590s for his other national history plays. *The Troublesome Reign*'s author reshapes chronology and invents episodes, alterations that *King John* generally adopts, and promotes conventional Protestant and national chauvinism, which *King John* mutes. From early in the English Reformation, John was seen as a proto-Protestant royal martyr who temporarily challenged Roman Catholicism by rejecting the papal choice for archbishop of Canterbury and heavily taxing the church. Hence he was thought to have anticipated Queen Elizabeth's father, Henry VIII, whose break with Rome and expropriation of the monasteries initiated the Reformation. But Shakespeare weakens the connection to Henry, toning down the rhetoric of *The Troublesome Reign* by more closely following Holinshed, who combines the Protestant view with a centuries-old Catholic hostility to John. While the anonymous play portrays monks engaged in outrageous sexual conduct, Shakespeare omits the scene and calls John's ecclesiastical tax policy pillaging. Similarly, although John's submission to Rome is lamented in *King John*, Shakespeare hardly makes the decision catastrophic. But he does retain some of *The Troublesome Reign*'s anti-Catholicism—for instance, in John's defense of an English church. Overall, however, the play's Protestantism is unmilitant: *King John* offers scant comfort to Catholics but little more to Protestants. This outlook may reflect Shakespeare's antipathy to Christian theological controversy and perhaps his partly Catholic family background and education.

Shakespeare also softens *The Troublesome Reign*'s English national chauvinism, despite concluding with the Bastard's patriotic credo:

> This England never did, nor never shall,
> Lie at the proud foot of a conqueror
> But when it first did help to wound itself.
> Now these her princes are come home again,
> Come the three corners of the world in arms
> And we shall shock them. Naught shall make us rue
> If England to itself do rest but true.
>
> (5.7.112–18)

These lines are more ambiguous than they first appear. Although they oppose foreign conquest of England, the play has considered the possibility that such domination is preferable to continued rule by a murderous English monarch. Moreover, the "But when" in the first sentence and the "if" in the third temper optimism, especially given the prior conduct of the aristocracy.

This skeptical view of traditional authority—ecclesiastical and secular alike—shapes the characterization of *King John*. Most striking is the relative inattention to John himself, the figure whose "life and death" the play claims to dramatize. The resulting vacuum is filled by women and a bastard, personages generally peripheral to dynastic history. Nowhere in Shakespeare's two historical tetralogies do women play so active a role. In the first act, John's mother, Queen Eleanor, challenges the French ambassador even before her son has a chance to do so. She then recognizes the Bastard as the illegitimate offspring of her dead son King Richard I, the Lionheart, John's oldest brother and predecessor on the throne, and (1.1.150) recruits her newly found grandson into royal service.

In Acts 2 and 3, the verbal dispute between John and Arthur (represented by the King of France) is partly carried out by proxy. Eleanor and especially Arthur's mother, Constance, whose role Shakespeare expanded from his sources, are more active than their children and (with the Bastard) rhetorically dominate the stage—especially in their confrontation in Act 2, Scene 1 and in Constance's subsequent lamentations for her son. Going beyond the common female role—victim of history—these women attempt to direct the action. Moreover, Constance and Eleanor question each other's sexual honor—an issue broached earlier when the Bastard's mother acknowledges her adulterous affair with King Richard. This recurrent concern underscores the uncertainly of biologically legitimate patriarchal succession. Hereditary descent from father to son accords a central role to women, whose sexual fidelity is considered necessary to that descent but unreliable. *King John* emphasizes the dubious fidelity of women but denies any consequence for hereditary succession. Although the mothers' attacks on each other weaken traditional notions of male legitimacy and Constance powerfully points up the unprincipled maneuvering of the two kings, she changes no one's mind, and midway through the play both she and Eleanor disappear from the plot. Their offstage deaths are reported shortly thereafter.

With them go the challenges they pose but not necessarily all they represent. Rather than executing Arthur, Hubert protects the boy, assuming a nurturing, arguably maternal, role. The Bastard's relationship to John late in the play is similar, and Prince Henry sheds tears over his dying father. Pandolf calls the Church "our Holy mother" (3.1.67,

King John's tomb in Worcester Cathedral. From Francis Sandford, A *Genealogical History of the Kings and Queens of England* (1707).

182), and the Bastard taxes the treasonous lords for "ripping up the womb / Of your dear mother England" (5.2.152–53). But it is unclear how effective these surrogates prove. Following the mothers' deaths, the sons become increasingly inept. They are memorable less in themselves than for the way that physical imagery running through *King John,* often as personification, is reliteralized in the accounts of their suffering. Arthur leaps to his accidental death when the "Good ground" of England, which he hopes does "not break my limbs," proves to be inhospitable "stones" (4.3.2, 6, 9). Earlier, the motif of fire and heat is picked up in the threat to burn out Arthur's eyes, a threat echoed in, to use John's words, the "tyrant fever [that] burns me up" and the poison that produces "so hot a summer in my bosom" (5.3.14, 5.7.30). More generally, John's stunned response to his mother's death helps explain the transformation in his behavior from confident leadership to helpless passivity. By the last part of the play, he is neither tragic nor even entirely villainous but simply beside the point, his fall coinciding with the Bastard's rise.

That rise enables a defense of illegitimacy. An almost entirely unhistorical personage in the least historical of Shakespeare's history plays, the Bastard is the work's most prominent character. Although critics have traced the development of his character, he is arguably less a coherent fictional figure than a series of discontinuous theatrical functions. His changes seem dictated more by twists of the plot than shifts in personality. The Bastard initially embodies a mischievous popular culture. Theatrically, he descends from the devilish Vice figure, a character in the earlier English morality plays. The Vice combined a commitment to evil, an intimacy with the audience, and a penchant for fun. Similarly, the Bastard speaks to and for the audience in verbally playful asides and soliloquies, denouncing the moral failings of the powerful while cheerfully conceding that he, too, is out for himself. He takes pleasure in promoting discord, and he appears immune to bodily harm, an immunity that wins him repeated description as the devil.

Unlike Shakespeare's earlier transmutations of the Vice such as Richard III, however, the Bastard is obviously a positive character. Thus, there is another side to this figure, which becomes dominant only later in the play. After John deems him legitimate and the Bastard rejects his patrimony in order to be knighted and recognized as King Richard's illegitimate son, his simultaneous financial fall and social rise allow the identification of royalty with illegitimacy. His unswerving loyalty contrasts with the self-serving deal between John and the King of France, a deal that the Bastard memorably denounces as "commodity," or self-interest (2.1.562–99). Later, that loyalty casts a harsh light on the English aristocrats' treasonous alliance with the French. The Bastard thus becomes more responsible, if less entertaining—a transformation managed by keeping the character offstage for five hundred lines. Horrified by the death of Arthur, whom he now views as the legitimate monarch, but persuaded that it was accidental, he undertakes the defense of crown and realm alike, even as John declines. In this endeavor, he proves the ethical center of a world otherwise almost devoid of positive value.

The Bastard owes this authority to his social and theatrical range. As the reembodiment of his biological father, he reflects both badly and well on the King. It is the Bastard rather than John who exacts family vengeance by killing the Duke of Austria, in this play—but not historically—slayer of King Richard. And it is the Bastard who offers the appropriate response to the death and possible murder of Arthur, for which the King bears partial—arguably full—responsibility. By comparison, John looks at best mediocre and at worst evil. Yet the Bastard's presence also suggests that the spirit of Richard guards the throne and, hence, that John is the right person for the job. As the Bastard insists in referring to John, "his royalty doth speak in me" (5.2.129).

Thus a man whose birth is illegitimate validates the fitness to rule of a man whose claim to the crown is already disputed in *The Troublesome Reign*. Shakespeare further weakens John's legal position, which is based on King Richard's will naming him successor. When Constance asserts Arthur's right to the throne, Eleanor retorts, "I can produce / A will that bars the title of thy son" (2.1.191–92). But a will is trumped by the rule of succession, which stipulates that the crown go to the firstborn male or his oldest male descendant. Here that is Arthur, son of the deceased Geoffrey, younger brother of Richard but, crucially, older brother of John. Hence, when John explains why he will prevail against the French and Arthur—"Our strong possession and our right for us" (1.1.39)—Eleanor cautions, "Your strong possession much more than your right" (line 40). Her denial of legality has authority because she supports John. John unwittingly concedes the decisiveness of order of birth when he awards the Falconbridge inheritance to the illegitimate Bastard rather than to the Bastard's younger, legitimate brother, whose claim is based only on his father's will. Even though Arthur is, therefore, legitimate and John is not, legitimacy and fitness are not synonymous. After undermining John's hereditary right, Shakespeare complicates the question. He departs from his sources by making Arthur a helpless child heavily dependent on his mother, the King of France, and the Duke of Austria. Arthur also has no interest in being King: his unfitness to rule—recognized by most commentators on *King John*—means that John's "strong possession" carries real weight.

But by ordering Arthur's murder, John squanders his authority, thereby also weakening the play's conflict between hereditary legitimacy and rightful rule. *King John*'s skepticism about the meaningfulness of historical process thus undermines this central theme. A similar fate is reserved even for the Bastard, despite his crucial role in recognizing John's heir and articulating a vision of national unity. In Holinshed, John "lost a great part of his army" to drowning; in *The Troublesome Reign*, the Bastard informs John that the sea has "swallowed up the most of all our men." *King John* has the Bastard narrate this event twice, both times making him more responsible for the debacle—"half my power," "the best part of my power" (5.6.40, 5.7.61). Ineptitude is soon replaced by irrelevance: the Bastard opts for war after others have already negotiated peace. Although he is not simply shunted aside by the unpredictable concatenation of historical events, the resolution has less to do with human intention and achievement than with the collapse of both contending parties.

Where does this leave England? Temporally, *King John* differs from Shakespeare's other history plays of the 1590s: it treats the early thirteenth rather than the late fourteenth and fifteenth centuries. Standing alone rather than in a tetralogy, it does not develop a dynastic sense of "England" by depicting the sequence of reigns. Sociologically, the play is also atypical. John's reign is remembered for the Magna Carta and—without historical warrant—Robin Hood. Both concern resistance to royal tyranny—by the aristocracy and the lower class, respectively. Although these stories were available in the 1590s, neither appears in the play. The lords rebel late in the action, but the balance of power between king and nobility remains secondary. And despite a brief reference to popular unrest, *King John* accords the English people an even more marginal role in constituting the nation. This treatment of aristocracy and populace contrasts with Shakespeare's approach in his history plays of the next three years from the second tetralogy, *1* and *2 Henry IV* and *Henry V*.

King John points elsewhere. Richard the Lionheart's legacy is dispersed among three of his blood relatives—John, Arthur, and the Bastard—none of whom is a fully adequate successor. Like the Bastard, Constance and Eleanor are part of the royal family. But these three characters, who, as noted earlier, belong to peripheral groups, suggest an expansion of outlook, a shift from dynasty to nation and, hence, a repudiation of absolutist rule. That expansion is implied by the importance accorded in Act 2 to the political will of the citizens of Angers, who are asked to decide which claimant is their legitimate king, and arguably by the valorization of humane feeling and personal loyalty late in the play. Yet the Bastard's social rise from obscurity to protector of England suggests a partial analogue to the sixteenth-century emergence of a nonhereditary political elite to fill crucial positions in the new state bureaucracy. On this reading, the play ends not with an expanded, less authoritarian view of the polity, but with a redeployed ruling apparatus. If so, this reorganization of the state remains barely realized in *King John*. So, too, does a properly national sense of England. It may be that no national perspective was fully available without the traditional legitimacy of dynastic succession. The second tetralogy may be seen as an effort to fuse the people and the crown. *King John*, however, devoid of climactic battle or concluding marriage, is more effective at undermining than at reconstituting authority: it is here that its distinctiveness lies.

The play may thus have provided its initial audiences with a compelling projection back into the thirteenth century of the charged issue of the legitimacy of Queen Elizabeth and competing claims of Mary, Queen of Scots. First, just as John's monarchical claim depends on Richard's will, the will of Henry VIII named Elizabeth heir. But the legitimacy of appointing one's successors by will had been challenged even in Henry's lifetime. Second, Shakespeare's John is accused of being a bastard and excommunicated by the pope; Elizabeth was declared a bastard by her father and excommunicated by the pope. And just as Arthur is the son of John's older brother, Mary, Queen of Scots, was the daughter of Henry's older sister. Elizabeth's legal claim to the crown was thus arguably weaker than Mary's.

Fourth, Arthur's cause is championed by King Philip of France; Mary, too, enjoyed the support of foreign Catholic monarchs, including King Philip II of Spain. Fifth, after ordering Arthur's death, John tries to absolve himself of the crime that he commissioned but did not commit; in 1587, Elizabeth ordered Mary's execution and then distanced herself from the judicial murder. Sixth, Arthur's death provokes an invasion from France to impose foreign Catholic rule. The invaders are led by the Dauphin, whose claim to the English crown rests on his marriage to John's niece, Blanche. Analogous motives led Philip II, widowed husband of Mary—the older sister of Elizabeth and her predecessor as queen—to launch the Spanish Armada the year after Mary's death. Finally, in *King John*, England is saved by a providential storm that destroys much of the French navy. So, too, a storm wrecked the Armada, a catastrophe interpreted by the victors as God's deliverance of Protestant England from enemies intent on conquest and Catholic rule.

Although these summaries oversimplify theater and history alike, they suggest the explosive issues that Shakespeare dramatized—the struggle with the papacy, the threat of invasion, and especially the problem of legitimate rule. There were risks in questioning Elizabeth's royal legitimacy or accusing her of murdering the rightful queen—even by covert historical analogy. Yet *King John* raises these matters not to resolve them but to meditate on their complexity. John both is and is not Arthur's murderer; he both is and is not the legitimate king.

Finally, the enigmatic logic of *King John*'s plot has affected its theatrical fortunes. Since the eighteenth century, the play has been cut to render its uncertain nationalism unambiguous. In the nineteenth century, its discontinuities and powerful confrontations between characters encouraged productions in which narrative sweep was sacrificed to pageantry and individual scenes, especially involving Constance. *King John* has also proven useful for political allegory in times of crisis. It was prominent in the battle against the censorship legislation of the 1737 Licensing Act, and it was marshaled to support loyalist opposition to the Catholic Jacobite invasion of England in 1745. It served similar ends in the French and Indian War fifteen years later, during the Napoleonic Wars at the beginning of the nineteenth century, as a justification for British imperialism during the Boer War in South Africa in 1899, and as a rallying cry before and during World War II. A 1961 production took the contested city of Angers as an image of Berlin, recently divided between East and West, and subsequent decades saw performances in several Eastern European Communist countries. Although *King John* was the first of Shakespeare's plays to be filmed (in 1899, an extremely brief version consisting of three scenes—John's temptation of Hubert, Constance's lamentation, and John's death scene), the work's theatrical standing declined in the twentieth century. There may be promise, however, in the recent rebellion against politically orthodox interpretations in criticism and performance alike. The 1988–89 production directed by Deborah Warner is noteworthy for its often satiric view of male authority in an unstable world. Perhaps a revival of interest depends less on the play's pageantry or jingoism than on its disabused view of power and its refusal to find reassurance in the interconnected, yet uncertain, sequence of historical events.

WALTER COHEN

TEXTUAL NOTE

The initial printing of *The Life and Death of King John* was in the First Folio of 1623 (F). That text probably goes back to an authorial manuscript, or "foul papers," from 1596 that was subsequently copied between 1609 and 1623 by two scribes. Their transcript, though not a promptbook, seems to have been designed with future theatrical performance in mind. The second scribe moved further from Shakespeare's manuscript toward stage-ready copy than did the first. In response to a 1606 law prohibiting oaths, the scribes presumably sanitized Shakespeare's language, replacing, for instance, "God" with "heaven."

The *Norton Shakespeare* reverses that process, restoring what Shakespeare wrote but retaining other scribal innovations, such as the introduction of act and scene divisions. In F, these are messy and illogical, perhaps in part because two compositors set the type for the play. This edition follows earlier editors in treating F's "Scaena Secunda" as 2.1 and its "Actus Secundus" as 2.2, even though this is not the only reasonable solution. Beginning at the present edition's 2.1.325, F starts calling the Citizen of Angers "Hubert." The shift may indicate a desire to double the parts (have the same actor play both roles) or conflate the two characters. If the latter, the extant text does not complete the job: the two men do not seem like the same person. Accordingly, this edition emends F to keep the two characters separate.

Partly on the basis of *King John*'s recourse to rhetoric reminiscent of the Spanish Armada era (1588), a few scholars place its composition in 1590 or earlier and see it as a source for the anonymous play *The Troublesome Reign of John, King of England* (published in 1591). Yet a direct link between the wording of two stage directions in *The Troublesome Reign* and their analogues in *King John* is easily explained only if the anonymous play came first and Shakespeare was familiar with it. Shakespeare could have read the relevant stage directions in the 1591 edition of *The Troublesome Reign*, but it is not clear how the author of *The Troublesome Reign* could have seen Shakespeare's unpublished stage directions. Stylistic and metrical tests, which date *King John* to roughly 1596, support this hypothesis.

SELECTED BIBLIOGRAPHY

Anderson, Thomas. "'Legitimation, name, and all is gone': Bastardy and Bureaucracy in Shakespeare's *King John*." *Journal for Early Modern Cultural Studies* 4.2 (Fall/Winter 2004): 35–61. The Bastard's rise as indicative less of monarchical power than of the emergence of a new model of impersonal bureaucratic efficiency.

Braunmuller, A. R. "*King John* and Historiography." *English Literary History* 55 (1988): 309–32. Conflict between theater and historical writing, exemplified in the Bastard's ahistorical character and Arthur's death.

Burckhardt, Sigurd. *Shakespearean Meanings*. Princeton: Princeton University Press, 1968. 116–43. *King John* as a modern, rather than traditional, play, rejecting divine sanction for both religious and secular authority.

Candido, Joseph, ed. "*King John*." Shakespeare: The Critical Tradition series. Atlantic Highlands, N.J.: Athlone, 1996. Selection from criticisms of the play, 1790–1919; focus on individual characters and emotionally powerful scenes.

Cousin, Geraldine. *King John*. Manchester: Manchester University Press, 1994. Performance history, including 1984 BBC film (see below).

Curren-Aquino, Deborah T., ed. "*King John*": *New Perspectives*. Newark: University of Delaware Press, 1989. Twelve essays, various perspectives, but generally seeing the play as an experiment with the form of the national history play.

Dusinberre, Juliet. "*King John* and Embarrassing Women." *Shakespeare Survey* 42 (1989): 37–52. Women as a structurally unifying force in the first three acts. The play disintegrates with their disappearance.

Howard, Jean E., and Phyllis Rackin. *Engendering a Nation: A Feminist Account of Shakespeare's English Histories*. London: Routledge, 1997. 119–33. *King John* as a challenge to patriarchal, dynastic orthodoxy through skeptical women's voices.

Shirley, Frances A., ed. "*King John*" and "*Henry VIII*": *Critical Essays*. New York: Garland, 1988. The twelve essays on *King John,* mostly from the 1930s to 1960s, are diverse in outlook but generally more concerned with structural and national unity than is recent criticism.

Vaughan, Virginia Mason. "*King John*." *A Companion to Shakespeare's Works*. Vol. 2: *The Histories*. Ed. Richard Dutton and Jean E. Howard. Malden, Mass.: Blackwell, 2003. 379–94. Overview of the play, seen as advocating limits on absolute secular or religious power.

FILMS

King John. 1899. Dir. Walter Pfeffer Dando and William K. L. Dickson. UK. 2 min. The first Shakespeare film, a black-and-white silent. See Introduction.

The Life and Death of King John. 1984. Dir. David Giles. UK. 155 min. A relatively conservative BBC production notable for Claire Bloom's innovative, coolly rational Constance.

The Life and Death of King John

THE PERSONS OF THE PLAY

KING JOHN of England
QUEEN ELEANOR, his mother
LADY FALCONBRIDGE
Philip the BASTARD, later knighted as Sir Richard Plantagenet,
    her illegitimate son by King Richard I (Cœur-de-lion)
Robert FALCONBRIDGE, her legitimate son
James GURNEY, her attendant
Lady BLANCHE of Spain, niece of King John
PRINCE HENRY, son of King John
HUBERT, a follower of King John
Earl of SALISBURY
Earl of PEMBROKE
Earl of ESSEX
Lord BIGOT
KING PHILIP of France
LOUIS THE DAUPHIN, his son
ARTHUR, Duke of Brittaine, nephew of King John
Lady CONSTANCE, his mother
Duke of AUSTRIA (Limoges)
CHÂTILLON, ambassador from France to England
Count MELUN
A CITIZEN of Angers
Cardinal PANDOLF, a legate from the Pope
PETER OF POMFRET, a prophet
HERALDS
EXECUTIONERS
MESSENGERS
SHERIFF
Lords, soldiers, attendants

1.1

[*Flourish.*] *Enter* KING JOHN, QUEEN ELEANOR,[1] [*and the*
Earls of] PEMBROKE, ESSEX, *and* SALISBURY; *with the*[m]
CHÂTILLON *of France*

KING JOHN Now say, Châtillon, what would France with us?[2]
CHÂTILLON Thus, after greeting, speaks the King of France,
  In my behaviour,° to the majesty—   *person*
  The borrowed° majesty—of England here.   *usurped*
5 QUEEN ELEANOR A strange beginning: 'borrowed majesty'?
KING JOHN Silence, good mother, hear the embassy.°   *message*
CHÂTILLON Philip of France, in right and true behalf

1.1 Location: John's court in London.
1. This scene, which occupies the first act, is unhistorical. The youngest son of Henry II and "Queen Eleanor" (Eleanor of Aquitaine), John (1167–1216) succeeded his brother, the famed crusader Richard I (the Lionheart), in 1199 and ruled until his death. Eleanor of Aquitaine (c. 1122–1204) was Queen first of France and then of England. See "A Shakespearean Genealogy," on the front endpapers.
2. What does (the King of) France want with us?

Of thy deceasèd brother Geoffrey's[3] son,
Arthur Plantagenet,[4] lays most lawful claim
10 To this fair island and the territories,
To Ireland, Poitou, Anjou, Touraine, Maine;[5]
Desiring thee to lay aside the sword
Which sways° usurpingly these several titles,°   *rules / separate lands*
And put the same into young Arthur's hand,
15 Thy nephew and right royal sovereign.
KING JOHN   What follows if we disallow of this?
CHÂTILLON   The proud control° of fierce and bloody war,   *compulsion*
To enforce these rights so forcibly withheld—
KING JOHN   Here have we war for war, and blood for blood,
20 Controlment for controlment: so answer France.
CHÂTILLON   Then take my king's defiance from my mouth,
The farthest limit of my embassy.
KING JOHN   Bear mine° to him, and so depart in peace.   *my defiance*
Be thou as lightning in the eyes of France,
25 For ere thou canst report,[6] I will be there;
The thunder of my cannon° shall be heard.   *(anachronism)*
So hence. Be thou the trumpet of our wrath,
And sullen presage° of your own decay.°—   *gloomy omen / downfall*
An honourable conduct° let him have;   *escort*
30 Pembroke, look to't.—Farewell, Châtillon.
      Exeunt CHÂTILLON *and* PEMBROKE
QUEEN ELEANOR   What now, my son? Have I not ever° said   *always*
How that ambitious Constance[7] would not cease
Till she had kindled France and all the world
Upon° the right and party of her son?   *On behalf of*
35 This might have been prevented and made whole°   *settled*
With very easy arguments of love,°   *friendly discussions*
Which now the manage° of two kingdoms must   *government*
With fearful-bloody issue° arbitrate.   *outcome*
KING JOHN   Our strong possession and our right for us.°   *on our side*
QUEEN ELEANOR [*aside to* KING JOHN]   Your strong possession
40   much more than your right,
Or else it must go wrong with you and me:
So much my conscience whispers in your ear,
Which none but heaven and you and I shall hear.
     Enter a SHERIFF [*who whispers to* ESSEX]
ESSEX   My liege,° here is the strangest controversy,   *lord*
45 Come from the country to be judged by you,
That e'er I heard. Shall I produce the men?
KING JOHN   Let them approach.—   [*Exit* SHERIFF]

---

3. Geoffrey was older than John and younger than Richard I; he died before Henry II. Because of changes in the laws of inheritance, John's claims to the throne would have been weaker in Shakespeare's lifetime— and are so represented—than they were in his own day, the early thirteenth century.
4. "Plantagenet" was the family name of most English monarchs from the accession of Henry II in 1154 to the deposition of Richard III in 1485. The historical Arthur was in his late teens; Shakespeare makes him much younger.

5. Except for Ireland, English territories in western and central France. Historically, it was these French territories, rather than the English crown itself, that Arthur claimed.
6. Before you can deliver your message (pun on noise of thunder or cannon).
7. Arthur's mother, Geoffrey's widow in Shakespeare and in his main source, *The Troublesome Reign of King John*. Historically, Constance remarried twice after Geoffrey's death.

Our abbeys and our priories shall pay[8]

This expeditious charge.°   *sudden cost (of war)*

    Enter Robert FALCONBRIDGE *and Philip [the* BASTARD,[9]

    with the Sheriff]

                What men are you?

50   BASTARD   Your faithful subject I, a gentleman

Born in Northamptonshire, and eldest son,

As I suppose, to Robert Falconbridge,

A soldier, by the honour-giving hand

Of Cœur-de-lion° knighted in the field.   *Richard the Lionheart*

55   KING JOHN   What art thou?

FALCONBRIDGE   The son and heir to that same Falconbridge.

KING JOHN   Is that the elder, and art thou the heir?

You came not of one mother then, it seems.

BASTARD   Most certain of one mother, mighty King—

60   That is well known—and, as I think, one father.

But for the certain knowledge of that truth

I put you o'er to° heaven, and to my mother.   *refer you to*

Of that° I doubt as all men's children may.   *(truth)*

QUEEN ELEANOR   Out on thee,° rude man! Thou dost shame thy   *Away with you*

    mother

65   And wound her honour with this diffidence.°   *distrust*

BASTARD   I, Madam? No, I have no reason for it.

That is my brother's plea and none of mine,

The which if he can prove, a pops me out°   *he deprives me of*

At least from fair five hundred pound a year.

70   Heaven guard my mother's honour, and my land!

KING JOHN   A good blunt fellow.—Why, being younger born,

Doth he lay claim to thine inheritance?

BASTARD   I know not why, except to get the land;

But once he slandered me with bastardy.

75   But whe'er° I be as true° begot or no,   *whether / legitimately*

That still I lay upon my mother's head;°   *I let my mother answer*

But that I am as well begot, my liege—

Fair fall the bones that took the pains for me[1]—

Compare our faces and be judge yourself.

80   If old Sir Robert did beget us both

And were our father, and this son like him,

O old Sir Robert, father, on my knee

I give heaven thanks I was not like to thee.

KING JOHN   Why, what a madcap hath heaven lent us here!

85   QUEEN ELEANOR[2]   He hath a trick° of Cœur-de-lion's face;   *distinguishing trait*

The accent of his tongue affecteth° him.   *resembles*

Do you not read some tokens of my son

In the large composition° of this man?   *openness; build*

KING JOHN   Mine eye hath well examinèd his parts,°   *attributes*

And finds them perfect Richard.

90   [*To Robert* FALCONBRIDGE]   Sirrah,° speak: *(used to inferiors)*

What doth move you to claim your brother's land?

---

8. Alluding to John's much-resented taxation of the
monastic orders.
9. Drawing upon a passing reference in Holinshed's
Chronicles, The Troublesome Reign invents a major role
for this character, a role that Shakespeare further

expands.
1. May good fortune befall the bones (of the dead
man) who went to the trouble of begetting me.
2. The Queen may speak the following lines privately
to John.

BASTARD   Because he hath a half-face° like my father!   *profile; thin face*
     With half that face³ would he have all my land,
     A half-faced groat⁴ five hundred pound a year.
95 FALCONBRIDGE   My gracious liege, when that my father lived,
     Your brother° did employ my father much—   *(Richard)*
  BASTARD   Well, sir, by this you cannot get my land.
     Your tale must be how he employed my mother.
  FALCONBRIDGE   And once dispatched him in an embassy
100   To Germany, there with the Emperor
     To treat of high affairs touching that time.
     Th'advantage of his absence took the King,
     And in the meantime sojourned at my father's,
     Where how he did prevail I shame to speak.
105   But truth is truth: large lengths of seas and shores
     Between my father and my mother lay,
     As I have heard my father speak himself,
     When this same lusty° gentleman was got.°   *vigorous / conceived*
     Upon his deathbed he by will bequeathed
110   His lands to me, and took it on his death°   *solemnly swore*
     That this my mother's son was none of his;
     And if he were, he came into the world
     Full fourteen weeks before the course of time.
     Then, good my liege, let me have what is mine,
115   My father's land, as was my father's will.
  KING JOHN   Sirrah, your brother is legitimate.°   *(legally correct)*
     Your father's wife did after wedlock bear him,
     And if she did play false, the fault was hers,
     Which fault lies on the hazards of° all husbands   *is a risk for*
120   That marry wives. Tell me, how if my brother,
     Who, as you say, took pains to get this son,
     Had of your father claimed this son for his?
     In sooth, good friend, your father might have kept
     This calf, bred from his cow, from all the world;
125   In sooth he might. Then if he were my brother's,
     My brother might not claim him, nor your father,
     Being none of his, refuse him.⁵ This concludes:
     My mother's son did get your father's heir;
     Your father's heir must have your father's land.
130 FALCONBRIDGE   Shall then my father's will be of no force
     To dispossess that child which is not his?
  BASTARD   Of no more force to dispossess me, sir,
     Than was his will° to get me, as I think.   *legal instrument; lust*
  QUEEN ELEANOR   Whether hadst° thou rather be: a Falconbridge,   *Which would*
135   And like thy brother to enjoy thy land,
     Or the reputed son of Cœur-de-lion,
     Lord of thy presence,° and no land beside?   *yourself*
  BASTARD   Madam, an if° my brother had my shape,   *an If=if*
     And I had his, Sir Robert's his° like him,   *Sir Robert's*
140   And if my legs were two such riding-rods,°   *their riding switches*
     My arms such eel-skins stuffed, my face so thin
     That in mine ear I durst not stick a rose

---

3. Half of his father's face, since Falconbridge inherits maternal features as well; "face" is also "impudence." 4. A coin showing the monarch's head in profile; also Falconbridge, who as a person is worth only as much as a groat (4 pence), despite his inheritance. 5. *nor . . . him:* nor could your father, though not the biological father to the Bastard, disown him.

Lest men should say 'Look where three-farthings goes!',[6]
And, to° his shape, were heir to all this land,   *in addition to*
145 Would I might never stir from off this place.[7]
I would give it every foot° to have this face;   *every foot of it*
It would not be Sir Nob in any case.[8]
QUEEN ELEANOR   I like thee well. Wilt thou forsake thy fortune,
Bequeath thy land to him, and follow me?
150 I am a soldier and now bound to France.
BASTARD   Brother, take you my land; I'll take my chance.
Your face hath got five hundred pound a year,
Yet sell your face for fivepence and 'tis dear.°—   *expensive*
Madam, I'll follow you unto the death.
155 QUEEN ELEANOR   Nay, I would have you go before me thither.
BASTARD   Our country manners give our betters way.[9]
KING JOHN   What is thy name?
BASTARD   Philip, my liege, so is my name begun:
Philip, good old Sir Robert's wife's eldest son.
160 KING JOHN   From henceforth bear his name whose form thou bear'st.
Kneel thou down Philip, but arise more great:
[*He knights the* BASTARD]
Arise Sir Richard and Plantagenet.[1]
BASTARD   Brother by th' mother's side, give me your hand.
My father gave me honour, yours gave land.
165 Now blessèd be the hour, by night or day,
When I was got, Sir Robert was away.
QUEEN ELEANOR   The very spirit of Plantagenet!
I am thy grandam, Richard; call me so.
BASTARD   Madam, by chance, but not by truth;° what though?°   *chastely / but so what?*
170 Something about,° a little from the right,°   *a bit off / unlawful*
In at the window, or else o'er the hatch;[2]
Who dares not stir by day must walk° by night,   *go; rob (sexually)*
And have is have, however men do catch.[3]
Near or far off, well won is still well shot,[4]
175 And I am I, howe'er I was begot.
KING JOHN   Go, Falconbridge, now hast thou thy desire:
A landless knight° makes thee a landed squire.—   *(the Bastard)*
Come, madam, and come, Richard; we must speed
For France; for France, for it is more than need.
180 BASTARD   Brother, adieu. Good fortune come to thee,
For thou wast got i'th' way of honesty.
Exeunt all but [*the*] BASTARD
A foot of honour[5] better than I was,
But many a many foot of land the worse.
Well, now can I make any Joan° a lady.   *lower-class woman*

6. A rose appeared behind the Queen's head on a three-farthing coin, which was thin and of small value (less than a penny).
7. May I be struck dead here and now.
8. My appearance would not be that of Sir Robert under any circumstances. The speech is full of sexual innuendo. "Riding-rods" (line 140) and "eel-skins" (line 141) hint at sexual inadequacy associated with a thin penis. "Nob" (line 147) is also slang for "penis." "Rose" (line 142), "shape" (line 144), and "case" (line 147) may refer to the vagina; "riding" (line 140), "stuffed" (line 141), "stick a rose" (line 142), and "foot" (line 146) suggest copulation; and "stir" (line 145) can mean "sexually arouse."

9. The Bastard jokes that it's proper to let social superiors go first.
1. Perhaps the shift from blank verse to rhyme (lines 145–81), though not fully systematic, reinforces the Bastard's social elevation here.
2. Both phrases are proverbial for birth out of wedlock. *hatch:* the lower half of a divided door.
3. That is, possession is nine-tenths of the law.
4. Archery metaphor, with sexual innuendo, as with "stir" (line 172). The entire passage is also marked by mock-proverbial expressions.
5. A degree of status. The Bastard contrasts his aristocratic "honour" with Falconbridge's middle-class "honesty" (line 181).

185 'Good e'en, Sir Richard'—'God-a-mercy[6] fellow';
And if his name be George I'll call him Peter,
For new-made honour doth forget men's names;
'Tis too respective and too sociable
For your conversion.[7] Now your traveller,
190 He and his toothpick at my worship's mess;
And when my knightly stomach is sufficed,
Why then I suck my teeth[8] and catechize
My pickèd° man of countries. 'My dear sir,'   *affected; tooth-picked*
Thus leaning on mine elbow I begin,
195 'I shall beseech you—'. That is Question now;
And then comes Answer like an Absey book.°   *a school (ABC) primer*
'O sir,' says Answer, 'at your best command,
At your employment, at your service, sir.'
'No sir,' says Question, 'I, sweet sir, at yours.'
200 And so, ere Answer knows what Question would,°   *wishes*
Saving in dialogue of compliment,°   *Except empty flattery*
And talking of the Alps and Apennines,
The Pyrenean and the River Po,
It draws toward supper° in conclusion so.   *(another meal)*
205 But this is worshipful society,
And fits the mounting spirit° like myself;   *ambitious character*
For he is but a bastard to° the time   *no true child of*
That doth not smack of observation;°   *courtly obsequiousness*
And so am I°—whether I smack or no,   *so I intend*
210 And not alone in habit° and device,°   *clothes / heraldic emblem*
Exterior form, outward accoutrement,
But from the inward motion°—to deliver   *impulse*
Sweet, sweet, sweet poison° for the age's tooth;°   *flattery / appetite*
Which,° though I will not practise° to deceive,   *(flattery) / make a habit*
215 Yet to avoid deceit° I mean to learn;   *being deceived*
For it shall strew the footsteps of my rising.[9]

     Enter LADY FALCONBRIDGE *and James* GURNEY

But who comes in such haste in riding-robes?
What woman-post° is this? Hath she no husband   *female dispatch rider*
That will take pains to blow a horn[1] before her?
220 O me, 'tis my mother! How now, good lady?
What brings you here to court so hastily?
LADY FALCONBRIDGE   Where is that slave thy brother? Where is he
That holds in chase° mine honour up and down?   *Who hunts*
BASTARD   My brother Robert, old Sir Robert's son?
225 Colbrand the Giant,[2] that same mighty man?
Is it Sir Robert's son that you seek so?
LADY FALCONBRIDGE   Sir Robert's son, ay, thou unreverent boy,

---

6. God reward you: the patronizing reply of a social superior. The Bastard imagines himself, newly promoted, encountering a social inferior who says "Good evening." His soliloquy continues in this vein, parodying the affectation of courtiers and foreign travelers, in part through the ironic use of religious rhetoric—"conversion" (line 189, referring to his new rank), "my worship's mess" (line 190; "my worship" means both "a lord" and "the Lord"; "mess" means both "a dinner table" and "the Mass," the commemoration of Christ's Last Supper), and "catechize" (line 192; orally question, usually about religious principles).

7. *'Tis . . . conversion:* Remembering names is beneath the dignity of a newly created knight.
8. The Bastard defiantly cleans his teeth in the vulgar English fashion, rather than resorting to the traveler's and courtier's affectation of a toothpick.
9. For flattery will ease my ascent; awareness of deceptive flattery will do so.
1. Post horn announcing the rider's approach; also, the symbol of a cuckold.
2. Danish giant killed by Guy in the popular romance *Guy of Warwick.*

Sir Robert's son. Why scorn'st thou at Sir Robert?
He is Sir Robert's son, and so art thou.
230 BASTARD James Gurney, wilt thou give us leave° awhile?   *leave us*
GURNEY Good leave, good Philip.
BASTARD   Philip Sparrow,[3] James!
There's toys abroad;[4] anon I'll tell thee more.

                                      Exit James [GURNEY]

Madam, I was not old Sir Robert's son.
Sir Robert might have eat his part in me
235 Upon Good Friday, and ne'er broke his fast.
Sir Robert could do° well, marry° to confess,   *(sexual) / indeed*
Could a get° me! Sir Robert could not do it: *Could he have begotten*
We know his handiwork.° Therefore, good mother,   *(Falconbridge)*
To whom am I beholden for these limbs?
240 Sir Robert never holp° to make this leg.   *helped*
LADY FALCONBRIDGE Hast thou conspirèd with thy brother too,
That for thine own gain shouldst defend mine honour?
What means this scorn, thou most untoward° knave?   *unmannerly*
BASTARD Knight, knight, good mother, Basilisco-like![5]
245 What! I am dubbed; I have it° on my shoulder.   *(a sword tap)*
But, mother, I am not Sir Robert's son.
I have disclaimed Sir Robert; and my land,
Legitimation, name, and all is gone.
Then, good my mother, let me know my father;
250 Some proper man, I hope; who was it, mother?
LADY FALCONBRIDGE Hast thou denied thyself a Falconbridge?
BASTARD As faithfully as I deny the devil.
LADY FALCONBRIDGE King Richard Cœur-de-lion was thy father.
By long and vehement suit I was seduced
255 To make room for him in my husband's bed.
Heaven lay not my transgression to my charge!
Thou art the issue° of my dear° offence,   *result / costly; loving*
Which was so strongly urged past my defence.
BASTARD Now by this light, were I to get° again,   *be conceived*
260 Madam, I would not wish a better father.
Some sins do bear their privilege° on earth,   *are pardonable*
And so doth yours; your fault was not your folly.°   *your sin wasn't foolish*
Needs must you lay your heart at his dispose,°   *disposal*
Subjected tribute to commanding love,
265 Against whose fury and unmatchèd force
The aweless° lion could not wage the fight,   *fearless*
Nor keep his princely heart from Richard's hand.
He that perforce° robs lions of their hearts[6]   *by his strength*
May easily win a woman's. Ay, my mother,
270 With all my heart I thank thee for my father.
Who lives and dares but say thou didst not well
When I was got, I'll send his soul to hell.
Come, lady, I will show thee to my kin,
     And they shall say, when Richard me begot,

---

3. Recalling the popularity of Philip as a name for a mere bird, the Bastard considers the name beneath him.
4. There's trivial news (ironic).
5. The cowardly braggart Basilisco in an anonymous play *Solyman and Perseda*, probably from the early 1590s, calls himself a knight while his servant calls him a knave.
6. Alluding to Richard I's legendary feat of killing a lion by putting his hand down its throat and pulling out its heart (hence the epithet Cœur-de-lion, Lionheart).

275   If thou hadst said him nay, it had been sin.
        Who says it was, he lies: I say 'twas not.[7]

                                Exeunt

2.1

[Flourish.] Enter before Angers [at one door] PHILIP
King of France, LOUIS [THE] DAUPHIN, [Lady] CON-
STANCE, *and* ARTHUR [*Duke of Brittaine, with soldiers;
at another door the Duke of]* AUSTRIA [*wearing a lion's
hide, with soldiers*][1]

KING PHILIP   Before Angers well met, brave Austria.—
    Arthur, that great forerunner of thy blood,
    Richard° that robbed the lion of his heart   *(Arthur's uncle)*
    And fought the holy wars in Palestine,°   *Third Crusade (1189–92)*
5   By this brave duke came early to his grave;[2]
    And, for amends to his posterity,
    At our importance° hither is he come   *urgent request*
    To spread his colours,° boy, in thy behalf,   *battle flags*
    And to rebuke the usurpation
10   Of thy unnatural uncle, English John.
    Embrace him, love him, give him welcome hither.
ARTHUR [*to* AUSTRIA]   God shall forgive you Cœur-de-lion's death,
    The rather that° you give his offspring life,   *All the more because*
    Shadowing° their right under your wings of war.   *Protecting*
15   I give you welcome with a powerless hand,
    But with a heart full of unstainèd love.
    Welcome before the gates of Angers, Duke.
KING PHILIP   A noble boy. Who would not do thee right?
AUSTRIA [*kissing* ARTHUR]   Upon thy cheek lay I this zealous kiss
20   As seal to this indenture° of my love: *contract*
    That to my home I will no more return
    Till Angers and the right thou hast in France,
    Together with that pale, that white-faced shore,°   *chalk cliffs of Dover*
    Whose foot° spurns back the ocean's roaring tides   *(of the cliffs)*
25   And coops° from other lands her islanders,   *protects*
    Even till that England, hedged in with the main,°   *ocean*
    That water-wallèd bulwark, still° secure   *always*
    And confident from foreign purposes,
    Even till that utmost corner of the west
30   Salute thee for her king. Till then, fair boy,
    Will I not think of home, but follow arms.
CONSTANCE   O, take his mother's thanks, a widow's thanks,
    Till your strong hand shall help to give him strength
    To make a more° requital to your love.   *greater*
35   AUSTRIA   The peace of heaven is theirs that lift their swords
    In such a just and charitable war.
    KING PHILIP   Well then, to work! Our cannon shall be bent°   *aimed*

---

7. Not a sin; nought (nothing); naughty, and hence
something, a sin.
2.1 Location: Before the town wall of Angers.
1. This is "Scaena Secunda" in F (see the Textual
Note). The back of the stage represents the town wall,
with the town notionally behind it. The Citizen's entry
"upon the walls" (s.d. after line 200) is onto the upper
stage. Below the upper stage, central tiring-house doors
would probably represent the gates of Angers, the capital of John's French holdings. These remain closed; the
French and English armies appear from side entrances.
2. Austria, the "brave duke," imprisoned Richard, but
Richard was actually killed while besieging the castle of
the Viscount of Limoges in France. Shakespeare follows his main source in combining the two historical
figures in the character of Austria.

	Against the brows° of this resisting town.	walls
	Call for our chiefest men of discipline°	military skill
40	To cull the plots of best advantages.³	
	We'll lay before this town our royal bones,	
	Wade to the market-place in Frenchmen's blood,	
	But we will° make it subject to this boy.	In order to; unless we

CONSTANCE Stay for an answer to your embassy,
45 Lest unadvised° you stain your swords with blood.   *rashly*
My lord Châtillon may from England bring
That right in peace which here we urge° in war,   *seek*
And then we shall repent each drop of blood
That hot rash haste so indirectly° shed.   *wrongfully*

Enter CHÂTILLON

50 KING PHILIP A wonder, lady: lo upon thy wish
Our messenger Châtillon is arrived.—
What England° says, say briefly, gentle lord;   *the King of England*
We coldly° pause for thee. Châtillon, speak.   *calmly*

CHÂTILLON Then turn your forces from this paltry siege,
55 And stir them up against a mightier task.
England, impatient of your just demands,
Hath put himself in arms. The adverse winds,
Whose leisure I have stayed,° have given him time   *Which I had to wait out*
To land his legions all as soon as I.
60 His marches are expedient° to this town,   *coming quickly*
His forces strong, his soldiers confident.
With him along is come the Mother-Queen,
An Ate° stirring him to blood and strife;   *goddess of discord*
With her her niece,⁴ the Lady Blanche of Spain;
65 With them a bastard of the King's deceased;°   *of Richard's*
And all th'unsettled humours⁵ of the land—
Rash, inconsiderate,° fiery voluntaries,°   *imprudent / volunteers*
With ladies'° faces and fierce dragons' spleens°—   *beardless / tempers*
Have sold their fortunes at their native homes,
70 Bearing their birthrights proudly on their backs,⁶
To make a hazard of° new fortunes here.   *To take a chance on*
In brief, a braver choice of dauntless spirits
Than now the English bottoms° have waft o'er   *ships*
Did never float upon the swelling tide
75 To do offence and scathe° in Christendom.   *damage*

Drum beats

The interruption of their churlish drums
Cuts off more circumstance.° They are at hand;   *detail*
To parley or to fight therefore prepare.

KING PHILIP How much unlooked-for is this expedition!°   *military force; speed*
80 AUSTRIA By how much unexpected, by so much
We must awake endeavour for defence,
For courage mounteth with occasion.°   *necessity*
Let them be welcome then: we are prepared.

---

3. To pick the positions of greatest advantage (for the cannons).
4. Actually, Eleanor's granddaughter: "niece" is used in a broad sense.
5. Men of discontented spirits; masterless men of no fixed abode. The soldiers are seen as "humors" (physical elements of the body, which affect temperament) discharged from the body of England.
6. In the form of armor bought by selling their land ("birthrights" and "fortunes," line 69). "All his clothes are on his back" is proverbial.

Enter [*marching*] KING [JOHN] *of England,* [*the*] BAS-
TARD, QUEEN [ELEANOR], [*Lady*] BLANCHE, [*the Earl of*]
PEMBROKE, *and* [*soldiers*]

KING JOHN   Peace be to France, if France in peace permit
85   Our just and lineal° entrance to our own.°   *hereditary / Angers*
       If not, bleed France,° and peace ascend to heaven,   *let France bleed*
       Whiles we, God's wrathful agent, do correct°   *punish*
       Their proud contempt that beats his peace to heaven.
KING PHILIP   Peace be to England, if that war° return   *if the English forces*
90   From France to England, there to live in peace.
       England we love, and for that England's° sake   *that land's; Arthur's*
       With burden of our armour here we sweat.
       This toil of ours should be a work of thine;
       But thou from loving England art so far
95   That thou hast underwrought° his lawful king,   *undermined*
       Cut off the sequence of posterity,°   *the succession*
       Outfacèd infant state,° and done a rape   *Defied Arthur's right*
       Upon the maiden virtue of the crown.
       [*Pointing to* ARTHUR]
       Look here upon thy brother Geoffrey's face.
100   These eyes, these brows, were moulded out of his;
       This little abstract° doth contain that large°   *précis / full version*
       Which died in Geoffrey; and the hand of time
       Shall draw this brief° into as huge a volume.   *summary*
       That Geoffrey was thy elder brother born,
105   And this his son; England was Geoffrey's right,
       And this is Geoffrey's.° In the name of God,   *(son and heir)*
       How comes it then that thou art called a king,
       When living blood doth in these temples beat,
       Which owe° the crown that thou o'ermasterest?   *own*
110   KING JOHN   From whom hast thou this great commission, France,
       To draw my answer from thy articles?°   *charges*
KING PHILIP   From that supernal° judge that stirs good thoughts   *heavenly*
       In any breast of strong authority°   *In any powerful ruler*
       To look into the blots and stains of right.
115   That judge hath made me guardian to this boy,
       Under whose warrant I impeach° thy wrong,   *challenge*
       And by whose help I mean to chastise it.
KING JOHN   Alack, thou dost usurp authority.
KING PHILIP   Excuse it is to beat usurping down.[7]
120   QUEEN ELEANOR   Who is it thou dost call usurper, France?
CONSTANCE   Let me make answer: thy usurping son.
QUEEN ELEANOR   Out,° insolent! Thy bastard shall be king   *Begone*
       That thou mayst be a queen and check° the world.   *master*
CONSTANCE   My bed was ever° to thy son as true   *always*
125   As thine was to thy husband; and this boy
       Liker in feature to his father Geoffrey
       Than thou and John in manners, being as like
       As rain to water, or devil to his dam.°   *mother*
       My boy a bastard? By my soul I think
130   His father never was so true begot.
       It cannot be, an if° thou wert his mother.   *an if=if*

7. My (so-called) usurpation is excusable because I am using it to put down (real) usurpation.

QUEEN ELEANOR [*to* ARTHUR]   There's a good mother, boy, that
    blots° thy father.   *slanders*
CONSTANCE [*to* ARTHUR]   There's a good grandam, boy, that
    would blot thee.
AUSTRIA   Peace!
BASTARD   Hear the crier!⁸
AUSTRIA   What the devil art thou?
135   BASTARD   One that will play the devil, sir, with you,
    An a° may catch your hide⁹ and you alone.   *If he (I)*
    You are the hare° of whom the proverb goes,   *coward*
    Whose valour plucks dead lions by the beard.°   *(an insult)*
    I'll smoke your skin-coat° an I catch you right—   *thrash your hide*
140   Sirrah,° look to't—i'faith I will, i'faith!   *Boy (an insult)*
   BLANCHE   O, well did he° become that lion's robe   *(Richard)*
    That did disrobe the lion of that robe!
   BASTARD   It lies as sightly° on the back of him   *fitly*
    As great Alcides' shows¹ upon an ass.
145   But, ass, I'll take that burden from your back,
    Or lay on that° shall make your shoulders crack.   *that burden which*
   AUSTRIA   What cracker° is this same that deafs our ears   *boaster*
    With this abundance of superfluous breath?—
    King Philip, determine what we shall do straight.°   *immediately*
150   KING PHILIP   Women and fools,° break off your conference.—   *children*
    King John, this is the very sum of all:
    England and Ireland, Anjou,² Touraine, Maine,
    In right of Arthur do I claim of thee.
    Wilt thou resign them and lay down thy arms?
155   KING JOHN   My life as soon. I do defy thee, France.—
    Arthur of Brittaine, yield thee to my hand,
    And out of my dear love I'll give thee more
    Than e'er the coward hand of France can win.
    Submit thee, boy.
   QUEEN ELEANOR [*to* ARTHUR]   Come to thy grandam, child.
160   CONSTANCE [*to* ARTHUR]   Do, child, go to it° grandam, child.   *its*
    Give grandam kingdom, and it grandam will
    Give it a plum, a cherry, and a fig.°   *(obscene)*
    There's a good grandam.°   *(sarcastic baby talk)*
   ARTHUR   Good my mother, peace.
    I would that I were low laid in my grave.
165   I am not worth this coil° that's made for me.   *commotion*
    [*He weeps*]
   QUEEN ELEANOR   His mother shames him so, poor boy, he weeps.
   CONSTANCE   Now shame upon you, whe'er° she does or no!   *whether*
    His grandam's wrongs, and not his mother's shames,
    Draw those heaven-moving pearls from his poor eyes,
170   Which heaven shall take in nature° of a fee;   *as a kind*
    Ay, with these crystal beads° heaven shall be bribed   *tears*
    To do him justice and revenge on you.
   QUEEN ELEANOR   Thou monstrous slanderer of heaven and earth!

---

8. The Bastard mockingly compares Austria to an officer in a law court who calls for order.
9. The lion skin Austria wears, which, as a memento of
his father's death, antagonizes the Bastard.
1. As the lion skin of Hercules would appear (alluding
to his legendary size and strength, and to the proverbial

"ass in a lion's skin").
2. Here and at line 488, Shakespeare appears to confuse the province (Anjou) with the besieged town
(Angers; French: Angiers). Elsewhere, he maintains a
distinction, as do his sources.

CONSTANCE   Thou monstrous injurer of heaven and earth!
175   Call not me slanderer. Thou and thine usurp
The dominations, royalties° and rights   *royal powers*
Of this oppressèd boy. This is thy eld'st son's son,[3]
Infortunate in nothing but in thee.
Thy sins are visited° in this poor child;   *punished*
180   The canon of the law° is laid on him,   *biblical decree*
Being but the second generation
Removèd from thy sin-conceiving womb.[4]

KING JOHN   Bedlam,° have done.   *Lunatic*

CONSTANCE   I have but this to say:
That he° is not only plaguèd for her sin,°   *(Arthur) / (adultery)*
185   But God hath made her sin° and her the plague   *(John)*
On this removèd issue,° plaguèd for her   *(Arthur)*
And with her plague;[5] her sin his injury,
Her injury the beadle to her sin;
All punished in the person of this child,
190   And all for her.[6] A plague upon her!

QUEEN ELEANOR   Thou unadvisèd° scold, I can produce   *rash*
A will that bars the title of thy son.

CONSTANCE   Ay, who doubts that? A will, a wicked will,
A woman's will,[7] a cankered grandam's will!

195   KING PHILIP   Peace, lady; pause or be more temperate.
It ill beseems this presence° to cry aim   *royal assembly*
To[8] these ill-tunèd repetitions.—
Some trumpet summon hither to the walls
These men of Angers. Let us hear them speak
200   Whose title they admit, Arthur's or John's.

Trumpet sounds. Enter a CITIZEN[9] *upon the walls*

CITIZEN   Who is it that hath warned° us to the walls?   *summoned*

KING PHILIP   'Tis France for England.

KING JOHN   England for itself.
You men of Angers and my loving subjects—

KING PHILIP   You loving men of Angers, Arthur's subjects,
205   Our trumpet called you to this gentle parle°—   *parley*

KING JOHN   For our° advantage; therefore hear us first.   *(England's; John's)*
These flags of France that are advancèd here
Before the eye and prospect of your town,
Have hither marched to your endamagement.
210   The cannons have their bowels full of wrath,
And ready mounted are they to spit forth
Their iron indignation 'gainst your walls.
All preparation for a bloody siege
And merciless proceeding by these French
215   Confront your city's eyes, your winking° gates;   *closed (in sleep)*
And but for our approach, those sleeping stones

---

3. Oldest grandson; but perhaps deliberately meant to produce the false inference that Arthur is really the "eld'st son's [Richard's] son."
4. Implying sexual infidelity in the conception of John. These lines (especially 179) echo the Second Commandment (Exodus 20:5, "the law" of line 180): "visiting the iniquity of the fathers upon the children unto the third and fourth generation."
5. *plagued . . . plague:* punished because of and by her.
6. *her sin his injury . . . her:* her wrongful action is like a parish constable (a "beadle," who whipped petty criminals) urging on her son to afflict Arthur; all (Eleanor's

sin, John as its embodiment) are punished in Arthur, and all because of Eleanor.
7. Testament influenced by a woman (Eleanor; ironically, it was illegal for women to make wills themselves, for fear their husbands would influence them); a woman's desire (as in the proverbial "A woman will have her will").
8. *to cry aim / To:* to encourage.
9. Shakespeare may have taken some steps toward conflating this character with Hubert, who figures prominently later in the play (see note to line 325 and Textual Note), but no early text survives in which such an identification of characters has been fully effected.

	That as a waist° doth girdle you about,	*girdle*
	By the compulsion of their ordinance,°	*artillery*
	By this time from their fixèd beds of lime°	*their foundations*
220	Had been dishabited,[1] and wide havoc made	
	For bloody power to rush upon your peace.	
	But on the sight of us your lawful king,	
	Who painfully,° with much expedient° march,	*laboriously / hurried*
	Have brought a countercheck before your gates	
225	To save unscratched your city's threatened cheeks,	
	Behold the French, amazed,° vouchsafe° a parle;	*terrified / grant*
	And now instead of bullets wrapped in fire	
	To make a shaking fever in your walls,	
	They shoot but calm words folded up in smoke°	*deceit*
230	To make a faithless error° in your ears;	*lie*
	Which trust accordingly, kind citizens,	
	And let us in, your king, whose laboured° spirits,	*worn out*
	Forwearied in this action of swift speed,	
	Craves harbourage within your city walls.	

KING PHILIP   When I have said, make answer to us both.

[*He takes Arthur's hand*]

	Lo, in this° right hand, whose protection	*(Philip's)*
	Is most divinely vowed upon the right	
	Of him° it holds, stands young Plantagenet,	*(Arthur)*
	Son to the elder brother of this man°	*(John)*
240	And king o'er him and all that he enjoys.	
	For this downtrodden equity° we tread	*right*
	In warlike march these greens before your town,	
	Being no further enemy to you	
	Than the constraint° of hospitable zeal	*necessity*
245	In the relief of this oppressèd child	
	Religiously° provokes. Be pleasèd then	*Solemnly*
	To pay that duty which you truly owe	
	To him that owes° it, namely this young prince;	*has a right to*
	And then our arms, like to a muzzled bear,	
250	Save in aspect,° hath all offence° sealed up:	*appearance / aggression*
	Our cannons' malice vainly shall be spent	
	Against th'invulnerable clouds of heaven,	
	And with a blessèd and unvexed retire,°	*unmolested retreat*
	With unhacked swords and helmets all unbruised,	
255	We will bear home that lusty blood again	
	Which here we came to spout against your town,	
	And leave your children, wives, and you in peace.	
	But if you fondly° pass our proffered offer,	*foolishly*
	'Tis not the roundure° of your old-faced walls	*roundness; circumference*
260	Can hide you from our messengers of war,°	*cannonballs*
	Though all these English and their discipline°	*military skill*
	Were harboured in their rude° circumference.	*rugged*
	Then tell us, shall your city call us lord	
	In that behalf which° we have challenged it,	*in which; for whom*
265	Or shall we give the signal to our rage,	
	And stalk in blood to our possession?	

CITIZEN   In brief, we are the King of England's subjects.

| | For him and in his right we hold this town. | |

---

1. Dislodged, unclothed ("habit" picking up "waist," "girdle," line 217). Angers continues to be personified here ("cheeks," line 225; "fever," line 228) and later in the scene.

KING JOHN Acknowledge then the King, and let me in.

270 CITIZEN That can we not; but he that proves° the king,   *proves to be*
    To him will we prove loyal; till that time
    Have we rammed up our gates against the world.

KING JOHN Doth not the crown of England prove the king?
    And if not that, I bring you witnesses:

275   Twice fifteen thousand hearts of England's breed—

BASTARD [*aside*] Bastards and else.°   *others*

KING JOHN To verify our title with their lives.

KING PHILIP As many and as well-born bloods as those—

BASTARD [*aside*] Some bastards too.

280 KING PHILIP Stand in his face° to contradict his claim.   *against him*

CITIZEN Till you compound° whose right is worthiest,   *settle*
    We for the worthiest hold° the right from both.   *withhold*

KING JOHN Then God forgive the sin of all those souls
    That to their everlasting residence,

285   Before the dew of evening fall, shall fleet°   *leave their bodies*
    In dreadful trial of° our kingdom's king.   *contest to determine*

KING PHILIP Amen, Amen! Mount, chevaliers!° To arms!   *horsemen*

BASTARD Saint George that swinged° the dragon, and e'er since   *thrashed*
    Sits on's horseback at mine hostess' door,[2]

290   Teach us some fence!° [*To* AUSTRIA] Sirrah, were I at home   *swordsmanship*
    At your den, sirrah, with your lioness,°   *whore; wife*
    I would set an ox-head° to your lion's hide   *add cuckold's horns*
    And make a monster of you.

AUSTRIA   Peace, no more.

BASTARD O tremble, for you hear the lion roar!

295 KING JOHN Up higher to the plain, where we'll set forth
    In best appointment° all our regiments.   *readiness*

BASTARD Speed then, to take advantage of the field.°   *best battle positions*

KING PHILIP It shall be so, and at the other hill
    Command the rest to stand.[3] God and our right!°   *(English royal motto)*

            Exeunt [*severally*° KING JOHN *and* KING PHILIP *with their*   *separately*
            powers. The CITIZEN *remains on the walls*]
            [*Alarum.*] *Here, after excursions,*° *enter* [*at one door*] *the*   *onstage skirmishes*
            HERALD *of France, with* [*a*] *trumpet*[*er*], *to the gates*

300 FRENCH HERALD You men of Angers, open wide your gates
    And let young Arthur Duke of Brittaine in,
    Who by the hand of France this day hath made
    Much work for tears in many an English mother,
    Whose sons lie scattered on the bleeding ground;

305   Many a widow's husband grovelling lies,
    Coldly embracing the discoloured earth;
    And victory with little loss doth play
    Upon the dancing banners of the French,
    Who are at hand, triumphantly displayed,°   *drawn up*

310   To enter conquerors, and to proclaim
    Arthur of Brittaine England's king and yours.

            Enter [*at another door the*] *English* HERALD, *with* [*a*]
            trumpet[*er*]

ENGLISH HERALD Rejoice, you men of Angers, ring your bells!
    King John, your king and England's, doth approach,

---

2. The idea that St. George, England's patron saint, is ever on horseback yet never rides was proverbial. *at mine hostess' door*: on an inn sign.

3. Command the reserves to be in readiness. (This concludes an unheard conversation in parallel with John's.)

Commander of this hot malicious day.
315 Their armours that marched hence so silver-bright
Hither return all gilt° with Frenchmen's blood.   *smeared; golden*
There stuck no plume in any English crest°   *(on a helmet)*
That is removèd by a staff° of France;   *spear*
Our colours° do return in those same hands   *banners*
320 That did display them when we first marched forth;
And like a jolly troop of huntsmen come
Our lusty English, all with purpled hands
Dyed in the dying slaughter of their foes.
Open your gates and give the victors way.
325 CITIZEN[4]   Heralds, from off our towers we might° behold   *could*
From first to last the onset and retire
Of both your armies, whose equality
By our best eyes cannot be censurèd.°   *differentiated*
Blood hath bought blood and blows have answered blows,
330 Strength matched with strength and power confronted power.
Both are alike, and both alike we like.
One must prove greatest. While they weigh so even,
We hold our town for neither, yet for both.

> *Enter the two kings with their powers,° at several doors*   *armies*
> *[at one door* KING JOHN, *the* BASTARD, QUEEN ELEANOR
> *and Lady* BLANCHE, *with soldiers; at another door* KING
> PHILIP, LOUIS THE DAUPHIN, *and the Duke of* AUSTRIA
> *with soldiers]*[5]

KING JOHN   France, hast thou yet more blood to cast away?
335 Say, shall the current of our right run on,
Whose passage, vexed with thy impediment,
Shall leave his native channel° and o'erswell°   *normal course / flood*
With course disturbed even thy confining shores,
Unless thou let his silver water keep
340 A peaceful progress to the ocean?
KING PHILIP   England, thou hast not saved one drop of blood
In this hot trial more than we of France;
Rather, lost more. And by this hand I swear,
. That sways the earth this climate° overlooks,   *part of the sky*
345 Before we will lay down our just-borne arms,
We'll put thee down 'gainst whom these arms we bear,
Or add a royal number° to the dead,   *(Philip)*
Gracing the scroll that tells of this war's loss
With slaughter coupled to the name of kings.
350 BASTARD   Ha, majesty! How high thy glory towers
When the rich blood of kings is set on fire!
O, now doth Death line his dead chaps° with steel;   *deadly jaws*
The swords of soldiers are his teeth, his fangs;
And now he feasts, mousing° the flesh of men   *tearing; biting*
355 In undetermined differences° of kings.   *unresolved disputes*
Why stand these royal fronts° amazèd thus?   *faces*
Cry havoc,[6] Kings! Back to the stainèd field,
You equal potents,° fiery-kindled spirits!   *equally strong rulers*

---

4. This and subsequent speeches of the Citizen are attributed to Hubert in the earliest Folio text. See note to line 200.
5. F calls for "the two Kings with their powers"; this seems to exclude Constance and Arthur.
6. Order given to troops for pillaging and merciless slaughter.

Then let confusion° of one part° confirm   *let overthrow / side*
360   The other's peace; till then, blows, blood, and death!
    KING JOHN   Whose party do the townsmen yet admit?
    KING PHILIP   Speak, citizens, for England: who's your king?
    CITIZEN   The King of England, when we know the King.
    KING PHILIP   Know him in us,° that here hold up his right.   *me*
365   KING JOHN   In us, that are our own great deputy°   *representative*
      And bear possession of our person° here,   *represent my own claim*
      Lord of our presence,° Angers, and of you.   *myself*
    CITIZEN   A greater power than we denies all this,
      And, till it be undoubted, we do lock
370   Our former scruple in our strong-barred gates,
      Kinged of° our fear, until our fears resolved   *Commanded by*
      Be by some certain king, purged and deposed.
  BASTARD   By heaven, these scroyles° of Angers flout you, Kings,   *scoundrels*
      And stand securely on their battlements
375   As in a theatre, whence they gape and point
      At your industrious scenes and acts of death.
      Your royal presences° be ruled by me.   *persons*
      Do like the mutines of Jerusalem:[7]
      Be friends awhile, and both conjointly° bend   *together*
380   Your sharpest deeds of malice on this town.
      By east and west let France and England mount
      Their battering cannon, chargèd to° the mouths,   *loaded to*
      Till their soul-fearing° clamours have brawled° down   *terrifying / broken*
      The flinty ribs° of this contemptuous city.   *walls*
385   I'd play incessantly upon these jades,[8]
      Even till unfencèd° desolation   *unwalled*
      Leave them as naked as the vulgar° air.   *common*
      That done, dissever your united strengths,
      And part your mingled colours once again;
390   Turn face to face, and bloody point to point.
      Then in a moment Fortune shall cull° forth   *choose*
      Out of one side her happy minion,°   *darling*
      To whom in favour she shall give the day,°   *victory*
      And kiss him with a glorious victory.
395   How like you this wild counsel, mighty states?°   *rulers*
      Smacks it not something of the policy?°   *political cunning*
  KING JOHN   Now, by the sky that hangs above our heads,
      I like it well.—France, shall we knit° our powers,   *join*
      And lay this Angers even with the ground,
400   Then after fight who shall be king of it?
  BASTARD [*to* KING PHILIP]   An if thou hast the mettle of a king,
      Being wronged as we are by this peevish° town,   *obstinate*
      Turn thou the mouth of thy artillery,
      As we will ours, against these saucy° walls;   *presumptuous*
405   And when that we have dashed them to the ground,
      Why, then defy each other, and pell-mell°   *quickly*
      Make work upon ourselves, for[9] heaven or hell.
  KING PHILIP   Let it be so.—Say, where will you assault?

---

7. Warring factions of Jerusalem who temporarily united against besieging Roman forces in 70 C.E.
8. I'd unceasingly fire at (or torment) these wretches. (A "jade" was a decrepit horse or an insulting term for a woman—and hence a double insult when applied to a man.)
9. On behalf of; for the destination of.

KING JOHN   We from the west will send destruction
410   Into this city's bosom.
AUSTRIA   I from the north.
KING PHILIP   Our thunder° from the south   *cannon*
        Shall rain their drift of bullets° on this town.   *shower of cannonballs*
BASTARD [*to* KING JOHN]   O prudent discipline!° From north to south   *tactics*
415   Austria and France shoot in each other's mouth.
        I'll stir them to it. Come, away, away!
CITIZEN   Hear us, great Kings, vouchsafe a while to stay,
        And I shall show you peace and fair-faced league.
        Win you this city without stroke or wound;
420   Rescue those breathing lives to die in beds,
        That here come sacrifices for the field.
        Persever not, but hear me, mighty Kings.
KING JOHN   Speak on with favour;° we are bent° to hear.   *permission / willing*
CITIZEN   That daughter there of Spain, the Lady Blanche,
425   Is niece to England. Look upon the years°   *ages*
        Of Louis the Dauphin and that lovely maid.
        If lusty love should go in quest of beauty,
        Where should he find it fairer than in Blanche?
        If zealous° love should go in search of virtue,   *pious*
430   Where should he find it purer than in Blanche?
        If love ambitious sought a match of birth,
        Whose veins bound° richer blood than Lady Blanche?   *contain*
        Such as she is in beauty, virtue, birth,
        Is the young Dauphin every way complete;°   *perfect*
435   If not complete, O, say he is not she;
        And she again wants nothing—to name want—
        If want it be not that she is not he.[1]
        He is the half part of a blessèd man,
        Left to be finishèd by such as she;
440   And she a fair divided excellence,
        Whose fullness of perfection lies in him.
        O, two such silver currents when they join
        Do glorify the banks that bound them in,
        And two such shores to two such streams made one,
445   Two such controlling bounds, shall you be, Kings,
        To these two princes if you marry them.
        This union shall do more than battery can
        To our fast-closèd gates, for at this match,[2]
        With swifter spleen° than powder can enforce,   *passion*
450   The mouth of passage shall we fling wide ope,
        And give you entrance. But without this match
        The sea enragèd is not half so deaf,
        Lions more confident, mountains and rocks
        More free from motion, no, not Death himself
455   In mortal fury half so peremptory,°   *resolved*
        As we to keep this city.
BASTARD [*aside*]   Here's a stay°   *an obstacle; cease-fire*
        That shakes the rotten carcass of old Death
        Out of his rags.[3] Here's a large mouth,° indeed,   *(of a cannon or human)*

---

1. *If not . . . he:* The Dauphin is perfect insofar   2. Marriage; device for lighting gun "powder" (line
as he lacks Blanche, and vice versa. *wants:* lacks. *to:* if   449).
I must.   3. *That . . . rags:* That steals what belongs to death.

That spits forth Death and mountains, rocks and seas,
460 Talks as familiarly of roaring lions
As maids of thirteen do of puppy-dogs.
What cannoneer begot this lusty blood?
He speaks plain cannon: fire, and smoke, and bounce;°   *bang*
He gives the bastinado° with his tongue;   *a cudgeling*
465 Our ears are cudgelled; not a word of his
But buffets better than a fist of France.
Zounds!° I was never so bethumped with words   *God's wounds*
Since I first called my brother's father Dad.
QUEEN ELEANOR [*aside to* KING JOHN]   Son, list° to this conjunc-   *listen*
tion,° make this match,   *proposition*
470 Give with our niece a dowry large enough;
For, by this knot, thou shalt so surely tie
Thy now unsured assurance to the crown
That yon green° boy shall have no sun to ripe   *unripe; young*
The bloom that promiseth a mighty fruit.
475 I see a yielding in the looks of France;
Mark how they whisper. Urge them while their souls
Are capable of° this ambition,   *susceptible to*
Lest zeal,° now melted by the windy breath   *(on Arthur's behalf)*
Of soft petitions, pity, and remorse,
480 Cool and congeal° again to what it was.   *freeze*
CITIZEN   Why answer not the double majesties
This friendly treaty° of our threatened town?   *entreaty; proposal*
KING PHILIP   Speak England first, that hath been forward first
To speak unto this city: what say you?
485 KING JOHN   If that the Dauphin there, thy princely son,
Can in this book of beauty° read 'I love',   *(Blanche)*
Her dowry shall weigh equal with a queen;
For Anjou and fair Touraine, Maine, Poitou,[4]
And all that we upon this side the sea—
490 Except this city now by us besieged—
Find liable° to our crown and dignity,   *subject*
Shall gild her bridal bed, and make her rich
In titles, honours, and promotions,°   *elevations in rank*
As she in beauty, education, blood,
495 Holds hand with° any princess of the world.   *Is equal to*
KING PHILIP   What sayst thou, boy? Look in the lady's face.
LOUIS THE DAUPHIN   I do, my lord, and in her eye I find
A wonder, or a wondrous miracle,
The shadow of myself formed in her eye;
500 Which, being but the shadow of your son,
Becomes a sun and makes your son a shadow.[5]
I do protest I never loved myself
Till now enfixèd° I beheld myself   *imprinted*
Drawn in the flattering table° of her eye.   *surface*
[*He*] *whispers with* BLANCHE
505 BASTARD [*aside*]   Drawn in the flattering table of her eye,
Hanged in the frowning wrinkle of her brow,

4. The French territories claimed by both John and Arthur will go to the Dauphin.
5. *The shadow of myself . . . a shadow:* The Dauphin speaks in elaborate clichés of courtly love poetry: the conceit is common, as is the "sun/son" wordplay. He claims that his "shadow," from being a mere reflection or pale imitation of the King's son (or a shadow of the sun) in Blanche's eyes, becomes a "sun" because her eyes are so bright, with the result that the actual "son" becomes a mere "shadow" of his own reflection.

And quartered in her heart:[6] he doth espy
Himself love's traitor. This is pity now,
That hanged and drawn and quartered there should be
510 In such a love so vile a lout as he.
BLANCHE [to LOUIS THE DAUPHIN]   My uncle's will in this respect is mine.
If he see aught° in you that makes him like,   anything
That anything he sees which moves his liking
I can with ease translate it to my will;
515 Or if you will, to speak more properly,°   precisely
I will enforce it easily to my love.
Further I will not flatter you, my lord,
That all I see in you is worthy° love,   deserving of
Than this:[7] that nothing do I see in you,
520 Though churlish° thoughts themselves should be your judge,   grudging
That I can find should merit any hate.
KING JOHN   What say these young ones? What say you, my niece?
BLANCHE   That she is bound in honour still° to do   always
What you in wisdom shall vouchsafe° to say.   deign
525 KING JOHN   Speak then, Prince Dauphin, can you love this lady?
LOUIS THE DAUPHIN   Nay, ask me if I can refrain from love,
For I do love her most unfeignedly.
KING JOHN   Then do I give Volquessen,[8] Maine,
Poitou, and Anjou, these five provinces,
530 With her to thee, and this addition more:
Full thirty thousand marks° of English coin.   £20,000
Philip of France, if thou be pleased withal,°   with this
Command thy son and daughter to join hands.
KING PHILIP   It likes° us well.—Young princes, close your hands. pleases
535 AUSTRIA   And your lips too, for I am well assured
That I did so when I was first assured.°   betrothed
[LOUIS THE DAUPHIN and Lady BLANCHE join hands and kiss]
KING PHILIP   Now citizens of Angers, ope your gates.
Let in that amity which you have made,
For at Saint Mary's chapel presently°   immediately
540 The rites of marriage shall be solemnized.—
Is not the Lady Constance in this troop?
[Aside] I know she is not, for this match made up
Her presence would have interrupted much.
[Aloud] Where is she and her son? Tell me who knows.
545 LOUIS THE DAUPHIN   She is sad and passionate° at your highness' tent. sorrowful
KING PHILIP   And by my faith this league that we have made
Will give her sadness very little cure.—
Brother of England, how may we content
This widow lady? In her right we came,
550 Which we, God knows, have turned another way
To our own vantage.°   advantage
KING JOHN   We will heal up all,
For we'll create young Arthur Duke of Brittaine[9]
And Earl of Richmond, and this rich fair town
We make him lord of. Call the Lady Constance.

---

6. *Drawn . . . heart:* the Bastard alludes to the punishment of being hanged, drawn (disemboweled; but also,
painted, line 504), and quartered (cut in pieces; but also,
lodged) for treason. The rhyme scheme of lines 505–10
mimics the last six lines of a Shakespearean sonnet.

7. Taking up "Further," line 517.
8. Modern Vexin, northwest of Paris.
9. An inconsistency: Arthur already holds this title, as
John himself acknowledges (line 156).

555 Some speedy messenger bid her repair°   *come*
     To our solemnity.° I trust we shall,   *(marriage) ceremony*
     If not fill up the measure of her will,
     Yet in some measure satisfy her so
     That we shall stop her exclamation.°   *loud reproaches*
560 Go we as well as haste will suffer° us   *allow*
     To this unlooked-for, unprepared pomp.°   *ceremony*
                    [*Flourish.*] *Exeunt* [*all but the* BASTARD]
     BASTARD Mad world, mad kings, mad composition!°   *treaty*
     John, to stop Arthur's title in the whole,
     Hath willingly departed° with a part;   *parted*
565 And France, whose armour conscience buckled on,
     Whom zeal and charity brought to the field
     As God's own soldier, rounded° in the ear   *whispered to*
     With° that same purpose-changer,[1] that sly devil,   *By*
     That broker that still breaks the pate[2] of faith,
570 That daily break-vow, he that wins of° all,   *gets the best of*
     Of kings, of beggars, old men, young men, maids,—
     Who° having no external° thing to lose   *(maids) / material*
     But the word 'maid',° cheats° the poor maid of that—   *virginity / he cheats*
     That smooth-faced° gentleman, tickling° commodity;   *plausible / cajoling*
575 Commodity, the bias[3] of the world,
     The world who of itself is peisèd° well,   *balanced*
     Made to run even upon even ground,
     Till this advantage, this vile-drawing° bias,   *drawing to evil*
     This sway° of motion, this commodity,   *swayer; swerver*
580 Makes it take head° from all indifferency,°   *flee / impartiality*
     From all direction, purpose, course, intent;
     And this same bias, this commodity,
     This bawd,° this broker, this all-changing word,   *procurer*
     Clapped on the outward eye[4] of fickle France,
585 Hath drawn him from his own determined aid,
     From a resolved and honourable war,
     To a most base and vile-concluded peace.
     And why rail I on this commodity?
     But for° because he hath not wooed me yet—   *Only*
590 Not that I have the power to clutch° my hand   *clench (in refusal)*
     When his fair angels would salute[5] my palm,
     But for° my hand, as unattempted° yet,   *Because / untempted*
     Like a poor beggar raileth on the rich.
     Well, whiles I am a beggar I will rail,
595 And say there is no sin but to be rich,
     And being rich, my virtue then shall be
     To say there is no vice but beggary.
     Since kings break faith upon° commodity,   *on account of*
     Gain, be my lord, for I will worship thee.   *Exit*

1. "Purpose-changer," as well as the subsequent noun phrases in lines 568–70, is in apposition to those in line 574, in particular "commodity" (self-interest, profit seeking: that which translates everything into its market value to the exclusion of noneconomic considerations).
2. Cracks the skull (giving colloquial vigor to "breaks faith"). *broker:* go-between, procurer (leading to wordplay in "breaks" and "break-vow," lines 569–70).
3. Literally, in the game of bowls, the off-center weight of a bowl that causes it to veer from a straight course.
4. Fixed its hold on the outer edge of a bowl so as to make it swerve from a true course; suddenly caught the "outward eye" of self-interest as opposed to the inward eye of conscience. Both meanings are applicable to King Philip.
5. *angels would salute:* 10-shilling coins (with the archangel Michael on them) would kiss (greet); alluding to the Annunciation and Michael's "salute" to the Virgin Mary.

2.2

Enter [Lady] CONSTANCE, ARTHUR *[Duke of Brittaine],*
and [the Earl of] SALISBURY[1]

CONSTANCE *[to* SALISBURY*]*   Gone to be married? Gone to swear a peace?
    False blood to false blood joined! Gone to be friends?
    Shall Louis have Blanche, and Blanche those provinces?
    It is not so, thou hast misspoke, misheard.
5   Be well advised,° tell o'er thy tale again.   *Consider carefully*
    It cannot be, thou dost but say 'tis so.
    I trust I may not trust thee, for thy word
    Is but the vain breath of a common° man.   *(as opposed to royal)*
    Believe me, I do not believe thee, man;
10   I have a king's oath to the contrary.
    Thou shalt be punished for thus frighting me;
    For I am sick and capable of° fears;   *susceptible to*
    Oppressed with wrongs, and therefore full of fears;
    A widow husbandless, subject to fears;
15   A woman naturally born to fears;
    And though° thou now confess thou didst but jest,   *even if*
    With my vexed spirits I cannot take a truce,°   *make peace*
    But they will quake and tremble all this day.
    What dost thou mean by shaking of thy head?
20   Why dost thou look so sadly on my son?
    What means that hand upon that breast of thine?
    Why holds thine eye that lamentable rheum,°   *tears*
    Like a proud° river peering o'er his bounds?°   *swollen / banks*
    Be these sad signs confirmers of thy words?
25   Then speak again—not all thy former tale,
    But this one word: whether thy tale be true.
SALISBURY   As true as I believe you think them° false   *(the French and English)*
    That give you cause to prove my saying true.
CONSTANCE   O, if thou teach me to believe this sorrow,
30   Teach thou this sorrow how to make me die;
    And let belief and life encounter so
    As doth the fury of two desperate men
    Which in the very meeting fall and die.[2]
    Louis marry Blanche! *[To* ARTHUR*]* O boy, then where art thou?
35   France friend with England!—What becomes of me?
    [To SALISBURY*]* Fellow,° be gone, I cannot brook° thy sight;   *(an insult) / endure*
    This news hath made thee a most ugly man.
SALISBURY   What other harm have I, good lady, done,
    But spoke the harm that is by others done?
40 CONSTANCE   Which harm within itself so heinous is
    As it makes harmful all that speak of it.
ARTHUR   I do beseech you, madam, be content.°   *calm*
CONSTANCE   If thou that bidd'st me be content wert grim,
    Ugly and sland'rous to thy mother's womb,[3]
45   Full of unpleasing blots and sightless° stains,   *unsightly*
    Lame, foolish, crooked, swart,° prodigious,[4]   *dark*
    Patched° with foul moles and eye-offending marks,   *Blotched*
    I would not care, I then would be content,

2.2 Location: The French camp by Angers.
1. This is "Actus Secundus" in F (see Textual Note).
2. O . . . die: in this image, drawn from emblem-book representations of Fury, sorrow (or belief) dies as

Constance does.
3. Malformed babies were seen as a divine punishment for wickedness.
4. Monstrous (and thereby foretelling evil).

For then I should not love thee, no, nor thou
50   Become thy great birth, nor deserve a crown.
But thou art fair, and at thy birth, dear boy,
Nature and Fortune joined to make thee great.
Of Nature's gifts thou mayst with lilies boast,
And with the half-blown° rose. But Fortune, O,   *half-blossomed; young*
55   She is corrupted, changed, and won from thee;
Sh'adulterates° hourly with thine uncle John,   *prostitutes herself*
And with her golden hand hath plucked on° France   *enticed*
To tread down fair respect of sovereignty,°   *(Arthur's rights)*
And made his majesty the bawd to theirs.⁵
60   France is a bawd to Fortune and King John,
That strumpet Fortune, that usurping John.
[*To* SALISBURY] Tell me, thou fellow, is not France forsworn?°   *an oath breaker*
Envenom° him with words, or get thee gone   *Poison*
And leave those woes alone, which I alone
Am bound to underbear.°   *suffer under*
65   SALISBURY   Pardon me, madam,
I may not go without you to the Kings.
CONSTANCE   Thou mayst, thou shalt; I will not go with thee.
I will instruct my sorrows to be proud,
For grief is proud and makes his owner stoop.
[*She sits upon the ground*]
70   To me and to the state° of my great grief   *throne (ironic)*
Let kings assemble, for my grief's so great
That no supporter but the huge firm earth
Can hold it up. Here I and sorrows sit;
Here is my throne; bid kings come bow to it.
[*Exeunt* SALISBURY *and* ARTHUR]

3.1

[*Flourish.*] *Enter* KING JOHN [*and* KING PHILIP *of*]
France [*hand in hand;* LOUIS THE] DAUPHIN [*and Lady*]
BLANCHE, [*married;* QUEEN] ELEANOR, *Philip* [*the* BAS-
TARD, *and the Duke of*] AUSTRIA¹
KING PHILIP [*to* BLANCHE]   'Tis true,² fair daughter, and this blessèd day
Ever in France shall be kept festival.
To solemnize this day, the glorious sun
Stays in his course° and plays the alchemist,³   *Stands still*
5   Turning with splendour of his precious eye
The meagre cloddy earth to glittering gold.
The yearly course that brings this day about
Shall never see it but a holy day.
CONSTANCE [*rising*]   A wicked day, and not a holy day!
10   What hath this day deserved? What hath it done,
That it in golden letters should be set

---

5. And made Philip the go-between for John and Fortune.
3.1 Location: The French camp by Angers.
1. Shakespeare originally intended no act break,
though that division, which appears in F, probably indicates a pause in the performance when the play was
revived with act divisions. Salisbury and Arthur might
stay onstage, but they have no further part in the
scene's action. Their exit, if it occurs, may be followed
by a brief pause with Constance alone onstage. She
remains unobserved until line 9. F's stage directions
have her enter with the others at the start of the act,
perhaps because they merely list all the characters who
need to be onstage after a break in the action. But her
words of 2.2.67–74 are incompatible with her entry
here, which is therefore omitted.
2. King Philip enters in mid-conversation.
3. Alchemists sought to turn base metals such as lead
into gold.

	Among the high tides° in the calendar?	*great festivals*
	Nay, rather turn this day out of the week,	
	This day of shame, oppression, perjury.	
15	Or if it must stand still,° let wives with child	*remain*
	Pray that their burdens may not fall° this day,	*they not give birth*
	Lest that their hopes prodigiously⁴ be crossed;	
	But° on this day let seamen fear no wreck;	*Except*
	No bargains break that are not this day made;	
20	This day all things begun come to ill end,	
	Yea, faith itself to hollow falsehood change.	

KING PHILIP   By heaven, lady, you shall have no cause
To curse the fair proceedings of this day.
Have I not pawned° to you my majesty?°   *pledged / royal word*

CONSTANCE   You have beguiled me with a counterfeit°   *false coin or portrait*
Resembling majesty, which being touched and tried°   *tested for gold*
Proves valueless. You are forsworn, forsworn.
You came in arms to spill mine enemies' blood,
But now in arms° you strengthen it with yours.   *arm in arm; militarily*
The grappling vigour and rough frown of war
Is cold in amity and painted° peace,   *counterfeit*
And our oppression° hath made up° this league.   *affliction / possible*
Arm, arm, you heavens, against these perjured Kings!
A widow cries, be husband to me, God!
Let not the hours of this ungodly day
Wear out° the day in peace, but ere sun set   *Finish*
Set armèd discord 'twixt these perjured Kings.
Hear me, O hear me!

AUSTRIA   Lady Constance, peace.

CONSTANCE   War, war, no peace! Peace is to me a war.
O Limoges, O Austria,⁵ thou dost shame
That bloody spoil.° Thou slave, thou wretch, thou coward!   *(the lion skin)*
Thou little valiant, great in villainy;
Thou ever strong upon the stronger side;
Thou Fortune's champion, that dost never fight
But when her humorous ladyship° is by   *changeable Fortune*
To teach thee safety. Thou art perjured too,
And sooth'st up greatness.° What a fool art thou,   *flatter the powerful*
A ramping° fool, to brag and stamp, and swear   *showily threatening*
Upon my party!° Thou cold-blooded slave,   *cause*
Hast thou not spoke like thunder on my side,°   *behalf*
Been sworn my soldier, bidding me depend
Upon thy stars, thy fortune, and thy strength?
And dost thou now fall over° to my foes?   *defect*
Thou wear a lion's hide! Doff it, for shame,
And hang a calf's-skin⁶ on those recreant° limbs.   *cowardly; traitorous*

AUSTRIA   O, that a man should speak those words to me!

BASTARD   And hang a calf's-skin on those recreant limbs.

AUSTRIA   Thou dar'st not say so, villain, for thy life.

BASTARD   And hang a calf's-skin on those recreant limbs.

KING JOHN [*to the* BASTARD]   We like not this. Thou dost forget
thyself.°   *your rank; protocol*

---

4. By an ominously monstrous child.   6. Symbolizing cowardice or folly.
5. See note to 2.1.5.

Enter [Cardinal] PANDOLF

KING PHILIP   Here comes the holy legate of the Pope.[7]

PANDOLF   Hail, you anointed deputies of God.°—   *kings*
To thee, King John, my holy errand is.
I Pandolf, of fair Milan Cardinal,

65   And from Pope Innocent the legate here,
Do in his name religiously demand
Why thou against the Church, our Holy Mother,
So wilfully dost spurn,° and force perforce°   *kick / and forcibly*
Keep Stephen Langton, chosen° Archbishop   *(by the Pope)*

70   Of Canterbury, from that holy see.
This, in our foresaid Holy Father's name,
Pope Innocent, I do demand of thee.

KING JOHN   What earthy name to interrogatories
Can task the free breath of a sacred king?[8]

75   Thou canst not, Cardinal, devise a name
So slight, unworthy, and ridiculous
To charge me to an° answer, as the Pope.   *to make an*
Tell him this tale, and from the mouth of England
Add thus much more: that no Italian priest°   *the Pope*

80   Shall tithe or toll° in our dominions;   *collect church revenue*
But as we, under God, are supreme head,[9]
So, under him, that great supremacy°   *sovereignty*
Where we do reign we will alone uphold
Without th'assistance of a mortal hand.

85   So tell the Pope, all reverence set apart°   *rejected*
To him and his usurped authority.

KING PHILIP   Brother of England, you blaspheme in this.

KING JOHN   Though you and all the kings of Christendom
Are led so grossly by this meddling priest,

90   Dreading the curse that money may buy out,[1]
And by the merit of vile gold, dross, dust,
Purchase corrupted pardon of a man,[2]
Who in that sale sells pardon from himself;[3]
Though you and all the rest so grossly led

95   This juggling° witchcraft with revenue cherish;   *deceiving*
Yet I alone, alone do me oppose
Against the Pope, and count his friends my foes.

PANDOLF   Then by the lawful power that I have
Thou shalt stand cursed and excommunicate;°   *excommunicated*

100   And blessèd shall he be that doth revolt
From his allegiance to an heretic;
And meritorious shall that hand be called,
Canonizèd and worshipped as a saint,
That takes away by any secret course
Thy hateful life.

---

7. Shakespeare follows his main source in combining two papal legates in one, as he does in the use of Austria to represent two of Richard I's adversaries.
8. *What . . . king?*: What person holding an earthly title (the Pope or his deputy) can demand answers from a King who governs by divine right? John attributes to himself the divine authority he has just denied the Pope.
9. "Supreme head" of the English Church is the title adopted in 1534 by Henry VIII, Elizabeth's father, in defiance of the papacy. This passage is perhaps the most openly and anachronistically Protestant, anti-Catholic moment in the play.
1. Excommunication is the "curse" that a bribe can buy off, or reverse.
2. An allusion to the sale of indulgences, or papal dispensations for sin, by a member of the Catholic clergy ("a man").
3. The clergyman "sells" (gives up) hope of God's forgiveness for himself and is hence damned by his selling. The pardon he sells lacks efficacy because it comes "from himself," rather than from God.

105	CONSTANCE O lawful let it be	
	That I have room° with Rome to curse awhile.	*opportunity*
	Good Father Cardinal, cry thou 'Amen'	
	To my keen curses, for without my wrong°	*the wrongs done to me*
	There is no tongue hath power to curse him right.°	*properly*
110	PANDOLF There's law and warrant, lady, for my curse.	
	CONSTANCE And for mine too. When law can do no right,	
	Let it be lawful that law bar no wrong.°	*cursing*
	Law cannot give my child his kingdom here,	
	For he that holds his kingdom holds the law.	
115	Therefore, since law° itself is perfect wrong,	*(secular)*
	How can the law° forbid my tongue to curse?	*(ecclesiastical)*
	PANDOLF Philip of France, on peril of a curse,°	*excommunication*
	Let go the hand of that arch-heretic,	
	And raise the power of France upon his head,	
120	Unless he do submit himself to Rome.	
	QUEEN ELEANOR Look'st thou pale, France? Do not let go thy hand.	
	CONSTANCE [*to* KING JOHN] Look to it, devil, lest that France repent,	
	And by disjoining hands hell lose a soul.	
	AUSTRIA King Philip, listen to the Cardinal.	
125	BASTARD And hang a calf's-skin on his recreant limbs.	
	AUSTRIA Well, ruffian, I must pocket up° these wrongs,	*put up with*
	Because—	
	BASTARD Your breeches best may carry them.[4]	
	KING JOHN Philip, what sayst thou to the Cardinal?	
	CONSTANCE What should he say, but as° the Cardinal?	*the same as*
130	LOUIS THE DAUPHIN Bethink you, Father, for the difference	
	Is purchase of a heavy curse from Rome,	
	Or the light loss of England for a friend.	
	Forgo the easier.	
	BLANCHE That's the curse of Rome.	
	CONSTANCE O Louis, stand fast; the devil tempts thee here	
135	In likeness of a new untrimmèd° bride.	*virginal*
	BLANCHE The Lady Constance speaks not from her faith,	
	But from her need.	
	CONSTANCE [*to* KING PHILIP] O if thou grant my need,	
	Which only lives but by the death of faith,[5]	
	That need must needs infer this principle:[6]	
140	That faith would live again by death of need.°	*by the end of my woes*
	O, then tread down my need, and faith mounts up;	
	Keep my need up, and faith is trodden down.	
	KING JOHN The King is moved, and answers not to this.	
	CONSTANCE [*to* KING PHILIP] O, be removed from him, and answer well.	
145	AUSTRIA Do so, King Philip, hang no more in doubt.	
	BASTARD Hang nothing but a calf's-skin, most sweet lout.	
	KING PHILIP I am perplexed, and know not what to say.	
	PANDOLF What canst thou say but will perplex° thee more,	*trouble*
	If thou stand excommunicate and cursed?	
150	KING PHILIP Good Reverend Father, make my person yours,°	*put yourself in my place*
	And tell me how you would bestow yourself.°	*what you would do*
	This royal hand and mine are newly knit,°	*joined*

---

4. Probably, you may best carry them (the "wrongs" of line 126, or kicks) in the pocket of your breeches; possibly implying that Austria will be kicked in the breeches. 5. Which (my need) exists only because of your broken faith (the pledge to support Arthur) or my loss of faith in you; perhaps, which will live only if you break your faith (to the Church). 6. That need necessarily implies this truth.

And the conjunction of our inward souls
Married in league, coupled and linked together
155 With all religious strength of sacred vows;
The latest breath that gave the sound of words
Was deep-sworn faith, peace, amity, true love,
Between our kingdoms and our royal selves;
And even° before this truce, but new° before,   *just / only just*
160 No longer than we well could wash our hands°   *(of blood)*
To clap this royal bargain up of peace,[7]
God knows, they were besmeared and over-stained
With slaughter's pencil,° where Revenge did paint   *paintbrush*
The fearful difference° of incensèd kings;   *dispute*
165 And shall these hands, so lately purged of blood,
So newly joined in love, so strong in both,°   *(blood and love)*
Unyoke this seizure[8] and this kind regreet,°   *return of salutation*
Play fast and loose with faith, so jest with heaven,
Make such unconstant children of ourselves,
170 As now again to snatch our palm from palm,
Unswear faith sworn, and on the marriage-bed
Of smiling peace to march a bloody host,
And make a riot on the gentle brow
Of true sincerity? O holy sir,
175 My Reverend Father, let it not be so.
Out of your grace, devise, ordain, impose
Some gentle order, and then we shall be blessed
To do your pleasure and continue friends.
PANDOLF All form is formless, order orderless,
180 Save what is opposite to England's love.
Therefore to arms, be champion of our Church,
Or let the Church, our mother, breathe her curse,
A mother's curse, on her revolting son.
France, thou mayst hold° a serpent by the tongue,   *may more easily hold*
185 A crazèd lion by the mortal° paw,   *deadly*
A fasting tiger safer by the tooth,
Than keep in peace that hand which thou dost hold.
KING PHILIP I may disjoin my hand, but not my faith.
PANDOLF So mak'st thou faith an enemy to faith,[9]
190 And like a civil war, sett'st oath to oath,
Thy tongue against thy tongue. O, let thy vow,
First made to heaven, first be to heaven performed;
That is, to be the champion of our Church.
What since thou swor'st[1] is sworn against thyself,
195 And may not be performèd by thyself;
For that which thou hast sworn to do amiss
Is not amiss when it is truly done;[2]
And being not done where doing tends to ill,
The truth is then most done not doing it.
200 The better act of purposes mistook[3]
Is to mistake again; though indirect,°   *circuitous; wrong*
Yet indirection thereby grows direct,

7. To seal this royal peace treaty by shaking hands.
8. Of hands joined together.
9. You set your faith to John against your faith to the Church. The confusing rhetoric of this speech exemplifies the elaborate and sometimes equivocal reasoning known as casuistry that was practiced by sixteenth- century Catholics and hated by English Protestants.
1. What you've subsequently sworn (amity with John).
2. *For . . . done:* For it's not immoral to break an immoral vow. *truly done:* not done at all because it is immoral.
3. The better act when you've done wrong.

And falsehood falsehood cures, as fire cools fire
Within the scorchèd veins of one new burned.[4]
205 It is religion that doth make vows kept;°   *make us honor our vows*
But thou hast sworn against religion;
By what thou swear'st, against the thing thou swear'st;[5]
And mak'st an oath the surety for thy troth:[6]
Against an oath, the truth. Thou art unsure
210 To swear: swear'st only not to be forsworn—[7]
Else what a mockery should it be to swear!—
But thou dost swear only to be forsworn,
And most forsworn to keep what thou dost swear;[8]
Therefore thy later vows against thy first
215 Is in thyself rebellion to° thyself,   *against*
And better conquest never canst thou make
Than arm thy constant and thy nobler parts
Against these giddy loose suggestions;°   *dissolute temptations*
Upon° which better part° our prayers come in   *On behalf of / side*
220 If thou vouchsafe° them. But if not, then know   *accept*
The peril of our curses light on thee
So heavy as thou shalt not shake them off,
But in despair° die under their black weight.   *(because damned)*
AUSTRIA   Rebellion, flat rebellion!
BASTARD   Wilt not be?[9]
225 Will not a calf's-skin stop that mouth of thine?
LOUIS THE DAUPHIN   Father, to arms!
BLANCHE   Upon thy wedding day?
Against the blood that thou hast married?
What, shall our feast be kept with° slaughtered men?   *attended by*
Shall braying trumpets and loud churlish drums,
230 Clamours of hell, be measures° to our pomp?°   *music / celebration*
[*She kneels*]
O husband, hear me! Ay, alack, how new
Is 'husband' in my mouth! Even for that name
Which till this time my tongue did ne'er pronounce,
Upon my knee I beg, go not to arms
Against mine uncle.
235 CONSTANCE [*kneeling*]   O, upon my knee
Made hard with kneeling, I do pray to thee,
Thou virtuous Dauphin, alter not the doom°   *fate*
Forethought by heaven.[1]
BLANCHE [*to* LOUIS THE DAUPHIN]   Now shall I see thy love:
what motive may
240 Be stronger with thee than the name of wife?
CONSTANCE   That which upholdeth him that thee upholds:°   *who supports you*
His honour.—O thine honour, Louis, thine honour!
LOUIS THE DAUPHIN [*to* KING PHILIP]   I muse your majesty doth
seem so cold

4. *as fire . . . burned:* the theory that one fire cools
another was proverbial but false.
5. By your oath to John, you break your oath to your
religion, the basis for all other vows.
6. You make an oath the guarantee of your "troth"
(agreement with John); but with a pun on its opposite—
the "truth" (or religious faith) of the next line.
7. *Thou art . . . forsworn:* You waver over swearing, and
do so only not to break faith (with John).
8. *But thou . . . dost swear:* But your (secular) oath-

taking leads only to (religious) oath-breaking, especially in maintaining your oath to John.
9. Is it all in vain; won't you be quiet?
1. Constance self-interestedly treats as a single issue
John's two separate matters—Arthur's right to the
throne and Pandolf's insistence on papal right. The
belief that people are preordained for either salvation or
damnation ("doom / Forethought by heaven") is more
Protestant than Catholic.

When such profound respects° do pull you on.   *weighty considerations*

245 PANDOLF   I will denounce a curse upon his head.

KING PHILIP   Thou shalt not need.—England, I will fall from° thee.   *desert*

    [*He takes his hand from King John's hand.* BLANCHE

        and CONSTANCE *rise*]

CONSTANCE   O, fair return of banished majesty!

QUEEN ELEANOR   O, foul revolt of French inconstancy!

KING JOHN   France, thou shalt rue this hour within this hour.

250 BASTARD   Old Time the clock-setter, that bald sexton Time,

    Is it as he will?—Well then, France shall rue.²

BLANCHE   The sun's o'ercast with blood; fair day, adieu!

    Which is the side that I must go withal?°   *with*

    I am with both, each army hath a hand,

255   And in their rage, I having hold of both,

    They whirl asunder° and dismember me.   *dash apart*

    Husband, I cannot pray that thou mayst win.—

    Uncle, I needs must pray that thou mayst lose.—

    Father,° I may not wish the fortune thine.—   *Father-in-law (Philip)*

260   Grandam, I will not wish thy wishes thrive.

    Whoever wins, on that side shall I lose,

    Assurèd loss before the match be played.

LOUIS THE DAUPHIN   Lady, with me, with me thy fortune° lies.   *prosperity*

BLANCHE   There where my fortune° lives, there° my life dies.   *fate / (with Louis)*

KING JOHN [*to the* BASTARD]   Cousin, go draw our puissance°   *army*

265   together.—   *Exit the* BASTARD]

    France, I am burned up with inflaming wrath,

    A rage whose heat hath this condition:

    That nothing can allay,° nothing but blood,   *cure*

    The blood, and dearest-valued blood, of France.

270 KING PHILIP   Thy rage shall burn thee up, and thou shalt turn

    To ashes ere our blood shall quench that fire.

    Look to thyself, thou art in jeopardy.

KING JOHN   No more than he that threats.—To arms let's hie!°   *hasten*

                Exeunt [*severally*]

3.2

    Alarum;° excursions.° Enter [*the*] BASTARD, *with* [*the*   *Call to arms / battles*

    Duke of] *Austria's head*

BASTARD   Now, by my life, this day grows wondrous hot;

    Some airy devil¹ hovers in the sky

    And pours down mischief. Austria's head lie there,

    While Philip breathes.

        Enter [KING] JOHN, ARTHUR [*Duke of Brittaine, and*]

        HUBERT

5 KING JOHN   Hubert, keep this boy.—Philip,° make up!°   *(the Bastard) / press on*

    My mother is assailèd in our tent,

    And ta'en° I fear.   *captured*

BASTARD   My lord, I rescued her;

---

2. *Old . . . rue:* The sexton set the church clock and dug graves. Hence, the "hour" (line 249), or time, which was usually portrayed as bald, will indeed be fatal. "Time" and "rue" recall the punning proverb about herbs, "Thyme and rue grow both in one garden," in which the pleasant taste of thyme is contrasted with the bitterness of rue: the passage of time is accompa-nied by regret. Together the two lines mean something like "If things proceed according to the fatal effects of time, France will indeed be sorry, because time (thyme) and rue go together."

3.2 Location: Plains near Angers.

1. Aerial devils or spirits held to cause thunderstorms and subsequent death.

Her highness is in safety; fear you not.
But on, my liege, for very little pains

10   Will bring this labour to an happy end.

        Exeunt [KING JOHN *and the* BASTARD *at one door*,
               HUBERT *and* ARTHUR *at another door*]

3.3

      Alarum; excursions; retreat.° Enter [KING] JOHN,   *signal for retreat*
      [QUEEN] ELEANOR, ARTHUR [*Duke of Brittaine, the*] BAS-
      TARD, HUBERT, *lords* [*with soldiers*][1]

KING JOHN [*to* QUEEN ELEANOR]   So shall it be; your grace shall
    stay behind[2]

    So° strongly guarded. [*To* ARTHUR] Cousin,° look not sad;   *Thus / Kinsman*
    Thy grandam loves thee, and thy uncle will
    As dear be to thee as thy father was.

5 ARTHUR   O, this will make my mother die with grief.

KING JOHN [*to the* BASTARD]   Cousin, away for England! Haste before,°   *Go ahead*
    And ere our coming, see thou shake the bags
    Of hoarding abbots.[3] The fat ribs of peace
    Must by the hungry now be fed upon.

10   Imprisoned angels° set at liberty.[4]   *gold coins; spirits*
    Use our commission° in his° utmost force.   *(to tax) / its*

BASTARD   Bell, book, and candle[5] shall not drive me back
    When gold and silver becks° me to come on.   *beckons*
    I leave your highness.—Grandam, I will pray,

15   If ever I remember to be holy,
    For your fair safety. So I kiss your hand.

QUEEN ELEANOR   Farewell, gentle cousin.

KING JOHN   Coz, farewell.

                [*Exit the* BASTARD]

QUEEN ELEANOR   Come hither, little kinsman. Hark, a word.
    [*She takes* ARTHUR *aside*]

KING JOHN   Come hither, Hubert.
    [*He takes* HUBERT *aside*]

              O my gentle Hubert,

20   We owe thee much. Within this wall of flesh°   *(John's body)*
    There is a soul counts thee her creditor,
    And with advantage° means to pay thy love;   *interest*
    And, my good friend, thy voluntary oath°   *oath of allegiance*
    Lives in this bosom, dearly cherishèd.
    Give me thy hand.
    [*He takes Hubert's hand*]

25   I had a thing to say,
    But I will fit it with some better tune.°   *words; reward*
    By heaven, Hubert, I am almost ashamed
    To say what good respect° I have of thee.   *opinion*

HUBERT   I am much bounden° to your majesty.   *indebted*

3.3 Location: Scene continues.
1. F does not begin a new scene here, but it does empty
the stage—hence the scene division adopted here and
in most modern editions.
2. In France, to control the French possessions while
John returns to England.
3. *shake . . . abbots:* pillage the monasteries, which

have hoarded wealth. When Henry VIII made himself
head of the English Church, he confiscated monastic
treasure.
4. F places this line right after "abbots" (line 8), perhaps because a marginal addition in the foul papers was
misplaced in the scribal transcript.
5. Articles used in the rite of excommunication.

30 KING JOHN   Good friend, thou hast no cause to say so yet,
        But thou shalt have; and creep time ne'er so slow,
        Yet it shall come for me to do thee good.
        I had a thing to say—but let it go.
        The sun is in the heaven, and the proud day,
35   Attended with the pleasures of the world,
        Is all too wanton° and too full of gauds°   merry / playthings
        To give me audience.° If the midnight bell   For you to listen
        Did with his iron tongue and brazen mouth
        Sound on into the drowsy race° of night;   course
40   If this same were a churchyard° where we stand,   graveyard
        And thou possessèd° with a thousand wrongs;   obsessed
        Or if that surly spirit, melancholy,
        Had baked° thy blood and made it heavy, thick,   congealed
        Which else° runs tickling up and down the veins,   otherwise
45   Making that idiot,° laughter, keep° men's eyes   jester / stay in
        And strain their cheeks to idle merriment—
        A passion° hateful to my purposes—   mood
        Or if that thou couldst see me without eyes,
        Hear me without thine ears, and make reply
50   Without a tongue, using conceit° alone,   understanding
        Without eyes, ears, and harmful sound of words;
        Then in despite° of broad-eyed watchful day   defiance
        I would into thy bosom pour my thoughts.
        But, ah, I will not. Yet I love thee well,
55   And by my troth,° I think thou lov'st me well.   faith
    HUBERT   So well that what you bid me undertake,
        Though that° my death were adjunct to my act,   Even if
        By heaven, I would do it.
    KING JOHN   Do not I know thou wouldst?
        Good Hubert, Hubert, Hubert, throw thine eye
60   On yon young boy. I'll tell thee what, my friend,
        He is a very serpent in my way,
        And wheresoe'er this foot of mine doth tread,
        He lies before me. Dost thou understand me?
        Thou art his keeper.
    HUBERT   And I'll keep him so
65   That he shall not offend your majesty.
    KING JOHN   Death.
    HUBERT   My lord.
    KING JOHN   A grave.
    HUBERT   He shall not live.
    KING JOHN   Enough.
        I could be merry now. Hubert, I love thee.
        Well, I'll not say what I intend for thee.
        Remember. [To QUEEN ELEANOR] Madam, fare you well.
70   I'll send those powers° o'er to your majesty.   troops
    QUEEN ELEANOR   My blessing go with thee.
    KING JOHN [to ARTHUR]   For England, cousin, go.
        Hubert shall be your man, attend on you
        With all true duty.—On toward Calais, ho!
                    Exeunt [QUEEN ELEANOR, attended, at one door,
                              the rest at another door]

3.4

*Enter [*KING PHILIP *of*] France, [LOUIS THE] DAUPHIN,
[*Cardinal*] PANDOLF, [*and*] attendants*

KING PHILIP   So, by a roaring tempest on the flood,
A whole armada of convicted sail
Is scattered and disjoined from fellowship.[1]

PANDOLF   Courage and comfort; all shall yet go well.

5   KING PHILIP   What can go well when we have run° so ill?   *performed; run away*
Are we not beaten? Is not Angers lost,
Arthur ta'en prisoner, divers° dear friends slain,   *various*
And bloody England° into England gone,   *John*
O'erbearing interruption, spite[2] of France?

10   LOUIS THE DAUPHIN   What he hath won, that hath he fortified.
So hot a speed, with such advice disposed,°   *judgment regulated*
Such temperate° order in so fierce a cause,   *calm*
Doth want example.° Who hath read or heard   *lack precedent*
Of any kindred action like to this?

15   KING PHILIP   Well could I bear that England had this praise,
So° we could find some pattern° of our shame.   *If / precedent*

Enter CONSTANCE [*distracted,° with her hair about her*   *wild; mad*
ears]

Look who comes here! A grave° unto a soul,   *(Constance's body)*
Holding th'eternal spirit against her will[3]
In the vile prison of afflicted breath.°—   *life*

20   I prithee, lady, go away with me.

CONSTANCE   Lo, now, now see the issue° of your peace!   *outcome*

KING PHILIP   Patience, good lady; comfort, gentle Constance.

CONSTANCE   No, I defy all counsel, all redress,°   *comfort*
But that which ends all counsel, true redress:

25   Death, Death, O amiable, lovely Death!
Thou odoriferous° stench, sound rottenness!   *fragrant*
Arise forth from the couch of lasting° night,   *bed of everlasting*
Thou hate and terror to prosperity,
And I will kiss thy detestable bones,

30   And put my eyeballs in thy vaulty brows,[4]
And ring these fingers with thy household worms,[5]
And stop this gap of breath with fulsome dust,[6]
And be a carrion° monster like thyself.   *corpse-eating*
Come grin on me, and I will think thou smil'st,

35   And buss° thee as thy wife. Misery's love,   *kiss*
O, come to me!

KING PHILIP   O fair affliction,° peace!   *afflicted one*

CONSTANCE   No, no, I will not, having breath to cry.
O, that my tongue were in the thunder's mouth!
Then with a passion° would I shake the world,   *an emotional outcry*

40   And rouse from sleep that fell anatomy,°   *fierce skeleton*
Which cannot hear a lady's feeble voice,
Which scorns a modern invocation.°   *an ordinary plea*

PANDOLF   Lady, you utter madness, and not sorrow.

3.4 Location: The French camp by Angers.
1. *So . . . fellowship:* This French naval defeat is not in
Shakespeare's sources. It is probably a reference to the
Spanish Armada of 1588 (see the Introduction). *convicted sail:* doomed ships.
2. Overcoming hindrances, in spite.

3. *Holding . . . will:* that is, she wants to die.
4. Hollow forehead; the eye sockets of the imagined
skull of death's corpse.
5. And wear the worms that serve you and live inside
you as rings around my fingers.
6. And kiss this mouth with nauseous dust.

CONSTANCE   Thou art not holy to belie me so.
45   I am not mad: this hair I tear is mine;
     My name is Constance; I was Geoffrey's wife;
     Young Arthur is my son; and he is lost.
     I am not mad; I would to God I were,
     For then 'tis like° I should forget myself.   likely
50   O, if I could, what grief should I forget!
     Preach some philosophy to make me mad,
     And thou shalt be canonized, Cardinal.
     For, being not mad, but sensible° of grief,   subject to feelings
     My reasonable part produces reason
55   How I may be delivered of° these woes,   freed from
     And teaches me to kill or hang myself.
     If I were mad I should forget my son,
     Or madly think a babe of clouts° were he.   cloth doll
     I am not mad; too well, too well I feel
60   The different plague° of each calamity.   distinct affliction
KING PHILIP   Bind up those tresses. O, what love I note
     In the fair multitude of those her hairs!
     Where but by chance a silver drop° hath fallen,   tear
     Even to that drop ten thousand wiry friends°   hairs
65   Do glue themselves° in sociable grief,   mat together
     Like true, inseparable, faithful loves,
     Sticking together in calamity.
CONSTANCE   To England, if you will.[7]
KING PHILIP   Bind up your hairs.
CONSTANCE   Yes, that I will. And wherefore will I do it?
70   I tore them from their bonds, and cried aloud,
     'O that these hands could so redeem my son,
     As they have given these hairs their liberty!'
     But now I envy at their liberty,
     And will again commit them to their bonds,
75   Because my poor child is a prisoner.
         [She binds up her hair]
     And Father Cardinal, I have heard you say
     That we shall see and know our friends in heaven.
     If that be true, I shall see my boy again;
     For since the birth of Cain, the first male child,
80   To him that did but yesterday suspire,°   take his first breath
     There was not such a gracious creature born.
     But now will canker-sorrow eat my bud,[8]
     And chase the native beauty from his cheek;
     And he will look as hollow as a ghost,
85   As dim and meagre° as an ague's° fit,   pale and thin / fever's
     And so he'll die; and rising so again,
     When I shall meet him in the court of heaven,
     I shall not know him; therefore never, never
     Must I behold my pretty Arthur more.
90   PANDOLF   You hold too heinous a respect° of grief.   view
CONSTANCE   He talks to me that never had a son.
KING PHILIP   You are as fond of grief as of your child.

---

7. Apparently a reply to line 20, delayed because of Constance's distraction. Possibly the intervening passage is a
revision interpolated after the original composition.

8. But now sorrow, like a cankerworm, will eat my
flower (Arthur); this is proverbial.

CONSTANCE   Grief fills the room up of my absent child,
Lies in his bed, walks up and down with me,
95   Puts on his pretty looks, repeats his words,
Remembers° me of all his gracious parts,   *Reminds*
Stuffs out his vacant garments with his form;
Then have I reason to be fond of grief.
Fare you well. Had you such a loss as I,
100   I could give better comfort than you do.
        [*She unbinds her hair*]
I will not keep this form upon my head
When there is such disorder in my wit.
O Lord, my boy, my Arthur, my fair son,
My life, my joy, my food, my all the world,
105   My widow-comfort, and my sorrow's cure!   *Exit*
KING PHILIP   I fear some outrage,° and I'll follow her.   *(perhaps suicide)*
                                    Exit [*attended*]
LOUIS THE DAUPHIN   There's nothing in this world can make me joy.
Life is as tedious as a twice-told tale,
Vexing the dull ear of a drowsy man;
110   And bitter shame hath spoiled the sweet world's taste,
That° it yields naught but shame and bitterness.   *So that*
PANDOLF   Before the curing of a strong disease,
Even in the instant of repair and health,
The fit° is strongest. Evils that take leave,   *symptom*
115   On their departure most of all show evil.
What have you lost by losing of this day?
LOUIS THE DAUPHIN   All days of glory, joy, and happiness.
PANDOLF   If you had won it, certainly you had.
No, no; when Fortune means° to men most good,   *intends*
120   She looks upon them with a threat'ning eye.
'Tis strange to think how much King John hath lost
In this which he accounts so clearly won.
Are not you grieved that Arthur is his prisoner?
LOUIS THE DAUPHIN   As heartily as he is glad he hath him.
125   PANDOLF   Your mind is all as youthful as your blood.
Now hear me speak with a prophetic spirit,
For even the breath of what I mean to speak
Shall blow each dust,° each straw, each little rub,°   *speck / obstacle*
Out of the path which shall directly lead
130   Thy foot to England's throne. And therefore mark.
John hath seized Arthur, and it cannot be
That whiles warm life plays in that infant's veins
The misplaced° John should entertain an hour,   *usurping*
One minute, nay, one quiet breath of rest.
135   A sceptre snatched with an unruly hand
Must be as boisterously° maintained as gained;   *violently*
And he that stands upon a slipp'ry place
Makes nice of no vile hold to stay⁹ him up.
That John may stand, then Arthur needs must fall;
140   So be it, for it cannot be but so.
LOUIS THE DAUPHIN   But what shall I gain by young Arthur's fall?
PANDOLF   You, in the right of Lady Blanche your wife,
May then make all the claim that Arthur did.¹

9. Is not fussy about the vileness of any hold to keep.   1. In Shakespeare's sources but not historical.

LOUIS THE DAUPHIN   And lose it, life and all, as Arthur did.

145 PANDOLF   How green you are, and fresh in this old world!
John lays you plots;° the times conspire with you;   *plots to your benefit*
For he that steeps his safety in true° blood   *legitimate*
Shall find but bloody safety and untrue.[2]
This act, so vilely born, shall cool the hearts
150 Of all his people, and freeze up their zeal,°   *enthusiastic loyalty*
That none so small advantage shall step forth
To check his reign but they will cherish it;[3]
No natural exhalation° in the sky,   *meteor*
No scope° of nature, no distempered° day,   *effect / stormy*
155 No common wind, no customèd° event,   *everyday*
But they will pluck away his° natural cause,   *its*
And call them meteors,° prodigies, and signs,   *portents*
Abortives,[4] presages, and tongues of° heaven   *signs from*
Plainly denouncing vengeance upon John.
160 LOUIS THE DAUPHIN   Maybe he will not touch young Arthur's life,
But hold° himself safe in his prisonment.   *consider*
PANDOLF   O sir, when he shall hear of your approach,
If that young Arthur be not gone already,
Even at that news he dies; and then the hearts
165 Of all his people shall revolt from him,
And kiss the lips of unacquainted° change,   *unfamiliar*
And pick strong matter of° revolt and wrath   *reasons for*
Out of the bloody fingers' ends of John.
Methinks I see this hurly all on foot,°   *commotion all under way*
170 And O, what better matter breeds for you
Than I have named! The Bastard Falconbridge
Is now in England, ransacking the Church,
Offending charity. If but a dozen French
Were there in arms, they would be as a call°   *decoy; call to arms*
175 To train° ten thousand English to their side,   *draw*
Or as a little snow tumbled about
Anon becomes a mountain. O noble Dauphin,
Go with me to the King. 'Tis wonderful
What may be wrought out of their discontent
180 Now that their souls are top-full of offence.°   *grievances*
For England, go! I will whet on° the King.   *provoke*
LOUIS THE DAUPHIN   Strong reasons make strange actions. Let us go.
If you say ay, the King will not say no.   *Exeunt*

4.1

Enter HUBERT, *and* EXECUTIONERS [*with a rope and irons*]
HUBERT   Heat me these irons hot, and look thou stand
Within the arras.[1] When I strike my foot
Upon the bosom of the ground, rush forth
And bind the boy which you shall find with me
5   Fast to the chair. Be heedful. Hence, and watch!
EXECUTIONER   I hope your warrant will bear out° the deed.   *authorize*
HUBERT   Uncleanly° scruples: fear not you. Look to't!°   *Improper / Do it*
[*The* EXECUTIONERS *withdraw behind the arras*]

---

2. Compare Genesis 9:6: "Whoso sheddeth man's
blood, by man shall his blood be shed." *untrue*: untrust-
worthy.
3. *none . . . it*: they will seize the smallest opportunity

to dethrone him.
4. Untimely or monstrous births (seen as portents).
4.1 Location: A castle prison in England.
1. Behind the tapestry hangings.

Young lad, come forth, I have to say° with you.   *something to discuss*
    Enter ARTHUR [*Duke of Brittaine*]

ARTHUR   Good morrow, Hubert.

HUBERT   Good morrow, little Prince.

10   ARTHUR   As little prince, having so great a title
To be more prince, as may be.² You are sad.

HUBERT   Indeed I have been merrier.

ARTHUR   Mercy on me!
Methinks nobody should be sad but I.
Yet I remember, when I was in France,

15   Young gentlemen would be as sad as night
Only for wantonness.° By my christendom,°   *affectation / faith*
So° I were out of prison and kept sheep,   *If*
I should be as merry as the day is long;
And so I would be here, but that I doubt°   *fear*

20   My uncle practises° more harm to me.   *plots*
He is afraid of me, and I of him.
Is it my fault that I was Geoffrey's son?
No, indeed is't not, and I would to God
I were your son, so you would love me, Hubert.

25   HUBERT [*aside*]   If I talk to him, with his innocent prate°   *prattle*
He will awake my mercy, which lies dead;
Therefore I will be sudden, and dispatch.

ARTHUR   Are you sick, Hubert? You look pale today.
In sooth, I would° you were a little sick,   *Truly, I wish*

30   That I might sit all night and watch with you.
I warrant I love you more than you do me.

HUBERT [*aside*]   His words do take possession of my bosom.
    [*He shows* ARTHUR *a paper*]
Read here, young Arthur. [*aside*] How now: foolish rheum,°   *tears*
Turning dispiteous° torture out of door?   *pitiless*

35   I must be brief, lest resolution drop
Out at mine eyes in tender womanish tears.
[*To* ARTHUR] Can you not read it? Is it not fair writ?°   *legible; legal*

ARTHUR   Too fairly, Hubert, for so foul effect.
Must you with hot irons burn out both mine eyes?³

HUBERT   Young boy, I must.

ARTHUR   And will you?

40   HUBERT   And I will.

ARTHUR   Have you the heart? When your head did but ache
I knit my handkerchief about your brows,
The best I had—a princess wrought it° me,   *made it for*
And I did never ask it you° again—   *back from you*

45   And with my hand at midnight held your head,
And like the watchful minutes to the hour
Still and anon° cheered up the heavy time,⁴   *Continually*
Saying 'What lack you?' and 'Where lies your grief?'°   *pain*
Or 'What good love° may I perform for you?'   *loving deed*

50   Many a poor man's son would have lain still
And ne'er have spoke a loving word to you,

---

2. *As . . . be:* Although I have title to be a great prince (king), I am as little a prince as is possible.
3. The order to blind Arthur here is at odds with the death sentence of 3.3.66, as well as with Hubert's deci-

sion later in this scene (line 127) falsely to report Arthur's death, a decision he makes good on in 4.2.
4. The minutes are seen as breaking up the time to make it pass easily.

But you at your sick service had a prince.
Nay, you may think my love was crafty love,
And call it cunning. Do, an if you will.
55 If heaven be pleased that you must use me ill,
Why then you must. Will you put out mine eyes,
These eyes that never did, nor never shall,
So much as frown on you?

HUBERT   I have sworn to do it,
And with hot irons must I burn them out.

60 ARTHUR   Ah, none but in this iron age⁵ would do it.
The iron of itself, though heat° red hot,   *heated*
Approaching near these eyes would drink my tears,
And quench his° fiery indignation   *its*
Even in the matter° of mine innocence;   *substance; tears*
65 Nay, after that, consume° away in rust,   *dissolve*
But° for containing fire to harm mine eye.   *Merely*
Are you more stubborn-hard than hammered iron?
An if an angel should have come to me
And told me Hubert should put out mine eyes,
70 I would not have believed him; no tongue but Hubert's.
             [HUBERT *stamps his foot*]

HUBERT   Come forth!
             [*The* EXECUTIONERS *come forth*]
                   Do as I bid you do.

ARTHUR   O, save me, Hubert, save me! My eyes are out
Even with the fierce looks of these bloody men.

HUBERT [*to the* EXECUTIONERS]   Give me the iron, I say, and bind him here.
             [*He takes the iron*]

75 ARTHUR   Alas, what need you be so boisterous-rough?
I will not struggle; I will stand stone-still.
For God's sake, Hubert, let me not be bound.
Nay, hear me, Hubert! Drive these men away,
And I will sit as quiet as a lamb;
80 I will not stir, nor wince, nor speak a word,
Nor look upon the iron angerly.°   *angrily*
Thrust but these men away, and I'll forgive you,
Whatever torment you do put me to.

HUBERT [*to the* EXECUTIONERS]   Go stand within. Let me alone with him.

85 EXECUTIONER   I am best pleased to be from° such a deed.   *away from*
                   [*Exeunt* EXECUTIONERS]

ARTHUR   Alas, I then have chid° away my friend!   *scolded*
He hath a stern look, but a gentle heart.
Let him come back, that his compassion may
Give life to yours.

HUBERT   Come, boy, prepare yourself.

ARTHUR   Is there no remedy?

90 HUBERT   None but to lose your eyes.

ARTHUR   O God, that there were but a mote° in yours,   *speck of dust*
A grain, a dust, a gnat, a wandering hair,
Any annoyance in that precious sense,°   *sight*
Then, feeling what small things are boisterous° there,   *painful*
95 Your vile intent must needs seem horrible.

HUBERT   Is this your promise? Go to,° hold your tongue!   *Stop it (rebuke)*

---

5. Cruel, degenerate world, in contrast to the legendary "golden" and "silver" ages; with a play on the hot irons.

ARTHUR   Hubert, the utterance of a brace of tongues
     Must needs want pleading for a pair of eyes.⁶
     Let° me not hold my tongue, let me not, Hubert;   *Make*
100   Or, Hubert, if you will, cut out my tongue,
     So° I may keep mine eyes. O, spare mine eyes,   *If*
     Though to no use but still to look on you.
     Lo, by my troth,° the instrument is cold   *faith*
     And would not harm me.
HUBERT   I can heat it, boy.
105 ARTHUR   No, in good sooth:° the fire is dead with grief,   *truly*
     Being create° for comfort, to be° used   *created / at being*
     In undeserved extremes.° See else° yourself.   *extreme suffering / for*
     There is no malice in this burning coal;
     The breath of heaven hath blown his spirit° out,   *(dead person's) soul*
110   And strewed repentant ashes° on his head.   *(of a penitent sinner)*
HUBERT   But with my breath I can revive it, boy.
ARTHUR   An if you do, you will but make it blush
     And glow with shame of your proceedings, Hubert.
     Nay, it perchance will sparkle° in your eyes,   *cast sparks*
115   And like a dog that is compelled to fight,
     Snatch at his master that doth tarre° him on.   *set*
     All things that you should° use to do me wrong   *would*
     Deny their office;° only you do lack   *Disobey*
     That mercy which fierce fire and iron extends,
120   Creatures of note° for mercy-lacking uses.   *Things noteworthy*
HUBERT   Well, see to live.⁷ I will not touch thine eye
     For all the treasure that thine uncle owes.°   *owns*
     Yet am I sworn, and I did purpose, boy,
     With this same very iron to burn them out.
125 ARTHUR   O, now you look like Hubert. All this while
     You were disguisèd.
HUBERT   Peace, no more. Adieu.
     Your uncle must not know but° you are dead.   *otherwise than that*
     I'll fill these doggèd° spies with false reports;   *unfeeling*
     And, pretty child, sleep doubtless° and secure   *without fear*
130   That Hubert, for the wealth of all the world,
     Will not offend° thee.   *harm*
ARTHUR   O God! I thank you, Hubert.
HUBERT   Silence, no more. Go closely° in with me.   *secretly*
     Much danger do I undergo for thee.   *Exeunt*

4.2

*[Flourish.] Enter [KING] JOHN, [the Earls of] PEMBROKE
and SALISBURY, and other lords. [KING JOHN ascends the
throne]*

KING JOHN   Here once again we sit, once again crowned,¹
     And looked upon, I hope, with cheerful eyes.
PEMBROKE   This 'once again', but that your highness pleased,
     Was once superfluous.² You were crowned before,

---

6. *the utterance . . . eyes:* not even a pair of tongues
would be enough to plead for a pair of eyes.
7. Live, and retain your sight.
4.2 Location: John's court in England.
1. John has had a second coronation. Its purpose,

according to Shakespeare's main source, was to get the
English lords again to swear allegiance to him.
2. *but . . . superfluous:* but for the fact that you wanted
this second coronation, it would have been one too
many.

5   And that high royalty was ne'er plucked off,
     The faiths of men ne'er stainèd with revolt;
     Fresh expectation° troubled not the land   Hope of a new king
     With any longed-for change or better state.³
     SALISBURY   Therefore to be possessed with double pomp,
10   To guard° a title that was rich before,   adorn
     To gild refinèd gold, to paint the lily,
     To throw a perfume on the violet,
     To smooth the ice, or add another hue
     Unto the rainbow, or with taper-light°   candlelight
15   To seek the beauteous eye of heaven to garnish,°   the sun to adorn
     Is wasteful and ridiculous excess.
     PEMBROKE   But that your royal pleasure must be done,
     This act is as an ancient tale new-told,
     And in the last repeating troublesome,
20   Being urgèd at a time unseasonable.°   inappropriate
     SALISBURY   In this the antique and well-noted° face   familiar
     Of plain old form° is much disfigurèd,   custom
     And like a shifted wind unto a sail,
     It makes the course of thoughts to fetch about,°   change directions
25   Startles and frights consideration,⁴
     Makes sound opinion sick, and truth suspected
     For putting on so new a fashioned robe.⁵
     PEMBROKE   When workmen strive to do better than well,
     They do confound° their skill in covetousness;⁶   destroy
30   And oftentimes excusing of a fault
     Doth make the fault the worser by th'excuse;
     As patches set upon a little breach°   tear
     Discredit more in hiding of the fault
     Than did the fault before it was so patched.
35   SALISBURY   To this effect: before you were new-crowned
     We breathed our counsel,° but it pleased your highness   spoke our advice
     To overbear° it; and we are all well pleased,   overrule
     Since all and every part of what we would°   wish
     Doth make a stand° at what your highness will.°   stop; resist / desires
40   KING JOHN   Some reasons of this double coronation
     I have possessed you with,° and think them strong.   instructed you in
     And more, more strong, when lesser is my fear
     I shall endue° you with. Meantime but ask   supply
     What you would have reformed that is not well,
45   And well shall you perceive how willingly
     I will both hear and grant you your requests.⁷
     PEMBROKE   Then I, as one that am the tongue° of these   spokesman
     To sound° the purposes of all their hearts,   express
     Both for myself and them, but chief of all
50   Your safety, for the which myself and them
     Bend° their best studies,° heartily request   Direct / efforts
     Th'enfranchisement° of Arthur, whose restraint   release

---

3. Better government; better living conditions.
4. Encourages questions about John's claim to the throne.
5. For behaving so uncustomarily; for donning a coronation robe.

6. By greedily trying to do even better.
7. Lines 43–46 may allude to the historical King John's submission to the baronial demands spelled out in the Magna Carta. See also line 168 and 5.2.20–23.

	Doth move the murmuring lips of discontent	
	To break into this dangerous argument:	
55	If what in rest° you have, in right you hold,	*in peace*
	Why then your fears—which, as they say, attend	
	The steps of wrong—should move you to mew up°	*confine*
	Your tender kinsman, and to choke his days	
	With barbarous ignorance, and deny his youth	
60	The rich advantage of good exercise?°	*education*
	That the time's enemies may not have this	
	To grace occasions,° let it be our suit	*To justify opposition*
	That you have bid us ask, his liberty;	
	Which for our goods we do no further ask	
65	Than whereupon our weal, on you depending,	
	Counts it your weal he have his liberty.⁸	

Enter HUBERT

KING JOHN Let it be so. I do commit his youth
To your direction.—Hubert, what news with you?
[*He takes* HUBERT *aside*]

PEMBROKE   This is the man should do the bloody deed:

70	He showed his warrant to a friend of mine.	
	The image of a wicked heinous fault°	*crime*
	Lives in his eye; that close aspect° of his	*furtive appearance*
	Does show the mood of a much troubled breast;	
	And I do fearfully believe 'tis done	
75	What we so feared he had a charge to do.	

SALISBURY   The colour of the King doth come and go

	Between his purpose and his conscience,	
	Like heralds 'twixt two dreadful battles set.°	*armies set for battle*
	His passion is so ripe it needs must break.°	*burst (like a boil)*
80	PEMBROKE And when it breaks, I fear will issue thence	
	The foul corruption° of a sweet child's death.	*pus*

KING JOHN [*coming forward*]   We cannot hold° mortality's strong hand.   *hold back*

	Good lords, although my will to give is living,	
	The suit which you demand is gone and dead.	
85	He tells us Arthur is deceased tonight.°	*last night*

SALISBURY   Indeed we feared his sickness was past cure.

PEMBROKE   Indeed we heard how near his death he was,

	Before the child himself felt he was sick.	
	This must be answered,° either here or hence.°	*answered for / in heaven*
90	KING JOHN Why do you bend such solemn brows on me?	
	Think you I bear the shears of destiny?⁹	
	Have I commandment on the pulse of life?	

SALISBURY   It is apparent° foul play, and 'tis shame   *blatant*

	That greatness should so grossly offer° it.	*brazenly flaunt*
95	So thrive it in your game;¹ and so, farewell.	

PEMBROKE   Stay yet, Lord Salisbury; I'll go with thee,

	And find th'inheritance of this poor child,	
	His little kingdom of a forcèd° grave.	*violently imposed*
	That blood which owed° the breadth of all this isle	*owned (by right)*
100	Three foot of it doth hold. Bad world the while.°	*while such deeds occur*

---

8. *Which . . . liberty:* Which we ask for ourselves only insofar as concern for our benefit, which depends on you, leads to the conclusion that it is to your benefit to free him.

9. The shears with which, in Greek mythology, the Fates cut the thread of life.
1. May you suffer a similar fate.

This must not be thus borne. This will break out°   *break out in conflict*
To all our sorrows; and ere long, I doubt.°   *fear*
         Exeunt [PEMBROKE, SALISBURY, *and other lords*]
KING JOHN   They burn in indignation. I repent.
There is no sure foundation set on blood,
105   No certain life achieved by others' death.
         Enter [*a*] MESSENGER
A fearful eye thou hast. Where is that blood
That I have seen inhabit in those cheeks?
So foul a sky° clears not without a storm;   *(his face)*
Pour down thy weather: how goes all° in France?   *everything; everyone*
110 MESSENGER   From France to England. Never such a power
For any foreign preparation°   *military expedition*
Was levied in the body of a land.
The copy° of your speed is learned by them,   *example*
For when you should be told they do prepare,
115   The tidings comes that they are all arrived.
KING JOHN   O, where hath our intelligence° been drunk?   *spy network*
Where hath it slept? Where is my mother's ear,
That such an army could be drawn in France,
And she not hear of it?
MESSENGER   My liege, her ear
120   Is stopped with dust. The first of April died
Your noble mother. And as I hear, my lord,
The Lady Constance in a frenzy died
Three days before; but this from rumour's tongue
I idly heard; if true or false I know not.
125 KING JOHN   Withhold thy speed,° dreadful Occasion;°   *Slow down / events*
O, make a league with me till I have pleased
My discontented peers. What, Mother dead?
How wildly then walks my estate° in France!—   *fare my possessions*
Under whose conduct came those powers of France
130   That thou for truth giv'st out° are landed here?   *claim*
MESSENGER   Under the Dauphin.
         Enter [*the*] BASTARD *and* PETER OF POMFRET[2]
KING JOHN   Thou hast made me giddy
With these ill tidings. [*To the* BASTARD] Now, what says the world
To your proceedings?° Do not seek to stuff   *(monastic pillaging)*
My head with more ill news, for it is full.
135 BASTARD   But if you be afeard to hear the worst,
Then let the worst, unheard, fall on your head.
KING JOHN   Bear with me, cousin, for I was amazed°   *confused; stunned*
Under the tide;° but now I breathe again   *sea (of bad tidings)*
Aloft the flood, and can give audience
140   To any tongue, speak it of what it will.
BASTARD   How I have sped° among the clergymen   *fared*
The sums I have collected shall express.
But as I travelled hither through the land,
I find the people strangely fantasied,°   *full of peculiar ideas*
145   Possessed with rumours, full of idle° dreams,   *foolish*
Not knowing what they fear, but full of fear.
And here's a prophet that I brought with me
From forth the streets of Pomfret, whom I found

---

2. Modern Pontefract, west Yorkshire.

With many hundreds treading on his heels;
150 To whom he sung, in rude,° harsh-sounding rhymes,   *unpolished*
That ere the next Ascension Day³ at noon
Your highness should deliver up° your crown.   *give up*
KING JOHN Thou idle dreamer, wherefore didst thou so?
PETER OF POMFRET Foreknowing that the truth will fall out so.
155 KING JOHN Hubert, away with him! Imprison him,
And on that day, at noon, whereon he says
I shall yield up my crown, let him be hanged.
Deliver him to safety,° and return,   *custody*
For I must use thee. [*Exeunt* HUBERT *and* PETER OF POMFRET]
                    O my gentle cousin,
160 Hear'st thou the news abroad, who are arrived?
BASTARD The French, my lord: men's mouths are full of it.
Besides, I met Lord Bigot and Lord Salisbury
With eyes as red° as new-enkindled fire,   *(in rage)*
And others more, going to seek the grave
165 Of Arthur, whom they say is killed tonight°   *last night*
On your suggestion.
KING JOHN   Gentle kinsman, go
And thrust thyself into their companies.
I have a way to win their loves again.
Bring them before me.
BASTARD   I will seek them out.
170 KING JOHN Nay, but make haste, the better foot before.°   *go quickly*
O, let me have no subject° enemies   *subjects who are my*
When adverse foreigners affright my towns
With dreadful pomp of stout invasion!
Be Mercury, set feathers to thy heels,⁴
175 And fly like thought° from them to me again.   *(proverbially swift)*
BASTARD The spirit of the time° shall teach me speed.   *Exit*   *present occasion*
KING JOHN Spoke like a sprightful° noble gentleman!—   *spirited*
Go after him, for he perhaps shall need
Some messenger betwixt me and the peers,
180 And be thou he.
MESSENGER With all my heart, my liege.   [*Exit*]
KING JOHN My mother dead!
          Enter HUBERT
HUBERT My lord, they say five moons° were seen tonight,   *(an ominous portent)*
Four fixèd, and the fifth did whirl about
185 The other four in wondrous motion.
KING JOHN Five moons?
HUBERT   Old men and beldams° in the streets   *crones*
Do prophesy upon it dangerously.
Young Arthur's death is common in their mouths,
And when they talk of him they shake their heads,
190 And whisper one another in the ear;
And he that speaks doth grip the hearer's wrist,
Whilst he that hears makes fearful action,°   *shows fear*
With wrinkled brows, with nods, with rolling eyes.
I saw a smith stand with his hammer, thus,
195 The whilst his iron did on the anvil cool,

---

3. The Thursday, forty days after Easter, on which   4. Mercury, swift messenger of the Roman gods, wore
Christ is supposed to have ascended to heaven.   winged sandals.

With open mouth swallowing a tailor's news,
Who, with his shears and measure in his hand,
Standing on slippers which his nimble haste
Had falsely thrust upon contrary° feet,   *the wrong*
200 Told of a many thousand warlike French
That were embattailèd° and ranked in Kent.   *in battle order*
Another lean unwashed artificer°   *artisan*
Cuts off his° tale, and talks of Arthur's death.   *(the tailor's)*
KING JOHN Why seek'st thou to possess me with these fears?
205 Why urgest thou so oft young Arthur's death?
Thy hand hath murdered him. I had a mighty cause
To wish him dead, but thou hadst none to kill him.
HUBERT No had,° my lord? Why, did you not provoke me? *Hadn't I*
KING JOHN It is the curse of kings to be attended
210 By slaves that take their humours° for a warrant *whims*
To break within the bloody house of life,[5]
And on the winking° of authority   *hint; lapse*
To understand a law,° to know the meaning *To infer a command*
Of dangerous majesty, when perchance it frowns
215 More upon humour than advisèd respect.°   *considered opinion*
HUBERT Here is your hand° and seal for what I did. *signature*
   [*He shows a paper*]
KING JOHN O, when the last account 'twixt heaven and earth
Is to be made,[6] then shall this hand and seal
Witness against us to damnation!
220 How oft the sight of means to do ill deeds
Make deeds ill done! Hadst not thou been by,° *on hand*
A fellow by the hand of nature marked,°   *(by ugliness)*
Quoted,° and signed° to do a deed of shame, *Noted / marked*
This murder had not come into my mind.
225 But taking note of thy abhorred aspect,°   *appearance*
Finding thee fit for bloody villainy,
Apt, liable° to be employed in danger,° *suitable / doing harm*
I faintly broke° with thee of Arthur's death; *vaguely spoke*
And thou, to be endearèd to a king,
230 Made it no conscience° to destroy a prince. *no matter of conscience*
HUBERT My lord—
KING JOHN Hadst thou but shook thy head or made a pause
When I spake darkly° what I purposèd,   *insinuated*
Or turned an eye of doubt upon my face,
235 As° bid me tell my tale in express° words, *As if to / plain*
Deep shame had struck me dumb, made me break off,
And those thy fears might have wrought fears in me.
But thou didst understand me by my signs,
And didst in signs again parley° with sin;   *negotiate*
240 Yea, without stop, didst let thy heart consent,
And consequently thy rude° hand to act   *rough*
The deed which both our tongues held vile° to name. *refused*
Out of my sight, and never see me more!
My nobles leave me, and my state is braved,° *challenged*
245 Even at my gates, with ranks of foreign powers;
Nay, in the body of this fleshly land,°   *(John's body)*

---

5. The human body, which contains blood and which   6. *when . . . made*: when Judgment Day arrives.
murder makes bloody.

    This kingdom, this confine° of blood and breath,   *territory*
    Hostility and civil tumult reigns
    Between my conscience and my cousin's death.
250 HUBERT   Arm you against your other enemies;
    I'll make a peace between your soul and you.
    Young Arthur is alive. This hand of mine
    Is yet a maiden° and an innocent hand,   *virgin*
    Not painted with the crimson spots of blood.
255   Within this bosom never entered yet
    The dreadful motion° of a murderous thought;   *impulse*
    And you have slandered nature° in my form,°   *my nature / appearance*
    Which, howsoever rude exteriorly,
    Is yet the cover of a fairer mind
260   Than to be butcher of an innocent child.
    KING JOHN   Doth Arthur live? O, haste thee to the peers;
    Throw this report° on their incensèd° rage,   *(like water) / burning*
    And make them tame to their obedience.°   *(to John)*
    Forgive the comment that my passion made
265   Upon thy feature,° for my rage was blind,   *features*
    And foul imaginary eyes of blood[7]
    Presented thee more hideous than thou art.
    O, answer not, but to my closet° bring   *private room*
    The angry lords with all expedient° haste.   *quick*
270   I conjure° thee but slowly; run more fast.   *Exeunt [severally]*   *urge*

4.3

Enter ARTHUR *[Duke of Brittaine] on the walls [disguised as a ship-boy]*

    ARTHUR   The wall is high, and yet will I leap down.
    Good ground, be pitiful, and hurt me not.
    There's few or none do know me; if they did,
    This ship-boy's semblance° hath disguised me quite.°   *disguise / completely*
5   I am afraid, and yet I'll venture it.
    If I get down and do not break my limbs,
    I'll find a thousand shifts° to get away.   *stratagems*
    As good to die and go, as die and stay.
        [He leaps down]
    O me! My uncle's spirit is in these stones.
10   Heaven take my soul, and England keep my bones!   *[He] dies*

Enter [the Earls of] PEMBROKE *[and]* SALISBURY, *and*
[Lord] BIGOT

    SALISBURY   Lords, I will meet him° at Saint Edmundsbury.[1]   *(the Dauphin)*
    It is our safety,° and we must embrace   *means of safety*
    This gentle offer of the perilous time.
    PEMBROKE   Who brought that letter from the Cardinal?°   *Pandolf*
15   SALISBURY   The Count Melun, a noble lord of France,
    Who's private with° me of the Dauphin's love;   *Who has confided in*
    'Tis much more general° than these lines import.   *much greater*
    BIGOT   Tomorrow morning let us meet him then.
    SALISBURY   Or rather, then set forward, for 'twill be
20   Two long days' journey, lords, or ere° we meet.   *before*

---

7. John's, bloody from rage; Hubert's, bloody from guilt; Arthur's, bloody from murder.   **4.3** Location: Outside the castle.
1. Bury St. Edmunds, Suffolk (a place of pilgrimage).

Enter [the] BASTARD

BASTARD   Once more today well met, distempered° lords.   *ill-humored*
   The King by me requests your presence straight.°   *immediately*
SALISBURY   The King hath dispossessed himself of us.
   We will not line his thin bestainèd cloak
25   With our pure honours, nor attend the foot
   That leaves the print of blood where'er it walks.
   Return and tell him so; we know the worst.
BASTARD   Whate'er you think, good words I think were best.
SALISBURY   Our griefs and not our manners reason now.
30 BASTARD   But there is little reason in your grief.
   Therefore 'twere reason° you had manners now.   *reasonable*
PEMBROKE   Sir, sir, impatience hath his privilege.°   *its particular right*
BASTARD   'Tis true—to hurt his master, no man else.[2]
SALISBURY   This is the prison.
   [He sees Arthur's body]
                            What is he lies here?
35 PEMBROKE   O death, made proud with pure and princely beauty!
   The earth had not a hole° to hide this deed.   *grave*
SALISBURY   Murder, as° hating what himself hath done,   *as though*
   Doth lay it open° to urge on revenge.   *on public display*
BIGOT   Or when he° doomed this beauty to a grave,   *(murder)*
40   Found it too precious-princely for a grave.
SALISBURY *[to the* BASTARD*]*   Sir Richard, what think you? You have beheld.
   Or have you° read or heard; or could you think,   *Have you either*
   Or do you almost think, although you see,
   That you do see? Could thought, without this object,
45   Form such another?[3] This is the very top,
   The height, the crest,° or crest unto the crest,   *(atop a coat of arms)*
   Of murder's arms; this is the bloodiest shame,
   The wildest savagery, the vilest stroke
   That ever wall-eyed° wrath or staring rage   *glaring*
50   Presented to the tears of soft remorse.°   *pity*
PEMBROKE   All murders past do stand excused in° this, *in comparison with*
   And this, so sole° and so unmatchable,   *unique*
   Shall give a holiness, a purity,
   To the yet-unbegotten sin of times,°   *the future*
55   And prove a deadly bloodshed but a jest,
   Exampled by° this heinous spectacle.   *Given the precedent of*
BASTARD   It is a damnèd and a bloody work,
   The graceless° action of a heavy° hand—   *impious / an oppressive*
   If that it be the work of any hand.
60 SALISBURY   If that it be the work of any hand?
   We had a kind of light° what would ensue: *premonition*
   It is the shameful work of Hubert's hand,
   The practice° and the purpose of the King;   *plot*
   From whose obedience I forbid my soul,
65   Kneeling before this ruin of sweet life,
   And breathing to his breathless excellence
   The incense of a vow, a holy vow,
   Never to taste the pleasures of the world,

---

2. Angry words hurt no one but the speaker (proverbial).
3. *Or do . . . another:* Could you even approach the thought of what you actually see here? Without seeing Arthur's body, would it be possible to imagine such a sight?

Never to be infected with delight,
70 Nor conversant with ease and idleness,
Till I have set a glory to this hand°   *(his own; Arthur's)*
By giving it the worship° of revenge.   *honor*
PEMBROKE *and* BIGOT   Our souls religiously confirm thy words.

        Enter HUBERT

HUBERT   Lords, I am hot with haste in seeking you.
75 Arthur doth live; the King hath sent for you.
SALISBURY   O, he is bold, and blushes not at death!—
Avaunt,° thou hateful villain, get thee gone!   *Begone*
HUBERT   I am no villain.
SALISBURY   Must I rob the law?[4]
      [He draws his sword]
BASTARD   Your sword is bright,° sir; put it up° again.   *unused / sheathe it*
80 SALISBURY   Not till I sheathe it in a murderer's skin.
HUBERT *[drawing his sword]*   Stand back, Lord Salisbury, stand back, I say!
By heaven, I think my sword's as sharp as yours.
I would not have you, lord, forget yourself,[5]
Nor tempt° the danger of my true° defence,   *test / honest; able*
85 Lest I, by marking of° your rage, forget   *responding to*
Your worth, your greatness and nobility.
BIGOT   Out, dunghill! Dar'st thou brave° a nobleman?   *defy*
HUBERT   Not for my life; but yet I dare defend
My innocent life against an emperor.
SALISBURY   Thou art a murderer.
90 HUBERT   Do not prove me so;°   *(by making me kill)*
Yet° I am none. Whose tongue soe'er speaks false,   *Up to now*
Not truly speaks; who speaks not truly, lies.
PEMBROKE   Cut him to pieces!
BASTARD *[drawing his sword]*   Keep the peace, I say!
SALISBURY   Stand by,° or I shall gall° you, Falconbridge.   *aside / wound*
95 BASTARD   Thou wert better gall the devil, Salisbury.
If thou but frown on me, or stir thy foot,
Or teach thy hasty spleen° to do me shame,   *temper*
I'll strike thee dead. Put up thy sword betime,°   *immediately*
Or I'll so maul you and your toasting-iron°   *sword (belittling)*
100 That you shall think the devil is come from hell.
BIGOT   What wilt thou do, renownèd Falconbridge,
Second° a villain and a murderer?   *Back up*
HUBERT   Lord Bigot, I am none.
BIGOT   Who killed this prince?
HUBERT   'Tis not an hour since I left him well.
105 I honoured him, I loved him, and will weep
My date° of life out for his sweet life's loss.   *term*
SALISBURY   Trust not those cunning waters of his eyes,
For villainy is not without such rheum,
And he, long traded° in it, makes it seem   *experienced*
110 Like rivers of remorse and innocency.
Away with me, all you whose souls abhor
Th'uncleanly savours° of a slaughter-house,   *odors*
For I am stifled with this smell of sin.
BIGOT   Away toward Bury,° to the Dauphin there.   *Bury St. Edmunds*

---

4. Deprive the law of its due by killing Hubert.
5. Lose self-control; forget your rank (it not being honorable for a lord to challenge a commoner, or vice
versa, as lines 85–86 suggest).

115	PEMBROKE There, tell the King, he may enquire° us out.	seek

Exeunt Lords [PEMBROKE, SALISBURY, *and* BIGOT]

BASTARD   Here's a good world! Knew you of this fair work?
Beyond the infinite and boundless reach
Of mercy, if thou didst this deed of death
Art thou damned, Hubert.

120   HUBERT   Do but hear me, sir.
BASTARD   Ha! I'll tell thee what:
Thou'rt damned as black—nay nothing is so black—
Thou art more deep damned than Prince Lucifer;
There is not yet so ugly a fiend of hell
125   As thou shalt be if thou didst kill this child.
HUBERT   Upon my soul—
BASTARD   If thou didst but consent
To this most cruel act, do but despair;⁶
And if thou want'st° a cord, the smallest thread   lack
That ever spider twisted from her womb
130   Will serve to strangle thee; a rush° will be a beam   reed
To hang thee on; or wouldst thou° drown thyself,   if you wish to
Put but a little water in a spoon
And it shall be, as all the ocean,
Enough to stifle such a villain up.
135   I do suspect thee very grievously.
HUBERT   If I in act, consent, or sin of thought
Be guilty of the stealing that sweet breath
Which was embounded° in this beauteous clay,°   enclosed / (Arthur's body)
Let hell want pains enough to torture me.
I left him well.
140   BASTARD   Go bear him in thine arms.
I am amazed,° methinks, and lose my way   bewildered
Among the thorns and dangers of this world.

[HUBERT *takes up* ARTHUR *in his arms*]

How easy dost thou take all England up!
From forth° this morsel of dead royalty,   Out of
145   The life, the right, and truth of all this realm
Is fled to heaven, and England now is left
To tug and scramble, and to part by th' teeth
The unowed interest⁷ of proud swelling state.
Now for the bare-picked bone of majesty
150   Doth doggèd° war bristle his angry crest,⁸   cruel
And snarleth in the gentle eyes of peace;
Now powers from home° and discontents at home   foreign armies
Meet in one line,° and vast confusion waits,°   rank / chaos awaits
As doth a raven on a sick-fall'n beast,
155   The imminent decay of wrested pomp.°   usurped power
Now happy he whose cloak and cincture° can   belt
Hold out this tempest. Bear away that child,
And follow me with speed. I'll to the King.
A thousand businesses are brief in hand,°   need urgent action
160   And heaven itself doth frown upon the land. *Exeunt* [*severally*]

---

6. Lose all hope of salvation and hence commit suicide.
7. Contested or unowned possession; obedience ("interest") that is not due ("unowed"), because John lacks legitimacy.
8. Dog's hackles (hairs on neck and back); crest on a coat of arms.

5.1

[*Flourish.*] *Enter* KING JOHN *and* [*Cardinal*] PANDOLF,
[*with*] *attendants*

KING JOHN [*giving* PANDOLF *the crown*]   Thus have I yielded up
    into your hand
    The circle of my glory.

PANDOLF [*giving back the crown*]   Take again
    From this my hand, as holding of° the Pope,   *as land rented from*
    Your sovereign greatness and authority.

5   KING JOHN   Now keep your holy word: go meet the French,
    And from his Holiness° use all your power   *the Pope*
    To stop their marches 'fore we are enflamed.
    Our discontented counties° do revolt,   *shires; nobles*
    Our people quarrel with obedience,
10   Swearing allegiance and the love of soul
    To stranger° blood, to foreign royalty.   *foreign*
    This inundation of mistempered humour
    Rests by you only to be qualified.[1]
    Then pause not, for the present time's so sick
15   That present° med'cine must be ministered,   *immediate*
    Or overthrow incurable ensues.

PANDOLF   It was my breath° that blew this tempest up,   *words*
    Upon your stubborn usage of the Pope,
    But since you are a gentle convertite,°   *convert*
20   My tongue shall hush again this storm of war
    And make fair weather in your blust'ring land.
    On this Ascension Day, remember well,
    Upon your oath of service to the Pope,
    Go I to make the French lay down their arms.

                      Exeunt [*all but* KING JOHN][2]

25 KING JOHN   Is this Ascension Day? Did not the prophet
    Say that before Ascension Day at noon
    My crown I should give off?[3] Even so I have.
    I did suppose it should be on constraint,
    But, heaven be thanked, it is but voluntary.

         Enter BASTARD

30 BASTARD   All Kent hath yielded; nothing there holds out
    But Dover Castle. London hath received,
    Like a kind host, the Dauphin and his powers.°   *army*
    Your nobles will not hear you, but are gone
    To offer service to your enemy;
35   And wild amazement hurries° up and down   *confusion drives*
    The little number of your doubtful° friends. *untrustworthy; fearful*

KING JOHN   Would not my lords return to me again
    After they heard young Arthur was alive?

BASTARD   They found him dead and cast into the streets,
40   An empty casket, where the jewel of life
    By some damned hand was robbed and ta'en away.

KING JOHN   That villain Hubert told me he did live.

BASTARD   So on my soul he did, for aught he knew.
    But wherefore do you droop? Why look you sad?

5.1 Location: John's court.
1. *This . . . qualified:* Only you can cure this surge of
diseased behavior.

2. F leaves the attendants onstage with John. But even
in that case, this speech could easily be a soliloquy.
3. See 4.2.147–52.

45 Be great in act as you have been in thought.
Let not the world see fear and sad distrust
Govern the motion of a kingly eye.
Be stirring as the time,[4] be fire with° fire;   against
Threaten the threat'ner, and outface the brow
50 Of bragging horror. So shall inferior eyes,
That borrow their behaviours from the great,
Grow great by your example, and put on
The dauntless spirit of resolution.
Away, and glisten like the god of war
55 When he intendeth to become the field.°   adorn the battlefield
Show boldness and aspiring confidence.
What, shall they seek the lion in his den
And fright him there, and make him tremble there?
O, let it not be said! Forage,° and run   Range (for prey)
60 To meet displeasure farther from the doors,
And grapple with him ere he come so nigh.
KING JOHN   The legate of the Pope hath been with me,
And I have made a happy peace with him,
And he hath promised to dismiss the powers
Led by the Dauphin.
65 BASTARD   O inglorious league!
Shall we, upon the footing of our land,°   standing on our own soil
Send fair-play orders,° and make compromise,   equitable conditions
Insinuation,° parley, and base truce   Ingratiating proposals
To arms invasive?° Shall a beardless boy,   invading
70 A cockered silken wanton,° brave our fields   spoiled dandyish child
And flesh his spirit[5] in a warlike soil,
Mocking the air with colours idly° spread,   carelessly
And find no check? Let us, my liege, to arms!
Perchance the Cardinal cannot make your peace,
75 Or if he do, let it at least be said
They saw we had a purpose of defence.
KING JOHN   Have thou the ordering of this present time.
BASTARD   Away, then, with good courage! [Aside] Yet I know
Our party may well meet a prouder foe.[6]   Exeunt

5.2

*Enter [marching] (in arms) [LOUIS THE] DAUPHIN, [the
Earl of] SALISBURY, [Count] MELUN, [the Earl of] PEM-
BROKE, [and Lord] BIGOT, [with] soldiers*
LOUIS THE DAUPHIN   My Lord Melun, let this[1] be copied out,
And keep it safe for our remembrance.
Return the precedent° to these lords again,   original copy
That having our fair order° written down,   arrangements
5 Both they and we, perusing o'er these notes,
May know wherefore we took the sacrament[2]
And keep our faiths firm and inviolable.
SALISBURY   Upon our sides it never shall be broken.
And, noble Dauphin, albeit we swear

---

4. Be as vigorous as the times demand.
5. Initiate himself in bloodshed (in the "soil," as a sword is "fleshed" in a body).
6. Is well able to handle an even stronger enemy than the French; may be up against an enemy more power-

ful than we are.
5.2 Location: St. Edmundsbury (Bury St. Edmunds) in Suffolk.
1. This agreement with the English lords.
2. The Mass, taken as a solemn dedication to the task.

10	A voluntary zeal° and an unurgèd° faith	*commitment / unforced*
	To your proceedings, yet believe me, Prince,	
	I am not glad that such a sore of time	
	Should seek a plaster° by contemned° revolt,	*bandage / despised*
	And heal the inveterate canker° of one wound	*infection*
15	By making many. O, it grieves my soul	
	That I must draw this metal° from my side	*(his sword)*
	To be a widow-maker! O, and there	
	Where honourable rescue and defence	
	Cries out upon³ the name of Salisbury!	
20	But such is the infection of the time,	
	That for the health and physic° of our right,	*cure*
	We cannot deal but with the very hand	
	Of stern injustice and confusèd wrong.⁴	
	And is't not pity, O my grievèd friends,	
25	That we the sons and children of this isle	
	Was born to see so sad an hour as this,	
	Wherein we step after a stranger,° march	*foreigner*
	Upon her gentle bosom, and fill up	
	Her enemies' ranks? I must withdraw and weep	
30	Upon the spot° of this enforcèd cause—	*place; stain*
	To grace the gentry of a land remote,	
	And follow unacquainted colours° here.	*unfamiliar banners*
	What, here? O nation, that thou couldst remove;°	*move elsewhere*
	That Neptune's arms° who clippeth thee about°	*the sea / embraces you*
35	Would bear thee from the knowledge of thyself	
	And gripple° thee unto a pagan shore,	*join*
	Where these two Christian armies might combine	
	The blood of malice in a vein of league,°	*(against a pagan foe)*
	And not to spend° it so unneighbourly.	*shed*
40	LOUIS THE DAUPHIN A noble temper° dost thou show in this,	*disposition*
	And great affections,° wrestling in thy bosom,	*emotions; loyalties*
	Doth make an earthquake of nobility.°	*out of a noble nature*
	O, what a noble combat hast thou fought	
	Between compulsion° and a brave respect!°	*necessity / patriotism*
45	Let me wipe off this honourable dew	
	That silverly doth progress on thy cheeks.	
	My heart hath melted at a lady's tears,	
	Being an ordinary inundation;	
	But this effusion of such manly drops,	
50	This shower blown up by tempest of the soul,	
	Startles mine eyes, and makes me more amazed	
	Than had I seen the vaulty° top of heaven	*arched*
	Figured quite o'er° with burning meteors.⁵	*Adorned thoroughly*
	Lift up thy brow, renownèd Salisbury,	
55	And with a great heart heave away this storm;	
	Commend° these waters to those baby eyes	*Leave*
	That never saw the giant° world enraged,	*grown-up*
	Nor met with Fortune other than at feasts,	
	Full warm of° blood, of mirth, of gossiping.	*with*
60	Come, come, for thou shalt thrust thy hand as deep	

3. Exclaim against; appeal to.
4. *We . . . wrong*: We cannot act except with unjust means; or, possibly, we cannot act except against the
unjust hand of John.
5. Meteors were seen as portents of disaster.

Into the purse of rich prosperity
As Louis himself. So, nobles, shall you all
That knit your sinews° to the strength of mine.   *join your powers*
    [*A trumpet sounds*]
And even there methinks an angel⁶ spake!
      Enter [*Cardinal*] PANDOLF

65   Look where the holy legate comes apace,
To give us warrant from the hand of heaven,°   *the Pope; God*
And on our actions set the name of right
With holy breath.
  PANDOLF   Hail, noble prince of France!
The next° is this. King John hath reconciled   *next thing I have to say*

70   Himself to Rome; his spirit is come in°   *has submitted*
That so stood out against the Holy Church,
The great metropolis and See of Rome;
Therefore thy threat'ning colours° now wind up,°   *banners / put away*
And tame the savage spirit of wild war,

75   That like a lion fostered up at hand°   *by human hand*
It may lie gently at the foot of peace,
And be no further harmful than in show.
  LOUIS THE DAUPHIN   Your grace shall pardon me: I will not back.°   *go back*
I am too high-born to be propertied,°   *manipulated*

80   To be a secondary° at control,   *subordinate*
Or useful serving-man and instrument
To any sovereign state° throughout the world.   *(the papacy)*
Your breath first kindled the dead coal of wars
Between this chastised kingdom and myself,

85   And brought in matter° that should feed this fire;   *fuel*
And now 'tis far too huge to be blown out
With that same weak wind which enkindled it.
You taught me how to know the face of right,°   *my rightful claim*
Acquainted me with interest° to this land,   *my claim*

90   Yea, thrust this enterprise into my heart;
And come ye now to tell me John hath made
His peace with Rome? What is that peace to me?
I, by the honour of my marriage bed,
After young Arthur, claim this land for mine;

95   And now it is half conquered, must I back
Because that John hath made his peace with Rome?
Am I Rome's slave? What penny hath Rome borne,°   *contributed*
What men provided, what munition sent
To underprop° this action? Is't not I   *support*

100   That undergo this charge? Who else but I,
And such as to my claim are liable,°   *are liable to me*
Sweat in this business and maintain° this war?   *pay for*
Have I not heard these islanders shout out
'Vive le Roi!' as I have banked their towns?

105   Have I not here the best cards for the game,
To win this easy match played for a crown?

---

6. The trumpet, an editorial addition, is seen as an angel's affirmation of the Dauphin's speech. The stage direction may not be necessary, however. "Angel" might also mean "gold coin," developing the money imagery of lines 61–63—"purse of rich prosperity," "nobles" (also a coin), and perhaps "sinews" (where "sinews of war" connotes money). The Dauphin's point, perhaps made in an aside, would be that money talks in persuading the English peers to join his cause.

And shall I now give o'er the yielded set?[7]
No, no, on my soul, it never shall be said.
PANDOLF   You look but on the outside of this work.
110   LOUIS THE DAUPHIN   Outside or inside, I will not return
Till my attempt° so much be glorified   warlike enterprise
As to my ample hope was promisèd
Before I drew° this gallant head of war,°   gathered / army
And culled° these fiery spirits from the world   picked out
115   To outlook conquest° and to win renown   To defy defeat
Even in the jaws of danger and of death.
[A trumpet sounds]
What lusty° trumpet thus doth summon us?   vigorous
Enter [the] BASTARD
BASTARD   According to the fair play° of the world,   code of chivalry
Let me have audience; I am sent to speak.
120   My holy lord of Milan, from the King
I come to learn how you have dealt for him,
And as° you answer I do know the scope   according to how
And warrant limited unto my tongue.
PANDOLF   The Dauphin is too wilful-opposite,°   stubbornly hostile
125   And will not temporize with° my entreaties.   will not heed
He flatly says he'll not lay down his arms.
BASTARD   By all the blood that ever fury breathed,
The youth says well. Now hear our English king,
For thus his royalty doth speak in me.
130   He is prepared, and reason too he should.°   as he should be
This apish and unmannerly approach,
This harnessed masque and unadvisèd revel,[8]
This unhaired° sauciness and boyish troops,   youthful
The King doth smile at, and is well prepared
135   To whip this dwarfish war, these pigmy arms,
From out the circle° of his territories.   confines
That hand which had the strength even at your door
To cudgel you and make you take the hatch,°   beat a hasty retreat
To dive like buckets in concealèd wells,
140   To crouch in litter° of your stable planks,   animal's bedding
To lie like pawns° locked up in chests and trunks,   pawned goods
To hug° with swine, to seek sweet safety out   bed down
In vaults and prisons, and to thrill° and shake   shiver
Even at the crying of your nation's crow,°   the cock
145   Thinking his voice an armèd Englishman;
Shall that victorious hand be feebled here
That in your chambers° gave you chastisement?   your own home
No! Know the gallant monarch is in arms,
And like an eagle o'er his eyrie towers°   soars over his nest
150   To souse° annoyance that comes near his nest.   swoop down on
[To the English lords]
And you degenerate, you ingrate revolts,°   ungrateful rebels
You bloody Neros, ripping up the womb
Of your dear mother England,[9] blush for shame;

---

7. 'Vive . . . set: The Dauphin uses an extended card-playing metaphor, including "Vive le Roi" ("Long live the King"), "banked" (put in the bank, won; but also, sailed by the banks of or perhaps besieged), "cards," "game," "match played," "crown" (the coin as a stake in a card game; John's crown), and "yielded set" (the hand already won).
8. This courtly entertainment in armor and rashly undertaken revelry.
9. The Roman Emperor Nero was supposed to have murdered his mother by ripping open her womb.

For your own ladies and pale-visaged maids
155 Like Amazons¹ come tripping after drums;
Their thimbles into armèd gauntlets° change,   steel-plated gloves
Their needles to lances, and their gentle hearts
To fierce and bloody inclination.°   disposition
LOUIS THE DAUPHIN   There end thy brave,° and turn thy face°   defiance / return
in peace.
160 We grant thou canst outscold us. Fare thee well:
We hold our time too precious to be spent
With such a brabbler.°   quarreler
PANDOLF   Give me leave to speak.
BASTARD   No, I will speak.
LOUIS THE DAUPHIN   We will attend° to neither.—   listen
Strike up the drums, and let the tongue of war
165 Plead for our interest and our being here.
BASTARD   Indeed your drums, being beaten, will cry out;
And so shall you, being beaten. Do but start
An echo with the clamour of thy drum,
And even at hand a drum is ready braced°   ready to be struck
170 That shall reverberate all as loud as thine.
Sound but another, and another shall
As loud as thine rattle the welkin's° ear,   sky's
And mock° the deep-mouthed thunder; for at hand,   outrival
Not trusting to this halting° legate here,   wavering
175 Whom he hath used rather for sport than need,
Is warlike John; and in his forehead sits
A bare-ribbed Death, whose office° is this day   task
To feast upon whole thousands of the French.
LOUIS THE DAUPHIN   Strike up our drums to find this danger out.
180 BASTARD   And thou shalt find it, Dauphin, do not doubt.
[*Drums beat.*] *Exeunt* [*the* BASTARD *at one door,*
all the rest, marching, at another door]

5.3

Alarum. Enter [KING] JOHN [*at one door*] *and* HUBERT
[*at another door*]
KING JOHN   How goes the day with us? O, tell me, Hubert.
HUBERT   Badly, I fear. How fares your majesty?
KING JOHN   This fever that hath troubled me so long
Lies heavy on me. O, my heart is sick!
Enter a MESSENGER
5 MESSENGER   My lord, your valiant kinsman Falconbridge
Desires your majesty to leave the field,
And send him word by me which way you go.
KING JOHN   Tell him toward Swineshead,° to the abbey there.   (in Lincolnshire)
MESSENGER   Be of good comfort, for the great supply°   reinforcements
10 That was expected by the Dauphin here
Are wrecked three nights ago on Goodwin Sands.°   shoals off Kent
This news was brought to Richard,° but even now   (the Bastard)
The French fight coldly and retire themselves.°   retreat
KING JOHN   Ay me, this tyrant fever burns me up,

---

1. Female warriors of classical legend.   5.3 Location: The battlefield.

15   And will not let me welcome this good news.
          Set on toward Swineshead. To my litter straight;°   *portable bed at once*
          Weakness possesseth me, and I am faint.   *Exeunt*

5.4

          [Alarum.] Enter [the Earls of] SALISBURY *[and]* PEM-
          BROKE, *and [Lord]* BIGOT
SALISBURY   I did not think the King so stored° with friends.   *well provided*
PEMBROKE   Up once again; put spirit in the French.
          If they miscarry,° we miscarry too.   *fail*
SALISBURY   That misbegotten devil Falconbridge,
5   In spite of spite,° alone upholds the day.°   *everything / battle*
PEMBROKE   They say King John, sore° sick, hath left the field.   *grievously*
          Enter [Count] MELUN, *wounded [led by a soldier]*
MELUN   Lead me to the revolts° of England here.   *rebels*
SALISBURY   When we were happy, we had other names.
PEMBROKE   It is the Count Melun.
SALISBURY   Wounded to death.
10   MELUN   Fly, noble English, you are bought and sold.°   *betrayed*
          Unthread the rude eye of rebellion,[1]
          And welcome home again discarded faith;
          Seek out King John and fall before his feet,
          For if the French be lords of° this loud° day   *win / hectic*
15   He° means to recompense the pains you take   *(Louis)*
          By cutting off your heads. Thus hath he sworn,
          And I with him, and many more with me,
          Upon the altar at Saint Edmundsbury,
          Even on that altar where we swore to you
20   Dear amity and everlasting love.
SALISBURY   May this be possible? May this be true?
MELUN   Have I not hideous death within my view,
          Retaining but a quantity of life,
          Which bleeds away, even as a form of wax
25   Resolveth from his figure° 'gainst the fire?   *Melts out of shape*
          What in the world should make me now deceive,
          Since I must lose the use of all deceit?
          Why should I then be false, since it is true
          That I must die here, and live hence° by truth?   *in the next world*
30   I say again, if Louis do win the day,
          He is forsworn° if e'er those eyes of yours   *perjured*
          Behold another daybreak in the east;
          But even this night, whose black contagious breath
          Already smokes about the burning cresset°   *suspended torch*
35   Of the old, feeble, and day-wearied sun,
          Even this ill night your breathing shall expire,
          Paying the fine of rated° treachery   *assessed (as penalty)*
          Even with a treacherous fine° of all your lives,   *payment; end*
          If Louis by your assistance win the day.
40   Commend me to one Hubert with your king.
          The love of him, and this respect° besides,   *consideration*
          For that° my grandsire was an Englishman,   *Because*

5.4 Location: Scene continues.   down which you've been led (like a thread that has been
1. Turn back from the barbarous path of rebellion   inserted into the needle's eye and must be pulled out).

Awakes my conscience to confess all this;
In lieu° whereof, I pray you bear me hence   *recompense*
45   From forth the noise and rumour° of the field,   *tumult*
Where I may think the remnant of my thoughts
In peace, and part this body and my soul
With contemplation and devout desires.
SALISBURY   We do believe thee; and beshrew° my soul   *woe to*
50   But° I do love the favour° and the form   *Unless / look*
Of this most fair occasion; by the which
We will untread° the steps of damnèd flight,°   *retrace / desertion*
And like a bated° and retirèd flood,   *an abated*
Leaving our rankness° and irregular course,   *flooding*
55   Stoop low within those bounds we have o'erlooked,°   *overflowed; ignored*
And calmly run on in obedience
Even to our ocean, to our great King John.
My arm shall give thee help to bear thee hence,
For I do see the cruel pangs of death
60   Right in thine eye.—Away, my friends! New flight,°   *change of allegiance*
And happy newness that intends old right.[2]   *Exeunt*

5.5

[*Alarum; retreat.*] Enter [LOUIS THE] DAUPHIN, *and his*
                                    train
LOUIS THE DAUPHIN   The sun of heaven, methought, was loath to set,
But stayed and made the western welkin blush,
When English measured° backward their own ground   *crossed*
In faint retire.° O, bravely came we off,[1]   *weak retreat*
5   When with a volley of our needless° shot,   *unnecessary*
After such bloody toil, we bid good night,
And wound our tatt'ring colours clearly up,[2]
Last in the field and almost lords of it.
                    Enter a MESSENGER
MESSENGER   Where is my prince the Dauphin?
LOUIS THE DAUPHIN   Here. What news?
10   MESSENGER   The Count Melun is slain; the English lords
By his persuasion are again fall'n off;°   *changed in allegiance*
And your supply° which you have wished so long   *supplies*
Are cast away and sunk on Goodwin Sands.
LOUIS THE DAUPHIN   Ah, foul shrewd° news! Beshrew° thy very   *harmful / Curse*
                    heart!
15   I did not think to be so sad tonight
As this hath made me. Who was he that said
King John did fly an hour or two before
The stumbling night[3] did part our weary powers?
MESSENGER   Whoever spoke it, it is true, my lord.
20   LOUIS THE DAUPHIN   Well, keep good quarter° and good care tonight.   *guard*
The day shall not be up so soon as I,
To try the fair adventure° of tomorrow.   *Exeunt*   *chance*

---

2. That intends to restore the ancient right—John's   2. We rolled our tattered (waving) banners up without
claim to rule and our just conduct.   obstruction from the English.
5.5 Location: Scene continues.   3. That is, night that causes stumbling.
1. We acquitted ourselves valiantly.

5.6

Enter [the] BASTARD *[with a light] and* HUBERT *[with a pistol], severally*

HUBERT   Who's there? Speak, ho! Speak quickly, or I shoot.

BASTARD   A friend. What art thou?

HUBERT   Of the part° of England.   side

BASTARD   Whither dost thou go?

HUBERT   What's that to thee?
    Why may not I demand of thine affairs
5   As well as thou of mine?

BASTARD   Hubert, I think.

HUBERT   Thou hast a perfect° thought.   correct
    I will upon all hazards° well believe   against all odds
    Thou art my friend that know'st my tongue so well.
    Who art thou?

10 BASTARD   Who thou wilt. An if thou please,
    Thou mayst befriend me so much as to think
    I come one way° of the Plantagenets.   by one parent

HUBERT   Unkind remembrance![1] Thou and eyeless° night   blind
    Have done me shame. Brave soldier, pardon me
15   That any accent° breaking from thy tongue   sound
    Should 'scape the true acquaintance of mine ear.

BASTARD   Come, come, sans compliment.° What news abroad?   no formalities

HUBERT   Why, here walk I in the black brow of night
    To find you out.

BASTARD   Brief, then, and what's the news?

20 HUBERT   O my sweet sir, news fitting to the night:
    Black, fearful, comfortless, and horrible.

BASTARD   Show me the very wound of this ill news;
    I am no woman, I'll not swoon at it.

HUBERT   The King, I fear, is poisoned by a monk.
25   I left him almost speechless, and broke out°   hurried away
    To acquaint you with this evil, that you might
    The better arm you to the sudden time°   for this emergency
    Than if you had at leisure° known of this.   later

BASTARD   How did he take it?° Who did taste to° him?   (poison) / (the food) for

30 HUBERT   A monk, I tell you, a resolvèd villain,[2]
    Whose bowels suddenly burst out. The King
    Yet° speaks, and peradventure may recover.   Still

BASTARD   Who didst thou leave to tend his majesty?

HUBERT   Why, know you not? The lords are all come back,
35   And brought Prince Henry[3] in their company,
    At whose request the King hath pardoned them,
    And they are all about his majesty.

BASTARD   Withhold thine indignation, mighty heaven,
    And tempt us not to bear above our power.[4]
40   I'll tell thee, Hubert, half my power this night,
    Passing these flats, are taken° by the tide.   drowned
    These Lincoln Washes[5] have devourèd them;

5.6 Location: Near Swineshead Abbey.
1. Bad memory (criticizing himself for not recognizing the Bastard).
2. A "resolvèd villain" since, as the person whose job it was to protect the King by tasting his food, he knowingly took poison himself just so that he could succeed in poisoning the King.

3. John's son; later, King Henry III.
4. And don't push us (or me) past our power to endure. "Bear above our power" may hint at the Bastard's previous thoughts, here put aside, of assuming the throne himself.
5. The tides of the Wash (tidal flatlands south of Lincolnshire).

Myself, well mounted, hardly° have escaped.   *barely; with trouble*
Away before!° Conduct me to the King.   *Go on ahead*
45   I doubt° he will be dead or ere° I come.   *Exeunt*   *fear / before*

5.7

Enter PRINCE HENRY, [*the Earl of*] SALISBURY, *and*
[*Lord*] BIGOT

PRINCE HENRY   It is too late. The life of all his blood
Is touched° corruptibly, and his pure° brain,   *infected / (once) lucid*
Which some suppose the soul's frail dwelling-house,
Doth by the idle° comments that it makes   *foolish*
5   Foretell the ending of mortality.°   *mortal life*
      Enter [*the Earl of*] PEMBROKE
PEMBROKE   His highness yet doth speak, and holds belief
That being brought into the open air,
It would allay the burning quality
Of that fell° poison which assaileth him.   *savage*
10 PRINCE HENRY   Let him be brought into the orchard here.—
                   [*Exit Lord* BIGOT][1]
Doth he still rage?
PEMBROKE   He is more patient
Than when you left him. Even° now, he sung.   *Just*
PRINCE HENRY   O, vanity° of sickness! Fierce extremes°   *delusion / (of pain)*
In their continuance will not feel themselves.[2]
15 Death, having preyed upon the outward parts,°   *the body*
Leaves them invincible,° and his siege is now   *(because overcome)*
Against the mind; the which he pricks and wounds
With many legions of strange fantasies,
Which in their throng and press to that last hold°   *stronghold (the mind)*
20 Confound° themselves. 'Tis strange that death should sing.   *Destroy*
I am the cygnet° to this pale faint swan,   *young swan*
Who chants a doleful hymn to his own death,[3]
And from the organ-pipe° of frailty sings   *voice box*
His soul and body to their lasting rest.
25 SALISBURY   Be of good comfort, Prince, for you are born
To set a form upon that indigest°   *chaos*
Which he hath left so shapeless and so rude.°   *formless*
    [KING] JOHN [*is*] *brought in* [*with Lord* BIGOT *attending*]
KING JOHN   Ay marry, now° my soul hath elbow-room;   *now being outdoors*
It would not out at° windows nor at doors.   *go out through*
30 There is so hot a summer in my bosom
That all my bowels crumble up to dust;
I am a scribbled form, drawn with a pen
Upon a parchment, and against° this fire°   *before / (of poison)*
Do I shrink up.
PRINCE HENRY   How fares your majesty?
35 KING JOHN   Poisoned, ill fare!° Dead, forsook, cast off;   *food; state of things*
And none of you will bid the winter come
To thrust his icy fingers in my maw,°   *stomach; mouth; throat*
Nor let my kingdom's rivers take their course
Through my burned bosom, nor entreat the north

5.7 Location: The orchard of Swineshead Abbey.
1. F has no stage direction. Someone must fetch John:
either Bigot here or Pembroke after line 12.

2. By continuing for a long time will cease to be felt.
3. John's swan song; swans were thought to sing only
as they died.

40 To make his bleak winds kiss my parchèd lips
And comfort me with cold. I do not ask you much;
I beg cold° comfort, and you are so strait°   *slight; cooling / mean*
And so ingrateful you deny me that.
PRINCE HENRY   O, that there were some virtue° in my tears   *remedial power*
That might relieve you!
45 KING JOHN   The salt in them is hot.
Within me is a hell, and there the poison
Is, as a fiend, confined to tyrannize
On unreprievable condemnèd blood.
          Enter [the] BASTARD
BASTARD   O, I am scalded with my violent motion°   *haste*
50 And spleen° of speed to see your majesty!   *impetuosity*
KING JOHN   O cousin, thou art come to set° mine eye.   *close*
The tackle° of my heart is cracked and burnt,   *rigging (heartstrings)*
And all the shrouds° wherewith my life should sail   *sail ropes*
Are turnèd to one thread, one little hair;
55 My heart hath one poor string to stay° it by,   *support*
Which holds but till thy news be utterèd,
And then all this thou seest is but a clod
And module° of confounded° royalty.   *counterfeit / destroyed*
BASTARD   The Dauphin is preparing° hitherward,   *coming*
60 Where God He knows how we shall answer him;
For in a° night the best part of my power,   *a single*
As I upon° advantage did remove,   *to gain*
Were in the Washes all unwarily
Devourèd by the unexpected flood.
          [KING JOHN *dies*]
65 SALISBURY   You breathe these dead° news in as dead an ear.   *fatal*
          [*To* KING JOHN] My liege, my lord!—But° now a king, now thus.   *Just*
PRINCE HENRY   Even so must I run on, and even so stop.
What surety of the world, what hope, what stay,°   *support; continuation*
When this was now a king and now is clay?
70 BASTARD [*to* KING JOHN]   Art thou gone so? I do but stay behind
To do the office° for thee of revenge,   *duty*
And then my soul shall wait on° thee to heaven,   *follow*
As it on earth hath been thy servant still.°   *always*
          [*To the lords*] Now, now, you stars° that move in your right spheres,[4]   *(the nobles)*
75 Where be your powers?° Show now your mended faiths,°   *armies / loyalties*
And instantly return with me again,
To push destruction and perpetual shame
Out of the weak door of our fainting° land.   *dispirited*
Straight° let us seek, or straight we shall be sought.   *Immediately*
80 The Dauphin rages at our very heels.
SALISBURY   It seems you know not, then, so much as we.
The Cardinal Pandolf is within at rest,
Who half an hour since came from the Dauphin,
And brings from him such offers of our peace
85 As we with honour and respect may take,
With purpose presently° to leave this war.   *immediately*
BASTARD   He will the rather do it when he sees
Ourselves well-sinewed° to our own defence.   *strongly armed*
SALISBURY   Nay, 'tis in a manner done already,

4. Proper orbits, around the King, as the stars were thought to orbit the earth.

90 For many carriages° he hath dispatched   *vehicles*
   To the sea-side, and put his cause and quarrel
   To the disposing of the Cardinal,
   With° whom yourself, myself, and other lords,   *To*
   If you think meet,° this afternoon will post°   *fit / hurry*
95 To consummate° this business happily.   *conclude*
   BASTARD   Let it be so.—And you, my noble prince,
   With other princes° that may best be spared,   *nobles*
   Shall wait upon° your father's funeral.   *attend*
   PRINCE HENRY   At Worcester must his body be interred,
   For so he willed it.
100 BASTARD   Thither shall it then,
   And happily° may your sweet self put on   *with good fortune*
   The lineal state° and glory of the land,   *inherited kingship*
   To whom with all submission, on my knee,
   I do bequeath° my faithful services   *give*
105 And true subjection everlastingly.
                        [*He kneels*]
   SALISBURY   And the like tender° of our love we make,   *offer*
   To rest° without a spot° for evermore.   *remain / blemish*
                 [SALISBURY, PEMBROKE *and* BIGOT *kneel*]
   PRINCE HENRY   I have a kind of soul that would give thanks,
   And knows not how to do it but with tears.
                        [*He weeps*]
110 BASTARD [*rising*]   O, let us pay the time but needful° woe,   *only the necessary*
   Since it hath been beforehand with our griefs.⁵
   This England never did, nor never shall,
   Lie at the proud foot of a conqueror
   But° when it first did help to wound itself.   *Except*
115 Now these her princes are come home again,
   Come the three corners of the world⁶ in arms
   And we shall shock° them. Naught shall make us rue   *resist; repel*
   If England to itself do rest but true.
                  [*Flourish.*] *Exeunt* [*with the body*]

---

5. Since we have already suffered and grieved—   ing is now over.
perhaps with the additional implication that the suffer-   6. England itself is seen as the fourth corner.

I Henry IV

A roadside inn that fails to provide chamber pots for its customers, a castle in Wales where a magician summons spirits to be his musicians, the royal palace in London from which the King of England launches a campaign against rebel forces—these are but a few of the disparate venues where the action of *1 Henry IV* occurs. With this drama, the Shakespearean history play broadens out to encompass a rich diversity of languages, characters, and locales. Nothing in Shakespeare's earlier English histories quite anticipates this one. The great prose chronicles of the sixteenth century, such as Raphael Holinshed's *Chronicles of England, Scotland, and Ireland* (second edition, 1587), which Shakespeare consulted and whose materials he freely adapted and supplemented, stand behind all his history plays. The earlier plays, however, like the chronicles, focus primarily on the world of court and battlefield in which the monarch and his nobles appear as history's significant players, their rivalries and their achievements the focal point of the action. Common people such as Jack Cade have roles in these works, but their stories are typically subordinated to the monarchical plot. In *1 Henry IV*, something different happens. Several lines of action unfold at once, each connected to particular geographical locales, and each commenting upon, without simply displacing, the others. Henry IV, who had seized the throne from Richard II, is the play's title character, but from the start he is a beleaguered figure kept from his dream of making a Crusade to the Holy Land by discontent and rebellion among his nobles, especially the Percy family, and burdened with an oldest son, Prince Hal, who acts more like a prodigal child than the heir to the throne. The King appears in some key scenes, but for long stretches the action focuses on other characters and on places, like a common London tavern, that the King would never deign to visit.

Some events take place in the north of England, in the Northumberland stronghold of the Percy family. The play is set in the early fifteenth century, but even in the late sixteenth century the north of England was popularly regarded as lawless, wild, and linked to marginalized Catholic practices and beliefs, its nobility not fully incorporated into the increasingly centralized state being constructed by the Tudor monarchs. In 1569, members of the Percy family had been prominent in the Northern Rebellion, an attempt to overthrow Queen Elizabeth and put Mary Queen of Scots, a Catholic, on the throne. In drawing his portrait of the Percys, Shakespeare makes their champion, Hotspur, an impassioned embodiment of medieval chivalry, eager above all for honor and for the glory to be won in battle. While the historical Hotspur was actually much older than the King's son, Prince Hal, Shakespeare follows Samuel Daniel's poem *The Civile Wars Between the Two Houses of Lancaster and York* (1595) in making him Hal's coequal in years and his rival for preeminence in the kingdom. He is joined in rebellion by other figures from the threatening territories on the perimeter of England: by the Earl of Douglas, a formidable Scottish warrior, and by the Welshman Owain Glyndŵr, a self-proclaimed magician with a fiery temper, a lyrical temperament, and a daughter who marries Edmund Mortimer, the man presented in this play as Richard II's designated heir to the throne. Wales thus harbors both rebellion and the man who was arguably the legitimate King of England.

Another of the play's crucial locales is a tavern in Eastcheap, a commercial district in the east of London. This tavern is Prince Hal's second home where he comes to drink and amuse himself, and particularly to carouse with Falstaff, the dissipated knight who is the young Prince's tutor in folly, his intimate friend, and surrogate father. In Eastcheap, Hal rubs elbows with commoners such as Mistress Quickly, the Hostess,

The historical Owain Glyndŵr claimed the title of Prince of Wales. His great seal, both sides of which are shown here, bears the inscription "Owain, by the grace of God, prince of Wales" and depicts four upreared (rampant) lions, the coat of arms of the Gwynedd dynasty, to which Glyndŵr belonged.

and with Francis, the inarticulate apprentice tapster. Shakespeare took his cue about Hal's presence amid this crew from the many popular accounts of the Prince's dissolute youth, especially from a play printed in 1598 called *The Famous Victories of Henry the Fifth,* some version of which seems to have been staged in the late 1580s. It depicts not only episodes from Hal's madcap youth but also his eventual reformation and assumption of the throne. Shakespeare elaborated extensively on this story of youthful prodigality. Mistress Quickly, for example, is entirely his invention, and the character of Falstaff, while loosely modeled on a figure in *The Famous Victories,* is utterly transformed by Shakespeare into what has remained one of the great comic creations of the English theater. Witty, opportunistic, and utterly indifferent to the decorum expected of a knight of advanced years, Falstaff makes the tavern a place of perpetual play and the antithesis of the duty-driven world of the court. That the Prince seems irresistibly drawn to Eastcheap makes others, especially his father, question his fitness to rule, but the high-spirited playfulness of Falstaff's world suggests why the Prince might take refuge there from the demands of his public role and the exacting expectations of the King, his father.

One of the objections to English popular theater voiced by a contemporary poet, Sir Philip Sidney, was that it mingled clowns with kings in a way that violated codes of aesthetic and social decorum; these codes insisted on the strict separation of high and low subject matter, language, and people. In contrast to Sidney's dicta, *1 Henry IV* is thoroughly hybrid in its mingling of the high matter of rebellion and affairs of state with the low matter of drinking, jokes, and highway robbery. The play is also a temporal hybrid in that the tavern scenes seem to take place not in the early fifteenth century, when Henry IV was struggling to secure his rule, but more nearly in the late sixteenth century, when Shakespeare was actually writing his play. In the tavern scenes, for example, characters make fun of plays and modes of writing popular in the 1570s and 1580s, such as Thomas Preston's ranting tyrant play *Cambyses* (1569) and the baroquely ornate rhetoric popularized by John Lyly in his *Euphues* (1578). The tavern world is also filled with references to the commodities that passed through London's markets in the late sixteenth century. The characters there drink sack, Madeira, and bastard—popular alcoholic beverages, some (such as Madeira) imported from as far away as an island off the coast of west Africa; and they refer to articles of clothing, such as the Spanish-leather wallets and leather jerkins with crystal buttons, worn by London's aspiring mercantile classes. Eastcheap itself, where the tavern is located, was a major market street in Shakespeare's London, and the tavern scenes are steeped in references to the commercial culture, including the theatrical culture, of early modern England.

There is every indication, however, that if a Sidney would have found the hybridity of the play a problem, ordinary consumers did not. Judging by its publication history, in its own time *1 Henry IV* was one of Shakespeare's most popular plays. It appeared in two quarto versions in 1598 and then in five more before the First Folio was printed in 1623. Even after that, individual quarto editions of the play continued to appear. Part of its popularity undoubtedly derived from the fact that with *1 Henry IV,* the Shakespearean history play began to supplement chronicle history, which focuses on monarchs, nobles, and affairs of state, with chorography: that is, with a mode of writing popular in the late sixteenth century that described and surveyed the land of England focusing on the products, the terrain, and the customs of England's various regions. *1 Henry IV* is a chorography in the sense that while the play's distinct lines of action comment on one another, each is defined in relation to specific places, customs, and social groups. The commercial, bawdy world of the tavern, with its cast of lowlife characters and its rituals of drinking and play, is very different from the more formal milieu of Westminster, where the King and his nobles are immersed in the tasks of statecraft, and different again from the world of passion and magic centered in Glyndŵr's Welsh castle. Through the multiple plots, the spectator watching the play experiences the illusion of complex temporal simultaneity and social and geographic heterogeneity. Thus in successive scenes, the rebels, in Wales, plot the dismemberment of England and listen to a song sung in Welsh (3.1); King Henry, in Westminster, berates his wayward son (3.2); Falstaff, in Eastcheap, tries to cheat Mistress Quickly by claiming that his ring was stolen in her tavern (3.3). All these actions go on cotemporally but in widely disparate locales, creating a theatrical illusion of the diversity encompassed by the ongoing life of the nation and its bordering regions.

But the play's complex elaboration of difference also makes evident its monarch's central problem: how to maintain control over and enforce unity upon the territories over which he claims dominion but which threaten to break away or assert a worrisome autonomy. As in *Henry V,* Shakespeare here dramatizes the tension between efforts at nation building and the cultural, religious, and political differences that promote fragmentation. The problem of furthering national unity is especially pressing for Henry IV because he did not lineally inherit the throne; he seized it from Richard II. He is on shaky ground, then, should he attempt to unify England under the banner of his own legitimacy. In fact, for much of the play, Henry is a king in search of a strategy of rule. He had hoped to unify his people and quiet his conscience for his part in Richard's deposition and death by undertaking a Crusade to recover Jerusalem for European Christianity. But trouble at home keeps him from enacting his plan as rebellion bubbles up on the Scottish border, on the Welsh border, in the northern counties, and even in the Church, in the person of the Archbishop of York. The land seethes with the murmurings of rebels.

In the England of the 1590s, the monarch's most pressing problem of control was posed by Ireland; there, after 1595, the Earl of Tyrone led the challenge to English rule. Like Glyndŵr, Tyrone was educated in England and in some accounts was even Glyndŵr's descendant. While Ireland is not directly depicted in *1 Henry IV,* Hotspur verbally links Wales and Ireland. Urged to listen to a song sung in Welsh, he says that he would rather hear his hunting dog "howl in Irish" (3.1.232), thereby confirming the common English view that Welsh and Irish were equally barbarous languages. More important, Wales stands in the play as a displaced image of the contemporary Irish situation. In the popular imagination, Wales often seemed a foreign place of mystery and danger, even though it had been officially incorporated in England in the 1530s and the Welsh language banned as unnatural and barbarous. In *1 Henry IV,* Wales represents the threat not only of rebellion but also of effeminization and seduction. Mortimer, the supposed heir to the English throne, falls in love with Glyndŵr's daughter, promises to learn her language, and never appears on the battlefield against Henry's forces. In essence, he "goes native," a persistent fear voiced by the English concerning their soldiers and settlers in Ireland. The English had long worried that through prolonged contact with the Irish, English men and women might adopt their barbarous ways and forfeit their English identity. They even feared that their children, in drinking the milk of Irish wet nurses, could be transformed into people more Irish than English.

In *1 Henry IV*, the threat posed by the dangerous Welsh borderlands and by the northern Percy faction directly challenges the King's authority. Hampered by the questionable means by which he came to the throne, Henry ultimately finds force and guile the most effective instruments for maintaining his power. He can win battles, and he is willing to use deception to improve his position. At Shrewsbury, his major battle against the rebels, a number of Henry's nobles dress like the King, frustrating the enemy's ability to identify the true King and encouraging Henry's own forces by the seeming ubiquity of their monarch. Perpetual battle, however, is a costly way to rule, and having many nobles dress like him runs counter to Henry's stated belief that the King should be seldom seen in order to be the more wondered at when he does appear. To have many men marching in the King's clothing and answering to the King's name might, in fact, subversively suggest that "King" is a part any man could play, given the right accoutrements.

Prince Hal faces the pressing task of finding better strategies for ruling the changed world his father brought into being by his deposition of King Richard. He cannot assume that his kingship will be uncontested simply because he is Henry's son. A usurper's offspring has more legitimacy than a usurper, but not much. Rather, Hal must *make* himself King by a convincing performance of the part, and he must beat out those who would be his rivals, such as Harry Hotspur. Viewed one way, *1 Henry IV* is a study in the political and theatrical skills necessary for rule in a world where the inevitability and assumed legitimacy of inherited kingship has been called into question. In 1532, Niccolò Machiavelli's *The Prince,* a manual of practical statecraft, was published and quickly became notorious throughout Europe. Machiavelli taught rulers how to maintain their power through a mixture of guile, alliance, warfare, and personal force of character. Popularly viewed as irreligious and amoral, Machiavelli nonetheless was a byword for political pragmatism.

In his sophisticated manipulation of power, Hal shows himself a good student of Machiavelli, and the Machiavellian strand of his characterization has caused a split in critical assessments of him. To many, Hal personifies the ideal English king, the perfect mean between the self-indulgence of a Falstaff and the impassioned inflexibility of a Hotspur. He is thus an object of desire and emulation. Other critics focus on what they perceive as a lack of humanity at the heart of this consummate politician and recoil from his calculated use of other people to serve his own ends. For example, at the end of the first scene in which he appears, Hal in soliloquy speaks about his tavern mates:

> I know you all, and will a while uphold
> The unyoked humour of your idleness.
> Yet herein will I imitate the sun,
> Who doth permit the base contagious clouds
> To smother up his beauty from the world,
> That when he please again to be himself,
> Being wanted he may be more wondered at
> By breaking through the foul and ugly mists
> Of vapours that did seem to strangle him.
>
> (1.2.173–81)

These lines reveal the calculation that is one part of this character's representation. Comparing himself to the royal symbol, the sun, Hal casts his companions as the contaminating clouds and ugly mists that temporarily obscure his own radiance. Hal is chillingly disdainful of those he elsewhere treats as boon companions, but he also finds their baseness *useful,* since it will set in high relief his own glory, once he has cast them off.

Hal is an interesting dramatic character and not merely a personification of political expediency, however, precisely because his calculated use of his companions does not necessarily preclude his being attracted to them and to the world of play and good fellowship that they represent. In *1 Henry IV,* Hal is not yet King, and the moment of repudiation is not yet upon him. In this play, he can both enjoy his time in Eastcheap and also acquire skills there that he will need when he ascends his father's troubled throne. In the tavern, for example, he and Falstaff take turns playing King and Prince in a theatrical staging of the prodigal Hal's encounter with his reproving father. Hal rehearses the cadences and the sentiments of royal speech, trying out a part, learning to inhabit it convincingly. But it is not just his own part he masters. Unlike his father, Hal does not hold himself aloof from his would-be subjects. His ventures into Eastcheap are in part a mapping of one corner of England, a survey of the customs and strange languages of this locale. To Ned Poins he boasts that having been instructed by three tapsters in the terminology of drinking, "I can drink with any tinker in his own language during my life" (2.5.16–17).

In the tavern, Hal also meditates on the strange tongue of his great rival, Hotspur, whose impatient but impassioned speech Hal parodies:

> I am not yet of Percy's mind, the Hotspur of the North—he that kills me some six or seven dozen of Scots at a breakfast, washes his hands, and says to his wife, 'Fie upon this quiet life! I want work.' 'O my sweet Harry,' says she, 'how many hast thou killed today?' 'Give my roan horse a drench,' says he, and answers, 'Some fourteen,' an hour after; 'a trifle, a trifle.' I prithee call in Falstaff. I'll play Percy, and that damned brawn shall play Dame Mortimer his wife. (2.5.94–101)

Learning the language of others and rehearsing their tongues is, for Hal, one of the arts of power. He can—and later he will—repudiate some of those whose language and customs he has imbibed, making the repudiation a justification for his own rule. Knowing disorderliness, the King will use his office to punish it. He can also appropriate the language of others, as at Shrewsbury he appropriates the chivalric accents of Hotspur; or he can co-opt others to serve his own purposes by speaking to them in a tongue they can comprehend. By his own account, Hal is beloved of the tapsters who have taught him their language, and they have promised that when he is king, he "shall command all the good lads in Eastcheap" (2.5.12–13). Many of them he will eventually command in his wars in France. It can be argued, therefore, that there is a profound instrumentality to Hal's sojourn outside the court milieu that should be his "natural" home. He is acquiring theatrical skills, linguistic skills, and above all a knowledge of the diverse corners of an England he must rule by a mixture of charm, guile, and strategic severity—demonizing some subjects to win the loyalty of others, outstripping rivals by outdoing them at their own particular strengths.

Yet Hal is only part of this play, and *1 Henry IV*'s uniqueness consists in good part in the way it plays off one dramatic perspective, one line of action, against another. The young Prince is certainly the focus of the play's narrative of reform, and he is the only character who can move with seeming ease among the worlds of tavern, court, and battlefield. Yet even as he surveys and judges those around him, the play's structure of geographical juxtapositions and its vivid depiction of other characters and other modes of being invite the audience to submit the Prince himself to critical scrutiny. Consider, for example, 3.1 and 3.2, the scenes at the center of the play that take the audience first to Glyndŵr's castle in Wales, where he, Hotspur, Mortimer, and Worcester are plotting their rebellion, and then to the King's palace at Westminster to which Henry has summoned his son. The first scene graphically establishes the kingdom-cleaving threat posed by the rebels. They have a map and are planning how they will divide the territory of England into three parts. But the scene also establishes the danger, mystery, and beauty of this borderland. Glyndŵr is a man trained in occult arts who boasts that the earth shook at his birth and that he can summon spirits to do his bidding. Hotspur scoffs, but when Glyndŵr's daughter promises to sing in Welsh, Glyndŵr says:

> Do so, and those musicians that shall play to you
> Hang in the air a thousand leagues from hence,
> And straight they shall be here. Sit and attend.
> (3.1.220–22)

Three lines later, music plays, its origins a mystery. When Glyndŵr speaks, Wales seems a land of enchantment, haunted by spirits.

Wales is also a place where women are integral to the action as they seldom are elsewhere in the play. Except for Mistress Quickly, Kate Percy and Glyndŵr's daughter are the play's only two female characters; and 3.1, the play's only scene in which two women are onstage at the same time, is set in Wales and is largely Shakespeare's invention. In the chronicles, Glyndŵr, Mortimer, and Hotspur's proposed division of conquered territory is negotiated by representatives in the Archbishop of Bangor's house. By contrast, in 1 *Henry IV* it occurs at Glyndŵr's home with the women present. In short, Shakespeare went to some trouble to link the rebels with women—more specifically, with wives and daughters. The question is why. In part, the choice portrays the rebels, unlike the Lancastrians, as having private as well as public lives. Glyndŵr is fond of his daughter and worries about her happiness. Mortimer dotes on this same daughter and seems to have married her for love as much as for political alliance. Hotspur's affection for his wife is displayed through the teasing banter with which he persistently addresses her. Scornful of mooning lovers, he nonetheless is careful to take his wife with him when he journeys to Wales.

The passions so nakedly on display in 3.1 clearly signal the rebels' vulnerabilities. In the patriarchal thought of the period, men were presented as superior to women because they were supposedly more rational and less subject to their passions. If men loved women too much, they risked becoming effeminate—that is, *like* a woman in placing desire above reason, especially if that desire kept a man from performing his public duties, such as going to war. Hotspur prizes his masculinity and the public honor to be won in battle. He is contemptuous of the affected courtier who appeared at Holmedon after the fighting, demanding Hotspur's prisoners (1.3.28–68). In his dealings with his wife, Hotspur seems to use banter and jokes to maintain control of his affection for her. He would not, for a woman, forgo the man-to-man erotics of battle when, "hot horse to horse" (4.1.123), he clashes against the bosom of Prince Hal. Mortimer, by contrast, simply succumbs to the charms of the Welsh woman. He never appears in battle: Wales and a wife swallow him up.

This Welsh world of danger, mystery, and passion sits strangely against the world of calculation that unfolds immediately thereafter, when in 3.2 King Henry castigates Prince Hal for his dissolute life and together they discuss strategies of monarchical self-presentation. The throne room is a place not of enchantment but of business. No women are shown at court, and passion manifests itself most strongly as the desire to rule. Father and son are both preoccupied with the tactics and strategies by which they can most effectively command the loyalty of subjects. While Henry fears his son misunderstands the task before him, Hal shows that he is every bit as astute as his father. But after the high emotions and alluring lyricism of the Welsh scene, the throne room at Westminster can seem a pragmatic and claustrophobic space. In concentrating their energies on rule, Henry and Hal here are divorced from many things that give the rebel world its charm.

Falstaff and the tavern pose a different challenge to the values of Westminster. As critics have shown, the fat man's tutoring of Hal in riotous living mimics the pedagogical relationship of master to student that was sometimes eroticized in the early modern period. Much of the poignancy of the play's depiction of the friendship between the two comes from the tension between their apparent intimacy and the Prince's stated intention to repudiate his companion. Falstaff's threat to monarchical values is obvious. Against the future-oriented calculations of Hal and his father, he insists on living in the present. As his huge body testifies, he demands the immediate gratification of physical desires. To eat, drink, and jest—these are pleasures that for Falstaff brook no delay. Hal can discipline himself. He is thin, as Falstaff points out, and he can plot a personal reformation sometime far in the future and work toward that end. Falstaff cannot or will not; and yet, while a figure of disorder, he has for many readers been the play's most interesting and memorable character. Aside from Hamlet, no other

Falstaff and Prince Hal. Pen and watercolor drawing on paper by William Blake (c. 1780).

Shakespearean figure has attracted as much critical attention as the fat knight.

When Shakespeare first wrote the play, he called this character Sir John Oldcastle. The choice was unfortunate, for the Cobham family, descendants of the historical Oldcastle, protested. William Brooke, the tenth Baron Cobham, had been Lord Chamberlain from August 1596 to March 1597, the very months when most scholars believe Shakespeare completed *1 Henry IV.* Since the Lord Chamberlain oversaw the licensing of plays through the office of the Master of the Revels, Cobham was in an especially favorable position to object to this comic rendition of his ancestor. Shakespeare apparently changed the character's name in response to this act of censorship, though traces of his original intentions can be discerned, including the fact that in 1.2.37–38 Falstaff is still referred to as "my old lad of the castle." In addition, in the first complete Quarto of *1 Henry IV,* there are a few traces of the fact that Peto once bore the name "Harvey," and Bardolph the name "Russell." Again, the objections of powerful figures may have forced changes. "Russell" was the family name of the prominent earls of Bedford, and "Harvey" the name of the stepfather of the Earl of Southampton.

Recently, some critics (including the editors of the Oxford text) have argued that the names "Peto," "Bardolph," and "Falstaff" should be replaced by the names Shakespeare originally intended—namely, "Harvey," "Russell," and "Oldcastle." They suggest that such a replacement would undo an act of censorship that thwarted Shakespeare's original intentions. This edition retains the substituted names primarily because these are the names Shakespeare consistently used after the initial act of censorship, and they have become part of the textual and dramatic history of this and other plays. While it is important to point out that an act of censorship occurred, to "undo" it creates new erasures in the textual and cultural history of the play. For Shakespeare, "Falstaff," not "Oldcastle," became the word linking the various textual manifestations of his fat knight as he appeared both in *1* and *2 Henry IV* and then in *The Merry Wives of Windsor.*

It is of interest, however, to ask why Shakespeare first used the name "Oldcastle" in his play. The historical Oldcastle was a knight who served Henry IV in battle in both France and Wales, but who was also a Lollard; that is, he was connected with the religious group often seen as a forerunner of English Protestantism for its critiques of the Catholic Church and its advocacy of a vernacular Bible to be made available to lay people. At first, Henry IV treated Oldcastle's religious views leniently, but eventually Oldcastle was sent to the Tower of London and condemned as a heretic by the Archbishop of Canterbury. He escaped, and Henry was warned that Oldcastle was leading an armed force against him. Oldcastle was captured in 1417 and eventually hung in chains and then burned on the gallows.

This knight suggests Shakespeare's portrait of the chivalric heroes Prince Hal and Hotspur at the battle of Shrewsbury. From Henry Peacham's *Minerva Britanna* (1612).

In the sixteenth century, how one viewed Oldcastle depended largely on one's religious perspective. To many zealous Protestants, such as John Foxe, Oldcastle was a Protestant hero, a victim of Catholic oppression rather than a traitor; Foxe included Oldcastle in his *Book of Martyrs*. But by the 1590s, Lollards were also sometimes linked with "extremist" Protestant groups pushing for radical reforms in the Church of England. Making a well-known Lollard martyr a fat figure of disorder therefore did not necessarily signal Catholic sympathies. It might simply be a way of suggesting the hypocrisy of zealous reformers. In other plays, especially in his portrait of Malvolio in *Twelfth Night*, Shakespeare makes fun of "Puritans" who claimed a greater righteousness and strictness of life than their more moderate contemporaries. In *1 Henry IV*, Falstaff's language is liberally studded with biblical quotations, most of which he misapplies or contradicts by his behavior. Thus he tells Hal that one must labor in one's vocation (1.2.92–93), an injunction found in 1 Corinthians 7:20 and in Ephesians 4:1. But the vocation in which *he* would labor is that of thief—not exactly what Protestant divines meant when discussing the virtues of a vocation. Moreover, by making Falstaff so obviously a glutton and lover of sack, Shakespeare could be making fun of the hypocrisy of Puritans, as Ben Jonson was to do in *Bartholomew Fair* and Thomas Middleton in *A Chaste Maid in Cheapside*.

The name Shakespeare fastened upon to replace Oldcastle had its own history. The historical Fastolf (1378?–1459) was a courageous officer in Henry VI's war in France, though in some chronicles he appears erroneously to have been called a coward, a detail that Shakespeare repeats in *1 Henry VI*. Having once used the name without repercussion in the former play, Shakespeare may have felt it was safe to employ it as a replacement for "Oldcastle" and to play upon the figure's reputation for cowardice.

Yet it may be a mistake to connect Shakespeare's character too strictly to any historical counterpart. As scholarship has shown, Falstaff is a rich amalgam of popular and literary traditions. In part, he resembles the irreverent Vice figure from the medieval morality plays. Traditionally, the Vice, a comic and clever character, tempted the hero to sin while voices of virtue or duty tried to steer him along a more reputable path. In *1 Henry IV*, Hal is torn between his allegiances to Falstaff and his father, to vice and virtue, to the tavern and the court. Falstaff also conjures up the topsy-turvy world of Carnival in which rulers were temporarily displaced and the body's pleasures (eating, drinking, breaking wind, having sex) were celebrated before the arrival of abstemious Lent. The unending jokes about Falstaff's fat paunch highlight his symbolic connection to bodily excess, and his contempt for the law and for military duty make him the antithesis of the King and a perpetual emblem of disorder. In creating Falstaff, Shakespeare also drew on the figure from classical tradition of the braggart warrior who is really a coward. At Shrewsbury, Falstaff plays the coward, and yet he falsely claims credit for having killed Hotspur. The gap between his words and his deeds is enormous, though in this instance, as in many others, the Prince graciously does not reveal this lie for what it is. Above all, however, Falstaff embodies traditions of popular critique associated with the stage clown. In early productions, Will Kemp, the famous clown in Shakespeare's company, probably played the part. Sometimes speaking from a downstage position near the audience, the clown traditionally poked fun at upstage author-ity figures. Falstaff does so in spades, whether mocking the elevated speech of King Henry or twitting Hal for being so skinny. But Falstaff is more than a gadfly or a para-site swollen fat on others' folly. He also embodies a mode of being in the world that serves as a powerful alternative both to the calculations of Hal and to Hotspur's head-long, death-courting pursuit of honor. For example, before the Battle of Shrewsbury Falstaff meditates witheringly on just what honor means and on its value:

> Can honour set-to a leg? No. Or an arm? No. Or take away the grief of a wound? No. Honour hath no skill in surgery, then? No. What is honour? A word. What is in that word 'honour'? What is that 'honour'? Air. A trim reckoning! Who hath it? He that died o'Wednesday. Doth he feel it? No. Doth he hear it? No. 'Tis insensible then? Yea, to the dead. But will it not live with the living? No. Why? Detraction will not suffer it. Therefore I'll none of it. Honour is a mere scutcheon. And so ends my catechism. (5.1.130–39)

Others, like Hotspur, find honor worth dying for, and generations of men have gone into battle believing the same thing. But for Falstaff, honor is worth the loss of neither a leg nor a life. During the ensuing battle, Falstaff carries a bottle of sack in his pistol case and ingloriously feigns death when attacked by Douglas. But though Hotspur and others are slain, Falstaff rises up. He embraces neither honor nor death, but life, and many readers and theatergoers have cheered his choice while others have been repulsed by his opportunism and cowardice.

Shrewsbury, then, is not only the place where the play's disparate strands of action come together as the King, Prince Hal, Hotspur, and even Falstaff assemble in one spot; it is also where the audience is invited to judge the relative worth of the values embraced by these different characters. Among those who fare well is Prince Hal. Shrewsbury is perhaps his happiest hour. During the battle, he finds a way to redeem his reputation and distinguish himself from Falstaff without being forced to repudiate his friend, just as he kills Hotspur while paying homage to his courage. But the equipoise of this battle's conclusion is precarious. Hal is not yet king and must still delay his assumption of the throne. Falstaff has not reformed and probably never will. And the rebels have not been destroyed. Hotspur is dead, but the Archbishop of York, Glyndŵr, and Mortimer are still in arms. In other words, it is an illusion that Hal has carried all before him. In the corners and crevices of the realm, dissension and differ-ence remain. In such conditions, the work of rule is a performance with no end.

JEAN E. HOWARD

TEXTUAL NOTE

The first quarto edition of *1 Henry IV* was printed in 1598. Only a fragment, compris-ing 1.3.199 through 2.3.19 of a single copy, now remains. This Quarto, usually desig-nated as Q0 but in the Oxford edition called Q1, was the basis for a second quarto edition printed later in 1598. This text, Q2, serves as the control text for most modern editions. The manuscript behind Q1 does not seem to have been marked up for the the-ater, so it was probably not the promptbook. The manuscript was either a corrected copy of Shakespeare's "foul papers" or, more probably, a transcription of them made by a pro-fessional scribe. This manuscript was prepared with unusual care, perhaps to show that changes required by the Master of the Revels had been made in the text. Originally, the characters Falstaff, Peto, and Bardolph had been assigned the names "Oldcastle," "Har-vey," and "Russell." Objections from the Cobham family, descendants of Oldcastle, and perhaps from other powerful people seem to have forced Shakespeare to change these names (see the Introduction for a fuller discussion of this act of censorship).

Five other quarto editions were published, in 1599, 1604, 1608, 1613, and 1622, before the publication of the First Folio (F) in 1623. These all derive from Q2 and have no independent authority. The Folio text derives from the 1613 Quarto, but act and scene divisions were added, speech prefixes and stage directions altered, and oaths were softened or removed and biblical allusions altered in compliance with the 1606 edict forbidding profanity on the stage. The party responsible for these changes is uncertain. Some changes may have been made by the compositors who set the text or by someone acting as editor (perhaps John Heminges or Henry Condell, Shakespeare's fellow share-holders in the King's Men who oversaw the production of the First Folio). The Oxford editors plausibly argue that these changes may in part derive from a manuscript pre-pared by the same scribe who prepared a similarly "literary" manuscript for *2 Henry IV*—that is, a manuscript less attuned to playhouse requirements than to the ration-alization of the text as a written document. This scribal manuscript may itself have derived from a promptbook whose theatrical features were largely obscured by the tran-scription. The Oxford editors also believe that a few of the changes made in F may reflect Shakespeare's own revisions of Q.

The act and scene divisions of F are followed except for the marking of new scenes at 2.3 and 5.3. The latter scene break, regularly inserted in most modern editions, indi-cates a clearing of the stage in the middle of the Battle of Shrewsbury; 2.3 is added to mark the moment at Gad's Hill when, Falstaff and his friends having led off the travel-ers they have captured, Hal and Poins come onstage disguised in their buckram suits.

As explained in the Introduction, for this play Norton is using the names "Falstaff," "Peto," and "Bardolph" (rather than Oxford's "Oldcastle," "Harvey," and "Russell"). Consequently, Oxford speech prefixes and stage directions, and in a few places the Oxford text, have been silently altered where these three characters are concerned in order to return to the names and language appearing in the printed quarto texts of 1598. Textual deviations from Q are marked in the variants, and Norton's standardiza-tion of quarto speech prefixes is delineated immediately before those variants. In par-ticular, "Falstaff," rather than Oxford's "Sir John," has been used in speech prefixes in this play as well as in *2 Henry IV*.

SELECTED BIBLIOGRAPHY

Barber, C. L. "Rule and Misrule in *Henry IV*." *Shakespeare's Festive Comedy: A Study of Dramatic Form and Its Relation to Social Custom.* Princeton: Princeton University Press, 1959. 192–221. Explores the ritual subtext of *Henry IV, Parts I and II*, argu-ing that Falstaff becomes a scapegoat whose banishment rids the community of bad luck.

Barker, Roberta. "Tragical-Comical-Historical Hotspur." *Shakespeare Quarterly* 54 (2003): 288–307. Examines how Hotspur has been interpreted through the cen-turies and argues that the role is central to the play's examination of masculine hero-ism.

Greenblatt, Stephen. "Invisible Bullets." *Shakespearean Negotiations: The Circulation of Social Energy in Renaissance England.* Berkeley: University of California Press, 1988. 21–65. Discusses how Renaissance texts such as Thomas Hariot's *A Brief and True Report of the New Found Land of Virginia* and Shakespeare's *1 Henry IV* sub-vert their culture's dominant values regarding religious belief and political author-ity and yet contain or mitigate the doubts they raise.

Greenfield, Matthew. "*1 Henry IV*: Metatheatrical Britain." *British Identities and En-glish Renaissance Literature.* Ed. David J. Baker and Willy Maley. New York: Cam-bridge University Press, 2002. 71–80. Discusses the interplay of different characters, locales, and genres in the play, arguing that it fails to create a single onstage community but instead reveals the distance between groups.

Highley, Christopher. "Wales, Ireland, and *1 Henry IV*." *Renaissance Drama*, n.s., 21 (1990): 91–114. Discusses England's Elizabethan wars in Ireland as a subtext for

1 Henry IV and Glyndŵr as a displaced image of the Irish leader Hugh O'Neill, Earl of Tyrone.

Howard, Jean E., and Phyllis Rackin. "Gender and Nation: Anticipations of Modernity in the Second Tetralogy." *Engendering a Nation: A Feminist Account of Shakespeare's English Histories*. London: Routledge, 1997. 137–215. Focuses on the disruptive role of women in the play, both the Welsh women, including Glyndŵr's daughter, and the women of the Eastcheap tavern.

Kastan, David Scott. "'The King Hath Many Marching in His Coats'; or, What Did You Do During the War, Daddy?" *Shakespeare Left and Right*. Ed. Ivo Kamps. New York: Routledge, 1991. 241–58. Argues that the theater does not just reproduce the political ideologies of the powerful but instead makes space for unauthorized and heterogeneous views, including, in *Henry IV*, the view that kingship itself is just a role.

Laroque, François. "Shakespeare's 'Battle of Carnival and Lent': The Falstaff Scenes Reconsidered (*1* and *2 Henry IV*)." *Shakespeare and Carnival: After Bakhtin*. Ed. Ronald Knowles. New York: St. Martin's, 1998. 83–96. Discusses the connections between Shakespeare's *Henry IV* plays and the opposition in Carnival between the fat and the lean, Falstaff and the Prince.

McMillin, Scott. *Henry IV, Part One*. Shakespeare in Performance series. Manchester: Manchester University Press, 1991. Analyzes theatrical, film, and television performances of *1 Henry IV* in the second half of the twentieth century, arguing that this is the period when Hal, rather than Falstaff or Hotspur, became the focus of critical and theatrical attention.

Mullaney, Steven. "The Rehearsal of Cultures." *The Place of the Stage: License, Play, and Power in Renaissance England*. Chicago: University of Chicago Press, 1988. 60–87. Discusses the sixteenth-century fascination with collecting artifacts from distant cultures and argues that the stage also represented and rehearsed otherness.

FILMS

Chimes at Midnight. 1965. Dir. Orson Welles. UK. 115 min. In black and white, the film combines scenes from several plays to focus on Falstaff and his relationship with Prince Hal. An imaginative and moving adaptation, it boasts memorable performances by Welles as Falstaff, John Gielgud as Henry IV, and Keith Baxter as the Prince.

Henry IV, Part I. 1979. Dir. David Giles. UK. 155 min. A BBC-TV production with strong performances by Anthony Quayle as Falstaff and Tim Pigott-Smith as Hotspur in an otherwise dutifully faithful version of the play.

My Own Private Idaho. 1991. Dir. Gus Van Sant. USA. 102 min. Set in modern-day Portland, Oregon, and loosely based on the *Henry IV* plays, the film stars River Phoenix and Keanu Reeves as two young men who for a time join William Richert, the Falstaff figure, in a life of dissipation.

The History of Henry the Fourth

THE PERSONS OF THE PLAY

KING HENRY IV

PRINCE HARRY, Prince of Wales,
  familiarly known as Hal

Lord JOHN OF LANCASTER

    } King Henry's sons

Earl of WESTMORLAND

Sir Walter BLUNT

Earl of WORCESTER

Percy, Earl of NORTHUMBERLAND, his brother

Henry Percy, known as HOTSPUR,
  Northumberland's son

Kate, LADY PERCY, Hotspur's wife

Lord Edmund MORTIMER, called Earl of March,
  Lady Percy's brother

LADY MORTIMER, his wife

Owain GLYNDŴR, Lady Mortimer's father

Earl of DOUGLAS

Sir Richard VERNON

Scrope, ARCHBISHOP of York

SIR MICHAEL, a member of the Archbishop's
  household

    } rebels against King Henry

Sir John FALSTAFF

Edward (Ned) POINS

BARDOLPH

PETO

Mistress Quickly, HOSTESS of
  a tavern in Eastcheap

FRANCIS, a drawer

VINTNER

    } associates of Prince Harry

GADSHILL

CARRIERS

CHAMBERLAIN

OSTLER

TRAVELLERS

SHERIFF

MESSENGERS

SERVANT

Lords, soldiers

1.1

Enter KING [HENRY], *Lord* JOHN OF LANCASTER, [*and
the*] *Earl of* WESTMORLAND, *with other* [*lords*]

KING HENRY So shaken as we are, so wan with care,
  Find we° a time for frighted peace to pant   *Let us find*
  And breathe short-winded accents° of new broils   *words*

1.1 Location: The palace, London.

606

To be commenced in strands afar remote.[1]
5   No more the thirsty entrance° of this soil   *parched mouth*
    Shall daub her lips with her own children's blood.
    No more shall trenching° war channel° her fields,   *cutting / furrow*
    Nor bruise her flow'rets with the armèd hoofs
    Of hostile paces.° Those opposèd eyes,   *horses' footsteps*
10 Which, like the meteors of a troubled heaven,[2]
    All of one nature, of one substance bred,
    Did lately meet in the intestine° shock   *internal*
    And furious close° of civil butchery,   *hand-to-hand combat*
    Shall now in mutual well-beseeming° ranks   *orderly*
15 March all one way, and be no more opposed
    Against acquaintance, kindred, and allies.
    The edge of war, like an ill-sheathèd knife,
    No more shall cut his master. Therefore, friends,
    As far as to the sepulchre of Christ—
20 Whose soldier now, under whose blessèd cross
    We are impressèd° and engaged to fight—   *conscripted*
    Forthwith a power of English shall we levy,
    Whose arms were moulded in their mothers' womb
    To chase these pagans in those holy fields
25 Over whose acres walked those blessèd feet
    Which fourteen hundred years ago were nailed,
    For our advantage, on the bitter cross.
    But this our purpose now is twelve month old,
    And bootless° 'tis to tell you we will go.   *useless*
30 Therefor° we meet not now. Then let me hear   *On that account*
    Of you, my gentle cousin° Westmorland,   *my noble kinsman*
    What yesternight our Council did decree
    In forwarding this dear expedience.°   *urgent undertaking*
WESTMORLAND   My liege, this haste was hot in question,°   *under urgent debate*
35 And many limits of the charge[3] set down
    But yesternight, when all athwart° there came   *at cross-purposes*
    A post° from Wales, loaden with heavy news,   *messenger*
    Whose worst was that the noble Mortimer,
    Leading the men of Herefordshire to fight
40 Against the irregular and wild Glyndŵr,[4]
    Was by the rude hands of that Welshman taken,
    A thousand of his people butcherèd,
    Upon whose dead corpse'° there was such misuse,   *corpses*
    Such beastly shameless transformation,[5]
45 By those Welshwomen done as may not be
    Without much shame retold or spoken of.
KING HENRY   It seems then that the tidings of this broil
    Brake° off our business for the Holy Land.   *Broke*

1. On distant shores. King Henry is alluding to the Holy Land, to which he vowed to lead a crusade at the close of *Richard II*.
2. Unusual events in the sky, such as comets or shooting stars, were thought to portend strife and disaster.
3. Many particulars concerning responsibilities and expenses.
4. In most editions, Glyndŵr's name is given as "Glendower," an anglicized version of the Welsh word used in this text. Glyndŵr is probably "irregular" in the sense of using guerrilla tactics in his warfare; possibly, the word alludes to his alleged sorcery.
5. Mutilation. Holinshed's 1587 *Chronicles*, one of Shakespeare's sources, says the Welsh women's acts on this occasion were too shameful to relate, but contemporary editor Abraham Fleming, in the same edition of the *Chronicles*, includes an account of another battle in which Welsh women cut off the sexual organs and the noses of conquered enemies and put them, respectively, in the mouths and anuses of those enemies.

WESTMORLAND   This matched with other did, my gracious lord,

50   For more uneven° and unwelcome news   *disturbing*

      Came from the north, and thus it did import:

      On Holy-rood day⁶ the gallant Hotspur there—

      Young Harry Percy—and brave Archibald,

      That ever valiant and approvèd° Scot,   *worthy*

55   At Holmedon⁷ met,

      Where they did spend a sad and bloody hour,

      As by° discharge of their artillery   *As judging by*

      And shape of likelihood° the news was told;   *And probable outcome*

      For he that brought them° in the very heat   *(the news)*

60   And pride° of their contention did take horse,   *height*

      Uncertain of the issue° any way.   *outcome*

KING HENRY   Here is a dear, a true industrious friend,

      Sir Walter Blunt,⁸ new lighted from his horse,

      Stained with the variation of each soil

65   Betwixt that Holmedon and this seat° of ours;   *dwelling*

      And he hath brought us smooth° and welcome news.   *agreeable*

      The Earl of Douglas is discomfited.

      Ten thousand bold Scots, two-and-twenty knights,

      Balked° in their own blood did Sir Walter see   *Heaped up; thwarted*

70   On Holmedon's plains. Of prisoners Hotspur took

      Mordake the Earl of Fife and eldest son

      To beaten Douglas,⁹ and the Earl of Athol,

      Of Moray, Angus, and Menteith;

      And is not this an honourable spoil,

75   A gallant prize? Ha, cousin, is it not?

WESTMORLAND   In faith, it is a conquest for a prince to boast of.

KING HENRY   Yea, there thou mak'st me sad, and mak'st me sin

      In envy that my lord Northumberland

      Should be the father to so blest a son—

80   A son who is the theme of honour's tongue,

      Amongst a grove the very straightest plant,

      Who is sweet Fortune's minion° and her pride—   *favorite*

      Whilst I by looking on the praise of him

      See riot and dishonour stain the brow

85   Of my young Harry. O, that it could be proved

      That some night-tripping fairy¹ had exchanged

      In cradle clothes our children where they lay,

      And called mine Percy, his Plantagenet! ²

      Then would I have his Harry, and he mine.

90   But let him° from my thoughts. What think you, coz,° *let him go / kinsman*

      Of this young Percy's pride? The prisoners

      Which he in this adventure hath surprised°   *captured*

      To his own use³ he keeps, and sends me word

---

6. Holy Cross Day, September 14.

7. Holmedon (also spelled "Humbleton") in Northumberland was the site in 1402 of a Scottish invasion of England.

8. It is not clear whether Blunt comes onstage now. He could have entered at the beginning of the scene; alternatively, as in this edition, he may not come onstage at all. Blunt has no lines in the scene, and Henry could at this point receive a letter containing Blunt's news or could be reporting news he has already learned. "Here" would thus refer in a general way to Blunt's being at

court.

9. Mordrake was not actually Douglas's son, but an understandable misreading of Holinshed led Shakespeare to believe he was.

1. It was popularly believed that fairies stole beautiful children and left bad or malformed ones in their place.

2. Henry was descended from the Plantagenet dynasty; and the Percys were a distinguished family from the north of England to which Hotspur belonged.

3. Prisoners were routinely used as a source of revenue.

I shall have none but Mordake Earl of Fife.

95 WESTMORLAND   This is his uncle's teaching. This is Worcester,
Malevolent to you in all aspects,[4]
Which makes him prune[5] himself, and bristle up
The crest of youth against your dignity.

KING HENRY   But I have sent for him to answer this;
100 And for this cause awhile we must neglect
Our holy purpose to Jerusalem.
Cousin, on Wednesday next our Council we
Will hold at Windsor. So inform the lords.
But come yourself with speed to us again,
105 For more is to be said and to be done
Than out of anger can be utterèd.

WESTMORLAND   I will, my liege.

Exeunt [KING HENRY, LANCASTER, *and other lords
at one door*; WESTMORLAND *at another door*]

1.2

Enter [HARRY][1] *Prince of Wales and Sir John* FALSTAFF[2]

FALSTAFF   Now, Hal, what time of day is it, lad?

PRINCE HARRY   Thou art so fat-witted° with drinking of old   *thick-witted*
sack,[3] and unbuttoning thee after supper, and sleeping upon
benches after noon, that thou hast forgotten to demand that
5 truly which thou wouldst truly know. What a devil hast thou to
do with the time of the day? Unless hours were cups of sack, and
minutes capons,[4] and clocks the tongues of bawds, and dials°   *clock faces; sundials*
the signs of leaping-houses,° and the blessed sun himself a   *brothels*
fair hot wench in flame-coloured taffeta,[5] I see no reason why
10 thou shouldst be so superfluous° to demand the time of the day.   *needlessly curious*

FALSTAFF   Indeed you come near me° now, Hal, for we that take   *are near the mark*
purses go by the moon and the seven stars,[6] and not 'By Phoe-
bus, he, that wand'ring knight so fair'.[7] And I prithee, sweet
wag,° when thou art a king, as God save thy grace—'majesty'   *mischievous boy*
15 I should say, for grace[8] thou wilt have none—

PRINCE HARRY   What, none?

FALSTAFF   No, by my troth, not so much as will serve to be prologue to an egg and butter.[9]

PRINCE HARRY   Well, how then? Come, roundly,° roundly.   *to the point*

20 FALSTAFF   Marry° then, sweet wag, when thou art king let not   *By Mary (a mild oath)*
us that are squires of the night's body[1] be called thieves of the

4. Habitually hostile to you. The line suggests that Worcester is a planet whose influence is always harmful, whatever his position, or "aspect," in the sky.
5. A term from falconry suggesting the hawk's trimming of its feathers as preparation for action.
1.2 Location: A room in the Prince's apartments, London.
1. F's stage direction reads, "Henry Prince of Wales"; Q reads, "prince of Wales." Norton speech prefixes refer to this character as "Prince Harry," and the same designation is used, as here, in stage directions.
2. See Introduction and Textual Note for a discussion of Falstaff's name.
3. Spanish white wine.
4. Castrated male chickens (an Elizabethan delicacy).
5. Silk cloth, which in some contexts was associated

6. The constellation known as the Pleiades. *go by the moon*: go about at moonlight; tell time by the light of the moon.
7. Evidently a line from a contemporary ballad or romance about Phoebus, the sun god of classical mythology.
8. Virtue; with a pun also on "grace" as meaning "God's favor" and "a prayer before meals." Falstaff asserts that Hal has none of these and so must be called "your majesty," rather than "your grace," which was also a title of honor.
9. *egg and butter*: a mere snack needing only the shortest grace.
1. Let not we who steal by night. Falstaff alludes to the attendants of knights known as "squires of the body."

day's beauty. Let us be 'Diana's foresters',[2] 'gentlemen of the
shade', 'minions of the moon', and let men say we be men of
good government,° being governed, as the sea is, by our noble   *conduct*

25 and chaste mistress the moon, under whose countenance° we   *face; protection*
steal.

PRINCE HARRY   Thou sayst well, and it holds well° too, for the   *the comparison is apt*
fortune of us that are the moon's men doth ebb and flow like
the sea, being governed as the sea is by the moon. As for proof

30 now: a purse of gold most resolutely snatched on Monday
night, and most dissolutely spent on Tuesday morning; got
with swearing 'lay by!',[3] and spent with crying 'bring in!';[4] now
in as low an ebb as the foot of the ladder, and by and by in as
high a flow as the ridge° of the gallows.[5]   *crossbar*

35 FALSTAFF   By the Lord, thou sayst true, lad; and is not my Hostess of the tavern a most sweet wench?

PRINCE HARRY   As the honey of Hybla,[6] my old lad of the cas-
tle;[7] and is not a buff jerkin[8] a most sweet robe of durance?°   *durability; imprisonment*

FALSTAFF   How now, how now, mad wag? What, in thy quips

40 and thy quiddities?° What a plague have I to do with a buff   *quibbles (wordplay)*
jerkin?

PRINCE HARRY   Why, what a pox[9] have I to do with my Hostess
of the tavern?

FALSTAFF   Well, thou hast called her to a reckoning[1] many a

45 time and oft.

PRINCE HARRY   Did I ever call for thee to pay thy part?[2]

FALSTAFF   No, I'll give thee thy due, thou hast paid all there.

PRINCE HARRY   Yea, and elsewhere so far as my coin would
stretch;[3] and where it would not, I have used my credit.

50 FALSTAFF   Yea, and so used it that were it not here apparent that
thou art heir apparent—but I prithee, sweet wag, shall there
be gallows standing in England when thou art king, and resolution thus fubbed[4] as it is with the rusty curb of old father
Antic° the law? Do not thou when thou art king hang a thief.   *buffoon*

55 PRINCE HARRY   No, thou shalt.

FALSTAFF   Shall I? O, rare! By the Lord, I'll be a brave° judge!   *fine; well-dressed*

PRINCE HARRY   Thou judgest false already. I mean thou shalt
have the hanging of the thieves, and so become a rare hangman.

60 FALSTAFF   Well, Hal, well; and in some sort it jumps° with my   *agrees*
humour° as well as waiting in the court,[5] I can tell you.   *temperament*

PRINCE HARRY   For obtaining of suits?[6]

---

2. Hunters by moonlight; thieves. In classical mythology, Diana was goddess of the moon.
3. A thief's cry similar to "Hands up!"
4. A tavern customer's call for more food or wine.
5. The Prince's speech is riddled with sexual slang,
including "purse" (line 30) as meaning "vagina" or
"scrotum"; "snatched" (line 30) as "forcibly had sexual
relations with"; "spent" (line 31) as "exhausted by sexual activity"; "lay by" (line 32) as "lie back"; "spent with"
(line 32) as "reached orgasm with"; and "low" (line 33)
and "high" (line 34) as referring to a penis, first limp
and then erect.
6. Region of Sicily renowned for its honey.
7. Slang for "roisterer"; also a play on the name "Old-

castle" (see Introduction).
8. Leather jacket often worn by jailers.
9. The equivalent of "what the devil." The pox literally
was plague or syphilis.
1. You have asked that she present the bill; asked that
she show her value sexually.
2. To pay your bill; to use your penis.
3. So far as my money would go; so far as my ability to
engender, or "coin," a child would take me.
4. And valor (of thieves) thus thwarted.
5. Being in attendance at the royal court or at the court
of justices.
6. Petitions; clothing. The hangman was entitled to
claim the victims' clothing.

FALSTAFF   Yea, for obtaining of suits, whereof the hangman
hath no lean wardrobe. 'Sblood,[7] I am as melancholy as a gib
65 cat,° or a lugged bear.[8]   *tomcat*

PRINCE HARRY   Or an old lion, or a lover's lute.

FALSTAFF   Yea, or the drone of a Lincolnshire bagpipe.

PRINCE HARRY   What sayst thou to a hare,[9] or the melancholy of
Moor-ditch?[1]

70 FALSTAFF   Thou hast the most unsavoury similes, and art
indeed the most comparative,° rascalliest sweet young Prince.   *quick at comparisons*
But Hal, I prithee trouble me no more with vanity.° I would   *worthless things*
to God thou and I knew where a commodity° of good names°   *supply / reputations*
were to be bought. An old lord of the Council rated me the
75 other day in the street about you, sir, but I marked him not;
and yet he talked very wisely, but I regarded him not; and yet
he talked wisely, and in the street too.

PRINCE HARRY   Thou didst well, for wisdom cries out in the
streets, and no man regards it.[2]

80 FALSTAFF   O, thou hast damnable iteration,[3] and art indeed
able to corrupt a saint. Thou hast done much harm upon me,
Hal, God forgive thee for it. Before I knew thee, Hal, I knew
nothing; and now am I, if a man should speak truly, little better than one of the wicked. I must give over this life, and I will
85 give it over. By the Lord, an° I do not, I am a villain. I'll be   *if*
damned for never a° king's son in Christendom.   *for no*

PRINCE HARRY   Where shall we take a purse tomorrow, Jack?

FALSTAFF   Zounds,[4] where thou wilt, lad! I'll make one;° an I do   *I'll take part*
not, call me villain and baffle me.[5]

90 PRINCE HARRY   I see a good amendment of life in thee, from
praying to purse-taking.

FALSTAFF   Why, Hal, 'tis my vocation,° Hal. 'Tis no sin for a   *calling*
man to labour in his vocation.[6]

Enter POINS

Poins! Now shall we know if Gadshill[7] have set a match.° O,   *planned a theft*
95 if men were to be saved by merit,[8] what hole in hell were hot
enough for him? This is the most omnipotent villain that ever
cried 'Stand!' to a true° man.   *an honest*

PRINCE HARRY   Good morrow, Ned.

POINS   Good morrow, sweet Hal. [*To* FALSTAFF]   What says
100 Monsieur Remorse? What says Sir John, sack-and-sugar
Jack?[9] How agrees the devil and thee about thy soul, that thou
soldest him on Good Friday[1] last, for a cup of Madeira[2] and a
cold capon's leg?

---

7. By His blood (an oath alluding to Christ's crucifixion).
8. A baited bear. In a popular form of entertainment,
bears were led in chains and set upon by dogs.
9. The hare's sadness was proverbial. Its flesh, when
eaten, was supposed to generate melancholy.
1. An open sewer outside the walls of London.
2. A biblical allusion to Proverbs 1:20–24.
3. You have a soul-endangering way of reading Scripture. This is one of several speeches in which Falstaff
uses a language associated with Puritans.
4. By Christ's wounds (a strong oath).
5. And subject me to public disgrace. Falstaff alludes
to the practice of "baffling," in which perjured knights
or effigies of them were hung upside down in public
places.

6. Allusion to 1 Corinthians 7:20 and Ephesians 4:1.
Falstaff is misusing the biblical injunction to work at
one's vocation to justify robbery.
7. A thief named after Gad's Hill, the place where he
practices his robberies. This hill, near Rochester on the
road from Canterbury to London, was notorious for
highway robberies.
8. By good works (as opposed to salvation by God's
grace).
9. "Jack" is a nickname for "John," but the word also
means "a drinking vessel" or "a knave." Falstaff likes
sugar in his sack, or sweet white wine.
1. The strictest of fast days in the Christian calendar.
2. A white wine exported from Madeira, an island off
the coast of west Africa.

PRINCE HARRY   Sir John stands to° his word, the devil shall have   *keeps*
105   his bargain, for he was never yet a breaker of proverbs: he will
give the devil his due.

POINS   [*to* FALSTAFF]   Then art thou damned for keeping thy
word with the devil.

PRINCE HARRY   Else he had been damned for cozening° the   *cheating*
110   devil.

POINS   But my lads, my lads, tomorrow morning by four o'clock
early, at Gads Hill, there are pilgrims going to Canterbury
with rich offerings, and traders riding to London with fat
purses. I have visors° for you all; you have horses for your-   *masks*
115   selves. Gadshill lies° tonight in Rochester. I have bespoke°   *lodges / ordered*
supper tomorrow night in Eastcheap.³ We may do it as secure°   *safely*
as sleep. If you will go, I will stuff your purses full of crowns;
if you will not, tarry at home and be hanged.

FALSTAFF   Hear ye, Edward, if I tarry at home and go not, I'll
120   hang you for going.

POINS   You will, chops?°   *fat cheeks*

FALSTAFF   Hal, wilt thou make one?

PRINCE HARRY   Who, I rob? I a thief? Not I, by my faith.

FALSTAFF   There's neither honesty,° manhood, nor good fel-   *honor*
125   lowship in thee, nor thou camest not of the blood royal, if
thou darest not stand for° ten shillings.⁴   *fight for; be worth*

PRINCE HARRY   Well then, once in my days I'll be a madcap.

FALSTAFF   Why, that's well said.

PRINCE HARRY   Well, come what will, I'll tarry at home.

130   FALSTAFF   By the Lord, I'll be a traitor then, when thou art king.

PRINCE HARRY   I care not.

POINS   Sir John, I prithee leave the Prince and me alone. I will
lay him down such reasons for this adventure that he shall go.

FALSTAFF   Well, God give thee the spirit of persuasion and him
135   the ears of profiting, that what thou speakest may move and
what he hears may be believed, that the true prince may, for
recreation' sake, prove a false thief; for the poor abuses of the
time want countenance.⁵ Farewell. You shall find me in
Eastcheap.

140   PRINCE HARRY   Farewell, the latter spring; farewell, All-hallown
summer.⁶   [*Exit* FALSTAFF]

POINS   Now, my good sweet honey lord, ride with us tomorrow.
I have a jest to execute that I cannot manage alone. Falstaff,
Peto, Bardolph, and Gadshill shall rob those men that we
145   have already waylaid—yourself and I will not be there—and
when they have the booty, if you and I do not rob them, cut
this head off from my shoulders.

PRINCE HARRY   But how shall we part with them in setting forth?

POINS   Why, we will set forth before or after them and appoint
150   them a place of meeting, wherein it is at our pleasure to fail.
And then will they adventure upon the exploit themselves,
which they shall have no sooner achieved but we'll set upon
them.

3. A street and market district in London, evidently the location of the play's tavern.
4. A 10-shilling coin was called a "royal," thus punning on the Prince's "blood royal."
5. Lack encouragement (from those of high rank).

6. Addressing Falstaff as youth in age (a second spring) and likening him to a period of unusually mild weather (a second summer) occurring around All Hallows' Day, November 1.

PRINCE HARRY   Ay, but 'tis like that they will know us by our
155   horses, by our habits,° and by every other appointment,° to be   *clothing / item*
      ourselves.
      POINS   Tut, our horses they shall not see—I'll tie them in the
      wood; our visors we will change after we leave them; and, sir-
      rah,[7] I have cases of buckram for the nonce,[8] to immask° our   *hide*
160   noted° outward garments.   *known*
      PRINCE HARRY   But I doubt they will be too hard for us.[9]
      POINS   Well, for two of them, I know them to be as true-bred
      cowards as ever turned back; and for the third, if he fight
      longer than he sees reason, I'll forswear arms. The virtue of
165   this jest will be the incomprehensible° lies that this same fat   *boundless*
      rogue will tell us when we meet at supper: how thirty at least
      he fought with, what wards,° what blows, what extremities he   *parries*
      endured; and in the reproof° of this lives the jest.   *disproof*
      PRINCE HARRY   Well, I'll go with thee. Provide us all things nec-
170   essary, and meet me tomorrow night in Eastcheap; there I'll
      sup. Farewell.
      POINS   Farewell, my lord.   *Exit*
      PRINCE HARRY   I know you all, and will a while uphold
      The unyoked humour° of your idleness.   *unbridled whims*
175   Yet herein will I imitate the sun,
      Who doth permit the base contagious° clouds   *disease-carrying*
      To smother up his beauty from the world,
      That° when he please again to be himself,   *So that*
      Being wanted° he may be more wondered at   *Having been missed*
180   By breaking through the foul and ugly mists
      Of vapours that did seem to strangle him.
      If all the year were playing holidays,
      To sport would be as tedious as to work;
      But when they seldom come, they wished-for come,
185   And nothing pleaseth but rare accidents.°   *exceptional events*
      So when this loose behaviour I throw off
      And pay the debt I never promisèd,
      By how much better than my word I am,
      By so much shall I falsify men's hopes;°   *expectations*
190   And like bright metal on a sullen ground,°   *dull background*
      My reformation, glitt'ring o'er my fault,
      Shall show more goodly and attract more eyes
      Than that which hath no foil to set it off.
      I'll so offend to° make offence a skill,°   *as to / an art*
195 · Redeeming time[1] when men think least I will.   *Exit*

1.3

Enter the KING, [*the Earls of*] NORTHUMBERLAND [*and*]
WORCESTER, HOTSPUR, *Sir Walter* BLUNT, *with other*
[*lords*]

KING HENRY [*to* HOTSPUR, NORTHUMBERLAND, *and* WORCESTER]
   My blood hath been too cold and temperate,
   Unapt° to stir at these indignities,   *Slow*

7. A familiar form of address, conventionally used with social inferiors.
8. I have suits of coarse cloth for the purpose.
9. But I fear they will be more than we can manage.
1. Making amends for misspent time. Injunctions to

redeem time were both proverbial and biblical: see Ephesians 5:16 or Colossians 4:5.
1.3. Location: A royal residence, probably Windsor Castle.

And you have found me,° for accordingly   *discovered this fact*
You tread upon my patience; but be sure
5   I will from henceforth rather be myself,°   *(i.e., my royal self)*
Mighty and to be feared, than my condition,[1]
Which hath been smooth as oil, soft as young down,
And therefore lost that title of° respect   *claim to*
Which the proud soul ne'er pays but to the proud.
10 WORCESTER   Our house,[2] my sovereign liege, little deserves
The scourge of greatness to be used on it,
And that same greatness too, which our own hands
Have holp° to make so portly.°   *helped / majestic*
NORTHUMBERLAND [*to the* KING]   My lord—
KING HENRY   Worcester, get thee gone, for I do see
15   Danger and disobedience in thine eye.
O sir, your presence is too bold and peremptory,°   *proud*
And majesty might never yet endure
The moody frontier[3] of a servant brow.
You have good leave° to leave us. When we need   *full permission*
20   Your use and counsel we shall send for you. *Exit* WORCESTER
You were about to speak.
NORTHUMBERLAND   Yea, my good lord.
Those prisoners in your highness' name demanded,
Which Harry Percy here at Holmedon took,
Were, as he says, not with such strength denied
25   As was delivered° to your majesty,   *reported*
Who either through envy° or misprision°   *malice / error*
Was guilty of this fault, and not my son.
HOTSPUR [*to the* KING]   My liege, I did deny no prisoners;
But I remember, when the fight was done,
30   When I was dry° with rage and extreme toil,   *thirsty*
Breathless and faint, leaning upon my sword,
Came there a certain lord, neat and trimly dressed,
Fresh as a bridegroom, and his chin, new-reaped,[4]
Showed° like a stubble-land at harvest-home.[5]   *Looked*
35   He was perfumèd like a milliner,[6]
And 'twixt his finger and his thumb he held
A pouncet-box,[7] which ever and anon
He gave his nose and took't away again—
Who° therewith angry, when it next came there   *(the nose)*
40   Took it in snuff[8]—and still he smiled and talked;
And as the soldiers bore dead bodies by,
He called them untaught knaves, unmannerly
To bring a slovenly° unhandsome corpse   *base; nasty*
Betwixt the wind and his nobility.
45   With many holiday and lady° terms   *dainty and effeminate*
He questioned me; amongst the rest demanded
My prisoners in your majesty's behalf.
I then, all smarting with my wounds being cold—
To be so pestered with a popinjay!°—   *parrot; vain dandy*

---

1. My natural (mild) temperament.
2. The Percy family, which had supported Henry against Richard II.
3. The angry expression (punning on "frontier" as meaning both "forehead" and "military fortifications").
4. Newly trimmed. London in the 1590s witnessed a fashion for close-shaved beards.
5. At the end of harvest (when the fields are cut back to stubble).
6. Seller of finely scented apparel such as bonnets, ribbons, and gloves. The name derives from the fact that these goods were often imports from Milan.
7. Perfume box with a perforated lid.
8. Took offense at it; inhaled it.

50	Out of my grief° and my impatience	*pain*
	Answered neglectingly,° I know not what—	*negligently*
	He should, or should not—for he made me mad	
	To see him shine so brisk, and smell so sweet,	
	And talk so like a waiting gentlewoman	
55	Of guns, and drums, and wounds, God save the mark!⁹	
	And telling me the sovereign'st° thing on earth	*best*
	Was parmacity¹ for an inward bruise,	
	And that it was great pity, so it was,	
	This villainous saltpetre² should be digged	
60	Out of the bowels of the harmless earth,	
	Which many a good tall° fellow had destroyed	*brave*
	So cowardly, and but for these vile guns	
	He would himself have been a soldier.	
	This bald unjointed° chat of his, my lord,	*This trivial incoherent*
65	Made me to answer indirectly, as I said,	
	And I beseech you, let not his report	
	Come current° for an accusation	*Be taken as valid*
	Betwixt my love and your high majesty.	

BLUNT [*to the* KING]   The circumstance considered, good my lord,

70	Whate'er Lord Harry Percy then had said	
	To such a person, and in such a place,	
	At such a time, with all the rest retold,	
	May reasonably die, and never rise	
	To do him wrong or any way impeach	
75	What then he said, so° he unsay it now.	*if*

KING HENRY   Why, yet he doth deny° his prisoners,   *refuse to hand over*

	But with proviso and exception	
	That we at our own charge shall ransom straight°	*immediately*
	His brother-in-law the foolish Mortimer,³	
80	Who, on my soul, hath wilfully betrayed	
	The lives of those that he did lead to fight	
	Against that great magician, damned Glyndŵr—	
	Whose daughter, as we hear, the Earl of March	
	Hath lately married. Shall our coffers, then,	
85	Be emptied to redeem a traitor home?	
	Shall we buy treason, and indent with fears⁴	
	When they have lost and forfeited themselves?	
	No, on the barren mountains let him starve;	
	For I shall never hold that man my friend	
90	Whose tongue shall ask me for one penny cost	
	To ransom home revolted° Mortimer—	*rebellious*

HOTSPUR   Revolted Mortimer?

	He never did fall off,° my sovereign liege,	*change allegiance*
	But by the chance of war. To prove that true	
95	Needs no more but one tongue for all those wounds,	
	Those mouthèd° wounds, which valiantly he took	*gaping; eloquent*

---

9. God keep evil away (an expression of indignation).
1. Spermaceti, an oily substance from the sperm whale that was used in various medicines and potions. The spelling "parmacity" probably derives from the ointment's association with the Italian city of Parma.
2. The main ingredient of gunpowder.
3. Shakespeare follows Holinshed's *Chronicles* in confusing or conflating two Edmund Mortimers. One was

captured by Glyndŵr and later became Glyndŵr's son-in-law and Hotspur's brother-in-law. The other, the fifth Earl of March, was his nephew and claimed the English throne as a descendant of Lionel, Duke of Clarence, third son of Edward III. This Mortimer was the one named by Richard II as his presumptive heir.
4. And bargain with those whom we have reason to fear.

When on the gentle Severn's⁵ sedgy° bank,   *marshy*
In single opposition, hand to hand,
He did confound° the best part of an hour   *consume*
100 In changing hardiment° with great Glyndŵr.   *matching valor*
Three times they breathed,° and three times did they drink,   *rested*
Upon agreement, of swift Severn's flood,
Who, then affrighted with their bloody looks,
Ran fearfully among the trembling reeds,
105 And hid his crisp° head in the hollow bank,   *rippled*
Bloodstainèd with these valiant combatants.
Never did bare and rotten policy°   *cunning*
Colour° her working with such deadly wounds,   *Disguise*
Nor never could the noble Mortimer
110 Receive so many, and all willingly.
Then let not him be slandered with revolt.⁶
KING HENRY Thou dost belie° him, Percy, thou dost belie him. *misrepresent*
He never did encounter with Glyndŵr. I tell thee,
He durst as well have met the devil alone
115 As Owain Glyndŵr for an enemy.
Art thou not ashamed? But, sirrah, henceforth
Let me not hear you speak of Mortimer.
Send me your prisoners with the speediest means,
Or you shall hear in such a kind from me
120 As will displease you.—My lord Northumberland,
We license your departure with your son.
[*To* HOTSPUR] Send us your prisoners, or you'll hear of it.
     Exeunt [*all but* HOTSPUR *and* NORTHUMBERLAND]
HOTSPUR An if° the devil come and roar for them   *An if=If*
I will not send them. I will after straight°   *go after him at once*
125 And tell him so, for I will ease my heart,
Although it be with hazard of my head.
NORTHUMBERLAND What, drunk with choler?° Stay and pause awhile. *anger*
     Enter [*the Earl of*] WORCESTER
Here comes your uncle.
HOTSPUR   Speak of Mortimer?
Zounds, I will speak of him, and let my soul
130 Want mercy° if I do not join with him.   *Be damned*
In his behalf I'll empty all these veins,
And shed my dear blood drop by drop in the dust,
But I will lift the downfall° Mortimer   *downfallen*
As high in the air as this unthankful King,
135 As this ingrate and cankered° Bolingbroke.⁷   *corrupted*
NORTHUMBERLAND [*to* WORCESTER] Brother, the King hath
     made your nephew mad.
WORCESTER Who struck this heat up after I was gone?
HOTSPUR He will forsooth have all my prisoners;
And when I urged the ransom once again
140 Of my wife's brother, then his cheek looked pale,
And on my face he turned an eye of death,°   *a menacing look*
Trembling even at the name of Mortimer.

---

5. The Severn River flows from Wales into Bristol Channel in England.
6. With the accusation of having revolted.
7. Henry's family name. Hotspur's use of it suggests his unwillingness to acknowledge Henry as King.

WORCESTER   I cannot blame him: was not he proclaimed
    By Richard, that dead is, the next of blood?°   *heir to the throne*
145 NORTHUMBERLAND   He was; I heard the proclamation.
    And then it was when the unhappy° King,   *unfortunate*
    Whose wrongs in us° God pardon, did set forth   *done by us*
    Upon his Irish expedition,[8]
    From whence he, intercepted,° did return   *interrupted*
150   To be deposed, and shortly murderèd.
  WORCESTER   And for whose death we in the world's wide mouth
    Live scandalized° and foully spoken of.   *disgraced*
  HOTSPUR   But soft,° I pray you; did King Richard then   *wait*
    Proclaim my brother° Edmund Mortimer   *brother-in-law*
    Heir to the crown?
155 NORTHUMBERLAND   He did; myself did hear it.
  HOTSPUR   Nay, then I cannot blame his cousin[9] King
    That wished him on the barren mountains starve.
    But shall it be that you that set the crown
    Upon the head of this forgetful man,
160   And for his sake wear the detested blot
    Of murderous subornation,[1] shall it be
    That you a world of curses undergo,
    Being the agents or base second means,
    The cords, the ladder, or the hangman, rather?
165   O, pardon me that I descend so low
    To show the line and the predicament
    Wherein you range[2] under this subtle° King!   *cunning*
    Shall it for shame be spoken in these days,
    Or fill up chronicles in time to come,
170   That men of your nobility and power
    Did gage° them both in an unjust behalf,°   *pledge / cause*
    As both of you, God pardon it, have done:
    To put down Richard, that sweet lovely rose,
    And plant this thorn, this canker,[3] Bolingbroke?
175   And shall it in more shame be further spoken
    That you are fooled, discarded, and shook off
    By him for whom these shames ye underwent?
    No; yet time serves° wherein you may redeem   *is available*
    Your banished honours, and restore yourselves
180   Into the good thoughts of the world again,
    Revenge the jeering and disdained° contempt   *disdainful*
    Of this proud King, who studies day and night
    To answer° all the debt he owes to you   *satisfy*
    Even with the bloody payment of your deaths.
    Therefore, I say—
185 WORCESTER   Peace, cousin, say no more.
    And now I will unclasp a secret book,
    And to your quick-conceiving discontents
    I'll read you matter deep and dangerous,
    As full of peril and adventurous spirit

---

8. As Shakespeare dramatizes in *Richard II*, Bolingbroke returned to England from exile in France while
Richard was at war in Ireland.
9. Punning on "cozen" (cheat).
1. Of assisting with a murder.
2. *To . . . range:* To show the degree and category into

which you might be classified (with a pun on "line" as
meaning "hangman's rope" and on "predicament" as
meaning "an unpleasant situation").
3. Wild and inferior kind of rose; also, cankerworm
(which destroys plants), or ulcerated sore.

190   As to o'erwalk° a current roaring loud   *walk across*
    On the unsteadfast footing of a spear.
  HOTSPUR   If he fall in, good night, or sink or swim.⁴
    Send danger from the east unto the west,
    So° honour cross it from the north to south;   *Provided*
195   And let them grapple. O, the blood more stirs
    To rouse a lion than to start a hare!
  NORTHUMBERLAND [*to* WORCESTER]   Imagination of some great exploit
    Drives him beyond the bounds of patience.
  HOTSPUR   By heaven, methinks it were an easy leap
200   To pluck bright honour from the pale-faced moon,
    Or dive into the bottom of the deep,
    Where fathom-line⁵ could never touch the ground,
    And pluck up drownèd honour by the locks,
    So he that doth redeem her thence might wear,
205   Without corrival,° all her dignities.   *competitor*
    But out upon this half-faced fellowship!°   *paltry sharing of honors*
  WORCESTER [*to* NORTHUMBERLAND]   He apprehends a world of
      figures⁶ here,
    But not the form of what he should attend.°   *pay attention to*
    [*To* HOTSPUR] Good cousin, give me audience for a while,
210   And list° to me.   *listen*
  HOTSPUR   I cry you mercy.°   *I beg your pardon*
  WORCESTER   Those same noble Scots⁷
    That are your prisoners—
  HOTSPUR   I'll keep them all.
    By God, he shall not have a Scot of them;
    No, if a scot would save his soul he shall not.
    I'll keep them, by this hand.
215   WORCESTER   You start away,
    And lend no ear unto my purposes.
    Those prisoners you shall keep.
  HOTSPUR   Nay, I will; that's flat.
    He said he would not ransom Mortimer,
    Forbade my tongue to speak of Mortimer;
220   But I will find him when he lies asleep,
    And in his ear I'll hollo 'Mortimer!'
    Nay, I'll have a starling shall be taught to speak
    Nothing but 'Mortimer', and give it him
    To keep his anger still° in motion.   *constantly*
225   WORCESTER   Hear you, cousin, a word.
  HOTSPUR   All studies here I solemnly defy,°   *renounce*
    Save how to gall and pinch° this Bolingbroke.   *torture*
    And that same sword-and-buckler⁸ Prince of Wales—
    But that I think his father loves him not
230   And would be glad he met with some mischance—
    I would have him poisoned with a pot of ale.⁹
  WORCESTER   Farewell, kinsman. I'll talk to you
    When you are better tempered to attend.

---

4. Farewell to him, whether he sinks or manages to swim for a short time.
5. A weighted line used in testing the depth of the sea.
6. Figures of speech; fantasies.
7. Inhabitants of Scotland (with a pun in the following lines on "scot" as meaning "a small sum").
8. In Elizabethan England, the sword and buckler, or small shield, were associated with ordinary fighting men. A prince should use rapier and dagger.
9. A drink associated with the common people.

NORTHUMBERLAND [*to* HOTSPUR]   Why, what a wasp-stung and
       impatient fool
235   Art thou to break into this woman's mood,[1]
    Tying thine ear to no tongue but thine own!
HOTSPUR   Why, look you, I am whipped and scourged with rods,
    Nettled and stung with pismires,° when I hear   *ants*
    Of this vile politician° Bolingbroke.   *schemer*
240   In Richard's time—what d'ye call the place?
    A plague upon't, it is in Gloucestershire.
    'Twas where the madcap Duke his uncle kept—
    His uncle York—where I first bowed my knee
    Unto this king of smiles, this Bolingbroke.[2]
245   'Sblood, when you and he came back from Ravenspurgh.[3]
NORTHUMBERLAND   At Berkeley castle.
HOTSPUR   You say true.
    Why, what a candy deal of° courtesy   *quantity of sweet*
    This fawning greyhound then did proffer me!
    'Look when° his infant fortune came to age',   *Whenever; as soon as*
250   And 'gentle Harry Percy', and 'kind cousin'.
    O, the devil take such cozeners!°—God forgive me.   *cheaters*
    Good uncle, tell your tale; I have done.
WORCESTER   Nay, if you have not, to't again.
    We'll stay° your leisure.   *await*
HOTSPUR   I have done, i'faith.
255   WORCESTER   Then once more to your Scottish prisoners.
    Deliver them up° without their ransom straight;   *Release them*
    And make the Douglas'[4] son your only mean°   *agent; means*
    For powers° in Scotland, which, for divers reasons   *raising an army*
    Which I shall send you written, be assured
260   Will easily be granted. [*To* NORTHUMBERLAND] You, my lord,
    Your son in Scotland being thus employed,
    Shall secretly into the bosom creep
    Of that same noble prelate well-beloved,
    The Archbishop.
HOTSPUR   Of York, is't not?
WORCESTER   True, who bears hard°   *resents*
265   His brother's death at Bristol, the Lord Scroop.[5]
    I speak not this in estimation,°   *as a guess*
    As what I think might be, but what I know
    Is ruminated, plotted, and set down,
    And only stays° but to behold the face   *waits*
270   Of that occasion that shall bring it on.
HOTSPUR   I smell it; upon my life, it will do well!
NORTHUMBERLAND   Before the game is afoot thou still lett'st slip.[6]
HOTSPUR   Why, it cannot choose but be a noble plot—
    And then the power° of Scotland and of York   *army*
    To join with Mortimer, ha?
275   WORCESTER   And so they shall.

---

1. Alluding to the commonplace that women were, by nature, unable to hold their tongues.
2. This event is depicted in *Richard II* 2.3.20–56.
3. Bolingbroke's landing place at the mouth of the Humber River in Yorkshire upon his return from exile.
4. The "the" before Douglas's name indicates that he is head of a Scottish clan or noble family.
5. Richard Scroop (or le Scrope), the Archbishop of York and an ally of the rebels in this play, was actually a distant cousin of William Scroop, Earl of Wiltshire, who was a favorite of Richard II and was executed by Henry IV in 1399. His death is mentioned in *Richard II* 3.2.
6. Before the quarry is even in the field, you always let loose the dogs. This image from hunting implies that Hotspur habitually jumps the gun.

HOTSPUR   In faith, it is exceedingly well aimed.

WORCESTER   And 'tis no little reason bids us speed
  To save our heads by raising of a head;°   *an army*
  For, bear ourselves as even° as we can,   *carefully*
280 The King will always think him in our debt,
  And think we think ourselves unsatisfied
  Till he hath found a time to pay us home.°   *repay us fully*
  And see already how he doth begin
  To make us strangers to his looks of love.

285 HOTSPUR   He does, he does. We'll be revenged on him.

WORCESTER   Cousin, farewell. No further go in this
  Than I by letters shall direct your course.
  When time is ripe, which will be suddenly,°   *soon*
  I'll steal to Glyndŵr and Lord Mortimer,
290 Where you and Douglas and our powers at once,
  As I will fashion it, shall happily meet,
  To bear our fortunes in our own strong arms,
  Which now we hold at° much uncertainty.   *with*

NORTHUMBERLAND   Farewell, good brother. We shall thrive, I
  trust.

295 HOTSPUR [*to* WORCESTER]   Uncle, adieu. O, let the hours be short
  Till fields° and blows and groans applaud our sport!   *battlefields*

  Exeunt [WORCESTER *at one door,*
  NORTHUMBERLAND *and* HOTSPUR *at another door*]

2.1

Enter a CARRIER,[1] *with a lantern in his hand*

FIRST CARRIER   Heigh-ho! An't° be not four by the day,° I'll be   *If it / in the morning*
  hanged. Charles's Wain[2] is over the new chimney, and yet our
  horse° not packed. What, ostler![3]   *horses*

OSTLER [*within*]   Anon,° anon!   *Right away*

5 FIRST CARRIER   I prithee, Tom, beat cut's saddle,[4] put a few
  flocks in the point.[5] Poor jade is wrung in the withers,[6] out of
  all cess.°   *measure*

  Enter another CARRIER

SECOND CARRIER   Peas and beans° are as dank here as a dog,   *(horse feed)*
  and that is the next way to give poor jades the bots.° This   *intestinal worms*
10 house is turned upside down since Robin Ostler died.

FIRST CARRIER   Poor fellow never joyed since the price of oats
  rose; it was the death of him.

SECOND CARRIER   I think this be the most villainous house in all
  London road for fleas. I am stung like a tench.[7]

15 FIRST CARRIER   Like a tench? By the mass, there is ne'er a king
  christen° could be better bit than I have been since the first   *Christian king*
  cock.°   *midnight*

2.1 Location: An innyard in Rochester, Kent.
1. One who transports goods for hire.
2. The constellation now known as the Plow or the Great Bear.
3. One who attends to horses at an inn.
4. Soften the horse's saddle. "Cut" was a term for a horse with a docked tail or a gelding; here, it may be the

horse's name.
5. Put a few tufts of wood in the saddle's pommel (to soften it).
6. The poor old horse is extremely sore in the ridge between its shoulder blades.
7. A spotted fish whose markings may have looked like flea bites.

SECOND CARRIER   Why, they will allow us ne'er a jordan,° and   *chamber pot*
then we leak° in your chimney, and your chamber-lye° breeds   *urinate / urine*
20   fleas like a loach.[8]
FIRST CARRIER   What, ostler! Come away, and be hanged, come
away!
SECOND CARRIER   I have a gammon of bacon° and two races°   *a ham / roots*
of ginger to be delivered as far as Charing Cross.[9]
25   FIRST CARRIER   God's body, the turkeys in my pannier° are   *basket*
quite starved! What, ostler! A plague on thee, hast thou never
an eye in thy head? Canst not hear? An° 'twere not as good deed   *If*
as drink to break the pate° on thee, I am a very villain. Come,   *skull*
and be hanged! Hast no faith° in thee?   *responsibility*
          Enter GADSHILL
30   GADSHILL   Good morrow, carriers. What's o'clock?
FIRST CARRIER   I think it be two o'clock.
GADSHILL   I prithee lend me thy lantern to see my gelding in the
stable.
FIRST CARRIER   Nay, by God, soft.° I know a trick worth two of   *wait*
35   that, i'faith.
GADSHILL [*to* SECOND CARRIER]   I pray thee, lend me thine.
SECOND CARRIER   Ay, when? Canst tell?[1] 'Lend me thy lantern,'
quoth a.° Marry, I'll see thee hanged first.   *says he*
GADSHILL   Sirrah carrier, what time do you mean to come to
40   London?
SECOND CARRIER   Time enough to go to bed with a candle, I
warrant° thee.—Come, neighbour Mugs, we'll call up the   *assure*
gentlemen. They will along° with company, for they have great   *travel*
charge.°   *Exeunt* [CARRIERS]   *have valuable cargo*
45   GADSHILL   What ho, chamberlain![2]
          Enter CHAMBERLAIN
CHAMBERLAIN   'At hand' quoth Pickpurse.[3]
GADSHILL   That's even as fair° as "'At hand" quoth the cham-   *good*
berlain', for thou variest no more from picking of purses than
giving direction doth from labouring:[4] thou layest the plot°   *plan*
50   how.
CHAMBERLAIN   Good morrow, Master Gadshill. It holds current
that° I told you yesternight. There's a franklin in the   *holds true what*
Weald[5] of Kent hath brought three hundred marks[6] with him
in gold. I heard him tell it to one of his company last night at
55   supper—a kind of auditor, one that hath abundance of charge
too, God knows what. They are up already, and call for eggs
and butter; they will away presently.
GADSHILL   Sirrah, if they meet not with Saint Nicholas's
clerks,[7] I'll give thee this neck.
60   CHAMBERLAIN   No, I'll none of it; I pray thee keep that for the
hangman, for I know thou worshippest Saint Nicholas as truly
as a man of falsehood may.

---

8. A fish. The comparison means that urine breeds
fleas either as a loach breeds loaches or as a loach
breeds fleas. There was a popular belief that some fish
spawned flies or fleas.
9. A marketplace between London and Westminster.
1. A retort similar to "Never."
2. Bedroom attendant. In popular discourse, chamberlains were notorious for their complicity with thieves.
3. "I am at your disposal," as the thief said (evidently a

popular tag).
4. For you are not more different from a pickpocket
than an overseer is from a laborer.
5. There's a small landowner in the wooded region.
6. Coins worth two-thirds of a pound each.
7. Slang for "highway robbers." St. Nicholas was variously regarded as the patron saint of travelers and of
thieves.

GADSHILL   What talkest thou to me of the hangman? If I hang,
I'll make a fat pair of gallows, for if I hang, old Sir John hangs
65   with me, and thou knowest he's no starveling. Tut, there are
other Trojans[8] that thou dreamest not of, the which° for sport'   who
sake are content to do the profession° some grace, that would,   (of robbery)
if matters should be looked into, for their own credit' sake
make all whole.° I am joined with no foot-landrakers,[9] no   set things right
70   long-staff sixpenny strikers,[1] none of these mad mustachio
purple-hued maltworms,[2] but with nobility and tranquillity,
burgomasters and great 'oyez'-ers;[3] such as can hold in,° such   can keep a secret
as will strike sooner than speak, and speak sooner than drink,
and drink sooner than pray. And yet, zounds, I lie, for they
75   pray continually to their saint the commonwealth; or rather,
not pray to her, but prey on her; for they ride up and down[4]
on her and make her their boots.°   booty; footwear
CHAMBERLAIN   What, the commonwealth their boots? Will she
hold out water in foul way?[5]
80   GADSHILL   She will, she will, justice hath liquored her.[6] We steal
as in a castle,° cocksure; we have the recipe of fern-seed,[7] we   in complete safety
walk invisible.
CHAMBERLAIN   Nay, by my faith, I think you are more beholden
to the night than to fern-seed for your walking invisible.
85   GADSHILL   Give me thy hand; thou shalt have a share in our
purchase,° as I am a true man.   plunder
CHAMBERLAIN   Nay, rather let me have it as you are a false thief.
GADSHILL   Go to, 'homo'° is a common name to all men. Bid the   man
ostler bring my gelding out of the stable. Farewell, you muddy°   stupid
90   knave.   Exeunt [severally]°   separately

2.2

Enter PRINCE [HARRY], POINS, PETO [and BARDOLPH][1]
POINS   Come, shelter, shelter!
               [Exeunt PETO and BARDOLPH at another door]
I have removed Falstaff's horse, and he frets° like a gummed   worries; frays
velvet.[2]
PRINCE HARRY   Stand close!°   [Exit POINS]   concealed
         Enter FALSTAFF
5   FALSTAFF   Poins! Poins, and be hanged! Poins!
PRINCE HARRY   Peace, ye fat-kidneyed rascal! What a brawling
dost thou keep!
FALSTAFF   Where's Poins, Hal?
PRINCE HARRY   He is walked up to the top of the hill. I'll go seek
10   him.   [Exit]

---

8. Slang for "roisterers."
9. Highwaymen who travel on foot (rather than on horse).
1. Thieves who carried crude weapons and robbed for small sums.
2. These drunkards with wild mustaches and purple faces.
3. Court officials who cried "Oyez," or "Hear ye."
4. They travel (with a pun on "ride" as meaning "to mount sexually").
5. Will she keep water out (off your feet) on a muddy

road; will she protect you in difficulty?
6. Greased her (as one waterproofs leather); bribed her.
7. Popularly supposed to make those who wore it invisible.
2.2 Location: The highway, Gad's Hill.
1. For a discussion of the names of "Bardolph" and "Peto," see the Textual Note and Introduction.
2. Like cheap velvet treated with gum. Gummed velvet was shiny but wore out quickly.

FALSTAFF   I am accursed to rob in that thief's company. The
rascal hath removed my horse and tied him I know not where.
If I travel but four foot by the square° further afoot, I shall   *(a measuring tool)*
break my wind.° Well, I doubt not but to die a fair death, for[3]   *be breathless; fart*
all this—if I scape hanging for killing that rogue. I have for-
sworn his company hourly any time this two-and-twenty
years, and yet I am bewitched with the rogue's company. If the
rascal have not given me medicines° to make me love him, I'll   *love potions*
be hanged. It could not be else: I have drunk medicines.
Poins! Hal! A plague upon you both! Bardolph! Peto! I'll starve
ere I'll rob a foot further. An 'twere not as good a deed as drink
to turn true man° and to leave these rogues, I am the veriest   *repent; turn informer*
varlet that ever chewed with a tooth. Eight yards of uneven
ground is threescore and ten miles afoot with me, and the
stony-hearted villains know it well enough. A plague upon't
when thieves cannot be true one to another!
          They whistle. [Enter PRINCE HARRY, POINS, PETO, *and*
          BARDOLPH]*[4]
Whew! A plague upon you all! Give me my horse, you rogues,
give me my horse, and be hanged!
PRINCE HARRY   Peace, ye fat-guts. Lie down, lay thine ear close
to the ground, and list if thou canst hear the tread of travellers.
FALSTAFF   Have you any levers to lift me up again, being down?
'Sblood, I'll not bear my own flesh so far afoot again for all the
coin in thy father's exchequer. What a plague mean ye to colt°   *trick*
me thus?
PRINCE HARRY   Thou liest: thou art not colted, thou art
uncolted.°   *unhorsed*
FALSTAFF   I prithee, good Prince Hal, help me to my horse,
good king's son.
PRINCE HARRY   Out, ye rogue, shall I be your ostler?
FALSTAFF   Hang thyself in thine own heir-apparent garters![5] If
I be ta'en, I'll peach° for this. An I have not ballads made on   *inform against you*
you all and sung to filthy tunes,[6] let a cup of sack be my poi-
son. When a jest is so forward, and afoot too![7] I hate it.
          Enter GADSHILL *[visored]*°   *wearing a mask*
GADSHILL   Stand!
FALSTAFF   So I do, against my will.
POINS   O, 'tis our setter,° I know his voice. Gadshill, what   *one who sets up a crime*
news?
GADSHILL[8]   Case ye,° case ye, on with your visors! There's   *Disguise yourselves*
money of the King's coming down the hill; 'tis going to the
King's exchequer.
FALSTAFF   You lie, ye rogue, 'tis going to the King's tavern.

3. Die a natural death, despite.
4. It is not clear exactly when the Prince and his companions show themselves to the frustrated Falstaff.
They can all enter here, or the Prince and Poins could
enter at line 28 and Bardolph and Peto at the same time
as Gadshill at line 43.
5. Falstaff's version of the proverb "He may hang himself in his own garters." As the heir to the throne, the
Prince was a member of the Order of the Garter, the
highest order of English knighthood.
6. Ballads on topical themes were sung by ballad
singers and sold cheaply as broadsides in streets, the-

aters, and other public places.
7. When a plot (to rob) is so advanced and goes so well;
when a joke (on me) goes so far and makes me go on
foot.
8. In Q, this speech is assigned to Bardolph; but Poins
has just asked Gadshill a question, so one expects an
answer to come from him. It has been conjectured that
the confusion here may reflect confusion in Shakespeare's foul papers about whether Bardolph and Gadshill were to be two characters or one. See note to
2.5.159.

GADSHILL   There's enough to make° us all.   *make fortunes for*
FALSTAFF   To be hanged.
        [*They put on visors*]
PRINCE HARRY   Sirs, you four shall front° them in the narrow   *confront*
55   lane. Ned Poins and I will walk lower. If they scape from your
        encounter, then they light on us.
PETO   How many be there of them?
GADSHILL   Some eight or ten.
FALSTAFF   Zounds, will they not rob us?
60   PRINCE HARRY   What, a coward, Sir John Paunch?
FALSTAFF   Indeed I am not John of Gaunt[9] your grandfather,
        but yet no coward, Hal.
PRINCE HARRY   Well, we leave that to the proof.°   *test*
POINS   Sirrah Jack, thy horse stands behind the hedge. When
65   thou needest him, there thou shalt find him. Farewell, and
        stand fast.
FALSTAFF   Now cannot I strike him if I should be hanged.
PRINCE HARRY [*aside to* POINS]   Ned, where are our disguises?
POINS [*aside to the* PRINCE]   Here, hard by. Stand close.
        [*Exeunt the* PRINCE *and* POINS]
70   FALSTAFF   Now, my masters, happy man be his dole,[1] say I;
        every man to his business.
        [*They stand aside.*]
        Enter the TRAVELLERS [*amongst them the* CARRIERS]
FIRST TRAVELLER   Come, neighbour, the boy shall lead our
        horses down the hill. We'll walk afoot a while, and ease their
        legs.
75   THIEVES [*coming forward*]   Stand!
SECOND TRAVELLER   Jesus bless us!
FALSTAFF   Strike, down with them, cut the villains' throats! Ah,
        whoreson caterpillars,[2] bacon-fed knaves! They hate us youth.
        Down with them, fleece them!
80   FIRST TRAVELLER   O, we are undone, both we and ours for ever!
FALSTAFF   Hang ye, gorbellied° knaves, are ye undone? No, ye   *potbellied*
        fat chuffs;[3] I would your store° were here. On, bacons,° on!   *all you own / fat men*
        What, ye knaves! Young men must live. You are grand-jurors,[4]
        are ye? We'll jure ye, faith.
        Here they rob them and bind them. Exeunt [*the* THIEVES
        with the TRAVELLERS]

2.3

        Enter PRINCE [HARRY] *and* POINS [*disguised in buckram
        suits*]
PRINCE HARRY   The thieves have bound the true° men; now   *honest*
        could thou and I rob the thieves, and go merrily to London. It
        would be argument° for a week, laughter for a month, and a   *topic for discussion*
        good jest for ever.
5   POINS   Stand close; I hear them coming.
        [*They stand aside*]
        Enter [FALSTAFF, BARDOLPH, PETO, *and* GADSHILL, *with
        the travellers' money*]

9. Henry IV's father. Falstaff puns on "Gaunt" as meaning "lean"; in fact, his name is derived from "Ghent,"
his birthplace.
1. Proverbial expression meaning "Good luck to everyone."
2. Parasites. *whoreson:* an insult derived from "whore's

son."
3. Rude, churlish fellows; misers.
4. Referring to the fact that only prosperous citizens
served on grand juries.
2.3 Location: Scene continues.

FALSTAFF Come, my masters, let us share, and then to horse
before day. An° the Prince and Poins be not two arrant cowards, there's no equity stirring.° There's no more valour in that
Poins than in a wild duck.   *If*
                                                                                                                   justice to be found

As they are sharing, the PRINCE *and* POINS *set upon*
them

10 PRINCE HARRY Your money!
POINS Villains!

They all [GADSHILL, BARDOLPH, *and* PETO] *run away*
[*severally*] *and* FALSTAFF, *after a blow or two,* [*roars and*]
runs away too, leaving the booty behind them

PRINCE HARRY Got with much ease. Now merrily to horse.
The thieves are all scattered, and possessed with fear
So strongly that they dare not meet each other.
15 Each takes his fellow for an officer.
Away, good Ned. Falstaff sweats to death,
And lards° the lean earth as he walks along.   *drips fat on*
Were't not for laughing, I should pity him.
POINS How the fat rogue roared!   *Exeunt* [*with the booty*]

2.4

Enter HOTSPUR, *reading a letter*

HOTSPUR 'But for mine own part, my lord, I could be well con-
tented to be there, in respect of° the love I bear your house.'°—   *because of / family*
He could be contented; why is he not then? In respect of the
love he bears our house! He shows in this he loves his own barn
5 better than he loves our house. Let me see some more.—'The
purpose you undertake is dangerous'— Why, that's certain: 'tis
dangerous to take a cold, to sleep, to drink; but I tell you, my
lord fool, out of this nettle danger we pluck this flower safety.—
'The purpose you undertake is dangerous, the friends you have
10 named uncertain, the time itself unsorted,° and your   *unsuitable*
whole plot too light for the counterpoise of° so great an   *to counterbalance*
opposition.'— Say you so, say you so? I say unto you again, you
are a shallow, cowardly hind,° and you lie. What a lack-brain   *peasant*
is this! By the Lord, our plot is a good plot as ever was laid,
15 our friends true and constant; a good plot, good friends, and
full of expectation; an excellent plot, very good friends. What
a frosty-spirited rogue is this! Why, my lord of York° commends   *(Archbishop Scrope)*
the plot and the general course of the action. Zounds, an I
were now by this rascal, I could brain him with his lady's fan!
20 Is there not my father, my uncle, and myself? Lord Edmund
Mortimer, my lord of York, and Owain Glyndŵr? Is there not
besides the Douglas? Have I not all their letters, to meet me
in arms by the ninth of the next month? And are they not
some of them set forward already? What a pagan rascal is this,
25 an infidel! Ha, you shall see now, in very sincerity of fear and
cold heart will he to the King, and lay open all our proceedings! O, I could divide myself and go to buffets[1] for moving°   *urging*
such a dish of skim-milk with so honourable an action! Hang
him! Let him tell the King we are prepared; I will set forward
30 tonight.

Enter his Lady [LADY PERCY]

2.4 Location: The Percys' home, Warkworth Castle, in
Northumberland.

1. I could split myself into two and fall to blows with
myself.

How now, Kate? I must leave you within these two hours.

LADY PERCY   O my good lord, why are you thus alone?
For what offence have I this fortnight been
A banished woman from my Harry's bed?

35   Tell me, sweet lord, what is't that takes from thee
Thy stomach,° pleasure, and thy golden sleep?   *appetite*
Why dost thou bend thine eyes upon the earth,
And start so often when thou sitt'st alone?
Why hast thou lost the fresh blood in thy cheeks,

40   And given my treasures and my rights² of thee
To thick-eyed° musing and curst melancholy?   *vacantly staring*
In thy faint° slumbers I by thee have watched,   *restless*
And heard thee murmur tales of iron wars,
Speak terms of manège° to thy bounding steed,   *horsemanship*

45   Cry 'Courage! To the field!' And thou hast talked
Of sallies and retires,° of trenches, tents,   *advances and retreats*
Of palisadoes,³ frontiers,° parapets,   *ramparts*
Of basilisks, of cannon, culverin,⁴
Of prisoners ransomed, and of soldiers slain,

50   And all the currents of a heady° fight.   *headlong*
Thy spirit within thee hath been so at war,
And thus hath so bestirred thee in thy sleep,
That beads of sweat have stood upon thy brow
Like bubbles in a late-disturbèd° stream;   *recently disturbed*

55   And in thy face strange motions have appeared,
Such as we see when men restrain their breath
On some great sudden hest.° O, what portents are these?   *command*
Some heavy° business hath my lord in hand,   *serious; sad*
And I must know it, else he loves me not.

HOTSPUR   What ho!

[*Enter* SERVANT]

60   Is Gilliams with the packet gone?

SERVANT   He is, my lord, an hour ago.

HOTSPUR   Hath Butler brought those horses from the sheriff?

SERVANT   One horse, my lord, he brought even now.

HOTSPUR   What horse? A roan, a crop-ear, is it not?

SERVANT   It is, my lord.

65   HOTSPUR   That roan shall be my throne.
Well, I will back him straight.—O, *Esperance!*⁵—
Bid Butler lead him forth into the park.

LADY PERCY   But hear you, my lord.

HOTSPUR   What sayst thou, my lady?

LADY PERCY   What is it carries you away?

HOTSPUR   Why, my horse,
My love, my horse.

70   LADY PERCY   Out, you mad-headed ape!
A weasel⁶ hath not such a deal of spleen°   *impulsiveness; anger*
As you are tossed with.
In faith, I'll know your business, Harry, that I will.

---

2. Marriage rights. Alluding to the belief that husbands and wives owe a mutual marriage debt that obliges them regularly to engage in sexual relations with one another.
3. Pointed stakes driven into the ground as defensive barriers.
4. *basilisks:* large cannons, named after a deadly

mythological reptile. *culverin:* a name for both a kind of long cannon and a firearm noted for its ability to fire over a long range.
5. Referring to the Percy motto *Esperance ma comforte,* or "Hope is my reliance."
6. Weasels were proverbially quarrelsome.

I fear my brother Mortimer doth stir

75   About his title, and hath sent for you

   To line° his enterprise; but if you go—   *strengthen*

HOTSPUR   So far afoot? I shall be weary, love.

LADY PERCY   Come, come, you paraquito,° answer me   *little parrot*

   Directly to this question that I ask.

80   In faith, I'll break thy little finger,° Harry,   *(euphemism for "penis")*

   An if thou wilt not tell me all things true.

HOTSPUR   Away, away, you trifler! Love? I love thee not,

   I care not for thee, Kate. This is no world

   To play with maumets[7] and to tilt° with lips.   *duel*

85   We must have bloody noses and cracked crowns,[8]

   And pass them current,[9] too. God's me,° my horse!—   *God save me*

   What sayst thou, Kate? What wouldst thou have with me?

LADY PERCY   Do you not love me? Do you not indeed?

   Well, do not, then, for since you love me not

90   I will not love myself. Do you not love me?

   Nay, tell me if you speak in jest or no.

HOTSPUR   Come, wilt thou see me ride?

   And when I am a-horseback,[1] I will swear

   I love thee infinitely. But hark you, Kate.

95   I must not have you henceforth question me

   Whither I go, nor reason whereabout.°   *discuss about what*

   Whither I must, I must; and, to conclude,

   This evening must I leave you, gentle Kate.

   I know you wise, but yet no farther wise

100 Than Harry Percy's wife; constant you are,

   But yet a woman;[2] and for secrecy

   No lady closer,° for I well believe   *more secretive*

   Thou wilt not utter what thou dost not know.

   And so far will I trust thee, gentle Kate.

105 LADY PERCY   How, so far?

HOTSPUR   Not an inch further. But hark you, Kate,

   Whither I go, thither shall you go too.

   Today will I set forth, tomorrow you.

   Will this content you, Kate?

LADY PERCY   It must, of force.°   *Exeunt*   *of necessity*

2.5

Enter PRINCE [HARRY]

PRINCE HARRY   Ned, prithee come out of that fat° room, and   *stuffy*
   lend me thy hand to laugh a little.

   Enter POINS [*at another door*]

POINS   Where hast been, Hal?

PRINCE HARRY   With three or four loggerheads,° amongst three   *blockheads*
5   or fourscore hogsheads.° I have sounded the very bass-string of   *casks for liquor*
   humility. Sirrah, I am sworn brother to a leash of drawers,° and   *group of three tapsters*
   can call them all by their christen names, as 'Tom', 'Dick', and
   'Francis'. They take it already, upon their salvation, that

---

7. Breasts; dolls; false gods. The term derived from "mahomet," whom English Protestants viewed as a false god worshipped by heathen peoples.
8. Punning on "cracked crowns" as meaning "broken heads" and "counterfeit currency." Hotspur may be alluding to the acts of rape associated with warfare: "nose" is slang for "penis," and a "cracked crown" can mean a "whore" or "deflowered woman."
9. Establish them as the norm; let them circulate.
1. On my horse; having sexual intercourse.
2. Women were assumed to be great talkers who could keep no secrets.
2.5 Location: An inn in Eastcheap, London.

though I be but Prince of Wales yet I am the king of courtesy,
10 and tell me flatly I am no proud jack° like Falstaff, but a   *fellow*
Corinthian,[1] a lad of mettle, a good boy—by the Lord, so they
call me; and when I am King of England I shall command all
the good lads in Eastcheap. They call drinking deep 'dyeing
scarlet',[2] and when you breathe in your watering[3] they cry
15 'Hem!' and bid you 'Play it off!'° To conclude, I am so good a   *Drink up*
proficient in one quarter of an hour that I can drink with any
tinker° in his own language during my life. I tell thee, Ned,   *itinerant pot mender*
thou hast lost much honour that thou wert not with me in this
action. But, sweet Ned—to sweeten which name of Ned I give
20 thee this penny-worth of sugar,[4] clapped even now into my
hand by an underskinker,° one that never spake other English   *assistant tapster*
in his life than 'Eight shillings and sixpence', and 'You are welcome', with this shrill addition, 'Anon,° anon, sir! Score° a   *At once / Chalk up*
pint of bastard[5] in the Half-moon!'[6] or so. But, Ned, to drive
25 away the time till Falstaff come, I prithee do thou stand in
some by-room, while I question my puny° drawer to what end   *inexperienced*
he gave me the sugar, and do thou never leave calling 'Francis!', that his tale to me may be nothing but 'Anon!' Step aside,
and I'll show thee a precedent.°   [*Exit* POINS]   *give you a foretaste*
30 POINS [*within*]   Francis!
PRINCE HARRY   Thou art perfect.
POINS [*within*]   Francis!
         Enter [FRANCIS, *a*] *drawer*
FRANCIS   Anon, anon, sir!—Look down into the Pomegranate,[7]
  Ralph!
35 PRINCE HARRY   Come hither, Francis.
FRANCIS   My lord.
PRINCE HARRY   How long hast thou to serve,[8] Francis?
FRANCIS   Forsooth, five years, and as much as to—
POINS [*within*]   Francis!
40 FRANCIS   Anon, anon, sir!
PRINCE HARRY   Five year! By'r Lady,[9] a long lease for the clink-
ing of pewter. But Francis, darest thou be so valiant as to play
the coward with thy indenture,° and show it a fair pair of   *contract*
heels, and run from it?
45 FRANCIS   O Lord, sir, I'll be sworn upon all the books° in En-   *(Bibles)*
gland, I could find in my heart—
POINS [*within*]   Francis!
FRANCIS   Anon, sir!
PRINCE HARRY   How old art thou, Francis?
50 FRANCIS   Let me see, about Michaelmas[1] next I shall be—
POINS [*within*]   Francis!
FRANCIS   Anon, sir! [*To the* PRINCE] Pray, stay a little, my lord.

---

1. A rich, licentious man. In contemporary texts, ancient Corinth was famous for wealth and sensuality.
2. Referring to the ruddy complexion associated with drunkards or to the fact that urine, a product of drink, was used to dye wool.
3. When you pause to breathe in your drink.
4. Tapsters sold sugar to sweeten wine.
5. A Spanish wine, so named because it was mixed or adulterated with honey.
6. Name of the inn room to which the wine is to be charged.
7. Name of another room in the inn.
8. Serve as apprentice. Apprenticeship typically began at age twelve or fourteen and lasted seven years.
9. By our Lady (an oath invoking the Virgin Mary).
1. September 29, a holy day honoring the archangel Michael and signifying to tradespeople the close of an accounting period.

PRINCE HARRY   Nay, but hark you, Francis. For the sugar thou
  gavest me, 'twas a pennyworth, was't not?
55 FRANCIS   O Lord, I would it had been two!
PRINCE HARRY   I will give thee for it a thousand pound. Ask me
  when thou wilt, and thou shalt have it—
POINS [within]   Francis!
FRANCIS   Anon, anon!
60 PRINCE HARRY   Anon, Francis? No, Francis, but tomorrow,
  Francis; or, Francis, o' Thursday; or, indeed, Francis, when
  thou wilt. But Francis.
FRANCIS   My lord.
PRINCE HARRY   Wilt thou rob this leathern-jerkin, crystal-
65 button, knot-pated, agate-ring, puke-stocking, caddis-garter,
  smooth-tongue, Spanish-pouch?[2]
FRANCIS   O Lord, sir, who do you mean?
PRINCE HARRY   Why, then, your brown bastard is your only
  drink![3] For look you, Francis, your white canvas doublet will
70 sully.° In Barbary,[4] sir, it cannot come to° so much.   *get dirty / be worth*
FRANCIS   What, sir?
POINS [within]   Francis!
PRINCE HARRY   Away, you rogue! Dost thou not hear them call?
  [As he departs POINS and the PRINCE] both call him. The
  Drawer stands amazed, not knowing which way to go.
  Enter VINTNER°   *Innkeeper*
VINTNER   What, standest thou still, and hearest such a calling?
75 Look to the guests within.   [Exit FRANCIS]
  My lord, old Sir John with half a dozen more are at the door.
  Shall I let them in?
PRINCE HARRY   Let them alone a while, and then open the door.
                                                          [Exit VINTNER]
  Poins!
80 POINS [within]   Anon, anon, sir!
  Enter POINS
PRINCE HARRY   Sirrah, Falstaff and the rest of the thieves are at
  the door. Shall we be merry?
POINS   As merry as crickets, my lad. But hark ye, what cunning
  match° have you made with this jest of the drawer? Come,   *game*
85 what's the issue?°   *outcome*
PRINCE HARRY   I am now of all humours that have showed
  themselves humours[5] since the old days of goodman° Adam to   *(title for a farmer)*
  the pupil° age of this present twelve o'clock at midnight.   *youthful*
  [Enter FRANCIS]
  What's o'clock, Francis?
90 FRANCIS   Anon, anon, sir!   [Exit at another door]

2. Referring (satirically) to Francis's employer, who
would be robbed of Francis's labor if the apprentice
were to run away. This employer is imagined as dressing in the manner of an upwardly mobile Londoner,
wearing a leather jacket ("jerkin") with crystal buttons
and keeping his hair close-cropped ("knot-pated"). He
also wears a signet ring with a carved agate, dark
("puke") stockings, and garters made from caddis ribbon (a cheaper alternative to silk). He has a simpering
style of speech and carries a vintner's pouch made of
Spanish leather.

3. The best of all drinks; the only drink you'll get (if you
stay in the tavern). This entire speech seems meant to
mystify Francis while obliquely warning him that he
will get dirty and be poor if he fulfills his apprenticeship.
4. North African region from which England acquired
sugar.
5. That is, I am in the mood for anything. Renaissance
medical theory held that four body fluids, or humors,
determined by their relative proportions the health,
temperament, and moods of an individual.

PRINCE HARRY That ever this fellow should have fewer words
than a parrot, and yet the son of a woman! His industry is
upstairs and downstairs, his eloquence the parcel of a reck-
oning.° I am not yet of Percy's mind, the Hotspur of the   *items of a bill*
95   North—he that kills me° some six or seven dozen of Scots at   *he that slays*
a breakfast, washes his hands, and says to his wife, 'Fie upon
this quiet life! I want work.' 'O my sweet Harry,' says she, 'how
many hast thou killed today?' 'Give my roan horse a drench,'°   *dose of medicine*
says he, and answers, 'Some fourteen,' an hour after; 'a trifle,
100 a trifle.' I prithee call in Falstaff. I'll play Percy, and that
damned brawn° shall play Dame Mortimer his wife. 'Rivo!'⁶   *fat boar*
says the drunkard. Call in Ribs, call in Tallow.°   *fat drippings*

Enter FALSTAFF [*with sword and buckler,* BARDOLPH,
PETO, *and* GADSHILL, *followed by* FRANCIS, *with wine*]

POINS Welcome, Jack. Where hast thou been?
FALSTAFF A plague of all cowards, I say, and a vengeance too,
105 marry and amen!—Give me a cup of sack, boy.—Ere I lead
this life long, I'll sew netherstocks,° and mend them and foot°   *stockings / making a new*
them too. A plague of all cowards!—Give me a cup of sack,   *foot for*
rogue. Is there no virtue extant?
He drinketh
PRINCE HARRY Didst thou never see Titan° kiss a dish of   *the sun*
110 butter— pitiful hearted Titan—that melted at the sweet tale
of the sun's? If thou didst, then behold that compound.⁷
FALSTAFF [*to* FRANCIS] You rogue, here's lime⁸ in this sack too.
There is nothing but roguery to be found in villainous man,
yet a coward is worse than a cup of sack with lime in it.
[*Exit* FRANCIS]⁹
115 A villainous coward! Go thy ways, old Jack, die when thou
wilt. If manhood, good manhood, be not forgot upon the face
of the earth, then am I a shotten herring.¹ There lives not
three good men unhanged in England, and one of them is fat
and grows old, God help the while.° A bad world, I say. I would   *these times*
120 I were a weaver²—I could sing psalms, or anything. A plague
of all cowards, I say still.
PRINCE HARRY How now, woolsack, what mutter you?
FALSTAFF A king's son! If I do not beat thee out of thy kingdom
with a dagger of lath,³ and drive all thy subjects afore thee like
125 a flock of wild geese, I'll never wear hair on my face more. You,
Prince of Wales!
PRINCE HARRY Why, you whoreson round man, what's the
matter?
FALSTAFF Are not you a coward? Answer me to that. And Poins
130 there?
POINS Zounds, ye fat paunch, an ye call me coward, by the
Lord I'll stab thee.

6. An exclamation associated with boisterous drinking.
7. Combination; that is, the melted butter (referring to
Falstaff).
8. Often added to bad wine to make it dry and
sparkling.
9. Neither Q nor F indicates when Francis leaves the
stage. He plays no further part in the action after this,
so an exit here avoids the problem of having a character onstage with no obvious function.

1. A herring that has spawned its roe and is thus very
thin.
2. Weavers were reputed to sing the Psalms of the
Bible at work. Many were Puritans, and some had emi-
grated from the zealously Protestant Low Countries.
3. A wooden dagger, which was the weapon associated
with the Vice figure in medieval morality plays (see note
to line 413).

FALSTAFF   I call thee coward? I'll see thee damned ere I call
thee coward, but I would give a thousand pound I could run
135 as fast as thou canst. You are straight enough in the shoulders;
you care not who sees your back. Call you that backing of your
friends? A plague upon such backing! Give me them that will
face me. Give me a cup of sack. I am a rogue if I drunk today.
PRINCE HARRY   O villain, thy lips are scarce wiped since thou
140 drunkest last.
FALSTAFF   All is one for that.°   *It doesn't matter*
  He drinketh
A plague of all cowards, still say I.
PRINCE HARRY   What's the matter?
FALSTAFF   What's the matter? There be four of us here have
145 ta'en a thousand pound this day morning.°   *this morning*
PRINCE HARRY   Where is it, Jack, where is it?
FALSTAFF   Where is it? Taken from us it is. A hundred upon
poor four of us.
PRINCE HARRY   What, a hundred, man?
150 FALSTAFF   I am a rogue if I were not at half-sword° with a dozen   *dueling closely*
of them, two hours together. I have scaped by miracle. I am
eight times thrust through the doublet,° four through the hose,°   *short jacket / breeches*
my buckler° cut through and through, my sword hacked like   *shield*
a handsaw. *Ecce signum.*[4]
  [*He shows his sword*]
155 I never dealt better since I was a man. All would not do.[5] A
plague of all cowards! [*Pointing to* GADSHILL, PETO, *and* BAR-
DOLPH] Let them speak. If they speak more or less than truth,
they are villains and the sons of darkness.
PRINCE HARRY[6]   Speak, sirs, how was it?
160 GADSHILL   We four set upon some dozen—
FALSTAFF [*to the* PRINCE]   Sixteen at least, my lord.
GADSHILL   And bound them.
PETO   No, no, they were not bound.
FALSTAFF   You rogue, they were bound every man of them, or
165 am a Jew else, an Hebrew Jew.
GADSHILL   As we were sharing, some six or seven fresh men set
upon us.
FALSTAFF   And unbound the rest; and then come in the other.
PRINCE HARRY   What, fought you with them all?
170 FALSTAFF   All? I know not what you call all, but if I fought not
with fifty of them, I am a bunch of radish. If there were not
two- or three-and-fifty upon poor old Jack, then am I no two-
legged creature.
PRINCE HARRY   Pray God you have not murdered some of them.
175 FALSTAFF   Nay, that's past praying for. I have peppered° two of   *made it hot for*
them. Two I am sure I have paid°—two rogues in buckram   *killed*
suits. I tell thee what, Hal, if I tell thee a lie, spit in my face,
call me horse. Thou knowest my old ward°—   *posture of defense*
  [*He stands as to fight*]

---

4. Behold the evidence (Latin).
5. All I did was not enough; the whole group was insuf-
ficient opposition.
6. This is a second place (see 2.2.48) where textual
confusion surrounds the character of Gadshill. In Q,
this line is assigned to Gadshill and the following line
to Russell (whose name was changed to "Bardolph" as

a result of censorship; see Introduction). In F, this line
is assigned to the Prince and the following line to Gadshill. The next two speeches here assigned to Gadshill
were also given to Russell in Q. The F assignment of
these lines to Gadshill may indicate that at some point
Shakespeare divided between two characters a role
originally designed for one.

here I lay,° and thus I bore my point.° Four rogues in buckram   *stood / sword point*
180   let drive at me.
PRINCE HARRY   What, four? Thou saidst but two even now.
FALSTAFF   Four, Hal, I told thee four.
POINS   Ay, ay, he said four.
FALSTAFF   These four came all afront,° and mainly° thrust at me.   *abreast / mightily*
185   I made me no more ado, but took all their seven points in my
target,° thus.   *shield*
         [*He wards himself with his buckler*]
PRINCE HARRY   Seven? Why, there were but four even now.
FALSTAFF   In buckram?
POINS   Ay, four in buckram suits.
190   FALSTAFF   Seven, by these hilts,° or I am a villain else.   *sword handle*
PRINCE HARRY [*aside to* POINS]   Prithee, let him alone. We shall
have more anon.
FALSTAFF   Dost thou hear me, Hal?
PRINCE HARRY   Ay, and mark° thee too, Jack.   *pay attention to; count*
195   FALSTAFF   Do so, for it is worth the listening to. These nine in
buckram that I told thee of—
PRINCE HARRY [*aside to* POINS]   So, two more already.
FALSTAFF   Their points[7] being broken—
POINS [*aside to the* PRINCE]   Down fell their hose.
200   FALSTAFF   Began to give me ground. But I followed me° close,   *I followed*
came in foot and hand, and, with a thought,° seven of the eleven   *swift as thought*
I paid.
PRINCE HARRY [*aside to* POINS]   O monstrous! Eleven buckram
men grown out of two!
205   FALSTAFF   But, as the devil would have it, three misbegotten
knaves in Kendal green[8] came at my back and let drive at me;
for it was so dark, Hal, that thou couldst not see thy hand.
PRINCE HARRY   These lies are like their father that begets
them—gross as a mountain, open, palpable. Why, thou clay-
210   brained guts, thou knotty-pated° fool, thou whoreson obscene   *blockheaded*
greasy tallow-catch[9]—
FALSTAFF   What, art thou mad? Art thou mad? Is not the truth
the truth?
PRINCE HARRY   Why, how couldst thou know these men in
215   Kendal green when it was so dark thou couldst not see thy
hand? Come, tell us your reason. What sayst thou to this?
POINS   Come, your reason, Jack, your reason.
FALSTAFF   What, upon compulsion? Zounds, an I were at the
strappado,[1] or all the racks[2] in the world, I would not tell you
220   on compulsion. Give you a reason on compulsion? If reasons
were as plentiful as blackberries, I would give no man a reason upon compulsion, I.
PRINCE HARRY   I'll be no longer guilty of this sin. This sanguine°   *red-faced*
coward, this bed-presser,° this horse-back-breaker, this huge hill   *licentious man*
225   of flesh—

---

7. Sword points, but Poins takes it as meaning "fasten-
ings for hose."
8. A coarse green cloth made in Kendal, Cumbria. It
was associated with poor country people, especially
forest dwellers, as well as outlaws.
9. Greasy lump of fat (gathered by butchers for candle

making).
1. A torture device in which victims were lifted off the
ground by ropes attached to their hands, which were
tied behind their backs, and then let fall.
2. A torture device in which victims' limbs were pulled
apart.

FALSTAFF 'Sblood, you starveling, you elf-skin, you dried neat's°   *ox's*
tongue, you bull's pizzle, you stock-fish[3]—O, for breath to utter
what is like thee!— you tailor's yard,[4] you sheath, you bow-
case, you vile standing tuck[5]—

230 PRINCE HARRY Well, breathe awhile, and then to't again, and
when thou hast tired thyself in base comparisons, hear me
speak but this.

POINS Mark, Jack.

PRINCE HARRY We two saw you four set on four, and bound
235 them, and were masters of their wealth.—Mark now how a
plain tale shall put you down.—Then did we two set on you
four, and, with a word, outfaced you from your prize, and have
it; yea, and can show it you here in the house. And Falstaff,
you carried your guts away as nimbly, with as quick dexterity,
240 and roared for mercy, and still run and roared, as ever I heard
bull-calf. What a slave art thou, to hack thy sword as thou
hast done, and then say it was in fight! What trick, what
device, what starting-hole° canst thou now find out to hide   *refuge*
thee from this open and apparent shame?

245 POINS Come, let's hear, Jack; what trick hast thou now?

FALSTAFF By the Lord, I knew ye as well as he that made ye.
Why, hear you, my masters. Was it for me to kill the heir-
apparent? Should I turn upon the true prince? Why, thou
knowest I am as valiant as Hercules;[6] but beware instinct. The
250 lion will not touch the true prince[7]—instinct is a great matter. I was now a coward on instinct. I shall think the better of
myself and thee during my life—I for a valiant lion, and thou
for a true prince. But by the Lord, lads, I am glad you have the
money.—[*Calling*] Hostess, clap to the doors.—Watch to-
255 night, pray tomorrow.[8] Gallants, lads, boys, hearts of gold, all
the titles of good fellowship come to you! What, shall we be
merry, shall we have a play extempore?

PRINCE HARRY Content, and the argument° shall be thy running   *subject*
away.

260 FALSTAFF Ah, no more of that, Hal, an thou lovest me.

      Enter HOSTESS

HOSTESS O Jesu, my lord the Prince!

PRINCE HARRY How now, my lady the Hostess, what sayst thou
to me?

HOSTESS Marry, my lord, there is a nobleman of the court at door
265 would speak with you. He says he comes from your father.

PRINCE HARRY Give him as much as will make him a royal
man,[9] and send him back again to my mother.

FALSTAFF What manner of man is he?

HOSTESS An old man.

---

3. *bull's pizzle:* a bull's penis that when dried and stretched was used as a whip. *stock-fish:* dried cod.
4. Tailors were popularly imagined to lack virility. Falstaff puns on "yard" as referring both to a tailor's measuring stick and to his penis.
5. *sheath:* empty case (punning on "sheath" as meaning "foreskin"). *bow-case:* a long, thin case for unstrung bows. *standing tuck:* a stiff rapier (with a pun on "standing" as meaning "sexually erect").

6. In classical mythology, a hero who performed prodigious acts of strength and courage.
7. A popular belief derived from classical texts.
8. Falstaff alludes here to Matthew 26:41: "Watch and pray, that ye enter not into temptation." He puns on "watch" as meaning "keep vigil" and "carouse" and on "pray" as meaning "prey."
9. Punning on "nobles" and "royals" as names of coins, the latter being more valuable.

270 FALSTAFF   What doth gravity out of his bed at midnight? Shall
     I give him his answer?

PRINCE HARRY   Prithee do, Jack.

FALSTAFF   Faith, and I'll send him packing.   *Exit*

PRINCE HARRY   Now, sirs; [*to* GADSHILL] by'r Lady, you fought
275 fair—so did you, Peto, so did you, Bardolph. You are lions
     too—you ran away upon instinct, you will not touch the true
     prince; no, fie!

BARDOLPH   Faith, I ran when I saw others run.

PRINCE HARRY   Faith, tell me now in earnest, how came Fal-
280 staff's sword so hacked?

PETO   Why, he hacked it with his dagger, and said he would
     swear truth out of England[1] but he would make you believe it
     was done in fight, and persuaded us to do the like.

BARDOLPH   Yea, and to tickle our noses with speargrass,[2] to make
285 them bleed; and then to beslubber our garments with it, and
     swear it was the blood of true men. I did that° I did not this   *what*
     seven year before—I blushed to hear his monstrous devices.

PRINCE HARRY   O villain, thou stolest a cup of sack eighteen years
     ago, and wert taken with the manner,° and ever since thou hast   *caught in the act*
290 blushed extempore.° Thou hadst fire[3] and sword on thy side,   *spontaneously*
     and yet thou rannest away. What instinct hadst thou for it?

BARDOLPH [*indicating his face*]   My lord, do you see these mete-
     ors? Do you behold these exhalations?[4]

PRINCE HARRY   I do.

295 BARDOLPH   What think you they portend?°   *signify*

PRINCE HARRY   Hot livers,[5] and cold° purses.   *empty*

BARDOLPH   Choler,[6] my lord, if rightly taken.°   [*Exit*][7]   *understood*

PRINCE HARRY   No, if rightly taken, halter.[8]

          Enter FALSTAFF

     Here comes lean Jack; here comes bare-bone. How now, my
300 sweet creature of bombast?[9] How long is't ago, Jack, since
     thou sawest thine own knee?

FALSTAFF   My own knee? When I was about thy years, Hal, I was
     not an eagle's talon in the waist; I could have crept into any
     alderman's thumb-ring. A plague of sighing and grief—it blows
305 a man up like a bladder. There's villainous news abroad. Here
     was Sir John Bracy from your father; you must to the court in
     the morning. That same mad fellow of the North, Percy, and
     he of Wales that gave Amamon° the bastinado,° and made Luc-   *(a devil) / a beating*
     ifer cuckold,[1] and swore the devil his true liegeman° upon the   *subject*
310 cross of a Welsh hook[2]—what a plague call you him?

---

1. Swear so excessively that Truth, imagined as an allegorical figure, would run out of England to escape him.
2. A plant with sharply pointed leaves.
3. A reference to Bardolph's red face, the focus of the
jests that follow.
4. "Meteors" and "exhalations" refer to the red
blotches on Bardolph's face, here compared to disturbances in the heavens.
5. Short tempers; livers inflamed by drink.
6. The humor associated with an angry disposition.
7. Neither Q nor F marks an exit for Bardolph here,
but both indicate that he reenters at line 439. The nec-

essary exit might well follow this discussion of his
inflamed face.
8. No, if rightly arrested, a noose. The Prince forces a
legal reading on the previous line, playing on "choler"
as "collar," or "noose," and taking "taken" to mean
"arrested."
9. Cotton padding; pompous speech.
1. Slept with the devil's own wife; gave the devil his
horns (the proverbial sign of a cuckold).
2. A heavy weapon with a crooked end, lacking the
cross shape on which oaths were usually made.

POINS   Owain Glyndŵr.

FALSTAFF   Owain, Owain, the same; and his son-in-law Mortimer, and old Northumberland, and that sprightly Scot of Scots
Douglas, that runs a-horseback up a hill perpendicular—

315 PRINCE HARRY   He that rides at high speed and with his pistol
kills a sparrow flying.

FALSTAFF   You have hit it.

PRINCE HARRY   So did he never the sparrow.

FALSTAFF   Well, that rascal hath good mettle in him; he will not
320 run.

PRINCE HARRY   Why, what a rascal art thou, then, to praise him
so for running!

FALSTAFF   A-horseback, ye cuckoo, but afoot he will not budge
a foot.

325 PRINCE HARRY   Yes, Jack, upon instinct.

FALSTAFF   I grant ye, upon instinct. Well, he is there too, and
one Mordake, and a thousand blue-caps° more. Worcester is   Scottish soldiers
stolen away tonight. Thy father's beard is turned white with the
news. You may buy land now as cheap as stinking mackerel.

330 PRINCE HARRY   Why then, it is like, if there come a hot June and
this civil buffeting hold,° we shall buy maidenheads as they buy   continue
hobnails: by the hundreds.³

FALSTAFF   By the mass, lad, thou sayst true; it is like we shall
have good trading that way. But tell me, Hal, art not thou hor-
335 rible afeard? Thou being heir-apparent, could the world pick
thee out three such enemies again as that fiend Douglas, that
spirit Percy, and that devil Glyndŵr? Art thou not horribly
afraid? Doth not thy blood thrill° at it?   shudder

PRINCE HARRY   Not a whit, i'faith. I lack some of thy instinct.

340 FALSTAFF   Well, thou wilt be horribly chid tomorrow when thou
comest to thy father. If thou love me, practise an answer.

PRINCE HARRY   Do thou stand for° my father, and examine me   impersonate
upon the particulars of my life.

FALSTAFF   Shall I? Content. This chair shall be my state,° this   throne
345 dagger my sceptre, and this cushion my crown.

        [He sits]

PRINCE HARRY   Thy state is taken for a joint-stool,⁴ thy golden
sceptre for a leaden dagger, and thy precious rich crown for a
pitiful bald crown.

FALSTAFF   Well, an° the fire of grace be not quite out of thee,   if
350 now shalt thou be moved. Give me a cup of sack to make my
eyes look red, that it may be thought I have wept; for I must
speak in passion, and I will do it in King Cambyses' vein.⁵

PRINCE HARRY   [bowing]   Well, here is my leg.°   bow

FALSTAFF   And here is my speech. [To PETO, POINS, and GADS-
355 HILL] Stand aside, nobility.

HOSTESS   O Jesu, this is excellent sport, i'faith.

FALSTAFF   Weep not, sweet Queen,⁶ for trickling tears are vain.

---

3. Alluding to rape as a practice of war or to the notion
that women would be likely to relinquish their virginity
cheaply during wartime.
4. A stool made of wooden pieces fitted or joined
together.
5. In the exaggerated rhetorical style associated with

such early Elizabethan plays as *Cambyses,* a tragedy
about a despotic Persian king.
6. Possibly addressed to the Hostess, with a pun on
"quean" as slang for "whore."

HOSTESS O the Father, how he holds his countenance!°	*keeps a straight face*
FALSTAFF For God's sake, lords, convey° my tristful° Queen,	*lead away / sad*
360 For tears do stop° the floodgates of her eyes.	*fill*
HOSTESS O Jesu, he doth it as like one of these harlotry° players	*vagabond; scurvy*

HOSTESS   O the Father, how he holds his countenance!°   *keeps a straight face*
FALSTAFF   For God's sake, lords, convey° my tristful° Queen,   *lead away / sad*
360   For tears do stop° the floodgates of her eyes.   *fill*
HOSTESS   O Jesu, he doth it as like one of these harlotry° players   *vagabond; scurvy*
        as ever I see!
FALSTAFF   Peace, good pint-pot; peace, good tickle-brain.[7]—
        Harry, I do not only marvel where thou spendest thy time, but
365   also how thou art accompanied. For though the camomile,°   *an herb*
        the more it is trodden on, the faster it grows, yet youth, the
        more it is wasted, the sooner it wears.[8] That thou art my son
        I have partly thy mother's word, partly my own opinion, but
        chiefly a villainous trick° of thine eye, and a foolish hanging   *trait*
370   of thy nether° lip, that doth warrant° me. If then thou be son   *lower / assure*
        to me, here lies the point. Why, being son to me, art thou so
        pointed at?° Shall the blessed sun of heaven prove a micher,°   *criticized / truant*
        and eat blackberries?—A question not to be asked. Shall the
        son of England prove a thief, and take purses?—A question to
375   be asked. There is a thing, Harry, which thou hast often heard
        of, and it is known to many in our land by the name of pitch.°   *sticky, black tar*
        This pitch, as ancient writers do report, doth defile.[9] So doth
        the company thou keepest. For Harry, now I do not speak to
        thee in drink, but in tears; not in pleasure, but in passion; not
380   in words only, but in woes also. And yet there is a virtuous
        man whom I have often noted in thy company, but I know not
        his name.
PRINCE HARRY   What manner of man, an it like your majesty?
FALSTAFF   A goodly, portly man, i'faith, and a corpulent; of a
385   cheerful look, a pleasing eye, and a most noble carriage;° and,   *bearing*
        as I think, his age some fifty, or, by'r Lady, inclining to three-
        score. And now I remember me, his name is Falstaff. If that
        man should be lewdly given,° he deceiveth me; for, Harry, I   *be lustful*
        see virtue in his looks. If, then, the tree may be known by the
390   fruit, as the fruit by the tree,[1] then peremptorily I speak it—
        there is virtue in that Falstaff. Him keep with; the rest ban-
        ish. And tell me now, thou naughty varlet, tell me, where hast
        thou been this month?
PRINCE HARRY   Dost thou speak like a king? Do thou stand for
395   me, and I'll play my father.
FALSTAFF [*standing*]   Depose me. If thou dost it half so gravely,
        so majestically both in word and matter, hang me up by the
        heels for a rabbit sucker,° or a poulter's hare.[2]   *an unweaned rabbit*
PRINCE HARRY [*sitting*]   Well, here I am set.°   *seated*
400 FALSTAFF   And here I stand. [*To the others*] Judge, my masters.
PRINCE HARRY   Now, Harry, whence come you?
FALSTAFF   My noble lord, from Eastcheap.
PRINCE HARRY   The complaints I hear of thee are grievous.

---

7. Slang term for a strong alcoholic drink, and hence
for the drinker.
8. Falstaff's entire speech is a parody of the previously
fashionable ornate rhetoric exemplified by John Lyly's
Euphues (1578).

9. See Ecclesiasticus 13:1 (also cited in Lyly's
Euphues).
1. An allusion to Matthew 12:33 (which also appears
in Lyly's *Euphues*).
2. A hare sold in a poultry shop.

FALSTAFF 'Sblood, my lord, they are false. [*To the others*] Nay,
I'll tickle ye for° a young prince, i'faith.   *amuse you as*
PRINCE HARRY Swearest thou, ungracious boy? Henceforth ne'er
look on me. Thou art violently carried away from grace. There
is a devil haunts thee in the likeness of an old fat man; a tun°   *large barrel*
of man is thy companion. Why dost thou converse° with that   *associate*
trunk of humours,³ that bolting-hutch° of beastliness, that   *bin for coarse meal*
swollen parcel of dropsies,⁴ that huge bombard° of sack, that   *leather wine vessel*
stuffed cloak-bag° of guts, that roasted Manningtree⁵ ox with   *suitcase*
the pudding° in his belly, that reverend Vice,⁶ that grey Iniquity,   *stuffing*
that father Ruffian, that Vanity in Years? Wherein is he good,°   *virtuous; proficient*
but to taste sack and drink it? Wherein neat and cleanly,° but   *deft*
to carve a capon and eat it? Wherein cunning, but in craft?
Wherein crafty, but in villainy? Wherein villainous, but in all
things? Wherein worthy, but in nothing?
FALSTAFF I would your grace would take me with you.° Whom   *explain what you mean*
means your grace?
PRINCE HARRY That villainous, abominable misleader of youth,
Falstaff; that old white-bearded Satan.
FALSTAFF My lord, the man I know.
PRINCE HARRY I know thou dost.
FALSTAFF But to say I know more harm in him than in myself
were to say more than I know. That he is old, the more the
pity, his white hairs do witness it. But that he is, saving your
reverence,⁷ a whoremaster, that I utterly deny. If sack and
sugar be a fault, God help the wicked. If to be old and merry
be a sin, then many an old host° that I know is damned. If to   *innkeeper*
be fat be to be hated, then Pharaoh's lean kine⁸ are to be
loved. No, my good lord, banish Peto, banish Bardolph, banish Poins, but for sweet Jack Falstaff, kind Jack Falstaff, true
Jack Falstaff, valiant Jack Falstaff, and therefore more valiant
being, as he is, old Jack Falstaff,
Banish not him thy Harry's company,
Banish not him thy Harry's company.
Banish plump Jack, and banish all the world.
PRINCE HARRY I do; I will.
[*Knocking within. Exit* HOSTESS.]⁹
Enter BARDOLPH, *running*
BARDOLPH O my lord, my lord, the sheriff with a most mon-
strous watch° is at the door.   *group of constables*
FALSTAFF Out, ye rogue! Play out the play! I have much to say
in the behalf of that Falstaff.
Enter the HOSTESS

---

3. A chest full of body fluids, whose excess, according to Renaissance medical theory, was extremely unhealthy.
4. Diseases characterized by retention of water.
5. Market town in Essex, noted for the Manningtree Fair, where a roasted ox may have been part of the festivities.
6. An irreverent, comic, and (usually) youthful character representing evil and sin in the medieval morality

plays. Sometimes named "Iniquity."
7. If you will excuse the expression.
8. In a biblical story in Genesis 41:18–21, Pharaoh dreams of seven lean cows ("kine") that portend seven years of famine.
9. Neither F nor Q marks an exit for the Hostess, but both indicate her reentry at line 443. It makes sense for her to exit here to see about the commotion at her door.

HOSTESS   O Jesu! My lord, my lord!

445   PRINCE HARRY   Heigh, heigh, the devil rides upon a fiddlestick![1]
        What's the matter?

HOSTESS   The sheriff and all the watch are at the door. They are
        come to search the house. Shall I let them in?

FALSTAFF   Dost thou hear, Hal? Never call a true piece of gold

450   a counterfeit—thou art essentially made, without seeming so.[2]

PRINCE HARRY   And thou a natural coward without instinct.

FALSTAFF   I deny your major.° If you will deny[3] the sheriff, so.   *main premise*
        If not, let him enter. If I become° not a cart° as well as another   *adorn / hangman's cart*
        man, a plague on my bringing up. I hope I shall as soon be

455   strangled with a halter as another.

PRINCE HARRY   Go, hide thee behind the arras.° The rest walk up   *tapestry wall hanging*
        above. Now, my masters, for a true face and good conscience.
                [*Exeunt* POINS, BARDOLPH, *and* GADSHILL]

FALSTAFF   Both which I have had, but their date is out;° and   *has expired*
        therefore I'll hide me.
                [*He withdraws behind the arras*]

460   PRINCE HARRY [*to* HOSTESS]   Call in the sheriff.   [*Exit* HOSTESS]
                Enter SHERIFF *and* [*a*] CARRIER
        Now, master sheriff, what is your will with me?

SHERIFF   First, pardon me, my lord. A hue and cry[4]
        Hath followed certain men unto this house.

PRINCE HARRY   What men?

465   SHERIFF   One of them is well known, my gracious lord,
        A gross, fat man.

CARRIER   As fat as butter.

PRINCE HARRY   The man, I do assure you, is not here,
        For I myself at this time have employed him.
        And, sheriff, I will engage° my word to thee   *pledge*

470   That I will by tomorrow dinner-time
        Send him to answer thee, or any man,
        For anything he shall be charged withal.
        And so let me entreat you leave the house.

SHERIFF   I will, my lord. There are two gentlemen

475   Have in this robbery lost three hundred marks.

PRINCE HARRY   It may be so. If he have robbed these men,
        He shall be answerable. And so, farewell.

SHERIFF   Good night, my noble lord.

PRINCE HARRY   I think it is good morrow, is it not?

480   SHERIFF   Indeed, my lord, I think it be two o'clock.
                Exeunt [SHERIFF *and* CARRIER]

PRINCE HARRY   This oily rascal is known as well as Paul's.°   *St. Paul's Cathedral*
        Go call him forth.

PETO   Falstaff!
                [*He draws back the arras, revealing* FALSTAFF *asleep*]
                Fast asleep

---

1. That is, what a row about nothing.
2. A famously difficult passage. Falstaff may be insisting he is true gold, not a counterfeit (and so should not
be turned over to the watch) just as Hal is a true Prince

("essentially made") despite appearances.
3. If you will refuse to let in.
4. A group of citizens who pursue a criminal.

Behind the arras, and snorting like a horse.
PRINCE HARRY Hark how hard he fetches breath. Search his
485 pockets.

        [PETO] *searcheth his pocket and findeth certain papers.*
        [*He closeth the arras and cometh forward*]

What hast thou found?
PETO   Nothing but papers, my lord.
PRINCE HARRY Let's see what they be. Read them.
PETO [*reads*] Item: a capon.   *2s. 2d.*
        Item: sauce.   *4d.*
490   Item: sack, two gallons.   *5s. 8d.*
        Item: anchovies and sack after supper.   *2s. 6d.*
        Item: bread.   *ob.*°   *obolus (halfpenny)*
PRINCE HARRY O monstrous! But one halfpennyworth of bread
    to this intolerable deal° of sack! What there is else, keep close;   *quantity*
495   we'll read it at more advantage.° There let him sleep till day.   *a better opportunity*
    I'll to the court in the morning. We must all to the wars, and
    thy place shall be honourable. I'll procure this fat rogue a
    charge of foot,[5] and I know his death will be a march of twelve
    score.[6] The money shall be paid back again, with advantage.°   *interest*
500 Be with me betimes° in the morning; and so good morrow,   *early*
    Peto.
PETO Good morrow, good my lord.   *Exeunt* [*severally*]

3.1

Enter HOTSPUR, [*the Earl of*] WORCESTER, *Lord* MORTI-
MER, [*and*] *Owain* GLYNDŴR [*with a map*]
MORTIMER These promises are fair, the parties sure,
    And our induction° full of prosperous hope.[1]   *beginning*
HOTSPUR Lord Mortimer and cousin Glyndŵr,
    Will you sit down? And uncle Worcester?
        [MORTIMER, GLYNDŴR, *and* WORCESTER *sit*]
5   A plague upon it, I have forgot the map!
GLYNDŴR No, here it is. Sit, cousin Percy, sit,
    Good cousin Hotspur;
        [HOTSPUR *sits*]
                For by that name
    As oft as Lancaster[2] doth speak of you,
    His cheek looks pale, and with a rising sigh
    He wisheth you in heaven.
10 HOTSPUR   And you in hell,
    As oft as he hears Owain Glyndŵr spoke of.
GLYNDŴR I cannot blame him. At my nativity
    The front° of heaven was full of fiery shapes,   *forehead*
    Of burning cressets;[3] and at my birth

---

5. Command of an infantry company.
6. I know it will kill him to march twelve times twenty
yards or paces.
3.1 Location: Glyndŵr's castle, Wales. According to
Holinshed's *Chronicles,* the events of this scene take
place in the house of the Archdeacon of Bangor; but he
is not present in Shakespeare's scene, and Glyndŵr acts
as host throughout.
1. Full of the hope of prospering.
2. Referring to Henry's title as Duke and hence implying a denial of the legitimacy of his kingship.
3. Metal baskets of fire suspended from long poles;
meteors.

15   The frame and huge foundation of the earth
        Shaked like a coward.
    HOTSPUR   Why, so it would have done
        At the same season if your mother's cat
        Had but kittened, though yourself had never been born.
    GLYNDŴR   I say the earth did shake when I was born.
20 HOTSPUR   And I say the earth was not of my mind
        If you suppose as fearing you it shook.
    GLYNDŴR   The heavens were all on fire, the earth did tremble—
    HOTSPUR   O, then the earth shook to see the heavens on fire,
        And not in fear of your nativity.
25   Diseasèd nature oftentimes breaks forth
        In strange eruptions; oft the teeming° earth   *fertile*
        Is with a kind of colic pinched and vexed
        By the imprisoning of unruly wind
        Within her womb, which for enlargement° striving   *release*
30   Shakes the old beldam° earth, and topples down   *grandmother*
        Steeples and moss-grown towers. At your birth
        Our grandam earth, having this distemp'rature,°   *disorder*
        In passion shook.
    GLYNDŴR   Cousin, of many men
        I do not bear these crossings.° Give me leave   *contradictions*
35   To tell you once again that at my birth
        The front of heaven was full of fiery shapes,
        The goats ran from the mountains, and the herds
        Were strangely clamorous to the frighted fields.
        These signs have marked me extraordinary,
40   And all the courses of my life do show
        I am not in the roll of common men.
        Where is he living, clipped in with° the sea   *encircled by*
        That chides the banks° of England, Scotland, Wales,   *shores*
        Which° calls me pupil or hath read to° me?   *Who / tutored*
45   And bring him out° that is but woman's son   *show me any man*
        Can trace° me in the tedious ways of art,[4]   *follow*
        And hold me pace° in deep experiments.   *keep up with me*
    HOTSPUR [*standing*]   I think there's no man speaketh better Welsh.[5]
        I'll to dinner.
50 MORTIMER   Peace, cousin Percy, you will make him mad.
    GLYNDŴR   I can call spirits from the vasty deep.°   *lower world*
    HOTSPUR   Why, so can I, or so can any man;
        But will they come when you do call for them?
    GLYNDŴR   Why, I can teach you, cousin, to command the devil.
55 HOTSPUR   And I can teach thee, coz, to shame the devil,
        By telling truth: 'Tell truth, and shame the devil'.
        If thou have power to raise him, bring him hither,
        And I'll be sworn I have power to shame him hence.
        O, while you live, tell truth and shame the devil.
60 MORTIMER   Come, come, no more of this unprofitable chat.
    GLYNDŴR   Three times hath Henry Bolingbroke made head°   *raised an army*
        Against my power;° thrice from the banks of Wye   *army*

---

4. The long, laborious ways of magic.   monly meant to use a strange, unintelligible language.
5. The Welsh language was often described by English   Hotspur implies that Glyndŵr speaks nonsense.
writers as a barbaric one, and "to speak Welsh" com-

And sandy-bottomed Severn have I sent him
Bootless° home, and weather-beaten back.[6]   *Unsuccessful*
65 HOTSPUR Home without boots, and in foul weather too!
How scapes he agues,° in the devil's name?   *fevers*
GLYNDŴR Come, here's the map. Shall we divide our right,°   *what we are entitled to*
According to our threefold order ta'en?[7]
MORTIMER The Archdeacon hath divided it
70 Into three limits° very equally.   *regions*
England from Trent and Severn hitherto°   *to here*
By south and east is to my part assigned;
All westward—Wales beyond the Severn shore
And all the fertile land within that bound—
75 To Owain Glyndŵr; [*to* HOTSPUR] and, dear coz, to you
The remnant northward lying off from Trent.
And our indentures tripartite° are drawn,   *in triplicate*
Which, being sealèd interchangeably[8]—
A business that this night may execute°—   *may be done tonight*
80 Tomorrow, cousin Percy, you and I
And my good lord of Worcester will set forth
To meet your father and the Scottish power,
As is appointed us, at Shrewsbury.
My father,° Glyndŵr, is not ready yet,   *father-in-law*
85 Nor shall we need his help these fourteen days.
Within that space you may have drawn together
Your tenants, friends, and neighbouring gentlemen.
GLYNDŴR A shorter time shall send me to you, lords;
And in my conduct° shall your ladies come,   *escort*
90 From whom you now must steal and take no leave;
For there will be a world of water shed
Upon the parting of your wives and you.
HOTSPUR Methinks my moiety° north from Burton here   *portion*
In quantity equals not one° of yours.   *either*
95 See how this river comes me cranking in,[9]
And cuts me from the best of all my land
A huge half-moon, a monstrous cantle,° out.   *piece*
I'll have the current in this place dammed up,
And here the smug° and silver Trent shall run   *smooth*
100 In a new channel fair and evenly.
It shall not wind with such a deep indent,
To rob me of so rich a bottom° here.   *lowland plain*
GLYNDŴR Not wind? It shall, it must; you see it doth.
MORTIMER Yea, but mark how he bears his course, and runs me up°   *turns upward*
105 With like advantage on the other side,
Gelding the opposèd continent[1] as much
As on the other side it takes from you.
WORCESTER Yea, but a little charge° will trench° him here,   *expense / rechannel*
And on this north side win this cape of land,
110 And then he runs straight and even.
HOTSPUR I'll have it so; a little charge will do it.

---

6. According to Holinshed, Glyndŵr used magic to
raise storms that frustrated Henry's attacks.
7. *threefold:* either an agreement made in triplicate
(see line 77) or an agreement having three parts (see
the rebels' plan to divide the island into three pieces at

lines 68–76). *order ta'en:* agreement made.
8. Bearing the seals of all three nobles.
9. Comes bending in on my shores.
1. Cutting a vital piece from ("gelding") the opposite
bank.

GLYNDŴR   I'll not have it altered.

HOTSPUR   Will not you?

GLYNDŴR   No, nor you shall not.

115 HOTSPUR   Who shall say me nay?

GLYNDŴR   Why, that will I.

HOTSPUR   Let me not understand you, then: speak it in Welsh.

GLYNDŴR   I can speak English, lord, as well as you;
      For I was trained up in the English court,
120   Where, being but young, I framèd to the harp
      Many an English ditty lovely well,
      And gave the tongue a helpful ornament²—
      A virtue that was never seen in you.

HOTSPUR   Marry, and I am glad of it, with all my heart.
125   I had rather be a kitten and cry 'mew'
      Than one of these same metre ballad-mongers.³
      I had rather hear a brazen canstick turned,⁴
      Or a dry wheel grate on the axle-tree,°   axle
      And that would set my teeth nothing on edge,
130   Nothing so much as mincing° poetry.   affected
      'Tis like the forced gait of a shuffling° nag.   hobbled

GLYNDŴR   Come, you shall have Trent turned.

HOTSPUR   I do not care. I'll give thrice so much land
      To any well-deserving friend;
135   But in the way of bargain—mark ye me—
      I'll cavil on° the ninth part of a hair.   quibble about
      Are the indentures drawn? Shall we be gone?

GLYNDŴR   The moon shines fair. You may away by night.
      I'll haste the writer, and withal°   simultaneously
140   Break with° your wives of your departure hence.   Inform
      I am afraid my daughter will run mad,
      So much she doteth on her Mortimer.   *Exit*

MORTIMER   Fie, cousin Percy, how you cross my father!

HOTSPUR   I cannot choose. Sometime he angers me
145   With telling me of the moldwarp⁵ and the ant,
      Of the dreamer Merlin⁶ and his prophecies,
      And of a dragon and a finless fish,
      A clip-winged griffin⁷ and a moulten° raven,   moulted
      A couching lion and a ramping cat,⁸
150   And such a deal of skimble-skamble° stuff   stupid
      As puts me from my faith.⁹ I tell you what,
      He held me last night at the least nine hours
      In reckoning up the several devils' names
      That were his lackeys. I cried, 'Hum!' and, 'Well, go to!',
155   But marked him not a word. O, he is as tedious
      As a tired horse, a railing wife,
      Worse than a smoky house. I had rather live

2. And gave the English language the ornament of a musical setting; and supplemented the English lyrics with pleasing music.
3. Sellers or writers of ballads.
4. A brazen candlestick scraped and polished on a lathe after casting. John Stow's *Survey of London* (1598) records contemporary complaints about the noise of candlestick making.
5. Mole. Holinshed records a prophecy whereby Henry, figured as a mole, would be overthrown by a

dragon, a lion, and a wolf, representing Glyndŵr, Percy, and Mortimer, respectively.
6. Legendary Welsh prophet, wizard, and bard at King Arthur's court.
7. A fabulous beast, part lion and part eagle.
8. Alluding to the heraldic terms "couchant" and "rampant," which mean "crouching" and "rearing fiercely." Hotspur is making fun of Glyndŵr's heraldic preoccupations.
9. As makes me a skeptic, even of religion.

With cheese and garlic, in a windmill, far,
Than feed on cates° and have him talk to me   *delicacies*
160 In any summer house° in Christendom.   *luxurious residence*
    MORTIMER   In faith, he is a worthy gentleman,
    Exceedingly well read, and profited°   *proficient*
    In strange concealments,° valiant as a lion,   *In occult arts*
    And wondrous affable, and as bountiful
165 As mines of India. Shall I tell you, cousin?
    He holds your temper in a high respect,
    And curbs himself even of his natural scope°   *freedom of speech*
    When you come 'cross° his humour; faith, he does.   *contradict*
    I warrant you, that man is not alive
170 Might so have tempted° him as you have done   *provoked*
    Without the taste of danger and reproof.
    But do not use it oft, let me entreat you.
    WORCESTER [*to* HOTSPUR]   In faith, my lord, you are too wilful-blame,°   *stubborn*
    And since your coming hither have done enough
175 To put him quite besides° his patience.   *out of*
    You must needs learn, lord, to amend this fault.
    Though sometimes it show greatness, courage, blood°—   *spirit; noble birth*
    And that's the dearest grace° it renders you—   *best distinction*
    Yet oftentimes it doth present° harsh rage,   *show*
180 Defect of manners, want of government,
    Pride, haughtiness, opinion,° and disdain,   *self-conceit*
    The least of which haunting a nobleman
    Loseth men's hearts, and leaves behind a stain
    Upon the beauty of all parts besides,°   *all other qualities*
185 Beguiling° them of commendation.   *Depriving*
    HOTSPUR   Well, I am schooled. Good manners be your speed!°   *give you success*
        Enter GLYNDŴR *with the Ladies* [LADY PERCY *and Morti-*
        mer's wife]
    Here come our wives, and let us take our leave.
        [*Mortimer's wife weeps, and speaks to him in Welsh*]
    MORTIMER   This is the deadly spite° that angers me: *vexation*
    My wife can speak no English, I no Welsh.
190 GLYNDŴR   My daughter weeps she'll not part with you.
    She'll be a soldier, too; she'll to the wars.
    MORTIMER   Good father, tell her that she and my aunt Percy[1]
    Shall follow in your conduct speedily.
        GLYNDŴR *speaks to her in Welsh, and she answers*
        him in the same
    GLYNDŴR   She is desperate here,° a peevish self-willed harlotry,°   *on this point / hussy*
195 One that no persuasion can do good upon.
        The lady speaks in Welsh
    MORTIMER   I understand thy looks. That pretty Welsh°   *(i.e., her tears)*
    Which thou down pourest from these swelling heavens°   *overflowing eyes*
    I am too perfect° in, and but for shame   *proficient*
    In such a parley° should I answer thee.   *In a similar language*
        The lady [*kisses him, and speaks*] *again in Welsh*
200 MORTIMER   I understand thy kisses, and thou mine,
    And that's a feeling disputation;[2]
    But I will never be a truant, love,

---

1. Kate, Lady Percy. Her historical counterpart was the   2. A conversation rooted in emotions or in touch.
sister, not the aunt, of Glyndŵr's son-in-law.

Till I have learnt thy language, for thy tongue
Makes Welsh as sweet as ditties highly° penned,   eloquently
205   Sung by a fair queen in a summer's bower
With ravishing division,° to her lute.   embellishments
GLYNDŴR   Nay, if you melt,° then will she run mad.   weep
    The lady [sits on the rushes³ and] speaks again in Welsh
MORTIMER   O, I am ignorance itself in this!
GLYNDŴR   She bids you on the wanton° rushes lay you down   luxurious
210   And rest your gentle head upon her lap,⁴
And she will sing the song that pleaseth you,
And on your eyelids crown the god of sleep,
Charming your blood with pleasing heaviness,°   sleepiness
Making such difference 'twixt wake and sleep
215   As is the difference betwixt day and night
The hour before the heavenly-harnessed team⁵
Begins his golden progress in the east.
MORTIMER   With all my heart, I'll sit and hear her sing.
By that time will our book,° I think, be drawn.   document
    [*He sits, resting his head on the Welsh lady's lap*]
220 GLYNDŴR   Do so, and those musicians that shall play to you
Hang in the air a thousand leagues from hence,
And straight they shall be here. Sit and attend.
HOTSPUR   Come, Kate, thou art perfect in lying down.°   expert at lovemaking
Come, quick, quick, that I may lay my head in thy lap.⁶
225 LADY PERCY [*sitting*]   Go, ye giddy goose!
    [HOTSPUR *sits, resting his head on Lady Percy's lap.*]
    The music plays⁷
HOTSPUR   Now I perceive the devil understands Welsh;
And 'tis no marvel, he is so humorous.°   eccentric; whimsical
By'r Lady, he's a good musician.
LADY PERCY   Then should you be nothing but musical,
230   For you are altogether governed by humours.°   whims
Lie still, ye thief, and hear the lady sing in Welsh.
HOTSPUR   I had rather hear Lady my brach° howl in Irish.   female hunting dog
LADY PERCY   Wouldst thou have thy head broken?
HOTSPUR   No.
235 LADY PERCY   Then be still.
HOTSPUR   Neither—'tis a woman's fault.⁸
LADY PERCY   Now God help thee!
HOTSPUR   To the Welsh lady's bed.
LADY PERCY   What's that?
240 HOTSPUR   Peace; she sings.
    Here the lady sings a Welsh song
HOTSPUR   Come, Kate, I'll have your song too.
LADY PERCY   Not mine, in good sooth.°   truth
HOTSPUR   Not yours, in good sooth! Heart,° you swear like a   By God's heart
comfit-maker's° wife: 'Not you, in good sooth!' and 'As true as   confectioner's
245   I live!' and
'As God shall mend me!' and 'As sure as day!';

---

3. Used as a floor covering, both in houses and on the theater stage.
4. Often a euphemism for the genitals.
5. The sun was supposedly carried in a chariot drawn by horses.
6. "Head" was slang for "penis" and "lap" for "vagina."

7. Instrumental music would probably be played in a so-called music house behind the upper stage in the Elizabethan theater and so might well seem to "hang in the air" (see lines 220–21).
8. No, I won't be still—it is a woman's trait (and I am a man).

And giv'st such sarcenet[9] surety for thy oaths
As if thou never walk'st further than Finsbury.[1]
Swear me, Kate, like a lady as thou art,
250 A good mouth-filling oath, and leave 'in sooth'
And such protest of pepper gingerbread[2]
To velvet-guards and Sunday citizens.[3]
Come, sing.
LADY PERCY   I will not sing.
255 HOTSPUR 'Tis the next° way to turn tailor,[4] or be redbreast   *quickest*
teacher.° [*Rising*] An the indentures be drawn, I'll away within   *or teach birds to sing*
these two hours; and so come in when ye will.   *Exit*
GLYNDŴR   Come, come, Lord Mortimer. You are as slow
As hot Lord Percy is on fire to go.
260 By this° our book is drawn. We'll but seal,   *now*
And then to horse immediately.
MORTIMER [*rising*]   With all my heart.
[*The ladies rise, and all*] *exeunt*

3.2

Enter KING [HENRY], PRINCE [HARRY], *and* [*lords*]
KING HENRY   Lords, give us leave—the Prince of Wales and I
Must have some private conference—but be near at hand,
For we shall presently have need of you.   *Exeunt lords*
I know not whether God will have it so
5 For some displeasing service I have done,
That in his secret doom° out of my blood°   *judgment / lineage*
He'll breed revengement and a scourge for me,
But thou dost in thy passages° of life   *course*
Make me believe that thou art only marked
10 For° the hot vengeance and the rod of heaven   *To be*
To punish my mistreadings. Tell me else,
Could such inordinate° and low desires,   *unsuitable*
Such poor, such bare, such lewd, such mean attempts,°   *base undertakings*
Such barren pleasures,[1] rude society,
15 As thou art matched withal° and grafted to,   *with*
Accompany the greatness of thy blood,
And hold their level° with thy princely heart?   *And claim equality*
PRINCE HARRY   So please your majesty, I would I could
Quit° all offences with as clear excuse   *Clear myself of*
20 As well as I am doubtless° I can purge   *certain*
Myself of many I am charged withal;
Yet such extenuation let me beg
As, in reproof° of many tales devised—   *upon disproof*
Which oft the ear of greatness needs must hear
25 By smiling pickthanks° and base newsmongers°—   *flatterers / gossips*
I may, for some things true wherein my youth
Hath faulty wandered and irregular,
Find pardon on my true submission.°   *admission of guilt*
KING HENRY   God pardon thee! Yet let me wonder, Harry,

9. Flimsy (from the name of a fine silk).
1. Finsbury Fields, north of London, was a popular resort for London's middling classes. Hotspur implies that Kate's mild oaths make her sound like a burgher's wife.
2. Watered-down oaths. Gingerbread was cheaply available at fairs and markets, and sometimes pepper was used as an inexpensive substitute for ginger.

3. Citizens who doff their work clothes and dress up only on Sundays. *To velvet-guards:* To those, like citizens' wives, whose clothes are trimmed ("guarded") with velvet.
4. Tailors were noted for singing.
3.2 Location: The palace, London.
1. Unprofitable habits; nonreproductive erotic pursuits.

30　At thy affections,° which do hold a wing　　　　　　　　　*inclinations*
　　Quite from² the flight of all thy ancestors.
　　Thy place in Council thou hast rudely³ lost—
　　Which by thy younger brother is supplied—
　　And art almost an alien to the hearts
35　Of all the court and princes of my blood.
　　The hope and expectation of thy time°　　　　　　　　*time of life; youth*
　　Is ruined, and the soul of every man
　　Prophetically do forethink thy fall.
　　Had I so lavish of my presence been,
40　So common-hackneyed⁴ in the eyes of men,
　　So stale and cheap to vulgar company,
　　Opinion,° that did help me to the crown,　　　　　　　*Public opinion*
　　Had still kept loyal to possession,⁵
　　And left me in reputeless° banishment,　　　　　　　　*inglorious*
45　A fellow of no mark nor likelihood.°　　　　　　　*promise of success*
　　By being seldom seen, I could not stir
　　But, like a comet, I was wondered at,
　　That men would tell their children 'This is he.'
　　Others would say 'Where, which is Bolingbroke?'
50　And then I stole all courtesy from heaven,⁶
　　And dressed myself in such humility
　　That I did pluck allegiance from men's hearts,
　　Loud shouts and salutations from their mouths,
　　Even in the presence of the crownèd King.
55　Thus did I keep my person fresh and new,
　　My presence like a robe pontifical°—　　　　　　　*churchman's rich dress*
　　Ne'er seen but wondered at—and so my state,°　　　*magnificence; royalty*
　　Seldom but sumptuous, showed like a feast,
　　And won by rareness such solemnity.
60　The skipping King, he ambled up and down
　　With shallow jesters and rash bavin° wits,　　　　　　　*brushwood*
　　Soon kindled and soon burnt, carded his state,⁷
　　Mingled his royalty with cap'ring fools,
　　Had his great name profanèd with their scorns,°　　*by their scornful manners*
65　And gave his countenance,° against his name,⁸　　　　　*approval*
　　To laugh at gibing boys, and stand the push°　　*tolerate the impudence*
　　Of every beardless vain comparative;°　　　　　　　　　*wit*
　　Grew a companion to the common streets,
　　Enfeoffed° himself to popularity,　　　　　　　　　*Surrendered*
70　That, being daily swallowed by men's eyes,
　　They surfeited with honey, and began
　　To loathe the taste of sweetness, whereof a little
　　More than a little is by much too much.
　　So when he had occasion to be seen,
75　He was but as the cuckoo is in June,⁹
　　Heard, not regarded, seen but with such eyes
　　As, sick and blunted with community,°　　　　　　　*familiarity*

2. *which . . . from:* which do fly a course contrary to.
3. By violence. Perhaps alluding to the story, dramatized in *The Famous Victories of Henry V,* that Prince
Hal boxed the Lord Chief Justice on the ear and was
subsequently punished.
4. Cheapened. A hackney was a horse available for
common hire.
5. The possessor of the throne (Richard II).

6. That is, surpassed heaven itself for graciousness.
7. Adulterated his royal dignity. The term refers to a
process ("carding") whereby wool or liquids were mixed
with inferior substances.
8. To the detriment of his reputation.
9. Referring to a proverbial saying, "No one regards the
June cuckoo's song."

Afford no extraordinary gaze
Such as is bent on sun-like majesty
80 When it shines seldom in admiring eyes,
But rather drowsed and hung their eyelids down,
Slept in his face,° and rendered such aspect°   *before his eyes / looks*
As cloudy° men use to their adversaries,   *sullen*
Being with his presence glutted, gorged, and full.
85 And in that very line,° Harry, standest thou;   *category*
For thou hast lost thy princely privilege
With vile participation.° Not an eye   *base companionship*
But is a-weary of thy common sight,
Save mine, which hath desired to see thee more,
90 Which now doth that° I would not have it do—   *what*
Make blind itself with foolish tenderness.
      [*He weeps*]

PRINCE HARRY   I shall hereafter, my thrice-gracious lord,
Be more myself.

KING HENRY   For all the world,
As thou art to this hour was Richard then,
95 When I from France set foot at Ravenspurgh,
And even as I was then is Percy now.
Now by my sceptre, and my soul to boot,
He hath more worthy interest° to the state   *more claim by worth*
Than thou, the shadow° of succession;   *mere image*
100 For, of° no right, nor colour° like to right,   *having / pretext*
He doth fill fields with harness° in the realm,   *armor*
Turns head° against the lion's° armèd jaws,   *Leads a revolt / king's*
And, being no more in debt to years than thou,
Leads ancient lords and reverend bishops on
105 To bloody battles, and to bruising arms.
What never-dying honour hath he got
Against renownèd Douglas!—whose high deeds,
Whose hot incursions and great name in arms,
Holds from all soldiers chief majority°   *preeminence*
110 And military title capital[1]
Through all the kingdoms that acknowledge Christ.
Thrice hath this Hotspur, Mars° in swaddling-clothes,   *god of war*
This infant warrior, in his enterprises
Discomfited° great Douglas; ta'en him once;   *Defeated*
115 Enlargèd° him; and made a friend of him   *Released*
To fill the mouth of deep defiance up,[2]
And shake the peace and safety of our throne.
And what say you to this? Percy, Northumberland,
The Archbishop's grace of York, Douglas, Mortimer,
120 Capitulate° against us, and are up.°   *Combine / up in arms*
But wherefore do I tell these news to thee?
Why, Harry, do I tell thee of my foes,
Which° art my near'st and dearest enemy?—   *Who*
Thou that art like enough, through vassal° fear,   *servile*
125 Base inclination, and the start of spleen,°   *fit of temper*
To fight against me under Percy's pay,
To dog his heels, and curtsy at his frowns,

---

1. And claim to the title of principal (capital) warrior.
2. To add volume to the voice of deep defiance; to fill up the appetite of deep defiance.

To show how much thou art degenerate.

PRINCE HARRY Do not think so; you shall not find it so.
130 And God forgive them that so much have swayed
Your majesty's good thoughts away from me.
I will redeem all this on Percy's head,
And in the closing of some glorious day
Be bold to tell you that I am your son;
135 When I will wear a garment all of blood,
And stain my favours° in a bloody mask,   *features*
Which, washed away, shall scour my shame with it.
And that shall be the day, whene'er it lights,°   *comes*
That this same child of honour and renown,
140 This gallant Hotspur, this all-praisèd knight,
And your unthought-of Harry chance to meet.
For every honour sitting on his helm,
Would they were multitudes, and on my head
My shames redoubled; for the time will come
145 That I shall make this northern youth exchange
His glorious deeds for my indignities.
Percy is but my factor,° good my lord,   *agent*
To engross up° glorious deeds on my behalf;   *amass*
And I will call him to so strict account
150 That he shall render every glory up,
Yea, even the slightest worship of his time,°   *honor of his life*
Or I will tear the reckoning from his heart.
This, in the name of God, I promise here,
The which if he be pleased I shall perform,
155 I do beseech your majesty may salve°   *heal*
The long-grown wounds of my intemperature;°   *disorder; intemperance*
If not, the end of life cancels all bonds,
And I will die a hundred thousand deaths
Ere break the smallest parcel of this vow.
160 **KING HENRY** A hundred thousand rebels die in this.
Thou shalt have charge° and sovereign trust herein.   *military command*

Enter [Sir Walter] BLUNT

How now, good Blunt? Thy looks are full of speed.
BLUNT So hath the business that I come to speak of.
Lord Mortimer of Scotland[3] hath sent word
165 That Douglas and the English rebels met
The eleventh of this month at Shrewsbury.
A mighty and a fearful head° they are,   *army*
If promises be kept on every hand,
As ever offered foul play in a state.
170 **KING HENRY** The Earl of Westmorland set forth today,
With him my son Lord John of Lancaster,
For this advertisement° is five days old.   *news*
On Wednesday next, Harry, you shall set forward.
On Thursday we ourselves will march.
175 Our meeting is Bridgnorth,[4] and, Harry, you
Shall march through Gloucestershire, by which account,°   *calculation*
Our business valuèd,° some twelve days hence   *taken into account*
Our general forces at Bridgnorth shall meet.

---

3. A Scottish lord who is unrelated to Glyndŵr's son-in-law.   4. A town about 20 miles southeast of Shrewsbury.

Our hands are full of business; let's away.
180 Advantage feeds him fat[5] while men delay.   *Exeunt*

3.3

Enter FALSTAFF [*with a truncheon*° *at his waist*], *and*   officer's club
BARDOLPH

FALSTAFF   Bardolph, am I not fallen away° vilely since this last   shrunk
action?[1] Do I not bate?° Do I not dwindle? Why, my skin hangs   grow thin
about me like an old lady's loose gown. I am withered like an
old apple-john.[2] Well, I'll repent, and that suddenly, while I
5 am in some liking.° I shall be out of heart[3] shortly, and then I   in the mood
shall have no strength to repent. An I have not forgotten what
the inside of a church is made of, I am a peppercorn, a brewer's
horse°—the inside of a church! Company, villainous company,   an old workhorse
hath been the spoil of me.
10 BARDOLPH   Sir John, you are so fretful you cannot live long.
FALSTAFF   Why, there is it. Come, sing me a bawdy song, make
me merry. I was as virtuously given° as a gentleman need to   inclined
be: virtuous enough; swore little; diced not—above seven
times a week; went to a bawdy-house not—above once in a
15 quarter—of an hour; paid money that I borrowed—three or
four times; lived well, and in good compass.° And now I live   limits
out of all order, out of all compass.
BARDOLPH   Why, you are so fat, Sir John, that you must needs be
out of all compass,° out of all reasonable compass, Sir John.   circumference; girth
20 FALSTAFF   Do thou amend thy face, and I'll amend my life.
Thou art our admiral,° thou bearest the lantern in the poop[4]—   flagship
but 'tis in the nose of thee. Thou art the Knight of the Burn-
ing Lamp.[5]
BARDOLPH   Why, Sir John, my face does you no harm.
25 FALSTAFF   No, I'll be sworn; I make as good use of it as many a
man doth of a death's head,[6] or a *memento mori*.[7] I never see
thy face but I think upon hell-fire and Dives that lived in
purple—for there he is in his robes, burning, burning.[8] If thou
wert any way given to virtue, I would swear by thy face; my
30 oath should be 'By this fire that's God's angel!' But thou art
altogether given over,° and wert indeed, but for the light in thy   dedicated to vice
face, the son of utter darkness. When thou rannest up Gads
Hill in the night to catch my horse, if I did not think thou hadst
been an *ignis fatuus* or a ball of wildfire,[9] there's no purchase
35 in money. O, thou art a perpetual triumph,° an everlasting   torchlight procession
bonfire-light! Thou hast saved me a thousand marks[1] in links°   small torches
and torches, walking with thee in the night betwixt tavern and

---

5. Opportunities (for rebellion) flourish; the superior
position (of the rebels) improves.
3.3 Location: The inn in Eastcheap, London.
1. This last military engagement (referring to the Gad's
Hill episode).
2. A kind of apple often eaten long after picking, when
its skin was shriveled.
3. Disinclined; weary.
4. The ship's main deck.
5. Parodying figures from popular romance such as
Amadis, the Knight of the Burning Sword.
6. A skull, or representation of a skull, such as was
engraved as an emblem of mortality on seal rings.
7. An object serving as a reminder of mortality (Latin
for "remember you must die").

8. Referring to a biblical parable about a rich man
"clothed in purple and fine linen" who regularly refused
to feed the beggar Lazarus and was ultimately forced to
suffer in hell for his sin (Luke 16:19–23); also referring
to Bardolph's body as bearing the signs of venereal disease. "Burning" implies "on fire with lust" as well as
"infected with syphilitic sores."
9. A flaming explosive used in warfare or in fireworks;
skin marked by erysipelas, an inflammatory disease.
ignis fatuus (Latin for "foolish fire"): a phenomenon in
which phosphorescent light appears on marshy ground;
a false hope.
1. Considerable money (each mark was worth two-
thirds of a pound).

tavern—but the sack that thou hast drunk me° would have   *drunk (at my cost)*
bought me lights as good cheap° at the dearest chandler's² in   *as cheaply*
40   Europe. I have maintained that salamander³ of yours with fire
any time this two-and-thirty years, God reward me for it.

BARDOLPH   'Sblood, I would my face were in your belly!⁴

FALSTAFF   God-a-mercy! So should I be sure to be heartburnt.

Enter HOSTESS

How now, Dame Partlet⁵ the hen, have you enquired yet who
45   picked my pocket?

HOSTESS   Why, Sir John, what do you think, Sir John? Do you
think I keep thieves in my house? I have searched, I have
enquired; so has my husband, man by man, boy by boy, ser-
vant by servant. The tithe° of a hair was never lost in my house   *tenth part*
50   before.

FALSTAFF   Ye lie, Hostess: Bardolph was shaved and lost many
a hair,⁶ and I'll be sworn my pocket was picked. Go to, you are
a woman, go.

HOSTESS   Who, I? No, I defy thee! God's light, I was never
55   called so in mine own house before.

FALSTAFF   Go to, I know you well enough.

HOSTESS   No, Sir John, you do not know me,⁷ Sir John; I know
you, Sir John. You owe me money, Sir John, and now you pick
a quarrel to beguile me of it. I bought you a dozen of shirts to
60   your back.

FALSTAFF   Dowlas,° filthy dowlas. I have given them away to   *Coarse linen*
bakers' wives; they have made bolters° of them.   *sieves*

HOSTESS   Now as I am a true woman, holland° of eight shillings   *fine linen*
an ell.° You owe money here besides, Sir John: for your diet,   *a measure of 45 inches*
65   and by-drinkings,° and money lent you, four-and-twenty pound.   *drinks between meals*

FALSTAFF [*pointing at* BARDOLPH]   He had his part of it. Let him
pay.

HOSTESS   He? Alas, he is poor; he hath nothing.

FALSTAFF   How, poor? Look upon his face. What call you rich?
70   Let them coin his nose, let them coin his cheeks, I'll not pay
a denier.⁸ What, will you make a younker° of me? Shall I not   *novice; gull*
take mine ease in mine inn, but I shall have my pocket picked?
I have lost a seal-ring of my grandfather's worth forty mark.

HOSTESS   O Jesu, [*to* BARDOLPH] I have heard the Prince tell
75   him, I know not how oft, that that ring was copper.

FALSTAFF   How? The Prince is a jack,° a sneak-up.° [*Raising*   *rascal / sly villain*
his truncheon] 'Sblood, an he were here I would cudgel him
like a dog if he would say so.

Enter PRINCE [HARRY *and* PETO], *marching; and* FAL-
STAFF *meets* [*them*], *playing upon his truncheon like a*
fife

How now, lad, is the wind in that door,° i'faith? Must we all   *quarter*
80   march?

BARDOLPH   Yea, two and two, Newgate fashion.⁹

---

2. The most expensive candle maker's.
3. A fabled lizard capable of living in fire. The implication is that Falstaff has maintained the salamander Bardolph with the "fires" of sack or lust.
4. Equivalent to "Stick it down your throat" (a proverbial retort to an insult).
5. A traditional name for hens and for women supposed to talk too much.

6. Had his beard cut; was cheated or robbed of his
money; lost his hair because of syphilis.
7. That is, you don't know how honest I am; you don't
have sexual knowledge of me.
8. French copper coin of little value.
9. Bound like convicts taken to and from London's
Newgate prison.

HOSTESS   My lord, I pray you hear me.

PRINCE HARRY   What sayst thou, Mistress Quickly? How doth
    thy husband?

I love him well; he is an honest man.

85   HOSTESS   Good my lord, hear me!

FALSTAFF   Prithee, let her alone, and list to me.

PRINCE HARRY   What sayst thou, Jack?

FALSTAFF   The other night I fell asleep here behind the arras,
    and had my pocket picked. This house is turned bawdy-
90   house: they pick pockets.

PRINCE HARRY   What didst thou lose, Jack?

FALSTAFF   Wilt thou believe me, Hal, three or four bonds of
    forty pound apiece, and a seal-ring of my grandfather's.

PRINCE HARRY   A trifle, some eightpenny matter.

95   HOSTESS   So I told him, my lord; and I said I heard your grace
    say so; and, my lord, he speaks most vilely of you, like a foul-
    mouthed man as he is, and said he would cudgel you.

PRINCE HARRY   What? He did not!

HOSTESS   There's neither faith, truth, nor womanhood in me
100   else.

FALSTAFF   There's no more faith in thee than in a stewed
    prune,[1] nor no more truth in thee than in a drawn fox;[2] and,
    for womanhood, Maid Marian[3] may be the deputy's wife of
    the ward to° thee. Go, you thing,[4] go!   *compared to*

105   HOSTESS   Say, what thing, what thing?

FALSTAFF   What thing? Why, a thing to thank God on.

HOSTESS   I am no thing to thank God on. I would thou shouldst
    know it, I am an honest man's wife; and setting thy knight-
    hood aside, thou art a knave to call me so.

110   FALSTAFF   Setting thy womanhood aside, thou art a beast to say
    otherwise.

HOSTESS   Say, what beast, thou knave, thou?

FALSTAFF   What beast? Why, an otter.

PRINCE HARRY   An otter, Sir John? Why an otter?

115   FALSTAFF   Why? She's neither fish nor flesh;[5] a man knows not
    where to have her.[6]

HOSTESS   Thou art an unjust man in saying so. Thou or any
    man knows where to have me, thou knave, thou.

PRINCE HARRY   Thou sayst true, Hostess, and he slanders thee
120   most grossly.

HOSTESS   So he doth you, my lord, and said this other day you
    owed him a thousand pound.

PRINCE HARRY [*to* FALSTAFF]   Sirrah, do I owe you a thousand
    pound?

125   FALSTAFF   A thousand pound, Hal? A million! Thy love is worth
    a million; thou owest me thy love.

HOSTESS   Nay, my lord, he called you 'jack' and said he would
    cudgel you.

FALSTAFF   Did I, Bardolph?

---

1. Symbol of a bawd. Brothels often displayed a dish of
stewed prunes in the window.
2. A hunted fox drawn out from its hiding spot; a dead
fox dragged to lay a false trail.
3. A disreputable character, usually played by a cross-
dressed man, in the boisterous May games and morris
dances denounced by Puritan preachers. The figure is

here juxtaposed to the respectable wife of the deputy of
the ward.
4. A euphemism for "female genitalia."
5. The otter's unusual appearance led to debates about
whether it was a fish or an animal.
6. How to understand her; how to have sexual relations
with her.

130 BARDOLPH Indeed, Sir John, you said so.

FALSTAFF Yea, if he said my ring was copper.

PRINCE HARRY I say 'tis copper; darest thou be as good as thy
word now?

FALSTAFF Why, Hal, thou knowest as thou art but man I dare,
135 but as thou art prince, I fear thee as I fear the roaring of the
lion's whelp.°   cub

PRINCE HARRY And why not as the lion?

FALSTAFF The King himself is to be feared as the lion. Dost
thou think I'll fear thee as I fear thy father? Nay, an I do, I pray
140 God my girdle break.

PRINCE HARRY O, if it should, how would thy guts fall about thy
knees! But sirrah, there's no room for faith, truth, nor honesty
in this bosom of thine; it is all filled up with guts and midriff.
Charge an honest woman with picking thy pocket? Why, thou
145 whoreson impudent embossed rascal,[7] if there were anything
in thy pocket but tavern reckonings, memorandums of bawdy-
houses, and one poor pennyworth of sugar-candy to make thee
long-winded°—if thy pocket were enriched with any other   to give you energy
injuries[8] but these, I am a villain. And yet you will stand to it,°   persist
150 you will not pocket up° wrong. Art thou not ashamed?   keep quiet about

FALSTAFF Dost thou hear, Hal? Thou knowest in the state of
innocency Adam fell, and what should poor Jack Falstaff do
in the days of villainy? Thou seest I have more flesh than
another man, and therefore more frailty. You confess, then,
155 you picked my pocket.

PRINCE HARRY It appears so by the story.

FALSTAFF Hostess, I forgive thee. Go make ready breakfast.
Love thy husband, look to thy servants, cherish thy guests.
Thou shalt find me tractable to any honest reason; thou seest
160 I am pacified still.° Nay, prithee, be gone.   Exit HOSTESS   always
Now, Hal, to the news at court. For the robbery, lad, how is
that answered?°   settled

PRINCE HARRY O, my sweet beef, I must still be good angel to
thee. The money is paid back again.

165 FALSTAFF O, I do not like that paying back; 'tis a double labour.

PRINCE HARRY I am good friends with my father, and may do
anything.

FALSTAFF Rob me the exchequer the first thing thou dost, and
do it with unwashed hands° too.   do it at once

170 BARDOLPH Do, my lord.

PRINCE HARRY I have procured thee, Jack, a charge of foot.°   an infantry command

FALSTAFF I would it had been of horse! Where shall I find one°   someone
that can steal well? O, for a fine thief of the age of two-and-
twenty or thereabouts! I am heinously unprovided.° Well, God   ill equipped
175 be thanked for these rebels—they offend none but the virtuous.
I laud them, I praise them.

PRINCE HARRY Bardolph.

BARDOLPH My lord?

PRINCE HARRY [giving letters] Go bear this letter to Lord John
of Lancaster,
180 To my brother John; this to my lord of Westmorland.

---

7. *embossed rascal:* bloated rogue; hunted deer,   8. Any other things whose loss causes you injury.
exhausted and foaming at the mouth.

[Exit BARDOLPH]

Go, Peto, to horse, to horse, for thou and I
Have thirty miles to ride yet ere dinner time.   *[Exit* PETO]
Jack, meet me tomorrow in the Temple Hall[9]
At two o'clock in the afternoon.
185   There shalt thou know thy charge, and there receive
Money and order for their furniture.°   *equipment*
The land is burning, Percy stands on high,
And either we or they must lower lie.   *[Exit]*

FALSTAFF   Rare words! Brave world! *[Calling]* Hostess, my
      breakfast, come!—
190   O, I could wish this tavern were my drum![1]   *Exit*

4.1

Enter HOTSPUR *and [the Earls of]* WORCESTER *and*
DOUGLAS

HOTSPUR   Well said, my noble Scot! If speaking truth
In this fine age were not thought flattery,
Such attribution° should the Douglas have   *praise*
As not a soldier of this season's stamp°   *coinage*
5   Should go so general current° through the world.   *be so widely accepted*
By God, I cannot flatter, I do defy
The tongues of soothers,° but a braver place   *flatterers*
In my heart's love hath no man than yourself.
Nay, task° me to my word, approve° me, lord.   *hold / test*
10   DOUGLAS   Thou art the king of honour.
No man so potent breathes upon the ground
But I will beard° him.   *defy*
HOTSPUR   Do so, and 'tis well.

Enter a MESSENGER *with letters*

What letters hast thou there? I can but thank you.
MESSENGER   These letters come from your father.
15   HOTSPUR   Letters from him? Why comes he not himself?
MESSENGER   He cannot come, my lord, he is grievous sick.
HOTSPUR   Zounds, how has he the leisure to be sick
In such a jostling° time? Who leads his power?   *turbulent*
Under whose government° come they along?   *command*
20   MESSENGER   His letters bears his mind, not I, my lord.

[HOTSPUR *reads the letter*]

WORCESTER   I prithee tell me, doth he keep his bed?
MESSENGER   He did, my lord, four days ere I set forth;
And at the time of my departure thence
He was much feared° by his physicians.   *feared for*
25   WORCESTER   I would the state of time° had first been whole°   *of the times / healthy*
Ere he by sickness had been visited.
His health was never better worth° than now.   *of more value*
HOTSPUR   Sick now? Droop now? This sickness doth infect
The very life-blood of our enterprise.
30   'Tis catching° hither, even to our camp.   *infectious*
He writes me here that inward sickness stays him,
And that his friends by deputation°   *through deputies*

---

9. One of the Inns of Court, London's law schools.
1. A disputed passage. Perhaps Falstaff means he
wishes that he could stay at the tavern rather than go to
war or that he could make the tavern ring with the noise
of his departure. He puns on "taborn" (tabor), a kind of
drum used to call soldiers to battle.
4.1 Location: The rebel camp near Shrewsbury.

	Could not so soon be drawn;° nor did he think it meet°	*assembled / suitable*
	To lay so dangerous and dear a trust	
35	On any soul removed° but on his own.	*not directly involved*
	Yet doth he give us bold advertisement°	*counsel*
	That with our small conjunction° we should on,	*joint force*
	To see how fortune is disposed to us;	
	For, as he writes, there is no quailing now,	
40	Because the King is certainly possessed°	*informed*
	Of all our purposes. What say you to it?	

WORCESTER   Your father's sickness is a maim to us.
HOTSPUR   A perilous gash, a very limb lopped off.

	And yet, in faith, it is not. His present want°	*absence*
45	Seems more than we shall find it. Were it good	
	To set° the exact wealth of all our states°	*stake / resources*
	All at one cast,° to set so rich a main¹	*throw of the dice*
	On the nice hazard° of one doubtful hour?	*precarious chance*
	It were not good, for therein should we read	
50	The very bottom and the sole² of hope,	
	The very list,° the very utmost bound,	*limit*
	Of all our fortunes.	

DOUGLAS   Faith, and so we should, where now remains

	A sweet reversion°—we may boldly spend	*future inheritance*
55	Upon the hope of what is to come in.	
	A comfort of retirement³ lives in this.	

HOTSPUR   A rendezvous, a home to fly unto,

	If that the devil and mischance look big°	*threateningly*
	Upon the maidenhead° of our affairs.	*virgin state; start*

WORCESTER   But yet I would your father had been here.

60	The quality and hair° of our attempt	*character*
	Brooks° no division. It will be thought	*Tolerates*
	By some that know not why he is away	
	That wisdom, loyalty, and mere° dislike	*absolute*
65	Of our proceedings kept the Earl from hence;	
	And think how such an apprehension	
	May turn the tide of fearful faction,°	*timid support*
	And breed a kind of question in our cause.	
	For, well you know, we of the off'ring° side	*challenging*
70	Must keep aloof from strict arbitrement,°	*rigorous judgment*
	And stop all sight-holes, every loop° from whence	*loophole*
	The eye of reason may pry in upon us.	
	This absence of your father's draws° a curtain	*opens*
	That shows the ignorant a kind of fear	
	Before not dreamt of.	

HOTSPUR   You strain too far.

75	I rather of his absence make this use:	
	It lends a lustre, and more great opinion,°	*prestige*
	A larger dare° to our great enterprise,	*daring*
	Than if the Earl were here; for men must think	
80	If we without his help can make a head°	*raise an army*
	To push against a kingdom, with his help	
	We shall o'erturn it topsy-turvy down.	
	Yet° all goes well, yet all our joints° are whole.	*So far / limbs*

---

1. A stake in gambling; an army.   3. Refuge to which one can retreat.
2. Undersurface (as of a shoe), with a pun on "soul."

DOUGLAS   As heart can think, there is not such a word
85   Spoke of in Scotland as this term of fear.
            Enter Sir Richard VERNON
HOTSPUR   My cousin Vernon! Welcome, by my soul!
VERNON   Pray God my news be worth a welcome, lord.
    The Earl of Westmorland, seven thousand strong,
    Is marching hitherwards; with him Prince John.
HOTSPUR   No harm. What more?
90 VERNON   And further I have learned
    The King himself in person is set forth,
    Or hitherwards intended speedily,
    With strong and mighty preparation.
HOTSPUR   He shall be welcome too. Where is his son,
95   The nimble-footed madcap Prince of Wales,
    And his comrades that daffed° the world aside   tossed
    And bid it pass?
VERNON   All furnished,° all in arms,   equipped
    All plumed like ostriches,⁴ that with the wind
    [   ]
100   Baiting° like eagles having lately bathed,   Beating their wings
    Glittering in golden coats like images,°   gilded statues
    As full of spirit as the month of May,
    And gorgeous as the sun at midsummer;
    Wanton° as youthful goats, wild as young bulls.   Frisky
105   I saw young Harry with his beaver° on,   visor; helmet
    His cuishes° on his thighs, gallantly armed,   armor for the thighs
    Rise from the ground like feathered Mercury,⁵
    And vaulted with such ease into his seat
    As if an angel dropped down from the clouds
110   To turn and wind° a fiery Pegasus,⁶   wheel about
    And witch° the world with noble horsemanship.   bewitch
HOTSPUR   No more, no more! Worse than the sun in March,
    This praise doth nourish agues.⁷ Let them come!
    They come like sacrifices in their trim,°   fine trappings
115   And to the fire-eyed maid of smoky war°   Bellona, goddess of war
    All hot and bleeding will we offer them.
    The mailèd° Mars shall on his altar sit   dressed in armor
    Up to the ears in blood. I am on fire
    To hear this rich reprisal° is so nigh,   prize
120   And yet not ours! Come, let me taste° my horse,   test; try
    Who is to bear me like a thunderbolt
    Against the bosom of the Prince of Wales.
    Harry to Harry shall, hot horse to horse,
    Meet and ne'er part till one drop down a corpse.
    O, that Glyndŵr were come!
125 VERNON   There is more news.
    I learned in Worcester, as I rode along,
    He cannot draw° his power this fourteen days.   assemble
DOUGLAS   That's the worst tidings that I hear of yet.

---

4. Some editors follow Q in printing "estridges" (goshawks, a kind of hawk) here. Various emendations have been proposed for this and the following lines. The Oxford editors assume a line has been lost, as the brackets indicate.
5. The Roman messenger of the gods, often repre-

sented as a young man with winged sandals or a winged hat.
6. A winged horse of classical myth.
7. The March sun was popularly imagined as warm enough to kindle feverish diseases ("agues") without being strong enough to dispel them.

WORCESTER   Ay, by my faith, that bears a frosty sound.

130 HOTSPUR   What may the King's whole battle° reach unto?   *army*

VERNON   To thirty thousand.

HOTSPUR   Forty let it be.

My father and Glyndŵr being both away,

The powers° of us may serve so great a day.   *armies*

Come, let us take a muster speedily.

135 Doomsday is near: die all, die merrily.

DOUGLAS   Talk not of dying; I am out of° fear   *free from*

Of death or death's hand for this one half year.   *Exeunt*

4.2

Enter FALSTAFF *and* BARDOLPH

FALSTAFF   Bardolph, get thee before to Coventry; fill me a bottle of sack. Our soldiers shall march through. We'll to Sutton
Coldfield[1] tonight.

BARDOLPH   Will you give me money, captain?

5 FALSTAFF   Lay out,° lay out.   *Use your own*

BARDOLPH   This bottle makes an angel.[2]

FALSTAFF   [*giving* BARDOLPH *money*] An if° it do, take it for thy   *An if=If*
labour; an if it make twenty, take them all; I'll answer the
coinage.[3] Bid my lieutenant Peto meet me at town's end.

10 BARDOLPH   I will, captain. Farewell.   *Exit*

FALSTAFF   If I be not ashamed of my soldiers, I am a soused
gurnet.° I have misused the King's press[4] damnably. I have got   *a pickled fish*
in exchange of one hundred and fifty soldiers three hundred
and odd pounds. I press me° none but good householders, yeo-   *I draft*
15 men's sons, enquire me out contracted° bachelors, such as had   *engaged to be wed*
been asked twice on the banns,[5] such a commodity° of warm   *quantity*
slaves[6] as had as lief° hear the devil as a drum, such as fear the   *willingly*
report of a caliver° worse than a struck° fowl or a hurt wild   *musket / wounded*
duck. I pressed me none but such toasts and butter,° with hearts   *such weaklings*
20 in their bellies no bigger than pins' heads, and they have
bought out their services;[7] and now my whole charge consists
of ensigns, corporals, lieutenants, gentlemen of companies[8]—
slaves as ragged as Lazarus[9] in the painted cloth,° where the   *cheap wall hangings*
glutton's dogs licked his sores—and such as indeed were never
25 soldiers, but discarded unjust° servingmen, younger sons to   *dishonest*
younger brothers, revolted° tapsters, and ostlers trade-fallen,°   *runaway / out of work*
the cankers° of a calm world and a long peace, ten times more   *cankerworms; parasites*
dishonourable-ragged than an old feazed ensign;° and such   *tattered flag*
have I to fill up the rooms of them as° have bought out their   *places of those who*
30 services, that you would think that I had a hundred and fifty
tattered prodigals lately come from swine-keeping, from eating
draff and husks.[1] A mad fellow met me on the way and told me
I had unloaded all the gibbets° and pressed the dead bodies.   *gallows*

4.2 Location: The road approaching Coventry.
1. Town about 20 miles northwest of Coventry in Warwickshire.
2. Brings my outlay to several shillings (an "angel").
Falstaff retorts by punning on "makes" as meaning
"earns a profit of."
3. I'll be responsible for the money coined.
4. Commission for conscripting soldiers.
5. Proclamations made on three consecutive Sundays
affirming one's intent to marry.

6. Well-off or comfort-loving cowards.
7. They have paid me to excuse them from military service.
8. Gentlemen volunteers who were not officers.
9. For the story of Lazarus and the rich man, see note
to 3.3.28.
1. Alluding to the biblical parable of the prodigal son,
who longs to eat swill ("draff") and corn husks meant
for pigs after he has squandered his inheritance in
debauchery (see Luke 15:11–16).

No eye hath seen such scarecrows. I'll not march through Cov-
35   entry with them, that's flat. Nay, and the villains march wide
betwixt the legs, as if they had gyves° on, for indeed I had the   *fetters*
most of them out of prison. There's not a shirt and a half in all
my company; and the half-shirt is two napkins tacked together
and thrown over the shoulders like a herald's coat without
40   sleeves; and the shirt, to say the truth, stolen from my host° at   *innkeeper*
Saint Albans, or the red-nose innkeeper of Daventry.² But that's
all one; they'll find linen enough on every hedge.³

      Enter PRINCE [HARRY] *and the Lord[Earl] of* WESTMOR-
      LAND

PRINCE HARRY   How now, blown Jack?⁴ How now, quilt?
FALSTAFF   What, Hal! How now, mad wag? What a devil dost
45   thou in Warwickshire? My good lord of Westmorland, I cry
you mercy!° I thought your honour had already been at   *I beg your pardon*
Shrewsbury.
WESTMORLAND   Faith, Sir John, 'tis more than time that I were
there, and you too; but my powers are there already. The King,
50   I can tell you, looks for us all. We must away° all night.   *must march*
FALSTAFF   Tut, never fear° me. I am as vigilant as a cat to steal   *worry about*
cream.
PRINCE HARRY   I think to steal cream indeed, for thy theft hath
already made thee butter.⁵ But tell me, Jack, whose fellows are
55   these that come after?
FALSTAFF   Mine, Hal, mine.
PRINCE HARRY   I did never see such pitiful rascals.
FALSTAFF   Tut, tut, good enough to toss,⁶ food for powder,° food   *cannon fodder*
for powder. They'll fill a pit as well as better. Tush, man, mor-
60   tal men, mortal men.
WESTMORLAND   Ay, but Sir John, methinks they are exceeding
poor and bare,° too beggarly.   *threadbare*
FALSTAFF   Faith, for their poverty, I know not where they had
that, and for their bareness, I am sure they never learned that
65   of me.
PRINCE HARRY   No, I'll be sworn, unless you call three fingers in
the ribs⁷ bare. But sirrah, make haste. Percy is already in the
field.   *Exit*
FALSTAFF   What, is the King encamped?
70   WESTMORLAND   He is, Sir John. I fear we shall stay too long.
                                                  [Exit]
FALSTAFF   Well, to the latter end of a fray
And the beginning of a feast
Fits a dull fighter and a keen guest.   *Exit*

4.3

      Enter HOTSPUR, [*the Earls of*] WORCESTER [*and*] DOUG-
      LAS, *and* [*Sir Richard*] VERNON
HOTSPUR   We'll fight with him tonight.
WORCESTER   It may not be.

---

2. Saint Albans is a town north of London, Daventry a
town southeast of Coventry.
3. Where laundresses set it out to dry.
4. Punning on "jack" as referring to what many Elizabethan soldiers wore: a quilted jacket covered with
leather or cloth and worn over iron plates. *blown:*
swollen; short-winded.

5. The riches ("cream") you have stolen have made you
rich, or turned you into fat.
6. Good enough to be tossed on pikes.
7. Three fingers of fat over the ribs. A finger was a measure of three-quarters of an inch.
4.3 Location: The rebels' camp, Shrewsbury.

DOUGLAS You give him then advantage.

VERNON   Not a whit.

HOTSPUR Why say you so? Looks he not for supply?°   *reinforcements*

VERNON So do we.

HOTSPUR   His is certain; ours is doubtful.

5 WORCESTER Good cousin, be advised. Stir not tonight.

VERNON [*to* HOTSPUR] Do not, my lord.

DOUGLAS   You do not counsel well.

You speak it out of fear and cold heart.

VERNON Do me no slander, Douglas. By my life—

And I dare well maintain it with my life—

10 If well-respected° honour bid me on,   *well-considered*

I hold as little counsel with weak fear

As you, my lord, or any Scot that this day lives.

Let it be seen tomorrow in the battle

Which of us fears.

15 DOUGLAS Yea, or tonight.

VERNON   Content.

HOTSPUR Tonight, say I.

VERNON Come, come, it may not be. I wonder much,

Being men of such great leading° as you are,   *leadership*

20 That you foresee not what impediments

Drag back our expedition.° Certain horse°   *rapid progress / cavalry*

Of my cousin Vernon's are not yet come up.

Your uncle Worcester's horse came but today,

And now their pride° and mettle is asleep,   *spirit*

25 Their courage with hard labour tame and dull,

That not a horse is half the half himself.

HOTSPUR So are the horses of the enemy

In general journey-bated° and brought low.   *weary from travel*

The better part of ours are full of rest.

30 WORCESTER The number of the King exceedeth our.

For God's sake, cousin, stay° till all come in.   *wait*

The trumpet sounds a parley[1] [*within*]. *Enter
Sir Walter* BLUNT

BLUNT I come with gracious offers from the King,

If you vouchsafe me hearing and respect.

HOTSPUR Welcome, Sir Walter Blunt; and would to God

35 You were of our determination.°   *on our side*

Some of us love you well, and even those some°   *those same persons*

Envy your great deservings and good name,

Because you are not of our quality,°   *party*

But stand against us like an enemy.

40 BLUNT And God defend° but still I should stand so,   *forbid*

So long as out of limit° and true rule   *bounds of allegiance*

You stand against anointed majesty.

But to my charge. The King hath sent to know

The nature of your griefs,° and whereupon   *grievances*

45 You conjure from the breast of civil peace

Such bold hostility, teaching his duteous land

Audacious cruelty. If that the King

Have any way your good deserts forgot,

Which he confesseth to be manifold,

---

1. Summons to a conference with the enemy.

50 He bids you name your griefs, and with all speed
    You shall have your desires, with interest,
    And pardon absolute for yourself and these
    Herein misled by your suggestion.°   *instigation*
    HOTSPUR The King is kind, and well we know the King
55 Knows at what time to promise, when to pay.
    My father and my uncle and myself
    Did give him that same royalty he wears;
    And when he was not six-and-twenty strong,
    Sick in the world's regard, wretched and low,
60 A poor unminded° outlaw sneaking home,   *insignificant*
    My father gave him welcome to the shore;
    And when he heard him swear and vow to God
    He came but to be Duke of Lancaster,
    To sue his livery,² and beg his peace
65 With tears of innocency and terms of zeal,
    My father, in kind heart and pity moved,
    Swore him assistance, and performed it too.
    Now when the lords and barons of the realm
    Perceived Northumberland did lean to him,
70 The more and less came in with cap and knee,³
    Met him in boroughs, cities, villages,
    Attended him on bridges, stood in lanes,⁴
    Laid gifts before him, proffered him their oaths,
    Gave him their heirs as pages, followed him,
75 Even at the heels, in golden° multitudes.   *resplendent*
    He presently, as greatness knows itself,°   *recognizes its power*
    Steps me° a little higher than his vow   *Steps*
    Made to my father while his blood° was poor   *spirit*
    Upon the naked shore at Ravenspurgh,
80 And now forsooth takes on him to reform
    Some certain edicts and some strait° decrees   *strict*
    That lie too heavy on the commonwealth,
    Cries out upon abuses, seems to weep
    Over his country's wrongs; and by this face,°   *outward show*
85 This seeming brow of justice, did he win
    The hearts of all that he did angle for;
    Proceeded further, cut me off° the heads   *cut off*
    Of all the favourites that the absent King
    In deputation° left behind him here   *As deputies*
90 When he was personal° in the Irish war.   *engaged in person*
    BLUNT Tut, I came not to hear this.
    HOTSPUR   Then to the point.
    In short time after, he deposed the King,
    Soon after that deprived him of his life,
    And in the neck of that tasked° the whole state;   *And immediately taxed*
95 To make that worse, suffered his kinsman March⁵—
    Who is, if every owner were well placed,⁶
    Indeed his king—to be engaged° in Wales,   *held hostage*
    There without ransom to lie forfeited;°   *unredeemed*

2. To plead for the restitution of his lands (which Richard II had seized when John of Gaunt, Bolingbroke's
father, died).
3. Those of both high and low social status deferen-
tially presented themselves (with cap in hand and
bended knee).
4. Stood in rows along the roadways.
5. The Earl of March. For his claim to the throne, see
note to 1.3.79.
6. If everyone had possessions according to his entitle-
ment.

Disgraced me in my happy victories,
100 Sought to entrap me by intelligence,°   *spying*
Rated° mine uncle from the Council-board,   *Drove away*
In rage dismissed my father from the court,
Broke oath on oath, committed wrong on wrong,
And in conclusion drove us to seek out
105 This head of safety,[7] and withal° to pry   *also*
Into his title, the which we find
Too indirect° for long continuance.   *irregular*
BLUNT Shall I return this answer to the King?
HOTSPUR Not so, Sir Walter. We'll withdraw awhile.
110 Go to the King, and let there be impawned°   *pledged*
Some surety for a safe return again;
And in the morning early shall mine uncle
Bring him our purposes. And so, farewell.
BLUNT I would you would accept of grace and love.
HOTSPUR And maybe so we shall.
115 BLUNT   Pray God you do.

Exeunt [HOTSPUR, WORCESTER, DOUGLAS, *and*
VERNON *at one door,* BLUNT *at another door*]

4.4

Enter the ARCHBISHOP *of York, and* SIR MICHAEL

ARCHBISHOP [*giving letters*] Hie, good Sir Michael, bear this sealèd brief°   *dispatch*
With wingèd haste to the Lord Marshal,
This to my cousin Scrope, and all the rest
To whom they are directed. If you knew
5 How much they do import, you would make haste.
SIR MICHAEL My good lord,
I guess their tenor.
ARCHBISHOP   Like enough you do.
Tomorrow, good Sir Michael, is a day
Wherein the fortune of ten thousand men
10 Must bide the touch;° for, sir, at Shrewsbury,   *stand the test*
As I am truly given to understand,
The King with mighty and quick-raisèd power
Meets with Lord Harry. And I fear, Sir Michael,
What with the sickness of Northumberland,
15 Whose power was in the first proportion,°   *magnitude*
And what with Owain Glyndŵr's absence thence,
Who with them was a rated sinew[1] too,
And comes not in, overruled by prophecies,
I fear the power of Percy is too weak
20 To wage an instant° trial with the King.   *immediate*
SIR MICHAEL Why, my good lord, you need not fear; there is Douglas
And Lord Mortimer.
ARCHBISHOP   No, Mortimer is not there.
SIR MICHAEL But there is Mordake, Vernon, Lord Harry Percy;
And there is my lord of Worcester, and a head°   *troop*
25 Of gallant warriors, noble gentlemen.
ARCHBISHOP And so there is; but yet the King hath drawn
The special head of all the land together—

---

7. That is, safety in these gathered forces.   1. A much-valued source of strength.
4.4 Location: The Archbishop's palace, York.

The Prince of Wales, Lord John of Lancaster,
The noble Westmorland, and warlike Blunt,
30 And many more corrivals,° and dear° men   *associates / noble*
Of estimation° and command in arms.   *reputation*
SIR MICHAEL   Doubt not, my lord, they shall be well opposed.
ARCHBISHOP   I hope no less, yet needful 'tis to fear;
And to prevent the worst, Sir Michael, speed.
35 For if Lord Percy thrive not, ere the King
Dismiss his power he means to visit us,
For he hath heard of our confederacy,
And 'tis but wisdom to make strong against him;
Therefore make haste. I must go write again
40 To other friends; and so farewell, Sir Michael.   *Exeunt [severally]*

5.1

Enter KING [HENRY], PRINCE [HARRY], *Lord* JOHN OF LAN-
CASTER, [*the*] *Earl of* WESTMORLAND, *Sir Walter* BLUNT,
and FALSTAFF

KING HENRY   How bloodily the sun begins to peer
Above yon bulky hill! The day looks pale
At his distemp'rature.°   *sick appearance*
PRINCE HARRY   The southern wind
Doth play the trumpet to his° purposes,   *(the sun's)*
5 And by his hollow whistling in the leaves
Foretells a tempest and a blust'ring day.
KING HENRY   Then with the losers let it sympathize,°   *accord*
For nothing can seem foul to those that win.
           The trumpet sounds [a parley within]. Enter [the Earl
           of] WORCESTER [*and Sir Richard* VERNON][1]
How now, my lord of Worcester? 'Tis not well
10 That you and I should meet upon such terms
As now we meet. You have deceived our trust,
And made us doff our easy robes of peace
To crush our old limbs in ungentle steel.
This is not well, my lord, this is not well.
15 What say you to it? Will you again unknit
This churlish knot of all-abhorrèd war,
And move in that obedient orb[2] again
Where you did give a fair and natural light,
And be no more an exhalèd meteor,[3]
20 A prodigy of fear,° and a portent   *A fearful omen*
Of broachèd mischief° to the unborn times?   *Of evil set flowing*
WORCESTER   Hear me, my liege.
For mine own part, I could be well content
To entertain the lag-end° of my life   *latter end*
25 With quiet hours; for I protest,
I have not sought the day of this dislike.°   *discord*
KING HENRY   You have not sought it? How comes it, then?
FALSTAFF   Rebellion lay in his way, and he found it.

5.1 Location: King Henry's camp at Shrewsbury.
1. Neither Q nor F indicates that Vernon accompanies
Worcester in this scene, but it seems lacking in ceremony
for Worcester to go to King Henry's camp alone. Also, in
the next scene, Worcester discusses with Vernon what the
King has said and whether to inform Hotspur, making it
appear that Vernon was present at this meeting.

2. Orbit. Henry, drawing on a conventional analogy
between social and cosmological order, compares
Worcester to a star or a planet that, in Ptolemaic cos-
mology, should move properly in its sphere (orbit)
around the earth.
3. Meteors were thought to be made of gas exhaled by
the sun and were considered bad omens.

PRINCE HARRY   Peace, chewet,° peace!   *jackdaw; chatterer*

30 WORCESTER [*to the* KING]   It pleased your majesty to turn your looks
  Of favour from myself and all our house;
  And yet I must remember° you, my lord,   *remind*
  We were the first and dearest of your friends.
  For you my staff of office did I break
35 In Richard's time, and posted° day and night   *rode swiftly*
  To meet you on the way and kiss your hand
  When yet you were in place° and in account° *social status / esteem*
  Nothing so strong and fortunate as I.
  It was myself, my brother, and his son
40 That brought you home, and boldly did outdare
  The dangers of the time. You swore to us,
  And you did swear that oath at Doncaster,
  That you did nothing purpose° 'gainst the state,   *intend*
  Nor claim no further than your new-fall'n right,[4]
45 The seat° of Gaunt, dukedom of Lancaster.   *estate*
  To this we swore our aid, but in short space
  It rained down fortune show'ring on your head,
  And such a flood of greatness fell on you,
  What with our help, what with the absent King,
50 What with the injuries° of a wanton° time,   *evils / lawless*
  The seeming sufferances° that you had borne,   *wrongs*
  And the contrarious° winds that held the King   *adverse*
  So long in his unlucky Irish wars
  That all in England did repute him dead;
55 And from this swarm of fair advantages
  You took occasion to be quickly wooed
  To gripe° the general sway into your hand,   *seize*
  Forgot your oath to us at Doncaster,
  And being fed by us, you used us so
60 As that ungentle gull,° the cuckoo's bird,   *rude young bird*
  Useth the sparrow[5]—did oppress our nest,
  Grew by our feeding to so great a bulk
  That even our love° durst not come near your sight *we who loved you*
  For fear of swallowing.° But with nimble wing *being swallowed*
65 We were enforced for safety' sake to fly
  Out of your sight, and raise this present head,
  Whereby we stand opposèd° by such means *in opposition to you*
  As you yourself have forged against yourself,
  By unkind usage, dangerous° countenance,   *threatening*
70 And violation of all faith and troth
  Sworn to us in your younger enterprise.
 KING HENRY   These things indeed you have articulate,°   *expressed*
  Proclaimed at market crosses,[6] read in churches,
  To face° the garment of rebellion   *adorn*
75 With some fine colour° that may please the eye *hue; pretext*
  Of fickle changelings° and poor discontents,   *turncoats*
  Which gape and rub the elbow[7] at the news
  Of hurly-burly innovation;°   *rebellion*

---

4. The right newly descended to you (upon the death of your father).

5. The female cuckoo lays its eggs in the nests of smaller birds such as the sparrow, who raises the cockoo's young until they grow so large they threaten the sparrow and her nest.

6. Crosses set up in marketplaces, often atop polygonal structures with open archways on each of the sides and vaulted within.

7. And hug themselves with crossed arms (conventional expression of delight).

And never yet did insurrection want°   *lack*
80 Such water-colours to impaint his cause,
Nor moody beggars starving for a time
Of pell-mell° havoc and confusion.   *chaotic*
PRINCE HARRY   In both our armies there is many a soul
Shall pay full dearly for this encounter
85 If once they join in trial.° Tell your nephew   *combat*
The Prince of Wales doth join with all the world
In praise of Henry Percy. By my hopes,
This present enterprise set off his head,°   *not counted against him*
I do not think a braver gentleman,
90 More active-valiant or more valiant-young,
More daring, or more bold, is now alive
To grace this latter age with noble deeds.
For my part, I may speak it to my shame,
I have a truant been to chivalry;
95 And so I hear he doth account me too.
Yet this, before my father's majesty:
I am content that he shall take the odds°   *have the advantage*
Of his great name and estimation,°   *reputation*
And will, to save the blood on either side,
100 Try fortune with him in a single fight.
KING HENRY   And, Prince of Wales, so dare we venture thee,
Albeit° considerations infinite   *Were it not that*
Do make against it. No, good Worcester, no.
We love our people well; even those we love
105 That are misled upon your cousin's° part;   *kinsman's*
And will they take the offer of our grace,°   *mercy*
Both he and they and you, yea, every man
Shall be my friend again, and I'll be his.
So tell your cousin, and bring me word
110 What he will do. But if he will not yield,
Rebuke and dread correction wait on° us,   *serve*
And they shall do their office. So be gone.
We will not now be troubled with reply.
We offer fair; take it advisedly.
                    Exeunt WORCESTER [*and* VERNON]
115 PRINCE HARRY   It will not be accepted, on my life.
The Douglas and the Hotspur both together
Are confident against the world in arms.
KING HENRY   Hence, therefore, every leader to his charge,
For on their answer will we set on them,
120 And God befriend us as our cause is just!
            Exeunt. Manent° *Prince* [HARRY] *and* FALSTAFF   *Remain*
FALSTAFF   Hal, if thou see me down in the battle, and bestride
me,° so.° 'Tis a point of friendship.   *stand over me / good*
PRINCE HARRY   Nothing but a colossus[8] can do thee that friend-
ship. Say thy prayers, and farewell.
125 FALSTAFF   I would 'twere bed-time, Hal, and all well.
PRINCE HARRY   Why, thou owest God a death.   [*Exit*]
FALSTAFF   'Tis not due yet. I would be loath to pay him before
his day. What need I be so forward with him that calls not on
me? Well, 'tis no matter; honour pricks° me on. Yea, but how   *spurs*

8. Referring to a massive statue of Apollo that purportedly stood over the entrance to the harbor in ancient Rhodes and was referred to as the Colossus of Rhodes.

130   if honour prick me off° when I come on? How then? Can hon-
    our set-to° a leg? No. Or an arm? No. Or take away the grief   *mend*
    of a wound? No. Honour hath no skill in surgery, then? No.
    What is honour? A word. What is in that word 'honour'? What
    is that 'honour'? Air. A trim reckoning!° Who hath it? He that   *A nice summing up*
135   died o'Wednesday. Doth he feel it? No. Doth he hear it? No.
    'Tis insensible[1] then? Yea, to the dead. But will it not live with
    the living? No. Why? Detraction° will not suffer° it. Therefore   *Slander / allow*
    I'll none of it. Honour is a mere scutcheon.[2] And so ends my
    catechism.   *Exit*

5.2

Enter [the Earl of] WORCESTER *and Sir Richard*
    VERNON

WORCESTER   O no, my nephew must not know, Sir Richard,
    The liberal and kind offer of the king.
VERNON   'Twere best he did.
WORCESTER   Then are we all undone.
    It is not possible, it cannot be,
5   The King should keep his word in loving us.
    He will suspect us still,° and find a time   *always*
    To punish this offence in other faults.
    Supposition all our lives shall be stuck full of eyes,[1]
    For treason is but trusted like the fox,
10   Who, ne'er so° tame, so cherished, and locked up,   *no matter how*
    Will have a wild trick of his ancestors.
    Look how we can, or° sad or merrily,   *whether*
    Interpretation will misquote our looks,
    And we shall feed like oxen at a stall,
15   The better cherished still the nearer death.
    My nephew's trespass may be well forgot;
    It hath the excuse of youth and heat of blood,
    And an adopted name of privilege[2]—
    A hare-brained Hotspur, governed by a spleen.°   *hot temper*
20   All his offences live upon my head,
    And on his father's. We did train° him on,   *lead*
    And, his corruption being ta'en from us,
    We as the spring° of all shall pay for all.   *source*
    Therefore, good cousin, let not Harry know
25   In any case the offer of the King.
VERNON   Deliver what you will; I'll say 'tis so.
    Enter HOTSPUR [*and the Earl of* DOUGLAS]
    Here comes your cousin.
HOTSPUR   My uncle is returned.
    Deliver up[3] my Lord of Westmorland.
    Uncle, what news?
30 WORCESTER   The King will bid you battle presently.
DOUGLAS   Defy him by the Lord of Westmorland.
HOTSPUR   Lord Douglas, go you and tell him so.

---

9. Selects me to die; marks me off the list.
1. Imperceptible to the senses.
2. Heraldic shield exhibited at funerals displaying the deceased person's coat of arms.
5.2 Location: The rebels' camp.
1. The King's suspicion will cause him constantly to spy on us. Worcester is referring to an allegorical rep-

resentation of Suspicion dressed in a coat of eyes or to secret agents similar to those whom Elizabeth's government maintained.
2. A nickname, "Hotspur," which may excuse his rashness.
3. Release (as the hostage for the safe return of Worcester and Vernon).

DOUGLAS   Marry, and shall, and very willingly.   *Exit*

WORCESTER   There is no seeming° mercy in the King.   *semblance of*

35 HOTSPUR   Did you beg any? God forbid!

WORCESTER   I told him gently of our grievances,
Of his oath-breaking, which he mended thus:
By now forswearing that he is forsworn.
He calls us 'rebels', 'traitors', and will scourge
40 With haughty arms this hateful name in us.

          Enter [the Earl of] DOUGLAS

DOUGLAS   Arm, gentlemen, to arms, for I have thrown
A brave° defiance in King Henry's teeth—   *proud*
And Westmorland that was engaged° did bear it—   *held as hostage*
Which cannot choose but bring him quickly on.

WORCESTER [*to* HOTSPUR]   The Prince of Wales stepped forth
45   before the King
And, nephew, challenged you to single fight.

HOTSPUR   O, would the quarrel lay upon our heads,
And that no man might draw short breath today
But I and Harry Monmouth![4] Tell me, tell me,
50 How showed his tasking?° Seemed it in contempt?   *challenge*

VERNON   No, by my soul, I never in my life
Did hear a challenge urged more modestly,
Unless a brother should a brother dare
To gentle° exercise and proof of arms.[5]   *noble*
55 He gave you all the duties of° a man,   *respect due to*
Trimmed up your praises[6] with a princely tongue,
Spoke your deservings like a chronicle,
Making you ever better than his praise
By still° dispraising praise valued with you;[7]   *constantly*
60 And, which became him like a prince indeed,
He made a blushing cital° of himself,   *mention*
And chid his truant youth with such a grace
As if he mastered there a double spirit
Of teaching and of learning instantly.°   *simultaneously*
65 There did he pause; but let me tell the world,
If he outlive the envy° of this day,   *malice*
England did never owe° so sweet a hope,   *own*
So much misconstrued in his wantonness.°   *self-indulgence*

HOTSPUR   Cousin, I think thou art enamourèd
70 On° his follies. Never did I hear   *Of*
Of any prince so wild a liberty.°   *such unrestrained license*
But be he as he will, yet once ere night
I will embrace him with a soldier's arm,
That he shall shrink under my courtesy.
75 Arm, arm, with speed! And fellows, soldiers, friends,
Better consider what you have to do
Than I, that have not well the gift of tongue,
Can lift your blood[8] up with persuasion.

          Enter a MESSENGER

MESSENGER   My lord, here are letters for you.

80 HOTSPUR   I cannot read them now.   [*Exit* MESSENGER]

---

4. Harry of Monmouth, the town in Wales where the Prince was born.
5. Trial of skill at weapons.
6. Embellished his praises of you.

7. As measured against you (because your merit exceeds all praise).
8. Rebelliousness; self-indulgence.

O gentlemen, the time of life is short.
To spend that shortness basely were too long
If life did ride upon a dial's point,
Still ending at the arrival of an hour.⁹
85 An if we live, we live to tread on kings;
If die, brave death when princes die with us!
Now for our consciences: the arms are fair
When the intent of bearing them is just.

Enter another MESSENGER

MESSENGER My lord, prepare; the King comes on apace. [*Exit*]
90 HOTSPUR I thank him that he cuts me from my tale,
For I profess not° talking, only this: *am not skilled at*
Let each man do his best. And here draw I
A sword whose temper° I intend to stain   *tempered steel*
With the best blood that I can meet withal
95 In the adventure of this perilous day.
Now *Esperance!*¹ Percy! And set on!
Sound all the lofty instruments of war,
And by that music let us all embrace,
For, heaven to earth,² some of us never shall
100 A second time do such a courtesy.

The trumpets sound. Here they embrace. [*Exeunt*]

5.3

KING [HENRY] *enters with his power. Alarum*¹ [*and exeunt*] *to the battle. Then enter* [*the Earl of*] DOUGLAS,
and Sir Walter BLUNT [*disguised as the* KING]

BLUNT What is thy name, that in the battle thus
Thou crossest me? What honour dost thou seek
Upon my head?
DOUGLAS   Know then my name is Douglas,
And I do haunt thee in the battle thus
5 Because some tell me that thou art a king.
BLUNT They tell thee true.
DOUGLAS The Lord of Stafford dear today hath bought
Thy likeness,² for instead of thee, King Harry,
This sword hath ended him. So shall it thee,
10 Unless thou yield thee as my prisoner.
BLUNT I was not born a yielder, thou proud Scot,
And thou shalt find a king that will revenge
Lord Stafford's death.

They fight. DOUGLAS *kills* BLUNT. *Then enter* HOTSPUR

HOTSPUR O Douglas, hadst thou fought at Holmedon thus,
15 I never had triumphed upon a Scot.
DOUGLAS All's done, all's won: here breathless lies the King.
HOTSPUR Where?
DOUGLAS Here.
HOTSPUR This, Douglas? No, I know this face full well.
20 A gallant knight he was; his name was Blunt—

9. *To spend . . . hour*: that is, If life only lasted an hour (*dial's point*: hand of a clock), it would still be too long if it were basely spent.
1. Hope (the Percy motto; see note to 2.4.66).
2. The odds are as great as the distance from heaven to earth.

5.3 Location: The remaining scenes take place on the battlefield at Shrewsbury.
1. A call to arms, usually sounded on drum or trumpets.
2. *hath . . . likeness*: has paid for impersonating you; has paid for his resemblance to you.

Semblably furnished° like the King himself.   *Similarly equipped*

DOUGLAS [*to Blunt's body*]   A fool go with thy soul,[3] whither it goes!

A borrowed title hast thou bought too dear.

Why didst thou tell me that thou wert a king?

25 HOTSPUR   The king hath many marching in his coats.[4]

DOUGLAS   Now by my sword, I will kill all his coats.

I'll murder all his wardrobe, piece by piece,

Until I meet the King.

HOTSPUR   Up and away!

Our soldiers stand full fairly for the day.[5]

Exeunt [leaving Blunt's body]

Alarum. Enter FALSTAFF

30 FALSTAFF   Though I could scape shot-free[6] at London, I fear

the shot here. Here's no scoring[7] but upon the pate.—Soft,

who are you?— Sir Walter Blunt. There's honour for you.

Here's no vanity. I am as hot as molten lead, and as heavy too.

God keep lead out of me; I need no more weight than mine

35 own bowels. I have led my ragamuffins where they are pep-

pered; there's not three of my hundred and fifty left alive, and

they are for the town's end,[8] to beg during life.

Enter PRINCE [HARRY]

But who comes here?

PRINCE HARRY   What, stand'st thou idle here? Lend me thy sword.

40 Many a noble man lies stark and stiff

Under the hoofs of vaunting enemies,

Whose deaths as yet are unrevenged. I prithee

Lend me thy sword.

FALSTAFF   O Hal, I prithee give me leave to breathe awhile.

45 Turk Gregory[9] never did such deeds in arms

As I have done this day. I have paid° Percy,   *settled with (killed)*

I have made him sure.[1]

PRINCE HARRY   He is indeed,

And living to kill thee. I prithee

Lend me thy sword.

FALSTAFF   Nay, before God, Hal,

50 If Percy be alive thou gett'st not my sword;

But take my pistol if thou wilt.

PRINCE HARRY   Give it me. What, is it in the case?

FALSTAFF   Ay, Hal;

'Tis hot, 'tis hot. There's that will sack a city.

The PRINCE *draws it out, and finds it to be a bottle of*
sack

PRINCE HARRY   What, is it a time to jest and dally now?

He throws the bottle at him. Exit

55 FALSTAFF   Well, if Percy be alive, I'll pierce him. If he do come

in my way, so; if he do not, if I come in his willingly, let him

make a carbonado[2] of me. I like not such grinning° honour as   *menacing*

---

3. May the title of "fool" go with your soul (for impersonating the King).
4. In his surcoat, or loose robes of rich material,
embroidered with the royal coat of arms and worn over
armor.
5. Our soldiers look as though they will win the day.
6. Escape without paying the tavern bill ("shot"), with
a pun in the following line on "shot" as ammunition
(projectiles, cannon shot, etc.).
7. Recording of debts by means of "scores," or notches

on a board (customary in taverns); wounding or cutting.
8. By the town gates, where people often begged.
9. A conflation of the idea of the Turk, taken to be a
cruel and fierce fighter and an enemy of Protestant England, and either Pope Gregory VII or Pope Gregory
XIII, both regarded as violent and cruel by Protestant
writers.
1. I have killed him; but the Prince takes "sure" to
mean "secure."
2. Meat slashed to grill.

Sir Walter hath. Give me life, which if I can save, so; if not, honour comes unlooked for, and there's an end.

Exit [with Blunt's body]

5.4

Alarum. Excursions. Enter KING [HENRY], PRINCE
[HARRY, *wounded*], *Lord* JOHN OF LANCASTER, *and* [the]
Earl of WESTMORLAND

KING HENRY   I prithee, Harry, withdraw thyself, thou bleed'st too much.
Lord John of Lancaster, go you with him.

JOHN OF LANCASTER   Not I, my lord, unless I did bleed too.

PRINCE HARRY [*to the* KING]   I beseech your majesty, make up,°   *go forward*
5   Lest your retirement do amaze° your friends.   *alarm*

KING HENRY   I will do so. My lord of Westmorland,
Lead him to his tent.

WESTMORLAND [*to the* PRINCE]   Come, my lord, I'll lead you to your tent.

PRINCE HARRY   Lead me, my lord? I do not need your help,
10   And God forbid a shallow scratch should drive
The Prince of Wales from such a field as this,
Where stained[1] nobility lies trodden on,
And rebels' arms triumph in massacres.

JOHN OF LANCASTER   We breathe° too long. Come, cousin Westmorland,   *rest*
15   Our duty this way lies. For God's sake, come.

[*Exeunt* LANCASTER *and* WESTMORLAND]

PRINCE HARRY   By God, thou hast deceived me, Lancaster;
I did not think thee lord of such a spirit.
Before I loved thee as a brother, John,
But now I do respect thee as my soul.

20 KING HENRY   I saw him hold Lord Percy at the point°   *sword point*
With lustier maintenance° than I did look for   *more valiant bearing*
Of such an ungrown warrior.

PRINCE HARRY   O, this boy lends mettle to us all!   *Exit*

Enter [the Earl of] DOUGLAS

DOUGLAS   Another king! They grow like Hydra's heads.[2]
25   I am the Douglas, fatal to all those
That wear those colours on them. What art thou
That counterfeit'st the person of a king?

KING HENRY   The King himself, who, Douglas, grieves at heart
So many of his shadows° thou hast met   *likenesses*
30   And not the very King. I have two boys
Seek° Percy and thyself about the field;   *Who seek*
But seeing thou fall'st on me so luckily,
I will assay° thee; and defend thyself.   *challenge*

DOUGLAS   I fear thou art another counterfeit;
35   And yet, in faith, thou bear'st thee like a king.
But mine° I am sure thou art, whoe'er thou be,   *(my prize of war)*
And thus I win thee.

They fight. The KING *being in danger, enter* PRINCE
[HARRY]

PRINCE HARRY   Hold up thy head, vile Scot, or thou art like
Never to hold it up again. The spirits

5.4
1. Bloodstained; disgraced by defeat.
2. A monster in classical mythology that grew two

heads whenever one was cut off. The hydra was a common image of political disorder.

40   Of valiant Shirley, Stafford, Blunt, are in my arms.
        It is the Prince of Wales that threatens thee,
        Who never promiseth but he means to pay.
                They fight. DOUGLAS *flieth*
        Cheerly, my lord! How fares your grace?
        Sir Nicholas Gawsey hath for succour sent,
45   And so hath Clifton. I'll to Clifton straight.
        KING HENRY   Stay and breathe awhile.
        Thou hast redeemed thy lost opinion,°   *reputation*
        And showed thou mak'st some tender of° my life,   *have some regard for*
        In this fair rescue thou hast brought to me.
50   PRINCE HARRY   O God, they did me too much injury
        That ever said I hearkened for° your death.   *desired*
        If it were so, I might have let alone
        The insulting° hand of Douglas over you,   *scornful*
        Which would have been as speedy in your end
55   As all the poisonous potions in the world,
        And saved the treacherous labour of your son.
        KING HENRY   Make up° to Clifton; I'll to Sir Nicholas Gawsey.   *Go forward*
                                                    Exit
                Enter HOTSPUR
        HOTSPUR   If I mistake not, thou art Harry Monmouth.
        PRINCE HARRY   Thou speak'st as if I would deny my name.
        HOTSPUR   My name is Harry Percy.
60   PRINCE HARRY   Why then, I see
        A very valiant rebel of the name.
        I am the Prince of Wales; and think not, Percy,
        To share with me in glory any more.
        Two stars keep not their motion in one sphere,[3]
65   Nor can one England brook° a double reign   *endure*
        Of Harry Percy and the Prince of Wales.
        HOTSPUR   Nor shall it, Harry, for the hour is come
        To end the one of us, and would to God
        Thy name in arms were now as great as mine.
70   PRINCE HARRY   I'll make it greater ere I part from thee,
        And all the budding honours on thy crest°   *helmet; coat of arms*
        I'll crop° to make a garland for my head.   *cut*
        HOTSPUR   I can no longer brook thy vanities.°   *empty boasts*
                They fight.
                Enter FALSTAFF
        FALSTAFF   Well said, Hal! To it, Hal! Nay, you shall find no boy's
75   play here, I can tell you.
                Enter DOUGLAS. *He fighteth with* FALSTAFF, *who falls*
                down as if he were dead. [*Exit* DOUGLAS.] *The* PRINCE
                killeth [HOTSPUR]
        HOTSPUR   O Harry, thou hast robbed me of my youth.
        I better brook the loss of brittle life
        Than those proud titles thou hast won of me.
        They wound my thoughts worse than thy sword my flesh.
80   But thoughts, the slaves of life, and life, time's fool,
        And time, that takes survey of all the world,
        Must have a stop.° O, I could prophesy,   *an end*

---

3. Alluding to the theory that stars moved in concentric spheres around a center. Only one star could occupy a
single sphere.

But that the earthy and cold hand of death
Lies on my tongue. No, Percy, thou art dust,
85 And food for—   [*He dies*]
  PRINCE HARRY For worms, brave Percy. Fare thee well, great heart.
Ill-weaved ambition, how much art thou shrunk!
When that this body did contain a spirit,
A kingdom for it was too small a bound,
90 But now two paces of the vilest earth
Is room enough. This earth that bears thee dead
Bears not alive so stout° a gentleman.   *valiant*
If thou wert sensible° of courtesy,   *conscious*
I should not make so dear° a show of zeal;°   *heartfelt / emotion*
95 But let my favours[4] hide thy mangled face,
      [*He covers Hotspur's face*]
And even in thy behalf I'll thank myself
For doing these fair rites of tenderness.
Adieu, and take thy praise with thee to heaven.
Thy ignominy sleep with thee in the grave,
100 But not remembered in thy epitaph.
      He spieth FALSTAFF *on the ground*
What, old acquaintance! Could not all this flesh
Keep in a little life? Poor Jack, farewell.
I could have better spared a better man.
O, I should have a heavy° miss of thee,   *sad; weighty*
105 If I were much in love with vanity.
Death hath not struck so fat a deer today,
Though many dearer in this bloody fray.
Embowelled[5] will I see thee by and by.
Till then, in blood by noble Percy lie.   *Exit*
      FALSTAFF *riseth up*
110 FALSTAFF Embowelled? If thou embowel me today, I'll give you
leave to powder° me, and eat me too, tomorrow. 'Sblood, 'twas   *pickle in salt*
time to counterfeit, or that hot termagant[6] Scot had paid me,
scot and lot° too. Counterfeit? I lie, I am no counterfeit. To   *in full*
die is to be a counterfeit, for he is but the counterfeit of a man
115 who hath not the life of a man. But to counterfeit dying when
a man thereby liveth is to be no counterfeit, but the true and
perfect image of life indeed. The better part of valour is discretion, in the which better part° I have saved my life. Zounds,   *role*
I am afraid of this gunpowder Percy, though he be dead. How
120 if he should counterfeit too, and rise? By my faith, I am afraid
he would prove the better counterfeit. Therefore I'll make him
sure; yea, and I'll swear I killed him. Why may not he rise as
well as I? Nothing confutes me but eyes,[7] and nobody sees
me. Therefore, sirrah, [*stabbing* HOTSPUR] with a new wound
125 in your thigh, come you along with me.
      He takes up HOTSPUR *on his back.*
      Enter PRINCE [HARRY] *and* [*Lord*] JOHN OF LANCASTER
  PRINCE HARRY Come, brother John. Full bravely hast thou fleshed

---

4. Ornaments such as plumes or gloves worn into battle.
5. Prepared for embalming and burial as noblemen
were; disemboweled in the manner of a hunted deer.
6. A quarrelsome or shrewish person; the name of an

imaginary deity who, according to medieval morality
plays, was worshipped by followers of Mohammed.
7. No one could confute my story but an eyewitness.

Thy maiden sword.[8]

JOHN OF LANCASTER   But soft; whom have we here?
Did you not tell me this fat man was dead?

PRINCE HARRY   I did; I saw him dead,
Breathless and bleeding on the ground.

130   [*To* FALSTAFF]   Art thou alive?
Or is it fantasy° that plays upon our eyesight?   *hallucination*
I prithee speak; we will not trust our eyes
Without our ears. Thou art not what thou seem'st.

FALSTAFF   No, that's certain: I am not a double man.° But if I   *ghost; two men*
135   be not Jack Falstaff, then am I a jack.° There is Percy. If your   *knave*
father will do me any honour, so; if not, let him kill the next
Percy himself. I look to be either earl or duke, I can assure you.

PRINCE HARRY   Why, Percy I killed myself, and saw thee dead.

FALSTAFF   Didst thou? Lord, Lord, how this world is given to
140   lying! I grant you I was down and out of breath, and so was he;
but we rose both at an instant,° and fought a long hour by   *simultaneously*
Shrewsbury clock. If I may be believed, so; if not, let them that
should reward valour bear the sin upon their own heads. I'll
take't on my death° I gave him this wound in the thigh. If the   *swear on my deathbed*
145   man were alive and would deny it, zounds, I would make him
eat a piece of my sword.

JOHN OF LANCASTER   This is the strangest tale that e'er I heard.

PRINCE HARRY   This is the strangest fellow, brother John.
[*To* FALSTAFF] Come, bring your luggage nobly on your back.
150   For my part, if a lie may do thee grace,°   *get you favor*
I'll gild it with the happiest° terms I have.   *most favorable*
      A retreat is sounded
The trumpet sounds retreat; the day is our.
Come, brother, let us to the highest° of the field   *highest ground*
To see what friends are living, who are dead.
                   Exeunt [*the* PRINCE *and* LANCASTER]
155   FALSTAFF   I'll follow, as they say, for reward. He that rewards me,
God reward him. If I do grow great, I'll grow less; for I'll purge,[9]
and leave sack, and live cleanly, as a nobleman should do.
                   Exit [*bearing Hotspur's body*]

5.5

The trumpets sound. Enter KING [HENRY], PRINCE
[HARRY], *Lord* JOHN OF LANCASTER, [*the*] *Earl of* WEST-
MORLAND, *with* [*the Earl of*] WORCESTER *and* [*Sir Rich-
ard*] VERNON, *prisoners* [*and soldiers*]

KING HENRY   Thus ever did rebellion find rebuke.
Ill-spirited Worcester, did not we send grace,
Pardon, and terms of love to all of you?
And wouldst thou turn our offers contrary,
5   Misuse the tenor° of thy kinsman's trust?   *Abuse the substance*
Three knights upon our party slain today,
A noble earl, and many a creature else,

---

8. *Full . . . sword:* How courageously or splendidly
have you initiated in bloodshed your untried weapon
(fought your first battle). The phrase alludes to hunting
practices in which hawks or hounds were "fleshed," or
made eager for prey by the taste of blood. Also alluding,
by way of the slang meaning of "sword" as "penis," to a
man's first sexual encounters with the flesh of others.
9. I'll take laxatives (to reduce my weight); I'll repent.

Had been alive this hour
If like a Christian thou hadst truly borne
10   Betwixt our armies true intelligence.°   *information*
WORCESTER   What I have done my safety urged me to,
    And I embrace this fortune patiently,
    Since not to be avoided it falls on me.
KING HENRY   Bear Worcester to the death, and Vernon too.
15   Other offenders we will pause upon.°   *reflect upon*
              Exeunt WORCESTER *and* VERNON [*guarded*]
    How goes the field?
PRINCE HARRY   The noble Scot Lord Douglas, when he saw
    The fortune of the day quite turned from him,
    The noble Percy slain, and all his men
20   Upon the foot of fear,° fled with the rest;   *Fleeing in fear*
    And falling from a hill he was so bruised
    That the pursuers took him. At my tent
    The Douglas is, and I beseech your grace
    I may dispose of him.
25   KING HENRY   With all my heart.
PRINCE HARRY   Then, brother John of Lancaster,
    To you this honourable bounty° shall belong.   *act of generosity*
    Go to the Douglas, and deliver him
    Up to his pleasure ransomless and free.
30   His valours shown upon our crests° today   *helmets*
    Have taught us how to cherish such high deeds
    Even in the bosom of our adversaries.
JOHN OF LANCASTER   I thank your grace for this high courtesy,
    Which I shall give away immediately.
35   KING HENRY   Then this remains, that we divide our power.
    You, son John, and my cousin Westmorland,
    Towards York shall bend you° with your dearest speed   *direct your course*
    To meet Northumberland and the prelate Scrope,
    Who, as we hear, are busily in arms.
40   Myself and you, son Harry, will towards Wales,
    To fight with Glyndŵr and the Earl of March.
    Rebellion in this land shall lose his sway,
    Meeting the check of such another day;
    And since this business so fair is done,
45   Let us not leave° till all our own be won.   *leave off*
            Exeunt [*the* KING, *the* PRINCE, *and their power*
            at one door, LANCASTER, WESTMORLAND, *and their*
            power at another door]

The Second Part of Henry IV

The title page of the 1600 Quarto of *2 Henry IV* describes the play as *The Second Part of Henry the Fourth, Continuing to His Death, and Coronation of Henry the Fifth. With the Humours of Sir John Falstaff, and Swaggering Pistol*. Its first focus is the "high" historical matter of the reign of Kings. For this part of the play, Shakespeare drew primarily on the second edition of Raphael Holinshed's *Chronicles of England, Scotland, and Ireland* (1587), although he probably consulted other sources, including Samuel Daniel's *First Four Books of the Civil Wars Between the Two Houses of Lancaster and York* (1595). In regard to this historical material, the title page particularly highlights the delicate moment of succession when one King dies and another is crowned. Shakespeare's audience was facing such a moment at the end of the 1590s. Elizabeth I was old, having been on the English throne since 1558; she had never married, and she had no heirs. The uncertainties of the coming succession may have, by contrast, heightened the pleasure of watching Henry IV followed upon the throne by his male heir, Henry V—the King who, whatever his father's sins in seizing the crown from Richard II, had become in the popular imagination a symbol of kingly perfection and English masculinity. With his customary subtlety, Shakespeare complicates and somewhat darkens the popular image of the wayward prince who undergoes a miraculous transformation, but Hal's coronation nonetheless is the end point toward which the play inexorably moves.

Besides its royal plot, the play also deals in some decidedly "low" and mostly unhistorical matter, suggested on the title page by mention of the "humours" of Falstaff and the presence of swaggering Pistol. These characters hold pride of place alongside Henry IV and Henry V, indicating the popularity of the antic parts of the play—Falstaff's jokes and his flouting of authority or Pistol's madly bombastic language. Some of the matter for the play's comic scenes probably derives from *The Famous Victories of Henry the Fifth*, a popular play about the life of Henry V first published in 1598 but believed to have been performed well before that date. In *2 Henry IV*, Prince Hal does not mingle with the comic figures as freely as he did in *1 Henry IV*; in fact, he appears only once, in 2.4, in the Eastcheap tavern where Falstaff holds court. Nonetheless, the total number of low, unhistorical characters expands considerably in this play. Pistol is a new character, and Mistress Quickly is joined in her Eastcheap tavern by Doll Tearsheet, a prostitute whose name graphically suggests one consequence of unrestrained fornication. Further, a number of country characters are introduced: the Gloustershire justices of the peace, Shallow and Silence; Shallow's servant, Davy; and the five rural recruits (Mouldy, Bullcalf, Wart, Feeble, and Shadow) whom Falstaff considers for conscription into the army. *2 Henry IV* is the only history play of which more than half is written in prose, and much of that richly varied prose occurs in the numerous scenes involving these humble figures Shakespeare added to the historical narrative of one king's death and another's coronation.

2 Henry IV was probably written soon after the very popular *1 Henry IV*, which was published in 1598 but probably written and staged in 1596–97. The Quarto was published in 1600, but there is a reference to the character of Justice Silence in Ben Jonson's *Every Man out of His Humour,* published in 1599. *2 Henry IV* was therefore probably performed sometime between February 1598, when *1 Henry IV* was entered in the Stationers' Register with no indication that it was the first part of a two-part play, and early in 1599. It is likely that censorship of Shakespeare's original naming of Falstaff as "Oldcastle," Bardolph as "Russell," and Peto as "Harvey" (see Introduction to *1 Henry IV*) had occurred before Shakespeare completed *2 Henry IV,* although a few

THE
Second part of Henrie
the fourth, continuing to his death,
and coronation of Henrie
the fift.

With the humours of sir Iohn Falstaffe, *and swaggering*
Pistoll.

As it hath been sundrie times publikely
acted by the right honourable, the Lord
Chamberlaine his seruants.

Written by William Shakespeare.

LONDON
Printed by V.S. for Andrew Wise, and
William Aspley.
1600.

Title page of the 1600 Quarto of *The Second part of Henrie the fourth* . . . , promising to combine royal history and the comic events involving Falstaff and his tavern companions.

traces of the original names appear in the speech prefixes and stage directions in the first two acts of the quarto text. Shakespeare may have interrupted his composition of *2 Henry IV* to write *The Merry Wives of Windsor,* a play that could have been performed as early as 1597. If so, he would have written the last acts of *2 Henry IV* well after the censorship of the offending names in *1 Henry IV* had occurred, and he would consequently have altered the names in the final acts of the play.

Narrowing down the play's date of composition, however, does not answer the question of why Shakespeare wrote two plays dealing with the reign of Henry IV. Some critics believe that the playwright once intended to encompass all the material of both plays in one, but in writing *1 Henry IV* he found he had room to depict only the events up to the Battle of Shrewsbury and Hal's emergence as a chivalric hero through his defeat of Hotspur. Therefore, what was "left over" was, in effect, put into *2 Henry IV* with the patchwork addition of enough comic material to scrape together a play. It is also possible that Shakespeare intended to dramatize only the events now in *1 Henry IV,* but that having done so, he was encouraged by his success to add another chapter to the story of Hal's reformation and gradual progression toward the throne. Alternatively, Shakespeare may have planned two plays from the beginning, intending to undertake two quite different explorations of the prodigal narrative by which the wild Prince becomes first a chivalric hero and eventually the King of England.

Whatever the original impetus for writing it, the finished play now called *2 Henry IV* has an integrity of its own and a set of preoccupations that clearly distinguishes it from *1 Henry IV.* The rebels, for example, are a less flamboyant crew than in the earlier play, and they are not vanquished in combat as at Shrewsbury; rather, at Gaultres, Prince John tricks them into laying down their weapons. Policy, not chivalry, wins the day. Hal's challenge, moreover, is no longer to prove himself the prince of chivalry, with the rebel Henry Percy (Hotspur) as his main antagonist. Rather, he must show himself fit for civil rule. Hence the importance in *2 Henry IV* of the Lord Chief Justice, a figure who in popular accounts of Hal's life had had the Prince imprisoned for impudently giving him a box on the ear. This event is not dramatized in either of Shakespeare's *Henry IV* plays, as it had been in *The Famous Victories,* but it is several times alluded to. In *2 Henry IV,* the Chief Justice emerges as the main foil to the disorderly Falstaff. Upon hearing that Henry IV is dead and Hal is King, the fat knight exclaims, "The laws of England are at my commandment" (5.3.125–26). It seems quite possible that under Henry V, law will give way before the appetites and desires of individual subjects. Hal and the Chief Justice do not share the stage until 5.2, but their encounter is a pivotal moment in the text, revealing whether Hal will recognize and honor the authority of the Chief Justice or follow Falstaff in flouting the law.

Also unique to this play is its pervasive concern with the passing of time. As Hastings says at the end of Act 1, "We are time's subjects" (1.3.110); arguably, he sounds the play's central theme. Even the King, to whom so many are subject, is himself subject to time. Shakespeare portrays him as old and sick, though the historical Henry successfully ruled England for ten years after the Battle of Shrewsbury. His sickness and the urgency of the rebel threat pressure the Prince, forcing him to realize that his idle days in the tavern are numbered and that if he lingers longer, he will "profane the precious time" (2.4.330), time he should spend coming to terms with his father and defending a kingdom still threatened by rebels. Even the irrepressible Falstaff now feels time's hand. He enters the play in 1.2 asking what the doctor has said about the urine he has sent for examination, and to Quickly and Tearsheet he confesses, "I am old, I am old" (2.4.243). If *1 Henry IV* is an expansive work, infused with a feeling of infinite play and infinite possibility, *2 Henry IV* has a melancholy, autumnal aura. It is a play of limits and constrictions. Shallow intones: "Death, as the Psalmist saith, is certain to all; all shall die" (3.2.33–34). Through its many images of sickness, disease, and old age, the play is permeated with intimations of mortality.

The play's portrayal of Prince Hal shares in the somber mood that suffuses all of *2 Henry IV.* When the audience first sees him, he is with Poins (2.2), brooding on the impasse to which his own actions have brought him. Rather than keeping a controlling distance from his tavern companion, Hal ruefully acknowledges what he shares with common men. Tired, he desires nothing more exalted than small beer, the common drink of every London apprentice. He admits that he should not, because of his rank, be intimate with Poins; and yet he confesses that he is, revealing how thoroughly he knows his companion's wardrobe and using Poins as a sounding board for his misgivings about his own behavior and its consequences. While the scene's mood changes when Bardolph enters with an absurdly pompous letter from Falstaff, its fretful beginning indicates a new strain in Shakespeare's depiction of Hal's progress toward the throne. In *1 Henry IV*, everything seemed easy for the Prince. He announced a course of reform and enacted it with little apparent cost to himself. In *2 Henry IV*, Shakespeare constructs a more sober Prince who articulates anxiety about the gap between his plebeian taste for small beer and the grandeur of the office he will assume, a Prince who knows that to have acted the wastrel in order to make a dazzling reform may have cost him his father's affection and made it impossible to express his love for the King without appearing a hypocrite. In the opening acts of *2 Henry IV*, Hal's capacity for self-critique and for uncertainty makes him more vulnerable, and perhaps more likable, than the shiny and assured paragon of *1 Henry IV*.

Shakespeare also shows changes in Hal's father, King Henry IV, who in Part 2 reveals a new capacity for introspection. In 3.1, speaking about the burdens of office, he acknowledges the costs of his success and admits that at the start of his reign he could little foresee the changes time would effect in him and in his plans and alliances. Yet like his son, in the end Henry finds his office worth the cost. Power may bring burdens, but for both characters it is irresistible. Each sentimentally envies common men (whose poverty and powerlessness they do not share), but neither renounces the office of King. And neither ever gives up the attempt to control his destiny. Having contemplated the many unforeseen changes of his reign, Henry IV finally breaks off his reverie to plan a campaign against the rebels:

> Are these things then necessities?
> Then let us meet them like necessities;
> And that same word even now cries out on us.
> They say the Bishop and Northumberland
> Are fifty thousand strong.
>
> (3.1.87–91)

This is the pragmatic voice of rule, the blunt determination that Shakespeare attributes both to Prince Hal and to his father.

Yet despite (and perhaps because of) their similarities, Shakespeare makes the relationship of Henry and Hal a troubled one. Part of the complexity of *2 Henry IV* is that while it tellingly anatomizes how these Kings, father and then son, acquire and maintain power, it simultaneously creates the impression of a psychodrama between the two of them that, though inseparable from their political roles, is never fully understood by either. Hal, despite telling Poins he loves his father, does not appear in the King's presence until the end of Act 4, when Henry is on his deathbed. Then, with what has seemed to many to be unseemly haste, Hal, believing his father dead, takes the crown from the sleeping King's pillow and sets it on his own head. Is this, as the King fears, Hal's acting out of a fantasy of parricide? Or, as Hal protests, is it his attempt to come to terms with the burdens of office that have hastened his father's death and that will now fall to him?

In part, the relationship between Hal and Henry is complicated by the guilt each feels about the politically useful and carefully managed "wildness" that each has employed. Hal, of course, has cultivated wildness as a prelude to reform. It is the foil by which he aims to set off his achievement of perfect chivalry and justice. But it is important to remember that to come by his throne, Henry himself had to enact the wildness of usurpation, seizing the crown from a lawfully anointed king, an act Shakespeare depicted in *Richard II*. To be sure, once in the seat of rule, Henry repudiated such wildness and embraced the law, justifying his own reign in part by presenting himself as the bulwark against disorder—that of the rebels and even that of his son. There is no doubt that Hal displays prodigal behavior, spending time in the tavern rather than at court, but his father dwells on and exaggerates his son's lawlessness, picturing England's distress when ruled by a man who "from curbed licence plucks / The muzzle of restraint" (4.3.258–59). This preoccupation with Hal's lawlessness may signal Henry's guilt about his own act of usurpation, for which he has long planned a penitential crusade to the Holy Land (a crusade that we eventually learn would *also* have the effect of distracting his nobles from thoughts of rebellion at home). But Henry does not seem able to see the ways in which his son's tactics resemble his own. Truly his father's child, Hal angles for power with an unerring sense of when to embrace wildness and when to repudiate it. Just as Henry's act of seizing the crown raises the specter of parricide, Henry's obsession with curbing Hal's wildness hints at castration. Without seeming fully to realize the consequences of his own actions, the King would cut off one source of Hal's power, even though he himself once embraced disorder and still needs it to justify his rule.

In Henry's last conversation with Hal and at his death, father and son switch positions in the discourse of "wildness" that runs through the play. The King has been the principle of order, the Prince the ungovernable prodigal. On his deathbed, however, the King acknowledges to Hal:

> God knows, my son,
> By what bypaths and indirect crook'd ways
> I met this crown; and I myself know well
> How troublesome it sat upon my head.
> To thee it shall descend with better quiet,
> Better opinion, better confirmation;
> For all the soil of the achievement goes
> With me into the earth.
>
> (4.3.311–18)

He represents himself as a man stained by his own errancy, but one whose sins can be buried with his death. Hal picks up the theme when he announces after his father's death, "My father is gone wild into his grave" (5.2.122), as if Henry himself embodied the principle of disorder, now buried. Yet Hal continues, suddenly making problematic whose wildness the grave holds:

> For in his tomb lie my affections;
> And with his spirits sadly I survive
> To mock the expectation of the world.
>
> (5.2.123–25)

Now it is *Hal's* wildness that the grave holds, his father's sober spirits that live on in the son. Shedding his prodigality is now not an act of disempowerment but its opposite. The wild Prince has become the order-loving King. It will now be his turn to repudiate those who live outside the compass of the law, beginning with Falstaff.

Critics have argued that *2 Henry IV* looks forward to the tragedies in its somber tone and its focus upon the tortured self-divisions of the King and his son. There is truth in this claim, but one must also recognize that while the play allows the audience to read doubt and self-division in Henry and the Prince, at the end it moves to install Hal unambiguously in the position of the reformed Prince and law-abiding King. Hal's apparent self-division holds the attention of the audience just as his carefully managed reform wins the admiration of his subjects. But when the time is right, whatever the "personal" cost, he embraces the law in the person of the Chief Justice while burying wildness in the person of his father and publicly repudiating it in the person of Falstaff. In so doing, he shows an unerring instinct for the improvisations that allow him to acquire and retain power.

But though Hal publicly repudiates wildness, the play does not. Wildness surges up unpredictably, not only in the actions of the rebels but also in the actions and particularly in the unruly language of those many "minor" characters who are Shakespeare's additions to his historical sources and whose existence is signaled on the title page by reference to the humors of Falstaff and swaggering Pistol. In the late sixteenth century, the English language was undergoing expansion and entering a period of vibrant linguistic experimentation. Many writers were interested in making English a fit language in which to write verse that would rival the achievements of classical literature. They experimented with imitating the verse forms used by Latin writers in particular; they also coined new words, and they attempted to purge English of uncouth or infelicitous elements. But it was not just poets who affected the language. Trade brought new products to England, and those products had to have names. Foreign visitors, merchants, and workers were a common sight in the London landscape, and they, of course, brought their languages with them. Foreign terms were regularly absorbed into the English vernacular. Meanwhile, the theater offered auditors the high-sounding rhetoric of kings and tyrants, while London preachers made their reputations with dazzling displays of oratorical power.

This atmosphere generated an infectious excitement about language, and not all of this excitement was easy to control. Rhetorical handbooks proliferated, each sketching out the styles and figures of speech appropriate to different occasions, and each also listing rhetorical "vices," examples of indecorous or ungrammatical or infelicitous speech. *2 Henry IV* could be considered a casebook of linguistic vices. The minor characters speak a wild farrago of tongues that defy the desire for linguistic order. Swaggering Pistol is a case in point. Much of his speech is composed of scraps of rhetoric he has picked up from going to the London theater, especially, perhaps, to the Rose, where Edward Alleyn, chief actor for the Admiral's Men, specialized in a highly rhetorical and hyperbolic acting style that Pistol seems both to channel and to parody. Pistol, for example, imagines himself as Tamburlaine, the overreaching hero of Marlowe's two-part play about a Scythian shepherd who became one of the great military conquerors of all time. Alleyn was famous for this role, and Pistol's swaggering style aspires to Alleyn's (and Tamburlaine's) rhetorical pyrotechnics. Pistol, however, mangles his references to Marlowe's hero, intermingling what he can remember of Tamburlaine's speeches with a mishmash of fine-sounding names and lines from drinking songs, as when he proclaims:

> Shall pack-horses
> And hollow pampered jades of Asia,
> Which cannot go but thirty mile a day,
> Compare with Caesars and with cannibals,
> And Trojan Greeks?
> Nay, rather damn them with King Cerberus,
> And let the welkin roar. Shall we fall foul for toys?
> (2.4.140–46)

Pistol's "mistakes" are pervasive. First he imitates what he can remember of the moment when Tamburlaine taunts the conquered kings whom he has put in harness to draw his chariot. But then he veers into nonsense, mistaking "cannibal" for "Hannibal," the heroic leader of Carthage; describing Greeks as Trojans, while in *The Iliad* the Greeks and Trojans were two peoples at war with one another; then attributing a crown to Cerberus, the three-headed dog who guarded the gates of hell; and ending with a tag from a drinking song: "And let the welkin roar." The sheer exuberance of the speech is partly what makes it pleasurable—Pistol's delight in the sound of big words, whatever those words may mean—along with the lawless incongruity with which one bit of remembered rhetoric is stitched onto the next. Self-mockingly, but also self-importantly, the passage points to the power of the theater to intoxicate spectators with fine rhetoric. Choleric, explosive, overflowing with the excesses of stage rhetoric, Pistol is a wild card in the play's quest for order and the rule of law.

He is not alone. The play opens with a prologue spoken by Rumour, whose business is telling lies, substituting the untrue for the true. That Shakespeare prefaced the play with this figure indicates his concern with the vagaries and waywardness of language. Sometimes language is maliciously used to deceive, as with Rumour or Prince John's double-edged speech at Gaultres. Sometimes, as with Pistol's bombast, it is used to evoke delight in how words sound, regardless of what they mean. At other times, as with Falstaff's puns, language reveals the double and triple meanings that can be activated from a simple utterance. To take a single example, consider Falstaff's anger in 1.2 at the prosperous merchant who refuses to give him twenty-two yards of satin without his providing adequate security—that is, adequate goods or money to cover the debt. To his Page

The Rumour of Shakespeare's Induction is derived from the classical figure of Fame, here depicted as covered with ears (to gather reports from all quarters) and blowing a horn (to broadcast news abroad). From Vicenzo Cartari, *Imagines deorum* (1581).

Falstaff sputters, "Well, he may sleep in security, for he hath the horn of abundance, and the lightness of his wife shines through it; and yet cannot he see, though he have his own lanthorn to light him" (1.2.39–42). The subversive wittiness of this passage depends on Falstaff's punning on the fact that "horn" can mean the horn lanterns sold by merchants, the cornucopia that is a symbol of abundance, or the horns of a man who has been sexually betrayed by his wife, while "lightness" can mean both illumination and sexual promiscuity. On the surface, Falstaff is grudgingly admitting that the merchant is rich and graced with a wife. But the puns tell another story: that of a blind cuckold whose wife's sexual infidelity is visible to everyone but himself. In Falstaff's mouth, language is a slippery thing and often a devastating tool for confounding an enemy.

One of the play's most remarkable rhetoricians, Mistress Quickly, did not make it to the title page of the Quarto, but her verbal blunders are another example of language's unpredictable qualities. Quickly is not the same person she was in *1 Henry IV*. For one thing, she seems to have lost the husband who was mentioned often, though never glimpsed, in the previous play; and she has acquired a new companion in the person of the prostitute Doll Tearsheet. Unmarried, economically independent, and associated with the criminality of prostitution and perhaps of murder (in 5.4, the women are accused with Pistol of having beaten a man to death), Quickly emerges as a figure of disorder who must be purged from a reformed commonwealth. In part, she represents linguistic anarchy. Her signature utterance is the malapropism, the verbal blunder by which one word is mistaken for another. For example, telling the Chief Justice of Falstaff's whereabouts, she says he was "indited," meaning "invited," to dinner (2.1.24). The malapropism is interesting because it is a kind of lawless speech in which the speaker is guided by the sound of words, or by a private logic, rather than by the usual rules of sense. Quickly, for example, in mistaking "indicted" for "invited" has blundered into her own kind of sense, since she would indeed like to see Falstaff indicted, or brought to legal judgment, for the debts he owes her. Malapropisms, to those who know better, make the speaker appear foolish. Yet they also can disrupt the institutions that depend on clear and predictable communication. Not even the Chief Justice knows quite what to make of Quickly, so persistently does her speech elude the net of common sense, enveloping her in a tangle of meanings—some obscene, some suggestively significant—that she may or may not intend. Sir Francis Bacon called revenge "wild justice"; the malapropism might be called "wild speech," so thoroughly does it defy semantic predictability.

The distinctiveness of the prose assigned to the comic figures in *2 Henry IV* is one of the play's most striking features. It highlights Shakespeare's ability to delineate character by means of linguistic differences. Shallow's mindless repetition of simple words, Falstaff's puns, Quickly's malapropisms, and Pistol's bombast are all ways of individuating these figures. They also suggest the fecundity of speech in Henry's England and register, at the linguistic level, a wild disorder no principle of decorum or law can entirely contain. By means of the double entendre, much of what characters speak in the tavern world alludes to the body and its pleasures, even while they intend or appear to talk of something else. For example, Quickly, complaining of Falstaff to the Chief Justice, says, "He stabbed me in mine own house, most beastly, in good faith. A cares not what mischief he does; if his weapon be out, he will foin like any devil, he will spare neither man, woman, nor child" (2.1.12–15). "Foin" means "thrust" or "strike." Overtly, Quickly describes a Falstaff who takes out his sword or dagger and indiscriminately stabs whoever happens to be handy. Indirectly, and perhaps inadvertently, she describes a Falstaff who, when his sexual "weapon," or penis, is out, will indiscriminately engage in sex with whoever happens to be near. The tavern scenes teem with similar instances of sexualized speech or, more accurately, speech that tells two stories at the same time, one of them a story of sex: its pleasures and diseases and persistence. The bawdy doubleness of tavern

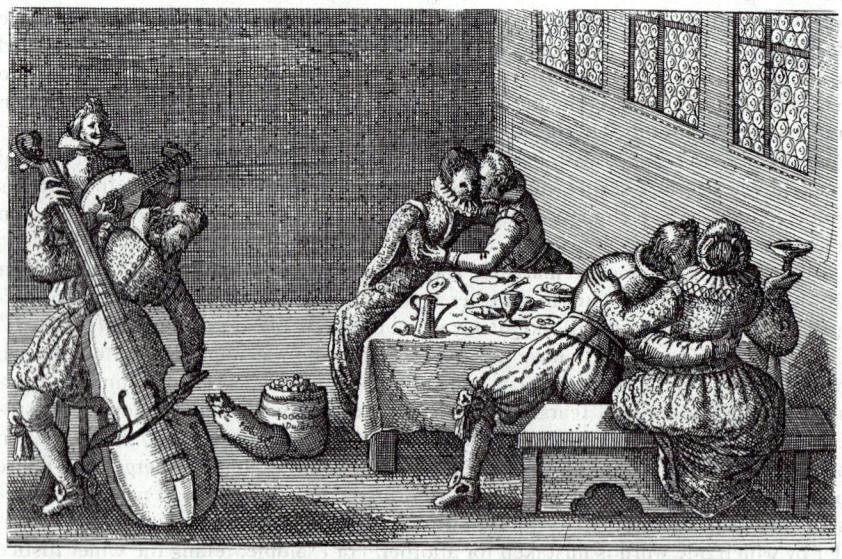

A seventeenth-century tavern scene recalling Mistress Quickly's Eastcheap tavern. From Peter Rollos, *Le Centre de l'amour* (1630?).

prose contrasts sharply with the elevated poetry in which the King most often speaks. Worrying, planning, commanding, the King constructs himself as a bulwark against disorder. But the disorderly, bombastic, vibrant, and lewd speech of the tavern suggests at the level of language the difficulties of controlling the manifold energies of his subjects.

Thinking about the play's control of or its failure to control unsanctioned energies provides a context for considering what traditionally has been the most discussed aspect of *2 Henry IV*: the Prince's final public repudiation of Falstaff. In this play, Falstaff is kept separate from the Prince except for the one scene (2.4) in which the Prince disguises himself as a tavern barman and overhears Falstaff talking with Doll and Quickly. Moreover, the exploitative side of Falstaff is more fully displayed here than in the earlier play. He leeches off Quickly; he takes bribes to release able-bodied men from service in the army; he worms a thousand pounds from Shallow. Yet he is still able, as in the stunning speech in which he indicts Prince John for cold-bloodedness (4.2.78–111), to offer a telling critique of his betters and to embody a frank physicality they eschew. Given Falstaff's wit and his centrality to the pleasure afforded by both *1* and *2 Henry IV,* the new King's repudiation of him—"I know thee not, old man. Fall to thy prayers" (5.5.45)—continues to trouble critics and audiences. Certainly, how the moment is staged can mitigate or harshen its implications. In Terry Hands's 1975 Royal Shakespeare Company production, for example, the newly crowned King came onstage in glittering gold and masked, the epitome of detached and heartless power. In other productions, he rejects his former friend with a sob, emphasizing his own sense of loss and his continuing affection for Falstaff. But however it is staged, there is little doubt that the new King, whatever his "personal" feelings, has turned Falstaff away to consolidate his power.

The final scene, however, is not the play's last word: it is followed by an Epilogue. It is likely that this Epilogue was spoken by the company's clown, in this case Will Kemp, a famed comic actor who in this play is believed to have played Falstaff. It is especially likely that Kemp spoke the Epilogue because of the several references in it to the actor's willingness to use his legs, or to dance, should his words not prove agreeable. Kemp was a skilled dancer, and when he left Shakespeare's company in 1599, he undertook a famous morris dance from London to Norwich. The Epilogue gives the common actor who had played Falstaff the play's last word and its final display of physical skill. At Shrewsbury, Hal had thought Falstaff dead, but, faking death, the fat man had arisen. In *2 Henry IV,* the old knight is banished from the King's presence in the play's final scene, but in the Epilogue, the actor who had played him reappears— soliciting the audience's applause, denying that Falstaff is a representation of the Lollard martyr Sir John Oldcastle (see the Introduction to *1 Henry IV*) and kicking up his heels in a virtuoso display of dancing skill. If in the play proper the forces of order have attempted to demonize the energies associated with popular culture and the low life of the tavern, in the Epilogue those energies have free rein. The body of the common actor holds center stage as Kemp, throwing aside the character Falstaff's mantle of age, delights the audience with a jig.

The Epilogue has another effect. It pluralizes the "authorities" to which the theater is beholden. With its references to the Oldcastle controversy and its final allusion to praying for Queen Elizabeth, the Epilogue acknowledges the power embodied in the person of the monarch and in the state's censorship apparatus. But it also refers to pleasing both the gentlewomen and the gentlemen of the audience—in other words, the paying customers who came to the theater for all sorts of pleasures. If the title page of the Quarto is to be believed, readers, and probably audiences, were as much delighted by the irrepressible and irresponsible antics of Falstaff and swaggering Pistol as by the sober reformation of Hal and the suffering of his father, just as they were undoubtedly as delighted by the mangling of the King's English as by its decorous deployment. In short, while in this play the rule of law officially triumphs over the forces of disorder, the comic actor has the last dance, and theater finds a way to offer pleasures in excess of what the sober historical narrative allows.

Jean E. Howard

TEXTUAL NOTE

2 Henry IV was entered in the Stationers' Register on August 23, 1600, and first printed in a quarto version dated that same year. This Quarto had two issues, the first of which, QA, lacks the present 3.1, in which the sleepless King Henry meditates on the passage of time and the ironies of history. In QB, this scene is included. The text was not printed again until it appeared in a significantly different version in the First Folio of 1623 (F). The Folio text contains eight fairly substantial passages, totaling about 160 lines, not found in Q (A or B). It also differs from the quarto text in a number of other ways: oaths have been excised; punctuation, syntax, and certain aspects of style have been regularized; stage directions have been altered, and in several scenes the names of characters have been "massed" together in an initial stage direction, even if some of these characters only enter at a later point in the scene; some quarto lines are missing, and new part lines appear, as does a table of "The Actors Names" listing all the speaking parts.

The important debate about the play's textual history concerns the relation of Q to F. Q shows signs—such as the use of a number of different speech prefixes for the same character—of having been printed directly from the author's "foul papers," which do not appear to have been marked up for use in a theatrical performance. One explanation for the absence of 3.1 in QA is that the scene was marked for excision in the foul papers, either because it was politically sensitive or to reduce the length of the play. Others have argued that the scene was written on a separate manuscript leaf that became detached from its proper place in the foul papers and so was overlooked by the compositor. The Oxford editors believe that this scene was added by Shakespeare *after* the rest of the manuscript had been written as the first step in his ongoing reworking of the play. They postulate that the compositor who set this part of QA missed the marks indicating where the scene was to be added to the foul papers.

F, by contrast, shows signs of having been prepared by a professional scribe in its regularization of a number of aspects of the text, though these changes also introduce errors and obscure the exact nature of the manuscript underlying the transcription. The excision of oaths is undoubtedly a result of the 1606 statute against profanity on the stage. Some further changes found in F may be due to the special problems facing the compositors setting the text. It appears that too little space had been allocated in F for setting this play in type. Consequently, a group of four additional sheets was added, but the compositor still had to omit words, compressing one part of the text, and to add words and phrases, expanding other parts of the text, in order to fit the play into its allotted space. It is possible that the list of "The Actors Names" was added to fill up a blank page.

Some editors argue that the eight substantial passages found in F but missing from Q were originally present in the manuscript used for setting Q but were marked for excision, either because they were politically sensitive or for theatrical reasons such as the need to reduce the length of the speeches assigned to actors doubling in two roles. These editors grant priority to the quarto text (which appears to be printed from Shakespeare's foul papers and which does not contain the errors and changes made by the scribe who prepared the Folio manuscript), but they usually add the eight additional passages on the grounds that they were originally part of the manuscript behind the Quarto.

The Oxford editors work from different assumptions; specifically, they argue that beginning with 3.1, Shakespeare himself made a series of revisions to the play, perhaps recording these in the fair copy that was to serve as the promptbook. They argue that he did so as part of a consistent strategy to augment the historical portions of the play and to connect it more fully to *Richard II* and *1 Henry IV*. They agree that two of the eight additional Folio passages represent cuts in the quarto text because they deal with the politically sensitive matter of rebellion, but they also hold that the remaining six are Shakespeare's later *additions* to the play. They further argue that some of the other changes in F, such as the deletion of specific lines, show authorial intervention in the interest of making the play more stageworthy. The Oxford editors therefore postulate that the scribe who produced the copy used for setting F, while having a copy of Q to consult, was working primarily from a theatrical promptbook that registered some authorial revisions to the quarto version of the play, though the theatrical nature of that promptbook has been obscured by the "literary" habits of the scribe. As a consequence, this edition of the play, while using Q as its control text, accepts a higher number of Folio readings than is true for many other editions in an attempt to reproduce the stage version of the play the Oxford editors believe underlies F.

The eight substantial new passages found in F deserve further discussion. Interestingly, all of them involve figures who are of the rebels' party. The Oxford editors agree that two of them were censored because they too compellingly justified rebellion. These are 1.1.188–208, Morton's speech announcing that the Archbishop of York has joined the rebellion, using the murder of Richard II as partial justification, and 4.1.55–79, the Archbishop's speech justifying the rebels' position and exclaiming against the King's indifference to their grievances. Other passages are in greater dispute. For example, 2.3.23–45, part of Lady Percy's magnificent speech in praise of Hotspur, does not appear in Q. Is this because Shakespeare had not yet written it? Or had it been cut from the original manuscript because the praise of Hotspur could be read as indirect praise of the Earl of Essex, the dashing, headstrong noble whose triumphal return from a 1599 campaign against the Irish Shakespeare was to anticipate with excitement in *Henry V*—but who in actuality returned home in disgrace and shortly thereafter led an abortive rebellion against Elizabeth? Or was it cut because the boy actor playing Lady Percy also was to play Doll Tearsheet in the next scene and had to have the number of lines he spoke reduced? Each of the eight additional Folio passages, which include 1.1.165–78, 1.3.21–24, 1.3.36–55, 1.3.85–108, and 4.1.101–37 (as well as the three passages already mentioned), is flagged in the notes so that readers can consider each case for themselves. The principal passages deleted from this text but present in Q and in most modern editions of the text are indented and printed as inset passages at the points where they appeared in Q.

Apart from Act 4, this text follows Folio act and scene divisions, although in F the Induction is marked as a separate scene. As for Act 4, F divides it into two scenes, and in many modern editions it is divided into five scenes; this edition divides it into three, ignoring the interpolated scene breaks often added by modern editors after 4.1.226, when Prince John marches onstage to speak with the rebels at Gaultres and after 4.3.132, when the King is carried to the Jerusalem Chamber. It retains, however, the interpolated break after 4.1.349 in which Falstaff enters with Coleville after Prince John has departed the stage, on the grounds that unlike the other two instances, this is a place where the stage is cleared and the action is therefore not continuous. It also retains the Folio scene break (now 4.3) when King Henry first comes onstage sick and in his bed.

SELECTED BIBLIOGRAPHY

Calderwood, James L. *Metadrama in Shakespeare's Henriad: "Richard II" to "Henry V."* Berkeley: University of California Press, 1979. Esp. 88–104. Examines Hal's rejection of Falstaff and the fat knight's inability to escape from history into comic invulnerability.

Crewe, Jonathan. "Reforming Prince Hal: The Sovereign Inheritor in *2 Henry IV.*" *Renaissance Drama*, n.s., 21 (1990): 225–42. Discusses the play's obsession with Hal's reform and the role of the father's death in effecting that reform.

Goldberg, Jonathan. "Hal's Desire, Shakespeare's Idaho." *Shakespeare's Hand*. Minneapolis: University of Minnesota Press, 2003. 222–52. Uses Gus Van Sant's film *My Own Private Idaho* to explore sex and gender relations in *1* and *2 Henry IV*, including Hal's potentially sodomitical relations with Falstaff.

Hodgdon, Barbara. "'Let the End Try the Man': *1* and *2 Henry IV*." *The End Crowns All: Closure and Contradiction in Shakespeare's History*. Princeton: Princeton University Press, 1991. 151–84. Discusses the play's problematic ending and different ways it has been staged.

Knights, L. C. "Time's Subjects: The Sonnets and *King Henry IV, Part II*." *Some Shakespearean Themes*. London: Chatto & Windus, 1959. 45–64. Explores the play's themes of time and change as prefigured in the sonnets.

Levine, Nina. "Extending Credit in the *Henry IV* Plays." *Shakespeare Quarterly* 51 (2000): 403–31. Discusses the pervasiveness and ideological complexity of the language of credit in both *Henry IV* plays.

MacDonald, Ronald R. "Uses of Diversity: Bakhtin's Theory of Utterance and Shakespeare's Second Tetralogy." *"Henry IV, Parts One and Two."* Ed. Nigel Wood. Theory in Practice series. Buckingham, Eng.: Open University Press, 1995. 65–91. Uses Bakhtin's theories of language to discuss the heteroglossia, or profusion of disparate voices, in this play.

Rackin, Phyllis. "Historical Kings/Theatrical Clowns." *Stages of History: Shakespeare's English Chronicles*. Ithaca, N.Y.: Cornell University Press, 1990. 201–47. Explores in all the histories the threat to authority embodied in the disorderly conduct and subversive speech of common men and of Falstaff.

Ruiter, David. "'The Unquiet Time' of *2 Henry IV*: Festivity and Order in Flux." *Shakespeare's Festive History: Feasting, Festivity, Fasting, and Lent in the Second Henriad*. Aldershot, Eng.: Ashgate, 2003. 103–41. Probes the difficulties Hal encounters in staging the reform he has so long planned.

Wiles, David. *Shakespeare's Clown: Actor and Text in the Elizabethan Playhouse*. New York: Cambridge University Press, 1987. Esp. "Kemp's Jigs" (43–60) and "Falstaff" (116–35). Argues that Falstaff's role is the clown's part and that it was originally played by Will Kemp, a notable clown in Shakespeare's company who was also famous for his dancing of jigs.

Young, David P., ed. *Twentieth Century Interpretations of "Henry IV, Part II": A Collection of Critical Essays*. Englewood Cliffs, N.J.: Prentice-Hall, 1968. Wide-ranging collection of classic essays from the mid-twentieth century.

FILM

Henry IV, Part II. 1979. Dir. David Giles. UK. 155 min. Judicious cuts and a strong performance by Anthony Quayle as Falstaff strengthen this sober BBC-TV version of the play.

The Second Part of Henry the Fourth

RUMOUR, the Presenter
EPILOGUE
KING HENRY IV
PRINCE HARRY, later crowned King Henry V ⎫
PRINCE JOHN of Lancaster ⎪ sons of
Humphrey, Duke of GLOUCESTER ⎬ King Henry IV
Thomas, Duke of CLARENCE ⎭
Percy, Earl of NORTHUMBERLAND, of the rebels' party
LADY NORTHUMBERLAND
LADY PERCY, their son Hotspur's widow
TRAVERS, Northumberland's servant
MORTON, a bearer of news from Shrewsbury
Scrope, ARCHBISHOP of York ⎫
LORD BARDOLPH ⎪
Thomas, Lord MOWBRAY, the Earl Marshal ⎬ rebels against
Lord HASTINGS ⎪ King Henry IV
Sir John COLEVILLE ⎭
LORD CHIEF JUSTICE
His SERVANT
GOWER, a Messenger
Sir John FALSTAFF ⎫
His PAGE ⎪
BARDOLPH ⎪
POINS ⎬ 'irregular humorists'
Ensign PISTOL ⎪
PETO ⎭
MISTRESS QUICKLY, hostess of a tavern
DOLL TEARSHEET, a whore
SNARE ⎫
    ⎬ sergeants
FANG ⎭
Neville, Earl of WARWICK ⎫
Earl of SURREY ⎪
Earl of WESTMORLAND ⎬ supporters of King Henry
HARCOURT ⎪
Sir John Blunt ⎭
Robert SHALLOW ⎫ country justices
SILENCE ⎭
DAVY, Shallow's servant
Ralph MOULDY ⎫
Simon SHADOW ⎪
Thomas WART ⎬ men levied to fight for King Henry
Francis FEEBLE ⎪
Peter BULLCALF ⎭
PORTER of Northumberland's household
DRAWERS

BEADLES
GROOMS
MESSENGER
Sneak and other musicians
Lord Chief Justice's men, soldiers and attendants

Induction

Enter RUMOUR[1] [*in a robe*] *painted full of tongues*

RUMOUR　Open your ears; for which of you will stop°		*plug up*
The vent of hearing° when loud Rumour speaks?		*The ear*
I from the orient° to the drooping west,		*east*
Making the wind my post-horse,° still° unfold		*hired horse / continually*

5 The acts commencèd on this ball of earth.
Upon my tongues continual slanders ride,
The which in every language I pronounce,
Stuffing the ears of men with false reports.
I speak of peace, while covert enmity
10 Under the smile of safety wounds the world;
And who but Rumour, who but only I,
Make fearful musters and prepared defence[2]

| Whiles the big° year, swoll'n with some other griefs, | *pregnant* |

Is thought with child by the stern tyrant war,
15 And no such matter? Rumour is a pipe
Blown by surmises, Jealousy's conjectures,
And of so easy and so plain a stop[3]

| That the blunt° monster with uncounted° heads, | *stupid / innumerable* |

The still-discordant wav'ring multitude,

20　Can play upon it. But what° need I thus	*why*
My well-known body to anatomize°	*dissect; lay open*
Among my household?° Why is Rumour here?	*(the theater audience)*

I run before King Harry's victory,
Who in a bloody field by Shrewsbury[4]
25 Hath beaten down young Hotspur and his troops,
Quenching the flame of bold rebellion
Even with the rebels' blood. But what mean I
To speak so true at first? My office is
To noise abroad that Harry Monmouth[5] fell
30 Under the wrath of noble Hotspur's sword,
And that the King before the Douglas' rage
Stooped his anointed head as low as death.

| This have I rumoured through the peasant° towns | *rural* |

Between that royal field of Shrewsbury

| 35　And this worm-eaten hold° of raggèd stone, | *stronghold* |

Induction Location: Outside Northumberland's castle at Warkworth.

1. A personification, possibly based on Virgil's "Fama," depicted as a female monster with many eyes, ears, and tongues who circulated both true and false accounts of events. See *Aeneid* 4.179–90.
2. Cause soldiers, prompted by fear, to assemble and defenses to be made ready. These lines may be topical: fear of imminent Spanish invasion led the Privy Council to mobilize militia forces frequently throughout the latter years of Elizabeth's reign.
3. And whose "stops," or openings, are so easy to play upon. The ease with which Rumour's pipe can be played means that even the common people can do it.

In the next lines, Rumour refers to these commoners as a many-headed monster, a common derogatory image of the people, especially when they aspire to participation in governance. By contrast, the proper head of the realm was held to be the single sovereign.
4. In Shakespeare's rendition of the Battle of Shrewsbury, staged in *1 Henry IV,* Prince Hal kills Henry Percy (Hotspur), and his forces capture the Scottish Earl of Douglas, two of the principal leaders of rebellion. In 1.1 of this play, the announcement of Henry Percy's death invokes considerable wordplay on his nickname, his "hot" spur being transformed into a "cold" spur by death.
5. Prince Hal was called Harry Monmouth in honor of his birthplace, Monmouth, in Wales.

Where Hotspur's father, old Northumberland,
Lies crafty-sick.° The posts come tiring on,⁶   *pretending to be ill*
And not a man of them brings other news
Than they have learnt of me. From Rumour's tongues
40 They bring smooth comforts false, worse than true wrongs.

                                        Exit

1.1

Enter LORD BARDOLPH¹ *at one door.* [*He crosses the*
stage to another door]

LORD BARDOLPH
Who keeps the gate here, ho?
            Enter PORTER [*above*]²
                                Where is the Earl?
PORTER What shall I say you are?
LORD BARDOLPH   Tell thou the Earl
That the Lord Bardolph doth attend° him here.   *await*
PORTER His lordship is walked forth into the orchard.
5 Please it your honour knock but at the gate,
And he himself will answer.
            Enter the Earl NORTHUMBERLAND [*at the other door, as*
            sick, with a crutch and coif]°   *nightcap*
LORD BARDOLPH   Here comes the Earl.

                                [*Exit* PORTER]

NORTHUMBERLAND What news, Lord Bardolph? Every minute now
Should be the father of some stratagem.
The times are wild; contention, like a horse
10 Full of high feeding,° madly hath broke loose,   *overly rich food*
And bears down all before him.
LORD BARDOLPH   Noble Earl,
I bring you certain news from Shrewsbury.
NORTHUMBERLAND Good, an° God will.   *if*
LORD BARDOLPH   As good as heart can wish.
The King is almost wounded to the death;
15 And, in the fortune° of my lord your son,   *good luck*
Prince Harry slain outright; and both the Blunts³
Killed by the hand of Douglas; young Prince John
And Westmorland and Stafford fled the field;
And Harry Monmouth's brawn,° the hulk Sir John,   *fattened pig*
20 Is prisoner to your son. O, such a day,
So fought, so followed,° and so fairly won,   *carried through*
Came not till now to dignify the times
Since Caesar's fortunes!°   *successes*
NORTHUMBERLAND   How is this derived?
Saw you the field? Came you from Shrewsbury?
25 LORD BARDOLPH I spake with one, my lord, that came from thence,
A gentleman well bred and of good name,
That freely rendered me these news for true.

---

6. The messengers, exhausting themselves, gallop on.
1.1. Location: Scene continues.
1. A nobleman associated with the rebel Percy faction;
Falstaff's companion with the same name is unrelated.
2. Having the Porter enter on the upper playing
space is conjectural, but it effectively suggests that

Northumberland is in a stronghold where his retainers
are wary of intruders. The upper stage, however, does
not appear to have been used elsewhere in the play.
3. In *1 Henry IV*, only one Blunt, Sir Walter, dies at
Shrewsbury.

Enter TRAVERS

NORTHUMBERLAND   Here comes my servant Travers, who I sent
On Tuesday last to listen after news.

30 LORD BARDOLPH   My lord, I overrode° him on the way,   *overtook*
And he is furnished with no certainties
More than he haply° may retail from me.   *perhaps*

NORTHUMBERLAND   Now, Travers, what good tidings comes with you?

TRAVERS   My lord, Lord Bardolph turned me back[4]

35 With joyful tidings, and being better horsed
Outrode me. After him came spurring hard
A gentleman almost forspent° with speed,   *worn out*
That stopped by me to breathe° his bloodied horse.   *rest*
He asked the way to Chester,[5] and of him

40 I did demand what news from Shrewsbury.
He told me that rebellion had ill luck,
And that young Harry Percy's spur was cold.
With that he gave his able horse the head,
And, bending forward, struck his armèd heels

45 Against the panting sides of his poor jade°   *worn-out horse*
Up to the rowel-head;[6] and starting so,
He seemed in running to devour the way,
Staying° no longer question.   *Awaiting*

NORTHUMBERLAND   Ha? Again:
Said he young Harry Percy's spur was cold?

50 Of Hotspur, 'Coldspur'? that rebellion
Had met ill luck?

LORD BARDOLPH   My lord, I'll tell you what:
If my young lord your son have not the day,
Upon mine honour, for a silken point°   *lace for tying a garment*
I'll give my barony. Never talk of it.

55 NORTHUMBERLAND   Why should the gentleman that rode by Travers
Give then such instances of loss?

LORD BARDOLPH   Who, he?
He was some hilding° fellow that had stol'n   *worthless*
The horse he rode on, and, upon my life,
Spoke at a venture.°   *at random*

Enter MORTON

Look, here comes more news.

60 NORTHUMBERLAND   Yea, this man's brow, like to a title leaf,
Foretells the nature of a tragic volume.[7]
So looks the strand° whereon the imperious flood   *shore*
Hath left a witnessed usurpation.[8]
Say, Morton, didst thou come from Shrewsbury?

65 MORTON   I ran from Shrewsbury, my noble lord,
Where hateful death put on his ugliest mask
To fright our party.

---

4. In Q, Travers says that Sir John Umfreuile, not Lord
Bardolph, turned him back. Since Lord Bardolph reports
having met Travers on the road, most critics agree that
Umfreuile and Lord Bardolph are the same character
whose name got changed at some point. At 1.1.161, Q
assigns one line to "Umfr.," another indication that a
character with this name was once to figure in the play.
This line does not appear in F or in the present text.
5. A town north of Shrewsbury.
6. The spiked wheel at the end of the spur.

7. Alluding to the descriptive title pages of early modern printed books, which often indicated the principal
actions of the work and sometimes characterized them
as tragic or comic. For an example, see the descriptive
title page of the quarto version of this play, reprinted in
the Introduction.
8. *whereon . . . usurpation:* where the sea has left evidence of its conquest (of the land). The comparison is
between Morton's brow, wrinkled by sorrow, and sand
furrowed by the sea's encroachment.

NORTHUMBERLAND   How doth my son and brother?[9]
      Thou tremblest, and the whiteness in thy cheek
      Is apter than thy tongue to tell thy errand.
70   Even such a man, so faint, so spiritless,
      So dull, so dead in look, so woebegone,
      Drew Priam's curtain[1] in the dead of night,
      And would have told him half his Troy was burnt;
      But Priam found the fire ere he his tongue,
75   And I my Percy's death ere thou report'st it.
      This thou wouldst say: 'Your son did thus and thus,
      Your brother thus; so fought the noble Douglas',
      Stopping° my greedy ear with their bold deeds;   *Filling*
      But in the end, to stop° my ear indeed,   *plug up; obstruct*
80   Thou hast a sigh to blow away this praise,
      Ending with 'Brother, son, and all are dead.'
   MORTON   Douglas is living, and your brother yet;
      But for my lord your son—
NORTHUMBERLAND   Why, he is dead.
      See what a ready tongue suspicion hath!
85   He that but fears the thing he would not know
      Hath by instinct knowledge from others' eyes
      That what he feared is chanced.° Yet speak, Morton.   *has happened*
      Tell thou an earl his divination lies,[2]
      And I will take it as a sweet disgrace,
90   And make thee rich for doing me such wrong.
   MORTON   You are too great to be by me gainsaid,
      Your spirit is too true, your fears too certain.
NORTHUMBERLAND   Yet for all this, say not that Percy's dead.
      I see a strange confession in thine eye—
95   Thou shak'st thy head, and hold'st it fear or sin
      To speak a truth. If he be slain, say so.
      The tongue offends not that reports his death;
      And he doth sin that doth belie the dead,
      Not he which says the dead is not alive.
100   Yet the first bringer of unwelcome news
      Hath but a losing office,° and his tongue   *thankless duty*
      Sounds ever after as a sullen° bell   *mournful*
      Remembered knolling a departing friend.
   LORD BARDOLPH   I cannot think, my lord, your son is dead.
105 MORTON [*to* NORTHUMBERLAND]   I am sorry I should force you to believe
      That which I would to God I had not seen;
      But these mine eyes saw him in bloody state,
      Rend'ring faint quittance,[3] wearied and out-breathed,°   *out of breath*
      To Harry Monmouth, whose swift wrath beat down
110   The never-daunted Percy to the earth,
      From whence with life he never more sprung up.
      In few,° his death, whose spirit lent a fire   *In short*
      Even to the dullest peasant in his camp,

9. The Earl of Worcester, who helped lead the rebellion staged in *1 Henry IV*.
1. Opened Priam's bed curtain. Priam was King of Troy during the Trojan War. This may allude to a scene from Virgil's *Aeneid* in which Hector appears to Aeneas, not Priam, in a dream, warning him of danger. Aeneas

wakes to find Troy in flames.
2. Tell me, who am an earl, that in my prophecy I lie. To say a social superior lies would normally be a grave offense, but Northumberland would be happy to be proven wrong.
3. Repayment (return of blows).

Being bruited° once, took fire and heat away	reported
115 From the best-tempered courage⁴ in his troops;	
For from his metal° was his party steeled,	steel; courage
Which once in him abated,° all the rest	blunted
Turned on themselves,⁵ like dull and heavy lead;	
And, as the thing that's heavy in itself	
120 Upon enforcement° flies with greatest speed,	When forced into motion
So did our men, heavy in Hotspur's loss,	
Lend to this weight such lightness with their fear	
That arrows fled not swifter toward their aim	
Than did our soldiers, aiming at their safety,	
125 Fly from the field. Then was that noble Worcester	
Too soon ta'en prisoner; and that furious Scot	
The bloody Douglas, whose well-labouring sword	
Had three times slain th'appearance of the King,⁶	
Gan vail his stomach,⁷ and did grace° the shame	sanction
130 Of those that turned their backs, and in his flight,	
Stumbling in fear, was took. The sum of all	
Is that the King hath won, and hath sent out	
A speedy power° to encounter you, my lord,	quick-moving army
Under the conduct° of young Lancaster	command
135 And Westmorland. This is the news at full.	

NORTHUMBERLAND   For this I shall have time enough to mourn.

In poison there is physic;° and these news,	medicine
Having been° well, that would have made me sick,	If I had been
Being sick, have in some measure made me well;	
140 And, as the wretch whose fever-weakened joints,	
Like strengthless hinges, buckle under life,⁸	
Impatient of his fit, breaks like a fire	
Out of his keeper's° arms, even so my limbs,	nurse's
Weakened with grief, being now enraged with grief,	
Are thrice themselves.	

[He casts away his crutch]

145 Hence therefore, thou nice° crutch!	unmanly
A scaly° gauntlet now with joints of steel	mailed
Must glove this hand.	

[He snatches off his coif]

And hence, thou sickly coif!	
Thou art a guard too wanton° for the head	effeminate; luxurious
Which princes fleshed with conquest⁹ aim to hit.	
150 Now bind my brows with iron, and approach	
The ragged'st° hour that time and spite dare bring	roughest
To frown upon th'enraged Northumberland!	
Let heaven kiss earth! Now let not nature's hand	
Keep the wild flood confined! Let order die!	
155 And let this world no longer be a stage	
To feed contention in a ling'ring act;¹	

---

4. Courage of the finest quality. The implicit comparison is to steel that had been tempered, or made strong, by extreme heat.
5. Bent backward (like soft metal); fled.
6. In *1 Henry IV*, at the Battle of Shrewsbury, members of the rebel faction slew several noblemen dressed in the King's coats whom they mistook for Henry himself. See *1 Henry IV* 5.3.1–13 and 5.4.24–37.

7. Began to lose courage (stomach).
8. Collapse from the burden of living.
9. Which princes made eager for bloody victories by having tasted raw flesh (been victorious). Hounds were "fleshed," given a taste of raw meat, to prepare them for the hunt.
1. *And let . . . act*: And let the world stop being a stage where strife is encouraged in a prolonged action.

But let one spirit of the first-born Cain[2]
Reign in all bosoms, that each heart being set
On bloody courses, the rude scene may end,
160   And darkness be the burier of the dead!
LORD BARDOLPH   Sweet Earl, divorce not wisdom from your honour.
MORTON   The lives of all your loving complices°   *associates*
Lean on your health, the which, if you give o'er
To stormy passion, must perforce decay.[3]
165   You cast th'event° of war, my noble lord,   *calculated the outcome*
And summed° the account of chance, before you said   *added up*
'Let us make head'.° It was your presurmise   *raise an army*
That in the dole° of blows your son might drop.   *dealing out*
You knew he walked o'er perils on an edge,°   *a narrow blade*
170   More likely to fall in than to get o'er.
You were advised° his flesh was capable   *aware*
Of wounds and scars, and that his forward spirit
Would lift him where most trade of° danger ranged.°   *dealing in / was displayed*
Yet did you say, 'Go forth'; and none of this,
175   Though strongly apprehended, could restrain
The stiff-borne° action. What hath then befall'n?   *stubbornly pursued*
Or what doth this bold enterprise bring forth,
More than that being° which was like to be?   *event*
LORD BARDOLPH   We all that are engagèd to° this loss   *involved in*
180   Knew that we ventured on such dangerous seas
That if we wrought out life was ten to one;[4]
And yet we ventured for the gain proposed,
Choked the respect of° likely peril feared;   *Refused to consider*
And since we are o'erset,° venture again.   *overthrown*
185   Come, we will all put forth body and goods.
MORTON   'Tis more than time; and, my most noble lord,
I hear for certain, and dare speak the truth,[5]
The gentle Archbishop of York is up°   *up in arms*
With well-appointed powers.° He is a man   *well-equipped forces*
190   Who with a double surety binds his followers.[6]
My lord, your son had only but the corpse,°   *mere bodies*
But shadows and the shows of men, to fight;
For that same word 'rebellion' did divide
The action of their bodies from their souls,
195   And they did fight with queasiness, constrained,
As men drink potions, that their weapons only
Seemed on our side; but, for their spirits and souls,
This word 'rebellion', it had froze them up,
As fish are in a pond. But now the Bishop
200   Turns insurrection to religion.
Supposed sincere and holy in his thoughts,
He's followed both with body and with mind,
And doth enlarge his rising[7] with the blood
Of fair King Richard, scraped from Pomfret stones;[8]

2. In the Bible, the first human being to be born and the murderer of his brother.
3. Lines 165–78 are not included in Q. (See Textual Note.)
4. The odds were ten to one against our preserving life.
5. Lines 188–208 are missing from Q. It is generally agreed that these lines were cut for political reasons.
6. Referring to the fact that the Archbishop, unlike Hotspur, might use his religious as well as his temporal authority to secure his soldiers' fidelity.
7. And increases the size or enhances the reputation of his rebellion.
8. Alluding to Henry IV's responsibility for the murder of Richard at Pontefract Castle (Pomfret), as staged in Act 5 of *Richard II*. Richard's blood is treated as a holy saint's relic.

205 Derives from heaven his quarrel and his cause;
Tells them he doth bestride° a bleeding land   *protect by standing over*
Gasping for life under great Bolingbroke;°   *(Henry IV)*
And more and less° do flock to follow him.   *people of all ranks*
NORTHUMBERLAND   I knew of this before, but, to speak truth,
210 This present grief had wiped it from my mind.
Go in with me, and counsel every man
The aptest way for safety and revenge.
Get posts° and letters, and make° friends with speed.   *messengers / gather*
Never so few, and never yet more need.   *Exeunt*

1.2

Enter Sir John FALSTAFF, [followed by] his PAGE bearing
his sword and buckler°   *shield*

FALSTAFF   Sirrah,[1] you giant, what says the doctor to my water?°   *urine*
PAGE   He said, sir, the water itself was a good healthy water,
but, for the party that owed° it, he might have more diseases   *owned*
than he knew for.°   *was aware of*
5 FALSTAFF   Men of all sorts take a pride to gird° at me. The brain   *mock*
of this foolish-compounded clay,[2] man, is not able to invent
anything that tends to laughter more than I invent, or is
invented on me. I am not only witty in myself, but the cause
that wit is in other men. I do here walk before thee like a sow
10 that hath o'erwhelmed° all her litter but one. If the Prince put   *crushed*
thee into my service for any other reason than to set me off,[3]
why then, I have no judgement. Thou whoreson mandrake,[4]
thou art fitter to be worn in my cap than to wait at my heels. I
was never manned with° an agate[5] till now; but I will set you   *attended by*
15 neither in gold nor silver, but in vile apparel, and send you
back again to your master for a jewel—the juvenal° the Prince   *youth*
your master, whose chin is not yet fledge.°   *covered with down*
I will sooner have a
beard grow in the palm of my hand than he shall get one off
his cheek; and yet he will not stick° to say his face is a face-   *hesitate*
20 royal.[6] God may finish it when he will; 'tis not a hair amiss yet.
He may keep it still at° a face-royal, for a barber shall never   *at the value of*
earn sixpence out of it. And yet he'll be crowing as if he had
writ man° ever since his father was a bachelor. He may keep   *called himself a man*
his own grace,° but he's almost out of mine, I can assure him. *title (Prince); favor*
25 What said Master Dumbleton about the satin for my short
cloak and slops?[7]
PAGE   He said, sir, you should procure him better assurance
than Bardolph. He would not take his bond and yours; he
liked not the security.
30 FALSTAFF   Let him be damned like the glutton![8] Pray God his

1.2 Location: A street in London.
1. Form of address to a social inferior.
2. Clay compounded with foolishness (an image derived from the biblical account of the first human being as formed out of clay).
3. To make me stand out by contrast. The page is tiny, and Falstaff is huge.
4. An herb with a forked root that was popularly supposed to resemble a miniature man. It was believed to shriek when pulled from the ground and to have aphrodisiacal powers. *whoreson*: an insult, derived from the phrase "whore's son."

5. A small jewel often carved with images of people and worn in caps.
6. The face of royalty (with a pun on "royal," a coin worth 10 shillings and stamped with the monarch's face).
7. Baggy knee breeches, fashionable in Elizabethan London.
8. Referring to the biblical parable of Dives, a rich glutton who ignored the pleas of the beggar Lazarus and at death was condemned to hell, where he implored Lazarus to dip his finger in water and lay it on his tongue to cool the flames (see Luke 16:19–31).

tongue be hotter! A whoreson Achitophel,⁹ a rascally yea-
forsooth knave,¹ to bear a gentleman in hand° and then stand   *lead a gentleman on*
upon security! The whoreson smooth-pates² do now wear noth-
ing but high shoes and bunches of keys at their girdles;³ and if
35   a man is through with them in honest taking-up,⁴ then they
must stand upon security. I had as lief° they would put rats-   *gladly*
bane° in my mouth as offer to stop it with security. I looked a°   *rat poison / that he*
should have sent me two and twenty yards of satin, as I am a
true knight,⁵ and he sends me 'security'! Well, he may sleep in
40   security, for he hath the horn of abundance, and the lightness
of his wife shines through it;⁶ and yet cannot he see, though he
have his own lanthorn to light him. Where's Bardolph?
PAGE   He's gone in Smithfield⁷ to buy your worship a horse.
FALSTAFF   I bought him in Paul's,⁸ and he'll buy me a horse in
45   Smithfield. An° I could get me but a wife in the stews,° I were   *If / brothels*
manned, horsed, and wived.
            Enter [the] LORD CHIEF JUSTICE *and [his]* SERVANT
PAGE   Sir, here comes the nobleman that committed° the Prince   *imprisoned*
for striking him about Bardolph.⁹
FALSTAFF [*moving away*]   Wait close;° I will not see him.¹   *concealed*
50   LORD CHIEF JUSTICE [*to his* SERVANT]   What's he that goes there?
SERVANT   Falstaff, an't please your lordship.
LORD CHIEF JUSTICE   He that was in question° for the robbery?²   *under investigation*
SERVANT   He, my lord; but he hath since done good service at
Shrewsbury, and, as I hear, is now going with some charge° to   *command of soldiers*
55   the Lord John of Lancaster.
LORD CHIEF JUSTICE   What, to York? Call him back again.
SERVANT   Sir John Falstaff!
FALSTAFF   Boy, tell him I am deaf.
PAGE [*to the* SERVANT]   You must speak louder; my master is
60   deaf.
LORD CHIEF JUSTICE   I am sure he is to the hearing of anything
good. [*To the* SERVANT] Go pluck him by the elbow; I must
speak with him.
SERVANT   Sir John!
65   FALSTAFF   What, a young knave and begging! Is there not wars?³
Is there not employment? Doth not the King lack subjects? Do
not the rebels want soldiers? Though it be a shame to be on
any side but one, it is worse shame to beg than to be on the

---

9. A biblical figure, King David's trusted counselor, who betrayed him by supporting the treason of the king's son (2 Samuel 15).
1. A villainous knave who appears to be agreeable. A "yea-forsooth" knave makes promises with mild oaths (but then breaks them).
2. Alluding disparagingly to the fashion among trades-men, especially Puritans, for short hair.
3. Wear the most fashionable shoes and display a mass of keys (habits suggesting pride and conspicuous con-sumption).
4. If a man makes a deal with them for a purchase on credit.
5. Referring to Tudor sumptuary codes, which pre-scribed the fabrics that could be worn by people of differ-ent social ranks. As a knight, Falstaff can wear satin.
6. For he is rich and his wife's promiscuity is visible to all, with puns on "horn" as referring to the horn lanterns sold by merchants; to a symbol of overflowing

plenty (a cornucopia); and to cuckoldry (deceived hus-bands were said to wear horns). "Lightness" can mean both illumination and sexual promiscuity.
7. A district northwest of London's city walls, used as a market for animals.
8. St. Paul's Cathedral in London, where masterless men presented themselves for employment.
9. Alluding to the apocryphal account of the youthful Prince's assault on the Lord Chief Justice, staged in *The Famous Victories of Henry V*, the anonymous play from which Shakespeare's is partly derived.
1. Falstaff's determination not to acknowledge the Lord Chief Justice presumably causes him to turn his back on the magistrate or walk off in another direction.
2. The Gadshill robbery, in which Falstaff took part. See *1 Henry IV* 2.2.
3. Alluding to the Elizabethan practice of mass con-scription of impoverished men.

worst side, were it worse than the name of rebellion can tell
70 how to make° it.   *regard*

SERVANT   You mistake me, sir.

FALSTAFF   Why, sir, did I say you were an honest man? Setting
my knighthood and my soldiership aside, I had lied in my
throat° if I had said so.   *deliberately lied*

75 SERVANT   I pray you, sir, then set your knighthood and your soldiership aside, and give me leave to tell you you lie in your
throat if you say I am any other than an honest man.

FALSTAFF   I give thee leave to tell me so? I lay aside that which
grows to me?° If thou gettest any leave of me, hang me. If thou   *is part of me*
80 takest leave, thou wert better be hanged. You hunt counter.[4]
Hence, avaunt!°   *be gone*

SERVANT   Sir, my lord would speak with you.

LORD CHIEF JUSTICE   Sir John Falstaff, a word with you.

FALSTAFF   My good lord! God give your lordship good time of
85 day. I am glad to see your lordship abroad. I heard say your
lordship was sick. I hope your lordship goes abroad by advice.°   *by medical advice*
Your lordship, though not clean past your youth, have yet some
smack of age in you, some relish of the saltness of time in you;
and I most humbly beseech your lordship to have a reverent
90 care of your health.

LORD CHIEF JUSTICE   Sir John, I sent for you before your expedition to Shrewsbury.

FALSTAFF   An't please your lordship, I hear his majesty is
returned with some discomfort from Wales.[5]

95 LORD CHIEF JUSTICE   I talk not of his majesty. You would not
come when I sent for you.

FALSTAFF   And I hear, moreover, his highness is fallen into this
same whoreson apoplexy.°   *paralysis*

LORD CHIEF JUSTICE   Well, God mend him! I pray you, let me
100 speak with you.

FALSTAFF   This apoplexy is, as I take it, a kind of lethargy, an't
please your lordship, a kind of sleeping in the blood, a
whoreson tingling.

LORD CHIEF JUSTICE   What° tell you me of it? Be it as it is.   *Why*

105 FALSTAFF   It hath it original° from much grief, from study, and   *its origin*
perturbation of the brain. I have read the cause of his effects in
Galen.[6] It is a kind of deafness.

LORD CHIEF JUSTICE   I think you are fallen into the disease, for
you hear not what I say to you.

110 FALSTAFF   Very well, my lord, very well. Rather, an't please you,
it is the disease of not listening, the malady of not marking, that
I am troubled withal.°   *with*

LORD CHIEF JUSTICE   To punish you by the heels[7] would amend
the attention of your ears, and I care not if I do become your
115 physician.

FALSTAFF   I am as poor as Job,[8] my lord, but not so patient. Your
lordship may minister the potion of imprisonment to me in

---

4. You pursue the scent of the game in the wrong
direction.
5. Some discouragement from Wales (where the King
promised to fight Glyndŵr and Mortimer at the end of
1 Henry IV).
6. Ancient Greek physician whose anatomical texts were
widely translated and printed in early modern Europe.

Galen was commonly regarded as the chief authority in
human physiology.
7. By putting your feet in the stocks or in shackles.
8. A biblical figure who, in the Book of Job, patiently
endured the many adversities with which God afflicted
him, including poverty.

respect of° poverty; but how I should be your patient to follow   *on account of*
your prescriptions, the wise may make some dram of a scruple,
120   or indeed a scruple itself.⁹

LORD CHIEF JUSTICE   I sent for you, when there were matters
against you for your life,¹ to come speak with me.

FALSTAFF   As I was then advised by my learned counsel in the
laws of this land-service,° I did not come.   *military duty*

125   LORD CHIEF JUSTICE   Well, the truth is, Sir John, you live in
great infamy.

FALSTAFF   He that buckles himself in my belt cannot live in less.

LORD CHIEF JUSTICE   Your means are very slender, and your waste
is great.

130   FALSTAFF   I would it were otherwise; I would my means were
greater and my waist slenderer.

LORD CHIEF JUSTICE   You have misled the youthful Prince.

FALSTAFF   The young Prince hath misled me. I am the fellow
with the great belly, and he my dog.²

135   LORD CHIEF JUSTICE   Well, I am loath to gall° a new-healed   *to injure by rubbing*
wound. Your day's service at Shrewsbury hath a little gilded
over your night's exploit on Gads Hill. You may thank th'unquiet time for your quiet o'erposting° that action.   *passing swiftly over*

FALSTAFF   My lord—

140   LORD CHIEF JUSTICE   But since all is well, keep it so. Wake not a
sleeping wolf.

FALSTAFF   To wake a wolf is as bad as smell a fox.°   *as being suspicious*

LORD CHIEF JUSTICE   What! You are as a candle, the better part
burnt out.

145   FALSTAFF   A wassail candle,³ my lord, all tallow°—if I did say of   *animal fat*
wax,⁴ my growth would approve° the truth.   *attest to*

LORD CHIEF JUSTICE   There is not a white hair in your face but
should have his effect° of gravity.   *manifestation*

FALSTAFF   His effect of gravy, gravy, gravy.⁵

150   LORD CHIEF JUSTICE   You follow the young Prince up and down
like his ill angel.°   *evil spirit*

FALSTAFF   Not so, my lord; your ill angel is light,⁶ but I hope he
that looks upon me will take me without weighing. And yet in
some respects, I grant, I cannot go.° I cannot tell, virtue is of so   *walk; be circulated*
155   little regard in these costermongers' times⁷ that true valour is
turned bearherd;⁸ pregnancy° is made a tapster, and his quick   *mental agility*
wit wasted in giving reckonings;° all the other gifts appertinent°   *tavern bills / belonging*
to man, as the malice of this age shapes them, are not worth a
gooseberry. You that are old consider not the capacities of us
160   that are young. You do measure the heat of our livers with the
bitterness of your galls.⁹ And we that are in the vanguard° of   *most advanced stage*
our youth, I must confess, are wags too.

9. The wise may feel a particle of doubt. Drams and scruples were small weights used to measure medicines in apothecary shops.
1. For which your life was at stake.
2. An obscure allusion. It may refer to the man in the moon, a mythical figure who supposedly carried a bush and was accompanied by a dog.
3. A large fat candle used at holiday festivities.
4. Beeswax, with pun on "wax" as meaning "grow."
5. Grease; sweat. Falstaff implies that sweat should drop from his face as fat (gravy) drops from hot meat.
6. Your bad coin weighs less. Falstaff puns on "angel" as the name of a gold coin that could illegally be clipped so that it weighed less than it should.
7. In these commercial times. A costermonger sold trifling commodities such as fruits and vegetables.
8. Keeper of bears, such as those used for the popular entertainment of bearbaiting.
9. You measure the strength of our passions by the bitterness of your melancholy. The liver was believed to be the seat of youthful passions, and bile or gall produced the melancholy and anger characteristic of old age.

LORD CHIEF JUSTICE   Do you set down your name in the scroll
of youth, that are written down old with all the characters° of   *letters; signs*

165   age? Have you not a moist eye, a dry hand, a yellow cheek, a
white beard, a decreasing leg, an increasing belly? Is not your
voice broken, your wind short, your chin double, your wit single, and every part about you blasted with antiquity? And will
you yet call yourself young? Fie, fie, fie, Sir John!

170 FALSTAFF   My lord, I was born about three of the clock in the
afternoon with a white head, and something a° round belly.   *a somewhat*
For my voice, I have lost it with hallowing° and singing of   *shouting to hounds*
anthems. To approve° my youth further, I will not. The truth   *prove*
is, I am only old in judgement and understanding; and he that

175   will caper° with me for a thousand marks,[1] let him lend me the   *dance (in competition)*
money, and have at him! For the box of th'ear that the Prince
gave you, he gave it like a rude° prince, and you took it like a   *violent; an uncivilized*
sensible lord.[2] I have checked him for it, and the young lion
repents—[*aside*] marry,° not in ashes and sackcloth, but in new   *by the Virgin Mary (oath)*

180   silk and old sack.[3]

LORD CHIEF JUSTICE   Well, God send the Prince a better companion!

FALSTAFF   God send the companion a better prince! I cannot rid
my hands of him.

185 LORD CHIEF JUSTICE   Well, the King hath severed you and
Prince Harry. I hear you are going with Lord John of Lancaster against the Archbishop and the Earl of Northumberland.

FALSTAFF   Yea, I thank your pretty sweet wit for it. But look° you   *see that*

190   pray, all you that kiss my lady Peace at home, that our armies
join not in a hot day; for, by the Lord, I take but two shirts out
with me, and I mean not to sweat extraordinarily. If it be a hot
day and I brandish anything but my bottle, would I might never
spit white again.[4] There is not a dangerous action° can peep   *military action*

195   out his head but I am thrust upon it. Well, I cannot last ever.
But it was alway yet the trick° of our English nation, if they   *habit*
have a good thing, to make it too common. If ye will needs say
I am an old man, you should give me rest. I would to God my
name were not so terrible to the enemy as it is. I were better to

200   be eaten to death with a rust than to be scoured to nothing with
perpetual motion.

LORD CHIEF JUSTICE   Well, be honest, be honest, and God bless
your expedition.

FALSTAFF   Will your lordship lend me a thousand pound to fur-

205   nish me forth?

LORD CHIEF JUSTICE   Not a penny, not a penny. You are too
impatient to bear crosses.[5] Fare you well. Commend me to my
cousin Westmorland.

                    [*Exeunt* LORD CHIEF JUSTICE *and his* SERVANT]

---

1. A unit of money; one mark was equal to two-thirds
of a pound.
2. Like a reasonable lord; like a lord capable of feeling
pain. For the story of Hal's striking the Chief Justice,
see note to 1.2.48.
3. A Spanish white wine that improved with age.

4. A disputed passage. Perhaps, may I never drink
again (white spit was thought to be the result of heavy
drinking).
5. To endure afflictions like a good Christian; to carry
silver coins, which bear the sign of a cross.

FALSTAFF   If I do, fillip° me with a three-man beetle.⁶ A man can   *strike*
210   no more separate age and covetousness than a° can part young   *he*
       limbs and lechery; but the gout⁷ galls the one and the pox
       pinches° the other, and so both the degrees prevent my   *syphilis torments*
       curses.⁸ Boy!
PAGE   Sir.
215   FALSTAFF   What money is in my purse?
PAGE   Seven groats° and two pence.   *coins worth fourpence*
FALSTAFF   I can get no remedy against this consumption of the
       purse. Borrowing only lingers and lingers it out, but the disease
       is incurable. [*Giving letters*] Go bear this letter to my lord of
220   Lancaster; this to the Prince; this to the Earl of Westmorland;
       and this to old Mistress Ursula,⁹ whom I have weekly sworn to
       marry since I perceived the first white hair of my chin. About
       it. You know where to find me.   [*Exit* PAGE]¹
       A pox of this gout!—or a gout of this pox!—for the one or the
225   other plays the rogue with my great toe. 'Tis no matter if I do
       halt;° I have the wars for my colour,° and my pension shall   *limp / pretext*
       seem the more reasonable. A good wit will make use of any-
       thing. I will turn diseases to commodity.°   *Exit*   *profit*

1.3

Enter the ARCHBISHOP [*of York*], *Thomas* MOWBRAY [*the*]
*Earl Marshal,*¹ *Lord* HASTINGS, *and* LORD BARDOLPH
ARCHBISHOP OF YORK   Thus have you heard our cause and
            known our means,
       And, my most noble friends, I pray you all
       Speak plainly your opinions of our hopes.
       And first, Lord Marshal, what say you to it?
5   MOWBRAY   I well allow the occasion of our arms,²
       But gladly would be better satisfied
       How in our means° we should advance ourselves   *with our resources*
       To look with forehead bold and big enough
       Upon the power and puissance° of the King.   *strength*
10   HASTINGS   Our present musters grow upon the file°   *according to our list*
       To five-and-twenty thousand men of choice,°   *choice men*
       And our supplies° live largely in the hope   *reinforcements*
       Of great Northumberland, whose bosom burns
       With an incensèd fire of injuries.
15   LORD BARDOLPH   The question then, Lord Hastings, standeth thus:
       Whether our present five-and-twenty thousand
       May hold up head° without Northumberland.   *May succeed*
HASTINGS   With him we may.

6. A huge sledgehammer designed to be lifted by three laborers at once.
7. A disease characterized by painful inflammation of the joints, often of the toe joints in particular, and associated with the excessive consumption of rich food and alcohol. Falstaff is bothered by gout, and it may have been the reason he sent his urine to be examined by the doctor at the beginning of this scene.
8. So both conditions (age and youth) anticipate my curses. Venereal disease torments young lecherous men; gout afflicts old men.
9. A name nowhere else mentioned in this play. It could be the first name of Mistress Quickly. It may also be an inadvertent reference to the Ursula of *Much Ado About Nothing*, a play also printed in 1600.
1. Neither Q nor F marks a separate exit for the Page. F indicates a plural "Exeunt" at the end of the scene, suggesting that Falstaff and the Page exit together. But clearly the fat knight's concluding lines are a private meditation on his diseases best spoken after he has sent the Page off to deliver his letters.
1.3 Location: The Archbishop's palace in York.
1. The officer in charge of arranging royal ceremonies.
2. I grant the justice of our taking arms.

LORD BARDOLPH   Yea, marry, there's the point;
But if without him we be thought too feeble,
20   My judgement is, we should not step too far[3]
Till we had his assistance by the hand;
For in a theme° so bloody-faced as this,   matter
Conjecture, expectation, and surmise
Of aids uncertain should not be admitted.
25 ARCHBISHOP OF YORK   'Tis very true, Lord Bardolph, for indeed
It was young Hotspur's case at Shrewsbury.
LORD BARDOLPH   It was, my lord; who lined° himself with hope,   strengthened
Eating the air on promise of supply,[4]
Flatt'ring himself with project of a power°   expectation of an army
30   Much smaller° than the smallest of his thoughts;   smaller in actuality
And so, with great imagination
Proper to madmen, led his powers to death,
And winking° leapt into destruction.   shutting his eyes
HASTINGS   But by your leave, it never yet did hurt
35   To lay down likelihoods and forms of hope.[5]
LORD BARDOLPH   Yes, if this present quality° of war—   condition
Indeed the instant° action, a cause on foot°—   present / in motion
Lives so in hope; as in an early spring
We see th'appearing buds, which to prove° fruit   mature into
40   Hope gives not so much warrant as despair
That frosts will bite them.[6] When we mean to build
We first survey the plot,[7] then draw the model;°   design
And when we see the figure° of the house,   design
Then must we rate the cost of the erection,
45   Which if we find outweighs ability,
What do we then but draw anew the model
In fewer offices,° or, at least,° desist   rooms / worst
To build at all? Much more in this great work—
Which is almost to pluck a kingdom down
50   And set another up—should we survey
The plot of situation and the model,
Consent° upon a sure foundation,   Agree
Question surveyors,° know our own estate,°   architects / resources
How able such a work to undergo,
55   To weigh against his opposite;[8] or else
We fortify in paper and in figures,
Using the names of men instead of men,
Like one that draws the model of an house
Beyond his power to build it, who, half-through,
60   Gives o'er, and leaves his part-created cost[9]
A naked subject° to the weeping clouds,   An exposed object
And waste for churlish winter's tyranny.
HASTINGS   Grant that our hopes, yet° likely of fair birth,   still
Should be stillborn, and that we now possessed
65   The utmost man of expectation,[1]

3. Lines 21–24 are not present in Q.
4. Sustaining himself on nothing but the promise of
aid; believing the empty words he had heard concerning promised aid.
5. And hopeful plans. Lines 36–55 are not present in Q.
6. *as in . . . them:* an obscure passage. Bardolph may
mean that optimism in this instance is ill advised, just
as it is ill advised to hope that early spring buds will

mature into fruit rather than be killed by frost.
7. Plan. What follows is an elaboration on a biblical
parable in Luke 14:28–30 about a wise builder.
8. *To weigh . . . opposite:* To put in the balance against
contrary arguments. Bardolph is urging the rebels to
evaluate their strengths against their weaknesses.
9. And leaves his costly building half completed.
1. The last man whom we can expect.

I think we are a body strong enough,
  Even as we are, to equal with the King.
LORD BARDOLPH What, is the King but five-and-twenty thousand?
HASTINGS To us no more, nay, not so much, Lord Bardolph;
70 For his divisions, as the times do brawl,°   *are full of conflict*
  Are in three heads: one power against the French,
  And one against Glyndŵr, perforce a third
  Must take up us.° So is the unfirm King   *oppose us*
  In three divided, and his coffers sound
75 With hollow poverty and emptiness.
ARCHBISHOP OF YORK That he should draw his several° strengths together   *separate*
  And come against us in full puissance
  Need not be dreaded.
HASTINGS   If he should do so,
  He leaves his back unarmed, the French and Welsh
80 Baying him at the heels.[2] Never fear that.
LORD BARDOLPH Who is it like° should lead his forces hither?   *likely*
HASTINGS The Duke of Lancaster and Westmorland;
  Against the Welsh, himself and Harry Monmouth;
  But who is substituted° 'gainst the French   *delegated*
  I have no certain notice.[3]
85 ARCHBISHOP OF YORK   Let us on,
  And publish° the occasion of our arms.   *make public*
  The commonwealth is sick of their own choice;
  Their over-greedy love hath surfeited.[4]
  An habitation giddy and unsure
90 Hath he that buildeth on the vulgar° heart.   *common*
  O thou fond° many, with what loud applause   *foolish*
  Didst thou beat° heaven with blessing Bolingbroke,   *assail*
  Before he was what thou wouldst have him be!
  And being now trimmed° in thine own desires,   *decked out*
95 Thou, beastly feeder, art so full of him
  That thou provok'st thyself to cast him up.
  So, so, thou common dog, didst thou disgorge
  Thy glutton bosom of the royal Richard;
  And now thou wouldst eat thy dead vomit up,
100 And howl'st to find it. What trust is in these times?
  They that when Richard lived would have him die
  Are now become enamoured on his grave.
  Thou that threw'st dust upon his goodly head,
  When through proud London he came sighing on
105 After th'admirèd heels of Bolingbroke,
  Cri'st now, 'O earth, yield us that king again,
  And take thou this!' O thoughts of men accursed!
  Past and to come seems best; things present, worst.
MOWBRAY Shall we go draw our numbers° and set on?   *gather our forces*
110 HASTINGS We are time's subjects, and time bids be gone.   *Exeunt*

---

2. That is, following him like hunting dogs.   4. Became sick through overindulgence.
3. Lines 85–108 are not present in Q.

2.1

Enter [MISTRESS QUICKLY *the*] *hostess of* [*a*] *tavern, and
an officer,* FANG [*followed at a distance by another officer*], SNARE[1]

MISTRESS QUICKLY   Master Fang, have you entered the action?°   *begun the lawsuit*
FANG   It is entered.
MISTRESS QUICKLY   Where's your yeoman?° Is't a lusty[2] yeoman?   *assistant*
Will a stand to't?[3]
5   FANG   Sirrah!—Where's Snare?
MISTRESS QUICKLY   O Lord, ay, good Master Snare.
SNARE [*coming forward*]   Here, here.
FANG   Snare, we must arrest Sir John Falstaff.
MISTRESS QUICKLY   Yea, good Master Snare, I have entered him[4]
10   and all.
SNARE   It may chance° cost some of us our lives, for he will stab.   *perhaps*
MISTRESS QUICKLY   Alas the day, take heed of him; he stabbed[5]
me in mine own house, most beastly, in good faith. A cares not
what mischief he does; if his weapon° be out, he will foin° like   *dagger; penis / thrust*
15   any devil, he will spare neither man, woman, nor child.
FANG   If I can close[6] with him, I care not for his thrust.
MISTRESS QUICKLY   No, nor I neither. I'll be at your elbow.
FANG   An I but fist° him once, an a come but within my   *seize; masturbate*
vice°—   *grasp*
20   MISTRESS QUICKLY   I am undone by his going, I warrant you; he's
an infinitive thing upon my score.[7] Good Master Fang, hold
him sure. Good Master Snare, let him not scape. A comes continuantly to Pie Corner[8]—saving your manhoods—to buy a
saddle,[9] and he is indited° to dinner to the Lubber's Head[1] in   *(for "invited")*
25   Lombard Street, to Master Smooth's the silkman. I pray you,
since my exion is entered,[2] and my case° so openly known to   *lawsuit; vagina*
the world, let him be brought in to his answer. A hundred mark
is a long one° for a poor lone woman to bear; and I have borne,[3]   *huge account*
and borne, and borne, and have been fobbed off, and fobbed
30   off, and fobbed off, from this day to that day, that it is a shame
to be thought on. There is no honesty in such dealing, unless
a woman should be made an ass and a beast, to bear every
knave's wrong.

Enter Sir John FALSTAFF, BARDOLPH, *and the* [PAGE][4]

2.1 Location: Eastcheap, a street and market in London.
1. That Snare should linger behind Fang is suggested by the subsequent lines in which Fang cannot locate his fellow officer. Perhaps Snare is slow and lazy; or perhaps he deliberately lags behind to sniff out trouble and "ensnare" villains.
2. Sturdy; lustful. The following lines are full of sexual puns.
3. Will he fight vigorously? Will he maintain an erect penis?
4. I have brought suit against him, with a pun on "entered him" as meaning "had sexual relations with him." The phrase usually denotes a man's sexual entry into a woman.
5. With a pun on "stabbed" as meaning "sexually penetrated."
6. Fight hand to hand; clinch.
7. "Infinitive" is Quickly's malapropism, or verbal blunder, for "infinite." She implies that the board ("score")

on which her accounts are tallied has innumerable markings corresponding to Falstaff's debts to her.
8. Piecorner was an area of Smithfield named for its cooks' shops and known for its commerce in horses and sex. *continually:* blunder for "continually" or "incontinently."
9. With a pun on "saddle" as also meaning "female genitalia."
1. Blunder for "Libbard's," an Elizabethan form of "Leopard's." The silk merchant's shop sign evidently contained the image of a leopard's head.
2. Since my legal action has begun, with a pun on "entered" suggesting sexual penetration.
3. Endured, with a pun on "have borne" as meaning "have supported the weight of a partner in sexual relations."
4. As here, Q's stage directions sometimes refer to "the boy" rather than "the page." These have been standardized to "Page" throughout.

Yonder he comes, and that arrant° malmsey-nose⁵ knave Bar-   *notorious*
35   dolph with him. Do your offices,° do your offices, Master Fang   *duties*
  and Master Snare; do me,⁶ do me, do me your offices.
FALSTAFF   How now, whose mare's dead? What's the matter?
FANG   Sir John, I arrest you at the suit of Mistress Quickly.
FALSTAFF [*drawing*]   Away, varlets! Draw, Bardolph! Cut me off
40   the villain's head! Throw the quean° in the channel!°   *whore / street gutter*
    [BARDOLPH *draws*]
MISTRESS QUICKLY   Throw me in the channel? I'll throw thee in
  the channel!
    [*A brawl*]
  Wilt thou, wilt thou, thou bastardly rogue? Murder, murder!
  Ah, thou honeysuckle⁷ villain, wilt thou kill God's officers, and
45   the King's? Ah, thou honeyseed° rogue! Thou art a honeyseed,   *(for "homicidal")*
  a man-queller, and a woman-queller.
FALSTAFF   Keep them off, Bardolph!
FANG   A rescue,⁸ a rescue!
MISTRESS QUICKLY   Good people, bring a rescue or two. Thou
50   wot,° wot thou? Thou wot, wot'a? Do, do, thou rogue, do, thou   *You will*
  hempseed!⁹
PAGE   Away, you scullion,° you rampallian,° you fustilarian!¹ I'll   *kitchen wench / ruffian*
  tickle your catastrophe!²
    Enter [the] LORD CHIEF JUSTICE *and his men*
LORD CHIEF JUSTICE   What is the matter? Keep the peace here,
55   ho!
    [*Brawl ends.* FANG *seizes* FALSTAFF]³
MISTRESS QUICKLY   Good my lord, be good to me; I beseech you,
  stand to me.⁴
LORD CHIEF JUSTICE   How now, Sir John? What, are you brawling here?
  Doth this become your place,° your time° and business?   *social place / age*
60   You should have been well on your way to York.
  [*To* FANG] Stand from him, fellow. Wherefore hang'st thou
  upon him?
MISTRESS QUICKLY   O my most worshipful lord, an't° please your   *if it*
  grace, I am a poor widow of Eastcheap, and he is arrested at
  my suit.
65 LORD CHIEF JUSTICE   For what sum?
MISTRESS QUICKLY   It is more than for some, my lord, it is for all,
  all I have. He hath eaten me out of house and home. He hath
  put all my substance into that fat belly of his; [*to* FALSTAFF] but
  I will have some of it out again, or I will ride thee a-nights like
70   the mare.⁵

---

5. Red-nosed from drinking alcohol. Malmsey was a strong red wine named after its place of origin in Greece and available from Spain, Portugal, and their colonies as well as Greece.
6. Do your jobs for me, with a pun on "do me" as slang for "have sexual relations with me."
7. For "homicidal," with a pun on "honey" as slang for "sexual pleasure."
8. A cry for help in resisting arrest. Fang fears Falstaff is being rescued, but Quickly in the next line takes "res-cue" to mean "reinforcements" and seems to call for the rescue Fang is trying to stop.
9. Another version of "homicide," with an allusion to the hangman's hempen rope.

1. Fat, unkempt woman.
2. Expression meaning "I'll whip your rear end."
3. There are considerable opportunities for comic stage business here. Someone has to be hanging on Falstaff at this point, because at line 61, the Lord Chief Justice tells a "fellow" to let go. Perhaps Fang has twined him-self around Falstaff's legs or has even (living up to his name) lodged his teeth in Falstaff's clothing or anatomy.
4. Support me; be sexually erect for me.
5. Referring to a kind of goblin supposed to produce nightmares by sitting on the chest of a sleeper, with puns on "ride" as meaning "mount sexually" and on "mare" as a disparaging term for "woman."

FALSTAFF   I think I am as like to ride the mare, if I have any
vantage of ground to get up.°   *mount*
LORD CHIEF JUSTICE   How comes this, Sir John? Fie, what man
of good temper would endure this tempest of exclamation? Are
75   you not ashamed, to enforce a poor widow to so rough a course
to come by her own?
FALSTAFF [*to the Hostess*]   What is the gross sum that I owe thee?
MISTRESS QUICKLY   Marry, if thou wert an honest man, thyself,
and the money too. Thou didst swear to me upon a parcel-gilt°   *partly gilded*
80   goblet, sitting in my Dolphin chamber,° at the round table, by   *(an inn room)*
a sea-coal fire,⁶ upon Wednesday in Wheeson° week, when the   *Whitsun (Pentecost)*
Prince broke thy head for liking° his father to a singing-man of   *likening*
Windsor⁷—thou didst swear to me then, as I was washing thy
wound, to marry me, and make me my lady thy wife. Canst
85   thou deny it? Did not goodwife Keech⁸ the butcher's wife
come in then, and call me 'Gossip⁹ Quickly'—coming in to
borrow a mess of° vinegar, telling us she had a good dish of   *some*
prawns, whereby thou didst desire to eat some, whereby I told
thee they were ill for a green° wound? And didst thou not,   *fresh*
90   when she was gone downstairs, desire me to be no more so
familiarity° with such poor people, saying that ere long they   *(for "familiar")*
should call me 'madam'?¹ And didst thou not kiss me, and bid
me fetch thee thirty shillings? I put thee now to thy book-oath;°   *oath on the Bible*
deny it if thou canst.
[*She weeps*]
95   FALSTAFF   My lord, this is a poor mad soul, and she says up and
down the town that her eldest son is like you. She hath been
in good case,° and the truth is, poverty hath distracted her.²   *prosperous*
But for these foolish officers, I beseech you I may have
redress against them.
100   LORD CHIEF JUSTICE   Sir John, Sir John, I am well acquainted
with your manner of wrenching the true cause the false way. It
is not a confident brow,° nor the throng of words that come   *countenance*
with such more than impudent sauciness from you, can thrust
me from a level° consideration. You have, as it appears to me,   *just*
105   practised upon the easy-yielding spirit of this woman, and made
her serve your uses both in purse and in person.
MISTRESS QUICKLY   Yea, in truth, my lord.
LORD CHIEF JUSTICE   Pray thee, peace.   [*To* FALSTAFF] Pay her
the debt you owe her, and unpay the villainy you have done
110   with her. The one you may do with sterling money, and the
other with current° repentance.   *genuine*
FALSTAFF   My lord, I will not undergo this sneap° without reply.   *reproof*
You call honourable boldness 'impudent sauciness'; if a man
will make curtsy and say nothing, he is virtuous. No, my lord,
115   my humble duty° remembered, I will not be your suitor. I say   *due respect to you*
to you I do desire deliverance from these officers, being upon
hasty employment in the King's affairs.
LORD CHIEF JUSTICE   You speak as having power to do wrong;

---

6. Fire generated from charcoal shipped by sea rather
than by the inferior, locally produced charcoal.
7. One of the professional singers in the chapel at
Windsor, a royal residence west of London.
8. "Goodwife" was the title of a married woman.
"Keech" meant "a lump of animal fat."

9. Familiar form of address for a female friend, derived
from "godmother," the name for the female guardian of
a newly christened child.
1. A form of address for a knight's wife; a whore.
2. Driven her mad.

but answer in th'effect of your reputation,° and satisfy the poor   *as befits your status*
120   woman.
FALSTAFF [*drawing apart*]   Come hither, hostess.
       [*She goes to him*]
       Enter M[*aster*] GOWER, *a messenger*
LORD CHIEF JUSTICE   Now, Master Gower, what news?
GOWER   The King, my lord, and Harry Prince of Wales
    Are near at hand; the rest the paper tells.
       [LORD CHIEF JUSTICE *reads the paper, and converses*
       apart with GOWER]
125 FALSTAFF   As I am a gentleman!
MISTRESS QUICKLY   Faith, you said so before.
FALSTAFF   As I am a gentleman! Come, no more words of it.
MISTRESS QUICKLY   By this heavenly ground I tread on, I must be
    fain° to pawn both my plate and the tapestry of my dining-   *content*
130   chambers.
FALSTAFF   Glasses, glasses, is the only drinking;[3] and for thy
    walls, a pretty slight drollery,° or the story of the Prodigal,[4] or   *comic painting*
    the German hunting in waterwork,[5] is worth a thousand of
    these bed-hangers° and these fly-bitten tapestries. Let it be ten   *bed curtains*
135   pound if thou canst. Come, an 'twere not for thy humours,°   *moods*
    there's not a better wench in England. Go, wash thy face, and
    draw° the action. Come, thou must not be in this humour with   *withdraw*
    me. Dost not know me? Come, I know thou wast set on to this.
MISTRESS QUICKLY   Pray thee, Sir John, let it be but twenty
140   nobles.[6] I'faith, I am loath to pawn my plate, so God save me,
    la!
FALSTAFF   Let it alone; I'll make other shift.° You'll be a fool   *I'll manage otherwise*
    still.°   *always*
MISTRESS QUICKLY   Well, you shall have it, though I pawn my
145   gown. I hope you'll come to supper. You'll pay me altogether?
FALSTAFF   Will I live? [*To* BARDOLPH *and the* PAGE] Go with her,
    with her. Hook on,° hook on!   *Stick to her*
MISTRESS QUICKLY   Will you have Doll[7] Tearsheet meet you at
    supper?
150 FALSTAFF   No more words; let's have her.
       Exeunt [MISTRESS QUICKLY, BARDOLPH,
       the PAGE, FANG *and* SNARE]
LORD CHIEF JUSTICE [*to* GOWER]   I have heard better news.
FALSTAFF   What's the news, my good lord?
LORD CHIEF JUSTICE [*to* GOWER]   Where lay the King tonight?°   *last night*
GOWER   At Basingstoke,[8] my lord.
155 FALSTAFF [*to* LORD CHIEF JUSTICE]   I hope, my lord, all's well.
    What is the news, my lord?
LORD CHIEF JUSTICE [*to* GOWER]   Come all his forces back?
GOWER   No; fifteen hundred foot, five hundred horse,
    Are marched up to my lord of Lancaster
160   Against Northumberland and the Archbishop.
FALSTAFF [*to* LORD CHIEF JUSTICE]   Comes the King back from
       Wales, my noble lord?

---

3. Glass drinking vessels began to replace metal tankards in the late sixteenth century.
4. Alluding to a biblical parable about a profligate son who repents, which was a frequent subject for cheap painted cloths. See Luke 15:11–32.
5. A hunting scene of German or Dutch origin painted on a wall in imitation of tapestry.
6. Gold coins. Twenty were worth about 6 pounds.
7. A common name for a prostitute.
8. A town 46 miles west of London.

LORD CHIEF JUSTICE [*to* GOWER] You shall have letters of me
    presently.°   *at once*
Come, go along with me, good Master Gower.
    [*They are going*]
FALSTAFF My lord!
165   LORD CHIEF JUSTICE What's the matter?
FALSTAFF Master Gower, shall I entreat you with me to dinner?
GOWER I must wait upon my good lord here, I thank you, good
    Sir John.
LORD CHIEF JUSTICE Sir John, you loiter here too long, being
170   you are to take soldiers up° in counties as you go.   *levy soldiers*
FALSTAFF Will you sup with me, Master Gower?
LORD CHIEF JUSTICE What foolish master taught you these man-
    ners, Sir John?
FALSTAFF Master Gower, if they become me not, he was a fool
175   that taught them me.⁹ [*To* LORD CHIEF JUSTICE] This is the
    right fencing grace,° my lord—tap for tap, and so part fair.°   *style / on good terms*
LORD CHIEF JUSTICE Now the Lord lighten° thee; thou art a   *enlighten; make thin*
    great fool.   *Exeunt* [LORD CHIEF JUSTICE *and* GOWER *at one*
                                          door, FALSTAFF *at another*]

2.2

    Enter PRINCE HARRY *and* POINS¹
PRINCE HARRY Before God, I am exceeding weary.
POINS Is't come to that? I had thought weariness durst not have
    attached° one of so high blood.   *laid hold of*
PRINCE HARRY Faith, it does me, though it discolours the com-
5   plexion of my greatness² to acknowledge it. Doth it not show
    vilely in me to desire small° beer?   *weak*
POINS Why, a prince should not be so loosely studied° as to   *disposed*
    remember so weak a composition.
PRINCE HARRY Belike then my appetite was not princely got; for,
10   by my troth, I do now remember the poor creature small beer.
    But indeed, these humble considerations make me out of love
    with my greatness. What a disgrace is it to me to remember thy
    name!³ Or to know thy face tomorrow! Or to take note how
    many pair of silk stockings thou hast—videlicet° these, and   *namely*
15   those that were thy peach-coloured ones! Or to bear° the inven-   *remember*
    tory of thy shirts—as one for superfluity,° and another for use.   *as a spare*
    But that the tennis-court keeper knows better than I, for it is a
    low ebb of linen with thee when thou keepest not racket° there;   *do not play*
    as thou hast not done a great while, because the rest of thy low
20   countries have made a shift to eat up thy holland.⁴

---

9. Falstaff suggests that the habit of ignoring others is
something he learned from a fool, namely the Chief
Justice, who a few lines earlier would not answer Falstaff's questions.
2.2 Location: Prince Hal's dwelling.
1. Q's stage direction reads: "Enter the Prince, Poynes,
Sir John Russel, with other." This is the only place in Q
where the name "Russel" is employed instead of "Bardolph," but it indicates that Shakespeare had been working on some portion of this play before he was forced to
change "Oldcastle" to "Falstaff," "Russell" to "Bardolph,"
and "Harvey" to "Peto" (see Introduction to *1 Henry IV*).
2. It mars my noble countenance (by turning it pale
from weakness or red from shame).
3. Men of high rank should not be on familiar terms
with, or remember the names of, those below them in

status.
4. Because the brothels ("low countries") have contrived
to eat up all the money you would have spent on linen
("holland"). With puns on "low countries" as also meaning "sexual organs" and "the Netherlands" as well as
"brothels"; and with a pun on "holland" as referring to
the country of Holland as well as to the fine linen made
there. Poins has spent his money either on whores or on
providing linen for the babies he has prodigally fathered.
His lack of shirts makes it impossible for him to play at
the tennis courts, where players sweat so much that
shirts were frequently changed. Lines 20.1–20.4, which
follow, do not appear in F but are in Q. The Oxford editors assume they were cut by Shakespeare during revision of the play.

20.1 *And God knows whether those that bawl out the ruins of*
thy linen⁵ shall inherit his kingdom⁶—but the midwives
say the children are not in the fault, whereupon the world
increases, and kindreds are mightily strengthened.

POINS   How ill it follows, after you have laboured so hard, you
should talk so idly! Tell me, how many good young princes
would do so, their fathers lying so sick as yours is?

PRINCE HARRY   Shall I tell thee one thing, Poins?

25 POINS   Yes, faith, and let it be an excellent good thing.

PRINCE HARRY   It shall serve among wits of no higher breeding
than thine.

POINS   Go to, I stand the push of° your one thing that you'll tell.   *I can tolerate*

PRINCE HARRY   Marry, I tell thee, it is not meet° that I should be   *appropriate*

30 sad now my father is sick; albeit I could tell to thee, as to one
it pleases me, for fault° of a better, to call my friend, I could be   *lack*
sad; and sad indeed too.

POINS   Very hardly,° upon such a subject.   *With great difficulty*

PRINCE HARRY   By this hand, thou thinkest me as far in the devil's

35 book as thou and Falstaff, for obduracy° and persistency. Let   *stubbornness*
the end try the man. But I tell thee, my heart bleeds inwardly
that my father is so sick; and keeping such vile company as
thou art hath, in reason, taken from me all ostentation° of   *signs*
sorrow.

40 POINS   The reason?

PRINCE HARRY   What wouldst thou think of me if I should weep?

POINS   I would think thee a most princely hypocrite.

PRINCE HARRY   It would be every man's thought, and thou art a
blessed fellow to think as every man thinks. Never a man's

45 thought in the world keeps the roadway⁷ better than thine.
Every man would think me an hypocrite indeed. And what
accites° your most worshipful thought to think so?   *induces*

POINS   Why, because you have been so lewd,° and so much   *base*
engrafted° to Falstaff.   *attached*

50 PRINCE HARRY   And to thee.

POINS   By this light, I am well spoke on;° I can hear it with mine   *of*
own ears. The worst that they can say of me is that I am a
second brother,⁸ and that I am a proper fellow of my hands;°   *a good fighter*
and those two things I confess I cannot help.

Enter BARDOLPH [*followed by the* PAGE]

55 By the mass, here comes Bardolph.

PRINCE HARRY   And the boy that I gave Falstaff. A° had him from   *He*
me Christian, and look if the fat villain have not transformed
him ape.⁹

BARDOLPH   God save your grace!

60 PRINCE HARRY   And yours, most noble Bardolph!

POINS   [*to* BARDOLPH]   Come, you virtuous ass, you bashful fool,
must you be blushing?¹ Wherefore blush you now? What a

---

5. The bastard children who are wrapped in your old
shirts.
6. Go to heaven. With allusions to Matthew 25:34
("Come, ye blessed of my Father, inherit the kingdom
prepared for you from the foundation of the world") and
19:14 ("Suffer little children, and forbid them not, to
come unto me: for of such is the kingdom of heaven").
7. Adheres to the popular viewpoint.

8. That is, a younger brother (and therefore without
prospect of inheritance).
9. Made him look ridicuous, like an ape or a monkey
rather than a human being. Falstaff has perhaps
dressed the Page in an outlandish livery or uniform.
1. The jokes in this portion of the scene often refer to
Bardolph's notoriously red face. The color may be due to
drink, venereal disease, or some form of acne or rosacea.

maidenly man at arms are you become! Is't such a matter° to   *so difficult*
get a pottle-pot's maidenhead?[2]

65 PAGE A calls me e'en now, my lord, through a red lattice,[3] and
  I could discern no part of his face from the window. At last I
  spied his eyes, and methought he had made two holes in the
  ale-wife's red petticoat, and so peeped through.

PRINCE HARRY [*to* POINS] Has not the boy profited?°   *(from Falstaff)*

70 BARDOLPH [*to the* PAGE] Away, you whoreson upright rabbit,
  away!

PAGE Away, you rascally Althea's[4] dream, away!

PRINCE HARRY Instruct us, boy; what dream, boy?

PAGE Marry, my lord, Althea dreamt she was delivered of a
75   firebrand, and therefore I call him her dream.

PRINCE HARRY [*giving him money*] A crown's-worth of good
  interpretation! There 'tis, boy.

POINS O, that this good blossom could be kept from cankers!° *cankerworms*
  [*Giving the* PAGE *money*] Well, there is sixpence to preserve
80   thee.

BARDOLPH An° you do not make him hanged among you, the   *If*
  gallows shall be wronged.

PRINCE HARRY And how doth thy master, Bardolph?

BARDOLPH Well, my good lord. He heard of your grace's coming
85   to town. There's a letter for you.

POINS Delivered with good respect.° And how doth the Mar- *(said ironically)*
  tlemas[5] your master?

BARDOLPH In bodily health, sir.
  [PRINCE HARRY *reads the letter*]

POINS Marry, the immortal part° needs a physician, but that   *the soul*
90   moves not him. Though that be sick, it dies not.

PRINCE HARRY I do allow this wen° to be as familiar with me as   *wart*
  my dog; and he holds his place,° for look you how he writes. *maintains his position*
  [*He gives* POINS *the letter*][6]

POINS 'John Falstaff, knight'.—Every man must know that,° as *(Falstaff's rank)*
  oft as he has occasion to name himself; even like those that are
95   kin to the King, for they never prick their finger but they say
  'There's some of the King's blood spilt.' 'How comes that?' says
  he that takes upon him not to conceive.° The answer is as ready *understand*
  as a borrower's cap:[7] 'I am the King's poor cousin,° sir.'   *relative*

PRINCE HARRY Nay, they will be kin to us, or they will fetch it° *derive kinship*
100   from Japhet.[8] [*Taking the letter*] But the letter. 'Sir John Falstaff, knight, to the son of the King nearest his father, Harry
  Prince of Wales, greeting.'

POINS Why, this is a certificate!°   *legal document*

PRINCE HARRY Peace!— 'I will imitate the honourable Romans
105   in brevity.'

POINS [*taking the letter*] Sure he means brevity in breath, short

---

2. To open and drain a two-quart tankard of ale (with
implicit comparison to penetrating a virgin).
3. Sign of an alehouse window.
4. A conflation of two dreams from classical mythology.
It was Hecuba, the Queen of Troy, who, when pregnant
with Paris, dreamed she gave birth to a firebrand that set
fire to her city. Althaea was told that her newborn son,
Meleager, would live only as long as a brand in the fire
was not consumed, so she snatched it from the hearth.
5. Fatted cattle or pigs that were slaughtered on

November 11, the feast day of St. Martin (Martlemas).
6. The reading of the letter is another occasion for
comic horseplay. The Prince and Poins may pass it back
and forth, or Poins may read it over Prince Harry's
shoulder, or snatch it away.
7. As readily produced as the cap of one looking for
money.
8. One of Noah's sons (Genesis 10:2–5), imagined to
be the common ancestor of all Europeans.

winded. [*Reads*] 'I commend me to thee, I commend thee, and I leave thee. Be not too familiar with Poins, for he misuses thy favours so much that he swears thou art to marry his sister Nell.
110 Repent at idle times as thou mayst. And so, farewell.

> Thine by yea and no⁹—which is as much as to say, as thou usest him—Jack Falstaff with my familiars,° John *friends* with my brothers and sisters, and Sir John with all Europe.'

115 My lord, I'll steep this letter in sack and make him eat it.

PRINCE HARRY   That's to make him eat twenty of his words. But do you use me thus, Ned? Must I marry your sister?

POINS   God send the wench no worse fortune, but I never said so.

120 PRINCE HARRY   Well, thus we play the fools with the time, and the spirits of the wise sit in the clouds and mock us. [*To* BAR- DOLPH] Is your master here in London?

BARDOLPH   Yea, my lord.

PRINCE HARRY   Where sups he? Doth the old boar feed in the
125 old frank?¹

BARDOLPH   At the old place, my lord, in Eastcheap.

PRINCE HARRY   What company?

PAGE   Ephesians, my lord, of the old church.²

PRINCE HARRY   Sup any women with him?

130 PAGE   None, lord, but old Mistress Quickly and Mistress Doll Tearsheet.

PRINCE HARRY   What pagan° may that be?   *heathen; prostitute*

PAGE   A proper gentlewoman, sir, and a kinswoman of my mas- ter's.

135 PRINCE HARRY   Even such kin as the parish heifers are to the town bull. Shall we steal upon them, Ned, at supper?

POINS   I am your shadow, my lord; I'll follow you.

PRINCE HARRY   Sirrah, you, boy, and Bardolph, no word to your master that I am yet come to town. [*Giving money*] There's for
140 your silence.

BARDOLPH   I have no tongue, sir.

PAGE   And for mine, sir, I will govern it.

PRINCE HARRY   Fare you well; go.

> [*Exeunt* BARDOLPH *and the* PAGE]

This Doll Tearsheet should be some road.³

145 POINS   I warrant you, as common as the way between Saint Albans⁴ and London.

PRINCE HARRY   How might we see Falstaff bestow° himself   *behave* tonight in his true colours, and not ourselves be seen?

POINS   Put on two leathern jerkins° and aprons, and wait upon   *jackets*
150 him at his table like drawers.°   *tavern servants*

PRINCE HARRY   From a god to a bull—a heavy declension°—it   *a sad degradation* was Jove's case.⁵ From a prince to a prentice—a low transfor-

---

9. Parodying the mild oaths associated with Puritans.
1. Pigsty. Possibly a reference to Eastcheap's famous tavern the Boar's Head.
2. Carousers of the usual kind. The Page alludes to the biblical account of the Ephesians, whom St. Paul admonished against lust and drunkenness before their conversion, with a possible reference to Catholics

(members of "the old church"), whom English Protestants accused of moral laxity.
3. Some common prostitute. "Road" is slang for "vagina."
4. Town on the heavily traveled road north from London.
5. Referring to Jove's transformation into a bull before his rape of Europa.

mation—that shall be mine; for in everything the purpose
must weigh with° the folly. Follow me, Ned.   *Exeunt*   match

2.3

Enter [the Earl of] NORTHUMBERLAND, LADY [NORTHUM-
BERLAND] *and* LADY PERCY[1]

NORTHUMBERLAND   I pray thee, loving wife and gentle
    daughter,°   *daughter-in-law*
Give even way° unto my rough affairs.   *Allow free scope*
Put not you on the visage of the times
And be like them to Percy troublesome.

5   LADY NORTHUMBERLAND   I have given over; I will speak no more.
Do what you will; your wisdom be your guide.
NORTHUMBERLAND   Alas, sweet wife, my honour is at pawn,
And, but° my going, nothing can redeem it.   *except by*
LADY PERCY   O yet, for God's sake, go not to these wars!

10   The time was, father, that you broke your word[2]
When you were more endeared° to it than now—   *bound*
When your own Percy, when my heart's dear Harry,
Threw many a northward look to see his father
Bring up his powers; but he did long in vain.

15   Who then persuaded you to stay at home?
There were two honours lost, yours and your son's.
For yours, the God of heaven brighten it!
For his, it stuck upon him as the sun
In the grey° vault of heaven, and by his light   *pale blue*

20   Did all the chivalry° of England move   *chivalrous warriors*
To do brave acts. He was indeed the glass°   *mirror*
Wherein the noble youth did dress themselves.[3]
He had no legs that practised not his gait;[4]
And speaking thick,[5] which nature made his blemish,

25   Became the accents of the valiant;
For those that could speak low and tardily°   *slowly*
Would turn their own perfection to abuse
To seem like him. So that in speech, in gait,
In diet, in affections° of delight,   *choice*

30   In military rules, humours of blood,°   *disposition*
He was the mark° and glass, copy° and book,   *target / example*
That fashioned others. And him—O wondrous him!
O miracle of men!—him did you leave,
Second to none, unseconded° by you,   *unsupported*

35   To look upon the hideous god of war
In disadvantage, to abide a field°   *confront a battle*
Where nothing but the sound of Hotspur's name
Did seem defensible;° so you left him.   *to provide a defense*
Never, O never do his ghost the wrong

40   To hold your honour more precise and nice°   *exacting*
With others than with him. Let them alone.

2.3 Location: Outside Northumberland's castle at
Warkworth.
1. Q's stage direction designates the women only as
wives: "Enter Northumberland, his wife, and the wife
to Harry Percie."
2. Alluding to Northumberland's absence from the
Battle of Shrewsbury. See *1 Henry IV.*

3. Lines 23–45 do not appear in Q.
4. There was no man able to walk who did not try to
move as Hotspur did.
5. Speaking rapidly. The phrase has often been taken to
mean that Hotspur had a speech defect. A long stage
tradition made him a stutterer.

The Marshal and the Archbishop are strong.
Had my sweet Harry had but half their numbers,
Today might I, hanging on Hotspur's neck,
Have talked of Monmouth's° grave.   *Prince Hal's*

45 NORTHUMBERLAND   Beshrew your heart,
Fair daughter, you do draw my spirits from me
With new lamenting ancient oversights.
But I must go and meet with danger there,
Or it will seek me in another place,
And find me worse provided.

50 LADY NORTHUMBERLAND   O fly to Scotland,
Till that the nobles and the armèd commons
Have of their puissance° made a little taste.   *strength*

LADY PERCY   If they get ground and vantage of the King,
Then join you with them like a rib of steel,
55 To make strength stronger; but, for all our loves,
First let them try themselves. So did your son.
He was so suffered.° So came I a widow,   *allowed to proceed*
And never shall have length of life enough
To rain upon remembrance with mine eyes,[6]
60 That it may grow and sprout as high as heaven
For recordation° to my noble husband.   *As a memorial*

NORTHUMBERLAND   Come, come, go in with me. 'Tis with my mind
As with the tide swelled up unto his height,
That makes a still stand,° running neither way.   *standstill*
65 Fain would I go to meet the Archbishop,
But many thousand reasons hold me back.
I will resolve for Scotland. There am I
Till time and vantage° crave my company.   *Exeunt*   *opportunity*

2.4

[*A table and chairs set forth.*][1] *Enter a* DRAWER° [*with*   *servant in a tavern*
wine and another DRAWER *with a dish of apple-johns*][2]

FIRST DRAWER   What the devil hast thou brought there—apple-
johns? Thou knowest Sir John cannot endure an apple-john.

SECOND DRAWER   Mass,[3] thou sayst true. The Prince once set a
dish of apple-johns before him; and told him, there were five
5   more Sir Johns; and, putting off his hat, said 'I will now take
my leave of these six dry, round, old, withered knights.' It
angered him to the heart. But he hath forgot that.

FIRST DRAWER   Why then, cover,° and set them down; and see if   *spread the cloth*
thou canst find out Sneak's noise.° Mistress Tearsheet would   *band of musicians*
10   fain hear some music.   [*Exit the* SECOND DRAWER]

[*The* FIRST DRAWER *covers the table.*]
[*Enter the* SECOND DRAWER]

6. To rain tears upon his memory, here imagined as a
plant—perhaps rosemary, the conventional symbol of
remembrance.
2.4 Location: A tavern, perhaps the Boar's Head, in
Eastcheap.
1. Changes were made to this scene at some point. In
Q, dialogue occurs between Francis and "a Drawer or
two." At 2.4.13, Q's stage direction reads: "Enter Will."
This character has no lines, and probably his part was
later deleted. In F, the dialogue is somewhat rearranged

and occurs between two drawers, as here. However
many servants are onstage, though, the point of their
scurrying about is to create excitement about Falstaff's
arrival and the trick to be played on him.
2. A kind of apple that could be kept for two years and
was meant to be eaten when the skin was wrinkled and
shriveled up.
3. An oath derived from the name of the Catholic
church service.

SECOND DRAWER   Sirrah, here will be the Prince and Master
    Poins anon,° and they will put on two of our jerkins and aprons,   *soon*
    and Sir John must not know of it. Bardolph hath brought word.
FIRST DRAWER   By the mass, here will be old utis!° It will be an   *merrymaking; a din*
15 excellent stratagem.
SECOND DRAWER   I'll see if I can find out Sneak.   *Exeunt*
            Enter MISTRESS QUICKLY *and* DOLL TEARSHEET [*drunk*]
MISTRESS QUICKLY   I'faith, sweetheart, methinks now you are in
    an excellent good temperality.° Your pulsidge⁴ beats as extraor-   *(for "temper")*
    dinarily as heart would desire, and your colour, I warrant you,
20 is as red as any rose, in good truth, la; but i'faith, you have
    drunk too much canaries,⁵ and that's a marvellous searching°   *strong*
    wine, and it perfumes the blood ere we can say 'What's this?'
    How do you now?
DOLL TEARSHEET   Better than I was.—Hem!
25 MISTRESS QUICKLY   Why, that's well said! A good heart's worth
    gold.
            Enter Sir John FALSTAFF
    Lo, here comes Sir John.
FALSTAFF [*sings*]   'When Arthur first in court'⁶—[*Calls*] Empty
    the jordan!°—[*Sings*] 'And was a worthy king'—How now, Mis-   *chamber pot*
30 tress Doll?
MISTRESS QUICKLY   Sick of a qualm,° yea, good faith.   *fainting fit*
FALSTAFF   So is all her sect;° an they be once in a calm,⁷ they   *kind; sex*
    are sick.
DOLL TEARSHEET   A pox damn you, you muddy rascal!⁸ Is that
35 all the comfort you give me?
FALSTAFF   You make fat rascals, Mistress Doll.
DOLL TEARSHEET   I make them? Gluttony and diseases make
    them; I make them not.
FALSTAFF   If the cook help to make the gluttony, you help to
40 make the diseases, Doll. We catch of you,° Doll, we catch of   *are infected by you*
    you; grant that, my poor virtue, grant that.
DOLL TEARSHEET   Yea, Jesu, our chains and our jewels.⁹
FALSTAFF   'Your brooches, pearls, and ouches'¹—for to serve
    bravely is to come halting off,² you know; to come off the
45 breach with his pike bent bravely,³ and to surgery bravely; to
    venture upon the charged chambers⁴ bravely.
MISTRESS QUICKLY   By my troth, this is the old fashion. You two
    never meet but you fall to some discord. You are both, i' good
    truth, as rheumatic° as two dry toasts; you cannot one bear with   *(for "choleric")*
50 another's confirmities.° What the goodyear, one must bear,⁵ [*to*   *(for "infirmities")*
    DOLL] and that must be you. You are the weaker vessel, as they
    say, the emptier vessel.

---

4. For "pulse."
5. Sweet wine from the Canary Islands.
6. Lines from the ballad "Sir Lancelot du Lake."
7. Quiet; not sexually active (punning on "qualm" in
the prior line).
8. You dull knave. A "rascal" was a young, lean deer.
They were called "muddy" when sluggish and out of
season. In his next speech, Falstaff will accuse Doll of
making even lean deer fat, probably by tempting them
to gluttony and vice.
9. Yes, you steal ("catch") our valuables.
1. Perhaps a line from a ballad, with puns on the three
items of jewelry as slang for the carbuncles and sores

that result from venereal disease.
2. To fight bravely is to return limping; to engage in vigorous sex is to be wounded in the process.
3. To come away from the gap in the fortifications (the
breech) with one's weapon finely bent (with puns on
"breech" as slang for "female genitalia" and "pike" as
slang for "penis").
4. Interior of a mine loaded with munitions; the sexually aroused interior of a woman.
5. Endure; carry goods; support the weight of a sexual
partner; give birth. *What the goodyear:* a phrase probably meaning "What the devil."

DOLL TEARSHEET   Can a weak empty vessel bear such a huge full
hogshead?° There's a whole merchant's venture° of Bordeaux   *cask / cargo*
55   stuff° in him; you have not seen a hulk better stuffed in the   *wine*
hold.— Come, I'll be friends with thee, Jack. Thou art going
to the wars, and whether I shall ever see thee again or no there
is nobody cares.
        Enter [a] DRAWER
DRAWER   Sir, Ensign⁶ Pistol's below, and would speak with you.
60   DOLL TEARSHEET   Hang him, swaggering° rascal, let him not   *blustering; quarreling*
come hither. It is the foul-mouthedest rogue in England.
MISTRESS QUICKLY   If he swagger, let him not come here. No, by
my faith! I must live among my neighbours; I'll no swaggerers.
I am in good name and fame with the very best. Shut the door;
65   there comes no swaggerers here. I have not lived all this while
to have swaggering now. Shut the door, I pray you.
FALSTAFF   Dost thou hear, hostess?
MISTRESS QUICKLY   Pray ye pacify yourself, Sir John. There
comes no swaggerers here.
70   FALSTAFF   Dost thou hear? It is mine ensign.
MISTRESS QUICKLY   Tilly-fally,° Sir John, ne'er tell me. Your   *Nonsense*
ensign-swaggerer comes not in my doors. I was before Master
Tisick⁷ the debuty° t'other day, and, as he said to me—'twas no   *(for "deputy")*
longer ago than Wed'sday last, i' good faith—'Neighbour
75   Quickly,' says he—Master Dumb our minister was by then—
'Neighbour Quickly,' says he, 'receive those that are civil, for,'
said he, 'you are in an ill name.' Now a said so, I can tell
whereupon.⁸ 'For,' says he, 'you are an honest woman, and well
thought on; therefore take heed what guests you receive.
80   Receive,' says he, 'no swaggering companions.' There comes
none here. You would bless you° to hear what he said. No, I'll   *feel fortunate*
no swaggerers.
FALSTAFF   He's no swaggerer, hostess—a tame cheater,⁹ i'faith.
You may stroke him as gently as a puppy greyhound. He'll not
85   swagger with a Barbary hen,° if her feathers turn back in any   *guinea hen; prostitute*
show of resistance.—Call him up, drawer.   [*Exit* DRAWER]
MISTRESS QUICKLY   Cheater¹ call you him? I will bar no honest
man my house, nor no cheater, but I do not love swaggering,
by my troth, I am the worse when one says 'swagger'. Feel,
90   masters, how I shake, look you, I warrant you.
DOLL TEARSHEET   So you do, hostess.
MISTRESS QUICKLY   Do I? Yea, in very truth do I, an 'twere° an   *as if I were*
aspen leaf. I cannot abide swaggerers.
        Enter PISTOL, BARDOLPH, *and [the]* PAGE
PISTOL   God save you, Sir John.
95   FALSTAFF   Welcome, Ensign Pistol. Here, Pistol, I charge you²
with a cup of sack. Do you discharge³ upon mine hostess.
PISTOL   I will discharge upon her, Sir John, with two bullets.°   *(slang for "testicles")*
FALSTAFF   She is pistol-proof, sir, you shall not hardly offend°   *injure*
her.

---

6. A military title for the army's standard-bearer.
7. The name signifies a hacking cough.
8. Now I can tell why he ("a") said so.
9. A decoy in a scheme to defraud people.
1. Quickly apparently understands the word as

"escheator," an officer responsible for returning to the
crown property whose title had lapsed.
2. Toast to you; load you with ammunition (punning on
Pistol's name); arouse you sexually.
3. Return the toast; empty the cup; shoot; ejaculate.

100 MISTRESS QUICKLY   Come, I'll drink no proofs, nor no bullets. I'll
drink no more than will do me good, for no man's pleasure, I.
PISTOL   Then to you, Mistress Dorothy! I will charge° you.   *toast; arouse; order*
DOLL TEARSHEET   Charge me? I scorn you, scurvy companion.
What, you poor, base, rascally, cheating, lack-linen mate!°   *fellow who has no linen*
105 Away, you mouldy rogue, away! I am meat for your master.[4]
PISTOL   I know you, Mistress Dorothy.
DOLL TEARSHEET   Away, you cutpurse° rascal, you filthy bung,[5]   *thieving; castrated*
away! By this wine, I'll thrust my knife in your mouldy chaps°   *cheeks; buttocks*
an you play the saucy cuttle with me![6]
[*She brandishes a knife*]
110 Away, you bottle-ale rascal, you basket-hilt stale juggler,[7] you!
[PISTOL *draws his sword*]
Since when, I pray you, sir? God's light, with two points[8] on
your shoulder! Much!
PISTOL   God let me not live, but I will murder your ruff° for this.   *starched collar*
MISTRESS QUICKLY   No, good Captain Pistol; not here, sweet cap-
115 tain.
DOLL TEARSHEET   Captain? Thou abominable damned cheater,
art thou not ashamed to be called 'captain'? An captains were
of my mind, they would truncheon° you out, for taking their   *cudgel*
names upon you before you have earned them. You a captain?
120 You slave! For what? For tearing a poor whore's ruff in a bawdy-
house! He a captain? Hang him, rogue, he lives upon mouldy
stewed prunes[9] and dried cakes. A captain? God's light, these
villains will make the word 'captain' odious; therefore captains
had need look to't.
125 BARDOLPH   Pray thee, go down, good ensign.
FALSTAFF   Hark thee hither, Mistress Doll.
[*He takes her aside*]
PISTOL   Not I! I tell thee what, Corporal Bardolph, I could tear
her! I'll be revenged of her.
PAGE   Pray thee, go down.
130 PISTOL   I'll see her damned first
To Pluto's damned lake,° by this hand,[1]   *(the lake of hell)*
To th'infernal deep,
Where Erebus,° and tortures vile also.   *the underworld*
'Hold hook and line!' say I.
135 Down, down, dogs; down, Fates.
Have we not Hiren here?[2]
MISTRESS QUICKLY   Good Captain Pizzle,° be quiet. 'Tis very   *Penis*
late, i'faith. I beseek you now, aggravate° your choler.   *(for "moderate")*
PISTOL   These be good humours indeed!
140 Shall pack-horses

4. That is, I am superior to you; with a pun on "meat" as meaning "a body available for sexual pleasure."
5. Thief; anus.
6. If you continue to abuse me (with a pun on "cuttle" as signifying both "knife" and "cuttlefish," which was supposed to vomit a black liquid to conceal itself from enemies).
7. You imposter with a cheap, outdated sword. Basket-work hilts were used on inexpensive weapons or those used only for practice.
8. Tags for fastening armor.
9. Available in brothels as a supposed preventative of

venereal disease, with a pun on "stew" as meaning "brothel."
1. In this and subsequent speeches, Pistol rants in an affected style that recalls and parodies the language of sensational plays from the 1590s and earlier, which were often set in non-European locales and involved military and erotic adventures.
2. Apparently a line from *The Turkish Mohamet and Hiren [Irene] the Fair Greek,* a lost play by George Peele. Pistol may be referring to his sword as "Hiren" with a pun on "iron."

And hollow pampered jades of Asia,[3]
Which cannot go but thirty mile a day,
Compare with Caesars and with cannibals,[4]
And Trojan Greeks?
145 Nay, rather damn them with King Cerberus,[5]
And let the welkin° roar. Shall we fall foul for toys?[6]   *heavens*
MISTRESS QUICKLY   By my troth, captain, these are very bitter
words.
BARDOLPH   Be gone, good ensign; this will grow to a brawl anon.
150 PISTOL   Die men like dogs! Give crowns like pins![7]
Have we not Hiren here?
MISTRESS QUICKLY   O' my word, captain, there's none such here.
What the goodyear, do you think I would deny her? For God's
sake, be quiet.
155 PISTOL   Then feed and be fat, my fair Calipolis.[8]
Come, give's some sack.
Si fortune me tormente, sperato me contento.[9]
Fear we broadsides?[1] No; let the fiend give fire!°   *shoot*
Give me some sack; and, sweetheart, lie thou there.
    [*He lays down his sword*]
160 Come we to full points here? And are etceteras nothings?[2]
    [*He drinks*]
FALSTAFF   Pistol, I would be quiet.
PISTOL   Sweet knight, I kiss thy neaf.° What, we have seen the   *fist*
seven stars![3]
DOLL TEARSHEET   For God's sake, thrust him downstairs. I can-
165 not endure such a fustian° rascal.   *worthless*
PISTOL   Thrust him downstairs? Know we not Galloway nags?[4]
FALSTAFF   Quoit° him down, Bardolph, like a shove-groat shil-   *Throw*
ling.[5] Nay, an a do° nothing but speak nothing, a shall be   *if he does*
nothing here.
170 BARDOLPH [*to* PISTOL]   Come, get you downstairs.
PISTOL [*taking up his sword*]   What, shall we have incision?
    Shall we imbrue?°   *steep in blood*
Then death rock me asleep, abridge my doleful days.
Why then, let grievous, ghastly, gaping wounds
Untwine the Sisters Three.[6] Come, Atropos, I say!
175 MISTRESS QUICKLY   Here's goodly stuff toward!°   *about to happen*
FALSTAFF   Give me my rapier, boy.
DOLL TEARSHEET   I pray thee, Jack, I pray thee, do not draw.
FALSTAFF [*taking his rapier and speaking to* PISTOL]   Get you downstairs.
    [FALSTAFF, BARDOLPH, *and* PISTOL *brawl*]

---

3. A garbled allusion to Marlowe's *2 Tamburlaine*
4.3.1–2, in which Tamburlaine taunts the Kings whom
he has captured and whom he uses in lieu of horses to
draw his chariot.
4. Pistol may mean "Hannibals." Hannibal was a
famous general of Carthage.
5. In classical mythology, the three-headed dog guard-
ing the underworld.
6. Quarrel over trifles.
7. Alluding to Tamburlaine's extravagance in distribut-
ing the crowns of conquered Kings among his followers.
8. Echoing Peele's *Battle of Alcazar,* in which the
Moorish King Muly Mahomet offers his starving wife
the raw flesh of a lion he has just killed.

9. If fortune torments me, hope contents me (a motto
that Pistol renders in a mixture of Italian, French, and
Spanish).
1. Shots fired from the side of a ship.
2. That is, have we come to a stop? Is there no further
satisfaction to be had in the rest (the "etceteras")? Pistol puns on "etceteras" and "nothings" as slang for
"female genitalia."
3. We have caroused all night (with an allusion to the
Ursa Major constellation).
4. Small Scottish horses; prostitutes.
5. Shilling coin used in a game like shuffleboard.
6. The three Fates of Greek mythology: Clotho, Lach-
esis, and Atropos. Atropos cut the thread of life.

MISTRESS QUICKLY   Here's a goodly tumult! I'll forswear keeping
house afore I'll be in these tirrits° and frights!   *(for "terrors" or "fits")*

[FALSTAFF *thrusts at* PISTOL]

So!

[PISTOL *thrusts at* FALSTAFF]

Murder, I warrant now! Alas, alas, put up your naked weapons,
put up your naked weapons!

[*Exit* PISTOL, *pursued by* BARDOLPH]

DOLL TEARSHEET   I pray thee, Jack, be quiet; the rascal's gone.
Ah, you whoreson little valiant villain, you!

MISTRESS QUICKLY   [*to* FALSTAFF] Are you not hurt i'th' groin?
Methought a made a shrewd° thrust at your belly.   *vicious*

[*Enter* BARDOLPH]

FALSTAFF   Have you turned him out o'doors?

BARDOLPH   Yea, sir. The rascal's drunk. You have hurt him, sir,
i'th' shoulder.

FALSTAFF   A rascal, to brave° me!   *defy*

DOLL TEARSHEET   Ah, you sweet little rogue, you! Alas, poor ape,
how thou sweatest! Come, let me wipe thy face; come on, you
whoreson chops.° Ah rogue, i'faith, I love thee. Thou art as   *fat cheeks*
valorous as Hector of Troy,⁷ worth five of Agamemnon,⁸ and
ten times better than the Nine Worthies.⁹ Ah, villain!

FALSTAFF   A rascally slave! I will toss the rogue in a blanket.¹

DOLL TEARSHEET   Do, an thou darest for thy heart. An thou dost,
I'll canvas° thee between a pair of sheets.   *toss*

Enter music[ians]

PAGE   The music is come, sir.

FALSTAFF   Let them play.—Play, sirs!

[*Music plays*]

Sit on my knee, Doll. A rascal bragging slave! The rogue fled
from me like quicksilver.°   *mercury*

DOLL TEARSHEET   I'faith, and thou followed'st him like a church.° *(i.e., sedately)*
Thou whoreson little tidy° Bartholomew boar-pig,² when wilt   *plump*
thou leave fighting o'days, and foining° o'nights, and begin to   *thrusting*
patch up thine old body for heaven?

Enter PRINCE [HARRY] and POINS, disguised [as drawers]

FALSTAFF   Peace, good Doll, do not speak like a death's-head,³
do not bid me remember mine end.

DOLL TEARSHEET   Sirrah, what humour's° the Prince of?   *disposition is*

FALSTAFF   A good shallow young fellow. A would have made a
good pantler;° a would ha' chipped° bread well.   *pantry worker / cut*

DOLL TEARSHEET   They say Poins has a good wit.

FALSTAFF   He a good wit? Hang him, baboon! His wit's as thick
as Tewkesbury⁴ mustard; there's no more conceit° in him than   *intellect*
is in a mallet.

DOLL TEARSHEET   Why does the Prince love him so, then?

FALSTAFF   Because their legs are both of a bigness, and a° plays   *he*
at quoits⁵ well, and eats conger and fennel,⁶ and drinks off can-

---

7. The greatest Trojan warrior in Homer's *Iliad*.
8. Leader of the Greeks in the battle for Troy.
9. Nine legendary brave men: three Christians—
Arthur, Charlemagne, Godfrey of Boulogne; three
pagans—Hector, Alexander, Julius Caesar; and three
Jews—Joshua, David, Judas Maccabaeus.
1. A punishment for cowardice.
2. A roasted pig associated with an annual London carnival held on August 24, St. Bartholomew's Day.

3. Skull or representation of a skull used as a reminder
of mortality.
4. Market town in Gloucestershire famed for its mustard.
5. A game involving the throwing of a heavy iron ring
toward a target on the ground.
6. Conger eel, a heavy, hard-to-digest food, was served
with fennel.

220 dles' ends for flap-dragons,[7] and rides the wild mare[8] with the
     boys, and jumps upon joint-stools, and swears with a good
     grace, and wears his boot very smooth like unto the sign of the
     leg,[9] and breeds no bate° with telling of discreet stories, and   *discord*
     such other gambol° faculties a has that show a weak mind and   *sportive*
225 an able body; for the which the Prince admits him; for the
     Prince himself is such another—the weight of a hair will turn
     the scales between their avoirdupois.°   *weight*

PRINCE HARRY [*aside to* POINS] Would not this nave° of a wheel   *hub*
     have his ears cut off?

230 POINS Let's beat him before his whore.

PRINCE HARRY Look whe'er the withered elder[1] hath not his poll°   *head*
     clawed like a parrot.[2]

POINS Is it not strange that desire should so many years outlive
     performance?

235 FALSTAFF Kiss me, Doll.
          [*They kiss*]

PRINCE HARRY [*aside to* POINS] Saturn and Venus[3] this year in
     conjunction! What says th'almanac to that?

POINS And look whether the fiery Trigon[4] his man be not lisping
     to his master's old tables,° his note-book, his counsel-keeper![5]   *writing tablets*

240 FALSTAFF [*to* DOLL] Thou dost give me flattering busses.°   *kisses*

DOLL TEARSHEET By my troth, I kiss thee with a most constant
     heart.

FALSTAFF I am old, I am old.

DOLL TEARSHEET I love thee better than I love e'er a scurvy
245 young boy of them all.

FALSTAFF What stuff° wilt have a kirtle° of? I shall receive money   *material / skirt*
     o'Thursday; shalt° have a cap tomorrow.—A merry song!   *you shall*
          [*The music plays again*]
     Come, it grows late; we'll to bed. Thou'lt forget me when I am
     gone.

250 DOLL TEARSHEET By my troth, thou'lt set me a-weeping an thou
     sayst so. Prove° that ever I dress myself handsome till thy re-   *If you ever prove*
     turn—well, hearken° a'th' end.   *judge*

FALSTAFF Some sack, Francis.

PRINCE *and* POINS [*coming forward*] Anon, anon, sir.

255 FALSTAFF Ha, a bastard son of the King's!—And art not thou
     Poins his brother?°   *the brother of Poins*

PRINCE HARRY Why, thou globe of sinful continents,[6] what a life
     dost thou lead!

FALSTAFF A better than thou: I am a gentleman, thou art a
260 drawer.

PRINCE HARRY Very true, sir, and I come to draw you out by the
     ears.

MISTRESS QUICKLY O, the Lord preserve thy grace! By my troth,

---

7. Referring to a tavern game in which one drank
liquor on which burning objects (flapdragons) had been
set afloat.
8. Plays at a form of leapfrog; has sexual relations with
a woman.
9. As in the sign over the bootmaker's shop (depicting
a well-booted leg).
1. Sapless elder tree; impotent old man.
2. Doll may here be running her hands through Falstaff's hair.

3. The planets governing old age and love.
4. The signs of the zodiac were divided into four sets of
three (trigons). Aries, Leo, and Sagittarius are the "fiery
trigon," being hot and dry. Poins alludes to Bardolph's
red face.
5. Apparently Bardolph is wooing Quickly, here
referred to as Falstaff's confidante and the keeper of his
secrets.
6. World composed of sinful lands; a vast receptacle of
sin.

welcome to London! Now the Lord bless that sweet face of
265 thine! O Jesu, are you come from Wales?

FALSTAFF [*to* PRINCE HARRY]   Thou whoreson mad compound of
majesty! By this light°—flesh and corrupt blood, thou art wel-   *(a conventional oath)*
come.

DOLL TEARSHEET   How, you fat fool? I scorn you.

270 POINS [*to* PRINCE HARRY]   My lord, he will drive you out of your
revenge and turn all to a merriment, if you take not the heat.°   *don't act at once*

PRINCE HARRY [*to* FALSTAFF   You whoreson candlemine° you,   *storehouse of tallow*
how vilely did you speak of me now, before this honest,° virtu-   *chaste*
ous, civil gentlewoman!

275 MISTRESS QUICKLY   God's blessing of your good heart, and so she
is, by my troth!

FALSTAFF [*to* PRINCE HARRY]   Didst thou hear me?

PRINCE HARRY   Yea, and you knew me as you did when you ran
away by Gads Hill;[7] you knew I was at your back, and spoke it
280 on purpose to try my patience.

FALSTAFF   No, no, no, not so, I did not think thou wast within
hearing.

PRINCE HARRY   I shall drive you, then, to confess the wilful
abuse, and then I know how to handle you.

285 FALSTAFF   No abuse, Hal; o'mine honour, no abuse.

PRINCE HARRY   Not? To dispraise me, and call me 'pantler' and
'bread-chipper' and I know not what?

FALSTAFF   No abuse, Hal.

POINS   No abuse?

290 FALSTAFF   No abuse, Ned, i'th' world, honest Ned, none. I dis-
praised him before the wicked, that the wicked might not fall
in love with him; [*to* PRINCE HARRY] in which doing I have
done the part of a careful° friend and a true subject, and thy   *caring*
father is to give me thanks for it. No abuse, Hal; none, Ned,
295 none; no, faith, boys, none.

PRINCE HARRY   See now whether pure fear and entire cowardice
doth not make thee wrong this virtuous gentlewoman to close
with° us. Is she of the wicked? Is thine hostess here of the   *in order to pacify*
wicked? Or is thy boy of the wicked? Or honest Bardolph,
300 whose zeal burns in his nose, of the wicked?

POINS [*to* FALSTAFF]   Answer, thou dead elm, answer.

FALSTAFF   The fiend hath pricked down Bardolph irrecover-
able,[8] and his face is Lucifer's privy° kitchen, where he doth   *private*
nothing but roast malt-worms.° For the boy, there is a good   *weevils; drunkards*
305 angel about him, but the devil outbids him,° too.   *(the good angel)*

PRINCE HARRY   For the women?

FALSTAFF   For one of them, she's in hell already, and burns°   *infects with syphilis*
poor souls. For th'other, I owe her money, and whether she be
damned for that I know not.[9]

310 MISTRESS QUICKLY   No, I warrant you.

FALSTAFF   No, I think thou art not; I think thou art quit for° that.   *acquitted of*
Marry, there is another indictment upon thee, for suffering
flesh to be eaten in thy house, contrary to the law,[1] for the
which I think thou wilt howl.

7. Referring to events staged in Act 2 of *1 Henry IV*.
8. Marked Bardolph as beyond redemption.
9. Referring to the view that usury (lending money at
interest) was a sin.

1. Alluding to laws enacted against eating meat during
the Christian penitential days known as Lent as well as
to laws against the sex trade, with a pun on "house" as
"brothel."

315 MISTRESS QUICKLY All victuallers° do so. What's a joint of mut-   *innkeepers; bawds*
ton° or two in a whole Lent?   *piece of lamb; whore*
PRINCE HARRY You, gentlewoman—
DOLL TEARSHEET What says your grace?
FALSTAFF His grace says that which his flesh rebels against.[2]
PETO knocks at door [within]
320 MISTRESS QUICKLY Who knocks so loud at door? [*Calls*] Look to
th' door there, Francis.
Enter PETO
PRINCE HARRY Peto, how now, what news?
PETO The King your father is at Westminster;
And there are twenty weak and wearied posts°   *messengers*
325 Come from the north; and as I came along
I met and overtook a dozen captains,
Bareheaded, sweating, knocking at the taverns,
And asking every one for Sir John Falstaff.
PRINCE HARRY By heaven, Poins, I feel me much to blame
330 So idly to profane the precious time,
When tempest of commotion, like the south°   *the south wind*
Borne° with black vapour, doth begin to melt   *Laden*
And drop upon our bare unarmèd heads.—
Give me my sword and cloak.—Falstaff, good night.
Exeunt PRINCE [HARRY] and POINS
335 FALSTAFF Now comes in the sweetest morsel of the night, and
we must hence and leave it unpicked.
[*Knocking within. Exit BARDOLPH*]
More knocking at the door!
[*Enter BARDOLPH*]
How now, what's the matter?
BARDOLPH You must away to court, sir, presently.°   *at once*
340 A dozen captains stay° at door for you.   *wait*
FALSTAFF [*to the PAGE*] Pay the musicians, sirrah. Farewell, host-
ess; farewell, Doll. You see, my good wenches, how men of
merit are sought after. The undeserver° may sleep, when the   *unimportant officer*
man of action is called on. Farewell, good wenches. If I be not
345 sent away post,° I will see you again ere I go.   *hastily*
[*Exeunt musicians*]
DOLL TEARSHEET [*weeping*] I cannot speak. If my heart be not
ready to burst—well, sweet Jack, have a care of thyself.
FALSTAFF Farewell, farewell!
Exit [with BARDOLPH, PETO, and the PAGE]
MISTRESS QUICKLY Well, fare thee well. I have known thee these
350 twenty-nine years come peascod-time,[3] but an honester and
truer-hearted man—well, fare thee well.
[*Enter BARDOLPH*]
BARDOLPH Mistress Tearsheet!
MISTRESS QUICKLY What's the matter?
BARDOLPH Bid Mistress Tearsheet come to my master.   [*Exit*]
355 MISTRESS QUICKLY O run, Doll; run, run, good Doll!
Exeunt [DOLL at one door, MISTRESS QUICKLY at another door]

2. Implying that the Prince's virtuous speech can't hide   3. The time of year when peas form in the pod (early
a body filled with lust for Tearsheet.   spring).

3.1

Enter KING [HENRY] *in his nightgown,*° *with a page*   dressing gown
KING HENRY [*giving letters*]   Go call the Earls of Surrey and of Warwick.
    But ere they come, bid them o'er-read these letters
    And well consider of them. Make good speed.   *Exit* [*page*]
    How many thousand of my poorest subjects
5   Are at this hour asleep? O sleep, O gentle sleep,
    Nature's soft nurse, how have I frighted° thee,   frightened
    That thou no more wilt weigh my eyelids down
    And steep my senses in forgetfulness?
    Why rather, sleep, liest thou in smoky cribs,°   hovels
10   Upon uneasy pallets° stretching thee,   hard straw beds
    And hushed with buzzing night-flies to thy slumber,
    Than in the perfumed chambers of the great,
    Under the canopies of costly state,°   splendor
    And lulled with sound of sweetest melody?
15   O thou dull° god, why li'st thou with the vile°   drowsy / lowly
    In loathsome beds, and leav'st the kingly couch
    A watch-case,° or a common 'larum-bell?   sentry box
    Wilt thou upon the high and giddy mast
    Seal up the ship-boy's eyes, and rock his brains
20   In cradle of the rude° imperious surge,   rough
    And in the visitation of the winds,
    Who take the ruffian billows by the top,
    Curling their monstrous heads, and hanging them
    With deafing° clamour in the slippery clouds,   deafening
25   That, with the hurly,° death itself awakes?   tumult
    Canst thou, O partial sleep, give thy repose
    To the wet sea-boy in an hour so rude,°   wild
    And in the calmest and most stillest night,
    With all appliances° and means to boot,°   devices / as well
30   Deny it to a king? Then happy low,° lie down.   happy humble people
    Uneasy lies the head that wears a crown.
    Enter [*the Earls of*] WARWICK *and* SURREY
WARWICK   Many good morrows to your majesty!
KING HENRY   Is it good morrow, lords?
WARWICK   'Tis one o'clock, and past.
KING HENRY   Why then, good morrow to you all, my lords.
35   Have you read o'er the letter that I sent you?
WARWICK   We have, my liege.°   sovereign
KING HENRY   Then you perceive the body of our kingdom,
    How foul it is, what rank° diseases grow,   loathsome
    And with what danger near the heart of it.
40 WARWICK   It is but as a body yet distempered,°   sick
    Which to his former strength may be restored
    With good advice and little medicine.
    My lord Northumberland will soon be cooled.
KING HENRY   O God, that one might read the book of fate,
45   And see the revolution of the times[1]
    Make mountains level, and the continent,°   dry land
    Weary of solid firmness, melt itself
    Into the sea; and other times to see

3.1 Location: The palace at Westminster.   1. The changes that time will bring.

The beachy girdle of° the ocean   *girdle of beaches around*

50 Too wide for Neptune's[2] hips; how chance's mocks

And changes fill the cup of alteration

With divers° liquors![3]   *various*

52.1   *O, if this were seen,*

The happiest youth, viewing his progress through,°   *through life*

What perils past, what crosses° to ensue,   *afflictions*

Would shut the book and sit him down and die.

           'Tis not ten years gone

Since Richard and Northumberland, great friends,

Did feast together; and in two year after

55 Were they at wars. It is but eight years since

This Percy° was the man nearest my soul,   *(Northumberland)*

Who like a brother toiled in my affairs,

And laid his love and life under my foot,°   *at my disposal*

Yea, for my sake, even to° the eyes of Richard   *before*

60 Gave him defiance. But which of you was by—

[*To* WARWICK] You, cousin Neville,[4] as I may remember—

When Richard, with his eye brimful of tears,

Then checked and rated° by Northumberland,   *chided*

Did speak these words,[5] now proved a prophecy?—

65 'Northumberland, thou ladder by the which

My cousin Bolingbroke ascends my throne'—

Though then, God knows, I had no such intent,

But that necessity so bowed the state

That I and greatness were compelled to kiss—

70 'The time shall come'—thus did he follow it—

'The time will come that foul sin, gathering head,[6]

Shall break into corruption'; so went on,

Foretelling this same time's condition,

And the division of our amity.

75 WARWICK   There is a history in all men's lives

Figuring° the natures of the times deceased;°   *Showing / past*

The which observed, a man may prophesy,

With a near aim, of the main chance° of things   *general probability*

As yet not come to life, who° in their seeds   *which*

80 And weak beginnings lie intreasurèd.°   *stored*

Such things become the hatch and brood° of time;   *progeny and offspring*

And by the necessary form of this[7]

King Richard might create a perfect guess

That great Northumberland, then false to him,

85 Would of that seed grow to a greater falseness,

Which should not find a ground to root upon

Unless on you.

KING HENRY   Are these things then necessities?

Then let us meet them like necessities;

2. In classical mythology, the god of the sea. Here the seashore is depicted as a girdle worn by Neptune. That the girdle is too wide or too large indicates that the sea is retreating from the land, in contrast to the prior image of land being absorbed into the ocean.
3. The following three and a half lines (52.1–52.4) do not appear in F, though they are in the 1600 quarto version of the play.
4. An apparent error. The King is addressing the Earl

of Warwick, whose surname was Beauchamp, not Neville. Shakespeare may be confusing him with Richard Neville, an important character in his plays on the life of Henry VI.
5. See *Richard II* 5.1, in which similar lines are spoken, though neither Bolingbroke nor Warwick was present.
6. Coming to maturity; coming to a head, like pus on a sore.
7. And by this requisite pattern (of cause and effect).

And that same word even now cries out on° us.   *denounces*
90   They say the Bishop and Northumberland
    Are fifty thousand strong.
WARWICK   It cannot be, my lord.
    Rumour doth double, like the voice and echo,
    The numbers of the feared. Please it your grace
    To go to bed? Upon my soul, my lord,
95   The powers that you already have sent forth
    Shall bring this prize in very easily.
    To comfort you the more, I have received
    A certain instance° that Glyndŵr is dead.   *proof*
    Your majesty hath been this fortnight ill,
100 And these unseasoned° hours perforce must add   *irregular*
    Unto your sickness.
KING HENRY   I will take your counsel.
    And were these inward° wars once out of hand,   *civil*
    We would, dear lords, unto the Holy Land.   *Exeunt*

3.2

Enter Justice SHALLOW *and Justice* SILENCE

SHALLOW   Come on, come on, come on! Give me your hand,
    sir, give me your hand, sir. An early stirrer, by the rood!° And   *cross*
    how doth my good cousin° Silence?   *kinsman*
SILENCE   Good morrow, good cousin Shallow.
5 SHALLOW   And how doth my cousin your bedfellow? And your
    fairest daughter and mine, my god-daughter Ellen?
SILENCE   Alas, a black ouzel,¹ cousin Shallow.
SHALLOW   By yea and no, sir, I dare say my cousin William is
    become a good scholar. He is at Oxford still, is he not?
10 SILENCE   Indeed, sir, to my cost.
SHALLOW   A° must then to the Inns o' Court² shortly. I was once   *He*
    of Clement's Inn,³ where I think they will talk of mad Shallow
    yet.
SILENCE   You were called 'lusty Shallow' then, cousin.
15 SHALLOW   By the mass, I was called anything; and I would have
    done anything indeed, too, and roundly,° too. There was I, and   *thoroughly*
    little John Doit of Staffordshire, and black George Barnes, and
    Francis Pickbone, and Will Squeal, a Cotswold man; you had
    not four such swinge-bucklers° in all the Inns o' Court again.   *swashbucklers*
20   And I may say to you, we knew where the bona-robas° were,   *well-dressed prostitutes*
    and had the best of them all at commandment. Then was Jack
    Falstaff, now Sir John, a boy, and page to Thomas Mowbray,
    Duke of Norfolk.
SILENCE   This Sir John, cousin, that comes hither anon° about   *soon*
25   soldiers?
SHALLOW   The same Sir John, the very same. I see him break
    Scoggin's⁴ head at the court gate when a was a crack,° not thus   *young fellow*
    high. And the very same day did I fight with one Samson Stock-

---

3.2 Location: Outside Justice Shallow's house in
Gloucestershire.
1. Blackbird. Women with black hair and/or complex-
ions were often viewed as "foul" rather than "fair."
2. Prestigious legal schools in London that admitted
men to the bar.

3. One of the Inns of Chancery, less prestigious legal
colleges.
4. A buffoon (possibly referring to Edward IV's court
jester of that name and famous as the main character
of *Scogin's Jests*, a popular Elizabethan jestbook).

fish, a fruiterer, behind Gray's Inn.[5] Jesu, Jesu, the mad days
30   that I have spent! And to see how many of my old acquaintance
are dead.

SILENCE   We shall all follow, cousin.

SHALLOW   Certain, 'tis certain; very sure, very sure. Death, as the
Psalmist saith, is certain to all; all shall die. How° a good yoke   *What's the price of*
35   of bullocks at Stamford fair?

SILENCE   By my troth, I was not there.

SHALLOW   Death is certain. Is old Double of your town living
yet?

SILENCE   Dead, sir.

40   SHALLOW   Jesu, Jesu, dead! A° drew a good bow; and dead! A   *He*
shot a fine shoot. John o' Gaunt° loved him well, and betted   *(Henry IV's father)*
much money on his head. Dead! A would have clapped i'th'
clout at twelve score,[6] and carried you a forehand shaft a fourteen and fourteen and a half,[7] that it would have done a man's
45   heart good to see. How a score of ewes now?

SILENCE   Thereafter as they be.[8] A score of good ewes may be
worth ten pounds.

SHALLOW   And is old Double dead?

Enter BARDOLPH *and* [*the* PAGE][9]

SILENCE   Here come two of Sir John Falstaff's men, as I think.

50   SHALLOW   Good morrow, honest gentlemen.

BARDOLPH   I beseech you, which is Justice Shallow?

SHALLOW   I am Robert Shallow, sir, a poor esquire of this county,
and one of the King's Justices of the Peace. What is your good
pleasure with me?

55   BARDOLPH   My captain, sir, commends him° to you—my captain   *sends his respects*
Sir John Falstaff, a tall° gentleman, by heaven, and a most gal-   *valiant*
lant leader.

SHALLOW   He greets me well, sir. I knew him a good backsword
man.° How doth the good knight? May I ask how my lady his   *fencer*
60   wife doth?

BARDOLPH   Sir, pardon, a soldier is better accommodated than
with a wife.

SHALLOW   It is well said, in faith, sir, and it is well said indeed,
too. 'Better accommodated'—it is good; yea, indeed is it. Good
65   phrases are surely, and ever were, very commendable. 'Accommodated'—it comes of '*accommodo*'. Very good, a good phrase.

BARDOLPH   Pardon, sir, I have heard the word—'phrase' call you
it?—By this day, I know not the phrase; but I will maintain the
word with my sword to be a soldier-like word, and a word of
70   exceeding good command,° by heaven. 'Accommodated'; that   *fit for many uses*
is, when a man is, as they say, accommodated; or when a man
is being whereby a may be thought to be accommodated;
which is an excellent thing.

Enter Sir John FALSTAFF

SHALLOW   It is very just.° Look, here comes good Sir John. [*To*   *true*
75   FALSTAFF] Give me your hand, give me your worship's good

5. One of the Inns of Court.
6. Hit the target from 240 yards.
7. He could shoot an arrow straight, to 280 or 290
yards. A "forehand shaft" is an arrow shot in a straight
line rather than with the curved trajectory common for
long shots.
8. The price depends on their quality.

9. In F, Bardolph enters with "his Boy." In Q, he enters
"and one with him." It is reasonable to assume, but not
certain, that Falstaff's page is Bardolph's companion.
The use of a boy actor for this part would allow the
number of adult actors required for the rest of the
scene to be reduced by one.

hand. By my troth, you like well,° and bear your years very well.   *you are thriving*
Welcome, good Sir John.

FALSTAFF I am glad to see you well, good Master Robert Shallow. [*To* SILENCE] Master Surecard, as I think.

80 SHALLOW No, Sir John, it is my cousin Silence, in commission[1]
with me.

FALSTAFF Good Master Silence, it well befits you should be of
the peace.

SILENCE Your good worship is welcome.

85 FALSTAFF Fie, this is hot weather, gentlemen. Have you provided me here half a dozen sufficient° men?   *able*

SHALLOW Marry, have we, sir. Will you sit?

FALSTAFF Let me see them, I beseech you.
    [*He sits*]

SHALLOW Where's the roll,° where's the roll, where's the roll?   *list*

90 Let me see, let me see, let me see; so, so, so, so, so. Yea, marry,
sir: 'Ralph Mouldy'. [*To* SILENCE] Let them appear as I call,
let them do so, let them do so. Let me see, [*calls*] where is
Mouldy?
    [*Enter* MOULDY][2]

MOULDY Here, an't please you.

95 SHALLOW What think you, Sir John? A good-limbed fellow,
young, strong, and of good friends.°   *well connected*

FALSTAFF Is thy name Mouldy?

MOULDY Yea, an't please you.

FALSTAFF 'Tis the more time° thou wert used.   *well past time*

100 SHALLOW Ha, ha, ha, most excellent, i'faith! Things that are
mouldy lack use. Very singular good, in faith, well said, Sir
John, very well said.

FALSTAFF Prick him.°   *Mark his name*

MOULDY I was pricked[3] well enough before, an you could have

105 let me alone. My old dame° will be undone now for one to do   *wife*
her husbandry[4] and her drudgery. You need not to have
pricked me; there are other men fitter to go out than I.

FALSTAFF Go to, peace, Mouldy. You shall go, Mouldy; it is
time you were spent.°   *used up*

110 MOULDY Spent?

SHALLOW Peace, fellow, peace. Stand aside; know you where
you are?
    [MOULDY *stands aside*]
For th'other, Sir John, let me see: 'Simon Shadow'—

FALSTAFF Yea, marry, let me have him to sit under. He's like to

115 be a cold° soldier.   *dead; cowardly*

SHALLOW [*calls*] Where's Shadow?
    [*Enter* SHADOW]

SHADOW Here, sir.

FALSTAFF Shadow, whose son art thou?

SHADOW My mother's son, sir.

120 FALSTAFF Thy mother's son! Like enough, and thy father's
shadow.° So the son of the female is the shadow° of the male—   *likeness / faint copy*

---

1. Having a position (as justice of the peace).
2. In F, the recruits enter at the beginning of the scene with Silence and Shallow. But they have nothing to do until this point in the scene. It is better to have them all enter with Mouldy and be called forward one by one, or,
as here, to enter separately as each name is called.
3. Vexed; provided with a penis.
4. Will be lacking someone to perform the sexual duties of a husband; will be lacking someone to do the work of the farm.

it is often so indeed—but not of the father's substance.[5]

SHALLOW Do you like him, Sir John?

FALSTAFF Shadow will serve for summer. Prick him, for we have
125 a number of shadows[6] fill up the muster book.

    [SHADOW *stands aside*]

SHALLOW [*calls*] 'Thomas Wart.'

FALSTAFF Where's he?

    [*Enter* WART]

WART Here, sir.

FALSTAFF Is thy name Wart?

130 WART Yea, sir.

FALSTAFF Thou art a very ragged wart.

SHALLOW Shall I prick him, Sir John?

FALSTAFF It were superfluous, for his apparel is built° upon his   *pieced together*
back, and the whole frame stands upon pins.[7] Prick him no
135 more.

SHALLOW Ha, ha, ha, you can do it, sir, you can do it! I commend you well.

    [WART *stands aside*]

[*Calls*] 'Francis Feeble.'

    [*Enter* FEEBLE]

FEEBLE Here, sir.

140 SHALLOW What trade art thou, Feeble?

FEEBLE A woman's tailor,[8] sir.

SHALLOW Shall I prick him, sir?

FALSTAFF You may, but if he had been a man's tailor, he'd ha'
pricked[9] you. [*To* FEEBLE] Wilt thou make as many holes in an
145 enemy's battle° as thou hast done in a woman's petticoat?   *army*

FEEBLE I will do my good will,° sir; you can have no more.   *do my best*

FALSTAFF Well said, good woman's tailor; well said, courageous
Feeble! Thou wilt be as valiant as the wrathful dove or most
magnanimous° mouse. Prick the woman's tailor. Well, Master   *brave*
150 Shallow; deep, Master Shallow.

FEEBLE I would Wart might have gone, sir.

FALSTAFF I would thou wert a man's tailor, that thou mightst
mend him and make him fit to go.° I cannot put him to a   *to serve; to have sex*
private soldier[1] that is the leader of so many thousands.° Let   *(of lice)*
155 that suffice, most forcible Feeble.

FEEBLE It shall suffice, sir.

FALSTAFF I am bound to thee, reverend Feeble.

    [FEEBLE *stands aside*]

Who is next?

SHALLOW [*calls*] 'Peter Bullcalf o'th' green.'

160 FALSTAFF Yea, marry, let's see Bullcalf.

    [*Enter* BULLCALF]

BULLCALF Here, sir.

FALSTAFF Fore God, a likely° fellow! Come, prick Bullcalf till   *promising*
he roar again.

---

5. Not born from the father's body (because born from the mother's); not the father's true son.

6. Fictitious names that officers recorded in order to collect additional pay from the crown.

7. The whole structure depends upon pegs ("pins"); stands upon legs ("pins").

8. Women's tailors were bywords for effeminacy and cowardice.

9. Dressed; stabbed; penetrated.

1. Make him a private soldier; offer him sexually to a private soldier.

BULLCALF   O Lord, good my lord captain!
165 FALSTAFF   What, dost thou roar before thou'rt pricked?
BULLCALF   O Lord, sir, I am a diseased man.
FALSTAFF   What disease hast thou?
BULLCALF   A whoreson cold, sir; a cough, sir, which I caught
with ringing in the King's affairs[2] upon his coronation day, sir.
170 FALSTAFF   Come, thou shalt go to the wars in a gown.° We will   *dressing gown*
have away° thy cold, and I will take such order° that thy friends   *get rid / measures*
shall ring for thee.[3]
          [BULLCALF *stands aside*]
Is here all?
SHALLOW   There is two more called than your number. You
175 must have but four here,[4] sir, and so I pray you go in with me
to dinner.
FALSTAFF   Come, I will go drink with you, but I cannot tarry°   *stay for*
dinner. I am glad to see you, by my troth, Master Shallow.
SHALLOW   O, Sir John, do you remember since we lay all night
180 in the Windmill in Saint George's Field?[5]
FALSTAFF   No more of that, good Master Shallow, no more of
that.
SHALLOW   Ha, 'twas a merry night! And is Jane Nightwork alive?
FALSTAFF   She lives, Master Shallow.
185 SHALLOW   She never could away with° me.   *tolerate*
FALSTAFF   Never, never. She would always say she could not
abide Master Shallow.
SHALLOW   By the mass, I could anger her to th' heart. She was
then a bona-roba. Doth she hold her own well?
190 FALSTAFF   Old, old, Master Shallow.
SHALLOW   Nay, she must be old; she cannot choose but be old;
certain she's old; and had Robin Nightwork by old Nightwork
before I came to Clement's Inn.
SILENCE   That's fifty-five year ago.
195 SHALLOW   Ha, cousin Silence, that thou hadst seen that that this
knight and I have seen! Ha, Sir John, said I well?
FALSTAFF   We have heard the chimes at midnight, Master
Shallow.
SHALLOW   That we have, that we have, that we have; in faith, Sir John, we
200 have. Our watchword was 'Hem° boys!' Come, let's to dinner;   *Drink up*
come, let's to dinner. Jesus, the days that we have seen! Come,
come.   *Exeunt* [SHALLOW, SILENCE, *and* FALSTAFF]
BULLCALF [*coming forward*]   Good Master Corporate° Bardolph,   *(for "Corporal")*
stand° my friend, and here's four Harry ten shillings in French   *act as*
205 crowns for you.[6] In very truth, sir, I had as lief° be hanged, sir,   *willingly*
as go. And yet for mine own part, sir, I do not care; but rather
because I am unwilling, and, for mine own part, have a desire
to stay with my friends. Else, sir, I did not care, for mine own
part, so much.
210 BARDOLPH [*taking the money*]   Go to; stand aside.
          [BULLCALF *stands aside*]

2. Ringing the church bells in the King's honor.
3. In your place; at your death.
4. An inconsistency: there have been five, not six, recruits called.
5. A region of London south of the Thames near Southwark, known as a market for sex. "The Windmill" was the name of a brothel or an inn.

6. An elaborate way of offering a bribe. The reference to "Harry ten shillings" is anachronistic; shillings originated during Henry VII's reign and by the 1590s had been devalued to half their original worth. Therefore, Bullcalf is offering about 1 pound to be paid in French crowns (coins worth 4 shillings each).

MOULDY [*coming forward*] And, good Master Corporal Captain, for my old dame's sake stand my friend. She has nobody to do anything about her when I am gone, and she is old and cannot help herself. You shall have forty,° sir.   *(shillings)*

215 BARDOLPH Go to; stand aside.

[MOULDY *stands aside*]

FEEBLE By my troth, I care not. A man can die but once. We owe God a death. I'll ne'er bear a base mind. An't be my destiny, so; an't be not, so. No man's too good to serve's° prince.   *serve his* And let it go which way it will, he that dies this year is quit for°   *released from* (*dying*)

220 the next.

BARDOLPH Well said; thou'rt a good fellow.

FEEBLE Faith, I'll bear no base mind.

Enter [Sir John] FALSTAFF[, SHALLOW, *and* SILENCE]

FALSTAFF Come, sir, which men shall I have?

SHALLOW Four of which you please.

225 BARDOLPH [*to* FALSTAFF] Sir, a word with you. [*Aside to him*] I have three pound to free Mouldy and Bullcalf.

FALSTAFF Go to, well.

SHALLOW Come, Sir John, which four will you have?

FALSTAFF Do you choose for me.

230 SHALLOW Marry, then: Mouldy, Bullcalf, Feeble, and Shadow.

FALSTAFF Mouldy and Bullcalf. For you, Mouldy, stay at home till you are past service;[7] and for your part, Bullcalf, grow till you come unto it.[8] I will none of you.

[*Exeunt* BULLCALF *and* MOULDY]

SHALLOW Sir John, Sir John, do not yourself wrong. They are

235 your likeliest men, and I would have you served with the best.

FALSTAFF Will you tell me, Master Shallow, how to choose a man? Care I for the limb, the thews,° the stature, bulk, and big   *strength* assemblance° of a man? Give me the spirit, Master Shallow.   *composition* Here's Wart; you see what a ragged appearance it is? A shall

240 charge you and discharge you° with the motion of a pewterer's   *load and fire* hammer,° come off and on swifter than he that gibbets on the   *with a steady motion* brewer's bucket.[9] And this same half-faced° fellow Shadow;   *thin-faced* give me this man. He presents no mark° to the enemy; the   *target* foeman may with as great aim level at° the edge of a penknife.   *fire against*

245 And for a retreat, how swiftly will this Feeble the woman's tailor run off! O, give me the spare men, and spare me the great ones.—Put me a caliver° into Wart's hand, Bardolph.   *musket*

BARDOLPH [*giving* WART *a caliver*] Hold, Wart. Traverse°—thas,   *March* thas, thas!

[WART *marches*]

250 FALSTAFF [*to* WART] Come, manage me your caliver. So; very well. Go to, very good, exceeding good. O, give me always a little, lean, old, chapped, bald shot!° Well said, i'faith, Wart;   *marksman* thou'rt a good scab. Hold; [*giving a coin*] there's a tester° for   *sixpence* thee.

255 SHALLOW He is not his craft's master; he doth not do it right. I remember at Mile-End Green,[1] when I lay° at Clement's   *lodged*

---

7. Past the time of military duty; past the time of sexual potency.

8. That is, grow until you come into the time of military service; the time of sexual potency. Falstaff plays on the fact that Bullcalf is a *calf*, not a *bull*.

9. Retreat and advance, or raise and lower your gun, faster than he who hangs pails on each end of the wooden bar (gibbet) that a brewer carries on his shoulders.

1. Open land east of London used as a training ground for citizen militias and for fairs and shows.

Inn—I was then Sir Dagonet in Arthur's show²—there was a
little quiver° fellow, and a would manage you his piece thus, *nimble*
and a would about and about, and come you in° and come you *thrust at you*
in. 'Ra-ta-ta!' would a say; 'Bounce!'° would a say; and away *Bang*
again would a go; and again would a come. I shall ne'er see
such a fellow.

FALSTAFF These fellows will do well, Master Shallow. God keep
you, Master Silence; I will not use many words with you. Fare
you well, gentlemen both; I thank you. I must° a dozen mile *must go*
tonight.—Bardolph, give the soldiers coats.

SHALLOW Sir John, the Lord bless you; God prosper your affairs!
God send us peace! As you return, visit my house; let our old
acquaintance be renewed. Peradventure I will with ye to the
court.

FALSTAFF Fore God, would you would!

SHALLOW Go to, I have spoke at a word.° God keep you! *spoken sincerely*

FALSTAFF Fare you well, gentle gentlemen.

Exeunt [SHALLOW *and* SILENCE]

On, Bardolph, lead the men away.

[*Exeunt* BARDOLPH, WART, SHADOW, *and* FEEBLE]

As I return, I will fetch off° these justices. I do see the bottom *defraud*
of Justice Shallow. Lord, Lord, how subject we old men are to
this vice of lying! This same starved justice hath done nothing
but prate to me of the wildness of his youth and the feats he
hath done about Turnbull Street;³ and every third word a lie,
duer paid° to the hearer than the Turk's tribute.⁴ I do remem- *sooner paid*
ber him at Clement's Inn, like a man made after supper of a
cheese paring. When a was naked, he was for all the world like
a forked radish,⁵ with a head fantastically carved upon it with a
knife. A was so forlorn° that his dimensions, to any thick° sight, *thin / imperfect*
were invisible. A was the very genius° of famine.⁶ *spirit*

> *yet lecherous as a monkey; and the whores called him*
> *'mandrake'. A came ever in the rearward of the fashion,*
> *and sung those tunes to the overscutched hussies°* that *worn-out whores*
> *he heard the carmen° whistle, and sware they were his* *wagoners*
> *fancies or his good-nights.°* *his own love songs*

And now is this Vice's dagger⁷ become a squire, and talks as familiarly of John o' Gaunt as if he had been sworn brother to him,
and I'll be sworn a ne'er saw him but once, in the Tilt-yard,° *tournament arena*
and then he° burst his° head for crowding among the marshal's *(Gaunt) / (Shallow's)*
men. I saw it, and told John o' Gaunt he beat his own
name;⁸ for you might have trussed° him and all his apparel into *packed*
an eel-skin. The case of a treble hautboy° was a mansion for *oboe*
him, a court. And now has he land and beeves.° Well, I'll be *oxen*
acquainted with him if I return; and't shall go hard but I'll
make him a philosopher's two stones to me.⁹ If the young dace° *small fish*

---

2. Referring to his role as King Arthur's fool in an
archery pageant in which each participant took the
name of one of the knights of the Round Table.
3. An area of Smithfield associated with criminal activities.
4. Money extracted from those the Turkish Sultan conquered or who engaged in trade with him. The penalty
for failure to pay was death, so presumably money was
paid punctually. Shallow is even quicker to tell lies.
5. A mandrake root, said to resemble a man's body. See

note to 1.2.12.
6. The following inset lines (285.1–285.5) appear in Q
but not in F.
7. The wooden dagger used by the Vice, a comic character in medieval morality plays.
8. Attacked someone very gaunt or thin.
9. I'll make him twice as valuable to me as the philosopher's stone that was supposed to transmute base
metals into gold, with a pun on "stones" as meaning
"testicles."

be a bait for the old pike, I see no reason in the law of nature
but I may snap at him. Let time shape, and there an end.

Exit

4.1

Enter [in arms] the ARCHBISHOP [*of York*], [*Thomas*]
MOWBRAY, [*Lord*] HASTINGS, [*and*] COLEVILLE[1] *within
the Forest of Gaultres*[2]

ARCHBISHOP OF YORK   What is this forest called?

HASTINGS   'Tis Gaultres Forest, an't° shall please your grace. *if it*

ARCHBISHOP OF YORK   Here stand, my lords, and send discoverers° forth *scouts*
To know the numbers of our enemies.

HASTINGS   We have sent forth already.

5   ARCHBISHOP OF YORK   'Tis well done.
My friends and brethren in these great affairs,
I must acquaint you that I have received
New-dated° letters from Northumberland, *Recent*
Their cold intent, tenor, and substance, thus:

10   Here doth he wish his person, with such powers
As might hold sortance° with his quality,° *accord / rank*
The which he could not levy; whereupon
He is retired to ripe° his growing fortunes *ripen*
To Scotland, and concludes in hearty prayers

15   That your attempts may overlive the hazard
And fearful meeting of their opposite.° *enemy*

MOWBRAY   Thus do the hopes we have in him touch ground
And dash themselves to pieces.

Enter a MESSENGER

HASTINGS   Now, what news?

MESSENGER   West of this forest, scarcely off a mile,

20   In goodly form° comes on the enemy; *battle array*
And, by the ground they hide,° I judge their number *cover*
Upon or near the rate of thirty thousand.

MOWBRAY   The just proportion° that we gave them out.° *exact size / estimated*
Let us sway on, and face them in the field.

Enter [the Earl] of WESTMORLAND

25   ARCHBISHOP OF YORK   What well-appointed leader fronts° us here? *confronts*

MOWBRAY   I think it is my lord of Westmorland.

WESTMORLAND   Health and fair greeting from our general,
The Prince, Lord John and Duke of Lancaster.

ARCHBISHOP OF YORK   Say on, my lord of Westmorland, in peace,
What doth concern your coming.

30   WESTMORLAND   Then, my lord,
Unto your grace do I in chief address
The substance of my speech. If that rebellion
Came like itself, in base and abject routs,° *lowborn disorderly bands*
Led on by bloody youth, guarded° with rags, *adorned*

35   And countenanced° by boys and beggary; *approved*
I say, if damned commotion so appeared

4.1 Location: Gaultres Forest in Yorkshire.
1. In F, this initial stage direction includes Westmorland, who actually enters later in the scene, and
Coleville, a rebel captured by Falstaff in 4.2. Most editors delete both figures from the initial stage direction.
The Oxford editors speculate that Coleville is the captain

who at 4.1.295–97 is sent to tell the rebel army to disperse after peace is made, so they include him in the
scene from the beginning.
2. Gaultres was a royal forest north and west of York.
In Holinshed's *Chronicles* and in Q and F, it is spelled
"Gaultree," a spelling adopted in most editions.

In his true native and most proper shape,
You, reverend father, and these noble lords
Had not been here to dress the ugly form
40   Of base and bloody insurrection
With your fair honours. You, Lord Archbishop,
Whose see° is by a civil peace maintained,   *diocese*
Whose beard the silver hand of peace hath touched,
Whose learning and good letters° peace hath tutored,   *scholarship*
45   Whose white investments figure° innocence,   *robes represent*
The dove and very blessèd spirit of peace,
Wherefore do you so ill translate° yourself   *transform*
Out of the speech of peace that bears such grace
Into the harsh and boist'rous tongue of war,
50   Turning your books to graves, your ink to blood,
Your pens to lances, and your tongue divine
To a loud trumpet and a point° of war?   *signal*
ARCHBISHOP OF YORK   Wherefore do I this? So the question stands.
Briefly, to this end: we are all diseased,³
55   And with our surfeiting° and wanton hours   *overfeeding*
Have brought ourselves into a burning fever,
And we must bleed° for it—of which disease   *be bled as a cure*
Our late King Richard, being infected, died.
But, my most noble lord of Westmorland,
60   I take not on me here as a physician,
Nor do I as an enemy to peace
Troop in the throngs of military men;
But rather show° a while like fearful war   *appear*
To diet rank° minds, sick of happiness,   *swollen; overindulged*
65   And purge th'obstructions which begin to stop
Our very veins of life. Hear me more plainly.
I have in equal balance justly weighed
What wrongs our arms may do, what wrongs we suffer,
And find our griefs heavier than our offences.
70   We see which way the stream of time doth run,
And are enforced from our most quiet shore
By the rough torrent of occasion;°   *events*
And have the summary of all our griefs,
When time shall serve, to show in articles,°   *an itemized list*
75   Which long ere this we offered to the King,
And might by no suit gain our audience.
When we are wronged, and would unfold our griefs,
We are denied access unto his person
Even by those men that most have done us wrong.
80   The dangers of the days but newly gone,
Whose memory is written on the earth
With yet° appearing blood, and the examples   *still*
Of every minute's instance,° present now,   *Occurring every minute*
Hath put us in these ill-beseeming° arms,   *unsuitable*
85   Not to break peace, or any branch of it,
But to establish here a peace indeed,
Concurring both in name and quality.
WESTMORLAND   Whenever yet was your appeal denied?

---

3. Lines 55–79 are missing from Q, perhaps because they state the case for rebellion too forcefully.

Wherein have you been gallèd° by the King?   *vexed; grieved*
90 What peer hath been suborned to grate on° you,   *induced to annoy*
That you should seal° this lawless bloody book   *license*
Of forged rebellion with a seal divine?[4]
ARCHBISHOP OF YORK   My brother general, the commonwealth
I make my quarrel in particular.[5]
95 WESTMORLAND   There is no need of any such redress;
Or if there were, it not belongs to you.
MOWBRAY   Why not to him in part, and to us all
That feel the bruises of the days before,
And suffer the condition of these times
100 To lay a heavy and unequal° hand   *unjust*
Upon our honours?[6]
WESTMORLAND   O my good Lord Mowbray,
Construe the times to° their necessities,   *according to*
And you shall say indeed it is the time,
And not the King, that doth you injuries.
105 Yet for your part, it not appears° to me,   *it does not appear*
Either from the King or in the present time,
That you should have an inch of any ground
To build a grief on. Were you not restored
To all the Duke of Norfolk's signories,°   *properties*
110 Your noble and right well-remembered father's?
MOWBRAY   What thing in honour had my father lost
That need to be revived and breathed° in me?   *brought to life*
The King that loved him, as the state stood then,
Was force perforce° compelled to banish him;   *against his will*
115 And then that Henry Bolingbroke and he,
Being mounted and both rousèd° in their seats,   *raised*
Their neighing coursers daring of the spur,[7]
Their armèd staves in charge,[8] their beavers° down,   *helmet visors*
Their eyes of fire sparkling through sights° of steel,   *visor slits*
120 And the loud trumpet blowing them together,
Then, then, when there was nothing could have stayed°   *kept*
My father from the breast of Bolingbroke—
O, when the King did throw his warder° down,   *staff of command*
His own life hung upon the staff he threw;
125 Then threw he down himself and all their lives
That by indictment° and by dint of sword   *legal accusations*
Have since miscarried under Bolingbroke.
WESTMORLAND   You speak, Lord Mowbray, now you know not what.
The Earl of Hereford° was reputed then   *(Bolingbroke)*
130 In England the most valiant gentleman.
Who knows on whom fortune would then have smiled?
But if your father had been victor there,
He ne'er had borne it out of Coventry;[9]
For all the country in a general voice
135 Cried hate upon him, and all their prayers and love

4. Alluding to bishops as official licensers of books with the ability to exercise censorship. Westmorland accuses the Archbishop of *not* censoring the book of rebellion.
5. *My . . . particular*: these two lines are obscure. York seems to be saying he is making the cause of the commonwealth his own because all men are his brothers.
6. The second half of line 101 and lines 102–37 do not appear in Q. They recount a version of events depicted in Shakespeare's *Richard II* in which Richard stopped a formal combat between Thomas Mowbray, father of the Mowbray of this play, and Bolingbroke, now Henry IV.
7. Daring the spur to prick them forward.
8. Their steel-tipped lances ready for the charge.
9. He never would have carried away the prize from Coventry (where the duel was to take place).

Were set on Hereford, whom they doted on
And blessed and graced, indeed, more than the King.
But this is mere digression from my purpose.
Here come I from our princely general
140   To know your griefs, to tell you from his grace
That he will give you audience; and wherein
It shall appear that your demands are just,
You shall enjoy them, everything set off°   *forgotten*
That might so much as think you enemies.
145 MOWBRAY   But he hath forced us to compel this offer,
And it proceeds from policy,° not love.   *political cunning*
WESTMORLAND   Mowbray, you overween° to take it so.   *presume too much*
This offer comes from mercy, not from fear;
For lo, within a ken° our army lies,   *the field of vision*
150   Upon mine honour, all too confident
To give admittance to a thought of fear.
Our battle° is more full of names° than yours,   *army / titled men*
Our men more perfect in the use of arms,
Our armour all as strong, our cause the best.
155   Then reason will° our hearts should be as good.   *it follows that*
Say you not then our offer is compelled.
MOWBRAY   Well, by my will we shall admit no parley.°   *discussion of terms*
WESTMORLAND   That argues but the shame of your offence.
A rotten case° abides no handling.   *cause*
160 HASTINGS   Hath the Prince John a full commission,
In very ample virtue° of his father,   *With full authority*
To hear and absolutely to determine
Of what° conditions we shall stand upon?   *whatever*
WESTMORLAND   That is intended° in the general's name.   *indicated*
165   I muse° you make so slight a question.   *wonder*
ARCHBISHOP OF YORK   Then take, my lord of Westmorland, this schedule;°   *document*
For this contains our general grievances.
Each several° article herein redressed,   *individual*
All members of our cause, both here and hence,
170   That are ensinewed° to this action   *tightly bound (by sinews)*
Acquitted° by a true substantial form,°   *Pardoned / binding act*
And present execution of our wills
To us and to our purposes consigned,[1]
We come within our awe-full banks again,[2]
175   And knit our powers to the arm of peace.
WESTMORLAND [*taking the schedule*]   This will I show the general.
       Please you, lords,
In sight of both our battles we may meet,
And either end in peace—which God so frame°—   *bring to pass*
Or to the place of diff'rence° call the swords   *conflict*
Which must decide it.
180 ARCHBISHOP OF YORK   My lord, we will do so.   *Exit* WESTMORLAND
MOWBRAY   There is a thing within my bosom tells me
That no conditions of our peace can stand.
HASTINGS   Fear you not that. If we can make our peace

---

1. *And . . . consigned:* And immediate ("present") fulfillment of our demands allowed us. The emendation to "consigned" of Q's and F's "confinde" allows three parallel clauses to follow one another, each dealing with one of the rebels' conditions for putting down their arms.
2. We come again within the bounds of respect (with the suggestion of a flooded river returning to its banks).

Upon such large° terms and so absolute   *liberal*
185 As our conditions shall consist° upon,   *insist*
Our peace shall stand as firm as rocky mountains.
MOWBRAY   Yea, but our valuation° shall be such   *the value we are held in*
That every slight and false-derivèd° cause,   *wrongly attributed*
Yea, every idle, nice,° and wanton° reason,   *petty / frivolous*
190 Shall to the King taste of this action,°   *(of rebellion)*
That, were our royal faiths martyrs in love,[3]
We shall be winnowed with so rough a wind
That even our corn shall seem as light as chaff,
And good from bad find no partition.°   *distinction*
195 ARCHBISHOP OF YORK   No, no, my lord; note this. The King is weary
Of dainty and such picking° grievances,   *trivial*
For he hath found to end one doubt° by death   *fear*
Revives two greater in the heirs of life;
And therefore will he wipe his tables° clean,   *tablets*
200 And keep no tell-tale to his memory
That may repeat and history° his loss   *retell*
To new remembrance; for full well he knows
He cannot so precisely weed this land
As his misdoubts° present occasion.   *suspicions*
205 His foes are so enrooted with his friends
That, plucking to unfix an enemy,
He doth unfasten so and shake a friend;
So that this land, like an offensive wife
That hath enraged him on to offer strokes,°   *attempt beatings*
210 As he is striking, holds his infant up,
And hangs resolved correction in the arm
That was upreared to execution.[4]
HASTINGS   Besides, the King hath wasted all his rods°   *means of punishment*
On late° offenders, that he now doth lack   *recent*
215 The very instruments of chastisement;
So that his power, like to a fangless lion,
May offer,° but not hold.   *threaten*
ARCHBISHOP OF YORK   'Tis very true.
And therefore be assured, my good Lord Marshal,
If we do now make our atonement° well,   *reconciliation*
220 Our peace will, like a broken limb united,
Grow stronger for the breaking.
MOWBRAY   Be it so.
     Enter WESTMORLAND
Here is returned my lord of Westmorland.
WESTMORLAND   The Prince is here at hand. Pleaseth your lordship
To meet his grace just° distance 'tween our armies?   *equal*
225 MOWBRAY   Your grace of York, in God's name then set forward.
ARCHBISHOP OF YORK   Before, and greet his grace!—My lord, we come.
     [*They march over the stage.*]
     Enter PRINCE JOHN [*with one or more soldiers carrying wine*]
PRINCE JOHN   You are well encountered here, my cousin Mowbray.
Good day to you, gentle lord Archbishop;

3. So that even if our loyalty to the King made us lov-   4. *And . . . execution:* And so punishment that was
ing martyrs.   about to be executed is held in suspended action.

And so to you, Lord Hastings, and to all.
230　My lord of York, it better showed with you
　　When that your flock, assembled by the bell,
　　Encircled you to hear with reverence
　　Your exposition on the holy text,
　　Than now to see you here an iron° man,　　　　　　　　　*armored; a fierce*
235　Cheering a rout° of rebels with your drum,　　　　　　　*disorderly band*
　　Turning the word° to sword, and life to death.　　　　　　*(Scripture)*
　　That man that sits within a monarch's heart
　　And ripens in the sunshine of his favour,
　　Would he° abuse the countenance° of the King,　　　*Should he / favor*
240　Alack, what mischiefs might he set abroach°　　　　　　　*afoot*
　　In shadow° of such greatness! With you, Lord Bishop,　　*Under cover*
　　It is even so. Who hath not heard it spoken
　　How deep you were within the books of God—
　　To us, the speaker in his° parliament,　　　　　　　　　*(God's)*
245　To us, th'imagined voice of God himself,
　　The very opener° and intelligencer°　　　　　　*interpreter / informer*
　　Between the grace, the sanctities of heaven
　　And our dull workings?° O, who shall believe　　　*ignorant thoughts*
　　But you misuse the reverence of your place,
250　Employ the countenance and grace of heav'n
　　As a false favourite doth his prince's name
　　In deeds dishonourable? You have ta'en up,°　　　　　*enlisted*
　　Under the counterfeited zeal of⁵ God,
　　The subjects of his substitute, my father;
255　And, both against the peace of heaven and him,
　　Have here upswarmèd them.⁶

ARCHBISHOP OF YORK　　　　　　　　Good my lord of Lancaster,
　　I am not here against your father's peace;
　　But, as I told my lord of Westmorland,
　　The time misordered doth, in common sense,
260　Crowd us and crush us to this monstrous form,
　　To hold our safety up. I sent your grace
　　The parcels° and particulars of our grief,　　　　　　*items; details*
　　The which hath been with scorn shoved from the court,
　　Whereon this Hydra son⁷ of war is born;
265　Whose dangerous eyes may well be charmed asleep⁸
　　With grant° of our most just and right desires,　　　*the granting*
　　And true obedience, of this madness cured,
　　Stoop tamely to the foot of majesty.

MOWBRAY　　If not, we ready are to try our fortunes
　　To the last man.
270　HASTINGS　　　　And though we here fall down,
　　We have supplies° to second our attempt.　　　　　*reinforcements*
　　If they miscarry, theirs shall second them;
　　And so success of° mischief shall be born,　　　　　　*from*
　　And heir from heir shall hold this quarrel up,
275　Whiles° England shall have generation.°　　　*As long as / offspring*

5. Under the pretense of zeal toward God; under the pretense of God's approval.
6. Have raised them up in angry swarms (like bees).
7. Hydra-like offspring. The Archbishop alludes to the many-headed monster of classical mythology, which was almost impossible to kill because its heads grew again as fast as they were cut off.
8. Alluding to another monster of classical mythology, the hundred-eyed Argus, which Hermes overcame by charming it to sleep.

PRINCE JOHN   You are too shallow, Hastings, much too shallow,
  To sound the bottom of the after-times.°   *future*
WESTMORLAND   Pleaseth your grace to answer them directly
  How far forth you do like their articles?
280 PRINCE JOHN   I like them all, and do allow° them well,   *grant*
  And swear here, by the honour of my blood,
  My father's purposes have been mistook,
  And some about him have too lavishly°   *freely*
  Wrested his meaning and authority.
285   [*To the* ARCHBISHOP] My lord, these griefs shall be with speed redressed;
  Upon my soul they shall. If this may please you,
  Discharge your powers unto their several counties,
  As we will ours; and here between the armies
  Let's drink together friendly and embrace,
290   That all their eyes may bear those tokens home
  Of our restorèd love and amity.
ARCHBISHOP OF YORK   I take your princely word for these redresses.
PRINCE JOHN   I give it you, and will maintain my word;
  And thereupon I drink unto your grace.
      [*He drinks*]
295 HASTINGS [*to* COLEVILLE]   Go, captain, and deliver to the army
  This news of peace. Let them have pay, and part.
  I know it will well please them. Hie thee,° captain.   *Get thee gone*
                              Exit [COLEVILLE]
ARCHBISHOP OF YORK   To you, my noble lord of Westmorland!
      [*He drinks*]
WESTMORLAND [*drinking*]   I pledge your grace. An if you knew what pains
300 I have bestowed to breed this present peace,
  You would drink freely; but my love to ye
  Shall show itself more openly hereafter.
ARCHBISHOP OF YORK   I do not doubt you.
WESTMORLAND   I am glad of it.
  [*Drinking*] Health to my lord and gentle cousin Mowbray!
305 MOWBRAY   You wish me health in very happy season,°   *at an apt moment*
  For I am on the sudden something ill.
ARCHBISHOP OF YORK   Against° ill chances men are ever merry;   *Before*
  But heaviness° foreruns the good event.   *sorrow*
WESTMORLAND   Therefore be merry, coz,° since sudden sorrow   *kinsman*
310 Serves to say thus: some good thing comes tomorrow.
ARCHBISHOP OF YORK   Believe me, I am passing° light in spirit.   *exceptionally*
MOWBRAY   So much the worse, if your own rule be true.
                              Shout [*within*]
PRINCE JOHN   The word of peace is rendered. Hark how they
      shout.
MOWBRAY   This had° been cheerful after victory.   *would have*
315 ARCHBISHOP OF YORK   A peace is of the nature of a conquest,
  For then both parties nobly are subdued,
  And neither party loser.
PRINCE JOHN [*to* WESTMORLAND]   Go, my lord,
  And let our army be dischargèd too.   *Exit* [WESTMORLAND]
  [*To the* ARCHBISHOP] And, good my lord, so please you, let our trains°   *troops*
320 March by us, that we may peruse the men
  We should have coped withal.°   *fought against*
ARCHBISHOP OF YORK   Go, good Lord Hastings,
  And ere they be dismissed, let them march by.   *Exit* [HASTINGS]

PRINCE JOHN   I trust, lords, we shall lie° tonight together.   *lodge*
          Enter [the Earl of] WESTMORLAND *[with captains]*
  Now, cousin, wherefore stands our army still?
325 WESTMORLAND   The leaders, having charge from you to stand,
  Will not go off until they hear you speak.
PRINCE JOHN   They know their duties.
          Enter [Lord] HASTINGS
HASTINGS *[to the* ARCHBISHOP*]*   Our army is dispersed.
  Like youthful steers unyoked, they take their courses,
  East, west, north, south; or, like a school broke up,
330   Each hurries toward his home and sporting place.
WESTMORLAND   Good tidings, my lord Hastings, for the which
  I do arrest thee, traitor, of high treason;
  And you, Lord Archbishop, and you, Lord Mowbray,
  Of capital treason I attach° you both.   *arrest*
       [The captains guard HASTINGS, *the* ARCHBISHOP, *and*
       MOWBRAY*]*
335 MOWBRAY   Is this proceeding just and honourable?
WESTMORLAND   Is your assembly so?
ARCHBISHOP OF YORK   Will you thus break your faith?
PRINCE JOHN   I pawned° thee none.   *pledged*
  I promised you redress of these same grievances
340   Whereof you did complain; which, by mine honour,
  I will perform with a most Christian care.
  But for you rebels, look to taste the due
  Meet° for rebellion and such acts as yours.   *Appropriate*
  Most shallowly did you these arms° commence,   *military exploits*
345   Fondly° brought here, and foolishly sent hence.—   *Foolishly*
  Strike up our drums, pursue the scattered stray.°   *stragglers*
  God, and not we, hath safely fought today.
  Some guard these traitors to the block of death,
  Treason's true bed and yielder up of breath.   *Exeunt*

4.2

Alarum. Excursions. Enter [Sir John] FALSTAFF *and*
  COLEVILLE
FALSTAFF   What's your name, sir, of what condition° are you,   *social status*
  and of what place, I pray?
COLEVILLE   I am a knight, sir, and my name is Coleville of the
  Dale.
5 FALSTAFF   Well then, Coleville is your name, a knight is your
  degree,° and your place the Dale. Coleville shall be still your   *rank*
  name, a traitor your degree, and the dungeon your place—a
  place deep enough, so shall you be still Coleville of the Dale.
COLEVILLE   Are not you Sir John Falstaff?
10 FALSTAFF   As good a man as he, sir, whoe'er I am. Do ye yield,
  sir, or shall I sweat for you? If I do sweat, they are the drops° of   *tears*
  thy lovers,° and they weep for thy death; therefore rouse up fear   *friends*
  and trembling, and do observance° to my mercy.   *pay homage (kneel)*
COLEVILLE *[kneeling]*   I think you are Sir John Falstaff, and in
15   that thought yield me.
FALSTAFF *[aside]*   I have a whole school of tongues in this belly
  of mine, and not a tongue of them all speaks any other word

4.2 Location: Scene continues.

but my name. An I had but a belly of any indifferency,° I were   *of moderate size*
simply the most active fellow in Europe. My womb,° my   *belly*
20 womb, my womb undoes me.

       Enter PRINCE JOHN, [*the Earl of*] WESTMORLAND, [*Sir
       John Blunt,*] *and* [*other lords and soldiers*]

Here comes our general.

PRINCE JOHN   The heat° is past; follow no further now.   *chase*

       [*A*] *retreat* [*is sounded*]

Call in the powers, good cousin Westmorland.

                                [*Exit* WESTMORLAND]

Now, Falstaff, where have you been all this while?
25 When everything is ended, then you come.
These tardy tricks of yours will, on my life,
One time or other break some gallows' back.[1]

FALSTAFF   I would be sorry, my lord, but it should be thus. I
never knew yet but rebuke and check° was the reward of valour.   *censure*
30 Do you think me a swallow, an arrow, or a bullet? Have I in
my poor and old motion the expedition° of thought? I have   *speed*
speeded hither with the very extremest° inch of possibility; I   *utmost*
have foundered° nine-score and odd posts;° and here, travel-   *made lame / horses*
tainted as I am, have in my pure and immaculate valour taken
35 Sir John Coleville of the Dale, a most furious knight and valorous enemy. But what of that? He saw me, and yielded, that I
may justly say, with the hook-nosed fellow of Rome, 'I came,
saw, and overcame.'[2]

PRINCE JOHN   It was more of his courtesy than your deserving.

40 FALSTAFF   I know not. Here he is, and here I yield him; and I
beseech your grace, let it be booked with the rest of this day's
deeds; or, by the Lord, I will have it in a particular ballad[3] else,
with mine own picture on the top on't, Coleville kissing my
foot; to the which course if I be enforced, if you do not all show
45 like gilt twopences to me,[4] and I in the clear sky of fame o'er-
shine you as much as the full moon doth the cinders of the
element,° which show like pins' heads to her, believe not the   *the stars*
word of the noble. Therefore let me have right, and let desert
mount.°   *merit be rewarded*

50 PRINCE JOHN   Thine's too heavy to mount.

FALSTAFF   Let it shine then.

PRINCE JOHN   Thine's too thick° to shine.   *opaque; dim*

FALSTAFF   Let it do something, my good lord, that may do me
good, and call it what you will.

PRINCE JOHN   Is thy name Coleville?

55 COLEVILLE   It is, my lord.

PRINCE JOHN   A famous rebel art thou, Coleville.

FALSTAFF   And a famous true subject took him.

COLEVILLE   I am, my lord, but as my betters are
That led me hither. Had they been ruled by me,
60 You should have won them dearer° than you have.   *at greater cost*

FALSTAFF   I know not how—they sold themselves, but thou
Like a kind fellow gav'st thyself away,
And I thank thee for thee.

---

1. Cause you to be hanged, which will break the gallows.
2. Referring to Julius Caesar, whose portrait and imperial exploits would be familiar to Elizabethans through
Thomas North's translation of Plutarch.

3. Ballad specifically about me. Ballads often reported
contemporary scandals and events.
4. If you do not all look like counterfeits when compared with me.

Enter [the Earl of] WESTMORLAND

PRINCE JOHN   Have you left pursuit?

WESTMORLAND   Retreat is made, and execution stayed.°   stopped

65   PRINCE JOHN   Send Coleville with his confederates
To York, to present° execution.   immediate
Blunt, lead him hence, and see you guard him sure.

Exit [Blunt,] with COLEVILLE

And now dispatch we toward the court, my lords.
I hear the King my father is sore° sick.   severely

70   [*To* WESTMORLAND] Our news shall go before us to his majesty,
Which, cousin, you shall bear to comfort him;
And we with sober speed will follow you.

FALSTAFF   My lord, I beseech you give me leave to go
Through Gloucestershire, and when you come to court

75   Stand,° my good lord, pray, in your good report.   Let me stand

PRINCE JOHN   Fare you well, Falstaff. I in my condition°   position
Shall better speak of you than you deserve.

Exeunt [all but FALSTAFF]

FALSTAFF   I would you had but the wit; 'twere better than your
dukedom. Good faith, this same young sober-blooded boy doth

80   not love me, nor a man cannot make him laugh. But that's no
marvel; he drinks no wine. There's never none of these demure
boys come to any proof;° for thin drink° doth so overcool their   turn out well / beer
blood, and making many fish meals, that they fall into a kind
of male green-sickness;[5] and then when they marry, they get

85   wenches.° They are generally fools and cowards—which some   beget females
of us should be too, but for inflammation.[6] A good sherry-sack°   Spanish sherry
hath a two-fold operation in it. It ascends me into the brain,
dries me there[7] all the foolish and dull and crudy° vapours   coagulated
which environ° it, makes it apprehensive,° quick, forgetive,[8]   surround / witty

90   full of nimble, fiery, and delectable shapes, which, delivered
o'er to the voice, the tongue, which is the birth, becomes excellent wit. The second property of your excellent sherry is the
warming of the blood, which, before cold and settled,° left the   stagnant
liver[9] white and pale, which is the badge of pusillanimity and

95   cowardice. But the sherry warms it, and makes it course from
the inwards to the parts' extremes;° it illuminateth the face,   extremities
which, as a beacon, gives warning to all the rest of this little
kingdom, man, to arm; and then the vital commoners and
inland° petty spirits[1] muster me° all to their captain, the heart; internal / assemble

100   who, great and puffed up with his retinue, doth any deed of
courage. And this valour comes of sherry. So that skill in the
weapon is nothing without sack, for that that sets it a-work; and
learning a mere hoard of gold kept by a devil,[2] till sack com-
mences it and sets it in act and use.[3] Hereof comes it that

---

5. An anemic condition that affected young women in puberty and that was supposed to be cured through sexual activity. Throughout this speech, Falstaff indicts John for lacking the heat necessary for masculine valor and the begetting of male children. Diet was believed to affect the balance of the four humors, or fluids, that determined temperament and the relative "heat" of the body.
6. The passions that alcohol inflames.
7. It ascends into the brain and to my benefit dries up.

8. Inventive.
9. The supposed seat of the passions.
1. Alluding to the medical doctrine of "vital spirits," or highly refined fluids, that were supposed to suffuse the blood.
2. Referring to the popular belief that hidden treasures were guarded by evil spirits.
3. Until sack sets learning free; confers a degree upon learning (punning on "commencement" and "act," two terms used for the granting of a university degree).

105 Prince Harry is valiant; for the cold blood he did naturally
inherit of his father he hath, like lean,° sterile, and bare land,   *barren*
manured, husbanded,° and tilled, with excellent endeavour of   *cultivated*
drinking good, and good store of fertile sherry, that he is
become very hot and valiant. If I had a thousand sons, the first
110 human principle I would teach them should be to forswear
thin potations, and to addict themselves to sack.

        Enter BARDOLPH

How now, Bardolph?

BARDOLPH   The army is dischargèd all and gone.

FALSTAFF   Let them go. I'll through Gloucestershire, and there
115 will I visit Master Robert Shallow, Esquire. I have him already
tempering[4] between my finger and my thumb, and shortly will
I seal with him.[5] Come, away!   *Exeunt*

4.3

    Enter KING [HENRY *in his bed,*[1] *attended by the Earl of*]
    WARWICK, *Thomas Duke of* CLARENCE, *Humphrey*
    [*Duke*] *of* GLOUCESTER [*and others*]

KING HENRY   Now, lords, if God doth give successful end
To this debate° that bleedeth at our doors,   *conflict*
We will our youth lead on to higher fields,[2]
And draw no swords but what are sanctified.
5 Our navy is addressed,° our power collected,   *prepared*
Our substitutes in absence well invested,°   *installed in office*
And everything lies level to° our wish;   *in accordance with*
Only we want a little personal strength,
And pause us till these rebels now afoot
10 Come underneath the yoke of government.

WARWICK   Both which we doubt not but your majesty
Shall soon enjoy.

KING HENRY   Humphrey, my son of Gloucester,
Where is the Prince your brother?

GLOUCESTER   I think he's gone to hunt, my lord, at Windsor.

KING HENRY   And how accompanied?

15 GLOUCESTER   I do not know, my lord.

KING HENRY   Is not his brother Thomas of Clarence with him?

GLOUCESTER   No, my good lord, he is in presence here.

CLARENCE   What would my lord and father?

KING HENRY   Nothing but well to thee, Thomas of Clarence.
20 How chance thou art not with the Prince thy brother?
He loves thee, and thou dost neglect him, Thomas.
Thou hast a better place in his affection
Than all thy brothers. Cherish it, my boy,
And noble offices° thou mayst effect   *duties*
25 Of mediation, after I am dead,
Between his greatness and thy other brethren.
Therefore omit° him not, blunt not his love,   *neglect*
Nor lose the good advantage of his grace

---

4. Softening like warm sealing wax.
5. Mold him to my use; conclude with him.
4.3 Location: The Jerusalem Chamber, the palace at Westminster. (This room is actually in Westminster Abbey.)

1. Henry may enter walking or carried in a chair or, as here, in a bed thrust out from behind the stage. The use of a bed emphasizes the severity of his illness.
2. That is, those of Palestine, where the King proposes to lead a crusade.

By seeming cold or careless of his will;
30   For he is gracious, if he be observed;°   *shown respect*
He hath a tear for pity, and a hand
Open as day for melting° charity.   *compassionate*
Yet notwithstanding, being incensed, he is flint,
As humorous° as winter, and as sudden   *changeable*
35   As flaws congealèd° in the spring° of day.   *As snowflakes / dawn*
His temper therefore must be well observed.
Chide him for faults, and do it reverently,
When you perceive his blood inclined to mirth;
But being moody, give him line and scope°   *free range*
40   Till that his passions, like a whale on ground,
Confound° themselves with working. Learn this, Thomas,   *Exhaust*
And thou shalt prove a shelter to thy friends,
A hoop of gold³ to bind thy brothers in,
That the united vessel of their blood,⁴
45   Mingled with venom of suggestion°—   *malicious gossip*
As force perforce the age will pour it in—
Shall never leak, though it do work as strong
As aconitum⁵ or rash gunpowder.
CLARENCE   I shall observe him with all care and love.
50   KING HENRY   Why art thou not at Windsor with him, Thomas?
CLARENCE   He is not there today; he dines in London.
KING HENRY   And how accompanied? Canst thou tell that?
CLARENCE   With Poins and other his continual° followers.   *constant*
KING HENRY   Most subject is the fattest° soil to weeds,   *richest*
55   And he, the noble image of my youth,
Is overspread with them; therefore my grief
Stretches itself beyond the hour of death.
The blood weeps from my heart when I do shape
In forms imaginary th'unguided days°   *days lacking a ruler*
60   And rotten times that you shall look upon
When I am sleeping with my ancestors;
For when his headstrong riot hath no curb,
When rage° and hot blood are his counsellors,   *passion*
When means° and lavish manners meet together,   *opportunity*
65   O, with what wings shall his affections° fly   *desires; inclinations*
Towards fronting peril and opposed decay?⁶
WARWICK   My gracious lord, you look beyond° him quite.   *misjudge*
The Prince but studies his companions,
Like a strange tongue,° wherein, to gain the language,   *foreign language*
70   'Tis needful that the most immodest word
Be looked upon and learnt, which once attained,
Your highness knows, comes to no further use
But to be known and hated; so, like gross° terms,   *vulgar; common*
The Prince will in the perfectness of time
75   Cast off his followers, and their memory
Shall as a pattern or a measure live
By which his grace must mete° the lives of other,°   *appraise / others*
Turning past evils to advantages.

---

3. A barrel with a golden hoop; a golden ring.   5. Monkshood, an especially virulent poison.
4. The vessel—a vial or chalice—that holds their blood.   6. Toward the peril and destruction that confront him.

KING HENRY 'Tis seldom when the bee doth leave her comb
    In the dead carrion.[7]
            Enter [the Earl of] WESTMORLAND
80   Who's here? Westmorland?
WESTMORLAND Health to my sovereign, and new happiness
    Added to that that I am to deliver!
    Prince John your son doth kiss your grace's hand.
    Mowbray, the Bishop Scrope, Hastings, and all
85   Are brought to the correction of your law.
    There is not now a rebel's sword unsheathed,
    But peace puts forth her olive everywhere.
    The manner how this action hath been borne
    Here at more leisure may your highness read,
90   With every course° in his° particular.   *stage in the action / its*
    [*He gives the* KING *papers*]
KING HENRY O Westmorland, thou art a summer bird
    Which ever in the haunch° of winter sings   *hind part*
    The lifting up of day.°   *dawn*
            Enter HARCOURT
                     Look, here's more news.
HARCOURT From enemies heaven keep your majesty;
95   And when they stand against you, may they fall
    As those that I am come to tell you of!
    The Earl Northumberland and the Lord Bardolph,
    With a great power of English and of Scots,
    Are by the sheriff of Yorkshire overthrown.
100   The manner and true order of the fight
    This packet, please it you, contains at large.
    [*He gives the* KING *papers*]
KING HENRY And wherefore should these good news make me sick?
    Will fortune never come with both hands full,
    But write her fair words still in foulest letters?
105   She either gives a stomach° and no food—   *an appetite*
    Such are the poor in health—or else a feast,
    And takes away the stomach—such are the rich,
    That have abundance and enjoy it not.
    I should rejoice now at this happy news,
110   And now my sight fails, and my brain is giddy.
    O me! Come near me now; I am much ill.
    [*He swoons*]
GLOUCESTER Comfort, your majesty!
CLARENCE   O my royal father!
WESTMORLAND My sovereign lord, cheer up yourself, look up.°   *take courage*
WARWICK Be patient, princes; you do know these fits
115   Are with his highness very ordinary.
    Stand from him, give him air; he'll straight be well.
CLARENCE No, no, he cannot long hold out° these pangs.   *endure*
    Th'incessant care and labour of his mind
    Hath wrought the mure° that should confine it in   *made the wall*
120   So thin that life looks through and will break out.
GLOUCESTER The people fear° me, for they do observe   *frighten*

---

7. *'Tis . . . carrion:* It is rare that the bee who has placed her honeycomb in a carcass abandons it. (So the new King will be unlikely to abandon his old pleasures.)

Unfathered heirs and loathly births of nature.[8]
The seasons change their manners, as° the year   *as if*
Had found some months asleep and leaped them over.

125 CLARENCE   The river° hath thrice flowed, no ebb between,   *(the Thames)*
And the old folk, time's doting chronicles,
Say it did so a little time before
That our great grandsire Edward° sicked and died.   *(Edward III)*

WARWICK   Speak lower, princes, for the King recovers.

130 GLOUCESTER   This apoplexy will certain be his end.

KING HENRY   I pray you take me up and bear me hence
Into some other chamber; softly, pray.
    [*The* KING *is carried over the stage in his bed*]
Let there be no noise made, my gentle friends,
Unless some dull° and favourable hand   *restful*

135 Will whisper music to my weary spirit.

WARWICK   Call for the music in the other room.
              [*Exit one or more. Still° music within*]   *Soft*

KING HENRY   Set me the crown upon my pillow here.
    [CLARENCE *takes the crown from the King's head, and*
    sets it on his pillow][9]

CLARENCE   His eye is hollow, and he changes° much.   *(in complexion)*
    [*A noise within*]

WARWICK   Less noise, less noise!
    Enter PRINCE HARRY

PRINCE HARRY   Who saw the Duke of Clarence?

140 CLARENCE   I am here, brother, full of heaviness.°   *sadness*

PRINCE HARRY   How now, rain within doors, and none abroad?
How doth the King?

GLOUCESTER   Exceeding ill.

PRINCE HARRY   Heard he the good news yet? Tell it him.

GLOUCESTER   He altered much upon the hearing it.

145 PRINCE HARRY   If he be sick with joy, he'll recover without physic.

WARWICK   Not so much noise, my lords! Sweet prince, speak low.
The King your father is disposed to sleep.

CLARENCE   Let us withdraw into the other room.

WARWICK   Will't please your grace to go along with us?

150 PRINCE HARRY   No, I will sit and watch here by the King.
         [*Exeunt all but the* KING *and* PRINCE HARRY]
Why doth the crown lie there upon his pillow,
Being so troublesome a bedfellow?
O polished perturbation,° golden care,   *source of unease*
That keep'st the ports° of slumber open wide   *gates (the eyes)*

155 To many a watchful° night!—Sleep with it° now; *wakeful / (the crown)*
Yet not so sound, and half so deeply sweet,
As he whose brow with homely biggen° bound   *nightcap*
Snores out the watch of night.[1] O majesty,
When thou dost pinch thy bearer, thou dost sit

160 Like a rich armour worn in heat of day,
That scald'st with safety.—By his gates of breath°   *his lips*
There lies a downy feather which stirs not.
Did he suspire,° that light and weightless down *If he breathed*

---

8. Children supernaturally begotten and malformed offspring resulting from normal conception.
9. It is unclear who removes the crown: the weakened King or his son Clarence, who is the next to speak.

1. Nighttime. "Watch" alludes to the periods of sentry duty into which the night was divided.

Perforce must move.—My gracious lord, my father!—
165 This sleep is sound indeed. This is a sleep
That from this golden rigol° hath divorced   *ring*
So many English kings.—Thy due from me
Is tears and heavy sorrows of the blood,
Which nature, love, and filial tenderness
170 Shall, O dear father, pay thee plenteously.
My due from thee is this imperial crown,
Which, as immediate from° thy place and blood,   *as next in line to*
Derives itself° to me.   *Descends*
                    [*He puts the crown on his head*]
                              Lo where it sits,
Which God shall guard; and put the world's whole strength
175 Into one giant arm, it shall not force
This lineal° honour from me. This from thee   *hereditary*
Will I to mine leave, as 'tis left to me.   *Exit*
                    [*Music ceases. The* KING *awakes*]
KING HENRY   Warwick, Gloucester, Clarence!
          Enter [*the Earl of*] WARWICK, [*and the Dukes of*]
          GLOUCESTER [*and*] CLARENCE
CLARENCE   Doth the King call?
WARWICK   What would your majesty? How fares your grace?
180 KING HENRY   Why did you leave me here alone, my lords?
CLARENCE   We left the Prince my brother here, my liege,
     Who undertook to sit and watch by you.
KING HENRY   The Prince of Wales? Where is he? Let me see him.
WARWICK   This door is open; he is gone this way.
185 GLOUCESTER   He came not through the chamber where we stayed.
KING HENRY   Where is the crown? Who took it from my pillow?
WARWICK   When we withdrew, my liege, we left it here.
KING HENRY   The Prince hath ta'en it hence. Go seek him out.
     Is he so hasty that he doth suppose
190 My sleep my death?
     Find him, my lord of Warwick; chide him hither.   [*Exit* WARWICK]
     This part° of his conjoins° with my disease,   *act / unites*
     And helps to end me. See, sons, what things you are,
     How quickly nature falls into revolt
195 When gold becomes her object!
     For this the foolish over-careful fathers
     Have broke their sleep with thoughts, their brains with care,
     Their bones with industry; for this they have
     Engrossèd° and piled up the cankered° heaps   *Gathered / diseased*
200 Of strange-achievèd gold;[2] for this they have
     Been thoughtful° to invest their sons with arts   *careful*
     And martial exercises; when, like the bee
     Culling from every flower the virtuous sweets,
     Our thighs packed with wax, our mouths with honey,
205 We bring it to the hive; and, like the bees,
     Are murdered for our pains. This bitter taste
     Yields his engrossments to the ending father.[3]
                    Enter [*the Earl of*] WARWICK

---

2. Gold gained in foreign lands or by unnatural or unusual means.

3. *This . . . father:* This bitter taste is all the dying father's amassing of wealth amounts to.

Now where is he that will not stay so long
Till his friend sickness have determined° me?   *put an end to*
210 WARWICK My lord, I found the Prince in the next room,
Washing with kindly° tears his gentle° cheeks   *filial / noble*
With such a deep demeanour,° in great sorrow,   *sad countenance*
That tyranny, which never quaffed° but blood,   *drank*
Would, by beholding him, have washed his knife
215 With gentle eye-drops.° He is coming hither.   *tears*
KING HENRY But wherefore did he take away the crown?
            Enter PRINCE HARRY [*with the crown*]
Lo where he comes.—Come hither to me, Harry.
[*To the others*] Depart the chamber; leave us here alone.
            Exeunt [*all but the* KING *and* PRINCE HARRY]
PRINCE HARRY I never thought to hear you speak again.
220 KING HENRY Thy wish was father, Harry, to that thought.
I stay too long by thee, I weary thee.
Dost thou so hunger for mine empty chair
That thou wilt needs invest thee with my honours
Before thy hour be ripe? O foolish youth,
225 Thou seek'st the greatness that will overwhelm thee!
Stay but a little, for my cloud of dignity°   *fragile greatness*
Is held from falling with so weak a wind°   *(his breath)*
That it will quickly drop. My day is dim.
Thou hast stol'n that which after some few hours
230 Were thine without offence, and at my death
Thou hast sealed up° my expectation.   *confirmed*
Thy life did manifest thou loved'st me not,
And thou wilt have me die assured of it.
Thou hid'st a thousand daggers in thy thoughts,
235 Whom° thou hast whetted on thy stony heart   *Which*
To stab at half an hour of my life.
What, canst thou not forbear me° half an hour?   *grant me but*
Then get thee gone and dig my grave thyself,
And bid the merry bells ring to thine ear
240 That thou art crownèd, not that I am dead.
Let all the tears that should bedew my hearse°   *coffin*
Be drops of balm⁴ to sanctify thy head.
Only compound° me with forgotten dust.   *mix*
Give that which gave thee life unto the worms.
245 Pluck down my officers, break my decrees;
For now a time is come to mock at form°—   *decorum*
Harry the Fifth is crowned. Up, vanity!
Down, royal state!° All you sage counsellors, hence!   *ceremony*
And to the English court assemble now
250 From every region, apes° of idleness!   *fools*
Now, neighbour confines,° purge you of your scum!   *bordering regions*
Have you a ruffian that will swear, drink, dance,
Revel the night, rob, murder, and commit
The oldest sins the newest kind of ways?
255 Be happy; he will trouble you no more.
England shall double gild° his treble guilt,   *paint over*
England shall give him office, honour, might;

---

4. The consecrated oils with which new monarchs were anointed during their coronation.

For the fifth Harry from curbed licence⁵ plucks
The muzzle of restraint, and the wild dog
260 Shall flesh his tooth on° every innocent.   *taste the flesh of*
O my poor kingdom, sick with civil blows!°   *domestic conflicts*
When that my care could not withhold° thy riots,°   *control / strife*
What wilt thou do when riot is thy care?⁶
O, thou wilt be a wilderness again,
265 Peopled with wolves, thy old inhabitants.
PRINCE HARRY   O pardon me, my liege! But for my tears,
The moist impediments unto my speech,
I had forestalled this dear° and deep rebuke   *grievous*
Ere you with grief had spoke and I had heard
270 The course of it so far. There is your crown;
        [*He returns the crown and kneels*]
And He° that wears the crown immortally   *(God)*
Long guard it yours! If I affect° it more   *desire*
Than as your honour and as your renown,
Let me no more from this obedience rise,
275 Which my most true and inward duteous spirit
Teacheth this prostrate and exterior° bending.   *outward*
God witness with me, when I here came in
And found no course of breath within your majesty,
How cold it struck my heart. If I do feign,
280 O, let me in my present wildness° die,   *sinfulness*
And never live to show th'incredulous world
The noble change that I have purposèd.°   *intended*
Coming to look on you, thinking you dead,
And dead almost, my liege, to think you were,
285 I spake unto this crown as having sense,°   *as if it had senses*
And thus upbraided it: 'The care on thee depending⁷
Hath fed upon the body of my father;
Therefore thou best of gold art worst of gold.
Other, less fine in carat, is more precious,
290 Preserving life in medicine potable;⁸
But thou, most fine, most honoured, most renowned,
Hast eat thy bearer up.' Thus, my royal liege,
Accusing it, I put it on my head,
To try° with it, as with an enemy   *struggle*
295 That had before my face murdered my father,
The quarrel of a true inheritor.°   *legitimate heir*
But if it did infect my blood with joy
Or swell my thoughts to any strain of pride,
If any rebel or vain spirit of mine
300 Did with the least affection of° a welcome   *inclination toward*
Give entertainment to the might of it,
Let God for ever keep it from my head,
And make me as the poorest vassal is,
That doth with awe and terror kneel to it.
305 KING HENRY   O my son,
God put it in thy mind to take it hence,

---

5. *Licence*: excessive freedom. The image is of a wild dog that has been curbed, kept under restraint, until his muzzle is removed and chaos ensues.
6. When debauchery (in the person of Hal) is your caretaker; when strife becomes your concern (rather than mine after my death).
7. The trouble that comes along with the crown.
8. Gold in a drinkable solution ("potable") was widely considered healthful.

That thou mightst win the more thy father's love,
Pleading so wisely in excuse of it!
Come hither, Harry; sit thou by my bed,
310 And hear, I think, the very latest° counsel   last
That ever I shall breathe.
       [PRINCE HARRY *rises from kneeling and sits by the bed*]
                              God knows, my son,
By what bypaths and indirect crook'd ways
I met this crown; and I myself know well
How troublesome it sat upon my head.
315 To thee it shall descend with better quiet,
Better opinion,° better confirmation;   public support
For all the soil° of the achievement goes   stain
With me into the earth. It seemed in me
But as an honour snatched with boist'rous hand;
320 And I had many living to upbraid
My gain of it by their assistances,⁹
Which daily grew to quarrel and to bloodshed,
Wounding supposèd peace. All these bold fears°   fearful acts
Thou seest with peril I have answerèd;
325 For all my reign hath been but as a scene
Acting that argument.° And now my death   theme
Changes the mood, for what in me was purchased¹
Falls upon thee in a more fairer sort,
So thou the garland wear'st successively.²
330 Yet though thou stand'st more sure than I could do,
Thou art not firm enough, since griefs are green,°   grievances are fresh
And all thy friends—which thou must make thy friends—
Have but their stings and teeth newly ta'en out,
By whose fell° working I was first advanced,   cruel
335 And by whose power I well might lodge a fear
To be again displaced; which to avoid
I cut them off, and had a purpose now
To lead out many to the Holy Land,
Lest rest and lying still might make them look°   examine
340 Too near° unto my state. Therefore, my Harry,   Too closely
Be it thy course to busy giddy° minds   restless
With foreign quarrels, that action° hence borne out   military exploits
May waste° the memory of the former days.   obliterate
More would I, but my lungs are wasted so
345 That strength of speech is utterly denied me.
How I came by the crown, O God forgive,
And grant it may with thee in true peace live!
PRINCE HARRY   My gracious liege,
You won it, wore it, kept it, gave it me;
350 Then plain and right must my possession be,
Which I with more than with a common pain°   effort
'Gainst all the world will rightfully maintain.
       Enter [PRINCE] JOHN *of Lancaster [followed by the Earl*
       of] WARWICK [*and others*]
KING HENRY   Look, look, here comes my John of Lancaster.

---

9. *And . . . assistances:* And many were living who made
demands on me and reproved me on the strength of the
fact that they had helped me to seize the throne.

1. Was acquired by acts, not by inheritance.
2. So that you wear the sign of victory (the crown) by
right of succession.

PRINCE JOHN   Health, peace, and happiness to my royal father!
355   KING HENRY   Thou bring'st me happiness and peace, son John;
But health, alack, with youthful wings is flown
From this bare withered trunk. Upon thy sight
My worldly business makes a period.°   *an end*
Where is my lord of Warwick?
PRINCE HARRY   My lord of Warwick!
[WARWICK *comes forward to the* KING]
360   KING HENRY   Doth any name particular belong
Unto the lodging° where I first did swoon?   *room*
WARWICK   'Tis called Jerusalem, my noble lord.
KING HENRY   Laud be to God! Even there my life must end.
It hath been prophesied to me many years
365   I should not die but in Jerusalem,
Which vainly I supposed the Holy Land;
But bear me to that chamber; there I'll lie;
In that Jerusalem shall Harry die.
Exeunt [bearing the KING *in his bed]*

5.1

Enter SHALLOW, SILENCE,[1] *[Sir John]* FALSTAFF, BAR-
DOLPH, *and [the]* PAGE
SHALLOW *[to* FALSTAFF*]*   By cock and pie,[2] you shall not away
tonight.—What, Davy, I say!
FALSTAFF   You must excuse me, Master Robert Shallow.
SHALLOW   I will not excuse you; you shall not be excused;
5   excuses shall not be admitted; there is no excuse shall serve;
you shall not be excused.—Why, Davy!
[*Enter* DAVY]
DAVY   Here, sir.
SHALLOW   Davy, Davy, Davy; let me see, Davy; let me see.
William Cook—bid him come hither.—Sir John, you shall not
10   be excused.
DAVY   Marry, sir, thus: those precepts° cannot be served. And   *warrants*
again,° sir: shall we sow the headland[3] with wheat?   *Moreover*
SHALLOW   With red wheat, Davy. But for William Cook; are there
no young pigeons?
15   DAVY   Yes, sir. Here is now the smith's note° for shoeing and   *bill*
plough-irons.
SHALLOW   Let it be cast° and paid. Sir John, you shall not be   *calculated*
excused.
DAVY   Sir, a new link° to the bucket must needs be had; and, sir,   *chain*
20   do you mean to stop any of William's wages, about the sack he
lost at Hinkley[4] Fair?
SHALLOW   A° shall answer° it. Some pigeons, Davy, a couple of   *He / pay for*
short-legged hens, a joint of mutton, and any pretty little tiny
kickshaws,° tell William Cook.   *fancy dishes*
25   DAVY   Doth the man of war stay all night, sir?
SHALLOW   Yea, Davy. I will use him well; a friend i'th' court is

---

5.1 Location: Shallow's house in Gloucestershire.
1. F includes Silence in this scene; Q does not. If present, he lives up to his name, getting no lines.
2. A mild oath. "Cock" was a euphemism for "God,"
and "pie" was a colloquial word for the collection of

rules by which the pre-Reformation Church ordered
the Church calendar.
3. Unplowed strip of land between two plowed fields.
4. A market town near Coventry.

better than a penny in purse. Use his men well, Davy, for they
are arrant knaves, and will backbite.°   *slander*
DAVY   No worse than they are back-bitten,° sir, for they have mar-   *(by fleas)*
30   vellous° foul linen.   *amazingly*
SHALLOW   Well conceited,° Davy. About thy business, Davy.   *quipped*
DAVY   I beseech you, sir, to countenance° William Visor of   *favor*
Wo'ncot against Clement Perks o'th' Hill.[5]
SHALLOW   There is many complaints, Davy, against that Visor.
35   That Visor is an arrant knave, on my knowledge.
DAVY   I grant your worship that he is a knave, sir; but yet God
forbid, sir, but a knave should have some countenance at his
friend's request. An honest man, sir, is able to speak for himself,
when a knave is not. I have served your worship truly, sir, this
40   eight years. An I cannot once or twice in a quarter bear out° a   *support*
knave against an honest man, I have little credit with your worship. The knave is mine honest friend, sir; therefore I beseech
you let him be countenanced.
SHALLOW   Go to; I say he shall have no wrong. Look about,
45   Davy.   [*Exit* DAVY]
Where are you, Sir John? Come, off with your boots.— Give
me your hand, Master Bardolph.
BARDOLPH   I am glad to see your worship.
SHALLOW   I thank thee with all my heart, kind Master Bardolph.
50   [*To the* PAGE] And welcome, my tall° fellow.—Come, Sir John.   *valiant*
FALSTAFF   I'll follow you, good Master Robert Shallow.
                     [*Exit* SHALLOW *with* SILENCE]
Bardolph, look to our horses.   [*Exit* BARDOLPH *with the* PAGE]
If I were sawed into quantities,° I should make four dozen of   *pieces*
such bearded hermits' staves as Master Shallow. It is a wonder-
55   ful thing to see the semblable coherence° of his men's spirits   *close correspondence*
and his. They, by observing him, do bear themselves like
foolish justices; he, by conversing° with them, is turned into a   *associating*
justice-like servingman. Their spirits are so married in con-
junction, with the participation of society,° that they flock   *by close association*
60   together in consent like so many wild geese. If I had a suit to
Master Shallow, I would humour his men with the imputation
of being near their master; if to his men, I would curry° with   *employ flattery*
Master Shallow that no man could better command his ser-
vants. It is certain that either wise bearing or ignorant carriage°   *demeanor*
65   is caught as men take° diseases, one of another; therefore let   *catch*
men take heed of their company. I will devise matter enough
out of this Shallow to keep Prince Harry in continual laughter
the wearing out of six fashions—which is four terms,[6] or two
actions°—and a shall laugh without intervallums.[7] O, it is   *lawsuits*
70   much that a lie with a slight oath, and a jest with a sad° brow,   *serious*
will do with a fellow that never had the ache in his shoulders![8]
O, you shall see him laugh till his face be like a wet cloak ill
laid up![9]
SHALLOW [*within*]   Sir John!
75   FALSTAFF   I come, Master Shallow; I come, Master Shallow.
                                     Exit

---

5. Possibly Stinchcombe Hill, not far from "Wo'ncot"
(the local pronunciation of Woodmancot in Gloucestershire).
6. Alluding to the four divisions of the judicial year.

7. Time between terms.
8. With someone who has not experienced old age or
troubles.
9. *ill laid up*: carelessly put away (so that it is wrinkled).

5.2

Enter the Earl of WARWICK [*at one door*], *and the* LORD
CHIEF JUSTICE [*at another door*]

WARWICK   How now, my Lord Chief Justice, whither away?
LORD CHIEF JUSTICE   How doth the King?
WARWICK   Exceeding well: his cares are now all ended.
LORD CHIEF JUSTICE   I hope not dead.
WARWICK   He's walked the way of nature,
5   And to our purposes he lives no more.
LORD CHIEF JUSTICE   I would his majesty had called me with him.
   The service that I truly did his life
   Hath left me open to all injuries.
WARWICK   Indeed I think the young King loves you not.
10   LORD CHIEF JUSTICE   I know he doth not, and do arm myself
   To welcome the condition° of the time,   *(new) circumstances*
   Which cannot look more hideously upon me
   Than I have drawn it in my fantasy.
      Enter [PRINCE] JOHN *of Lancaster,* [*and the Dukes of*]
      CLARENCE *and* GLOUCESTER
WARWICK   Here come the heavy issue° of dead Harry.   *sad offspring*
15   O, that the living Harry had the temper
   Of he the worst of these three gentlemen!
   How many nobles then should hold their places,
   That must strike sail° to spirits of vile sort!°   *submit / low rank*
LORD CHIEF JUSTICE   O God, I fear all will be overturned.
20   PRINCE JOHN   Good morrow, cousin Warwick, good morrow.
GLOUCESTER *and* CLARENCE   Good morrow, cousin.
PRINCE JOHN   We meet like men that had forgot to speak.
WARWICK   We do remember, but our argument°   *subject matter*
   Is all too heavy to admit much talk.
25   PRINCE JOHN   Well, peace be with him that hath made us heavy!
LORD CHIEF JUSTICE   Peace be with us, lest we be heavier!
GLOUCESTER   O good my lord, you have lost a friend indeed;
   And I dare swear you borrow not that face
   Of seeming sorrow—it is sure your own.
PRINCE JOHN [*to* LORD CHIEF JUSTICE]   Though no man be
30   assured what grace to find,°   *favor he will find*
   You stand in coldest expectation.
   I am the sorrier; would 'twere otherwise.
CLARENCE [*to* LORD CHIEF JUSTICE]   Well, you must now speak
      Sir John Falstaff fair,
   Which swims against your stream of quality.°   *character; rank*
35   LORD CHIEF JUSTICE   Sweet princes, what I did I did in honour,
   Led by th'impartial conduct of my soul;
   And never shall you see that I will beg
   A raggèd° and forestalled remission.[1]   *base*
   If truth and upright innocency fail me,
40   I'll to the King my master, that is dead,
   And tell him who hath sent me after him.
      Enter PRINCE HARRY [*as King*]
WARWICK   Here comes the Prince.
LORD CHIEF JUSTICE   Good morrow, and God save your majesty!

5.2 Location: The palace at Westminster.
1. Either a pardon sure to be denied or a pardon secured in advance (by an act of submission).

PRINCE HARRY   This new and gorgeous garment, majesty,
45   Sits not so easy on me as you think.
      Brothers, you mix your sadness with some fear.
      This is the English not the Turkish court;
      Not Amurath an Amurath succeeds,[2]
      But Harry Harry. Yet be sad, good brothers,
50   For, by my faith, it very well becomes you.
      Sorrow so royally in you appears
      That I will deeply° put the fashion on,   *solemnly*
      And wear it in my heart. Why then, be sad;
      But entertain no more of it, good brothers,
55   Than a joint burden laid upon us all.
      For me, by heaven, I bid you be assured
      I'll be your father and your brother too.
      Let me but bear° your love, I'll bear your cares.   *have; carry*
      Yet weep that Harry's dead, and so will I;
60   But Harry lives that shall convert those tears
      By number° into hours of happiness.   *One by one*
PRINCE JOHN, GLOUCESTER, *and* CLARENCE   We hope no other
            from your majesty.
PRINCE HARRY   You all look strangely on me, [*to* LORD CHIEF
            JUSTICE] and you most.
      You are, I think, assured I love you not.
65 LORD CHIEF JUSTICE   I am assured, if I be measured rightly,
      Your majesty hath no just cause to hate me.
PRINCE HARRY   No? How might a prince of my great hopes forget
      So great indignities you laid upon me?
      What—rate,° rebuke, and roughly send to prison   *chide*
70   Th'immediate heir of England? Was this easy?
      May this be washed in Lethe[3] and forgotten?
LORD CHIEF JUSTICE   I then did use the person° of your father.   *act as a deputy*
      The image of his power lay then in me;
      And in th'administration of his law,
75   Whiles I was busy for the commonwealth,
      Your highness pleasèd to forget my place,°   *rank; position*
      The majesty and power of law and justice,
      The image of the King whom I presented,
      And struck me in my very seat of judgement;
80   Whereon, as° an offender to your father,   *as you were*
      I gave bold way to my authority
      And did commit° you. If the deed were ill,   *imprison*
      Be you contented, wearing now the garland,°   *crown*
      To have a son set your decrees at naught—
85   To pluck down justice from your awe-full° bench,   *awe-inspiring*
      To trip the course of law, and blunt the sword
      That guards the peace and safety of your person,
      Nay, more, to spurn at your most royal image,
      And mock your workings in a second body?°   *representative*
90   Question your royal thoughts, make the case yours,
      Be now the father, and propose° a son;   *imagine*
      Hear your own dignity so much profaned,

---

2. An English name for the Turkish Sultan Murad III,
who had his brothers executed upon his succession in
1574. Turks were bywords for cruelty and tyranny in
early modern England.
3. The river in Hades that induced forgetfulness.

See your most dreadful laws so loosely slighted,
Behold yourself so by a son disdained;
95 And then imagine me taking your part,
And in your power soft° silencing your son.   *gently*
After this cold considerance, sentence me;
And, as you are a king, speak in your state°   *role as monarch*
What I have done that misbecame my place,
100 My person, or my liege's sovereignty.
PRINCE HARRY   You are right Justice,° and you weigh this well.   *perfect justice*
Therefore still bear the balance and the sword;[4]
And I do wish your honours may increase
Till you do live to see a son of mine
105 Offend you and obey you as I did.
So shall I live to speak my father's words:
'Happy am I that have a man so bold
That dares do justice on my proper° son,   *own*
And not less happy having such a son
110 That would deliver up his greatness so
Into the hands of justice.' You did commit° me,   *imprison*
For which I do commit° into your hand   *place*
Th'unstainèd sword that you have used° to bear,   *were accustomed*
With this remembrance:° that you use the same   *reminder*
115 With the like bold, just, and impartial spirit
As you have done 'gainst me. There is my hand.
You shall be as a father to my youth;
My voice shall sound° as you do prompt mine ear,   *speak*
And I will stoop and humble my intents
120 To your well-practised wise directions.—
And princes all, believe me, I beseech you,
My father is gone wild into his grave,
For in his tomb lie my affections;°   *wild passions*
And with his spirits sadly I survive
125 To mock° the expectation of the world,   *defy*
To frustrate prophecies, and to raze out
Rotten opinion, who hath writ me down
After my seeming.[5] The tide of blood° in me   *of passion*
Hath proudly flowed in vanity till now.
130 Now doth it turn, and ebb back to the sea,
Where it shall mingle with the state of floods,°   *the majesty of the sea*
And flow henceforth in formal majesty.
Now call we our high court of Parliament,
And let us choose such limbs° of noble counsel   *members*
135 That the great body of our state may go
In equal rank with the best-governed nation;
That war, or peace, or both at once, may be
As things acquainted and familiar to us;
[*to* LORD CHIEF JUSTICE] In which you, father, shall have foremost hand.
140 [*To all*] Our coronation done, we will accite,°   *summon*
As I before remembered, all our state;°   *nobility*
And, God consigning to° my good intents,   *endorsing*
No prince nor peer shall have just cause to say,
'God shorten Harry's happy life one day.'   *Exeunt*

4. The traditional emblems of justice.   5. According to my (false) appearance.

5.3

[*A table and chairs set forth.*] *Enter Sir John* FALSTAFF,
SHALLOW, SILENCE, DAVY [*with vessels for the table*],
BARDOLPH, *and* [*the*] PAGE

SHALLOW [*to* FALSTAFF]   Nay, you shall see my orchard, where,
in an arbour, we will eat a last year's pippin[1] of mine own
grafting, with a dish of caraways,[2] and so forth—come, cousin
Silence—and then to bed.

5   FALSTAFF   Fore God, you have here a goodly dwelling and a rich.

SHALLOW   Barren, barren, barren; beggars all, beggars all, Sir
John. Marry, good air.—Spread, Davy; spread, Davy.
[DAVY *begins to spread the table*]
Well said,° Davy.   *done*

FALSTAFF   This Davy serves you for good uses; he is your serving-
10   man and your husband.°   *steward*

SHALLOW   A good varlet,° a good varlet, a very good varlet, Sir   *servant*
John.—By the mass, I have drunk too much sack at supper.—A
good varlet. Now sit down, now sit down. [*To* SILENCE] Come,
cousin.

15   SILENCE   Ah, sirrah, quoth-a,° we shall   *said he*
[*sings*]   Do nothing but eat and make good cheer,
              And praise God for the merry year,
              When flesh is cheap and females dear,
              And lusty lads roam here and there
20   So merrily,
              And ever among so merrily.

FALSTAFF   There's a merry heart, good Master Silence! I'll give
you a health° for that anon.   *drink a toast to you*

SHALLOW   Good Master Bardolph!—Some wine, Davy.

25   DAVY [*to* FALSTAFF]   Sweet sir, sit. [*To* BARDOLPH] I'll be with you
anon. [*To* FALSTAFF] Most sweet sir, sit. Master page, good master page, sit.
[*All but* DAVY *sit.* DAVY *pours wine*]
Proface![3] What you want° in meat, we'll have in drink; but you   *lack*
must bear;° the heart's all.   *be forbearing*

30   SHALLOW   Be merry, Master Bardolph and my little soldier there,
be merry.

SILENCE [*sings*]   Be merry, be merry, my wife has all,
                     For women are shrews, both short and tall,
                     'Tis merry in hall when beards wags all,
35   And welcome merry shrovetide.[4]
Be merry, be merry.

FALSTAFF   I did not think Master Silence had been a man of this
mettle.°   *boldness*

SILENCE   Who, I? I have been merry twice and once ere now.
Enter DAVY [*with a dish of apples*]

40   DAVY   There's a dish of leather-coats° for you.   *russet apples*

SHALLOW   Davy!

DAVY   Your worship! I'll be with you straight. [*To* FALSTAFF] A
cup of wine, sir?

5.3 Location: Shallow's garden in Gloucestershire.
1. A kind of apple traditionally kept for a year before
eating.
2. Caraway seeds or sweet biscuits containing these
seeds, often eaten with apples.

3. A greeting used as a welcome to a meal, from an Italian phrase meaning "May it do you good."
4. The season of festivities preceding the Christian
penitential season, Lent.

SILENCE [*sings*] A cup of wine
45   That's brisk and fine,
                         And drink unto thee, leman° mine,   *sweetheart*
                         And a merry heart lives long-a.
FALSTAFF Well said, Master Silence.
SILENCE And we shall be merry; now comes in the sweet o'th'
50   night.
FALSTAFF Health and long life to you, Master Silence!
      [*He drinks*]
SILENCE Fill the cup and let it come. I'll pledge you a mile to
      th' bottom.[5]
SHALLOW Honest Bardolph, welcome! If thou want'st anything
55   and wilt not call, beshrew thy heart! [*To the* PAGE] Welcome,
      my little tiny thief, and welcome indeed, too!—I'll drink to
      Master Bardolph, and to all the cavalieros° about London.   *fine fellows*
      [*He drinks*]
DAVY I hope to see London once ere I die.
BARDOLPH An I might see you there, Davy!
60 SHALLOW By the mass, you'll crack° a quart together, ha, will   *drink*
      you not, Master Bardolph?
BARDOLPH Yea, sir, in a pottle-pot.°   *two-quart glass*
SHALLOW By God's liggens,[6] I thank thee. The knave will stick
      by thee, I can assure thee that; a will not out;° 'tis true-bred.   *drop out*
65 BARDOLPH And I'll stick by him, sir.
SHALLOW Why, there spoke a king! Lack nothing, be merry!
      One knocks at [*the*] *door* [*within*]
      Look who's at door there, ho! Who knocks?   [*Exit* DAVY]
      [SILENCE *drinks*]
FALSTAFF [*to* SILENCE] Why, now you have done me right![7]
SILENCE [*sings*] Do me right,
70   And dub me knight—
                         Samingo.[8]
      Is't not so?
FALSTAFF 'Tis so.
SILENCE Is't so?—Why then, say an old man can do somewhat.
      [*Enter* DAVY]
75 DAVY An't please your worship, there's one Pistol come from the
      court with news.
FALSTAFF From the court? Let him come in.
      Enter PISTOL
      How now, Pistol?
PISTOL Sir John, God save you.
80 FALSTAFF What wind blew you hither, Pistol?
PISTOL Not the ill wind which blows no man to good.
      Sweet knight, thou art now one of the greatest men in this
      realm.
SILENCE By'r Lady, I think a be—but goodman° Puff of Bar'son.[9]   *except for yeoman*
85 PISTOL Puff?
      Puff in thy teeth, most recreant coward base!—

---

5. I'll drink to the bottom of the cup, even if it were a
mile.
6. An obscure oath, possibly derived from "by God's
(eye)lid."
7. Done me justice (by drinking well).
8. Translated lines from a French drinking song,

"Monsieur Mingo." "Sa" may be a mispronunciation of
"Sir." "Mingo" means "I urinate."
9. Referring either to Barcheston, a town 10 miles
south of Stratford, or Barston, a town between Coventry and Solihull.

Sir John, I am thy Pistol and thy friend,
And helter-skelter have I rode to thee,
And tidings do I bring, and lucky joys,
90   And golden times, and happy news of price.
FALSTAFF   I pray thee now, deliver them like a man of this world.
PISTOL   A foutre° for the world and worldlings base!   *fig*
I speak of Africa and golden joys.
FALSTAFF   O base Assyrian knight,[1] what is thy news?
95   Let King Cophetua[2] know the truth thereof.
SILENCE [*singing*]   'And Robin Hood, Scarlet, and John.'[3]
PISTOL   Shall dunghill curs confront the Helicons?[4]
And shall good news be baffled?°   *disgraced*
Then Pistol lay thy head in Furies'[5] lap.
100   SHALLOW   Honest gentleman, I know not your breeding.
PISTOL   Why then, lament therefor.
SHALLOW   Give me pardon, sir. If, sir, you come with news from
the court, I take it there's but two ways: either to utter them, or
conceal them. I am, sir, under the King in some authority.
105   PISTOL   Under which king, besonian?° Speak, or die.   *beggarly fellow*
SHALLOW   Under King Harry.
PISTOL   Harry the Fourth, or Fifth?
SHALLOW   Harry the Fourth.
PISTOL   A foutre for thine office!
Sir John, thy tender lambkin now is king.
Harry the Fifth's the man. I speak the truth.
110   When Pistol lies, do this, [*making the fig*][6] and fig me,
Like the bragging Spaniard.
FALSTAFF   What, is the old King dead?
PISTOL   As nail in door. The things I speak are just.°   *true*
FALSTAFF   Away, Bardolph, saddle my horse! Master Robert
Shallow, choose what office thou wilt in the land; 'tis thine.
115   Pistol, I will double-charge thee[7] with dignities.
BARDOLPH   O joyful day!
I would not take a knighthood for my fortune.
PISTOL   What, I do bring good news?
FALSTAFF [*to* DAVY]   Carry Master Silence to bed.
                          [*Exit* DAVY *with* SILENCE]
120   Master Shallow—my lord Shallow—be what thou wilt, I am
fortune's steward—get on thy boots; we'll ride all night.—O
sweet Pistol!—Away, Bardolph!   [*Exit* BARDOLPH]
Come, Pistol, utter more to me, and withal° devise something   *at the same time*
to do thyself good. Boot, boot, Master Shallow! I know the
125   young King is sick for me. Let us take any man's horses—the
laws of England are at my commandment. Blessed are they
that have been my friends, and woe to my Lord Chief Justice.
PISTOL   Let vultures vile seize on his lungs also!

---

1. Adopting Pistol's elevated rhetorical style, Falstaff calls him a knight of Assyria, an Asian empire that the Elizabethans associated with pillage and robbery.
2. Alluding to the African King who marries a beggar in the popular ballad "A Beggar and a King."
3. A line from the ballad "Robin Hood and the Jolly Pinder of Wakesfield."
4. That is, "the true Muses." Pistol conflates the Muses of classical mythology with Mt. Helicon, part of the

Parnassus mountain range on which they dwelt.
5. Then let Pistol appeal to the goddesses of revenge.
6. An obscene gesture, known as "the Spanish fig," in which the thumb is put between the fore and middle fingers in a way meant to be suggestive of genitalia and sex acts. In the next line, Pistol refers to a "bragging" (lying) Spaniard who was "figged."
7. Load you (with honors) twice over; load you like a gun twice over, with a pun on Pistol's name.

130 'Where is the life that late I led?'[8] say they.
Why, here it is. Welcome these pleasant days.　　　　*Exeunt*

5.4

Enter Beadles, [dragging in MISTRESS] QUICKLY *and*
DOLL TEARSHEET[1]

MISTRESS QUICKLY　No, thou arrant knave! I would to God that I
might die, that I might have thee hanged. Thou hast drawn my
shoulder out of joint.

FIRST BEADLE　The constables have delivered her over to me;
5　and she shall have whipping-cheer,[2] I warrant her. There hath
been a man or two killed about her.[3]

DOLL TEARSHEET　Nut-hook,[4] nut-hook, you lie! Come on, I'll
tell thee what, thou damned tripe-visaged° rascal, an° the child　　*flabby-faced / if*
I go with do miscarry,[5] thou wert better thou hadst struck thy
10　mother, thou paper-faced° villain.　　*white-faced*

MISTRESS QUICKLY　O the Lord, that Sir John were come! He
would make this a bloody day to somebody. But I pray God the
fruit of her womb miscarry!

FIRST BEADLE　If it do, you shall have a dozen of cushions again;
15　you have but eleven now.[6] Come, I charge you both go with
me, for the man is dead that you and Pistol beat amongst you.

DOLL TEARSHEET　I'll tell you what, you thin man in a censer,[7] I
will have you as soundly swinged° for this, you bluebottle[8]　　*beaten*
rogue, you filthy famished correctioner! If you be not swinged,
20　I'll forswear half-kirtles.°　　*give up wearing skirts*

FIRST BEADLE　Come, come, you she knight-errant, come!

MISTRESS QUICKLY　O God, that right should thus o'ercome might!
Well, of sufferance° comes ease.　　*from suffering*

DOLL TEARSHEET　Come, you rogue, come; bring me to a justice.

25　MISTRESS QUICKLY　Ay, come, you starved bloodhound.

DOLL TEARSHEET　Goodman death, goodman bones!

MISTRESS QUICKLY　Thou atomy,° thou!　　*(for "anatomy"; skeleton)*

DOLL TEARSHEET　Come, you thin thing; come, you rascal.°　　*lean deer*

FIRST BEADLE　Very well.　　*Exeunt*

5.5

Enter two GROOMS[, *strewing rushes*[1]]

FIRST GROOM　More rushes, more rushes!

SECOND GROOM　The trumpets have sounded twice.

FIRST GROOM　'Twill be two o'clock ere they come from the coronation.　　*Exeunt*

---

8. A line from a lost poem or ballad.
5.4 Location: A street in London.
1. Q says, "Enter Sinklo and three or foure officers."
Sinklo was probably an actor's name. He was evidently
very thin, for this scene contains a number of unflat-
tering references to one of the officer's skinniness.
2. That is, a whipping for her entertainment or supper
("cheer"). Beadles (the parish officers responsible for
enforcing laws) commonly meted out this punishment
for prostitution.
3. Because of her; in her company.
4. A hook for pulling nuts from trees; the arresting

constable.
5. Women who were pregnant might escape the full
force of the law until after they gave birth.
6. Implying that Tearsheet feigns pregnancy by carrying one of Quickly's pillows under her gown.
7. You figure of a man embossed on the lid of a pot for
burning incense.
8. Alluding to the blue tunics worn by beadles.
5.5 Location: A public place near Westminster Abbey.
1. Floor coverings, here strewn on the ground before
the King's entrance.

Enter [Sir John] FALSTAFF, SHALLOW, PISTOL, BAR-
DOLPH, *and [the]* PAGE²

5   FALSTAFF   Stand here by me, Master Robert Shallow. I will make
the King do you grace.° I will leer upon him as a comes by,   *honor*
and do but mark the countenance that he will give me.

  PISTOL   God bless thy lungs, good knight.

  FALSTAFF   Come here, Pistol; stand behind me. [*To* SHALLOW]
10   O, if I had had time to have made new liveries,³ I would have
bestowed° the thousand pound I borrowed of you! But 'tis no   *spent*
matter; this poor show doth better; this doth infer° the zeal I   *imply*
had to see him.

  SHALLOW   It doth so.

15   FALSTAFF   It shows my earnestness of affection—

  PISTOL   It doth so.

  FALSTAFF   My devotion—

  PISTOL   It doth, it doth, it doth.

  FALSTAFF   As it were, to ride day and night, and not to deliberate,
20   not to remember, not to have patience to shift me°—   *change my clothes*

  SHALLOW   It is most certain.

  FALSTAFF   But to stand stained with travel and sweating with
desire to see him, thinking of nothing else, putting all affairs
in oblivion, as if there were nothing else to be done but to see
25   him.

  PISTOL   'Tis *semper idem*, for *absque hoc nihil est*:⁴ 'tis all in every
part.

  SHALLOW   'Tis so indeed.

  PISTOL   My knight, I will inflame thy noble liver,
30   And make thee rage.
Thy Doll, and Helen⁵ of thy noble thoughts,
Is in base durance° and contagious° prison,   *imprisonment / noxious*
Haled° thither   *Dragged*
By most mechanical° and dirty hand.   *menial*
35   Rouse up Revenge from ebon den° with fell Alecto's snake,⁶   *dark cave (hell)*
For Doll is in. Pistol speaks naught but truth.

  FALSTAFF   I will deliver her.
      [*Shouts within.*] *Trumpets sound*

  PISTOL   There roared the sea, and trumpet-clangour sounds!
      Enter KING HARRY *the Fifth,* [PRINCE JOHN *of Lancaster,*
      the Dukes of CLARENCE *and* GLOUCESTER, *the*] LORD
      CHIEF JUSTICE [*and others*]

  FALSTAFF   God save thy grace, King Hal, my royal Hal!
40   PISTOL   The heavens thee guard and keep, most royal imp° of fame!   *offspring*

  FALSTAFF   God save thee, my sweet boy!

  KING HARRY   My Lord Chief Justice, speak to that vain° man.   *foolish*

  LORD CHIEF JUSTICE [*to* FALSTAFF]   Have you your wits? Know
    you what 'tis you speak?

  FALSTAFF   My king, my Jove,⁷ I speak to thee, my heart!

---

2. In Q, Falstaff and his friends enter after "Trumpets
sound, and the King, and his train passe over the stage."
There are thus two royal processions, one before Falstaff enters and one later in the scene. F contains only
the latter procession, which immediately precedes the
climactic moment when Hal rejects Falstaff.
3. Uniforms such as those worn by the retainers in a
noble household.

4. The first Latin motto, "ever the same," was associated with Queen Elizabeth; the second means "apart
from this, there is nothing."
5. The famously beautiful woman whose abduction by
Paris is said to have started the Trojan War.
6. Alecto was one of the Furies of classical mythology;
her head was covered with snakes.
7. In classical mythology, the ruler of the gods.

45   KING HARRY   I know thee not, old man. Fall to thy prayers.
How ill white hairs becomes a fool and jester!
I have long dreamt of such a kind of man,
So surfeit-swelled,° so old, and so profane;   *bloated from excess*
But being awake, I do despise my dream.
50   Make less thy body hence,° and more thy grace.   *henceforth*
Leave gormandizing;° know the grave doth gape   *gluttony*
For thee thrice wider than for other men.
Reply not to me with a fool-born jest.
Presume not that I am the thing I was,
55   For God doth know, so shall the world perceive,
That I have turned away my former self;
So will I those that kept me company.
When thou dost hear I am as I have been,
Approach me, and thou shalt be as thou wast,
60   The tutor and the feeder of my riots.
Till then I banish thee, on pain of death,
As I have done the rest of my misleaders,
Not to come near our person by ten mile.
For competence of life[8] I will allow you,
65   That lack of means enforce you not to evils;
And as we hear you do reform yourselves,
We will, according to your strengths and qualities,°   *attainments*
Give you advancement. [*To* LORD CHIEF JUSTICE] Be it your
     charge, my lord,
To see performed the tenor of our word. [*To his train*] Set on!
                    Exeunt KING [HARRY *and his train*]
70   FALSTAFF   Master Shallow, I owe you a thousand pound.
SHALLOW   Yea, marry, Sir John; which I beseech you to let me
have home with me.
FALSTAFF   That can hardly be, Master Shallow. Do not you
grieve at this. I shall be sent for in private to him. Look you, he
75   must seem thus to the world. Fear not your advancements. I
will be the man yet that shall make you great.
SHALLOW   I cannot perceive how, unless you give me your doublet and stuff me out with straw. I beseech you, good Sir John,
let me have five hundred of my thousand.
80   FALSTAFF   Sir, I will be as good as my word. This that you heard
was but a colour.°   *pretense*
SHALLOW   A colour[9] I fear that you will die in, Sir John.
FALSTAFF   Fear no colours. Go with me to dinner. Come, Lieutenant Pistol; come, Bardolph. I shall be sent for soon at
85   night.
             Enter [*the* LORD CHIEF] JUSTICE *and* PRINCE JOHN [*with
             officers*]
LORD CHIEF JUSTICE [*to officers*]   Go carry Sir John Falstaff to
     the Fleet.°   *(a London prison)*
Take all his company along with him.
FALSTAFF   My lord, my lord!
LORD CHIEF JUSTICE   I cannot now speak. I will hear you soon.—
90   Take them away.

---

8. An allowance sufficient to supply life's necessities.   9. Punning on "collar" as meaning "hangman's noose."

PISTOL   *Si fortuna me tormenta, spero me contenta.*[1]

Exeunt. Manent° Lancaster [PRINCE JOHN]   *Remain*
and [LORD] CHIEF JUSTICE

PRINCE JOHN   I like this fair proceeding of the King's.
He hath intent his wonted° followers   *customary*
Shall all be very well provided for,
95   But all are banished till their conversations°   *conduct*
Appear more wise and modest to the world.
LORD CHIEF JUSTICE   And so they are.
PRINCE JOHN   The King hath called his parliament, my lord.
LORD CHIEF JUSTICE   He hath.
100   PRINCE JOHN   I will lay odds that, ere this year expire,
We bear our civil swords and native fire[2]
As far as France. I heard a bird so sing,
Whose music, to my thinking, pleased the King.
Come, will you hence?   *Exeunt*

Epilogue

[*Enter* EPILOGUE]

EPILOGUE   First my fear, then my curtsy,° last my speech.   *bow*
My fear is your displeasure; my curtsy, my duty; and my
speech to beg your pardons. If you look for a good speech now,
5   you undo° me; for what I have to say is of mine own making,   *ruin*
and what indeed I should say will, I doubt,° prove mine own   *fear*
marring. But to the purpose, and so to the venture.° Be it   *hazard*
known to you, as it is very well, I was lately here in the end of
a displeasing play, to pray your patience for it, and to promise
10   you a better. I did mean indeed to pay you with this; which, if
like an ill venture[1] it come unluckily home, I break,° and you,   *go bankrupt*
my gentle creditors, lose. Here I promised you I would be, and
here I commit my body to your mercies. Bate° me some, and   *Excuse*
I will pay you some, and, as most debtors do, promise you infi-
15   nitely.[2]
If my tongue cannot entreat you to acquit me, will you command me to use my legs? And yet that were but light payment,
to dance out of your debt. But a good conscience will make
any possible satisfaction, and so would I. All the gentlewomen
20   here have forgiven me; if the gentlemen will not, then the gentlemen do not agree with the gentlewomen, which was never
seen before in such an assembly.
One word more, I beseech you. If you be not too much
cloyed with fat meat, our humble author will continue the story
25   with Sir John in it,[3] and make you merry with fair Catherine of
France; where, for anything I know, Falstaff shall die of a
sweat[4]—unless already a° be killed with your hard opinions.   *he*

1. See note to 2.4.157.
2. Our swords used up to now in civil war and our native zeal.
Epilogue
1. An unlucky commercial speculation, especially in a cargo at sea.
2. Q here inserts the lines "and so I kneele downe before you; but indeed, to pray for the Queene," which

conclude the Epilogue in F. This is one of several indications that the Epilogue was rewritten and expanded at some point, but that in Q these lines, with their reference to the Queen, were not moved to their proper place at the end of the speech.
3. In fact, Sir John Falstaff does not appear in *Henry V*, the play here anticipated.
4. A sweating sickness; the plague; a venereal disease.

For Oldcastle[5] died a martyr, and this is not the man. My tongue is weary; when my legs are too, I will bid you good night, and so kneel down before you—but, indeed, to pray for 30 the Queen.

[*He dances, then kneels for applause. Exit*]

---

5. Alluding to the fact that Sir John was originally called "Oldcastle" in *1 Henry IV.* See the Introduction to that play.

Henry V

From a military point of view, Henry V was perhaps the most capable king England ever had. In 1414, reviving an English royal claim on the French throne, Henry invaded France. The following year, he won the Battle of Agincourt against impossible odds, forcing the King of France to declare him his heir and marry him to his daughter. Not surprisingly, Henry's story was a favorite with his English compatriots. It was lovingly chronicled by the historians Raphael Holinshed (died c. 1580) and Edward Hall (d. 1547), and probably dramatized once or more by other playwrights before Shakespeare brought his own version to the stage in 1599.

Shakespeare's *Henry V* is the last written of a set of eight plays on medieval English history. His first four history plays had dealt with the tumultuous years between 1422 and 1485, when England was first at war with France and then, after 1455, embroiled in a civil war—the Wars of the Roses. Shakespeare wrote another four plays several years later, presenting the events of 1398 to 1420 that led up to these long wars over the royal succession. *Richard II* depicts Henry Bolingbroke's successful rebellion against Richard II and his coronation as Henry IV. The next two plays describe the troubled reign of the usurper, whose former allies turn against him and whose son keeps company with thieves. At the end of *2 Henry IV,* the King dies and young Prince Hal ascends the throne as Henry V, quickly belying his wastrel reputation and proving himself an astute leader in the play that bears his name. In the final lines of *Henry V,* however, the Chorus foresees Henry's imminent death, after which civil strife will break out once again.

Henry V is, therefore, one of a group of plays rather than a freestanding work. It refers constantly to events before and after its own temporal limits, events familiar to Shakespeare's audience from plays they had already seen performed. These references complicate the play's tone considerably. The Chorus's final predictions, for instance, darken the otherwise straightforwardly triumphal conclusion. Surely our awareness of the internecine strife that precedes and follows Henry's reign reinforces our admiration for him—he prospers where others have failed and will again fail, miserably. At the same time, *Henry V* is haunted by problems merely deferred, not resolved; in the long view, its hero's success looks transitory, even futile.

In 1599, such complexities may have seemed especially pertinent. England was mobilizing for a major campaign against Ireland to be led by Elizabeth's dashing young favorite, the Earl of Essex. *Henry V* registers both the patriotic excitement generated by the prospect of a military venture in foreign parts and the dread of war in a notoriously difficult environment (in the event, Essex's expedition was a disaster). These acutely mixed feelings were symptomatic of more general disputes about England's foreign policy. For much of the sixteenth century, England had attempted merely to defend its borders, but as it became wealthier and more powerful, expansion seemed feasible again. Ireland and the Netherlands beckoned; so did the New World, where France and Spain had already established colonies. Henry V's foray into France typified the kind of aggressive enterprise some of Shakespeare's contemporaries wished their nation to underwrite and others denounced as wasteful and dangerous.

Given the circumstances in which *Henry V* was originally written, it is not surprising that it has generated striking interpretive disagreements or that the play continues to be viewed through the lens of contemporary events. In Laurence Olivier's film version, made during World War II, *Henry V* is a vindication of England's excellence, and the victory at Agincourt a hopeful precedent for success in a justified

Henricus v. From John Rastell, *The Pastyme of People* (1529).

European war. Kenneth Branagh's 1989 film, on the other hand, reflects the murkier experience of more recent conflicts: the American intervention in Vietnam, the British in the Falkland Islands. Did Shakespeare intend the play as a paean to militarism or as an exposé of war's pointless brutality? Is Henry supposed to be a heroic or a repellent character? Is the war in France justified or purely expedient?

Henry's impressive leadership is repeatedly emphasized by the Chorus, by his followers, and even occasionally by his enemies. He not merely copes with, but triumphs over, the difficult circumstances bequeathed him: uniting his disputatious people against an external enemy, spending their aggressions abroad instead of at home, and gaining himself a kingdom to boot. He displays unshakeable personal courage in the campaign in France, in the smaller skirmishes as well as in the desperate moments before Agincourt. His "Once more unto the breach" speech (3.1.1–34) and his prophetic vision of aged veterans boasting to their compatriots on St. Crispin's Day (4.3.41ff.) have often been held up as models of inspirational eloquence.

On the other hand, *Henry V* clear-sightedly acknowledges, as had *Richard II* and *1* and *2 Henry IV,* that the factors that render someone an effective king are not necessarily morally admirable ones. Even while Shakespeare displays Henry's charisma to the full, he refuses to be entirely dazzled by his allure. In the early sixteenth century, Machiavelli had introduced Renaissance political thinkers to the notion that success as a ruler might be separable from, or even inimical to, what was conventionally considered virtuous behavior. A successful leader, he argued, needed the traits of both the fox and the lion: in other words, he had to know how to use deception and violence to achieve his ends. Shakespeare's Henry is certainly no monster of iniquity, but his career poses some of the same questions that Machiavelli raised in *The Prince.* What is the relationship of political success to personal goodness? Should princes be judged by moral rules different from those that apply to the rest of mankind?

A closer look at *Henry V* reveals a play not only deeply equivocal but self-consciously so. The capstone of Shakespeare's years of experimentation in the history play form, *Henry V* seems profoundly aware of the way generic constraints bear in upon its hero. Comedy and tragedy form themselves upon the rhythms of an individual life, ending in marriage or in death. History plays, by contrast, even when they seem to concentrate on the fortunes of a single character, dramatize the life of a nation, or at least its governing class. Characters in history plays are conceived as an endless generational succession, inheriting a political and historical situation from their ancestors and passing it down to their descendants. When one person dies, another steps into his place. The King's marriage represents not merely a natural culmination of his personal story, but one episode in a family's attempt to perpetuate a dynasty.

The young King Henry V is, therefore, both more and less than a talented and intelligent individual. One of a series, like the play that bears his name, he must come to terms with what it means to be part of a family line, what it means for one's "career" to begin before birth and end long after death. And Henry's family line is, of course, a tangled matter. His dubious title to the English throne reflects some of the instabilities in the concept of inheritance: what can it mean to acquire name and title "legitimately" from a man who stole the throne? The passing of property and title from one generation to the next might seem to reflect facts of nature, but it is also, as the Archbishop of Canterbury's discussion of "Salic law" reveals in 1.2, a matter of custom, a cultural construction. Inheritance can be altered as well by force or by negotiation: Henry IV compelled Richard to abdicate, and Henry V's victory at Agincourt requires the French King to recognize an English conqueror rather than his own son as heir to the French throne.

Troubles over the way proper generational sequence ought to be defined resonate throughout the play. War, in particular, seems intimately tied up with questions of lineage. Battlefield heroics can reinforce and clarify the relationship between fathers and sons. King Charles of France, for instance, describes Henry's belligerence as his birthright:

> The kindred of him hath been fleshed upon us,
> And he is bred out of that bloody strain
> That haunted us in our familiar paths.
> Witness our too-much-memorable shame
> When Crécy battle fatally was struck,
> And all our princes captived by the hand
> Of that black name, Edward, Black Prince of Wales,
> Whiles that his mountant sire, on mountain standing,
> Up in the air, crowned with the golden sun,
> Saw his heroical seed and smiled to see him
> Mangle the work of nature and deface
> The patterns that by God and by French fathers
> Had twenty years been made.
>
> (2.4.50–62)

Henry's great-uncle, Edward the Black Prince, butchers the French while the Prince's father, King Edward III, gladly looks on. There seem to be no mothers in this entirely male domain, merely God and fathers in alliance, so that Edward III himself seems rather improbably deified, "up in the air, crowned with the golden sun." Henry, in his stirring speech to his troops at Harfleur, evidences a similar pattern of assumptions:

> On, on, you noblest English,
> Whose blood is fet from fathers of war-proof,
> Fathers that like so many Alexanders
> Have in these parts from morn till even fought,
> And sheathed their swords for lack of argument.
> Dishonor not your mothers; now attest
> That those whom you called fathers did beget you.
>
> (3.1.17–23)

Mothers get a mention from Henry, as they did not from the French King, but they contribute nothing of their own nature to their offspring: their function is merely to duplicate the fathers in the next generation. Any discrepancy between the achievement of the fathers and the achievement of the sons, in fact, "dishonors" the mothers by implying that they must have slept with men other than their husbands, because the only explanation for such an inconsistency is that the biological father must be different from the acknowledged one. Once again, fathers set demanding precedents for sons eager to emulate their exploits but inevitably threatened by the possibility of falling short. The French King and Henry imagine inheritance, which might seem a passive process, as a strenuous endeavor.

If battle clarifies the pedigrees of winners, it simultaneously obscures those of the losers. In practical terms, of course, Henry's victory debars the Dauphin, the French heir apparent, from assuming his father's title. More generally, however, as both Henry and the French King insist, defeat in battle disrupts familial affinity, defacing paternal patterns, dishonoring mothers. Negotiating with Harfleur's governor, Henry predicts the consequences of the town's refusal to surrender quietly:

> why, in a moment look to see
> The blind and bloody soldier with foul hand
> Defile the locks of your shrill-shrieking daughters;
> Your fathers taken by the silver beards,
> And their most reverend heads dashed to the walls;
> Your naked infants spitted upon pikes,
> Whiles the mad mothers with their howls confused
> Do break the clouds, as did the wives of Jewry
> At Herod's bloody-hunting slaughtermen.
>
> (3.3.110–18)

On the face of it, it might seem surprising for a general to characterize his own troops as rapists and murderers, or implicitly to compare himself with the infanticidal King Herod, one of the Bible's wickedest villains. Yet Henry's rhetorical tactics are entirely deliberate: by describing his soldiers' potential victims as members of families—as daughters, fathers, infants, mothers—he heightens the impact of their violence. The rampaging army, he implies, will shatter not merely individuals but whole networks of affiliation. The speech effectively intimidates his auditors, who give up without a fight.

Soldiers using a battering ram. From Flavius Vegetius Renatus, *The Foure Bookes of Flavius Vegetius Renatus: Briefelye contayninge a plaine forme, and perfect knowledge of martiall policye* . . . (1572).

Unfortunately, even soldiers in the "winning" camp, insofar as they are vulnerable to the enemy, are liable to similar familial disasters. Exeter's description of war's misfortunes exempts neither side from calamity, from

> the widows' tears, the orphans' cries,
> The dead men's blood, the pining maidens' groans,
> For husbands, fathers, and betrothèd lovers . . . .
> (2.4.106–08)

Although Henry's invasion leaves the French more bloodied and tearful than the English, the English, too, suffer emotional and practical losses. Henry's soldiers are wasted by disease, hanged, occasionally even killed in battle. In 4.1, the common soldier worries, in an age without veteran's benefits, of dying with "wives left poor behind them" and "children rawly left" (lines 132–34). Henry's insistence on his inheritance rights, in other words, may disrupt not only his enemies' but his subordinates'. If infants are slaughtered, daughters raped, fathers torn from dependents, how can families be reconstituted? How can legitimate inheritance possibly be determined?

The difficulties of succession and inheritance are issues for Shakespeare the playwright as well as for his protagonist. Just as the character Henry V must strive to match and excel the patterns set by his ancestors, so the play *Henry V* must concern itself with what it means to be a sequel in two different senses: the way in which it represents actual historical events in a necessarily diminished theatrical form, and the way in which it must struggle to gratify an audience whose expectations had been formed by three exceedingly popular plays in the same series. At the beginning of every act, a Chorus pointedly emphasizes the play's self-conscious lack of realism:

> Can this cock-pit hold
> The vasty fields of France? Or may we cram
> Within this wooden O the very casques
> That did affright the air at Agincourt?
> (Prologue, lines 11–14)

Of course, *Henry V* is no more implausible than most other Renaissance plays. But in a sense, the theatrical anxieties of *Henry V* are cognate with the personal anxieties of its hero; the play is afraid of degenerating from its precursors, proving an inadequate replica of a distinguished original. And just as Henry V seems to overcompensate, not merely living up to his illustrious predecessors but going beyond them, so, too, *Henry V*, like many sequels, copes with its belatedness by a strategy of overstatement. It exaggerates some of the themes and issues of the earlier plays. In *1 Henry IV*, Hotspur, Prince Hal's valiant antagonist, epitomized many of the traditional ideals of chivalry—a word derived from the French *cheval*, "horse." In *Henry V*, Bourbon, one of Henry's new opponents, writes a sonnet to his horse that begins "Wonder of nature"—for, he says, "my horse is my mistress" (3.7.36–37, 40). Hotspur's chivalry, caricatured to the point of ridiculousness, degenerates in *Henry V* into bestiality jokes made at the expense of a blustering fop.

Shakespeare dramatizes Henry's success, in other words, not merely by magnifying his exploits but by minimizing the threat from possible competitors. Although the enemies of Henry's adulthood are technically more formidable than the enemies of his adolescence, they are characterized as bumbling and laughable, so that Henry's victory over them seems virtually preordained. Henry's allies seem similarly diminished. Falstaff, who dominated much of *1* and *2 Henry IV*, dies without reappearing in *Henry V*, leaving his cronies Bardolph, Nim, and Pistol to accompany Henry to France. They are joined by Fluellen, a Welsh soldier; MacMorris, an Irish one; Jamy, a Scots one; and Williams, a rural English one. This miscellany is proof of Henry's charisma; while in the previous plays the Irish, Scots, and Welsh were up in arms, Henry V successfully enlists them in his cause—not by homogenizing their differences, but by inspiring their allegiance to him even as they quarrel furiously with one another. Henry's triumph at Agincourt, Shakespeare claims, involves all the peoples of the British Isles. At the same time, these loyal adherents are given little of Falstaff's subversive wit, presumably because Falstaff's wholesale critique of military valor would undercut too thoroughly the premises of Henry's royal magnetism. Even the bluff yeoman Williams, who complains of the disproportionate suffering common people undergo to satisfy the ambitions of their betters, does not dissent from the fundamental principle of social and military hierarchy: to disobey one's superiors, he claims, "were against all proportion of subjection" (4.1.138). For better or worse, everyone seems to agree, the subject's life is at the ruler's disposal.

Shakespeare's excision of Falstaff's skeptical intelligence from *Henry V* means that there is no one within the play to point out the ironies of many of the turns of the plot. Presumably, though no one comments explicitly upon it, the venality of the clerics who finance Henry's expedition to France is sufficiently clear to the audience. Likewise, when Gower loyally remarks that Henry, unlike Alexander, never killed any of his friends, we are likely to think back to Falstaff's death, attributed earlier to Henry's neglect, and also to reflect that of Henry's other Eastcheap chums only Pistol has survived the "great victory" at Agincourt. Elsewhere it is unclear how or even whether the audience is expected to grasp an irony. In 1.1, Henry decides to press his claim on the French throne through the female line of descent. Shortly thereafter, he executes three erstwhile friends for conspiring against his life. In fact their plot was inspired by the conviction that Henry's title to the English throne was obstructed by the Earl of Mortimer's daughter, the Earl of Cambridge's wife. In other words, Henry employs against the French a principle that, if it were enforced against him, would strip him of both English and French kingdoms. Yet the point is made so obliquely that only a spectator cognizant of the tangled Plantagenet genealogy is likely to catch it.

As the stature of Henry's foes and associates diminishes, the ethical problems posed by his exploits are correspondingly aggravated. As we have already seen, Henry's self-assertion necessarily occurs at the expense of others, thereby raising the question of the extent to which his interests ought to take precedence over competing claims. Neither we nor Henry can be certain whether his exceptional situation and abilities exempt him from the criteria by which common persons are judged. In fact, Henry's unusual gifts as a leader render the uncertainty more pointed. Richard II disregarded common folk, and Henry IV deliberately avoided them; but Henry V inspires them by his capacity to immerse himself sympathetically in their lives. His insistence upon his ordinariness becomes a strategy of rule—part of what he is loved for during his lifetime and what becomes legendary after his death. But then, when he insists on seeing himself as a unique case nonetheless, he seems not merely to be asserting a King's usual prerogatives, but to be inconsistently or hypocritically making special allowances for himself.

This unresolved ambivalence becomes obvious in 4.1, when Henry disguises himself as a commoner and ventures among his rank and file. Initially, he argues for the essential similarity between himself and his followers.

> I think the King is but a man, as I am. The violet smells to him as it doth to me; the element shows to him as it doth to me. All his senses have but human conditions. His ceremonies laid by, in his nakedness he appears but a man, and though his affections are higher mounted than ours, yet when they stoop, they stoop with the like wing. (lines 99–104)

The ordinary soldiers, Williams and Bates, are unconvinced, pointing out that if they lose the battle, the King will be ransomed while they will be killed. On the other hand, they note, because they are required to obey the King under any circumstances, they need not concern themselves with the justice of the King's cause: their blood will be on Henry's head if he is waging an unjust war. The common soldiers see the King as unlike themselves, with special responsibilities that compensate for his special privileges. Henry responds indignantly:

> The King is not bound to answer the particular endings of his soldiers, the father of his son, nor the master of his servant, for they purpose not their deaths when they propose their services. Besides, there is no king, be his cause never so spotless, if it come to the arbitrament of swords, can try it out with all unspotted soldiers. Some, peradventure, have on them the guilt of premeditated and contrived murder; some, of beguiling virgins with the broken seals of perjury; some, making the wars their bulwark, that have before gored the gentle bosom of peace with pillage and robbery.
> (lines 146–55)

Henry resists accepting the extraordinary moral burden his followers would confer upon him. Yet his refusal is based not on his earlier assertion of the shared humanity of king and subject, but on a conviction of the king's special position. He distinguishes sharply and problematically between the king's "superior" violence—the violence of war—and the violence of individual subjects, which is merely criminal. After the soldiers leave, Henry exclaims bitterly:

> Upon the King.
> 'Let us our lives, our souls, our debts, our care-full wives,
> Our children, and our sins, lay on the King.'
> We must bear all. O hard condition,
> Twin-born with greatness: subject to the breath
> Of every fool, whose sense no more can feel
> But his own wringing. What infinite heartsease
> Must kings neglect that private men enjoy?
> (lines 212–19)

It is hard to take this self-pity seriously, given that Henry attempts to deflect all blame for his actions onto enemies and inferiors, even while accepting as his due the rewards that accrue to him by virtue of his exceptional status.

On the other hand, Shakespeare also shows effectively the King's genuine isolation from ordinary pleasures of work and play that normal people can take for granted. Though he repudiates Falstaff, the King retains a distinctly sportive quality; but the moral and practical gap that yawns between the ascendant Henry and his correspondingly diminished associates complicates the effect of his playfulness. In 2.2, with a typical flourish, he pretends to hand the traitors Scrope, Grey, and Cambridge their military commissions, after feigning to inquire about mercy for traitors. Actually, he gives them letters showing that he knows of their plot. This is splendid theater, but it is also quite chilling: Henry plays with his guilty victims as a cat plays with a mouse. His joke signifies not true contest, but absolute control.

Elsewhere, too, Henry's power tips the balance of hostility and affection that usually characterizes practical jokes in a markedly aggressive direction. In disguise on the eve of the Battle of Agincourt, he argues with the commoner Williams, as we have already seen, over the question of the king's responsibility for his subjects. He and Williams exchange gloves so they will be able to resume the quarrel after the battle. In 4.7, with victory assured, Henry gives Williams's glove to Fluellen to see what Williams will do when he sees it again. When Williams attacks Fluellen, Henry stops the fight, pretending to be angry at the insult to himself. Williams—technically guilty of the capital crime of mutiny—defends himself boldly enough, and Henry, thinking to be generous, returns Williams's glove to him filled with coins. Yet Williams fails to thank Henry, and when Fluellen attempts to add to the gift, he spurns it angrily. It is unclear from the script whether Williams eventually accepts the gold; either way, Henry's power contaminates what he wants to see as a game. While in the earlier plays Prince Hal always had the advantage of rank, it was still possible for Falstaff to give him almost as

Game of tennis. From Johann Amos Comenius, *Orbis Sensualium Pictus* (1659).

good as he got. Now that Henry is king and Falstaff is dead, Henry is always the winner, and so the game is no game at all. Arguably, in fact, Henry goes to war with France because he misses a sense of *competition*—because the fate of the effective king is that he cannot find real opposition at home.

Henry's wooing of Catherine in 5.2 is typified by the same dubious sense of fun. This scene, often quite endearing onstage, is also entirely beside the point. We hear from the Chorus in 3.0 that the French King offered Catherine to Henry before his forces arrived in France, but he rejected the offer because the suggested dowry—some "petty and unprofitable dukedoms"—did not suffice. Nonetheless, in 5.2, Henry calls Catherine his "capital demand" and presents himself to her as a wooer. He pretends that Catherine is free to reject him, even though the marriage is already arranged as part of the peace treaty. Rather like Williams, Catherine refuses to play along: when he asks, "Canst thou love me?" she replies, "I cannot tell." "Wilt thou have me?" "Dat is as it shall please de *roi mon père*" (lines 183ff.). Is Catherine being coy, or is she simply speaking the literal truth? In the game as Henry constructs it, Catherine's refusals can as easily be interpreted as coquettishness as real denial. In other words, even if she refuses to play Henry's game, she necessarily plays it anyhow. In *Henry V*, Shakespeare must cope with a knotty dramatic problem: how to interest an audience in a man who has, or wins, everything—whose life seems an unbroken series of successes. In the final scene as in the rest of the play, Shakespeare fascinates us by exhibiting the inevitably equivocal nature of kingly glory.

KATHARINE EISAMAN MAUS

TEXTUAL NOTE

Henry V exists in the 1623 First Folio (F) version and in a quarto version first issued in 1600 and reprinted in 1602 and 1619. The Folio version is generally accepted as the most authoritative text and was probably derived from Shakespeare's "foul papers," or manuscript, but there are also signs that the compositor consulted the 1619 Quarto

(Q3) when setting up the Folio text. F is not, however, a wholly reliable source; it contains a fairly large number of readings rejected by modern editors, probably the result of a compositor misreading a handwritten text. The Oxford editors argue that Q, although printed much earlier than F and obviously corrupt in some respects, actually represents a later stage of the text and may therefore incorporate some of Shakespeare's second thoughts and modifications. They believe that Q is based on memorial reconstruction by actors who played the parts of Exeter and Gower, for the text is far more reliable when these characters are onstage than for other scenes.

The quarto text also has a slightly different cast of characters than Folio's: F's Bedford is Q's Clarence, F's Westmoreland is Q's Warwick, and speeches assigned in F to Britain and to the Dauphin in the Agincourt scenes are given to Bourbon in Q. The most important substitution is the last, Bourbon's replacement of the Dauphin in 3.7, 4.2, and 4.5. In F, the Dauphin's substantial role sets him up as Henry's personal adversary, much as Hotspur was in 1 Henry IV. Also in F, the Dauphin's amply demonstrated folly seems to warrant his eventual displacement by Henry. The quarto speech assignments, on the other hand, are consistent with King Charles's order in 3.5 that the Dauphin remain with him at Rouen. In Q, the Dauphin's absence from the battlefield, rather than his extravagantly frivolous presence, implies his unfitness for rule.

Although most editors accept the Folio speech assignments, Gary Taylor, editor of the Oxford text, argues that Shakespeare in fact vacillated about whether to include the Dauphin in the Agincourt scenes and that Q represents his final decision not to do so. In consequence, although F remains the Oxford control text, Taylor adopts many more readings from Q than do most editors. In this respect, the Oxford *Henry V* seems to depart from the editors' usual policy of not conflating distinctly different texts of the same play (the policy that produces the two *King Lears* later in this volume). Taylor provides information on the tangled textual history of the play and a full explanation of his editorial choices in his single-volume edition of *Henry V* (Oxford: Clarendon, 1982).

SELECTED BIBLIOGRAPHY

Altman, Joel. "'Vile Participation': The Amplification of Violence in the Theatre of *Henry V.*" *Shakespeare Quarterly* 42 (1991): 1–32. *Henry V* in the context of contemporary political and religious issues—in particular, the debate over the nature of Communion.

Barton, Anne. "The King Disguised: Shakespeare's *Henry V* and the Comical History." *The Triple Bond: Plays, Mainly Shakespearean, in Performance.* Ed. Joseph G. Price. University Park: Pennsylvania State University Press, 1975. 92–117. Sees *Henry V* in a tradition of Elizabethan plays that combine history and comedy.

Cormack, Bradin. "'If We Be Conquered': Legal Nationalism and the France of Shakespeare's English Histories." *A Power to Do Justice: Jurisdiction and Early English Literature.* Chicago: University of Chicago Press, 2007. Shakespeare's treatment of France and the French language in terms of sixteenth-century English anxieties about national identity.

Danson, Lawrence. "*Henry V*: King, Chorus, and Critics." *Shakespeare Quarterly* 34 (1983): 27–43. King Henry as an actor; the Chorus as a means of drawing attention to the relationship between history and theater.

Dollimore, Jonathan, and Alan Sinfield. "History and Ideology, Masculinity and Miscegenation." *Faultlines: Cultural Materialism and the Politics of Dissident Reading.* By Alan Sinfield. Berkeley: University of California Press, 1992. 109–42. Imperialist and masculinist attitudes reinforce one another in the play.

Greenblatt, Stephen. "Invisible Bullets: Renaissance Authority and Its Subversion, *Henry IV* and *Henry V.*" *Political Shakespeare: New Essays in Cultural Materialism.* Ed. Jonathan Dollimore and Alan Sinfield. Manchester: Manchester University

Press, 1985. 18–47. Theater and the glamour of a royal power that incorporates what seems to undermine it.

Ornstein, Robert. "Henry V." A Kingdom for a Stage: The Achievement of Shakespeare's History Plays. Cambridge, Mass.: Harvard University Press, 1972. 175–202. Henry V as an equivocal celebration of the King's victories.

Quint, David. "Alexander the Pig: Shakespeare on History and Poetry." Boundary 2 10 (1982): 49–63. Shakespeare's relation to Renaissance humanists' conceptions of history.

Rabkin, Norman. "Rabbits, Ducks, and Henry V." Shakespeare Quarterly 28 (1977): 279–96. Henry V as an unresolvably ambiguous play.

Wells, Stanley, with Gary Taylor. Modernizing Shakespeare's Spelling [Wells], with Three Studies in the Text of "Henry V" [Taylor]. Oxford: Clarendon, 1979. Provides the scholarly rationale for the textual editing of the Oxford/Norton version of the play.

FILMS

Henry V. 1944. Dir. Laurence Olivier. UK. 137 min. Colorful, patriotic version made near the end of World War II, with Oliver as a very sympathetic king. Intelligently translates the play's theatrical self-consciousness to the film medium.

Henry V. 1979. Dir. David Giles. UK. 163 min. This BBC-TV production retains more features of a stage production than do the elaborate Olivier and Branagh versions. David Gwillim is a pleasant but resolute hero.

Henry V. 1989. Dir. Kenneth Branagh. UK. 137 min. Harsher and more violent than the Olivier version, with an elaborate reenactment of the Battle of Agincourt. Branagh stars as a grimly driven Henry.

The Life of Henry the Fifth

THE PERSONS OF THE PLAY

CHORUS

KING HARRY V of England, claimant to the French throne

Duke of GLOUCESTER ⎫
Duke of CLARENCE ⎬ his brothers

Duke of EXETER, his uncle

Duke of YORK

SALISBURY

WESTMORLAND

WARWICK

Archbishop of CANTERBURY

Bishop of ELY

Richard, Earl of CAMBRIDGE ⎫
Henry, Lord SCROPE of Masham ⎬ traitors
Sir Thomas GREY ⎭

PISTOL ⎫
NIM ⎬ formerly Falstaff's companions
BARDOLPH ⎭

BOY, formerly Falstaff's page

HOSTESS, formerly Mistress Quickly, now Pistol's wife

Captain GOWER, an Englishman

Captain FLUELLEN, a Welshman

Captain MACMORRIS, an Irishman

Captain JAMY, a Scot

Sir Thomas ERPINGHAM

John BATES ⎫
Alexander COURT ⎬ English soldiers
Michael WILLIAMS ⎭

HERALD

KING CHARLES VI of France

ISABEL, his wife and queen

The DAUPHIN, their son and heir

CATHERINE, their daughter

ALICE, an old gentlewoman

The CONSTABLE of France ⎫
Duke of BOURBON ⎪
Duke of ORLÉANS ⎪
Duke of BERRI ⎬ French noblemen at Agincourt
Lord RAMBURES ⎪
Lord GRANDPRÉ ⎭

Duke of BURGUNDY

MONTJOY, the French Herald

GOVERNOR of Harfleur

French AMBASSADORS to England

Prologue

*Enter [*chorus *as*] *Prologue*

CHORUS   O for a muse of fire, that would ascend
                The brightest heaven of invention:°   *imagination*
                A kingdom for a stage, princes to act,
                And monarchs to behold the swelling° scene.   *expansive; splendid*
5   Then should the warlike Harry, like himself,
                Assume the port° of Mars,° and at his heels,   *bearing / god of war*
                Leashed in like hounds, should famine, sword, and fire
                Crouch for employment. But pardon, gentles° all,   *gentlefolk*
                The flat unraisèd° spirits that hath dared   *uninspired*
10   On this unworthy scaffold° to bring forth   *platform*
                So great an object. Can this cock-pit° hold   *small cockfighting arena*
                The vasty fields of France? Or may we cram
                Within this wooden O° the very casques°   *round theater / helmets*
                That did affright the air at Agincourt?[1]
15   O pardon: since a crookèd figure[2] may
                Attest° in little place a million,   *Represent*
                And let us, ciphers° to this great account,°   *zeroes / sum; story*
                On your imaginary forces° work.   *powers of imagination*
                Suppose within the girdle of these walls
20   Are now confined two mighty monarchies,
                Whose high uprearèd and abutting fronts°   *frontiers*
                The perilous narrow ocean° parts asunder.   *(English Channel)*
                Piece out our imperfections with your thoughts:
                Into a thousand parts divide one man,
25   And make imaginary puissance.°   *power*
                Think, when we talk of horses, that you see them,
                Printing their proud hoofs i'th' receiving earth;
                For 'tis your thoughts that now must deck° our kings,   *equip*
                Carry them here and there, jumping o'er times,
30   Turning th'accomplishment of many years
                Into an hourglass—for the which supply,°   *to supplement which*
                Admit me Chorus to this history,
                Who Prologue-like your humble patience pray
                Gently to hear, kindly to judge, our play.   *Exit*

1.1

*Enter the [*Archbishop*] of* CANTERBURY *and [the Bishop
of]* ELY

CANTERBURY   My lord, I'll tell you. That self° bill is urged   *same*
                Which in th'eleventh year of the last king's reign
                Was like,° and had indeed against us passed,   *likely*
                But that the scrambling and unquiet time
5   Did push it out of farther question.°   *consideration*
ELY   But how, my lord, shall we resist it now?
CANTERBURY   It must be thought on. If it pass against us,
                We lose the better half of our possession,
                For all the temporal lands[1] which men devout
10   By testament have given to the Church
                Would they strip from us—being valued thus:

---

1. Site of Henry's famous victory over the French in 1415.
2. A zero, which multiplies a digit's value by ten.

crookèd: curved.
1.1 Location: In Henry's court.
1. Land devoted to secular uses.

As much as would maintain, to the King's honour,
Full fifteen earls and fifteen hundred knights,
Six thousand and two hundred good esquires;[2]
15 And, to relief of lazars° and weak age,   *lepers*
Of indigent faint souls past corporal° toil,   *bodily*
A hundred almshouses right well supplied;
And to the coffers of the King beside
A thousand pounds by th' year. Thus runs the bill.
20 ELY   This would drink deep.
CANTERBURY   'Twould drink the cup and all.
ELY   But what prevention?
CANTERBURY   The King is full of grace and fair regard.°   *kindly inclination*
ELY   And a true lover of the holy Church.
25 CANTERBURY   The courses of his youth promised it not.
The breath no sooner left his father's body
But that his wildness, mortified° in him,   *struck dead*
Seemed to die too. Yea, at that very moment
Consideration° like an angel came   *Spiritual reflection*
30 And whipped th'offending Adam° out of him,   *innate depravity*
Leaving his body as a paradise
T'envelop and contain celestial spirits.
Never was such a sudden scholar made;
Never came reformation in a flood
35 With such a heady currance° scouring faults;   *headlong current*
Nor never Hydra-headed[3] wilfulness
So soon did lose his seat°—and all at once—   *throne*
As in this king.
ELY   We are blessèd in the change.
CANTERBURY   Hear him but reason in divinity°   *theology*
40 And, all-admiring, with an inward wish
You would desire the King were made a prelate;°   *an important clergyman*
Hear him debate of commonwealth affairs,
You would say it hath been all-in-all his study;
List° his discourse of war, and you shall hear   *Listen to*
45 A fearful battle rendered you in music;
Turn him to any cause of policy,°   *political issue*
The Gordian knot[4] of it he will unloose,
Familiar° as his garter—that when he speaks,   *Offhandedly*
The air, a chartered libertine,° is still,   *licensed freedman*
50 And the mute wonder lurketh in men's ears
To steal his sweet and honeyed sentences:
So that the art and practic part of life
Must be the mistress to this theoric.[5]
Which is a wonder how his grace should glean it,
55 Since his addiction° was to courses vain,   *inclination*
His companies° unlettered, rude, and shallow,   *companions*
His hours filled up with riots,° banquets, sports,   *reveling*
And never noted in him any study,
Any retirement, any sequestration°   *removal*
60 From open haunts and popularity.[6]

---

2. Gentlemen below knightly rank.
3. Many-headed (the Hydra was a monstrous snake, killed by Hercules).
4. It was foretold that whoever untied the intricate Gordian knot would rule Asia; Alexander the Great cut it with his sword.
5. *the art . . . theoric:* practical experience must have taught him the theory.
6. From public places and unrefined companions.

ELY   The strawberry grows underneath the nettle,
      And wholesome berries thrive and ripen best
      Neighboured by fruit of baser quality;
      And so the Prince obscured his contemplation
65   Under the veil of wildness—which, no doubt,
      Grew like the summer grass, fastest by night,
      Unseen, yet crescive in his faculty.[7]
CANTERBURY   It must be so, for miracles are ceased,[8]
      And therefore we must needs admit the means°   natural causes
      How things are perfected.
70 ELY   But, my good lord,
      How now for mitigation of this bill
      Urged by the Commons? Doth his majesty
      Incline to it, or no?
CANTERBURY   He seems indifferent,
      Or rather swaying more upon our part
75   Than cherishing th'exhibitors[9] against us;
      For I have made an offer to his majesty,
      Upon our spiritual convocation[1]
      And in regard of causes now in hand,
      Which I have opened° to his grace at large: expounded
80   As touching France, to give a greater sum
      Than ever at one time the clergy yet
      Did to his predecessors part withal.°   with
ELY   How did this offer seem received, my lord?
CANTERBURY   With good acceptance of his majesty,
85   Save that there was not time enough to hear,
      As I perceived his grace would fain° have done,   gladly
      The severals[2] and unhidden passages°   channels of descent
      Of his true titles to some certain dukedoms,
      And generally to the crown and seat of France,
90   Derived from Edward,° his great-grandfather.   King Edward III
ELY   What was th'impediment that broke this off?
CANTERBURY   The French ambassador upon that instant
      Craved audience—and the hour I think is come
      To give him hearing. Is it four o'clock?
95 ELY   It is.
CANTERBURY   Then go we in, to know his embassy°—   message
      Which I could with a ready guess declare
      Before the Frenchman speak a word of it.
ELY   I'll wait upon you, and I long to hear it.   *Exeunt*

1.2

Enter KING [HARRY, *the Dukes of* GLOUCESTER], CLARENCE, *and*
EXETER, [*and the Earls of*] WARWICK [*and*] WESTMORLAND
KING HARRY   Where is my gracious lord of Canterbury?
EXETER   Not here in presence.
KING HARRY   Send for him, good uncle.
WESTMORLAND   Shall we call in th'ambassador, my liege?

---

7. Yet growing according to its natural ability.
8. Protestants believed that no miracles occurred after scriptural times (anachronistic in the mouth of a medieval archbishop).
9. Parliamentary sponsors of the bill.

1. On behalf of the assembled clergy.
2. Legal means by which land is conveyed in separate parts to different heirs.
1.2 Location: The royal court.

KING HARRY   Not yet, my cousin.[1] We would be resolved,
5   Before we hear him, of some things of weight
         That task° our thoughts, concerning us and France.   exercise

         Enter [Archbishop of CANTERBURY *and Bishop of* ELY]

CANTERBURY   God and his angels guard your sacred throne,
         And make you long become° it.   adorn
KING HARRY   Sure we thank you.
         My learnèd lord, we pray you to proceed,
10   And justly and religiously unfold
         Why the law Salic[2] that they have in France
         Or° should or should not bar us in our claim.   Either
         And God forbid, my dear and faithful lord,
         That you should fashion, wrest, or bow your reading,[3]
15   Or nicely charge° your understanding soul   foolishly burden
         With opening titles miscreate,[4] whose right
         Suits not in native colours° with the truth;   Does not accord
         For God doth know how many now in health
         Shall drop their blood in approbation°   confirmation
20   Of what your reverence shall incite us to.
         Therefore take heed how you impawn° our person,   pledge
         How you awake our sleeping sword of war;
         We charge you in the name of God take heed.
         For never two such kingdoms did contend
25   Without much fall of blood, whose guiltless drops
         Are every one a woe, a sore complaint
         'Gainst him whose wrongs gives edge unto the swords
         That makes such waste in brief mortality.°   short-lived humankind
         Under this conjuration° speak, my lord,   injunction
30   For we will hear, note, and believe in heart
         That what you speak is in your conscience washed
         As pure as sin with baptism.
CANTERBURY   Then hear me, gracious sovereign, and you peers
         That owe your selves, your lives, and services
35   To this imperial throne. There is no bar
         To make against your highness' claim to France
         But this, which they produce from Pharamond:°   legendary French King
         '*In terram Salicam mulieres ne succedant*'—
         'No woman shall succeed in Salic[5] land'—
40   Which 'Salic land' the French unjustly gloss°   interpret
         To be the realm of France, and Pharamond
         The founder of this law and female bar.[6]
         Yet their own authors faithfully affirm
         That the land Salic is in Germany,
45   Between the floods° of Saale and of Elbe,   rivers
         Where, Charles the Great having subdued the Saxons,
         There left behind and settled certain French
         Who, holding in disdain the German women
         For some dishonest° manners of their life,   unchaste
50   Established there this law: to wit, no female
         Should be inheritrix in Salic land—
         Which Salic, as I said, 'twixt Elbe and Saale,

---

1. Kinsman; complimentary form of address from King   4. With explicating false property rights.
to nobles.   5. Referring to an ancient Frankish tribe that lived
2. Explained below, lines 35ff.   beside the Rhine River.
3. Should shape, pervert, or bend your interpretation. 6. And prohibition of female inheritance.

Is at this day in Germany called Meissen.
Then doth it well appear the Salic Law
55   Was not devisèd for the realm of France.
Nor did the French possess the Salic land
Until four hundred one-and-twenty years
After defunction° of King Pharamond,   *death*
Idly° supposed the founder of this law,   *Foolishly*
60   Who died within the year of our redemption°   A.D.
Four hundred twenty-six; and Charles the Great°   *Charlemagne*
Subdued the Saxons, and did seat° the French   *establish*
Beyond the river Saale, in the year
Eight hundred five. Besides, their writers say,
65   King Pépin, which deposèd Childéric,
Did, as heir general[7]—being descended
Of Blithild, which was daughter to King Clotaire—
Make claim and title to the crown of France.
Hugh Capet also—who usurped the crown
70   Of Charles the Duke of Lorraine, sole heir male
Of the true line and stock of Charles the Great—
To fine° his title with some shows of truth,   *complete; purify*
Though in pure truth it was corrupt and naught,
Conveyed himself as heir to th' Lady Lingard,
75   Daughter to Charlemain, who was the son
To Louis the Emperor, and Louis the son
Of Charles the Great. Also, King Louis the Ninth,
Who was sole heir to the usurper Capet,
Could not keep quiet in his conscience,
80   Wearing the crown of France, till satisfied
That fair Queen Isabel, his grandmother,
Was lineal of ° the Lady Ermengarde,   *descended from*
Daughter to Charles, the foresaid Duke of Lorraine;
By the which marriage, the line of Charles the Great
85   Was reunited to the crown of France.
So that, as clear as is the summer's sun,
King Pépin's title and Hugh Capet's claim,
King Louis his° satisfaction, all appear   *(Louis's)*
To hold in right and title of the female;
90   So do the kings of France unto this day,
Howbeit they would hold up this Salic Law
To bar your highness claiming from the female,
And rather choose to hide them in a net°   *complexities*
Than amply to embar° their crookèd titles,   *frankly to rule out*
95   Usurped from you and your progenitors.
KING HARRY   May I with right and conscience make this claim?
CANTERBURY   The sin upon my head, dread sovereign.
For in the Book of Numbers° is it writ,   *Numbers 27:8*
'When the son dies, let the inheritance
100   Descend unto the daughter.' Gracious lord,
Stand for your own; unwind your bloody flag;
Look back into your mighty ancestors.
Go, my dread lord, to your great-grandsire's tomb,
From whom you claim;[8] invoke his warlike spirit,

7. One who inherits through either the male or female   8. Edward III claimed the French throne through his
line.   mother, Isabella.

105 And your great-uncle's, Edward the Black Prince,
Who on the French ground played a tragedy,
Making defeat° on the full power of France, *(at Crécy, in 1346)*
Whiles his most mighty father° on a hill *(Edward III)*
Stood smiling to behold his lion's whelp
110 Forage in blood of French nobility.
O noble English, that could entertain° *encounter*
With half their forces the full pride of France,
And let another half stand laughing by,
All out of work, and cold for° action. *for want of*
115 ELY Awake remembrance of those valiant dead,
And with your puissant° arm renew their feats. *powerful*
You are their heir, you sit upon their throne,
The blood and courage that renownèd them° *made them famous*
Runs in your veins—and my thrice-puissant liege
120 Is in the very May-morn of his youth,
Ripe for exploits and mighty enterprises.
EXETER Your brother kings and monarchs of the earth
Do all expect that you should rouse yourself
As did the former lions of your blood.
125 WESTMORLAND They know your grace hath cause; and means and might,
So hath your highness. Never king of England
Had nobles richer and more loyal subjects,
Whose hearts have left their bodies here in England
And lie pavilioned° in the fields of France. *encamped*
130 CANTERBURY O let their bodies follow, my dear liege,
With blood and sword and fire, to win your right.
In aid whereof, we of the spiritualty° *clergy*
Will raise your highness such a mighty sum
As never did the clergy at one time
135 Bring in to any of your ancestors.
KING HARRY We must not only arm t'invade the French,
But lay down our proportions⁹ to defend
Against the Scot, who will make raid upon us
With all advantages.° *Given any opportunity*
140 CANTERBURY They of those marches,° gracious sovereign, *borderlands*
Shall be a wall sufficient to defend
Our inland from the pilfering borderers.
KING HARRY We do not mean the coursing snatchers° only, *mounted raiders*
But fear the main intendment° of the Scot, *hostile intention*
145 Who hath been still a giddy° neighbour to us. *always an unreliable*
For you shall read that my great-grandfather
Never unmasked his power unto France
But that the Scot on his unfurnished° kingdom *unprotected*
Came pouring like the tide into a breach° *gap in a dike*
150 With ample and brim fullness of his force
Galling° the gleanèd° land with hot assays,° *Hurting / depleted / attacks*
Girding with grievous siege castles and towns,
That England, being empty of defence,
Hath shook and trembled at the bruit° thereof. *noise*
155 CANTERBURY She hath been then more feared than harmed, my liege.
For hear her but exampled° by herself : *given an example*
When all her chivalry hath been in France

9. Decide the distribution of our forces.

And she a mourning widow of her nobles,
She hath herself not only well defended
160 But taken and impounded as a stray
The King of Scots,[1] whom she did send to France
To fill King Edward's fame with prisoner kings
And make your chronicle as rich with praise
As is the ooze and bottom of the sea
165 With sunken wrack° and sumless treasures.[2]   shipwrecks
A LORD   But there's a saying very old and true:
              'If that you will France win,
                  Then with Scotland first begin.'
For once the eagle England being in prey,°   out hunting
170 To her unguarded nest the weasel Scot
Comes sneaking, and so sucks her princely eggs,
Playing the mouse in absence of the cat,
To 'tame[3] and havoc° more than she can eat.   spoil
EXETER   It follows then the cat must stay at home.
175 Yet that is but a crushed° necessity,   forced
Since we have locks to safeguard necessaries
And pretty° traps to catch the petty thieves.   clever
While that the armèd hand doth fight abroad,
Th'advisèd° head defends itself at home.   well-advised
180 For government, though high and low and lower,[4]
Put into parts,[5] doth keep in one consent,°   harmony
Congreeing° in a full and natural close,°   Coming together / cadence
Like music.
CANTERBURY   True. Therefore doth heaven divide
The state of man in divers functions,
185 Setting endeavour in continual motion;
To which is fixèd, as an aim or butt,°   target
Obedience. For so work the honey-bees,
Creatures that by a rule in nature teach
The act of order to a peopled kingdom.
190 They have a king,[6] and officers of sorts,
Where some like magistrates correct at home;
Others like merchants venture trade abroad;
Others like soldiers, armèd in their stings,
Make boot upon° the summer's velvet buds,   Plunder
195 Which pillage they with merry march bring home
To the tent royal of their emperor,
Who busied in his majesty surveys
The singing masons building roofs of gold,
The civil citizens lading° up the honey,   weighing
200 The poor mechanic° porters crowding in   menial
Their heavy burdens at his narrow gate,
The sad-eyed justice with his surly hum
Delivering o'er to executors° pale   executioners
The lazy yawning drone. I this infer:
205 That many things, having full reference
To one consent,[7] may work contrariously.°   disparately

1. David II of Scotland, taken prisoner in 1346, when
Edward III was in France; actually, he was imprisoned
in London.
2. Incalculable riches.
3. Attame, or meddle with.

4. That is, composed of three social classes.
5. Divided into different functions.
6. The queen bee was thought to be male.
7. *having . . . consent:* united by a common purpose.

As many arrows, loosèd several ways,°   *from different places*
Fly to one mark, as many ways meet in one town,
As many fresh streams meet in one salt sea,
210   As many lines close in the dial's° centre,   *sundial's*
So may a thousand actions once afoot
End in one purpose, and be all well borne
Without defect. Therefore to France, my liege.
Divide your happy England into four,
215   Whereof take you one quarter into France,
And you withal shall make all Gallia° shake.   *France*
If we with thrice such powers left at home
Cannot defend our own doors from the dog,
Let us be worried,° and our nation lose   *savaged*
220   The name° of hardiness and policy.[8]   *reputation*
KING HARRY   Call in the messengers sent from the Dauphin.[9]
                                   [Exit one or more]
Now are we well resolved, and by God's help
And yours, the noble sinews of our power,
France being ours we'll bend it to our awe,°   *make it submit to us*
225   Or break it all to pieces. Or° there we'll sit,   *Either*
Ruling in large and ample empery°   *sovereignty*
O'er France and all her almost kingly dukedoms,
Or lay these bones in an unworthy urn,
Tombless, with no remembrance over them.
230   Either our history shall with full mouth
Speak freely of our acts, or else our grave,
Like Turkish mute,[1] shall have a tongueless mouth,
Not worshipped with a waxen epitaph.[2]
         Enter AMBASSADORS *of France [with a tun]*°   *chest; barrel*
Now are we well prepared to know the pleasure
235   Of our fair cousin Dauphin, for we hear
Your greeting is from him, not from the King.
AMBASSADOR   May't please your majesty to give us leave
Freely to render what we have in charge,
Or shall we sparingly show you far off [3]
240   The Dauphin's meaning and our embassy?
KING HARRY   We are no tyrant, but a Christian king,
Unto whose grace our passion is as subject
As is our wretches fettered in our prisons.
Therefore with frank and with uncurbèd plainness
Tell us the Dauphin's mind.
245   AMBASSADOR   Thus then in few:°   *short*
Your highness lately sending into France
Did claim some certain dukedoms, in the right
Of your great predecessor, King Edward the Third.
In answer of which claim, the Prince our master
250   Says that you savour° too much of your youth,   *show traces*
And bids you be advised, there's naught in France
That can be with a nimble galliard° won: *lively dance*
You cannot revel into dukedoms there.
He therefore sends you, meeter° for your spirit,   *more appropriate*

---

8. Political discernment.   and deprived of speech.
9. Title of the French heir apparent.   2. Not dignified with (even) a perishable memorial.
1. Turkish harem attendants were reportedly castrated   3. Show you in an abridged and roundabout way.

255   This tun of treasure, and in lieu of this
             Desires you let the dukedoms that you claim
             Hear no more of you. This the Dauphin speaks.
    KING HARRY   What treasure, uncle?
    EXETER *[opening the tun]*   Tennis balls, my liege.
    KING HARRY   We are glad the Dauphin is so pleasant° with us.   *jocular*
260   His present and your pains we thank you for.
             When we have matched our rackets to these balls,
             We will in France, by God's grace, play a set
             Shall strike his father's crown° into the hazard.[4]   *royal crown; coin*
             Tell him he hath made a match with such a wrangler
265   That all the courts of France will be disturbed
             With chases.[5] And we understand him well,
             How he comes o'er° us with our wilder days,   *taunts*
             Not measuring what use we made of them.
             We never valued this poor seat° of England,   *throne*
270   And therefore, living hence,° did give ourself   *away from court*
             To barbarous licence—as 'tis ever common
             That men are merriest when they are from home.
             But tell the Dauphin I will keep my state,°   *dignity; territory*
             Be like a king, and show my sail of greatness
275   When I do rouse me in° my throne of France.   *about*
             For that have I laid by my majesty
             And plodded like a man for working days,
             But I will rise there with so full a glory
             That I will dazzle all the eyes of France,
280   Yea strike the Dauphin blind to look on us.
             And tell the pleasant Prince this mock of his
             Hath turned his balls to gunstones,° and his soul   *cannonballs*
             Shall stand sore chargèd° for the wasteful vengeance   *heavily burdened*
             That shall fly from them—for many a thousand widows
285   Shall this his mock mock out of their dear husbands,
             Mock mothers from their sons, mock castles down;
             Ay, some are yet ungotten and unborn
             That shall have cause to curse the Dauphin's scorn.
             But this lies all within the will of God,
290   To whom I do appeal, and in whose name
             Tell you the Dauphin I am coming on
             To venge me° as I may, and to put forth   *avenge myself*
             My rightful hand in a well-hallowed cause.
             So get you hence in peace. And tell the Dauphin
295   His jest will savour but of shallow wit
             When thousands weep more than did laugh at it.—
             Convey them with safe conduct.—Fare you well.
                           Exeunt AMBASSADORS
    EXETER   This was a merry message.
    KING HARRY   We hope to make the sender blush at it.
300   Therefore, my lords, omit no happy hour
             That may give furth'rance to our expedition;
             For we have now no thought in us but France,
             Save those to God, that run before our business.

---

4. Jeopardy; aperture in the back wall of an Elizabethan tennis court.
5. Military pursuit; in tennis, second impact of a
missed return, rated by its proximity to the back wall (a
disputable point, hence "wrangler" in line 264).

Therefore let our proportions for these wars
305 Be soon collected, and all things thought upon
That may with reasonable swiftness add
More feathers to our wings; for, God before,⁶
We'll chide this Dauphin at his father's door.
Therefore let every man now task his thought,
310 That this fair action may on foot be brought.

Exeunt. Flourish

2.0

Enter CHORUS

CHORUS Now all the youth of England are on fire,
And silken° dalliance in the wardrobe lies;   *luxurious*
Now thrive the armourers, and honour's thought
Reigns solely in the breast of every man.
5 They sell the pasture now to buy the horse,
Following the mirror° of all Christian kings   *exemplar*
With wingèd heels, as English Mercuries.¹
For now sits expectation in the air
And hides a sword from hilts unto the point
10 With crowns imperial, crowns° and coronets,   *titles; coins*
Promised to Harry and his followers.
The French, advised by good intelligence°   *espionage*
Of this most dreadful preparation,
Shake in their fear, and with pale policy°   *feeble intrigue*
15 Seek to divert the English purposes.
O England!—model° to thy inward greatness,   *small replica*
Like little body with a mighty heart,
What mightst thou do, that honour would thee do,
Were all thy children kind and natural?
20 But see, thy fault France hath in thee found out:
A nest of hollow² bosoms, which he fills
With treacherous crowns; and three corrupted men—
One, Richard, Earl of Cambridge; and the second
Henry, Lord Scrope of Masham; and the third
25 Sir Thomas Grey, knight, of Northumberland—
Have, for the gilt³ of France—O guilt indeed!—
Confirmed conspiracy with fearful° France;   *frightened*
And by their hands this grace of kings must die,
If hell and treason hold° their promises,   *keep*
30 Ere he take ship for France, and in Southampton.
Linger your patience on, and we'll digest
Th'abuse of distance, force—perforce—a play.⁴
The sum is paid, the traitors are agreed,
The King is set from London, and the scene
35 Is now transported, gentles, to Southampton.
There is the playhouse now, there must you sit,
And thence to France shall we convey you safe,
And bring you back, charming the narrow seas
To give you gentle pass—for if we may
40 We'll not offend one stomach⁵ with our play.

---

6. With God leading us; if God leads us.
2.0
1. Messenger of the gods; patron of thieves.
2. Hypocritical; empty (as receptacles for money).
3. Gold; gold leaf (suggesting superficiality).

4. *digest . . . play*: incorporate (and make acceptable) a violation of the unity of place, and stuff a play with events.
5. Offend anyone; make anyone seasick.

But till the King come forth, and not till then,
Unto Southampton do we shift our scene.   *Exit*

2.1

Enter Corporal NIM *and Lieutenant* BARDOLPH

BARDOLPH Well met, Corporal Nim.

NIM Good morrow, Lieutenant Bardolph.

BARDOLPH What, are Ensign° Pistol and you friends yet?   flag bearer

NIM For my part, I care not. I say little, but when time shall
5   serve, there shall be smiles—but that shall be as it may. I dare
     not fight, but I will wink° and hold out mine iron.° It is a simple   close my eyes / sword
     one, but what though?° It will toast cheese, and it will endure   of that
     cold, as another man's sword will—and there's an end.

BARDOLPH I will bestow a breakfast to make you friends, and
10   we'll be all three sworn brothers to France. Let't be so, good
     Corporal Nim.

NIM Faith, I will live so long as I may, that's the certain of it,
     and when I cannot live any longer, I will do as I may. That is
     my rest, that is the rendezvous° of it.   last word?

15   BARDOLPH It is certain, corporal, that he is married to Nell
     Quickly, and certainly she did you wrong, for you were troth-
     plight° to her.   betrothed

NIM I cannot tell. Things must be as they may. Men may sleep,
     and they may have their throats about them at that time, and
20   some say knives have edges. It must be as it may. Though
     Patience be a tired mare, yet she will plod. There must be con-
     clusions. Well, I cannot tell.

Enter [Ensign] PISTOL *and* HOSTESS *Quickly*

BARDOLPH Good morrow, Ensign Pistol.¹ [*To* NIM] Here comes
     Ensign Pistol and his wife. Good Corporal, be patient here.

25   NIM How now, mine host° Pistol?   tavern keeper; pimp

PISTOL Base tick, call'st thou me host? Now by Gad's lugs°   God's ears
     I swear I scorn the term. Nor shall my Nell keep lodgers.

HOSTESS No, by my troth, not long, for we cannot lodge and
     board a dozen or fourteen gentlewomen that live honestly by
30   the prick° of their needles, but it will be thought we keep a   (unwittingly obscene)
     bawdy-house straight.

[NIM *draws his sword*]

O well-a-day,° Lady!² If he be not hewn now, we shall see wilful   alas
adultery° and murder committed.   (for "assault")

[PISTOL *draws his sword*]

BARDOLPH Good lieutenant, good corporal, offer nothing° here.   don't fight

35   NIM Pish.

PISTOL Pish for thee, Iceland dog.° Thou prick-eared cur of   small, hairy breed
     Iceland.

HOSTESS Good Corporal Nim, show thy valour, and put up°   away
     your sword.

[*They sheathe their swords*]

NIM Will you shog off ?° I would have you *solus*.³   move along

40   PISTOL 'Solus', egregious dog? O viper vile!
     The *solus* in thy most marvellous face,

2.1 Location: Eastcheap, a slum section of London,
site of the tavern scenes in *1* and *2 Henry IV*. Bardolph,
Pistol, and Hostess Quickly were featured in the *Henry
IV* plays; Nim (slang for "thief") is a new character.

1. Sixteenth-century pistols were notoriously noisy and
inaccurate.
2. By our Lady, a mild oath.
3. Alone; unmarried.

The *solus* in thy teeth, and in thy throat,
And in thy hateful lungs, yea in thy maw pardie[4]—
And which is worse, within thy nasty mouth.

45 I do retort° the *solus* in thy bowels,   *send back*
For I can take,° and Pistol's cock is up,[5]   *take fire; strike*
And flashing fire will follow.

NIM   I am not Barbason,° you cannot conjure me.[6] I have an   *(the name of a devil)*
humour° to knock you indifferently well. If you grow foul with   *inclination*
50 me, Pistol, I will scour you with my rapier, as I may, in fair
terms.° If you would walk off, I would prick your guts a little,   *pretty thoroughly*
in good terms, as I may, and that's the humour of it.

PISTOL   O braggart vile, and damnèd furious wight!°   *creature*
The grave doth gape and doting death is near.
55 Therefore ex-hale.°   *draw (your sword)*

     [PISTOL *and* NIM] *draw* [*their swords*]

BARDOLPH   Hear me, hear me what I say.

     [*He draws his sword*]

He that strikes the first stroke, I'll run him up to the hilts, as I
am a soldier.

PISTOL   An oath of mickle° might, and fury shall abate.   *great*

     [*They sheathe their swords*]

60 [*To* NIM] Give me thy fist,° thy forefoot to me give.   *(i.e., hand)*
Thy spirits are most tall.°   *valiant*

NIM   I will cut thy throat one time or other, in fair terms, that is
the humour of it.

PISTOL   *Couple a gorge*,[7]
65 That is the word. I thee defy again.
O hound of Crete, think'st thou my spouse to get?
No, to the spital[8] go,
And from the powd'ring tub[9] of infamy
Fetch forth the lazar kite of Cressid's kind,[1]
70 Doll Tearsheet[2] she by name, and her espouse.
I have, and I will hold, the quondam° Quickly   *former*
For the only she, and—*pauca*,° there's enough. Go to.   *few (words)*

     Enter the BOY [*running*]

BOY   Mine host Pistol, you must come to my master,° and you,   *(Sir John Falstaff)*
hostess. He is very sick, and would to bed.—Good Bardolph,
75 put thy face between his sheets, and do the office of a warming-
pan.[3]—Faith, he's very ill.

BARDOLPH   Away, you rogue!

HOSTESS   By my troth, he'll yield the crow a pudding[4] one of
these days. The King has killed his heart.[5] Good husband,
80 come home presently.°   *Exit* [*with* BOY]   *right away*

BARDOLPH   Come, shall I make you two friends? We must to
France together. Why the devil should we keep knives to cut
one another's throats?

PISTOL   Let floods o'erswell,[6] and fiends for food howl on!

85 NIM   You'll pay me the eight shillings I won of you at betting?

---

4. *in thy maw pardie:* in your stomach, indeed (old-fashioned).
5. Pistol's trigger is cocked (unwittingly obscene).
6. Frighten me with big words.
7. Corrupt French for "Cut the throat."
8. Hospital; in Elizabethan times, a filthy, disease-ridden place occupied by indigents near death.
9. Sweat bath, used in treating syphilis.

1. The diseased, scavenging whore (Cressida, a faithless Trojan woman, was a pattern of female wickedness).
2. A prostitute who appears in *2 Henry IV.*
3. Referring to Bardolph's "fiery" complexion.
4. He'll feed the crows (after his death).
5. By rejecting him, in the last scene of *2 Henry IV.*
6. Let destruction reign (perhaps an unidentified quotation).

PISTOL   Base is the slave that pays.

NIM   That now I will have. That's the humour of it.

PISTOL   As manhood shall compound.° Push home.   *valor will determine*

[PISTOL *and* NIM] *draw* [*their swords*]

BARDOLPH [*drawing his sword*]   By this sword, he that makes the

90   first thrust, I'll kill him. By this sword, I will.

PISTOL   Sword is an oath,[7] and oaths must have their course.

[*He sheathes his sword*]

BARDOLPH   Corporal Nim, an° thou wilt be friends, be friends.   *if*

An thou wilt not, why then be enemies with me too. Prithee,

put up.

95   NIM   I shall have my eight shillings?

PISTOL   A noble° shalt thou have, and present pay,[8]   *6 shillings 8 pence*

And liquor likewise will I give to thee,

And friendship shall combine, and brotherhood.

I'll live by Nim, and Nim shall live by me.

100   Is not this just? For I shall sutler[9] be

Unto the camp, and profits will accrue.

Give me thy hand.

NIM   I shall have my noble?

PISTOL   In cash, most justly paid.

105   NIM   Well then, that's the humour of 't.

[NIM *and* BARDOLPH *sheathe their swords*]

Enter HOSTESS [*Quickly*]

HOSTESS   As ever you come of women, come in quickly to Sir
John. Ah, poor heart, he is so shaked of a burning quotidian-
tertian,[1] that it is most lamentable to behold. Sweet men, come
to him.   [*Exit*]

110   NIM   The King hath run bad humours on° the knight, that's the   *shows ill will toward*
even° of it.   *truth*

PISTOL   Nim, thou hast spoke the right.
His heart is fracted° and corroborate.[2]   *broken*

NIM   The King is a good king, but it must be as it may. He passes

115   some humours and careers.°   *behaves strangely*

PISTOL   Let us condole° the knight—for, lambkins, we will live.   *console*

Exeunt

2.2

Enter [*Duke of*] EXETER, [*Duke of* GLOUCESTER,] *and*
[*Earl of*] WESTMORLAND

GLOUCESTER   Fore God, his grace is bold to trust these traitors.

EXETER   They shall be apprehended by and by.

WESTMORLAND   How smooth and even they do bear themselves,
As if allegiance in their bosoms sat,

5   Crownèd with faith and constant loyalty.

GLOUCESTER   The King hath note of all that they intend,
By interception which they dream not of.

EXETER   Nay, but the man that was his bedfellow,[1]
Whom he hath dulled and cloyed° with gracious favours—   *tired and sated*

10   That he should for a foreign purse so sell
His sovereign's life to death and treachery.

---

7. Punning on "'s word," by God's word.
8. And immediate payment.
9. Seller of provisions (notoriously dishonest).
1. Dangerous fever (the Hostess conflates quotidian
fever, which recurs daily, with tertian fever, which

recurs every third day).
2. Confirmed (error for "corrupted").
2.2 Location: Southampton, a port in the south of England.
1. It was common for men to share a bed.

Sound trumpets. Enter KING [HARRY, *Lord*] SCROPE,
[*Earl of*] CAMBRIDGE, *and* [*Sir Thomas*] GREY

KING HARRY   Now sits the wind fair, and we will aboard.
My lord of Cambridge, and my kind lord of Masham,
And you, my gentle knight, give me your thoughts.
15   Think you not that the powers we bear with us
Will cut their passage through the force of France,
Doing the execution° and the act   *destruction*
For which we have in head° assembled them?   *an army*
SCROPE   No doubt, my liege, if each man do his best.
20   KING HARRY   I doubt not that, since we are well persuaded
We carry not a heart with us from hence
That grows not in a fair consent with ours,
Nor leave not one behind that doth not wish
Success and conquest to attend on us.
25   CAMBRIDGE   Never was monarch better feared and loved
Than is your majesty. There's not, I think, a subject
That sits in heart-grief and uneasiness
Under the sweet shade of your government.
GREY   True. Those that were your father's enemies
30   Have steeped their galls° in honey, and do serve you   *bitterness*
With hearts create of duty and of zeal.
KING HARRY   We therefore have great cause of thankfulness,
And shall forget the office° of our hand   *use*
Sooner than quittance° of desert and merit,   *payment*
35   According to their weight and worthiness.
SCROPE   So service shall with steelèd sinews toil,
And labour shall refresh itself with hope,
To do your grace incessant services.
KING HARRY   We judge no less.—Uncle of Exeter,
40   Enlarge° the man committed° yesterday   *Release / imprisoned*
That railed against our person. We consider
It was excess of wine that set him on,
And on his more advice° we pardon him.   *sober reconsideration*
SCROPE   That's mercy, but too much security.°   *complacency*
45   Let him be punished, sovereign, lest example
Breed, by his sufferance,° more of such a kind.   *by pardoning him*
KING HARRY   O let us yet be merciful.
CAMBRIDGE   So may your highness, and yet punish too.
GREY   Sir, you show great mercy if you give him life,
50   After the taste of much correction.
KING HARRY   Alas, your too much love and care of me
Are heavy orisons° 'gainst this poor wretch.   *weighty pleas*
If little faults proceeding on distemper°   *from drunkenness*
Shall not be winked at,° how shall we stretch our eye   *overlooked*
55   When capital crimes, chewed, swallowed, and digested,[2]
Appear before us? We'll yet° enlarge that man,   *nonetheless*
Though Cambridge, Scrope, and Grey, in their dear° care   *loving*
And tender preservation of our person,
Would have him punished. And now to our French causes.
Who are the late[3] commissioners?
60   CAMBRIDGE   I one, my lord.
Your highness bade me ask for it° today.   *(the commission)*

---

2. That is, crimes thoroughly premeditated.   3. Newly appointed (to govern during Henry's absence).

SCROPE So did you me, my liege.

GREY   And I, my royal sovereign.

KING HARRY Then Richard, Earl of Cambridge, there is yours;
There yours, Lord Scrope of Masham, and sir knight,
65 Grey of Northumberland, this same is yours.
Read them, and know I know your worthiness.—
My lord of Westmorland, and Uncle Exeter,
We will aboard tonight.—Why, how now, gentlemen?
What see you in those papers, that you lose
70 So much complexion?—Look ye how they change:
Their cheeks are paper.—Why, what read you there
That have so cowarded and chased your blood
Out of appearance?°   sight

CAMBRIDGE   I do confess my fault,
And do submit me to your highness' mercy.

75 GREY *and* SCROPE To which we all appeal.

KING HARRY The mercy that was quick° in us but late   alive
By your own counsel is suppressed and killed.
You must not dare, for shame, to talk of mercy,
For your own reasons turn into your bosoms,
80 As dogs upon their masters, worrying° you.—   tearing
See you, my princes and my noble peers,
These English monsters?⁴ My lord of Cambridge here,
You know how apt our love was to accord°   agree
To furnish him with all appurtenants°   privileges
85 Belonging to his honour; and this vile man
Hath for a few light crowns lightly conspired
And sworn unto the practices° of France   plots
To kill us here in Hampton. To the which
This knight,° no less for bounty bound to us   (Grey)
90 Than Cambridge is, hath likewise sworn. But O
What shall I say to thee, Lord Scrope, thou cruel,
Ingrateful, savage, and inhuman creature?
Thou that didst bear the key of all my counsels,
That knew'st the very bottom of my soul,
95 That almost mightst ha' coined me into gold
Wouldst thou ha' practised on° me for thy use: conspired against
May it be possible that foreign hire
Could out of thee extract one spark of evil
That might annoy my finger? 'Tis so strange
100 That though the truth of it stands off as gross°   clearly
As black on white, my eye will scarcely see it.
Treason and murder ever kept together,
As two yoke-devils sworn to either's purpose,
Working so grossly in a natural° cause   (for devils)
105 That admiration° did not whoop° at them;   astonishment / cry out
But thou, 'gainst all proportion,° didst bring in   natural order
Wonder to wait on° treason and on murder.   consort with
And whatsoever cunning fiend it was
That wrought upon thee so preposterously°   unnaturally
110 Hath got the voice° in hell for excellence.   vote
And other devils that suggest° by treasons   seduce
Do botch and bungle up° damnation   clumsily conceal

---

4. "Monsters" were usually imported freaks.

With patches, colours,° and with forms, being fetched° *pretexts / derived*
From glist'ring semblances of piety;
115 But he that tempered° thee, bade thee stand up,° *molded / rebel*
Gave thee no instance° why thou shouldst do treason, *motive*
Unless to dub thee with the name[5] of traitor.
If that same demon that hath gulled° thee thus *duped*
Should with his lion gait walk the whole world,
120 He might return to vasty Tartar° back *to huge hell*
And tell the legions,° 'I can never win *armies of devils*
A soul so easy as that Englishman's.'
O how hast thou with jealousy° infected *suspicion*
The sweetness of affiance.° Show men dutiful? *trust*
125 Why so didst thou. Seem they grave and learned?
Why so didst thou. Come they of noble family?
Why so didst thou. Seem they religious?
Why so didst thou. Or are they spare in diet,
Free from gross passion, or° of mirth or anger, *either*
130 Constant in spirit, not swerving with the blood,° *passion*
Garnished and decked in modest complement,° *appearance*
Not working with the eye without the ear,
And but in purgèd° judgement trusting neither? *purified*
Such, and so finely boulted,° didst thou seem. *sifted*
135 And thus thy fall hath left a kind of blot
To mark the full-fraught° man, and best endowed, *packed (with excellences)*
With some suspicion. I will weep for thee,
For this revolt of thine methinks is like
Another fall of man.—Their faults are open.° *obvious*
140 Arrest them to the answer of the law,
And God acquit them of their practices.
EXETER   I arrest thee of high treason, by the name of Richard,
Earl of Cambridge.—I arrest thee of high treason, by the name
of Henry, Lord Scrope of Masham.—I arrest thee of high trea-
145 son, by the name of Thomas Grey, knight, of Northumberland.
SCROPE   Our purposes God justly hath discovered,° *revealed*
And I repent my fault more than my death,
Which I beseech your highness to forgive
Although my body pay the price of it.
150 CAMBRIDGE   For me, the gold of France did not seduce,
Although I did admit it as a motive
The sooner to effect what I intended.[6]
But God be thankèd for prevention,
Which heartily in sufferance° will rejoice, *suffering punishment*
155 Beseeching God and you to pardon me.
GREY   Never did faithful subject more rejoice
At the discovery of most dangerous treason
Than I do at this hour joy o'er myself,
Prevented from a damnèd enterprise.
160 My fault, but not my body, pardon, sovereign.
KING HARRY   God 'quit° you in his mercy. Hear your sentence. *acquit*
You have conspired against our royal person,
Joined with an enemy proclaimed and fixed,

5. To knight you with the title.
6. The Earl of Cambridge was heir of Edmund Mortimer through his wife, Edmund's sister, and Mortimer arguably had a better claim to the English throne than did Henry himself. Henry's adherence to a principle of inheritance "through the female line" is hardly absolute.

And from his coffers
165   Received the golden earnest of° our death,   *advance payment for*
  Wherein you would have sold your king to slaughter,
  His princes and his peers to servitude,
  His subjects to oppression and contempt,
  And his whole kingdom into desolation.
170   Touching our person seek we no revenge,
  But we our kingdom's safety must so tender,°   *regard*
  Whose ruin you have sought, that to her laws
  We do deliver you. Get ye therefore hence,
  Poor miserable wretches, to your death;
175   The taste whereof, God of his mercy give
  You patience to endure, and true repentance
  Of all your dear° offences.—Bear them hence.   *grievous*

                Exeunt [the traitors, guarded]

  Now lords for France, the enterprise whereof
  Shall be to you, as us, like° glorious.   *equally*
180   We doubt not of a fair and lucky war,
  Since God so graciously hath brought to light
  This dangerous treason lurking in our way
  To hinder our beginnings. We doubt not now
  But every rub° is smoothèd on our way.   *obstacle*
185   Then forth, dear countrymen. Let us deliver
  Our puissance° into the hand of God,   *power*
  Putting it straight in expedition.°   *at once in action*
  Cheerly to sea, the signs° of war advance: *flags*
  No king of England, if not king of France.   *Flourish. Exeunt*

2.3

Enter [Ensign] PISTOL, *[Corporal]* NIM, *[Lieutenant]*
BARDOLPH, BOY, *and* HOSTESS *[Quickly]*

HOSTESS   Prithee, honey, sweet husband, let me bring° thee to   *accompany*
  Staines.[1]
PISTOL   No, for my manly heart doth erne.° Bardolph,   *grieve*
  Be blithe; Nim, rouse thy vaunting veins; boy, bristle
5   Thy courage up. For Falstaff he is dead,
  And we must erne therefore.
BARDOLPH   Would I were with him, wheresome'er he is, either
  in heaven or in hell.
HOSTESS   Nay, sure he's not in hell. He's in Arthur's bosom,[2] if
10   ever man went to Arthur's bosom. A° made a finer end, and   *He*
  went away an° it had been any christom[3] child. A parted ev'n   *as if*
  just between twelve and one, ev'n at the turning o'th' tide—for
  after I saw him fumble with the sheets, and play with flowers,°   *(on the bedclothes)*
  and smile upon his finger's end, I knew there was but one way.
15   For his nose was as sharp as a pen, and a babbled of green
  fields.[4] 'How now, Sir John?' quoth I. 'What, man! Be o' good
  cheer.' So a cried out, 'God, God, God', three or four times.
  Now I, to comfort him, bid him a should not think of God; I
  hoped there was no need to trouble himself with any such

2.3 Location: Eastcheap.
1. Town on the road to Southampton.
2. Mistake for "Abraham's bosom," heaven.
3. Error for "chrisom," just christened.
4. Falstaff was reciting the Twenty-third Psalm ("The

Lord is my shepherd"), but Hostess Quickly does not
recognize it. The text is corrupt at this point, reading "a
Table of green fields," and was corrected by the
eighteenth-century editor Lewis Theobald in a famous
emendation.

20 thoughts yet. So a bade me lay more clothes on his feet. I put
my hand into the bed and felt them, and they were as cold as
any stone. Then I felt to his knees, and so up'ard and up'ard,
and all was as cold as any stone.

NIM   They say he cried out of sack.[5]

25 HOSTESS   Ay, that a did.

BARDOLPH   And of women.

HOSTESS   Nay, that a did not.

BOY   Yes, that a did, and said they were devils incarnate.

HOSTESS   A could never abide carnation, 'twas a colour he never
30 liked.

BOY   A said once the devil would have him about women.

HOSTESS   A did in some sort, indeed, handle° women—but then   *discuss*
he was rheumatic,[6] and talked of the Whore of Babylon.[7]

BOY   Do you not remember, a saw a flea stick upon Bardolph's
35 nose, and a said it was a black soul burning in hell-fire.

BARDOLPH   Well, the fuel[8] is gone that maintained that fire.
That's all the riches I got in his service.

NIM   Shall we shog?° The King will be gone from Southampton.   *be off*

PISTOL   Come, let's away.—My love, give me thy lips.
        [*He kisses her*]
40 Look to my chattels and my movables.°   *personal property*
Let senses rule. The word is 'Pitch and pay'.°   *Cash down, no credit*
Trust none, for oaths are straws, men's faiths are wafer-cakes,°   *fragile*
And Holdfast is the only dog,[9] my duck.°   *darling*
Therefore *caveto*° be thy counsellor.   *beware*
45 Go, clear thy crystals.°—Yokefellows in arms,   *wipe your eyes*
Let us to France, like horseleeches, my boys,
To suck, to suck, the very blood to suck!

BOY [*aside*]   And that's but unwholesome food, they say.

PISTOL   Touch her soft mouth, and march.

50 BARDOLPH   Farewell, hostess.
        [*He kisses her*]

NIM   I cannot kiss, that is the humour of it, but adieu.

PISTOL [*to* HOSTESS]   Let housewifery appear. Keep close,° I   *Stay indoors; be thrifty*
thee command.

HOSTESS   Farewell! Adieu!   *Exeunt* [*severally*]°   *separately*

2.4

Flourish. Enter KING [CHARLES *the Sixth of France*], *the*
DAUPHIN, [*the* CONSTABLE,] *and the Dukes of* BERRI *and*
[BOURBON]

KING CHARLES   Thus comes the English with full power upon us,
And more than carefully it us concerns
To answer royally in our defences.
Therefore the Dukes of Berri and of Bourbon,
5 Of Brabant and of Orléans shall make forth,
And you Prince Dauphin, with all swift dispatch
To line° and new-repair our towns of war   *garrison*

---

5. *of sack*: against wine, formerly one of Falstaff's great
indulgences.
6. Error for "lunatic," delirious.
7. The scarlet woman of Revelation, identified by
Protestants with the Catholic Church.

8. That is, Falstaff's liquor.
9. Alluding to the proverb "Brag is a good dog, but
Holdfast is better."
2.4 Location: France, where the remainder of the play
takes place. The King's court at Rouen.

With men of courage and with means defendant.°   *of defense*
For England° his approaches makes as fierce   *the King of England*
10   As waters to the sucking of a gulf.°   *whirlpool*
It fits us then to be as provident
As fear may teach us, out of late° examples   *recent*
Left by the fatal and neglected[1] English
Upon our fields.

DAUPHIN   My most redoubted° father,   *formidable*
15   It is most meet° we arm us 'gainst the foe,   *proper*
For peace itself should not so dull a kingdom—
Though war, nor no known quarrel, were in question—
But that defences, musters, preparations
Should be maintained, assembled, and collected
20   As° were a war in expectation.   *As if*
Therefore, I say, 'tis meet we all go forth
To view the sick and feeble parts of France.
And let us do it with no show of fear,
No, with no more than if we heard that England
25   Were busied with a Whitsun morris dance[2]
For, my good liege, she is so idly° kinged,   *frivolously*
Her sceptre so fantastically° borne   *irrationally*
By a vain, giddy, shallow, humorous° youth,   *capricious*
That fear attends her not.

CONSTABLE   O peace, Prince Dauphin.
30   You are too much mistaken in this king.
Question your grace the late° ambassadors   *recent*
With what great state he heard their embassy,
How well supplied with agèd counsellors,
How modest in exception,° and withal   *objecting*
35   How terrible° in constant resolution,   *fearsome*
And you shall find his vanities forespent°   *his former follies*
Were but the outside of the Roman Brutus,[3]
Covering discretion with a coat of folly,
As gardeners do with ordure° hide those roots   *manure*
40   That shall first spring and be most delicate.

DAUPHIN   Well, 'tis not so, my Lord High Constable.
But though° we think it so, it is no matter.   *if*
In cases of defence 'tis best to weigh°   *consider*
The enemy more mighty than he seems.
45   So the proportions of defence are filled[4]—
Which, of a weak and niggardly projection,°   *scale*
Doth like a miser spoil his coat with scanting°   *skimping*
A little cloth.

KING CHARLES   Think we King Harry strong.
And princes, look you strongly arm to meet him.
50   The kindred of him hath been fleshed[5] upon us,
And he is bred out of that bloody strain
That haunted us in our familiar paths.
Witness our too-much-memorable shame

---

1. The fatally underestimated, at the Battles of Crécy (1346) and Poitiers (1356).
2. Folk dance celebrating Whitsuntide, a summer holiday.
3. Lucius Junius Brutus pretended idiocy to disarm the tyrant Lucius Tarquinius Superbus, against whom he led a successful revolt.
4. A proper defense is mounted.
5. Have been given their first taste of blood.

When Crécy battle fatally was struck,°   *fought*
55   And all our princes captived by the hand
      Of that black name, Edward, Black Prince of Wales,
      Whiles that his mountant° sire, on mountain standing,   *ascendant*
      Up in the air, crowned with the golden sun,
      Saw his heroical seed and smiled to see him
60   Mangle the work of nature and deface
      The patterns that by God and by French fathers
      Had twenty years been made. This is a stem
      Of that victorious stock, and let us fear
      The native° mightiness and fate° of him.   *hereditary / fortune*
            Enter a MESSENGER
65   MESSENGER   Ambassadors from Harry, King of England,
      Do crave admittance to your majesty.
      KING CHARLES   We'll give them present audience. Go and bring them.
                                                                    [*Exit* MESSENGER]
      You see this chase is hotly followed, friends.
      DAUPHIN   Turn head[6] and stop pursuit. For coward dogs
70   Most spend their mouths° when what they seem to threaten   *bark the loudest*
      Runs far before them. Good my sovereign,
      Take up the English short, and let them know
      Of what a monarchy you are the head.
      Self-love, my liege, is not so vile a sin
      As self-neglecting.
            Enter [Duke of] EXETER [*attended*]
75   KING CHARLES   From our brother England?
      EXETER   From him, and thus he greets your majesty:
      He wills you, in the name of God Almighty,
      That you divest yourself and lay apart°   *aside*
      The borrowed glories that by gift of heaven,
80   By law of nature and of nations, 'longs°   *belongs*
      To him and to his heirs, namely the crown,
      And all wide-stretchèd honours that pertain
      By custom and the ordinance of times°   *laws of ages*
      Unto the crown of France. That you may know
85   'Tis no sinister° nor no awkward° claim,   *illegitimate / oblique*
      Picked from the worm-holes of long-vanished days,
      Nor from the dust of old oblivion raked,
      He sends you this most memorable line,°   *pedigree*
      In every branch truly demonstrative,°   *conclusive*
90   Willing you over-look° this pedigree,   *Wishing you to look over*
      And when you find him evenly derived°   *directly descended*
      From his most famed of famous ancestors,
      Edward the Third, he bids you then resign
      Your crown and kingdom, indirectly° held   *unjustly*
95   From him, the native and true challenger.°   *claimant*
      KING CHARLES   Or else what follows?
      EXETER   Bloody constraint. For if you hide the crown
      Even in your hearts, there will he rake for it.
      Therefore in fierce tempest is he coming,
100   In thunder and in earthquake, like a Jove,
      That if requiring° fail, he will compel;   *requesting*

6. Make a stand (a hunting term).

And bids you, in the bowels° of the Lord,	*compassion*
Deliver up the crown, and to take mercy	
On the poor souls for whom this hungry war	
105 Opens his vasty jaws; and on your head	
Turns he the widows' tears, the orphans' cries,	
The dead men's blood, the pining maidens' groans,	
For husbands, fathers, and betrothèd lovers	
That shall be swallowed in this controversy.	
110 This is his claim, his threat'ning, and my message—	
Unless the Dauphin be in presence here,	
To whom expressly I bring greeting too.	
KING CHARLES For us, we will consider of this further.	
Tomorrow shall you bear our full intent	
Back to our brother England.	
115 DAUPHIN For the Dauphin,	
I stand here for him. What to him from England?	
EXETER Scorn and defiance, slight regard, contempt;	
And anything that may not misbecome	
The mighty sender, doth he prize° you at.	*assess*
120 Thus says my king: an if° your father's highness	*an if=if*
Do not, in grant° of all demands at large,°	*concession / in full*
Sweeten the bitter mock you sent his majesty,	
He'll call you to so hot an answer for it	
That caves and womby vaultages° of France	*hollow caverns*
125 Shall chide your trespass and return your mock	
In second accent° of his ordinance.°	*echo / artillery*
DAUPHIN Say if my father render fair return	
It is against my will, for I desire	
Nothing but odds° with England. To that end,	*strife*
130 As matching to his youth and vanity,°	*frivolity*
I did present him with the Paris° balls.	*tennis*
EXETER He'll make your Paris Louvre° shake for it,	*French royal palace*
Were it the mistress° court of mighty Europe.	*principal (in tennis)*
And be assured, you'll find a diff'rence,	
135 As we his subjects have in wonder found,	
Between the promise of his greener° days	*younger*
And these he masters now: now he weighs time	
Even to the utmost grain.° That you shall read	*smallest unit*
In your own losses, if he stay in France.	
140 KING CHARLES [*rising*] Tomorrow shall you know our mind at full.	
Flourish[7]	
EXETER Dispatch us with all speed, lest that our king	
Come here himself to question our delay—	
For he is footed° in this land already.	*come ashore*
KING CHARLES You shall be soon dispatched with fair conditions.	
145 A night is but small breath° and little pause	*small time*
To answer matters of this consequence. *Exeunt. Flourish*	

---

7. Fanfare (to signal the end of the interview; Exeter unceremoniously continues).

3.0

Enter CHORUS

CHORUS Thus with imagined wing° our swift scene flies   *wings of imagination*
In motion of no less celerity
Than that of thought. Suppose that you have seen
The well-appointed° king at Dover pier   *well-equipped*
5   Embark his royalty, and his brave fleet
With silken streamers the young Phoebus fanning.[1]
Play with your fancies,° and in them behold   *imagination*
Upon the hempen tackle ship-boys climbing;
Hear the shrill whistle,° which doth order give   *(of the ship's captain)*
10 To sounds confused; behold the threaden° sails,   *woven of thread*
Borne with th'invisible and creeping wind,
Draw the huge bottoms° through the furrowed sea,   *hulls*
Breasting the lofty surge. O do but think
You stand upon the rivage° and behold   *shore*
15 A city on th'inconstant billows dancing—
For so appears this fleet majestical,
Holding due course to Harfleur.[2] Follow, follow!
Grapple° your minds to sternage° of this navy,   *Fasten / the sterns*
And leave your England, as dead midnight still,
20 Guarded with grandsires, babies, and old women,
Either past or not arrived to pith° and puissance.   *strength*
For who is he, whose chin is but enriched
With one appearing hair, that will not follow
These culled° and choice-drawn cavaliers to France?   *select*
25 Work, work your thoughts, and therein see a siege.
Behold the ordnance° on their carriages,   *cannons*
With fatal mouths gaping on girded° Harfleur.   *encircled*
Suppose th'ambassador from the French comes back,
Tells Harry that the King doth offer him
30 Catherine his daughter, and with her, to° dowry,   *as*
Some petty and unprofitable dukedoms.
The offer likes° not, and the nimble gunner   *pleases*
With linstock° now the devilish cannon touches,   *lighting stick*
         Alarum, and chambers° go off   *small cannon*
And down goes all before them. Still be kind,
35 And eke out our performance with your mind.   *Exit*

3.1

Alarum. Enter KING [HARRY *and the English army, with*]
scaling ladders

KING HARRY Once more unto the breach,[1] dear friends, once more,
Or close the wall up with our English dead.
In peace there's nothing so becomes a man
As modest stillness and humility,
5   But when the blast of war blows in our ears,
Then imitate the action of the tiger.
Stiffen the sinews, conjure up the blood,
Disguise fair nature with hard-favoured rage.
Then lend the eye a terrible aspect,

3.0
1. *the . . . fanning*: fluttering toward the rising sun.
2. French port on the mouth of the Seine.

3.1 Location: Before Harfleur.
1. Gap in the fortifications, created by artillery bombardment.

10	Let it pry° through the portage² of the head	peer
	Like the brass cannon, let the brow o'erwhelm° it	overhang
	As fearfully as doth a gallèd° rock	worn
	O'erhang and jutty° his confounded° base,	jut out over / ruined
	Swilled° with the wild and wasteful° ocean.	Washed / destructive
15	Now set the teeth and stretch the nostril wide,	
	Hold hard the breath, and bend up every spirit	
	To his full height. On, on, you noblest English,	
	Whose blood is fet° from fathers of war-proof,°	fetched / proven in war
	Fathers that like so many Alexanders³	
20	Have in these parts from morn till even fought,	
	And sheathed their swords for lack of argument.°	opposition
	Dishonour not your mothers; now attest	
	That those whom you called fathers did beget you.	
	Be copy° now to men of grosser° blood,	example / less noble
25	And teach them how to war. And you, good yeomen,°	men below noble rank
	Whose limbs were made in England, show us here	
	The mettle° of your pasture; let us swear	quality
	That you are worth your breeding—which I doubt not,	
	For there is none of you so mean and base	
30	That hath not noble lustre in your eyes.	
	I see you stand like greyhounds in the slips,°	leashes
	Straining upon the start. The game's afoot.	
	Follow your spirit, and upon this charge	
	Cry, 'God for Harry! England and Saint George!'°	patron saint of England

Alarum, and chambers go off. [*Exeunt*]

3.2

Enter NIM, BARDOLPH, [*Ensign*] PISTOL, *and* BOY

BARDOLPH   On, on, on, on, on! To the breach, to the breach!

NIM	Pray thee corporal, stay. The knocks are too hot, and for	
	mine own part I have not a case° of lives. The humour of it is	set
	too hot, that is the very plainsong° of it.	plain truth
5 PISTOL	'The plainsong' is most just,° for humours do abound.	apt

Knocks go and come, God's vassals drop and die,

[*sings*]   And sword and shield
                         In bloody field
                              Doth win immortal fame.

| 10 BOY | Would I were in an alehouse in London. I would give all | |
| | my fame for a pot of ale, and safety. | |

PISTOL [*sings*]   And I.
                      If wishes would prevail with me°   *in my case*
                      My purpose should not fail with me
| 15 | But thither would I hie.°   go |

BOY [*sings*]   As duly
                         But not as truly
                              As bird doth sing on bough.

Enter [*Captain*] FLUELLEN *and beats them in*

FLUELLEN	God's plud!¹ Up to the breaches, you dogs! Avaunt,	
20	you cullions!²	
PISTOL	Be merciful, great duke, to men of mould.³	

---

2. Portholes (that is, eye sockets).
3. Alexander the Great was said to have wept because no worlds remained for him to conquer.
3.2 Scene continues.

1. Blood (Fluellen's Welsh accent substitutes "p" for "b," and also "f" for "v" and "ch" for "j").
2. Be off, you wretches. *cullions:* testicles.
3. Earth (that is, mortal men).

Abate thy rage, abate thy manly rage,
Abate thy rage, great duke. Good bawcock,⁴ bate
Thy rage. Use lenity,° sweet chuck.   *leniency*

25 NIM These be good humours!⁵
          [FLUELLEN *begins to beat* NIM]
          Your honour runs bad humours.°   *Exeunt [all but the* BOY]   *is ill tempered*

    BOY As young as I am, I have observed these three swashers.° I   *swashbucklers*
          am boy to them all three, but all they three, though they should
          serve me, could not be man⁶ to me, for indeed three such
30   antics° do not amount to a man. For Bardolph, he is white-   *buffoons*
          livered° and red-faced—by the means whereof a° faces it out,   *cowardly / he*
          but fights not. For Pistol, he hath a killing tongue and a quiet
          sword—by the means whereof a breaks words, and keeps whole
          weapons. For Nim, he hath heard that men of few words are
35   the best men, and therefore he scorns to say his prayers, lest a
          should be thought a coward. But his few bad words are
          matched with as few good deeds—for a never broke any man's
          head but his own, and that was against a post, when he was
          drunk. They will steal anything, and call it 'purchase'.⁷ Bar-
40   dolph stole a lute case, bore it twelve leagues,° and sold it for   *about 36 miles*
          three halfpence. Nim and Bardolph are sworn brothers in
          filching,° and in Calais⁸ they stole a fire shovel. I knew by that   *stealing*
          piece of service the men would carry coals.⁹ They would have
          me as familiar with men's pockets as their gloves or their hand-
45   kerchiefs—which makes° much against my manhood, if I   *offends*
          should take from another's pocket to put into mine, for it is
          plain pocketing up of wrongs.¹ I must leave them, and seek
          some better service. Their villainy goes against my weak stom-
          ach, and therefore I must cast it up.°   *Exit*   *vomit it; leave it*

3.3

Enter [Captain] GOWER *[and Captain* FLUELLEN,
meeting]

GOWER Captain Fluellen, you must come presently° to the   *immediately*
        mines.¹ The Duke of Gloucester would speak with you.

FLUELLEN To the mines? Tell you the Duke it is not so good to
        come to the mines. For look you, the mines is not according to
5   the disciplines° of the war. The concavities° of it is not suffi-   *tactics; art / depth*
        cient. For look you, th'athversary, you may discuss unto the
        Duke, look you, is digt° himself, four yard under, the coun-   *digged (dug)*
        termines.² By Cheshu,° I think a will plow° up all, if there is not   *Jesu / blow*
        better directions.

10 GOWER The Duke of Gloucester, to whom the order° of the   *supervision*
        siege is given, is altogether directed by an Irishman, a very val-
        iant gentleman, i'faith.

FLUELLEN It is Captain MacMorris, is it not?

GOWER I think it be.

15 FLUELLEN By Cheshu, he is an ass, as³ in the world. I will verify

---

4. Fine chap (French *beau coq*).
5. This is fine behavior (sarcastic).
6. Punning on the sense "personal servant."
7. Booty (seized in combat).
8. French port town.
9. Do dirty work; tolerate insults.

1. Pocketing stolen goods; putting up with insults
(unmanly behavior).
3.3 Location: Outside Harfleur.
1. Tunnels dug to undermine a besieged fortress.
2. Tunnels dug to undermine enemy "mines."
3. *he is an ass, as:* he is as big an ass as there is.

as much in his beard.° He has no more directions in the true   *to his face*
disciplines of the wars, look you—of the *Roman* disciplines—
than is a puppy dog.

         Enter [Captain] MACMORRIS *and Captain* JAMY

GOWER   Here a comes, and the Scots captain, Captain Jamy,
20 with him.

FLUELLEN   Captain Jamy is a marvellous falorous° gentleman,   *valorous*
that is certain, and of great expedition° and knowledge in   *quick-wittedness*
th'anciant wars, upon my particular knowledge of his directions.
By Cheshu, he will maintain his argument as well as any mili-
25 tary man in the world, in the disciplines of the pristine wars of
the Romans.

JAMY   I say gud day, Captain Fluellen.

FLUELLEN   Good e'en to your worship, good Captain James.

GOWER   How now, Captain MacMorris, have you quit the
30 mines? Have the pioneers given o'er?°   *diggers stopped work*

MACMORRIS   By Chrish law,⁴ 'tish ill done. The work ish give
over, the trumpet sound the retreat. By my hand I swear, and
my father's soul, the work ish ill done, it ish give over. I would
have blowed up the town, so Chrish save me law, in an hour.
35 O 'tish ill done, 'tish ill done, by my hand 'tish ill done.

FLUELLEN   Captain MacMorris, I beseech you now, will you
vouchsafe° me, look you, a few disputations with you, as partly   *allow*
touching or concerning the disciplines of the war, the Roman
wars, in the way of argument, look you, and friendly communi-
40 cation? Partly to satisfy my opinion and partly for the satisfaction, look you, of my mind. As touching the direction of the
military discipline, that is the point.

JAMY   It sall be vary gud, gud feith, gud captains bath,° and I sall   *both*
quite° you with gud leve, as I may pick occasion. That sall I,   *requite; answer*
45 marry.

MACMORRIS   It is no time to discourse, so Chrish save me. The
day is hot, and the weather and the wars and the King and the
dukes. It is no time to discourse. The town is besieched. An the
trumpet call us to the breach, and we talk and, be Chrish, do
50 nothing, 'tis shame for us all. So God sa'° me, 'tis shame to   *save*
stand still, it is shame by my hand. And there is throats to be
cut, and works to be done, and there ish nothing done, so
Christ sa' me law.

JAMY   By the mess,° ere these eyes of mine take themselves to   *By the mass (an oath)*
55 slumber, ay'll de gud service, or I'll lig° i'th' grund for it. Ay   *lie*
owe Got a death, and I'll pay't as valorously as I may, that sall I
suirely do, that is the brief and the long. Marry, I wad full fain
heard° some question 'tween you twae.°   *eagerly have heard / two*

FLUELLEN   Captain MacMorris, I think, look you, under your
60 correction, there is not many of your nation—

MACMORRIS   Of my nation? What ish my nation? Ish a villain
and a bastard and a knave and a rascal? What ish my nation?
Who talks of my nation?

FLUELLEN   Look you, if you take the matter otherwise than is
65 meant, Captain MacMorris, peradventure I shall think you do
not use me with that affability as in discretion you ought to use

---

4. La (adds force to an utterance).

me, look you, being as good a man as yourself, both in the
disciplines of war and in the derivation of my birth, and in
other particularities.

70 MACMORRIS I do not know you so good a man as myself. So
Chrish save me, I will cut off your head.

GOWER Gentlemen both, you will mistake each other.

JAMY Ah, that's a foul fault.

A *parley*⁵ [*is sounded*]

GOWER The town sounds a parley.

75 FLUELLEN Captain MacMorris, when there is more better
opportunity to be required, look you, I will be so bold as to tell
you I know the disciplines of war. And there is an end.   *Exit*

[*Flourish.*] *Enter* KING [HARRY] *and all his train before
the gates*

KING HARRY How yet resolves the Governor of the town?
This is the latest parle° we will admit.   last parley
80 Therefore to our best mercy give yourselves,
Or like to men proud of° destruction   glorying in
Defy us to our worst. For as I am a soldier,
A name that in my thoughts becomes me best,
If I begin the batt'ry° once again   bombardment
85 I will not leave the half-achievèd Harfleur
Till in her ashes she lie burièd.
The gates of mercy shall be all shut up,
And the fleshed° soldier, rough and hard of heart,   inflamed
In liberty of bloody hand shall range
90 With conscience wide° as hell, mowing like grass   permissive
Your fresh fair virgins and your flow'ring infants.
What is it then to me if impious war
Arrayed in flames like to the prince of fiends
Do with his smirched complexion all fell° feats   cruel
95 Enlinked to waste° and desolation?   destruction
What is't to me, when you yourselves are cause,
If your pure maidens fall into the hand
Of hot and forcing violation?
What rein can hold licentious wickedness
100 When down the hill he holds° his fierce career?°   maintains / gallop
We may as bootless° spend our vain command   unprofitably
Upon th'enragèd soldiers in their spoil
As send precepts° to the leviathan°   summons / sea monster
To come ashore. Therefore, you men of Harfleur,
105 Take pity of your town and of your people
Whiles yet my soldiers are in my command,
Whiles yet the cool and temperate wind of grace
O'erblows° the filthy and contagious clouds⁶   Disperses
Of heady° murder, spoil, and villainy.   headstrong
110 If not—why, in a moment look to see
The blind and bloody soldier with foul hand
Defile the locks of your shrill-shrieking daughters;
Your fathers taken by the silver beards,
And their most reverend heads dashed to the walls;
115 Your naked infants spitted° upon pikes,   impaled
Whiles the mad mothers with their howls confused

5. Trumpet call requesting negotiation.   6. Pestilence was believed to drop from the sky.

Do break the clouds, as did the wives of Jewry[7]
At Herod's bloody-hunting slaughtermen.
What say you? Will you yield, and this avoid?
120 Or, guilty in defence, be thus destroyed?
        Enter GOVERNOR [*on the wall*]
GOVERNOR   Our expectation hath this day an end.
The Dauphin, whom of succours we entreated,
Returns° us that his powers are yet not ready   *Replies to*
To raise so great a siege. Therefore, dread King,
125 We yield our town and lives to thy soft mercy.
Enter our gates, dispose of us and ours,
For we no longer are defensible.
KING HARRY   Open your gates.   [*Exit* GOVERNOR]
        Come, Uncle Exeter,
Go you and enter Harfleur. There remain,
130 And fortify it strongly 'gainst the French.
Use mercy to them all. For us, dear uncle,
The winter coming on, and sickness growing
Upon our soldiers, we will retire to Calais.
Tonight in Harfleur will we be your guest;
135 Tomorrow for the march are we addressed.°   *ready*
        [*The gates are opened.*] *Flourish, and* [*they*] *enter the town*

3.4

        Enter [*Princess*] CATHERINE *and* ALICE, *an old gentle-
        woman*

CATHERINE   Alice, tu as été en Angleterre, et tu bien parles
le langage.[1]
ALICE   Un peu, madame.
CATHERINE   Je te prie, m'enseignez. Il faut que j'apprenne à
5 parler. Comment appelez-vous la main en anglais?
ALICE   La main? Elle est appelée *de hand*.
CATHERINE   *De hand*. Et les doigts?
ALICE   Les doigts? Ma foi, j'oublie les doigts, mais je me souviendrai. Les doigts—je pense qu'ils sont appelés *de fingres*. Oui, *de*
10 *fingres*.
CATHERINE   La main, *de hand*; les doigts, *de fingres*. Je pense que
je suis la bonne écolière; j'ai gagné deux mots d'anglais vite-
ment. Comment appelez-vous les ongles?
ALICE   Les ongles? Nous les appelons *de nails*.
15 CATHERINE   *De nails*. Écoutez—dites-moi si je parle bien: *de
hand, de fingres, et de nails*.

---

7. Judaea; see Matthew 2:16–18.
3.4 Location: The French King's palace.
1. A translation of this French scene follows, with editorial comments in brackets.

CATHERINE   Alice, you've been in England, and you speak the language well.
ALICE   A little, madam.
CATHERINE   Please teach me. I must learn to speak it. What do you call *la main* in English?
ALICE   *La main*? It is called "de hand."
CATHERINE   De hand. And *les doigts*?
ALICE   *Les doigts*? Faith, I forget *les doigts*, but I'll remember. *Les doigts*—I think they're called "de fingres." Yes, de fingres.
CATHERINE   *Le main*, de hand; *les doigts*, de fingres. I think I'm a good scholar; I've learned two words of English quickly. What do you call *les ongles*?
ALICE   *Les ongles*? We call them "de nails."
CATHERINE   De nails. Listen—tell me if I speak well: de hand, de fingres, and de nails.

ALICE C'est bien dit, madame. Il est fort bon anglais.

CATHERINE Dites-moi l'anglais pour le bras.

ALICE *De arma*, madame.

20 CATHERINE Et le coude?

ALICE *D'elbow.*

CATHERINE *D'elbow.* Je m'en fais la répétition de tous les mots
que vous m'avez appris dès à présent.

ALICE Il est trop difficile, madame, comme je pense.

25 CATHERINE Excusez-moi, Alice. Écoutez: *d'hand, de fingre, de
nails, d'arma, de bilbow.*

ALICE *D'elbow,* madame.

CATHERINE O Seigneur Dieu, je m'en oublie! *D'elbow.* Comment appelez-vous le col?

30 ALICE *De nick,* madame.

CATHERINE *De nick.* Et le menton?

ALICE *De chin.*

CATHERINE *De sin.* Le col, *de nick*; le menton, *de sin.*

ALICE Oui. Sauf votre honneur, en vérité vous prononcez les

35 mots aussi droit que les natifs d'Angleterre.

CATHERINE Je ne doute point d'apprendre, par la grâce de Dieu,
et en peu de temps.

ALICE N'avez-vous y déjà oublié ce que je vous ai enseigné?

CATHERINE Non, et je réciterai à vous promptement: *d'hand, de*

40 *fingre, de mailès*—

ALICE *De nails,* madame.

CATHERINE *De nails, de arma, de ilbow*—

ALICE Sauf votre honneur, *d'elbow.*

CATHERINE Ainsi dis-je. *D'elbow, de nick, et de sin.* Comment

45 appelez-vous les pieds et la robe?

ALICE *De foot,* madame, et *de cown.*

CATHERINE *De foot* et *de cown?* O Seigneur Dieu! Ils sont les
mots de son mauvais, corruptible, gros, et impudique, et non
pour les dames d'honneur d'user. Je ne voudrais prononcer ces

50 mots devant les seigneurs de France pour tout le monde. Foh!
De foot et *de cown!* Néanmoins, je réciterai une autre fois ma

---

ALICE That's well said, madam. It is very good English.

CATHERINE Tell me the English for *le bras.*

ALICE "De arma," madam.

CATHERINE And *le coude?*

ALICE "D'elbow."

CATHERINE D'elbow. I'll repeat all the words you have taught me so far.

ALICE It is too difficult, madam, in my opinion.

CATHERINE Excuse me, Alice. Listen: d'hand, de fingre, de nails, d'arma, de bilbow.

ALICE D'elbow, madam.

CATHERINE O Lord God, I forgot. D'elbow. What do you call *le col?*

ALICE "De nick," madam.

CATHERINE De nick. And *le menton?*

ALICE "De chin."

CATHERINE De sin. *Le col,* de nick; *le menton,* de sin.

ALICE Yes. Saving your honor, to tell the truth you pronounce the words just as properly as the native English.

CATHERINE I don't doubt that I'll learn, with God's help, and in a short time.

ALICE Haven't you already forgotten what I have taught you?

CATHERINE No, I shall recite to you right now: d'hand, de fingre, de mailès—

ALICE De nails, madam.

CATHERINE De nails, de arma, de ilbow—

ALICE Saving your honor, d'elbow.

CATHERINE That's what I said. D'elbow, de nick, and de sin. What do you call *les pieds* and *la robe?*

ALICE "De foot," madam, and "de cown" [gown].

CATHERINE De foot and de cown? O Lord God, those are evil-sounding words, easily misconstrued, vulgar, and
immodest, and not for respectable ladies to use. [They sound like the French *foutre,* "fuck," and *con,* "cunt."] I
wouldn't speak those words in front of French gentlemen for all the world. Ugh! de foot and de cown! Still, I shall

leçon ensemble. *D'hand, de fingre, de nails, d'arma, d'elbow,
de nick, de sin, de foot, de cown.*

ALICE   Excellent, madame!

55   CATHERINE   *C'est assez pour une fois. Allons-nous à dîner.*

Exeunt

3.5

Enter KING [CHARLES *the Sixth] of France,* DAUPHIN,
CONSTABLE, [DUKE *of*] BOURBON, *and others*

KING CHARLES   'Tis certain he hath passed the River Somme.

CONSTABLE   And if he be not fought withal,° my lord,   *with*
   Let us not live in France; let us quit all
   And give our vineyards to a barbarous people.

5   DAUPHIN   *O Dieu vivant!*° Shall a few sprays[1] of us,   *O living God*
   The emptying of our fathers' luxury,[2]
   Our scions,° put in wild and savage stock,   *grafts*
   Spirt° up so suddenly into the clouds   *Sprout*
   And over-look their grafters?

10   BOURBON   Normans, but bastard Normans, Norman bastards!
   Mort de ma vie,° if they march along   *Death of my life*
   Unfought withal, but I will sell my dukedom
   To buy a slobb'ry° and a dirty farm   *muddy*
   In that nook-shotten[3] isle of Albion.°   *England*

15   CONSTABLE   *Dieu de batailles!*° Where° have they this mettle?   *God of battles / Whence*
   Is not their climate foggy, raw, and dull,
   On whom as in despite° the sun looks pale,   *contempt*
   Killing their fruit with frowns? Can sodden° water,   *boiled; to make ale*
   A drench for sur-reined jades[4]—their barley-broth—
20   Decoct° their cold blood to such valiant heat?   *Boil, to purify*
   And shall our quick blood, spirited with wine,
   Seem frosty? O for honour of our land
   Let us not hang like roping° icicles   *ropelike*
   Upon our houses' thatch, whiles a more frosty people
25   Sweat drops of gallant youth in our rich fields—
   'Poor' may we call them,° in their native lords.   *(the fields)*

DAUPHIN   By faith and honour,
   Our madams mock at us and plainly say
   Our mettle is bred out,° and they will give   *is exhausted*
30   Their bodies to the lust of English youth,
   To new-store France with bastard warriors.

BOURBON   They bid us, 'To the English dancing-schools,
   And teach lavoltas° high and swift corantos'[5]—   *leaping dance*
   Saying our grace is only in our heels,
35   And that we are most lofty runaways.

KING CHARLES   Where is Montjoy the herald? Speed° him hence.   *Quickly send*
   Let him greet England with our sharp defiance.
   Up, princes, and with spirit of honour edged
   More sharper than your swords, hie° to the field.   *go*
40   Charles Delabret, High Constable of France,
   You Dukes of Orléans, Bourbon, and of Berri,
   Alençon, Brabant, Bar, and Burgundy,

---

recite my entire lesson once more. D'hand, de fingre, de nails, d'arma, d'elbow, de nick, de sin, de foot, de cown.
ALICE   Excellent, madam!
CATHERINE   That's enough for one time. Let's go to dinner.

3.5 Location: The French King's court.   3. With an indented shore.
1. Offshoots (bastards).   4. A tonic for overworked horses.
2. The discharge ("emptying") of our forefathers' lust.   5. Running dance.

Jaques Châtillion, Rambures, Vaudemont,
Beaumont, Grandpré, Roussi, and Fauconbridge,
45 Foix, Lestrelles, Boucicault, and Charolais,
High dukes, great princes, barons, lords, and knights,
For your great seats now quit you° of great shames.
Bar Harry England, that sweeps through our land
With pennons° painted in the blood of Harfleur;   *banners*
50 Rush on his host, as doth the melted snow
Upon the valleys, whose low vassal seat
The Alps doth spit and void his rheum° upon.   *empty its moisture*
Go down upon him, you have power enough,
And in a captive chariot into Rouen
Bring him our prisoner.
55 CONSTABLE   This becomes the great.°   *befits noblemen*
Sorry am I his numbers are so few,
His soldiers sick and famished in their march,
For I am sure when he shall see our army
He'll drop his heart into the sink° of fear   *pit*
60 And, fore achievement,° offer us his ransom.   *instead of battle*
KING CHARLES   Therefore, Lord Constable, haste on Montjoy,
And let him say to England that we send
To know what willing ransom he will give.—
Prince Dauphin, you shall stay with us in Rouen.
65 DAUPHIN   Not so, I do beseech your majesty.
KING CHARLES   Be patient, for you shall remain with us.—
Now forth, Lord Constable, and princes all,
And quickly bring us word of England's fall. *Exeunt* [*severally*]

3.6

Enter Captains GOWER *and* FLUELLEN [*meeting*]

GOWER   How now, Captain Fluellen, come you from the bridge?
FLUELLEN   I assure you there is very excellent services committed at the bridge.
GOWER   Is the Duke of Exeter safe?
5 FLUELLEN   The Duke of Exeter is as magnanimous as Agamemnon,[1] and a man that I love and honour with my soul and my heart and my duty and my live and my living and my uttermost power. He is not, God be praised and blessed, any hurt in the world, but keeps the bridge most valiantly, with excellent disci-
10 pline. There is an ensign lieutenant there at the pridge, I think in my very conscience he is as valiant a man as Mark Antony, and he is a man of no estimation° in the world, but I did see   *fame*
him do as gallant service.
GOWER   What do you call him?
15 FLUELLEN   He is called Ensign Pistol.
GOWER   I know him not.

Enter Ensign PISTOL

FLUELLEN   Here is the man.
PISTOL   Captain, I thee beseech to do me favours.
The Duke of Exeter doth love thee well.
20 FLUELLEN   Ay, I praise God, and I have merited some love at his hands.

---

6. *For . . . you:* In defense of your high ranks, now revenge yourselves.

3.6 Location: The English camp.
1. Greek general in the Trojan War.

PISTOL   Bardolph, a soldier firm and sound of heart,
        Of buxom° valour, hath by cruel fate   *lively*
        And giddy Fortune's furious fickle wheel,
25   That goddess blind that stands upon the rolling restless stone—
FLUELLEN   By your patience, Ensign Pistol: Fortune is painted
        blind, with a muffler° afore her eyes, to signify to you that For-   *blindfold*
        tune is blind. And she is painted also with a wheel, to signify to
        you—which is the moral of it—that she is turning and incon-
30   stant and mutability and variation. And her foot, look you, is
        fixed upon a spherical stone, which rolls and rolls and rolls.
        In good truth, the poet makes a most excellent description of
        it; Fortune is an excellent moral.°   *symbolic emblem*
PISTOL   Fortune is Bardolph's foe and frowns on him,
35   For he hath stol'n a pax,² and hangèd must a° be.   *he*
        A damnèd death—
        Let gallows gape for dog, let man go free,
        And let not hemp³ his windpipe suffocate.
        But Exeter hath given the doom° of death   *sentence*
40   For pax of little price.
        Therefore go speak, the Duke will hear thy voice,
        And let not Bardolph's vital thread be cut
        With edge of penny cord and vile reproach.
        Speak, captain, for his life, and I will thee requite.
45 FLUELLEN   Ensign Pistol, I do partly understand your meaning.
PISTOL   Why then rejoice therefor.
FLUELLEN   Certainly, ensign, it is not a thing to rejoice at. For
        if, look you, he were my brother, I would desire the Duke to
        use his good pleasure, and put him to executions. For disci-
50   pline ought to be used.
PISTOL   Die and be damned! and *fico*⁴ for thy friendship.
FLUELLEN   It is well.
PISTOL   The fig of Spain.
FLUELLEN   Very good.
55 PISTOL   I say the fig within thy bowels and thy dirty maw.   *Exit*
FLUELLEN   Captain Gower, cannot you hear it lighten and
        thunder?
GOWER   Why, is this the ensign you told me of? I remember him
        now. A bawd, a cutpurse.°   *thief*
60 FLUELLEN   I'll assure you, a uttered as prave words at the pridge
        as you shall see in a summer's day. But it is very well. What he
        has spoke to me, that is well, I warrant you, when time is serve.
GOWER   Why 'tis a gull,° a fool, a rogue, that now and then goes   *simpleton*
        to the wars, to grace himself at his return into London under
65   the form of a soldier. And such fellows are perfect in the great
        commanders' names, and they will learn° you by rote where   *teach*
        services were done— at such and such a sconce,° at such a   *fortification*
        breach, at such a convoy, who came off bravely, who was shot,
        who disgraced, what terms the enemy stood on—and this they
70   con° perfectly in the phrase of war, which they trick up° with   *memorize / adorn*
        new-tuned° oaths. And what a beard of the General's cut and a   *newly coined*
        horrid suit of the camp⁵ will do among foaming bottles and ale-

---

2. Small tablet with a crucifix stamped on it.   the thumb between two fingers.
3. Of which ropes were made.   5. *horrid . . . camp*: frightening soldier's attire.
4. Spanish for "fig"; obscene gesture made by thrusting

washed wits is wonderful to be thought on. But you must learn
to know such slanders° of the age, or else you may be marvel-   *disgraces*
lously mistook.

FLUELLEN   I tell you what, Captain Gower, I do perceive he is
not the man that he would gladly make show to the world he
is. If I find a hole in his coat,° I will tell him my mind.   *means of exposing him*
            [*A drum is heard*]
Hark you, the King is coming, and I must speak with him from
the pridge.
            Enter KING [HARRY] *and his poor soldiers,* [*with*] *drum*
            and colours°   *drummer and flag bearer*
God pless your majesty.

KING HARRY   How now, Fluellen, com'st thou from the bridge?

FLUELLEN   Ay, so please your majesty. The Duke of Exeter has
very gallantly maintained the pridge. The French is gone off,
look you, and there is gallant and most prave passages.° Marry,   *altercations*
th'athversary was have possession of the pridge, but he is
enforced to retire, and the Duke of Exeter is master of the
pridge. I can tell your majesty, the Duke is a prave man.

KING HARRY   What men have you lost, Fluellen?

FLUELLEN   The perdition° of th'athversary hath been very great,   *loss*
reasonable great. Marry, for my part I think the Duke hath lost
never a man, but one that is like to be executed for robbing a
church, one Bardolph, if your majesty know the man. His face
is all bubuncles and whelks° and knobs and flames o' fire, and   *abscesses and pimples*
his lips blows at his nose, and it is like a coal of fire, sometimes
plue and sometimes red. But his nose is executed,⁶ and his
fire's out.

KING HARRY   We would have all such offenders so cut off, and
we here give express charge that in our marches through the
country there be nothing compelled from the villages, nothing
taken but° paid for, none of the French upbraided or abused in   *unless*
disdainful language. For when lenity° and cruelty play for a   *leniency*
kingdom, the gentler gamester is the soonest winner.
            Tucket.° Enter MONTJOY   *Trumpet call*

MONTJOY   You know me by my habit.°   *herald's coat*

KING HARRY   Well then, I know thee. What shall I know of thee?

MONTJOY   My master's mind.

KING HARRY   Unfold it.

MONTJOY   Thus says my King:
'Say thou to Harry of England, though we seemed dead, we did
but sleep. Advantage° is a better soldier than rashness. Tell   *Circumspection*
him, we could have rebuked him at Harfleur, but that we
thought not good to bruise an injury° till it were full ripe. Now   *squeeze a pimple*
we speak upon our cue,° and our voice is imperial. England   *at the proper time*
shall repent his folly, see his weakness, and admire our suffer-
ance.° Bid him therefore consider of his ransom, which must   *wonder at our patience*
proportion the losses we have borne, the subjects we have lost,
the disgrace we have digested°—which in weight to re-answer,°   *endured / compensate*
his pettiness would bow under. For our losses, his exchequer°   *King's treasury*
is too poor; for th'effusion of our blood, the muster⁷ of his kingdom too faint a number; and for our disgrace, his own person
kneeling at our feet but a weak and worthless satisfaction. To
this add defiance, and tell him for conclusion he hath betrayed

---

6. Slit (in the pillory before he is hanged).   7. Entire population, assembled for military service.

his followers, whose condemnation is pronounced.'
So far my King and master; so much my office.
KING HARRY   What is thy name? I know thy quality.°   *rank*
MONTJOY   Montjoy.
125   KING HARRY   Thou dost thy office fairly. Turn thee back
And tell thy king I do not seek him now,
But could be willing to march on to Calais
Without impeachment,° for to say the sooth°—   *hindrance / truth*
Though 'tis no wisdom to confess so much
130   Unto an enemy of craft and vantage°—   *cunning and superiority*
My people are with sickness much enfeebled,
My numbers lessened, and those few I have
Almost no better than so many French;
Who when they were in health—I tell thee herald,
135   I thought upon one pair of English legs
Did march three Frenchmen. Yet forgive me, God,
That I do brag thus. This your air of France
Hath blown that vice in me. I must repent.
Go, therefore, tell thy master here I am;
140   My ransom is this frail and worthless trunk,°   *body*
My army but a weak and sickly guard.
Yet, God before, tell him we will come on,
Though France himself and such another neighbour
Stand in our way. There's for thy labour, Montjoy.[8]
145   Go bid thy master well advise himself.
If we may pass, we will; if we be hindered,
We shall your tawny ground with your red blood
Discolour. And so, Montjoy, fare you well.
The sum of all our answer is but this:
150   We would not seek a battle as we are,
Nor as we are we say we will not shun it.
So tell your master.
MONTJOY   I shall deliver so. Thanks to your highness.   *Exit*
GLOUCESTER   I hope they will not come upon us now.
155   KING HARRY   We are in God's hand, brother, not in theirs.
March to the bridge. It now draws toward night.
Beyond the river we'll encamp ourselves,
And on tomorrow bid them march away.   *Exeunt*

3.7

Enter the CONSTABLE, *Lord* RAMBURES, [*Dukes of*]
ORLÉANS [*and*] BOURBON,[1] *with others*
CONSTABLE   Tut, I have the best armour of the world. Would it
were day.
ORLÉANS   You have an excellent armour. But let my horse have
his due.
5   CONSTABLE   It is the best horse of Europe.
ORLÉANS   Will it never be morning?
BOURBON   My lord of Orléans and my Lord High Constable, you
talk of horse and armour?
ORLÉANS   You are as well provided of both as any prince in the
10   world.
BOURBON   What a long night is this! I will not change my horse

---

8. Henry generously "tips" the enemy herald.
3.7 Location: The French camp near Agincourt.

1. As in Q; F has "Dauphin" in this scene and in 4.2
and 4.5. See Textual Note.

with any that treads but on four pasterns.° Ah ha! He bounds   *hooves*
from the earth as if his entrails were hares—*le cheval volant,*
the Pegasus, *qui a les narines de feu!*[2] When I bestride him, I
15   soar, I am a hawk; he trots the air, the earth sings when he
touches it,[3] the basest horn° of his hoof is more musical than   *lowest part (with pun)*
the pipe of Hermes.[4]

ORLÉANS   He's of the colour of the nutmeg.

BOURBON   And of the heat of the ginger.[5] It is a beast for Per-
20   seus. He is pure air and fire, and the dull elements of earth and
water never appear in him, but only in patient stillness while
his rider mounts him. He is indeed a horse, and all other jades°   *nags*
you may call beasts.

CONSTABLE   Indeed, my lord, it is a most absolute° and excellent   *perfect*
25   horse.

BOURBON   It is the prince of palfreys.° His neigh is the bidding   *warhorses*
of a monarch, and his countenance enforces homage.

ORLÉANS   No more, cousin.

BOURBON   Nay, the man hath no wit, that cannot from the ris-
30   ing of the lark to the lodging of the lamb vary deserved praise
on my palfrey. It is a theme as fluent° as the sea. Turn the sands   *flowing; abundant*
into eloquent tongues, and my horse is argument° for them all.   *subject*
'Tis a subject for a sovereign to reason on, and for a sovereign's
sovereign to ride on, and for the world, familiar to us and
35   unknown, to lay apart their particular functions, and wonder at
him. I once writ a sonnet in his praise, and began thus: 'Wonder of nature!—'

ORLÉANS   I have heard a sonnet begin so to one's mistress.

BOURBON   Then did they imitate that which I composed to my
40   courser, for my horse is my mistress.

ORLÉANS   Your mistress bears well.[6]

BOURBON   *Me* well, which is the prescribed praise and perfection
of a good and particular° mistress.   *private*

CONSTABLE   Nay, for methought yesterday your mistress
45   shrewdly° shook your back.   *severely*

BOURBON   So perhaps did yours.

CONSTABLE   Mine was not bridled.

BOURBON   O then belike she was old and gentle, and you rode
like a kern° of Ireland, your French hose° off, and in your strait   *soldier / wide breeches*
50   strossers.°   *tights*

CONSTABLE   You have good judgement in horsemanship.

BOURBON   Be warned by me then: they that ride so, and ride not
warily, fall into foul bogs. I had rather have my horse to my
mistress.

55   CONSTABLE   I had as lief have my mistress a jade.°   *horse; whore*

BOURBON   I tell thee, Constable, my mistress wears his own
hair.[7]

CONSTABLE   I could make as true a boast as that, if I had a sow
to my mistress.

60   BOURBON   '*Le chien est retourné à son propre vomissement, et la*

2. The flying horse . . . with nostrils of fire. Pegasus was
a mythological flying horse, ridden by the hero Perseus.
3. When Pegasus struck Mount Helicon with his hoof,
the fountain of the Muses sprang forth.
4. Greek messenger god, whose sweet playing on the
pipe charmed the many-eyed guard Argus, allowing the
imprisoned Io to escape.

5. Horses' colors supposedly suggested their disposi-
tions: "nutmeg" meant "pleasant and nimble"; "ginger"
meant "hot and skittish."
6. Carries weight (with obscene innuendo).
7. Implying that the constable's mistress does not, having lost it to syphilis.

truie lavée au bourbier.[8] Thou makest use of anything.

CONSTABLE   Yet do I not use my horse for my mistress, or any
such proverb so little kin to the purpose.

RAMBURES   My Lord Constable, the armour that I saw in your
65   tent tonight, are those stars or suns upon it?

CONSTABLE   Stars, my lord.

BOURBON   Some of them will fall tomorrow, I hope.

CONSTABLE   And yet my sky shall not want.

BOURBON   That may be, for you bear a many superfluously,
70   and 'twere more honour some were away.

CONSTABLE   Even as your horse bears your praises, who would
trot as well were some of your brags dismounted.

BOURBON   Would I were able to load him with his desert! Will
it never be day? I will trot tomorrow a mile, and my way shall
75   be paved with English faces.

CONSTABLE   I will not say so, for fear I should be faced out of
my way.° But I would it were morning, for I would fain° be about   turned aside / gladly
the ears of the English.

RAMBURES   Who will go to hazard° with me for twenty prisoners?   wager

80   CONSTABLE   You must first go yourself to hazard, ere you have
them.

BOURBON   'Tis midnight. I'll go arm myself.   *Exit*

ORLÉANS   The Duke of Bourbon longs for morning.

RAMBURES   He longs to eat the English.

85   CONSTABLE   I think he will eat all he kills.

ORLÉANS   By the white hand of my lady, he's a gallant prince.

CONSTABLE   Swear by her foot, that she may tread out° the oath.   erase with her foot

ORLÉANS   He is simply the most active gentleman of France.

CONSTABLE   Doing is activity, and he will still be doing.

90   ORLÉANS   He never did harm that I heard of.

CONSTABLE   Nor will do none tomorrow. He will keep that good
name still.

ORLÉANS   I know him to be valiant.

CONSTABLE   I was told that by one that knows him better than
95   you.

ORLÉANS   What's he?

CONSTABLE   Marry, he told me so himself, and he said he cared
not who knew it.

ORLÉANS   He needs not; it is no hidden virtue in him.

100   CONSTABLE   By my faith, sir, but it is. Never anybody saw it but
his lackey.[9] 'Tis a hooded valour, and when it appears it will
bate.[1]

ORLÉANS   'Ill will never said well.'

CONSTABLE   I will cap that proverb with 'There is flattery in
105   friendship.'

ORLÉANS   And I will take up that with 'Give the devil his due.'

CONSTABLE   Well placed! There stands your friend for the devil.
Have at the very eye° of that proverb with 'A pox of the devil!'   bull's-eye

ORLÉANS   You are the better at proverbs by how much 'a fool's
110   bolt° is soon shot'.   short, blunt arrow

8. "The dog is turned to his own vomit again and the
sow that was washed to her wallowing in the mire"
(quoting 2 Peter 2:22).
9. That is, the only person he is brave enough to beat

is his servant.
1. Beat its wings (like a hawk, which was kept "hooded"
until prey was sighted); also, abate.

CONSTABLE   You have shot over.°   overshot the target
ORLÉANS   'Tis not the first time you were overshot.°   defeated
　　　　Enter a MESSENGER
MESSENGER   My Lord High Constable, the English lie within
　　fifteen hundred paces of your tents.
115　CONSTABLE   Who hath measured the ground?
MESSENGER   The Lord Grandpré.
CONSTABLE   A valiant and most expert gentleman.
　　　　　　　　　　　　　　　　　　　　　　[Exit MESSENGER*]*
　　Would it were day! Alas, poor Harry of England. He longs not
　　for the dawning as we do.
120　ORLÉANS   What a wretched and peevish fellow is this King of
　　England, to mope° with his fat-brained followers so far out of   *wander*
　　his knowledge.
CONSTABLE   If the English had any apprehension,° they would   *sense*
　　run away.
125　ORLÉANS   That they lack—for if their heads had any intellectual
　　armour, they could never wear such heavy headpieces.
RAMBURES   That island of England breeds very valiant creatures.
　　Their mastiffs are of unmatchable courage.
ORLÉANS   Foolish curs, that run winking° into the mouth of a   *with closed eyes*
130　Russian bear[2], and have their heads crushed like rotten apples.
　　You may as well say, 'That's a valiant flea that dare eat his
　　breakfast on the lip of a lion.'
CONSTABLE   Just,° just. And the men do sympathize with the   *True*
　　mastiffs in robustious and rough coming on, leaving their wits
135　with their wives. And then, give them great meals of beef,[3] and
　　iron and steel, they will eat like wolves and fight like devils.
ORLÉANS   Ay, but these English are shrewdly° out of beef.   *badly*
CONSTABLE   Then shall we find tomorrow they have only stom-
　　achs° to eat, and none to fight. Now is it time to arm. Come,   *appetite*
140　shall we about it?
ORLÉANS   It is now two o'clock. But let me see—by ten
　　We shall have each a hundred Englishmen.   *Exeunt*

4.0

　　　　[Enter] CHORUS
CHORUS   Now entertain conjecture of° a time   *imagine*
　　When creeping murmur and the poring° dark   *pouring; eye-straining*
　　Fills the wide vessel of the universe.
　　From camp to camp through the foul womb of night
5　The hum of either army stilly sounds,
　　That° the fixed sentinels almost receive   *So that*
　　The secret whispers of each other's watch.
　　Fire answers fire, and through their paly° flames   *pale*
　　Each battle sees the other's umbered° face.   *shadowed*
10　Steed threatens steed, in high and boastful neighs
　　Piercing the night's dull ear, and from the tents
　　The armourers, accomplishing° the knights,   *equipping*
　　With busy hammers closing rivets up,
　　Give dreadful note of preparation.
15　The country cocks do crow, the clocks do toll

---

2. Referring to the sport of bearbaiting, in which dogs   3. A traditional English food.
were set upon bears chained to a post.   **4.0**

And the third hour of drowsy morning name.
Proud of their numbers and secure in soul,
The confident and overlusty French
Do the low-rated° English play at dice,[1]   *underrated*
20   And chide the cripple tardy-gaited night,
Who like a foul and ugly witch doth limp
So tediously away. The poor condemnèd English,
Like sacrifices, by their watchful fires
Sit patiently and inly° ruminate   *inwardly*
25   The morning's danger; and their gesture sad,
Investing° lank lean cheeks and war-worn coats,   *Accompanying*
Presented them unto the gazing moon
So many horrid ghosts. O now, who will behold
The royal captain of this ruined band
30   Walking from watch to watch, from tent to tent,
Let him cry, 'Praise and glory on his head!'
For forth he goes and visits all his host,°   *army*
Bids them good morrow with a modest smile
And calls them brothers, friends, and countrymen.
35   Upon his royal face there is no note°   *sign*
How dread an army hath enrounded° him;   *encircled*
Nor doth he dedicate° one jot of colour   *lose*
Unto the weary and all-watchèd night,
But freshly looks and overbears attaint[2]
40   With cheerful semblance and sweet majesty,
That every wretch, pining and pale before,
Beholding him, plucks comfort from his looks.
A largess universal,° like the sun,   *wealth available to all*
His liberal eye doth give to everyone,
45   Thawing cold fear, that mean and gentle° all   *lowborn and noble*
Behold, as may unworthiness define,[3]
A little touch of Harry in the night.
And so our scene must to the battle fly,
Where O for pity, we shall much disgrace,
50   With four or five most vile and ragged foils,°   *swords*
Right ill-disposed in brawl ridiculous,
The name of Agincourt. Yet sit and see,
Minding° true things by what their mock'ries be.   *Exit*   *Imagining*

4.1

Enter KING [HARRY] *and* [*Duke of*] GLOUCESTER [*then
the Duke of* CLARENCE]

KING HARRY   Gloucester, 'tis true that we are in great danger;
The greater therefore should our courage be.
Good morrow, brother Clarence. God Almighty!
There is some soul of goodness in things evil,
5   Would men observingly distil it out—
For our bad neighbour makes us early stirrers,
Which is both healthful and good husbandry.°   *economy*
Besides, they are our outward consciences,
And preachers to us all, admonishing
10   That we should dress us fairly° for our end.   *prepare adequately*

---

1. See 3.7.79.
2. And suppresses signs of exhaustion.
3. As far as their limited capacities permit.
4.1 Location: The English camp at Agincourt.

Thus may we gather honey from the weed
And make a moral of the devil himself.
            Enter [Sir Thomas] ERPINGHAM
Good morrow, old Sir Thomas Erpingham.
A good soft pillow for that good white head

15 Were better than a churlish turf of France.
ERPINGHAM   Not so, my liege. This lodging likes° me better,   *pleases*
      Since I may say, 'Now lie I like a king.'
KING HARRY   'Tis good for men to love their present pains
      Upon example.[1] So the spirit is eased,

20 And when the mind is quickened, out of doubt
      The organs, though defunct and dead before,
      Break up their drowsy grave and newly move
      With casted slough[2] and fresh legerity.°   *nimbleness*
      Lend me thy cloak, Sir Thomas.
            [*He puts on Erpingham's cloak*]
                              Brothers both,

25 Commend me to the princes in our camp.
      Do my good morrow° to them, and anon   *Say good morning*
      Desire them all to my pavilion.
GLOUCESTER   We shall, my liege.
ERPINGHAM   Shall I attend your grace?

30 KING HARRY   No, my good knight.
      Go with my brothers to my lords of England.
      I and my bosom must debate awhile,
      And then I would no other company.
ERPINGHAM   The Lord in heaven bless thee, noble Harry.

35 KING HARRY   God-a-mercy,° old heart, thou speak'st cheerfully.   *Thank you*
            Exeunt [all but KING HARRY]

            Enter PISTOL [*to him*]
PISTOL   *Qui vous là?*°   *Who goes there*
KING HARRY   A friend.
PISTOL   Discuss unto me: art thou officer,
      Or art thou base, common, and popular?°   *plebeian*

40 KING HARRY   I am a gentleman of a company.
PISTOL   Trail'st thou the puissant pike?°   *Are you an infantryman*
KING HARRY   Even so. What are you?
PISTOL   As good a gentleman as the Emperor.
KING HARRY   Then you are a better than the King.

45 PISTOL   The King's a bawcock and a heart-of-gold,
      A lad of life, an imp of fame,°   *a scion of noble stock*
      Of parents good, of fist most valiant.
      I kiss his dirty shoe, and from heartstring
      I love the lovely bully.° What is thy name?   *lovable swashbuckler*

50 KING HARRY   Harry *le roi.*°   *the King*
PISTOL   Leroi? A Cornish name. Art thou of Cornish crew?
KING HARRY   No, I am a Welshman.
PISTOL   Know'st thou Fluellen?
KING HARRY   Yes.

55 PISTOL   Tell him I'll knock his leek about his pate
      Upon Saint Davy's day.[3]
KING HARRY   Do not you wear your dagger in your cap that day,
      lest he knock that about yours.

---

1. By the pattern provided by others.
2. Old skin having been cast off (like a snake).

3. March 1, Welsh national holiday celebrating St.
David's victory over the Saxons.

PISTOL Art thou his friend?

60 KING HARRY And his kinsman too.

PISTOL The *fico*[4] for thee then.

KING HARRY I thank you. God be with you.

PISTOL My name is Pistol called.

KING HARRY It sorts° well with your fierceness.   *Exit* [PISTOL]   agrees
    Enter [*Captains*] FLUELLEN *and* GOWER [*severally.* KING
    HARRY *stands apart*]

65 GOWER Captain Fluellen!

FLUELLEN So! In the name of Jesu Christ, speak fewer. It is the
  greatest admiration° in the universal° world, when the true and   wonder / whole
  ancient prerogatifs and laws of the wars is not kept. If you
  would take the pains but to examine the wars of Pompey the
70 Great,[5] you shall find, I warrant you, that there is no tiddle-
  taddle nor pibble-babble° in Pompey's camp. I warrant you,   chattering
  you shall find the ceremonies of the wars, and the cares of it,
  and the forms of it, and the sobriety of it, and the modesty of
  it, to be otherwise.

75 GOWER Why, the enemy is loud. You hear him all night.

FLUELLEN If the enemy is an ass and a fool and a prating cox-
  comb,° is it meet,° think you, that we should also, look you, be   yammering fool / proper
  an ass and a fool and a prating coxcomb? In your own con-
  science now?

80 GOWER I will speak lower.

FLUELLEN I pray you and beseech you that you will.
                     Exeunt [FLUELLEN *and* GOWER]

KING HARRY Though it appear a little out of fashion,°   unconventional
  There is much care and valour in this Welshman.
    Enter three soldiers: John BATES, *Alexander* COURT, *and*
    Michael WILLIAMS

COURT Brother John Bates, is not that the morning which breaks
85 yonder?

BATES I think it be. But we have no great cause to desire the
  approach of day.

WILLIAMS We see yonder the beginning of the day, but I think
  we shall never see the end of it.—Who goes there?

90 KING HARRY A friend.

WILLIAMS Under what captain serve you?

KING HARRY Under Sir Thomas Erpingham.

WILLIAMS A good old commander and a most kind gentleman.
  I pray you, what thinks he of our estate?°   situation

95 KING HARRY Even as men wrecked upon a sand, that look to be
  washed off the next tide.

BATES He hath not told his thought to the King?

KING HARRY No, nor it is not meet he should. For though I speak
  it to you, I think the King is but a man, as I am. The violet
100 smells to him as it doth to me; the element shows° to him as it   the sky appears
  doth to me. All his senses have but human conditions.° His   limitations
  ceremonies laid by, in his nakedness he appears but a man,
  and though his affections° are higher mounted than ours, yet   desires
  when they stoop,[6] they stoop with the like wing. Therefore,
105 when he sees reason of fears,° as we do, his fears, out of doubt,   to fear

---

4. See 3.6.51.
5. Roman general, defeated by Julius Caesar.
6. Plummet down (term from falconry).

be of the same relish° as ours are. Yet, in reason, no man should possess him with[7] any appearance of fear, lest he, by showing it, should dishearten his army.

taste; kind

110 BATES He may show what outward courage he will, but I believe, as cold a night as 'tis, he could wish himself in Thames up to the neck. And so I would he were, and I by him, at all adventures,[8] so we were quit° here.

away from

KING HARRY By my troth,° I will speak my conscience of the King. I think he would not wish himself anywhere but where 115 he is.

oath

BATES Then I would he were here alone. So should he be sure to be ransomed, and a many poor men's lives saved.

KING HARRY I dare say you love him not so ill to wish him here alone, howsoever you speak this to feel° other men's minds. 120 Methinks I could not die anywhere so contented as in the King's company, his cause being just and his quarrel honourable.

test

WILLIAMS That's more than we know.

BATES Ay, or more than we should seek after. For we know 125 enough if we know we are the King's subjects. If his cause be wrong, our obedience to the King wipes the crime of it out of us.

WILLIAMS But if the cause be not good, the King himself hath a heavy reckoning to make, when all those legs and arms and 130 heads chopped off in a battle shall join together at the latter day,[9] and cry all, 'We died at such a place'—some swearing, some crying for a surgeon, some upon their wives left poor behind them, some upon the debts they owe, some upon their children rawly° left. I am afeard there are few die well that die 135 in a battle, for how can they charitably dispose of anything, when blood is their argument?° Now, if these men do not die well, it will be a black matter for the King that led them to it— who° to disobey were against all proportion of subjection.[1]

abruptly; poorly

business

whom

KING HARRY So, if a son that is by his father sent about merchan- 140 dise do sinfully miscarry upon the sea, the imputation of° his wickedness, by your rule, should be imposed upon his father, that sent him. Or if a servant, under his master's command transporting a sum of money, be assailed by robbers, and die in many irreconciled iniquities,° you may call the business of the 145 master the author of the servant's damnation. But this is not so. The King is not bound to answer the particular endings of his soldiers, the father of his son, nor the master of his servant, for they purpose not their deaths when they propose their services. Besides, there is no king, be his cause never so spotless, if it 150 come to the arbitrament° of swords, can try it out with all unspotted° soldiers. Some, peradventure,° have on them the guilt of premeditated and contrived murder; some, of beguiling virgins with the broken seals of perjury; some, making the wars their bulwark,° that have before gored the gentle bosom of 155 peace with pillage and robbery. Now, if these men have

blame for

unatoned sins

settlement

unblemished / perhaps

defense (against the law)

---

7. Induce him to experience.
8. Whatever might happen.
9. Last Judgment, when human beings are to be

resurrected in the body.
1. *against . . . subjection*: to defy all proper relationships of authority and subordination.

defeated the law and outrun native° punishment, though they
can outstrip men, they have no wings to fly from God. War is
his beadle.° War is his vengeance. So that here men are punished for before-breach° of the King's laws, in now the King's
160   quarrel. Where they feared the death, they have borne life
away; and where they would be safe, they perish. Then if they
die unprovided,° no more is the King guilty of their damnation
than he was before guilty of those impieties for the which they
are now visited.° Every subject's duty is the King's, but every
165   subject's soul is his own. Therefore should every soldier in the
wars do as every sick man in his bed: wash every mote° out of
his conscience. And dying so, death is to him advantage;° or
not dying, the time was blessedly lost wherein such preparation
was gained. And in him that escapes, it were not sin to think
170   that, making God so free an offer, he° let him outlive that day
to see his greatness and to teach others how they should prepare.

BATES   'Tis certain, every man that dies ill,° the ill upon his own
head. The King is not to answer it. I do not desire he
175   should answer for me, and yet I determine to fight lustily for
him.

KING HARRY   I myself heard the King say he would not be ransomed.

WILLIAMS   Ay, he said so, to make us fight cheerfully, but when
180   our throats are cut he may be ransomed, and we ne'er the
wiser.

KING HARRY   If I live to see it, I will never trust his word after.

WILLIAMS   You pay him then! That's a perilous shot out of an
elder-gun,° that a poor and a private displeasure can do against
185   a monarch. You may as well go about to turn the sun to ice
with fanning in his face with a peacock's feather. You'll never
trust his word after! Come, 'tis a foolish saying.

KING HARRY   Your reproof is something too round.° I should be
angry with you, if the time were convenient.

190 WILLIAMS   Let it be a quarrel between us, if you live.

KING HARRY   I embrace it.

WILLIAMS   How shall I know thee again?

KING HARRY   Give me any gage° of thine, and I will wear it in my
bonnet. Then if ever thou darest acknowledge it, I will make it
195   my quarrel.

WILLIAMS   Here's my glove. Give me another of thine.

KING HARRY   There.
      [They exchange gloves]

WILLIAMS   This will I also wear in my cap. If ever thou come to
me and say, after tomorrow, 'This is my glove', by this hand I
200   will take thee a box on the ear.

KING HARRY   If ever I live to see it, I will challenge it.

WILLIAMS   Thou darest as well be hanged.

KING HARRY   Well, I will do it, though I take thee in the King's
company.

205 WILLIAMS   Keep thy word. Fare thee well.

BATES   Be friends, you English fools, be friends. We have
French quarrels enough, if you could tell how to reckon.°

KING HARRY   Indeed, the French may lay twenty French crowns°
to one they will beat us, for they bear them on their shoulders.

---

at home

police officer
earlier breaking

unprepared

punished

speck
profit

(God)

in sin

a popgun

blunt

token

count
coins; heads

210 But it is no English treason to cut French crowns,[2] and tomor-
row the King himself will be a clipper.　　　　*Exeunt soldiers*
Upon the King.
'Let us our lives, our souls, our debts, our care-full wives,
Our children, and our sins, lay on the King.'
215 We must bear all. O hard condition,
Twin-born with greatness: subject to the breath
Of every fool, whose sense no more can feel
But his own wringing.° What infinite heartsease　　　　　　　　*pain*
Must kings neglect that private men enjoy?
220 And what have kings that privates have not too,
Save ceremony, save general ceremony?
And what art thou, thou idol ceremony?
What kind of god art thou, that suffer'st more
Of mortal griefs than do thy worshippers?
225 What are thy rents?° What are thy comings-in?°　　　　*revenues / income*
O ceremony, show me but thy worth.
What is thy soul of adoration?[3]
Art thou aught° else but place, degree, and form,　　　　　　*anything*
Creating awe and fear in other men?
230 Wherein thou art less happy, being feared,
Than they in fearing.
What drink'st thou oft, instead of homage sweet,
But poisoned flattery? O be sick, great greatness,
And bid thy ceremony give thee cure.
235 Think'st thou the fiery fever will go out
With titles blown from adulation?
Will it give place to flexure° and low bending?　　　　　　　　*bowing*
Canst thou, when thou command'st the beggar's knee,
Command the health of it? No, thou proud dream
240 That play'st so subtly with a king's repose;
I am a king that find° thee, and I know　　　　　　　　　　　　*expose*
'Tis not the balm, the sceptre, and the ball,°　　　*orb (royal accessory)*
The sword, the mace, the crown imperial,
The intertissued robe of gold and pearl,
245 The farcèd° title running fore the king,　　　　　　　　　　　　*stuffed*
The throne he sits on, nor the tide of pomp
That beats upon the high shore of this world—
No, not all these, thrice-gorgeous ceremony,
Not all these, laid in bed majestical,
250 Can sleep so soundly as the wretched slave
Who with a body filled and vacant mind
Gets him to rest, crammed with distressful bread;
Never sees horrid night, the child of hell,
But like a lackey° from the rise to set　　　　　　　　　　　　　*servant*
255 Sweats in the eye of Phoebus,° and all night　　　　　　　　　　*the sun*
Sleeps in Elysium;° next day, after dawn　　　　　*classical paradise*
Doth rise and help Hyperion° to his horse,　　　　*the sun's charioteer*
And follows so the ever-running year
With profitable labour to his grave.
260 And but for ceremony such a wretch,
Winding up days with toil and nights with sleep,

2. "Clipping" (line 211), or shaving, precious metal off　　3. What is the secret of the adoration you inspire?
coins was punishable as treason.

Had the forehand° and vantage of a king.   *advantage*
The slave, a member of the country's peace,
Enjoys it, but in gross brain little wots°   *thinks*
265   What watch the King keeps to maintain the peace,
Whose hours the peasant best advantages.°   *profits most from*
          Enter [Sir Thomas] ERPINGHAM
ERPINGHAM   My lord, your nobles, jealous of° your absence,   *concerned about*
Seek through your camp to find you.
KING HARRY   Good old knight,
Collect them all together at my tent.
I'll be before thee.
270   ERPINGHAM   I shall do't, my lord.   *Exit*
KING HARRY   O God of battles, steel my soldiers' hearts.
Possess them not with fear. Take from them now
The sense of reck'ning,° ere th'opposèd numbers   *ability to count*
Pluck their hearts from them. Not today, O Lord,
275   O not today, think not upon the fault
My father made in compassing the crown.⁴
I Richard's body have interrèd new,°   *buried anew*
And on it have bestowed more contrite tears
Than from it issued forcèd drops of blood.
280   Five hundred poor have I in yearly pay
Who twice a day their withered hands hold up°   *(in prayer)*
Toward heaven to pardon blood. And I have built
Two chantries,⁵ where the sad and solemn priests
Sing still for Richard's soul. More will I do,
285   Though all that I can do is nothing worth,
Since that my penitence comes after ill,°   *sin*
Imploring pardon.
          Enter the [Duke of] GLOUCESTER
GLOUCESTER   My liege.
KING HARRY   My brother Gloucester's voice? Ay.
290   I know thy errand, I will go with thee.
The day, my friends, and all things stay° for me.   *Exeunt*   *wait*

4.2

          Enter [Dukes of BOURBON *and]* ORLÉANS, *and [Lord]*
          RAMBURES
ORLÉANS   The sun doth gild our armour. Up, my lords!
BOURBON   *Monte cheval!*° My horse! *Varlet, lacquais!*° Ha!   *To horse / valet*
ORLÉANS   O brave spirit!
BOURBON   *Via les eaux et terre!*
5   ORLÉANS   *Rien plus? L'air et feu!*¹
BOURBON   *Cieux,*° Cousin Orléans!   *To the heavens*
          Enter CONSTABLE
Now, my Lord constable!
CONSTABLE   Hark how our steeds for present° service neigh.   *immediate*
BOURBON   Mount them and make incision in their hides,
10   That their hot blood may spin in English eyes
And dout° them with superfluous courage. Ha!   *extinguish*
RAMBURES   What, will you have them weep our horses' blood?

---

4. Henry's father usurped the throne from its rightful
possessor, Richard II.
5. Chapels where Masses for the dead were sung.
4.2. Location: The French camp.

1. Away over water and earth!
No more? Air and fire! (Playing on the four elements,
of which fire was the highest.)

How shall we then behold their natural tears?
   Enter MESSENGER
MESSENGER   The English are embattled,[2] you French peers.
15   CONSTABLE   To horse, you gallant princes, straight to horse!
    Do but behold yon poor and starvèd band,
    And your fair show° shall suck away their souls,   *appearance*
    Leaving them but the shells and husks of men.
    There is not work enough for all our hands,
20   Scarce blood enough in all their sickly veins
    To give each naked curtal-axe° a stain   *cutlass*
    That our French gallants shall today draw out
    And sheathe for lack of sport. Let us but blow on them,
    The vapour of our valour will o'erturn them.
25   'Tis positive 'gainst all exceptions,° lords,   *'Tis definitely true*
    That our superfluous lackeys and our peasants,
    Who in unnecessary action swarm
    About our squares of battle, were enough
    To purge this field of such a hilding° foe,   *worthless*
30   Though we upon this mountain's basis by°   *foot nearby*
    Took stand° for idle speculation,   *Stood still*
    But that our honours must not. What's to say?
    A very little little let us do
    And all is done. Then let the trumpets sound
35   The tucket sonance° and the note to mount,   *trumpet signal*
    For our approach shall so much dare the field
    That England shall couch down in fear and yield.
      Enter [*Lord*] GRANDPRÉ
GRANDPRÉ   Why do you stay so long, my lords of France?
    Yon island carrions,° desperate of their bones,   *cadavers*
40   Ill-favouredly become the morning field.
    Their ragged curtains° poorly are let loose   *banners*
    And our air shakes them passing scornfully.
    Big Mars° seems bankrupt in their beggared host   *god of war*
    And faintly through a rusty beaver° peeps.   *visor*
45   The horsemen sit like fixèd candlesticks
    With torchstaves° in their hands, and their poor jades   *tapers*
    Lob° down their heads, drooping the hides and hips,   *Hang*
    The gum down-roping° from their pale dead eyes,   *mucus dripping*
    And in their palled° dull mouths the gimmaled° bit   *pale / jointed*
50   Lies foul with chewed grass, still and motionless.
    And their executors,[3] the knavish crows,
    Fly o'er them all impatient for their hour.
    Description cannot suit itself in words
    To demonstrate the life of° such a battle   *depict realistically*
55   In life so lifeless as it shows itself.
   CONSTABLE   They have said their prayers, and they stay° for death.   *wait*
   BOURBON   Shall we go send them dinners and fresh suits
    And give their fasting horses provender,°   *food*
    And after° fight with them?   *afterward*
60   CONSTABLE   I stay but for my guidon.° To the field!   *pennant*
    I will the banner from a trumpet° take   *trumpeter*
    And use it for my haste. Come, come away!
    The sun is high, and we outwear° the day.   *Exeunt*   *waste*

---

2. Drawn into lines of battle.   3. Administrators of wills (who dispose of the remains
                 of the dead).

4.3

Enter [Dukes of] GLOUCESTER, [CLARENCE, and] EXE-
TER, [Earls of] SALISBURY and [WARWICK, and Sir
Thomas] ERPINGHAM, with all [the] host

GLOUCESTER   Where is the King?

CLARENCE   The King himself is rode to view their battle.°   *army*

WARWICK   Of fighting men they have full threescore thousand.°   *60,000*

EXETER   There's five to one. Besides, they all are fresh.

5   SALISBURY   God's arm strike with us! 'Tis a fearful odds.
       God b'wi' you, princes all. I'll to my charge.°   *command post*
       If we no more meet till we meet in heaven,
       Then joyfully, my noble Lord of Clarence,
       My dear Lord Gloucester, and my good Lord Exeter,
10   And [*to* WARWICK] my kind kinsman, warriors all, adieu.

CLARENCE   Farewell, good Salisbury, and good luck go with thee.

EXETER   Farewell, kind lord. Fight valiantly today—
       And yet I do thee wrong to mind° thee of it,   *remind*
       For thou art framed of the firm truth of valour.

                                        [*Exit* SALISBURY]

15   CLARENCE   He is as full of valour as of kindness,
       Princely in both.

                Enter KING; [HARRY, *behind*]

WARWICK   O that we now had here
       But one ten thousand of those men in England
       That do no work today.

KING HARRY   What's he that wishes so?
       My cousin Warwick? No, my fair cousin.
20   If we are marked to die, we are enough
       To do our country loss;° and if to live,   *For our country to lose*
       The fewer men, the greater share of honour.
       God's will, I pray thee wish not one man more.
       By Jove, I am not covetous for gold,
25   Nor care I who doth feed upon my cost;
       It ernes° me not if men my garments wear;   *grieves*
       Such outward things dwell not in my desires.
       But if it be a sin to covet honour
       I am the most offending soul alive.
30   No, faith, my coz,° wish not a man from England.   *kinsman*
       God's peace, I would not lose so great an honour
       As one man more methinks would share° from me   *deprive*
       For the best hope I have. O do not wish one more.
       Rather proclaim it presently° through my host°   *immediately / army*
35   That he which hath no stomach° to this fight,   *appetite; courage*
       Let him depart. His passport shall be made
       And crowns for convoy° put into his purse.   *money for transport*
       We would not die in that man's company
       That fears his fellowship° to die with us.   *duty as our companion*
40   This day is called the Feast of Crispian.[1]
       He that outlives this day and comes safe home
       Will stand a-tiptoe when this day is named
       And rouse him at the name of Crispian.
       He that shall see this day and live t'old age

4.3 Location: The English camp.
1. October 25, dedicated to the martyred brothers Crispin and Crispianus (or Crispinian).

45 Will yearly on the vigil° feast his neighbours   *eve of the saint's day*
    And say, 'Tomorrow is Saint Crispian.'
    Then will he strip his sleeve and show his scars
    And say, 'These wounds I had on Crispin's day.'
    Old men forget; yet all shall be forgot,
50 But he'll remember, with advantages,°   *embellishments*
    What feats he did that day. Then shall our names,
    Familiar in his mouth as household words—
    Harry the King, Bedford and Exeter,
    Warwick and Talbot, Salisbury and Gloucester—
55 Be in their flowing cups freshly remembered.
    This story shall the good man teach his son,
    And Crispin Crispian shall ne'er go by
    From this day to the ending of the world
    But we in it shall be rememberèd,
60 We few, we happy few, we band of brothers.
    For he today that sheds his blood with me
    Shall be my brother; be he ne'er so vile,°   *lowborn*
    This day shall gentle his condition.²
    And gentlemen in England now abed
65 Shall think themselves accursed they were not here,
    And hold their manhoods cheap whiles any speaks
    That fought with us upon Saint Crispin's day.

                    Enter [Earl of] SALISBURY

SALISBURY   My sovereign lord, bestow yourself° with speed.   *take your positions*
    The French are bravely in their battles° set   *battle lines*
70 And will with all expedience° charge on us.   *speed*
KING HARRY   All things are ready if our minds be so.
WARWICK   Perish the man whose mind is backward now.
KING HARRY   Thou dost not wish more help from England, coz?
WARWICK   God's will, my liege, would you and I alone,
75 Without more help, could fight this royal battle.
KING HARRY   Why now thou hast unwished five thousand men,
    Which likes° me better than to wish us one.—   *pleases*
    You know your places. God be with you all.

                    Tucket. Enter MONTJOY

MONTJOY   Once more I come to know of thee, King Harry,
80 If for thy ransom thou wilt now compound°   *make terms*
    Before thy most assurèd overthrow.
    For certainly thou art so near the gulf
    Thou needs must be englutted.° Besides, in mercy   *swallowed*
    The Constable desires thee thou wilt mind°   *remind*
85 Thy followers of repentance, that their souls
    May make a peaceful and a sweet retire
    From off these fields where, wretches, their poor bodies
    Must lie and fester.
KING HARRY   Who hath sent thee now?
90 MONTJOY   The Constable of France.
KING HARRY   I pray thee bear my former answer back.
    Bid them achieve° me, and then sell my bones.   *get*
    Good God, why should they mock poor fellows thus?
    The man that once did sell the lion's skin
95 While the beast lived, was killed with hunting him.³

---

2. Shall raise him to gentlemanly rank.   3. *The man . . . him*: alluding to one of Aesop's fables.

A many of our bodies shall no doubt
Find native° graves, upon the which, I trust,   (English)
Shall witness live in brass of this day's work.
And those that leave their valiant bones in France,
100 Dying like men, though buried in your dunghills
They shall be famed. For there the sun shall greet them
And draw their honours reeking° up to heaven,   *steaming; stinking*
Leaving their earthly parts to choke your clime,
The smell whereof shall breed a plague in France.
105 Mark then abounding valour in our English,
That, being dead, like to the bullets grazing°   *ricocheting*
Break out into a second course of mischief,
Killing in relapse of mortality.°   *another fatal outbreak*
Let me speak proudly. Tell the Constable
110 We are but warriors for the working day.°   *workaday warriors*
Our gayness and our gilt are all besmirched
With rainy marching in the painful field.
There's not a piece of feather° in our host—   *decorative plume*
Good argument, I hope, we will not fly—
115 And time hath worn us into slovenry.°   *filth*
But by the mass, our hearts are in the trim.°   *fine shape*
And my poor soldiers tell me, yet ere night
They'll be in fresher robes, as they will pluck
The gay new coats o'er your French soldiers' heads,
120 And turn them out of service.⁴ If they do this—
As if God please, they shall—my ransom then
Will soon be levied.⁵ Herald, save thou thy labour.
Come thou no more for ransom, gentle herald.
They shall have none, I swear, but these my joints—
125 Which if they have as I will leave 'em them,
Shall yield them little. Tell the Constable.
MONTJOY I shall, King Harry. And so fare thee well.
Thou never shalt hear herald any more.
KING HARRY   I fear thou wilt once more come for a ransom.

                                          Exit [MONTJOY]

        Enter [*Duke of* YORK]
130 YORK My lord, most humbly on my knee I beg
The leading of the vanguard.
KING HARRY   Take it, brave York.—Now soldiers, march away,
And how thou pleasest, God, dispose the day.   *Exeunt*

4.4

      Alarum. Excursions.° *Enter* PISTOL, [*a*] FRENCH SOL-   *Skirmishes*
      DIER, [*and the*] BOY
PISTOL Yield, cur.
FRENCH SOLDIER *Je pense que vous êtes le gentilhomme de bon
qualité.*¹
PISTOL *Qualité? 'Calin o custure me!*²
5 Art thou a gentleman? What is thy name? Discuss.
FRENCH SOLDIER *O Seigneur Dieu!*°   *O Lord God*
PISTOL [*aside*] O Seigneur Dew should be a gentleman.—

---

4. Dismiss them, stripped of their servant's uniforms.
5. Collected (from the French themselves).
4.4. Location: The battlefield.

1. I think you are a gentleman of high rank.
2. The Irish refrain of a popular ballad, meaning "I am a girl from beside the Suir."

Perpend° my words, O Seigneur Dew, and mark: *Weigh*
O Seigneur Dew, thou diest, on point of fox,°   *sword*

10   Except, O Seigneur, thou do give to me
Egregious° ransom.   *Extraordinary*

FRENCH SOLDIER   *O prenez miséricorde! Ayez pitié de moi!*[3]

PISTOL   'Moy' shall not serve, I will have forty 'moys',[4]
Or I will fetch thy rim° out at thy throat   *stomach lining*

15   In drops of crimson blood.

FRENCH SOLDIER   *Est-il impossible d'échapper la force de ton bras?*[5]

PISTOL   Brass, cur? Thou damnèd and luxurious° mountain goat,   *lecherous*
Offer'st me brass?

FRENCH SOLDIER   *O pardonne-moi!*

20   PISTOL   Sayst thou me so? Is that a ton of moys?—
Come hither boy. Ask me this slave in French
What is his name.

BOY   *Écoutez: comment êtes-vous appelé?*[6]

FRENCH SOLDIER   *Monsieur le Fer.*

25   BOY   He says his name is Master Fer.

PISTOL   Master Fer? I'll fer him, and firk° him, and ferret° him.   *beat / savage*
Discuss the same in French unto him.

BOY   I do not know the French for fer and ferret and firk.

PISTOL   Bid him prepare, for I will cut his throat.

30   FRENCH SOLDIER   *Que dit-il, monsieur?*°   *What does he say, sir*

BOY   *Il me commande à vous dire que vous faites vous prêt, car ce
soldat ici est disposé tout à cette heure de couper votre gorge.*°   *(translates Pistol)*

PISTOL   *Oui, couper la gorge, par ma foi,*[7]
Peasant, unless thou give me crowns, brave crowns;

35   Or mangled shalt thou be by this my sword.

FRENCH SOLDIER   *O je vous supplie, pour l'amour de Dieu, me
pardonner. Je suis le gentilhomme de bonne maison. Gardez ma
vie, et je vous donnerai deux cents écus*°   *(translated by the boy)*

PISTOL   What are his words?

40   BOY   He prays you to save his life. He is a gentleman of a good
house, and for his ransom he will give you two hundred
crowns.

PISTOL   Tell him, my fury shall abate, and I the crowns will take.

FRENCH SOLDIER   *Petit monsieur, que dit-il?*[8]

45   BOY   *Encore qu'il est contre son jurement de pardonner aucun
prisonnier; néanmoins, pour les écus que vous lui ci promettez, il
est content à vous donner la liberté, le franchisement.*

FRENCH SOLDIER [*kneeling to* PISTOL]   *Sur mes genoux je vous
donne mille remerciements, et je m'estime heureux que j'ai

50   tombé entre les mains d'un chevalier, comme je pense, le plus
brave, vaillant, et treis-distingué seigneur d'Angleterre.*°   *(translated by the boy)*

PISTOL   Expound unto me, boy.

BOY   He gives you upon his knees a thousand thanks, and he
esteems himself happy that he hath fallen into the hands of

55   one, as he thinks, the most brave, valorous, and thrice-worthy
seigneur of England.

PISTOL   As I suck blood, I will some mercy show.
Follow me.

---

3. O take pity! Have pity on me!   6. Listen: what's your name?
4. Pistol mistakes *moi* for the name of a coin.   7. Yes, cut your throat, by my faith.
5. Is it impossible to escape the strength of your arm?   8. Little sir, what says he?

BOY   *Suivez-vous le grand capitaine.*⁹

> [*Exeunt* PISTOL *and* FRENCH SOLDIER]

60   I did never know so full a voice issue from so empty a heart.
     But the saying is true: 'The empty vessel makes the greatest
     sound.' Bardolph and Nim had ten times more valour than this
     roaring devil i'th' old play, that everyone may pare his nails
     with a wooden dagger,¹ and they are both hanged, and so
65   would this be, if he durst steal anything adventurously.° I must   *recklessly*
     stay with the lackeys with the luggage of our camp. The French
     might have a good prey of us, if he knew of it, for there is none
     to guard it but boys.   *Exit*

4.5

> *Enter* CONSTABLE, [*Dukes of*] ORLÉANS [*and*] BOURBON,
> *and* [*Lord*] RAMBURES

CONSTABLE   *O diable!*

ORLÉANS   *O Seigneur! Le jour est perdu, tout est perdu!*

BOURBON   *Mort de ma vie!*¹ All is confounded,° all.   *lost*
     Reproach and everlasting shame
5   Sits mocking in our plumes.

> *A short alarum*

     O méchante fortune!°—[*To* RAMBURES] Do not run away.   *evil fate*

ORLÉANS   We are enough yet living in the field
     To smother up the English in our throngs,
     If any order might be thought upon.

10   BOURBON   The devil take order. Once more back again!
     And he that will not follow Bourbon now,
     Let him go home, and with his cap in hand
     Like a base leno° hold the chamber door   *pimp*
     Whilst by a slave no gentler° than my dog   *better born*
15   His fairest daughter is contaminated.

CONSTABLE   Disorder that hath spoiled° us friend° us now.   *ruined / befriend*
     Let us on heaps go offer up our lives.

BOURBON   I'll to the throng.
     Let life be short, else shame will be too long.²   *Exeunt*

4.6

> *Alarum. Enter* KING [HARRY] *and his train,*° *with pris-*   *followers*
> oners

KING HARRY   Well have we done, thrice-valiant countrymen.
     But all's not done; yet keep the French the field.

> [*Enter the Duke of* EXETER]

EXETER   The Duke of York commends him to your majesty.

KING HARRY   Lives he, good uncle? Thrice within this hour
5   I saw him down, thrice up again and fighting.
     From helmet to the spur, all blood he was.

EXETER   In which array, brave soldier, doth he lie,
     Larding° the plain. And by his bloody side,   *Moistening*
     Yokefellow to his honour-owing° wounds,   *honorable*
10   The noble Earl of Suffolk also lies.

---

9. Follow the great captain.
1. Allegorical "Vice" characters in old-fashioned morality plays were typically armed with wooden daggers.
4.5 Location: The battlefield.
1. O the devil!

O God! The day is lost, all is lost!
Death of my life!

2. See Additional Passages at end of play for the Folio
and quarto versions of this scene.
4.6 Location: The battlefield.

Suffolk first died, and York, all haggled over,°   *hacked up*
Comes to him, where in gore he lay insteeped,°   *soaked*
And takes him by the beard, kisses the gashes
That bloodily did yawn upon his face,
15   And cries aloud, "Tarry, dear cousin Suffolk.
My soul shall thine keep company to heaven.
Tarry, sweet soul, for mine, then fly abreast,
As in this glorious and well-foughten field
We kept together in our chivalry.'
20   Upon these words I came and cheered him up.
He smiled me in the face, raught° me his hand,   *reached*
And with a feeble grip says, 'Dear my lord,
Commend my service to my sovereign.'
So did he turn, and over Suffolk's neck
25   He threw his wounded arm, and kissed his lips,
And so espoused to death, with blood he sealed
A testament of noble-ending love.
The pretty and sweet manner of it forced
Those waters from me which I would have stopped.
30   But I had not so much of man in me,
And all my mother° came into mine eyes   *(feminine) tenderness*
And gave me up to tears.

KING HARRY   I blame you not,
For hearing this I must perforce compound°   *come to terms*
With mistful eyes, or they will issue° too.   *weep*
Alarum
35   But hark, what new alarum is this same?
The French have reinforced their scattered men.
Then every soldier kill his prisoners.
    [*The soldiers kill their prisoners*][1]
Give the word through.

PISTOL   *Coup' la gorge.*°   *Exeunt*   *Cut the throat*

4.7

Enter [Captains] FLUELLEN *and* GOWER

FLUELLEN   Kill the poys and the luggage! 'Tis expressly against
the law of arms. 'Tis as arrant a piece of knavery, mark you
now, as can be offert. In your conscience now, is it not?

GOWER   'Tis certain there's not a boy left alive. And the cowardly
5   rascals that ran from the battle ha' done this slaughter. Besides,
they have burned and carried away all that was in the King's
tent; wherefore the King most worthily hath caused every soldier to cut his prisoner's throat. O 'tis a gallant king.

FLUELLEN   Ay, he was porn at Monmouth.° Captain Gower,   *(in Wales)*
10   what call you the town's name where Alexander the Pig was
born?

GOWER   Alexander the Great.

FLUELLEN   Why I pray you, is not 'pig' great? The pig or the
great or the mighty or the huge or the magnanimous are all
15   one reckonings, save the phrase is a little variations.°   *(for "varied")*

GOWER   I think Alexander the Great was born in Macedon. His
father was called Philip of Macedon, as I take it.

FLUELLEN   I think it is e'en Macedon where Alexander is porn.

1. This may or may not be done onstage.   **4.7** Location: Before Henry's pavilion.

I tell you, captain, if you look in the maps of the world I warrant
20   you sall find, in the comparisons between Macedon and Monmouth, that the situations, look you, is both alike. There is a
river in Macedon, and there is also moreover a river at Monmouth. It is called Wye at Monmouth, but it is out of my prains
what is the name of the other river—but 'tis all one, 'tis alike as
25   my fingers is to my fingers, and there is salmons in both. If you
mark Alexander's life well, Harry of Monmouth's life is come
after it indifferent well.[1] For there is figures° in all things. Alex-   *comparisons*
ander, God knows, and you know, in his rages and his furies
and his wraths and his cholers° and his moods and his displea-   *angers*
30   sures and his indignations, and also being a little intoxicates in
his prains, did in his ales and his angers, look you, kill his best
friend Cleitus—

GOWER   Our King is not like him in that. He never killed any of
his friends.

35 FLUELLEN   It is not well done, mark you now, to take the tales
out of my mouth ere it is made an end and finished. I speak
but in the figures and comparisons of it. As Alexander killed his
friend Cleitus, being in his ales and his cups, so also Harry
Monmouth, being in his right wits and his good judgements,
40   turned away the fat knight with the great-belly doublet—he was
full of jests and gipes° and knaveries and mocks—I have forgot   *gibes*
his name.

GOWER   Sir John Falstaff.

FLUELLEN   That is he. I'll tell you, there is good men porn at
45   Monmouth.

GOWER   Here comes his majesty.

> *Alarum. Enter* KING HARRY *and* [*the English army*], *with*
> [*Duke of*] BOURBON, [*Duke of* ORLÉANS, *and other*] *pris-*
> *oners.*[2] *Flourish*

KING HARRY   I was not angry since I came to France
Until this instant. Take a trumpet, herald;
Ride thou unto the horsemen on yon hill.
50   If they will fight with us, bid them come down,
Or void° the field: they do offend our sight.   *leave*
If they'll do neither, we will come to them,
And make them skirr° away as swift as stones   *scurry*
Enforcèd° from the old Assyrian slings.   *Driven*
55   Besides, we'll cut the throats of those we have,
And not a man of them that we shall take
Shall taste our mercy. Go and tell them so.

> *Enter* MONTJOY

EXETER   Here comes the herald of the French, my liege.

GLOUCESTER   His eyes are humbler than they used to be.

60 KING HARRY   How now, what means this, herald? Know'st thou not
That I have fined° these bones of mine for ransom?   *pledged*
Com'st thou again for ransom?

MONTJOY   No, great King.
I come to thee for charitable licence,°   *permission*
That we may wander o'er this bloody field
65   To book° our dead and then to bury them,   *register*

---

1. *is . . . well:* resembles it fairly well.
2. This is a second batch of prisoners, captured after the French counterattack.

To sort our nobles from our common men—
For many of our princes, woe the while,
Lie drowned and soaked in mercenary blood.[3]
So do our vulgar° drench their peasant limbs   *common people*
70 In blood of princes, and our wounded steeds
Fret fetlock°-deep in gore, and with wild rage   *ankle*
Jerk out their armèd heels at their dead masters,
Killing them twice. O give us leave, great King,
To view the field in safety, and dispose
Of their dead bodies.
75 KING HARRY   I tell thee truly, herald,
I know not if the day be ours or no,
For yet a many of your horsemen peer°   *appear*
And gallop o'er the field.
MONTJOY   The day is yours.
KING HARRY   Praisèd be God, and not our strength, for it.
80 What is this castle called that stands hard by?
MONTJOY   They call it Agincourt.
KING HARRY   Then call we this the field of Agincourt,
Fought on the day of Crispin Crispian.
FLUELLEN   Your grandfather of famous memory, an't° please   *if it*
85 your majesty, and your great-uncle Edward the Plack Prince of
Wales, as I have read in the chronicles, fought a most prave
pattle here in France.
KING HARRY   They did, Fluellen.
FLUELLEN   Your majesty says very true. If your majesties is
90 remembered of it, the Welshmen did good service in a garden
where leeks did grow, wearing leeks in their Monmouth caps,[4]
which your majesty know to this hour is an honourable badge
of the service. And I do believe your majesty takes no scorn to
wear the leek upon Saint Tavy's day.
95 KING HARRY   I wear it for a memorable honour,
For I am Welsh, you know, good countryman.
FLUELLEN   All the water in Wye° cannot wash your majesty's   *Welsh river*
Welsh plood out of your pody, I can tell you that. God pless it
and preserve it, as long as it pleases his grace, and his majesty
100 too.
KING HARRY   Thanks, good my countryman.
FLUELLEN   By Jeshu, I am your majesty's countryman. I care not
who know it, I will confess it to all the world. I need not to be
ashamed of your majesty, praised be God, so long as your maj-
105 esty is an honest man.
KING HARRY   God keep me so.
      Enter WILLIAMS [*with a glove in his cap*]
                 Our heralds go with him.
Bring me just notice° of the numbers dead   *accurate record*
On both our parts.
       Exeunt [MONTJOY, GOWER, *and English*] *heralds*
            Call yonder fellow hither.
EXETER [*to* WILLIAMS]   Soldier, you must come to the King.
110 KING HARRY   Soldier, why wearest thou that glove in thy cap?
WILLIAMS   An't please your majesty, 'tis the gage° of one that I   *token*
should fight withal, if he be alive.

---

3. Common soldiers, unlike noblemen, fought for pay.   4. Tall, tapering caps without brims.

KING HARRY   An Englishman?

WILLIAMS   An't please your majesty, a rascal, that swaggered with
me last night—who, if a live, and ever dare to challenge this
glove, I have sworn to take him a box o'th' ear; or if I can see
my glove in his cap—which he swore, as he was a soldier, he
would wear if a lived—I will strike it out soundly.

KING HARRY   What think you, Captain Fluellen? Is it fit this soldier keep his oath?

FLUELLEN   He is a craven° and a villain else, an't please your   *coward*
majesty, in my conscience.

KING HARRY   It may be his enemy is a gentleman of great sort,
quite from the answer of his degree.⁵

FLUELLEN   Though he be as good a gentleman as the devil is,
as Lucifer and Beelzebub° himself, it is necessary, look your   *Satan*
grace, that he keep his vow and his oath. If he be perjured, see
you now, his reputation is as arrant a villain and a Jack-sauce°   *saucy knave*
as ever his black shoe trod upon God's ground and his earth,
in my conscience, law.

KING HARRY   Then keep thy vow, sirrah, when thou meetest the
fellow.

WILLIAMS   So I will, my liege, as I live.

KING HARRY   Who serv'st thou under?

WILLIAMS   Under Captain Gower, my liege.

FLUELLEN   Gower is a good captain, and is good knowledge and
literatured° in the wars.   *well read*

KING HARRY   Call him hither to me, soldier.

WILLIAMS   I will, my liege.   *Exit*

KING HARRY [*giving him Williams's other glove*]   Here, Fluellen,
wear thou this favour for me and stick it in thy cap. When
Alençon and myself were down together, I plucked this glove
from his helm. If any man challenge this, he is a friend to
Alençon and an enemy to our person. If thou encounter any
such, apprehend° him, an° thou dost me love.   *arrest / if*

FLUELLEN   Your grace does me as great honours as can be
desired in the hearts of his subjects. I would fain° see the man   *gladly*
that has but two legs that shall find himself aggriefed at this
glove, that is all; but I would fain see it once. An't please God
of his grace, that I would see.

KING HARRY   Know'st thou Gower?

FLUELLEN   He is my dear friend, an't please you.

KING HARRY   Pray thee, go seek him and bring him to my tent.

FLUELLEN   I will fetch him.   *Exit*

KING HARRY   My lord of Warwick and my brother Gloucester,
Follow Fluellen closely at the heels.
The glove which I have given him for a favour
May haply purchase him a box o'th' ear.
It is the soldier's. I by bargain should
Wear it myself. Follow, good cousin Warwick.
If that the soldier strike him, as I judge
By his blunt bearing he will keep his word,
Some sudden mischief may arise of it,
For I do know Fluellen valiant
And touched with choler,° hot as gunpowder,   *made angry*

---

5. Quite above responding to a challenge from one of Williams's rank.

And quickly will return an injury.°   *insult*
Follow, and see there be no harm between them.
Go you with me, uncle of Exeter.   *Exeunt [severally]*

4.8

Enter [Captain] GOWER *and* WILLIAMS
WILLIAMS   I warrant° it is to knight you, captain.   *I'm sure*
              Enter [Captain] FLUELLEN
FLUELLEN   God's will and his pleasure, captain, I beseech you
    now, come apace° to the King. There is more good toward you,   *quickly*
    peradventure,° than is in your knowledge to dream of.   *perhaps*
5 WILLIAMS   Sir, know you this glove?
FLUELLEN   Know the glove? I know the glove is a glove.
WILLIAMS *[plucking the glove from Fluellen's cap]*   I know this,
    and thus I challenge it.
              [He] strikes [FLUELLEN]
FLUELLEN   God's plood, and his! An arrant traitor as any's in the
10   universal world, or in France, or in England.
GOWER *[to* WILLIAMS*]*   How now, sir? You villain!
WILLIAMS   Do you think I'll be forsworn?
FLUELLEN   Stand away, Captain Gower. I will give treason his
    payment into plows, I warrant you.
15 WILLIAMS   I am no traitor.
FLUELLEN   That's a lie in thy throat. I charge you in his majesty's
    name, apprehend him. He's a friend of the Duke Alençon's.
              Enter [Earl of] WARWICK *and [Duke of]* GLOUCESTER
WARWICK   How now, how now, what's the matter?
FLUELLEN   My lord of Warwick, here is—praised be God for it—
20   a most contagious° treason come to light, look you, as you shall   *noxious*
    desire in a summer's day.
              Enter KING [HARRY] *and [Duke of]* EXETER
    Here is his majesty.
KING HARRY   How now, what is the matter?
FLUELLEN   My liege, here is a villain and a traitor that, look your
25   grace, has struck the glove which your majesty is take out of
    the helmet of Alençon.
WILLIAMS   My liege, this was my glove—here is the fellow° of   *mate*
    it—and he that I gave it to in change promised to wear it in his
    cap. I promised to strike him, if he did. I met this man with my
30   glove in his cap, and I have been as good as my word.
FLUELLEN   Your majesty hear now, saving your majesty's man-
    hood, what an arrant rascally beggarly lousy knave it is. I hope
    your majesty is pear° me testimony and witness, and will   *(for "will bear")*
    avouchment° that this is the glove of Alençon that your maj-   *(for "vouch")*
35   esty is give me, in your conscience now.
KING HARRY   Give me thy glove, soldier.
    Look, here is the fellow of it.
    'Twas I indeed thou promisèd'st to strike,
    And thou hast given me most bitter terms.°   *words*
40 FLUELLEN   An't please your majesty, let his neck answer for it, if
    there is any martial law in the world.
KING HARRY   How canst thou make me satisfaction?
WILLIAMS   All offences, my lord, come from the heart. Never
    came any from mine that might offend your majesty.

4.8 Location: Before Henry's pavilion.

45   KING HARRY It was ourself thou didst abuse.

WILLIAMS Your majesty came not like yourself. You appeared to
me but as a common man. Witness the night, your garments,
your lowliness. And what your highness suffered under that
shape, I beseech you take it for your own fault, and not mine,
50   for had you been as I took you for, I made no offence. Therefore I beseech your highness pardon me.

KING HARRY Here, Uncle Exeter, fill this glove with crowns
And give it to this fellow.—Keep it, fellow,
And wear it for an honour in thy cap
55   Till I do challenge it.—Give him the crowns.
—And captain, you must needs be friends with him.

FLUELLEN By this day and this light, the fellow has mettle
enough in his belly.—Hold, there is twelve pence for you, and
I pray you to serve God, and keep you out of prawls and prab-
60   bles and quarrels and dissensions, and I warrant you it is the
better for you.

WILLIAMS I will none of your money.

FLUELLEN It is with a good will. I can tell you, it will serve you
to mend your shoes. Come, wherefore should you be so pash-
65   ful? Your shoes is not so good. 'Tis a good shilling, I warrant
you, or I will change it.[1]

          Enter [an English] HERALD

KING HARRY Now, herald, are the dead numbered?

HERALD Here is the number of the slaughtered French.

KING HARRY What prisoners of good sort° are taken, uncle?   *high rank*
70   EXETER Charles, Duke of Orléans, nephew to the King;
Jean, Duke of Bourbon, and Lord Boucicault;
Of other lords and barons, knights and squires,
Full fifteen hundred, besides common men.

KING HARRY This note doth tell me of ten thousand French
75   That in the field lie slain. Of princes in this number
And nobles bearing banners,° there lie dead   *coats of arms*
One hundred twenty-six; added to these,
Of knights, esquires, and gallant gentlemen,
Eight thousand and four hundred, of the which
80   Five hundred were but yesterday dubbed knights.
So that in these ten thousand they have lost
There are but sixteen hundred mercenaries;
The rest are princes, barons, lords, knights, squires,
And gentlemen of blood and quality.
85   The names of those their nobles that lie dead:
Charles Delabret, High Constable of France;
Jaques of Châtillion, Admiral of France;
The Master of the Crossbows, Lord Rambures;
Great-Master of France, the brave Sir Guiscard Dauphin;
90   Jean, Duke of Alençon; Antony, Duke of Brabant,
The brother to the Duke of Burgundy;
And Édouard, Duke of Bar; of lusty earls,
Grandpré and Roussi, Fauconbridge and Foix,
Beaumont and Marle, Vaudemont and Lestrelles.
95   Here was a royal fellowship of death.

---

1. Williams may or may not take the money.

Where is the number of our English dead?
    [He is given another paper]
Edward the Duke of York, the Earl of Suffolk,
Sir Richard Keighley, Davy Gam Esquire;
None else of name,° and of all other men   *high rank*
100 But five-and-twenty. O God, thy arm was here,
And not to us, but to thy arm alone
Ascribe we all. When, without stratagem,
But in plain shock° and even play of battle,   *confrontation*
Was ever known so great and little loss
105 On one part and on th'other? Take it God,
For it is none but thine.
EXETER   'Tis wonderful.
KING HARRY   Come, go we in procession to the village,
And be it death proclaimèd through our host
To boast of this, or take that praise from God
110 Which is his only.
FLUELLEN   Is it not lawful, an't please your majesty, to tell how
    many is killed?
KING HARRY   Yes, captain, but with this acknowledgement,
That God fought for us.
115 FLUELLEN   Yes, in my conscience, he did us great good.
KING HARRY   Do we all holy rites:
Let there be sung *Non nobis* and *Te Deum*,[2]
The dead with charity enclosed in clay;°   *buried with pious love*
And then to Calais, and to England then,
120 Where ne'er from France arrived more-happy° men.   *Exeunt*   *more fortunate*

5.0

Enter CHORUS
CHORUS   Vouchsafe° to those that have not read the story   *Allow*
That I may prompt them—and of such as have,
I humbly pray them to admit th'excuse
Of time, of numbers, and due course of things,
5 Which cannot in their huge and proper life
Be here presented. Now we bear the King
Toward Calais. Grant him there; there seen,
Heave him away upon your wingèd thoughts
Athwart the sea. Behold, the English beach
10 Pales-in° the flood, with men, maids, wives, and boys,   *Fences in*
Whose shouts and claps out-voice the deep-mouthed sea,
Which like a mighty whiffler[1] fore the King
Seems to prepare his way. So let him land,
And solemnly see him set on to London.
15 So swift a pace hath thought, that even now
You may imagine him upon Blackheath,[2]
Where that his lords desire him to have borne
His bruisèd helmet and his bended sword
Before him through the city; he forbids it,
20 Being free from vainness and self-glorious pride,
Giving full trophy, signal, and ostent°   *honor for the victory*

---

2. *Non nobis* is Psalm 115, beginning "Not unto us, O
Lord, not unto us, but unto thy name give the glory." *Te
Deum* is a canticle of thanks beginning "We praise thee,
O God."

5.0
1. Official who cleared the way for a procession.
2. Open space outside London.

Quite from himself, to God. But now behold,
In the quick forge and working-house of thought,
How London doth pour out her citizens.

25 The Mayor and all his brethren, in best sort,°   *clothing*
Like to the senators of th'antique Rome
With the plebeians° swarming at their heels,   *commoners*
Go forth and fetch their conqu'ring Caesar in—
As, by a lower but high-loving likelihood,³

30 Were now the General of our gracious Empress⁴—
As in good time he may—from Ireland coming,
Bringing rebellion brochèd° on his sword,   *impaled*
How many would the peaceful city quit
To welcome him! Much more, and much more cause,

35 Did they this Harry. Now in London place him;
As yet the lamentation of the French
Invites the King of England's stay at home.
The Emperor's coming⁵ in behalf of France,
To order peace between them [

40   ]⁶ and omit
All the occurrences, whatever chanced,
Till Harry's back-return again to France.⁷
There must we bring him, and myself have played
The interim by remeb'ring° you 'tis past.   *reminding*

45 Then brook° abridgement, and your eyes advance,   *tolerate*
After your thoughts, straight back again to France.   *Exit*

5.1

Enter [Captain] GOWER *and [Captain]* FLUELLEN *[with
a leek in his cap and a cudgel]*

GOWER   Nay, that's right. But why wear you your leek today?
Saint Davy's day is past.

FLUELLEN   There is occasions and causes why and wherefore in
all things. I will tell you, ass my friend, Captain Gower. The

5   rascally scald° beggarly lousy pragging knave Pistol—which you   *scabby*
and yourself and all the world know to be no petter than a
fellow, look you now, of no merits—he is come to me, and
prings me pread and salt yesterday,° look you, and bid me eat   *(on St. Davy's Day)*
my leek. It was in a place where I could not breed no con-

10   tention with him, but I will be so bold as to wear it in my cap
till I see him once again, and then I will tell him a little piece
of my desires.

Enter [Ensign] PISTOL

GOWER   Why, here a° comes, swelling like a turkey-cock.   *he*

FLUELLEN   'Tis no matter for his swellings nor his turkey-

15   cocks.—God pless you Ensign Pistol, you scurvy lousy knave,
God pless you.

PISTOL   Ha, art thou bedlam?° Dost thou thirst, base Trojan,°   *crazy / villain*
To have me fold up Parca's¹ fatal web?
Hence! I am qualmish° at the smell of leek.   *nauseated*

---

3. Lovingly anticipated probability.
4. *General . . . Empress:* Earl of Essex (see Introduction).
5. Sigismund; the Holy Roman Emperor, attempted,
and failed, to negotiate a peace between France and
England.

6. A line is evidently missing here.
7. Henry invaded France a second and third time, in
1417 and 1421; Act 5 begins in the latter year.
5.1 Location: The English camp.
1. The Parcae were the mythological Fates who spun
and cut the thread of life.

20 FLUELLEN   I peseech you heartily, scurvy lousy knave, at my
     desires and my requests and my petitions, to eat, look you, this
     leek. Because, look you, you do not love it, nor your affections
     and your appetites and your digestions does not agree with it, I
     would desire you to eat it.
25 PISTOL   Not for Cadwallader° and all his goats.   *last Welsh king*
   FLUELLEN   There is one goat for you. [*He*] *strikes* [PISTOL] Will
     you be so good, scald° knave, as eat it?   *worthless*
   PISTOL   Base Trojan, thou shalt die.
   FLUELLEN   You say very true, scald knave, when God's will is. I
30   will desire you to live in the mean time, and eat your victuals.° *food*
     Come, there is sauce for it. [*He strikes him*] You called me
     yesterday 'mountain-squire',° but I will make you today a   *(Wales is moutainous)*
     'squire of low degree'. I pray you, fall to. If you can mock a leek
     you can eat a leek.
     [*He strikes him*]
35 GOWER   Enough, captain, you have astonished° him.   *stunned*
   FLUELLEN   By Jesu, I will make him eat some part of my leek, or
     I will peat his pate° four days and four nights.—Bite, I pray you. *head*
     It is good for your green° wound and your ploody coxcomb.°   *fresh/head*
   PISTOL   Must I bite?
40 FLUELLEN   Yes, certainly, and out of doubt and out of question
     too, and ambiguities.
   PISTOL   By this leek, I will most horribly revenge—
     [FLUELLEN *threatens him*]
     I eat and eat—I swear—
   FLUELLEN   Eat, I pray you. Will you have some more sauce to
45   your leek? There is not enough leek to swear by.
   PISTOL   Quiet thy cudgel,° thou dost see I eat.   *wooden club*
   FLUELLEN   Much good do you, scald knave, heartily. Nay, pray
     you throw none away. The skin is good for your broken cox-
     comb. When you take occasions to see leeks hereafter, I pray
50   you mock at 'em, that is all.
   PISTOL   Good.
   FLUELLEN   Ay, leeks is good. Hold you, there is a groat° to heal   *fourpence*
     your pate.
   PISTOL   Me, a groat?
55 FLUELLEN   Yes, verily,° and in truth you shall take it, or I have   *truly*
     another leek in my pocket which you shall eat.
   PISTOL   I take thy groat in earnest° of revenge.   *advance payment*
   FLUELLEN   If I owe you anything, I will pay you in cudgels. You
     shall be a woodmonger, and buy nothing of me but cudgels.
60   God b'wi' you, and keep you, and heal your pate.   *Exit*
   PISTOL   All hell shall stir for this.
   GOWER   Go, go, you are a counterfeit cowardly knave. Will you
     mock at an ancient tradition, begun upon an honourable
     respect and worn as a memorable trophy of predeceased
65   valour, and dare not avouch° in your deeds any of your words?   *prove*
     I have seen you gleeking and galling° at this gentleman twice   *jesting and annoying*
     or thrice. You thought, because he could not speak English in
     the native garb, he could not therefore handle an English cud-
     gel. You find it otherwise. And henceforth let a Welsh correc-
70   tion teach you a good English condition. Fare ye well.   *Exit*
   PISTOL   Doth Fortune play the hussy° with me now?   *whore*
     News have I that my Nell is dead

I'th' spital of a malady of France,°   *venereal disease*
And there my rendezvous° is quite cut off.   *refuge*
75 Old I do wax, and from my weary limbs
Honour is cudgelled. Well, bawd° I'll turn,   *pimp*
And something lean to cutpurse of quick hand.
To England will I steal, and there I'll steal,
And patches will I get unto these cudgelled scars,
80 And swear I got them in the Gallia° wars.   *Exit*   *French*

5.2

Enter at one door KING [HARRY, *Dukes of*] EXETER [*and*
CLARENCE, *Earl of*] WARWICK, *and other lords; at
another,* KING [CHARLES *the Sixth*] *of France,* QUEEN ISA-
BEL, *the Duke of* BURGUNDY, *and other French,* [*among
them Princess*] CATHERINE [*and* ALICE]

KING HARRY   Peace to this meeting, wherefor° we are met.   *for which*
Unto our brother France and to our sister,
Health and fair time of day. Joy and good wishes
To our most fair and princely cousin Catherine;
5 And as a branch and member of this royalty,
By whom this great assembly is contrived,
We do salute you, Duke of Burgundy.
And princes French, and peers, health to you all.
KING CHARLES   Right joyous are we to behold your face.
10 Most worthy brother England, fairly met.
So are you, princes English, every one.
QUEEN ISABEL   So happy be the issue,° brother England,   *outcome*
Of this good day and of this gracious meeting,
As we are now glad to behold your eyes—
15 Your eyes which hitherto have borne in them,
Against the French that met them in their bent,°   *glance*
The fatal balls° of murdering basilisks.[1]   *eyeballs; cannonballs*
The venom of such looks we fairly hope
Have lost their quality,° and that this day   *nature*
20 Shall change all griefs and quarrels into love.
KING HARRY   To cry amen to that, thus we appear.
QUEEN ISABEL   You English princes all, I do salute you.
BURGUNDY   My duty to you both, on equal love,
Great Kings of France and England. That I have laboured
25 With all my wits, my pains, and strong endeavours,
To bring your most imperial majesties
Unto this bar° and royal interview,   *court*
Your mightiness on both parts best can witness.
Since, then, my office hath so far prevailed
30 That face to face and royal eye to eye
You have congreeted,° let it not disgrace me   *met*
If I demand, before this royal view,
What rub° or what impediment there is   *hindrance*
Why that the naked, poor, and mangled peace,
35 Dear nurse of arts, plenties, and joyful births,
Should not in this best garden of the world,
Our fertile France, put up her lovely visage?
Alas, she hath from France too long been chased,

5.2 Location: The French court.   1. Fabulous animals able to kill with a glance.

And all her husbandry° doth lie on heaps,   *agriculture*
40 Corrupting in it° own fertility.   *its*
Her vine, the merry cheerer of the heart,
Unprunèd dies; her hedges even-plashed°   *interwoven*
Like prisoners wildly overgrown with hair
Put forth disordered twigs; her fallow leas°   *unplanted fields*
45 The darnel, hemlock, and rank fumitory°   *kinds of weeds*
Doth root upon, while that the coulter° rusts   *plow*
That should deracinate° such savagery.   *root out*
The even mead°—that erst brought sweetly forth   *meadow*
The freckled cowslip, burnet, and green clover—
50 Wanting the scythe, all uncorrected, rank,
Conceives by idleness,° and nothing teems   *Breeds worthless things*
But hateful docks, rough thistles, kecksies, burs,°   *(all are weeds)*
Losing both beauty and utility.
An° all our vineyards, fallows, meads, and hedges,   *And if*
55 Defective in their natures, grow to wildness,
Even so our houses and ourselves and children
Have lost, or do not learn for want of time,
The sciences° that should become° our country,   *knowledge/adorn*
But grow like savages—as soldiers will
60 That nothing do but meditate on blood—
To swearing and stern looks, diffused° attire,   *disordered*
And everything that seems unnatural.
Which to reduce into our former favour[2]
You are assembled, and my speech entreats
65 That I may know the let° why gentle peace   *impediment*
Should not expel these inconveniences
And bless us with her former qualities.
KING HARRY   If, Duke of Burgundy, you would the peace
Whose want gives growth to th'imperfections
70 Which you have cited, you must buy that peace
With full accord to all our just demands,
Whose tenors° and particular effects   *general principles*
You have enscheduled briefly in your hands.
BURGUNDY   The King hath heard them, to the which as yet
There is no answer made.
75 KING HARRY   Well then, the peace,
Which you before so urged, lies in his answer.
KING CHARLES   I have but with a cursitory° eye   *cursory*
O'erglanced the articles. Pleaseth your grace
To appoint some of your council presently
80 To sit with us once more, with better heed
To re-survey them, we will suddenly
Pass our accept and peremptory° answer.   *approved and definite*
KING HARRY   Brother, we shall.—Go, Uncle Exeter
And brother Clarence, and you, brother Gloucester;
85 Warwick and Huntingdon, go with the King,
And take with you free power to ratify,
Augment, or alter, as your wisdoms best
Shall see advantageable for our dignity,
Anything in or out of our demands,
90 And we'll consign° thereto.—Will you, fair sister,   *agree*

2. To revert to our old appearance.

Go with the princes, or stay here with us?

QUEEN   Our gracious brother, I will go with them.

Haply° a woman's voice may do some good   *Perhaps*

When articles too nicely° urged be stood on.   *punctiliously*

95 KING HARRY   Yet leave our cousin Catherine here with us.

She is our capital° demand, comprised   *chief*

Within the fore-rank of our articles.

QUEEN   She hath good leave.

        Exeunt [all but] KING HARRY, CATHERINE, *and* [ALICE]

        the gentlewoman

KING HARRY   Fair Catherine, and most fair,

Will you vouchsafe to teach a soldier terms

100 Such as will enter at a lady's ear

And plead his love-suit to her gentle heart?

CATHERINE   Your majesty shall mock at me. I cannot speak your

England.

KING HARRY   O fair Catherine, if you will love me soundly with

105 your French heart, I will be glad to hear you confess it brokenly

with your English tongue. Do you like me, Kate?

CATHERINE *Pardonnez-moi,*° I cannot tell vat is 'like me'.   *Excuse me*

KING HARRY   An angel is like you, Kate, and you are like an

angel.

110 CATHERINE [*to* ALICE]   *Que dit-il?—que je suis semblable à les*

anges?

ALICE   *Oui, vraiment—sauf votre grâce—ainsi dit-il.*[3]

KING HARRY   I said so, dear Catherine, and I must not blush to

affirm it.

115 CATHERINE   *O bon Dieu!*° *Les langues des hommes sont pleines*   *O good God*

de tromperies.°   *(translated below)*

KING HARRY   What says she, fair one? That the tongues of men

are full of deceits?

ALICE   *Oui,* dat de tongeus of de mans is be full of deceits—dat

120 is de Princess.

KING HARRY   The Princess is the better Englishwoman. I'faith,

Kate, my wooing is fit for thy understanding. I am glad thou

canst speak no better English, for if thou couldst, thou wouldst

find me such a plain king that thou wouldst think I had sold

125 my farm to buy my crown. I know no ways to mince it in love,

but directly to say, 'I love you'; then if you urge me farther than

to say, 'Do you in faith?', I wear out my suit. Give me your

answer, i'faith do, and so clap° hands and a bargain. How say   *shake*

you, lady?

130 CATHERINE   *Sauf votre honneur,*° me understand well.   *Save your honor*

KING HARRY   Marry, if you would put me to verses, or to dance

for your sake, Kate, why, you undid me. For the one I have

neither words nor measure,° and for the other I have no   *meter*

strength in measure°—yet a reasonable measure in strength. If *talent for dancing*

135 I could win a lady at leap-frog, or by vaulting into my saddle

with my armour on my back, under the correction of bragging

be it spoken, I should quickly leap into a wife. Or if I might

buffet° for my love, or bound my horse for her favours, I could   *box*

lay on like a butcher, and sit like a jackanapes,° never off. But   *monkey*

140 before God, Kate, I cannot look greenly,° nor gasp out my elo-   *abashed*

---

3. What does he say? That I am like an angel? Yes, truly, save your grace, he says that.

quence, nor I have no cunning in protestation—only downright oaths, which I never use till urged, nor never break for
urging. If thou canst love a fellow of this temper,° Kate, whose   *makeup*
face is not worth sunburning, that never looks in his glass° for   *mirror*
145   love of anything he sees there, let thine eye be thy cook. I speak
to thee plain soldier: if thou canst love me for this, take me. If
not, to say to thee that I shall die, is true—but for thy love, by
the Lord, no. Yet I love thee, too. And while thou livest, dear
Kate, take a fellow of plain and uncoined° constancy, for he   *not in common use*
150   perforce must do thee right, because he hath not the gift to
woo in other places. For these fellows of infinite tongue, that
can rhyme themselves into ladies' favours, they do always reason themselves out again. What! A speaker is but a prater,° a   *chatterer*
rhyme is but a ballad; a good leg will fall, a straight back will
155   stoop, a black beard will turn white, a curled pate will grow
bald, a fair face will wither, a full eye will wax° hollow, but a   *become*
good heart, Kate, is the sun and the moon—or rather the sun
and not the moon, for it shines bright and never changes, but
keeps his course truly. If thou would have such a one, take me;
160   and take me, take a soldier; take a soldier, take a king. And
what sayst thou then to my love? Speak, my fair—and fairly, I
pray thee.

CATHERINE   Is it possible dat I sould love de *ennemi* of France?

KING HARRY   No, it is not possible you should love the enemy of
165   France, Kate. But in loving me, you should love the friend of
France, for I love France so well that I will not part with a
village of it, I will have it all mine; and Kate, when France is
mine, and I am yours, then yours is France, and you are mine.

CATHERINE   I cannot tell vat is dat.

170 KING HARRY   No, Kate? I will tell thee in French—which I am
sure will hang upon my tongue like a new-married wife about
her husband's neck, hardly to be shook off. *Je quand suis le
possesseur de France, et quand vous avez le possession de moi*—
let me see, what then? Saint Denis be my speed!—*donc vôtre
175   est France, et vous êtes mienne*.[4] It is as easy for me, Kate, to
conquer the kingdom as to speak so much more French. I shall
never move° thee in French, unless it be to laugh at me.   *persuade*

CATHERINE *Sauf votre honneur, le français que vous parlez, il est
meilleur que l'anglais lequel je parle*.[5]

180 KING HARRY   No, faith, is't not, Kate. But thy speaking of my
tongue, and I thine, most truly-falsely, must needs be granted
to be much at one.° But Kate, dost thou understand thus much   *alike; united*
English? Canst thou love me?

CATHERINE I cannot tell.

185 KING HARRY   Can any of your neighbours tell, Kate? I'll ask them.
Come, I know thou lovest me, and at night when you come
into your closet° you'll question this gentlewoman about me,   *bedchamber*
and I know, Kate, you will to her dispraise those parts° in me   *qualities*
that you love with your heart. But good Kate, mock me merci-
190   fully—the rather, gentle princess, because I love thee cruelly.
If ever thou be'st mine, Kate—as I have a saving faith within
me tells me thou shalt—I get thee with scrambling,° and thou   *fighting*

4. Translation of the last part of his previous speech.
5. Saving your honor, the French you speak is better than the English I speak.

must therefore needs prove a good soldier-breeder. Shall not
thou and I, between Saint Denis and Saint George,[6] com-
195 pound a boy, half-French half-English, that shall go to Con-
stantinople and take the Turk by the beard? Shall we not? What
sayst thou, my fair flower-de-luce?[7]

CATHERINE I do not know dat.

KING HARRY No, 'tis hereafter to know, but now to promise. Do
200 but now promise, Kate, you will endeavour for your French
part of such a boy, and for my English moiety° take the word   half
of a king and a bachelor. How answer you, *la plus belle Cather-*
ine du monde, mon très chère et divine déesse?[8]

CATHERINE Your *majesté 'ave faux*° French enough to deceive   false
205 de most *sage demoiselle*° dat is *en France.*   maiden

KING HARRY Now fie upon my false French! By mine honour,
in true English, I love thee, Kate. By which honour I dare not
swear thou lovest me, yet my blood° begins to flatter me that   instinct
thou dost, notwithstanding the poor and untempering° effect of uningratiating
210 my visage. Now beshrew° my father's ambition! He was think-   curse
ing of civil wars when he got me; therefore was I created with
a stubborn outside, with an aspect° of iron, that when I come   a face
to woo ladies I fright them. But in faith, Kate, the elder I wax
the better I shall appear. My comfort is that old age, that ill
215 layer-up° of beauty, can do no more spoil upon my face. Thou   preserver
hast me, if thou hast me, at the worst, and thou shalt wear me,
if thou wear me, better and better; and therefore tell me, most
fair Catherine, will you have me? Put off your maiden blushes,
avouch the thoughts of your heart with the looks of an empress,
220 take me by the hand and say, 'Harry of England, I am thine'—
which word thou shalt no sooner bless mine ear withal, but I
will tell thee aloud, 'England is thine, Ireland is thine, France
is thine, and Henry Plantagenet is thine'—who, though I speak
it before his face, if he be not fellow° with the best king; thou   equal
225 shalt find the best king of good fellows. Come, your answer in
broken music°—for thy voice is music and thy English broken. music in parts
Therefore, queen of all, Catherine, break thy mind to me in
broken English: wilt thou have me?

CATHERINE Dat is as it shall please de *roi mon père.*°   King my father

230 KING HARRY Nay, it will please him well, Kate. It shall please
him, Kate.

CATHERINE Den it sall also content me.

KING HARRY Upon that I kiss your hand, and I call you my
queen.

235 CATHERINE *Laissez, mon seigneur, laissez, laissez! Ma foi, je ne*
veux point que vous abbaissez votre grandeur en baisant la main
d'une de votre seigneurie indigne serviteur. Excusez-moi, je vous
supplie, mon treis-puissant seigneur.[9]

KING HARRY Then I will kiss your lips, Kate.

240 CATHERINE *Les dames et demoiselles pour être baisées devant*
leurs noces, il n'est pas la coutume de France.°   (translated below)

KING HARRY [*to* ALICE] Madam my interpreter, what says she?

ALICE Dat it is not be de *façon pour les*° ladies of France—I   fashion for the
cannot tell vat is *baiser en*° Anglish.   "kiss" in

---

6. Patron saints of France and England.
7. Fleur-de-lis, French national emblem.
8. The most beautiful Catherine in the world, my very
dear and divine goddess.

9. Stop, my lord, stop, stop! My faith, I do not want you
to lower your grandeur by kissing the hand of one of
your humble servants. Excuse me, I beseech you, my
very powerful lord.

245   KING HARRY   To kiss.

     ALICE   Your *majesté entend* bettre *que moi.*[1]

     KING HARRY   It is not a fashion for the maids in France to kiss
       before they are married, would she say?

     ALICE   *Oui, vraiment.*°   *Yes, truly*

250   KING HARRY   O Kate, nice° customs curtsy to great kings. Dear   *fastidious*
       Kate, you and I cannot be confined within the weak list° of a   *barrier*
       country's fashion. We are the makers of manners, Kate, and the
       liberty that follows our places stops the mouth of all find-faults,
       as I will do yours, for upholding the nice fashion of your coun-
255   try in denying me a kiss. Therefore, patiently and yielding. [*He
       kisses her*] You have witchcraft in your lips, Kate. There is more
       eloquence in a sugar touch of them than in the tongues of the
       French Council, and they should sooner persuade Harry of
       England than a general petition of monarchs. Here comes
260   your father.

               Enter KING [CHARLES, QUEEN ISABEL, *the Duke of* BUR-
              GUNDY,] *and the French* [*and*] *English lords*

     BURGUNDY   God save your majesty. My royal cousin, teach you
       our princess English?

     KING HARRY   I would have her learn, my fair cousin, how per-
       fectly I love her, and that is good English.

265   BURGUNDY   Is she not apt?

     KING HARRY   Our tongue is rough, coz,° and my condition is not   *kinsman*
       smooth, so that having neither the voice nor the heart of flattery
       about me I cannot so conjure up the spirit of love in her that
       he will appear in his true likeness.

270   BURGUNDY   Pardon the frankness of my mirth, if I answer you for
       that. If you would conjure in her, you must make a circle;[2] if
       conjure up love in her in his true likeness, he must appear
       naked and blind.° Can you blame her then, being a maid yet   (*like Cupid, god of love*)
       rosed over with the virgin crimson of modesty, if she deny the
275   appearance of a naked blind boy in her naked seeing self? It
       were, my lord, a hard condition for a maid to consign to.

     KING HARRY   Yet they do wink° and yield, as love is blind and   *close their eyes*
       enforces.

     BURGUNDY   They are then excused, my lord, when they see not
280   what they do.

     KING HARRY   Then, good my lord, teach your cousin to consent
       winking.

     BURGUNDY   I will wink on her to consent, my lord, if you will
       teach her to know my meaning. For maids, well summered
285   and warm kept, are like flies at Bartholomew-tide:° blind,   *August 24*
       though they have their eyes. And then they will endure han-
       dling, which before would not abide looking on.

     KING HARRY   This moral ties me over to time and a hot summer,
       and so I shall catch the fly, your cousin, in the latter end,[3] and
290   she must be blind too.

     BURGUNDY   As love is, my lord, before that it loves.

     KING HARRY   It is so. And you may, some of you, thank love for
       my blindness, who cannot see many a fair French city for one
       fair French maid that stands in my way.

---

1. Your majesty understands better than I.   devils).
2. By embracing her (sorcerers drew circles to call up   3. At last; in the backside.

295 KING CHARLES Yes, my lord, you see them perspectively,[4] the
cities turned into a maid—for they are all girdled with maiden
walls that war hath never entered.
KING HARRY Shall Kate be my wife?
KING CHARLES So please you.
300 KING HARRY I am content, so the maiden° cities you talk of may   *unconquered*
wait on her: so the maid that stood in the way for my wish shall
show me the way to my will.
KING CHARLES We have consented to all terms of reason.
KING HARRY Is't so, my lords of England?
305 WARWICK The King hath granted every article:
His daughter first, and so in sequel all,
According to their firm proposèd natures.
EXETER Only he hath not yet subscribèd° this: *signed to*
where your majesty demands that the King of France, having
310 any occasion to write for matter of grant,° shall name your high-   *in formal documents*
ness in this form and with this addition: [*reads*] in French,
Notre très cher fils Henri, Roi d'Angleterre, Héritier de France,
and thus in Latin, *Praeclarissimus filius noster Henricus, Rex
Angliae et Haeres Franciae.*[5]
315 KING CHARLES Nor this I have not, brother, so denied,
But your request shall make me let it pass.
KING HARRY I pray you then, in love and dear alliance,
Let that one article rank with the rest,
And thereupon give me your daughter.
320 KING CHARLES Take her, fair son, and from her blood raise up
Issue° to me, that the contending kingdoms   *Offspring*
Of France and England, whose very shores look pale
With envy of each other's happiness,
May cease their hatred, and this dear conjunction°   *loving union*
325 Plant neighbourhood° and Christian-like accord   *neighborliness*
In their sweet bosoms, that never war advance
His bleeding sword 'twixt England and fair France.
ALL Amen.
KING HARRY Now welcome, Kate, and bear me witness all
330 That here I kiss her as my sovereign Queen.
         Flourish
QUEEN ISABEL God, the best maker of all marriages,
Combine your hearts in one, your realms in one.
As man and wife, being two, are one in love,
So be there 'twixt your kingdoms such a spousal
335 That never may ill office° or fell° jealousy,   *bad action / cruel*
Which troubles oft the bed of blessèd marriage,
Thrust in between the paction° of these kingdoms   *agreement*
To make divorce of their incorporate league;
That English may as French, French Englishmen,
340 Receive each other, God speak this 'Amen'.
ALL Amen.
KING HARRY Prepare we for our marriage. On which day,
My lord of Burgundy, we'll take your oath,
And all the peers', for surety of our leagues.

---

4. In a lens that produces optical illusions.
5. Our very dear son Henry, King of England, heir of France.

345   Then shall I swear to Kate, and you to me,
       And may our oaths well kept and prosp'rous be.

                                    Sennet.° Exeunt   Ceremonial trumpet call

Epilogue

Enter CHORUS[1]

CHORUS   Thus far with rough and all-unable pen
          Our bending° author hath pursued the story,   (over a desk)
       In little room confining mighty men,
          Mangling by starts the full course of their glory.
5   Small time, but in that small most greatly lived
          This star of England. Fortune made his sword,
       By which the world's best garden he achieved,
          And of it left his son imperial lord.
       Henry the Sixth, in infant bands° crowned king   swaddling clothes
10   Of France and England, did this king succeed,
       Whose state so many had the managing
          That they lost France and made his England bleed,
       Which oft our stage hath shown[2]—and, for their sake,
       In your fair minds let this acceptance take.°   [*Exit*]   this play find favor

Additional Passages

The Dauphin / Bourbon variant, which usually involves only the speech prefixes,
has several consequences for the dialogue and structure of 4.5. Following are the
edited Folio and quarto versions of this scene.

A. Folio

       Enter CONSTABLE, ORLÉANS, BOURBON, DAUPHIN, *and*
       RAMBURES

CONSTABLE   *O diable!*
ORLÉANS   *O Seigneur! Le jour est perdu, tout est perdu.*
DAUPHIN   *Mort de ma vie!* All is confounded, all.
       Reproach and everlasting shame
5   Sits mocking in our plumes.
          A short alarum
       O méchante fortune! Do not run away.   [*Exit* RAMBURES]
CONSTABLE   Why, all our ranks are broke.
DAUPHIN   O perdurable shame! Let's stab ourselves:
       Be these the wretches that we played at dice for?
10   ORLÉANS   Is this the king we sent to for his ransom?
BOURBON   Shame, an eternall shame, nothing but shame!
       Let us die in pride. In once more, back again!
       And he that will not follow Bourbon now,
       Let him go home, and with his cap in hand
15   Like a base leno hold the chamber door,
       Whilst by a slave no gentler than my dog
       His fairest daughter is contaminated.
CONSTABLE   Disorder that hath spoiled us, friend us now,
       Let us on heaps go offer up our lives.
20   ORLÉANS   We are enough yet living in the field
       To smother up the English in our throngs,

---

1. The following lines form a sonnet.
2. In *1 Henry VI, The First Part of the Contention (2*   *Henry VI), Richard Duke of York (3 Henry VI),* and *Richard III.*

If any order might be thought upon.
BOURBON   The devil take order now. I'll to the throng.
Let life be short, else shame will be too long.   *Exeunt*

B. Quarto

    Enter the four French lords: [*the* CONSTABLE, ORLÉANS,
    BOURBON, *and* GEBON]

GEBON   O *diabello!*°   devil
CONSTABLE   *Mort de ma vie!*
ORLÉANS   O what a day is this!
BOURBON   *O jour de honte,*° all is gone, all is lost.   day of shame
5 CONSTABLE   We are enough yet living in the field
To smother up the English,
If any order might be thought upon.
BOURBON   A plague of order! Once more to the field!
And he that will not follow Bourbon now,
10 Let him go home, and with his cap in hand,
Like a base leno hold the chamber door,
Whilst by a slave no gentler than my dog
His fairest daughter is contaminated.
CONSTABLE   Disorder that hath spoiled us, right us now.
15 Come we in heaps, we'll offer up our lives
Unto these English, or else die with fame.
BOURBON   Come, come along.
Let's die with honour, our shame doth last too long.   *Exeunt*

Sir Thomas More: *Passages Attributed to Shakespeare*

The play *Sir Thomas More* was originally composed between late 1592 and mid-1595, probably in 1592–93, by Anthony Munday, Henry Chettle, and perhaps a third writer (Thomas Dekker?). Sometime later, perhaps in 1593–94 or 1603–04, Shakespeare seems to have participated in its revision. The original version was designed for Lord Strange's Men, who presumably intended to stage it at their regular theater, the Rose. Drawing on Raphael Holinshed's *Chronicles of England, Scotland, and Ireland* (1587), Nicholas Harpsfield's *Life and Death of Sir Thomas Moore,* and Thomas Stapleton's Latin biography *Vita Thomae Mori,* the play conforms to the popular tragic model known in Latin as *de casibus virorum illustrium* (on the fall of illustrious men). It follows the career of More—leading English Renaissance humanist and author of *Utopia,* Lord Chancellor of England and persecutor of Protestants, and, finally, Catholic martyr when the religious tide turned. The work focuses on his success as sheriff in peacefully quelling the anti-alien London riots of May Day 1517; his elevation to the post of Lord Chancellor; and his eventual execution for refusing to subscribe to certain of the King's articles. Throughout and especially at the end, the witty and wise protagonist is treated with almost uncritical admiration.

Strange's Men specialized in plays on English subjects with a loosely nationalist appeal; they also liked to live dangerously. *Sir Thomas More* was doubly dangerous. First, even though it carefully converts the issue that led to More's death (papal versus royal supremacy of the church) into a less concrete conflict between worldly authority and individual conscience that would appeal to a Puritan-leaning audience, it sympathetically dramatizes the life of a Catholic martyr killed by Henry VIII, the father of the ruling Protestant monarch, Queen Elizabeth. Second, although it shows More successfully preventing popular protest that historically he was unable to control, the play exploits contemporary antiforeign resentment, which was noticeable by late 1592 and led to rioting and harsh government reprisals between 1593 and 1595. On neither issue does the absolute monarch end up looking particularly good. Before the first performance, however, the censor, Sir Edmund Tilney, Master of the Revels, demanded substantial rewriting, in particular a toning down of the attack on foreigners and the elimination of the scene dramatizing the 1517 rebellion against them. Apparently before the manuscript could be revised, an outbreak of plague closed the theaters for most of the period from mid-1592 to mid-1594, and the actors abandoned the play.

Early in the seventeenth century, the text was revised for performance—possibly at the Fortune, the regular theater of Lord Admiral's Men/Prince Henry's Men, conceivably at the Globe by Shakespeare's company, the Lord Chamberlain's Men/King's Men. (On James I's accession in 1603, Prince Henry and his father, the King, assumed the patronage of the Lord Admiral's and Lord Chamberlain's companies.) The play fit the strategy of the Lord Admiral's Men in the years immediately after 1600, when they specialized in revivals from the Strange's repertory of the early 1590s and the Admiral's own of 1594–97. Also, during the same period, both the Lord Admiral's and the Lord Chamberlain's Men mounted a number of plays set during the reign of Henry VIII. A new monarch and the absence of the dangerous political context of the 1590s allowed the revisers to imagine how they might take account of the censor's earlier concerns. But they could not disregard the fact that the play as originally written required more actors than were in either company, and they adapted the text accordingly. No record of performance exists.

For the original version, Anthony Munday (manuscript Hand S) had copied out the entire text, modifying the work of his collaborator(s). The revision, which also significantly improved the quality of the play, was undertaken by Henry Chettle (Hand A), Thomas Dekker (Hand E), probably Thomas Heywood (Hand B), a playhouse scribe (Hand C), and very probably Shakespeare (Hand D). The result, "The Booke of Sir Thomas Moore" (British Library, MS Harleian 7368)—where "Booke" means theatrical promptbook—is arguably the messiest and most extensively revised dramatic manuscript

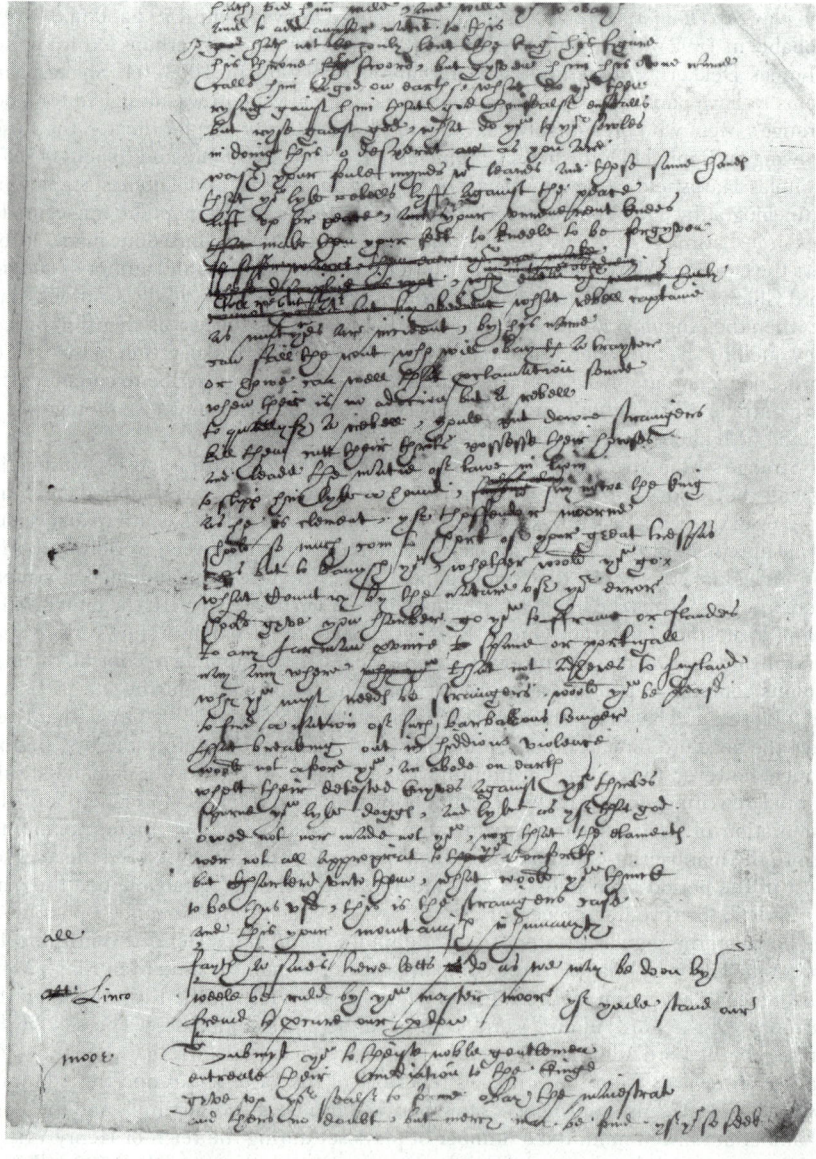

From Anthony Munday and others, "The Booke of Sir Thomas Moore" (British Library MS Harleian 7368), fol. 9a. This is the most legible of the pages believed to be in Shakespeare's hand.

of the age. It was not printed until the nineteenth century. It is worth emphasizing the existence of other possible explanations—three in particular—of the text besides the one offered here. The revisions may have occurred immediately following the initial composition of the play, either before or after Tilney's censorship. Second, a small minority denies that Shakespeare is Hand D. Third and most striking, it has been argued that Hand D, whatever his identity, was one of the original playwrights rather than a reviser.

Hand D is present in the first of the two passages printed here, Add.II.D (Addition II, Hand D; 8^r, 8^v, 9^r), which was subsequently edited by Hand C, partly to make it conform to the other revisions. If Add.II.D is Shakespearean, it is by far the longest extant specimen of Shakespeare's handwriting and as such is of considerable scholarly, as well as theatrical and literary, value. It shows what a Shakespearean first draft looks like and, hence, some of the challenges a scribe or printer had to contend with. The attribution to Shakespeare is based on resemblances to his other extant handwriting (almost exclusively signatures), spelling similarities to printed texts that probably are directly based on manuscripts in Shakespeare's hand, and stylistic affinities. The text printed here excludes the emendations that Hand C made to Add.II.D. Normally, this edition opts for the theatrical, rather than the authorial, version of a play on the grounds that Shakespeare was aware of and accepted the revisions introduced by his acting company when preparing his manuscript for the stage. In this instance, however, his involvement in rehearsal and performance is less likely than usual. The second passage included here, Add.III (folio 11*^{b}), is in Hand C and is attributed to Shakespeare, with somewhat less confidence, on stylistic grounds. Normally, as well, this edition prints an entire play rather than a fragment. Here, however, Shakespeare's contribution is small and his involvement probably late—long after the play had been conceptualized and, indeed, written. The entire play is available, however, online at the *Norton Shakespeare* Web site.

Add.II.D constitutes almost the first two-thirds of what one modern edition calls Scene 6 and another Act 2, Scene 3. Earlier in the play, the citizens of London, angered by the high-handed, legally protected behavior of foreigners, prepare to take bloody revenge. Here, More, acting on behalf of a state otherwise prepared to meet force with force, talks the assembled crowd out of violence and into submission to the King. Shakespeare's revision belittles the protesters, depriving them of an individuality they possessed earlier in the play and reducing them to the idiotic fear of disease-causing foreign vegetables (the parsnip and the pumpkin, lines 10–19). Although the rhetoric of More's arguments for obedience is clever and even arresting in its evocation of "the wretched strangers" leaving England (line 81), the claims are orthodox and traditional. They may represent changes from the original manuscript and, like the imagery, certainly have parallels in Shakespeare's other plays, most tellingly in Ulysses' speech on degree in 1.3 of *Troilus and Cressida* (probably from 1602). Even though the lines seem at least partly designed to reassure the censor, their political implications also point in a different direction. Once the crowd has listened to More, whom they already trust and respect, they willingly submit to royal authority. The text demonstrates the fundamental decency of the common folk. And More's brilliant success provides a plausible, if historically inaccurate, explanation of his appointment as Lord Chancellor.

Like Ulysses' speech, however, More's is undermined by the rest of the play. The passage also engages in powerfully ironic foreshadowing at the expense of the monarchy. More promises,

> Submit you to these noble gentlemen,
> Entreat their mediation to the King,
> Give up yourself to form, obey the magistrate,
> And there's no doubt but mercy may be found,
> If you so seek it.

(lines 157–61)

There is, however, a "doubt": Lincoln goes to the scaffold, his noble death anticipating More's own fate. More also insists that

> . . . to the King God hath his office lent
> . . . .
> . . . What do you then,
> Rising 'gainst him that God himself installs,
> But rise 'gainst God?
> (lines 107, 113–15)

The equation of God and King, the divine sanction for royal authority—these are the principles that More repudiates at the cost of his life. A similar effect is achieved in Add.III, which opens Scene 8 of one modern edition and Act 3, Scene 1, of another. Newly named Lord Chancellor, More soliloquizes on the suddenness of his ascent, in which he sees evidence of a providential force at odds with explanations based on "our fortunes" (line 2; Fortune is usually represented in *de casibus* tragedy by the image of the turning wheel). This view leads him to predict, accurately, that "to be great / Is" to be "greatly undone" (lines 19–21)—where the greatness of the undoing can refer both to the height from which he falls and to the stature of the cause for which he goes to his death.

Walter Cohen

SELECTED BIBLIOGRAPHY

Fox, Alistair. "The Paradoxical Design of *The Book of Sir Thomas More.*" *Renaissance and Reformation/Renaissance et Réforme* n.s. 5 (1981): 162–73. Includes discussion of the symbolic resonance of the dramatic interlude that More puts on for the Lord Mayor (Scene 9).

Gabrieli, Vittorio. "*Sir Thomas More:* Sources, Characters, Ideas." *Moreana* 23 (June 1986): 17–43. The central study of the play's sources.

Howard-Hill, T. H., ed. *Shakespeare and "Sir Thomas More": Essays on the Play and Its Shakespearian Interest.* Cambridge, Eng.: Cambridge University Press, 1989. A collection of articles dealing with both authorship issues and critical interpretation.

Levine, Nina S. "Citizens' Games: Differentiating Collaboration and *Sir Thomas More.*" *Shakespeare Quarterly* 58 (2007): 31–64. Investigates the analogy between collaborative authorship and the subject of that collaboration, rebellious citizen solidarity.

Masten, Jeffrey. "More or Less: Editing the Collaborative." *Shakespeare Studies* 29 (2001): 109–31. Argues for including the full play, rather than just the Shakespearean portions, in editions of Shakespeare, thus avoiding a practice that underemphasizes the unity of the work.

McMillin, Scott. *The Elizabethan Theatre and "The Book of Sir Thomas More."* Ithaca, N.Y.: Cornell University Press, 1987. Interprets the play in the context of theatrical practice at the time, arguing that Shakespeare was part of the collaboration that originally composed the play rather than one of its revisers.

Munday, Anthony, and others. Revised by Henry Chettle, Thomas Dekker, Thomas Heywood, and William Shakespeare. *Sir Thomas More: A Play.* Ed. Vittorio Gabrieli and Giorgio Melchiori. The Revels Plays series. Manchester: Manchester University Press, 1990. Annotated modern edition of the play.

Wentersdorf, Karl P. "On 'Momtanish Inhumanyty' in *Sir Thomas More.*" *Studies in Philology* 103 (2006): 178–85. Argues that More criticizes the citizens' hostility to foreigners as Muslim inhumanity.

Sir Thomas More: *Passages Attributed to Shakespeare*

Add.II.D

[*John*] LINCOLN [*a broker*],° DOLL, BETTS, [SHERWIN (*a*   *buying and selling agent*
goldsmith*), and prentices*° *armed; Thomas* MORE (*sheriff*   *apprentices*
of the City of London), the other sheriff, Sir Thomas
PALMER, *Sir Roger* CHOLMELEY,] *and a* SERJEANT-*at-
arms* [*stand aloof*]

LINCOLN [*to the prentices*]   Peace, hear me! He that will not see°   *tolerate*
a red herring at a Harry groat,° butter at eleven pence a pound,   *cost of fourpence*
meal at nine shillings a bushel, and beef at four nobles a stone,
list[1] to me.
5   OTHER   It will come to that pass if strangers be suffered.[2] Mark
him.
LINCOLN   Our country is a great eating country; argo,[3] they eat
more in our country than they do in their own.
OTHER   By a halfpenny loaf a day, troy weight.°   *standard measure*
10   LINCOLN   They bring in strange roots,[4] which is merely° to the   *entirely*
undoing of poor prentices, for what's a sorry parsnip[5] to a good
heart?
OTHER   Trash, trash. They breed sore eyes, and 'tis enough to
infect the city with the palsy.
15   LINCOLN   Nay, it has infected it with the palsy, for these bastards
of dung[6]—as you know, they grow in dung—have infected us,
and it is our infection will make the city shake, which partly
comes through the eating of parsnips.
OTHER   True, and pumpions° together.   *pumpkins*
SERJEANT [*coming forward*]   What say you to the mercy of the
20   King?
Do you refuse it?
LINCOLN   You would have us upon th'hip,° would you? No,   *at a disadvantage*
marry, do we not. We accept of the King's mercy; but we will
show no mercy upon the strangers.
25   SERJEANT   You are the simplest things
That ever stood in such a question.[7]
LINCOLN   How say you now? Prentices 'simple'? [*To the pren-
tices*] Down with him!
ALL   Prentices simple! Prentices simple!

Add.II.D Location: St. Martin's Lane, London; May Day
1517.
1. *noble*: gold coin worth 6 shillings 8 pence. *stone*: 14
pounds. *list*: listen. These prices would have seemed high
to a contemporary audience.
2. If foreigners ("strangers" means "foreigners" throughout the scene) are allowed (to remain in London).
3. As Lincoln says, England had a reputation for gluttony. *argo*: for Latin *ergo* (therefore).

4. Foreign vegetables.
5. Lincoln confuses parsnips with potatoes, which were
introduced to England from the Americas in the 1580s
and were rumored to cause disease.
6. Illegitimate growths made still more repugnant by
their association with excrement; perhaps merely abusive.
7. Stood their ground in such circumstances (against
the King's wishes).

Enter the Lord MAYOR, [*the Earl of*] SURREY, [*and the Earl of*] SHREWSBURY

30 SHERIFF [*to the prentices*]   Hold in the King's name! Hold!

SURREY [*to the prentices*]   Friends, masters, countrymen—

MAYOR [*to the prentices*]   Peace ho, peace! I charge you, keep
    the peace!

SHREWSBURY [*to the prentices*]   My masters, countrymen—

SHERWIN   The noble Earl of Shrewsbury, let's hear him.

35 BETTS   We'll hear the Earl of Surrey.

LINCOLN   The Earl of Shrewsbury.

BETTS   We'll hear both.

ALL   Both, both, both, both!

LINCOLN   Peace, I say peace! Are you men of wisdom, or what
40   are you?

SURREY   What you will have them,° but not men of wisdom.   *Whatever you call them*

SOME   We'll not hear my Lord of Surrey.

OTHERS   No, no, no, no, no! Shrewsbury, Shrewsbury!

MORE [*to the nobles and officers*]   Whiles they are o'er the bank
    of their obedience,
45 Thus will they bear down all things.[8]

LINCOLN [*to the prentices*]   Sheriff More speaks. Shall we hear
    Sheriff More speak?

DOLL   Let's hear him. A keeps a plentiful shrievaltry,[9] and a
    made my brother Arthur Watchins Sergeant Safe's yeoman.°   *assistant*
50 Let's hear Sheriff More.

ALL   Sheriff More, More, More, Sheriff More!

MORE   Even by the rule you have among yourselves,
    Command still audience.°   *quiet hearing*

SOME   Surrey, Surrey!

55 OTHERS   More, More!

LINCOLN *and* BETTS   Peace, peace, silence, peace!

MORE   You that have voice and credit with the number,°   *the crowd*
    Command them to a stillness.

LINCOLN   A plague on them! They will not hold their peace.
60 The devil cannot rule them.

MORE   Then what a rough and riotous charge° have you,   *people in your care; duty*
    To lead those that the devil cannot rule.
    [*To the prentices*] Good masters, hear me speak.

DOLL   Ay, by th' mass, will we. More, thou'rt a good house-
65 keeper,[1] and I thank thy good worship for my brother Arthur
    Watchins.

ALL   Peace, peace!

MORE   Look, what you do offend you cry upon,[2]
    That is the peace. Not one of you here present,
70 Had there such fellows lived when you were babes
    That could have topped the peace as now you would,
    The peace wherein you have till now grown up
    Had been ta'en from you, and the bloody times
    Could not have brought you to the state of men.[3]

8. The image is of water flooding over the banks (of obedience), destroying everything in its path.
9. He ("A") is a generous sheriff.
1. Patron; head of a well-to-do household.
2. By yelling "peace" (though you call for peace), you break the peace. More's speeches to the crowd, especially lines 79–94, echo Ulysses' speech on degree in *Troilus*

and Cressida 1.3.74–137, in particular lines 110–24. Both of these sincere expositions of orthodoxy are ironized by the ensuing events.
3. *Not one . . . men:* If such peace breakers as you had been around when you were children, you wouldn't have had peaceful times to grow up in, and you wouldn't have lived to become men.

75   Alas, poor things, what is it you have got,
    Although we grant you get the thing you seek?
   BETTS   Marry, the removing of the strangers, which cannot
    choose but much advantage the poor handicrafts° of the city.   *craftspeople*
   MORE   Grant them removed, and grant that this your noise
80   Hath chid down all the majesty of England.[4]
    Imagine that you see the wretched strangers,
    Their babies at their backs, with their poor luggage
    Plodding to th' ports and coasts for transportation,
    And that you sit as kings in your desires,[5]
85   Authority quite silenced by your brawl
    And you in ruff of your opinions clothed:[6]
    What had you got? I'll tell you. You had taught
    How insolence and strong hand° should prevail,   *force*
    How order should be quelled—and by this pattern
90   Not one of you should live an agèd man,
    For other ruffians as their fancies wrought
    With selfsame hand, self reasons, and self right
    Would shark° on you, and men like ravenous fishes   *prey*
    Would feed on one another.
95   DOLL   Before God, that's as true as the gospel.
   BETTS   Nay, this'° a sound fellow, I tell you. Let's mark° him.   *this is / listen to*
   MORE   Let me set up before your thoughts, good friends,
    One supposition,° which if you will mark   *proposition*
    You shall perceive how horrible a shape
100   Your innovation° bears. First, 'tis a sin   *rebellion*
    Which oft th'apostle° did forewarn us of,   *Paul (Romans 13:1–5)*
    Urging obedience to authority;
    And 'twere no error if I told you all
    You were in arms 'gainst God.
105   ALL   Marry, God forbid that!
   MORE   Nay, certainly you are.
    For to the King God hath his office lent
    Of dread,° of justice, power and command,   *fearful respect*
    Hath bid him rule and willed you to obey;
110   And to add ampler majesty to this,
    He hath not only lent the King his figure,
    His throne and sword, but given him his own name,
    Calls him a god on earth. What do you then,
    Rising 'gainst him that God himself installs,
115   But rise 'gainst God?[7] What do you to your souls
    In doing this? O desperate as you are,
    Wash your foul minds with tears, and those same hands
    That you like rebels lift against the peace
    Lift up for peace; and your unreverent knees,
120   Make them your feet. To kneel to be forgiven
    Is safer wars than ever you can make,
    Whose discipline is riot.[8]

---

4. *grant that . . . England*: suppose your action overthrew the state.
5. You get what you want; your wishes are obeyed.
6. And you wearing the clothes ("ruff" was a fancy starched collar; also, the highest pride) befitting the rank and authority you think you deserve (alluding to Elizabethan sumptuary laws, which determined, according to rank and income, the clothes one was permitted to wear).
7. More argues in this speech that the monarch's authority has divine sanction—ironically, a position that, as the end of the play reveals, he later repudiated at the cost of his life.
8. *Is . . . riot*: Is a safer means of fighting (for your goals) than your rebellion.

In, in, to your obedience!⁹ Why, even your hurly°   riot
Cannot proceed but by obedience.
125   What rebel captain,
        As mut'nies are incident,° by his name   about to happen
        Can still the rout?° Who will obey a traitor?   quiet the rabble
        Or how can well that proclamation sound,
        When there is no addition° but 'a rebel'   title of rank
130   To qualify° a rebel? You'll put down strangers,   signify
        Kill them, cut their throats, possess their houses,
        And lead the majesty of law in lyam°   on a leash
        To slip° him like a hound—alas, alas!   release
        Say now the King,
135   As he is clement° if th'offender mourn,°   merciful / repent
        Should so much come too short of your great trespass¹
        As but to banish you: whither would you go?
        What country, by° the nature of your error,   in light of
        Should give you harbour? Go you to France or Flanders,
140   To any German province, Spain or Portugal,
        Nay, anywhere that not adheres² to England—
        Why, you must needs° be strangers. Would you be pleased   necessarily
        To find a nation of such barbarous temper
        That breaking out in hideous violence
145   Would not afford you an abode on earth,
        Whet° their detested knives against your throats,   But would whet
        Spurn you like dogs, and like as if that God
        Owed° not nor made not you, nor that the elements   Owned
        Were not all appropriate° to your comforts   suitable
150   But chartered unto° them, what would you think   reserved only for
        To be thus used? This is the strangers' case,
        And this your mountainish³ inhumanity.
ONE [to the others]   Faith, a° says true. Let's do as we may be   he
        done by.⁴
155   ANOTHER [to MORE]   We'll be ruled by you, Master More, if
        you'll stand our friend to procure our pardon.
MORE   Submit you to these noble gentlemen,
        Entreat their mediation to the King,
        Give up yourself to form,° obey the magistrate,   correct behavior
160   And there's no doubt but mercy may be found,
        If you so seek it.⁵

Add.III

Enter [Sir Thomas] MORE
MORE   It is in heaven that I am thus and thus,¹
        And that which we profanely term our fortunes
        Is the provision of the power above,
        Fitted and shaped just to that strength of nature
5   Which we are born withal.° Good God, good God,   with
        That I from such an humble bench² of birth

9. Get back within the boundaries of your obedience.
1. Should reduce by so much the punishment for your
great offense.
2. Anywhere whose customs don't conform.
3. Gross, coarse. Possibly a contraction of Mahometan-
ish, or Muslim.
4. Proverbial. From the Sermon on the Mount (Matthew
7:12 and Luke 6:31).

5. In the event, More's intercession is unable to save Lincoln, whose noble death on the scaffold foreshadows
More's own and, like his, reflects badly on the King—the
dying men's loyal words notwithstanding.
Add.III   Location: The chancery staterooms in Westminster.
1. It is up to heaven that I am one thing and then another.
2. Legal position; foot of the table: hence, origin.

Should step as 'twere up to my country's head
And give the law out there; ay, in my father's life
To take prerogative and tithe of knees[3]
From elder kinsmen, and him bind by my place
To give the smooth and dexter way to me[4]
That owe it him by nature!° Sure these things,   *by birth*
Not physicked° by respect, might turn our blood   *regulated*
To much corruption. But More, the more thou hast
Either of honour, office, wealth and calling,
Which might accite° thee to embrace and hug them,   *entice*
The more do thou e'en° serpents' natures think them: *even*
Fear their gay skins, with thought of their sharp stings,
And let this be thy maxim: to be great
Is, when the thread of hazard is once spun,
A bottom great wound up, greatly undone.[5]

10 (line 10)
15 (line 15)
20 (line 20)

3. *To . . . knees*: To have preeminence and the deference of having others curtsy.
4. *and him . . . me*: and for my rank to force ("bind") someone ("him") to yield the right-hand side and the smooth part of the road.
5. *to be great . . . undone*: worldly power, when the thread that Fortune ("hazard") allots has been all wound up onto a big spool ("bottom"; or, when the hazards of reaching a high position have been surmounted), simply means a greater fall (or, falling only for something important). In Greek mythology, the end of a life occurred when the Fates cut a person's thread. Regardless of the exact interpretation of the passage, it accurately predicts More's fate.

All Is True (Henry VIII)

All Is True (*Henry VIII*; 1613) is the Shakespearean play that brought down the house. During a performance on June 29, 1613, when it "had beene acted not passing 2 or 3 times before," "certain Chambers" (small cannons) were shot off. The thatch of the Globe Theatre ignited, and the building burned down. Contemporary accounts disagree about whether the accident occurred early in the play, when King Henry participates in "a Masque at the Cardinal Wolsey's house" and the stage direction reads "Chambers discharged" (1.4.50), or, more improbably, when it "was almost ended." Apparently there was only one injury, to a man who "was scalded with the fire by adventuring in to save a child which otherwise had been burnt." Another version claims that the injured man "had his breeches set on fire, that would perhaps have broyled him, if he had not by the benefit of a provident wit put it out with bottle Ale." (See the Henry Wotton letter, page 848.)

All Is True does indeed show "a provident wit" and "save a child," though perhaps not in the fashion the two commentators had in mind. In reviewing some of the important events of the reign of Henry VIII, and in parading many of its central historical figures before the audience, the play ultimately reveals the workings of a divine providence that watches over England and assures the birth of the future Queen Elizabeth. It achieves this effect through the mixing of dramatic genres: in *All Is True*, the national history play meets the tragicomic romance. Known as *Henry VIII* at least since 1623, the text is a collaborative effort of Shakespeare and John Fletcher—with Shakespeare apparently the senior partner. It draws on narratives of relatively recent English history—primarily Raphael Holinshed's *Chronicles of England, Scotland, and Ireland* (1587 ed.), Shakespeare's main source for his earlier English history plays, and, for much of Act 5, John Foxe's epic of Protestant propaganda, *Book of Martyrs*. In so doing, the playwrights returned to a genre that Shakespeare had dominated during its heyday in the 1590s. By contrast, tragicomic romance, influenced by late Renaissance elite Italian theater, was very much in vogue in 1613, thanks largely to the recent works of Shakespeare, Francis Beaumont, and Fletcher.

The Shakespearean history play focuses on dynastic instabilities and civil conflicts of the late fourteenth and fifteenth centuries, and especially on the national implications of struggles between aristocratic factions. Shakespearean romance characteristically deploys a fictional plot in which long suffering and separation (often across the sea) are transcended through the virtuous daughter, who redeems her father, and through magical interventions that produce providential outcomes. The synthesis of romance and history in *All Is True* thus emphasizes a providential interpretation of English history. The resulting implication—that the antagonisms of earlier history are justified by the felicity of the present reign—risks chauvinistic sycophancy. Yet *All Is True* also challenges this celebratory interpretation: it is in the tension between these two tendencies that the play's interest lies.

The historical narrative, which combines close reliance on the sources with chronological compression and rearrangement, spans more than fifteen years. Its principal structural unit, first alluded to in the Prologue (lines 25–30), is *de casibus* tragedy, which recounts the fall of illustrious figures and resembles the morality play's abstractly allegorical focus on virtue and vice. The wheel of fortune is the form's dominant, cyclical image: what goes up must come down. Providential romance, however, is more linear and unidirectional: you start in one place and end somewhere else. Moreover, it ends in felicity rather than disaster. *All Is True* reconciles these apparently incompatible movements through an elegant structural trick: it makes a series of local *de casibus* tragedies serve a single overarching providential purpose that does not emerge until the very end. Much of the play accordingly seems to have nothing to do with a transcendently ordered pattern. It does not even concern the ups and downs of monarchs and their rivals, as in Shakespeare's earlier histories. Instead, we witness the successive falls of people close to Henry VIII—Buckingham, Katherine, and Cardinal Wolsey—and the near fall of Cranmer, Archbishop of Canterbury. Each gets a day in court—his or her fifteen minutes of fame—before passing from the scene. These downfalls, like other events in the play, are rendered through stirring speeches and pageantry that recall the spectacle of the contemporary court theatrical form known as the "masque" (see 1.4), which for centuries made the work a success on the stage and which left their mark on film versions of Henry's reign, even those not based on *All Is True* (see the list of films).

Initially, the repetitive *de casibus* structure doesn't seem to be heading anywhere. Yet the linguistic patterning suggests a larger purpose. Beginning with the Prologue's invocation of tears and pity (lines 5–6), the play emphasizes suffering, the burden of life, acquiescence in defeat, forgiveness of one's foes, patience, religious serenity, and an understanding of the fall from power as part of a natural pattern like life itself. Cardinal Wolsey's undoing offers a striking instance of the transformation of conflict into reconciliation. Surrey correctly blames Wolsey for the execution of Buckingham, Surrey's father-in-law. Taunting the Cardinal at the moment of his ruin, he is finally rebuked:

> LORD CHAMBERLAIN   O, my lord,
> Press not a falling man too far. 'Tis virtue.
> His faults lie open to the laws. Let them,
> Not you, correct him. My heart weeps to see him
> So little of his great self.
> SURREY   I forgive him.
>   (3.2.333–37)

Once the lords have left, Wolsey, in a deviation from Holinshed, gets a moving repentance. Discovering his religious vocation only following the collapse of his secular

Now, to let matters of State sleep, I will entertain you at the present with what hath happened this week at the banks side. The Kings Players had a new Play, called *All is true*, representing some principall pieces of the raign of *Henry* 8. which was set forth with many extraordinary circumstances of Pomp and Majesty, even to the matting of the stage; the Knights of the Order, with their Georges and Garter, the Guards with their embroidered Coats, and the like: sufficient in truth within a while to make greatness very familiar, if not ridiculous. Now, King *Henry* making a Masque at the Cardinal *Wolsey's* house, and certain Chambers being shot off at his entry, some of the paper, or other stuff wherewith one of them was stopped, did light on the thatch, where being thought at first but an idle smoak, and their eyes more attentive to the show, it kindled inwardly, and ran round like a train, consuming within less then an hour the whole house to the very grounds.

This was the fatal period of that vertuous fabrique, wherein yet nothing did perish, but wood and straw, and a few forsaken cloaks; only one man had his breeches set on fire, that would perhaps have broyled him, if he had not by the benefit of a provident wit put it out with bottle Ale. The rest when we meet: till when, I protest every minute is the siege of Troy. Gods dear blessings till then and ever be with you.

Your poor Uncle and
faithful servant,

HENRY WOTTON.

One of several accounts of the burning of the Globe Theatre. From a letter of July 2, 1613, in *Letters of Sir Henry Wotton to Sir Edmund Bacon* (1661).

career, the hitherto villainous Cardinal experiences a shift in outlook that aligns him with his victims, Buckingham and Katherine. Asked how he feels, Wolsey replies:

> Why, well—
> Never so truly happy, my good Cromwell.
> I know myself now, and I feel within me
> A peace above all earthly dignities,
> A still and quiet conscience.
>
> (3.2.377–81)

Thus, like Buckingham's and Katherine's precipitous descents, but also like Adam and Eve's, Wolsey's fall is a fortunate one.

The Cardinal considers his former responsibilities "a burden / Too heavy for a man that hopes for heaven" (3.2.385–86). But not too heavy for a woman: the burden is delivered at the end of the play when Queen Anne gives birth to the future Queen Elizabeth—the moment toward which all previous events have been tending. The critic Northrop Frye noted in the play "an invisible but omnipotent and ruthless providence who is ready to tear the whole social and religious structure of England to pieces in order to get Queen Elizabeth born." Buckingham has a serious claim to the crown, so he must be removed. Katherine's defect is that she is not the queen who will bear Elizabeth. Wolsey, who favors a diplomatically useful French alliance for Henry and hence opposes the king's marriage to Anne, unwittingly brings them together at a party he hosts (1.4). The individual tragedies are thus both personally and politically fortunate. Elizabeth's birth promises not only her own reign but also that of her successor, King James I, England's sovereign at the time of *All Is True*. Praise of these two monarchs is accompanied by compliments to James's daughter Elizabeth, who was married in February 1613. Archbishop Cranmer's concluding prophecy makes the link explicit:

> when
> The bird of wonder dies—the maiden phoenix—
> Her ashes new create another heir
> As great in admiration as herself.
>
> (5.4.39–42)

Although Queen Elizabeth is the "maiden phoenix" and James the heir, James's daughter was also compared to the phoenix at the time of her marriage.

This connection also lays to rest Henry's persistent desire for a male heir. That absent royal son earlier justifies Henry's divorce of Katherine:

> methought
> I stood not in the smile of heaven. . . .
> . . . .
> I weighed the danger which my realms stood in
> By this my issue's fail, and that gave to me
> Many a groaning throe.
>
> (2.4.183–96)

Henry assumes the burden himself, experiencing "many a groaning throe" as if he could deliver the son that Katherine cannot. When Anne takes on the burden, Henry reveals his ongoing anxiety:

> KING HENRY   Is the Queen delivered?
> Say, 'Ay, and of a boy.'
> OLD LADY   Ay, ay, my liege,
> And of a lovely boy. The God of heaven
> Both now and ever bless her! 'Tis a girl
> Promises boys hereafter.
>
> (5.1.163–67)

Cardinal Wolsey is forced "to render up the great seal" to Norfolk and Suffolk (3.2.230). From George Cavendish, *The Life and Death of Cardinal Wolsey* (1557).

The Old Lady's flattery reveals the truth: Elizabeth *is* "a girl / Promises boys hereafter." In having James succeed her, she fulfills the properly self-effacing function of women in this patriarchal fantasy and delivers to Henry what Anne could not—a male heir.

Providence also enters the play through the standard sea journeys of Shakespearean romance, journeys that typically bring separation, suffering, and a transformation whose association with water links it to baptism. Set entirely in England, *All Is True* seems remote from such concerns. Yet the aquatic and nautical imagery of destruction pervades the play. The "hideous storm" immediately following the conclusion of the Anglo-French treaty is a "tempest" that prophesies the dissolution of the alliance (1.1.90–92). Buckingham metaphorically warns against false friends, who,

> when they once perceive
> The least rub in your fortunes, fall away
> Like water from ye, never found again
> But where they mean to sink ye.
>
> (2.1.129–32)

Henry finds himself "hulling in / The wild sea of my conscience" over his marriage to Katherine (2.4.196–97), who worries about her "shipwrecked" ladies-in-waiting. Wolsey's foes are "rav'nous fishes" who ineffectually attack his "new trimmed" "vessel" (1.2.80–81). Wolsey himself is a "rock" that threatens Buckingham and will protect Henry "against the chiding flood" of danger and rebellion (1.1.113; 3.2.198). He is a boat that "coasts / And hedges" but will "founder" (3.2.38–39, 40). He has swum "far beyond my depth" and is at "the mercy / Of a rude stream that must for ever hide me" (3.2.362, 364–65). He has borne "a load would sink a navy" (3.2.384), but he tells Cromwell that he, who "sounded all the depths and shoals of honour, / Found thee a way, out of his wreck, to rise in" (3.2.437–38). Approaching death, Wolsey is "broken with the storms of state" (4.2.21).

Positive associations with water and the sea are often connected with colonialism, important in the London of 1613 because of western Europe's unprecedented global expansion beginning in the fifteenth century and, in particular, because of the very recent establishment of England's first permanent settlement in the New World. The English nobility in France were so opulently attired that they "made Britain India"

(1.1.21)—an image of fabulous wealth that evokes both the West and East Indies, both the Caribbean and the vast region extending from India to Southeast Asia. "Our King has all the Indies in his arms" (4.1.45) when he embraces Anne, "a very fresh fish" at court (2.3.87). At her public appearance, "such a noise arose / As the shrouds make at sea in a stiff tempest" (4.1.73–74). The perilous journeys and shipwrecks are redeemed by Elizabeth's watery baptism, which has the crowd appeal of "some strange Indian with the great tool" (5.3.32)—a phrase that unites ethnic exoticism and sexual titillation. Speaking of James, Cranmer predicts,

> Wherever the bright sun of heaven shall shine,
> His honour and the greatness of his name
> Shall be, and make new nations.
>
> (5.4.50–52)

The capital of the "new nation" is Jamestown and the nation itself Virginia, named for "the maiden phoenix" who died "yet a virgin" (5.4.40, 60)—James's predecessor, the infant Elizabeth.

Although the providential logic that leads first Elizabeth and then James to the throne often works against human intentions, Henry takes an increasingly active role in securing the destined end. The crucial moment is Cranmer's trial. Just before it begins, the stage direction reads *"Enter* KING [HENRY] . . . *at a window, above"* (5.2.18). There, seeing but unseen, he is quasi-divine, as he himself suggests in angrily observing the council's humiliation of Cranmer: "Is this the honour they do one another? / 'Tis well there's one above 'em yet" (5.2.25–26). The "one above 'em" can be either God or the King, a distinction the scene blurs. This elevated perspective presumably pleased James, who held an absolutist, divine-right view of monarchy. Henry's intervention later in the scene to protect Cranmer preserves the man who later established the doctrinal basis of the English Reformation. As suggested by Cranmer's prophetic promise about Elizabeth's reign—"God shall be truly known" (5.4.36)—this religious outcome is also part of the providential pattern. Yet except in Cranmer's conflict with the Catholic Gardiner, who accuses him of being "a sectary" and Cromwell of being "a favourer / Of this new sect" (5.2.104, 114–15), and in Wolsey's dismissive description of Anne as "a spleeny Lutheran" (3.2.100), little is made of the central event of Henry's reign: the break with Rome. The characters are judged not by their religious sympathies but by their integrity. Accordingly, the outstanding figures are an English Protestant, Cranmer, and a Spanish Catholic, Katherine. The notion of conscience, which is far more prominent here than in Hollinshed's *Chronicles* and which Protestants used against the papacy to repudiate blind adherence to any human doctrinal authority, is deployed by the playwrights to judge Catholics and Protestants alike. This impartiality may be more the work of Shakespeare than of Fletcher (see the Textual Note); in any case, the overall result is the characteristic national reconciliation of Shakespeare's history plays.

National reconciliation also transcends class antagonism, an issue largely absent from the sources. Like the other lords, the Duke of Buckingham resents the usurpation of the nobility's traditional power by the proud "beggar" Wolsey, a "butcher's cur" (1.1.122, 120): the Cardinal's father was supposedly a butcher. Despite these humble origins, Wolsey adopts the aristocratic outlook of the position he has risen to. He opposes Henry's marriage to Anne, who came from the gentry rather than the nobility and who had been one of Katherine's ladies-in-waiting: "A knight's daughter / To be her mistress' mistress? The Queen's queen?" (3.2.95–96). But the play also posits a harmony between upper class and lower that can be disturbed only by self-serving intermediaries who mistreat humble folk. Buckingham is betrayed to Wolsey by his surveyor, whom he fired for oppressing his tenants. Katherine gets Henry to repeal a tax levied by Wolsey that is so onerous it drives the poor to rebellion. Interclass unity is affirmed in the popular excitement about the baby Elizabeth, which the play refracts through the lower-class prose of the exasperated Porter (5.3)—a prose noteworthy in a play composed overwhelmingly in blank verse. Similarly, at Anne's earlier coronation, one of the gentlemen, who play the role of a chorus absent from the sources, remarks,

> The citizens,
> I am sure, have shown at full their royal minds—
> As, let 'em have their rights, they are ever forward.
> (4.1.7–9)

And, in slightly different fashion, Cranmer renders hereditary class hierarchy a thing of the past. "Those about" Elizabeth "from her shall read the perfect ways of honour, / And by those claim their greatness, not by blood" (5.4.36–38).

Yet as recent productions have emphasized, *All Is True* offers a critical account of Henry's reign. In particular, the play implicitly suggests the costs of the Elizabethan Protestant succession. Even though only Buckingham is executed, *All Is True* makes that execution resonate. The innocent and virtuous Katherine is given a strength of character, consequent impressiveness, and spiritual coronation absent both from Holinshed's portrayal and from her successor, Anne. Yet Henry's "princely commendations" to the dying Katherine are "like a pardon after execution" (4.2.119, 122). As Katherine is succeeded by Anne, so Wolsey is replaced by Sir Thomas More, Cromwell, and Cranmer (3.2.392–460). All four of these successors were later executed, as the audience well knew. Wolsey hopes that More will "do justice / For truth's sake and his conscience" (lines 397–98)—principles that were to cost the Catholic More his life. Anne actually predicts her own fate in lamenting Katherine's mistreatment:

> Much better
> She ne'er had known pomp; though't be temporal,
> Yet if that quarrel, fortune, do divorce
> It from the bearer, 'tis a sufferance panging
> As soul and bodies severing.
> (2.3.12–16)

Wolsey advises Cromwell:

> Be just, and fear not.
> Let all the ends thou aim'st at be thy country's,
> Thy God's, and truth's. Then if thou fall'st, O Cromwell,
> Thou fall'st a blessèd martyr.
> (3.2.447–50)

Gardiner's anti-Protestant attacks on Cranmer and Cromwell foreshadow his later success in sending both men to their death. Even Elizabeth's christening evokes execution: "Belong to th' gallows, and be hanged" (5.3.5).

Ambivalence extends as well to the centrally providential characters. No man utters anything but praise for the "beauty and honour" of that "angel" Anne Boleyn (2.3.76, 4.1.44). Skepticism about her "honour" is instead voiced by a woman. When Anne denies any desire for political advancement, the Old Lady calls this position "hypocrisy," ridicules Anne's pliant "conscience," and finds her claim "strange" (2.3.26, 32, 36). Yet Anne does become queen, without an explanation of her supposed change of heart but with a suggestive pun on "quean" (whore) characteristic of the entire sexualized exchange and of Anne's earlier banter (1.4.46–49). The scene with the Old Lady, apparently invented by Shakespeare, thus sullies Anne before she becomes a purely ceremonial figure reduced to bearing royal children. Moreover, Elizabeth's conception before Henry and Anne's marriage may be alluded to in the "great-bellied women" at Anne's coronation and the "fry of fornication" at Elizabeth's christening (4.1.78, 5.3.33–34).

As for Henry himself, although he is repeatedly praised by his victims (2.1.87–95, 3.2.381–93, 4.2.161–65), his increasing attention to government raises retrospective questions about his earlier behavior. The Henry of the play, more troubling than Holinshed's, seems oddly abstracted, either culpably unaware or disingenuously disavowing knowledge of foreign affairs, taxation, and treason. He often seems the Teflon king, to whom no blame sticks. The self-destructive zigzags in foreign policy—alliance with

Henry VIII, age fifty-two, in the posthumous portrait engraved by Cornelis Metsys in 1548. Gardiner's unsuccessful attack on Cranmer probably occurred around this time.

France, alliance with Spain, attempted alliance with France—are Wolsey's doings, not his: the buck stops elsewhere. Moreover, his interventions are not fully reassuring. His charges against Wolsey ignore major issues to focus on personal, peripheral concerns. Even his protection of Cranmer is necessary only because Henry allows his biased council to proceed in the first place. Indeed, the play suggests that the law serves the man with power, whether Wolsey or the King.

Explicit skepticism about Henry is produced by his divorce proceedings. *All Is True* shows a man "afflicted" by a "wounded conscience," by "conscience, conscience," by "my conscience" (2.2.62, 74, 142; 2.4.167, 179, 200). But earlier, at Wolsey's banquet, it shows a man attracted to Anne Boleyn: "The fairest hand I ever touched. O beauty, / Till now I never knew thee" (1.4.76–77). This meeting is the play's invention. A disabused view is openly voiced later:

> LORD CHAMBERLAIN   It seems the marriage with his brother's wife
>   Has crept too near his conscience.
>   SUFFOLK   No, his conscience
>   Has crept too near another lady.
>
>   (2.2.15–17)

Even apologists for Henry's behavior suspect his motives. Overwhelmed by the sight of Anne, the Second Gentleman remarks, "I cannot blame his conscience" (4.1.47). It is hard to determine whether such criticism undermines the providential pattern or renders the pattern's transcendence of such formidable obstacles all the more miraculous. Like many Shakespearean plays, *All Is True* opposes means and ends, showing and telling, dramatized plot and asserted conclusion, pity and jubilation.

The critique of Henry may have been targeted at James as well, despite the play's closing compliment to him. The satire on French fashion (1.3) ridicules behavior at James's court in which the King participated. Like Henry, James neglected affairs of state, to the dismay of his subjects. His court was riven by factionalism; his absolutist view of monarchy at times resulted in a subordination of law to royal desire. Yet the crucial contemporary parallels lie elsewhere. In urging punishment of Cranmer's Protestantism, Gardiner warns that laxity leads to falling dominoes:

> Commotions, uproars—with a general taint
> Of the whole state, as of late days our neighbours,
> The upper Germany, can dearly witness.
>
>   (5.2.62–64)

The reference is to the Peasants' War in Germany (1524–26), in which the German aristocracy massacred perhaps 100,000 peasants. The danger of popular unrest in England is suggested by the court's fear of "loud rebellion" and the unruly "rabble" (1.2.30,

5.3.65). Similarly, the rowdies at Elizabeth's christening are "your faithful friends o'th' suburbs" (5.3.66). The suburbs were the location of the outdoor "public" theaters, such as the Globe, where *All Is True* was performed. The Porter remarks, "These are the youths that thunder at a playhouse, and fight for bitten apples, that no audience but the tribulation of Tower Hill or the limbs of Limehouse, their dear brothers, are able to endure" (5.3.55–58). The comparison is between the unruly apprentices who come to the theater and the rough crowds who attend public executions or frequent the dockyards. A christening recalls an execution; an ostensibly orthodox play in a suburban theater emphasizes the criminal character of suburb and audience alike.

It is thus the interaction between *All Is True* and its audience that undermines orthodoxy. This interaction is self-reflexive, or metadramatic, in character. That is, while providing a plausibly realistic dramatization of events, the play simultaneously indicates that it is merely a play, just a dramatization, by calling attention to the venue of performance—the "suburbs," the "playhouse," the "audience." As we have seen, however, this self-referentiality is the very opposite of apolitical aesthetic detachment. Furthermore, the Globe, which is surely the playhouse referred to in this scene, is not the only commercial theater that acquires thematic resonance in *All Is True*. By the time of the composition of the play, Shakespeare's acting company, the King's Men, divided its time—in the summer working at the Globe, in the winter at the Blackfriars, a more elite indoor, "private" theater in London itself rather than the suburbs. When Henry decides upon a judicial proceeding to determine whether or not his marriage to Katherine should be annulled, he also specifies a location for the event:

> The most convenient place I can think of
> For such receipt of learning is Blackfriars.
> (2.2.137–38)

Two scenes later, that is where the hearing is held, with the result that the audience of the play sits in judgment in the very place where the decision was actually rendered almost a century earlier, in 1529.

By placing the affluent audience of the Blackfriars in a position where it evaluates the conduct of a king, did *All Is True* undermine aristocratic and royal authority? Perhaps not as much as when the play was performed in the outdoor theater. According to Sir Henry Wotton, a spectator at the fateful performance when the Globe burned down, the work represented "some principall pieces of the raign of *Henry* 8 which was set forth with many extraordinary circumstances of Pomp and Majesty . . . sufficient in truth within a while to make greatness very familiar, if not ridiculous." Rather than dazzling into awestruck submission, the play's pageantry reduced the mystique of monarchy, turning the politically disenfranchised popular audience into moral arbiters of royal power. James's favorite, the Duke of Buckingham, may have felt as much when, in 1628, he commissioned a performance of *All Is True*, only to walk out after his namesake's beheading. In 1649, a Parliament driven by popular pressure emulated the play by staging an execution of its own. This time, however, the victim was James I's own son: the man on the scaffold was the King.

WALTER COHEN

TEXTUAL NOTE

Although the play was initially printed in the First Folio of 1623 (F) under the title *The Famous History of the Life of Henry the Eight* and today is generally known as *Henry VIII*, comments on early performances suggest that it was originally called *All Is True*. Perhaps the compilers of the Folio changed its title to make it conform to the pattern of using monarchs' names for the English history plays: it is placed at the end of this group of plays. Or perhaps John Fletcher, Shakespeare's collaborator on the play, is responsible for the switch (see below). The text is based not on an authorial manuscript but on a scribal copy; either the authorial or the scribal version may have been slightly revised for theatrical performance. F's division into acts and scenes is followed in the present edition; some editors, however, introduce a scene division after 5.2.34.

All Is True probably has links to the marriage on February 14, 1613, of Princess Elizabeth, King James's daughter, to the German Prince Frederick, the Elector Palatine. If so, it might have been written in late 1612. Unlike other plays by Shakespeare, it was not performed at court as part of the wedding festivities, but the text's reference to Blackfriars suggests that it could have been staged during the same period at that theater. But the accidental burning of the Globe Theatre at one of the first performances of the play on June 29, 1613, makes composition following the marriage, with the initial performance at the Globe in June 1613, equally likely. (See the Introduction.)

F attributes the play to Shakespeare. But beginning in the eighteenth century and especially since 1850, many critics have concluded that John Fletcher, who succeeded Shakespeare as the principal dramatist of the King's Men, collaborated on *All Is True*. External evidence for this position is inferential and inconclusive. Toward the end of his career, as perhaps at the beginning, Shakespeare seems to have turned to collaboration— in *Pericles*, the lost *Cardenio*, and *The Two Noble Kinsmen*. In the last two plays, dating from 1612–14, he apparently worked with Fletcher. On the other hand, these plays were all excluded from F by the editors, who were Shakespeare's fellow actors in the King's Men. Even though a minority of scholars continues to believe that Shakespeare was the sole author of *All Is True*, the internal stylistic and linguistic evidence strongly suggests that Fletcher wrote at least one-quarter of the piece—primarily 1.3–4, 3.1, and 5.2–4. (He seems to have written a little more than half of *The Two Noble Kinsmen*.) Yet the problem of attribution is not that simple. Shakespeare may have had some role in 3.1 and especially 5.2–4. Fletcher is likely to have played a part in 2.1–2 and 4.1–2. The unusually full stage directions may also be his work. Fletcher's sections of the play arguably have a more pro-Protestant outlook than Shakespeare's relatively balanced and uncommitted treatment of religious controversy. Finally, scholarly skepticism about the attribution of certain scenes (notably 2.1 and 4.1) to either Shakespeare or Fletcher has led to speculation about a third author. Francis Beaumont, who regularly collaborated with Fletcher, has been proposed, but the suggestion remains conjectural.

In short, both the broad conception of the play and most of the "big" scenes appear to be Shakespeare's.

SELECTED BIBLIOGRAPHY

Bergeron, David M. *Shakespeare's Romances and the Royal Family.* Lawrence: University Press of Kansas, 1985. 203–22. Links the play politically to James I and his family, and generically more to the late romances than to the earlier English history plays.

Frye, Susan. "Queens and the Structure of History in *Henry VIII.*" *A Companion to Shakespeare's Works*, Vol. 4: *Poems, Problem Comedies, Late Plays.* Ed. Richard Dutton and Jean E. Howard. Malden, Mass.: Blackwell, 2003. 427–44. Parallels between the courts of Henry VIII and James I, centered on Queens struggling with a succession of male favorites.

Healy, Thomas. "History and Judgement in *Henry VIII.*" *Shakespeare's Late Plays: New Readings.* Ed. Jennifer Richards and James Knowles. Edinburgh: Edinburgh University Press, 1999. 158–75. Argues that the play is structured to encourage the audience to respond with judgment rather than emotion to the conflicting possible interpretations of history.

Hodgdon, Barbara. *The End Crowns All: Closure and Contradiction in Shakespeare's History.* Princeton: Princeton University Press, 1991. 212–34. Focuses on Elizabeth as the concluding figure of the play, uniting masquelike and anti-masquelike (or carnivalesque) elements.

Kermode, Frank. "What Is Shakespeare's *Henry VIII* About?" *Shakespeare, The Histo-ries: A Collection of Critical Essays.* Ed. Eugene M. Waith. Englewood Cliffs, N.J.: Prentice-Hall, 1965. 168–79. Henry as God's deputy and the agent of England's future felicity, by means of a morality structure involving the successive falls of the other leading figures.

Knight, G. Wilson. *The Crown of Life: Essays in Interpretation of Shakespeare's Final Plays.* London: Oxford University Press, 1947. 256–336. Sees the play as Shake-speare's culminating work, moving from order through tragic falls to concluding ritual.

McMullan, Gordon, ed. *King Henry VIII (All Is True).* London: Arden Shakespeare, 2000. Outstanding scholarly edition with a book-length critical introduction.

Noling, Kim H. "Grubbing Up the Stock: Dramatizing Queens in *Henry VIII*." *Shake-speare Quarterly* 39 (1988): 291–306. Katherine's strong stage positions contrasted with Anne's relatively weak role, including dissociation from her daughter, Elizabeth—all in the service of flattering male monarchs, Henry and James.

Shirley, Frances A., ed. *"King John" and "Henry VIII": Critical Essays.* New York: Gar-land, 1988. Twelve essays on the play from nineteenth- and twentieth-century the-atrical and literary criticism.

Wegemer, Gerard. "Henry VIII on Trial: Confronting Malice and Conscience in Shake-speare's *All Is True*." *Renascence* 52 (2000): 111–30. Argues that, in addition to the public trials structuring the play, covert trials of Thomas More and of Henry him-self produce a critical view of the monarch.

FILMS

The Private Life of Henry VIII. 1933. Dir. Alexander Korda. UK. 97 min. Unrelated to *All Is True.* Starring Charles Laughton.

A Man for All Seasons. 1966. Dir. Fred Zinnemann. UK. 120 min. Unrelated to *All Is True.* Based on Robert Bolt's play about Sir Thomas More's religious conflict over Henry's decision to divorce Katherine and wed Anne. Stellar cast, including Paul Scofield in the title role; Oscars for Best Actor, Director, Picture.

Anne of the Thousand Days. 1969. Dir. Charles Jarrott. UK. 145 min. Unrelated to *All Is True.* On Anne Boleyn's rise and fall. Distinguished cast, including Geneviève Bujold as Anne and Richard Burton as Henry.

Henry VIII. 1979. Dir. Kevin Billington. UK. 166 min. Highly praised BBC production minimizing the pomp and ceremony in plays or films on Henry and his age, in favor of a contrast between public political life and inwardness and morality, focused on Katherine, played by Claire Bloom.

All Is True

THE PERSONS OF THE PLAY

PROLOGUE
KING HENRY the Eighth
Duke of BUCKINGHAM
Lord ABERGAVENNY ⎫ his sons-in-law
Earl of SURREY ⎭
Duke of NORFOLK
Duke of SUFFOLK
LORD CHAMBERLAIN
LORD CHANCELLOR
Lord SANDS (also called Sir William SANDS)
Sir Thomas LOVELL
Sir Anthony DENNY
Sir Henry GUILDFORD
CARDINAL WOLSEY
Two SECRETARIES
BUCKINGHAM'S SURVEYOR
CARDINAL CAMPEIUS
GARDINER, the King's new secretary, later Bishop of Winchester
His PAGE
Thomas CROMWELL
CRANMER, Archbishop of Canterbury
QUEEN KATHERINE, later KATHERINE, Princess Dowager
GRIFFITH, her gentleman usher
PATIENCE, her waiting-woman
Other WOMEN
Six spirits, who dance before Katherine in a vision
A MESSENGER
Lord CAPUTIUS
ANNE Boleyn
An OLD LADY
BRANDON ⎫
SERJEANT-at-arms ⎬ who arrest Buckingham and Abergavenny
Sir Nicholas VAUX ⎫
Tipstaves ⎪
Halberdiers ⎬ after Buckingham's arraignment
Common people ⎭
Two vergers ⎫
Two SCRIBES ⎪
Archbishop of Canterbury ⎪
Bishop of LINCOLN ⎪
Bishop of Ely ⎪
Bishop of Rochester ⎬ appearing at the Legatine Court
Bishop of Saint Asaph ⎪
Two priests ⎪
Serjeant-at-arms ⎪
Two noblemen ⎪
A CRIER ⎭

Three GENTLEMEN
Two judges
Choristers
Lord Mayor of London
Garter King-of-Arms
Marquis Dorset
Four Barons of the Cinque Ports
Stokesley, Bishop of London
Old Duchess of Norfolk
Countesses
} appearing in the Coronation

A DOORKEEPER
Doctor BUTTS, the King's physician
Pursuivants, pages, footboys, grooms
} At Cranmer's trial

A PORTER
His MAN
Two aldermen
Lord Mayor of London
GARTER King-of-Arms
Six noblemen
Old Duchess of Norfolk, godmother
The child, Princess Elizabeth
Marchioness Dorset, godmother
} at the Christening

EPILOGUE
Ladies, gentlemen, a SERVANT, guards, attendants, trumpeters

Prologue

[*Enter* PROLOGUE]

PROLOGUE   I come no more to make you laugh. Things now
    That bear a weighty and a serious brow,
    Sad, high, and working,° full of state° and woe—   *full of pathos / grandeur*
    Such noble scenes as draw the eye to flow
5   We now present. Those that can pity here
    May, if they think it well, let fall a tear.
    The subject will deserve it. Such as give
    Their money out of hope they may believe,
    May here find truth, too. Those that come to see
10   Only a show or two, and so agree
    The play may pass, if they be still, and willing,
    I'll undertake may see away their shilling
    Richly in two short hours.[1] Only they
    That come to hear a merry bawdy play,
15   A noise of targets,° or to see a fellow   *shields*
    In a long motley coat guarded[2] with yellow,
    Will be deceived. For, gentle hearers, know
    To rank our chosen truth with such a show
    As fool and fight is, beside forfeiting
20   Our own brains, and the opinion that we bring
    To make that only true we now intend,[3]

Prologue
1. *Those . . . hours:* If those who come only for a spectacle ("show") and approve the play on those terms are quiet and willing, I promise they'll get their shilling's worth (the price of more expensive, genteel seating) in two hours (plays ran two to three hours).
2. Ornamented on its border. The fool's "motley," or

patchwork, coat may refer to other plays about Henry's life, including Samuel Rowley's *When You See Me, You Know Me* (1605), which featured Henry's fool, Will Summers, and was reprinted and perhaps revived in 1613.
3. *beside . . . intend:* in addition to wasting our mental labor, and our intention of presenting an entirely truthful representation.

Will leave us never an understanding⁴ friend.
Therefore, for goodness' sake, and as you are known
The first and happiest hearers° of the town,   *finest audience*
25 Be sad° as we would make ye. Think ye see   *grave*
The very persons of our noble story
As they were living; think you see them great,°   *of high rank*
And followed with the general throng and sweat
Of thousand friends; then, in a moment, see
30 How soon this mightiness meets misery.
And if you can be merry then, I'll say
A man may weep upon his wedding day.   [*Exit*]

1.1

[*A cloth of state throughout the play.*]¹ *Enter the Duke
of* NORFOLK *at one door; at the other* [*door enter*] *the
Duke of* BUCKINGHAM *and the Lord* ABERGAVENNY

BUCKINGHAM [*to* NORFOLK]   Good morrow, and well met. How have ye done
Since last we saw° in France?   *met*
NORFOLK   I thank your grace,
Healthful, and ever since a fresh° admirer   *an eager*
Of what I saw there.²
BUCKINGHAM   An untimely ague
5 Stayed me a prisoner in my chamber³ when
Those suns of glory, those two lights of men,
Met in the vale of Ardres.
NORFOLK   'Twixt Guisnes and Ardres.⁴
I was then present, saw them salute on horseback,
Beheld them when they lighted,° how they clung   *got off*
10 In their embracement as° they grew together,   *as if*
Which had they,° what four throned ones could have weighed⁵   *if they had*
Such a compounded one?
BUCKINGHAM   All the whole time
I was my chamber's prisoner.
NORFOLK   Then you lost
The view of earthly glory. Men might say
15 Till this time pomp was single, but now married
To one above itself.⁶ Each following day
Became the next day's master, till the last
Made former wonders its.⁷ Today the French,
All clinquant° all in gold, like heathen gods   *glittering*
20 Shone down the English; and tomorrow they
Made Britain India.⁸ Every man that stood
Showed like a mine. Their dwarfish pages were

---

4. Punning reference to the lower-class groundlings, who are literally "understanding" in the sense of "standing under" the raised stage.
1.1. Location: The court at London.
1. A seat under a canopy for the King or Cardinal Wolsey, perhaps onstage throughout the play. The original Globe performances also had "matting" (a woven straw floor-covering) on the stage.
2. The reference is to the rendezvous of Henry VIII and Francis I of France near Calais in June 1520, at the Field of the Cloth of Gold, named for the sumptuous displays by the two Kings.
3. Actually, Buckingham was present, if reluctantly (because of the expense), at the Field of the Cloth of

Gold. The fictional "ague," or fever, allows the dramatist to show Buckingham responding to Norfolk's detailed description.
4. Guisnes belonged to England, Ardres to France.
5. Been as heavy as.
6. *Till . . . itself:* The pomp of each King now joins ("marries") that of the other, making a greater pomp than either alone could display.
7. *Each . . . its:* Each day learned wonders from the previous one, making the last day the most wonderful of all. *master:* standard.
8. *they . . . India:* the English made Britain look as (fabulously) rich as India or the West Indies.

As cherubim, all gilt;[9] the *mesdames*,° too,   *ladies*
Not used to toil, did almost sweat to bear
25 The pride° upon them, that° their very labour   *fancy adornment / so that*
Was to them as a painting.[1] Now this masque
Was cried° incomparable, and th'ensuing night   *said to be*
Made it a fool and beggar. The two kings
Equal in lustre, were now best, now worst,
30 As presence did present them.[2] Him in eye
Still him in praise,[3] and being present both,
'Twas said they saw but one, and no discerner
Durst wag his tongue in censure.[4] When these suns—
For so they phrase 'em—by their heralds challenged
35 The noble spirits to arms, they did perform
Beyond thought's compass, that former fabulous story
Being now seen possible enough, got credit
That *Bevis* was believed.[5]
BUCKINGHAM   O, you go far!
NORFOLK   As I belong to worship,° and affect   *the aristocracy*
40 In honour honesty,[6] the tract of ev'rything
Would by a good discourser lose some life
Which action's self was tongue to.[7] All was royal.
To the disposing° of it naught rebelled.   *arrangement*
Order gave each thing view. The office did
45 Distinctly his full function.[8]
BUCKINGHAM   Who did guide—
I mean, who set the body and the limbs
Of this great sport° together, as you guess?   *show*
NORFOLK   One, certes, that promises no element[9]
In such a business.
BUCKINGHAM   I pray you who, my lord?
50 NORFOLK   All this was ordered by the good discretion
Of the right reverend Cardinal of York.°   *(Wolsey)*
BUCKINGHAM   The devil speed° him! No man's pie is freed   *ruin*
From his ambitious finger. What had he
To do in these fierce° vanities? I wonder   *excessive*
55 That such a keech[1] can, with his very bulk,
Take up the rays o'th' beneficial sun,°   *(Henry)*
And keep it from the earth.
NORFOLK   Surely, sir,
There's in him stuff that puts° him to these ends.   *spurs*
For being not propped by ancestry, whose grace
60 Chalks successors their way,[2] nor called upon
For high feats done to th' crown, neither allied
To eminent assistants,° but spider-like,   *ministers of state*
Out of his self-drawing° web, a° gives us note   *spun from himself / he*

9. Gold-plated statues of cherubim, often found in churches.
1. Made them rosy, as if with makeup.
2. According to who was present.
3. *Him . . . praise*: To the King on display at the time went all the acclaim.
4. *no . . . censure*: no one watching dared say one outshone the other.
5. *they did . . . believed*: their performance was such that stories formerly deemed mere fables, now looking possible, gained plausibility. Even *Sir Bevis of Hampton* (Southampton), a popular medieval romance, was

believed.
6. *and . . . honesty*: and honorably love truth.
7. *the tract . . . to*: the events surpass their telling.
8. *Order . . . Distinctly*: Careful organization made everything appropriately visible. Each responsible person properly fulfilled his role.
9. One, without doubt, who seems out of place.
1. Hunk of fat from a slaughtered animal. Wolsey was said to be a butcher's son.
2. *ancestry . . . way*: noble ancestors, whose honorable qualities mark the way for future generations.

The force of his own merit makes his way—
65 A gift that heaven gives for him which buys
A place next to the King.

ABERGAVENNY   I cannot tell
What heaven hath given him—let some graver eye
Pierce into that; but I can see his pride
Peep through each part of him. Whence has he that?°   (such pride)
70 If not from hell, the devil is a niggard°   selfish
Or has given all before,° and he° begins   already / (Wolsey)
A new hell in himself.

BUCKINGHAM   Why the devil,
Upon this French going out,° took he upon him   journey
Without the privity° o'th' King t'appoint   private sanction
75 Who should attend on him? He makes up the file°   roll
Of all the gentry, for the most part such
To whom as great a charge as little honour
He meant to lay upon;³ and his own letter,
The honourable board of council out,
Must fetch him in, he papers.⁴

80 ABERGAVENNY   I do know
Kinsmen of mine—three at the least—that have
By this so sickened° their estates that never   wasted
They shall abound as formerly.

BUCKINGHAM   O, many
Have broke their backs with laying manors on 'em⁵
85 For this great journey. What did this vanity
But minister communication of
A most poor issue?⁶

NORFOLK   Grievingly I think
The peace between the French and us not values°   does not merit
The cost that did conclude it.

BUCKINGHAM   Every man,
90 After the hideous storm that followed, was
A thing inspired, and, not consulting,° broke   without conferring
Into a general° prophecy—that this tempest,   collective
Dashing the garment of this peace, aboded°   prophesied
The sudden breach on't.°   of it

NORFOLK   Which is budded out°—   has occurred
95 For France hath flawed° the league, and hath attached°   betrayed / seized
Our merchants' goods at Bordeaux.

ABERGAVENNY   Is it therefore°   on this account
Th'ambassador is silenced?

NORFOLK   Marry is't.°   Of course it is

ABERGAVENNY   A proper title of a° peace, and purchased   A fine thing to call
At a superfluous rate.°   too high a cost

BUCKINGHAM   Why, all this business
Our reverend Cardinal carried.°   oversaw

100 NORFOLK   Like it° your grace,   May it please
The state takes notice of the private difference

---

3. *To whom . . . upon:* (Wolsey gave) places of little
honor to the noblemen on whom he laid the greatest
expense for the display.
4. *and . . . papers:* and with the council ignored ("out"),
his own summons ("letter") forces every person he lists
("papers") to comply.
5. *many . . . 'em:* many have sold off their estates—and

thus bankrupted themselves—to pay for a costly
wardrobe; with a pun on "manners."
6. *What . . . issue:* What did such wasteful expense do
but bankrupt their own children ("poor issue"); or
encourage talk for a trivial outcome ("poor issue")?

Betwixt you and the Cardinal. I advise you—
And take it from a heart that wishes towards you
Honour and plenteous safety—that you read°   assess
105 The Cardinal's malice and his potency
Together; to consider further that
What his high hatred would effect wants° not   lacks
A minister° in his power. You know his nature,   An agent
That he's revengeful; and I know his sword
110 Hath a sharp edge—it's long, and't may be said
It reaches far; and where 'twill not extend
Thither he darts it. Bosom up° my counsel,   Keep secret; take to heart
You'll find it wholesome. Lo, where comes that rock
That I advise your shunning.
                    Enter CARDINAL WOLSEY, *the purse*[7] *[containing the*
                    great seal] borne before him. [Enter with him] certain
                    of the guard, and two SECRETARIES *with papers. The*
                    CARDINAL *in his passage fixeth his eye on* BUCKINGHAM
                    and BUCKINGHAM *on him, both full of disdain*
CARDINAL WOLSEY [*To a* SECRETARY]   The Duke of Buckingham's
115   surveyor,° ha?   overseer of an estate
Where's his examination?°   testimony
SECRETARY   Here, so please you.
CARDINAL WOLSEY   Is he in person ready?
SECRETARY   Ay, please your grace.
CARDINAL WOLSEY   Well, we shall then know more, and Buckingham
Shall lessen this big° look.   pompous
                    Exeunt CARDINAL [WOLSEY] *and his train*
120 BUCKINGHAM   This butcher's cur is venom-mouthed, and I
Have not the power to muzzle him; therefore best
Not wake him in his slumber. A beggar's book°   learning
Outworths a noble's blood.°   inherited privilege
NORFOLK   What, are you chafed?°   annoyed
Ask God for temp'rance; that's th'appliance only°   the only medicine
Which your disease requires.
125 BUCKINGHAM   I read in's looks
Matter against me, and his eye reviled
Me as his abject° object. At this instant   discarded
He bores° me with some trick. He's gone to th' King—   pierces; defrauds
I'll follow, and outstare him.
NORFOLK   Stay, my lord,
130 And let your reason with your choler° question°   anger/dispute
What 'tis you go about. To climb steep hills
Requires slow pace at first. Anger is like
A full hot° horse who, being allowed his way,   feisty
Self-mettle° tires him. Not a man in England   His own disposition
135 Can advise me like you. Be to yourself
As you would to your friend.[8]
BUCKINGHAM   I'll to the King,
And from a mouth of honour[9] quite cry down
This Ipswich° fellow's insolence, or proclaim   (Wolsey's birthplace)
There's difference in no persons.°   Rank no longer matters

---

7. A special bag that held the "great seal," part of the   a friend to do.
Lord Chancellor's insignia of office.   9. An aristocratic, virtuous mouth.
8. *Be . . . friend:* Don't do anything you wouldn't advise

NORFOLK   Be advised.°   *Be careful*

140 Heat not a furnace for your foe so hot
That it do singe yourself. We may outrun
By violent swiftness that which we run at,°   *toward*
And lose by over-running. Know you not
The fire that mounts° the liquor till't run o'er   *swells (by boiling)*
145 In seeming to augment it wastes it? Be advised.
I say again there is no English soul
More stronger to direct you than yourself,
If with the sap of reason you would quench
Or but allay° the fire of passion.   *abate*
BUCKINGHAM   Sir,
150 I am thankful to you, and I'll go along
By your prescription; but this top-proud° fellow—   *proudest of all*
Whom from the flow of gall I name not, but
From sincere motions[1]—by intelligence,°   *covert information*
And proofs as clear as founts° in July when   *springs*
155 We see each grain of gravel, I do know
To be corrupt and treasonous.
NORFOLK   Say not 'treasonous'.
BUCKINGHAM   To th' King I'll say't, and make my vouch° as strong   *case*
As shore of rock. Attend: this holy fox,
Or wolf, or both—for he is equal° rav'nous   *as*
160 As he is subtle, and as prone to mischief
As able to perform't, his mind and place°   *high position*
Infecting one another, yea, reciprocally—
Only to show his pomp as well in France
As here at home, suggests° the King our master   *tempts*
165 To this last° costly treaty, th'interview°   *latest / the meeting*
That swallowed so much treasure and, like a glass,
Did break i'th' rinsing.
NORFOLK   Faith, and so it did.
BUCKINGHAM   Pray give me favour,° sir. This cunning Cardinal, *let me continue*
The articles o'th' combination° drew   *terms of the treaty*
170 As himself pleased, and they were ratified
As he cried 'Thus let be', to as much end°   *effect*
As give a crutch to th' dead. But our count-Cardinal[2]
Has done this, and 'tis well for worthy Wolsey,
Who cannot err, he did it. Now this follows—
175 Which, as I take it, is a kind of puppy
To th'old dam,° treason—Charles the Emperor,[3]   *bitch; mother*
Under pretence to see the Queen his aunt°—   *(Katherine)*
For 'twas indeed his colour,° but he came   *alibi*
To whisper° Wolsey—here makes visitation.   *meet covertly with*
180 His fears were that the interview betwixt
England and France might through their amity
Breed him some prejudice, for from this league
Peeped harms that menaced him. Privily° he   *Clandestinely*
Deals with our Cardinal and, as I trow°—   *believe*
185 Which I do well, for I am sure the Emperor
Paid ere he promised, whereby his suit was granted

---

1. *Whom . . . motions*: Whom I name not from a rancorous impulse but from pure motives.
2. Church leader assuming secular, aristocratic rank

(compare "King-Cardinal," 2.2.18).
3. Charles V, Holy Roman Emperor and King of Spain.

Ere it was asked—but when the way was made,
And paved with gold, the Emperor thus desired
That he° would please to alter the King's course   *(Wolsey)*
190   And break the foresaid peace. Let the King know,
As soon he shall by me, that thus the Cardinal
Does buy and sell his° honour as he° pleases,   *(Henry's) / (Wolsey)*
And for his own advantage.
NORFOLK   I am sorry
To hear this of him, and could wish he were
Something mistaken° in't.   *Partly misrepresented*
195   BUCKINGHAM   No, not a syllable.
I do pronounce him in that very shape
He shall appear in proof.°   *in practice*
          Enter BRANDON, *a* SERJEANT-*at-arms before him, and*
                  two or three of the guard
BRANDON   Your office, serjeant, execute it.
SERJEANT   Sir.
[*To* BUCKINGHAM] My lord the Duke of Buckingham and Earl
200   Of Hereford, Stafford, and Northampton, I
Arrest thee of high treason in the name
Of our most sovereign King.
BUCKINGHAM [*to* NORFOLK]   Lo° you, my lord,   *Look*
The net has fall'n upon me. I shall perish
Under device and practice.°   *trickery and schemes*
BRANDON   I am sorry
205   To see you ta'en from liberty to look on⁴
The business present. 'Tis his highness' pleasure
You shall to th' Tower.
BUCKINGHAM   It will help me nothing
To plead mine innocence, for that dye is on me
Which makes my whit'st part black. The will of heav'n
210   Be done in this and all things. I obey.
O, my lord Abergavenny, fare you well.
BRANDON   Nay, he must bear you company.
[*To* ABERGAVENNY]   The King
Is pleased you shall to th' Tower till you know
How he determines further.
ABERGAVENNY   As the Duke said,
215   The will of heaven be done and the King's pleasure
By me obeyed.
BRANDON   Here is a warrant from
The King t'attach° Lord Montague and the bodies   *to seize*
Of the duke's confessor, John de la Car,
One Gilbert Perk, his chancellor—
BUCKINGHAM   So, so;
220   These are the limbs o'th' plot. No more, I hope.
BRANDON   A monk o'th' Chartreux.°   *Carthusian*
BUCKINGHAM   O, Nicholas Hopkins?
BRANDON   He.
BUCKINGHAM   My surveyor is false. The o'er-great Cardinal
Hath showed him gold. My life is spanned° already.   *marked out*
225   I am the shadow of poor Buckingham,

---

4. *to look on:* and (sorry) to behold.

Whose figure even this instant cloud puts on
By dark'ning my clear sun.[5] [*To* NORFOLK] My lord, farewell.
Exeunt [NORFOLK at one door, BUCKINGHAM and
ABERGAVENNY under guard at another]

1.2

Cornetts. Enter KING HENRY leaning on Cardinal
[Wolsey]'s shoulder. [Enter with them Wolsey's two SEC-
RETARIES,] the nobles, and Sir Thomas LOVELL. [The
KING ascends to his seat under the cloth of state;] CAR-
DINAL [WOLSEY] places himself under the King's feet°   below the throne
on his right side

KING HENRY [*to* WOLSEY]   My life itself and the best heart° of it   *essential core*
Thanks you for this great care. I stood i'th' level°   *line of fire*
Of a full-charged confederacy,° and give thanks   *loaded conspiracy*
To you that choked it. Let be called before us
5   That gentleman of Buckingham's.° In person   *(the surveyor)*
I'll hear him his confessions justify,°   *verify*
And point by point the treasons of his master
He shall again relate.
CRIER (*within*)   Room for the Queen, ushered by the Duke of Norfolk.
Enter QUEEN [KATHERINE, the Duke of] NORFOLK, and
[the Duke of] SUFFOLK. She kneels. KING [HENRY]
riseth from his state,° takes her up, and kisses her   throne

10   QUEEN KATHERINE   Nay, we must longer kneel. I am a suitor.
KING HENRY   Arise, and take place by us.
[He] placeth [her] by him

                                                  Half your suit
Never name to us. You have half our power,
The other moiety° ere you ask is given.   *half*
Repeat your will° and take it.   *State your wish*
QUEEN KATHERINE   Thank your majesty.
15   That you would love yourself, and in that love
Not unconsidered leave your honour nor
The dignity of your office, is the point
Of my petition.
KING HENRY   Lady mine, proceed.
QUEEN KATHERINE   I am solicited,° not by a few,   *apprised*
20   And those of true condition,° that your subjects   *loyal character*
Are in great grievance. There have been commissions
Sent down among 'em[1] which hath flawed° the heart   *broken*
Of all their loyalties; wherein, although,
My good lord Cardinal, they vent reproaches
25   Most bitterly on you, as putter-on
Of these exactions,° yet the King our master—   *taxes*
Whose honour heaven shield from soil°—even he escapes not   *blemish*
Language unmannerly, yea, such which breaks
The sides[2] of loyalty, and almost appears
In loud rebellion.
30   NORFOLK   Not 'almost appears'—
It doth appear; for upon these taxations

---

5. A cloud having overshadowed my former glory and
come between me and my king ("sun" may refer to
either Buckingham or Henry).
1.2 Location: A council chamber at court.

1. *There . . . 'em:* They have received writs authorizing
the collection of taxes.
2. *which . . . sides:* which oversteps the limits.

The clothiers all, not able to maintain
The many to them 'longing,° have put off°   *they employ / let go*
The spinsters, carders, fullers,³ weavers, who,
35   Unfit for other life, compelled by hunger
And lack of other means, in desperate manner
Daring th'event to th' teeth,⁴ are all in uproar,
And danger serves among them.

KING HENRY   Taxation?
Wherein, and what taxation? My lord Cardinal,
40   You that are blamed for it alike with us,
Know you of this taxation?

CARDINAL WOLSEY   Please you, sir,
I know but of a single° part in aught°   *(his own) / anything*
Pertains to th' state, and front but in that file
Where others tell steps with me.⁵

QUEEN KATHERINE   No, my lord?
45   You know no more than others? But you frame
Things that are known alike, which are not wholesome
To those which would not know them, and yet must
Perforce be their acquaintance.⁶ These exactions
Whereof my sovereign would have note,° they are   *knowledge*
50   Most pestilent to th' hearing, and to bear 'em
The back is sacrifice to° th' load. They say   *broken by*
They are devised by you, or else you suffer
Too hard an exclamation.°   *a complaint*

KING HENRY   Still exaction!
The nature of it? In what kind, let's know,
Is this exaction?

55   QUEEN KATHERINE   I am much too venturous
In tempting your patience, but am boldened
Under your promised pardon. The subjects' grief °   *grievance*
Comes through commissions which compels from each
The sixth part of his substance° to be levied   *wealth*
60   Without delay, and the pretence for this
Is named your wars in France. This makes bold mouths.
Tongues spit their duties out, and cold hearts freeze
Allegiance in them. Their curses now
Live where their prayers did, and it's come to pass
65   This tractable obedience is a slave
To each incensèd will.⁷ I would your highness
Would give it quick consideration, for
There is no primer° business.   *more pressing*

KING HENRY   By my life,
This is against our pleasure.

CARDINAL WOLSEY   And for me,
70   I have no further gone in this than by
A single voice,⁸ and that not passed me but
By learnèd approbation° of the judges. If I am   *approval*
Traduced° by ignorant tongues, which neither know   *Slandered*

3. All involved in wool production: "spinsters" spun the wool; "carders" combed through, extracting impurities; and "fullers" beat the wool to thicken and cleanse it.
4. Refusing adamantly to comply with the result.
5. *front . . . me*: I walk at the front of a line only of those who have power equal to my own (literally, who march in step behind me). Wolsey is denying that he is responsible.

6. *But . . . acquaintance*: But you originate measures that all know, that harm even those who would rather not accept them yet must.
7. *This . . . will*: Each subject's formerly compliant obedience is dominated by his anger.
8. *I . . . voice*: I have only cast my single vote; I have concurred with a unanimous vote.

My faculties° nor person yet will be   *abilities*
75 The chronicles of my doing, let me say
'Tis but the fate of place,° and the rough brake°   *rank / thicket*
That virtue must go through. We must not stint°   *halt*
Our necessary actions in the fear
To cope° malicious censurers, which ever,   *Of facing*
80 As rav'nous fishes, do a vessel follow
That is new trimmed,° but benefit no further   *newly rigged*
Than vainly longing. What we oft do best,
By sick interpreters, once weak ones, is
Not ours or not allowed;⁹ what° worst, as oft,   *what we do*
85 Hitting a grosser quality,° is cried up   *Appealing to the base*
For our best act. If we shall stand still,
In fear our motion¹ will be mocked or carped at,
We should take root here where we sit,
Or sit state-statues only.²
KING HENRY   Things done well,
90 And with a care, exempt themselves from fear;
Things done without example,° in their issue°   *precedent / effects*
Are to be feared. Have you a precedent
Of this commission? I believe not any.
We must not rend our subjects from our laws
95 And stick them in our will.° Sixth part of each?   *use them at our whim*
A trembling contribution! Why, we take
From every tree lop,° bark, and part o'th' timber,   *branches*
And though we leave it with a root, thus hacked
The air will drink the sap. To every county
100 Where this is questioned° send our letters with   *challenged*
Free pardon to each man that has denied°   *refused*
The force of this commission. Pray look to't—
I put it to your care.
CARDINAL WOLSEY [*to a* SECRETARY]   A word with you.
Let there be letters writ to every shire
Of the King's grace° and pardon.   *mercy*
105 [*Aside to the* SECRETARY]   The grievèd commons
Hardly° conceive of me. Let it be noised°   *Severely / rumored*
That through our intercession this revokement
And pardon comes. I shall anon advise you
Further in the proceeding.   *Exit* SECRETARY
        Enter [BUCKINGHAM'S] SURVEYOR
110 QUEEN KATHERINE [*to the* KING]   I am sorry that the Duke of Buckingham
Is run in° your displeasure.   *Has provoked*
KING HENRY   It grieves many.
The gentleman is learnèd, and a most rare speaker,
To nature none more bound;³ his training such
That he may furnish and instruct great teachers
115 And never seek for aid out of ° himself. Yet see,   *outside of*
When these so noble benefits shall prove
Not well disposed,° the mind growing once corrupt,   *employed*
They turn to vicious forms ten times more ugly
Than ever they were fair. This man so complete,°   *accomplished*

---

9. *What . . . allowed:* Formerly foolish, now corrupt
("sick") observers never attribute to us or approve in us
what we do best.
1. For fear our proposal (or action).

2. Or become nothing but decorative statues of leaders.
3. No man has been given greater gifts by nature.

120 Who was enrolled 'mongst wonders—and when we
    Almost with ravished° list'ning could not find   *spellbound*
    His hour of speech a minute—he, my lady,
    Hath into monstrous habits° put the graces   *shapes; behavior; clothes*
    That once were his, and is become as black
125 As if besmeared in hell. Sit by us. You shall hear—
    This was his gentleman in trust of him—
    Things to strike honour sad.
    [*To* WOLSEY]   Bid him recount
    The fore-recited practices° whereof   *schemes*
    We cannot feel too little, hear too much.
    CARDINAL WOLSEY [*to the* SURVEYOR]   Stand forth, and with bold
130   spirit relate what you
    Most like a careful subject have collected°   *gathered as evidence*
    Out of° the Duke of Buckingham.   *(by observing)*
    KING HENRY [*to the* SURVEYOR]   Speak freely.
    BUCKINGHAM'S SURVEYOR   First, it was usual with him, every day
    It would infect his speech, that if the King
135 Should without issue die, he'll carry it so°   *arrange so as*
    To make the sceptre his. These very words
    I've heard him utter to his son-in-law,
    Lord Abergavenny, to whom by oath he menaced
    Revenge upon the Cardinal.
    CARDINAL WOLSEY [*to the* KING]   Please your highness note
140 His dangerous conception in this point,
    Not friended by his wish to your high person.[4]
    His will is most malignant, and it stretches
    Beyond you to your friends.
    QUEEN KATHERINE   My learned Lord Cardinal,
    Deliver all with charity.
    KING HENRY [*to the* SURVEYOR]   Speak on.
145 How grounded he his title to the crown
    Upon our fail?° To this point hast thou heard him *childlessness; death*
    At any time speak aught?
    BUCKINGHAM'S SURVEYOR   He was brought to this
    By a vain prophecy of Nicholas Hopkins.
    KING HENRY   What was that Hopkins?
    BUCKINGHAM'S SURVEYOR   Sir, a Chartreux friar,
150 His confessor, who fed him every minute
    With words of sovereignty.
    KING HENRY   How know'st thou this?
    BUCKINGHAM'S SURVEYOR   Not long before your highness sped to France,
    The Duke being at the Rose,[5] within the parish
    Saint Lawrence Poutney, did of me demand
155 What was the speech° among the Londoners   *gossip*
    Concerning the French journey. I replied
    Men feared the French would prove perfidious,
    To the King's danger; presently° the Duke   *at once*
    Said 'twas the fear indeed, and that he doubted°   *suspected*
160 'Twould prove the verity of certain words
    Spoke by a holy monk that oft, says he,
    'Hath sent to me, wishing me to permit

---

4. Since he has not been granted ("friended by") his   5. Manor owned by Buckingham just outside London.
wish that the King die without an heir.

John de la Car, my chaplain, a choice hour°   *a suitable time*
To hear from him a matter of some moment;
165 Whom after under the confession's seal
He solemnly had sworn, that what he spoke
My chaplain to no creature living but
To me should utter, with demure° confidence   *grave*
This pausingly ensued: "neither the King nor's heirs",
170 Tell you the Duke, "shall prosper. Bid him strive
To win the love o'th' commonalty.° The Duke   *common people*
Shall govern England."'
QUEEN KATHERINE   If I know you well,
You were the Duke's surveyor, and lost your office
On the complaint o'th' tenants. Take good heed
175 You charge not in your spleen° a noble person   *spite*
And spoil° your nobler soul. I say, take heed;   *ruin*
Yes, heartily beseech you.
KING HENRY   Let him on.°   *continue*
[*To the* SURVEYOR] Go forward.
BUCKINGHAM'S SURVEYOR   On my soul I'll speak but truth.
I told my lord the Duke, by th' devil's illusions
180 The monk might be deceived, and that 'twas dangerous
To ruminate on this so far until
It forged him some design which, being believed,
It was much like to do.⁶ He answered, 'Tush,
It can do me no damage', adding further
185 That had the King in his last sickness failed,°   *died*
The Cardinal's and Sir Thomas Lovell's heads
Should have gone off.
KING HENRY   Ha? What, so rank?° Ah, ha!   *rotten*
There's mischief in this man. Canst thou say further?
BUCKINGHAM'S SURVEYOR   I can, my liege.
KING HENRY   Proceed.
BUCKINGHAM'S SURVEYOR   Being at Greenwich,
190 After your highness had reproved the Duke
About Sir William Bulmer—
KING HENRY   I remember
Such a time, being my sworn servant,
The Duke retained him his.° But on—what hence?   *for his own*
BUCKINGHAM'S SURVEYOR   'If ', quoth he, 'I for this had been committed'—
195 As to the Tower, I thought—'I would have played
The part my father⁷ meant to act upon
Th'usurper Richard who, being at Salisbury,
Made suit to come in's presence; which if granted,
As he made semblance of his duty,° would   *seemed to kneel*
Have put his knife into him.'
200 KING HENRY   A giant traitor!
CARDINAL WOLSEY [*to the* QUEEN]   Now, madam, may° his highness   *can*
      live in freedom,
And this man out of prison?
QUEEN KATHERINE   God mend all.

---

6. *until . . . do:* until the Duke's ruminations made him imagine ("forged him") some scheme that, if he believed in it (and hence in the Monk's prophecy), he would probably undertake.
7. The Duke of Buckingham during Richard III's reign.

KING HENRY [*to the* SURVEYOR]　There's something more would
　　　out of thee—what sayst?
BUCKINGHAM'S SURVEYOR　After 'the Duke his father', with 'the knife',
205　He stretched him,° and with one hand on his dagger,　　　　*stood up straight*
　　Another spread on's breast, mounting° his eyes,　　　　　　*raising up*
　　He did discharge a horrible oath whose tenor
　　Was, were he evil used,° he would outgo　　　　　　　　*poorly treated*
　　His father by as much as a performance°　　　　　　　*true performance*
　　Does an irresolute purpose.
210　KING HENRY　　　　　　　There's his period°—　　　　*ultimate goal*
　　To sheathe his knife in us. He is attached.°　　　　　　*arrested*
　　Call him to present° trial. If he may　　　　　　　　　*immediate*
　　Find mercy in the law, 'tis his; if none,
　　Let him not seek't of us. By day and night,
215　He's traitor to th' height.°　　　　[*Flourish.*] *Exeunt*　*to the greatest degree*

1.3

Enter [the] LORD CHAMBERLAIN *and Lord* SANDS
LORD CHAMBERLAIN　Is't possible the spells of France should juggle°　*enchant*
　　Men into such strange mysteries?°　　　　　　　　*outlandish conduct*
SANDS　　　　　　　　　New customs,
　　Though they be never so ridiculous—
　　Nay, let 'em be unmanly°—yet are followed.　　　　　　*effeminate*
5　LORD CHAMBERLAIN　As far as I see, all the good our English
　　Have got by the late voyage° is but merely　　　　　　*(to France)*
　　A fit or two o'th' face.° But they are shrewd ones,　*Odd new expressions*
　　For when they hold 'em° you would swear directly　*maintain these looks*
　　Their very noses had been counsellors
10　To Pépin or Clotharius, they keep state so.[1]
SANDS　They have all new legs,° and lame ones; one would take it,　*new walks and bows*
　　That never see 'em pace° before, the spavin　　　　　*saw them walk*
　　Or spring-halt reigned among 'em.[2]
LORD CHAMBERLAIN　　　　　Death,° my lord,　　　*By God's death*
　　Their clothes are after such a pagan cut to't
　　That sure they've worn out Christendom.[3]
　　　　Enter Sir Thomas LOVELL
15　　　　　　　　　　　How now—
　　What news, Sir Thomas Lovell?
LOVELL　　　　　　　Faith, my lord,
　　I hear of none but the new proclamation
　　That's clapped upon the court gate.
LORD CHAMBERLAIN　　　　　What is't for?
LOVELL　The reformation of our travelled gallants
20　That fill the court with quarrels, talk, and tailors.
LORD CHAMBERLAIN　I'm glad 'tis there. Now I would pray our '*messieurs*'
　　To think an English courtier may be wise
　　And never see the Louvre.°　　　　　　　*French king's palace*
LOVELL　　　　　　　They must either,
　　For so run the conditions, leave those remnants

1.3 Location: The court.
1. *To . . . so:* To sixth- and seventh-century kings of France, their noses ("they") have such dignified (but convoluted) postures.
2. *the spavin . . . 'em:* they seem to be lame. *spavin:* swelling in horses' legs. *spring-halt:* spasms in horses'

legs.
3. *Their . . . Christendom:* They have run out of the fashions of Christendom and have moved on to pagan habits. This mockery reflects contemporary anxieties about the "effeminacy" of imported Continental fashions. *are after:* have.

25　　Of fool and feather° that they got in France,	*folly and adornment*
With all their honourable points of ignorance[4]	
Pertaining thereunto—as fights and fireworks,°	*whoring*
Abusing better men than they can be	
Out of a foreign wisdom, renouncing clean	
30　　The faith they have in tennis and tall stockings,	
Short blistered breeches, and those types of travel[5]—	
And understand again like honest men,	
Or pack° to their old playfellows. There, I take it,	*return*
They may, *cum privilegio, 'oui'* away	
35　　The lag end of their lewdness[6] and be laughed at.	

SANDS 　'Tis time to give 'em physic,° their diseases 　　*medicine*
Are grown so catching.

LORD CHAMBERLAIN 　　　　What a loss our ladies
Will have of these trim vanities!° 　　　　　*well-dressed fops*

LOVELL 　　　　　　　　　Ay, marry,° 　　　　*indeed*
There will be woe indeed, lords. The sly whoresons
40　　Have got a speeding° trick to lay down° ladies. 　　*an expeditious / seduce*
A French song and a fiddle has no fellow.° 　　　*equal*

SANDS 　The devil fiddle 'em! I am glad they are going,
For sure there's no converting of 'em.° Now 　　*changing their ways*
An honest country lord, as I am, beaten
45　　A long time out of play,° may bring his plainsong° 　　*love / unadorned tune*
And have an hour of hearing, and, by'r Lady,
Held current° music, too. 　　　　　*modern; stylish*

LORD CHAMBERLAIN 　　　　Well said, Lord Sands.
Your colt's tooth is not cast yet?[7]

SANDS 　　　　　　　　No, my lord,
Nor shall not while I have a stump.° 　　　*(of a tooth—sexual)*

LORD CHAMBERLAIN [*to* LOVELL] 　　Sir Thomas,
Whither were you a-going?

50　　LOVELL 　　　　　　　To the Cardinal's.
Your lordship is a guest too.

LORD CHAMBERLAIN 　　　O, 'tis true.
This night he makes° a supper, and a great one, 　　　*holds*
To many lords and ladies. There will be
The beauty of this kingdom, I'll assure you.

55　　LOVELL 　That churchman bears a bounteous mind indeed,
A hand as fruitful° as the land that feeds us. 　　*benevolent*
His dews° fall everywhere. 　　　*(pun on "dues," taxes)*

LORD CHAMBERLAIN 　　　No doubt he's noble.
He had a black mouth that said other of him.[8]

SANDS 　He may, my lord; he's wherewithal.° In him 　　*he can afford to*
60　　Sparing° would show a worse sin than ill doctrine.° 　　*Stinginess / heresy*
Men of his way° should be most liberal. 　　　*profession*
They are set here for examples.

LORD CHAMBERLAIN 　　　　True, they are so,
But few now give so great ones.° My barge stays.° 　　*examples / waits*
Your lordship shall along.° [*To* LOVELL] Come, good Sir Thomas, 　　*join me*

---

4. Which, in their ignorance, they consider honorable.
5. *Abusing . . . travel:* They must stop "abusing" their betters out of a misplaced faith in French wisdom, and start "renouncing" French habits like tennis, tall stockings, puffed breeches, and such marks of travel (which were affected by Henry VIII and James I, as well as James's courtiers).

6. *They . . . lewdness:* They may, with immunity ("*cum privilegio*"), indulge their remaining decadence by copying the French. *oui:* yes.
7. You haven't abandoned your youthful lasciviousness ("colt's tooth") yet?
8. Anyone who denies this generosity must have an evil mouth.

65   We shall be late else, which I would not be,
      For I was spoke to,° with Sir Henry Guildford,   *invited*
      This night to be comptrollers.°   *stewards*
SANDS   I am your lordship's. *Exeunt*

                              1.4
      Hautboys.[1] *[Enter servants with] a small table for* CAR-
      DINAL *[*WOLSEY *which they place] under the [cloth of]*
      state, [and] a longer table for the guests. Then enter at
      one door ANNE *Boleyn and divers other ladies and gen-*
      tlemen as guests, [and] at another door enter Sir Henry
      GUILDFORD
GUILDFORD   Ladies, a general welcome from his grace
      Salutes ye all. This night he dedicates
      To fair content and you. None here, he hopes,
      In all this noble bevy,° has brought with her   *company*
5   One care abroad. He would have all as merry
      As feast, good company, good wine, good welcome
      Can make good people.
            Enter [the] LORD CHAMBERLAIN, *Lord* SANDS, *and [Sir*
            Thomas] LOVELL
      [*To the* LORD CHAMBERLAIN] O, my lord, you're tardy.
      The very thought of this fair company
      Clapped wings to me.
LORD CHAMBERLAIN   You are young, Sir Harry Guildford.
10   SANDS   Sir Thomas Lovell, had the Cardinal
      But half my lay° thoughts in him, some of these   *secular*
      Should find a running banquet,[2] ere they rested,
      I think would better please 'em. By my life,
      They are a sweet society of fair ones.
15   LOVELL   O, that your lordship were but now confessor
      To one or two of these.
SANDS   I would I were.
      They should find easy penance.
LOVELL   Faith, how easy?
SANDS   As easy as a down bed would afford it.
LORD CHAMBERLAIN   Sweet ladies, will it please you sit?
      [*To* GUILDFORD]   Sir Harry,
20   Place you° that side, I'll take the charge of this.   *Arrange seating on*
            [*They sit about the longer table. A noise within*]
      His grace is ent'ring. Nay, you must not freeze—
      Two women placed together makes cold weather.
      My lord Sands, you are one will keep 'em waking.°   *spirited*
      Pray sit between these ladies.
SANDS   By my faith,
      And thank your lordship.
            [*He sits between* ANNE *and another*]
25   By your leave, sweet ladies.
      If I chance to talk a little wild, forgive me.
      I had it from my father.
ANNE   Was he mad, sir?

1.4 Location: Westminster, a hall in York Place.   2. Light refreshments; furtive, stolen pleasures.
1. Early reeded wind instrument, ancestor of the oboe.

SANDS   O, very mad; exceeding mad—in love, too.
But he would bite° none. Just as I do now,   *(sign of madness)*
He would kiss you twenty with a breath.[3]
        [*He kisses her*]

30 LORD CHAMBERLAIN   Well said,° my lord.   *done*
So now you're fairly seated. Gentlemen,
The penance lies on you if these fair ladies
Pass away frowning.

SANDS   For my little cure,°   *duty; (of souls)*
35 Let me alone.
            Hautboys. Enter CARDINAL WOLSEY [*who*] *takes his*
            [*seat at the small table under the*] *state°*   *chair of state*

CARDINAL WOLSEY   You're welcome, my fair guests. That noble lady
Or gentleman that is not freely merry
Is not my friend. This, to confirm my welcome,
And to you all, good health!
            [*He drinks*]

SANDS   Your grace is noble.
40 Let me have such a bowl may° hold my thanks,   *as may*
And save me so much talking.

CARDINAL WOLSEY   My lord Sands,
I am beholden to you. Cheer° your neighbours.   *Amuse*
Ladies, you are not merry! Gentlemen,
Whose fault is this?

SANDS   The red wine first must rise
45 In their fair cheeks, my lord, then we shall have 'em
Talk us to silence.

ANNE   You are a merry gamester,°   *fellow; gambler*
My lord Sands.

SANDS   Yes, if I make my play.[4]
Here's to your ladyship; and pledge it,° madam,   *drink to it*
For 'tis to such a thing—

ANNE   You cannot show me.°   *(sexual)*

SANDS [*to* WOLSEY]   I told your grace they would talk anon.
            Drum and trumpet. Chambers discharged[5]

50 CARDINAL WOLSEY   What's that?

LORD CHAMBERLAIN [*to the* SERVANTS]
Look out there, some of ye.   [*Exit a* SERVANT]

CARDINAL WOLSEY   What warlike voice,
And to what end is this? Nay, ladies, fear not.
By all the laws of war you're privileged.°   *safe from harm*
            Enter [*the*] SERVANT

LORD CHAMBERLAIN   How now—what is't?

SERVANT   A noble troop of strangers,
55 For so they seem. They've left their barge and landed,
And hither make as° great ambassadors   *come like*
From foreign princes.

CARDINAL WOLSEY   Good Lord Chamberlain,
Go give 'em welcome—you can speak the French tongue.
And pray receive 'em nobly, and conduct 'em

---

3. He would kiss you twenty times with a single breath.
4. If I win my hand (at cards or love).
5. Small cannon fired. The firing of this cannon in a

June 29, 1613, performance of the play probably caused the fire that destroyed the Globe Theatre. See the Introduction.

60   Into our presence where this heaven of beauty
        Shall shine at full upon them. Some attend him.
                    [*Exit* CHAMBERLAIN, *attended*]
                All rise, and [*some servants*] *remove* [*the*] *tables*
        You have now a broken banquet, but we'll mend it.
        A good digestion to you all, and once more
        I shower a welcome on ye—welcome all.
                Hautboys. Enter, ushered by the LORD CHAMBERLAIN,
                King [HENRY] *and others as masquers habited like shep-*
                herds. They pass directly before CARDINAL [WOLSEY]
                and gracefully salute him
65   A noble company. What are their pleasures?
    LORD CHAMBERLAIN   Because they speak no English, thus they prayed
        To tell your grace, that, having heard by fame°   rumor
        Of this so noble and so fair assembly
        This night to meet here, they could do no less,
70   Out of the great respect they bear to beauty,
        But leave their flocks, and, under your fair conduct,°   *if you'll permit me*
        Crave leave to view these ladies, and entreat
        An hour of revels⁶ with 'em.
    CARDINAL WOLSEY   Say, Lord Chamberlain,
        They have done my poor house grace, for which I pay 'em
75   A thousand thanks, and pray 'em take their pleasures.
                [*The masquers*] *choose ladies.* [*The*] KING [*chooses*]
                ANNE *Boleyn*
    KING HENRY [*to* ANNE]   The fairest hand I ever touched. O beauty,
        Till now I never knew thee.
                Music. [*They*] *dance*
    CARDINAL WOLSEY [*to the* LORD CHAMBERLAIN]   My lord.
    LORD CHAMBERLAIN   Your grace.
80   CARDINAL WOLSEY   Pray tell 'em thus much from me.
        There should be one amongst 'em by his person
        More worthy this place° than myself, to whom,   *chair of state*
        If I but knew him, with my love and duty
        I would surrender it.
    LORD CHAMBERLAIN   I will, my lord.
                [*He*] *whisper*[*s with the masquers*]
    CARDINAL WOLSEY   What say they?
85   LORD CHAMBERLAIN   Such a one they all confess
        There is indeed, which they would have your grace
        Find out, and he will take it.°   *(the place of honor)*
    CARDINAL WOLSEY [*standing*]   Let me see then.
        By all your good leaves, gentlemen, here I'll make
        My royal choice.
                [*He bows before the* KING]
    KING HENRY [*unmasking*]   Ye have found him, Cardinal.
90   You hold a fair assembly. You do well, lord.
        You are a churchman, or I'll tell you, Cardinal,
        I should judge now unhappily.⁷
    CARDINAL WOLSEY   I am glad
        Your grace is grown so pleasant.°   *merry*
    KING HENRY   My Lord Chamberlain,
        Prithee come hither.

---

6. Entertainment; perhaps, more specifically, the danc-   7. I would judge such ostentatiousness unfavorably.
ing with the audience of the actors in a court masque.

[*Gesturing towards* ANNE] What fair lady's that?
LORD CHAMBERLAIN   An't° please your grace, Sir Thomas   *If it*
95   Boleyn's daughter—
The Viscount Rochford—one of her highness' women.
KING HENRY   By heaven, she is a dainty one. [*To* ANNE] Sweetheart,
    I were unmannerly to take you out°   *(to dance)*
    And not to kiss you [*kisses her*]. A health,° gentlemen;   *toast*
    [*He drinks*]
100   Let it go round.
CARDINAL WOLSEY   Sir Thomas Lovell, is the banquet ready
    I'th' privy chamber?
LOVELL   Yes, my lord.
CARDINAL WOLSEY [*to the* KING]   Your grace
    I fear with dancing is a little heated.
KING HENRY   I fear too much.
105   CARDINAL WOLSEY   There's fresher air, my lord,
    In the next chamber.
KING HENRY   Lead in your ladies, every one. [*To* ANNE] Sweet partner,
    I must not yet forsake you. [*To* WOLSEY] Let's be merry,
    Good my lord Cardinal. I have half a dozen healths
110   To drink to these fair ladies, and a measure°   *majestic dance*
    To lead 'em once again, and then let's dream
    Who's best in favour.⁸ Let the music knock it.°   *strike it up*
                                    Exeunt with trumpets

                                    2.1
            Enter two GENTLEMEN, *at several° doors*   *separate*
FIRST GENTLEMAN   Whither away so fast?
SECOND GENTLEMAN   O, God save ye.
    Ev'n to the hall° to hear what shall become   *Westminster Hall*
    Of the great Duke of Buckingham.
FIRST GENTLEMAN   I'll save you
    That labour, sir. All's now done but the ceremony
    Of bringing back the prisoner.
5   SECOND GENTLEMAN   Were you there?
FIRST GENTLEMAN   Yes, indeed was I.
SECOND GENTLEMAN   Pray speak what has happened.
FIRST GENTLEMAN   You may guess quickly what.
SECOND GENTLEMAN   Is he found guilty?
FIRST GENTLEMAN   Yes, truly is he, and condemned upon't.
SECOND GENTLEMAN   I am sorry for't.
10   FIRST GENTLEMAN   So are a number more.
SECOND GENTLEMAN   But pray, how passed it?°   *how did the trial go*
FIRST GENTLEMAN   I'll tell you in a little.° The great Duke   *concisely*
    Came to the bar, where to his accusations
    He pleaded still not guilty, and allegèd°   *offered up*
15   Many sharp reasons to defeat the law.°   *the crown's case*
    The King's attorney, on the contrary,
    Urged on the examinations,° proofs,° confessions,   *depositions / statements*
    Of divers witnesses, which the Duke desired
    To him brought *viva voce*° to his face—   *in person*
20   At which appeared against him his surveyor,
    Sir Gilbert Perk his chancellor, and John Car,

---

8. Who's most popular with the ladies; who's best   **2.1** Location: A street in Westminster.
looking.

Confessor to him, with that devil-monk,
Hopkins, that made this mischief.
SECOND GENTLEMAN   That was he
That fed him with his prophecies.
FIRST GENTLEMAN   The same.
25   All these accused him strongly, which he fain[1]
Would have flung from him, but indeed he could not.
And so his peers, upon this evidence,
Have found him guilty of high treason. Much
He spoke, and learnèdly, for life, but all
30   Was either pitied in him or forgotten.[2]
SECOND GENTLEMAN   After all this, how did he bear himself?
FIRST GENTLEMAN   When he was brought again to th' bar to hear
His knell rung out, his judgement,° he was stirred   *sentence*
With such an agony he sweat extremely,
35   And something spoke in choler,° ill and hasty;   *anger*
But he fell to° himself again, and sweetly   *got control of*
In all the rest showed a most noble patience.
SECOND GENTLEMAN   I do not think he fears death.
FIRST GENTLEMAN   Sure he does not.
He never was so womanish. The cause
He may a little grieve at.
40   SECOND GENTLEMAN   Certainly
The Cardinal is the end° of this.   *source*
FIRST GENTLEMAN   'Tis likely
By all conjectures: first, Kildare's attainder,
Then deputy of Ireland,[3] who, removed,
Earl Surrey was sent thither—and in haste, too,
Lest he should help his father.°   *father-in-law*
45   SECOND GENTLEMAN   That trick of state
Was a deep envious° one.   *deeply spiteful*
FIRST GENTLEMAN   At his return
No doubt he will requite it. This is noted,
And generally:° whoever the King favours,   *by all*
The Card'nal instantly will find employment—
And far enough from court, too.
50   SECOND GENTLEMAN   All the commons
Hate him perniciously° and, o' my conscience,   *want him dead*
Wish him ten fathom deep. This Duke as much
They love and dote on, call him 'bounteous Buckingham,
The mirror° of all courtesy[4]—   *exemplar*
          Enter [the Duke of] BUCKINGHAM *from his arraign-*
          ment, tipstaves before him, the axe with the edge
          towards him, halberd[ier]s on each side, accompanied
          with Sir Thomas LOVELL, *Sir Nicholas* VAUX, *Sir*
          [William] SANDS,[5] *and common people*
FIRST GENTLEMAN   Stay there, sir,
55   And see the noble ruined man you speak of.

---

1. Which accusations he gladly.
2. *all . . . forgotten:* (Buckingham's defense) either was fruitless or brought only pity.
3. Thomas Fitzgerald, Earl of Kildare, Lord Lieutenant of Ireland, lost his estates and position ("attainder") and was sentenced to death by Wolsey.
4. Polished manners, but also courtliness more generally.
5. *tipstaves:* court-appointed officers who carried

tipstaves, staffs tipped with metal. *halberdiers:* guards who carried halberds, long-handled weapons with both spear tips and battle-ax blades. "Sir William Sands" is called "Lord Sands" in the stage directions at the beginning of 1.3 and at 1.4.7. The discrepancy occurs because the play violates chronology here: Henry and Anne actually met years after Buckingham's trial, and Sands became a baron in the interim.

SECOND GENTLEMAN Let's stand close° and behold him.   *aside; silent*
      [They stand apart]
BUCKINGHAM *[to the common people]*   All good people,
    You that thus far have come to pity me,
    Hear what I say, and then go home and lose° me.   *forget*
    I have this day received a traitor's judgement,°   *sentence*
60   And by that name must die. Yet, heaven bear witness,
    And if I have a conscience let it sink° me,   *destroy*
    Even as the axe falls, if I be not faithful.
    The law I bear no malice for my death.
    'T has done, upon the premises,° but justice.   *evidence*
65   But those that sought it I could wish more° Christians.   *truer*
    Be what they will, I heartily forgive 'em.
    Yet let 'em look° they glory not in mischief,   *beware*
    Nor build their evils on the graves of great men,[6]
    For then my guiltless blood must cry against 'em.
70   For further life in this world I ne'er hope,
    Nor will I sue, although the King have mercies
    More than I dare make faults.° You few that loved me,   *commit misdeeds*
    And dare be bold to weep for Buckingham,
    His noble friends and fellows, whom to leave
75   Is only bitter to him, only dying,[7]
    Go with me like good angels to my end,
    And, as the long divorce° of steel falls on me,   *(of body and soul)*
    Make of your prayers one sweet sacrifice,°   *offering*
    And lift my soul to heaven. *[To the guard]* Lead on, i' God's name.
80 LOVELL   I do beseech your grace, for charity,
    If ever any malice in your heart
    Were hid against me, now to forgive me frankly.
BUCKINGHAM   Sir Thomas Lovell, I as free forgive you
    As I would be forgiven. I forgive all.
85   There cannot be those numberless offences
    'Gainst me that I cannot take° peace with. No black envy°   *make / spite*
    Shall mark my grave. Commend me to his grace,
    And if he speak of Buckingham, pray tell him
    You met him half in heaven. My vows and prayers
90   Yet are the King's, and, till my soul forsake,°   *depart (my body)*
    Shall cry for blessings on him. May he live
    Longer than I have time to tell° his years;   *count*
    Ever beloved and loving may his rule be;
    And, when old time° shall lead him to his end,   *old age*
95   Goodness and he fill up one monument.°   *share one tomb*
LOVELL   To th' waterside I must conduct your grace,
    Then give my charge up to Sir Nicholas Vaux,
    Who undertakes° you to your end.   *leads*
VAUX *[to an attendant]*   Prepare there—
    The Duke is coming. See the barge be ready,
100   And fit it with such furniture° as suits   *trappings*
    The greatness of his person.
BUCKINGHAM   Nay, Sir Nicholas,
    Let it alone. My state[8] now will but mock me.
    When I came hither I was Lord High Constable

---

6. Nor advance their evil designs through plotting the downfall of noblemen.
7. *His . . . dying:* Leaving his friends is the only bitter part of Buckingham's sentence, the only death.
8. status; "furniture" (line 100).

And Duke of Buckingham; now, poor Edward Bohun.⁹
105   Yet I am richer than my base accusers,
That never knew what truth meant. I now seal it,°   *attest to truth*
And with that blood will make 'em one day groan for't.
My noble father, Henry of Buckingham,
Who first raised head° against usurping Richard,   *an army*
110   Flying for succour to his servant Banister,
Being distressed, was by that wretch betrayed,
And without trial fell. God's peace be with him.
Henry the Seventh succeeding, truly pitying
My father's loss, like a most royal prince,
115   Restored me to my honours, and out of ruins
Made my name once more noble. Now his son,
Henry the Eighth, life, honour, name, and all
That made me happy, at one stroke has taken
For ever from the world. I had my trial,
120   And must needs say a noble one; which makes me
A little happier than my wretched father.
Yet thus far we are one in fortunes: both
Fell by our servants, by those men we loved most—
A most unnatural and faithless service.
125   Heaven has an end° in all. Yet, you that hear me,   *a purpose*
This from a dying man receive as certain—
Where you are liberal of your loves and counsels,
Be sure you be not loose;° for those you make friends   *unrestrained*
And give your hearts to, when they once perceive
130   The least rub° in your fortunes, fall away   *obstacle*
Like water from ye, never found again
But where they mean to sink° ye. All good people   *destroy*
Pray for me. I must now forsake ye. The last hour
Of my long weary life is come upon me.
135   Farewell, and when you would say something that is sad,
Speak how I fell. I have done, and God forgive me.
           Exeunt [the] Duke [of BUCKINGHAM] *and train*
           [*The two* GENTLEMEN *come forward*]
FIRST GENTLEMAN   O, this is full of pity, sir; it calls,
I fear, too many curses on their heads
That were the authors.
SECOND GENTLEMAN   If the Duke be guiltless,
140   'Tis full of woe. Yet I can give you inkling°   *forewarning*
Of an ensuing evil, if it fall,°   *should occur*
Greater than this.
FIRST GENTLEMAN   Good angels keep it from us.
What may it be? You do not doubt my faith,¹ sir?
SECOND GENTLEMAN   This secret is so weighty, 'twill require
A strong faith to conceal it.
145   FIRST GENTLEMAN   Let me have it—
I do not talk much.
SECOND GENTLEMAN   I am confident;°   *I trust you*
You shall, sir. Did you not of late days hear
A buzzing° of a separation   *gossip*
Between the King and Katherine?
FIRST GENTLEMAN   Yes, but it held not.°   *did not persist*

9. Actually Edward Stafford; Shakespeare copies Holinshed's mistake.
1. "Faith" (here and in line 145) picks up the religious language of "curses" (line 138) and "angels" (line 142), while suggesting fidelity, loyalty, trustworthiness, and, as line 146 suggests, discretion.

150 For when the King once heard it, out of anger
He sent command to the Lord Mayor straight
To stop the rumour and allay° those tongues   *suppress*
That durst disperse it.

SECOND GENTLEMAN   But that slander, sir,
Is found a truth now, for it grows again
155 Fresher than e'er it was, and held° for certain   *believed*
The King will venture at it. Either the Cardinal
Or some about him near° have, out of malice   *his confidants*
To the good Queen, possessed him with a scruple°   *doubt*
That will undo her. To confirm this, too,
160 Cardinal Campeius² is arrived, and lately,
As all think, for this business.

FIRST GENTLEMAN   'Tis the Cardinal;
And merely to revenge him on the Emperor³
For not bestowing on him at his asking
The Archbishopric of Toledo this is purposed.

SECOND GENTLEMAN   I think you have hit the mark.° But is't not   *guessed correctly*
165   cruel
That she should feel the smart° of this? The Cardinal   *pain*
Will have his will, and she must fall.

FIRST GENTLEMAN   'Tis woeful.
We are too open° here to argue this.   *exposed*
Let's think in private more.   *Exeunt*

2.2

Enter [the] LORD CHAMBERLAIN *[with a] letter*

LORD CHAMBERLAIN *[reads]* 'My lord, the horses your lordship
sent for, with all the care I had, I saw well chosen, ridden, and
furnished.° They were young and handsome, and of the best   *trained and equipped*
breed in the north. When they were ready to set out for Lon-
5 don, a man of my lord Cardinal's, by commission and main
power,¹ took 'em from me with this reason—his master would be
served before a subject, if not before the King; which stopped
our mouths, sir.'
I fear he will indeed. Well, let him have them.
10 He will have all, I think.

Enter to the LORD CHAMBERLAIN *the Dukes of* NORFOLK
and SUFFOLK

NORFOLK   Well met, my Lord Chamberlain.

LORD CHAMBERLAIN   Good day to both your graces.

SUFFOLK   How is the King employed?

LORD CHAMBERLAIN   I left him private,°   *alone*
Full of sad° thoughts and troubles.   *grave*

NORFOLK   What's the cause?

15 LORD CHAMBERLAIN   It seems the marriage with his brother's wife
Has crept too near his conscience.

SUFFOLK   No, his conscience
Has crept too near another lady.

---

2. Henry had to get a special dispensation from the
Pope before marrying Katherine, because her previous
husband was Prince Arthur, Henry's brother, who died
a year after the marriage took place. Wolsey had Cardinal Laurence Campeius (Lorenzo Campeggio) come to
London as a papal legate in 1528 to reopen debate

about the marriage and to aid his plot to have it
annulled.
3. Charles V, Holy Roman Emperor and King of Spain,
was Katherine's nephew.
2.2 Location: The court at London.
1. By warrant and superior strength.

NORFOLK   'Tis so.
This is the Cardinal's doing. The King-Cardinal,
That blind priest, like the eldest son of fortune,

20   Turns what he list.[2] The King will know him° one day.   *(for what he is)*
SUFFOLK   Pray God he do. He'll never know himself else.
NORFOLK   How holily he° works in all his business,   *(Wolsey)*
And with what zeal! For now he has cracked the league
Between us and the Emperor, the Queen's great-nephew,[3]

25   He dives into the King's soul and there scatters
Dangers, doubts, wringing° of the conscience,   *affliction*
Fears, and despairs—and all these for his marriage.
And out of all these, to restore the King,
He counsels a divorce—a loss of her

30   That like a jewel has hung twenty years
About his neck, yet never lost her lustre;
Of her that loves him with that excellence°   *great virtue*
That angels love good men with; even of her
That, when the greatest stroke° of fortune falls,   *severest blow*

35   Will bless the King[4]—and is not this course° pious?°   *(of action)* / *(ironic)*
LORD CHAMBERLAIN   Heaven keep me from such counsel! 'Tis most true—
These news are everywhere, every tongue speaks 'em,
And every true heart weeps for't. All that dare
Look into these affairs see this main end°—   *ultimate aim*

40   The French king's sister.[5] Heaven will one day open
The King's eyes, that so long have slept, upon
This bold bad man.
SUFFOLK   And free us from his slavery.
NORFOLK   We had need pray,

45   And heartily, for our deliverance,
Or this imperious man will work us all
From princes into pages. All men's honours
Lie like one lump° before him, to be fashioned   *(of clay)*
Into what pitch° he please.   *stature*
SUFFOLK   For me, my lords,

50   I love him not, nor fear him—there's my creed.
As I am made without him, so I'll stand,[6]
If the King please. His curses and his blessings
Touch me alike; they're breath I° not believe in.   *I do*
I knew him, and I know him; so I leave him
To him that made him proud—the Pope.

55 NORFOLK   Let's in,
And with some other business put the King
From these sad thoughts that work too much upon him.
[*To the* LORD CHAMBERLAIN] My lord, you'll bear us company?
LORD CHAMBERLAIN   Excuse me,
The King has sent me otherwhere. Besides,

60   You'll find a most unfit time to disturb him.
Health to your lordships.

---

2. *The King-Cardinal . . . list:* Like Fortune, his mother, Wolsey blindly turns the wheel of fortune as he likes ("list").
3. Wolsey has now broken the alliance between Henry and Charles V to get additional revenge on Charles: see 2.1.161–64. Previously (1.1.176–93), to gain favor with Charles, he engineered the breaking of the treaty with France sealed at the Field of the Cloth of Gold.

4. Prophetic: Katherine does later "bless the King" who has repudiated her (4.2.164).
5. Henry's marriage to the Duchess of Alençon will reunite the English and French Kings, thus still further injuring Charles V. See 3.2.86–87.
6. Since not Wolsey but the King granted my nobility of rank, I'll remain firm in my position.

NORFOLK   Thanks, my good Lord Chamberlain.
                         Exit [*the*] LORD CHAMBERLAIN
            KING [HENRY] *draws the curtain,*[7] *and sits reading pensively*

SUFFOLK   How sad° he looks! Sure he is much afflicted.°   *grave / distressed*
KING HENRY   Who's there? Ha?
NORFOLK   Pray God he be not angry.
KING HENRY   Who's there, I say? How dare you thrust yourselves
65   Into my private meditations!
     Who am I? Ha?
NORFOLK   A gracious king that pardons all offences
     Malice ne'er meant. Our breach of duty this way°   *in this respect*
     Is business of estate,° in which we come   *state*
     To know your royal pleasure.
70   KING HENRY   Ye are too bold.
     Go to, I'll make ye know your times of business.
     Is this an hour for temporal affairs? Ha?
            Enter [CARDINAL] WOLSEY *and* [CARDINAL] CAMPEIUS,
            [*the latter*] *with a commission*
     Who's there? My good lord Cardinal? O, my Wolsey,
     The quiet° of my wounded conscience,   *ease*
     Thou art a cure° fit for a king.   *balm; curate (priest)*
75   [*To* CAMPEIUS]   You're welcome,
     Most learnèd reverend sir, into our kingdom.
     Use us, and it. [*To* WOLSEY] My good lord, have great care
     I be not found a talker.[8]
CARDINAL WOLSEY   Sir, you cannot.
     I would your grace would give us but an hour
     Of private conference.
80   KING HENRY [*to* NORFOLK *and* SUFFOLK]   We are busy; go.
            [NORFOLK *and* SUFFOLK *speak privately to one another*
            as they depart]
NORFOLK   This priest has no pride in him!°   *(more irony)*
SUFFOLK   Not to speak of.
     I would not be so sick, though, for his place[9]—
     But this cannot continue.
NORFOLK   If it do
     I'll venture one have-at-him.°   *thrust (in fencing)*
SUFFOLK   I another.
                Exeunt NORFOLK *and* SUFFOLK
CARDINAL WOLSEY [*to the* KING]   Your grace has given a precedent°   *model*
85   of wisdom
     Above all princes in committing freely
     Your scruple to the voice of Christendom.[1]
     Who can be angry now? What envy reach you?
     The Spaniard,° tied by blood and favour to her,   *Charles V*
90   Must now confess, if they have any goodness,
     The trial just and noble. All the clerks°—   *clerics*
     I mean the learnèd ones in Christian kingdoms—
     Have their free voices.° Rome, the nurse of judgement,   *may vote freely*

---

7. Almost certainly drawn by an attendant. The King's chamber is upstage in the discovery space, a curtained-off, perhaps recessed area at the back of the stage.
8. *have . . . talker:* make sure my offer of hospitality counts for more than mere words.

9. I would not want to be afflicted with such pride, even for his exalted position.
1. *voice of Christendom:* the papal legate Campeius and the representatives of the great European universities who have come to England to hear the case.

Invited by your noble self, hath sent
95 One general tongue° unto us: this good man,   *representative voice*
This just and learnèd priest, Card'nal Campeius,
Whom once more I present unto your highness.
KING HENRY [*embracing* CAMPEIUS] And once more in mine
    arms I bid him welcome,
And thank the holy conclave° for their loves.   *College of Cardinals*
100 They have sent me such a man I would have wished for.
CARDINAL CAMPEIUS Your grace must needs deserve all strangers'° loves,   *foreigners'*
You are so noble. To your highness' hand
I tender my commission,
    [*He gives the commission to the* KING]
    [*to* WOLSEY]   by whose virtue,
The Court of Rome commanding, you, my lord
105 Cardinal of York, are joined with me their servant
In the unpartial° judging of this business.   *impartial*
KING HENRY Two equal° men. The Queen shall be acquainted°   *fair / apprised*
Forthwith for what you come. Where's Gardiner?
CARDINAL WOLSEY   I know your majesty has always loved her
110 So dear in heart not to deny her that°   *that which*
A woman of less place° might ask by law—   *rank*
Scholars allowed freely to argue for her.
KING HENRY Ay, and the best she shall have, and my favour
To him that does best, God forbid else. Cardinal,
115 Prithee call Gardiner to me, my new secretary.[2]
    [CARDINAL WOLSEY *goes to the door and calls* GARDINER]
I find him a fit fellow.
        Enter GARDINER
CARDINAL WOLSEY [*aside to* GARDINER]   Give me your hand. Much joy
    and favour to you.
You are the King's now.
GARDINER [*aside to* WOLSEY]   But to be commanded
For ever by your grace, whose hand has raised me.
120 KING HENRY Come hither, Gardiner.
    [*The* KING] *walks* [*with* GARDINER] *and whispers* [*with*
    him]
CARDINAL CAMPEIUS [*to* WOLSEY]   My lord of York, was not one
    Doctor Pace[3]
In this man's place before him?
CARDINAL WOLSEY   Yes, he was.
CARDINAL CAMPEIUS Was he not held a learnèd man?
CARDINAL WOLSEY   Yes, surely.
CARDINAL CAMPEIUS Believe me, there's an ill opinion spread then,
    Even of yourself, lord Cardinal.
125 CARDINAL WOLSEY   How? Of me?
CARDINAL CAMPEIUS They will not stick° to say you envied him,   *scruple*
And fearing he would rise, he was so virtuous,
Kept him a foreign man still,° which so grieved him   *always abroad*
That he ran mad and died.
CARDINAL WOLSEY   Heav'n's peace be with him—
130 That's Christian care enough. For living murmurers°   *malcontents*

---

2. Stephen Gardiner, former secretary to Wolsey, became Henry's secretary in July 1529 through Wolsey's preferment, and Bishop of Winchester in 1531.
3. Richard Pace, the King's former secretary, was now sent frequently abroad by Wolsey on diplomatic business, apparently as punishment for becoming too close to the King.

There's places of rebuke. He was a fool,
For he would needs be virtuous.
   [*Gesturing towards* GARDINER]   That good fellow,
If I command him, follows my appointment.°   *orders*
I will have none so near⁴ else. Learn this, brother:
135 We live not to be griped° by meaner persons.   *grasped; brought down*
  KING HENRY [*to* GARDINER]   Deliver this with modesty° to th'   *Announce this mildly*
      Queen.   *Exit* GARDINER
The most convenient place that I can think of
For such receipt of⁵ learning is Blackfriars;
There ye shall meet about this weighty business.
140 My Wolsey, see it furnished.° O, my lord,   *fitted out properly*
Would it not grieve an able° man to leave   *a (sexually) vigorous*
So sweet a bedfellow? But conscience, conscience—
O, 'tis a tender place,° and I must leave her.   *Exeunt*   *(conscience); (sexual)*

2.3

Enter ANNE *Boleyn and an* OLD LADY

  ANNE   Not for that neither. Here's the pang that pinches°—   *pain that torments*
His highness having lived so long with her, and she
So good a lady that no tongue could ever
Pronounce dishonour of her—by my life,
5 She never knew harm-doing—O now, after
So many courses of the sun° enthronèd,   *years*
Still° growing in a majesty and pomp the which   *Ever*
To leave a thousandfold more bitter than
'Tis sweet at first t'acquire—after this process,
10 To give her the avaunt,° it is a pity   *boot*
Would move a monster.
  OLD LADY   Hearts of most hard temper°   *constitution*
Melt and lament for her.
  ANNE   O, God's will! Much better
She ne'er had known pomp; though't be temporal,°   *only of this world*
Yet if that quarrel,° fortune, do divorce   *quarreler*
15 It from the bearer, 'tis a sufferance panging°   *as painful*
As soul and bodies severing.
  OLD LADY   Alas, poor lady!
She's a stranger° now again.   *foreigner*
  ANNE   So much the more
Must pity drop upon her. Verily,
I swear, 'tis better to be lowly born
20 And range with humble livers in content
Than to be perked up in a glist'ring grief¹
And wear a golden sorrow.
  OLD LADY   Our content
Is our best having.°   *possession*
  ANNE   By my troth° and maidenhead,   *faith*
I would not be a queen.
  OLD LADY   Beshrew me,° I would—   *Devil take me*
25 And venture maidenhead for't; and so would you,
For all this spice° of your hypocrisy.   *sample*
You, that have so fair parts° of woman on you,   *qualities; beauty*

---

4. I want no one else on such intimate terms with the King.
5. For hearing such scholarly disputation, or such scholars.

2.3 Location: The Queen's apartments at court.
1. 'tis . . . grief: it's better to be born poor and to occupy a lowly rank happily than to be unhappy despite one's riches (literally, to be dressed up in a glittering sadness).

Have, too, a woman's heart which ever yet
Affected° eminence, wealth, sovereignty;   *Craved*
30 Which, to say sooth,° are blessings; and which gifts,   *truth*
Saving your mincing,° the capacity   *Despite your affectation*
Of your soft cheveril° conscience would receive   *kid leather (pliant)*
If you might please to stretch it.

ANNE   Nay, good troth.[2]

OLD LADY   Yes, troth and troth. You would not be a queen?

35 ANNE   No, not for all the riches under heaven.

OLD LADY   'Tis strange. A threepence bowed would hire me,
Old as I am, to queen it.[3] But I pray you,
What think you of a duchess? Have you limbs
To bear that load of title?

ANNE   No, in truth.

40 OLD LADY   Then you are weakly made. Pluck off[4] a little;
I would not be a young count in your way
For more than blushing comes to.[5] If your back
Cannot vouchsafe this burden,[6] 'tis too weak
Ever to get a boy.

ANNE   How you do talk!
45 I swear again, I would not be a queen
For all the world.

OLD LADY   In faith, for little England
You'd venture an emballing;[7] I myself
Would for Caernarfonshire,[8] although there 'longed°   *belonged*
No more to th' crown but that. Lo, who comes here?

    Enter [the] LORD CHAMBERLAIN

50 LORD CHAMBERLAIN   Good morrow, ladies. What were't worth to know
The secret of your conference?°   *conversation*

ANNE   My good lord,
Not your demand; it values not° your asking.   *does not merit*
Our mistress' sorrows we were pitying.

LORD CHAMBERLAIN   It was a gentle business, and becoming
55 The action of good women. There is hope
All will be well.

ANNE   Now I pray God, amen.

LORD CHAMBERLAIN   You bear a gentle mind, and heav'nly blessings
Follow such creatures. That you may, fair lady,
Perceive I speak sincerely, and high note's
60 Ta'en of your many virtues, the King's majesty
Commends his good opinion of you,° and   *Sends his compliments*
Does purpose° honour to you no less flowing°   *intend / copious*
Than Marchioness of Pembroke; to which title
A thousand pound a year annual support
Out of his grace he adds.

65 ANNE   I do not know
What kind of my obedience I should tender.

---

2. Faith (exclamatory); perhaps a pun on "trot," a demeaning term for an old woman.
3. *A threepence . . . it*: A bent ("bowed") and hence worthless coin would convince me to be a Queen. Sexual puns ("queen"—"quean," or whore; "bowed"—bawd) continue through the scene.
4. Come lower in rank; undress.
5. *I . . . to*: Perhaps: If you persist in this "way" (path; being unable to bear the load of being duchess; condi-

tion of virginity), a "count" (an earl, the rank below duke) will get no more from you than blushes. Also: I would give up being a young virginal cunt ("count") like you with no more than a blush.
6. Cannot bear these honors. "Burden," like "bear" (line 39), suggests both intercourse and childbearing.
7. *for . . . emballing*: for England you'd accept investiture with the royal emblem of ball and scepter (you'd get laid).
8. Particularly poor Welsh county.

More than my all is nothing; nor my prayers
Are not° words duly hallowed, nor my wishes   *no more than*
More worth than empty vanities; yet prayers and wishes
70 Are all I can return. Beseech your lordship,
Vouchsafe° to speak my thanks and my obedience,   *Condescend*
As from a blushing handmaid to his highness,
Whose health and royalty I pray for.
LORD CHAMBERLAIN   Lady,
I shall not fail t'approve° the fair conceit°   *endorse / opinion*
75 The King hath of you. [*Aside*] I have perused her well.
Beauty and honour in her are so mingled
That they have caught the King, and who knows yet
But from this lady may proceed a gem
To lighten⁹ all this isle. [*To* ANNE] I'll to the King
80 And say I spoke with you.
ANNE   My honoured lord.
                    Exit [the] LORD CHAMBERLAIN
OLD LADY   Why, this it is—see, see!
I have been begging sixteen years in court,
Am yet a courtier beggarly,° nor could   *still begging*
85 Come pat betwixt too early and too late
For any suit of pounds;¹ and you—O, fate!—
A very fresh fish here—fie, fie upon
This compelled° fortune!—have your mouth filled up   *forced upon you*
Before you open it.
ANNE   This is strange to me.
90 OLD LADY   How tastes it? Is it bitter? Forty pence, no.²
There was a lady once—'tis an old story—
That would not be a queen, that would she not,
For all the mud in Egypt.³ Have you heard it?
ANNE   Come, you are pleasant.°   *merry; joking*
OLD LADY   With your theme I could
95 O'ermount the lark. The Marchioness of Pembroke?
A thousand pounds a year, for pure° respect?   *mere*
No other obligation? By my life,
That promises more thousands. Honour's train
Is longer than his foreskirt.⁴ By this time
100 I know your back will bear a duchess. Say,
Are you not stronger than you were?
ANNE   Good lady,
Make yourself mirth with your particular fancy,°   *private fantasies*
And leave me out on't. Would I had no being,
If this salute° my blood a jot. It faints me°   *agitates / I faint*
105 To think what follows.⁵
The Queen is comfortless, and we forgetful
In our long absence. Pray do not deliver
What here you've heard to her.
OLD LADY   What do you think me—
                    Exeunt

9. To bring light to (alluding to Elizabeth), with religious connotations. Gems were believed to emit light.
1. *nor . . . pounds:* nor could I arrive at just the right moment to succeed in any petition for money.
2. I'll bet a small sum (conventionally, 40 pence) that it isn't.
3. For all the wealth (in this case, the fertile land, or

"mud") of Egypt.
4. *That . . . foreskirt:* Future rewards will exceed present ones, just as a noblewoman's dress is longer in back than in front.
5. "What follows," ultimately, is Anne's execution at Henry's order in 1536, on the charge of adultery.

2.4

Trumpets: sennet.° [*Then*] *cornetts. Enter two vergers*[1]   *fanfare*
with short silver wands; next them two SCRIBES *in the*
habit of doctors;[2] *after them the* [*Arch*]*bishop of Can-*
terbury alone; after him the Bishops of LINCOLN, *Ely,*
Rochester, and Saint Asaph; next them, with some small
distance, follows a gentleman bearing [*both*] *the purse*
[*containing*] *the great seal and a cardinal's hat; then*
two priests bearing each a silver cross; then a gentleman
usher, bare-headed, accompanied with a serjeant-at-
arms bearing a silver mace;° *then two gentlemen bear-*   *ceremonial staff*
ing two great silver pillars; after them, side by side, the
two cardinals, [WOLSEY *and* CAMPEIUS; *then*] *two noble-*
men with the sword and mace. The KING [*ascends to his*
seat] *under the cloth of state; the two cardinals sit*
under him as judges; the QUEEN [*attended by* GRIFFITH
her gentleman usher] *takes place some distance from*
the KING; *the Bishops place themselves on each side the*
court in [*the*] *manner of a consistory,°* *below them,*   *church court*
the SCRIBES. *The lords sit next the Bishops. The rest of*
the attendants stand in convenient order about the stage

CARDINAL WOLSEY   Whilst our commission from Rome is read
    Let silence be commanded.

KING HENRY   What's the need?
    It hath already publicly been read,
    And on all sides th'authority allowed.°   *accepted*
    You may then spare that time.

5   CARDINAL WOLSEY   Be't so. Proceed.

SCRIBE [*to the* CRIER]   Say, 'Henry, King of England, come into the court'.

CRIER   Henry, King of England, come into the court.

KING HENRY   Here.

SCRIBE [*to the* CRIER]   Say, 'Katherine, Queen of England, come
    into the court'.

10   CRIER   Katherine, Queen of England, come into the court.
        The QUEEN *makes no answer,* [*but*] *rises out of her chair,*
        goes about the court, comes to the KING, *and kneels at*
        his feet. Then [*she*] *speaks*

QUEEN KATHERINE   Sir, I desire you do me right and justice,
    And to bestow your pity on me; for
    I am a most poor woman, and a stranger,°   *foreigner*
    Born out of your dominions, having here
15   No judge indifferent,° nor no more assurance   *impartial*
    Of equal° friendship and proceeding.° Alas, sir,   *just / legal order*
    In what have I offended you? What cause
    Hath my behaviour given to your displeasure
    That thus you should proceed to put me off,°   *abandon me*
20   And take your good grace° from me? Heaven witness   *good will; yourself*
    I have been to you a true and humble wife,
    At all times to your will conformable,

2.4 Location: A hall in Blackfriars.
1. Officials who carry the verge (a staff symbolizing the
authority of office) before a bishop or other dignitary.
2. Furred black gown and flat caps of doctors of law.

Ever in fear to kindle your dislike,
Yea, subject to your countenance, glad or sorry
25 As I saw it inclined. When was the hour
I ever contradicted your desire,
Or made it not mine too? Or which of your friends
Have I not strove to love, although I knew
He were mine enemy? What friend of mine
30 That had to him derived° your anger did I   incurred
Continue in my liking? Nay, gave notice
He was from thence discharged? Sir, call to mind
That I have been your wife in this obedience
Upward of twenty years, and have been blessed
35 With many children by you.[3] If, in the course
And process of this time, you can report—
And prove it, too—against mine honour aught,°   anything
My bond to wedlock, or my love and duty
Against° your sacred person, in God's name   Toward
40 Turn me away, and let the foul'st contempt
Shut door upon me, and so give me up
To the sharp'st kind of justice. Please you, sir,
The King your father was reputed for
A prince most prudent, of an excellent
45 And unmatched wit° and judgement. Ferdinand   wisdom
My father, King of Spain, was reckoned one
The wisest[4] prince that there had reigned by many
A year before. It is not to be questioned
That they had gathered a wise council to them
50 Of every realm, that did debate this business,
Who deemed our marriage lawful. Wherefore I humbly
Beseech you, sir, to spare me till I may
Be by my friends in Spain advised, whose counsel
I will implore. If not, i'th' name of God,
Your pleasure be fulfilled.
55 CARDINAL WOLSEY   You have here, lady,
And of your choice, these reverend fathers, men
Of singular integrity and learning,
Yea, the elect o'th' land, who are assembled
To plead your cause. It shall be therefore bootless°   pointless
60 That longer you desire° the court, as well   beg (for a delay)
For your own quiet,° as to rectify   peace of mind
What is unsettled in the King.
CARDINAL CAMPEIUS   His grace
Hath spoken well and justly. Therefore, madam,
It's fit this royal session do proceed,
65 And that without delay their arguments
Be now produced and heard.
QUEEN KATHERINE [to WOLSEY]   Lord Cardinal,
To you I speak.
CARDINAL WOLSEY   Your pleasure, madam.
QUEEN KATHERINE   Sir,
I am about to weep, but thinking that
We are a queen, or long have dreamed so, certain°   without doubt

3. Queen Katherine bore five of Henry's children. All   4. was . . . wisest: was judged the very wisest.
but one, later Queen Mary, died at birth or in infancy.

70 The daughter of a king, my drops of tears
I'll turn to sparks of fire.

CARDINAL WOLSEY   Be patient yet.

QUEEN KATHERINE   I will when you are humble! Nay, before,
Or God will punish me. I do believe,
Induced° by potent circumstances, that   *Convinced*
75 You are mine enemy, and make my challenge°   *legal objection that*
You shall not be my judge. For it is you
Have blown this coal betwixt my lord and me,
Which God's dew quench. Therefore I say again,
I utterly abhor,° yea, from my soul,   *loathe; reject*
80 Refuse you for my judge, whom yet once more
I hold my most malicious foe, and think not
At all a friend to truth.

CARDINAL WOLSEY   I do profess°   *declare*
You speak not like yourself, who ever yet°   *always*
Have stood to° charity, and displayed th'effects   *upheld*
85 Of disposition gentle and of wisdom
O'er-topping woman's power. Madam, you do me wrong.
I have no spleen° against you, nor injustice   *malevolence*
For you or any. How far I have proceeded,
Or how far further shall, is warranted
90 By a commission from the consistory,°   *College of Cardinals*
Yea, the whole consistory of Rome. You charge me
That I 'have blown this coal'. I do deny it.
The King is present. If it be known to him
That I gainsay my deed,° how may he wound,   *deny what took place*
95 And worthily,° my falsehood—yea, as much   *justly*
As you have done my truth. If he know
That I am free of your report, he knows
I am not of your wrong.⁵ Therefore in him
It lies to cure° me, and the cure is to   *absolve*
100 Remove these thoughts from you. The which before
His highness shall speak in,° I do beseech   *about*
You, gracious madam, to unthink your speaking,
And to say so no more.

QUEEN KATHERINE   My lord, my lord—
I am a simple woman, much too weak
105 T'oppose your cunning. You're meek and humble-mouthed;
You sign your place and calling, in full seeming,
With meekness and humility⁶—but your heart
Is crammed with arrogancy, spleen,° and pride.   *malice*
You have by fortune and his highness' favours
110 Gone slightly° o'er low steps, and now are mounted   *effortlessly*
Where powers are your retainers, and your words,
Domestics to you, serve your will as't please
Yourself pronounce their office.⁷ I must tell you,
You tender more° your person's honour than   *have more regard for*
115 Your high profession spiritual, that again
I do refuse you for my judge, and here,

5. *If . . . wrong:* If he agrees that I am innocent ("free") of your accusation, then he knows that I have done you no wrong; and that I have no part in the wrong you do me by thus accusing me.
6. *You . . . humility:* You mark your office and role with great outward display of meekness and humility.
7. *and now . . . office:* and now have attained a place where men of authority ("powers") serve you, and your words are like attendants ("domestics"), which transform into deeds anything you pronounce as your will.

Before you all, appeal unto the Pope,
To bring my whole cause 'fore his holiness,
And to be judged by him.
She curtsies to the KING *and* [*begins*] *to depart*

CARDINAL CAMPEIUS   The Queen is obstinate,
120   Stubborn° to justice, apt to accuse it, and   *Impervious*
Disdainful to be tried by't. 'Tis not well.
She's going away.

KING HENRY [*to the* CRIER]   Call her again.

CRIER   Katherine, Queen of England, come into the court.

GRIFFITH [*to the* QUEEN]   Madam, you are called back.

QUEEN KATHERINE   What° need you note it? Pray you keep your   *Why*
125   way.°   *keep going*
When *you* are called, return. Now the Lord help.
They vex me past my patience. Pray you, pass on.
I will not tarry; no, nor ever more
Upon this business my appearance make
In any of their courts.
Exeunt QUEEN [KATHERINE] *and her attendants*

130   **KING HENRY**   Go thy ways, Kate.
That man i'th' world who shall report he has
A better wife, let him in naught be trusted
For speaking false in that. Thou art alone—
If thy rare qualities, sweet gentleness,
135   Thy meekness saint-like, wife-like government,°   *restraint*
Obeying in commanding,[8] and thy parts°   *qualities*
Sovereign and pious else° could speak thee out°—   *besides / describe you*
The queen of earthly queens. She's noble born,
And like her true nobility she has
Carried° herself towards me.   *Conducted*

140   **CARDINAL WOLSEY**   Most gracious sir,
In humblest manner I require° your highness   *entreat*
That it shall please you to declare in hearing
Of all these ears—for where I am robbed and bound,
There must I be unloosed, although not there
145   At once and fully satisfied°—whether ever I   *given recompense*
Did broach this business to your highness, or
Laid any scruple in your way which might
Induce you to the question on't,° or ever   *of it*
Have to you, but with thanks to God for such
150   A royal lady, spake one the least° word that might   *the very least*
Be to the prejudice of her present state,
Or touch° of her good person?   *censure*

KING HENRY   My lord Cardinal,
I do excuse you;° yea, upon mine honour,   *forgive you fully*
I free you from't. You are not° to be taught   *do not require*
155   That you have many enemies that know not
Why they are so, but, like to village curs,
Bark when their fellows do. By some of these
The Queen is put in anger. You're excused.
But will you be more justified?° You ever   *vindicated*
160   Have wished the sleeping of this business, never desired
It to be stirred, but oft have hindered, oft,

8. Acting like an obedient wife even as you rule like a Queen.

The passages° made toward it. On my honour   *proceedings*
I speak my good lord Card'nal to this point,
And thus far clear him.⁹ Now, what moved me to't,°   *convinced me of it*
165 I will be bold with time and your attention.
Then mark th'inducement.° Thus it came—give heed to't.   *what influenced me*
My conscience first received a tenderness,°   *sensitivity*
Scruple, and prick, on° certain speeches uttered   *from*
By th' Bishop of Bayonne, then French Ambassador,
170 Who had been hither sent on the debating
A marriage 'twixt the Duke of Orléans¹ and
Our daughter Mary. I'th' progress of this business,
Ere a determinate resolution,° he—   *decisive settlement*
I mean the Bishop—did require a respite
175 Wherein he might the King his lord advertise°   *make aware*
Whether our daughter were legitimate,
Respecting this our marriage with the dowager,
Sometimes° our brother's wife. This respite shook   *Formerly*
The bosom of my conscience, entered me,
180 Yea, with a spitting° power, and made to tremble   *piercing*
The region of my breast; which forced such way
That many mazed considerings did throng
And prest in with this caution.² First, methought
I stood not in the smile of heaven, who had
185 Commanded nature that my lady's womb,
If it conceived a male child by me, should
Do no more offices of life to't than
The grave does yield to th' dead. For her male issue
Or° died where they were made, or shortly after   *Either*
190 This world had aired them.° Hence I took a thought *given life to; shown*
This was a judgement on me that my kingdom,
Well worthy the best heir³ o'th' world, should not
Be gladded° in't by me. Then follows that   *made joyful*
I weighed the danger which my realms stood in
195 By this my issue's fail,° and that gave to me   *lack; death*
Many a groaning throe.° Thus hulling in⁴   *pang (of pregnancy)*
The wild sea of my conscience, I did steer
Toward this remedy, whereupon we are
Now present here together—that's to say
200 I meant to rectify my conscience, which
I then did feel full sick, and yet° not well,   *still*
By all the reverend fathers of the land
And doctors learned. First I began in private
With you, my lord of Lincoln.⁵ You remember
205 How under my oppression I did reek°   *sweat*
When I first moved° you.   *appealed to*
LINCOLN   Very well, my liege.
KING HENRY   I have spoke long. Be pleased yourself to say
How far you satisfied me.

---

9. *I speak . . . Him*: Here the King speaks to the court as a whole, announcing that up to this point he exonerates the Cardinal of any wrongdoing.
1. Second son of King Francis I of France, he later became Henry II of France.
2. *many . . . caution*: many confused thoughts crowded in at this warning.
3. Pun on "aired" (line 190).
4. Floating aimlessly, like a ship adrift in the current that is not making use of its sails.
5. The Bishop of Lincoln, according to Holinshed, was the King's confessor.

LINCOLN   So please your highness,
The question did at first so stagger me,
210 Bearing a state of mighty moment° in't   *so weighty, urgent a matter*
And consequence of dread,° that I committed   *dire consequences*
The daring'st counsel which I had to doubt,[6]
And did entreat your highness to this course
Which you are running here.
KING HENRY [*to Canterbury*]   I then moved you,
215 My lord of Canterbury, and got your leave
To make this present summons. Unsolicited
I left no reverend person in this court,
But by particular consent proceeded
Under your hands and seals.[7] Therefore, go on,
220 For no dislike i'th' world against the person
Of the good Queen, but the sharp thorny points
Of my allegèd° reasons, drives this forward.   *advanced by me*
Prove but our marriage lawful, by my life
And kingly dignity, we are contented
225 To wear our mortal state to come with her,
Katherine, our queen, before the primest° creature   *most perfect*
That's paragoned o'°th' world.   *considered a model by*
CARDINAL CAMPEIUS   So please your highness,
The Queen being absent, 'tis a needful fitness°   *only appropriate*
That we adjourn this court till further° day.   *a later*
230 Meanwhile must be an earnest motion°   *plea*
Made to the Queen to call back her appeal
She intends unto his holiness.
KING HENRY [*aside*]   I may perceive
These cardinals trifle with me. I abhor
This dilatory sloth and tricks of Rome.
235 My learned and well-belovèd servant, Cranmer,
Prithee return.[8] With thy approach I know
My comfort comes along. [*Aloud*] Break up the court.
I say, set on.°   *Exeunt in manner as they entered*   *proceed*

3.1
Enter QUEEN [KATHERINE] *and her women, as at work*
QUEEN KATHERINE   Take thy lute, wench. My soul grows sad with troubles.
Sing, and disperse 'em if thou canst. Leave° working.   *Cease*
GENTLEWOMAN [*sings*]   Orpheus[1] with his lute made trees,
And the mountain tops that freeze,
5   Bow themselves when he did sing.
To his music plants and flowers
Ever sprung, as° sun and showers   *as if*
There had made a lasting spring.
Everything that heard him play,
10   Even the billows of the sea,
Hung their heads, and then lay by.°   *were still*

6. *I committed . . . doubt*: I distrusted even the boldest
advice I myself could offer.
7. With your written agreement.
8. The King here apostrophizes Thomas Cranmer, who
is not present but is traveling on the Continent collecting opinions on the status of Henry and Katherine's

marriage. See 3.2.401–02 for mention of his return and
his elevation to the position of Archbishop of Canterbury.
3.1 Location: The Queen's apartments at court.
1. In Greek mythology, he was famous for the power of
his music.

In sweet music is such art,
Killing care and grief of heart
Fall asleep, or hearing, die.

Enter [GRIFFITH,] *a gentleman*

15 QUEEN KATHERINE   How now?
GRIFFITH   An't please your grace, the two great cardinals
Wait in the presence.°   reception chamber
QUEEN KATHERINE   Would they speak with me?
GRIFFITH   They willed me say so, madam.
QUEEN KATHERINE   Pray their graces
To come near.   [*Exit* GRIFFITH]
What can be their business
20 With me, a poor weak woman, fall'n from favour?
I do not like their coming, now I think on't;
They should be good men, their affairs as righteous—
But all hoods make not monks.²

Enter the two cardinals, WOLSEY *and* CAMPEIUS [*ushered
by* GRIFFITH]

CARDINAL WOLSEY   Peace to your highness.
QUEEN KATHERINE   Your graces find me here part of a housewife—
25 I would be all,³ against° the worst may happen.   in case
What are your pleasures with me, reverend lords?
CARDINAL WOLSEY   May it please you, noble madam, to withdraw
Into your private chamber, we shall give you
The full cause of our coming.
QUEEN KATHERINE   Speak it here.
30 There's nothing I have done yet, o' my conscience,
Deserves a corner.° Would all other women   subterfuge
Could speak this with as free° a soul as I do.   innocent
My lords, I care not—so much I am happy°   favored
Above a number°—if my actions   many
35 Were tried by ev'ry tongue, ev'ry eye saw 'em,
Envy and base opinion° set against 'em,   Spite and base gossip
I know my life so even.° If your business   uniformly virtuous
Seek me out and that way I am wife in,⁴
Out with it boldly. Truth loves open dealing.
40 CARDINAL WOLSEY   *Tanta est erga te mentis integritas, Regina serenissima*⁵—
QUEEN KATHERINE   O, good my lord, no Latin.
I am not such a truant° since my coming°   so idle / (to England)
As not to know the language I have lived in.
A strange° tongue makes my cause more strange° suspicious—   foreign / unusually
45 Pray, speak in English. Here are some will thank you,
If you speak truth, for their poor mistress' sake.
Believe me, she has had much wrong. Lord Cardinal,
The willing'st° sin I ever yet committed   most premeditated
May be absolved in English.
CARDINAL WOLSEY   Noble lady,
50 I am sorry my integrity should breed—
And service to his majesty and you—
So deep suspicion, where all faith° was meant.   loyalty
We come not by the way° of accusation,   for the sake

2. Proverbial: religious trappings do not ensure piety.
3. I would like to be not just partly but completely a housewife.
4. *If . . . in:* If your business concerns me and my behavior as wife.
5. So great is the integrity of (my) mind toward you, most serene Queen (Latin).

To taint that honour every good tongue blesses,
55 Nor to betray you any way° to sorrow—   *by any means*
You have too much, good lady—but to know
How you stand minded° in the weighty difference   *Your deliberation*
Between the King and you, and to deliver,°   *recount*
Like free° and honest men, our just opinions   *unprejudiced*
And comforts to your cause.
60 CARDINAL CAMPEIUS   Most honoured madam,
My lord of York, out of his noble nature,
Zeal, and obedience he still bore° your grace,   *has always borne*
Forgetting, like a good man, your late censure
Both of his truth and him—which was° too far—   *went*
65 Offers, as I do, in a sign of peace,
His service and his counsel.
QUEEN KATHERINE [*aside*]   To betray me.
[*Aloud*] My lords, I thank you both for your good wills.
Ye speak like honest men—pray God ye prove so.
But how to make ye suddenly° an answer   *without deliberation*
70 In such a point of weight, so near° mine honour—   *bound up with*
More near my life, I fear—with my weak wit,°   *comprehension*
And to such men of gravity and learning,
In truth I know not. I was set° at work   *sitting*
Among my maids, full little—God knows—looking
75 Either for such men or such business.
For her sake that I have been⁶—for I feel
The last fit° of my greatness—good your graces,   *spell*
Let me have time and counsel for my cause.
Alas, I am a woman friendless, hopeless.
80 CARDINAL WOLSEY   Madam, you wrong the King's love with these fears.
Your hopes and friends are infinite.
QUEEN KATHERINE   In England
But little for my profit.° Can you think, lords,   *of little use to me*
That any Englishman dare give me counsel,
Or be a known friend 'gainst his highness' pleasure—
85 Though he be grown so desperate° to be honest—   *rash enough*
And live a subject?° Nay, forsooth, my friends,   *survive in this land*
They that must weigh out° my afflictions,   *offset*
They that my trust must grow to, live not here.
They are, as all my other comforts, far hence,
In mine own country, lords.
90 CARDINAL CAMPEIUS   I would your grace
Would leave your griefs and take my counsel.
QUEEN KATHERINE   How, sir?
CARDINAL CAMPEIUS   Put your main cause into the King's protection.
He's loving and most gracious. 'Twill be much
Both for your honour better and your cause,
95 For if the trial of the law o'ertake ye
You'll part away° disgraced.   *leave*
CARDINAL WOLSEY [*to the* QUEEN]   He tells you rightly.
QUEEN KATHERINE   Ye tell me what ye wish for both—my ruin.
Is this your Christian counsel? Out upon ye!
Heaven is above all yet—there sits a judge
That no king can corrupt.

6. For the sake of the woman—the Queen—I once was.

100	CARDINAL CAMPEIUS Your rage mistakes° us.	*misrepresents*
	QUEEN KATHERINE The more shame for ye! Holy men I thought ye,	
	Upon my soul, two reverend cardinal virtues⁷—	
	But cardinal sins and hollow hearts I fear ye.	
	Mend° 'em, for shame, my lords! Is this your comfort?	*Reform*
105	The cordial° that ye bring a wretched lady,	*restoring medicine*
	A woman lost° among ye, laughed at, scorned?	*ruined*
	I will not wish ye half my miseries—	
	I have more charity. But say I warned ye.	
	Take heed, for heaven's sake take heed, lest at once°	*all at once*
110	The burden of my sorrows fall upon ye.	
	CARDINAL WOLSEY Madam, this is a mere distraction.°	*utter madness; evasion*
	You turn the good we offer into envy.°	*malevolence*
	QUEEN KATHERINE Ye turn me into nothing. Woe upon ye,	
	And all such false professors.° Would you have me—	*(of religion)*
115	If you have any justice, any pity,	
	If ye be anything but churchmen's habits°—	*vestments*
	Put my sick cause into his hands that hates me?	
	Alas, he's banished me his bed already—	
	His love, too, long ago. I am old, my lords,	
120	And all the fellowship I hold now with him	
	Is only my obedience. What can happen	
	To me above° this wretchedness? All your studies	*beyond*
	Make me accursèd like this.⁸	*immediate*
	CARDINAL CAMPEIUS Your fears are worse.°	*(than reality)*
	QUEEN KATHERINE Have I lived thus long—let me speak° myself,	*represent*
125	Since virtue finds no friends—a wife, a true one?	
	A woman, I dare say, without vainglory,°	*conceit*
	Never yet branded with suspicion?	
	Have I with all my full affections	
	Still° met the King, loved him next° heav'n, obeyed him,	*Always / next to*
130	Been out of fondness superstitious° to him,	*overly devoted*
	Almost forgot my prayers to content him?	
	And am I thus rewarded? 'Tis not well, lords.	
	Bring me a constant woman to her husband,	
	One that ne'er dreamed a joy beyond his pleasure,	
135	And to that woman when she has done most,	
	Yet will I add an° honour, a great patience.	*another*
	CARDINAL WOLSEY Madam, you wander from° the good we aim at.	*misinterpret*
	QUEEN KATHERINE My lord, I dare not make myself so guilty	
	To give up willingly that noble title	
140	Your master wed me to. Nothing but death	
	Shall e'er divorce my dignities.	
	CARDINAL WOLSEY Pray, hear me.	
	QUEEN KATHERINE Would I had never trod this English earth,	
	Or felt the flatteries that grow upon it.	
	Ye have angels' faces, but heaven knows your hearts.	
145	What will become of me now, wretched lady?	
	I am the most unhappy woman living.	
	[*To her women*] Alas, poor wenches, where are now your forturnes?	

---

7. The cardinal virtues (justice, temperance, prudence, and fortitude, with a play on their rank), which, along with the three theological virtues (faith, hope, and charity), constitute the seven virtues. These oppose the seven deadly ("cardinal," punning on "carnal") sins

referred to in the next line.

8. *All . . . this*: All your endeavors (and inquiries) bring me only these miseries; I defy you, with all your clerical learning, to imagine a more terrible fate than this.

Shipwrecked upon a kingdom where no pity,
No friends, no hope, no kindred weep for me?
150   Almost no grave allowed me? Like the lily,
That once was mistress of the field and flourished,
I'll hang my head and perish.

CARDINAL WOLSEY   If your grace
Could but be brought to know our ends° are honest,   *intentions*
You'd feel more comfort. Why should we, good lady,
155   Upon what cause, wrong you? Alas, our places,°   *official duties*
The way of our profession, is against it.
We are to cure such sorrows, not to sow 'em.
For goodness' sake, consider what you do,
How you may hurt yourself, ay, utterly
160   Grow from the King's acquaintance by this carriage.°   *behavior*
The hearts of princes kiss obedience,
So much they love it, but to stubborn spirits
They swell and grow as terrible as storms.
I know you have a gentle noble temper,°   *temperament*
165   A soul as even° as a calm. Pray, think us   *unwavering*
Those we profess—peacemakers, friends, and servants.

CARDINAL CAMPEIUS   Madam, you'll find it so. You wrong your virtues
With these weak women's fears. A noble spirit,
As yours was put° into you, ever casts   *given*
170   Such doubts as false coin from it. The King loves you.
Beware you lose it not. For° us, if you please   *As for*
To trust us in your business, we are ready
To use our utmost studies in your service.

QUEEN KATHERINE   Do what ye will, my lords, and pray forgive me.
175   If I have used° myself unmannerly,   *behaved*
You know I am a woman, lacking wit°   *understanding*
To make a seemly answer to such persons.
Pray do my service° to his majesty.   *give my respects*
He has my heart yet, and shall have my prayers
180   While I shall have my life. Come, reverend fathers,
Bestow your counsels on me. She now begs
That° little thought, when she set footing here,°   *Who / (in England)*
She should have bought her dignities so dear.   *Exeunt*

3.2

Enter the Duke of NORFOLK, [*the*] *Duke of* SUFFOLK,
Lord SURREY, *and* [*the*] LORD CHAMBERLAIN

NORFOLK   If you will now unite in your complaints,
And force them with a constancy,° the Cardinal   *persevere in them*
Cannot stand under them. If you omit°   *neglect*
The offer of this time,° I cannot promise   *This opportunity*
5   But that you shall sustain more new disgraces
With these you bear already.

SURREY   I am joyful
To meet the least occasion that may give me
Remembrance of my father-in-law the Duke,°   *(of Buckingham)*
To be revenged on him.°   *(Wolsey)*

SUFFOLK   Which of the peers
10   Have uncontemned gone° by him, or at least   *not been disdained*
Strangely neglected?° When did he regard   *snubbed as a stranger*

3.2 Location: The court.

The stamp of nobleness in any person
Out of° himself?   *Aside from*
LORD CHAMBERLAIN   My lords, you speak your pleasures.
What he deserves of you and me I know;
15   What we can do to him—though now the time
Gives way to° us—I much fear. If you cannot   *Favors*
Bar his access to th' King, never attempt
Anything on° him, for he hath a witchcraft   *against*
Over the King in's tongue.
NORFOLK   O, fear him not.
20   His spell in that is out.° The King hath found   *past*
Matter against him that for ever mars
The honey of his language. No, he's settled,
Not to come off, in his displeasure.[1]
SURREY   Sir,
I should be glad to hear such news as this
Once every hour.
25   NORFOLK   Believe it, this is true.
In the divorce his contrary proceedings°   *double-dealing*
Are all unfolded,° wherein he appears   *exposed*
As I would wish mine enemy.
SURREY   How came
His practices° to light?   *schemes*
SUFFOLK   Most strangely.
SURREY   O, how, how?
30   SUFFOLK   The Cardinal's letters to the Pope miscarried,°   *went astray; got diverted*
And came to th'eye o'th' King, wherein was read
How that the Cardinal did entreat his holiness
To stay° the judgement o'th' divorce, for if   *delay*
It did take place, 'I do', quoth he, 'perceive
35   My king is tangled in affection to
A creature° of the Queen's, Lady Anne Boleyn'.   *servant*
SURREY   Has the King this?
SUFFOLK   Believe it.
SURREY   Will this work?
LORD CHAMBERLAIN   The King in this perceives him how he coasts°   *sails indirectly*
And hedges° his own way. But in this point   *moves secretly*
40   All his tricks founder, and he brings his physic°   *medicine*
After his patient's death. The King already
Hath married the fair lady.
SURREY   Would he had.
SUFFOLK   May you be happy in your wish, my lord,
For I profess you have it.
SURREY   Now all my joy
Trace the conjunction.°   *Follow the union*
SUFFOLK   My amen to't.
45   NORFOLK   All men's.
SUFFOLK   There's order given for her coronation.
Marry, this is yet but young,° and may be left   *recent*
To some ears unrecounted. But, my lords,
She is a gallant° creature, and complete°   *an excellent / perfect*
50   In mind and feature. I persuade me,° from her   *am sure*
Will fall some blessing to this land which shall
In it be memorized.[2]

1. No, Wolsey is stuck, with no way out, in Henry's displeasure. Or: No, Henry is firm, with no possibility of changing, in his displeasure toward Wolsey.
2. Be made memorable (alluding to Elizabeth).

SURREY   But will the King
  Digest° this letter of the Cardinal's?   *Tolerate*
  The Lord forbid!

NORFOLK   Marry, amen.

SUFFOLK   No, no—
55 There be more wasps that buzz about his nose
  Will make this sting the sooner. Cardinal Campeius
  Is stol'n away to Rome; hath ta'en no leave;
  Has left the cause o'th' King unhandled,° and   *unsettled*
  Is posted° as the agent of our Cardinal   *Has rushed*
60 To second all his plot. I do assure you
  The King cried 'Ha!'³ at this.

LORD CHAMBERLAIN   Now God incense him,
  And let him cry 'Ha!' louder.

NORFOLK   But, my lord,
  When returns Cranmer?

SUFFOLK   He is returned in his opinions, which
65 Have satisfied the King for his divorce,
  Together with all famous colleges,
  Almost, in Christendom.⁴ Shortly, I believe,
  His second marriage shall be published,° and   *announced publicly*
  Her coronation. Katherine no more
70 Shall be called 'Queen', but 'Princess Dowager',
  And 'widow to Prince Arthur'.

NORFOLK   This same Cranmer's
  A worthy fellow, and hath ta'en much pain°   *great pains*
  In the King's business.

SUFFOLK   He has, and we shall see him
  For it an archbishop.

NORFOLK   So I hear.

SUFFOLK   'Tis so.

  Enter [CARDINAL] WOLSEY *and* CROMWELL
  The Cardinal.

75 NORFOLK   Observe, observe—he's moody.
  [*They stand apart and observe* WOLSEY *and* CROMWELL]

CARDINAL WOLSEY [*to* CROMWELL]   The packet,° Cromwell—   *parcel of letters*
  gave't you the King?

CROMWELL   To his own hand, in's bedchamber.

CARDINAL WOLSEY   Looked he
  O'th' inside of the paper?°   *wrapper*

CROMWELL   Presently°   *Immediately*
  He did unseal them, and the first he viewed
80 He did it with a serious mind; a heed°   *concerned look*
  Was in his countenance. You he bade
  Attend him here this morning.

CARDINAL WOLSEY   Is he ready
  To come abroad?

CROMWELL   I think by this° he is.   *by this time*

85 CARDINAL WOLSEY Leave me a while.   *Exit* CROMWELL
  [*Aside*] It shall be to the Duchess of Alençon,
  The French King's sister—he shall marry her.

---

3. Henry's characteristic expression of impatience and part of his legend in the Renaissance. See, for instance, 1.2.187 and 2.2.63, 66.
4. *He . . . Christendom:* Cranmer has sent ahead the opinions concerning the King's marriage that he collected on the Continent, and the results have satisfied both the King and most learned clerics.

Anne Boleyn? No, I'll no Anne Boleyns for him.
There's more in't than fair visage. Boleyn?
90 No, we'll no Boleyns. Speedily I wish
To hear from Rome. The Marchioness of Pembroke?
        [*The nobles speak among themselves*]
NORFOLK   He's discontented.
SUFFOLK   Maybe he hears the King
Does whet his anger to° him.   °against
SURREY   Sharp enough,
Lord, for thy justice.
CARDINAL WOLSEY [*aside*]   The late° Queen's gentlewoman? A   °former
95   knight's daughter
To be her mistress' mistress? The Queen's queen?
This candle burns not clear;° 'tis I must snuff it,   °bright
Then out it goes. What though I know her virtuous
And well deserving? Yet I know her for
100 A spleeny Lutheran,[5] and not wholesome° to   °beneficial
Our cause, that she should lie i'th' bosom of
Our hard-ruled° King. Again, there is sprung up   °hard-to-advise
An heretic, an arch-one, Cranmer, one°   °one who
Hath crawled into the favour of the King
And is his oracle.[6]
        [*The nobles speak among themselves*]
105 NORFOLK   He is vexed at something.
        Enter KING [HENRY] *reading a schedule*° [*and* LOVELL   °scroll
        with him]
SURREY   I would 'twere something that would fret the string,
The master-cord on's heart![7]
SUFFOLK   The King, the King!
KING HENRY [*aside*]   What piles of wealth hath he accumulated
To his own portion?° And what expense by th' hour   °share
110 Seems to flow from him? How i'th' name of thrift
Does he rake this together? [*To the nobles*] Now, my lords,
Saw you the Cardinal?
NORFOLK   My lord, we have
Stood here observing him. Some strange commotion°   °rebellion
Is in his brain. He bites his lip, and starts,
115 Stops on a sudden, looks upon the ground,
Then lays his finger on his temple, straight°   °immediately
Springs out into fast gait, then stops again,
Strikes his breast hard, and anon he casts
His eye against the moon. In most strange postures
We have seen him set himself.
120 KING HENRY   It may well be
There is a mutiny in's mind. This morning
Papers of state he sent me to peruse
As I required, and wot° you what I found   °know
There, on my conscience put unwittingly?
125 Forsooth, an inventory thus importing°   °delineating
The several parcels of his plate,[8] his treasure,

---

5. Passionate Lutheran. It is possible that Wolsey objected to Henry's marriage to Anne on religious grounds, as well as on the class grounds that he outlines in this speech.
6. is his oracle: is considered by Henry to be divinely inspired.

7. would . . . heart: would eat through ("fret") the heart-strings (tying Henry to Wolsey), with a musical allusion: "fret" (fingering bar), "string," and "cord" (chord).
8. plate: gold and silver functional household equipment that also stored and displayed wealth.

Rich stuffs, and ornaments of household which
I find at such proud rate° that it outspeaks   *high value*
Possession of a subject.⁹

NORFOLK   It's heaven's will.

130   Some spirit put this paper in the packet
To bless your eye withal.°   *with*

KING HENRY   If we did think
His contemplation were above the earth
And fixed on spiritual object, he should still
Dwell in his musings. But I am afraid

135   His thinkings are below the moon,° not worth   *mundane*
His serious considering.

            [The] KING *takes his seat [and] whispers [with]* LOVELL,
            who [then] goes to the CARDINAL

CARDINAL WOLSEY   Heaven forgive me!
[To the KING*]* Ever God bless your highness!

KING HENRY   Good my lord,
You are full of heavenly stuff,¹ and bear the inventory
Of your best graces in your mind, the which

140   You were now running o'er. You have scarce time
To steal from spiritual leisure a brief span
To keep your earthly audit. Sure, in that,
I deem you an ill husband, and am glad
To have you therein my companion.²

CARDINAL WOLSEY   Sir,

145   For holy offices I have a time; a time
To think upon the part of business which
I bear i'th' state; and nature does require
Her times of preservation which, perforce,
I, her frail son, amongst my brethren mortal,
Must give my tendance to.°   *take care of*

150 KING HENRY   You have said well.

CARDINAL WOLSEY   And ever may your highness yoke together,
As I will lend you cause, my doing well
With my well-saying.

KING HENRY   'Tis well said again,
And 'tis a kind of good deed to say well—

155   And yet words are no deeds. My father loved you.
He said he did, and with his deed did crown°   *make good*
His word upon you. Since I had my office,
I have kept you next° my heart, have not alone   *nearest to*
Employed you where high profits might come home,

160   But pared my present havings° to bestow   *given up possessions*
My bounties upon you.

CARDINAL WOLSEY *[aside]*   What should this mean?

SURREY *[aside]*   The Lord increase this business!

KING HENRY   Have I not made you
The prime° man of the state? I pray you tell me   *principal*
If what I now pronounce you have found true,

---

9. *a . . . subject*: it inventories more wealth than is fit
for a subject.
1. Godly qualities, but Henry's ironic language ("stuff,"
"steal," "audit") refers to both worldly and spiritual
matters.
2. Henry jokes that both he and Wolsey are "ill husbands," Wolsey because he cannot manage ("husband")

his household resources (ostensibly, he is otherworldly,
but really he is a greedy spendthrift) and because he
now opposes Henry's remarriage, and perhaps Henry
because he has literally been a poor husband to Katherine. Henry is being ironic, however, and may merely
mean that he has husbanded his resources badly in
trusting them to Wolsey.

165 And, if you may confess it, say withal
If you are bound to us or no. What say you?
CARDINAL WOLSEY My sovereign, I confess your royal graces°   favors
Showered on me daily have been more than could
My studied purposes requite,° which went   conscious efforts repay
170 Beyond all man's endeavours. My endeavours
Have ever come too short of my desires,°   aspirations
Yet filed° with my abilities. Mine own ends°   matched / aims
Have been mine so that° evermore they pointed   only insofar as
To th' good of your most sacred person and
175 The profit of the state. For your great graces
Heaped upon me, poor undeserver, I
Can nothing render but allegiant° thanks,   loyal
My prayers to heaven for you, my loyalty,
Which ever has and ever shall be growing,
Till death, that winter, kill it.
180 KING HENRY   Fairly answered.
A loyal and obedient subject is
Therein illustrated. The honour of it
Does pay the act of it, as, i'th' contrary,
The foulness is the punishment.³ I presume
185 That as my hand has opened° bounty to you,   freely offered
My heart dropped love, my power rained honour, more
On you than any, so your hand and heart,
Your brain, and every function of your power,
Should, notwithstanding that° your bond of duty,°   despite / (to Rome)
190 As 'twere in love's particular,° be more   peculiar intimacy
To me, your friend, than any.
CARDINAL WOLSEY   I do profess
That for your highness' good I ever laboured
More than mine own; that am, have,° and will be—   have been
Though all the world should crack° their duty to you,   forswear
195 And throw it from their soul, though perils did
Abound, as thick as thought could make 'em, and
Appear in forms more horrid—yet, my duty,
As doth a rock against the chiding° flood,   roaring
Should the approach of this wild river break,°   check
And stand unshaken yours.
200 KING HENRY   'Tis nobly spoken.
Take notice, lords, he has a loyal breast,
For you have seen him open't. [To WOLSEY] Read o'er this,
     [He gives him a paper]
And after this [giving him another paper], and then to breakfast with
What appetite you have.
                              Exit KING [HENRY], frowning upon the
                              CARDINAL. The nobles throng after
                              [the KING], smiling and whispering
CARDINAL WOLSEY   What should this mean?
205 What sudden anger's this? How have I reaped° it?   acquired
He parted frowning from me, as if ruin
Leaped from his eyes. So looks the chafèd° lion   angry
Upon the daring huntsman that has galled° him,   wounded

---

3. *The honour . . . punishment:* The reward for loyalty and obedience is the honor they bring. Similarly, disloyalty and corruption are their own punishment, causing the subject dishonor.

Then makes him nothing.° I must read this paper—   *slaughters the hunter*
I fear, the story of his anger.
    [*He reads one of the papers*]
210   'Tis so.
This paper has undone° me. 'Tis th'account   *ruined*
Of all that world° of wealth I have drawn together   *vast quantity*
For mine own ends—indeed, to gain the popedom,
And fee° my friends in Rome. O negligence,   *pay off*
215 Fit for a fool to fall by! What cross° devil   *perverse*
Made me put this main° secret in the packet   *most important*
I sent the King? Is there no way to cure this?
No new device to beat this from his brains?
I know 'twill stir him strongly. Yet I know
220 A way, if it take right,° in spite of fortune   *if it succeed*
Will bring me off° again. What's this?   *save me*
    [*He reads the other paper*]
                        'To th' Pope'?
The letter, as I live, with all the business
I writ to's holiness. Nay then, farewell.
I have touched the highest point of all my greatness,
225 And from that full meridian° of my glory   *a star's highest point*
I haste now to my setting. I shall fall
Like a bright exhalation° in the evening,   *shooting star*
And no man see me more.
    Enter to [CARDINAL] WOLSEY *the Dukes of* NORFOLK
    and SUFFOLK, *the Earl of* SURREY, *and the* LORD CHAM-
    BERLAIN
NORFOLK   Hear the King's pleasure, Cardinal, who commands you
230 To render up the great seal presently°   *immediately*
Into our hands, and to confine yourself
To Asher House, my lord of Winchester's,
Till you hear further from his highness.
CARDINAL WOLSEY   Stay—
Where's your commission,° lords? Words cannot carry *written warrant*
Authority so weighty.
235 SUFFOLK   Who dare cross° 'em   *challenge*
Bearing the King's will from his mouth expressly?
CARDINAL WOLSEY   Till I find more than will or words to do it—
I mean your malice—know, officious lords,
I dare and must deny it. Now I feel
240 Of what coarse metal° ye are moulded—envy.°⁴   *(also) mettle*
How eagerly ye follow my disgraces
As if it fed ye, and how sleek° and wanton° *obsequious / impetuous*
Ye appear in everything may bring my ruin!
Follow your envious courses, men of malice.
245 You have Christian warrant for 'em, and no doubt
In time will find their fit rewards.⁵ That seal
You ask with such a violence,° the King,   *vehemence*
Mine and your master, with his own hand gave me,
Bade me enjoy it, with the place° and honours,   *position*
250 During my life; and, to confirm his goodness,
Tied it by letters patents.° Now, who'll take it?   *open letters*
SURREY   The King that gave it.

---

4. Malice; jealousy.
5. *You . . . rewards:* You emulate other, equally unjust Christians and will reap their "rewards" (punishments).

CARDINAL WOLSEY   It must be himself then.

SURREY   Thou art a proud traitor, priest.

CARDINAL WOLSEY   Proud lord, thou liest.

Within these forty hours Surrey durst better

Have burnt that tongue than said so.

255 **SURREY**   Thy ambition,

Thou scarlet sin,[6] robbed this bewailing land

Of noble Buckingham, my father-in-law.

The heads of all thy brother cardinals

With thee and all thy best parts° bound together   *attributes*

260 Weighed° not a hair of his. Plague of° your policy,°   *Equaled / on / scheming*

You sent me deputy for Ireland,

Far from his succour, from the King, from all

That might have mercy on the fault thou gav'st him;°   *charged him wtih*

Whilst your great goodness, out of holy pity,

Absolved him with an axe.

265 **CARDINAL WOLSEY**   This, and all else

This talking lord can lay upon my credit,°   *good reputation*

I answer is most false. The Duke by law

Found his deserts. How innocent I was

From° any private malice in his end,   *Of*

270 His noble jury and foul cause can witness.

If I loved many words, lord, I should tell you

You have as little honesty as honour,

That° in the way of loyalty and truth   *I who*

Toward the King, my ever royal master,

275 Dare mate° a sounder man than Surrey can be,   *rival*

And all that love his follies.

SURREY   By my soul,

Your long coat, priest, protects you; thou shouldst feel

My sword i'th' life-blood of thee else. My lords,

Can ye endure to hear this arrogance,

280 And from this fellow?° If we live thus tamely,   *(contemptuous)*

To be thus jaded° by a piece of scarlet,   *cowed*

Farewell nobility. Let his grace go forward

And dare us with his cap, like larks.[7]

CARDINAL WOLSEY   All goodness

Is poison to thy stomach.

SURREY   Yes, that goodness

285 Of gleaning all the land's wealth into one,

Into your own hands, Card'nal, by extortion;

The goodness of your intercepted packets

You writ to th' Pope against the King; your goodness—

Since you provoke me—shall be most notorious.

290 My lord of Norfolk, as you are truly noble,

As you respect the common good, the state

Of our despised nobility, our issues°—   *sons*

Whom if he° live will scarce be gentlemen—   *(Wolsey)*

Produce the grand sum of his sins, the articles°   *charges against him*

295 Collected from his life. [*To* WOLSEY] I'll startle you

---

6. *scarlet:* referring to the cardinal's robes; see line 281
and 3.1.103. *scarlet sin:* egregious sin in the Bible; see
Isaiah 1:18.

7. And befuddle us with his scarlet cap, as larks are
caught by dazzling them with scarlet cloth.

Worse than the sacring-bell when the brown wench
Lay kissing in your arms,[8] lord Cardinal.
CARDINAL WOLSEY [*aside*]   How much, methinks, I could despise this man,
But that I am bound in charity against it.
300 NORFOLK [*to* SURREY]   Those articles, my lord, are in the King's hand;°   *possession*
But thus° much—they are foul ones.   *I'll tell you this*
CARDINAL WOLSEY   So much fairer
And spotless shall mine innocence arise
When the King knows my truth.°   *loyalty*
SURREY   This cannot save you.
I thank my memory I yet remember
305 Some of these articles, and out they shall.
Now, if you can blush and cry 'Guilty', Cardinal,
You'll show a little honesty.
CARDINAL WOLSEY   Speak on, sir;
I dare your worst objections.° If I blush,   *accusations*
It is to see a nobleman want° manners.   *lack*
310 SURREY   I had rather want those than my head. Have at you!°   *(a challenge)*
First, that without the King's assent or knowledge
You wrought to be a legate,[9] by which power
You maimed the jurisdiction of all bishops.
NORFOLK [*to* WOLSEY]   Then, that in all you writ to Rome, or else
315 To foreign princes, '*Ego et Rex meus*'[1]
Was still° inscribed—in which you brought the King   *always*
To be your servant.
SUFFOLK [*to* WOLSEY]   Then, that without the knowledge
Either of King or Council, when you went
Ambassador to the Emperor,° you made bold   *Charles V*
320 To carry into Flanders the great seal.
SURREY [*to* WOLSEY]   Item,° you sent a large commission°   *Next / delegation*
To Gregory de Cassado, to conclude,
Without the King's will or the state's allowance,°   *consent*
A league between his highness and Ferrara.
325 SUFFOLK [*to* WOLSEY]   That out of mere° ambition you have caused   *pure*
Your holy hat to be stamped on the King's coin.[2]
SURREY [*to* WOLSEY]   Then, that you have sent innumerable substance°— *untold riches*
By what means got, I leave to your own conscience—
To furnish° Rome, and to prepare the ways   *supply; bribe*
330 You have for dignities to the mere undoing°   *complete destruction*
Of all the kingdom. Many more there are,
Which since they are of you, and odious,
I will not taint my mouth with.
LORD CHAMBERLAIN   O, my lord,
Press° not a falling man too far. 'Tis virtue.°   *Oppress / (not to)*
335 His faults lie open to° the laws. Let them,   *exposed before*
Not you, correct him. My heart weeps to see him
So little of his great self.
SURREY   I forgive him.

---

8. *I'll . . . arms:* The small "sacring bell" was rung at Mass
when the priest elevated the consecrated Host. Surrey
imagines Wolsey surprised with a country girl ("brown"
because tanned or dirty from working, or perhaps ugly or
promiscuous) when he should have been at Mass.
9. You schemed to be a papal representative.
1. I and my King. Norfolk accuses Wolsey of putting himself before the King and of making the King his dependent. Technically, however, the Latin word order is correct
and means "my King and I," thus making it less offensive.
2. Allowed to produce half groats and half pennies with
his insignia in his home diocese of York, Wolsey had his
cardinal's hat stamped on a groat, thereby usurping the
King's monopoly on coins of larger denominations.

SUFFOLK   Lord Cardinal, the King's further pleasure is—
      Because all those things you have done of late,
340   By your power legantine within this kingdom,
      Fall into th' compass of a praemunire³—
      That therefore such a writ be sued° against you,   served
      To forfeit all your goods, lands, tenements,
      Chattels,° and whatsoever, and to be   Personal property
345   Out of the King's protection. This is my charge.
NORFOLK [to WOLSEY]   And so we'll leave you to your meditations
      How to live better. For your stubborn answer
      About the giving back the great seal to us,
      The King shall know it and, no doubt, shall thank you.
350   So fare you well, my little good lord Cardinal. *Exeunt all but* WOLSEY
CARDINAL WOLSEY   So farewell—to the little good you bear me.
      Farewell, a long farewell, to all my greatness!
      This is the state of man. Today he puts forth
      The tender leaves of hopes; tomorrow blossoms,
355   And bears his blushing° honours thick upon him;   resplendent
      The third day comes a frost, a killing frost,
      And when he thinks, good easy° man, full surely   trusting
      His greatness is a-ripening, nips his root,
      And then he falls, as I do. I have ventured,
360   Like little wanton boys that swim on bladders,⁴
      This many summers in a sea of glory,
      But far beyond my depth; my high-blown pride
      At length broke under me, and now has left me
      Weary, and old with service, to the mercy
365   Of a rude stream° that must for ever hide me.   turbulent current
      Vain pomp and glory of this world, I hate ye!
      I feel my heart new opened. O, how wretched
      Is that poor man that hangs on princes' favours!
      There is betwixt that smile we would aspire to,
370   That sweet aspect of princes, and their ruin,⁵
      More pangs and fears than wars or women have,
      And when he falls, he falls like Lucifer,°   (from heaven to hell)
      Never to hope again.
                  Enter CROMWELL, [*who then*] *stand*[*s*] *amazed*
                              Why, how now, Cromwell?
CROMWELL   I have no power to speak, sir.
CARDINAL WOLSEY   What, amazed
375   At my misfortunes? Can thy spirit wonder
      A great man should decline?°   fall from power
            [CROMWELL *begins to weep*]
                              Nay, an° you weep   if
      I am fall'n indeed.
CROMWELL   How does your grace?
CARDINAL WOLSEY   Why, well—
      Never so truly happy, my good Cromwell.
      I know myself now, and I feel within me

---

3. Having made himself a papal legate, Wolsey is subject to punishment because he has broken the law of
praemunire—that is, he has appealed to an outside
(here, papal) court when the offense fell under the
jurisdiction of English courts. Wolsey is thus charged

with elevating the Pope's authority over his sovereign's.
4. Like frolicsome little boys who stay afloat (only by)
using inflated membranes from an animal's body.
5. *their ruin:* the destruction they cause.

380 A peace above all earthly dignities,
A still and quiet conscience. The King has cured me.
I humbly thank his grace, and from these shoulders,
These ruined pillars,⁶ out of pity, taken
A load would sink a navy—too much honour.
385 O, 'tis a burden, Cromwell, 'tis a burden
Too heavy for a man that hopes for heaven.
CROMWELL   I am glad your grace has made that right use of it.
CARDINAL WOLSEY   I hope I have. I am able now, methinks,
Out of a fortitude of soul I feel,
390 To endure more miseries and greater far
Than my weak-hearted enemies dare offer.
What news abroad?
CROMWELL   The heaviest and the worst
Is your displeasure° with the King.   *disgrace*
CARDINAL WOLSEY   God bless him.
CROMWELL   The next is that Sir Thomas More is chosen
Lord Chancellor in your place.
395 CARDINAL WOLSEY   That's somewhat sudden.
But he's a learnèd man. May he continue
Long in his highness' favour, and do justice
For truth's sake and his conscience, that his bones,
When he has run his course and sleeps in blessings,
400 May have a tomb of orphans' tears wept on him.⁷
What more?
CROMWELL   That Cranmer is returned° with welcome,   *(from the Continent)*
Installed lord Archbishop of Canterbury.⁸
CARDINAL WOLSEY   That's news indeed.
CROMWELL   Last, that the Lady Anne,
Whom the King hath in secrecy long married,
405 This day was viewed in open as his queen,
Going to chapel, and the voice° is now   *gossip*
Only about her coronation.
CARDINAL WOLSEY   There was the weight that pulled me down.
     O, Cromwell,
The King has gone beyond° me. All my glories   *overreached*
410 In° that one woman I have lost for ever.   *Due to*
No sun shall ever usher forth mine honours,
Or gild again the noble troops° that waited   *retainers*
Upon my smiles. Go, get thee from me, Cromwell.
I am a poor fall'n man, unworthy now
415 To be thy lord and master. Seek the King—
That sun I pray may never set—I have told him
What and how true thou art. He will advance thee.
Some little memory of me will stir him.
I know his noble nature not to let
420 Thy hopeful service perish too. Good Cromwell,
Neglect him not. Make use° now, and provide   *Seize your chance*
For thine own future safety.
CROMWELL [*weeping*]   O, my lord,
Must I then leave you? Must I needs forgo°   *renounce*

6. Perhaps the pillars carried during Wolsey's triumphal entrance in 2.4.
7. The Lord Chancellor's duties included guardianship of all children under twenty-one, particularly

orphans. Henry had More beheaded in 1535 for his
Catholicism.
8. In 1533; Cranmer was beheaded by Henry's oldest
daughter, Queen Mary, in 1556 for his Protestantism.

So good, so noble, and so true a master?
425   Bear witness, all that have not hearts of iron,
With what a sorrow Cromwell leaves his lord.
The King shall have my service, but my prayers
For ever and for ever shall be yours.
CARDINAL WOLSEY [*weeping*]   Cromwell, I did not think to shed a tear
430   In all my miseries, but thou hast forced me,
Out of thy honest truth, to play the woman.°   *to weep*
Let's dry our eyes, and thus far hear me, Cromwell,
And when I am forgotten, as I shall be,
And sleep in dull cold marble, where no mention
435   Of me more must be heard of, say I taught thee—
Say Wolsey, that once trod the ways of glory,
And sounded° all the depths and shoals of honour,   *fathomed*
Found thee a way, out of his wreck,° to rise in,   *shipwreck*
A sure and safe one, though thy master missed it.
440   Mark but my fall, and that that ruined me.
Cromwell, I charge thee, fling away ambition.⁹
By that sin fell the angels. How can man, then,
The image of his maker, hope to win° by it?   *profit*
Love thyself last. Cherish those hearts that hate thee.
445   Corruption wins not more than honesty.
Still° in thy right hand carry gentle peace   *Ever*
To silence envious tongues. Be just, and fear not.
Let all the ends thou aim'st at be thy country's,
Thy God's, and truth's. Then if thou fall'st, O Cromwell,
450   Thou fall'st a blessèd martyr.¹
Serve the King. And prithee, lead me in—
There take an inventory of all I have:
To the last penny 'tis the King's. My robe,
And my integrity to heaven, is all
455   I dare now call mine own. O Cromwell, Cromwell,
Had I but served my God with half the zeal
I served my King, He would not in mine age
Have left me naked° to mine enemies.   *utterly exposed*
CROMWELL   Good sir, have patience.
CARDINAL WOLSEY   So I have. Farewell
460   The hopes of court; my hopes in heaven do dwell.   *Exeunt*

4.1

Enter [the] two GENTLEMEN *meeting one another. [The
first holds a paper]*
FIRST GENTLEMAN   You're well met once again.¹
SECOND GENTLEMAN   So are you.
FIRST GENTLEMAN   You come to take your stand here and behold
The Lady Anne pass from her coronation?
SECOND GENTLEMAN   'Tis all my business. At our last encounter
5   The Duke of Buckingham came from his trial.
FIRST GENTLEMAN   'Tis very true. But that time offered sorrow,
This, general joy.
SECOND GENTLEMAN   'Tis well. The citizens,

---

9. Cromwell did not take Wolsey's advice; Henry had
him beheaded in 1540 for treason and heresy after an
even more rapid rise and fall than Wolsey's.
1. As Cromwell was sometimes thought to be in

Shakespeare's time.
4.1 Location: A street in Westminster.
1. See 2.1.

I am sure, have shown at full their royal minds°—   *royalist allegiance*
As, let 'em have their rights, they are ever forward²—
10 In celebration of this day with shows,
Pageants, and sights of honour.
FIRST GENTLEMAN   Never greater,
Nor, I'll assure you, better taken,° sir.   *received*
SECOND GENTLEMAN   May I be bold to ask what that contains,
That paper in your hand?
FIRST GENTLEMAN   Yes, 'tis the list
15 Of those that claim their offices this day
By custom of the coronation.
The Duke of Suffolk is the first, and claims
To be High Steward; next, the Duke of Norfolk,
He to be Earl Marshal. You may read the rest.
[He gives him the paper]
20 SECOND GENTLEMAN   I thank you, sir. Had I not known those customs,
I should have been beholden to your paper.
But I beseech you, what's become of Katherine,
The Princess Dowager? How goes her business?
FIRST GENTLEMAN   That I can tell you too. The Archbishop
25 Of Canterbury, accompanied with other
Learnèd and reverend fathers of his order,
Held a late° court at Dunstable, six miles off   *Recently held a*
From Ampthill, where the Princess lay;° to which   *resided*
She was often cited° by them, but appeared not.   *summoned*
30 And, to be short, for not appearance, and
The King's late scruple, by the main assent°   *consensus*
Of all these learnèd men, she was divorced,
And the late marriage made of none effect,°   *null*
Since which she was removed to Kimbolton,
Where she remains now sick.
35 SECOND GENTLEMAN   Alas, good lady!
[Flourish of trumpets within]
The trumpets sound. Stand close.° The Queen is coming.   *aside*
*[Enter the coronation procession, which] pass[es] over
the stage in order and state. Hautboys [within,
play during the procession]*

THE ORDER OF THE CORONATION

1. [First, enter] trumpet[ers, who play] a lively flourish.
2. Then, [enter] two judges.
3. [Then, enter the] LORD CHANCELLOR, *with [both the]
purse [containing the great seal] and [the] mace [borne]
before him.*
*4. [Then, enter] choristers singing; [with them,]
music[ians playing.]*
*5. [Then, enter the Lord] Mayor of London bearing the
mace, [followed by] Garter [King-of-Arms° wearing] his*   *chief herald*
coat of arms and a gilt copper crown.
*6. [Then, enter] Marquis Dorset bearing a sceptre of
gold, [and wearing,] on his head, a demi-coronal of
gold [and, about his neck, a collar of esses].³ With him*

---

2. As, to give them their due, they are always eager to
demonstrate.

3. Heavy gold chain made of S-shaped links worn
around the neck by men of high office.

[enter] the Earl of SURREY bearing the rod of silver with
the dove, crowned with an earl's coronet, [and also wearing a] collar of esses.
7. [Next, enter the] Duke of SUFFOLK as High Steward,
in his robe of estate, [with] his coronet on his head,
[and] bearing a long white wand. With him, [enter] the
Duke of NORFOLK with the rod of marshalship [and] a
coronet on his head. [Each wears a] collar of esses.
8. [Then,] under a canopy borne by four [barons] of
the Cinque Ports,⁴ [enter] ANNE, the [new] Queen, in
her robe. Her hair, [which hangs loose,° is] richly   (a bridal custom)
adorned with pearl. [She wears a] crown. [Accompany-
ing] her on [either] side [are] the Bishops of London
and Winchester.
9. [Next, enter] the old Duchess of Norfolk, in a coronal
of gold wrought with flowers, bearing the Queen's train.
10. [Finally, enter] certain ladies or countesses, with
plain circlets of gold without flowers.
[The two GENTLEMEN comment on the procession as it
passes over the stage]

SECOND GENTLEMAN   A royal train,° believe me. These I know.   procession
Who's that that bears the sceptre?
FIRST GENTLEMAN   Marquis Dorset.
And that, the Earl of Surrey with the rod.
40   SECOND GENTLEMAN   A bold brave gentleman. That should be
The Duke of Suffolk?
FIRST GENTLEMAN   'Tis the same: High Steward.
SECOND GENTLEMAN   And that, my lord of Norfolk?
FIRST GENTLEMAN   Yes.
SECOND GENTLEMAN [seeing ANNE]   Heaven bless thee!
Thou hast the sweetest face I ever looked on.
Sir, as I have a soul, she is an angel.
45   Our King has all the Indies⁵ in his arms,
And more, and richer, when he strains° that lady.   embraces
I cannot blame his conscience.
FIRST GENTLEMAN   They that bear
The cloth of honour° over her are four barons   canopy
Of the Cinque Ports.
50   SECOND GENTLEMAN   Those men are happy,
And so are all° are near her.   all who
I take it she that carries up the train
Is that old noble lady, Duchess of Norfolk.
FIRST GENTLEMAN   It is. And all the rest are countesses.
55   SECOND GENTLEMAN   Their coronets say so. These are stars indeed—
FIRST GENTLEMAN   And sometimes falling ones.°   meteors; (sexual)
SECOND GENTLEMAN   No more of that.

Exit [the last of the procession,] and then
a great flourish of trumpets [within]
Enter a third GENTLEMAN [in a sweat]

FIRST GENTLEMAN   God save you, sir. Where have you been broiling?°   overheating
THIRD GENTLEMAN   Among the crowd i'th'Abbey, where a finger

---

4. By traditional prerogative, the barons of the Cinque
Ports (Hastings, Sandwich, Dover, Romney, and Hythe
on the southeast coast of England) carried a canopy
over the sovereign at state occasions.
5. The East and West Indies were considered sources
of great wealth. See 1.1.21.

Could not be wedged in more. I am stifled
60   With the mere rankness° of their joy.   *exuberance; odor*
SECOND GENTLEMAN   You saw the ceremony?
THIRD GENTLEMAN   That I did.
FIRST GENTLEMAN   How was it?
THIRD GENTLEMAN   Well worth the seeing.
SECOND GENTLEMAN   Good sir, speak° it to us.   *describe*
THIRD GENTLEMAN   As well as I am able. The rich stream
65   Of lords and ladies, having brought the Queen
To a prepared place in the choir,° fell off°   *company / drew back*
A distance from her, while her grace sat down
To rest a while—some half an hour or so—
In a rich chair of state, opposing° freely   *displaying*
70   The beauty of her person to the people.
Believe me, sir, she is the goodliest° woman   *fairest*
That ever lay by man; which when the people
Had the full view of, such a noise arose
As the shrouds° make at sea in a stiff tempest,   *ship's rigging*
75   As loud and to as many tunes. Hats, cloaks—
Doublets,° I think—flew up, and had their faces   *Short jackets*
Been loose, this day they had been lost. Such joy
I never saw before. Great-bellied women,
That had not half a week to go, like rams°   *battering rams*
80   In the old time of war, would shake the press,°   *crowd*
And make 'em reel before 'em. No man living
Could say 'This is my wife' there, all were woven
So strangely in one piece.
SECOND GENTLEMAN   But what followed?
THIRD GENTLEMAN   At length her grace rose, and with modest paces
85   Came to the altar, where she kneeled, and saint-like
Cast her fair eyes to heaven, and prayed devoutly,
Then rose again, and bowed her to the people,
When by the Archbishop of Canterbury
She had all the royal makings° of a queen,   *essential trappings*
90   As holy oil, Edward Confessor's crown,
The rod and bird of peace, and all such emblems
Laid nobly on her. Which performed, the choir,
With all the choicest music° of the kingdom,   *musicians*
Together sung *Te Deum*.[6] So she parted,°   *departed*
95   And with the same full state° paced back again   *ceremony*
To York Place, where the feast is held.
FIRST GENTLEMAN   Sir,
You must no more call it York Place—that's past,
For since the Cardinal fell, that title's lost.
'Tis now the King's, and called Whitehall.
THIRD GENTLEMAN   I know it,
100   But 'tis so lately altered that the old name
Is fresh about me.
SECOND GENTLEMAN   What two reverend bishops
Were those that went on each side of the Queen?
THIRD GENTLEMAN   Stokesley and Gardiner, the one of Winchester—

---

6. Hymn of praise and thanksgiving beginning *"Te Deum laudamus,"* "We praise thee, O Lord."

Newly preferred° from the King's secretary—   *promoted*
The other London.[7]

105 SECOND GENTLEMAN   He of Winchester
Is held no great good lover of the Archbishop's,
The virtuous Cranmer.

THIRD GENTLEMAN   All the land knows that.
However, yet there is no great breach. When it comes,
Cranmer will find a friend will not° shrink from him.   *who will not*

SECOND GENTLEMAN   Who may that be, I pray you?

110 THIRD GENTLEMAN   Thomas Cromwell,
A man in much esteem with th' King, and truly
A worthy friend. The King has made him
Master o'th' Jewel House,
And one already of the Privy Council.

SECOND GENTLEMAN   He will deserve more.

115 THIRD GENTLEMAN   Yes, without all doubt.
Come, gentlemen, ye shall go my way,
Which is to th' court, and there ye shall be my guests.
Something° I can command. As I walk thither   *Some influence*
I'll tell ye more.

FIRST *and* SECOND GENTLEMEN   You may command us, sir.

Exeunt

4.2

[*Three chairs.*] *Enter* KATHERINE *Dowager, sick, led
between* GRIFFITH *her gentleman usher, and* PATIENCE
her woman

GRIFFITH   How does your grace?

KATHERINE   O Griffith, sick to death.
My legs, like loaden° branches, bow to th' earth,   *heavily laden*
Willing to leave their burden. Reach a chair.
[*A chair is brought to her. She sits*]
So now, methinks, I feel a little ease.
5 Didst thou not tell me, Griffith, as thou led'st me,
That the great child of honour,° Cardinal Wolsey,   *(ironic)*
Was dead?

GRIFFITH   Yes, madam, but I think your grace,
Out of the pain you suffered, gave no ear to't.

KATHERINE   Prithee, good Griffith, tell me how he died.
10 If well, he stepped before me happily°   *aptly*
For my example.

GRIFFITH   Well, the voice° goes, madam.   *talk*
For after the stout Earl Northumberland
Arrested him at York, and brought him forward,
As a man sorely tainted,° to his answer,°   *disgraced / hearing*
15 He fell sick, suddenly, and grew so ill
He could not sit his mule.

KATHERINE   Alas, poor man.

GRIFFITH   At last, with easy roads,° he came to Leicester,   *stages of a journey*
Lodged in the abbey, where the reverend abbot,
With all his convent,° honourably received him,   *monastery*

7. John Stokesley was Bishop of London; already secretary to the King, Gardiner also became Bishop of

Winchester following Wolsey's demise.
4.2 Location: Katherine's apartments in Kimbolton.

20   To whom he gave these words: 'O father abbot,
             An old man broken with the storms of state
             Is come to lay his weary bones among ye.
             Give him a little earth,° for charity.'   *a resting place*
             So went to bed, where eagerly his sickness
25   Pursued him still, and three nights after this,
             About the hour of eight, which he himself
             Foretold should be his last, full of repentance,
             Continual meditations, tears, and sorrows,
             He gave his honours to the world again,
30   His blessèd part° to heaven, and slept in peace.   *soul*
     KATHERINE   So may he rest, his faults lie gently on him.
             Yet thus far, Griffith, give me leave to speak° him,   *describe*
             And yet with charity. He was a man
             Of an unbounded stomach,° ever ranking   *ambition*
35   Himself with princes; one that by suggestion°   *underhanded dealing*
             Tied° all the kingdom. Simony[1] was fair play.   *Shackled*
             His own opinion was his law. I'th' presence°   *King's chamber*
             He would say untruths, and be ever double°   *duplicitious*
             Both in his words and meaning. He was never,
40   But where he meant to ruin, pitiful.°   *merciful*
             His promises were, as he then was, mighty;
             But his performance, as he is now, nothing.
             Of his own body he was ill,° and gave   *sexually immoral*
             The clergy ill example.
     GRIFFITH   Noble madam,
45   Men's evil manners live in brass, their virtues
             We write in water.[2] May it please your highness
             To hear me speak his good now?
     KATHERINE   Yes, good Griffith,
             I were malicious else.
     GRIFFITH   This cardinal,
             Though from an humble stock, undoubtedly
50   Was fashioned to much honour. From his cradle
             He was a scholar, and a ripe and good one,
             Exceeding wise, fair-spoken, and persuading;°   *persuasive*
             Lofty and sour to them that loved him not,
             But to those men that sought him,° sweet as summer.   *befriended him*
55   And though he were unsatisfied° in getting°—   *insatiable / (riches)*
             Which was a sin—yet in bestowing, madam,
             He was most princely: ever witness for him
             Those twins of learning that he raised° in you,   *set up*
             Ipswich and Oxford[3]—one of which fell with him,
60   Unwilling to outlive the good that did it;
             The other, though unfinished, yet so famous,
             So excellent in art,° and still so rising,   *scholarship*
             That Christendom shall ever speak his virtue.
             His overthrow heaped happiness upon him,
65   For then, and not till then, he felt° himself,   *recognized*
             And found the blessèdness of being little.°   *humble*

---

1. Trading, for money or favors, in ecclesiastical offices.
2. *Men's . . . water:* Evil deeds are long remembered, good ones soon forgotten (proverbial).
3. Wolsey founded colleges at Ipswich and Oxford; the latter survives as Christ Church.

　　　　And to add greater honours to his age
　　　　Than man could give him, he died fearing God.
　　KATHERINE　After my death I wish no other herald,
70　　No other speaker of my living actions
　　　　To keep mine honour from corruption
　　　　But such an honest chronicler as Griffith.
　　　　Whom I most hated living,° thou hast made me,　　　　　　*while alive*
　　　　With thy religious truth and modesty,°　　　　　　　　　　*equanimity*
75　　Now in his ashes honour. Peace be with him.
　　　　[*To her woman*] Patience, be near me still, and set me lower.
　　　　I have not long to trouble thee. Good Griffith,
　　　　Cause the musicians play me that sad note°　　　　　　　*melody*
　　　　I named my knell, whilst I sit meditating
80　　On that celestial harmony I go to.[4]
　　　　　　Sad and solemn music. [KATHERINE *sleeps*]
　　GRIFFITH [*to the woman*]　She is asleep. Good wench, let's sit down quiet
　　For fear we wake her. Softly, gentle Patience.
　　　　　　[*They sit*]

　　　　　　　　　THE VISION

　　　Enter, solemnly tripping one after another, six person-
　　　ages clad in white robes, wearing on their heads gar-
　　　lands of bays, and golden visors on their faces.[5] [*They*
　　　carry] *branches of bays or palm in their hands. They first*
　　　congé° unto [KATHERINE], *then dance; and, at certain*　　　*bow*
　　　changes,° the first two hold a spare garland over her　　*dance movements*
　　　head at which the other four make reverent curtsies.
　　　Then the two that held the garland deliver the same to
　　　the other next two, who observe the same order in their
　　　changes and holding the garland over her head. Which
　　　done, they deliver the same garland to the last two who
　　　likewise observe the same order. At which, as it were by
　　　inspiration, she makes in her sleep signs of rejoicing, and
　　　holdeth up her hands to heaven. And so in their dancing
　　　vanish, carrying the garland with them. The music con-
　　　tinues

　　KATHERINE [*waking*]　Spirits of peace, where are ye? Are ye all gone,
　　　　And leave me here in wretchedness behind ye?
　　　　　　[GRIFFITH *and* PATIENCE *rise and come forward*]
　　GRIFFITH　Madam, we are here.
85　　KATHERINE　　　　　　　　　　　　It is not you I call for.
　　　　Saw ye none enter since I slept?
　　GRIFFITH　　　　　　　　　　　None, madam.
　　KATHERINE　No? Saw you not even now a blessèd troop
　　　　Invite me to a banquet, whose bright faces
　　　　Cast thousand beams upon me, like the sun?
90　　They promised me eternal happiness,
　　　　And brought me garlands, Griffith, which I feel
　　　　I am not worthy yet to wear. I shall,
　　　　Assuredly.

　　4. After death, the soul supposedly could hear the　　　5. White to signify purity; bay leaves ("bays") to indi-
　　music of the spheres (the heavenly bodies) as they　　cate triumph or joy; golden masks ("visors") perhaps to
　　revolved around the earth.　　　　　　　　　　　　　　suggest they are spirits.

GRIFFITH   I am most joyful, madam, such good dreams
　　　Possess your fancy.°　　　　　　　　　　　　　　　*Fill your imagination*

95　KATHERINE　　　　　　Bid the music° leave.　　　　　　*musicians*
　　　They are harsh and heavy° to me.　　　　　　　　　*tiresome*

　　　Music ceases

PATIENCE [*to* GRIFFITH]　　　　　Do you note
　　　How much her grace is altered on the sudden?
　　　How long her face is drawn? How pale she looks,
　　　And of an earthy colour? Mark her eyes?

GRIFFITH　She is going, wench. Pray, pray.

100　PATIENCE　　　　　　　　　　Heaven comfort her.

　　　Enter a MESSENGER

MESSENGER [*to* KATHERINE]
　　　An't like° your grace—　　　　　　　　　　　　　*If it please*

KATHERINE　　　　　　　You are a saucy fellow—
　　　Deserve we no more reverence?

GRIFFITH [*to the* MESSENGER]　　　You are to blame,
　　　Knowing she will not lose her wonted° greatness,　*forgo her usual*
　　　To use so rude behaviour. Go to, kneel.

MESSENGER [*kneeling before* KATHERINE]　I humbly do entreat
105　　　　your highness' pardon.
　　　My haste made me unmannerly. There is staying°　*waiting*
　　　A gentleman sent from the King to see you.

KATHERINE　Admit him entrance, Griffith. But this fellow
　　　Let me ne'er see again.　　　　　　　*Exit* MESSENGER

　　　　　Enter Lord CAPUTIUS [*ushered by* GRIFFITH]
　　　　　　　　　If my sight fail not,
110　You should be lord ambassador from the Emperor,°　*Charles V*
　　　My royal nephew, and your name Caputius.

CAPUTIUS　Madam, the same, [*bowing*] your servant.

KATHERINE　　　　　　　　　　O, my lord,
　　　The times and titles now are altered strangely
　　　With me since first you knew me. But I pray you,
　　　What is your pleasure with me?

115　CAPUTIUS　　　　　　　　Noble lady,
　　　First mine own service to your grace; the next,
　　　The King's request that I would visit you,
　　　Who grieves much for your weakness, and by me
　　　Sends you his princely commendations,°　　　　*compliments*
120　And heartily entreats you take good comfort.

KATHERINE　O, my good lord, that comfort comes too late,
　　　'Tis like a pardon after execution.
　　　That gentle physic,° given in time, had cured me;　*medicine*
　　　But now I am past all comforts here but prayers.
　　　How does his highness?

125　CAPUTIUS　　　　　　Madam, in good health.

KATHERINE　So may he ever do, and ever flourish
　　　When I shall dwell with worms, and my poor name
　　　Banished the kingdom. [*To her woman*] Patience, is that letter
　　　I caused you write yet sent away?

PATIENCE　　　　　　　No, madam.

130　KATHERINE [*to* CAPUTIUS]　Sir, I most humbly pray you to deliver
　　　This to my lord the King.

　　　　　[*The letter is given to* CAPUTIUS]

CAPUTIUS   Most willing,° madam.   *willingly*

KATHERINE   In which I have commended to his goodness
   The model° of our chaste loves, his young daughter⁶—   *image*
   The dews of heaven fall thick in blessings on her—
135   Beseeching him to give her virtuous breeding.°   *raise her virtuously*
   She is young, and of a noble modest nature.
   I hope she will deserve well—and a little
   To love her for her mother's sake, that loved him,
   Heaven knows how dearly. My next poor petition
140   Is that his noble grace would have some pity
   Upon my wretched women, that so long
   Have followed both my fortunes° faithfully;   *(good and bad)*
   Of which there is not one, I dare avow—
   And now I should not lie⁷—but will deserve,
145   For virtue and true beauty of the soul,
   For honesty° and decent carriage,°   *chastity / conduct*
   A right good husband. Let him be a noble,
   And sure those men are happy that shall have 'em.
   The last is for my men—they are the poorest,
150   But poverty could never draw 'em from me—
   That they may have their wages duly paid 'em,
   And something over to remember me by.
   If heaven had pleased to have given me longer life,
   And able° means, we had not parted thus.   *sufficient*
155   These are the whole contents; and, good my lord,
   By that you love the dearest in this world,
   As you wish Christian peace to souls departed,
   Stand these poor people's friend and urge the King
   To do me this last rite.°   *(also) right*

CAPUTIUS   By heaven I will,
160   Or let me lose the fashion of a man.°   *forfeit my humanity*

KATHERINE   I thank you, honest lord. Remember me
   In all humility unto his highness.
   Say his long trouble now is passing
   Out of this world. Tell him, in death I blessed him,
165   For so I will. Mine eyes grow dim. Farewell,
   My lord. Griffith, farewell.
   [*To her woman*]   Nay, Patience,
   You must not leave me yet. I must to bed.
   Call in more women. When I am dead, good wench,
   Let me be used° with honour. Strew me over   *treated*
170   With maiden° flowers, that all the world may know   *(signifying chastity)*
   I was a chaste wife to my grave. Embalm me,
   Then lay me forth.° Although unqueened, yet like   *prepare me for burial*
   A queen and daughter to a king inter me.
   I can° no more.   *can say or do*

                    Exeunt [CAPUTIUS *and* GRIFFITH *at one door;*
                    PATIENCE] *leading* KATHERINE [*at another*]

---

6. Mary was Katherine and Henry's only child who survived infancy (see 2.4.35 and note). She was Queen for five years (1553–58) before Elizabeth, her half sister.

7. Now, on the point of death, I would not (ought not to) lie. It was generally thought that people spoke truth on their deathbeds.

5.1

Enter [at one door] GARDINER, *Bishop of Winchester;*
before him, a PAGE *with a torch*

GARDINER   It's one o'clock, boy, is't not?

PAGE   It hath struck.

GARDINER   These should be hours for necessities,
Not for delights; times to repair° our nature   restore
With comforting repose, and not for us
To waste these times.

        [Enter at another door] Sir Thomas LOVELL *[meeting*
        them]

5   Good hour of night, Sir Thomas!
Whither so late?

LOVELL   Came you from the King, my lord?

GARDINER   I did, Sir Thomas, and left him at primero°   *a card game*
With the Duke of Suffolk.

LOVELL   I must to him too,
Before he go to bed. I'll take my leave.

10   GARDINER   Not yet, Sir Thomas Lovell—what's the matter?
It seems you are in haste. An if there be
No great offence° belongs to't, give your friend   *inappropriateness*
Some touch° of your late business. Affairs that walk,   *hint*
As they say spirits do, at midnight, have
15   In them a wilder nature than the business
That seeks dispatch° by day.   *to be done*

LOVELL   My lord, I love you,
And durst commend° a secret to your ear   *entrust*
Much weightier than this work.° The Queen's in labour—   *my affairs*
They say in great extremity—and feared°   *it is feared that*
She'll with the labour end.

20   GARDINER   The fruit she goes with
I pray for heartily, that it may find
Good time,° and live. But, for the stock,° Sir Thomas,   *Fortune / trunk (Anne)*
I wish it grubbed up° now.   *rooted out*

LOVELL   Methinks I could
Cry the amen,° and yet my conscience says   *Agree*
25   She's a good creature and, sweet lady, does
Deserve our better wishes.

GARDINER   But sir, sir,
Hear me, Sir Thomas. You're a gentleman
Of mine own way.[1] I know you wise, religious.
And let me tell you, it will ne'er be well—
30   'Twill not, Sir Thomas Lovell, take't of me—
Till Cranmer, Cromwell—her two hands—and she,
Sleep in their graves.

LOVELL   Now, sir, you speak of two
The most remarked° i'th' kingdom. As for Cromwell,   *regarded*
Beside that of the Jewel House is made Master
35   O'th' Rolls and the King's secretary. Further, sir,
Stands in the gap and trade° of more preferments   *open road*
With which the time will load him. Th'Archbishop

5.1 Location: London, a gallery at court.
1. Of my religious persuasion (Catholicism, as opposed to Anne's Lutheranism).

Is the King's hand and tongue, and who dare speak
One syllable against him?

GARDINER   Yes, yes, Sir Thomas—
40   There are that dare, and I myself have ventured
To speak my mind of him, and, indeed, this day,
Sir—I may tell it you, I think—I have
Incensed° the lords o'th' Council that he is—   °Angered
For so I know he is, they know he is—
45   A most arch heretic, a pestilence
That does infect the land; with which they, moved,°   °angered
Have broken with° the King, who hath so far   °revealed to
Given ear to our complaint, of his great grace
And princely care, foreseeing those fell mischiefs
50   Our reasons laid before him, hath° commanded   °that he has
Tomorrow morning to the Council board
He be convented.° He's a rank° weed, Sir Thomas,   °summoned / rotten
And we must root him out. From your affairs
I hinder you too long. Good night, Sir Thomas.
55   LOVELL   Many good nights, my lord; I rest° your servant.   °remain
                    Exeunt GARDINER and PAGE [at one door]
          Enter KING [HENRY] and SUFFOLK [at another door]
KING HENRY [to SUFFOLK]   Charles, I will play no more tonight.
My mind's not on't. You are too hard° for me.   °skillful
SUFFOLK   Sir, I did never win of you before.
KING HENRY   But little, Charles,
60   Nor shall not when my fancy's° on my play.   °attention is
Now, Lovell, from the Queen what is the news?
LOVELL   I could not personally deliver to her
What you commanded me, but by her woman
I sent your message, who returned her thanks
65   In the great'st humbleness, and desired your highness
Most heartily to pray for her.
KING HENRY   What sayst thou? Ha?
To pray for her? What, is she crying out?
LOVELL   So said her woman, and that her suffrance° made   °suffering
Almost each pang a death.
KING HENRY   Alas, good lady.
70   SUFFOLK   God safely quit° her of her burden, and   °release
With gentle travail,° to the gladding° of   °labor / making joyful
Your highness with an heir.
KING HENRY   'Tis midnight, Charles.
Prithee to bed, and in thy prayers remember
Th'estate° of my poor queen. Leave me alone,   °condition
75   For I must think of that which company
Would not be friendly to.²
SUFFOLK   I wish your highness
A quiet night, and my good mistress will°   °I will
Remember in my prayers.
KING HENRY   Charles, good night.   Exit SUFFOLK
          Enter Sir Anthony DENNY
Well, sir, what follows?
80   DENNY   Sir, I have brought my lord the Archbishop,
As you commanded me.

2. which . . . to: which requires privacy.

KING HENRY   Ha, Canterbury?
DENNY   Ay, my good lord.
KING HENRY   'Tis true—where is he, Denny?
DENNY   He attends your highness' pleasure.
KING HENRY   Bring him to us.
                                        [*Exit* DENNY]
LOVELL [*aside*]   This is about that which the Bishop° spake.   Gardiner
85   I am happily° come hither.   fortunately
              Enter CRANMER [*the Archbishop, ushered by*] DENNY
KING HENRY [*to* LOVELL *and* DENNY]   Avoid° the gallery.   Quit
              [DENNY *begins to depart.*] LOVELL *seems to stay*
     Ha? I have said. Be gone.
     What?   *Exeunt* LOVELL *and* DENNY
CRANMER [*aside*]   I am fearful. Wherefore° frowns he thus?   Why
     'Tis his aspect° of terror. All's not well.   countenance
90   KING HENRY   How now, my lord? You do desire to know
     Wherefore I sent for you.
CRANMER [*kneeling*]   It is my duty
     T'attend your highness' pleasure.
KING HENRY   Pray you, arise,
     My good and gracious Lord of Canterbury.
     Come, you and I must walk a turn together.
95   I have news to tell you. Come, come—give me your hand.
              [CRANMER *rises. They walk*]
     Ah, my good lord, I grieve at what I speak,
     And am right sorry to repeat what follows.
     I have, and most unwillingly, of late
     Heard many grievous°—I do say, my lord,   serious
100 Grievous—complaints of you, which, being considered,
     Have moved us and our Council that you shall
     This morning come before us, where I know
     You cannot with such freedom purge° yourself   with ease clear
     But that, till further trial in those charges
105 Which will require your answer, you must take
     Your patience to you,[3] and be well contented
     To make your house our Tower. You a brother of us,°   a fellow councillor
     It fits we thus proceed, or else no witness
     Would come against you.
CRANMER [*kneeling*]   I humbly thank your highness,
110 And am right glad to catch this good occasion
     Most throughly to be winnowed, where my chaff
     And corn shall fly asunder.[4] For I know
     There's none stands under° more calumnious tongues   is subject to
     Than I myself, poor man.
KING HENRY   Stand up, good Canterbury.
115 Thy truth and thy integrity is rooted
     In us, thy friend. Give me thy hand. Stand up.
     Prithee, let's walk.
              [CRANMER *rises. They walk*]
                    Now, by my halidom,°   by our Lady
     What manner of man are you? My lord, I looked°   predicted

---

3. *must . . . you:* must be patient.
4. *And am . . . asunder:* And I am glad to have the occasion thoroughly to see the bad ("chaff") separated from

the good ("corn," or wheat) in my character. See
Matthew 3:12 and Luke 3:17.

You would have given me your petition that
120   I should have ta'en some pains to bring together
Yourself and your accusers, and to have heard you
Without indurance° further.   *imprisonment*
CRANMER   Most dread liege,
The good° I stand on is my truth and honesty.   *virtue*
If they shall fail, I with mine enemies
125   Will triumph o'er my person, which I weigh not,
Being of those virtues vacant.⁵ I fear nothing°   *not at all*
What can be said against me.
KING HENRY   Know you not
How your state stands i'th' world, with the whole world?
Your enemies are many, and not small;° their practices   *insignificant*
130   Must bear the same proportion, and not ever
The justice and the truth o'th' question carries
The dew o'th' verdict with it.⁶ At what ease°   *How easily*
Might corrupt minds procure knaves as corrupt
To swear against you? Such things have been done.
135   You are potently° opposed, and with a malice   *powerfully*
Of as great size. Ween you of ° better luck,   *Do you anticipate*
I mean in perjured witness,° than your master,°   *evidence / Christ*
Whose minister you are, whiles here he lived
Upon this naughty° earth? Go to, go to.   *wicked*
140   You take a precipice for no leap of danger,
And woo your own destruction.
CRANMER   God and your majesty
Protect mine innocence, or I fall into
The trap is° laid for me.   *that is*
KING HENRY   Be of good cheer.
They shall no more prevail than we give way to.°   *let them*
145   Keep comfort to you, and this morning see
You do appear before them. If they shall chance,
In charging you with matters, to commit° you,   *imprison*
The best persuasions to the contrary
Fail not to use, and with what vehemency
150   Th'occasion shall instruct you. If entreaties
Will render you no remedy, [*giving his ring*] this ring
Deliver them, and your appeal to us
There make before them.
        [CRANMER *weeps*]
                              Look, the good man weeps.
He's honest, on mine honour. God's blest mother,
155   I swear he is true-hearted, and a soul
None better in my kingdom. Get you gone,
And do as I have bid you.   *Exit* CRANMER
                    He has strangled
His language in his tears.
        Enter [*the*] OLD LADY
LOVELL (*within*)   Come back! What mean you?
        [*Enter* LOVELL, *following her*]
OLD LADY   I'll not come back. The tidings that I bring

---

5. *If . . . vacant:* If I lack truth and honesty, I will agree
with my enemies in condemning myself, whom I do not
value in the absence of truth and honesty.
6. *their . . . it:* their schemes are equally numerous and

powerful, and justice and truth do not always prevail.
"Dew" suggests fecundity or generosity; there may also
be a sense of "due," implying justness.

160   Will make my boldness manners.° [*To the* KING] Now good angels   *into manners*
    Fly o'er thy royal head, and shade thy person
    Under their blessèd wings.

KING HENRY   Now by thy looks
    I guess thy message. Is the Queen delivered?
    Say, 'Ay, and of a boy.'

OLD LADY   Ay, ay, my liege,
165   And of a lovely boy. The God of heaven
    Both now and ever bless her! 'Tis a girl°   *Anne; Elizabeth*
    Promises boys hereafter. Sir, your queen
    Desires your visitation, and° to be   *and for you*
    Acquainted with this stranger. 'Tis as like you
    As cherry is to cherry.

KING HENRY   Lovell—
170   LOVELL   Sir?
KING HENRY   Give her an hundred marks.° I'll to the Queen.   *roughly 65 pounds*

                                        Exit

OLD LADY   An hundred marks? By this light, I'll ha' more.
    An ordinary groom is for° such payment.   *deserves*
    I will have more, or scold it out of him.
175   Said I for this the girl was like to him? I'll
    Have more, or else unsay't; and now, while 'tis hot,
    I'll put it to the issue.   *Exeunt*

5.2

Enter [pursuivants,° pages, footboys, and grooms. Then   *messengers*
enter] CRANMER, *Archbishop of Canterbury*

CRANMER   I hope I am not too late, and yet the gentleman
    That was sent to me from the council prayed me
    To make great haste. All fast?° What means this? [*Calling at*   *The doors closed*
      the door] Ho!
    Who waits there?

        Enter [a DOOR]KEEPER
             Sure you know me?

DOORKEEPER   Yes, my lord,
    But yet I cannot help you.
5   CRANMER   Why?

      Enter Doctor BUTTS [*passing over the stage*]

DOORKEEPER   Your grace must wait till you be called for.
CRANMER   So.
BUTTS [*aside*]   This is a piece of malice. I am glad
    I came this way so happily.° The King   *fortunately*
    Shall understand it presently.°   *Exit*   *immediately*
CRANMER [*aside*]   'Tis Butts,
10   The King's physician. As he passed along
    How earnestly he cast his eyes upon me!
    Pray heaven he sound° not my disgrace. For certain   *fathom; publicize*
    This is of purpose laid° by some that hate me—   *carried out*
    God turn their hearts, I never sought their malice—
15   To quench° mine honour. They would shame to make me   *destroy*
    Wait else at door, a fellow Councillor,
    'Mong boys, grooms, and lackeys. But their pleasures
    Must be fulfilled, and I attend with patience.

5.2 Location: Anteroom and council chamber at court.

Enter KING [HENRY] *and* [*Doctor*] BUTTS *at a window,*
above

BUTTS   I'll show your grace the strangest sight—

KING HENRY   What's that, Butts?

20   BUTTS   I think your highness saw this many a day.

KING HENRY   Body o'me, where is it?

BUTTS [*pointing at* CRANMER, *below*]   There, my lord.
The high promotion of his grace of Canterbury,
Who holds his state° at door, 'mongst pursuivants,   waits with dignity
Pages, and footboys.

KING HENRY   Ha? 'Tis he indeed.

25   Is this the honour they do one another?
'Tis well there's one above 'em[1] yet. I had thought
They had parted° so much honesty among 'em—   shared
At least good manners—as not thus to suffer
A man of his place° and so near our favour   rank

30   To dance attendance on their lordships' pleasures,
And at the door, too, like a post with packets!°   courier with letters
By holy Mary, Butts, there's knavery!
Let 'em alone, and draw the curtain close.
We shall hear more anon.

[CRANMER *and the* DOORKEEPER *stand to one side.*
Exeunt the lackeys]
[*Above,* BUTTS *partly draws the curtain close. Below,*][2] *a*
council table [*is*] *brought in* [*along*] *with chairs and*
stools, and placed under the [*cloth of*] *state. Enter* [*the*]
LORD CHANCELLOR, [*who*] *places himself at the upper*
end of the table, on the left hand, [*leaving*] *a seat void*
above him [*at the table's head*] *as*° *for Canterbury's seat.*   as if
[*The*] *Duke of* SUFFOLK, [*the*] *Duke of* NORFOLK, [*the*
Earl of] SURREY, [*the*] LORD CHAMBERLAIN, [*and*] GARDI-
NER, [*the Bishop of Winchester,*] *seat themselves in order*
on each side [*of the table*]. CROMWELL [*sits*] *at* [*the*]
lower end, [*and acts*] *as secretary*

35   LORD CHANCELLOR [*to* CROMWELL]   Speak to the business, master secretary.
Why are we met in council?

CROMWELL   Please your honours,
The chief cause concerns his grace of Canterbury.

GARDINER   Has he had° knowledge of it?   been given

CROMWELL   Yes.

NORFOLK [*to the* DOORKEEPER]   Who waits there?

DOORKEEPER [*coming forward*]
Without,° my noble lords?   Outside

GARDINER   Yes.

DOORKEEPER   My lord Archbishop;

40   And has done half an hour, to know your pleasures.

LORD CHANCELLOR   Let him come in.

DOORKEEPER [*to* CRANMER]   Your grace may enter now.

CRANMER *approaches the Council table*

LORD CHANCELLOR   My good lord Archbishop, I'm very sorry
To sit here at this present° and behold   moment

---

1. Both God and King, here implicitly linked.
2. Some editions begin a new scene here. But Cranmer
should be visible throughout, and the King and Butts
stay sequestered in the gallery above the stage until the
King's abrupt entrance.

That chair stand empty, but we all are men
45 In our own natures frail, and capable°   *prone to failings*
Of our flesh; few are angels; out of which frailty
And want° of wisdom, you, that best should teach us,   *lack*
Have misdemeaned yourself,° and not a little,   *behaved badly*
Toward the King first, then his laws, in filling
50 The whole realm, by your teaching and your chaplains'—
For so we are informed—with new opinions,
Diverse and dangerous, which are heresies,
And, not reformed, may prove pernicious.°   *lethal*
GARDINER   Which reformation must be sudden too,
55 My noble lords; for those that tame wild horses
Pace 'em not in their hands to make 'em gentle,[3]
But stop their mouths with stubborn bits and spur 'em
Till they obey the manège.° If we suffer,°   *training / allow*
Out of our easiness° and childish pity   *leniency*
60 To one man's honour, this contagious sickness,
Farewell all physic°—and what follows then?   *remedies*
Commotions, uproars—with a general taint
Of the whole state, as of late days our neighbours,
The upper Germany, can dearly witness,[4]
65 Yet freshly pitied in our memories.
CRANMER   My good lords, hitherto in all the progress
Both of my life and office, I have laboured,
And with no little study,° that my teaching   *effort*
And the strong course of my authority
70 Might go one way, and safely; and the end
Was ever to do well. Nor is there living—
I speak it with a single° heart, my lords—   *pure*
A man that more detests, more stirs against,°   *actively resists*
Both in his private conscience and his place,°   *office*
75 Defacers° of a public peace than I do.   *Destroyers*
Pray heaven the King may never find a heart
With less allegiance in it. Men that make
Envy and crooked malice nourishment
Dare bite the best. I do beseech your lordships
80 That, in this case of justice, my accusers,
Be what they will,° may stand forth face to face,   *Whoever they are*
And freely urge against° me.   *openly accuse*
SUFFOLK   Nay, my lord,
That cannot be. You are a Councillor,
And by that virtue° no man dare accuse you.   *by virtue of that*
GARDINER [*to* CRANMER]   My lord, because we have business of
85   more moment,°   *import*
We will be short° with you. 'Tis his highness' pleasure   *brief*
And our consent, for better trial of you,
From hence you be committed to the Tower
Where, being but a private man again,
90 You shall know many dare accuse you boldly,
More than, I fear, you are provided for.°   *ready for*
CRANMER   Ah, my good lord of Winchester, I thank you.
You are always my good friend. If your will pass,°   *is approved*

3. Do not put them through their paces with only a hand for restraint.
4. Alluding to Protestant sects in Germany who fomented uprisings in urban centers in the 1520s and 1530s (the Peasants' War, 1524–26, and perhaps the killing of the Münster Anabaptists in 1535).

I shall both find your lordship judge and juror,[5]
95   You are so merciful. I see your end°—   *aim*
     'Tis my undoing. Love and meekness, lord,
     Become a churchman better than ambition.
     Win straying souls with modesty again;
     Cast none away. That I shall clear myself,
100 Lay all the weight ye can upon my patience,
     I make as little doubt as you do conscience[6]
     In doing daily wrongs. I could say more,
     But reverence to your calling makes me modest.°   *temperate*
GARDINER   My lord, my lord—you are a sectary,°   *Protestant*
105 That's the plain truth. Your painted gloss discovers,
     To men that understand you, words and weakness.[7]
CROMWELL [*to* GARDINER]   My lord of Winchester, you're a little,
     By your good favour,° too sharp. Men so noble,   *If you'll excuse me*
     However faulty, yet should find° respect   *be offered*
110 For what they have been. 'Tis a cruelty
     To load° a falling man.   *burden further*
GARDINER   Good master secretary,
     I cry your honour mercy.[8] You may worst°   *least justifiably*
     Of all this table say so.
CROMWELL   Why, my lord?
GARDINER   Do not I know you for a favourer
     Of this new sect? Ye are not sound.°   *loyal; orthodox*
115 CROMWELL   Not sound?
GARDINER   Not sound, I say.
CROMWELL   Would you were half so honest!
     Men's prayers then would seek you, not their fears.
GARDINER   I shall remember this bold language.
CROMWELL   Do.
     Remember your bold life, too.
LORD CHANCELLOR   This is too much.
     Forbear, for shame, my lords.
GARDINER   I have done.
120 CROMWELL   And I.
LORD CHANCELLOR [*to* CRANMER]   Then thus for you, my lord. It
           stands agreed,
     I take it, by all voices,° that forthwith   *votes*
     You be conveyed to th' Tower a prisoner,
     There to remain till the King's further pleasure
125 Be known unto us. Are you all agreed, lords?
ALL THE COUNCIL   We are.
CRANMER   Is there no other way of mercy,
     But I must needs to° th' Tower, my lords?   *must go to*
GARDINER   What other
     Would you expect? You are strangely° troublesome.   *extraordinarily*
     Let some o'th' guard be ready there.
           Enter the guard
CRANMER   For me?
     Must I go like a traitor thither?
130 GARDINER [*to the guard*]   Receive° him,   *Take*
     And see him safe i'th' Tower.

---

5. Gardiner would both try (as "judge") and pass judgment (as "juror")—to Cranmer, an injustice.
6. I doubt no more than you act ethically.
7. *Your . . . weakness:* Your false exterior (or, perhaps,

your specious language) exposes, to men who can see
through you, empty words and human frailty.
8. I beg your pardon.

CRANMER   Stay, good my lords.
I have a little yet to say. Look there, my lords—
    [*He shows the King's ring*]
By virtue of that ring I take my cause
Out of the grips° of cruel men, and give it   *clutches*
135   To a most noble judge, the King my master.
LORD CHAMBERLAIN   This is the King's ring.
SURREY   'Tis no counterfeit.
SUFFOLK   'Tis the right ring, by heav'n. I told ye all
When we first put this dangerous stone a-rolling
'Twould fall upon ourselves.
NORFOLK   Do you think, my lords,
140   The King will suffer but the little finger
Of this man to be vexed?
LORD CHAMBERLAIN   'Tis now too certain.
How much more is his life in value with him!°   *esteemed by the King*
Would I were fairly out on't.°   *out of (the plot)*
    [*Exit* KING *with* BUTTS *above*]
CROMWELL   My mind gave me,°   *I suspected*
In seeking tales and informations
145   Against this man, whose honesty the devil
And his disciples only envy at,°   *covet; despise*
Ye blew the fire that burns ye. Now have at ye!°   *be on guard*
    Enter [*below,*] KING [HENRY] *frowning on them.*
    [*He*] *takes his seat*
GARDINER   Dread sovereign, how much are we bound to heaven
In daily thanks, that gave us such a prince,
150   Not only good and wise, but most religious.
One that in all obedience makes the church
The chief aim of his honour, and, to strengthen
That holy duty, out of dear respect,°   *sincere piety*
His royal self in judgement comes to hear
155   The cause betwixt her° and this great offender.   *(the Church)*
KING HENRY   You were ever good at sudden commendations,°   *extempore flattery*
Bishop of Winchester. But know I come not
To hear such flattery now; and in my presence
They are too thin and base to hide offences.
160   To me you cannot reach. You play the spaniel,
And think with wagging of your tongue to win me.
But whatsoe'er thou tak'st me for, I'm sure
Thou hast a cruel nature and a bloody.
    [*To* CRANMER] Good man, sit down.
    [CRANMER *takes his seat at the head of the Council*
    table]
                       Now let me see the proudest,
165   He° that dares most, but wag his finger at thee.   *The man*
By all that's holy, he had better starve°   *die*
Than but once think this place becomes thee not.
SURREY   May it please your grace—
KING HENRY   No, sir, it does not please me!
I had thought I had had men of some understanding
170   And wisdom of° my Council, but I find none.   *in*
Was it discretion, lords, to let this man,
This good man—few of you deserve that title—
This honest man, wait like a lousy footboy

	At chamber door? And one as great as you are?	
175	Why, what a shame° was this! Did my commission	*shameful act*
	Bid ye so far forget yourselves? I gave ye	
	Power as he was a Councillor to try him,	
	Not as a groom. There's some of ye, I see,	
	More out of malice than integrity,	
180	Would try him to the utmost, had ye mean;°	*the means*
	Which ye shall never have while I live.	

LORD CHANCELLOR   Thus far,
My most dread sovereign, may it like° your grace   *please*
To let my tongue excuse all. What was purposed°   *intended*
Concerning his imprisonment was rather—
185   If there be faith in men—meant for his trial
And fair purgation° to the world than malice,   *acquittal of suspicion*
I'm sure, in me.

KING HENRY   Well, well, my lords—respect him.
Take him and use him well, he's worthy of it.
I will say thus much for him—if a prince
190   May be beholden to a subject, I
Am for his love and service so to him.
Make me no more ado, but all embrace him.
Be friends, for shame, my lords. (*To* CRANMER) My lord of Canterbury,
I have a suit which you must not deny me:
195   That is a fair young maid that yet wants baptism—
You must be godfather, and answer for her.

CRANMER   The greatest monarch now alive may glory
In such an honour; how may I deserve it,
That am a poor and humble subject to you?

200 KING HENRY   Come, come, my lord—you'd spare your spoons.⁹
You shall have two noble partners with you—the old Duchess
of Norfolk and Lady Marquis Dorset. Will these please you?
[*To* GARDINER] Once more, my lord of Winchester, I charge you
Embrace and love this man.

GARDINER   With a true heart
And brother-love I do it.

          [GARDINER *and* CRANMER *embrace*]
205 CRANMER [*weeping*]   And let heaven
Witness how dear I hold this confirmation.

KING HENRY   Good man, those joyful tears show thy true heart.
The common voice,° I see, is verified   *opinion*
Of thee which says thus, 'Do my lord of Canterbury
210   A shrewd turn,° and he's your friend for ever.'   *An act of malice*
Come, lords, we trifle time away. I long
To have this young one made a Christian.
As I have made ye one, lords, one remain—
So I grow stronger, you more honour gain.   *Exeunt*

5.3

Noise and tumult within.° Enter PORTER [*with rushes*]   *offstage*
and his MAN [*with a broken cudgel*]

PORTER [*to those within*]   You'll leave° your noise anon, ye rascals.   *stop*
Do you take

---

9. The King teases Cranmer that he hesitates only because
he wants to spare himself the expense of christening
spoons, the customary gift from a godparent to a child.
5.3 Location: The palace yard.

The court for Paris Garden,[1] ye rude slaves?
Leave your gaping.°   *yelling*
ONE (*within*)   Good master porter, I belong to th' larder.°   *serve in the pantry*
5   PORTER   Belong to th' gallows, and be hanged, ye rogue!
Is this a place to roar in?
[*To his* MAN] Fetch me a dozen crab-tree staves, and strong ones,
[*Raising his rushes*] These are but switches to 'em.
[*To those within*]   I'll scratch your heads.
You must be seeing christenings? Do you look
10 For ale and cakes here, you rude rascals?
MAN   Pray, sir, be patient. 'Tis as much impossible,
Unless we sweep 'em from the door with cannons,
To scatter 'em as 'tis to make 'em sleep
On May-day morning[2]—which will never be.
15 We may as well push against Paul's° as stir 'em.   *St. Paul's Cathedral*
PORTER   How got they in, and be hanged?°   *(a curse or expletive)*
MAN   Alas, I know not. How gets the tide in?
As much as one sound cudgel° of four foot—   *club*
[*He raises his cudgel*]
You see the poor remainder°—could distribute,   *what's left of it*
I made no spare,° sir.   *spared no one*
20 PORTER   You did nothing, sir.
MAN   I am not Samson, nor Sir Guy, nor Colbrand,[3]
To mow 'em down before me; but if I spared any
That had a head to hit, either young or old,
He or she, cuckold or cuckold-maker,
25 Let me ne'er hope to see a chine° again—   *cut of beef*
And that I would not for a cow,° God save her!   *for anything*
ONE (*within*)   Do you hear, master porter?
PORTER   I shall be with you presently,
Good master puppy. [*To his* MAN] Keep the door close, sirrah.
MAN   What would you have me do?
30 PORTER   What should you do,
but knock 'em down by th' dozens? Is this Moorfields[4] to muster in? Or have we some strange Indian with the great tool
come to court,[5] the women so besiege us? Bless me, what a fry
of fornication[6] is at door! On my Christian conscience, this one
35 christening will beget a thousand. Here will be father, godfather, and all together.
MAN   The spoons° will be the bigger, sir. There is a fellow some-   *(for christening)*
what near the door, he should be a brazier° by his face, for o'   *brass worker*
my conscience twenty of the dog-days° now reign in's nose. All   *hottest summer days*
40 that stand about him are under the line[7]—they need no other
penance. That fire-drake° did I hit three times on the head, and   *fiery dragon*
three times was his nose discharged against me. He stands there
like a mortar-piece, to blow us.[8] There was a haberdasher's wife
of small wit near him, that railed upon me till her pinked por-

1. A park for bear- and bullbaiting located in Southwark,
a London suburb, where the Globe Theatre also stood.
2. On May Day, revelers rose before dawn for festivities
to greet spring.
3. Figures of legendary physical powers. In the Bible,
Samson is renowned for his strength; in the romance
tradition, Sir Guy of Warwick, who killed the Danish
giant Colebrand, was also known for his prowess.
4. Parkland outside London's walls where citizen

militias may have trained.
5. Indians brought to England and exhibited at court
excited popular fascination, here about their genitalia.
6. Crowd of would-be fornicators or bastards.
7. All those near him seem to be standing at the equa-
tor, his face is so red.
8. Like a cannon, ready to blow us up; ready to blow his
nose at us.

45   ringer⁹ fell off her head, for kindling such a combustion° in the   *tumult*

state. I missed the meteor° once, and hit that woman, who cried   *brazier*

out 'Clubs!',¹ when I might see from far some forty truncheon-

ers° draw to her succour, which were the hope o'th' Strand,²   *men with cudgels*

where she was quartered.° They fell on.° I made good my place.   *lived / attacked*

50   At length they came to th' broomstaff to° me. I defied 'em still,   *right next to*

when suddenly a file of boys behind 'em, loose shot,³ delivered

such a shower of pebbles that I was fain° to draw mine honour   *obliged*

in and let 'em win the work.° The devil was amongst 'em, I   *fort*

think, surely.

55 PORTER   These are the youths° that thunder at a playhouse, and   *apprentices*

fight for bitten apples, that no audience but the tribulation of

Tower Hill or the limbs of Limehouse,⁴ their dear brothers, are

able to endure. I have some of 'em in *limbo patrum*,⁵ and there

they are like to dance these three days, besides the running

60   banquet of two beadles that is to come.⁶

                 Enter [the] LORD CHAMBERLAIN

LORD CHAMBERLAIN   Mercy o' me, what a multitude are here!

They grow still, too—from all parts they are coming,

As if we kept a fair here! Where are these porters,

These lazy knaves? [*To the* PORTER *and his* MAN] You've made

     a fine hand,° fellows!   *nice work (ironic)*

65   There's a trim° rabble let in—are all these   *an elegant (ironic)*

Your faithful friends o'th' suburbs?⁷ we shall have

Great store of room, no doubt, left for the ladies

When they pass back from the christening!

PORTER   An't° please your honour,   *If it*

We are but men, and what so many may do,

70   Not being torn a-pieces, we have done.

An army cannot rule 'em.°   *keep them in order*

LORD CHAMBERLAIN   As I live,

If the King blame me for't, I'll lay ye all

By th' heels,° and suddenly—and on your heads   *In the stocks*

Clap round° fines for neglect. You're lazy knaves,   *large*

75   And here ye lie baiting of bombards° when   *you lie drinking*

Ye should do service.

          [*Flourish of trumpets within*]

                  Hark, the trumpets sound.

They're come, already, from the christening.

Go break among the press,° and find a way out   *crowd*

To let the troop pass fairly,° or I'll find   *fittingly*

80   A Marshalsea shall hold ye play⁸ these two months.

       [*As they leave, the* PORTER *and his* MAN *call within*]

PORTER   Make way there for the Princess!

---

9. Perforated small cap.

1. London apprentices would shout this when about to begin or end a street fight.

2. Fashionable shopping and residential part of London.

3. Marksmen (here, throwers) unattached to a company.

4. The tough crowds at the Tower for executions; or further east in Limehouse, a rough part of London near the docks.

5. In prison (literally, limbo of the fathers). Jewish patriarchs, because they predated Christ, at death went not to Christian heaven but to limbo, near hell, where

they remained until Judgment Day. With echoes of "limbs of Limehouse" (line 57).

6. *dance . . . come*: festive celebration ("dance") with dessert ("running banquet"); public whipping of prisoners (like a "running banquet," or dessert) after imprisonment (the main course) by minor law-enforcement officials ("beadles").

7. From the suburbs, areas outside London's city walls, beyond the city's legal jurisdiction, and hence considered lawless.

8. *I'll . . . play*: I'll shut you in the Marshalsea, a prison in Southwark.

MAN   You great fellow,[9]
Stand close up,° or I'll make your head ache.   *Move aside*
PORTER   You i'th' camlet,° get up o'th' rail—   *rough cloth*
I'll peck you o'er the pales else.[1]   *Exeunt*

5.4

Enter trumpet[er]s, sounding. Then [enter] two alder-
men, [the] Lord Mayor [of London], GARTER [King-of-
Arms], CRANMER [the Archbishop of Canterbury, the]
Duke of NORFOLK with his marshal's staff, [the] Duke of
SUFFOLK, two noblemen bearing great standing bowls for
the christening gifts; then [enter] four noblemen bearing
a canopy, under which [is] the Duchess of Norfolk, god-
mother, bearing the child [Elizabeth] richly habited in a
mantle, [whose] train [is] borne by a lady. Then follows
the Marchioness Dorset, the other godmother, and
ladies. The troop pass once about the stage and GARTER
speaks

GARTER   Heaven, from thy endless goodness send prosperous
life, long, and ever happy, to the high and mighty Princess of
England, Elizabeth.[1]
    Flourish. Enter KING [HENRY] and guard
CRANMER *[kneeling]*   And to your royal grace, and the good Queen!
5   My noble partners° and myself thus pray   *fellow godparents*
All comfort, joy, in this most gracious lady,
Heaven ever laid up to make parents happy,
May hourly fall upon ye.
KING HENRY   Thank you, good lord Archbishop.
What is her name?
CRANMER   Elizabeth.
KING HENRY   Stand up, lord.
    [CRANMER rises]
[To the child] With this kiss take my blessing—
    [He kisses the child]
10   God protect thee,
Into whose hand I give thy life.
CRANMER   Amen.
KING HENRY *[to CRANMER, old duchess, and Marchioness]*
My noble gossips,° you've been too prodigal.°   *godparents / generous*
I thank ye heartily. So shall this lady,
When she has so much English.
CRANMER   Let me speak, sir,
15 For heaven now bids me, and the words I utter
Let none think flattery, for they'll find 'em truth.
This royal infant—heaven still° move about her—   *always*
Though in her cradle, yet now promises
Upon this land a thousand thousand blessings
20 Which time shall bring to ripeness. She shall be—
But few now living can behold that goodness—
A pattern to all princes living with her,

9. Addressed to someone either onstage or in the audience.
1. *get . . . else*: get off the rail (the railing running
around the edge of the stage), or I'll throw you off.
5.4 Location: The court.
1. This formulaic speech is similar to one given at the 1613

wedding of King James I's daughter Elizabeth to Prince
Frederick, the Elector Palatine. This scene parallels the
christening celebration of one Princess Elizabeth, in
the play, to the wedding celebration of another, at the
time of the play's first production.

And all that shall succeed. Saba² was never
More covetous° of wisdom and fair virtue   *desirous*
25   Than this pure soul shall be. All princely graces
That mould up° such a mighty piece° as this is,   *produce / masterpiece*
With all the virtues that attend the good,
Shall still be doubled on her. Truth shall nurse her,
Holy and heavenly thoughts still counsel her.
30   She shall be loved and feared. Her own° shall bless her;   *own people*
Her foes shake like a field of beaten° corn,   *windswept*
And hang their heads with sorrow. Good grows with her.
In her days every man shall eat in safety
Under his own vine what he plants, and sing
35   The merry songs of peace to all his neighbours.
God shall be truly known,° and those about her   *(via Protestantism)*
From her shall read° the perfect ways of honour,   *learn*
And by those claim their greatness, not by blood.
Nor shall this peace sleep with her, but, as when
40   The bird of wonder dies—the maiden phoenix³—
Her ashes new create another heir
As great in admiration° as herself,   *deserving of wonder*
So shall she leave her blessèdness to one,°   *(James I)*
When heaven shall call her from this cloud of darkness,°   *earthly state*
45   Who from the sacred ashes of her honour
Shall star-like rise as great in fame as she was,
And so stand fixed. Peace, plenty, love, truth, terror,
That were the servants to this chosen infant,
Shall then be his, and, like a vine, grow to him.
50   Wherever the bright sun of heaven shall shine,
His honour and the greatness of his name
Shall be, and make new nations.⁴ He shall flourish,
And like a mountain cedar reach his branches
To all the plains about him. Our children's children
Shall see this, and bless heaven.
55   KING HENRY   Thou speakest wonders.
CRANMER   She shall be, to the happiness of England,
An agèd princess. Many days shall see her,
And yet no day without a deed° to crown it.   *an accomplishment*
Would I had known no more. But she must die—
60   She must, the saints must have her—yet a virgin,
A most unspotted lily shall she pass
To th' ground, and all the world shall mourn her.
KING HENRY   O lord Archbishop,
Thou hast made me now a man. Never before
65   This happy child did I get° anything.   *beget; achieve*
This oracle of comfort has so pleased me
That when I am in heaven I shall desire
To see what this child does, and praise my maker.
I thank ye all. To you, my good Lord Mayor,

2. The Queen of Sheba visited Solomon in Jerusalem in order to benefit from his wisdom, and thus became a model for wise (but presumably deferential) women. See 1 Kings 10:1–10.
3. Mythical Arabian bird, the only one of its kind, who, when it dies after a long life, regenerates itself from its own ashes. James I inherits the spirit of the phoenix, Queen Elizabeth—a spirit now, perhaps, being passed

on to his daughter Princess Elizabeth.
4. See Genesis 17:4: "A father of many nations have I made thee." The passage was frequently invoked in relation to Princess Elizabeth's marriage. The play here also compliments James on the "new nation" he has established in America, appropriately named Virginia after the "virgin" Queen Elizabeth (line 60).

70   And your good brethren, I am much beholden.
      I have received much honour by your presence,
      And ye shall find me thankful. Lead the way, lords.
      Ye must all see the Queen, and she must thank ye.
      She will be sick° else. This day, no man think   *unhappy*
75   He's business at his house, for all shall stay°—   *stop work*
      This little one shall make it holiday.   [*Flourish.*] *Exeunt*

Epilogue

[*Enter* EPILOGUE]

EPILOGUE   'Tis ten to one this play can never please
      All that are here. Some come to take their ease,
      And sleep an act or two; but those, we fear,
      We've frighted with our trumpets; so, 'tis clear,
5   They'll say 'tis naught.° Others to hear the city   *worth nothing*
      Abused extremely, and to cry 'That's witty!'[1]—
      Which we have not done neither; that,° I fear,   *such that*
      All the expected good° we're like to hear   *anticipated praise*
      For this play at this time is only in
10   The merciful construction of ° good women,   *interpretation by*
      For such a one we showed 'em. If they smile,
      And say ''Twill do', I know within a while
      All the best men are ours—for 'tis ill hap°   *luck*
      If they hold° when their ladies bid 'em clap.   [*Exit*]   *refrain*

Epilogue
1. "The city," both London and its citizens, was satirized in "city comedies" at the private theaters (as opposed to public playhouses like the Globe, whose leading dramatist here retaliates).

APPENDICES

APPENDICES

Early Modern Map Culture

In the early modern period, maps were often considered rare and precious objects, and seeing a map could be an important and life-changing event. This was so for Richard Hakluyt, whose book *The Principal Navigations, Voiages, Traffiques and Discoveries of the English Nation* (1598–1600) was the first major collection of narratives describing England's overseas trading ventures. Hakluyt tells how, as a boy still at school in London, he visited his uncle's law chambers and saw a book of cosmography lying open there. Perceiving his nephew's interest in the maps it contained, the uncle turned to a modern map and "pointed with his wand to all the known Seas, Gulfs, Bayes, Straights, Capes, Rivers, Empires, Kingdomes, Dukedomes, and Territories of ech part, with declaration also of their speciall commodities and particular wants, which by the benefit of traffike, and entercourse of merchants, are plentifully supplied. From the Mappe he brought me to the Bible, and turning to the 107 Psalme, directed mee to the 23 and 24 verses, where I read, that they which go downe to the sea in ships, and occupy [work] by the great waters, they see the works of the Lord, and his woonders in the deepe." This event, Hakluyt records, made so deep an impression upon him, that he vowed he would devote his life to the study of this kind of knowledge. *The Principal Navigations* was the result, a book that mixes a concern with the profit to be made from trade and from geographical knowledge with praise for the Christian god who made the "great waters" and, in Hakluyt's view, looked with special favor on the English merchants and sailors who voyaged over them.

In the early modern period, access to maps was far less easy than it is today. Before the advent of printing in the late fifteenth century, maps were drawn and decorated by hand. Because they were rare and expensive, these medieval maps were for the most part owned by the wealthy and the powerful. Sometimes adorned with pictures of fabulous sea monsters and exotic creatures, maps often revealed the Christian worldview of those who composed them. Jerusalem appeared squarely in the middle of many maps (called T and O maps), with Asia, Africa, and Europe, representing the rest of the known world, arranged symmetrically around the Holy City. Because they had not yet been discovered by Europeans, North and South America were not depicted.

Mapping practices changed markedly during the late fifteenth and sixteenth centuries both because of the advent of print and also because European nations such as Portugal and Spain began sending ships on long sea voyages to open new trade routes to the East and, eventually, to the Americas. During this period, monarchs competed to have the best cartographers supply them with accurate maps of their realms and especially of lands in Africa, Asia, or the Americas, where they hoped to trade or plant settlements. Such knowledge was precious and jealously guarded. The value of such maps and the secrecy that surrounded them are indicated by a story published in Hakluyt's *The Principal Navigations*. An English ship had captured a Portuguese vessel in the Azores, and a map was discovered among the ship's valuable cargo, which included spices, silks, carpets, porcelain, and other exotic commercial objects. The map was "inclosed in a case of sweete Cedar wood, and lapped up almost an hundred fold in fine calicut-cloth, as though it had been some incomparable jewell." The value of the map and what explains the careful way in which it was packed lay in the particular information it afforded the English about Portuguese trading routes. More than beautiful objects, maps like this one were crucial to the international race to find safe sea routes to the most profitable trading centers in the East.

In the sixteenth century, books of maps began to be printed, making them more affordable for ordinary people, though some of these books, published as big folio volumes, remained too dear for any but wealthy patrons to buy. Yet maps were increasingly a part of daily life, and printing made many of them more accessible. Playgoers in Shakespeare's audiences must have understood in general the value and uses of maps, for they appear as props in a number of his plays. Most famously, at the beginning of *King Lear,* the old king has a map brought onstage showing the extent of his kingdom. He then points on the map to the three separate parts into which he is dividing his realm to share among his daughters. The map, often unfurled with a flourish on a table or held up for view by members of Lear's retinue, signals the crucial relationship of the land to the monarch. He is his domains, and the map signifies his possession of them. To divide the kingdom, in essence to tear apart the map, would have been judged foolish and destructive by early modern political theorists. Similarly, in *1 Henry IV,* when rebels against the sitting monarch, Henry IV, plot to overthrow him, they bring a map onstage in order to decide what part of the kingdom will be given to each rebel leader. Their proposed dismemberment of the realm signifies the danger they pose. Treasonously, they would rend in pieces the body of the commonwealth.

Maps, of course, had other uses besides signifying royal domains. In some instances, they were used pragmatically to help people find their way from one place to another. A very common kind of map, a portolan chart, depicted in minute detail the coastline of a particular body of water. Used by sailors, these maps frequently were made by people native to the region they described. Many world or regional maps, because they were beautifully decorated and embellished with vivid colors, were used for decorative purposes. John Dee, a learned adviser to Queen Elizabeth and a great book collector, wrote that some people used maps "to beautifie their Halls, Parlers, Chambers, Galeries, Studies, or Libraries." He also spoke of more scholarly uses for these objects. They could, for example, be useful aids in the study of history or geography, enabling people to locate "thinges past, as battels fought, earthquakes, heavenly fyringes, and such occurents in histories mentioned." Today we make similar use of maps, like those included in this volume, when, in reading Shakespeare's plays, we resort to a map to find out where the Battle of Agincourt took place or where Othello sailed when he left Venice for Cyprus.

This edition of the *Norton Shakespeare* includes six maps. Three of them are modern maps drawn specifically to show the location of places important to Shakespeare's plays. They depict London, the British Isles and France, and the eastern Mediterranean. This edition also includes three early modern maps that indicate some of the different kinds of printed maps that people might have seen in Shakespeare's lifetime. The earliest is a map of London that appeared in a 1574 edition of a famous German atlas, *Civitates Orbis Terrarum (Cities of the World),* compiled by George Braun with engravings by Franz Hogenberg. This remarkable atlas includes maps and information on cities throughout Europe, Asia, and North Africa; the first of its six volumes appeared in 1572, the last in 1617. Being included in the volume indicated a city's status as a recognized metropolitan center. In a charming touch, Braun added to his city maps pictures of figures in local dress. At the bottom of the map of London, for example, there are four figures who appear to represent the city's prosperous citizens. In the center, a man in a long robe holds the hand of soberly dressed matron. On either side of them are younger and more ornately dressed figures. The young man sports a long sword and a short cloak, the woman a dress with elaborate skirts. In the atlas, the map is colored, and the clothes of the two young people echo one another in shades of green and red.

At the time the map was made, London was a rapidly expanding metropolis. In 1550, it contained about 55,000 people; by 1600, it would contain nearly 200,000. The map shows the densely populated old walled city north of the Thames River, in the middle of which was Eastcheap, the commercial district where, in Shakespeare's plays about the reign of Henry IV, Falstaff holds court in a tavern. The map also shows that by 1570 London was spreading westward beyond the wall toward Westminster Palace. This medieval structure, which appears on the extreme left side of the map, was where English monarchs resided when in London and where, at the end of *2 Henry IV,* the king dies in the fabled Jerusalem Chamber of the Westminster complex. On the far right of the map, one can see the Tower of London, where Edward IV's young sons were imprisoned by Richard III, an event depicted in Shakespeare's *The Tragedy of King Richard the Third*. The map also indicates the centrality of the Thames to London's commercial life. It shows the river full of boats, some of those on the east side of London Bridge large oceangoing vessels with several masts. South of the river, where many of the most famous London theaters, including Shakespeare's Globe, were to be constructed in the 1590s, there are relatively few buildings. By 1600, this would change, as Southwark, as it was known, came to be an increasingly busy entertainment, residential, and commercial district.

The map of the Christian Holy Lands at the eastern tip of the Mediterranean Sea had extremely wide distribution because it was included in the many editions of the Geneva Bible, an English translation of the Scriptures put together by a group of Puritan scholars working in Geneva in the 1550s. Moderately sized and priced, the Geneva Bible became the most popular Bible in English until the King James version was produced in 1611. Even after that date, many ordinary Protestant readers continued to use the popular Geneva Bible, which underwent refinements, changes, and additions throughout the second half of the sixteenth century, including in 1576 a new translation of the New Testament heavily indebted to the scholarship of the French theologian Théodore de Bèze.

The map included here is from a 1592 edition of this Bible, printed in London by Christopher Barker. The map was placed before Matthew, the first book of the New Testament, and it shows places mentioned in the first four Gospels (Matthew, Mark, Luke, and John), which collectively tell of the life and deeds of Jesus. It indicates, for example, the location of Bethlehem, where he was born; Nazareth, where he spent his youth; and Cana of Galilee, where he turned water into wine at a marriage. It suggests that, to the English reader, this particular territory was overwritten by and completely intertwined with Christian history. Yet in the Mediterranean Sea, on the left of the map, several large ships are visible, and they are reminders of another fact about this region: it was a vigorous trading arena where European Christian merchants did business with local merchants—Christian, Jew, and Muslim—and with traders bringing luxury goods by overland routes from the East. A number of Shakespeare's plays are set in this complex eastern Mediterranean region where several religious traditions laid claim to its territories and many commercial powers competed for preeminence. *Pericles,* for example, has a hero who is the ruler of Tyre, a city on the upper right side of the map. In the course of his wanderings, Pericles visits many cities along the eastern coasts of the Mediterranean. The conclusion of the play, in which the hero is reunited both with his long-lost daughter and the wife he believes dead, has seemed to many critics to share in a sense of Christian miracle, despite the fact of its ostensibly pagan setting. *The Comedy of Errors* and parts of *Othello* and of *Antony and Cleopatra* are also set in the eastern Mediterranean. One of Shakespeare's earliest plays, *The Comedy of Errors,* is an urban comedy in which the protagonists are merchants deeply involved in commercial transactions. It is also the first play in which Shakespeare mentions the Americas in an extended joke in which he compares parts of a serving woman's body to the countries on a map including Ireland, France, and the Americas. In *Othello,* the eastern Mediterranean island of Cyprus is represented as a tense Christian outpost defending Venetian interests against the Muslim Turks. In *Antony and Cleopatra,* Egypt figures as the site of Eastern luxury and also of imperial conquest, an extension of the Roman Empire. Clearly, this region was to Shakespeare and his audiences one of the most complex and most highly charged areas of the world: a site of religious, commercial, and imperial significance.

The map of Great Britain and Ireland comes from a 1612 edition of John Speed's *The Theatre of the Empire of Great Britaine,* an innovative atlas containing individual maps of counties and towns in England and Wales, as well as larger maps that include Scotland and Ireland. Speed was by trade a tailor who increasingly devoted his time to the study of history and cartography. Befriended by the antiquarian scholar William Camden, he eventually won patronage from Sir Fulke Greville, who gave him a pension that allowed him to devote full time to his scholarly endeavors. *The Theatre* was one product of this newfound freedom. The map included here is one of his most ambitious. It shows the entire British Isles, nominated by Speed as "The Kingdome of Great Britaine and Ireland," though at this time Ireland was far from under the control of the English crown and Scotland was still an independent kingdom, despite the fact that James I, a Scot by birth, had tried hard to forge a formal union between England and Scotland. This problem of the relationship of the parts of the British Isles to one another, and England's assertion of power over the others, is treated in *Henry V,* in which officers from Wales, Ireland, and Scotland are sharply delineated yet all depicted as loyal subjects of the English king.

One striking aspect of Speed's map is the balance it strikes between the two capital cities, London on the left, prominently featuring the Thames and London Bridge, and Edinburgh on the right. This would have pleased James, whose interest in his native country Shakespeare played to in his writing of *Macbeth,* based on material from Scottish history. Speed's map acknowledges the claims of the monarch to the territory it depicts. In the upper left corner, the British lion and the Scottish unicorn support a roundel topped with a crown. When James became king of England in 1603, he created this merged symbol of Scottish-English unity. The motto of the Royal Order of the Garter, "Honi soit qui mal y pense" (Shamed be he who thinks ill of it), is inscribed around the circumference. In the bottom left corner of the map, another locus of authority is established. Two cherubs, one holding a compass, the other a globe, sit beneath a banner on which is inscribed the words: "Performed by John Speede." If the territory is the monarch's, the craft that depicts it belongs to the tailor turned cartographer.

Today, maps are readily available from any gasoline station or on the Internet, but in early modern England they were still rare and valuable objects that could generate great excitement in those who owned or beheld them. Along with other precious items, maps were sometimes put on display in libraries and sitting rooms, but they had functions beyond the ornamental. They helped to explain and order the world, indicating who claimed certain domains, showing where the familiar stories of the Bible or of English history occurred, helping merchants find their way to distant markets. As John Dee, the early modern map enthusiast concluded, "Some, for one purpose: and some, for an other, liketh, loveth, getteth, and useth, Mappes, Chartes, and Geographicall Globes."

JEAN E. HOWARD

Ireland, Scotland, Wales, England, and Western France: Places Important to Shakespeare's Plays.

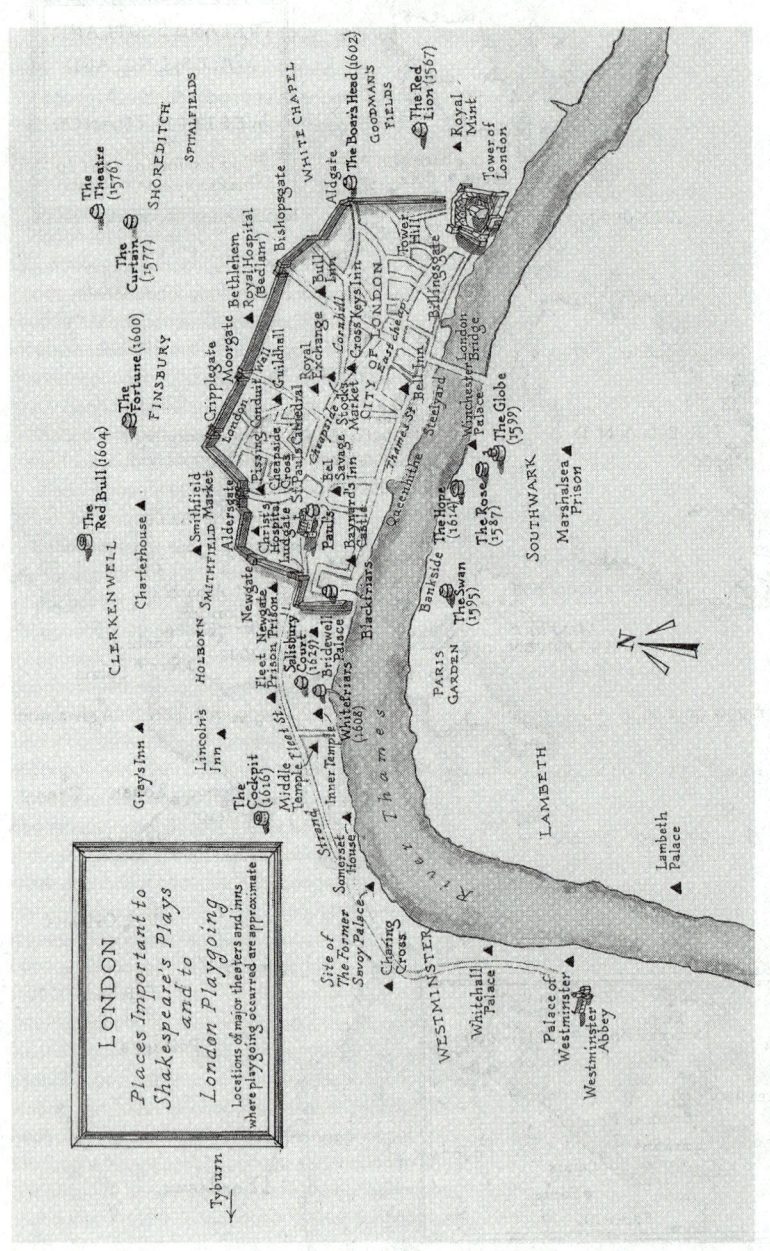

London: Places Important to Shakespeare's Plays and London Playgoing.

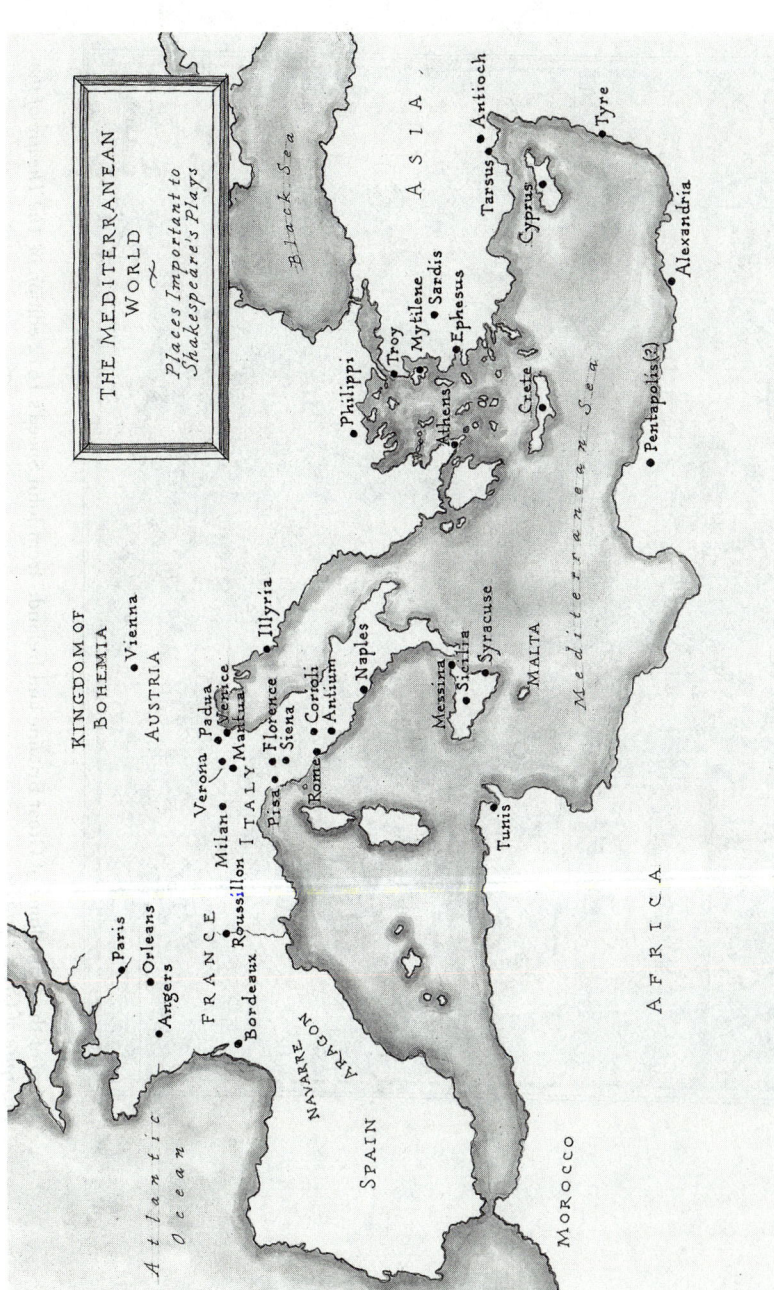

The Mediterranean World: Places Important to Shakespeare's Plays.

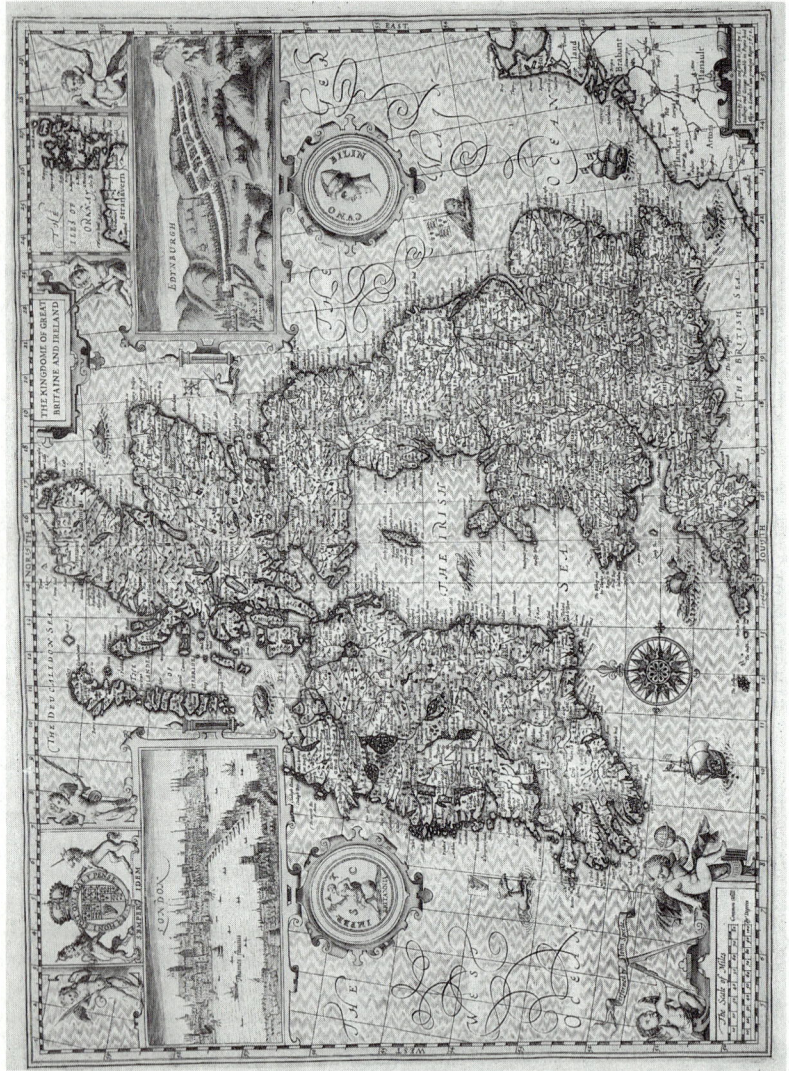

Map of the "Kingdome of Great Britaine and Ireland," from John Speed's 1612 edition of *The Theatre of the Empire of Great Britaine*.

Printed map of London, 1574, taken from a German atlas of European cities by George Braun and Franz Hogenberg.

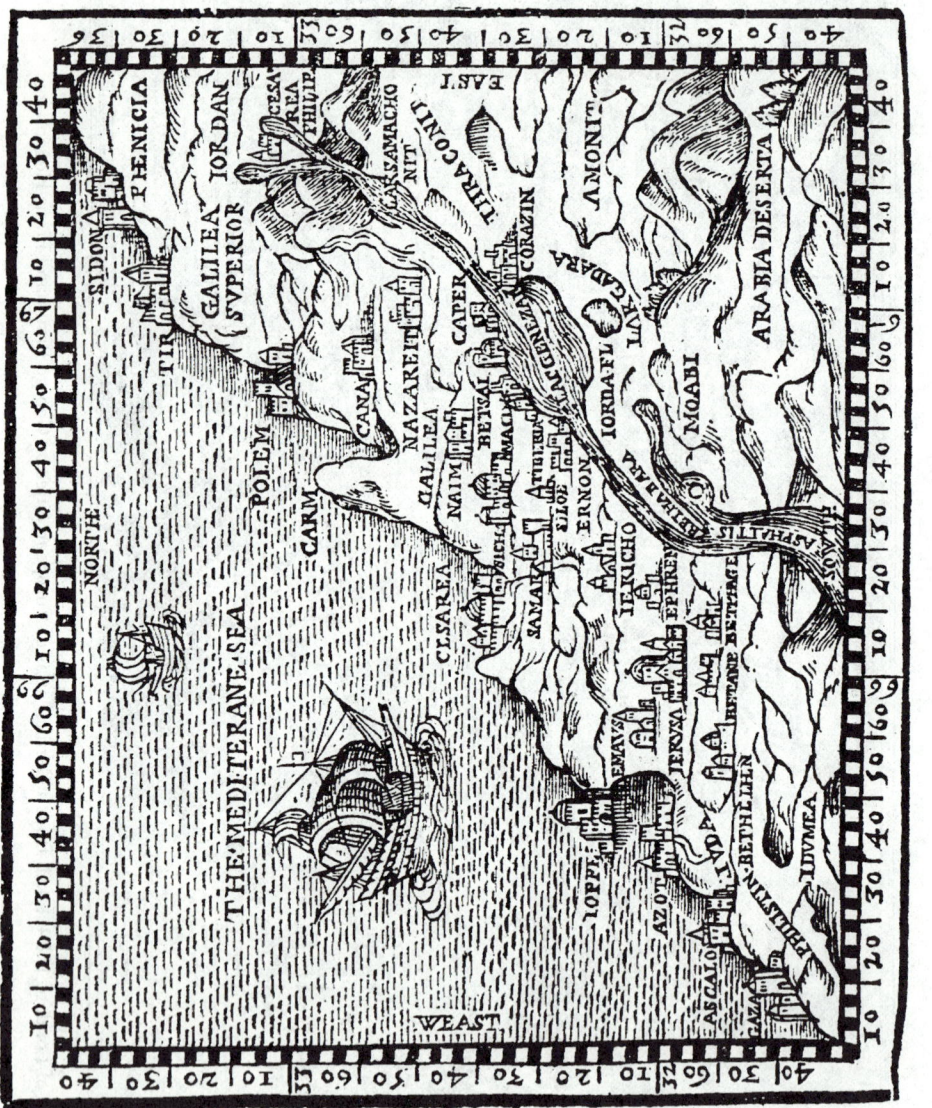

Map of the Holy Land, from the Théodore de Bèze Bible, printed in London, 1592.

Documents

This selection of documents provides a range of contemporary testimony about Shakespeare's character, his work, and the social and institutional conditions under which it was produced. In the absence of newspapers and reviewers, few references to the theater survive. The availability of such hints and fragments as are presented here serves as a mark of Shakespeare's distinction, for the theater was perceived by much of the literate population as ephemeral popular entertainment. The reports of spectators whose accounts we have are more like reviews than any other texts the period has to offer; hence the importance even of brief notes such as Nashe's or Platter's, and the particular value of extended accounts such as those of Simon Forman. The government documents included here offer a vivid glimpse of the institutional procedures by which the theater was regulated. The legal documents—a contract for the construction of a theater modeled on the Globe, and Shakespeare's will—provide the most detailed account available of the material conditions of his life and work. The extracts from criticism and other literary texts show the diversity of contemporary response to his art.

The source for each text is given at the end of the introductory headnote. Additional documents can be found at wwnorton.com/shakespeare.

WS: E. K. Chambers, *William Shakespeare: A Study of Facts and Problems*, 2 vols. (Oxford: Clarendon Press, 1930).
ES: E. K. Chambers, *The Elizabethan Stage*, 4 vols. (Oxford: Clarendon Press, 1923).

Robert Greene on Shakespeare (1592)

[Robert Greene (1560–1592), a prolific author of plays, romances, and pamphlets, attacked Shakespeare in his *Greenes, Groats-worth of Witte, bought with a million of Repentance.* Greene had studied at Cambridge, and his "M.A." was prominently displayed on his title pages. Shakespeare's lack of a university education is clearly one motive for the professional resentment of the following excerpt. Another is probably that Greene was poor and very ill and felt forsaken while writing the *Groats-worth of Witte;* the preface refers to it as his "Swanne-like song," and the narrative is framed as the repentance of a dying man. (Some scholars have held that the posthumously published work contains fabrications by a publisher attempting to capitalize on Greene's name.) The three colleagues Greene addresses are likely to be Christopher Marlowe, Thomas Nashe, and George Peele. The text is that of 1596, as printed in Alexander B. Grosart's *Life and Complete Works in Prose and Verse of Robert Greene,* vol. 12 (New York: Russell and Russell).]

> *To those Gentlemen his Quondam acquaintance,*
> *that spend their wits in making Plaies, R. G.*
> *wisheth a better exercise, and wisdome*
> *to prevent his extremities. . . .*

Base minded men al three of you, if by my miserie ye be not warned: for unto none of you (like me) fought those burres to cleave: those Puppits (I meane) that speake from our mouths, those Anticks garnisht in our colours. Is it not strange that I, to whom they al have beene beholding: is it not like that you, to whome they all have beene beholding, shall (were ye in that case that I am now) be both at once of them forsaken? Yes trust them not: for there is an upstart Crow, beautified with our feathers, that with his *Tygers heart wrapt in a Players hide,*[1] *supposes he is as well able to bumbast out a blanke verse as the best of you: and being an absolute Johannes fac totum,*[2] is in his owne conceit the onely Shake-scene in a countrie. O that I might intreate your rare wits to be imployed in more profitable courses: & let those Apes imitate your past excellence, and never more acquaint them with your admired inventions. I know the best husband[3] of you all will never prove an Usurer, and the kindest of them / all will never proove a kinde nurse: yet whilst you may, seeke you better Maisters; for it is pittie men of such rare wits, should be subject to the pleasures of such rude groomes.

Thomas Nashe on *1 Henry VI* (1592)

[Thomas Nashe (1567–1601), Greene's fellow playwright and pamphleteer, protests the attribution to himself of the *Groats-worth of Witte* in the preface to the 1592 edition of a pamphlet of his own, *Pierce Penilisse; His Supplication to the Devil.* The satire of *Pierce Penilisse* is more general and political than that of the *Groats-worth*, attacking the manners of the middle class. The allusion to the Talbot scenes of *1 Henry VI* (4.2–7) comes in a section subtitled "The defence of Playes." Talbot is supposed to have been played by Richard Burbage, later the leading actor of the Lord Chamberlain's and King's Men. The text is from Ronald B. McKerrow's 1904 edition of Nashe's *Works*, vol. 1 (London: Bullen).]

How would it have joyed brave *Talbot* (the terror of the French) to thinke that after he had lyne two hundred yeares in his Tombe, hee should triumphe againe on the Stage, and have his bones newe embalmed with the teares of ten thousand spectators at least (at severall times), who, in the Tragedian that represents his person, imagine they behold him fresh bleeding.

Francis Meres on Shakespeare (1598)

[Francis Meres (1565–1647) was educated at Cambridge and was active in London literary circles in 1597–98, after which he became a rector and schoolmaster in the country. The descriptions of Shakespeare are taken from a section on poetry in *Palladis Tamia, Wits Treasury,* a work largely consisting of translated classical quotations and exempla. Unlike the main body of the work, the subsections on poetry, painting, and music include comparisons of English artists to figures of antiquity. Meres goes on after the extract below to list Shakespeare among the best English writers for lyric, tragedy, comedy, elegy, and love poetry. The text is from Don Cameron Allen's 1933 edition of the section "Poetrie" (Urbana: University of Illinois).]

From XI

As the Greeke tongue is made famous and eloquent by *Homer, Hesiod, Euripedes, Aeschilus, Sophocles, Pindarus, Phocylides* and *Aristophanes*; and the Latine tongue by *Virgill, Ovid, Horace, Silius Italicus, Lucanus, Lucretius, Ausonius* and *Claudianus*: so the English tongue is mightily enriched, and gorgeouslie invested

---

1. A parody of *Richard Duke of York* (3 *Henry VI*) 1.4.138: "O tiger's heart wrapped in a woman's hide!" This obvious allusion and the following pun on Shakespeare's name make it certain that Shakespeare is the

"crow" described here.
2. Jack-of-all-trades. *conceit:* imagination.
3. Steward.

in rare ornaments and resplendent abiliments by Sir *Philip Sidney, Spencer, Daniel, Drayton, Warner, Shakespeare, Marlow* and *Chapman.*

From XIV

As the soule of *Euphorbus* was thought to live in *Pythagoras:* so the sweete wittie soule of Ovid lives in mellifluous & honytongued *Shakespeare,* witnes his *Venus and Adonis,* his *Lucrece,* his sugred Sonnets.

From XV

As *Plautus* and *Seneca* are accounted the best for Comedy and Tragedy among the Latines: so *Shakespeare* among yᵉ English is the most excellent in both kinds for the stage; for Comedy, witnes his *Gētlemē of Verona,* his *Errors,* his *Love labors lost,* his *Love labours wonne,*[1] his *Midsummers night dreame,* & his *Merchant of Venice:* for Tragedy his *Richard the 2. Richard the 3. Henry the 4. King John, Titus Andronicus* and his *Romeo* and *Juliet.*

As *Epius Stolo* said, that the Muses would speake with *Plautus* tongue, if they would speak Latin: so I say that the Muses would speak with *Shakespeares* fine filed phrase, if they would speake English.

Thomas Platter on *Julius Caesar* (September 21, 1599)

[Thomas Platter (b. 1574), a Swiss traveler, recorded his experience at the Globe playhouse in an account of his travels. The German text is printed in WS 2:322.]

Den 21 Septembris nach dem Imbissessen, etwan umb zwey vhren, bin ich mitt meiner geselschaft v̈ber daz wasser gefahren, haben in dem streüwinen Dachhaus die Tragedy vom ersten Keyser Julio Caesare mitt ohngefahr 15 personen sehen gar artlich agieren; zu endt der Comedien dantzeten sie ihrem gebraucht nach gar v̈berausz zierlich, ye zwen in mannes vndt 2 in weiber kleideren angethan, wunderbahrlich mitt einanderen.

On the 21st of September after lunch, about two o'clock, I crossed the water [the Thames] with my party, and we saw the tragedy of the first emperor Julius Caesar acted very prettily in the house with the thatched roof, with about fifteen characters; at the end of the comedy, according to their custom, they danced with exceeding elegance, two each in men's and two in women's clothes, wonderfully together.

[Translated by Noah Heringman]

Gabriel Harvey on *Hamlet, Venus and Adonis,* and *The Rape of Lucrece* (1598–1603)

[Gabriel Harvey (c. 1550–1631), a scholar perhaps best remembered as the particular friend of Spenser, gave the following account of Shakespeare and other contemporaries in a long manuscript note in his copy of Speght's 1598 edition of Chaucer. The date of the note is uncertain, but internal evidence makes it highly unlikely to be later than 1603. The references to Shakespeare are brief but suggestive, and the note is useful both in providing a context for the appreciation of Shakespeare and for its characteris-

1. The play—or at least the title—has not survived; a bookseller's record of the title does survive, however.

tically keen assessment of the state of modern literature. The text is from G. C. Moore Smith's edition of *Gabriel Harvey's Marginalia* (Stratford-upon-Avon: Shakespeare Head Press, 1913).]

And now translated Petrarch, Ariosto, Tasso, & Bartas himself deserve curious comparison with Chaucer, Lidgate, & owre best Inglish, auncient & moderne. Amongst which, the Countesse of Pembrokes Arcadia, & the Faerie Queene ar now freshest in request: & Astrophil, & Amyntas ar none of the idlest pastimes of sum fine humanists. The Earle of Essex much commendes Albions England:[1] and not unworthily for diverse notable pageants, before, & in the Chronicle. Sum Inglish, & other Histories nowhere more sensibly described, or more inwardly discovered. The Lord Mountjoy makes the like account of Daniels peece of the Chronicle,[2] touching the Usurpation of Henrie of Bullingbrooke, which in deede is a fine, sententious, & politique peece of Poetrie: as proffitable, as pleasurable. The younger sort takes much delight in Shakespeares Venus, & Adonis: but his Lucrece, & his tragedie of Hamlet, Prince of Denmarke, have it in them, to please the wiser sort. Or such poets: or better: or none.

> Vilia miretur vulgus: mihi flavus Apollo
> Pocula Castaliæ plena ministret aquæ:[3]

quoth Sir Edward Dier, betwene jest, & earnest. Whose written devises farr excell most of the sonets, and cantos in print. His Amaryllis, & Sir Walter Raleighs Cynthia, how fine & sweet inventions? Excellent matter of emulation for Spencer, Constable, France, Watson, Daniel, Warner, Chapman, Silvester, Shakespeare, & the rest of owr florishing metricians. I looke for much, aswell in verse, as in prose, from mie two Oxford frends, Doctor Gager, & M. Hackluit: both rarely furnished for the purpose: & I have a phansie to Owens new Epigrams, as pithie as elegant, as plesant as sharp, & sumtime as weightie as breife: & amongst so manie gentle, noble, & royall spirits meethinkes I see sum heroical thing in the clowdes: mie soveraine hope. Axiophilus[4] shall forgett himself, or will remember to leave sum memorials behinde him: & to make an use of so manie rhapsodies, cantos, hymnes, odes, epigrams, sonets, & discourses, as at idle howers, or at flowing fitts he hath compiled. God knowes what is good for the world, & fitting for this age.

Contract for the Building of the Fortune Theatre (1600)

[This contract was drawn up between Philip Henslowe and Edward Alleyn, partners in the venture, and Peter Street, the carpenter (or general contractor) in charge of the construction. In fact, Alleyn seems to have put up all the money, £440 for the work specified in the contract in addition to £80 for decoration and considerable sums to acquire the lot and surrounding properties. Alleyn faced opposition from residents of the neighborhood, but he had secured the favor of key supporters, so that he was able to proceed with the construction. As the new home of the Lord Admiral's Men, the Fortune did in fact become a center of disturbances, with complaints coming to the Middlesex Bench of assaults, petty thefts, and riotous behavior. Alleyn had been the leading actor of the Lord Admiral's Men, chief competitors of the Lord Chamberlain's Men, and the Fortune was conceived to compete with the Globe, meanwhile replacing the decaying and poorly situated Rose Theatre. The contract's

---

1. By William Warner (1586).
2. *The Ciuile Wars Between the Two Houses of Lancaster and Yorke* (1595).
3. "Let what is cheap excite the marvel of the crowd; for me may golden Apollo minister full cups from the

Castalian fount" (Ovid, *Amores* 1.15.35–36, Loeb translation). These lines also appear on the title page of Shakespeare's *Venus and Adonis* (1592–93).
4. Probably Harvey himself.

descriptions and frequent references to the Globe, given this background, can be seen as providing some of our best evidence on the nature of the Globe itself. The text is reprinted in *ES*, vol. 2.]

'This Indenture made the Eighte daie of Januarye 1599,[1] and in the Twoe and Fortyth yeare of the Reigne of our sovereigne Ladie Elizabeth, by the grace of god Queene of Englande, Fraunce and Irelande, defender of the Faythe, &c. betwene Phillipp Henslowe and Edwarde Allen of the parishe of Ste Saviours in Southwark in the Countie of Surrey, gentlemen, on thone parte, and Peeter Streete, Cittizen and Carpenter of London, on thother parte witnesseth That whereas the saide Phillipp Henslowe & Edward Allen, the daie of the date hereof, have bargayned, compounded & agreed with the saide Peter Streete ffor the erectinge, buildinge & settinge upp of a new howse and Stadge for a Plaiehouse in and uppon a certeine plott or parcell of grounde appoynted oute for that purpose, scytuate and beinge nere Goldinge lane in the parishe of Ste Giles withoute Cripplegate of London,[2] to be by him the saide Peeter Streete or somme other sufficyent woorkmen of his provideinge and appoyntemente and att his propper costes & chardges, for the consideracion hereafter in theis presentes expressed, made, erected, builded and sett upp in manner & forme followinge (that is to saie); The frame of the saide howse to be sett square[3] and to conteine ffowerscore foote of lawfull assize everye waie square withoutt and fiftie five foote of like assize square everye waie within, with a good suer and stronge foundacion of pyles, brick, lyme and sand bothe without & within, to be wroughte one foote of assize att the leiste above the grounde; And the saide fframe to conteine three Stories in heighth, the first or lower Storie to conteine Twelve foote of lawfull assize in heighth, the second Storie Eleaven foote of lawfull assize in heigh, and the third or upper Storie to conteine Nyne foote of lawfull assize in heigh; All which Stories shall conteine Twelve foote and a halfe of lawfull assize in breadth througheoute, besides a juttey forwardes in either of the saide twoe upper Stories of Tenne ynches of lawfull assize, with ffower convenient divisions for gentlemens roomes,[4] and other sufficient and convenient divisions for Twoe pennie roomes, with necessarie seates to be placed and sett, aswell in those roomes as througheoute all the rest of the galleries of the saide howse, and with suchelike steares, conveyances & divisions withoute & within, as are made & contryved in and to the late erected Plaiehowse on the Banck in the saide parishe of Ste Saviours called the Globe; With a Stadge and Tyreinge howse[5] to be made, erected & settupp within the saide fframe, with a shadowe or cover[6] over the saide Stadge, which Stadge shalbe placed & sett, as alsoe the stearecases of the saide fframe, in suche sorte as is prefigured in a plott[7] thereof drawen, and which Stadge shall conteine in length Fortie and Three foote of lawfull assize and in breadth to extende to the middle of the yarde[8] of the saide howse; The same Stadge to be paled in belowe with good, stronge and sufficyent newe oken bourdes, and likewise the lower Storie of the saide fframe withinside, and the same lower storie to be alsoe laide over and fenced with stronge yron pykes; And the saide Stadge to be in all other proporcions contryved and fashioned like unto the Stadge of the saide Plaie howse called the Globe; With convenient windowes and lightes glazed to the saide Tyreinge howse; And the saide fframe, Stadge and Stearecases to be covered with Tyle, and to have a sufficient gutter of lead to carrie & convey the water frome the coveringe of the saide Stadge to fall backwardes; And also all the saide fframe and the Stairecases thereof

1. 1600 (New Style).
2. *nere . . . London*: an area then in the northwest suburbs, literally outside Cripplegate and, like the Globe across the water, outside the jurisdiction of a City Council often inimical to the theater.
3. This square shape was unusual; the outlines of comparable theaters of the period were round or polygonal (with more than four sides).
4. Something like the VIP boxes of the present day.

5. "Attiring house," a dressing room and backstage area extending onto the rear of the stage.
6. A roof (known as "the heavens") partially covering the stage, supported by the pillars that also served as versatile pieces of scenery.
7. Plan.
8. *in breadth . . . yarde*: the stage would then extend about 27 feet into the yard, specified earlier as 55 feet square.

to be sufficyently enclosed withoute with lathe, lyme & haire, and the gentlemens roomes and Twoe pennie roomes to be seeled[9] with lathe, lyme & haire, and all the fflowers of the saide Galleries, Stories and Stadge to be bourded with good & sufficyent newe deale bourdes of the whole thicknes, wheare need shalbe; And the saide howse and other thinges beforemencioned to be made & doen to be in all other contrivitions, conveyances, fashions, thinge and thinges effected, finished and doen according to the manner and fashion of the saide howse called the Globe, saveinge only that all the princypall and maine postes of the saide fframe and Stadge forwarde shalbe square and wroughte palasterwise,[1] with carved proporcions called Satiers[2] to be placed & sett on the topp of every of the same postes, and saveinge alsoe that the said Peeter Streete shall not be chardged with anie manner of pay[ntin]ge in or aboute the saide fframe howse or Stadge or anie parte thereof, nor rendringe[3] the walls within, nor seeling anie more or other roomes then the gentlemens roomes, Twoe pennie roomes and Stadge before remembred. Nowe theiruppon the saide Peeter Streete dothe covenant, promise and graunte ffor himself, his executours and administratours, to and with the saide Phillipp Henslowe and Edward Allen and either of them, and thexecutours and administratours of them and either of them, by theis presentes in manner & forme followeinge (that is to saie); That he the saide Peeter Streete, his executours or assignes, shall & will att his or their owne propper costes & chardges well, woorkmanlike & substancyallie make, erect, sett upp and fully finishe in and by all thinges, according to the true meaninge of theis presentes, with good, stronge and substancyall newe tymber and other necessarie stuff, all the saide fframe and other woorkes whatsoever in and uppon the saide plott or parcell of grounde (beinge not by anie aucthoretie restrayned, and haveinge ingres, egres & regres to doe the same) before the ffyve & twentith daie of Julie next commeinge after the date hereof; And shall alsoe at his or theire like costes and chardges provide and finde all manner of woorkmen, tymber, joystes, rafters, boordes, dores, boltes, hinges, brick, tyle, lathe, lyme, haire, sande, nailes, lade, iron, glasse, woorkmanshipp and other thinges whatsoever, which shalbe needefull, convenyent & necessarie for the saide fframe & woorkes & everie parte thereof; And shall alsoe make all the saide fframe in every poynte for Scantlinges[4] lardger and bigger in assize then the Scantlinges of the timber of the saide newe erected howse called the Globe; And alsoe that he the saide Peeter Streete shall furthwith, aswell by himself as by suche other and soemanie woorkmen as shalbe convenient & necessarie, enter into and uppon the saide buildinges and woorkes, and shall in reasonable manner proceede therein withoute anie wilfull detraccion untill the same shalbe fully effected and finished. In consideracion of all which buildinges and of all stuff & woorkemanshipp thereto belonginge, the saide Phillipp Henslowe & Edward Allen and either of them, ffor themselves, theire, and either of theire executours & administratours, doe joynctlie & severallie covenante & graunte to & with the saide Peeter Streete, his executours & administratours by theis presentes, that they the saide Phillipp Henslowe & Edward Allen or one of them, or the executours administratours or assignes of them or one of them, shall & will well & truelie paie or cawse to be paide unto the saide Peeter Streete, his executours or assignes, att the place aforesaid appoynted for the erectinge of the saide fframe, the full somme of Fower hundred & Fortie Poundes of lawfull money of Englande in manner & forme followeinge (that is to saie), att suche tyme and when as the Tymberwoork of the saide fframe shalbe rayzed & sett upp by the saide Peeter Streete his executours or assignes, or within seaven daies then next followeinge, Twoe hundred & Twentie poundes, and att suche time and when as the saide fframe & woorkes shalbe fullie effected & ffynished as is aforesaide, or within seaven daies then next followeinge, thother Twoe hundred and Twentie poundes,

9. Coated both on the "ceiling" (a related word) and the walls.
1. Finished in the form of pilasters, ornamental columns in the classical style.
2. Satyrs. *proporcions*: figures.
3. Plastering.
4. Prescribed dimensions of the beams.

withoute fraude or coven.[5] Provided allwaies, and it is agreed betwene the saide parties, that whatsoever somme or sommes of money the saide Phillipp Henslowe &
Edward Allen or either of them, or thexecutours or assignes of them or either of them,
shall lend or deliver unto the saide Peter Streete his executours or assignes, or anie
other by his appoyntemente or consent, ffor or concerninge the saide woorkes or anie
parte thereof or anie stuff thereto belonginge, before the raizeinge & settinge upp of
the saide fframe, shalbe reputed, accepted, taken & accoumpted in parte of the firste
paymente aforesaid of the saide some of Fower hundred & Fortie poundes, and all
suche somme & sommes of money, as they or anie of them shall as aforesaid lend or
deliver betwene the razeinge of the saide fframe & finishinge thereof and of all the
rest of the saide woorkes, shalbe reputed, accepted, taken & accoumpted in parte of
the laste pamente aforesaid of the same somme of Fower hundred & Fortie poundes,
anie thinge abovesaid to the contrary notwithstandinge. In witnes whereof the parties abovesaid to theis presente Indentures Interchaungeably have sett theire handes
and seales. Geoven[6] the daie and yeare ffirste abovewritten.

P S

Sealed and delivered by the saide Peter Streete in the presence of me William Harris Pub[lic] Scr[ivener] And me Frauncis Smyth appr[entice] to the said Scr[ivener]
[*Endorsed:*] Peater Streat ffor The Building of the Fortune.

Augustine Phillips, Francis Bacon, et al. on *Richard II* (1601)

[These extracts from testimony submitted at the Earl of Essex's trial for treason, and
related documents, show that some of Essex's supporters had contracted with the Lord
Chamberlain's Men to revive *Richard II,* apparently in order to provide a model for the justified deposition of a monarch and thus propitiate the coup in which Essex planned to
depose Elizabeth. The play was performed on February 7, and "it was on the same day,"
according to E. K. Chambers, "that Essex received a summons to appear before the Privy
Council. This interrupted his plans for securing possession of the Queen's person and
arresting her ministers, and precipitated his futile outbreak of February 8." Augustine
Phillips was one of Shakespeare's colleagues in the Lord Chamberlain's Men. Sir Edward
Coke was, for a time, chief justice under King James. The last excerpt is a contemporary
record of a conversation between the queen and her archivist several months after Essex
was executed. The texts are from WS, vol. 2.]

From the Abstract of Evidence

The Erle of Essex is charged with high Treason, namely, That he plotted and
practised with the Pope and king of Spaine for the disposing and settling to himself Aswell the Crowne of England, as of the kingdom of Ireland.

From the Examination of Augustine Phillips, February 18, 1601

The Examination of Augustyne Phillypps servant unto the L Chamberlyne and
one of hys players taken the xviij[th] of Februarij 1600 upon hys oth
He sayeth that on Fryday last was sennyght or Thursday S[r] Charles Percy S[r]
Josclyne Percy and the L. Montegle with some thre more spak to some of the play-

---

5. Deceit.   6. Given.

ers in the presans of thys examinate to have the play of the deposyng and kyllyng of Kyng Rychard the second to be played the Saterday next promysyng to gete them xls. more then their ordynary to play yt. Wher thys Examinate and hys fellowes were determyned to have played some other play, holdyng that play of Kyng Richard to be so old & so long out of use as that they shold have small or no Company at yt. But at their request this Examinate and his fellowes were Content to play yt the Saterday and had their xls. more then their ordynary for yt and so played yt accordyngly

Augustine Phillipps

From the speech of Sir Edward Coke at Essex's trial, February 19

I protest upon my soul and conscience I doe beleeve she should not have long lived after she had been in your power. Note but the precedents of former ages, how long lived Richard the Second after he was surprised in the same manner? The pretence was alike for the removing of certain counsellors, but yet shortly after it cost him his life.

From [Francis Bacon's] "A Declaration of the . . . Treasons . . . by Robert late Earle of Essex"

The afternoone before the rebellion, Merricke,[1] with a great company of others, that afterwards were all in the action, had procured to bee played before them, the play of deposing King Richard the second. Neither was it casuall, but a play bespoken by Merrick. And not so onely, but when it was told him by one of the players, that the play was olde, and they should have losse in playing it, because fewe would come to it: there was fourty shillings extraordinarie given to play it, and so thereupon playd it was. So earnest hee was to satisfie his eyes with the sight of that tragedie which hee thought soone after his lord should bring from the stage to the state, but that God turned it upon their owne heads.

From a Memorandum in the Lambard family manuscript, August 4

. . . so her Majestie fell upon[2] the reign of King Richard II. saying, 'I am Richard II. know ye not that?'

W.L. 'Such a wicked imagination was determined and attempted by a most unkind Gent. the most adorned creature that ever your Majestie made.'

Her Majestie. 'He that will forget God, will also forget his benefactors; this tragedy was played 40^{tie} times in open streets and houses.'

John Manningham on *Twelfth Night* and *Richard III* (1602)

[John Manningham (d. 1622) kept a diary during his time as a law student at the Middle Temple, recording the witticisms of his colleagues and a rich variety of anecdotes. The vibrant and boisterous life of the Inns of Court is also illustrated by the *Gesta Grayorum* (see above). The February entry describes the festivities organized for Candlemas Day at the Middle Temple, while the second recounts an anecdote related to Manningham by one Mr. Touse (this name is difficult to read in the manuscript). As with all the documents in this section, any date before March 25 is assigned to the following year according to our calendar, so that 1601 here becomes 1602 (New Style).

---

1. Sir Gilly Merrick, one of Essex's supporters, was later tried separately for treason.
2. Came across (in reading). The memorandum describes a scene in which the queen is reading over the archives that have been in the keeping of her interlocutor, William Lambard.

The text is from the 1976 edition of Robert Sorlien (Hanover, N.H.: University Press of New England).]

Febr. 1601

2. At our feast wee had a play called "Twelve night, or what you will"; much like the commedy of errores, or Menechmi[1] in Plautus, but most like and neere to that in Italian called Inganni.[2] A good practise in it to make the steward beleeve his Lady widdowe[3] was in Love with him, by counterfayting a letter, as from his Lady, in generall termes, telling him what shee liked best in him, and prescribing his gesture in smiling, his apparraile, &c., and then when he came to practise, making him beleeve they tooke him to be mad.

Marche. 1601

13. . . . Upon a tyme when Burbidge played Rich[ard] 3. there was a Citizen grewe soe farr in liking with him, that before shee went from the play shee appointed him to come that night unto hir by the name of Ri[chard] the 3. Shakespeare, overhearing their conclusion, went before, was intertained, and at his game ere Burbidge came. Then message being brought that Richard the 3ᵈ. was at the dore, Shakespeare caused returne to be made that William the Conquerour was before Rich[ard] the 3. Shakespeare's name William. (Mr. Touse.)

Letters Patent Formalizing the Adoption of the Lord Chamberlain's Men as the King's Men (May 19, 1603)

[James I issued the warrant ordering this patent shortly after his coronation, enhancing the status of Shakespeare's company. As retainers of the royal household with the title of Grooms of the Chamber, they performed at the court with increasing frequency (177 times between 1603 and 1616) and assisted occasionally with other court functions; but, more important, they acted throughout the kingdom under the authority of the royal patent, whose scope the forceful wording below makes clear. The patent, bearing the Great Seal, was issued May 19 as ordered in the warrant of May 17. There is some evidence to suggest that James was particularly taken with Shakespeare's poetry, and the playwright's valorization of James's ancestry (as originating with Banquo) in *Macbeth* certainly suggests that Shakespeare cultivated his esteem. The text is from *ES*, vol. 2.]

Commissio specialis pro Laurencio Fletcher & Willelmo Shackespeare et aliis[2] — James by the grace of god &c. To all Justices, Maiors, Sheriffes, Constables, hedborowes,[1] and other our Officers and lovinge Subjectes greeting. Knowe yee that Wee of our speciall grace, certeine knowledge, & mere motion[3] have licenced and aucthorized and by theise presentes[4] doe licence and aucthorize theise our Servauntes Lawrence Fletcher, William Shakespeare, Richard Burbage, Augustyne Phillippes, John Heninges, Henrie Condell, William Sly, Robert Armyn, Richard Cowly, and the rest of theire Assosiates freely to use and exercise the Arte and faculty of playinge

---

1. Source for *The Comedy of Errors*.
2. The two plays with this exact title (1562 and 1592) seem less likely to be "most like" *Twelfth Night* than another Italian play, *Ingannati* (1537), which has characters named Fabio and Malevolti and makes reference to Twelfth Night (Epiphany).
3. Olivia is not a widow in the version of Shakespeare's play that has come down to us, though she is

so described in one of Shakespeare's principal sources for the play.
1. A parish officer similar to a petty constable.
2. *Commissio . . . aliis:* By special commission on behalf of . . . and others.
3. Inclination, desire.
4. The present document.

Comedies, Tragedies, histories, Enterludes, moralls,[5] pastoralls, Stageplaies, and Suche others like as theie have alreadie studied or hereafter shall use or studie, aswell for the recreation of our lovinge Subjectes, as for our Solace and pleasure when wee shall thincke good to see them, duringe our pleasure. And the said Commedies, tragedies, histories, Enterludes, Morralles, Pastoralls, Stageplayes, and suche like to shewe and exercise publiquely to theire best Commoditie,[6] when the infection of the plague shall decrease, aswell within theire nowe usual howse called the Globe within our County of Surrey, as alsoe within anie towne halls or Moute halls[7] or other conveniente places within the liberties and freedome of anie other Cittie, universitie, towne, or Boroughe whatsoever within our said Realmes and domynions. Willinge and Commaundinge you and everie of you, as you tender our pleasure, not onelie to permitt and suffer them herein without anie your lettes hindrances or molestacions during our said pleasure, but alsoe to be aidinge and assistinge to them, yf anie wronge be to them offered, And to allowe them such former Curtesies as hath bene given to men of theire place and quallitie,[8] and alsoe what further favour you shall shewe to theise our Servauntes for our sake wee shall take kindlie at your handes. In wytnesse whereof &c. witnesse our selfe at Westminster the nyntenth day of May

per breve de privato sigillo[9] &c.

Master of the Wardrobe's Account (March 1604)

[This entry offers us a rare glimpse of the players in the entourage of King James, sporting festive regalia in their capacity as Grooms of the Chamber. The royal procession took place March 15, 1604. The text is from WS, vol. 2.]

Red Clothe bought of sondrie persons and given by his Majestie to diverse persons against[1] his Majesties sayd royall proceeding through the Citie of London, viz.:— . . .

The Chamber . . .	
Fawkeners[2] &c. &c.	Red cloth
William Shakespeare	iiii yardes di.
Augustine Phillipps	"
Lawrence Fletcher	"
John Hemminges	"
Richard Burbidge	"
William Slye	"
Robert Armyn	"
Henry Cundell	"
Richard Cowley	"

Simon Forman on *Macbeth*, *Cymbeline*, and *The Winter's Tale* (1611)

[Simon Forman (1552–1611) was a largely self-educated physician and astrologer who rose from humble beginnings to establish a successful London practice. A large parcel of his manuscripts, including scientific and autobiographical material as well as the diary from which this account of the plays is taken, has survived, making his life one of the best-documented Elizabethan lives. These manuscripts provide

---

5. Morality plays.
6. Advantage.
7. Council chambers.
8. Profession.
9. In sum, from the privy seal.

1. For.
2. Obsolete form of "falconers," very likely the men who trained the falcons used for James's fowl-hunting expeditions. The falconers might owe their place in the retinue to James's well-known passion for hunting.

detailed information about Forman's many sidelines, such as the manufacture of talismans, alchemy, and necromancy, as well about his sex life. The text is from *WS*, vol. 2.]

The Bocke of Plaies and Notes therof per formane for Common Pollicie[1]

In Mackbeth at the Glob, 1610 ⟨1611⟩, the 20 of Aprill ♄ (Saturday), ther was to be observed, firste, howe Mackbeth and Bancko, 2 noble men of Scotland, Ridinge thorowe a wod, the ⟨r⟩ stode before them 3 women feiries or Nimphes, And saluted Mackbeth, sayinge, 3 tyms unto him, haille Mackbeth, king of Codon;[2] for thou shalt be a kinge, but shalt beget No kinges, &c. Then said Bancko, What all to Mackbeth And nothing to me. Yes, said the nimphes, haille to thee Bancko, thou shalt beget kinges, yet be no kinge. And so they departed & cam to the Courte of Scotland to Dunkin king of Scotes, and yt was in the dais of Edward the Confessor. And Dunkin bad them both kindly wellcome, And made Mackbeth forth with Prince of Northumberland,[3] and sent him hom to his own castell, and appointed Mackbeth to provid for him, for he would sup with him the next dai at night, & did soe. And Mackebeth contrived to kill Dunkin, & thorowe the persuasion of his wife did that night Murder the kinge in his own Castell, beinge his guest. And ther were many prodigies seen that night & the dai before. And when Mack Beth had murdred the kinge, the blod on his handes could not be washed of by Any meanes, nor from his wives handes, which handled the bloddi daggers in hiding them, By which means they became both moch amazed & Affronted. The murder being knowen, Dunkins 2 sonns fled, the on to England, the ⟨other to⟩ Walles, to save them selves, they being fled, they were supposed guilty of the murder of their father, which was nothinge so. Then was Mackbeth crowned kinge, and then he for feare of Banko, his old companion, that he should beget kinges but be no kinge him selfe, he contrived the death of Banko, and caused him to be Murdred on the way as he Rode. The next night, beinge at supper with his noble men whom he had bid to a feaste to the which also Banco should have com, he began to speake of Noble Banco, and to wish that he wer ther. And as he thus did, standing up to drincke a Carouse to him, the ghoste of Banco came and sate down in his cheier behind him. And he turninge About to sit down Again sawe the goste of Banco, which fronted him so, that he fell into a great passion of fear and fury, Utterynge many wordes about his murder, by which, when they hard that Banco was Murdred they Suspected Mackbet.

Then MackDove fled to England to the kinges sonn, And soe they Raised an Army, And cam into Scotland, and at Dunston Anyse overthrue Mackbet. In the meantyme whille Macdovee was in England, Mackbet slewe Mackdoves wife & children, and after in the battelle Mackdove slewe Mackbet.

Observe Also howe Mackbetes quen did Rise in the night in her slepe, & walke and talked and confessed all, & the docter noted her wordes.

Of Cimbalin king of England.

Remember also the storri of Cymbalin king of England, in Lucius tyme, howe Lucius Cam from Octavus Cesar for Tribut, and being denied, after sent Lucius with a greate Arme of Souldiars who landed at Milford haven, and Affter wer vanquished by Cimbalin, and Lucius taken prisoner, and all by means of 3 outlawes, of the which 2 of them were the sonns of Cimbalim, stolen from him when they were but 2 yers old by an old man whom Cymbalin banished, and he kept them as his own sonns 20 yers with him in A cave. And howe ⟨one⟩ of them slewe Clotan, that was the quens sonn, goinge to Milford haven to sek the love of Innogen the

---

1. *Common Pollicie:* practical use. Forman's title for his notes on plays is not printed in Chambers, but interpolated here from G. Blakemore Evans's transcription in the *Riverside Shakespeare*.

2. Cawdor.
3. Probably Forman's error; Duncan gives Macbeth the title Thane of Cawdor. Duncan's son Malcolm is the Prince of Northumberland.

kinges daughter, whom he had banished also for lovinge his daughter,[4] and howe
the Italian that cam from her love conveied him selfe into A Cheste, and said yt
was a chest of plate sent from her love & others, to be presented to the kinge. And
in the depest of the night, she being aslepe, he opened the cheste, & cam forth of
yt, And vewed her in her bed, and the markes of her body, & toke awai her braslet,
& after Accused her of adultery to her love, &c. And in thend howe he came with
the Romains into England & was taken prisoner, and after Reveled to Innogen,
Who had turned her self into mans apparrell & fled to mete her love at Milford
haven, & chanchsed to fall on the Cave in the wodes wher her 2 brothers were, &
howe by eating a sleping Dram they thought she had bin deed, & laid her in the
wodes, & the body of Cloten by her, in her loves apparrell that he left behind him,
& howe she was found by Lucius, &c.

In the Winters Talle at the glob 1611 the 15 of maye ☿ ⟨Wednesday⟩.

Observe ther howe Lyontes the kinge of Cicillia was overcom with Jelosy of his
wife with the kinge of Bohemia his frind that came to see him, and howe he contrived his death and wold have had his cup berer to have poisoned, who gave the
king of Bohemia warning therof & fled with him to Bohemia.

Remember also howe he sent to the Orakell of Appollo & the Annswer of
Apollo, that she was giltles and that the king was jelouse &c. and howe Except the
child was found Again that was loste the kinge should die without yssue, for the
child was caried into Bohemia & ther laid in a forrest & brought up by a sheppard
And the kinge of Bohemia his sonn maried that wentch & howe they fled into Cicillia to Leontes, and the sheppard having showed the letter of the nobleman by
whom Leontes sent a was ⟨away?⟩ that child and the jewells found about her, she
was knowen to be Leontes daughter and was then 16 yers old.

Remember also the Rog[5] that cam in all tottered like coll pixci[6] and howe he
feyned him sicke & to have bin Robbed of all that he had and howe he cosened the
por man of all his money, and after cam to the shep sher[7] with a pedlers packe &
ther cosened them Again of all their money And howe he changed apparrell with
the kinge of Bomia his sonn, and then howe he turned Courtier &c. Beware of
trustinge feined beggars or fawninge fellouss.

Sir Henry Wotton on *All Is True (Henry VIII)* and the Burning of the Globe (1613)

[Sir Henry Wotton (1568–1639), a highly educated poet and essayist, distinguished
diplomat, and finally provost of Eton College, wrote to his nephew Sir Edmund Bacon
shortly after the burning of the Globe. Chambers includes several other accounts of
this incident in *The Elizabethan Stage*, vol. 2, pp. 419ff. The event is also recorded in
John Stow's chronicles and was lamented by poets, including (several years later) Ben
Jonson, and held up by Puritan divines like Prynne as an intimation of God's wrath. The
excerpt below is from the earliest extant text, *Letters of Sir Henry Wotton to Sir Edmund
Bacon* (London, 1661), p. 29.]

Now, to let matters of State sleep, I will entertain you at the present with what
hath happened this week at the banks side. The Kings Players had a new Play, called
All is true, representing some principall pieces of the raign of *Henry* 8, which was set
forth with many extraordinary circumstances of Pomp and Majesty, even to the matting of the stage; the Knights of the Order, with their Georges and Garter, the Guards
with their embroidered Coats, and the like: sufficient in truth within a while to make

---

4. Morgan/Belarius is not banished in the version of
the play that comes down to us.
5. Rogue (Autolycus).

6. Probably "colt-pixie," a mischievous sprite or fairy.
7. Sheep shearing.

greatness very familiar, if not ridiculous. Now, King *Henry* making a Masque at the Cardinal, *Wolsey's* house, and certain Chambers[1] being shot off at his entry, some of the paper, or other stuff wherewith one of them was stopped, did light on the thatch, where being thought at first but an idle smoak, and their eyes more attentive to the show, it kindled inwardly, and ran round like a train, consuming within less then an hour the whole house to the very grounds.

This was the fatal period of that vertuous fabrique, wherein yet nothing did perish, but wood and straw, and a few forsaken cloaks; only one man had his breeches set on fire, that would perhaps have broyled him, if he had not by the benefit of a provident wit put it out with bottle Ale. The rest when we meet.

Ben Jonson on *The Tempest* (and *Titus Andronicus*) (1614)

[This extract from *Bartholomew Fair* contains one of several allusions to Shakespeare in the plays of his associate and sometime rival. The first paragraph alludes to the fashion for revenge plays such as Shakespeare's *Titus Andronicus* and Kyd's *Spanish Tragedy*, at its height roughly twenty-five years before *Bartholomew Fair* was written. The second paragraph refers disapprovingly to *The Tempest* (1613), first produced shortly before *Bartholomew Fair*. The text is that reprinted in *WS*, vol. 2, from the 1631 edition of Jonson's play (from the play's Induction).]

Hee that will sweare, *Jeronimo*, or *Andronicus* are the best playes, yet, shall passe unexcepted at,[1] heere, as a man whose Judgement shewes it is constant, and hath stood still, these five and twentie, or thirtie yeeres. . . .

If there bee never a *Servant-monster* i' the Fayre; who can helpe it? he[2] sayes; nor a nest of Antiques?[3] Hee is loth to make Nature afraid[4] in his *Playes*, like those that beget *Tales*, *Tempests*, and such like *Drolleries*, to mix his head with other mens heeles; let the concupisence of *Jigges* and *Dances*, raigne as strong as it will amongst you.[5]

Shakespeare's Will (March 25, 1616)

[Shakespeare probably dictated this will sometime around January 1616. The first draft seems to have been dated in January, and 1616 is the most likely inference for the year (see note 1). The final revision was certainly made on the date given, but no clean copy was prepared, so the manuscript contains a substantial number of insertions and deletions. The text here has been silently emended to assist in ease of reading. Deleted passages have been eliminated; the most significant of these is reproduced in the notes, where significant interlineations are also identified. Most of the altered passages, as Chambers writes, simply "correct slips, make the legal terminology more precise, or incorporate afterthoughts." The revision of the will was occasioned chiefly by the February marriage of Shakespeare's daughter Judith. Our text is adapted from E. A. J. Honigmann and Susan Brock, eds., *Playhouse Wills, 1558–1642* (Manchester: Manchester University Press, 1993). For a facsimile and thorough discussion of the will, see *WS* 2:169–80.]

1. Small pieces of artillery, used for firing salutes.
1. Uncriticized.
2. The author.
3. Variant spelling of "antics," grotesque or ludicrous representations, or the actors (such as the clowns in *The Tempest*) playing such parts.
4. Make nature afraid by inexact imitation or too much

fantasy.
5. *concupisence . . . you:* a reference to the dance generally incorporated into theatrical performance (see, for example, Platter's account above). Jonson suggests he is refusing to cater to the vulgar taste for more dancing in plays.

Testamentum willelmij Shackspeare

Vicesimo Quinto die martij Anno Regni Domini nostri Jacobi nunc Regis Anglie &c decimo quarto & Scotie xlixo Annoque domini 1616[1]

In the name of god Amen I William Shackspeare of Stratford upon Avon in the countie of warrwick gentleman in perfect health & memorie god be praysed doe make & Ordayne this my last will & testament in manner & forme followeing That ys to saye ffirst I Comend my Soule into the handes of god my Creator hoping & assuredlie beleeving through thonelie merittes of Jesus Christe my Saviour to be made partaker of lyfe everlastinge And my bodye to the Earth whereof yt ys made Item I Gyve & bequeath unto my Daughter Judyth One Hundred & ffyftie poundes of lawfull English money to be paied unto her in manner & forme followeing That ys to saye One Hundred Poundes in discharge of her marriage porcion[2] within one yeare after my Deceas with consideracion[3] after the Rate of twoe shillinges in the pound for soe long tyme as the same shalbe unpaied unto her after my deceas & the ffyftie poundes Residewe thereof upon her Surrendring of or gyving of such sufficient securitie as the overseers of this my Will shall like of to Surrender or graunnte All her[4] estate & Right that shall discend or come unto her after my deceas or that shee nowe hath of in or to one Copiehold tenemente with thappurtenaunces lyeing & being in Stratford upon Avon aforesaied in the saied countie of warrwick being parcell or holden of the mannour of Rowington unto my Daughter Susanna Hall & her heires for ever Item I Gyve & bequeath unto my saied Daughter Judith One Hundred & ffyftie Poundes more if shee or Anie issue of her bodie be Lyvinge att thend of three Yeares next ensueing the daie of the Date of this my Will during which tyme my executours to paie her consideracion from my deceas according to the Rate afore saied And if she dye within the saied terme without issue of her bodye then my will ys & I doe gyve & bequeath One Hundred Poundes thereof to my Neece Elizabeth Hall & the ffiftie Poundes to be sett fourth by my executours during the lief of my Sister Johane Harte & the use & proffitt thereof Cominge shalbe payed to my saied Sister Jone & after her deceas the saied l li[5] shall Remaine Amongst the children of my saied Sister Equallie to be Devided Amongst them But if my saied Daughter Judith be lyving att thend of the saied three Yeares or anie yssue of her bodye then my Will ys & soe I devise & bequeath the saied Hundred & ffyftie poundes to be sett out by my executours & overseers for the best benefitt of her & her issue & the stock[6] not to be paied unto her soe long as she shalbe marryed & Covert Baron[7] but my will ys that she shall have the consideracon yearelie paied unto her during her lief & after her deceas the saied stock and consideracion to bee paied to her children if she have Anie & if not to her executours or assignes she lyving the saied terme after my deceas Provided that if such husbond as she shall att thend of the saied three Yeares be marryed unto or attaine after doe sufficientle Assure unto her & thissue of her bodie landes Awnswereable to the porcion by this my will gyven unto her & to be adjudged soe by my executours & overseers then my will ys that the saied Cl li[8] shalbe paied to such husbond as shall make such assurance to his owne use Item I gyve & bequeath unto my saied sister Jone xx li & all my wearing Apparrell to be paied & Delivered within one yeare after my deceas And I doe Will & devise unto her the house with thappurtenaunces in Stratford wherein she dwelleth for her naturall lief under the yearelie Rent of xii d. Itm I gyve & bequeath unto her three sonns William Harte[9]

---

1. *Testamentum . . . 1616:* The Will of William Shakespeare (marginal heading). On the twenty-fifth day of March, in the fourteenth year of the reign of our lord James now King of England, etc., and of Scotland the forty-ninth, in the year of our Lord 1616. (The abbreviation for "January" is crossed out in the manuscript, "March" having been substituted at the time the will was revised.)

2. The phrase "in discharge of her marriage porcion" was inserted during the course of revision.

3. Compensation, or interest.

4. Susanna Hall's. (The preceding "All" marks the beginning of a new sentence.)

5. *l li:* £50.

6. Principal.

7. *Covert Baron:* under the protection of a husband.

8. *Cl li:* £150.

9. A blank in the manuscript. Shakespeare appears to have forgotten the name of one of his nephews, Thomas.

hart & Michaell Harte ffyve poundes A peece to be payed within one Yeare after my deceas[1] Item I gyve & bequeath unto her the saied Elizabeth Hall All my Plate (except my brod silver & gilt bole)[2] that I nowe have att the Date of this my Will Itm I gyve & bequeath unto the Poore of Stratford aforesaied tenn poundes to mr Thomas Combe my Sword to Thomas Russell Esquier ffyve poundes & to ffrauncis Collins of the Borough of Warrwick in the countie of Warrwick gentleman thirteene poundes Sixe shillinges & Eight pence to be paied within one Yeare after my Deceas Itm I gyve & bequeath to Hamlett Sadler xxvi s viii d[3] to buy him A Ringe to William Raynoldes gentleman xxvi s viii d to buy him A Ringe to my godson William Walker xx s in gold to Anthonye Nashe gentleman xxvi s viii d & to mr John Nashe xx vi s viii d & to my fellows John Hemynnges Richard Burbage & Henry Cundell xxvi s viii d A peece to buy them Ringes[4] Item I Gyve Will bequeath & Devise unto my Daughter Susanna Hall for better enabling of her to performe this my will & towardes the performans thereof All that Capitall messuage or tenemente[5] with thappurtenaunces in Stratford aforesaied Called the newe place Wherein I nowe Dwell & twoe messuages or tenementes with thappurtenaunces scituat lyeing & being in Henley streete within the borough of Stratford aforesaied And all my barnes stables Orchardes gardens landes tenementes & hereditamentes[6] Whatsoever scituat lyeing & being or to be had Receyved perceyved or taken within the townes Hamlettes villages ffieldes & groundes of Stratford upon Avon Oldstratford Bushopton & Welcombe or in anie of them in the saied countie of warrwick And alsoe All that Messuage or tenemente with thappurtenaunces wherein one John Robinson dwelleth scituat lyeing & being in the blackfriers in London nere the Wardrobe & all other my landes tenementes & hereditamentes Whatsoever To Have & to hold All & singuler the saied premisses with their Appurtenaunces unto the saied Susanna Hall for & During the terme of her naturall lief & after her Deceas to the first sonne of her bodie lawfullie Issueing & to the heires males of the bodie of the saied first Sonne lawfullie Issueinge & for defalt of such issue to the second Sonne of her bodie lawfullie issueinge & to the heires males of the bodie of the saied Second Sonne lawfullie issueinge & for defalt of such heires to the third Sonne of the bodie of the saied Susanna Lawfullie issueing & of the heries males of the bodie of the saied third sonne lawfullie issueing And for defalt of such issue the same soe to be & Remaine to the ffourth ffyfth sixte & Seaventh sonnes of her bodie lawfullie issueing one after Another & to the heires[7] Males of the bodies of the saied ffourth fifth Sixte & Seaventh sonnes lawfullie issueing in such manner as yt ys before Lymitted to be & Remaine to the first second & third Sonns of her bodie & to their heires males And for defalt of such issue the saied premisses to be & Remaine to my sayed Neece Hall[8] & the heires Males of her bodie Lawfullie yssueing for Defalt of such issue to my Daughter Judith & the heires Males of her bodie lawfullie issueinge And for Defalt of such issue to the Right heires of me the saied William

---

1. *unto . . . deceas:* this passage was inserted at the top of the second page, probably when the will was revised. The following lines, with which the page originally began, are crossed out in the original: "to be sett out for her within one Yeare after my Deceas by my executours with thadvise & direccions of my overseers for her best proffitt untill her Marriage & then the same with the increase thereof to be paied unto her." These lines evidently referred to Judith Shakespeare as unmarried.
2. This parenthetical clause is an insertion, and has sparked some debate about Shakespeare's opinion of Judith's marriage.
3. The "s" stands for "shillings," the "d" for "pence."
4. *to my fellows . . . Ringes:* Shakespeare's "fellows," or colleagues, Heminges, Burbage, and Condell, had worked with him in the Lord Chamberlain's Men and

King's Men for many years. Many other wills and documents of the period provide evidence of the practice of wearing mourning rings alluded to here.
5. Residence. *messuage:* dwelling house with its outbuildings or adjoining lands.
6. Heritable property.
7. In addition to the signature near the end, Shakespeare signed the will here, in the bottom right-hand corner of the second page.
8. Susanna Hall's daughter Elizabeth, actually Shakespeare's granddaughter (the sense of "niece" is less restricted in early modern usage). Elizabeth proved to be Susanna's only surviving child, and since Susanna was already thirty-three in 1616, the hypothetical series of seven sons preceding this mention of Elizabeth is doubly remarkable.

Shackspere for ever Itm I gyve unto my wief my second best bed[9] with the furniture Item I gyve & bequeath to my saied Daughter Judith my broad silver gilt bole All the Rest of my goodes Chattelles Leases plate Jewels & household stuffe Whatsoever after my dettes and Legasies paied & my funerall expences discharged I gyve Devise & bequeath to my Sonne in Lawe John Hall gentleman & my Daughter Susanna his wief Whom I ordaine & make executours of this my Last Will & testament And I doe intreat & Appoint the saied Thomas Russell Esquier & ffrauncis Collins gentleman to be overseers hereof And doe Revoke All former wills & publishe this to be my last Will & testament In Witnes Whereof I have here unto put my hand the Daie & Yeare first above Written. /   By me William Shakespeare witnes to the publishing hereof Fra: Collyns Julyus Shawe John Robinson Hamnet Sadler Robert Whattcott[1]

Front Matter from the First Folio of Shakespeare's Plays (1623)

[John Heminges and Henry Condell, friends and colleagues of Shakespeare, organized this first publication of his collected (thirty-six) plays. Eighteen of the plays had not appeared in print before, and for these the First Folio is the sole surviving source. Only *Pericles, The Two Noble Kinsmen,* and *Sir Thomas More* are not included in the volume. Four of the first twelve (printed) pages of the Folio are reproduced below in reduced facsimile. They include Jonson's brief address "To the Reader," Droeshout's portrait of Shakespeare, a table of contents, and a list of actors.]

9. This bequest to Shakespeare's wife, Anne, was inserted in the course of his revision of the will. She is not mentioned elsewhere in the will at least partly because, as Shakespeare's widow, she would be guaranteed a certain portion of the estate by law. The appearance of this inserted bequest is nevertheless strange enough to have evoked much speculation.

1. After Shakespeare's death, the will was endorsed here at the bottom of the third page with a Latin inscription indicating that the will had gone to probate before a magistrate on June 22, 1616.

To the Reader.

This Figure, that thou here feeſt put,
    It vvas for gentle Shakeſpeare cut;
Wherein the Grauer had a ſtrife
    with Nature, to out-doo the life :
O, could he but haue dravvne his vvit
    As vvell in braſſe, as he hath hit
His face ; the Print vvould then ſurpaſſe
    All, that vvas euer vvrit in braſſe.
But, ſince he cannot, Reader, looke
    Not on his Picture, but his Booke.

                                    B. I.

Mr. WILLIAM

SHAKESPEARES

COMEDIES,
HISTORIES, &
TRAGEDIES.

Published according to the True Originall Copies.

Martin Droeshout sculpsit London.

LONDON
Printed by Isaac Iaggard, and Ed. Blount. 1623.

A CATALOGVE

of the feuerall Comedies, Hiſtories, and Tragedies contained in this Volume.

The Workes of William Shakespeare,

containing all his Comedies, Histories, and
Tragedies: Truely set forth, according to their first
ORIGINALL.

The Names of the Principall Actors
in all these Playes.

Illiam Shakespeare.

Richard Burbadge.

John Hemmings.

Augustine Phillips.

William Kempt.

Thomas Poope.

George Bryan.

Henry Condell.

William Slye.

Richard Cowly.

John Lowine.

Samuell Crosse.

Alexander Cooke.

Samuel Gilburne.

Robert Armin.

William Ostler.

Nathan Field.

John Underwood.

Nicholas Tooley.

William Ecclestone.

Joseph Taylor.

Robert Benfield.

Robert Goughe.

Richard Robinson.

Iohn Shancke.

Iohn Rice.

John Milton on Shakespeare (1630)

[John Milton (1608–1674) was born in London and as a boy might conceivably have seen Shakespeare's company act. This poem first appeared prefixed to the Second Folio of Shakespeare's works in 1632 and again in the 1640 *Poems* of Shakespeare. The text is from the 1645 edition of Milton's *Poems*, as reprinted in *WS*, vol. 2, but the title given is from the Second Folio version.]

An Epitaph on the admirable Dramaticke Poet, W. Shakespeare

What needs my *Shakespear* for his honour'd Bones,
The labour of an age in piled Stones,
Or that his hallow'd reliques should be hid
Under a star-ypointing[1] *Pyramid?*
Dear son of memory, great heir of Fame,
What need'st thou such weak witnes of thy name?
Thou in our wonder and astonishment
Hast built thy self a live-long Monument.
For whilst toth' shame of slow-endeavouring art,
They easie numbers flow, and that each heart
Hath from the leaves of thy unvalu'd[2] Book,
Those Delphick[3] lines with deep impression took,
Then thou our fancy of itself bereaving,[4]
Dost make us Marble with too much conceaving;
And so Sepulcher'd in such pomp dost lie,
That Kings for such a Tomb would wish to die.

Ben Jonson on Shakespeare (1623–37)

[In addition to numerous allusions to Shakespeare in his plays, Ben Jonson (1573–1637) writes explicitly about his friend, colleague, and rival in a number of places, most significantly in the two commendatory poems prefixed to the First Folio (see above) and in the published extracts from his notebooks entitled *Timber: or, Discoveries; Made upon Men and Matter,* first published in his *Works* of 1640. It is impossible to date the original entries precisely; Chambers's conjecture is that the following entry on Shakespeare was made after 1630. The text is from the authoritative edition by C. H. Herford and Percy Simpson, vol. 8 (Oxford: Clarendon Press, 1952).]

Indeed, the multitude commend Writers, as they doe Fencers, or Wrastlers; who if they come in robustiously, and put for it, with a deale of violence, are received for the *braver-fellowes:* when many times their owne rudenesse is a cause of their disgrace; and a slight touch of their Adversary, gives all that boisterous force the foyle. But in these things, the unskilfull are naturally deceiv'd, and judging wholly by the bulke, thinke rude things greater then polish'd; and scatter'd more numerous, then compos'd: Nor thinke this only to be true in the sordid multitude, but the neater sort of our *Gallants:* for all are the multitude; only they differ in cloaths, not in judgement or understanding.

I remember, the Players have often mentioned it as an honour to *Shakespeare,*

1. Pointing to the stars.
2. Invaluable.
3. Reference to Apollo, god of poetry, whose most famous shrine was at Delphi.

4. *our . . . bereaving:* "our imaginations are rapt 'out of ourselves,' leaving behind our soulless bodies like statues"—Isabel MacCaffrey.

that in his writing, (whatsoever he penn'd) hee never blotted out line.[1] My answer hath beene, Would he had blotted a thousand. Which they thought a malevolent speech. [I had not told posterity this,] but for their ignorance, who choose that circumstance to commend their friend by, wherein he most faulted. And to justifie mine owne candor, (for I lov'd the man, and doe honour his memory (on this side Idolatry) as much as any.) Hee was (indeed) honest, and of an open, and free nature: had an excellent *Phantsie*[2]; brave notions, and gentle expressions: wherein hee flow'd with that facility, that sometime it was necessary he should be stop'd: *Sufflaminandus erat;*[3] as *Augustus* said of *Haterius*.[4] His wit was in his owne power; would the rule of it had beene so too. Many times hee fell into those things, could not escape laughter: As when hee said in the person of *Cæsar*, one speaking to him; *Cæsar, thou dost me wrong.* Hee replyed: *Cæsar did never wrong, but with just cause*[5]: and such like; which were ridiculous. But hee redeemed his vices, with his vertues. There was ever more in him to be praysed, then to be pardoned.

John Aubrey on Shakespeare (1681)

[What Chambers calls "the Shakespeare-mythos" was already well under way by the time John Aubrey (1626–1697) collected these anecdotes for the biographies in his *Brief Lives*, first anthologized in 1692. Aubrey's chief sources were prominent figures of the Restoration stage, which had seen increasingly popular revivals and adaptations of *Hamlet*, *The Tempest*, and many other plays of Shakespeare. Numerous actors and critics in the latter part of the seventeenth century helped to "rehabilitate" Shakespeare; if at the time of the Restoration his plays had seemed terribly musty and old-fashioned, by the 1680s his reputation as an author of lasting value was well established, thanks to the enthusiasm of Restoration playgoers. Aubrey's first source, Christopher Beeston, was the son of a one-time member of Shakespeare's company. William Davenant was a formidable entrepreneur as well as a dramatist, and Thomas Shadwell a prolific playwright perhaps best remembered as Dryden's King of Dullness. The text is from Chambers's transcription (*WS*, vol. 2), with a few silent emendations for ease of reading. Some of the material is from the published version of *Brief Lives*, and some of it from manuscript notes apparently used in writing the *Lives*.]

> the more to be admired q[uia][1] he was not a company keeper[2]
> lived in Shoreditch, wouldnt be debauched, & if invited to
> writ; he was in paine.[3]
>
> W. Shakespeare.

M[r]. William Shakespear. [*bay-wreath in margin*] was borne at Stratford upon Avon, in the County of Warwick; his father was a Butcher, & I have been told heretofore by some of the neighbours, that when he was a boy he exercised his father's Trade, but when he kill'd a Calfe, he would doe it in a *high style*, & make a Speech. There was at that time another Butcher's son in this Towne, that was held not at all inferior to him for a naturall witt, his acquaintance & coetanean,[4] but dyed young. This Wm. being inclined naturally to Poetry and acting, came to London I guesse about 18. and was an Actor at one of the Play-houses and did act

---

1. Compare Heminges and Condell's address to the reader in the First Folio: "And what he thought, he uttered with that easinesse, that wee have scarse received from him a blot in his papers."
2. Imagination.
3. "He needed the drag-chain" (adapted from Marcus Seneca's *Controversiae* 4, Preface).
4. Quintus Haterius, Roman rhetorician (d. 26 C.E.).
5. See *Julius Caesar* 3.1.47.

1. Because.
2. "Company keeper" can mean "libertine" or "reveler"; the general sense of the passage is that Shakespeare is "the more to be admired" for his temperance and modesty.
3. The embarrassment ("paine") at being asked to write is presumably due to the same alleged modesty.
4. Contemporary.

exceedingly well: now B. Johnson was never a good Actor, but an excellent Instructor. He began early to make essayes at Dramatique Poetry, which at that time was very lowe; and his Playes tooke well: He was a handsome well shap't man: very good company, and of a very readie and pleasant smooth Witt. The Humour[5] of . . . the Constable in a Midsomersnight's Dreame, he happened to take at Grendon [*In margin,* 'I thinke it was Midsomer night that he happened to lye there'.] in Bucks[6] which is the roade from London to Stratford, and there was living that Constable about 1642 when I first came to Oxon.[7] M[r]. Jos. Howe is of that parish and knew him. Ben Johnson and he did gather Humours of men dayly where ever they came. One time as he was at the Tavern at Stratford super[8] Avon, one Combes an old rich Usurer was to be buryed, he makes there this extemporary[9] Epitaph

> Ten in the Hundred[1] the Devill allowes
> But *Combes* will have twelve, he sweares & vowes:
> If any one askes who lies in this Tombe:
> Hoh! quoth the Devill, 'Tis my John o' Combe.

He was wont to goe to his native Country once a yeare. I thinke I have been told that he left 2 or 300[li] per annum[2] there and therabout: to a sister. [*In margin,* 'V.[3] his Epitaph in Dugdales Warwickshire'.] I have heard S[r] Wm. Davenant and M[r]. Thomas Shadwell (who is counted the best Comœdian we have now) say, that he had a most prodigious Witt, and did admire his naturall parts beyond all other Dramaticall writers. He was wont to say, That he never blotted out a line in his life: sayd Ben: Johnson, I wish he had blotted out a thousand. [*In margin,* 'B. Johnsons Underwoods'.] His Comœdies will remaine witt, as long as the English tongue is understood; for that he handles mores hominum;[4] now our present writers reflect so much upon particular persons, and coxcombeities, that 20 yeares hence, they will not be understood. Though as Ben: Johnson sayes of him, that he had but little Latine and lesse Greek, He understood Latine pretty well: for he had been in his younger yeares a Schoolmaster in the Countrey. [*In margin,* 'from M[r] —— Beeston'.]

S[r] William Davenant Knight Poet Laureate was borne in _____ street in the City of Oxford, at the Crowne Tavern. His father was John Davenant a Vintner there, a very grave and discreet Citizen: his mother was a very beautifull woman, & of a very good witt and of conversation extremely agreable. . . . M[r] William Shakespeare was wont to goe into Warwickshire once a yeare, and did commonly in his journey lye at this house in Oxon: where he was exceedingly respected. I have heard parson Robert D[avenant] say that here M[r] W. Shakespeare here gave him a hundred kisses. Now S[r] Wm. would sometimes when he was pleasant over a glasse of wine with his most intimate friends e.g. Sam: Butler (author of Hudibras) &c. say, that it seemed to him that he writt with the very spirit that Shakespeare,[5] and seemed contented enough to be thought his Son: he would tell them the story as above. in which way his mother had a very light report, whereby she was called a whore.

---

5. Character, personality.
6. Buckinghamshire.
7. Oxford.
8. Upon.
9. Extemporaneous.
1. 10-percent interest. (Combe is damned because he charges 12 percent on his loans, 2 percent above the maximum allowed for usury not to be a mortal sin.)
2. £300 a year.
3. See.
4. *for that . . . hominum:* because he treats of (general) human manners or customs.
5. A word such as "had" seems to be missing.

TIMELINE

TEXT	CONTEXT
	1558 Queen Mary I, a Roman Catholic, dies; her sister Elizabeth, raised Protestant, is proclaimed queen.
	1559 Church of England is reestablished under the authority of the sovereign with the passage of the Act of Uniformity and the Act of Supremacy.
1562 *The Tragedy of Gorboduc*, by Thomas Norton and Thomas Sackville, is performed; it is the first English play in blank verse.	**1563** The Church of England adopts the Thirty-nine Articles of Religion, detailing its points of doctrine and clarifying its differences both from Roman Catholicism and from more extreme forms of Protestantism.
	1564 William Shakespeare is born in Stratford to John and Mary Arden Shakespeare; he is christened a few days later, on April 23.
	1565 John Shakespeare is made an alderman of Stratford.
	1567 Mary Queen of Scots is imprisoned on suspicion of the murder of her husband, Lord Darnley. Their infant son, Charles James, is crowned James VI of Scotland.
	1568 John Shakespeare is elected Bailiff of Stratford, the town's highest office. Performances in Stratford by the Queen's Players and the Earl of Worcester's men.
	1572 An act is passed that severely punishes vagrants and wanderers, including actors not affiliated with a patron. Performances in Stratford by the Earl of Leicester's men.
	1574 The Earl of Warwick's and Earl of Worcester's men perform in Stratford.
	1576 James Burbage, father of Richard, later the leading actor in Shakespeare's company, builds the Theatre in Shoreditch, a suburb of London.
	1577 The Curtain Theatre opens in Shoreditch.

TEXT	CONTEXT
	1577–1580 Sir Francis Drake circumnavigates the globe.
	1578 Mary Shakespeare pawns her lands, suggesting that the family is in financial distress. Lord Strange's Men and Lord Essex's Men perform at Stratford.
	1580 A Jesuit mission is established in England with the aim of reconverting the nation to Roman Catholicism.
	1582 Shakespeare marries Anne Hathaway.
	1583 The birth of Shakespeare's older daughter, Susanna.
	1584 Sir Walter Ralegh establishes the first English colony in the New World at Roanoke Island in modern North Carolina; the colony fails.
	1585 The birth of Shakespeare's twin son and daughter, Hamnet and Judith. John Shakespeare is fined for not going to church.
	1586 Sir Philip Sidney dies from battle wounds.
1587 Thomas Kyd's *The Spanish Tragedy* (pub. c. 1592) and Christopher Marlowe's *Tamburlaine* (pub. 1590) are performed.	**1587** Mary Queen of Scots is executed for treason against Elizabeth I. Francis Drake defeats the Spanish fleet at Cádiz. John Shakespeare loses his position as an alderman. Philip Henslowe builds the Rose theater at Bankside, on the Thames.
	1588 The Spanish Armada attempts an invasion of England but is defeated.
1589 Robert Greene, *Friar Bacon and Friar Bungay*. Thomas Kyd, *Hamlet* (not extant; perhaps a source for Shakespeare's *Hamlet*). Christopher Marlowe, *The Jew of Malta*.	**1589** Shakespeare is probably affiliated with the amalgamated Lord Strange's and Lord Admiral's Men from about this time until 1594.
1590 Anonymous, *The True Chronicle History of King Leir, and his Three Daughters*.	**1590** James VI of Scotland marries Anne of Denmark, but believes himself to be bewitched on his honeymoon when he cannot consummate the marriage. Witch trials in Scotland.
1591 Shakespeare's *1, 2,* and *3 Henry VI* performed.	
	1592 The theatrical manager of the Admiral's Men, Philip Henslowe, begins his diary, continued until 1604, recording his business

TEXT	CONTEXT
	transactions, an important source for theater historians.
1592–1593 *Richard III.* *Venus and Adonis.* *The Comedy of Errors.* *Titus Andronicus.* *The Taming of the Shrew.*	From June 1592 to June 1594, London theaters are shut down because of the plague; acting companies tour the provinces.
1594 Shakespeare dedicates *The Rape of Lucrece* to Henry Wriothesley, Earl of Southampton.	**1594** Roderigo Lopez, Portuguese physician and a Jewish convert to Christianity, is executed on slight evidence for having plotted to poison Elizabeth I.
1594–1596 *A Midsummer Night's Dream.* *Richard II.* *Romeo and Juliet.*	The birth of James VI's first son, Henry.
	1595 Shakespeare lives in St. Helen's Parish, Bishopsgate, London. Shakespeare apparently becomes a sharer in (provides capital for) the newly re-formed Lord Chamberlain's Men. The Swan Theatre is built in Bankside. Hugh O'Neill, Earl of Tyrone, rebels against English rule in Ireland. Walter Ralegh explores Guiana, on the north coast of South America.
1596 *King John.* *The Merchant of Venice.* *1 Henry IV.*	**1596** John Shakespeare is granted a coat of arms; hence the title of "gentleman." William Shakespeare's son Hamnet dies.
1597 *The Merry Wives of Windsor.*	**1597** James Burbage builds the second Blackfriars Theatre. But the Lord Chamberlain's Men are not permitted to play in it, so they rent it to boys' companies for a number of years. The landlord refuses to renew the lease on the land under the Theatre in Shoreditch.
1598 *2 Henry IV.* *Much Ado About Nothing.* Ben Jonson, *Every Man in His Humor,* which lists Shakespeare as one of the actors.	**1598** The Edict of Nantes ends the French civil wars, granting toleration to Protestants. Materials from the demolished Theatre in Shoreditch are transported across the Thames to be used in building the Globe Theatre.
1599 *Henry V.* *Julius Caesar.* *As You Like it.*	**1599** The queen's favorite, Robert Devereux, Earl of Essex, leads an expedition to Ireland in March but returns home without permission in October and is imprisoned. Satires and other offensive books are prohibited by ecclesiastical order. Extant copies are gathered and burned. Two notorious satirists, Thomas Nashe and Gabriel Harvey, are forbidden to publish.

TEXT	CONTEXT
1600 *Hamlet.* Michael Drayton and several collaborators, who object to Shakespeare's depiction of Oldcastle-Falstaff in the *Henry IV* plays, write *The First Part of the True and Honorable History of the Life of Sir John Oldcastle, the Good Lord Cobham.*	**1600** The Earl of Essex is suspended from some of his offices and confined to house arrest. The birth of James VI's second son, Charles. The founding of the East India Company. Edward Alleyn and Philip Henslowe build the Fortune Theatre for the Lord Admiral's Men, competing with the Lord Chamberlain's Men at the Globe.
1601 "The Phoenix and the Turtle" published in Robert Chester's *Love's Martyr.* *Twelfth Night.* In the "War of the Theaters," Ben Jonson, John Marston, and Thomas Dekker write a series of satiric plays mocking one another.	**1601** The Earl of Essex leads some gentlemen against Elizabeth I, but the rising is quickly quelled. A few of the rebels, including Shakespeare's patron, the Earl of Southampton, arrange a staging of *Richard II* at the Globe, apparently to incite rebellion. Essex is convicted of treason and beheaded. Shakespeare's father dies.
1602 *Troilus and Cressida.*	**1602** Shakespeare makes substantial real-estate purchases in Stratford. The opening of the Bodleian Library in Oxford.
	1603 Queen Elizabeth dies; she is succeeded by her cousin, James VI of Scotland (now James I of England). Shakespeare's name appears for the last time in Ben Jonson's lists of actors, as a "principal tragedian" in *Sejanus.* Plague closes the London theaters from mid-1603 to April 1604. Hugh O'Neill surrenders in Ireland.
1604 *Measure for Measure.* *Othello.*	**1604** The conclusion of a peace with Spain makes travel across the Atlantic safer, encouraging plans for English colonies in the Americas.
1605 *All's Well That Ends Well.* *King Lear.*	**1605** The discovery of the Gunpowder Plot by some radical Catholics to blow up the Houses of Parliament during its opening ceremonies, when the royal family, Lords, and Commons are assembled in one place. The Red Bull Theatre built.
1606 *Macbeth.* *Antony and Cleopatra.* Ben Jonson, *Volpone.* Anonymous, *The Revenger's Tragedy.*	**1606** The London and Plymouth Companies receive charters to colonize Virginia. Parliament passes "An Act to Restrain Abuses of Players," prohibiting oaths or blasphemy onstage.
1607 *Timon of Athens.* *Pericles.*	**1607** An English colony is established in Jamestown, Virginia. Shakespeare's daughter Susanna marries John Hall. Shakespeare's brother Edmund (described as a player) dies.

TEXT	CONTEXT
1608 *Coriolanus.*	1608 The King's Men obtain permission to play at the second Blackfriars Theatre, a smaller indoor venue.
1609 *Cymbeline.* Unauthorized publication of the sonnets.	
1610 *The Winter's Tale.* Ben Jonson, *The Alchemist.*	1610 Henry is made Prince of Wales. Shakespeare probably returns to Stratford and settles there.

1611 *The Tempest.*
Francis Beaumont and John Fletcher,
  A King and No King.
Publication of the Authorized (King James)
  Bible.
	1611 Plantation of Ulster in Ireland, a colony of English and Scottish Protestants settled on land confiscated from Irish rebels.

1612 *All Is True (Henry VIII),* with John Fletcher. John Webster, *The White Devil.*	1612 Prince Henry dies.
1613 *The Two Noble Kinsmen,* with John Fletcher.	1613 Princess Elizabeth marries Frederick V, Elector Palatine. The Globe Theatre burns down during a performance of *All Is True.*
1614 Ben Jonson, *Bartholomew Fair.* John Webster, *The Duchess of Malfi.*	1614 Philip Henslowe and Jacob Meade build the Hope Theatre, used both for play performances and as a bearbaiting arena. The Globe Theatre reopens.
1616 Ben Jonson publishes *The Works of Benjamin Jonson,* the first collection of plays by an English author.	1616 William Harvey describes the circulation of the blood. Shakespeare's daughter Judith marries. Shakespeare dies on April 23.
1623 Members of the King's Men publish the First Folio of Shakespeare's plays.	

Textual Variants

THE FIRST PART OF THE CONTENTION
OF THE TWO FAMOUS HOUSES OF YORK
AND LANCASTER (THE SECOND PART
OF HENRY VI)

CONTROL TEXT: F, primarily, and Q1 for some passages: 1.1.54–70; 2.1.70 s.d.; 2.1.116–53 s.d.; 4.5 initial s.d.–4.6 initial s.d.; and most of 2.3, from s.d. following line 58 to initial s.d. in 2.4. In these five passages, readings taken from F are treated as variants of Q1 and marked as such. In addition, this edition prints some material from Q not in F but that derives, the Oxford editors believe, from a revised version of the Folio text. These passages are also marked in the variants because they are alterations to the control text. For discussion of the status of this text, see the Textual Note; for a much fuller collation and discussion of Quarto and Folio variants, see Oxford's *William Shakespeare: A Textual Companion.*

F: The Folio of 1623
Q1: The Quarto of 1594
Q2: The Quarto of 1600
Q3: The Quarto of 1619

s.p. KING HENRY [F's use of *King* has been changed throughout.]
s.p. QUEEN MARGARET [F's use of *Queen* has been changed throughout.]
s.p. CARDINAL BEAUFORT [F's use of *Cardinal* and *Winchester* has been standardized throughout.]
s.p. GLOUCESTER [F's use of *Gloucester* and *Humphrey* has been standardized throughout.]
s.p. DUCHESS [F's use of *Elianor* and *Duchess* has been standardized throughout.]
s.p. HORNER [F's use of *Armorer* has been changed throughout.]
s.p. BOLINGBROKE [F's spelling, *Bullingbrooke,* has been changed throughout.]
s.p. ASNATH [F's use of *Spirit* (in 1.4) has been changed.]
s.p. SIMPCOX'S WIFE [F's use of *Wife* (in 2.1) has been changed.]
s.p. CAPTAIN [F's use of *Lieutenant* (in 4.1) has been changed to Q's *Captain.*]
s.p. WHITMORE [F's use of *Whitmore* and *Walter* (in 4.1) has been standardized.]

s.p. FIRST REBEL [F's use of *Bevis* has been changed throughout.]
s.p. SECOND REBEL [F's use of *Holland* has been changed throughout.]
s.p. MESSENGER [F's use of *Michael* (in 4.2) has been changed.]
s.p. STAFFORD'S BROTHER [F's use of *Brother* (in 4.2) has been changed.]
s.p. WEAVER [F's use of *Smith* and *Weaver* has been standardized throughout.]
s.p. BUTCHER [F's use of *Dicke* and *Butcher* has been standardized throughout.]
s.p. REBEL [Q's use of *Robin* has been changed at 4.7.116 (Q is control text for this section).]
s.p. CLIFFORD [F's use of *Clifford* and *Old Clifford* has been standardized throughout.]
s.p. YOUNG CLIFFORD [F's use of *Clifford* and *Young Clifford* has been standardized throughout.]

Title: *The first part of the contention of the two famous / Houses, of Yorke and Lancaster* [Q running title] THE / First part of the Con- / tention betwixt the two famous Houses of Yorke / and Lancaster, with the death of the good / Duke Humphrey: / And the banishment and death of the Duke of / Suffolke, and the Tragicall end of the proud Cardinall / of Winchester, with the notable Rebellion / of Jacke Cade: / And the Duke of Yorkes first claime unto / the Crowne [Q title page] The second Part of Henry the Sixt, / with the death of the Good Duke / HUMFREY [F head title]

1.1.24–29 Th' . . . King [Q, not in F; for F's version of this speech, see inset passage in text.] **24 excess of** excessive **28 naught** nothing **35 s.p. LORDS** *kneel*[*ing*] *All kneel.* **44 René** Raynard [Q] Reignier [F] **47 it is further agreed between them** [Q; not in F] **49 fa–** [Q] *father* **54–70** [Q is control text for these lines.] **55 duchy of Anjou and the county of** Duches of *Anioy* and of **56 delivered** delivered over **63 I'th** [F] in the **89 had** hath **141 But I'll . . . speak.** [Q; not in F] **166 hoist** hoyse **175 Protector** [Q] Protectors **189 thee** [Q] the **196–97 The reverence . . . command.** [Q; not in F] **207 Then let's away** Then lets make hast away **250 surfeit in the** surfetting in **255 in** [Q] in in

1.2.19 hour thought **22 dream** dreames **38 are** [Q] wer **75 Jordan** *Jordane* **cunning witch of Eye** cunning witch [F]

1.3.6 s.p. FIRST PETITIONER *Peter* **33 master** Mistresse **34–36 usurer . . . usurper** [Q] Usurper **45 s.p. ALL PETITIONERS** *All* **72 haught** haughtie **94 their** the **104 helm** [Q] Helme. *Exit.* **146 I'd** [Q] I could [F] **149 pamper** hamper **154 fury** Fume **208 judge by** case judge **215 s.p. KING HENRY** Then . . . of Somerset [Q; not in F] **216–17 We make . . . foes.** We make your grace Regent over the French, / And to defend our rights gainst forraine foes, / And so do good unto the Realme of *France* [Q; not in F] **226 be** shall be

1.4.23 Asnath Asmath **31 Tell me what fate awaits** [Q2, Q3] what fates await **33 betide** [Q] befall **37–38** [For Q's version of these lines, see inset passage in text.] **42 deep** deeply **56–57 What have . . . posse.** [In F, York reads the prophecies aloud at this point; Q transposes this reading to the next scene and assigns it to King Henry at 2.1.177–87]. **56 s.d.** [He] reads [the writings] Reades. / The Duke yet lives, that Henry shall depose: / But him out-live, and dye a violent death. **57 Aeacidam** AEacida **posse** posso. / Well, to the rest: / Tell me what fate awaits the Duke of Suffolke? / By Water shall he dye, and take his end. / What shall betide the Duke of Somerset? / Let him shunne Castles, Safer shall he be upon the sandie Plaines, / Then where Castles mounted stand **58–59 These oracles are hardily attained / And hardly understood. Come, come, my lord,** Come, come, my Lords, These oracles are hardly attained / And hardly understood.

2.1.26 some such **37–43 s.p. GLOUCESTER . . . words.** [Q; not in F] **46 an if** And if **53 s.p. CARDINAL BEAUFORT** [F makes the line a continuation of Gloucester's prior speech.] **65 tell** and tell **74 sight** his sight **109 Alban** Albones **114 And . . . sir;** [Q] What Coulour is my Gowne of? / *Simpc⟨oxe⟩*. Black forsooth, **116–53** [Q is control text for this section.] **117 before** [F] ere a **many** [F] many, a one **118 s.p. SIMPCOX'S WIFE . . . life.** [F; not in Q] **119 Tell** [F] But tell **128 Simon** Sander Simpcox [F; not in Q] **129 Simon** Sander **thou** [not in Q] **131 our** all our **133 distinguish** distinguish of **135 Saint My Lords,** Saint Alban [F] Albones **136 Would** and would **138 that** [F] I would **141 We have, my lord, an if it please your grace.** Yes, my Lord, if it please your Grace. **144 Bring** Now fetch **stool** stoole hither by and by **145 o'er** over **147 am not able even to** am not able to **149 sirrah** Sir **150 Whip** Sirrah Beadle, whip **177–87** [Following Q, the Oxford editors move the reading of the prophecies from

1.4.56 to this location.] **176 And here's . . . them.** [Q; not in F] **177 s.p. KING HENRY** [Q] Yorke. **First . . . of him become?** become of him? [Q; not in F] **178–79 The Duke . . . death.** [after Q; not in F here] **180 God's will be done in all.** [Q; not in F] **Well, to the rest** [after F] **181–82 Tell . . . end.** [after Q; not in F here] **183–184 s.p. SUFFOLK . . . lie.** [Q; not in F] **185 s.p. KING HENRY** [Q; F assigns to York] **185–87 What . . . stand.** [after Q; not in F here]

2.2.6 out at full at full **26 well** all **28 Duke of York** Duke **41 Owain Glyndŵr** *Owen Glendour* **45 was son** was **46 son** Sonnes Sonne **56 John's** his **77 off** we off

2.3.3 sins sinne **19 grave** ground **30 helm Realme** **34 erst** [Q1, Q2] ere **35 willing** [Q] willingly **2.3.58–2.4.0** [In these lines, Q is control text for 2.3.58–75, 2.3.83–88, and 2.3.101–2.4.0] **78 an** if and if **88 well** [F; not in Q] **98 wame** way **99 enemy** Enemies

2.4.18 sheriffs [Q] Sherife **77, 103 s.p. FIRST SHERIFF** *Sh⟨erife⟩*, Sherife

3.1.78 wolf Wolves **98 Suffolk's Duke** [Q] *Suffolke* **137 my good** [Q] my **211 strains** strayes **264 conceit** deceit **319–30** [For the Q version of these lines, see inset passage in the text.] **330.2 'gainst** against **348 nurse** nourish **363 porcupine** Porpentine **381 coistrel** [Q] rascall [F]

3.2.14 Then draw the curtains close; away, be gone! Away, be gone **26 Meg** Nell **75 leper** Leaper **79 Queen Margaret** Dame *Eliaor* **ne'er** neere **82 wrecked** wrack'd **83, 85 winds** [Q] winde **100 Margaret** *Eliaor* **107 heart** Hart **116 witch** watch **120 Margaret** *Elinor* **223 born** borne **236 s.p. COMMONS . . . Suffolk! Down with Suffolk!** [Q; not in F; F s.d. reads *A noyse within.*] **243 s.p. COMMONS . . . the commons** [after Q; not in F] **272 s.p. COMMONS** *⟨within⟩* (*Commons within.*) **280 s.p. COMMONS** *⟨within⟩* Within. **310 enemies** [Q] enemy **312 Could** [Q] Would **320 My** mine **on** an **distraught** distract **334 turn** turnes **336 this** [Q] the **346 upon these lips** upon these **395 his** [Q] it's **402 By thee to die** [Q] To dye by thee

3.3.10 whe'er where

4.1.6 Clip Cleape **20 s.p. WHITMORE Cut** Cut **22** [line assumed missing] **33 thee** death **49 Jove sometime went disguised, and why not I?** [Q; not in F] **51 s.p. SUFFOLK** (*Suf.*) [Q; not in F] **52 The** [Q] *Suf⟨folke⟩*. The **53 jady** [Q] iaded **71 s.p. CAPTAIN . . . Ay** *Lieu. Poole, Sir Poole?* Lord, / I **77 shalt** [Q] shall **85 mother's bleeding** Mother-bleeding **93 are** and **113 s.p. CAPTAIN . . . rage.** [not in F] **114 s.p. SUFFOLK** [not in F] **116 s.p. CAPTAIN Walter–** s.p. WHITMORE Come *Lieu⟨tenant⟩*. Water: W. Come **118** *Paene*

Pine 121 **daunted** danted 134 s.p. SUF-
FOLK **Come** Come 135 **That** *Suf⟨folke⟩*.
That

4.2.30 **fall** fail 75 **Chatham** [Q] Chartam 80
He's Ha's 87 **that** [Q] it 90 **an** a 132 **an**
[Q] if 135 **testify** [Q1, Q2] testifie it 147
maimed main'd

4.3.6 **Thou** [Q1, Q2] and thou 6 **licence a**
License

4.4.20 **lamenting and mourning** lamenting
and mourning for 38 **Kenilworth** Killing-
worth 42 **trait'rous rabble hateth** Traitors
hateth 48 **almost** [Q; not in F] 57 **be**
betrayed betraid

4.5–4.6.0 [Q is control text for these lines.] 2
lord Scales Lord 2–3 **he and his men** they
3–4 **did withstand** withstand 8 **essayed** [F]
attempted 9 **Get you to Smithfield, there**
to gather head But get you to Smythfield,
and gather head 10 **will I** I will

4.6.5 **otherwise** [Q] other 7 **Zounds** [Q; not
in F] 10 **My** *Dicke.* My 11 **go on** [Q] go 12
afire [Q1, Q3] on fire

4.7.21 **serge** Surge 24 **Dauphin** Dolphine
39 **on** [Q] in 43 **their shirts** their shirt
48–51 *Bonum . . . well enough.* [Q] Away
with him, away with him, he speaks Latine.
63 **But** Kent 81 **caudle** Candle 81–82 **the**
health o' the help of 100 **to the Standard**
in Cheapside [Q; not in F] 101 **go to Mile**
End Green [Q; not in F] 113 **Married men**
[Q] Men 115 **s.d.–131 s.d.** *Enter . . .*
Sergeant [Q; not in F] 117 **quench** [Q3]
squench 124 **went and** went and and 131
proper paper 131 **brain** Brave 134–36 **He**
that . . . smock. [Q; not in F] 147 **What**
noise is this? What noise is this heare? 156
rebel rabble

4.8.27 **stout** Irish stout 34 **calmed** calme

4.9.6 **oe'r** on 18 **waning** warning 22 **Zounds**
Sounes [Q; not in F] 52 **Stand you all**
aside. [Q; not in F] 56 **God** [Q] love 74
bore bare

5.1.10 **sword** soule 72 **Iwis** I was 83 **wi'th'**
with th' 109 **Sirrah** Wold'st have me
kneele? First let me ask of thee, / If they can
brooke I bow a knee to man: / Sirrah **sons**
[Q] sonne 111 **for** of 147 **bearheard**
Berard 192 **or** and 195 **you** [Q] thee 199
household [Q] housed 205 **to** [Q] io [or
possibly "so"]

5.2.0–6 *Alarums . . . Somerset's body.* [After
F; F places this passage following 5.3.65.]

5.3.8 **s.p. CLIFFORD** Warwick . . . come. [Q;
not in F] 20–30 **s.p. YORK** Clifford . . .
York. [Q; not in F. For the F version of this
encounter, see inset passage in the text.] 20
Clifford Now Clifford 22 **know** now 25
not never 30.10 **oeuvres** *eumenes*

5.5.1–4 **How now, . . . rights.** [Q; not in F]
5.5.17 **s.d.–19** Enter . . . York [Q] But

Noble as he is, looke where he comes. / s.d.
Enter Salisbury 37 **drums** Drumme

RICHARD DUKE OF YORK (3 HENRY VI)

CONTROL TEXT: F

F: The Folio of 1623
O: The Octavo of 1595
Q2: The Quarto of 1600
Q3: The Quarto of 1619
Fa, Fb: Successive states of F incorporating
various print-shop corrections and changes

s.p. YORK [F's *Plantagenet* and *York* have been
standardized throughout.]

s.p. KING HENRY [F's *Henry* has been changed
throughout.]

s.p. QUEEN MARGARET [F's *Queen* and *Mar-*
garet have been changed throughout.]

s.p. PRINCE EDWARD [F's *Prince* and *Prince*
Edward have been standardized throughout.]

s.p. GEORGE/GEORGE OF CLARENCE [F's
Clarence has been changed to "George"
(1.1–3.1) and to "George of Clarence"
once he is granted the title Duke of
Clarence.]

s.p. RICHARD OF GLOUCESTER [F's
Richard has been changed after 3.1
once he is granted the title Duke of
Gloucester.]

s.p. KING EDWARD [F's *King* and *King Edward*
have been standardized from 3.2 to the end
of the play.]

s.p. LADY GRAY [F's *Widow, Lady Gray,* and
Gray have been standardized throughout.]

s.p. KING LOUIS [F's *Lewis* has been changed
throughout.]

s.p. LADY BONA [F's *Bona* has been changed
throughout.]

s.p. MESSENGER [F's *Gabriel* has been
changed at 1.2.49.]

s.p. SOLDIER [F's *Son* has been changed
throughout 2.5.]

s.p. SECOND SOLDIER [F's *Father* has been
changed throughout 2.5.]

s.p. FIRST GAMEKEEPER [F's *Sinklo* has been
changed throughout 3.1]

s.p. SECOND GAMEKEEPER [F's *Humfrey* has
been changed throughout 3.1.]

Title: The true Tragedie of Richard Duke / *of*
Yorke, and the good King / Henry the Sixt [O
head title] The true Tragedie of Richard /
Duke of Yorke, and the death of / good King
Henrie the Sixt, / *with the whole contention*
betweene / the two Houses
Lancaster / and Yorke, as it was sundrie times
/ acted by the Right Honoura- / ble the Earle
of Pem- / brooke his servants. [O title page]

The third Part of Henry the Sixt, / with the death of the Duke of / YORKE [F]

1.1.19 hap hope **69 s.p. EXETER** [O] *Westm⟨orland⟩* **78 mine** [O, Q2] my **83 and that's** [Q3] that's **105 Thy** [O] My **120–24 s.p. NORTHUMBERLAND . . . king** [O; for F, see inset passage in text.] **121 York** *Planta-genet* **122 both** both both **138 An** And **171 me** [O; not in F] **197 thine** [O, Q2] an **200 nor** neyther **255 the utter ruin** vtter ruine **260 with** [O; not in F] **262 from** [O] to **269 coast** cost

1.2.40 to Edmund Brook [O] vnto my **65 s.p. SIR JOHN** *John* **72 uncles** Vnckle

1.4.51 buckle [O] buckler **82 thy** [O] the **138 tiger's** Tygres **151 passions move** [O] passions moues

2.1.113 And, very well appointed as I thought, [O; not in F] **127 captains** [O] Captiues **131 an idle** [O] a lazie **144 his** [O] the

2.2.92 our brother out [O] out me **133 s.p. RICHARD** [O] *War⟨wicke⟩* **172 deniest** [O] denied'st

2.5.38 weeks [not in F] **119 E'en** Men

2.6.6 commixture [O] Commixtures **8 The common people swarm like summer flies,** [O; not in F] **42 s.p. EDWARD** [O] *Rich⟨ard⟩* **43 s.p. RICHARD A** [O] A **44 s.p. EDWARD . . . See** [O] See **44 And** [O] *Ed⟨ward⟩* And **60 his** [O] is **80 buy but** [O] buy

3.1.17 wast was **24 thee** the **sour adversity** sower Aduesaries **30 Is I:** **55 thou that** [O] thou **96 in the** the

3.2.3 lands [O] Land **28 whip me then** [O] then whip me **30 an** [O, Q2] if **32 them** [O] then **119 as** [O] your **123 honourably** [O] honourable

3.3.11 state Seat **33 An** And **124 eternal** [O] externall **156 Warwick, peace** Warwicke **202 ay I 228 I'll** [O] I

4.1.17 you [not in F] **28 my** [O, Q2] mine **91 thy** [O] the **133 near'st** [O, Q2] neere

4.2.2 sort people **12 come** welcome **15 towns** Towne

4.6.4 stands stand **8 Comes** Come

4.7.11 prisonment imprisonment **55 be confiscate** confiscate

4.8.67–74 Ay . . . fight. [O omits line 4.8.70 and the following stage direction and assigns the remainder of these lines to Montgomery. F divides them among Montgomery, Hastings, and a soldier.] **71 s.p. MONTGOMERY** [O] *Soul⟨dier⟩* **72 Ireland** [O] *Ireland, & c.* **73 And** [O] *Mount⟨gomerie⟩* And

4.9.12 stir stirre vp

5.1.68 bye buy **75 an** [O, Q2] if **78 an** in **80–83 s.p. GEORGE OF CLARENCE . . . WAR-WICKE** [O; not in F] **94 Jephthah** Iephah **102 brothers** [O] Brother

5.4.27 raggèd raged **35 York** [not in F] **82 s.d.–5.5.17** *Alarum . . . ambitious* **York.** [For the O version, see inset passage in the text.]

5.5.17.1 s.p. ALL THE LANCASTER PARTY *All* **17.2 Now** [F] Lo **17.5 Go, bear them hence** [F] Awaie **17.8 Edward** [F] Now *Edward* **49 The** [O; not in F] **76–77 butcher, / Hard-favoured Richard?** [O] butcher *Richard?*

5.6.46 tempests [O] Tempest **80 I had no father, I am like no father;** [O; not in F] **85 kept'st** keept'st **90–91 Henry . . . the rest,** [O, Q2] King *Henry,* and the Prince his Son are gone, / *Clarence* thy turne is next, and then the rest **90 art** [F; not in O]

5.7.5 renowned [O] Renowne **21 an** [O, Q2] if **25 and** [Fb] add [Fa] **thou** [O] that **27 kiss** [Fb] 'tis [Fa] **30 s.p. LADY GRAY** *Cla⟨rence⟩* **Thanks** [O] Thanke **42 rests** [Fb] tests [Fa]

THE FIRST PART OF HENRY THE SIXTH

CONTROL TEXT: F

F: The Folio of 1623

s.p. KING HENRY [F's use of *King* has been changed throughout.]

s.p. JOAN [F's use of *Joan, Pucelle,* and *Puzzel* (see note 4 to 1.6.85) has been standardized throughout.]

s.p. CHARLES [F's use of *Dolphin (Dauphin)* and *Charles* has been standardized throughout.]

s.p. RICHARD PLANTAGENET / RICHARD DUKE OF YORK [F's use of *York* and *Richard* has been standardized to "Richard Planta-genet" until 3.1.175–77, when he regains his title; thereafter, "Richard Duke of York" is used.]

s.p. WINCHESTER [F's use of *Winchester* and *Cardinal* has been standardized throughout.]

s.p. FASTOLF [F's use of *Falstaff* has been changed throughout (see note to 1.1.131).]

s.p. RENÉ [F's use of *Reigneir* and *Reignier* has been changed throughout.]

s.p. GLASDALE [F's spelling, *Glansdale,* has been changed throughout.]

s.p. ALENÇON [F's spelling, *Alanson,* has been changed throughout.]

1.1.50 marish Nourish **60 Rouen, Rheims,** Rheimes, **62 corpse** Coarse **89 s.p. SECOND MESSENGER** *Mess.* **94 René** *Reynold* **103 s.p. THIRD MESSENGER** *Mes.* **131 Fastolf** *Falstaffe* **132 vanguard** Vauward **157**

Fore **Orléans** for Orleance is **176 steal** send

1.2.21 flee fly

1.3.9 bred breed **78 five** fine **92 rites** rights **110 halcyon's** *Halcyons*

1.4.5 knocketh knocks **19 My lord** The Cardinall **29 vizier** *Vmphier* **36 If** Ile canuas thee in thy broad Cardinalls Hat, If **41 purple** Scarlet **48 I'll** I bishop's mitre Cardinalls Hat **55 cloakèd** Scarlet **72 s.p. OFFICER** [not in F] **77 Bishop** Cardinall **82 bishop is** Cardinall's

1.5.8 Prince's spials Princes espyals **10 Wont** Went

1.6.5 Duke Earle **11 pilled** pil'd **41 Glasdale** *Glansdale* **44 Lou** Lords **67 Bear . . . bury it** [F places after 1.6.64] **71 like thee, Nero,** like thee, **79 la Pucelle** *de Puzel* **85 *Pucelle* or pucelle** *Puzel* or *Pussel* **Dauphin** Dolphin

1.7.3 men them **29 style** Soyle

1.8.3 la Pucelle *de Puzel* **21 pyramid** Pyramis **22 of** or **29 la Pucelle** *de Puzel*

2.1.5 s.p. A SENTINEL *Sent.* **29 all together** altogether **38 s.p. SENTINELS** *Sent.*

2.2.6 centre Centure **20 Arc** Acre

2.3.21 seely silly

2.4.41 from the tree are cropped are cropt from the Tree **57 law** you **117 wiped** whipt **132 gentles** gentle

2.5.3 rack Wrack **6–7 Argue . . . Mortimer, / Nestor-like . . . care.** *Nestor*-like . . . Care, / Argue . . . Mortimer. **44** dis-ease Disease **71 King** [not in F] **75 the third** third **76 the King** hee **129 mine** ill my will

3.1.52 s.p. GLOUCESTER *Warw⟨icke⟩.* **53 s.p. WARWICK** [not in F, where this line and the prior three words, here assigned to Gloucester, are given to Warwick] **54 so** see **64 intertalk** enter talke **83 pebble** peeble **167 alone** all alone **175 gird** gyrt **203 should lose** loose

3.2.13 *Qui* Che

3.5.32 Goodbye God b'uy

4.1.14 thee the **19 Patay** *Poictiers* **48 my** [not in F] **180 I wist** I wish

4.2.3 captain Captaines **calls** call **15 s.p. GENERAL** *Cap.* **29 fire** ryue **34 due** dew

4.3.17 s.p. LUCY 2. *Mes.* **30 s.p. LUCY** *Mes.* **34 s.p. LUCY** *Mes.* **47 s.p. LUCY** *Mes.*

4.4.16 legions Regions **19 unadvantaged** in aduantage **26 and** [not in F] **27 René** *Reignard* **31 horse** hoast

4.5.39 shamed shame

4.7.70 *Maréchal* Marshall **89 have them** haue him **94 with them** with him

5.1.59 nor neither

5.2.17–18 s.p. JOAN Now . . . fear. / Of Now . . . feare. / *Pucel.* Of

5.3.8 speed and quick speedy and quicke

5.4.15 comest comst

5.5.4–5 And . . . side. / I . . . peace, I . . . peace, / And . . . side. 12 his her **18 stream** streames **24 here to hear** heere **41 random** randon **92 Assent** Consent **110 countries** Country **135 modestly** modestie

5.6.10 an't and **37 one** me, **49 Arc** *Aire* **68 ingling** iugling **70 we will** we'll

5.7.60 That [not in F]

THE TRAGEDY OF KING RICHARD THE THIRD

CONTROL TEXT: F (except for 3.1.0–148 and 5.5.4–end, for which the copy text is Q1)

F: The Folio of 1623
Q1: The Quarto of 1597
Q2: The Quarto of 1598
Q3: The Quarto of 1602
Q4: The Quarto of 1605
Q5: The Quarto of 1612
Q6: The Quarto of 1622

1.1–3.1 and 3.1.148–5.5.4

s.p. RICHARD GLOUCESTER [F's use of *Richard* and *Gloucester* has been standardized until 4.2.]

s.p. KING RICHARD [F's use of *King* and *Richard* has been standardized after 4.2.]

s.p. BRACKENBURY [F's use of *Brackenbury* and *Lieutenant* has been standardized throughout.]

s.p. LORD HASTINGS [F's use of *Hastings* has been changed throughout.]

s.p. LADY ANNE [F's use of *Anne* has been changed throughout.]

s.p. HALBERDIER [F uses *Gentleman*.]

s.p. QUEEN ELIZABETH [F's use of *Queen* has been standardized throughout.]

s.p. STANLEY [F's use of *Stanley* and *Derby* has been standardized throughout.]

s.p. QUEEN MARGARET [F's use of *Queen Margaret* and *Margaret* has been standardized throughout.]

s.p. A MURDERER, MURDERERS [F's use of *Villain* has been standardized throughout.]

s.p. FIRST MURDERER [F's use of *1 Murderer* and *1* has been standardized throughout.]

s.p. SECOND MURDERER [F's use of *2 Murderer* and *2* has been standardized throughout.]

s.p. KING EDWARD [F's use of *King* has been standardized throughout.]

s.p. BOY [F's use of *Boy* and *Edward* has been standardized until 3.1.]

s.p. DUCHESS OF YORK [F's use of *Duchess of York* and *Duchess* has been standardized throughout.]

s.p. GIRL [F's use of *Daughter* has been standardized throughout.]

s.p. FIRST CITIZEN [F's use of *1 Citizen* and *1* has been standardized throughout.]

s.p. SECOND CITIZEN [F's use of *2 Citizen* and *2* has been standardized throughout.]

s.p. THIRD CITIZEN [F's use of *3* has been standardized throughout.]

s.p. CARDINAL [F's use of *Archbishop* and *Cardinal* has been standardized throughout.]

s.p. MAYOR [F's use of *Lord Mayor* and *Mayor* has been standardized throughout.]

s.p. BISHOP OF ELY [F's use of *Ely* has been standardized throughout.]

s.p. ALL BUT RICHARD [F's use of *All* has been standardized throughout.]

s.p. SECOND MESSENGER, THIRD MESSENGER, FOURTH MESSENGER [F only uses *Messenger.*]

s.p. SIR CHRISTOPHER [F's use of *Christopher* has been standardized throughout.]

s.p. HENRY EARL OF RICHMOND [F's use of *Richmond* has been standardized throughout.]

3.1.0–148 and 5.5.4–end

s.p. KING RICHARD [Q's use of *King Richard* and *Richard* has been standardized throughout.]

s.p. PRINCE EDWARD [Q's use of *Prince* has been standardized throughout.]

s.p. GHOST OF PRINCE EDWARD, GHOST OF KING HENRY, GHOST OF CLARENCE, GHOSTS OF THE PRINCES, GHOST OF HASTINGS [Q's use of *Ghost* has been standardized throughout.]

s.p. GHOST OF GRAY [Q's use of *Gray* has been standardized throughout.]

s.p. GHOST OF VAUGHAN [Q's use of *Vaughan* has been standardized throughout.]

Title: *The Tragedy of King Richard the Third*]
THE TRAGEDY OF / King Richard the third. / Containing, / His treacherous Plots against his brother Clarence: / the pittiefull murther of his innocent nephewes: / his tyrannicall vsurpation: with the whole course / of his detested life, and most deserued death. [Q title page] The Tragedy of Richard the Third: / with the Landing of Earle Richmond, and the / Battell at Bosworth Field. [F head title]

1.1.26 spy [Q] see **49 Belike** O belike **52 for** [Q] but **67 Woodeville** *Woodeulle* **73 Mrs** Mistresse **74 ye** [Q] you **75 for his** for her **88 An't** and **92 jealous** [Q] ieaious **96 kin** kindred **104 I** [Q] I do **do withal** withal **113 dearer** deeper **116 or** [Q] or else **125 the** [Q1] this **134 prey** [Q] play **139 Paul** [Q] Iohn **146 haste** horse

1.2.15 Cursèd . . . hence, [F places the line after 1.2.16.] **39 stand** [Q] Stand'st **56 Ope** Open **60 deed** Deeds **61 supernatural** most vnnaturall **70 no** [Q] nor **78 a** [Q; not in F] **80 t'accuse** to curse **92 hand** [Q] hands **101 ye** [Q1] yee **120 of** that accursed **effect** and most accurst effect **126 rend** [Q] rent **127 sweet** [Q] y^t **154 drops.** [Q; F here adds twelve lines; see indented passage.] **Shamed** [Q, F (text)] For [F (catchword)] **189 s.p. RICHARD GLOUCESTER** [Q; not in F] **190 s.p. LADY ANNE . . . give.** [Q; not in F] **213 s.p. RICHARD GLOUCESTER . . . corpse.** [Q; not in F] **214 Blackfriars** white Friers **238** *denier* denier

1.3.6 If . . . me? [Q; F gives the line twice, spanning a page break.] **7 s.p. RIVERS** [Q] If he were dead, what would betide me on / Gray. [F (text)] *Gray.* [F (catchword)] **17 come** [Q1] comes **Lords** [Q] Lord **30 s.p. RIVERS** [Q] *Qu⟨een Elizabeth⟩.* **33 With** [Q1] What **43 are they** [Q] is it **complain** complaines **54 s.p. RIVERS** [Q] *Gray.* **whom** [Q1] who **68–69 that . . . it** that he may learne the ground **114 Tell . . . said,** [Q; not in F] **118 remember** [Q] do remember **153 may you** [Q] you may **155 Ah** A **160 of** [Q] off **166 go.** [Q; F here adds three lines; see indented passage.] **197 my** [Q] our **270 was** [Q] is **271 s.p. RICHARD GLOUCESTER** *Buc⟨kingham⟩.* **290 naught** not **302 s.p. HASTINGS** [Q] *Buc⟨kingham⟩.* **307 s.p. QUEEN ELIZABETH** [Q] *Mar⟨garet⟩.* **319 you my gracious lords** yours my gracious Lord **325 whom** [Q] who

1.4.19 sought thought **22 waters** [Q1] water **22–23 my . . . my** [Q1] mine . . . mine **25 Ten** [Q] A **26 ouches** anchors **29 those** [Q] the **32 Which** [Q] That **50 cried** [Q] spake **58 methoughts** [Q1] me thought **66 Brackenbury** [Q] Keeper, Keeper **68 me.** [Q; F here adds four lines; see indented passage.] **69 Keeper, I pray thee** Keeper, I prythee **90 of** [Q] from **96 I** [Q1] we **112 pray thee** [Q] prythee **119 'Swounds** [Q] Come **136 'Swounds** [Q; not in F] **177 to have redemption** [Q] for any goodnesse **178 By . . . sins,** [Q; not in F] **201 ye** [Q] you **225 And . . . other,** [Q; not in F] **227 of** [Q1] on **230 As** Right as **251–55 Which distress—** [F places the lines after 1.4.244.] **257 serve** [Q] do **261 guilty murder** done [Q] murther

2.1.5 in [Q] to **7 Hastings and Rivers** *Dorset and Riuers* **19 your** [Q] you **50 Brother** [Q] Gloster **57 unwittingly** [Q] vnwillingly **59 By** [Q] To **67 Of you . . . of you** [Q] Of you and you, Lord *Riuers* and of *Dorset* **68 me.—** [Q] me: / Of you Lord *Wooduill* and Lord *Scales*, of you, **70 Englishman** [Q] Englishmen **82 s.p. RIVERS** [Q] *King* **85 one** [Q] man **93 but** [Q] and **97 pray thee** [Q] prethee **105 slew** [Q] kill'd **108 at** [Q] and **131 once** [Q] onee

2.2.3 you [Q; not in F] **13 this** [Q] it **26 his** [Q] a **27 shapes** [Q] shape **39 mark** make **47 I** [Q; not in F] **83 weep** [Q] weepes **84–85 and . . . weep** [Q; not in F] **88 lamentation.** [F here adds twelve lines; see indented passage.] **105 hearts** [Q] hates **106 splinted** [Q, F] splinterd **110 king.** [Q; F here adds eighteen lines; see indented passage.] **112 Ludlow** [Q] London **114 weighty** [Q; not in F] **115 s.p. QUEEN . . . YORK** [not in F] **With . . . hearts.** [Q; not in F] **117 God's sake** [Q] God sake **124 Ludlow** [Q] London

2.3.35 make [Q] makes **43 Ensuing** [Q, F (catchword)] Pursuing [F (text)]

2.4.1 hear [Q1] heard **them** [not in F] **1–2 Northampton. / at Stony Stratford** [Q] Stony Stratford, / And at Northampton **9 young** [Q] good **12 nuncle** Vnkle **13 gross** great **21 s.p. CARDINAL Why** [Q] *Yor⟨k⟩*. And **26 pray thee** [Q] prythee **36 s.p. CARDINAL** [Q] *Dut.* (Duchess of York) **37 your son, Lord Dorset** a Messenger **38 Lord Marquis** [Q; not in F] **s.p. DORSET** [Q; throughout scene] *Mes⟨senger⟩.* **40 then** [Q; not in F] **42 And with them** and with them, / Sir **48 our** [Q] my **50 jet** [Q] Iutt **64 death** [Q] earth

3.1.0 [Right after this stage direction, F loses its independent authority until c. 3.1.148. Q1 is the control text in this interim; F is here a direct reprint of Q3, which contains errors that need to be corrected by reference to Q1.] **22 hastes** comes **24 In happy time** And in good time **39 Anon expect him** Anone expect him here **41 sacred** holy **46 not** but **52 my mind, he** mine opinion **53 'longs** is **54 You . . . charter** You breake no priuiledge nor charter there **59 I come** I go **74 liege. Lo:** **85 t'enrich** enrich **87 made** makes **88 yet** now **90 good** gratious **101 noble cousin** Cosen noble **102 uncle, well** Vnckle **107 He . . . you** then Then he . . . you **109 as** as in **110 render** giue **111 With all** [Q3–6, F] withall **113–14 give, / It being but** giue, / And being but **121 I'd** I **132 sharp, prodigal** sharpe, prouided **136 My . . . along** [Q, F; none of the many attempts to pad out this line carries any conviction.] **143 there** [not in Q] **148 and** [F, not in Q] **149 we** I **153 parlous** perillous **161 Lord William** William Lo: **166 Will not** [F; F regains its full authority at this line.] Will **170 purpose.** [Q; for F, see indented passage.] **174 your** [Q] the **188 My** Now my

3.2.1 from Lord from the lo: **3 my Lord Stanley** Stanley **17 councils** [Q] Councell **74**

you do [Q; not in F] **87 talked** [Q1] talke **91 follow presently** [Q] talke with this good fellow **92 Well met, Hastings** [Q] How now, Sirrha? **95 I met thee** [Q] thou met'st me **102 Hastings** [Q] fellow **103 God save your lordship** [Q] I thanke your

3.3.14 heads, [Q] Heads / When shee exclaim'd on *Hastings*, you, and I **16–17 Hastings . . . Richard** [Q] *Richard . . . Hastings*

3.4.4 that [Q] the **solemn** royall **9 methinks** [Q] we thinke **26 not you** [Q] you not **39 worshipful** [Q] worshipfully **55 likelihood** [Q] liuelyhood **58 s.p. STANLEY I . . . not.** [not in F] **65 whatsoe'er** [Q] whosoe're **68 See** [Q] Looke **78 Some see it done** [Q] *Louell* and *Ratcliffe,* looke that it be done **82 raze** [Q] rowse **83 But** [Q] And **94 s.p. CATESBY** *Ra⟨tcliffe⟩.* **98 th'air** aire **102 s.p. CATESBY** *Lou⟨ell⟩.*

3.5.4 wert [Q] were **6 Tremble . . . straw,** [F places the line after 3.5.7.] **12 s.p. RICHARD GLOUCESTER . . . Mayor** [Q] But what, is *Catesby* gone? / *Rich⟨ard⟩.* He is, and see he brings the Maior along **13 Let . . . him.** [Q; not in F] **19 innocence** [Q1] innocencie **20 O . . . Catesby** [Q] Be patient, they are friends: *Ratcliffe,* and *Louell.* **21 s.p. CATESBY** [Q] *Louell.* **31 attainture** attainder **32 The** Well, well, he was the **48 I** [Q] *Buck⟨ingham⟩. I* **50 s.p. RICHARD GLOUCESTER** [Q4; not in F] **54 we** [Q] I **hear** heard **56 treason** [Q] Treasons **60 word** [Q] words **64 cause** [Q1] case **82 listed** [Q] lusted **101 Now** [Q; for F, see indented passage.] **in** [Q] goe **103 notice** [Q] order

3.6.13 naught [Q1] nought

3.7.7 insatiate [Q] vnsatiate **14 face** forme **20 mine** [Q1] my **40 wisdoms** [Q] wisdome **43–44 s.p. BUCKINGHAM No . . . lord. / s.p. RICHARD GLOUCESTER** [Q; not in F] **49 build** [Q] make **50 request** [Q] requests **54 we'll** [Q] we **72 lolling** [Q, F] lulling **day-bed** [Q] Loue-Bed **101 request** [Q] requests **125 her** [Q] his **126 Her** [Q] His **127 Her** His **143 condition.** [Q; F here adds ten lines; see indented passage.] **160 no doubt, us** [Q] no doubt vs **203 equally** [Q, F] egallie **209 'Swounds, I'll** [Q] we will **210 s.p. RICHARD GLOUCESTER O . . . Buckingham.** [Q; not in F] **212 s.p. ANOTHER** [Q; not in F] **214 stone** stones **215 entreats** [Q] entreaties **230 kind** King **237 cousin** [Q] Cousins

4.1.46 counted England's Englands counted **57 in** [Q] with **75 made** [not in F] **96 racked** [Q, F] wrackt **teen.** [Q; F here adds seven lines; see indented passage.]

4.2.14 liege [Q] Lord **20 immediately** suddenlie **50 those parts beyond the seas** [Q] the parts **55 born** [Q] poore **73 there** [Q]

then 81 'Tis [Q] There is 84–85 s.p. KING RICHARD Shall . . . lord. [Q; not in F] 90 to [Q] vnto 101 perhaps. [Q; not in F] 101–19 s.p. BUCKINGHAM . . . today. [Q; not in F] 120 Why . . . no? [Q] May it please you to resolue me in my suit.

4.3.4 whom [Q] who 5 ruthless [Q1] ruthfull 8 two [Q] to 15 once [Q] one 31 at [Q] and 39 goodnight [Q] good night 40 Breton [Q, F] Brittaine 42 o'er [Q] on 45 Good news or bad [Q] Good or bad newes 46 Ely [Q] *Mourton* 53 leads [Q] leds 55 an and

4.4.10 unblown [Q] vnblowed 30 innocents' [Q] innocent 36 seniory [Q] signeurie 39 Tell . . . mine. [Q; not in F] 45 holpst hop'st 56 charnel [Q, F] carnal 64 Thy [Q] The quite [Q6] quit 77 plead pray 93 are [Q1] be 100 For queen . . . care [Q; F places the line after 4.4.101.] 107 wert [Q1] wast 112 weary [Q1] wearied 118 nights . . . days [Q1] night . . . day 127 client [Q1] Clients 128 recorders succeeders intestate [Q] intestine 141 Where [Q] Where't 175 in [Q] with 176 Hewer *Hower* 180 pray thee prythee 188 heavy [Q] greeuous 216 births [Q] Birth 221 life. [Q; F here adds fourteen lines; see indented passage.] 225 or [Q1–5] and 243 that it 254 would I [Q1] I would 260 sometimes [Q1] sometime 270 is [Q; not in F] 273 this. [Q; F here adds fifty-five lines; see indented passage.] 286 love [Q] low 295 s.p. KING RICHARD . . . past. [Q1; F places the line after 4.4.296.] 296 s.p. QUEEN ELIZABETH [Q1; not in F] 297 s.p. KING RICHARD [Q; not in F] 300 holy [Q] Lordly 301 lordly knightlie 307 that [Q] it 308 God . . . God's [Q] Heauen . . . Heavens 323 in [Q1] with 327 o'erpast [Q] repast 343 good [Q] deare 348 peevish-fond [Q] peeuish found 356 recomfiture [Q] recomforture 375 Ratcliffe *Catesby* 391 mile [Q] miles 395 renegade [Q, F] runnagate 398 Ely [Q] *Morton* 421 Ay, ay [Q] I 431 Courtenay [Q, F] Courtney 434 Guildfords [Q, F] Guilfords 441 flood . . . water [Q] Floods . . . Waters 445 Ratcliffe . . . gave him [Q] There is my Purse, to cure that Blow of thine 452 Breton [Q, F] Brittaine 458 Bretagne [Q, F] Brittaine 465 tidings, [Q1] Newes, but

4.5.2 this [Q] the 5 aid [Q] ayde. / So get thee gone: commend me to thy Lord 17–18 Tell . . . daughter. [Q; F places the lines after 4.5.5.] 17 Tell him [Q] Withall say, that

5.2.8 spoils spoild 11 Lies [Q] Is 12 Near [Q] Ne're 17 swords [Q] men

5.3.2 Why, how now, Catesby [Q] My Lord of Surrey 3 s.p. CATESBY [Q] Sur⟨rey⟩.

5.4.4 standard. [Q; F places 5.4.21–24 here and adds, "My Lord of Oxford, you Sir *William Brandon,* / And your Sir *Walter Her-*

bert stay with me."] 21–24 Give . . . power. [Q, F places the lines after 5.4.4.]

5.5.3 [Q1 is the control text for the remainder of the play, although a handful of Folio variants are considered or adopted, as derived from the damaged final leaves of the manuscript.] 8 sentinels [F] centinell 10 s.p. KING RICHARD Stir [F, Q (text)] Sturr [Q (catchword)] 11 s.p. CATESBY Rat⟨cliffe⟩. 19 Ratcliffe [Q6, F (italic)] Ratliffe 25 some a boule of 29 Leave me. Bid my guard watch. Bid my guard watch, leaue me. 30–31 About . . . tent, / Ratcliffe, and Ratliffe about . . . tent / And 32 sit [Q2] set 43 mortal-sharing mortal staring 53 sundered [Q3] sundried 72 tomorrow, / Prince . . . Sixth. to morrow. 84 Comforts Doth comfort 85 sit [Q2] set on [Q5] in 93 s.p. GHOST OF RIVERS [Q3] *King* on [Q5] in 97 pointless [not in Q] 99 Will [Q2] Wel 100 s.p. GHOSTS OF THE PRINCES [F] *Ghost*. 110 Hastings, then Hastings 137 am [Q2] and 140 Myself What my selfe 156 Nay [F] And 163 My Ratcliffe, my 167 all our friends prove our friends proue all 168 Ratcliffe O Ratcliffe 177 s.p. LORDS [Q3–6] Lo⟨rds⟩. 180 s.p. A LORD [Q] Lo⟨rd⟩. 189 s.p. A LORD [Q] Lo⟨rd⟩. 191 Much that I could say More than I haue said 193 on vpon 196 forces faces 199 friends gentlemen 212 foison fat pays shall paie 219–20 this . . . my my . . . this 221 to the 223 bold and boldlie, and

5.6.12 not [Q2] nor 25 placèd strongly shall be placed 27 multitude foote and horse 28 ourself [not in Q] 29 both sides either side 31 boot! [Q3] bootes 32 s.p. NORFOLK A good [F, Q (text)] A good [Q (catchword)] 33 paper [not in Q] 34 Jackie [Q, F] Iocky too so 37 each euery 47 Bretons [Q, F] Brittains 49 ventures aduentures 52 distain restraine 54 Bretagne [Q, F] Brittaine 55 milksop [Q6, F] milkesopt 74 young his sonne

5.8.8–9 s.p. KING . . . But [F, Q (text)] But [Q (catchword)] 9 young George Stanley, is he is yong George Stanley 13 s.p. STANLEY [F] Der⟨by⟩. [not in Q] 14 Ferrers Ferris 15 becomes become 27 that this 28 United Deuided 32 his thy 37 forth in

The Tragedy of King Richard the Second

CONTROL TEXT: Q1; additional matter from F

F: The Folio of 1623
Q1: The Quarto of 1597
Q2, Q3: Quartos of 1598

Q4: The Quarto of 1608
Q5: The Quarto of 1615
Q6: The Quarto of 1634

Title: The Tragedie of Richard II [Q] The life and death of King Richard the Second [F]

s.p. KING RICHARD King [to 5.1]

1.1.118 by my [F] by **152 gentlemen** [F] gentleman **157 time** [F] month **162–63 Harry, when? / Obedience bids** Harrie, when? Obedience bids, / Obedience bids [F] Harry? when obedience bids, / Obedience bids **186 down** [F] vp
1.2.1 Gloucester's [F]; Woodstockes **58 it** [Q2, F] is
1.3.33 comest [Q5] comes [Q1] com'st [F] **55 just** [F] right **127 swords** [F] sword **127–28 swords, / Which** [F; Q1 has a five-line passage after line 127 omitted in F, indented in this edition. See Textual Note.] **166 then** [F; not in Q] **174 you owe** [F] y'owe **215 night** [Q4, F] nightes **220 sudden** [F] sullen **231–32 father. / Alas** [F; Q has a four-line passage omitted in F, indented in this edition after line 235.] **251 travel** trauaile **256–57 return. / s.p. BOLINGBROKE** [F; Q has twenty-six lines omitted from F, indented in this edition after line 256.] **256.2 remember** remember me
1.4.7 grew [F] blew **19 cousin, cousin** [F] Coosens Coosin **22 Bushy, Bagot here, and Green** [Q6] Bushie, [Q1] Bushy: heere Bagot and Greene [F] **51–52 Enter Bushy / Bushy, what news?** [F] Enter Bushie with newes. [Q1] **58 in his** [F] in the [Q1] into the [Q2] **63 late!** [F] late, / Amen [indented]
2.1.18 whose taste the wise are feared whose taste the wise are found [Q1] Whose state the wise are found [Q2] his state: then there are sound [F] **48 as a** [Q4, F] as **70 reined** ragde **102 encagèd** [F] inraged **113 now, now not,** **115–16 And— / s.p. KING RICHARD** And thou, a [F] And thou / King. A **125 brother** [Q2] brothers **178 the** [F] a **233 that thou wouldst** thou wouldst [Q1] thou'dst [F] **255 his** [F] his noble **258 King's grown** [Q3, F] King growen **278 Port le** [F] le Port **281 Thomas . . . Arundel** [not in Q1, F; a line is missing, probably a result of censorship.] **284 Thomas Ramston** John Ramston **286 Coint** [F] Coines
2.2.12 At . . . With With . . . at **16 eye** [F] eyes **31 As thought—** As thought [Q1] As though [Q2, F] **59 broke** [Q2, F] broken **119 Castle** [F; not in Q1] **138 commoners** commons **148–49 s.p. BAGOT Farewell . . . / BUSHY Well** [continued to Green] Farewell . . . / Bush⟨ie⟩ Well [Q1] Bush⟨y⟩. Farewell . . . Well [F]
2.3.36 Hereford, [Q3] Herefords **98 the** [F; not in Q1] **124 kinsman** [F] cousin **157 to** [Q2, F] vnto
3.1.32 England. [F] England, Lords farewell.
3.2.1 Harlechly Barkloughly **28–29 all. / s.p. AUMERLE** [F; Q1 has four lines omitted in F, indented in this edition after line 28.] **31 friends** [F] power **36 bloody** [Q2, F] bouldy **51 from** [F] off from **80 sluggard** [F] coward **81 forty** [F] twenty **98 loss,** [F] and **130 offence** [F; not in Q1] **174 wail their present woes** [F] sit and wail theyr woes **199 faction** [F] partie
3.3.13 with you [F; not in Q1] **35 Upon** [F] on both **58–59 rain / My waters** [F] raigne. / My water's **90 is** [F] standes **118 a prince and** princesse [Q1] a Prince [Q3] a Prince, is [F] **126 We** [Q4, F] King. We **126 ourself** [F] our selues **170 mock** [F] laugh
3.4.11 joy grief 35 too [F] two **58 garden! We at** garden at [Q1] garden, at [Q3, F] **68 then** [not in Q1, F] **81 Cam'st** [Q2, F] them
4.1.21 him [Q3, F] them **50–51 foe. / s.p. SURREY** [F; Q1 has an eight-line passage omitted from F, indented in this edition after line 50.] **50.3 may** it may **50.4 sun to sun** sinne to sinne **67 my** [Q3, F; not in Q1] the [Q2] **92 Bishop of Carlisle** Bishop [Q3, F] B. [Q1] **103 of that name the fourth** [F] fourth of that name **136 you** [Q2, F] yon **136 rear** [F] raise **139 Prevent** Preuent it **145–308 May . . . fall** [F (and similarly Q4); not in Q1. Only departures from F are noted for these lines.] **227 upon** [Q4] vpon me **241 and** [Q4] a **245 Nor** [Q4] No, nor **309–10 On . . . yourselves** [Q4, F] Let it be so, and loe on wednesday next, / We solemnly proclaime our Coronation, / Lords be ready all [Q1] **322 I will** Ile
5.1.25 stricken [F] throwne **44 fall** [F] tale **66 friends** [F] men **78 queen** [F] wife **84 s.p. NORTHUMBERLAND** [F] King.
5.2.52 Hold these jousts and triumphs Hold those Iusts & Triumphs [F] do these iusts & triumphs hold **55 prevent it** preuent **78 by my life, my** by my life, by my [Q1] my life, my [Q2, F] **82 son** [F] Aumerle
5.3.1 tell [F] tell me **14 these** [F] those **21 days** [F] yeares **30 the** my **35 I may** [Q2, F] May **55 lest** lest thy **73 voiced** [Q3, F] voice **91 kneel** [F] walke **100 mouth** [Q2, F] month **109 s.p. KING HENRY** [Q2, F] yorke **142 so** [not in Q1, F] too [Q6]
5.4.3, 6 s.p. FIRST, SECOND [not in Q1, F] **3 Those** [F] These
5.5.13–14 faith . . . faith [F] word . . . word **33 treason makes** [F] treasons make **55 sounds that tell** sound that tells **56 that** [F] which **58 hours, and times** [F] times, and houres **65 a sign** [Q2, F] asigne **94 spurgalled** [F] Spurrde, galld

5.6.8 Salisbury, Spencer, Blunt [F] Oxford, Salisbury, Blunt [Q1] Oxford, Salisbury [Q2] **17 not** [Q2, F1] nor **43 through the** [F] through

THE LIFE AND DEATH OF KING JOHN

CONTROL TEXT: F

F: The Folio of 1623

s.p. KING JOHN [F's use of *King John*, *John*, and *England* has been standardized throughout.]

s.p. QUEEN ELEANOR [F most often uses *Eleanor*, but also *Queen*, *Queen Mother*, and *Old Queen*. The choice of speech prefix often corresponds to the immediate context; they have been standardized throughout.]

s.p. BASTARD [F uses *Philip* until line 138 and *Bastard* almost exclusively thereafter: standardized throughout.]

s.p. FALCONBRIDGE [F's use of *Robert* has been altered throughout.]

s.p. KING PHILIP [In many places, noted individually below, F confuses the King with the Dauphin (*Lewis*). Otherwise, F's use of *King*, *Philip*, and *France* has been standardized throughout.]

s.p. LOUIS THE DAUPHIN [F uses *Dauphin* (*Dolphin*) alone: expanded throughout.]

1.1.11 Poitou *Poyctiers* **161 arise** rise **188 'Tis too** 'Tis two **208 smack** smoake **237 Could a** Could **257 Thou** That

2.1.1, 18 s.p. KING PHILIP *Lewis* **63 Ate** Ace **113 breast** beast **144 shows** shooes **149 King Philip** King *Lewis* **150 s.p. KING PHILIP** *Lew⟨is⟩* **152 Anjou** *Angiers* **169 Draw** Drawes **215 Confront your** Comfort yours **325 s.p. CITIZEN** *Hubert.* **327 your** yonr **335 run** rome **362 who's** whose **368 s.p. CITIZEN** *Fra⟨nce⟩* **371 Kinged** Kings **425 niece** neere **435 complete, O** compleat of **488 Anjou** *Angiers* **489 side** fide **501 sun** sonne **524 shall** still **540 rites** rights **572 lose** loose

3.1.34 God heauens **36 day** daies **62 God** heauen **74 task** tast **81 God** heauen **122 it** that **162 God Heauen 185 crazèd** cased **208 troth** truth **210 swear'st** sweares **224 Wilt** Wil't

3.3.8–10 Of . . . liberty. Of hoording Abbots: imprisoned angells / Set at libertie: the fat ribs of peace / Must by the hungry now be fed vpon: **52 broad-eyed** brooded

3.4.44 art not art **48 God** heauen **64 Friends** fiends **110 world's** words **149 vilely born** euilly borne **182 make** makes

4.1.23 God heauen **63 his** this **77 God's** heauen **91 God** heauen **114 eyes** eye **131 God** heauen

4.2.1 again against **31 worser** worse **42 when** then **73 Does** Do **117 ear** care

4.3.16 Who's Whose **17 'Tis** Is **33 man** mans **147 scramble** scamble **156 cincture** center

5.1.54 glisten glister

5.2.36 gripple cripple **43 thou** [not in F] **133 unhaired** vn-heard **135 these** this **145 his** this

5.3.8 Swineshead *Swinsted*

5.4.34 cresset Crest

5.5.3 measured measure **7 tatt'ring** tott'ring

5.6.13 eyeless endles

5.7.16 invincible inuisible **17 mind** winde **21 cygnet** Symet **42 strait** straight **60 God** heauen **88 our own** our **108 kind of** kinde

THE HISTORY OF HENRY THE FOURTH (1 HENRY IV)

CONTROL TEXT: Q1 for 1.3.199–2.3.19, Q2 elsewhere

F: The Folio of 1623
Q1: Remaining fragment of the Quarto of 1598
Q2: The complete Quarto of 1598
Q3: The Quarto of 1599
Q4: The Quarto of 1604
Q5: The Quarto of 1608
Q6: The Quarto of 1613
Q5b, Q6b: Successive states of Q5 and Q6 incorporating various print-shop corrections and changes
Q7: The Quarto of 1622

Title: THE / HISTORY OF / HENRIE THE / FOURTH; / With the battell at Shrewsburie, / betweene the King and Lord / Henry Percy, surnamed / Henrie Hotspur of / the North. / With the humorous conceits of Sir / John Falstalffe [Q2 title page] The First Part of Henry the Fourth, / with the Life and Death of HENRY / Sirnamed HOT-SPURRE. [F head title]

s.p. KING HENRY [Q's use of *King* has been changed throughout.]

s.p. PRINCE HARRY [Q's use of *Prince* has been changed throughout.]

s.p. POINS [Q's use of *Poines* / *Poynes* has been standardized throughout.]

s.p. HOTSPUR [Q's use of *Hotspur* / *Percy* has been standardized throughout.]

s.p. FIRST TRAVELLER and SECOND TRAVELLER [Q's *Traveler* of 2.2 has been differentiated into two persons.]

s.p. LADY PERCY [Q's use of *Lady* has been changed throughout.]

s.p. BARDOLPH [Q's use of *Russell / Bardoll* has been standardized throughout.]

s.p. GLYNDŴR [Q's use of *Glendower* has been changed throughout.]

s.p. SIR MICHAEL [Q's use of *Sir M⟨ighell⟩* in 4.4 has been modernized.]

s.p. JOHN OF LANCASTER [Q's use of *Prince John / John / John of Lancaster* has been standardized throughout.]

1.1.39 Herefordshire [Q7, F] Herdforshire **40 Glyndŵr** Glendower [similarly throughout] **62 a dear** [Q5b, F] deere **71 the Earl** Earle **73 Moray** Murrey **75–76 not? / s.p. WESTMORLAND In faith, it is a not?** In faith it is. / *West⟨merland⟩.* A

1.2.70 similes [Q6]; smiles **71 sweet** [Q3, F]; sweer **100 John, sack-and-sugar Jack?** John Sacke, and Sugar Jacke? **114 visors** vizards **144 Peto, Bardolph** Harvey, Rossill **148 But how** [F] How **154 Ay** [F] Yea **158 visors** vizards **161 But** [F] Yea, but

1.3.12 too [F] to **25 was** [F] is **26 Who either through envy** [F] Either envie therefore **27 Was** [F] Is **52 or** [F] or he **65 Made me to answer** [F] I answered **83 the** [Q3, F] that **115 Owain** Owen [similarly throughout] **122 you'll** [F] you wil **126 Although it be with** [F] Albeit I make a **131 In his behalf** [F] Yea on his part **133 downfall** [F] down-trod **199 s.p. HOTSPUR** [Q6, F; no s.p. in Q1] **209–10 a while . . . me.** [F] a while. **237 whipped** [Q2, F] whip **240 d'ye** [F] do you **241 upon't** [F] upon it **253 to't** [F] to it **254 We'll** [F] We wil **264 is't** [F] is it **265 Bristol** Bristow **Scrope** Scroop **289 Lord** Lo: **292 our** [Q2, F] out

2.1.1 An't [F] An it **23 races** razes **38 quoth a** [F] quoth he **51 Weald** wild **64 he's** [F] he is **68 foot-landrakers** [Q4, F] footland rakers **71 'oyez'-ers** Oneyres **80 recipe** receyte

2.2.16 two-and-twenty [F] xxii: **25 upon't** [F] upon it **45–46 Gadshill, what news? / s.p. GADSHILL** Bardoll, what newes. / *Bar⟨doll⟩.* **46 visors** vizards **70, 78 s.p. FIRST TRAVELLER** [unnumbered in Q] **71 their** our **74 s.p. SECOND TRAVELLER** [unnumbered in Q]

2.4.2 respect [Q7, F] the respect **42 thee** the **48 ransomed** ransome **63 A roan** [Q4, F] Roane **78 to** unto **83 maumets** mammets

2.5.29 precedent [F] present **32 s.p. POINS** [Q5, F] *Prin⟨ce⟩.* **61 o' a** 110 sun's sonnes **159 s.p. PRINCE HARRY** [F] *Gad⟨shill⟩.* **160, 162, 166 s.p. GADSHILL** [F] *Ross⟨ill⟩.* **230 to't** [F] to it **303 talon** talent **311 Owain** O

346 joint-stool joynd stoole **358 Father** [F] father **359 tristful** trustfull **366 yet** [Q4, F] so **431 lean** [Q3, F] lane **478, 479 Good . . . good** God . . . god **487 s.p. PETO** [F; not in Q] **492 s.p. PRINCE HARRY** [F; not in Q]

3.1.48 speaketh speakes **67 here's** [F] here is **97 cantle** [F] scantle **126 metre** miter **129 on** an **152 the least** least **182 nobleman** [F] noble man **197 thou down pourest** thou powrest downe **228 he's** [F] he is

3.2.59 won wan **84 gorged** [Q3, F] gordge **96 then** [F] than **112 swaddling-clothes** swathling cloaths **156 intemperature** [F] intemperance **157 bonds** bands

3.3.30 that's [Q4] that **49 tithe** tight **65 four-and-twenty** [F] xxiiii. **107 no thing** [F] nothing **122 owed** ought **158 guests** [F] ghesse **173–4 two-and-twenty** [F] xxii. **184 o'clock of** clocke

4.1.18 jostling justling **20 my lord** my mind **31 sickness stays him** sicknesse **50 sole** soule **55 is** [F] tis **98 ostriches** Estridges **98–100 that with the wind / [. . .] / Baiting** that with the wind / Baited **106 cuishes** cushes **109 dropped** [Q3, F] drop **117 altar** [Q5, F] altars **124 corpse** coarse **127 cannot** [Q6b, F] can **128 yet** [Q6, F] it **135 merrily** [F] merely

4.2.3 Coldfield cop- / hill **14–15 yeomen's** Yeomans **22 ensigns** Ancients **28 feazed ensign** fazd ancient **31 tattered** tottered

4.3.23 horse [Q5, F] horses **26 the half** the halfe of **84 country's** [Q6b, F] Countrey

4.4.30 more mo

5.1.42, 58 Doncaster [F] Dancaster **83 our** [F] your **135 o' a** 136 will it [Q3, F] wil

5.2.3 undone [Q6, F] under one **10 ne'er** [F] never

5.3.1 in the in **22 A fool** Ah foole **35 ragamuffins** rag of Muffins **39 stand'st** [F] stands **42 as yet are** are yet **50 gett'st** [F] gets

5.4.57 Sir S. 67 Nor [F] Now **91 thee** the **97 rites** [F] rights **108 Embowelled** Inboweld **110 Embowelled** Inboweld **110 embowel** inbowel **144 take't on** [F] take it upon **147 e'er** [F] ever

THE SECOND PART OF HENRY THE FOURTH

CONTROL TEXT: Q; additional passages from F

F: The Folio of 1623

Q: The Quarto of 1600

QA: First issue of 1600 Q, lacking 3.1

QB: Second issue of 1600, containing 3.1

Title: THE / Second part of Henrie / the fourth, continuing to his death, / *and coronation of Henrie* / the fift. / With the humours of Sir John Fal- / *staffe, and swaggering* / Pistoll. [Q title page] The Second Part of Henry the Fourth, / Containing his Death: and the Coronation / of King Henry the Fift. [F head title]

s.p. LORD BARDOLPH [Q's use of *Bardolph* (for the nobleman) has been changed throughout.]

s.p. NORTHUMBERLAND [Q's use of *Earl / Northumberland* has been standardized throughout.]

s.p. FALSTAFF [Q's use of *Oldcastle / John / Sir John / Falstaff* has been standardized throughout.]

s.p. PAGE [Q's use of *Boy / Page* has been standardized throughout.]

s.p. LORD CHIEF JUSTICE [Q's use of *Lord / Justice* has been standardized throughout.]

s.p. ARCHBISHOP OF YORK [Q's use of *Bishop* has been changed throughout.]

s.p. MOWBRAY [Q's use of *Marshall / Mowbray* has been standardized throughout.]

s.p. MISTRESS QUICKLY [Q's use of *Hostess / Quickly* has been standardized throughout.]

s.p. GOWER [Q's use of *Gower / Messenger* has been standardized throughout.]

s.p. PRINCE HARRY [Q's use of *Prince / Harry* has been standardized throughout.]

s.p. LADY NORTHUMBERLAND [Q's use of *Wife* has been changed throughout.]

s.p. LADY PERCY [Q's use of *Kate* has been changed throughout.]

s.p. FIRST DRAWER and **SECOND DRAWER** [Q's use of *Francis* and *Drawer* has been changed throughout (with some speeches redistributed).]

s.p. DOLL TEARSHEET [Q's use of *Tere-sheet / Doll / Dorothy / Whoore* has been standardized throughout.]

s.p. PRINCE JOHN [Q's use of *John / Prince / Lancaster* has been standardized throughout.]

s.p. KING HENRY [Q's use of *King* has been changed throughout.]

s.p. GLOUCESTER [Q's use of *Humphrey / Gloucester* has been standardized throughout.]

s.p. FIRST and **SECOND GROOM** [Q's use of *Strewers of Rushes 1, 2,* and *3* has been changed throughout (with some speeches redistributed).]

s.p. FIRST BEADLE [Q's use of *Sinklo* has been changed throughout.]

The following variants record only where the Norton text departs from Q, the control text. 3.1, missing in QA, is based on QB, but

where material in QA was reset in QB, QA remains the authoritative text. F, however, contains eight lengthy passages (and some shorter ones) that do not appear in Q (1.1.165–78, 1.1.188–208, 1.3.21–24, 1.3.36–55, 1.3.85–108, 2.3.23–45, 4.1.55–79, 4.1.101–37). These are marked in the variants and are based on F Material originally in Q but absent in F (and in the Oxford text) is printed in the variants or in inset passages within this text. For a much fuller collation of Q and F, see Oxford's *William Shakespeare: A Textual Companion.*

Induction [F; heading not in Q] **s.p. RUMOUR** [not in Q] **13 griefs** [F] griefe **21 anatomize** anthomize **35 hold** hole **36 Where** [F] When

1.1.34 Lord Bardolph Sir John Umfreuile **41 ill** [F] bad **55 should the** [F] should that **59 a venture** a venter **96 say so** [F; not in Q] **103 knolling** [F] tolling **126 Too** [F] So **161 s.p. LORD BARDOLPH** [F] *Umfr⟨euile⟩.* This strained passion doth you wrong my lord. / *Bard⟨olfe⟩.* **163 Lean on your** [F] Leave on you **165–78 You . . . be?** [F; not in Q] **177 doth** hath **181 was** [F] twas **188–208 The . . . him.** [F; not in Q]

1.2.3 more moe **6 clay, man** clay-man **7 tends** [F] intends **10 o'erwhelmed** [F] overwhelmd **14 set** [F] in-set **25 Dumbleton** Dommelton [Q] *Dombledon* [Q] **26 slops** [F] my sloppes **31 rascally** [F] rascall **33 smooth-pates** [F] smoothy-pates **41 it;** [F] it: wheres Bardolf, **42 him. Where's Bardolph?** [F] him. **45 An** and **67 want** [F] need **88 age** [F] an ague **93 An't** andt **101 is, as I take it, a** [F] as I take it? is a **110 s.p. FALSTAFF** [F] Old⟨castle⟩. **131 waist** waste **slenderer** [F] slender **156 bearherd** Berod **158 this** [F] his **them, are** [F] the one **161 vanguard** vaward **176 th'ear** [F] the yeere **185–86 and Prince Harry** [not in Q] **192 my bottle, would** [F] a bottle. I would

1.3.21–24 Till . . . admitted. [F; not in Q] **26 case** [F] cause **28 on** [F] and **29 with** [F] in **36–55 Yes . . . else** [F; not in Q] **58 one on** [F] so **71 Are** [F] And **78 not** [F] not to **79 He . . . Welsh** [F] French and Welch he leaves his back unarmde, they **84 'gainst** [F] against **85–108 s.p. ARCHBISHOP OF YORK . . . worst.** [F; not in Q] **109 s.p. MOWBRAY** [F] *Bish⟨op⟩.*

2.1.18 An I and I **an a** and a **19 vice** [F] view **22–23 continuantly** [F] continually **25 Lombard** [F] Lumbert **29 fobbed** fubd **38 Sir John** [F; not in Q] **44 Ah** a **45 Ah** a **48 s.p. FANG** [F] *Offic⟨er⟩.* **52 s.p. PAGE** [F] *Boy* **66–67 all, all** [F] al **73 Fie, what** [F] what **95 mad** made **134 tapestries** [F] tapestrie **134–35 ten pound** [F] X £. **138 Come** [F]

come, come **152 good** [F; not in Q] **154 Basingstoke** [F] Billingsgate
2.2.14 hast—videlicet these [F] hast with these **15 ones** [F] once **19 thy** [F] the **20 made a shift to** [F; not in Q] **holland.** [F; Q here prints additional lines, and these are included as an inset passage after 2.2.20 of the text.] **23 lying** [F] being **yours** [F] yours at this time **28 you'll** [F] you will **49 engrafted** engraffed **65 A calls me e'en now** A calls me enow **68 red petticoat** peticote **70 rabbit** [F] rabble **72 Althea** [F] Althear **78 good** [F; not in Q] **81 An** And **82 be wronged** [F] have wrong **84 my good** [F] my **98 borrower's** borowed **106 Sure he** [F] He sure **112 familiars** [F] family **115 My lord . . .** [F; no speech prefix before this line] *Poynes* My lord . . . **144 road** rode **150 like** [F] as **151 declension** [F] descension **152 prince** [F] pince **153 everything** [F] enery thing
2.3.11 endeared [F] endeere **23–45 He . . . grave** [F; not in Q]
2.4.1 s.p. FIRST DRAWER [F] *Fran⟨cis⟩.* **3 s.p. SECOND DRAWER** [F] *Draw⟨er⟩.* **8 s.p. FIRST DRAWER** [F] *Fran⟨cis⟩.* **11 s.p. SECOND DRAWER** [F] *Francis.* **14 s.p. FIRST DRAWER** [F] *Dra⟨wer⟩.* **16 s.p. SECOND DRAWER** [F] *Francis.* **20 in good truth, la** in good truth, law **22 we** [F] one **32 an** and **38 them; I** [F] I **42 Yea, Jesu** Yea, joy **46 bravely.** bravely. / *Doll* Hang your selfe, you muddie Cunger, hang your selfe. **48–49 i'good truth** ygood truth **59 Ensign** Antient [similarly elsewhere] **71 your** [F] & your **113 this.** [F] this. / *Sir John* No more Pistol, I would not have you go off here, discharge your selfe of our company, Pistoll. **117 An** and **123 'captain' odious** [F] as odious as the word occupy, which was an excellent good worde before it was il sorted **133 Where** [F] with **135 Fates** [F] faters **144 Trojan** troiant **150 Die men** [F] Men **152 O' A** **168 an a** and a **189 o'a** **198 A** [F] Ah **207 o' . . . o'** a . . . a **213 ha' chipped** a chipt **223 boot** [F] bootes **228 the scales** [F] scales **240 master's** [F] master **248 o'Thursday** a thursday **251 By my troth, thou'lt** By my troth thou't an and **286 o' a** **293 him** [F] thee **306 outbids** [F] blinds **356 good Doll.** [F] good Doll, come, shee comes blubberd, yea? wil you come Doll?
3.1.1–103 [QB; not in QA] **18 mast** [F] masse **22 billows** [F] pillowes **26 thy** [F] them **27 sea-boy** [F] season **52 liquors!** [F; Q here contains additional lines printed in this text as an inset passage after this word.] **80 beginnings** [F] beginning
3.2.11 o' a 19 o' a 20 bona-robas [F] bona robes **35 Stamford** [F] Samforth **41 o' Gaunt** a Gaunt **42 i'th'** ith **50 s.p. SHAL-**

LOW [F] *Bardolfe* [QA] **61 accommodated** [F] accommodate **75 your** [F] your good **79 Surecard** [F] Soccard **90 so. Yea** so (so, so) yea **94 an't** and't **98 an't** and't **103 s.p. FAL-STAFF** Prick him. [F] *John prickes him.* [Q s.d. is indented from right-hand margin on same type line as "well said."] **104 an** and **122 not** [F] much **133 for his** [F] for **143 he'd ha'** hee'd a **165 thou'rt** [F] thou art **168 caught** [F] cought **174 There** [F] Here **181–82 good Master Shallow, no more of that** [F] master Shallow. **199 in** [F] that we have, in **200 Hem boys** [F] Hemboies **205 lief** [F] live **217 I'll ne'er** ile nere **217–18 An't . . . an't** and't . . . and't **252 chapped** chopt **263 will** wooll **268 As you** [F] at your **my house** [F] our house **274 On** [F] *Shal⟨low⟩.* On **285 invisible** invincible **famine.** [Q here contains additional lines printed in this text as an inset passage after this word.] **285.2 ever** [F] over **291 trussed** [F] thrust
4.1.34 rags rage **36 appeared** appeare **55–79 And . . . wrong.** [F; not in Q] **71 shore** there **80 days** [F] daie's **101–37 O . . . King.** [F; not in Q. The s.p. *"West."* is set before 4.1.138 in Q.] **114 force** forc'd **137 indeed** and did **173 to our** [F] our **consigned** confinde **178 And At** **234 Than** [F] That **man** [F] man talking **245 th'imagined** th'imagine **250 Employ** Imply **274 this** [F] his **292–93 redresses. s.p. / PRINCE JOHN I** [F] redresses, / I **295 s.p. HASTINGS** [F] *Prince* **327 Our . . . dispersed** [F] My lord, our army is disperst already **343 rebellion . . . yours.** [F] rebellion: **348 these** this **traitors** [F] traitour
4.2.2 I pray [F; not in Q] **37 Rome** [F] Rome, there cosin **62 gav'st away** [F] gavest away gratis **63 Have** [F] Now, have **75 pray** [F; not in Q] **78 but** [F; not in Q] **96 illumi-nateth** [F] illumineth **100 his** [F] this
4.3.32 melting [F] meeting **39 line** [F] time **52 accompanied? Canst thou tell that?** [F] accompanied **94 heaven** [F] heavens **104 write . . . letters** [F] wet . . . termes **120 and will break out** [F; not in Q] **132 chamber; softly, pray** [F] chamber **179 How fares your grace?** [F; not in Q] **183 him.** [F] him: he is not here. **203 Culling** [F] tol-ing **203–4 the virtuous sweets, / Our thighs** [F] Our thigh **209 have hands** [F] inward true and **275 true and inward** [F] inward true and **288 worst of** [F] worse then **289 fine in carat, is** [F] fine, in karrat **292 my** [F] my most **305 O my son** [F; not in Q] **306 put it** [F] put **348 My gracious leige** [F; not in Q]
5.1.1 pie [F] pie sir **8 Davy, Davy, Davy** [F] Davy, Davy, Davy, Davy **8–9 see. William** [F] see Davy, let me see, yea mary William **12 headland** [F] hade land **19 Sir** [F] Now

sir 21 Hinkley [F] Hunkly 29–30 marvellous [F] marvailes 33 o'th' a'th' 40 An and 46 Come, [F] come, come, come 49 all [F; not in Q]

5.2.21 s.p. GLOUCESTER and CLARENCE [F] Princ. ambo 46 mix [F] mixt 62 s.p. PRINCE . . . CLARENCE Bro. other [F] otherwise

5.3.3 grafting graffing 5 here a . . . and a [F] here . . . and 24 Good Master Bardolph! [F] Give master Bardolfe 46 thee the 52–53 to th' too'th 57 cavalieros [F] cabileros 59 An And 64 'tis a tis 75 An't And't 84 By'r Lady Birlady 86 in thy [F] ith thy 95 Cophetua Covetua 117 knighthood [F] Knight

5.4.8 an and 11 He [F] I 22 o'ercome overcom

5.5.1–3 s.p. FIRST GROOM, SECOND GROOM, FIRST GROOM [Q opens with s.d. Enter strewers of rushes. The first three speeches are assigned to 1, 2, and 3, each presumably a strewer.] 3 o' a 3–4 coronation. Exeunt / Enter coronation, dispatch, dispatch. / Trumpets sound, and the King, and his traine passe over the Stage; after them enter 5 Robert [F; not in Q] 14 s.p. SHALLOW [F] Pist⟨ol⟩. 21–22 most certain. / s.p. FALSTAFF But [F] best certaine: but 23 affairs [F] affaires else 26 absque obsque all [F; not in Q] 49 awake [F] awakt 53 fool-born fool-borne 69 our [F] my 82 I fear that [F] that I feare

Epilogue 9 did mean [F; in F, the Epilogue is set in italics] meant 13–14 infinitely. [F] infinitely: and so I kneele downe before you; but indeed, to pray for the Queene. 21 before [F; not in Q] 27 died a [F] died 29–30 and . . . Queen [F; in Q, these lines follow Epilogue 15] 29 kneel [F] I kneele

THE LIFE OF HENRY THE FIFTH

CONTROL TEXT: F; additional matter from Q1

F: The Folio of 1623
Q1: The Quarto of 1600
Q3: The Quarto of 1619

s.p. KING HARRY [F's use of King has been standardized throughout.]

s.p. KING CHARLES [F's use of King has been standardized throughout.]

1.2.38 succedant succedual 50 there [Q] then 72 fine [Q] find 74 heir [Q] th'Heire 77 Ninth Tenth 99 son man 115 those these 131 blood Bloods 147 unmasked his power [Q] went with his forces unto into

154 the bruit thereof the brute hereof [Q] th'ill neighborhood 163 your [Q] their 166 A LORD [Q] Bish⟨op of⟩ Ely. 183 True. [Q; not in F] 197 majesty [Q] Maiesties 208 Fly [Q] Come 212 end [Q] And 213 defect [Q] defeat 276 have I I haue [F] haue we [Q1] we haue [Q3] 284 from [Q] with 287 Ay, [Q] And

2.0.32—perforce—[not in F]

2.1.21 mare [Q] name 23 Good morrow, Ensign Pistol [Q; not in F] 25 NIM [Q; not in F] 26 Gad's lugs [Q] this hand 65 thee defy [Q] defie thee 72 enough. [Q] enough to 73 you your 95 s.p. NIM I shall have my eight shillings? Nim. I shal haue my eight shillings I woon of you at beating? [Q; not in F] 105 that's that

2.2.1 s.p. GLOUCESTER [Q; throughout scene] Bed⟨ford⟩. [F; throughout scene] 35 their [Q] the 84 him [Q; not in F] 85 vile [Q; not in F] 95 ha' [Q1] haue 104 a an 136 mark make the thee 144 Henry [Q] Thomas 154 heartily in sufferance in sufferance heartily 163 and fixed [Q; not in F] 172 have [Q; not in F] 173 ye [Q1] you

2.3.15 babbled Table 22 up'ard and up'ard vpward and vpward [Q] up-peer'd and upward 29 s.p. HOSTESS Woman. 35 hell-fire [Q1] Hell 41 word [Q1] world

2.4.4 Bourbon [Q] Britaine 33 agèd [Q] Noble 57 mountant Mountaine 75 England [Q1] of England 106 Turns he [Q] Turning 107 pining [Q] priuy 123 for [Q] of

3.0.6 fanning fayning

3.1.7 conjure commune 17 noblest Noblish 24 men me 32 Straining Straying

3.2.19 God's plud [Q; not in F] 19 breaches [Q] breach 26 runs wins

3.3 s.p. FLUELLEN [Q; throughout scene] Welch. [F; throughout scene] s.p. JAMY [Q; throughout scene] Scot. [F; throughout scene] s.p. MACMORRIS [Q; throughout scene] Irish. [F; throughout scene] 55–56 Aye owe Got a aye, or goe to 109 heady headly 112 Defile Desire 124 dread [Q] great

3.4.3 Un En 4 j'apprenne ie apprend 5 parler parlen Comment Comient 6 La main? Elle est appelée Le main il & appelle 7 Et les doigts [continued to Catherine] Alice. E le doyts. 8 s.p. ALICE Kat⟨herine⟩ 8–9 souviendrai souemeray 9 sont ont fingers. Oui fingres, ou 11 s.p. CATHERINE Alice. 12 la bonne écolière; j'ai le bon escholier. / Kat⟨herine⟩. I'ay 13 les le 14 Les Le 15 De nails. Ecoutez— De Nayles escoute: 19 arma Arme 20 le de 22 la répétition le repeticio 39 Non, et Nome 43 Sauf Sans honneur honeus 44 dis de 45 pieds pied la robe [Q] de roba 46 De foot Le foot 46, 47, 51, 53 cown con [Q] Count 47 De foot et de Le Foot, & le Ils Il 51 De foot et de Le

Foot & le **Néanmoins** *neant moys* **53** *foot, de foote, e de* [Q] *Foot, le*
3.5.10, 32 s.p. BOURBON [Q] *Brit⟨ain⟩.* **11 de** *du* **26** '**Poor**' **may we** Poore we **45 Foix** Loys **46 knights** Kings
3.6.23 Of and of **27 her** [Q] his **49 executions** [Q] execution **58 is this the ensign you told me of** [Q] this is an arrant counterfeit Rascall **82** cam'st **99 here** [Q; not in F] **102 lenity** [Q] Leuitie
3.7.7 s.p. BOURBON [Q; throughout scene] *Dolph⟨in⟩.* [F; throughout scene] **12 Ah** ha Ch'ha **14 qui** a *ches* **60** *vomissement* vemissement et est **61** *truie* leuye **83 Duke of Bourbon** [Q] Dolphin
4.0.16 name nam'd
4.1.92 Thomas Iohn **148 deaths** [Q] death **propose** purpose **173 s.p.** BATES **3.** *Lord.* [Q] *Will⟨iams⟩.* **227 adoration** odoration **267 or** of **280 have I** [Q] I haue **286 ill** all
4.2 s.p. BOURBON [Q; throughout scene] *Dolph⟨in⟩.* [F; throughout scene] **5** *plus?* puis **6** *Cieux* Cein **11 dout** doubt **25** '**gainst** against **35 sonance** Sonuance **46 hands** hand **47 drooping** dropping **49 palled** pale **60 guidon** Guard: on
4.3.2 s.p. CLARENCE *Bed⟨ford⟩.* **3 s.p.** WARWICK [Q; throughout scene] *West⟨merland⟩.* [F; throughout scene] **8 Clarence** [Q] Bedford **11, 15 s.p.** CLARENCE *Bed⟨ford⟩.* [F; speeches not in Q] **44 t'old** old **48 And . . . day.'** [Q; not in F] **106 grazing** crasing **118 as** or **119 your** [Q] the **129 come** come againe
4.4.4 *Qualité* '*Calin o* Qualtitie calmie **12 miséricorde** *miserecordie* **pitié** pité **14 Or** for **46** *prisonnier* prisonner *néanmoins* neant-mons **47** *lui ci* layt a *promettez* promets **48** *je se* **49** *remerciements* remercious **49–50** *j'ai tombé le* intombe **50 mains** main. **comme** [not in F] **pense** peuse **51** *treis-distingué* tres distinie **59** *Suivez* Saaue
4.5 [Both Bourbon and the Dauphin appear in this scene in F. Whereas in most instances the textual differences between Q and F merely involve speech prefixes, here they are more substantial. See Additional Passages, pp. 1520–21, for F and Q versions of this scene.] **2** *Seigneur* sigueur *perdu . . . perdu* perdia *. . . perdie* **3 s.p.** BOURBON [Q] *Dol⟨phin⟩.* **Mort de** Mor Dieu **7–9 We are . . . upon** [Q; F places after 4.5.17] **10 order** [Q] Order now **12 home** [Q] hence **13 leno** [Q] Pander **14 by a slave** [Q] a base slaue
4.6.14–15 face, / **And** [Q] face. / He **15 dear** [Q] my **39 s.p.** PISTOL *Coup' la gorge.* [Q; not in F]
4.7.18 e'en in **19 world** Orld **36 made an end** [Q] made **83 Crispian** Crispianus **102 countryman** [Q] Countrymen **115 a live** aliue **118 a lived** aliue **150 that I would see** that I might see

4.8.9 God's plood, and his Gode plut, and his [Q1] 'Sblud **23 what is** [Q1] what's **94 Vaudemont** Vandemont **98 Keighley** Ketly **107 we** me **118 in** [Q; no in F]
5.0.10 maids [not in F] **29 high-loving** by loving
5.1.13 a [Q1] hee **36 By Jesu** [Q1] I say **37 and four nights** [Q; not in F] **80 swear** [Q] swore
5.2.50 scythe, all Sythe, withall **169 vat** wat **172–73** *suis le possesseur sur le* possession **236** *grandeur* grandeus **237** *de votre seigneurie* nostre Seigneur **indigne** indignie **244 vat** wat **246** *entend* entendre **291 before that it** before it **297 never** [not in F] **305 s.p.** WARWICK *West⟨merland⟩.* **306 so** [not in F] **328** ALL Lords. **337 paction** Pation

SIR THOMAS MORE

CONTROL TEXT: British Library MS Harley 7368: Add.II.D. (fols. 8ʳ—9ʳ); Add.III (fol. 11*ᵛ)

Add.II.D s.d. [**John . . . aloof**] *Enter Lincoln. Doll. Clown. Georg betts williamson others And a sergaunt at armes* **27 now? Prentices** '**simple**'? now prenty prentisses symple **34 s.p.** SHERWIN [Hand D, crossed out] williamson [Hand C] **42 s.p.** SOME all **43 s.p.** OTHERS [Hand D, crossed out] **54 s.p.** SOME all **55 s.p.** OTHERS all **89 order** orderd (?) **153 s.p.** ONE all
Add.III 18 stings state

ALL IS TRUE (HENRY VIII)

CONTROL TEXT: F

F: The Folio of 1623

Title: The Famous History of the Life of King HENRY the Eight [main Title] *The Life of King Henry the Eight* [running title; see the Introduction]

s.p. PROLOGUE, EPILOGUE [Though treated in this edition as characters, F's THE PROLOGVE and THE EPILOGVE could be either speech prefixes or section headings.]
s.p. KING HENRY [F's *King* has been expanded throughout.]
s.p. LORD CHAMBERLAIN [F uses *Chamberlain* and *Lord Chamberlain*; standardized throughout.]
s.p. LORD CHANCELLOR [F's *Chancellor* has been expanded throughout.]
s.p. SANDS [F uses *Sands* and *Lord Sands*;

standardized throughout. See note to 2.1.54 stage direction.]

s.p.GUILDFORD [F's *Sir Henry Guilford* has been shortened throughout.]

s.p.CARDINAL WOLSEY [F uses *Cardinal* and *Wolsey*. The latter occurs primarily when Cardinal Campeius is also onstage, although even then Cardinal Wolsey is usually referred to in the dialogue as "Cardinal"; standardized throughout.]

s.p.BUCKINGHAM'S SURVEYOR [F's *Surveyor* has been expanded throughout.]

s.p.CARDINAL CAMPEIUS [F uses *Campeius*, presumably in part to distinguish him from Cardinal Wolsey; expanded throughout.]

s.p.PAGE [F's *Boy* has been changed throughout.]

Epilogue

s.p.QUEEN KATHERINE, KATHERINE [F uses *Queen* until she becomes the princess dowager (4.2), at which point it switches to *Katherine*. Similarly, this edition switches from "Queen Katherine" to "Katherine" at 4.2.]

s.p.GRIFFITH [F's *Gentleman Usher* (2.4), *Gentleman* (3.1), and *Griffith* have been standardized throughout. See notes below for more information.]

s.p.ANNE Boleyn [F uses *Anne* and *Anne Bullen*; standardized throughout.]

s.p.OLD LADY [F uses *Old Lady* more frequently than *Lady*; standardized throughout.]

s.p.LINCOLN [F uses *Lincoln* and *Bishop of Lincoln*; standardized throughout.]

s.p.GENTLEMEN [F's "1," "2," and "3" have been expanded to "First Gentleman," etc.]

Prologue s.d. / s.p. *Enter* PROLOGUE / PROLOGUE *THE PROLOGVE*. **11 pass, if** *passe: If*

1.1.7 Ardres . . . Guisnes . . . Ardres *Andren . . . Guynes . . . Arde* **23** *mesdames Madams* **42–48 to. All . . . function. s.p. BUCKINGHAM Who . . . together, as you guess? s.p. NORFOLK too.** / *Buc⟨kingham⟩. All . . . Function: who . . . together? / Nor⟨folk⟩.* As you guesse: [In F, Buckingham begins speaking at "All was Royal" (line 42) and continues through "together" (line 47). Norfolk then begins the following speech with the phrase "As you guesse" (line 47).] **63 web, a** Web. O **116, 117 s.p. SECRETARY** *Secr⟨etary⟩.* [We cannot be certain which secretary speaks which lines, since two enter with Wolsey and they are not distinguished by speech prefix.] **120 venom-mouthed** *venom'd-mouth'd* **154 July** *Inly* **167 rinsing** *wrenching* **183 Privily he** *Priuily* **200 Hereford** *Hertford* **211 Abergavenny** *Aburgany* **219 Perk, his chancellor** *Pecke,* his Councellour. [The emendation derives from Holin-

shed.] **221 Nicholas** *Michaell* [The emendation derives from Holinshed.] **227 lord** Lords

1.2.9 s.p. CRIER (within) Room . . . Norfolk. *A noyse within crying roome . . . Duke of Norfolke.* [In F, this entire sentence is a stage direction, and there is no speech prefix.] **68 business** *basenesse* **140 His** This **148, 149 Hopkins** *Henton.* [The emendation derives from Holinshed. At 1.1.221, the name is presented correctly.] **157 feared** *feare* **165 confession's** Commissions [The emendation derives from Holinshed.] **171 win** [not in F] **181 To** For this to **191 Bulmer** *Blumer* [The emendation derives from Holinshed.] **191 remember** remember of

1.3.13 Or A **21 'messieurs'** *Monsiours* **34 'oui'** *wee* **59 he's** Ha's

1.4.6 feast first

2.1.21 Perk *Pecke.* **54 s.d. William** *Walter* [The emendation derives from Holinshed.] **79 i'** a **87 mark** make

2.2.1 s.p. LORD CHAMBERLAIN [*reads*] [not in F]

2.3.59 note's notes **61 of you** of you, to you **87 fie, fie** fye, fye, fye

2.4.7, 10 come into the court &c. **11 s.p. QUEEN KATHERINE** [not in F] **124 s.p. GRIFFITH** *Gent⟨leman⟩ Vsh⟨er⟩.* [It seems reasonable to suppose that this gentleman is the same as the *Gentleman* who attends the queen at 3.1.14. s.d. and is referred to as *Gent⟨leman⟩* at 3.1.16, 18 s.p., later identified as *Griffith, her Gentleman Vsher* at 4.2.0 s.d. **171 A** And **188 does yield to th'** does to th' **196 throe** throw

3.1.3 s.p. GENTLEWOMAN [*sings*] SONG. [In F, no speech prefix precedes the song.] **16, 18 s.p. GRIFFITH** *Gent⟨leman⟩.* **60 your** our **118 he's** ha's **123 accursed** a Curse

3.2.58 Has Ha's **143 glad** gald **172 filed** fill'd **340 legantine** Legatiue **344 Chattels** Castles

4.1.20 s.p. SECOND GENTLEMAN I 56 s.p. FIRST GENTLEMAN [not in F, which gives all of lines 55–56 to "2." Here, FIRST GENTLEMAN speaks the beginning of line 56.] **103 Stokesley** *Stokeley* [The emendation derives from Holinshed.] **119 s.p. FIRST and SECOND GENTLEMEN** Both.

4.2.5 led'st lead'st **7 think** thanke **99 colour** cold **109 s.d. CAPUTIUS** *Capuchius*

5.1.37 time Lime **140 precipice** Precepit **158 s.p. LOVELL (within)** *Gent⟨leman⟩ within.*

5.2.7 piece Peere **119, 121 s.p. LORD CHANCELLOR** ⟨*Lord*⟩ *Cham⟨berlain⟩.* **126 s.p. ALL THE COUNCIL** *All.* **167 this** his **207 heart** hearts

5.3.2 Paris Parish **4, 27 s.p. ONE (within)** *Within.* **78 a way** away

5.4.37 ways way **70 your** you **75 He's** 'Has

Epilogue s.d. / s.p. *Enter* EPILOGUE / EPILOGUE THE EPILOGVE.

General Bibliography*

There is a huge and ever-expanding scholarly literature about Shakespeare and his culture. This general list and the lists that accompany the individual plays and the poems in this volume are only a small sampling of the available resources. Journals devoted to Shakespeare studies include *Shakespeare Bulletin*, *Shakespeare Jahrbuch* (Germany), *Shakespeare Quarterly*, *Shakespeare Studies*, and *Shakespeare Survey* (England); other journals, such as *English Literary History*, *English Literary Renaissance*, *Renaissance Quarterly*, *Representations*, or *Studies in English Literature*, also frequently publish essays on Shakespeare's works. The categories below are only approximate; many of the texts could properly belong in more than one category.

Guides and Companions to Shakespeare Studies

Callaghan, Dympna, ed. *A Feminist Companion to Shakespeare*. Malden, Mass.: Blackwell, 2000.

De Grazia, Margreta, and Stanley Wells, eds. *The Cambridge Companion to Shakespeare*. Cambridge, Eng.: Cambridge University Press, 2001.

Drakakis, John, ed. *Alternative Shakespeares*. 2nd ed. London: Routledge, 1985.

Dutton, Richard, and Jean E. Howard, eds. *A Companion to Shakespeare's Works*, I: *The Tragedies*. Malden, Mass.: Blackwell, 2003.

———, eds. *A Companion to Shakespeare's Works*, II: *The Histories*. Malden, Mass.: Blackwell, 2003.

———, eds. *A Companion to Shakespeare's Works*, III: *The Comedies*. Malden, Mass.: Blackwell, 2003.

———, eds. *A Companion to Shakespeare's Works*, IV: *Poems, Problem Comedies, Late Plays*. Malden, Mass.: Blackwell, 2003.

Hattaway, Michael, ed. *The Cambridge Companion to Shakespeare's History Plays*. Cambridge, Eng.: Cambridge University Press, 2002.

Hawkes, Terence, ed. *Alternative Shakespeares, Volume 2*. London: Routledge, 1996.

Hodgdon, Barbara, and W. B. Worthen, eds. *A Companion to Shakespeare and Performance*. Malden, Mass.: Blackwell, 2005.

Jackson, Russell, ed. *The Cambridge Companion to Shakespeare on Film*. 2nd ed. Cambridge, Eng.: Cambridge University Press, 2007.

Kasten, David Scott, ed. *A Companion to Shakespeare*. Malden, Mass.: Blackwell, 1999.

Kinney, Arthur F. *Shakespeare by Stages: An Historical Introduction*. Malden, Mass.: Blackwell, 2003.

Leggatt, Alexander, ed. *The Cambridge Companion to Shakespearean Comedy*. Cambridge, Eng.: Cambridge University Press, 2002.

McDonald, Russ, ed. *The Bedford Companion to Shakespeare: An Introduction with Documents*. 2nd ed. Houndmills, Basingstoke: Palgrave Macmillan, 2001.

———, ed. *Shakespeare: An Anthology of Criticism and Theory, 1945–2000*. Malden, Mass.: Blackwell, 2004.

McEachern, Claire, ed. *The Cambridge Companion to Shakespearean Tragedy*. Cambridge, Eng.: Cambridge University Press, 2002.

*Edited by Holger Schott Syme, Department of English, University of Toronto.

Schoenfeldt, Michael. *A Companion to Shakespeare's Sonnets.* Malden, Mass.: Blackwell, 2006.

Smith, Emma, ed. *Shakespeare's Comedies: A Guide to Criticism.* Malden, Mass.: Blackwell, 2003.

———, ed. *Shakespeare's Histories: A Guide to Criticism.* Malden, Mass.: Blackwell, 2003.

———, ed. *Shakespeare's Tragedies: A Guide to Criticism.* Malden, Mass.: Blackwell, 2003.

Wells, Stanley, and Lena Cowen Orlin, eds. *Shakespeare: An Oxford Guide.* Oxford: Oxford University Press, 2003.

Wells, Stanley, and Sarah Stanton, eds. *The Cambridge Companion to Shakespeare on Stage.* New York: Cambridge University Press, 2002.

Shakespeare's World

Social, Political, and Economic History

Amussen, Susan Dwyer. *An Ordered Society: Gender and Class in Early Modern England.* New York: Columbia University Press, 1993.

Archer, Ian W. *The Pursuit of Stability: Social Relations in Elizabethan London.* New York: Cambridge University Press, 1991.

Ariès, Philippe, and Georges Duby, general eds. *A History of Private Life,* Volume III: *Passions of the Renaissance.* Ed. Roger Chartier. Trans. Arthur Goldhammer. Cambridge, Mass.: Belknap Press, 1989.

Armitage, David, and Michael J. Braddick, eds. *The British Atlantic World, 1500–1800.* New York: Palgrave Macmillan, 2002.

Barry, Jonathan, ed. *The Tudor and Stuart Town: A Reader in English Urban History, 1530–1688.* London: Longman, 1990.

Barry, Jonathan, and Christopher Brooks. *The Middling Sort of People: Culture, Society and Politics in England, 1550–1800.* Houndmills, Basingstoke: Palgrave Macmillan, 1994.

Barthelmey, Anthony Gerard. *Black Face, Maligned Race: The Representation of Blacks in English Drama from Shakespeare to Southerne.* Baton Rouge: Louisiana State University Press, 1987.

Beier, A. L. *Masterless Men: The Vagrancy Problem in England, 1560–1640.* New York: Methuen, 1985.

Beier, A. L., and Roger Finlay, eds. *London 1500–1700: The Making of the Metropolis.* New York: Longman, 1986.

Ben-Amos, Ilana Krausman. *Adolescence and Youth in Early Modern England.* New Haven: Yale University Press, 1994.

Bridenbaugh, Carl. *Vexed and Troubled Englishmen, 1590–1642.* New York: Oxford University Press, 1976.

Brigden, Susan. *New Worlds, Lost Worlds: The Rule of the Tudors, 1485–1603.* New York: Viking, 2001.

Burgess, Glenn. *The Politics of the Ancient Constitution: An Introduction to English Political Thought, 1603–1642.* University Park: Pennsylvania State University Press, 1993.

Capp, Bernard S. *When Gossips Meet: Women, Family, and Neighbourhood in Early Modern England.* Oxford: Oxford University Press, 2003.

Clark, Alice. *Working Life of Women in the Seventeenth Century.* Introduction by Amy Louise Erickson. 1968. New York: Routledge, 1992.

Clay, C. G. A. *Economic Expansion and Social Change: England 1500–1700.* 2 vols. New York: Cambridge University Press, 1984.

Cressy, David. *Birth, Marriage, and Death: Ritual, Religion, and the Life-Cycle in Tudor and Stuart England.* Oxford: Oxford University Press, 1997.

Cruickshank, Charles Greig. *Elizabeth's Army*. 2nd ed. Oxford: Clarendon, 1966.

Elliot, John Huxtable. *The Old World and the New, 1492–1650*. New York: Cambridge University Press, 1970.

Ellis, Steven G. *Tudor Ireland: Crown, Community, and the Conflict of Cultures, 1470–1603*. London: Longman, 1985.

Elton, G. R. *England Under the Tudors*. 3rd ed. New York: Routledge, 1991.

———. *The Tudor Revolution in Government: Administrative Changes in the Reign of Henry VIII*. Cambridge, Eng.: Cambridge University Press, 1959.

Emmison, F. G. *Elizabethan Life*. Chelmsford: Essex County Council, 1970.

Erickson, Amy Louise. *Women and Property in Early Modern England*. New York: Routledge, 1993.

Finlay, Roger. *Population and Metropolis: The Demography of London, 1580–1650*. Cambridge, Eng.: Cambridge University Press, 1981.

Fletcher, Anthony. *Gender, Sex, and Subordination in England, 1500–1800*. New Haven: Yale University Press, 1995.

Fletcher, Anthony, and John Stevenson, eds. *Order and Disorder in Early Modern England*. New York: Cambridge University Press, 1985.

Gaskill, Malcolm. *Crime and Mentalities in Early Modern England*. New York: Cambridge University Press, 2000.

Gittings, Clare. *Death, Burial and the Individual in Early Modern England*. London: Croom Helm, 1984.

Gowing, Laura. *Common Bodies: Women, Touch and Power in Seventeenth-Century England*. New Haven: Yale University Press, 2003.

Griffiths, Paul. *Youth and Authority: Formative Experiences in England, 1560–1640*. Oxford: Clarendon, 1996.

Griffiths, Paul, Adam Fox, and Steve Hindle, eds. *The Experience of Authority in Early Modern England*. New York: St. Martin's, 1996.

Guy, John A. *Queen of Scots: The True Life of Mary Stuart*. Boston: Houghton Mifflin, 2004.

———, ed. *The Reign of Elizabeth I: Court and Culture in the Last Decade*. Cambridge, Eng.: Cambridge University Press, 1995.

———. *Tudor England*. New York: Oxford University Press, 1988.

Heal, Felicity, and Clive Holmes. *The Gentry in England and Wales, 1500–1700*. Basingstoke: Macmillan, 1994.

Herrup, Cynthia B. *The Common Peace: Participation and the Criminal Law in Seventeenth-Century England*. New York: Cambridge University Press, 1987.

Hindle, Steve. *The State and Social Change in Early Modern England, c.1550–1640*. New York: St. Martin's, 2000.

Hirst, Derek. *Authority and Conflict: England, 1603–1658*. Cambridge, Mass.: Harvard University Press, 1986.

Ingram, Martin. *Church Courts, Sex, and Marriage in England, 1570–1640*. New York: Cambridge University Press, 1987.

James, Mervyn. *Society, Politics and Culture: Studies in Early Modern England*. New York: Cambridge University Press, 1986.

King, John N. *Tudor Royal Iconography: Literature and Art in an Age of Religious Crisis*. Princeton: Princeton University Press, 1989.

Kishlansky, Mark A. *A Monarchy Transformed: Britain 1603–1714*. New York: Penguin Books, 1996.

Klein, Joan Larsen. *Daughters, Wives, and Widows: Writings by Men about Women and Marriage in England, 1500–1640*. Urbana: University of Illinois Press, 1992.

Lake, Peter, with Michael Questier. *The Anti-Christ's Lewd Hat: Protestants, Papists and Players in Post-Reformation England*. New Haven: Yale University Press, 2002.

Laslett, Peter. *The World We Have Lost: Further Explored*. 3rd ed. New York: Scribner, 1984.

Levin, Carole. *The Heart and Stomach of a King: Elizabeth I and the Politics of Sex and Power*. Philadelphia: University of Pennsylvania Press, 1994.

Lockyer, Roger. *The Early Stuarts: A Political History of England, 1603–1642.* 2nd ed. London: Longman, 1999.

MacCaffrey, Wallace T. *Elizabeth I: War and Politics, 1588–1603.* Princeton: Princeton University Press, 1992.

Manning, Roger B. *Village Revolts: Social Protest and Popular Disturbances in England, 1509–1640.* Oxford: Clarendon, 1988.

Matar, Nabil I. *Islam in Britain, 1558–1685.* New York: Cambridge University Press, 1998.

———. *Turks, Moors, and Englishmen in the Age of Discovery.* New York: Columbia University Press, 1999.

Mendelson, Sara Heller, and Patricia Crawford. *Women in Early Modern England, 1550–1720.* Oxford: Clarendon, 1998.

Moody, T. W., F. X. Martin, and F. J. Byrne, eds. *A New History of Ireland,* Volume 3: *Early Modern Ireland, 1534–1691.* Oxford: Oxford University Press, 2001.

Mukerji, Chandra. *From Graven Images: Patterns of Modern Materialism.* New York: Columbia University Press, 1983.

Neale, J. E. *Elizabeth I and Her Parliaments, 1559–1581.* London: Cape, 1971.

———. *Queen Elizabeth I.* London: Pimlico, 1998.

Nichols, John, ed. *The Progresses and Public Processions of Queen Elizabeth.* 3 vols. London: J. Nichols, 1823.

Palliser, D. M. *The Age of Elizabeth: England under the Later Tudors, 1547–1603.* 2nd ed. New York: Longman, 1992.

Parry, J. H. *The Age of Reconnaissance: Discovery, Exploration, and Settlement, 1450 to 1650.* New York: Praeger, 1969.

Pearson, Lu Emily Hess. *Elizabethans at Home.* Stanford: Stanford University Press, 1967.

Peck, Linda Levy. *Court Patronage and Corruption in Early Stuart England.* Boston: Unwin Hyman, 1990.

Peters, Christine. *Women in Early Modern Britain, 1450–1640.* New York: Palgrave Macmillan, 2004.

Pocock, J. G. A. *The Ancient Constitution and the Feudal Law: Study of English Historical Thought in the Seventeenth Century—A Reissue with a Retrospect.* Rev. ed. New York: Cambridge University Press, 1987.

Rappaport, Steve. *Worlds within Worlds: Structures of Life in Sixteenth-Century London.* New York: Cambridge University Press, 1989.

Sharpe, J. A. *Crime in Early Modern England, 1550–1750.* 2nd ed. New York: Longman, 1999.

———. *Early Modern England: A Social History, 1550–1760.* 2nd ed. London: Arnold, 1997.

Slack, Paul. *The Impact of Plague in Tudor and Stuart England.* Boston: Routledge and Kegan Paul, 1985.

———. *Poverty and Policy in Tudor and Stuart England.* New York: Longman, 1988.

———, ed. *Rebellion, Popular Protest, and the Social Order in Early Modern England.* New York: Cambridge University Press, 1984.

Stone, Lawrence. *The Causes of the English Revolution, 1529–1642.* New York: Routledge, 2002.

———. *The Crisis of the Aristocracy, 1558–1641.* Oxford: Clarendon, 1965.

———. *The Family, Sex and Marriage in England, 1500–1800.* New York: Harper & Row, 1979.

Thirsk, Joan. *Economic Policy and Projects: The Development of a Consumer Society in Early Modern England.* Oxford: Clarendon, 1978.

Thomas, Keith. *Religion and the Decline of Magic: Studies in Popular Beliefs in Sixteenth and Seventeenth Century England.* New York: Scribner, 1971.

Underdown, David. *Fire from Heaven: Life in an English Town in the Seventeenth Century.* London: HarperCollins, 1992.

———. *Revel, Riot, and Rebellion: Popular Politics and Culture in England, 1603–1660.* Oxford: Clarendon, 1985.

Williams, Penry. *The Later Tudors: England, 1547–1603*. New York: Oxford University Press, 1995.

Wrightson, Keith. *Earthly Necessities: Economic Lives in Early Modern Britain*. New Haven: Yale University Press, 2000.

———. *English Society, 1580–1680*. London: Hutchinson, 1982.

Yates, Frances Amelia. *Astraea: The Imperial Theme in the Sixteenth Century*. London: Routledge and Kegan Paul, 1975.

Zagorin, Perez. *Rebels and Rulers, 1500–1660*. 2 vols. New York: Cambridge University Press, 1982.

Intellectual and Religious History

Armitage, David. *The Ideological Origins of the British Empire*. New York: Cambridge University Press, 2000.

Baker, Herschel Clay. *The Race of Time: Three Lectures on Renaissance Historiography*. Toronto: University of Toronto Press, 1967.

Barkan, Leonard. *Nature's Work of Art: The Human Body as Image of the World*. New Haven: Yale University Press, 1975.

Bossy, John. *Christianity in the West, 1400–1700*. New York: Oxford University Press, 1985.

Bouwsma, William James. *John Calvin: A Sixteenth-Century Portrait*. New York: Oxford University Press, 1988.

Cassirer, Ernst. *The Individual and the Cosmos in Renaissance Philosophy*. Trans. Mario Domandi. Philadelphia: University of Pennsylvania Press, 1972.

Clark, Stuart. *Thinking with Demons: The Idea of Witchcraft in Early Modern Europe*. New York: Oxford University Press, 1997.

Collinson, Patrick. *The Birthpangs of Protestant England: Religion and Cultural Change in the Sixteenth and Seventeenth Centuries*. New York: St. Martin's, 1988.

———. *The Elizabethan Puritan Movement*. New York: Oxford University Press, 1990.

———. *The Religion of Protestants: The Church in English Society, 1559–1625*. Oxford: Clarendon, 1982.

Doran, Susan, and Christopher Durston. *Princes, Pastors, and People: The Church and Religion in England, 1500–1700*. Rev. ed. New York: Routledge, 2003.

Duffy, Eamon. *The Stripping of the Altars: Traditional Religion in England, c. 1400–c. 1580*. 2nd ed. New Haven: Yale University Press, 1992.

Gadd, Ian, and Alexandra Gillespie, eds. *John Stow (1525–1605) and the Making of the English Past*. London: British Library, 2004.

Haigh, Christopher. *English Reformations: Religion, Politics, and Society under the Tudors*. New York: Oxford University Press, 1993.

Hill, Christopher. *Society and Puritanism in Pre-Revolutionary England*. New York: Schocken Books, 1964.

Houlbrooke, Ralph A. *Death, Religion, and the Family in England, 1480–1700*. New York: Oxford University Press, 1998.

Kelly, Henry Ansgar. *Divine Providence in the England of Shakespeare's Histories*. Cambridge, Mass.: Harvard University Press, 1970.

Kilroy, Gerard. *Edmund Campion. Memory and Transcription*. Aldershot, Eng.: Ashgate, 2005.

Klaits, Joseph. *Servants of Satan: The Age of the Witch Hunts*. Bloomington: Indiana University Press, 1985.

Kristeller, Paul Oskar. *Renaissance Thought: The Classic, Scholastic, and Humanistic Strains*. New York: Harper & Row, 1961.

Levao, Ronald. *Renaissance Minds and Their Fictions: Cusanus, Sidney, Shakespeare*. Berkeley: University of California Press, 1985.

Levin, Harry. *The Myth of the Golden Age in the Renaissance*. Bloomington: University of Indiana Press, 1969.

Levy, Fred Jacob. *Tudor Historical Thought*. San Marino, Calif.: Huntington Library Press, 1967.

MacCulloch, Diarmaid. *The Later Reformation in England, 1547–1603*. 2nd ed. New York: Palgrave, 2001.

———. *The Reformation*. New York: Viking, 2004.

Mack, Peter, ed. *Renaissance Rhetoric*. New York: St. Martin's, 1994.

Marotti, Arthur F. *Religious Ideology and Cultural Fantasy: Catholic and Anti-Catholic Discourses in Early Modern England*. Notre Dame, Ind.: University of Notre Dame Press, 2005.

Marshall, Peter. *Beliefs and the Dead in Reformation England*. London: Oxford University Press, 2002.

Oldridge, Darren, ed. *The Witchcraft Reader*. London: Routledge, 2001.

Patterson, Annabel M. *Reading Holinshed's Chronicles*. Chicago: University of Chicago Press, 1994.

Popkin, Richard H. *The History of Skepticism from Erasmus to Spinoza*. Berkeley: University of California Press, 1979.

Sharpe, James. *Instruments of Darkness: Witchcraft in England 1550–1750*. New York: Penguin Books, 1996.

Shuger, Debora Kuller. *Habits of Thought in the English Renaissance: Religion, Politics, and the Dominant Culture*. Berkeley: University of California Press, 1990.

Sonnino, Lee A. *A Handbook to Sixteenth-Century Rhetoric*. London: Routledge and Kegan Paul, 1968.

Strong, Roy. *The Cult of Elizabeth: Elizabethan Portraiture and Pageantry*. London: Thames and Hudson, 1977.

———. *The English Icon: Elizabethan & Jacobean Portraiture*. New York: Pantheon Books, 1969.

Walsham, Alexandra. *Providence in Early Modern England*. New York: Oxford University Press, 1999.

Watt, Tessa. *Cheap Print and Popular Piety, 1560–1649*. New York: Cambridge University Press, 1991.

Wind, Edgar. *Pagan Mysteries in the Renaissance*. Rev. and enl. ed. London: Oxford University Press, 1980.

Woolf, D. R. *Reading History in Early Modern England*. New York: Cambridge University Press, 2000.

———. *The Social Circulation of the Past: English Historical Culture, 1500–1730*. New York: Oxford University Press, 2003.

Cultural History and Early Modern Cultural Studies

Aers, David, Bob Hodge, and Gunther Kress. *Literature, Language, and Society in England, 1589–1680*. Totowa, N.J.: Barnes & Noble Books, 1981.

Agnew, Jean-Christophe. *Worlds Apart: The Market and the Theater in Anglo-American Thought, 1550–1750*. New York: Cambridge University Press, 1986.

Andersen, Jennifer, and Elizabeth Sauer, eds. *Books and Readers in Early Modern England: Material Studies*. Philadelphia: University of Pennsylvania Press, 2001.

Bakhtin, Mikhail. *Rabelais and His World*. Trans. Hélène Iswolsky. Rev. ed. Bloomington: Indiana University Press, 1984.

Baldwin, Thomas Whitfield. *William Shakespere's Small Latine & Lesse Greeke*. Urbana: University of Illinois Press, 1944.

Barkan, Leonard. *The Gods Made Flesh: Metamorphosis & the Pursuit of Paganism*. New Haven: Yale University Press, 1986.

Barker, Francis. *The Tremulous Private Body: Essays on Subjection*. New York: Methuen, 1984.

Baron, Sabrina Alcorn, ed. *The Reader Revealed*. Washington, D.C.: Folger Shakespeare Library, 2001.

Bartels, Emily Carroll. *Spectacles of Strangeness: Imperialism, Alienation, and Marlowe*. Philadelphia: University of Pennsylvania Press, 1993.

Beilin, Elaine V. *Redeeming Eve: Women Writers of the English Renaissance*. Princeton: Princeton University Press, 1987.

Blank, Paula. *Broken English: Dialects and the Politics of Language in Renaissance Literature*. New York: Routledge, 1996.

Bloom, Gina. *Voice in Motion: Staging Gender, Shaping Sound in Early Modern England*. Philadelphia: Pennsylvania University Press, 2007.

Bray, Alan. *Homosexuality in Renaissance England*. Rev. ed. New York: Columbia University Press, 1995.

Brayman Hackel, Heidi. *Reading Material in Early Modern England: Print, Gender, and Literacy*. New York: Cambridge University Press, 2005.

Briggs, Julia. *This Stage-Play World: Texts and Contexts, 1580–1625*. 2nd ed. New York: Oxford University Press, 1997.

Bristol, Michael D. *Carnival and Theater: Plebeian Culture and the Structure of Authority in Renaissance England*. New York: Methuen, 1985.

Brotton, Jerry. *Trading Territories: Mapping the Early Modern World*. London: Reaktion Books, 1997.

Brown, Pamela Allen. *Better a Shrew than a Sheep: Women, Drama, and the Culture of Jest in Early Modern England*. Ithaca, N.Y.: Cornell University Press, 2003.

Burke, Peter. *Popular Culture in Early Modern Europe*. New York: New York University Press, 1978.

Burt, Richard, and John Michael Archer, eds. *Enclosure Acts: Sexuality, Property, and Culture in Early Modern England*. Ithaca, N.Y.: Cornell University Press, 1994.

Bushnell, Rebecca W. *A Culture of Teaching: Early Modern Humanism in Theory and Practice*. Ithaca, N.Y.: Cornell University Press, 1996.

Buxton, John. *Elizabethan Taste*. London: Macmillan, 1963.

Caldwell, John. *The Oxford History of English Music*. New York: Oxford University Press, 1991.

Carroll, William C. *Fat King, Lean Beggar: Representations of Poverty in the Age of Shakespeare*. Ithaca, N.Y.: Cornell University Press, 1996.

Clegg, Cyndia Susan. *Press Censorship in Elizabethan England*. New York: Cambridge University Press, 1997.

———. *Press Censorship in Jacobean England*. New York: Cambridge University Press, 2001.

Cox, John D. *The Devil and the Sacred in English Drama, 1350–1642*. New York: Cambridge University Press, 2000.

Crane, Mary Thomas. *Framing Authority: Sayings, Self, and Society in Sixteenth-Century England*. Princeton: Princeton University Press, 1993.

Crawford, Julie. *Marvelous Protestantism: Monstrous Births in Post-Reformation England*. Baltimore: Johns Hopkins University Press, 2005.

Cressy, David. *Literacy and the Social Order: Reading and Writing in Tudor and Stuart England*. New York: Cambridge University Press, 1980.

De Grazia, Margreta, Maureen Quilligan, and Peter Stallybrass, eds. *Subject and Object in Renaissance Culture*. New York: Cambridge University Press, 1996.

Diehl, Huston. *Staging Reform, Reforming the Stage: Protestantism and Popular Theater in Early Modern England*. Ithaca, N.Y.: Cornell University Press, 1997.

Dolan, Frances E. *Dangerous Familiars: Representations of Domestic Crime in England, 1550–1700*. Ithaca, N.Y.: Cornell University Press, 1994.

———. *Whores of Babylon: Catholicism, Gender, and Seventeenth-Century Print Culture*. Ithaca, N.Y.: Cornell University Press, 1999.

Eisenstein, Elizabeth L. *The Printing Press as an Agent of Change: Communications and Cultural Transformations in Early-Modern Europe*. 2 vols. New York: Cambridge University Press, 1979.

Ferguson, Margaret W. *Dido's Daughters: Literacy, Gender, and Empire in Early Modern England and France.* Chicago: University of Chicago Press, 2003.

Ferguson, Margaret W., Maureen Quilligan, and Nancy J. Vickers, eds. *Rewriting the Renaissance: The Discourses of Sexual Difference in Early Modern Europe.* Chicago: University of Chicago Press, 1986.

Fisher, Will. *Materializing Gender in Early Modern English Literature and Culture.* New York: Cambridge University Press, 2006.

Fleming, Juliet. *Graffiti and the Writing Arts of Early Modern England.* Philadelphia: University of Pennsylvania Press, 2001.

Frye, Susan. *Elizabeth I: The Competition for Representation.* New York: Oxford University Press, 1993.

Fumerton, Patricia. *Cultural Aesthetics: Renaissance Literature and the Practice of Social Ornament.* Chicago: University of Chicago Press, 1991.

———. *Unsettled: The Culture of Mobility and the Working Poor in Early Modern England.* Chicago: University of Chicago Press, 2006.

Gillies, John. *Shakespeare and the Geography of Difference.* New York: Cambridge University Press, 1994.

Goldberg, Jonathan. *James I and the Politics of Literature: Jonson, Shakespeare, Donne, and Their Contemporaries.* Baltimore: Johns Hopkins University Press, 1983.

———. *Writing Matter: From the Hands of the English Renaissance.* Stanford: Stanford University Press, 1990.

———, ed. *Queering the Renaissance.* Durham, N.C.: Duke University Press, 1994.

Greenblatt, Stephen. *Learning to Curse: Essays in Early Modern Culture.* New York: Routledge, 1990.

———. *Renaissance Self-Fashioning: From More to Shakespeare.* Chicago: University of Chicago Press, 1980.

———, ed. *New World Encounters.* Berkeley: University of California Press, 1993.

———, ed. *Representing the English Renaissance.* Berkeley: University of California Press, 1988.

Grout, Donald Jay, and Hermine Weigel Williams. *A Short History of Opera.* 4th ed. New York: Columbia University Press, 2003.

Hall, Kim F. *Things of Darkness: Economies of Race and Gender in Early Modern England.* Ithaca, N.Y.: Cornell University Press, 1995.

Harris, Jonathan Gil. *Foreign Bodies and the Body Politic: Discourses of Social Pathology in Early Modern England.* New York: Cambridge University Press, 1998.

Harvey, Elizabeth D., ed. *Sensible Flesh: On Touch in Early Modern Culture.* Philadelphia: University of Pennsylvania Press, 2003.

Haselkorn, Anne M., and Betty S. Travitsky, eds. *The Renaissance Englishwoman in Print: Counterbalancing the Canon.* Amherst: University of Massachusetts Press, 1990.

Helgerson, Richard. *Forms of Nationhood: The Elizabethan Writing of England.* Chicago: University of Chicago Press, 1992.

Henderson, Katherine Usher, and Barbara F. McManus. *Half Humankind: Contexts and Texts of the Controversy About Women in England, 1540–1640.* Urbana: University of Illinois Press, 1985.

Hendricks, Margo, and Patricia Parker, eds. *Women, "Race," and Writing in the Early Modern Period.* New York: Routledge, 1994.

Hillman, David, and Carla Mazzio, eds. *The Body in Parts: Fantasies of Corporeality in Early Modern Europe.* New York: Routledge, 1997.

Hoeniger, F. David. *Medicine and Shakespeare in the English Renaissance.* Newark: University of Delaware Press, 1992.

Huizinga, Johan. *The Autumn of the Middle Ages.* Trans. Rodney J. Payton and Ulrich Mammitzsch. Chicago: University of Chicago Press, 1996.

Hull, Suzanne W. *Chaste, Silent & Obedient: English Books for Women, 1475–1640.* San Marino, Calif.: Huntington Library, 1982.

Hutson, Lorna. *The Usurer's Daughter: Male Friendship and Fictions of Women in Sixteenth-Century England*. New York: Routledge, 1994.

Javitch, Daniel. *Poetry and Courtliness in Renaissance England*. Princeton: Princeton University Press, 1978.

Jones, Ann Rosalind, and Peter Stallybrass. *Renaissance Clothing and the Materials of Memory*. New York: Cambridge University Press, 2000.

Jordan, Constance. *Renaissance Feminism: Literary Texts and Political Models*. Ithaca, N.Y.: Cornell University Press, 1990.

Knapp, Jeffrey. *Shakespeare's Tribe: Church, Nation, and Theater in Renaissance England*. Chicago: University of Chicago Press, 2002.

Laqueur, Thomas Walter. *Making Sex: Body and Gender from the Greeks to Freud*. Cambridge, Mass.: Harvard University Press, 1990.

MacDonald, Joyce Green. *Women and Race in Early Modern Texts*. New York: Cambridge University Press, 2002.

Magnusson, Lynne. *Shakespeare and Social Dialogue: Dramatic Language and Elizabethan Letters*. New York: Cambridge University Press, 1999.

Manley, Lawrence. *Literature and Culture in Early Modern London*. New York: Cambridge University Press, 1995.

Marcus, Leah S. *The Politics of Mirth: Jonson, Herrick, Milton, Marvell, and the Defense of Old Holiday Pastimes*. Chicago: University of Chicago Press, 1986.

McJannet, Linda. *The Sultan Speaks: Dialogue in English Plays and Histories about the Ottoman Turks*. New York: Palgrave Macmillan, 2006.

Meron, Theodor. *Bloody Constraint: War and Chivalry in Shakespeare*. New York: Oxford University Press, 1998.

Miller, David Lee, Sharon O'Dair, and Harold Weber, eds. *The Production of English Renaissance Culture*. Ithaca, N.Y.: Cornell University Press, 1994.

Montrose, Louis. *The Subject of Elizabeth: Authority, Gender, and Representation*. Chicago: University of Chicago Press, 2006.

Neill, Michael. *Issues of Death: Mortality and Identity in English Renaissance Tragedy*. Oxford: Clarendon, 1997.

Netzloff, Mark. *England's Internal Colonies: Class, Capital, and the Literature of Early Modern English Colonialism*. New York: Palgrave Macmillan, 2003.

Orlin, Lena Cowen. *Private Matters and Public Culture in Post-Reformation England*. Ithaca, N.Y.: Cornell University Press, 1994.

———, ed. *Material London, ca. 1600*. Philadelphia: University of Pennsylvania Press, 2000.

Parry, Graham. *The Golden Age Restor'd: The Culture of the Stuart Court, 1603–42*. New York: St. Martin's, 1981.

Paster, Gail Kern. *The Body Embarrassed: Drama and the Disciplines of Shame in Early Modern England*. Ithaca, N.Y.: Cornell University Press, 1993.

———. *Humoring the Body: Emotions and the Shakespearean Stage*. Chicago: University of Chicago Press, 2004.

Paster, Gail Kern, Katherine Rowe, and Mary Floyd-Wilson, eds. *Reading the Early Modern Passions: Essays in the Cultural History of Emotion*. Philadelphia: University of Pennsylvania Press, 2004.

Patterson, Annabel M. *Censorship and Interpretation: The Conditions of Writing and Reading in Early Modern England*. Madison: University of Wisconsin Press, 1984.

Peck, Linda Levy. *Consuming Splendor: Society and Culture in Seventeenth-Century England*. New York: Cambridge University Press, 2005.

Platt, Peter G. *Reason Diminished: Shakespeare and the Marvelous*. Lincoln: University of Nebraska Press, 1997.

Pollard, Tanya. *Drugs and Theater in Early Modern England*. New York: Oxford University Press, 2005.

Sanders, Eve Rachele. *Gender and Literacy on Stage in Early Modern England*. New York: Cambridge University Press, 1998.

Sawday, Jonathan. *The Body Emblazoned: Dissection and the Human Body in Renaissance Culture*. New York: Routledge, 1995.

Schoenfeldt, Michael C. *Bodies and Selves in Early Modern England: Physiology and Inwardness in Spenser, Shakespeare, Herbert, and Milton*. New York: Cambridge University Press, 1999.

Schwyzer, Philip. *Literature, Nationalism, and Memory in Early Modern England and Wales*. New York: Cambridge University Press, 2004.

Shapiro, James. *Shakespeare and the Jews*. New York: Columbia University Press, 1996.

Sharpe, Kevin, and Peter Lake, eds. *Culture and Politics in Early Stuart England*. Stanford: Stanford University Press, 1993.

Sherman, William H. *John Dee: The Politics of Reading and Writing in the English Renaissance*. Amherst: University of Massachusetts Press, 1995.

Shuger, Debora. *Censorship and Cultural Sensibility: The Regulation of Language in Tudor-Stuart England*. Philadelphia: University of Pennsylvania Press, 2006.

Simon, Joan. *Education and Society in Tudor England*. Cambridge, Eng.: Cambridge University Press, 1966.

Singh, Jyotsna G. *Colonial Narratives/Cultural Dialogues: 'Discoveries' of India in the Language of Colonialism*. New York: Routledge, 1996.

Smith, Bruce R. *The Acoustic World of Early Modern England: Attending to the O-Factor*. Chicago: University of Chicago Press, 1999.

———. *Homosexual Desire in Shakespeare's England: A Cultural Poetics*. Chicago: University of Chicago Press, 1994.

Smuts, R. Malcolm. *Court Culture and the Origins of a Royalist Tradition in Early Stuart England*. Philadelphia: University of Pennsylvania Press, 1987.

Stallybrass, Peter, and Allon White. *The Politics and Poetics of Transgression*. Ithaca, N.Y.: Cornell University Press, 1986.

Traub, Valerie, M. Lindsay Kaplan, and Dympna Callaghan, eds. *Feminist Readings of Early Modern Culture: Emerging Subjects*. New York: Cambridge University Press, 1996.

Turner, Henry S. *The English Renaissance Stage: Geometry, Poetics, and the Practical Spatial Arts 1580–1630*. New York: Oxford University Press, 2006.

Turner, James Grantham, ed. *Sexuality and Gender in Early Modern Europe: Institutions, Texts, Images*. New York: Cambridge University Press, 1993.

Wall, Wendy. *Staging Domesticity: Household Work and English Identity in Early Modern Drama*. New York: Cambridge University Press, 2002.

Watson, Robert N. *The Rest Is Silence: Death as Annihilation in the English Renaissance*. Berkeley: University of California Press, 1994.

Whigham, Frank. *Ambition and Privilege: The Social Tropes of Elizabethan Courtesy Theory*. Berkeley: University of California Press, 1984.

Woodbridge, Linda. *Vagrancy, Homelessness, and English Renaissance Literature*. Urbana: University of Illinois Press, 2001.

———. *Women and the English Renaissance: Literature and the Nature of Womankind, 1540 to 1620*. Urbana: University of Illinois Press, 1984.

Shakespeare's Generic, Literary, and Theatrical Contexts

Alpers, Paul. *What Is Pastoral?* Chicago: University of Chicago Press, 1996.

Altman, Joel. *The Tudor Play of Mind: Rhetorical Inquiry and the Development of Elizabethan Drama*. Berkeley: University of California Press, 1978.

Barish, Jonas. *The Antitheatrical Prejudice*. Berkeley: University of California Press, 1981.

Bate, Jonathan. *Shakespeare and Ovid*. Oxford: Clarendon, 1993.

Bates, Catherine. *The Rhetoric of Courtship in Elizabethan Language and Literature*. New York: Cambridge University Press, 1992.

Beckwith, Sarah. *Signifying God: Social Relation and Symbolic Act in the York Corpus Christi Plays*. Chicago: University of Chicago Press, 2001.

Belsey, Catherine. *The Subject of Tragedy: Identity and Difference in Renaissance Drama*. New York: Methuen, 1985.

Bevington, David M. *From "Mankind" to Marlowe: Growth of Structure in the Popular Drama of Tudor England*. Cambridge, Mass.: Harvard University Press, 1962.

———. *Tudor Drama and Politics: A Critical Approach to Topical Meaning*. Cambridge, Mass.: Harvard University Press, 1968.

Bly, Mary. *Queer Virgins and Virgin Queans on the Early Modern Stage*. New York: Oxford University Press, 2000.

Bowers, Fredson Thayer. *Elizabethan Revenge Tragedy, 1587–1642*. Princeton: Princeton University Press, 1940.

Braden, Gordon. *Renaissance Tragedy and the Senecan Tradition: Anger's Privilege*. New Haven: Yale University Press, 1985.

Bruster, Douglas. *Drama and the Market in the Age of Shakespeare*. New York: Cambridge University Press, 1992.

Bullough, Geoffrey, ed. *Narrative and Dramatic Sources of Shakespeare*. 8 vols. New York: Columbia University Press, 1957–75.

Butler, Martin. *Theatre and Crisis, 1632–1642*. New York: Cambridge University Press, 1984.

Carroll, William C. *The Metamorphoses of Shakespearean Comedy*. Princeton: Princeton University Press, 1985.

Cartwright, Kent. *Theatre and Humanism: English Drama in the Sixteenth Century*. New York: Cambridge University Press, 1999.

Clubb, Louise George. *Italian Drama in Shakespeare's Time*. New Haven: Yale University Press, 1989.

Cohen, Walter. *Drama of a Nation: Public Theater in Renaissance England and Spain*. Ithaca, N.Y.: Cornell University Press, 1985.

Crewe, Jonathan. *Trials of Authorship: Anterior Forms and Poetic Reconstruction from Wyatt to Shakespeare*. Berkeley: University of California Press, 1990.

Danson, Lawrence. *Shakespeare's Dramatic Genres*. New York: Oxford University Press, 2000.

Dawson, Anthony B., and Paul Yachnin. *The Culture of Playgoing in Shakespeare's England: A Collaborative Debate*. New York: Cambridge University Press, 2001.

Dillon, Janette. *Language and Stage in Medieval and Renaissance England*. New York: Cambridge University Press, 1998.

Felperin, Howard. *Shakespearean Romance*. Princeton: Princeton University Press, 1972.

Finkelpearl, Philip J. *John Marston of the Middle Temple: An Elizabethan Dramatist in His Social Setting*. Cambridge, Mass.: Harvard University Press, 1969.

Gardiner, Harold C. *Mysteries' End: An Investigation of the Last Days of the Medieval Religious Stage*. New Haven: Yale University Press, 1946.

Halasz, Alexandra. *The Marketplace of Print: Pamphlets and the Public Sphere in Early Modern England*. New York: Cambridge University Press, 1997.

Harbage, Alfred. *Shakespeare and the Rival Traditions*. New York: Macmillan, 1952.

Hardison, O. B. *Christian Rite and Christian Drama in the Middle Ages: Essays in the Origin and Early History of Modern Drama*. Baltimore: Johns Hopkins University Press, 1965.

Heinemann, Margot. *Puritanism and Theatre: Thomas Middleton and Opposition Drama under the Early Stuarts*. New York: Cambridge University Press, 1980.

Honan, Park. *Christopher Marlowe: Poet & Spy*. New York: Oxford University Press, 2005.

Honigmann, E. A. J., ed. *Shakespeare and His Contemporaries: Essays in Comparison*. Manchester: Manchester University Press, 1986.

———, ed. *Shakespeare's Impact on His Contemporaries*. London: Macmillan, 1982.

Howard, Jean E. *Theater of a City: The Places of London Comedy, 1598–1642.* Philadelphia: University of Pennsylvania Press, 2007.

Hunter, G. K. *John Lyly: The Humanist as Courtier.* Cambridge, Mass.: Harvard University Press, 1962.

Jones, Emrys. *The Origins of Shakespeare.* Oxford: Clarendon, 1977.

———. *Scenic Form in Shakespeare.* Oxford: Clarendon, 1971.

Kastan, David Scott, and Peter Stallybrass, eds. *Staging the Renaissance: Reinterpretations of Elizabethan and Jacobean Drama.* New York: Routledge, 1991.

Kermode, Lloyd Edward, Jason Scott-Warren, and Martine van Elk, eds. *Tudor Drama Before Shakespeare, 1485–1590: New Directions for Research, Criticism, and Pedagogy.* New York: Palgrave Macmillan, 2004.

Kolve, V. A. *The Play Called Corpus Christi.* Stanford: Stanford University Press, 1966.

Leggatt, Alexander. *Citizen Comedy in the Age of Shakespeare.* Toronto: University of Toronto Press, 1973.

———. *Introduction to English Renaissance Comedy.* Manchester: Manchester University Press, 1999.

Levin, Harry. *Shakespeare and the Revolution of the Times: Perspectives and Commentaries.* New York: Oxford University Press, 1976.

Levith, Murray J. *Shakespeare's Italian Settings and Plays.* Basingstoke: Macmillan, 1989.

Lomax, Marion. *Stage Images and Traditions: Shakespeare to Ford.* New York: Cambridge University Press, 1987.

Martindale, Charles, and A. B. Taylor, eds. *Shakespeare and the Classics.* New York: Cambridge University Press, 2004.

Masten, Jeffrey. *Textual Intercourse: Collaboration, Authorship, and Sexualities in Renaissance Drama.* New York: Cambridge University Press, 1997.

McLuskie, Kathleen. *Renaissance Dramatists.* New York: Harvester Wheatsheaf, 1989.

McMillin, Scott. *The Elizabethan Theatre and the Book of Sir Thomas More.* Ithaca, N.Y.: Cornell University Press, 1987.

McMillin, Scott, and Sally-Beth MacLean. *The Queen's Men and Their Plays.* New York: Cambridge University Press, 1998.

McMullan, Gordon, and Jonathan Hope, eds. *The Politics of Tragicomedy: Shakespeare and After.* New York: Routledge, 1991.

Miola, Robert S. *Shakespeare's Reading.* New York: Oxford University Press, 2000.

———. *Shakespeare's Rome.* New York: Cambridge University Press, 1983.

Newcomb, Lori Humphrey. *Reading Popular Romance in Early Modern England.* New York: Columbia University Press, 2002.

Norbrook, David. *Poetry and Politics in the English Renaissance.* London: Routledge and Kegan Paul, 1984.

Orgel, Stephen. *The Illusion of Power: Political Theater in the English Renaissance.* Berkeley: University of California Press, 1975.

Peters, Julie Stone. *Theatre of the Book, 1480–1880: Print, Text, and Performance in Europe.* New York: Oxford University Press, 2000.

Riggs, David. *Ben Jonson: A Life.* Cambridge, Mass.: Harvard University Press, 1989.

———. *The World of Christopher Marlowe.* London: Faber and Faber, 2004.

Rose, Mark. *Shakespearean Design.* Cambridge, Mass.: Belknap Press, 1972.

Rose, Mary Beth. *The Expense of Spirit: Love and Sexuality in English Renaissance Drama.* Ithaca, N.Y.: Cornell University Press, 1988.

Salingar, Leo. *Dramatic Form in Shakespeare and the Jacobeans: Essays.* New York: Cambridge University Press, 1986.

———. *Shakespeare and the Traditions of Comedy.* New York: Cambridge University Press, 1974.

Schwyzer, Philip. *Archaeologies of English Renaissance Literature.* New York: Oxford University Press, 2007.

Shapiro, James. *Rival Playwrights: Marlowe, Jonson, Shakespeare.* New York: Columbia University Press, 1991.

Snyder, Susan. *The Comic Matrix of Shakespeare's Tragedies:* Romeo and Juliet, Hamlet, Othello, *and* King Lear. Princeton: Princeton University Press, 1979.

Spivack, Bernard. *Shakespeare and the Allegory of Evil: The History of a Metaphor in Relation to His Major Villains.* New York: Columbia University Press, 1958.

Thomas, Vivian. *The Moral Universe of Shakespeare's Problem Plays.* New York: Routledge, 1991.

Vickers, Brian, ed. *English Renaissance Literary Criticism.* New York: Oxford University Press, 1999.

Vitkus, Daniel. *Turning Turk: English Theater and the Multicultural Mediterranean, 1570–1630.* New York: Palgrave Macmillan, 2003.

Weimann, Robert. *Shakespeare and the Popular Tradition in the Theater: Studies in the Social Dimension of Dramatic Form and Function.* Ed. Robert Schwartz. Baltimore: Johns Hopkins University Press, 1978.

Whitney, Charles. *Early Responses to Renaissance Drama.* New York: Cambridge University Press, 2006.

Woolf, Rosemary. *The English Mystery Plays.* Berkeley: University of California Press, 1972.

The Playing Field: Theaters, Actors, Patrons, and the State

Astington, John H. *English Court Theatre, 1558–1642.* Cambridge, Eng.: Cambridge University Press, 1999.

———, ed. *The Development of Shakespeare's Theater.* New York: AMS Press, 1992.

Barroll, J. Leeds. *Politics, Plague, and Shakespeare's Theater: The Stuart Years.* Ithaca, N.Y.: Cornell University Press, 1991.

Beckerman, Bernard. *Shakespeare at the Globe, 1599–1609.* New York: Macmillan, 1962.

Bentley, Gerald Eades. *The Jacobean and Caroline Stage.* 7 vols. Oxford: Clarendon, 1941–68.

———. *The Profession of Dramatist in Shakespeare's Time, 1590–1642.* Princeton: Princeton University Press, 1971.

———. *The Profession of Player in Shakespeare's Time, 1590–1642.* Princeton: Princeton University Press, 1984.

Berry, Herbert. *Shakespeare's Playhouses.* Illustrated by C. Walter Hodges. New York: AMS Press, 1987.

Bradbrook, M. C. *The Rise of the Common Player: A Study of Actor and Society in Shakespeare's England.* Cambridge, Mass.: Harvard University Press, 1962.

Chambers, E. K. *The Elizabethan Stage.* 4 vols. Oxford: Clarendon, 1923.

———. *The Mediaeval Stage.* 2 vols. Oxford: Clarendon, 1903.

Clare, Janet. *Art Made Tongue-Tied by Authority: Elizabethan and Jacobean Dramatic Censorship.* 2nd ed. Manchester: Manchester University Press, 1999.

Cook, Ann Jennalie. *The Privileged Playgoers of Shakespeare's London: 1576–1642.* Princeton: Princeton University Press, 1981.

Cox, John D., and David Scott Kastan, eds. *A New History of Early English Drama.* New York: Columbia University Press, 1997.

Dessen, Alan C. *Elizabethan Stage Conventions and Modern Interpreters.* Cambridge, Eng.: Cambridge University Press, 1984.

———. *Recovering Shakespeare's Theatrical Vocabulary.* New York: Cambridge University Press, 1995.

Dessen, Alan C., and Leslie Thomson. *A Dictionary of Stage Directions in English Drama, 1580–1642.* New York: Cambridge University Press, 1999.

Dillon, Janette. *The Cambridge Introduction to Early English Theatre.* New York: Cambridge University Press, 2006.

Dutton, Richard. *Licensing, Censorship and Authorship in Early Modern England: Buggeswords.* Houndmills, Basingstoke: Palgrave Macmillan, 2000.

———. *Mastering the Revels: The Regulation and Censorship of English Renaissance Drama*. London: Macmillan, 1991.

Dutton, Richard, Alison Findlay, and Richard Wilson, eds. *Region, Religion, and Patronage: Lancastrian Shakespeare*. Manchester: Manchester University Press, 2003.

Erne, Lukas. *Shakespeare as Literary Dramatist*. New York: Cambridge University Press, 2003.

Foakes, R. A. *Illustrations of the English Stage, 1580–1642*. Stanford: Stanford University Press, 1985.

Gair, W. Reavley. *The Children of Paul's: The Story of a Theatre Company, 1553–1608*. New York: Cambridge University Press, 1982.

Greg, W. W., ed. *Dramatic Documents from the Elizabethan Playhouses: Stage Plots: Actor's Parts: Prompt Books*. 2 vols. Oxford: Clarendon, 1931.

Gurr, Andrew. *Playgoing in Shakespeare's London*. 3rd ed. New York: Cambridge University Press, 2004.

———. *The Shakespeare Company, 1594–1642*. New York: Cambridge University Press, 2004.

———. *The Shakespearian Playing Companies*. Oxford: Clarendon, 1996.

———. *The Shakespearean Stage, 1574–1642*. 3rd ed. New York: Cambridge University Press, 1992.

Gurr, Andrew, and John Orrell. *Rebuilding Shakespeare's Globe*. London: Weidenfeld & Nicolson, 1989.

Harris, Jonathan Gil, and Natasha Korda, eds. *Staged Properties in Early Modern Drama*. New York: Cambridge University Press, 2002.

Hattaway, Michael. *Elizabethan Popular Theatre: Plays in Performance*. London: Routledge and Kegan Paul, 1982.

Henslowe, Philip. *Henslowe's Diary*. Ed. R. A. Foakes. 2nd ed. New York: Cambridge University Press, 2002.

Hodges, C. Walter. *The Globe Restored: A Study of the Elizabethan Theatre*. New York: Norton, 1973.

Holland, Peter, and Stephen Orgel, eds. *From Performance to Print in Shakespeare's England*. New York: Palgrave Macmillan, 2006.

———, eds. *From Script to Stage in Early Modern England*. Houndmills, Basingstoke: Palgrave Macmillan, 2004.

Ingram, William. *The Business of Playing: The Beginnings of Adult Professional Theater in Elizabethan London*. Ithaca, N.Y.: Cornell University Press, 1992.

Kernan, Alvin. *Shakespeare, the King's Playwright: Theater in the Stuart Court, 1603–1613*. New Haven: Yale University Press, 1995.

King, T. J. *Shakespearean Staging, 1599–1642*. Cambridge, Mass.: Harvard University Press, 1971.

Knutson, Roslyn Lander. *Playing Companies and Commerce in Shakespeare's Time*. Cambridge, Eng.: Cambridge University Press, 2001.

———. *The Repertory of Shakespeare's Company, 1594–1613*. Fayetteville: University of Arkansas Press, 1991.

Laroque, François. *Shakespeare's Festive World: Elizabethan Seasonal Entertainment and the Professional Stage*. New York: Cambridge University Press, 1991.

Lopez, Jeremy. *Theatrical Convention and Audience Response in Early Modern Drama*. New York: Cambridge University Press, 2002.

MacIntyre, Jean. *Costumes and Scripts in the Elizabethan Theatres*. Edmonton: University of Alberta Press, 1992.

Milling, Jane, and Peter Thomson, eds. *The Cambridge History of British Theatre*, Vol. 1: *Origins to 1660*. New York: Cambridge University Press, 2004.

Mulryne, J. R., and Margaret Shewring, eds. *Shakespeare's Globe Rebuilt*. New York: Cambridge University Press, 1997.

Munro, Lucy. *Children of the Queen's Revels: A Jacobean Theatre Repertory*. New York: Cambridge University Press, 2005.

Palfrey, Simon, and Tiffany Stern. *Shakespeare in Parts*. Oxford: Oxford University Press, 2007.

Shapiro, Michael. *Children of the Revels: The Boy Companies of Shakespeare's Time and Their Plays*. New York: Columbia University Press, 1977.

Smith, Irwin. *Shakespeare's Blackfriars Playhouse: Its History and Its Design*. New York: New York University Press, 1964.

Stern, Tiffany. *Making Shakespeare: From Stage to Page*. New York: Routledge, 2004.

———. *Rehearsal from Shakespeare to Sheridan*. Oxford: Clarendon, 2000.

White, Paul Whitfield, and Suzanne Westfall, eds. *Shakespeare and Theatrical Patronage in Early Modern England*. New York: Cambridge University Press, 2002.

Wickham, Glynne. *Early English Stages, 1300 to 1660*. 4 vols. New York: Routledge, 2002.

Wickham, Glynne, Herbert Berry, and William Ingram, eds. *English Professional Theatre, 1530–1660*. New York: Cambridge University Press, 2000.

Shakespeare's Life

Alexander, Peter. *Shakespeare's Life and Art*. New ed. New York: New York University Press, 1961.

Bate, Jonathan. *The Genius of Shakespeare*. London: Picador, 1997.

Bradbrook, M. C. *Shakespeare: The Poet in His World*. New York: Columbia University Press, 1978.

Chambers, E. K. *William Shakespeare: A Study of Facts and Problems*. 2 vols. Oxford: Clarendon, 1930.

Duncan-Jones, Katherine. *Ungentle Shakespeare: Scenes from His Life*. London: Arden Shakespeare, 2001.

Eccles, Mark. *Shakespeare in Warwickshire*. Madison: University of Wisconsin Press, 1961.

Edwards, Philip. *Shakespeare: A Writer's Progress*. New York: Oxford University Press, 1986.

Fraser, Russell A. *Shakespeare, The Later Years*. New York: Columbia University Press, 1992.

———. *Young Shakespeare*. New York: Columbia University Press, 1988.

Greenblatt, Stephen. *Will in the World: How Shakespeare Became Shakespeare*. New York: Norton, 2004.

Greer, Germaine. *Shakespeare*. New York: Oxford University Press, 1986.

Honan, Park. *Shakespeare: A Life*. New York: Oxford University Press, 1998.

Honigmann, E. A. J. *Shakespeare: The Lost Years*. 2nd ed. Manchester: Manchester University Press, 1998.

Hotson, Leslie. *Shakespeare Versus Shallow*. Boston: Little, Brown, and Company, 1931.

Levi, Peter. *The Life and Times of William Shakespeare*. New York: Macmillan, 1988.

Matus, Irvin Leigh. *Shakespeare, The Living Record*. Houndmills, Basingstoke: Macmillan, 1991.

Reese, M. M. *Shakespeare: His World and His Work*. Rev. ed. London: Edward Arnold, 1980.

Sams, Eric. *The Real Shakespeare: Retrieving the Early Years, 1564–1594*. New Haven: Yale University Press, 1995.

Schmidgall, Gary. *Shakespeare and the Poet's Life*. Lexington: University Press of Kentucky, 1990.

Schoenbaum, Samuel. *Shakespeare's Lives*. New ed. New York: Oxford University Press, 1991.

———. *William Shakespeare: A Compact Documentary Life*. Rev. ed. New York: Oxford University Press, 1987.

Shapiro, James. *A Year in the Life of William Shakespeare: 1599*. New York: Harper-Collins, 2005.

Taylor, Gary. *Reinventing Shakespeare: A Cultural History, from the Restoration to the Present*. New York: Weidenfeld & Nicolson, 1989.

Thomson, Peter. *Shakespeare's Professional Career*. New York: Cambridge University Press, 1992.

Wells, Stanley. *Shakespeare: A Life in Drama*. New York: Norton, 1995.

———. *Shakespeare: For All Time*. London: Macmillan, 2002.

Wood, Michael. *In Search of Shakespeare*. London: BBC, 2003.

Critical Approaches

Classics of Shakespeare Criticism

Barber, C. L. *Shakespeare's Festive Comedy: A Study of Dramatic Form and Its Relation to Social Custom*. Princeton: Princeton University Press, 1959.

Bradley, A. C. *Shakespearean Tragedy: Lectures on* Hamlet, Othello, King Lear, Macbeth. 3rd ed. New York: St. Martin's Press, 1992.

Coleridge, Samuel Taylor. *Coleridge on Shakespeare: The Text of the Lectures of 1811–12*. Ed. R. A. Foakes. Charlottesville: University Press of Virginia, 1971.

———. *Shakespearean Criticism*. 2 vols. Ed. T. M. Raysor. 2nd ed. New York: Dutton, 1969.

Eliot, T. S. "Shakespeare and the Stoicism of Seneca." *Selected Essays, 1917–1932*. New ed. New York: Harcourt, Brace, 1950.

Empson, William. *The Structure of Complex Words*. 3rd ed. London: Chatto & Windus, 1977.

Frye, Northrop. *Fools of Time: Studies in Shakespearean Tragedy*. Toronto: University of Toronto Press, 1967.

———. *A Natural Perspective: The Development of Shakespearean Comedy and Romance*. New York: Columbia University Press, 1965.

Hazlitt, William. *Characters of Shakespear's Plays*. London, 1817.

Johnson, Samuel. *Samuel Johnson on Shakespeare*. Ed. H. R. Woudhuysen. New York: Penguin, 1989.

Jones, Ernest. *Hamlet and Oedipus*. New York: Norton, 1949.

Kermode, Frank, ed. *Four Centuries of Shakespearian Criticism*. 1965. New York: Avon, 1965.

Knight, G. Wilson. *The Wheel of Fire: Interpretations of Shakespearean Tragedy, with Three New Essays*. 4th ed. New York: Harper & Row, 1977.

Kott, Jan. *Shakespeare Our Contemporary*. Trans. Boleslaw Taborski. Garden City, N.Y.: Anchor Books, 1966.

Morgann, Maurice. *Shakespearean Criticism*. Ed. Daniel A. Fineman. Oxford: Clarendon, 1972.

Spurgeon, Caroline F. E. *Shakespeare's Imagery, and What It Tells Us*. New York: Macmillan, 1935.

Tillyard, E. M. W. *Shakespeare's History Plays*. London: Chatto and Windus, 1944.

Vickers, Brian, ed. *Shakespeare: The Critical Heritage*. 6 vols. London: Routledge and Kegan Paul, 1974–1981.

General Studies

Barton, Anne. *Essays, Mainly Shakespearean*. New York: Cambridge University Press, 1994.

Bloom, Harold. *Shakespeare: The Invention of the Human*. New York: Riverhead Books, 1998.

Burckhardt, Sigurd. *Shakespearean Meanings*. Princeton: Princeton University Press, 1968.

Garber, Marjorie. *Shakespeare After All*. New York: Pantheon, 2004.

Hibbard, G. R. *The Making of Shakespeare's Dramatic Poetry*. Toronto: University of Toronto Press, 1981.

Honigmann, E. A. J. *Myriad-Minded Shakespeare: Essays on the Tragedies, Problem Comedies, and Shakespeare the Man*. 2nd ed. New York: St. Martin's Press, 1998.

Jones, John. *Shakespeare at Work*. New York: Oxford University Press, 1995.

Nuttall, A. D. *Shakespeare the Thinker*. New Haven: Yale University Press, 2007.

Ryan, Kiernan. *Shakespeare*. 3rd ed. New York: Palgrave Macmillan, 2001.

Language and Style

Baxter, John. *Shakespeare's Poetic Styles: Verse into Drama*. London: Routledge and Kegan Paul, 1980.

Blake, N. F. *Shakespeare's Language: An Introduction*. New York: St. Martin's Press, 1983.

Cercignani, Fausto. *Shakespeare's Works and Elizabethan Pronunciation*. New York: Oxford University Press, 1981.

Clemen, Wolfgang. *Shakespeare's Soliloquies*. Trans. Charity Scott Stokes. New York: Methuen, 1987.

———. *The Development of Shakespeare's Imagery*. New York: Hill and Wang, 1962.

Danson, Lawrence. *Tragic Alphabet: Shakespeare's Drama of Language*. New Haven: Yale University Press, 1974.

Donawerth, Jane. *Shakespeare and the Sixteenth-Century Study of Language*. Urbana: University of Illinois Press, 1984.

Edwards, Philip, Inga-Stina Ewbank, and G. K. Hunter, eds. *Shakespeare's Styles: Essays in Honour of Kenneth Muir*. New York: Cambridge University Press, 1980.

Gross, Kenneth. *Shakespeare's Noise*. Chicago: University of Chicago Press, 2001.

Hope, Jonathan. *Shakespeare's Grammar*. London: Arden Shakespeare, 2003.

Houston, John Porter. *Shakespearean Sentences: A Study in Style and Syntax*. Baton Rouge: Louisiana State University Press, 1988.

Hussey, S. S. *The Literary Language of Shakespeare*. 2nd ed. New York: Longman, 1992.

Kökeritz, Helge. *Shakespeare's Pronunciation*. New Haven: Yale University Press, 1953.

Mahood, M. M. *Shakespeare's Wordplay*. London: Methuen, 1957.

McDonald, Russ. *Shakespeare and the Arts of Language*. New York: Oxford University Press, 2001.

———. *Shakespeare's Late Style*. New York: Cambridge University Press, 2006.

Miriam Joseph, Sister. *Shakespeare's Use of the Arts of Language*. New York: Columbia University Press, 1947.

Palfrey, Simon. *Late Shakespeare: A New World of Words*. Oxford: Clarendon, 1997.

Parker, Patricia. *Literary Fat Ladies: Rhetoric, Gender, Property*. New York: Methuen, 1987.

———. *Shakespeare from the Margins: Language, Culture, Context*. Chicago: University of Chicago Press, 1996.

Partridge, Eric. *Shakespeare's Bawdy: A Literary & Psychological Essay and a Comprehensive Glossary*. 3rd ed. New York: Routledge, 1991.

Trousdale, Marion. *Shakespeare and the Rhetoricians*. Chapel Hill: University of North Carolina Press, 1982.

Vickers, Brian. *The Artistry of Shakespeare's Prose*. London: Methuen, 1968.

———. "Shakespeare's Use of Rhetoric." *A New Companion to Shakespeare Studies*. Ed. Kenneth Muir and S. Schoenbaum. Cambridge, Eng.: Cambridge University Press, 1971. 83–98.

Wright, George T. *Shakespeare's Metrical Art*. Berkeley: University of California Press, 1988.

Young, David. *The Action to the Word: Structure and Style in Shakespearean Tragedy.* New Haven: Yale University Press, 1990.

Psychoanalytic Criticism

Adelman, Janet. *Suffocating Mothers: Fantasies of Maternal Origin in Shakespeare's Plays,* Hamlet to The Tempest. New York: Routledge, 1992.

Armstrong, Philip. *Shakespeare in Psychoanalysis.* New York: Routledge, 2001.

Berger, Harry Jr. *Making Trifles of Terrors: Redistributing Complicities in Shakespeare.* Stanford: Stanford University Press, 1997.

Charnes, Linda. *Notorious Identity: Materializing the Subject in Shakespeare.* Cambridge, Mass.: Harvard University Press, 1993.

Enterline, Lynn. *The Rhetoric of the Body from Ovid to Shakespeare.* Cambridge, Eng.: Cambridge University Press, 2000.

Fineman, Joel. *Shakespeare's Perjured Eye: The Invention of Poetic Subjectivity in the Sonnets.* Berkeley: University of California Press, 1986.

Freedman, Barbara. *Staging the Gaze: Postmodernism, Psychoanalysis, and Shakespearean Comedy.* Ithaca, N.Y.: Cornell University Press, 1991.

Garber, Marjorie. *Coming of Age in Shakespeare.* New York: Methuen, 1981.

———. *Shakespeare's Ghost Writers: Literature as Uncanny Causality.* New York: Methuen, 1987.

Girard, René. *A Theater of Envy: William Shakespeare.* New York: Oxford University Press, 1991.

Holland, Norman N. *Psychoanalysis and Shakespeare.* New York: Octagon, 1966.

Lupton, Julia Reinhard, and Kenneth Reinhard. *After Oedipus: Shakespeare in Psychoanalysis.* Ithaca, N.Y.: Cornell University Press, 1993.

Marshall, Cynthia. *The Shattering of the Self: Violence, Subjectivity, and Early Modern Texts.* Baltimore: Johns Hopkins University Press, 2002.

Mazzio, Carla, and Douglas Trevor, eds. *Historicism, Psychoanalysis, and Early Modern Culture.* New York: Routledge, 2000.

Pye, Christopher. *The Regal Phantasm: Shakespeare and the Politics of Spectacle.* New York: Routledge, 1990.

———. *The Vanishing: Shakespeare, the Subject, and Early Modern Culture.* Durham, N.C.: Duke University Press, 2000.

Schwartz, Murray M., and Coppélia Kahn, eds. *Representing Shakespeare: New Psychoanalytic Essays.* Baltimore: Johns Hopkins University Press, 1982.

Skura, Meredith Anne. *The Literary Use of the Psychoanalytic Process.* New Haven: Yale University Press, 1981.

———. *Shakespeare the Actor and the Purposes of Playing.* Chicago: University of Chicago Press, 1993.

Wheeler, Richard P. *Shakespeare's Development and the Problem Comedies: Turn and Counter-Turn.* Berkeley: University of California Press, 1981.

Zimmerman, Susan, ed. *Erotic Politics: Desire on the Renaissance Stage.* New York: Routledge, 1992.

Feminism, Gender Studies, and Queer Studies

Bamber, Linda. *Comic Women, Tragic Men: A Study of Gender and Genre in Shakespeare.* Stanford: Stanford University Press, 1982.

Barker, Deborah, and Ivo Kamps, eds. *Shakespeare and Gender: A History.* New York: Verso, 1995.

Boose, Lynda E. "The Father and the Bride in Shakespeare." *PMLA* 97 (1982): 325–47.

Callaghan, Dympna. *Shakespeare Without Women: Representing Gender and Race on the Renaissance Stage.* New York: Routledge, 2000.

————. *Women and Gender in Renaissance Tragedy: A Study of* King Lear, Othello, The Duchess of Malfi, *and* The White Devil. Atlantic Highlands, N.J.: Humanities Press International, 1989.

Chedgzoy, Kate, ed. *Shakespeare, Feminism and Gender.* Houndmills, Basingstoke: Palgrave Macmillan, 2001.

Dash, Irene G. *Wooing, Wedding, and Power: Women in Shakespeare's Plays.* New York: Columbia University Press, 1981.

DiGangi, Mario. *The Homoerotics of Early Modern Drama.* New York: Cambridge University Press, 1997.

Dusinberre, Juliet. *Shakespeare and the Nature of Women.* 3rd ed. New York: Palgrave Macmillan, 2003.

Erickson, Peter. *Patriarchal Structures in Shakespeare's Drama.* Berkeley: University of California Press, 1985.

French, Marilyn. *Shakespeare's Division of Experience.* New York: Summit Books, 1981.

Garner, Shirley Nelson, and Madelon Sprengnether, eds. *Shakespearean Tragedy and Gender.* Bloomington: Indiana University Press, 1996.

Goldberg, Jonathan. *Sodometries: Renaissance Texts, Modern Sexualities.* Stanford: Stanford University Press, 1992.

Howard, Jean E., and Phyllis Rackin. *Engendering a Nation: A Feminist Account of Shakespeare's English Histories.* New York: Routledge, 1997.

Jardine, Lisa. *Still Harping on Daughters: Women and Drama in the Age of Shakespeare.* 2nd ed. New York: Columbia University Press, 1989.

Kahn, Coppèlia. *Man's Estate: Masculine Identity in Shakespeare.* Berkeley: University of California Press, 1981.

————. *Roman Shakespeare: Warriors, Wounds, and Women.* New York: Routledge, 1997.

Korda, Natasha. *Shakespeare's Domestic Economies: Gender and Property in Early Modern England.* Philadelphia: University of Pennsylvania Press, 2002.

Lenz, Carolyn, Ruth Swift, Gayle Greene, and Carol Thomas Neely, eds. *The Woman's Part: Feminist Criticism of Shakespeare.* Urbana: University of Illinois Press, 1980.

Neely, Carol Thomas. *Broken Nuptials in Shakespeare's Plays.* New Haven: Yale University Press, 1985.

————. *Distracted Subjects: Madness and Gender in Shakespeare and Early Modern Culture.* Ithaca, N.Y.: Cornell University Press, 2004.

Newman, Karen. *Fashioning Femininity and English Renaissance Drama.* Chicago: University of Chicago Press, 1991.

Novy, Marianne. *Love's Argument: Gender Relations in Shakespeare.* Chapel Hill: University of North Carolina Press, 1984.

————, ed. *Women's Re-Visions of Shakespeare: On the Responses of Dickinson, Woolf, Rich, H.D., George Eliot, and Others.* Urbana: University of Illinois Press, 1990.

Orgel, Stephen. *Impersonations: The Performance of Gender in Shakespeare's England.* New York: Cambridge University Press, 1996.

Shapiro, Michael. *Gender in Play on the Shakespearean Stage: Boy Heroines and Female Pages.* Ann Arbor: University of Michigan Press, 1994.

Shepherd, Simon. *Amazons and Warrior Women: Varieties of Feminism in Seventeenth Century Drama.* New York: St. Martin's, 1981.

Traub, Valerie. *Desire and Anxiety: Circulations of Sexuality in Shakespearean Drama.* New York: Routledge, 1992.

————. *The Renaissance of Lesbianism in Eary Modern England.* New York: Cambridge University Press, 2002.

Wayne, Valerie, ed. *The Matter of Difference: Materialist Feminist Criticism of Shakespeare.* Ithaca, N.Y.: Cornell University Press, 1991.

Historical Approaches: Materialism, New Historicism, and Cultural Materialism

Archer, John Michael. *Citizen Shakespeare: Freemen and Aliens in the Language of the Plays*. New York: Palgrave Macmillan, 2005.

Arnold, Oliver. *The Third Citizen: Shakespeare's Theater and the Early Modern House of Commons*. Baltimore: Johns Hopkins University Press, 2007.

Belsey, Catherine. *Shakespeare and the Loss of Eden: The Construction of Family Values in Early Modern Culture*. New Brunswick, N.J.: Rutgers University Press, 1999.

Berry, Ralph. *Shakespeare and Social Class*. Atlantic Highlands, N.J.: Humanities Press International, 1988.

Bristol, Michael D. *Shakespeare's America, America's Shakespeare*. New York: Routledge, 1990.

Bruster, Douglas. *Shakespeare and the Question of Culture: Early Modern Literature and the Cultural Turn*. New York: Palgrave Macmillan, 2003.

Cox, John D. *Shakespeare and the Dramaturgy of Power*. Princeton: Princeton University Press, 1989.

Dollimore, Jonathan. *Radical Tragedy: Religion, Ideology, and Power in the Drama of Shakespeare and His Contemporaries*. 3rd ed. New York: Palgrave Macmillan, 2004.

Dollimore, Jonathan, and Alan Sinfield, eds. *Political Shakespeare: Essays in Cultural Materialism*. 2nd ed. Ithaca, N.Y.: Cornell University Press, 1994.

Dubrow, Heather, and Richard Strier, eds. *The Historical Renaissance: New Essays on Tudor and Stuart Literature and Culture*. Chicago: University of Chicago Press, 1988.

Eagleton, Terry. *William Shakespeare*. Malden, Mass.: Blackwell, 1986.

Greenblatt, Stephen. *Hamlet in Purgatory*. Princeton: Princeton University Press, 2001.

———. *Shakespearean Negotiations: The Circulation of Social Energy in Renaissance England*. Berkeley: University of California Press, 1988.

Hadfield, Andrew. *Shakespeare and Republicanism*. New York: Cambridge University Press, 2005.

Hawkes, Terence. *Meaning by Shakespeare*. New York: Routledge, 1992.

———. *That Shakespeherian Rag: Essays on a Critical Process*. New York: Methuen, 1986.

Holderness, Graham, ed. *The Shakespeare Myth*. Manchester: Manchester University Press, 1988.

———, ed. *Shakespeare's History Plays: Richard II to Henry V*. Houndmills, Basingstoke: Palgrave Macmillan, 1992.

Howard, Jean E. *The Stage and Social Struggle in Early Modern England*. New York: Routledge, 1994.

Howard, Jean E., and Scott Cutler Shershow, eds. *Marxist Shakespeares*. New York: Routledge, 2001.

Howard, Jean E., and Marion F. O'Connor, eds. *Shakespeare Reproduced: The Text in History and Ideology*. New York: Methuen, 1987.

Jardine, Lisa. *Reading Shakespeare Historically*. New York: Routledge, 1996.

Jordan, Constance. *Shakespeare's Monarchies: Ruler and Subject in the Romances*. Ithaca, N.Y.: Cornell University Press, 1997.

Kamps, Ivo, ed. *Materialist Shakespeare: A History*. New York: Verso, 1995.

Kastan, David Scott. *Shakespeare After Theory*. London: Routledge, 1999.

———. *Shakespeare and the Shapes of Time*. Hanover, N.H.: University Press of New England, 1982.

Mallin, Eric S. *Inscribing the Time: Shakespeare and the End of Elizabethan England*. Berkeley: University of California Press, 1995.

Marcus, Leah S. *Puzzling Shakespeare: Local Reading and Its Discontents*. Berkeley: University of California Press, 1988.

Maus, Katharine Eisaman. *Inwardness and Theater in the English Renaissance*. Chicago: University of Chicago Press, 1995.

Montrose, Louis. *The Purpose of Playing: Shakespeare and the Cultural Politics of the Elizabethan Theatre*. Chicago: University of Chicago Press, 1996.

Mullaney, Steven. *The Place of the Stage: License, Play, and Power in Renaissance England*. Chicago: University of Chicago Press, 1988.

Orgel, Stephen. *The Authentic Shakespear: and Other Problems of the Early Modern Stage*. New York: Routledge, 2002.

Patterson, Annabel. *Shakespeare and the Popular Voice*. Malden, Mass.: Blackwell, 1989.

Rackin, Phyllis. *Stages of History: Shakespeare's English Chronicles*. Ithaca, N.Y.: Cornell University Press, 1990.

Siemon, James R. *Word Against Word: Shakespearean Utterance*. Amherst: University of Massachusetts Press, 2002.

Sinfield, Alan. *Shakespeare, Authority, Sexuality: Unfinished Business in Cultural Materialism*. New York: Routledge, 2006.

Tennenhouse, Leonard. *Power on Display: The Politics of Shakespeare's Genres*. New York: Methuen, 1986.

Weimann, Robert. *Author's Pen and Actor's Voice: Playing and Writing in Shakespeare's Theatre*. Ed. Helen Higbee and William West. New York: Cambridge University Press, 2000.

Wells, Robin Headlam. *Shakespeare, Politics, and the State*. Houndmills, Basingstoke: Palgrave Macmillan, 1986.

Wilson, Richard. *Secret Shakespeare: Studies in Theatre, Religion and Resistance*. Manchester: Manchester University Press, 2004.

———. *Will Power: Essays on Shakespearean Authority*. Detroit: Wayne State University Press, 1993.

Postcolonial Criticism, Race, and Ethnicity

Alexander, Catherine M. S., and Stanley Wells, eds. *Shakespeare and Race*. New York: Cambridge University Press, 2000.

Cartelli, Thomas. *Repositioning Shakespeare: National Formations, Postcolonial Appropriations*. New York: Routledge, 1999.

de Sousa, Geraldo U. *Shakespeare's Cross-Cultural Encounters*. Houndmills, Basingstoke: Palgrave Macmillan, 2002.

Floyd-Wilson, Mary. *English Ethnicity and Race in Early Modern Drama*. New York: Cambridge University Press, 2003.

Hendricks, Margo. " 'Obscured by dreams:' Race, Empire, and Shakespeare's *A Midsummer Night's Dream*." *Shakespeare Quarterly* 47 (1996): 37–60.

Hulme, Peter. *Colonial Encounters: Europe and the Native Caribbean, 1492–1797*. New York: Methuen, 1986.

Knapp, Jeffrey. *An Empire Nowhere: England, America, and Literature from Utopia to The Tempest*. Berkeley: University of California Press, 1992.

Loomba, Ania. *Gender, Race, Renaissance Drama*. Manchester: Manchester University Press, 1989.

Loomba, Ania, and Martin Orkin, eds. *Post-colonial Shakespeares*. New York: Routledge, 1998.

Maley, Willy. *Nation, State, and Empire in English Renaissance Literature: Shakespeare to Milton*. New York: Palgrave Macmillan, 2003.

Vaughan, Virginia Mason. *Performing Blackness on English Stages, 1500–1800*. New York: Cambridge University Press, 2005.

Other Philosophical and Theoretical Approaches

Booth, Stephen. *King Lear, Macbeth, Indefinition, and Tragedy*. New Haven: Yale University Press, 1983.

Cavell, Stanley. *Disowning Knowledge in Seven Plays of Shakespeare*. Updated ed. New York: Cambridge University Press, 2003.

Engle, Lars. *Shakespearean Pragmatism: Market of His Time*. Chicago: University of Chicago Press, 1993.

Evans, Malcolm. *Signifying Nothing: Truth's True Contents in Shakespeare's Text*. Athens: University of Georgia Press, 1986.

Felperin, Howard. *The Uses of the Canon: Elizabethan Literature and Contemporary Theory*. New York: Oxford University Press, 1990.

Goldberg, Jonathan. *Shakespeare's Hand*. Minneapolis: University of Minnesota Press, 2003.

Grady, Hugh. *The Modernist Shakespeare: Critical Texts in a Material World*. Oxford: Clarendon, 1991.

———. *Shakespeare, Machiavelli, and Montaigne: Power and Subjectivity from Richard II to Hamlet*. Oxford: Oxford University Press, 2002.

Grady, Hugh, and Terence Hawkes, eds. *Presentist Shakespeares*. New York: Routledge, 2006.

Hawkes, Terence. *Shakespeare in the Present*. New York: Routledge, 2002.

Knapp, Robert S. *Shakespeare—The Theater and the Book*. Princeton: Princeton University Press, 1989.

Lukacher, Ned. *Daemonic Figures: Shakespeare and the Question of Conscience*. Ithaca, N.Y.: Cornell University Press, 1994.

Lupton, Julia Reinhard. *Citizen-Saints: Shakespeare and Political Theology*. Chicago: University of Chicago Press, 2005.

Parker, Patricia, and Geoffrey Hartman, eds. *Shakespeare and the Question of Theory*. New York: Methuen, 1985.

Pechter, Edward. *What Was Shakespeare?: Renaissance Plays and Changing Critical Practice*. Ithaca, N.Y.: Cornell University Press, 1995.

Rabkin, Norman. *Shakespeare and the Problem of Meaning*. Chicago: University of Chicago Press, 1981.

Schalkwyk, David. *Speech and Performance in Shakespeare's Sonnets and Plays*. Cambridge, Eng.: Cambridge University Press, 2002.

Textual Criticism and Bibliography

Allen, Michael J. B., and Kenneth Muir, eds. *Shakespeare's Plays in Quarto: A Facsimile Edition of Copies Primarily from the Henry E. Huntington Library*. Berkeley: University of California Press, 1981.

Blayney, Peter W. M. *The First Folio of Shakespeare*. Washington, D.C.: Folger Library Publications, 1991.

———. *The Texts of* King Lear *and Their Origins*. Vol. 1: *Nicholas Okes and the First Quarto*. New York: Cambridge University Press, 1982.

Bowers, Fredson. *On Editing Shakespeare*. Charlottesville: University Press of Virginia, 1966.

Brooks, Douglas A. *From Playhouse to Printing House: Drama and Authorship in Early Modern England*. New York: Cambridge University Press, 2000.

De Grazia, Margreta. "Homonyms Before and After Lexical Standardization." *Deutsche Shakespeare-Gesellschaft West* (Jahrbuch 1990): 143–56.

———. *Shakespeare Verbatim: The Reproduction of Authenticity and the 1790 Apparatus*. New York: Oxford University Press, 1991.

De Grazia, Margreta, and Peter Stallybrass. "The Materiality of the Shakespearean Text." *Shakespeare Quarterly* 44 (1993): 255–83.

Erne, Lukas, and Margaret Jane Kidnie, eds. *Textual Performances: The Modern Reproduction of Shakespeare's Drama*. New York: Cambridge University Press, 2004.

Franklin, Colin. *Shakespeare Domesticated: The Eighteenth-Century Editions*. Brookfield, Vt.: Gower Publishing Company, 1991.

Hinman, Charlton, ed. *The First Folio of Shakespeare*. 2nd ed. New York: Norton, 1996.

———. *The Printing and Proof-Reading of the First Folio of Shakespeare*. 2 vols. Oxford: Clarendon, 1963.

Honigmann, E. A. J. *The Stability of Shakespeare's Text*. London: E. Arnold, 1965.

Ioppolo, Grace. *Dramatists and Their Manuscripts in the Age of Shakespeare, Jonson, Middleton and Heywood: Authorship, Authority and the Playhouse*. New York: Routledge, 2006.

———. *Revising Shakespeare*. Cambridge, Mass.: Harvard University Press, 1991.

Irace, Kathleen O. *Reforming the "Bad" Quartos: Performance and Provenance of Six Shakespearean First Editions*. Newark: University of Delaware Press, 1994.

Jackson, MacDonald P. *Defining Shakespeare: Pericles as Test Case*. New York: Oxford University Press, 2003.

Kastan, David Scott. *Shakespeare and the Book*. New York: Cambridge University Press, 2001.

Lesser, Zachary. *Renaissance Drama and the Politics of Publication: Readings in the English Book Trade*. New York: Cambridge University Press, 2004.

Maguire, Laurie E. *Shakespearean Suspect Texts: The "Bad" Quartos and Their Contexts*. New York: Cambridge University Press, 1996.

Maguire, Laurie E., and Thomas L. Berger, eds. *Textual Formations and Reformations*. Newark: University of Delaware Press, 1998.

Marcus, Leah S. *Unediting the Renaissance: Shakespeare, Marlowe, Milton*. New York: Routledge, 1996.

McKerrow, Ronald B. *Prolegomena for the Oxford Shakespeare: A Study in Editorial Method*. Oxford: Clarendon, 1939.

McLeod, Randall, ed. *Crisis in Editing: Texts of the English Renaissance*. New York: AMS Press, 1994.

———. "UN *Editing* Shak-speare." *SubStance* 33/34 (1982): 26–55.

———[as Random Cloud]. "The Psychopathology of Everyday Art." *The Elizabethan Theatre IX*. Ed. G. R. Hibbard. Port Credit, Ontario: P. D. Meany, 1986. 100–68.

Murphy, Andrew. *Shakespeare in Print: A History and Chronology of Shakespeare Publishing*. New York: Cambridge University Press, 2003.

———, ed. *The Renaissance Text: Theory, Editing, Textuality*. Manchester: Manchester University Press, 2000.

Pollard, Alfred W. *Shakespeare's Folios and Quartos: A Study in the Bibliography of Shakespeare's Plays, 1594–1685*. London: Methuen, 1909.

Seary, Peter. *Lewis Theobald and the Editing of Shakespeare*. Oxford: Clarendon, 1990.

Taylor, Gary, and Michael Warren, eds. *The Division of the Kingdoms: Shakespeare's Two Versions of* King Lear. Oxford: Clarendon, 1986.

Urkowitz, Steven. *Shakespeare's Revision of* King Lear. Princeton: Princeton University Press, 1980.

Vickers, Brian. *Shakespeare, Co-Author: A Historical Study of Five Collaborative Plays*. New York: Oxford University Press, 2002.

Walker, Alice. *Textual Problems of the First Folio*: Richard III, King Lear, Troilus & Cressida, 2 Henry IV, Hamlet, Othello. Cambridge, Eng.: Cambridge University Press, 1953.

Wells, Stanley. *Re-Editing Shakespeare for the Modern Reader*. New York: Oxford University Press, 1984.

Wells, Stanley, and Gary Taylor. *Modernizing Shakespeare's Spelling*. Oxford: Clarendon, 1979.

———. *William Shakespeare: A Textual Companion*. Oxford: Clarendon, 1987.

Werstine, Paul. "A Century of 'Bad' Shakespeare Quartos." *Shakespeare Quarterly* 50 (1999): 310–33.

———. "Narratives about Printed Shakespeare Texts: 'Foul Papers' and 'Bad' Quartos." *Shakespeare Quarterly* 41 (1990): 65–86.

Williams, George Walton. *The Craft of Printing and the Publication of Shakespeare's Works*. Washington, D.C.: Folger Shakespeare Library, 1985.

Wilson, J. Dover. *The Manuscript of Shakespeare's "Hamlet" and the Problems of Its Transmission: An Essay in Critical Bibliography*. 2 vols. New York: Macmillan, 1934.

Shakespeare and Performance

Aebischer, Pascale. *Shakespeare's Violated Bodies: Stage and Screen Performance*. New York: Cambridge University Press, 2003.

Aebischer, Pascale, Edward J. Esche, and Nigel Wheale, eds. *Remaking Shakespeare: Performance Across Media, Genres, and Cultures*. New York: Palgrave Macmillan, 2003.

Bartholomeusz, Dennis. *"Macbeth" and the Players*. Cambridge, Eng.: Cambridge University Press, 1969.

Barton, John. *Playing Shakespeare*. London: Methuen, 1984.

Bate, Jonathan, and Russell Jackson, eds. *Shakespeare: An Illustrated Stage History*. New York: Oxford University Press, 1996.

Berger, Harry Jr. *Imaginary Audition: Shakespeare on Stage and Page*. Berkeley: University of California Press, 1989.

Berry, Francis. *The Shakespeare Inset: Word and Picture*. London: Routledge and Kegan Paul, 1965.

Berry, Ralph. *Changing Styles in Shakespeare*. Boston: Allen & Unwin, 1981.

Bevington, David M. *Action Is Eloquence: Shakespeare's Language of Gesture*. Cambridge, Mass.: Harvard University Press, 1984.

———. *This Wide and Universal Theater: Shakespeare in Performance, Then and Now*. Chicago: University of Chicago Press, 2007.

Branam, George Curtis. *Eighteenth-Century Adaptations of Shakespearean Tragedy*. Berkeley: University of California Press, 1956.

Bratton, Jacky, and Julie Hankey, gen. eds. The Shakespeare in Production Series. Cambridge, Eng.: Cambridge University Press, 1996–.

Brennan, Anthony. *Onstage and Offstage Worlds in Shakespeare's Plays*. New York: Routledge, 1989.

———. *Shakespeare's Dramatic Structures*. Boston: Routledge and Kegan Paul, 1986.

Brown, Ivor. *Shakespeare and the Actors*. London: Bodley Head, 1970.

Brown, John Russell. *Shakespeare and the Theatrical Event*. Houndmills, Basingstoke: Palgrave Macmillan, 2002.

———. *Shakespeare's Dramatic Style:* Romeo and Juliet, As You Like It, Julius Caesar, Twelfth Night, Macbeth. London: Heinemann, 1970.

Bulman, James C., ed. *Shakespeare, Theory, and Performance*. New York: Routledge, 1996.

Calderwood, James. *Shakespearean Metadrama: The Argument of the Play in* Titus Andronicus, Love's Labour's Lost, Romeo and Juliet, A Midsummer Night's Dream, *and* Richard II. Minneapolis: University of Minnesota Press, 1971.

Carlisle, Carol Jones. *Shakespeare from the Greenroom: Actors' Criticisms of Four Major Tragedies*. Chapel Hill: University of North Carolina Press, 1969.

Cohn, Ruby. *Modern Shakespeare Offshoots*. Princeton: Princeton University Press, 1976.

Dean, Winton. "Shakespeare in the Opera House." *Shakespeare Survey* 18 (1965): 75–93.

Dobson, Michael. *The Making of the National Poet: Shakespeare, Adaptation and Authorship, 1660–1769*. Oxford: Clarendon, 1992.

———, ed. *Performing Shakespeare's Tragedies Today: The Actor's Perspective*. New York: Cambridge University Press, 2006.

Downer, Alan S. *The Eminent Tragedian William Charles Macready*. Cambridge, Mass.: Harvard University Press, 1966.

Duffin, Ross W. *Shakespeare's Songbook*. New York: Norton, 2004.

Foulkes, Richard, ed. *Shakespeare and the Victorian Stage*. New York: Cambridge University Press, 1986.

Goldman, Michael. *Acting and Action in Shakespearean Tragedy*. Princeton: Princeton University Press, 1985.

Hirsch, James E. *The Structure of Shakespearean Scenes*. New Haven: Yale University Press, 1981.

Hogan, Charles Beecher, ed. *Shakespeare in the Theatre, 1701–1800*. 2 vols. Oxford: Clarendon, 1952–57.

Holland, Peter. *English Shakespeares: Shakespeare on the English Stage in the 1990's*. New York: Cambridge University Press, 1997.

Homan, Sidney, ed. *Shakespeare's "More Than Words Can Witness": Essays on Visual and Nonverbal Enactment in the Plays*. Lewisburg, Pa.: Bucknell University Press, 1980.

———, ed. *When the Theater Turns to Itself: The Aesthetic Metaphor in Shakespeare*. Lewiston, Pa.: Bucknell University Press, 1981.

Hoenselaars, Ton, ed. *Shakespeare's History Plays: Performance, Translation and Adaptation in Britain and Abroad*. Cambridge, Eng.: Cambridge University Press, 2004.

Howard, Jean E. *Shakespeare's Art of Orchestration: Stage Technique and Audience Response*. Urbana: University of Illinois Press, 1984.

Jones, Emrys. *Scenic Form in Shakespeare*. Oxford: Clarendon, 1971.

Kennedy, Dennis. *Looking at Shakespeare: A Visual History of Twentieth-Century Performance*. 2nd ed. New York: Cambridge University Press, 2001.

———, ed. *Foreign Shakespeare: Contemporary Performance*. New York: Cambridge University Press, 1993.

Marshall, Gail, and Adrian Poole, eds. *Victorian Shakespeare*. New York: Palgrave Macmillan, 2003.

McGuire, Philip C. *Speechless Dialect: Shakespeare's Open Silences*. Berkeley: University of California Press, 1985.

McGuire, Philip C., and David A. Samuelson. *Shakespeare: The Theatrical Dimension*. New York: AMS Press, 1979.

Mooney, Michael E. *Shakespeare's Dramatic Transactions*. Durham, N.C.: Duke University Press, 1990.

Mowat, Barbara A. *The Dramaturgy of Shakespeare's Romances*. Athens: University of Georgia Press, 1976.

Odell, George Clinton Densmore. *Shakespeare from Betterton to Irving*. 2 vols. New York: Scribner, 1920.

Parsons, Keith, and Pamela Mason, eds. *Shakespeare in Performance*. London: Salamander, 1995.

Poel, William. *Shakespeare in the Theater*. London: Sidgwick and Jackson, 1913.

Rosenberg, Marvin. *The Masks of King Lear*. Berkeley: University of California Press, 1972.

Rosenberg, Marvin, et al. *Clamorous Voices: Shakespeare's Women Today*. London: Women's Press, 1988.

Rutter, Carol, gen. ed. The Shakespeare in Performance Series. Manchester: Manchester University Press, 1982–.

Shattuck, Charles H. *Shakespeare on the American Stage*, vol. 1: *From the Hallams to Edwin Booth*. Washington, D.C.: Folger Shakespeare Library, 1976.

———. *Shakespeare on the American Stage*, vol. 2: *From Booth and Barrett to Sothern and Marlowe*. Washington, D.C.: Folger Shakespeare Library, 1987.

——. *The Shakespeare Promptbooks: A Descriptive Catalogue.* Urbana: University of Illinois Press, 1965.

Slater, Ann. *Shakespeare, the Director.* Totowa, N.J.: Barnes & Noble Books, 1982.

Smallwood, Robert, ed. *Players of Shakespeare.* 6 vols. New York: Cambridge University Press, 1985–2004.

——, gen. ed. The Shakespeare at Stratford series. London: Arden Shakespeare, 2002– .

Speaight, Robert. *Shakespeare on the Stage: An Illustrated History of Shakespearian Performance.* London: Collins, 1973.

——. *William Poel and the Elizabethan Revival.* Cambridge, Mass.: Harvard University Press, 1954.

Spencer, Hazelton. *Shakespeare Improved: The Restoration Versions in Quarto and On the Stage.* Cambridge, Mass.: Harvard University Press, 1927.

Styan, J. L. *The Shakespeare Revolution: Criticism and Performance in the Twentieth Century.* New York: Cambridge University Press, 1977.

——. *Shakespeare's Stagecraft.* Cambridge, Eng.: Cambridge University Press, 1967.

——. "Sight and Space: The Perception of Shakespeare on Stage and Screen." *Shakespeare, Pattern of Excelling Nature: Shakespeare Criticism in Honor of America's Bicentennial.* Ed. David Bevington and Jay L. Halio. Newark: University of Delaware Press, 1978.

Thompson, Marvin and Ruth, eds. *Shakespeare and the Sense of Performance.* Newark: University of Delaware Press, 1989.

Trewin, J. C. *Shakespeare on the English Stage, 1900–1964.* London: Barrie and Rockliff, 1964.

Wells, Stanley. *Royal Shakespeare: Four Major Productions at Stratford-upon-Avon.* Manchester: Manchester University Press, 1977.

——, ed. *Shakespeare in the Theatre: An Anthology of Criticism.* New York: Oxford University Press, 1997.

Worthen, William B. *Shakespeare and the Authority of Performance.* New York: Cambridge University Press, 1997.

——. *Shakespeare and the Force of Modern Performance.* New York: Cambridge University Press, 2003.

Shakespeare on Film

Ball, Robert Hamilton. *Shakespeare on Silent Film: A Strange Eventful History.* London: Allen & Unwin, 1968.

Burt, Richard, and Lynda E. Boose, eds. *Shakespeare the Movie: Popularizing the Plays on Film, TV, and Video.* New York: Routledge, 1997.

——. *Shakespeare the Movie II: Popularizing the Plays on Film, TV, Video, and DVD.* New York: Routledge, 2003.

Bristol, Michael D. *Big-Time Shakespeare.* New York: Routledge, 1996.

Buchanan, Judith. *Shakespeare on Film.* New York: Pearson Longman, 2005.

Buchman, Lorne Michael. *Still in Movement: Shakespeare on Screen.* New York: Oxford University Press, 1991.

Bulman, J. C., and H. R. Coursen, eds. *Shakespeare on Television: An Anthology of Essays and Reviews.* Hanover, N.H.: University Press of New England, 1988.

Burnett, Mark Thornton, and Ramona Wray, eds. *Shakespeare, Film, Fin de Siècle.* New York: St. Martin's, 2000.

Burt, Richard. *Shakespeare After Mass Media.* New York: Palgrave Macmillan, 2002.

Cartelli, Thomas, and Katherine Rowe, eds. *New Wave Shakespeare on Screen.* Malden, Mass.: Polity Press, 2007.

Crowl, Samuel. *Shakespeare at the Cineplex: The Kenneth Branagh Era.* Athens: Ohio University Press, 2003.

————. *Shakespeare and Film*. New York: Norton, 2008.

Davies, Anthony, and Stanley Wells, eds. *Shakespeare and the Moving Image: The Plays on Film and Television*. New York: Cambridge University Press, 1994.

Donaldson, Peter S. *Shakespearean Films/Shakespearean Directors*. Boston: Unwin Hyman, 1990.

Henderson, Diana E. *Collaborations with the Past: Reshaping Shakespeare Across Time and Media*. Ithaca, N.Y.: Cornell University Press, 2006.

————. *A Concise Companion to Shakespeare on Screen*. Malden, Mass.: Blackwell, 2007.

Hindle, Maurice. *Studying Shakespeare on Film*. New York: Palgrave Macmillan, 2007.

Kliman, Bernice W. *Hamlet: Film, Television, and Audio Performance*. Madison, N.J.: Fairleigh Dickinson University Press, 1988.

Lehmann, Courtney. *Shakespeare Remains: Theater to Film, Early Modern to Postmodern*. Ithaca, N.Y.: Cornell, 2002.

Lehmann, Courtney, and Lisa S. Starks, eds. *Spectacular Shakespeare: Critical Theory and Popular Cinema*. Madison, N.J.: Fairleigh Dickinson University Press, 2002.

Rothwell, Kenneth S. *A History of Shakespeare on Screen: A Century of Film and Television*. 2nd ed. Cambridge, Eng.: Cambridge University Press, 2004.

Glossary

STAGE TERMS

"Above"   The gallery on the upper level of the *frons scenae*. In open-air theaters, such as the Globe, this space contained the lords' rooms. The central section of the gallery was sometimes used by the players for short scenes. Indoor theaters such as Blackfriars featured a curtained alcove for musicians above the stage.

"Aloft"   See *"Above."*

Amphitheater   An open-air theater, such as the Globe.

Arras   See *Curtain.*

Cellerage   See *Trap.*

Chorus   In the works of Shakespeare and other Elizabethan playwrights, a single individual (not, as in Greek tragedy, a group) who speaks before the play (and often before each act), describing events not shown on stage as well as commenting on the action witnessed by the audience.

Curtain   Curtains, or arras (hanging tapestries), covered a part of the *frons scenae,* thus concealing the discovery space, and may also have been draped around the edge of the stage to conceal the open area underneath.

Discovery space   A central opening or alcove concealed behind a curtain in the center of the *frons scenae.* The curtain could be drawn aside to "discover" tableaux such as Portia's caskets, the body of Polonius, or the statue of Hermione. Shakespeare appears to have used this stage device only sparingly.

Doubling   The common practice of having one actor play multiple roles, so that a play with a large cast of characters might be performed by a relatively small company.

Dumb shows   Mimed scenes performed before a play (or before each act), summarizing or foreshadowing the plot. Dumb shows were popular in early Elizabethan drama; although they already seemed old-fashioned in Shakespeare's time, they were employed by writers up to the 1640s.

Epilogue   A brief speech or poem addressed to the audience by an actor after the play. In some cases, as in 2 *Henry IV,* the epilogue could be combined with, or could merge into, the jig.

Forestage   The front of the stage, closest to the audience.

Frons scenae   The wall at the back of the stage, behind which lay the players' tiring-house. The *frons scenae* of the Globe featured two doors flanking the central discovery space, with a gallery "above."

Gallery   Covered seating areas surrounding the open yard of the public amphitheaters. There were three levels of galleries at the Globe; admission to these seats cost an extra penny (in addition to the basic admission fee of one penny to the yard), and seating in the higher galleries another penny yet. In indoor theaters such as Blackfriars, where there was no standing room, gallery seating was less expensive than seating in the pit; indeed, seats nearest the stage were the most expensive.

Gatherers   Persons employed by the playing company to take money at the entrances to the theater.

Groundlings   Audience members who paid the minimum price of admission (one penny) to stand in the yard of the open-air theaters; also referred to as "understanders."

Heavens   The canopied roof over the stage in the open-air theaters, protecting the players and their costumes from rain. The "heavens" would be brightly decorated with sun, moon, and stars, and perhaps the signs of the zodiac.

Hut   A structure on the top of the cover over the stage, where stagehands produced the effects of thunder and lightning and operated the machinery by which gods, such as Jupiter in *Cymbeline,* descended through the trapdoor in the "heavens."

Jig   A song-and-dance performance by the clown and other members of the company at the conclusion of a play. These performances were frequently bawdy and were officially banned in 1612.

Lords' rooms   Partitioned sections of the gallery "above," where the most prestigious and expensive seats in the public playhouses were located. These rooms were designed not to provide the best view of the action on the stage below, but to make their privileged occupants conspicuous to the rest of the audience.

Open-air theaters   Unroofed public playhouses in the suburbs of London, such as The Theatre, the Rose, and the Globe.

Part   The character played by an actor. In Shakespeare's theater, actors were given a roll of paper called a "part" containing all of the speeches and all of the cues belonging to their character. The term "role," synonymous with "part," is derived from such rolls of paper.

Patrons   Important nobles and members of the royal family under whose protection the theatrical companies of London operated; players not in the service of patrons were punishable as vagabonds. The companies were referred to as their patrons' "Men" or "Servants." Thus the name of the company to which Shakespeare belonged for most of his career was first the Lord Chamberlain's Men, then was changed to the King's Men in 1603, when James I became their patron.

Pillars   The "heavens" were supported by two tall painted pillars or posts near the front of the stage. These occasionally played a role in stage action, allowing a character to "hide" while remaining in full view of the audience.

Pit   The area in front of the stage in indoor theaters such as Blackfriars, where the most expensive and prestigious bench seating was to be had.

Posts   See *Pillars.*

Proscenium   The space of the transparent "fourth wall," which divides the actors from the orchestra and audience in the standard modern theater. The stages on which Shakespeare's plays were first performed had no proscenium.

Rearstage   The back of the stage, farthest from the audience.

Repertory   The stock of plays a company had ready for performance at a given time. Companies generally performed a different play each day, often more than a dozen plays in a month and more than thirty in the course of the season.

Role See *Part.*

Sharers Senior actors holding shares in a joint-stock theatrical company; they paid for costumes, hired hands, and new plays, and they shared profits and losses equally. Shakespeare was not only a longtime "sharer" of the Lord Chamberlain's Men but, from 1599, a "housekeeper," the holder of a one-eighth share in the Globe playhouse.

Tiring-house The players' dressing (attiring) room, a structure located at the back of the stage and connected to the stage by two or more doors in the *frons scenae.*

Trap A trapdoor near the front of the stage that allowed access to the "cellarage" beneath and was frequently associated with hell's mouth. Another trapdoor in the "heavens" opened for the descent of gods to the stage below.

"Within" The tiring-house, from which offstage sound effects such as shouts, drums, and trumpets were produced.

Yard The central space in open-air theaters such as the Globe, into which the stage projected and in which audience members stood. Admission to the yard in the public theaters cost a penny, the cheapest admission available.

TEXTUAL TERMS

Aside See *Stage direction.*

Autograph Text written in the author's own hand. With the possible exception of a few pages of the collaborative play *Sir Thomas More,* no dramatic works or poems written in Shakespeare's hand are known to survive.

Canonical Of an author, the writings generally accepted as authentic. In the case of Shakespeare's dramatic works, only two plays that are not among the thirty-six plays contained in the First Folio, *Pericles* and *The Two Noble Kinsmen,* have won widespread acceptance into the Shakespearean canon. (This sense of "canonical" should not be confused with the use of "the canon" to denote the entire body of literary works, including but not limited to Shakespeare's, that have traditionally been regarded as fit objects of admiration and study.)

Catchword A word printed below the text at the bottom of a page, matching the first word on the following page. The catchword enabled the printer to keep the pages in their proper sequence. Where the catchword fails to match the word at the top of the next page, there is reason to suspect that something has been lost or misplaced.

Compositor A person employed in a print shop to set type. To speed the printing process, most of Shakespeare's plays were set by more than one compositor. Compositors frequently followed their own standards in spelling and punctuation. They inevitably introduced some errors into the text, often by selecting the wrong piece from the type case or by setting the correct letter upside down.

Conflation A version of a play created by combining readings from more than one substantive edition. Since the early eighteenth century, for example, most versions of *King Lear* and of several other plays by Shakespeare have been conflations of quarto and First Folio texts.

Control text The text upon which a modern edition is based.

Dramatis personae A list of the characters appearing in the play. In the First Folio such lists were printed at the end of some but not all of the plays. The editor Nicholas Rowe (1709) first provided lists of dramatis personae for all of Shakespeare's dramatic works.

Exeunt / Exit See *Stage direction*.

Fair copy A transcript of the "foul papers" made either by a scribe or by the playwright.

Folio A bookmaking format in which each large sheet of paper is folded once, making two leaves (four pages front and back). This format produced large volumes, generally handsome and expensive. The First Folio of Shakespeare's plays was printed in 1623.

Foul papers An author's first completed draft of a play, typically full of blotted-out passages and revisions. None of Shakespeare's foul papers is known to survive.

Licensing By an order of 1581, new plays could not be performed until they had received a license from the Master of the Revels. A separate license, granted by the Court of High Commission, was required for publication, though in practice plays were often printed without license. From 1610, the Master of the Revels had the authority to license plays for publication as well as for performance.

Manent / Manet See *Stage direction*.

Memorial reconstruction The conjectured practice of reconstructing the text of a play from memory. Companies touring in the provinces without access to promptbooks may have resorted to memorial reconstruction. This practice also provides a plausible explanation for the existence of the so-called bad Quartos.

Octavo A bookmaking format in which each large sheet of paper is folded three times, making eight leaves (sixteen pages front and back). Only one of Shakespeare's plays, *Richard Duke of York* (3 *Henry VI*, 1595), was published in octavo format.

Playbook See *Promptbook*.

Press variants Minor textual variations among books of the same edition, resulting from corrections made in the course of printing or from damaged or slipped type.

Promptbook A manuscript of a play (either foul papers or fair copy) annotated and adapted for performance by the theatrical company. The promptbook incorporated stage directions, notes on properties and special effects, and revisions, sometimes including those required by the Master of the Revels. Promptbooks are usually identifiable by the replacement of characters' names with actors' names.

Quarto A bookmaking format in which each large sheet of paper is folded twice, making four leaves (eight pages front and back). Quarto volumes were smaller and less expensive than books printed in the folio format.

Scribal copy A transcript of a play produced by a professional scribe (or "scrivener"). Scribes tended to employ their own preferred spellings and abbreviations and could be responsible for introducing a variety of errors.

Speech prefix (s.p.) The indication of the identity of the speaker of the following line or lines. Early editions of Shakespeare's plays often use different prefixes at different points to designate the same person. On occasion, the name of the actor who was to play the role appears in place of the name of the character.

Stage direction (s.d.)   The part of the text that is not spoken by any character but that indicates actions to be performed onstage. Stage directions in the earliest editions of Shakespeare's plays are sparse and are sometimes grouped together at the beginning of a scene rather than next to the spoken lines they should precede, accompany, or follow. By convention, the most basic stage directions were written in Latin. "Exit" indicates the departure of a single actor from the stage, "exeunt" the departure of more than one. "Manet" indicates that a single actor remains onstage, "manent" that more than one remains. Lines accompanied by the stage direction "aside" are spoken so as not to be heard by the others onstage. This stage direction appeared in some early editions of Shakespeare plays, but other means were also used to indicate such speech (such as placing the words within parentheses), and sometimes no indication was provided.

Stationers' Register   The account books of the Company of Stationers (of which all printers were legally required to be members), recording the fees paid for permission to print new works as well as the fines exacted for printing without permission. The Stationers' Register thus provides a valuable if incomplete record of publication in England.

Substantive text   The text of an edition based upon access to a manuscript, as opposed to a derivative text based only on an earlier edition.

Variorum editions   Comprehensive editions of a work or works in which the various views of previous editors and commentators are compiled.

General Introduction   Plague death bill: By permission of the Folger Shakespeare Library • Webbe: By permission of the British Library • Amman: Spencer Collection, The New York Public Library, Astor, Lenox and Tilden Foundation • *Swetnam* title page: By permission of The Huntington Library, San Marino, California • Pope as Antichrist: By permission of the Folger Shakespeare Library • de Heere: The National Museum of Wales • Armada portrait: By kind permission of Marquess of Tavistock and Trustees of the Bedford Estate • Boaistuau: By permission of The Huntington Library, San Marino, California • Mandeville: By permission of the Houghton Library, Harvard University • Funeral procession: Additional Ms. 35324, folio 37v. By permission of the British Library • Gheeraerts: By permission of the Trustees of Dulwich Picture Gallery • van den Broek: Fitzwilliam Museum, University of Cambridge • Swimming: Bodleian Library, University of Oxford, 4° G.17.Art • Panorama of London: By permission of the British Library • Tarleton: Harley 3885, folio 19. By permission of the British Library • Hanging: Pepys Library, Magdalene College, Cambridge • Syphilis victim: By permission of The Huntington Library, San Marino, California • *Spanish Tragedy* title page: By permission of the Folger Shakespeare Library • Stratford-upon-Avon: By permission of City of York Libraries • Cholmondeley sisters: Tate Gallery, London • Alleyn: By permission of the Trustees of Dulwich Picture Library • *If You Know Not Me* title page: By permission of The Huntington Library, San Marino, California • van der Straet: By permission of the Folger Shakespeare Library

The Shakespearean Stage   Braun and Hogenburg: 8.Tab.c.4. Bk.1.pl.1. By permission of the British Library • Hollar: Guildhall Library, Corporation of London • Interior of the "new" Globe: Courtesy of The International Shakespeare Globe Center Ltd. Photo: John Tramper • Exterior of the "new" Globe: Courtesy of The International Shakespeare Globe Center Ltd. Photo: Richard Kalina • *Frons scenae* of the "new" Globe: Courtesy of The International Shakespeare Globe Center Ltd. Photo: Richard Kalina • Oliver: The Burghley House Collection. Photograph: Courtauld Institute of Art • Peacham: Reproduced by permission of the Marquess of Bath, Longleat House, Warminster, Wiltshire, Great Britain. Photograph: Courtauld Institute of Art • de Witt: University Library, Utrecht, MS 842, f.132r • Middle Temple Hall: The Benchers of the Honorable Society of the Middle Temple, London • Hollar: Guildhall Library, Corporation of London

Shakespearean History   Anjou: By permission of V&A Images, Victoria and Albert Museum • King Henry IV: © National Portrait Gallery, London • Holbein: © National Portrait Gallery, London.

The First Part of the Contention (2 Henry VI)   Child king: Additional Ms. 48976, Figure 50. By permission of the British Library • Kemp: By permission of the Folger Shakespeare Library • Halle: By permission of the Folger Shakespeare Library

Richard Duke of York (3 Henry VI)   Halberd: Reproduced by permission of the Trustees of the Wallace Collection • Edward IV: The Royal Collection. © Her Majesty Queen Elizabeth II • Whitney: By permission of the Folger Shakespeare Library

1 Henry VI   Holinshed: Reproduced by permission of the Huntington Library, San Marino, California • Henry VI: By courtesy of the National Portrait Gallery, London • Joan of Arc: Giraudon/Art Resource, NY

Richard III   Richard III: By courtesy of the National Portrait Gallery, London • Sittow: By courtesy of the National Portrait Gallery, London • Vischer: By permission of the Folger Shakespeare Library

The Reign of King Edward the Third   Holinshed: Reproduced by permission of the Huntington Library, San Marino, California

Richard II   Rastell: C.15.e.6. By permission of the British Library • Holbein: Reproduced by courtesy of the Trustees, The National Gallery, London • Tempesta: © British Museum

King John   Coronation: Eton College Ms. 123. Reproduced by permission of the Provost and Fellows of Eton College • Tomb: Reproduced by permission of The Huntington Library, San Marino, California

1 Henry IV   Owain Glydŵr seal: By permission of The National Museum of Wales • William Blake: Photograph © Museum of Fine Arts, Boston • Peacham: By Permission of the Folger Shakespeare Library

2 Henry IV   1600 Quarto page: By permission of the Folger Shakespeare Library • Cartari: By permission of the Folger Shakespeare Library • Rollos: Spencer Collection, The New York Public Library, Astor, Lenox and Tilden Foundations, Photo: Robert D. Rubic

Henry V   Rastell: G6030. By permission of the British Library • Renatus: By permission of the Houghton Library, Harvard University • Comenius: By permission of the Folger Shakespeare Library

Sir Thomas Moore   From *The Booke of Sir Thomas Moore*: Harley 7368, folio 9. By permission of the British Library

All Is True (Henry VIII)   Wotton/Bacon letter: Bodleian Library, University of Oxford, Vet. A. 3.f.137 • Cavendish: Bodleian Library, University of Oxford, Douce 363 for. 71R • Metsys: © British Museum

Early Modern Map Culture   Speed: © British Library/HIP/Art Resource, NY • Braun and Hogenberg: HIP/Art Resource, NY. Museum of London, London, Great Britain

Contemporary Documents
First Folio front matter: *The Norton Facsimile of the First Folio of Shakespeare,* 2nd ed. (1996)